Lecture Notes in Computer Science 7485

Commenced Publication in 1973
Founding and Former Series Editors:
Gerhard Goos, Juris Hartmanis, and Jan van Leeuwen

Ivan Visconti   Roberto De Prisco (Eds.)

Security and Cryptography for Networks

8th International Conference, SCN 2012
Amalfi, Italy, September 5-7, 2012
Proceedings

 Springer

Volume Editors

Ivan Visconti
Roberto De Prisco
Università di Salerno
Dipartimento di Informatica
via Ponte don Melillo, 84084 Fisciano (SA), Italy
E-mail: {visconti, robdep}@dia.unisa.it

ISSN 0302-9743   e-ISSN 1611-3349
ISBN 978-3-642-32927-2   e-ISBN 978-3-642-32928-9
DOI 10.1007/978-3-642-32928-9
Springer Heidelberg Dordrecht London New York

Library of Congress Control Number: 2012945012

CR Subject Classification (1998): E.3, K.6.5, D.4.6, C.2.0, C.2, J.1

LNCS Sublibrary: SL 4 – Security and Cryptology

Typesetting: Camera-ready by author, data conversion by Scientific Publishing Services, Chennai, India

Printed on acid-free paper

Springer is part of Springer Science+Business Media (www.springer.com)

Preface

The 8th Conference on Security and Cryptography for Networks (SCN 2012) was held in Amalfi, Italy, during September 5–7, 2012. This biennial conference has traditionally been held in Amalfi, with the exception of the fifth edition which was held in nearby Maiori.

The world-wide use of computer networks, and in particular of the Internet, opens new challenges for the security of electronic and distributed transactions. Cryptography and information security must face both the theoretical and practical aspects of the above challenges, by providing concepts, techniques, applications, and practical experiences. The principal aim of SCN as a conference is to bring together researchers, practitioners, developers, and users interested in the above fields, to foster cooperation and to exchange techniques, tools, experiences, and ideas in the stunning Amalfi Coast setting.

The conference received 72 submissions in a broad range of cryptography and security areas. The selection of papers was a difficult task. This year we received many high-quality submissions and 31 of them were accepted for publication in these proceedings on the basis of quality, originality, and relevance to the conference's scope.

At least three Program Committee (PC) members—out of 28 world-renowned experts in the conference's various areas of interest—reviewed each submitted paper, while submissions co-authored by a PC member were subjected to the more stringent evaluation of five PC members.

In addition to the PC members, many external reviewers joined the review process in their particular areas of expertise. We were fortunate to have this knowledgeable and energetic team of experts, and are deeply grateful to all of them for their hard and thorough work, which included a very active discussion phase—almost as long as the initial individual reviewing period. The paper submission, review, and discussion processes were effectively and efficiently made possible by the Web-Submission-and-Review software, written by Shai Halevi, and hosted by the International Association for Cryptologic Research (IACR). Many thanks to Shai for his assistance with the system's various features and for his constant availability.

Given the perceived quality of the submissions, the PC decided also this year to give a Best-Paper Award, both to promote outstanding work in the fields of cryptography and information security and to keep encouraging high-quality submissions to SCN. "Deterministic Public Key Encryption and Identity-Based Encryption from Lattices in the Auxiliary-Input Setting" by Xiang Xie, Rue Xue, and Rui Zhang was conferred such distinction.

The program was further enriched by the invited talks of Yuval Ishai (Technion, Israel) and Giuseppe Persiano (Università di Salerno, Italy), top experts on the subjects of the conference.

We thank all the authors who submitted papers to this conference; the Organizing Committee members, colleagues, and student helpers for their valuable time and effort; and all the conference attendees who made this event a truly intellectually stimulating one through their active participation.

We finally thank the *Dipartimento di Informatica* of the University of Salerno, Italy, for the financial support.

September 2012   Ivan Visconti
                                                                    Roberto De Prisco

SCN 2012
The 8th Conference on Security and Cryptography for Networks

September 5–7, 2012, Amalfi, Italy

Program Chair

Ivan Visconti   Università di Salerno, Italy

Program Committee

Masayuki Abe   NTT, Japan
Amos Beimel   Ben-Gurion University, Israel
Carlo Blundo   Università di Salerno, Italy
Alexandra Boldyreva   Georgia Institute of Technology, USA
Xavier Boyen   PARC, USA
Dario Catalano   University of Catania, Italy
Melissa Chase   Microsoft Research Redmond, USA
Dana Dachman-Soled   Microsoft Research New England, USA
Stefan Dziembowski   University of Warsaw, Poland and Sapienza
                                     University of Rome, Italy
Pierre-Alain Fouque   ENS, France
Juan Garay   AT&T Labs-Research, USA
Vipul Goyal   Microsoft Research, India
Brett Hemenway   University of Michigan, USA
Martin Hirt   ETH Zurich, Switzerland
Dennis Hofheinz   Karlsruhe Institute of Technology, Germany
Stanislaw Jarecki   UCI, USA
Gregory Neven   IBM Research, Switzerland
Carles Padro   Nanyang Technological University, Singapore
Benny Pinkas   Bar Ilan University, Israel, and Google, USA
Bart Preneel   Katholieke Universiteit Leuven, Belgium
Matt Robshaw   Orange Labs, France
Alon Rosen   IDC Herzliya, Israel
abhi shelat   University of Virginia, USA
Francois-Xavier Standaert   UCL, Belgium
Dominique Unruh   University of Tartu, Estonia
Bogdan Warinschi   University of Bristol, UK
Daniel Wichs   IBM T.J. Watson Research Center, USA
Moti Yung   Google, USA and Columbia University, USA

General Chair

Roberto De Prisco   Università di Salerno, Italy

Organizing Committee

Aniello Castiglione   Università di Salerno, Italy
Paolo D'Arco   Università di Salerno, Italy

Steering Committee

Carlo Blundo   Università di Salerno, Italy
Alfredo De Santis   Università di Salerno, Italy
Ueli Maurer   ETH Zürich, Switzerland
Rafail Ostrovsky   University of California - Los Angeles, USA
Giuseppe Persiano   Università di Salerno, Italy
Jacques Stern   ENS Paris, France
Douglas Stinson   University of Waterloo, Canada
Gene Tsudik   University of California - Irvine, USA
Moti Yung   Google, USA and Columbia University, USA

External Reviewers

Shweta Agrawal   Clemente Galdi   Ilan Orlov
Giulia Alberini   Chaya Ganesh   Chris Peikert
Joël Alwen   Peter Gaži   Vanishree Rao
Gilad Asharov   Clint Givens   Mariana Raykova
Abhishek Banerjee   Dov Gordon   Elizabeth Quaglia
Steven Bellovin   Divya Gupta   Alessandra Scafuro
Charles Bouillaguet   Tibor Jager   Hakan Seyalioglu
David Cash   Jeremy Jean   Adam Smith
Iwen Coisel   Tomasz Kazana   Adam Stubblefield
Sandro Coretti   François Koeune   Björn Tackmann
Reza Curtmola   Stephan Krenn   Yevgeniy Vahlis
Gregory Demay   Huijia Lin   Jorge L. Villar
Patrick Derbez   Steve Lu   Keita Xagawa
Mario Di Raimondo   Christoph Lucas   Vassilis Zikas
Laila El Aimani   Benjamin Martin   Yunlei Zhao
Oriol Farràs   Christian Matt   Hong-Sheng Zhou
Dario Fiore   Irippuge Milinda Perera
Atsushi Fujioka   Miyako Ohkubo

Table of Contents

Cryptography from Lattices

Signature Schemes

Encryption Schemes I

Efficient Two-Party and Multi-Party Computation

Security in the UC Framework

Cryptanalysis

Encryption Schemes II

Efficient Constructions

Protocols and Combiners

Deterministic Public Key Encryption and Identity-Based Encryption from Lattices in the Auxiliary-Input Setting

Xiang Xie[1], Rui Xue[2], and Rui Zhang[2]

[1] Institute of Software, Chinese Academy of Sciences
[2] The State Key Laboratory of Information Security
Institute of Information Engineering, Chinese Academy of Sciences
xiexiang@is.iscas.ac.cn, {xuerui,r-zhang}@iie.ac.cn

Abstract. Deterministic public key encryption (D-PKE) provides an alternative to randomized public key encryption in various scenarios (e.g. search on encrypted data) where the latter exhibits inherent drawbacks. In CRYPTO'11, Brakerski and Segev formalized a framework for studying the security of deterministic public key encryption schemes with respect to auxiliary inputs. A trivial requirement is that the plaintext should not be efficiently recoverable from the auxiliary inputs.

In this paper, we present an efficient deterministic public key encryption scheme in the auxiliary-input setting from lattices. The public key size, ciphertext size and ciphertext expansion factor are improved compared with the scheme proposed by Brakerski and Segev. Our scheme is also secure even in the multi-user setting where related messages may be encrypted under multiple public keys. In addition, the security of our scheme is based on the hardness of the learning with errors (LWE) problem which remains hard even for quantum algorithms.

Furthermore, we consider deterministic identity-based public key encryption (D-IBE) in the auxiliary-input setting. The only known D-IBE scheme (without considering auxiliary inputs) in the standard model was proposed by Bellare et al. in EUROCRYPT'12. However, this scheme is only secure in the selective security setting, and Bellare et al. identified it as an open problem to construct adaptively secure D-IBE schemes. The second contribution of this work is to propose a D-IBE scheme from lattices that is adaptively secure.

Keywords: deterministic (identity-based) public key encryption, auxiliary inputs, lattices.

1 Introduction

The fundamental notion of *semantic security* for public key encryption schemes was introduced by Goldwasser and Micali [16]. While semantic security provides strong privacy guarantees, it inherently requires a *randomized* encryption algorithm. Unfortunately, randomized encryption only allows linear time search

I. Visconti and R. De Prisco (Eds.): SCN 2012, LNCS 7485, pp. 1–18, 2012.

[1,10] on outsourced databases, which is prohibitive when the databases are terabytes in size. Further, randomized encryption necessarily expand the length of the plaintext, which may be undesirable in some applications such as legacy code or in-place encryption.

Bellare, Bolyreva, and O'Neill [6] initiated the study of *deterministic* public key encryption schemes that were oriented to search on encrypted data. Clearly, in this setting, no meaningful notion of security can be achieved if the plaintext space is small. Therefore, Bellare et al. [6] required security to hold only when the plaintexts are drawn from a high min-entropic distribution. Very recently, Brakerski and Segev [11] introduced a framework for modeling the security of deterministic encryption schemes with respect to auxiliary inputs. This framework is a generalization of the one formalized by Bellare et al. [6] (and further in [7,9,18]) to the auxiliary-input setting, in which an adversary possibly obtains additional information that is related to encrypted plaintext, and might even fully determine the encrypted plaintext information theoretically. An immediate consequence of having a deterministic encryption algorithm is that no meaningful notion of security can be satisfied if the plaintext can be recovered from the adversary's auxiliary information. Therefore, their framework focuses on the case of *hard-to-invert* auxiliary inputs. Brakerski and Segev [11] proposed two schemes satisfy this notion of security. However, these two schemes have large public key size, ciphertext size and ciphertext expansion factor. One result of this work is to propose a new scheme from lattices with improved public key size, ciphertext size and ciphertext expansion factor.

A deterministic identity-based encryption (D-IBE) scheme is an identity-based encryption [22] scheme with deterministic encryption algorithm. Bellare et al. [8] extended the security definition under high min-entropy into the identity-based setting. D-IBE allows efficiently searchable identity-based encryption of database entries while maintaining the maximal possible privacy, bringing the key-management benefits of the identity-based setting. Bellare et al. proposed a D-IBE scheme by first constructing identity-based lossy trapdoor functions (IB-LTDFs). Due to the inherent limitation of IB-LTDFs, their scheme only achieves selective security, and in fact, it has been identified as an open problem to construct adaptively secure D-IBE schemes [8].

1.1   Our Contributions

In this work, we propose a D-PKE scheme in the auxiliary-input setting from lattices in the standard model. The security of our scheme is based on the hardness of the LWE problem, which is known to be as hard as worst-case lattice problems [21,19]. The public key size, ciphertext size and ciphertext expansion factor are better than the scheme in [11], while the private key size is almost the same. The computations involved in encryption of our scheme are matrix-vector multiplication and followed by a rounding step. Matrix-vector multiplication can be implemented very fast in parallel, and rounding operations can also be computed by small low-depth arithmetic circuits. Therefore, the encryption can be implemented very fast. In addition, our scheme is secure even in the multi-user setting (as in [11]) where related messages may be encrypted under multiple public keys. In this setting we obtain security, with respect to auxiliary inputs, for any polynomial number of messages and users as long as the messages are related by invertible linear transformations.

Furthermore, we extend the security definition in the auxiliary-input setting to D-IBE, and propose a D-IBE scheme in the standard model. The only known (selectively secure) D-IBE scheme (not under the auxiliary-input setting) in the standard model was proposed by Bellare, Kiltz, Peikert and Waters [8], based on IB-LTDFs.

Our D-IBE scheme is the first adaptively secure one in the auxiliary-input setting. In the full version, we also give a more efficient selectively secure D-IBE scheme in the auxiliary-input setting whose ciphertext size and ciphertext expansion factor are comparable to our D-PKE scheme. All our schemes are secure with respect to auxiliary inputs that are sub-exponentially hard to invert.

1.2   Overview of Our Approach

A crucial technique hurdle is that the hardness of the LWE problem depends essentially on adding *random, independent* errors to every output of a mod-q "parity" function. Indeed, without any error, parity functions are trivially easy to learn. Fortunately, Banerjee, Peikert and Rosen [5] introduced a "derandomized" LWE problem, i.e., generating the errors efficiently and deterministically, while preserving hardness.

The $\text{LWE}_{q,n,m,\alpha}$ assumption says that for any $m = \text{poly}(n)$, modulus q and error rate α: The pairs $(\mathbf{A}, \mathbf{A}^t\mathbf{s} + \mathbf{e})$, for random matrix $\mathbf{A} \leftarrow \mathbb{Z}_q^{n \times m}$, random vector $\mathbf{s} \leftarrow \mathbb{Z}_q^n$, and "small" random error terms $\mathbf{e} \leftarrow \mathbb{Z}^m$ of magnitude $\approx \alpha q$, are indistinguishable from $(\mathbf{A}, \mathbf{u})$, where $\mathbf{u}$ is uniformly random in $\mathbb{Z}_q^m$. The derandomization technique for LWE in [5] is very simple: instead of adding a small random error term to the vector $\mathbf{A}^t\mathbf{s} \in \mathbb{Z}_q^m$. They deterministically *round* it to the nearest element of a sufficiently "coarse" subgroup $\mathbb{Z}_p^m$ where $p \ll q$. In other words, the "error term" comes solely from deterministically rounding $\mathbf{A}^t\mathbf{s}$ to a relatively nearby value. Denoting the rounding operation as $\lfloor \mathbf{A}^t\mathbf{s} \rceil_p \in \mathbb{Z}_p^m$, Banerjee et al. call the problem of distinguishing $(\mathbf{A}, \lfloor \mathbf{A}^t\mathbf{s} \rceil_p)$ from uniform random samples the *learn with rounding* ($\text{LWR}_{q,p,n,m}$) problem. In [5], Banerjee et al. show that the $\text{LWR}_{q,p,n,m}$ is at least as hard as $\text{LWE}_{q,n,m,\alpha}$ for an error rate α proportional to $1/p$, and super-polynomial q ($q \gg p$).

In order to make our D-PKE scheme secure in the auxiliary-input setting, it seems that we need more than the pseudorandomness of $\text{LWR}_{q,p,n,m}$ with uniformly random secret. We hope the $\text{LWR}_{q,p,n,m}$ samples still to be uniformly random even given some auxiliary information of the secret. That is, we want $(\mathbf{A}, \lfloor \mathbf{A}^t\mathbf{s} \rceil_p, f(\mathbf{s})) \approx (\mathbf{A}, \mathbf{u}, f(\mathbf{s}))$ for any hard-to-invert function f. Analogous result of LWE problem was shown in [15], namely $(\mathbf{A}, \mathbf{A}^t\mathbf{s} + \mathbf{e}, f(\mathbf{s})) \approx (\mathbf{A}, \mathbf{u}, f(\mathbf{s}))$ for properly chosen parameters. We briefly explain this statement. LWE assumption implies that $\mathbf{A}^t$ can be substituted by $\mathbf{Z} = \mathbf{B} \cdot \mathbf{C} + \mathbf{E}$, where $\mathbf{B} \leftarrow \mathbb{Z}_q^{m \times d}$, $\mathbf{C} \leftarrow \mathbb{Z}_q^{d \times n}$, and $\mathbf{E} \in \mathbb{Z}^{m \times n}$ is the error matrix (d is determined by the function f). Considering the distribution $(\mathbf{B}, \mathbf{C}, \mathbf{E}, \mathbf{BCs} + \mathbf{Es} + \mathbf{e}, f(\mathbf{s}))$. If $\mathbf{s}$ is sampled from "small" subgroup in $\mathbb{Z}_q^n$ such as $\{0,1\}^n$, **Es** is "small". For sufficiently "large" **e**, the distribution of **e** statistically hides **Es**. Then we only need to consider the distribution $(\mathbf{B}, \mathbf{C}, \mathbf{E}, \mathbf{BCs} + \mathbf{e}, f(\mathbf{s}))$. According to the generalized Goldreich-Levin theorem of Dodis et al. in [13], the distributions of $(\mathbf{Cs}, f(\mathbf{s}))$ and $(\mathbf{u}, f(\mathbf{s}))$ are statistically close. Applying LWE again, we obtain the above statement.

Randomized IBE schemes from lattices have been proposed in [14,12,2,3,17]. We adopt some of the techniques in [2] to construct our D-IBE. A non-trivial problem is how to use the artificial abort technique. The artificial abort technique in [2] does not work here, because that method only works on polynomial q. But, to guarantee the security, here we need q to be super-polynomial. We solve this problem by extending the technique first appeared in [23]. We remark that some parts of the proofs of our schemes follow the framework of [5].

1.3   Related Works

Deterministic public key encryption for high min-entropic messages was introduced by Bellare, Boldyreva and O'Neill [6] who formalized a definitional framework, which was later refined and extended in [7,9,18]. Bellare et at. [6] presented two constructions in the random oracle model: The first relies on any semantically secure public key encryption scheme; whereas the second relies on the RSA function. Constructions in the standard model were then presented in [7,9], based on trapdoor permutations with (almost) uniformly plaintext space [7], and lossy trapdoor functions [9]. However these constructions fall short in the multi-message setting, where arbitrarily related messages are encrypted under the same public key. O'Neill [18] made a step forwards addressing this problem.

Deterministic public key encryption for auxiliary inputs was proposed by Brakerski and Segev [11]. In the auxiliary-input setting, Brakerski and Segev [11] proposed two constructions in the standard model. The first one is based on d-linear assumptions. This scheme is also secure in the multi-user setting, which solved an open problem in [6]. The second one is based on a rather general class of subgroup indistinguishability assumptions. These two schemes are secure with respect to auxiliary inputs that are sub-exponentially hard to invert.

Deterministic identity-based public key encryption was introduced by Bellare, Kiltz, Peikert and Waters [8]. Bellare et al. aimed to construct identity-based lossy trapdoor functions (IB-LTDFs), which is an extension of lossy trapdoor functions [20]. They built a selectively secure D-IBE as an application of IB-LTDFs. Bellare et al. gave two constructions of IB-LTDFs, while only the one based on Decision Linear Diffie-Hellman assumption can be used to get D-IBE schemes[1]. Since the inherent limitations of IB-LTDFs, it's hard to directly used to construct adaptively secure D-IBE schemes.

---

[1] The other identity-based lossy trapdoor function is based on LWE assumption.

2 Preliminaries

For an integer m, we denote $[m]$ as a integer set $\{1, ..., m\}$. We use bold capital letters to denote matrices, and bold lowercase letters to denote vectors. The notation $\mathbf{A}^t$ denotes the transpose of the matrix $\mathbf{A}$. When we say a matrix defined over $\mathbb{Z}_q$ has full rank, we mean that it has full rank modulo q. If $\mathbf{A}_1$ is an $n \times m$ matrix and $\mathbf{A}_2$ is an $n \times m'$ matrix, then $[\mathbf{A}_1|\mathbf{A}_2]$ denotes the $n \times (m+m')$ matrix formed by concatenating $\mathbf{A}_1$ and $\mathbf{A}_2$. If $\mathbf{x}_1$ is a vector of length m and $\mathbf{x}_2$ is of length m', then we let $[\mathbf{x}_1|\mathbf{x}_2]$ denote the length $m + m'$ vector formed by concatenating $\mathbf{x}_1$ and $\mathbf{x}_2$. When doing matrix-vector multiplication, we always view vectors as column vectors.

A function $\mathrm{negl}(\lambda)$ is *negligible*, if it vanishes faster than the inverse of any polynomial in λ. The *statistical distance* between two distributions X, Y over some finite or countable set S is defined as $\Delta(X, Y) = \frac{1}{2} \sum_{s \in S} \left| \Pr[X = s] - \Pr[Y = s] \right|$. X and Y are statistically indistinguishable if $\Delta(X, Y)$ is negligible.

For any integer modulus $q \geq 2$, $\mathbb{Z}_q$ denotes the quotient ring of integer modulo q, and we represent $\mathbb{Z}_q$ by the numbers $\{-\lfloor \frac{q-1}{2} \rfloor, ..., \lceil \frac{q-1}{2} \rceil\}$. We define a "rounding" function $\lfloor \cdot \rceil_p : \mathbb{Z}_q \to \mathbb{Z}_p$, where $q \geq p \geq 2$, as $\lfloor x \rceil_p = \lfloor (p/q) \cdot x \rceil$ mod p. We extend $\lfloor \cdot \rceil_p$ component-wise to vectors and matrices over $\mathbb{Z}_q$.

2.1 Lattices

A full-rank m-dimensional integer lattice $\Lambda \subseteq \mathbb{Z}^m$ is a discrete additive subgroup whose linear span is $\mathbb{R}^m$. Every integer lattice is generated as the $\mathbb{Z}$-linear combination of some basis of linearly independent vectors $\mathbf{B} = \{\mathbf{b}_1, ..., \mathbf{b}_m\} \subset \mathbb{Z}^m$, i.e., $\Lambda = \{\sum_{i=1}^m z_i \mathbf{b}_i : z_i \in \mathbb{Z}\}$. In this work we deal exclusively with "q-ary" lattices. For a matrix $\mathbf{A} \in \mathbb{Z}_q^{n \times m}$, define the integer lattices

$$\Lambda^\perp(\mathbf{A}) = \{\mathbf{z} \in \mathbb{Z}^m : \mathbf{A}\mathbf{z} = 0 \mod q\}.$$

Let $\mathbf{S} = \{\mathbf{s}_1, ..., \mathbf{s}_k\}$ be a set of vectors in $\mathbb{R}^m$. We use $\widetilde{\mathbf{S}} = \{\widetilde{\mathbf{s}_1}, ..., \widetilde{\mathbf{s}_k}\}$ to denote the Gram-Schmidt orthogonalization of the vectors $\mathbf{s}_1, ..., \mathbf{s}_k$. We use $\|\mathbf{S}\|$ to denote the length of the longest vector in $\mathbf{S}$, and $\|\mathbf{S}\|_\infty$ to denote the largest magnitude of the entries in $\mathbf{S}$. For a real-valued matrix $\mathbf{R}$, we let $s_1(\mathbf{R})$ denote the largest singular value of $\mathbf{R}$, i.e. $s_1(\mathbf{R}) = \max_{\|\mathbf{u}\|=1} \|\mathbf{R}\mathbf{u}\|$.

Let Λ be a discrete subset of $\mathbb{Z}^m$. For any vector $\mathbf{c} \in \mathbb{R}^m$ and any positive parameter $\sigma \in \mathbb{R}_{>0}$, let $\rho_{\sigma,\mathbf{c}}(\mathbf{x}) = \exp(-\pi\|\mathbf{x} - \mathbf{c}\|^2/\sigma^2)$ be the Gaussian function on $\mathbb{R}^m$ with center $\mathbf{c}$ and parameter σ. Let $\rho_{\sigma,\mathbf{c}}(\Lambda) = \sum_{\mathbf{x} \in \Lambda} \rho_{\sigma,\mathbf{c}}(\mathbf{x})$ be the discrete integral of $\rho_{\sigma,\mathbf{c}}$ over Λ, and let $\mathcal{D}_{\Lambda,\sigma,\mathbf{c}}$ be the discrete Gaussian distribution over Λ with center $\mathbf{c}$ and parameter σ. Specifically, for all $\mathbf{y} \in \Lambda$, we have $\mathcal{D}_{\Lambda,\sigma,\mathbf{c}}(\mathbf{y}) = \frac{\rho_{\sigma,\mathbf{c}}(\mathbf{y})}{\rho_{\sigma,\mathbf{c}}(\Lambda)}$. For notional convenience, $\rho_{\sigma,\mathbf{0}}$ and $\mathcal{D}_{\Lambda,\sigma,\mathbf{0}}$ are abbreviated as ρ_σ and $\mathcal{D}_{\Lambda,\sigma}$, respectively.

We recall the learning with errors (LWE) problem, a classic hard problem on lattices defined by Regev [21]. The (decisional) learning with errors problem $\mathrm{LWE}_{q,n,m,\alpha}$, in dimension n with error rate $\alpha \in (0, 1)$, stated in matrix form, is: given an input $(\mathbf{A}, \mathbf{b})$, where $\mathbf{A} \in \mathbb{Z}_q^{n \times m}$ for any $m = \mathrm{poly}(n)$ is uniformly random and $\mathbf{b} \in \mathbb{Z}_q^m$ is either of the form $\mathbf{b} = \mathbf{A}^t\mathbf{s} + \mathbf{e} \bmod q$ for uniform $\mathbf{s} \in \mathbb{Z}_q^n$ and $\mathbf{e} \leftarrow \mathcal{D}_{\mathbb{Z}^m, \alpha q}$ or is uniformly random (and independent of $\mathbf{A}$), distinguish which is the case, with non-negligible advantage. It is known that when $\alpha q \geq 2\sqrt{n}$, this decision problem is at least as hard as approximating several problems on n-dimensional lattices in the *worst-case* to within $\widetilde{O}(n/\alpha)$ factors with a quantum computer [21] or on a classical computer for a subset of these problems [19]. In the following, we list some useful facts that make our constructions work.

Lemma 1 ([17] Lemma 2.11). *Let* $x \leftarrow \mathcal{D}_{\mathbb{Z}, r}$ *with* $r > 0$, *then with overwhelming probability,* $|x| \leq r\sqrt{n}$.

Lemma 2 ([4] Lemma 2.1). *Let* q, n, m *be positive integers with* $q \geq 2$ *be prime, and* $m \geq n \lg q + \omega(\lg \lambda)$. *Let* $\mathbf{A} \leftarrow \mathbb{Z}_q^{n \times m}$ *and* $\mathbf{R} \leftarrow \{-1, 1\}^{m \times m}$. *Then* $(\mathbf{A}, \mathbf{A}\mathbf{R})$ *is statistically close to uniform.*

Lemma 3 ([2] Lemma 15). *Let* $\mathbf{R}$ *be a* $k \times m$ *matrix chosen at random from* $\{-1, 1\}^{k \times m}$. *Then with overwhelming probability,* $s_1(\mathbf{R}) \leq 12 \cdot \sqrt{k + m}$.

Lemma 4 ([4] Lemma 3.5). *Let* q, n, m *be positive integers with* $q \geq 2$ *and* $m \geq 6n \lg q$. *There is a probabilistic polynomial-time algorithm* TrapGen(q, n, m) *that outputs a pair* $(\mathbf{A}, \mathbf{T}) \in \mathbb{Z}_q^{n \times m} \times \mathbb{Z}^{m \times m}$ *such that* $\mathbf{A}$ *is statistically close to uniform in* $\mathbb{Z}_q^{n \times m}$ *and* $\mathbf{T}$ *is a basis for* $\Lambda^\perp(\mathbf{A})$, *satisfying* $\|\mathbf{T}\|_\infty \leq O(n \lg q)$ *and* $\|\widetilde{\mathbf{T}}\| \leq O(\sqrt{n \lg q})$ *(Alwen and Peikert assert that the constant hidden in the first* $O(\cdot)$ *is no more than 20).*

Lemma 5 ([2] Theorem 17). *Let* $q > 2, m > n, \mathbf{A}, \mathbf{B} \in \mathbb{Z}_q^{n \times m}, \mathbf{T}_\mathbf{A}$ *be a basis of* $\Lambda^\perp(\mathbf{A})$, *and* $\sigma \geq \|\widetilde{\mathbf{T}_\mathbf{A}}\| \cdot \omega(\sqrt{\log m})$. *There exists an efficient randomized algorithm* SampleLeft *that, takes as inputs* $\mathbf{A}, \mathbf{B}, \mathbf{T}_\mathbf{A}, \sigma$, *and outputs a basis* $\mathbf{S}$ *of* $\Lambda^\perp(\mathbf{U})$ *for* $\mathbf{U} = [\mathbf{A}|\mathbf{B}]$ *with* $\|\mathbf{S}\| \leq O(\sigma \cdot m)$ *whose distribution depends on* $\mathbf{U}, \sigma$.

Lemma 6 ([2] Theorem 18). *Let* $q > 2, m > n, \mathbf{A}, \mathbf{B} \in \mathbb{Z}_q^{n \times m}, \mathbf{B}$ *be full rank,* $\mathbf{R} \in \{-1, 1\}^{m \times m}, \mathbf{T}_\mathbf{B}$ *be a basis of* $\Lambda^\perp(\mathbf{B})$, *and* $\sigma \geq \|\widetilde{\mathbf{T}_\mathbf{B}}\| \cdot s_1(\mathbf{R}) \cdot \omega(\sqrt{\log m})$. *There exists an efficient randomized algorithm* SampleRight *that, takes as inputs* $\mathbf{A}, \mathbf{R}, \mathbf{B}, \mathbf{T}_\mathbf{B}, \sigma$, *and outputs a basis* $\mathbf{S}$ *of* $\Lambda^\perp(\mathbf{U})$ *for* $\mathbf{U} = [\mathbf{A}|\mathbf{A}\mathbf{R} + \mathbf{B}]$ *with* $\|\mathbf{S}\| \leq O(\sigma \cdot m)$ *whose distribution depends on* $\mathbf{U}, \sigma$. *Note that this algorithm still works if we replace* $\mathbf{B}$ *with* $k\mathbf{B}$ *or* $\mathbf{C}\mathbf{B}$, *where* $k \in \mathbb{Z}_q$ *is coprime with* q *and* $\mathbf{C} \in \mathbb{Z}_q^{n \times n}$ *is full-rank.*

We consider any auxiliary input $f(x)$ from which it is hard to recover the input x. We say that a function f is ϵ-hard-to-invert with respect to a distribution $\mathcal{D}$, if for every efficient algorithm $\mathcal{A}$ it holds that $\Pr[\mathcal{A}(f(x)) = x] \leq \epsilon$ over the choice of $x \leftarrow \mathcal{D}$ and the internal coin tosses of $\mathcal{A}$. We describe a useful statement as follow which is crucial to our constructions.

Lemma 7 ([15] Theorem 5). *Let* $k \lg t > \lg q + \omega(\lg \lambda), t = poly(\lambda)$. *Let* $\mathcal{D}$ *be any distribution over* $\mathbb{Z}_t^n$ *and* $f : \mathbb{Z}_t^n \to \{0, 1\}^*$ *be any (possibly randomized) function that is* $2^{-k \lg t}$*-hard-to-invert with respect to* $\mathcal{D}$. *For any super-polynomial* $q = q(\lambda)$, *and any* $m = poly(n)$, *any* $\alpha, \beta \in (0, 1)$ *such that* $\alpha/\beta = negl(\lambda)$.

$$(\mathbf{A}, \mathbf{A}^t\mathbf{s} + \mathbf{e}, f(\mathbf{s})) \approx (\mathbf{A}, \mathbf{u}, f(\mathbf{s})),$$

where $\mathbf{A} \leftarrow \mathbb{Z}_q^{n \times m}$, $\mathbf{s} \leftarrow \mathcal{D} \subseteq \mathbb{Z}_t^n$ and $\mathbf{u} \leftarrow \mathbb{Z}_q^m$ are uniformly random and $\mathbf{e} \leftarrow \mathcal{D}_{\mathbb{Z},\beta q}^m$. Assuming the $\mathrm{LWE}_{q,d,m,\alpha}$ assumption, where $d \triangleq \frac{k \lg t - \omega(\lg \lambda)}{\lg q}$.

For the case of simplicity, we denote the $\mathbf{Adv}_{LWE_{q,n,m,\beta,f}}(\lambda)$ as the advantage of any efficient distinguisher of the above two distribution in Lemma 7. According to Lemma 7, we know that $\mathbf{Adv}_{LWE_{q,n,m,\beta,f}}(\lambda)$ is negligible in λ. Assuming the $\mathrm{LWE}_{q,d,m,\alpha}$ assumption, where $d \triangleq \frac{k \lg t - \omega(\lg \lambda)}{\lg q}$.

2.2 Security Definition

In this section, we describe the security notions introduced in [11]. Brakerski and Segev [11] formalized three security notions with respect to auxiliary inputs, and proved that all these three are equivalent. Brakerski and Segev [11] also showed that for the case of blockwise-hard-to-invert (see [11] for a definition of blockwise-hard-to-invert function) auxiliary inputs, encrypting a single message is equivalent to encrypting multiple messages. For the case of simplicity, in this paper, we only consider the case of a single message. In the single message case, hard-to-invert function and the blockwise-hard-to-invert function are equivalent. Furthermore, we slightly extend the notion in [11]. We require the ciphertext is indistinguishable from uniformly random elements in the ciphertext space. This property implies the strong PRIV1-IND notion defined in [11] and recipient anonymity.

A deterministic public key encryption scheme consists of three algorithms: (KeyGen, Enc, Dec). The probabilistic KeyGen algorithm produces a secret key and a corresponding public key. The deterministic Enc algorithm uses the public key to map plaintexts into ciphertexts. The deterministic Dec algorithm uses the secret key to recover plaintexts from ciphertexts.

Definition 1. *A deterministic public key encryption scheme* D-PKE=(KeyGen, Enc,Dec) *is PRIV1-INDr-secure with respect to ϵ-hard-to-invert auxiliary inputs if for any probabilistic polynomial-time algorithm $\mathcal{A}$, for any efficiently sampleable distributions $\mathcal{M}$, and any efficiently computable $\mathcal{F} = \{f\}$ that is ϵ-hard-to-invert with respect to $\mathcal{M}$ such that the advantage of $\mathcal{A}$ in the following game is negligible.*

$$\mathbf{Adv}_{\mathrm{D\text{-}PKE},\mathcal{A},\mathcal{F}}^{PRIV1\text{-}INDr}(\lambda) = \Big| \Pr[(pk, sk) \leftarrow \mathrm{KeyGen}(\lambda); b \leftarrow \{0,1\}; m \leftarrow \mathcal{M}; f \leftarrow \mathcal{F};$$

$$c_0^* = \mathrm{Enc}(pk, m); c_1^* \leftarrow \mathcal{C}; b' \leftarrow \mathcal{A}(pk, c_b^*, f(m)) : b = b'] - 1/2 \Big|.$$

Where $\mathcal{C}$ is the ciphertext space. The probability is taken over the choices of $m \leftarrow \mathcal{M}$, $(pk, sk) \leftarrow \mathrm{KeyGen}(\lambda)$, and over the internal coin tosses of $\mathcal{A}$.

The multi-user setting of deterministic public key encryption is a straightforward extension of the above definition. Namely, for any efficient adversary $\mathcal{A}$, given polynomial many encryptions of the related messages under multiple public keys and auxiliary information of these message, can not distinguish them from uniformly random elements in the ciphertext space with the same auxiliary information.

A deterministic identity-based public key encryption consists of four algorithms: (IBE.Setup, IBE.KGen, IBE.Enc, IBE.Dec). The probabilistic IBE.Setup algorithm generates public parameters, denoted by PP, and a master key MSK. The possibly probabilistic IBE.KGen algorithm uses the master key to extract a private key sk_{id} corresponding to a given identity id. The deterministic IBE.Enc algorithm encrypts messages for a given identity. The deterministic IBE.Dec algorithm decrypts ciphertexts using the private key.

Definition 2. *A deterministic identity-based public key encryption scheme D-IBE=(IBE.Setup, IBE.KGen, IBE.Enc, IBE.Dec) is PRIV1-ID-INDr-secure with respect to ϵ-hard-to-invert auxiliary inputs if for any probabilistic polynomial-time algorithm $\mathcal{A}$, for any efficiently sampleable distribution $\mathcal{M}$, and any efficiently computable $\mathcal{F} = \{f\}$ that is ϵ-hard-to-invert with respect to $\mathcal{M}$, such that the advantage of $\mathcal{A}$ in the following game is negligible.*

$$\mathbf{Adv}_{\text{D-IBE},\mathcal{A},\mathcal{F}}^{PRIV1\text{-}ID\text{-}INDr}(\lambda) = \Big| \Pr[(PP, MSK) \leftarrow \text{IBE.Setup}(\lambda);$$

$$id^* \leftarrow \mathcal{A}^{\text{IBE.KGen}(\cdot)}(PP); b \leftarrow \{0,1\}; m \leftarrow \mathcal{M}; f \leftarrow \mathcal{F}; c_0^* = \text{IBE.Enc}(PP, id^*, m);$$

$$c_1^* \leftarrow \mathcal{C}; b' \leftarrow \mathcal{A}^{\text{IBE.KGen}(\cdot)}(PP, c_b^*, f(m)) : b = b'] - 1/2 \Big|.$$

Where $\mathcal{C}$ is the ciphertext space, and oracle IBE.KGen$(\cdot)$ on input id generates a private key sk_{id} for the identity id with the restriction that $\mathcal{A}$ is not allowed to query id^*. The probability is taken over the choices of $m \leftarrow \mathcal{M}$, $(PP, MSK) \leftarrow \text{IBE.Setup}(\lambda)$, $sk_{id} \leftarrow \text{IBE.KGen}(PP, id, MSK)$, and over the internal coin tosses of $\mathcal{A}$.

3   The D-PKE Scheme

In this section, we propose a deterministic public key encryption scheme in the auxiliary-input setting. Before going to the concrete scheme, we first give a useful lemma, i.e. a trapdoor to invert the rounding function.

Lemma 8. *Let p, q, n, m be positive integers with $q \geq p \geq 2$. Let $\mathbf{A} \in \mathbb{Z}_q^{n \times m}$ be full-rank, and $\mathbf{T}$ be a basis of $\Lambda^\perp(\mathbf{A})$ with $\|\mathbf{T}\|_\infty < p/m$. Given $\mathbf{c} = \lfloor \mathbf{A}^t \mathbf{x} \rceil_p$, where $\mathbf{x} \in \mathbb{Z}_t^n$ with $t \leq q$, there is a polynomial-time algorithm Invert$(\mathbf{c}, \mathbf{A}, \mathbf{T})$ that outputs $\mathbf{x}$.[2]*

Proof. Given $\mathbf{c} = \lfloor \mathbf{A}^t \mathbf{x} \rceil_p$, rewrite it into $\mathbf{c} = (p/q)\mathbf{A}^t\mathbf{x} + \mathbf{e} + p\mathbf{v}$, where $\mathbf{e} \in \mathbb{R}^m$ is an "error" vector with $\|\mathbf{e}\|_\infty \leq 1/2$, and $\mathbf{v} \in \mathbb{Z}^m$. Then compute $\mathbf{T}^t\mathbf{c} = (p/q)(\mathbf{AT})^t\mathbf{x} + \mathbf{T}^t\mathbf{e} + p\mathbf{T}^t\mathbf{v}$. Since $\mathbf{T}$ is a basis of $\Lambda^\perp(\mathbf{A})$, we have

$$\mathbf{T}^t\mathbf{c} = p\mathbf{v}' + \mathbf{T}^t\mathbf{e} + p\mathbf{T}^t\mathbf{v} = \mathbf{T}^t\mathbf{e} + p\mathbf{w},$$

---

[2] The strong trapdoor presented in [17] can be used here. However, we have to sample a "short" basis first, and we do not know how to "directly" use the strong trapdoor.

for some $\mathbf{v}', \mathbf{w} \in \mathbb{Z}^m$. Since $\mathbf{T}^t\mathbf{c}$ and $p\mathbf{w}$ are integer vectors, then $\mathbf{T}^t\mathbf{e}$ is an integer vector as well. Therefore, $\mathbf{T}^t\mathbf{c} = \mathbf{T}^t\mathbf{e} \mod p$. By the hypothesis of $\mathbf{T}$, we know $\|\mathbf{T}^t\mathbf{e}\|_\infty \leq 1/2 \cdot m \cdot \|\mathbf{T}\|_\infty < p/2$. Then we get that $\mathbf{T}^t\mathbf{e} \mod p = \mathbf{T}^t\mathbf{e}$, and obtain $\mathbf{e}$, since $\mathbf{T}$ is invertible in $\mathbb{R}$. We next compute $(q/p)(\mathbf{c} - \mathbf{e}) = \mathbf{A}^t\mathbf{x} + q\mathbf{v}$, then, $(q/p)(\mathbf{c} - \mathbf{e}) \mod q = \mathbf{A}^t\mathbf{x}$. Since $\mathbf{A}$ is full-rank modulo q, $\mathbf{x}$ can be recovered by Gaussian elimination.   □

The D-PKE scheme is described as follows. Set the parameters p, q, n, m as specified in Sec. 3.1.

- **Key Generation.** Algorithm $\mathsf{KeyGen}(\lambda)$ takes as input a security parameter λ. It uses the algorithm from Lemma 4 to generate a (nearly) uniform matrix and a trapdoor, i.e., $(\mathbf{A}, \mathbf{T}) \leftarrow \mathsf{TrapGen}(q, n, m)$. It outputs $pk = \mathbf{A} \in \mathbb{Z}_q^{n \times m}$ and $sk = \mathbf{T} \in \mathbb{Z}^{m \times m}$.

- **Encryption.** Algorithm $\mathsf{Enc}(pk, \mathbf{m})$ takes as input a public key $pk = \mathbf{A}$ and a message $\mathbf{m} \in \mathbb{Z}_t^n (\subset \mathbb{Z}_q^n)$. It outputs a ciphertext $\mathbf{c} = \lfloor \mathbf{A}^t\mathbf{m} \rceil_p \in \mathbb{Z}_p^m$.

- **Decryption.** Algorithm $\mathsf{Dec}(sk, \mathbf{c})$ takes as input a secret key $sk = \mathbf{T}$ and a ciphertext $\mathbf{c} \in \mathbb{Z}_p^m$. It first computes $\mathbf{m} \leftarrow \mathsf{Invert}(\mathbf{c}, \mathbf{A}, \mathbf{T})$. Then, if $\mathbf{m} \in \mathbb{Z}_t^n$ it outputs $\mathbf{m}$, and otherwise it outputs $\perp$.

3.1 Correctness and Parameters

For the system to work correctly, we need to ensure that: (1) $\mathsf{TrapGen}$ can operate (i.e. $m \geq 6n \lg q$); (2) Lemma 8 holds; (3) Lemma 7 holds. To satisfy these requirements we set the parameters (q, p, m, n) as follows:

$$n = \lambda, \quad q = \text{the prime nearest to } 2^{n^\delta}, \quad m = \lceil 6n^{1+\delta} \rceil, \quad p = \lceil 120n^{2+2\delta} \rceil,$$

where δ is constant between 0 and 1. Since $\mathbf{A}$ is uniformly random in $\mathbb{Z}_q^{n \times m}$ and $m \geq 6n^{1+\delta}$, with overwhelming probability this matrix will have rank n. According to the Lemma 7 and the Theorem 1 which we will give a proof in the next subsection. We obtain that the security of this scheme is based on the $\mathrm{LWE}_{q,d,m,\alpha}$, where $d \triangleq \frac{k \lg t - \omega(\lg \lambda)}{\lg q}$, and $1/\alpha = 2^{n^{\delta'}}$ $(0 < \delta' < \delta)$. Given the state of art algorithms, this problem is sub-exponentially hard. Furthermore, we can choose $k \lg t$ to be sub-linear. Therefore, our auxiliary inputs are sub-exponentially hard to invert.

The public key size, private key size, ciphertext size and ciphertext expansion factor in our scheme are $O(n^{2+2\delta})$, $O(n^{3+3\delta})$, $O(n^{1+\delta} \lg n)$, and $O(n^\delta \lg n / \lg t)$ respectively. To optimize the ciphertext expansion factor, we can choose $t = n$, which makes the ciphertext expansion factor to be $O(n^\delta)$. In [11], these values are $n^2|\mathbb{G}|$, n^3, $n|\mathbb{G}|$ and $|\mathbb{G}|$ respectively,[3] where $|\mathbb{G}|$ denotes the length of elements in group $\mathbb{G}$ with order 2^n, It's easy to see that $|\mathbb{G}| \geq n$.

---

[3] One can encrypt large messages (other that bits) to reduce the ciphertext expansion factor, but in this case, it needs much more exponent arithmetics to decrypt.

3.2 Security of the D-PKE Scheme

Theorem 1. *For any $k > (\lg q + \omega(\lg \lambda))/\lg t$, $t = poly(\lambda) \leq q$. The D-PKE scheme is PRIV1-INDr-secure with respect to $2^{-k \lg t}$-hard-to-invert auxiliary inputs. If Lemma 7 holds, where $1/\beta \geq m \cdot p \cdot n^{\omega(1)}$, $q = n^{\omega(1)}$, and $p = poly(\lambda)$.*

Proof. For any distribution $\mathcal{M}$ over $\mathbb{Z}_t^n$, let $\mathcal{F} = \{f\}$ be $2^{-k \lg t}$-hard-to-invert with respect to distribution $\mathcal{M}$. To prove this theorem, we define a series of games, and give a reduction from the Lemma 7 with respect to distribution $\mathcal{M}$.

Game G_0. This game is the original PRIV1-INDr game with adversary $\mathcal{A}$. By $\mathbf{X}_i$, we denote the event $b = b'$ in Game G_i. By definition, $|\Pr[\mathbf{X}_0] - 1/2| = \mathbf{Adv}_{\text{D-PKE},\mathcal{A},\mathcal{F}}^{PRIV1\text{-}INDr}(\lambda)$.

Game G_1. This game is identical to game G_0, except that the challenger choose $\mathbf{A}$ uniformly at random in $\mathbb{Z}_q^{n \times m}$, and uses $\mathbf{A}$ as the public key given to $\mathcal{A}$. According to Lemma 4, it follows that $|\Pr[\mathbf{X}_1] - \Pr[\mathbf{X}_0]| \leq \text{negl}(\lambda)$, for unbounded adversary $\mathcal{A}$.

Game G_2. This game is identical to game G_1, except the way to generate challenge ciphertext. The challenger samples $\mathbf{m} \leftarrow \mathcal{M}$, and samples $\mathbf{e} \leftarrow \mathcal{D}_{\mathbb{Z},\beta q}^m$. Let $\mathbf{b} = \mathbf{A}^t \mathbf{m} + \mathbf{e} \mod q$. The challenger sets $\mathbf{c}_0^* = \lfloor \mathbf{b} \rceil_p$, $\mathbf{c}_1^*$ as in game G_1, i.e. chosen at random in $\mathbb{Z}_p^m$. It outputs $(\mathbf{A}, \mathbf{c}_b^*, f(\mathbf{m}))$ to $\mathcal{A}$, but with one exception: we define a "bad event" Bad_2 to be

$$\text{Bad}_2 \triangleq \lfloor \mathbf{b} + [-B, B]^m \rceil_p \neq \{\lfloor \mathbf{b} \rceil_p\},$$

where $B = \beta q \sqrt{n}$. If Bad_2 occurs on any of $\mathbf{b}$, the challenger immediately abort the game.

If Bad_2 does not occur for the pair $(\mathbf{A}, \mathbf{b})$, then we have $\lfloor \mathbf{b} \rceil_p = \lfloor \mathbf{A}^t \mathbf{m} + \mathbf{e} \rceil_p = \lfloor \mathbf{A}^t \mathbf{m} \rceil_p$ with overwhelming probability over the choice of $\mathbf{e} \leftarrow \mathcal{D}_{\mathbb{Z},\beta q}^m$, because $\|\mathbf{e}\|_\infty \leq \beta q \sqrt{n}$ with overwhelming probability according to Lemma 1. It follows that for any attacker $\mathcal{A}$,

$$|\Pr[\mathbf{X}_2] - \Pr[\mathbf{X}_1]| \leq \Pr[\text{Bad}_2] + \text{negl}(\lambda).$$

We do not directly bound the probability of Bad_2 occurring in G_2, instead deferring it to the analysis of the next game, where we can show that it is indeed negligible.

Game G_3. In this game, the challenger chooses $\mathbf{b} \in \mathbb{Z}_q^m$ uniformly at random, and samples $\mathbf{m} \leftarrow \mathcal{M}$. It then sets $\mathbf{c}_0^* = \lfloor \mathbf{b} \rceil_p$, and chooses $\mathbf{c}_1^*$ uniformly at random in $\mathbb{Z}_p^m$. The challenger gives $(\mathbf{A}, \mathbf{c}_b^*, f(\mathbf{m}))$ to $\mathcal{A}$, subject to the same "bad event" Bad_3 and abort condition as described in the game G_2 above. Under Lemma 7, and by the fact "bad event" can be tested efficiently given $\mathbf{b}$,[4]

---

[4] Given $\mathbf{b} = (b_1, ..., b_m)$, for each b_i, one can compute $\lfloor b_i - B \rceil_p$ and $\lfloor b_i + B \rceil_p$ and tests these two values equal to $\lfloor b_i \rceil_p$ or not.

a straightforward reduction implies that $|\Pr[\mathbf{X}_3] - \Pr[\mathbf{X}_2]| \leq \mathrm{negl}(\lambda)$ for any efficient attacker $\mathcal{A}$. For the same reason, it also follows that

$$\left|\Pr[\mathsf{Bad}_3] - \Pr[\mathsf{Bad}_2]\right| \leq \mathrm{negl}(\lambda).$$

Now for each uniform $\mathbf{b}$, $\Pr[\mathsf{Bad}_3] \leq m(2B+1)p/q = \mathrm{negl}(\lambda)$, by assumption on q and β. It follows that

$$\Pr[\mathsf{Bad}_2] \leq \mathrm{negl}(\lambda) \quad \Rightarrow \quad |\Pr[\mathbf{X}_2] - \Pr[\mathbf{X}_1]| \leq \mathrm{negl}(\lambda).$$

Game G_4. This game is similar to game G_3, with $\mathbf{b}$ being chosen uniformly at random, $\mathbf{m}$ being sampled from $\mathcal{M}$, and Bad_4 being defined similarly. However, in this game the challenger always returns $(\mathbf{A}, \mathbf{c}_b^*, f(\mathbf{m}))$ to $\mathcal{A}$, even when Bad_4 occurs. By the analysis above, we have that for any adversary $\mathcal{A}$,

$$|\Pr[\mathbf{X}_4] - \Pr[\mathbf{X}_3]| \leq \Pr[\mathsf{Bad}_4] = \Pr[\mathsf{Bad}_3] \leq \mathrm{negl}(\lambda).$$

Since $f(\mathbf{m})$ is independent of $\mathbf{b}$ and the statistical distance between $U(\mathbb{Z}_q^{n \times m}, \mathbb{Z}_p^m)$ and $U(\mathbb{Z}_q^{n \times m}) \times \lfloor U(\mathbb{Z}_q^m) \rceil_p$ is at most $mp/q = \mathrm{negl}(\lambda)$ by assumption on q, so we have $|\Pr[\mathbf{X}_4] - 1/2| = \mathrm{negl}(\lambda)$ for any efficient adversary $\mathcal{A}$.

Finally, by the triangle inequality, we have $|\Pr[\mathbf{X}_0] - 1/2| \leq \mathrm{negl}(\lambda)$ for any efficient adversary $\mathcal{A}$, which completes the proof. $\square$

The Multi-user Setting. It's easy to extend the above theorem to multi-user setting where linear related messages $\mathbf{m}_1, ..., \mathbf{m}_k$ are encrypted under any polynomial number of public keys $\mathbf{A}_1, ..., \mathbf{A}_k$. Linear related messages mean that there exist invertible and efficiently computable matrices $\mathbf{V}_2, .., \mathbf{V}_k \subseteq \mathbb{Z}_q^{n \times n}$ and vectors $\mathbf{w}_2, ..., \mathbf{w}_k \in \mathbb{Z}_q^n$, such that $\mathbf{m}_i = \mathbf{V}_i \mathbf{m}_1 + \mathbf{w}_i$ $(2 \leq i \leq k)$. In this case, the joint distribution of ciphertexts is $(\lfloor \mathbf{A}_1^t \mathbf{m}_1 \rceil_p, ..., \lfloor \mathbf{A}_k^t \mathbf{m}_k \rceil_p)$. I.e., $(\lfloor \mathbf{A}_1^t \mathbf{m}_1 \rceil_p, \lfloor \mathbf{A}_2^t \mathbf{V}_2 \mathbf{m}_1 + \mathbf{A}_2^t \mathbf{w}_2 \rceil_p, ..., \lfloor \mathbf{A}_k^t \mathbf{V}_k \mathbf{m}_1 + \mathbf{A}_k^t \mathbf{w}_k \rceil_p)$. Since $\mathbf{V}_i$ is invertible and $\mathbf{A}_i$ is uniformly random for $2 \leq i \leq k$, then $\mathbf{A}_i \mathbf{V}_i$ is uniformly random. Because Lemma 7 holds for any $m = poly(n)$, $\mathbf{V}_i, \mathbf{w}_i$ are efficient computable, using the technique in the above proof, we can obtain that our D-PKE scheme is secure in the multi-user for linear related messages. Due to the space limitation, we omit the proof here.

4   The D-IBE Scheme

In this section, we describe our D-IBE scheme. Set the parameters p, q, n, m, σ as specified in Sec. 4.1. We treat an identity id as a non-zero sequence of ℓ bits, i.e, $id = (b_1, ..., b_\ell) \in \{0, 1\}^\ell \backslash \{0^\ell\}$.

- **Setup.** Algorithm $\mathtt{IBE.Setup}(\lambda)$ takes as input a security parameter λ. It uses the algorithm from Lemma 4 to generate $(\mathbf{A}_0, \mathbf{T}) \leftarrow \mathtt{TrapGen}(q, n, m)$. Select $\ell + 1$ uniformly random matrices $\mathbf{A}_1, ..., \mathbf{A}_\ell, \mathbf{B}$ in $\mathbb{Z}_q^{n \times m}$. It outputs $PP = (\mathbf{A}_0, \mathbf{A}_1, ..., \mathbf{A}_\ell, \mathbf{B})$, $MSK = \mathbf{T}$.

- **Key Generation.** Algorithm IBE.KGen(PP, MSK, id) takes as input public parameters PP, a master secret key MSK, and an identity $id \in \{0,1\}^{\ell}$. It first computes $\mathbf{F}_{id} = [\mathbf{A}_0 | \sum_{i=1}^{\ell} b_i \mathbf{A}_i + \mathbf{B}]$, then it uses the algorithm in Lemma 5 to generate a short basis of $\Lambda^{\perp}(\mathbf{F}_{id})$. I.e., $\mathbf{T}_{\mathbf{F}_{id}} \leftarrow \text{SampleLeft}(\mathbf{A}_0, \sum_{i=1}^{\ell} b_i \mathbf{A}_i + \mathbf{B}, \mathbf{T}, \sigma)$. It outputs $sk_{id} = \mathbf{T}_{\mathbf{F}_{id}}$.

- **Encryption.** Algorithm IBE.Enc($id, \mathbf{m}$) takes as input public parameters PP, an identity $id \in \{0,1\}^{\ell}$, and a message $\mathbf{m} \leftarrow \mathbb{Z}_t^n$. It first computes $\mathbf{F}_{id} = [\mathbf{A}_0 | \sum_{i=1}^{\ell} b_i \mathbf{A}_i + \mathbf{B}]$, then let $\mathbf{c} = \lfloor \mathbf{F}_{id}^t \mathbf{m} \rceil_p$. It outputs $\mathbf{c}$.

- **Decryption.** Algorithm IBE.Dec($PP, id, sk_{id}, \mathbf{c}$) takes as input public parameters PP, an identity id, a secret key sk_{id} and a ciphertext $\mathbf{c} \in \mathbb{Z}_p^{2m}$. It first computes $\mathbf{m} \leftarrow \text{Invert}(\mathbf{c}, \mathbf{F}_{id}, sk_{id})$. Then, if $\mathbf{m} \in \mathbb{Z}_t^n$ it outputs $\mathbf{m}$, and otherwise it outputs $\perp$.

4.1 Correctness of Parameters

To ensure the correctness condition, we require: (1) TrapGen can operate (i.e. $m \geq 6n \lg q$); (2) Lemma 8 holds; (3) Lemma 7 holds; (4) σ is sufficiently large for SampleLeft and SampleRight. To satisfy all these requirements, we set the parameters (q, p, m, n, σ) as follows:

$$n = \lambda, q = \text{ the prime nearest to } 2^{n^{\delta}}, m = \lceil 6n^{1+\delta} \rceil, \sigma = 6\ell n^{1.5+\delta}, p = \lceil 3\ell n^{3.5+3\delta} \rceil,$$

where δ is constant between 0 and 1. According to Lemma 7 and Theorem 2 which we will give a proof in the next subsection. We obtain an adaptively secure scheme whose security is based on the $\text{LWE}_{q,d,m,\alpha}$, where $d \triangleq \frac{k \lg t - \omega(\lg \lambda)}{\lg q}$, and $1/\alpha = 2^{n^{\delta'}}$ ($0 < \delta' < \delta$). Given the state of art algorithms, this problem is sub-exponentially hard. Furthermore, we can choose $k \lg t$ to be sub-linear. Therefore, our auxiliary inputs are sub-exponentially hard to invert.

The public key size, private key size, ciphertext size and ciphertext expansion factor in our scheme are $O(3(\ell + 2)n^{2+2\delta})$, $O(n^{3+3\delta})$, $O(2n^{1+\delta} \lg \ell n)$, and $O(n^{\delta} \lg \ell n / \lg t)$ respectively. To optimize the ciphertext expansion factor, we can choose $t = \ell n$, which makes the ciphertext expansion factor to be $O(n^{\delta})$.

Remark. We also give a more efficient selectively secure D-IBE, the security definition and the concrete construction are given in the full version.

4.2 Security of D-IBE

Theorem 2. *For any $k > (\lg q + \omega(\lg \lambda))/\lg t$, $t = poly(\lambda)$, prime integer $q = n^{\omega(1)}$, and $p = poly(\lambda)$. Assume an adversary $\mathcal{A}$ on D-IBE's PRIV1-ID-INDr security with respect to $2^{-k \lg t}$-hard-to-invert auxiliary inputs, makes at most $Q(\lambda)$ secret key queries. Then for every polynomial $S(\lambda)$ and $1/\beta \geq \ell m^2 \cdot p \cdot n^{\omega(1)}$ we have*

$$\mathbf{Adv}_{D\text{-}IBE,\mathcal{A},\mathcal{F}}^{PRIV1\text{-}ID\text{-}INDr}(\lambda) \leq \frac{2\mathbf{Adv}_{LWE_{q,n,m,\beta,f}}(\lambda)}{\Delta} + \frac{1}{S(\lambda)} + negl(\lambda)$$

where $\Delta = \frac{1}{8(\ell+1)Q}$, and f is any $2^{-k\lg t}$-hard-to-invert function.

According to Lemma 7 and because S is arbitrary, we obtain:

Corollary 1. *Let $q = n^{\omega(1)}$ be a prime integer, $p = poly(\lambda)$, $1/\beta \geq \ell m^2 \cdot p \cdot n^{\omega(1)}$, and $\alpha/\beta = negl(\lambda)$. Assuming $LWE_{q,d,m,\alpha}$ assumption with $d \triangleq \frac{k\lg t - \omega(\lg \lambda)}{\lg q}$, then for any $k > (\lg q + \omega(\lg \lambda))/\lg t$, $t = poly(\lambda)$, the D-IBE scheme is PRIV1-ID-INDr-secure with respect to $2^{-k\lg t}$-hard-to-invert auxiliary inputs.*

Proof. For any distribution $\mathcal{M}$ over $\mathbb{Z}_t^n$, let $\mathcal{F} = \{f\}$ be $2^{-k\lg t}$-hard-to-invert with respect to distribution $\mathcal{M}$. To prove this theorem, we define a series of games, and give a reduction from Lemma 7 with respect to distribution $\mathcal{M}$.

Game G_0. This game is the original PRIV1-ID-INDr game with adversary $\mathcal{A}$. We assume without loss of generality that $\mathcal{A}$ always makes exactly $Q = Q(\lambda)$ secret key queries. We denote these queries by id_j for $1 \leq j \leq Q$, and the challenge identity chosen by $\mathcal{A}$ as id^*. By $\mathbf{X}_i$, we denote the event $b = b'$ in Game G_i. By definition, $|\Pr[\mathbf{X}_0] - 1/2| = \mathbf{Adv}_{D\text{-}IBE,\mathcal{A},\mathcal{F}}^{PRIV1\text{-}ID\text{-}INDr}(\lambda)$. In the following, Let $\mathcal{ID}^Q = (id^*, id_1, ..., id_Q)$.

Game G_1. In this game, the challenger slightly changes the way to generate the matrices $\mathbf{A}_i, i \in [\ell]$ and $\mathbf{B}$. At the setup phase, the challenger first sets an integer $M = 4Q$, and chooses an integer k uniformly at random in between 0 and ℓ. It then chooses a random $\ell + 1$-length vector, $\mathbf{x} = (x', x_1, ..., x_\ell)$, where x' is chosen uniformly at random in $\{1, ..., M\}$ and x_i for $i \in [\ell]$ are chosen uniformly at random in $\mathbb{Z}_M$. We define $F(id) = (q - kM) + x' + \sum_{i=1}^{\ell} b_i x_i$, note that $-kM + x' \neq 0$. And we define a binary function $K(id)$ as

$$K(id) = \begin{cases} 0 & \text{if } x' + \sum_{i=1}^{\ell} b_i x_i = 0 \mod M \\ 1 & \text{otherwise.} \end{cases}$$

Next it chooses matrices $\mathbf{B}'$ uniformly at random in $\mathbb{Z}_q^{n \times m}$, and chooses $\mathbf{R}_i \leftarrow \{-1, 1\}^{m \times m}$ for $i \in [\ell]$. The challenger sets $\mathbf{B} = (q - kM + x')\mathbf{B}' \mod q$, and constructs $\mathbf{A}_i$ for $i \in [\ell]$ as $\mathbf{A}_i = \mathbf{A}_0\mathbf{R}_i + x_i\mathbf{B}'$. Since $\mathbf{B}'$ is uniform, and q is prime, then $\mathbf{B}$ is uniform (since $-kM + x' \mod q \neq 0$ for sufficiently large q). By Lemma 4, $\mathbf{A}_0$ is uniform with overwhelming probability, then according to Lemma 2, $\mathbf{A}_i$ is statistically close to uniform. Therefore, we have $|\Pr[\mathbf{X}_1] - \Pr[\mathbf{X}_0]| \leq negl(\lambda)$. Note that, in G_1,

$$\mathbf{F}_{id} = [\mathbf{A}_0 | \mathbf{A}_0 \sum_{i=1}^{\ell} b_i \mathbf{R}_i + (q - kM + x' + \sum_{i=1}^{\ell} b_i x_i)\mathbf{B}']$$

$$= [\mathbf{A}_0 | \mathbf{A}_0 \sum_{i=1}^{\ell} b_i \mathbf{R}_i + F(id)\mathbf{B}'] \mod q$$

Furthermore, $F(id) = 0 \mod q$ implies $K(id) = 0$, since q is super-polynomial, and ℓ and M are polynomials, we can assume $q \gg \ell M$ for any reasonable values of q, ℓ and M.

Game G_2. In this game, after the adversary has terminated, the challenger throws an event Good_2 independently with probability $\Delta = \frac{1}{8(\ell+1)Q}$. The challenger aborts the experiment (and outputs a uniformly random bit) if $\neg\mathsf{Good}_2$ occurs. We get

$$\Pr[\mathbf{X}_2] - 1/2 = \Pr[\mathsf{Good}_2](\Pr[\mathbf{X}_1] - 1/2) = \Delta \cdot (\Pr[\mathbf{X}_1] - 1/2).$$

Game G_3. In this game, the challenger changes the abort policy. We define a function as

$$\tau(\mathbf{x}, \mathcal{ID}^Q) = \begin{cases} 0 & \text{if } (\wedge_{i=1}^Q K(id_i) = 1) \wedge x' + \sum_{i=1}^\ell b_i^* x_i = kM \\ 1 & \text{otherwise.} \end{cases}$$

Let E denote the event that $\tau(\mathbf{x}, \mathcal{ID}^Q)$ evaluates to 0 for a given choice of $\mathbf{x}$. According to the analysis in [23] (Claim 2), we know that $p_E = \Pr[E] \geq \Delta = \frac{1}{8(\ell+1)Q}$. Ideally, we would like to replace event Good_2 from game G_2 with event E. Unfortunately, E might not be independent of $\mathcal{A}$'s view, so we use artificial abort techniques. That is, given the identities in all $\mathcal{ID}^Q$, we approximate p_E by sufficiently often sampling values of $\mathbf{x}$. Hoeffding's inequality yields that with $\lceil \lambda S/\Delta \rceil$ samples, we can obtain an approximation $\hat{p_E} \geq \Delta$ of p_E that satisfies $\Pr[|p_E - \hat{p_E}| \geq \Delta/S] \leq 1/2^\lambda$. Now the challenger finally aborts if E does not occur. But even if E occurs (which might be with probability $p_E \geq \Delta$), the challenger artificially enforces an abort with probability $1 - \Delta/\hat{p_E}$. We call Good_3 be the event the challenger does not abort. We always have

$$\Pr[\mathsf{Good}_3] = 1 - \left((1 - p_E) + p_E(1 - \Delta/\hat{p_E})\right) = \Delta \cdot p_E/\hat{p_E}.$$

Hence, except with probability $1/2^\lambda$,

$$|\Pr[\mathsf{Good}_3] - \Pr[\mathsf{Good}_2]| = |\Delta - \Delta \cdot p_E/\hat{p_E}| = \Delta \cdot |(p_E - \hat{p_E})/\hat{p_E}| \leq \Delta \cdot \Delta/S\hat{p_E} \leq \Delta/S.$$

Since the above inequality holds for arbitrary $\mathcal{ID}^Q$ except with probability $1/2^\lambda$, we obtain that the statistical distance between the output of game G_2 and G_3 is bounded by $\Delta/S + 2^{-\lambda}$. Hence, $|\Pr[\mathbf{X}_3] - \Pr[\mathbf{X}_2]| \leq \Delta/S + 2^{-\lambda}$.

Game G_4. In this game, the challenger makes the following conceptual change regarding secret key queries and challenge ciphertext. Namely, upon receiving a secret key query for $id \in \mathcal{ID}^Q \backslash id^*$, the challenger immediately aborts (with uniform output) if $K(id) = 0$. Upon receiving the challenge identity id^*, the challenger immediately aborts (with uniform output) if $x' + \sum_{i=1}^\ell b_i^* x_i \neq kM$. This change is purely conceptual: since $K(id) = 0$, for $id \in \mathcal{ID}^Q \backslash id^*$, or $x' + \sum_{i=1}^\ell b_i^* x_i \neq kM$, event E cannot occur, so the Game G_4 would eventually abort as well. We get $\Pr[\mathbf{X}_4] = \Pr[\mathbf{X}_3]$.

Game G_5. In this game, the challenger changes the ways to generate $\mathbf{A}_0, \mathbf{B}'$ and to answer secret key queries. By the change from game G_4, we may assume that $K(id) = 1$ for all $id \in \mathcal{ID}^Q \backslash id^*$ and $x' + \sum_{i=1}^{\ell} b_i^* x_i = kM$ for id^*. This implies that $F(id) \neq 0 \mod q$ for all $id \in \mathcal{ID}^Q \backslash id^*$, and $F(id^*) = 0 \mod q$. The challenger chooses $\mathbf{A}_0$ uniformly at random in $\mathbb{Z}_q^{n \times m}$ and use Lemma 4 to generate $\mathbf{B}'$ with a trapdoor $(\mathbf{B}', \mathbf{T}_{\mathbf{B}'}) \leftarrow \mathtt{TrapGen}(q, n, m)$. From Lemma 4 we know that the distribution of $\mathbf{A}_0, \mathbf{B}'$ are statistically close. Upon receiving a secret query for id, the challenge use the algorithm $\mathbf{T}_{\mathbf{F}_{id}} \leftarrow \mathtt{SampleRight}(\mathbf{A}_0, \sum_{i=1}^{\ell} b_i \mathbf{R}_i, \mathbf{B}', \mathbf{T}_{\mathbf{B}'}, \sigma)$, this could be done, since $F(id) \neq 0 \mod q$. This results in the same distribution of secret keys as in Game G_4 with sufficiently large σ, up to negligible statistical distance. Thus $|\Pr[\mathbf{X}_5] - \Pr[\mathbf{X}_4]| \leq \mathrm{negl}(\lambda)$. Note that, in this case the matrix of the challenge ciphertext is as $\mathbf{F}_{id^*} = [\mathbf{A}_0 | \mathbf{A}_0 \mathbf{R}^*]$, where $\mathbf{R}^* = \sum_{i=1}^{\ell} b_i^* \mathbf{R}_i$.

Game G_6. In this game, the challenger changes the way to generate challenge ciphertext. The challenger samples $\mathbf{m} \leftarrow \mathcal{M}$, and sample error vector $\mathbf{e} \leftarrow \mathcal{D}_{\mathbb{Z}, \beta q}^m$. we denote $\mathbf{b} = \mathbf{A}_0^t \mathbf{m} + \mathbf{e} \mod q$. It sets $\hat{\mathbf{c}} = [\mathbf{b}^t | \mathbf{b}^t \mathbf{R}^*]^t$ and let $\mathbf{c}_0^* = \lfloor \hat{\mathbf{c}} \rceil_p$, $\mathbf{c}_1^*$ be as in the game G_5, i.e. chosen at random in $\mathbb{Z}_p^{2m}$. The challenger returns $(\mathbf{c}_b^*, f(\mathbf{m}))$ to $\mathcal{A}$, but with one exception: we define a "bad event" Bad_6 to be

$$\mathsf{Bad}_6 \triangleq \lfloor \hat{\mathbf{c}} + [-B, B]^{2m} \rceil_p \neq \{ \lfloor \hat{\mathbf{c}} \rceil_p \},$$

where $B = \ell \beta q \sqrt{nm}$. If Bad_6 occurs on any of $\hat{\mathbf{c}}$, the challenger immediately abort the game.

Since $(\mathbf{R}^*)^t \mathbf{b} = (\mathbf{A}_0 \mathbf{R}^*)^t \mathbf{m} + (\mathbf{R}^*)^t \mathbf{e}$, and $\mathbf{R}^* = \sum_{i=1}^{\ell} b_i^* \mathbf{R}_i$, where $\mathbf{R}_i \in \{-1, 1\}^{m \times m}$, we have $\|(\mathbf{R}^*)^t \mathbf{e}\|_\infty \leq \ell \beta q \sqrt{nm}$ with overwhelming probability, since $\mathbf{e} \leftarrow \mathcal{D}_{\mathbb{Z}, \beta q}^m$ according to Lemma 1. If Bad_6 does not occur for some $\hat{\mathbf{c}}$, then we have

$$\lfloor \hat{\mathbf{c}} \rceil_p = \begin{bmatrix} \lfloor \mathbf{A}_0^t \mathbf{m} + \mathbf{e} \rceil_p \\ \lfloor (\mathbf{A}_0 \mathbf{R}^*)^t \mathbf{m} + (\mathbf{R}^*)^t \mathbf{e} \rceil_p \end{bmatrix} = \begin{bmatrix} \lfloor \mathbf{A}_0^t \mathbf{m} \rceil_p \\ \lfloor (\mathbf{A}_0 \mathbf{R}^*)^t \mathbf{m} \rceil_p \end{bmatrix} = \lfloor \mathbf{F}_{id^*}^t \mathbf{m} \rceil_p.$$

It immediately follows that for any adversary $\mathcal{A}$

$$\Pr[\mathbf{X}_6] - \Pr[\mathbf{X}_5] \leq \Pr[\mathsf{Bad}_6] + \mathrm{negl}(\lambda).$$

We do not directly bound the probability of Bad_6 occurring in game G_6, instead deferring it to the analysis of the next game, where we can show that it is negligible.

Game G_7. In this game the only difference is that challenger chooses $\mathbf{b} \in \mathbb{Z}_q^m$ uniformly at random, and samples $\mathbf{m} \leftarrow \mathcal{M}$. To generate the challenge ciphertext, it sets $\hat{\mathbf{c}} = [\mathbf{b}^t | \mathbf{b}^t \mathbf{R}^*]^t$, and let $\mathbf{c}_0^* = \lfloor \hat{\mathbf{c}} \rceil_p$. It returns $(\mathbf{c}_b^*, f(\mathbf{m}))$ to $\mathcal{A}$, subject to the same "bad event" Bad_7 and abort condition as described in the game G_6 above. Under Lemma 7 and by the fact "bad event" can be tested efficiently given $\hat{\mathbf{c}}$, this implies that $|\Pr[\mathbf{X}_7] - \Pr[\mathbf{X}_6]| \leq \mathbf{Adv}_{\mathrm{LWE}_{q,n,m,\beta,f}}$ for any efficient attacker $\mathcal{A}$. For the same reason, it also follows that

$$\left| \Pr[\mathsf{Bad}_7] - \Pr[\mathsf{Bad}_6] \right| \leq \mathbf{Adv}_{\mathrm{LWE}_{q,n,m,\beta,f}}.$$

Let us consider the pair $(\mathbf{b}^t, \mathbf{b}^t \mathbf{R}^*)$, where $\mathbf{b} \in \mathbb{Z}_q^m$ is uniformly random, $\mathbf{R}^* = \sum_{i=1}^{\ell} b_i^* \mathbf{R}_i$ and $\mathbf{R}_i$'s are pairwise independently chosen from $\{-1, 1\}^m$ at random. Since $id^* \neq 0^\ell$, there exists j, such that $b_j^* = 1$. By Lemma 2 (when $n = 1$), we have that $(\mathbf{b}^t, \mathbf{b}^t \mathbf{R}_j)$ is statistically close to $U(\mathbb{Z}_q^{2m})$. Because $\mathbf{R}_i$'s are pairwise independent, we obtain that $(\mathbf{b}^t, \mathbf{b}^t \mathbf{R}^*)$ is statistically close to $U(\mathbb{Z}_q^{2m})$. This means that $\hat{\mathbf{c}}$ is statistically close to $U(\mathbb{Z}_q^{2m})$, therefore for each uniform $\hat{\mathbf{c}}$, $\Pr[\mathsf{Bad}_7] \leq 2m(2B+1)p/q = \mathrm{negl}(\lambda)$, by assumption on q and β. It follows that

$$\Pr[\mathsf{Bad}_6] \leq \mathbf{Adv}_{\mathrm{LWE}_{q,n,m,\beta,f}} + \mathrm{negl}(\lambda)$$
$$\Rightarrow |\Pr[\mathbf{X}_6] - \Pr[\mathbf{X}_5]| \leq \mathbf{Adv}_{\mathrm{LWE}_{q,n,m,\beta,f}} + \mathrm{negl}(\lambda).$$

Game G_8. This game is similar to game G_7, with $\mathbf{b} \in \mathbb{Z}_q^{2m}$ being chosen uniformly at random, $\mathbf{m}$ being sampled from $\mathcal{M}$, and Bad_8 being defined similarly. However, in this game the challenger always returns $(\mathbf{c}_b^*, f(\mathbf{m}))$ to $\mathcal{A}$, even when Bad_8 occurs. By the analysis above, we have that for any adversary $\mathcal{A}$,

$$|\Pr[\mathbf{X}_8] - \Pr[\mathbf{X}_7]| \leq \Pr[\mathsf{Bad}_7] = \Pr[\mathsf{Bad}_6] \leq \mathrm{negl}(\lambda).$$

According to the analysis in Game$_7$, we know $\hat{\mathbf{c}}$ is uniformly random, up to negligible statistical distance. Since $f(\mathbf{m})$ is independent of $\hat{\mathbf{c}}$ and the statistical distance between $U(\mathbb{Z}_p^{2m})$ and $\lfloor U(\mathbb{Z}_q^{2m}) \rceil_p$ is at most $2mp/q = \mathrm{negl}(\lambda)$ by assumption on q, so we have $\Pr[\mathbf{X}_8] - 1/2 \leq \mathrm{negl}(\lambda)$ for any efficient adversary $\mathcal{A}$.

Finally, by the triangle inequality, we obtain the result of Theorem 2.   □

Acknowledgements. Xiang Xie would like to thank Chris Peikert for many helpful discussions. The authors would like to thank the anonymous reviewers for their valuable comments. Xiang Xie and Rui Xue are supported by the Fund of the National Natural Science Foundation of China under Grant No. 61170280, the Strategic Priority Research Program of the Chinese Academy of Sciences under Grant No. XDA06010701, and IIE's Cryptography Research Project. Rui Zhang is supported by the One Hundred Person Project of the Chinese Academy of Sciences, the Fund of the National Natural Science Foundation of China under Grant No. 61100225, and the Strategic Priority Research Program of the Chinese Academy of Sciences under Grant No. XDA06010701.

References

1. Abdalla, M., Bellare, M., Catalano, D., Kiltz, E., Kohno, T., Lange, T., Malone-Lee, J., Neven, G., Paillier, P., Shi, H.: Searchable Encryption Revisited: Consistency Properties, Relation to Anonymous IBE, and Extensions. In: Shoup, V. (ed.) CRYPTO 2005. LNCS, vol. 3621, pp. 205–222. Springer, Heidelberg (2005)
2. Agrawal, S., Boneh, D., Boyen, X.: Efficient Lattice (H)IBE in the Standard Model. In: Gilbert, H. (ed.) EUROCRYPT 2010. LNCS, vol. 6110, pp. 553–572. Springer, Heidelberg (2010)

3. Agrawal, S., Boneh, D., Boyen, X.: Lattice Basis Delegation in Fixed Dimension and Shorter-Ciphertext Hierarchical IBE. In: Rabin, T. (ed.) CRYPTO 2010. LNCS, vol. 6223, pp. 98–115. Springer, Heidelberg (2010)
4. Alwen, J., Peikert, C.: Generating shorter bases for hard random lattices. Theory of Computing Systems, 1–19 (2011)
5. Banerjee, A., Peikert, C., Rosen, A.: Pseudorandom Functions and Lattices. In: Pointcheval, D., Johansson, T. (eds.) EUROCRYPT 2012. LNCS, vol. 7237, pp. 719–737. Springer, Heidelberg (2012)
6. Bellare, M., Boldyreva, A., O'Neill, A.: Deterministic and Efficiently Searchable Encryption. In: Menezes, A. (ed.) CRYPTO 2007. LNCS, vol. 4622, pp. 535–552. Springer, Heidelberg (2007)
7. Bellare, M., Fischlin, M., O'Neill, A., Ristenpart, T.: Deterministic Encryption: Definitional Equivalences and Constructions without Random Oracles. In: Wagner, D. (ed.) CRYPTO 2008. LNCS, vol. 5157, pp. 360–378. Springer, Heidelberg (2008)
8. Bellare, M., Kiltz, E., Peikert, C., Waters, B.: Identity-Based (Lossy) Trapdoor Functions and Applications. In: Pointcheval, D., Johansson, T. (eds.) EUROCRYPT 2012. LNCS, vol. 7237, pp. 228–245. Springer, Heidelberg (2012)
9. Boldyreva, A., Fehr, S., O'Neill, A.: On Notions of Security for Deterministic Encryption, and Efficient Constructions without Random Oracles. In: Wagner, D. (ed.) CRYPTO 2008. LNCS, vol. 5157, pp. 335–359. Springer, Heidelberg (2008)
10. Boneh, D., Di Crescenzo, G., Ostrovsky, R., Persiano, G.: Public Key Encryption with Keyword Search. In: Cachin, C., Camenisch, J.L. (eds.) EUROCRYPT 2004. LNCS, vol. 3027, pp. 506–522. Springer, Heidelberg (2004)
11. Brakerski, Z., Segev, G.: Better Security for Deterministic Public-Key Encryption: The Auxiliary-Input Setting. In: Rogaway, P. (ed.) CRYPTO 2011. LNCS, vol. 6841, pp. 543–560. Springer, Heidelberg (2011)
12. Cash, D., Hofheinz, D., Kiltz, E., Peikert, C.: Bonsai Trees, or How to Delegate a Lattice Basis. In: Gilbert, H. (ed.) EUROCRYPT 2010. LNCS, vol. 6110, pp. 523–552. Springer, Heidelberg (2010)
13. Dodis, Y., Goldwasser, S., Tauman Kalai, Y., Peikert, C., Vaikuntanathan, V.: Public-Key Encryption Schemes with Auxiliary Inputs. In: Micciancio, D. (ed.) TCC 2010. LNCS, vol. 5978, pp. 361–381. Springer, Heidelberg (2010)
14. Gentry, C., Peikert, C., Vaikuntanathan, V.: Trapdoors for hard lattices and new cryptographic constructions. In: Proceedings of the 40th Annual ACM Symposium on Theory of Computing, pp. 197–206. ACM (2008)
15. Goldwasser, S., Kalai, Y., Peikert, C., Vaikuntanathan, V.: Robustness of the learning with errors assumption. In: Innovations in Computer Science (ICS) (2010)
16. Goldwasser, S., Micali, S.: Probabilistic encryption. Journal of Computer and System Sciences 28(2), 270–299 (1984)
17. Micciancio, D., Peikert, C.: Trapdoors for Lattices: Simpler, Tighter, Faster, Smaller. In: Pointcheval, D., Johansson, T. (eds.) EUROCRYPT 2012. LNCS, vol. 7237, pp. 700–718. Springer, Heidelberg (2012)
18. O'Neill, A.: Deterministic public-key encryption revisited. Technical report, Cryptology ePrint Archive, Report 2010/533 (2010)
19. Peikert, C.: Public-key cryptosystems from the worst-case shortest vector problem: extended abstract. In: Proceedings of the 41st Annual ACM Symposium on Theory of Computing, pp. 333–342. ACM (2009)
20. Peikert, C., Waters, B.: Lossy trapdoor functions and their applications. In: Proceedings of the 40th Annual ACM Symposium on Theory of Computing, pp. 187–196. ACM (2008)

21. Regev, O.: On lattices, learning with errors, random linear codes, and cryptography. In: Proceedings of the Thirty-Seventh Annual ACM Symposium on Theory of Computing, pp. 84–93. ACM (2005)
22. Shamir, A.: Identity-Based Cryptosystems and Signature Schemes. In: Blakely, G.R., Chaum, D. (eds.) CRYPTO 1984. LNCS, vol. 196, pp. 47–53. Springer, Heidelberg (1985)
23. Waters, B.: Efficient Identity-Based Encryption Without Random Oracles. In: Cramer, R. (ed.) EUROCRYPT 2005. LNCS, vol. 3494, pp. 114–127. Springer, Heidelberg (2005)

Ring Switching
in BGV-Style Homomorphic Encryption

Craig Gentry[1], Shai Halevi[1], Chris Peikert[2], and Nigel P. Smart[3]

[1] IBM Research
[2] Georgia Institute of Technology
[3] University of Bristol

Abstract. The security of BGV-style homomorphic encryption schemes over polynomial rings relies on rings of very large dimension. This large dimension is needed because of the large modulus-to-noise ratio in the key-switching matrices that are used for the top few levels of the evaluated circuit. However, larger noise (and hence smaller modulus-to-noise ratio) is used in lower levels of the circuit, so from a security standpoint it is permissible to switch to lower-dimension rings, thus speeding up the homomorphic operations for the lower levels of the circuit. However, implementing such ring-switching is nontrivial, since these schemes rely on the ring algebraic structure for their homomorphic properties.

A basic ring-switching operation was used by Brakerski, Gentry and Vaikuntanathan, over polynomial rings of the form $\mathbb{Z}[X]/(X^{2^n} + 1)$, in the context of bootstrapping. In this work we generalize and extend this technique to work over any cyclotomic ring and show how it can be used not only for bootstrapping but also during the computation itself (in conjunction with the "packed ciphertext" techniques of Gentry, Halevi and Smart).

1 Introduction

The last year has seen a rapid advance in the state of fully homomorphic encryption; yet despite these advances the existing schemes are still too inefficient for most practical purposes. In this paper we make another step forward in making such schemes more efficient. In particular we present a technique to reduce the dimension of the ring needed for homomorphic computation of the lower levels of a circuit. Our techniques apply to homomorphic encryption schemes over polynomial rings, such as the scheme of Brakerski et al. [4, 5, 3], as well as the variants due to Lòpez-Alt et al. [14] and Brakerski [2].

The most efficient variants of all these schemes work over polynomial rings of the form $\mathbb{Z}[X]/F(X)$, and in all of them the ring dimension (which is the degree of $F(X)$) must be set high enough to ensure security: to be able to handle depth-L circuits, these schemes must use key-switching matrices with modulus-to-noise ratio of $2^{\tilde{\Omega}(L \cdot \mathrm{polylog}(\lambda))}$, hence the ring dimension must also be $\tilde{\Omega}(L \cdot \mathrm{polylog}(\lambda))$ (even if we assume that ring-LWE [15] is hard to within

I. Visconti and R. De Prisco (Eds.): SCN 2012, LNCS 7485, pp. 19–37, 2012.

fully exponential factors).[1] In practice, the ring dimension for moderately deep circuits can easily be many thousands. For example, to be able to evaluate AES homomorphically, Gentry et al. used in [13] circuits of depth $L \geq 50$, with corresponding ring-dimension of over 50000.

As homomorphic operations proceed, the noise in the ciphertext grows (or the modulus shrinks, if we use the modulus-switching technique from [5, 3]), hence reducing the modulus-to-noise ratio. Consequently, it becomes permissible to start using lower-dimension rings in order to speed up further homomorphic computation. However, in the middle of the computation we already have evaluated ciphertexts over the big ring, and so we need a method for transforming these into small-ring ciphertexts that encrypt the same thing. Such a "ring switching" procedure was described by Brakerski et al. [3], in the context of reducing the ciphertext-size prior to bootstrapping. The procedure in [3], however, is specific to polynomial rings of the form $R_{2^n} = \mathbb{Z}[X]/(X^{2^{n-1}}+1)$, and moreover by itself it cannot be combined with the "packed evaluation" techniques of Gentry et al. [11]. Extending this procedure is the focus of this work.

1.1   Our Contribution

In this work we present two complementary techniques:

- We extend the procedure from [3] to any cyclotomic ring $R = \mathbb{Z}[X]/\Phi_m(X)$ for a composite m. This is important, since the tools from [11] for working with "packed" ciphertexts require that we work with an odd integer m. For $m = u \cdot w$, we show how to break a ciphertext over the big ring R into a collection of $u' = \varphi(m)/\varphi(w)$ ciphertexts over the smaller ring $R' = \mathbb{Z}[X]/\Phi_w(X)$, such that the plaintext encrypted in the original big-ring ciphertext can be recovered as a simple linear function of the plaintexts encrypted in the smaller-ring ciphertexts.
- We then show how to take a "packed" big-ring ciphertext that contains many plaintext values in its plaintext slots, and distribute these plaintext values among the plaintext slots of several small-ring ciphertexts. If the original big-ring ciphertext was "sparse" (i.e., if only few of its plaintext slots were used), then our technique yields just a small number of small-ring ciphertexts, only as many as needed to fit all the used plaintext slots.

The first technique on its own may be useful in the context of bootstrapping, but it is not enough to achieve our goal of reducing the computational overhead by switching to small-ring ciphertexts, since we still need to show how to perform homomorphic operations on the resulting small-ring ciphertexts. This is achieved by utilizing the second technique. To demonstrate the usefulness of the second technique, consider the application of homomorphic AES computation [13], where the original big-ring ciphertext contains only 16 plaintext values

---

[1] The schemes from [3, 2] can replace large rings by using higher-dimension vectors over smaller rings. But their most efficient variants use big rings and low-dimension vectors, since the complexity of their key-switching step is quadratic in the dimension of these vectors.

(corresponding to the 16 bytes of the AES state). If the small-ring ciphertexts has 16 or more plaintext slots, then we can convert the original big-ring ciphertext into a single small-ring ciphertext containing the same 16 bytes in its slots, then continue the computation on this smaller ciphertext.

1.2   An Overview of the Construction

Our starting point is the polynomial composition technique of Brakerski et al. [3]. When $m = u \cdot w$ then a polynomial of degree less than $\varphi(m)$, $a(X) = \sum_{i=0}^{\varphi(m)-1} a_i X^i$, can be broken into u polynomials of degree less than $\varphi(m)/u \leq \varphi(w)$, by splitting the coefficients of a according to their index modulo u. Namely, denoting by $a_{(k)}$ the polynomial with coefficients $a_k, a_{k+u}, a_{k+2u}, \ldots$, we have

$$a(X) = \sum_{k=0}^{u-1} \sum_{j=0}^{\varphi(w)-1} a_{k+uj} X^{k+uj} = \sum_{k=0}^{u-1} X^k \sum_{j=0}^{\varphi(w)-1} a_{k+uj} X^{uj} = \sum_{k=0}^{u-1} X^k a_{(k)}(X^u).$$

(1)

We note that this "very syntactic" transformation of splitting the coefficients of a high-degree polynomial into several low-degree polynomials, has the following crucial algebraic properties:

1. The end result is a collection of "parts" $a_{(k)}$, all from the small ring R' (which is a sub-ring of the big ring R, since $w|m$).
2. Recalling that $f(x) \mapsto f(x^u)$ is an embedding of R' inside R, we have the property that the original a can be recovered as a simple linear combination of (the embedding of) the parts $a_{(k)}$.
3. The transformation $T(a) = (a_{(0)}, \ldots, a_{(u-1)})$ is linear, and as such it commutes with the linear operations inside the decryption formula of BGV-type schemes: If $\mathfrak{s}$ is a big-ring secret key and c is (part of) a big-ring ciphertext, then decryption over the big ring includes computing $a = \mathfrak{s} \cdot c \in R$ (and later reducing $a \bmod q$ and $\bmod 2$). Due to linearity, the parts of a can be expressed in terms of the tensor product between the parts of $\mathfrak{s}$ and c over the small ring. Namely, $T(\mathfrak{s} \cdot c)$ is some linear function of $T(\mathfrak{s}) \otimes T(c)$.

In addition to these algebraic properties, in the case considered in [3] where m, w are powers of two, it turns out that this transformation also possesses the following geometric property:

4. If a is a "short" element of R (in the canonical embedding of R), then all the components $a_{(k)} \in R'$ of $T(a)$ are also short in the canonical embedding of R'.

The importance of this last property stems from the fact that a valid ciphertext in a BGV-type homomorphic encryption scheme must have short noise, namely its inner product with the unknown secret key must be a short ring element. Property 3 above is used to convert a big-ring ciphertext encrypting a (relative to a big-ring secret key $\mathfrak{s}$) into a collection of "syntactically correct" small-ring ciphertexts encrypting the $a_{(k)}$'s (relative to the small-ring secret key $T(\mathfrak{s})$), and Property 4 is used to argue that these small-ring ciphertexts are indeed valid.

Attempting to apply the same transformation in the case where m, w are not powers of two, it turns out that the algebraic properties all still hold, but perhaps the geometric property does not. In this work we therefore describe a different transformation $T(\cdot)$ for breaking a big-ring element into a vector of small-ring elements, that has all the properties 1-4 above,[2] for any integers m, w such that $w|m$. This transformation crucially uses the interpretation of R as a dimension-$\varphi(m)/\varphi(w)$ extension ring of R', and is described in Section 3.2. Another advantage of our transformation over the one from [3] is that it breaks a big-ring element $a \in R$ into only $u' = \varphi(m)/\varphi(w)$ small ring parts $a_{(k)}$, as opposed to $u = m/w$ parts for the transformation from [3].

A Key-Switching Optimization. One source of inefficiency in the ring-switching procedure of Brakerski et al. [3] is that using the tensor product $T(\mathfrak{s}) \otimes T(c)$ amounts essentially to having u small-ring ciphertexts, each of which is a dimension-u vector over the small ring. Brakerski et al. point out that we can use key-switching/dimension-reduction to convert these high dimension ciphertexts into low-dimension ciphertexts over the small ring, but processing u ciphertexts of dimension u inherently requires work quadratic in u. Instead, here we describe an alternative procedure that saves a factor of u in running time.

Before using $T(\cdot)$ to break the ciphertext into pieces, we apply key-switching over the big ring to get a ciphertext with respect to another secret key that happens to belong to the small ring R'. (We again recall that R' is a sub-ring of R). The transformation $T(\cdot)$ has the additional property that when applied to a small-ring element $\mathfrak{s}' \in R' \subset R$, the resulting vector $T(\mathfrak{s}')$ over R' has just a single non-zero entry, namely $\mathfrak{s}'$ itself. Hence $T(\mathfrak{s}') \otimes T(c)$ is the same as just $\mathfrak{s}' \cdot T(c)$, and this lets us work directly with low-dimension ciphertexts over the small ring (as opposed to ciphertexts of dimension u). This is described in Section 3.1, where we prove that key-switching into a key from the small subring is as secure as ring-LWE in that small subring.

Packed Ciphertexts. As sketched so far, the ring-switching procedure lets us convert a big-ring ciphertext encrypting an element $a \in R$ into a collection of u' small-ring ciphertexts encrypting the parts $a_{(k)} \in R'$. However, coming in the middle of homomorphic evaluation, we may need to get small-ring ciphertexts encrypting elements other than the $a_{(k)}$'s. Specifically, if the original a encodes several plaintext values in its plaintext slots (as in [18, 11]), we may want to get encryptions of small-ring elements that encode the very same values in their slots.

We note that the plaintext values encoded in the element $a \in R$ are the evaluations $a(\rho_i)$, where the ρ_i's are primitive m-th roots of unity in some extension field $\mathbb{F}_{2^d}$. (Equivalently, the evaluations $a(\rho_i)$ correspond to the residues

---

[2] An earlier version of the current work [10] used the same transformation as in [3], and patched the problem with the geometric property by "lifting" everything from the big ring $\mathbb{Z}[X]/\Phi_m(X)$ to the even bigger ring $\mathbb{Z}[X]/(X^m - 1)$, using techniques similar to [11, 7].

$a \bmod \mathfrak{p}_i$, where the $\mathfrak{p}_i = \langle 2, F_i(X) \rangle$ are the distinct prime ideal factors of $\langle 2 \rangle$ in the ring R. Hence the evaluation representation over $\mathbb{F}_{2^d}$ is just Chinese remaindering modulo 2 in R.)

Similarly, the plaintext values encoded in an element $b \in R'$ are the evaluations $b(\tau_j)$, where the τ_j's are primitive w-th roots of unity in $\mathbb{F}_{2^d}$ (equivalently, the residues of b modulo the prime ideal factors of 2 in R'). Our goal, then, is to decompose a big-ring ciphertext encrypting a into small-ring ciphertexts encrypting some b_k's, such that for every i there are some j, k for which $b_k(\tau_j) = a(\rho_i)$.

On a very high level, the approach that we take is to observe that the linear transformation $T(\cdot)$ for break big-ring elements into vectors of small-ring parts, must as a side-effect of induce some linear transformation (over $\mathbb{F}_{2^d}$) on the values in the plaintext slots. Hence after we apply T, we just need to compute homomorphically the inverse linear transformation (e.g., using the techniques from [11] for computing on packed ciphertexts), thereby recovering the original values.

2 Notation and Preliminaries

For any positive integer u we let $[u] = \{0, \ldots, u-1\}$.

2.1 Algebraic Background

Recall that an ideal (in an arbitrary commutative ring R) is an additive subgroup which is closed under multiplication by R. Below we typically denote ideals by $\mathfrak{p}, \mathfrak{q}$, etc. An R-ideal $\mathfrak{p}$ is prime if $ab \in \mathfrak{p}$ (for some $a, b \in R$) implies $a \in \mathfrak{p}$ or $b \in \mathfrak{p}$ (or both). When R' is a sub-ring of R and $\mathfrak{p}$ is an R'-ideal, we implicitly identify $\mathfrak{p}$ with its extension to R, namely the R-ideal $\mathfrak{p}R$. For an R-ideal $\mathfrak{p}$, the quotient ring $R_\mathfrak{p} = R/\mathfrak{p}R$ is a ring consisting of the residue classes $a + \mathfrak{p}$ for all $a \in R$, with the ring operations induced by R.

For any positive integer $m \geq 2$, let $\mathbb{K} = \mathbb{Q}(\zeta_m) \cong \mathbb{Q}[X]/\Phi_m(X)$ be the mth cyclotomic number field (of degree $\varphi(m)$), and $R = \mathbb{Z}[\zeta_m] \cong \mathbb{Z}[X]/\Phi_m(X)$ its ring of integers, where $\zeta_m = \exp(2\pi\sqrt{-1}/m)$ is the mth principal complex root of unity, and $\Phi_m(X) = \prod_{i \in \mathbb{Z}_m^*}(X - \zeta_m^i) \in \mathbb{Z}[X]$ is the mth cyclotomic polynomial. The elements ζ_m^j (equivalently, X^j) for $j \in [\varphi(m)]$ form a $\mathbb{Q}$-basis of $\mathbb{K}$ and a $\mathbb{Z}$-basis of R, called the "power basis." That is, any $a \in \mathbb{K}$ can be written uniquely as $a = \sum_{j=0}^{\varphi(m)-1} a_j \cdot \zeta_m^j$ for some $a_k \in \mathbb{Q}$, and $a \in R$ if and only if every $a_j \in \mathbb{Z}$.

There are $\varphi(m)$ ring homomorphisms from $\mathbb{K}$ to $\mathbb{C}$ that fix $\mathbb{Q}$ pointwise, called *embeddings*, which are denoted $\sigma_i \colon \mathbb{K} \to \mathbb{C}$ for $i \in \mathbb{Z}_m^*$ and characterized by $\sigma_i(\zeta_m) = \zeta_m^i$. (Equivalently, $\sigma_i(a(X)) = a(\zeta_m^i) \in \mathbb{C}$ when viewing $\mathbb{K}$ as $\mathbb{Q}(X)/\Phi_m(X)$.) We note that the σ_i are automorphisms of $\mathbb{K}$, when viewing it as a sub-field of $\mathbb{C}$. The (field) trace is a $\mathbb{Q}$-linear function $\mathrm{Tr}_{\mathbb{K}/\mathbb{Q}} \colon \mathbb{K} \to \mathbb{Q}$, which can be defined as the sum of the embeddings: $\mathrm{Tr}_{\mathbb{K}/\mathbb{Q}}(a) = \sum_{i \in \mathbb{Z}_m^*} \sigma_i(a)$.

The *canonical embedding* $\sigma \colon \mathbb{K} \to \mathbb{C}^{\varphi(m)}$ is the concatenation of all the embeddings, i.e., $\sigma(a) = (\sigma_i(a))_{i \in \mathbb{Z}_m^*}$, and it endows $\mathbb{K}$ with a canonical geometry. In particular, we define the Euclidean (ℓ_2) and ℓ_∞ norms on $\mathbb{K}$ as

$$\|a\| := \|\sigma(a)\| = \sqrt{\sum_i |\sigma_i(a)|^2} \quad \text{and} \quad \|a\|_\infty := \|\sigma(a)\|_\infty = \max_i |\sigma_i(a)|,$$

respectively. Note that $\|a \cdot b\| \le \|a\|_\infty \cdot \|b\|$ for any $a, b \in \mathbb{K}$, because the σ_i are ring homomorphisms.

For some $w|m$, let $u = m/w$ (so $\zeta_w = \zeta_m^u$) and $u' = \varphi(m)/\varphi(w)$, and let $\mathbb{K}' = \mathbb{Q}(\zeta_w) \subseteq \mathbb{K}$ and $R' = \mathbb{Z}[\zeta_w] \subseteq R$ be the wth cyclotomic number field and ring (respectively), with $\varphi(w)$ embeddings $\sigma_i' \colon \mathbb{K}' \to \mathbb{C}$ for $i \in \mathbb{Z}_w^*$ defining the canonical embedding $\sigma' \colon \mathbb{K}' \to \mathbb{C}^{\varphi(w)}$. Notice that when we restrict to the subfield $\mathbb{K}' = \mathbb{Q}(\zeta_m^u)$ of $\mathbb{K}$, for any $i \in \mathbb{Z}_m^*$ we have $\sigma_i = \sigma'_{i \bmod w}$, because $\sigma_i(\zeta_m^u) = \zeta_m^{u \cdot (i \bmod w)} = \sigma'_{i \bmod w}(\zeta_w)$.

Observe that using the polynomial representation in the small ring $R' \cong \mathbb{Z}[X]/\Phi_w(X)$, the element ζ_w is represented by the indeterminate X. However, using polynomial representation in the big ring, $R \cong \mathbb{Z}[X]/\Phi_m(X)$, the same ring element $\zeta_w = \zeta_m^u \in R' \subset R$ is represented by the monomial X^u. In general, if $r' \in R'$ is a small-ring element represented by the polynomial $b(X) \in \mathbb{Z}[X]/\Phi_w(X)$, then the same small-ring element is represented by the polynomial $a(X) = b(X^u) \bmod \Phi_m(X) \in \mathbb{Z}[X]/\Phi_m(X)$, when viewed as an element in the sub-ring R' of R. In other words, the mapping $f(X) \mapsto f(X^u) \bmod \Phi_m(X)$, mapping polynomials of degree less than $\varphi(w)$ into a subset of the polynomials of degree less than $\varphi(m)$, is a ring embedding of $\mathbb{Z}[X]/\Phi_w(X) \cong R'$ as a sub-ring of $\mathbb{Z}[X]/\Phi_m(X) \cong R$. Similarly, this mapping is also a field embedding of $\mathbb{Q}[X]/\Phi_w(X) \cong \mathbb{K}'$ as a subfield of $\mathbb{Q}[X]/\Phi_m(X) \cong \mathbb{K}$.

We will use extensively the fact that $\mathbb{K}$ is a degree-u' extension of $\mathbb{K}'$, i.e., $\mathbb{K} = \mathbb{K}'(\zeta_m)$, and similarly $R = R'[\zeta_m]$. The powers ζ_m^k for $k \in [u']$ (also called the "power basis") form a $\mathbb{K}'$-basis of $\mathbb{K}$, and an R'-basis of R. Looking ahead, our transformation $T(\cdot)$ for breaking a big ring element into small-ring components will just output the vector of coefficients of the big-ring element relative to the power basis.

One can verify that among all the embeddings σ_i of $\mathbb{K}$, exactly u' of them fix $\mathbb{K}'$ (not just $\mathbb{Q}$) pointwise. Specifically, these are the embeddings σ_i indexed by each $i = 1 \bmod w$. The intermediate trace function $\mathrm{Tr}_{\mathbb{K}/\mathbb{K}'} \colon \mathbb{K} \to \mathbb{K}'$ is a $\mathbb{K}'$-linear function, defined as the sum of all those $\mathbb{K}'$-fixing embeddings, i.e.,

$$\mathrm{Tr}_{\mathbb{K}/\mathbb{K}'}(a) = \sum_{i \in I} \sigma_i(a), \quad I = \{i \in \mathbb{Z}_m^* : i = 1 \bmod w\}.$$

A standard fact from field theory is that every $\mathbb{K}'$-linear map $L \colon \mathbb{K} \to \mathbb{K}'$ can be expressed as $L(x) = \mathrm{Tr}_{\mathbb{K}/\mathbb{K}'}(d \cdot x)$ for some $d \in \mathbb{K}$. Another standard fact is that the intermediate trace satisfies $\mathrm{Tr}_{\mathbb{K}/\mathbb{Q}} = \mathrm{Tr}_{\mathbb{K}'/\mathbb{Q}} \circ \mathrm{Tr}_{\mathbb{K}/\mathbb{K}'}$.

The following lemma relates the intermediate trace to the embeddings of $\mathbb{K}$ and $\mathbb{K}'$, and will be used later to show that our ciphertext decomposition from R to R' produces component ciphertexts having short error terms.

Lemma 1. *For any $a \in \mathbb{K}$ and $i \in \mathbb{Z}_w^*$,*

$$\sigma_i'(\mathrm{Tr}_{\mathbb{K}/\mathbb{K}'}(a)) = \sum_{j=i \bmod w} \sigma_j(a).$$

In matrix form, $\sigma'(\mathrm{Tr}_{\mathbb{K}/\mathbb{K}'}(a)) = P \cdot \sigma(a)$, where P is the $\varphi(w)$-by-$\varphi(m)$ matrix (with rows indexed by $i \in \mathbb{Z}_w^*$ and columns by $j \in \mathbb{Z}_m^*$) whose (i,j)th entry is 1 if $j = i \bmod w$, and is 0 otherwise.

Proof. Recall that for any $i' \in \mathbb{Z}_m^*$ such that $i' = i \bmod w$, the $\mathbb{K}'$-embedding σ_i' and the $\mathbb{K}$-embedding $\sigma_{i'}$ coincide on $\mathbb{K}'$. In particular, $\sigma_i'(\mathrm{Tr}_{\mathbb{K}/\mathbb{K}'}(a)) = \sigma_{i'}(\mathrm{Tr}_{\mathbb{K}/\mathbb{K}'}(a))$ because $\mathrm{Tr}_{\mathbb{K}/\mathbb{K}'}(a) \in \mathbb{K}'$. Then by definition of $\mathrm{Tr}_{\mathbb{K}/\mathbb{K}'}$ and linearity of $\sigma_{i'}$, we have

$$\sigma_i'(\mathrm{Tr}_{\mathbb{K}/\mathbb{K}'}(a)) = \sigma_{i'}\left(\sum_{j=1 \bmod w} \sigma_j(a)\right) = \sum_j \sigma_{i'}(\sigma_j(a)) = \sum_{j'=i \bmod w} \sigma_{j'}(a),$$

where for the last equality we have used $\sigma_{i'} \circ \sigma_j = \sigma_{i' \cdot j}$ and $i' \in \mathbb{Z}_m^*$, so $j' = i' \cdot j \in \mathbb{Z}_m^*$ runs over all indexes congruent to $i' = i \bmod w$ when $j \in \mathbb{Z}_m^*$ runs over all indexes congruent to 1 mod w. $\qquad\square$

2.2   The Big Ring-to-Small Ring Decomposition

As sketched in the introduction, our approach is rooted in the technique of decomposing an element of the "big" ring $R = \mathbb{Z}[\zeta_m]$ (or field $\mathbb{K}$) into several elements of the "small" ring $R' = \mathbb{Z}[\zeta_w]$ (or field $\mathbb{K}'$). Recall from Section 2.1 that $\mathbb{K} = \mathbb{K}'[\zeta_m]$ is a field extension of degree $u' = \varphi(m)/\varphi(w)$ over $\mathbb{K}'$, having power $\mathbb{K}'$-basis $\zeta_m^0, \ldots, \zeta_m^{u'-1}$. That is, any $a \in \mathbb{K}$ can be written uniquely as $a = \sum_{k=0}^{u'-1} a_k \cdot \zeta_m^k$ for some "coefficients" $a_k \in \mathbb{K}'$, and $a \in R$ if and only if every $a_k \in R'$. We define the decomposition map $T \colon \mathbb{K} \to (\mathbb{K}')^{u'}$ (which also maps R to $(R')^{u'}$) to simply output the vector of these coefficients:[3]

$$T(a) = (a_0, \ldots, a_{u'-1}). \tag{2}$$

We note a few simple but important properties of T:

1. It is $\mathbb{K}'$-linear (and hence also R'-linear): for any $a, b \in \mathbb{K}$ and $r' \in \mathbb{K}'$, $T(a+b) = T(a)+T(b)$ (i.e., T is an additive homomorphism), and $T(r' \cdot a) = r' \cdot T(a)$.
2. Any ideal $\mathfrak{p}$ in R' induces a bijective $R_{\mathfrak{p}}'$-linear map $T_{\mathfrak{p}} \colon R_{\mathfrak{p}} \to (R_{\mathfrak{p}}')^{u'}$, namely, $T_{\mathfrak{p}}(a + \mathfrak{p}R) = T_{\mathfrak{p}}(a) + (\mathfrak{p})^{u'} = (a_0 + \mathfrak{p}, \ldots, a_{u'-1} + \mathfrak{p})$.

---

[3] Alternatively, we could define T to output coefficients with respect to the "dual power" $\mathbb{K}'$-basis of $\mathbb{K}$, which would map the (fractional) dual ideal $R^\vee$ of R to $(R'^\vee)^{u'}$. That decomposition has better geometric properties and is more consonant with the ring-LWE problem as defined in [15], but it is more technically involved. We defer the details to the full version.

When using polynomial representations, the $\mathbb{K}'$-linearity of T must be interpreted relative to the embedding $f(X) \mapsto f(X^u)$ that maps the polynomial representation of $\mathbb{K}'$ into that of $\mathbb{K}$. Specifically, it means that for any polynomials $b(X) \in \mathbb{Q}[X]/\Phi_w(X)$ and $a(X) \in \mathbb{Q}[X]/\Phi_m(X)$, it holds that

$$T\big(b(X^u) \cdot a(X) \bmod \Phi_m(X) \big) = b(X) \cdot T\big(a(X)\big) \bmod \Phi_w(X). \qquad (3)$$

Another important property is that T maps short elements in R to vectors of relatively short elements in R' (where as always, "short" is with respect to the canonical embeddings).

Lemma 2. *For $a \in R$, let $T(a) = (a_0, \ldots, a_{u'-1})$. Then for any $k \in [u']$, we have $\|a_k\| \leq c_{m,w} \cdot \|a\|/\sqrt{u'}$, where $c_{m,w} \geq 1$ is a constant that depends only on m and w.*

Note that the $\sqrt{u'}$ term appearing above is merely a normalization factor associated with the fact that the power basis elements of R' are a $\sqrt{u'}$ factor shorter than those of R under the canonical embeddings, so the decomposition does *not* actually shrink the elements in any effective way.

Te constant $c_{m,w}$ turns out to depend only on the ratio $r = \mathrm{rad}(m)/\mathrm{rad}(w)$, where $\mathrm{rad}(n)$ denotes the radical of n, i.e., the product of all the prime divisors of n (without multiplicities). Hence we hereafter denote it by c_r rather than $c_{m,w}$. For typical values of $r = \mathrm{rad}(m)/\mathrm{rad}(w)$, the constant c_r is (somewhat) small, e.g., $c_1 = 1$ and $c_p = \sqrt{2 - 2/p}$ when p is a prime. (Hence if m and w share all the same prime divisors, the relevant constant is 1, and if m has only one additional prime divisor then the constant is smaller than $\sqrt{2}$.) Some other examples are $c_{3 \cdot 5 \cdot 7} \approx 17.4$ and $c_{5 \cdot 7 \cdot 11} \approx 155$. We also note that the constant factor c_r can actually be removed entirely, by following the framework of [15, 16] and defining T to work with the fractional ideals $R^\vee$ and $R'^\vee$ (as mentioned in Footnote 3); see the discussion after the proof of Lemma 2.

Proof (sketch). We first express T in terms of the intermediate field trace $\mathrm{Tr}_{\mathbb{K}/\mathbb{K}'}$, then use Lemma 1 to bound $\|a_k\|$. Recall that every $\mathbb{K}'$-linear map from $\mathbb{K}$ to $\mathbb{K}'$ can be expressed as $L(x) = \mathrm{Tr}_{\mathbb{K}/\mathbb{K}'}(d \cdot x)$ for some fixed $d \in \mathbb{K}$. Since T is $\mathbb{K}'$-linear, then for every $k \in [u']$ there exists $d_k \in \mathbb{K}$ such that $a_k = \mathrm{Tr}_{\mathbb{K}/\mathbb{K}'}(d_k \cdot a)$ (for all $a \in \mathbb{K}$). The elements d_k are "dual" to the power $\mathbb{K}'$-basis elements ζ_m^k: for every $j, k \in [u']$ we have $\mathrm{Tr}_{\mathbb{K}/\mathbb{K}'}(\zeta_m^j \cdot d_k) = 1$ if $j = k$ and $\mathrm{Tr}_{\mathbb{K}/\mathbb{K}'}(\zeta_m^j \cdot d_k) = 0$ if $j \neq k$.

Now by Lemma 1 and the fact that the σ_j are ring homomorphisms, we have

$$\sigma'(a_k) = P \cdot \sigma(d_k \cdot a) = P \cdot D \cdot \sigma(a),$$

where $D = \mathrm{diag}(\sigma(d_k))$. Notice that the rows of $P \cdot D$ are orthogonal (since each column has exactly one nonzero entry). The Euclidean norm of row $i \in \mathbb{Z}_w^*$ is $\|\mathbf{d}_{k,i}\|$, where $\mathbf{d}_{k,i} = (\sigma_j(d_k))_{j=i \bmod w} \in \mathbb{C}^{u'}$. Therefore, $\|a_k\| \leq \|a\| \cdot \max_i \|\mathbf{d}_{k,i}\|$.

It remains to bound $\max_{k,i} \|\mathbf{d}_{k,i}\|$. For each $i \in \mathbb{Z}_w^*$, denote by Z_i the matrix (of dimension $u' \times u'$) defined as $Z_i = (\sigma_j(\zeta_m^k))_{j=i \bmod w, k \in [u']}$. Then the $\mathbf{d}_{k,i}$'s are determined by the linear constraints $Z_i^t \cdot \mathbf{d}_{k,i} = \mathbf{e}_k$ (where $\mathbf{e}_k \in \mathbb{Z}^{u'}$ is k'th standard basis vector). From Galois theory it follows that $\|\mathbf{d}_{k,i}\|$ is actually the same for every $i \in \mathbb{Z}_w^*$. It can also be shown that $\max_k \|\mathbf{d}_{k,1}\| \cdot \sqrt{u'}$ depends only on $\mathrm{rad}(m)/\mathrm{rad}(w)$; we omit the details.   □

We note again that the constant c_r in Lemma 2 can be eliminated by defining the transformation T relative to a different basis, specifically the "dual" of the power basis, consisting of the vectors $d_0, d_1, \ldots, d_{u'-1}$ from the proof above. The proof then proceeds in the same way, but with the roles of d_k and ζ_m^k reversed. The tighter bound then follows by observing that the magnitude of each $\sigma_j(\zeta^k)$ is exactly one. One technical issue with using the dual basis, however, is that T no longer maps R to vectors over R'. Instead, it maps the dual ideal $R^\vee$ to vectors over $R'^\vee$, which introduces some additional algebraic subtleties but also turns out to have certain other advantages, as described in [15, 16]. We defer further details to the full version.

2.3   RLWE-Based Cryptosystems

Below and throughout this work, for a residue class $z + q\mathbb{Z} \in \mathbb{Z}_q$ we let $[z]_q \in \mathbb{Z}$ denote its canonical representative in the interval $[-q/2, q/2)$. (One can think of $[\cdot]_q$ as an operation that takes an arbitrary integer z and reduces it modulo q into the interval $[-q/2, q/2)$, so as to get the canonical representative of $z + q\mathbb{Z}$.) We extend this to a map from $R_q = R/qR$ to R, by applying the operation coefficient-wise to the input (viewed as a polynomial in coefficient representation). I.e., for $z = \sum_i z_i X^i \in R_q$ we get $[z]_q = \sum_i [z_i]_q \cdot X^i$. A standard fact is that if $z \in a + qR$ for some $a \in R$ that is sufficiently short relative to q and the dimension of R, then $[z]_q = a$. Throughout the paper we implicitly assume that q is chosen large enough to ensure that all of the operations we describe produce valid ciphertexts.

In a basic ring-LWE-based cryptosystem [15], secret keys and ciphertexts are elements of $(R_q)^2$ for some odd integer q, and moreover the secret key has the form $\mathbf{s} = (1, \mathfrak{s}) \bmod q$, where $\mathfrak{s} \in R$ is short. The plaintext space is the quotient ring $R_2 = R/2R$. A valid ciphertext $\mathbf{c} = (c_0, c_1) \in (R_q)^2$ that encrypts a plaintext $a \in R_2$ with respect to $\mathbf{s} = (1, \mathfrak{s})$ satisfies

$$\langle \mathbf{c}, \mathbf{s} \rangle = c_0 + \mathfrak{s} \cdot c_1 \in (a + 2e) + qR \tag{4}$$

for some sufficiently short $a + 2e \in R$. To decrypt, one just computes $[c_0 + \mathfrak{s} \cdot c_1]_q = a + 2e$ and reduces modulo 2 to recover the plaintext a. Additionally, Brakerski et al. [4, 3] showed that this system (with certain additions to the public key) supports additive and multiplicative homomorphisms.

Our ring-switching procedure will be given a ciphertext where Equation (4) holds over R (for some $\mathfrak{s} \in R$), and will output ciphertexts for which the equality holds over R' (for a different secret $\mathfrak{s}' \in R'$).

2.4   Plaintext Arithmetic

Following [18, 3, 11–13], we recall how to encode vectors over a certain finite field into the message spaces. A summary is provided in Figure 1 below.

For concreteness, we focus first on R', viewing it as $\mathbb{Z}[X]/\Phi_w(X)$. Let d' be the order of 2 in the multiplicative group $\mathbb{Z}_w^*$. Then $\Phi_w(X)$ factors modulo 2 into $\ell' = \varphi(w)/d'$ distinct irreducible (over $\mathbb{F}_2$) polynomials $F_i(X)$, each of degree d'. The ideal $2R'$ has factorization $2R' = \prod_{i=1}^{\ell'} \mathfrak{p}_i$, where $\mathfrak{p}_i = \langle 2, F_i(X) \rangle$ are distinct prime ideals. Since each $F_i(X)$ is irreducible modulo 2, each $R'/\mathfrak{p}_i R' = \mathbb{F}_2[X]/\langle F_i(X) \rangle$ is isomorphic to the finite field $\mathbb{F}_{2^{d'}}$. By the Chinese remainder theorem, we can therefore identify elements of R_2' with elements of $(\mathbb{F}_{2^{d'}})^{\ell'}$, as summarized by the following diagram of ring isomorphisms.

$$ R'/2R' \xleftarrow{\quad \text{CRT} \quad} \bigoplus_i (R'/\mathfrak{p}_i R') \xleftrightarrow{\qquad} (\mathbb{F}_{2^{d'}})^{\ell'} $$

For our ring-switching application we use a particular ring isomorphism between $R'/2R'$ and $(\mathbb{F}_{2^{d'}})^{\ell'}$, for some fixed representation of $\mathbb{F}_{2^{d'}}$. Consider the quotient group $\mathbb{Z}_w^*/\langle 2 \rangle$ (which has cardinality ℓ'), and fix a specific set of representatives for this quotient group, $U_w = \{j_0, j_1, \ldots, j_{\ell'-1}\} \subseteq \mathbb{Z}_w^*$, containing of exactly one member from every conjugacy class in $\mathbb{Z}_w^*/\langle 2 \rangle$.[4] Also fix a specific primitive w-th root of unity $\tau \in \mathbb{F}_{2^{d'}}$, and identify each element $a \in R_2'$ with the ℓ'-vector consisting of $a(\tau^j) \in \mathbb{F}_{2^{d'}}$ for all $j \in U_w$:

$$ a \in R_2' \longleftrightarrow \langle a(\tau^{j_1}), \ldots, a(\tau^{j_{\ell'}}) \rangle \in (\mathbb{F}_{2^{d'}})^{\ell'}. $$

Showing that this is indeed a bijection is standard. In one direction, from a we can compute all the values $a(\tau^{j_k})$. In the other direction we have the following simple claim:

Claim. For every vector $(\alpha_0, \alpha_1, \ldots, \alpha_{\ell'-1}) \in \mathbb{F}_{2^{d'}}^{\ell'}$, there is a unique polynomial $a \in R_2'$ such that over $\mathbb{F}_{2^{d'}}$ it holds that $a(\tau^{j_k}) = \alpha_k$ for all $k \in [\ell']$.

Proof. We identify R_2' with $\mathbb{F}_2[X]/\Phi_w(X) \subset \mathbb{F}_{2^{d'}}[X]/\Phi_w(X)$, and recall that a polynomial $a \in \mathbb{F}_{2^{d'}}[X]/\Phi_w(X)$ belongs to the subring R_2' if and only if $a(X^2) = a(X)^2$ (as an identity in R_2'). Given a vector of values $(\alpha_0, \alpha_1, \ldots, \alpha_{\ell'-1}) \in \mathbb{F}_{2^{d'}}^{\ell'}$, we can therefore deduce from $a(\tau^{j_k}) = \alpha_k$ the evaluations of a on the other members of the same conjugacy class, namely $a(\tau^{2j_k}) = \alpha_k^2$, $a(\tau^{4j_k}) = \alpha_k^4$, $a(\tau^{8j_k}) = \alpha_k^8$, etc. Since U_w is a complete set of representatives for the quotient group $\mathbb{Z}_w^*/\langle 2 \rangle$, we can get in this way the evaluations of $a(\tau^j)$ for all the indices $j \in \mathbb{Z}_w^*$. This gives us the evaluation of a at $\varphi(w)$ different points, from which a is uniquely defined (because $\mathbb{F}_{2^{d'}}$ is a field and a has degree less than $\varphi(w)$). $\square$

We thus view the evaluation of the plaintext element at τ^{j_k} as the k'th "plaintext slot," and note that arithmetic operations in the ring R_2' act on the plaintext slots in a componentwise manner.

---

[4] In other words, the sets $U_w, 2U_w, 4U_w, \ldots 2^{d'-1}U_w$ are all disjoint, and their union is the entire group $\mathbb{Z}_w^*$.

For $R \cong \mathbb{Z}[X]/\Phi_m(X)$ the analysis proceeds similarly. Let d be the order of 2 in the multiplicative group $\mathbb{Z}_m^*$, so $d'|d$, and let $\ell = \varphi(m)/d$. Recalling that $F_i(X^u)$ is the embedding of $F_i(X) \in R'$ into R, we denote the factorizaton of $F_i(X^u)$ into irreducible factors modulo 2 by $F_i(X^u) = \prod_j F_{i,j}(X)$. We note that each $F_i(X)$ factors into exactly ℓ/ℓ' distinct irreducible (mod 2) factors, each of degree d, and that the factorization of $\Phi_m(X)$ into irreducible factors mod 2 is $\Phi_m(X) = \prod_{i,j} F_{i,j}(X)$. Therefore, each prime ideal $\mathfrak{p}_i$ in R' factors further in R, into the product of the ℓ/ℓ' prime ideals $\mathfrak{p}_{i,j} = \langle 2, F_{i,j}(X) \rangle$, where each $R/\mathfrak{p}_{i,j}R$ is isomorphic to $\mathbb{F}_{2^d}$.

We use a concrete ring isomorphism between $R/2R$ and $(\mathbb{F}_{2^d})^\ell$ analogous to the one described above, using some representative set U_m of the quotient group $\mathbb{Z}_m^* / \langle 2 \rangle$ and a primitive m-th root of unity ρ, and considering the "plaintext slots" of $a \in R_2$ as the evaluations $a(\rho^i)$ for all $i \in U_m$. Of course, the analog of Claim 2.4 holds here too.

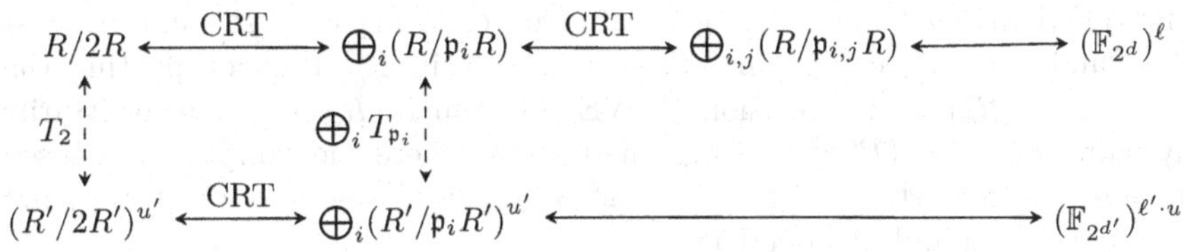

$$
\begin{array}{ccccccc}
R/2R & \xleftrightarrow{\text{CRT}} & \bigoplus_i (R/\mathfrak{p}_i R) & \xleftrightarrow{\text{CRT}} & \bigoplus_{i,j} (R/\mathfrak{p}_{i,j}R) & \longleftrightarrow & (\mathbb{F}_{2^d})^\ell \\
\big\updownarrow T_2 & & \big\updownarrow \bigoplus_i T_{\mathfrak{p}_i} & & & & \\
(R'/2R')^{u'} & \xleftrightarrow{\text{CRT}} & \bigoplus_i (R'/\mathfrak{p}_i R')^{u'} & & \longleftrightarrow & & (\mathbb{F}_{2^{d'}})^{\ell' \cdot u'}
\end{array}
$$

Fig. 1. Commutative diagram of various representations of the plaintext spaces, and morphisms between them. Solid lines are ring isomorphisms, and dashed lines are R'-linear homomorphisms (i.e., satisfying $T(x+y) = T(x) + T(y)$ and $T(rx) = rT(x)$ for all $r \in R'$).

3   The Ring-Switching Procedure

Given a big-ring ciphertext $\mathbf{c} \in (R_q)^2$ that encrypts a plaintext $a \in R_2$ relative to a big-ring secret key $\mathfrak{s} \in R$, our goal is to output u' small-ring ciphertexts $\mathbf{c}_k \in (R'_q)^2$ for $k \in [u']$, where each $\mathbf{c}_k$ encrypts $a_k \in R'_2$, namely the kth component $T(a)$, all relative to some small-ring secret key $\mathfrak{s}' \in R'$. The procedure consists of the following two steps:

1. **Key-switch.** We use the key-switching method from [5, 3] to switch to a ciphertext that is still over the big ring R, but which has a secret key $\mathfrak{s}' \in R'$ belonging to the small subring $R' \subseteq R$.
2. **Decompose.** We break the resulting big-ring ciphertext (over R_q) into u' small-ring ciphertexts (over R'_q) using the decomposition T_q. These ciphertexts will be valid with respect to the small-ring secret key $\mathfrak{s}' \in R'$, and will encrypt the components of $T(a)_k$ as desired (see Lemma 4).

3.1   Switching to a Small-Ring Secret Key

To enable this transformation, we include in the public key a "key switching hint," essentially encrypting the old big-ring key $\mathfrak{s}$ under the new small-ring key $\mathfrak{s}'$. Note that using such a small-ring secret key has security implications, since it severely reduces the dimension of the underlying LWE problem. In our case, however, the whole point of switching to a smaller ring is to get ciphertexts over a smaller dimension, so we are not actually losing any additional security by giving out the hint. Indeed, we show below that assuming the hardness of the decision-ring-LWE problem [15] over the small ring R_q', the key-switching hint is indistinguishable from uniformly random over R_q (even for a distinguisher that knows the old secret key $\mathfrak{s}$).

Ring-LWE. The ring-LWE (RLWE) problem [15] over R_q' is parameterized by an error distribution χ' over R', typically derived from a Gaussian and so highly concentrated on short elements.[5] For a "secret" element $\mathfrak{s}' \in R'$, a sample from the RLWE distribution $A_{\mathfrak{s}',\chi'}$ is generated by choosing $\alpha \in R_q'$ uniformly at random and $\epsilon \leftarrow \chi'$, computing $\beta \leftarrow \alpha \cdot \mathfrak{s}' + \epsilon$ in R_q', then outputting the pair $(\alpha, \beta) \in (R_q')^2$. The decision RLWE problem in R_q' is: given arbitrarily many pairs $(\alpha_i, \beta_i) \in (R_q')^2$, distinguish the case where the samples are chosen independently from $A_{\mathfrak{s}',\chi'}$ (for a single $\mathfrak{s}' \leftarrow \chi'$) from the case where they are uniformly random and independent.

To set up the key-switching technique, we first prove a lemma of independent interest about the hardness of RLWE over the big ring R_q when the secret is chosen according to χ' from the subring R'. Define an error distribution χ over R as $\chi = T^{-1}((\chi')^{u'})$, i.e., a sample from χ is generated by choosing independent $\epsilon_i \leftarrow \chi'$ for $i \in [u']$, and outputting $\epsilon = T^{-1}(\epsilon_0, \ldots, \epsilon_{u'-1}) = \sum_i \epsilon_i \cdot \zeta_m^i \in R$. Note that elements drawn from χ are short: because $\|\sigma(\zeta_m^i)\|_\infty = 1$ for all i, we have

$$\|\sigma(\epsilon_i \cdot \zeta_m^i)\| = \|\sigma(\epsilon_i)\| = \sqrt{u'} \cdot \|\sigma'(\epsilon_i)\|$$

(where as usual, the $\sqrt{u'}$ term is effectively a normalization factor between R' and R). Then by the triangle inequality, $\|\sigma(\epsilon)\| \le (u')^{3/2} \cdot B$, where B is an upper bound on every $\|\sigma'(\epsilon_i)\|$. (Tighter bounds can also be obtained when χ' is Gaussian, as is typical with RLWE.)

Lemma 3. *If the decision RLWE problem over R' with error distribution χ' is hard, then so is the decision RLWE problem over R with error distribution $\chi = T^{-1}((\chi')^{u'})$, but where the secret is chosen from χ', and in particular is in subring R'.*

Proof. It suffices to give a reduction that maps small-ring samples over $(R_q')^2$, drawn from $A_{\mathfrak{s}',\chi'}$ (respectively, the uniform distribution), to big-ring samples over $(R_q)^2$ with distribution $A_{\mathfrak{s}',\chi}$ (resp., the uniform distribution). To generate each output sample, the reduction takes u' fresh input samples $(\alpha_i, \beta_i) \in (R_q')^2$

---

[5] Or, following [15] more closely, χ' would be a distribution over the dual $R'^{\vee}$.

for $i \in [u']$, defines $\alpha' = (\alpha_i)_i, \beta' = (\beta_i)_i \in (R'_q)^{u'}$, and outputs $(\alpha, \beta) = (T_q^{-1}(\alpha'), T_q^{-1}(\beta')) \in R_q$.

Since T_q is a bijection, it is clear that the reduction maps the uniform distribution to the uniform distribution. On the other hand, if the samples $(\alpha_i, \beta_i = \alpha_i \cdot \mathfrak{s}' + \epsilon_i)$ are drawn from $A_{\mathfrak{s}', \chi'}$ for some $\mathfrak{s}' \leftarrow \chi'$, then α is still uniformly random, and moreover, letting $\epsilon' = (\epsilon_i)_i \in (R')^{u'}$ and by R'-linearity of T_q^{-1}, we have (over R_q)

$$\beta = T_q^{-1}(\alpha' \cdot \mathfrak{s}' + \epsilon') = T_q^{-1}(\alpha') \cdot \mathfrak{s}' + T^{-1}(\epsilon') = \alpha \cdot \mathfrak{s}' + \epsilon,$$

where $\epsilon = T^{-1}(\epsilon')$ is distributed according to χ by construction. So (α, β) is distributed according to $A_{\mathfrak{s}', \chi}$, as desired. $\square$

The Key-Switching Hint. Let $\mathfrak{s} \in R$ be the big-ring secret key, and $\mathfrak{s}' \in R' \subset R$ be the small-ring secret key that we want to switch to. To construct the key-switching hint, we independently draw $l = \lceil \log_2 q \rceil$ error terms $\epsilon_i \leftarrow \chi$ and uniformly random elements $\alpha_i \in R_q$, for $i \in [l]$. The hint consists of the all the pairs[6]

$$(\alpha_i, \beta_i = 2^i \cdot \mathfrak{s} - \alpha_i \cdot \mathfrak{s}' + 2\epsilon_i) \in (R_q)^2.$$

For security, note that by the form of the hint, it is immediate from Lemma 3 that for any big-ring secret key $\mathfrak{s} \in R$, the hint (even along with $\mathfrak{s}$) is computationally indistinguishable from uniform.

Since the errors ϵ_i are short, the hint is functional for key-switching, as described in [5]. Specifically, suppose we are given a valid ciphertext $\mathbf{c} = (c_0, c_1)$ relative to $\mathfrak{s}$, for which $c_0 + \mathfrak{s} \cdot c_1 = (a + 2e) \bmod q$ for some short $(a + 2e) \in R$. We decompose c_1 into its bitwise representation as $c_1 = \sum_{i \in [l]} 2^i d_i \bmod q$ for short elements $d_i \in R$ having 0-1 coefficients in the power basis. We then have the relation (over R_q)

$$\underbrace{c_0 + \sum_i d_i \beta_i}_{c_0'} + \underbrace{\sum_i d_i \alpha_i \cdot \mathfrak{s}'}_{c_1'} = c_0 + \sum_i d_i (2^i \mathfrak{s} + 2\epsilon_i) = c_0 + c_1 \cdot \mathfrak{s} + 2\sum_i d_i \epsilon_i$$

$$= a + 2(e + \sum_i d_i \epsilon_i).$$

Since $\sum_i d_i \epsilon_i \in R$ is short, (c_0', c_1') is a valid ciphertext encrypting a under $\mathfrak{s}'$, as desired.

3.2   Decomposing the Ciphertext

After switching to a small-ring secret key $\mathfrak{s}' \in R'$ in the previous step, the ciphertext is a pair $\mathbf{c} = (c_0, c_1) \in (R_q)^2$ such that

$$c_0 + \mathfrak{s}' \cdot c_1 \in (a + 2e) + qR,$$

---

[6] We could alternatively use the key-switching variant from [13], where the hint consists of a single pair (β, α), but with respect to a large modulus $Q \approx q^2 \cdot m$. The proof of security would then depend on the hardness of ring-LWE in R'_Q rather than in R'_q.

where $a + 2e \in R$ is sufficiently short. We decompose this ciphertext into u' ciphertexts $\mathbf{c}_k = (c_{k,0}, c_{k,1}) \in (R'_q)^2$ for $k \in [u']$, where for $b \in \{0, 1\}$, $T_q(c_b) = (c_{0,b}, \ldots, c_{u'-1,b})$. (Recall that $T_q \colon R_q \to (R'_q)^{u'}$ is the R'-linear bijection induced by the decomposition T defined in Section 2.2.)

Lemma 4. *If $\mathbf{c}$ is a valid encryption of plaintext $a \in R_2$ under secret key $\mathfrak{s}' \in R'$, then each $\mathbf{c}_k$ is a valid encryption of the kth component of $T_2(a) \in (R'_2)^{u'}$.*

Proof. Below we identify $\mathfrak{s}' \in R'$ with its mod-q equivalence class $\mathfrak{s}' + qR' \in R'_q$. Because T_q is R'_q-linear, we have

$$T_q(c_0) + \mathfrak{s}' \cdot T_q(c_1) = T_q(c_0 + \mathfrak{s}' \cdot c_1) = T(a + 2e) + (qR')^{u'},$$

where the multiplication of scalar $\mathfrak{s}' \in R'$ with $T_q(c_1) \in (R'_q)^{u'}$ is coordinate-wise. By Lemma 2, each component of $T(a+2e)$ has length bounded by $c_r \cdot \|a+2e\| / \sqrt{u'}$ (where the $\sqrt{u'}$ term is a normalization factor), so the "effective" lengths (relative to q and the dimension of R') grow by at most a fixed constant factor c_r, and are sufficiently small. Moreover, $T(a + 2e) \in T_2(a) \in (R'_2)^{u'}$, so the message encrypted by $\mathbf{c}_k$ is the kth component of $T_2(a)$. $\qquad\square$

4   Homomorphic Computation in the Small Ring

So far we have shown how to break a big-ring ciphertext, encrypting some big-ring element $a \in R_2$, into a collection of u' small-ring ciphertexts encrypting the small-ring elements $T(a) = (a_0, a_1, \ldots, a_{u'-1}) \in R'_2$. This, however, still falls short of our goal of speeding-up homomorphic computation by switching to small-ring ciphertexts. Indeed we have not shown how to use the encryption of the a_k's for further homomorphic computation.

Following the narrative of SIMD homomorphic computation from [18, 11–13], we view the big-ring plaintext element $a \in R_2$ as an encoding of a vector of plaintext values from the extension field $\mathbb{F}_{2^d}$ (with d the order of 2 in $\mathbb{Z}_m^*$). We therefore wish to obtain small-ring ciphertexts encrypting small-ring elements that encode of the same underlying $\mathbb{F}_{2^d}$ values.

One potential "algebraic issue" with this goal, is that it is not always possible to embed $\mathbb{F}_{2^d}$ values inside small-ring elements from R'_2. Recall that the extension degree d is determined by the order of 2 in $\mathbb{Z}_m^*$. But the order of 2 in $\mathbb{Z}_w^*$ may be smaller than d, in general it will be some d' that divides d. If $d' < d$ then we can only embed values from the sub-field $\mathbb{F}_{2^{d'}}$ in small-ring element from R'_2, and not the $\mathbb{F}_{2^d}$ values that we have encoded in the big-ring element a. For the rest of this section we only consider the special case where the order of 2 in both $\mathbb{Z}_m^*$ and $\mathbb{Z}_w^*$ is the same d, leaving the general case to the full version.

Even for the special case where the order of 2 in $\mathbb{Z}_m^*$ and $\mathbb{Z}_w^*$ is the same (and hence the "plaintext slots" in the small ring contain values from the same extension field as those in the big ring), we still need to tackle the issue that big ring elements have more plaintext slots than small ring elements. Specifically, big-ring elements have $\ell = \varphi(m)/d$ slots, whereas small-ring elements only have

$\ell' = \varphi(w)/d$ slots. The solution here is obvious: we just use more small-ring elements to hold all the plaintext slots that we need.

Note that if the original plaintext element a was "sparsely populated", holding only a few plaintext values in its slots, then we would like to generate only as many small-ring ciphertexts as needed to hold these few plaintext slots. A good example is the computation of the AES circuit in [13]: Since there are only 16 bytes in the AES state, we only use 16 slots in the plaintext element a. In this case, as long as we have at least 16 slots in small-ring elements, we can continue working with a single small-ring ciphertext (as opposed to the u' ciphertexts that the technique of the previous section gives us).

4.1   Ring-Switching with Plaintext Encoding

Below we describe our method for converting the plaintext encoding between the different rings, for the special case where the order of 2 is the same in $\mathbb{Z}_m^*$ and $\mathbb{Z}_w^*$. As sketched in the introduction, the basic observation underlying our approach is that the transformation $T(a) = (a_0, a_1, \ldots, a_{u'-1})$ that we apply to our plaintext when breaking a big-ring ciphertext into its small-ring parts, induces a linear transformation over the values in the plaintext slots. We then just finish-up the process by homomorphically computing the inverse linear transformation over the resulting small-ring ciphertexts (using "general purpose" techniques for computing on packed ciphertexts, such as in [11]), thereby restoring the plaintext slots to their original values.

As explained in Section 2.4, each plaintext slot in the big-ring element is associated with a member of the quotient group $\mathcal{Q}_m = \mathbb{Z}_m^*/\langle 2 \rangle$, and similar association holds between plaintext slots in small-ring elements and members of the quotient group $\mathcal{Q}_w = \mathbb{Z}_w^*/\langle 2 \rangle$. We thus begin by relating the structures and representations of these two quotient groups.

Below let $U_w \subseteq \mathbb{Z}_w^*$ be a representative set for $\mathcal{Q}_w$. i.e., a set containing exactly one index from each conjugacy class in $\mathbb{Z}_w^*/\langle 2 \rangle$. It is easy to see that when the order of 2 is the same in $\mathbb{Z}_m^*$ and $\mathbb{Z}_w^*$, then the set $U_m = \{j \in \mathbb{Z}_m^* : \exists i \in U_w \text{ s.t. } j \equiv i \pmod{w}\}$ is a representative set for $\mathcal{Q}_m$. Fixing in addition a primitive m'th root of unity $\rho \in \mathbb{F}_{2^d}$ and the particular primitive w'th root of unity $\tau = \rho^u$, we let the plaintext slots encoded in $a \in R_2$ be the evaluations $a(\rho^j) \in \mathbb{F}_{2^d}$ for $j \in U_m$, and similarly the plaintext slots encoded in $a' \in R'_2$ be the evaluations $a'(\tau^i)$ for $i \in U_w$.

We proceed to prove that under this representation, the transformation T from Section 2.2 induces an $\mathbb{F}_{2^d}$-linear transformation on the values in the $\mathbb{F}_{2^d}$ values in the plaintext slots. A key lemma is the following:

Lemma 5. *Let $m = u \cdot w$ for odd integers u, w, such that the order of 2 is the same in $\mathbb{Z}_m^*$ and in $\mathbb{Z}_w^*$. Let U_w be a representative set of $\mathcal{Q}_w = \mathbb{Z}_w^*/\langle 2 \rangle$, and fix the representative set of $\mathcal{Q}_m = \mathbb{Z}_m^*/\langle 2 \rangle$ to be $U_m = \{j \in \mathbb{Z}_m^* : \exists i \in U_w \text{ s.t. } j \equiv i \pmod{w}\}$. Denote the order of 2 (in both $\mathbb{Z}_m^*$ and $\mathbb{Z}_w^*$) by d, let $\rho \in \mathbb{F}_{2^d}$ be a primitive m'th root of unity, and fix the particular primitive w'th root of unity $\tau = \rho^u$.*

Finally, fix an arbitrary value $\alpha \in \mathbb{F}_{2^d}$ and let $a(X)$ be the (unique) polynomial in $\mathbb{F}_2[X]/\Phi_m(X)$ that satisfies $a(\rho^j) = \alpha$ for all $j \in U_m$.

Then a is of the form $a(X) = b(X^u) \bmod (\Phi_m(X), 2)$ for some polynomial $b(X) \in \mathbb{F}_2[X]/\Phi_2(X)$ satisfying $b(\tau^i) = \alpha$ for all $i \in U_w$. In particular a, b represent the same element $r' \in R'_2 \subset R_2$.

Proof. We first note that a polynomial $a(X)$ as above is indeed unique, due to Claim 2.4. Similarly a polynomial $b(X) \in \mathbb{F}_2[X]/\Phi_2(X)$ satisfying $b(\tau^i) = \alpha$ for all $i \in U_w$ is also uniquely determined. Denoting $c(X) \stackrel{\text{def}}{=} b(X^u) \bmod (\Phi_m(X), 2) \in R_2$, it is only left to show that $c(X) = a(X)$.

Clearly both c and a are polynomials in $R_2 \cong \mathbb{F}_2[X]/\Phi_m(X) \subset \mathbb{F}_{2^d}[X]/\Phi_m(X)$, so it is sufficient to show that they agree when evaluated on $\rho^j \in \mathbb{F}_{2^d}$ for all $j \in U_m$ (again by Claim 2.4). By definition of U_m, for every $j \in U_m$ there exists $i \in U_w$ such that $j \equiv i \pmod{w}$, hence we get

$$c(\rho^j) = b(\rho^{u \cdot j}) = b(\tau^j) = b(\tau^i) = \alpha = a(\rho^j). \qquad \square$$

(We note that the fact that 2 has the same order modulo w and m is used in the assertion that the set U_m as above is a representative set for $\mathcal{Q}_m$.)

Corollary 1. *With notations as in Lemma 5 and the transformation $T: R_2 \to (R'_2)^{u'}$ from Section 2.2, if a, b are as in Lemma 5 then for any element $x \in R_2$ we have $T_2(a \cdot x \in R_2) = b \cdot T(x) \in (R'_2)^{u'}$.*

Proof. Follows immediately from the R'_2-linearity of T_2 and the fact that the polynomials $a \in \mathbb{F}_2[X]/\Phi_m(X)$ and $b \in \mathbb{F}_2[X]/\Phi_w(X)$ represent the same element $r' \in R'_2 \subseteq R_2$ (since $a(X) = b(X^u) \bmod (\Phi_m(X), 2)$). $\qquad \square$

Given Corollary 1, the rest of the proof follows quite easily. Consider now the encoding functions that map R_2 elements into the vector of $\mathbb{F}_{2^d}$ values that are encoded in all their slots. Namely, for $a \in R_2$ denote by $\mathsf{Enc}_m(a) \in \mathbb{F}_{2^d}^{\ell}$ the vector of values $a(\rho^j)$ for $j \in U_m$. Similarly consider the encoding of a vector of R'_2 elements into the $\mathbb{F}_{2^d}$ values that are encoded in all the slots of all the elements. That is, for a vector $a = (a_0, a_1, \ldots, a_{u'-1}) \in (R'_2)^{u'}$, denote by $\mathsf{Enc}_w(a)$ the vector of values $a_k(\tau^i)$ for $i \in U_w$ and $k \in [u']$. We note that the dimensions of $\mathsf{Enc}_m(a)$ and $\mathsf{Enc}_w(T_2(a))$ are the same, namely they both have dimension $\ell = \varphi(m)/d = u' \cdot \varphi(w)/d$.

Lemma 6. *There exists an invertible linear transformation L over $\mathbb{F}_{2^d}$ such that for any $a \in R_2$ it holds that $\mathsf{Enc}_w(T_2(a)) = L(\ \mathsf{Enc}_m(a)\ )$.*

Proof. Recalling that the encoding functions are bijections (by Claim 2.4), we thus define $L(x) \stackrel{\text{def}}{=} \mathsf{Enc}_w(T_2(\mathsf{Enc}_m^{-1}(x)))$, and note that L must be invertible, because $T_2(\cdot)$ is also a bijection.

It remains only to show that L is $\mathbb{F}_{2^d}$-linear. The property $L(x) + L(y) = L(x + y)$ follows immediately from the facts that the same property holds for each of $T_2(\cdot)$, $\mathsf{Enc}_m(\cdot)$, and $\mathsf{Enc}_w(\cdot)$. We next use Lemma 5 and Corollary 1 to show the property $L(\alpha \cdot x) = \alpha \cdot L(x)$.

Fix a vector $x \in \mathbb{F}_{2^d}^{\ell}$ and a value $\alpha \in \mathbb{F}_{2^d}$, and let $a \in \mathbb{F}_2[X]/\Phi_m(X) \cong R_2$ be the element that has α in all of its plaintext slots, $a = \mathsf{Enc}_m^{-1}(\alpha^{\ell})$. Similarly let $x = \mathsf{Enc}_m^{-1}(\boldsymbol{x})$. Observe that since multiplication in R_2 implies pointwise multiplication on the slots, then the product $a \cdot x \in R_2$ encodes in its slots exactly α times the slots of x. In other words, we have $\mathsf{Enc}_m^{-1}(\alpha \cdot \boldsymbol{x} \in \mathbb{F}_{2^d}^{\ell}) = a \cdot x \in R_2$.

Since a has the same element α in all its slots then it satisfies the condition of Lemma 5 and Corollary 1. Let $b \in \mathbb{F}_2[X]/\Phi_w(X) \cong R_2'$ be the polynomial promised by Lemma 5. Then from Corollary 1 we have that $T_2(a \cdot x) = b \cdot T(x)$. Moreover Lemma 5 tells us that b also have the values α in all its slots. Since multiplication in R_2' also implies pointwise multiplication on the slots, i.e., $\mathsf{Enc}_w(b \cdot \boldsymbol{y}) = \alpha \cdot \mathsf{Enc}_w(\boldsymbol{y})$ for every $\boldsymbol{y} \in (R_2')^{u'}$. In particular,

$$\mathsf{Enc}_w(T_2(a \cdot x)) = \mathsf{Enc}_w(b \cdot T_2(x)) = \alpha \cdot \mathsf{Enc}_w(x),$$

or in other words $L(\alpha \cdot \boldsymbol{x}) = \alpha \cdot L(\boldsymbol{x})$, as needed.   □

Our strategy for recovering the original values in the plaintext space after ring-switching is to first use the transformation T to break a big-ring ciphertexts into a collection of small-ring ciphertexts. By Lemma 6 this operation has the side effect of transforming the slots according to the invertible $\mathbb{F}_{2^d}$-linear transformation L, so we compute homomorphically the inverse transformation L^{-1} on the slots, using the tools from [11] for computing on packed ciphertexts.

If we only need a few of the slots in a (as in the AES example), then we can compute only the relevant rows of L^{-1}, thereby getting at the end of the process only as many small-ring ciphertexts as required to encode all the plaintext slots that we are interested in.

Remarks. Note that the *only* properties of T that we used in this work are the properties 1-4 that were described in the introduction. Namely, all we need is a transformation $T: R \to (R')^*$ which is injective and R_2'-linear, and that maps small R elements into small R' vectors. There could be many such transformations, and they could offer different tradeoffs in practice. (For example, the transformation in a previous version of this work [10], which was based on the coefficient-splitting technique from [3], turns out to include a very sparse linear transformations L, making the homomorphic computation of L^{-1} at the end must easier.) Also, as mentioned in Section 2.2, in some cases we can use a K_2'-linear transformation $T: \mathbb{K} \to (\mathbb{K}')^*$ even if it does not map R-elements to R'-vectors.

We also note that Lemma 5 (and consequently Corollary 1 and Lemma 6) can be extended also to the case where the order of 2 modulo w is smaller than its order modulo m, as long as we only consider elements $a \in R_2$ that have values from the smaller field $\mathbb{F}_{2^{d'}}$ in their plaintext slots. We defer details of this extension to the full version.

Acknowledgments. The first and second authors are supported by the Intelligence Advanced Research Projects Activity (IARPA) via Department of Interior National Business Center (DoI/NBC) contract number D11PC20202. The U.S. Government is authorized to reproduce and distribute reprints for Governmental purposes notwithstanding any copyright annotation thereon. Disclaimer: The views and conclusions contained herein are those of the authors and should not be interpreted as necessarily representing the official policies or endorsements, either expressed or implied, of IARPA, DoI/NBC, or the U.S. Government.

The third author is supported by the National Science Foundation under CAREER Award CCF-1054495, by the Alfred P. Sloan Foundation, and by the Defense Advanced Research Projects Agency (DARPA) and the Air Force Research Laboratory (AFRL) under Contract No. FA8750-11-C-0098. The views expressed are those of the authors and do not necessarily reflect the official policy or position of the National Science Foundation, the Sloan Foundation, DARPA or the U.S. Government.

The fourth author is supported by the European Commission through the ICT Programme under Contract ICT-2007-216676 ECRYPT II and via an ERC Advanced Grant ERC-2010-AdG-267188-CRIPTO, by EPSRC via grant COED–EP/I03126X, and by a Royal Society Wolfson Merit Award. The views and conclusions contained herein are those of the authors and should not be interpreted as necessarily representing the official policies or endorsements, either expressed or implied, of the European Commission or EPSRC.

References

1. Applebaum, B., Cash, D., Peikert, C., Sahai, A.: Fast Cryptographic Primitives and Circular-Secure Encryption Based on Hard Learning Problems. In: Halevi, S. (ed.) CRYPTO 2009. LNCS, vol. 5677, pp. 595–618. Springer, Heidelberg (2009)
2. Brakerski, Z.: Fully Homomorphic Encryption without Modulus Switching from Classical GapSVP. In: Safavi-Naini, R. (ed.) CRYPTO 2012. LNCS, vol. 7417, pp. 868–886. Springer, Heidelberg (2012), http://eprint.iacr.org/2012/078
3. Brakerski, Z., Gentry, C., Vaikuntanathan, V.: Fully homomorphic encryption without bootstrapping. In: Innovations in Theoretical Computer Science (ITCS 2012) (2012), http://eprint.iacr.org/2011/277
4. Brakerski, Z., Vaikuntanathan, V.: Fully Homomorphic Encryption from Ring-LWE and Security for Key Dependent Messages. In: Rogaway, P. (ed.) CRYPTO 2011. LNCS, vol. 6841, pp. 505–524. Springer, Heidelberg (2011)
5. Brakerski, Z., Vaikuntanathan, V.: Efficient fully homomorphic encryption from (standard) LWE. In: FOCS 2011. IEEE Computer Society (2011)
6. Damgård, I., Pastro, V., Smart, N.P., Zakarias, S.: Multiparty Computation from Somewhat Homomorphic Encryption. In: Safavi-Naini, R. (ed.) CRYPTO 2012. LNCS, vol. 7417, pp. 643–662. Springer, Heidelberg (2012), http://eprint.iacr.org/2011/535
7. Ducas, L., Durmus, A.: Ring-LWE in Polynomial Rings. In: Fischlin, M., Buchmann, J., Manulis, M. (eds.) PKC 2012. LNCS, vol. 7293, pp. 34–51. Springer, Heidelberg (2012), http://eprint.iacr.org/2012/235
8. Gama, N., Nguyen, P.Q.: Predicting Lattice Reduction. In: Smart, N.P. (ed.) EUROCRYPT 2008. LNCS, vol. 4965, pp. 31–51. Springer, Heidelberg (2008)
9. Gentry, C.: Fully homomorphic encryption using ideal lattices. In: Mitzenmacher, M. (ed.) STOC 2009, pp. 169–178. ACM (2009)
10. Gentry, C., Halevi, S., Peikert, C., Smart, N.P.: Ring Switching in BGV-Style Homomorphic Encryption (preliminary version) (2012) (manuscript), http://eprint.iacr.org/2012/240

11. Gentry, C., Halevi, S., Smart, N.P.: Fully Homomorphic Encryption with Polylog Overhead. In: Pointcheval, D., Johansson, T. (eds.) EUROCRYPT 2012. LNCS, vol. 7237, pp. 465–482. Springer, Heidelberg (2012), http://eprint.iacr.org/2011/566

12. Gentry, C., Halevi, S., Smart, N.P.: Better Bootstrapping in Fully Homomorphic Encryption. In: Fischlin, M., Buchmann, J., Manulis, M. (eds.) PKC 2012. LNCS, vol. 7293, pp. 1–16. Springer, Heidelberg (2012), http://eprint.iacr.org/2011/680

13. Gentry, C., Halevi, S., Smart, N.P.: Homomorphic Evaluation of the AES Circuit. In: Safavi-Naini, R. (ed.) CRYPTO 2012. LNCS, vol. 7417, pp. 850–867. Springer, Heidelberg (2012), http://eprint.iacr.org/2012/099

14. Lòpez-Alt, A., Tromer, E., Vaikuntanathan, V.: On-the-Fly Multiparty Computation on the Cloud via Multikey Fully Homomorphic Encryption. In: STOC 2012. ACM (2012)

15. Lyubashevsky, V., Peikert, C., Regev, O.: On Ideal Lattices and Learning with Errors over Rings. In: Gilbert, H. (ed.) EUROCRYPT 2010. LNCS, vol. 6110, pp. 1–23. Springer, Heidelberg (2010)

16. Lyubashevsky, V., Peikert, C., Regev, O.: A toolkit for Ring-LWE cryptography (2012) (manuscript)

17. Lindner, R., Peikert, C.: Better Key Sizes (and Attacks) for LWE-Based Encryption. In: Kiayias, A. (ed.) CT-RSA 2011. LNCS, vol. 6558, pp. 319–339. Springer, Heidelberg (2011)

18. Nigel, P.: Smart and Frederik Vercauteren. Fully homomorphic SIMD operations (2011) (manuscript), http://eprint.iacr.org/2011/133

Zero-Knowledge Proofs with Low Amortized Communication from Lattice Assumptions

Ivan Damgård[1,*] and Adriana López-Alt[2]

[1] Aarhus University
[2] New York University

Abstract. We construct zero-knowledge proofs of plaintext knowledge (PoPK) and correct multiplication (PoPC) for the Regev encryption scheme with low amortized communication complexity. Previous constructions of both PoPK and PoPC had communication cost linear in the size of the public key (roughly quadratic in the lattice dimension, ignoring logarithmic factors). Furthermore, previous constructions of PoPK suffered from one of the following weaknesses: either the message and randomness space were restricted, or there was a *super-polynomial* gap between the size of the message and randomness that an honest prover chose and the size of which an accepting verifier would be convinced. The latter weakness was also present in the existent PoPC protocols.

In contrast, $O(n)$ proofs (for lattice dimension n) in our PoPK and PoPC protocols have communication cost linear in the public key. Thus, we improve the *amortized* communication cost of each proof by a factor linear in the lattice dimension. Furthermore, we allow the message space to be $\mathbb{Z}_p$ and the randomness distribution to be the discrete Gaussian, both of which are natural choices for the Regev encryption scheme. Finally, in our schemes there is no gap between the size of the message and randomness that an honest prover chooses and the size of which an accepting verifier is convinced.

Our constructions use the "MPC-in-the-head" technique of Ishai et al. (STOC 2007). At the heart of our constructions is a protocol for proving that a value is bounded by some publicly known bound. This uses Lagrange's Theorem that states that any positive integer can be expressed as the sum of four squares (an idea previously used by Boudot (EUROCRYPT 2000)), as well as techniques from Cramer and Damgård (CRYPTO 2009).

1 Introduction

The problem of secure multiparty computation (MPC) [19,6,12,31] is central in the field of modern cryptography. In this problem, N parties $\mathcal{P}_1, \ldots, \mathcal{P}_N$ holding

---

* The first author acknowledges support from the Danish National Research Foundation and The National Science Foundation of China (under the grant 61061130540) for the Sino-Danish Center for the Theory of Interactive Computation, within which part of this work was performed; and also from the CFEM research center (supported by the Danish Strategic Research Council) within which part of this work was performed.

I. Visconti and R. De Prisco (Eds.): SCN 2012, LNCS 7485, pp. 38–56, 2012.
© Springer-Verlag Berlin Heidelberg 2012

private inputs $x_1, \ldots, x_N$, respectively, wish to compute a function $f(x_1, \ldots, x_N)$ on their inputs without revealing any information apart from the output of the evaluation (in particular, they wish to keep their inputs secret from the other parties). Solutions to this problem abound in the literature. Many of these solutions use the circuit rerandomization technique of Beaver [3] (see e.g. [20,23,4,21,14,5,8,15], among many others). Circuit rerandomization requires players to hold (additive) secret sharings of many random triples (a, b, c) such that $c = a \cdot b$ in some finite field. Traditionally, these triples are created using zero-knowledge proofs.

Bendlin et al. [8] use zero-knowledge proofs of plaintext knowledge (PoPK) and correct multiplication (PoCM) for this purpose. To see how this is done, consider the 2-party setting as an example. To obtain an additive secret sharing of random values a, b, players $\mathcal{P}_1$ and $\mathcal{P}_2$ can each choose random values u_1, v_1 and u_2, v_2, respectively, and define $a = u_1 + u_2$ and $b = v_1 + v_2$. Obtaining an additive secret sharing of $c = a \cdot b$ is more involved. First, notice that $c = a \cdot b = (u_1 + u_2) \cdot (v_1 + v_2) = u_1 v_1 + u_1 v_2 + u_2 v_1 + u_2 v_2$. If $\mathcal{P}_1$ and $\mathcal{P}_2$ could obtain an additive sharing of each product $u_i v_j = y_{ij} + z_{ij}$ then they could obtain a sharing for c by simply adding each of these shares: $c = (y_{11} + y_{12} + y_{21} + y_{22}) + (z_{11} + z_{12} + z_{21} + z_{22})$. Thus, the problem reduces to having $\mathcal{P}_1$ and $\mathcal{P}_2$ obtain an additive sharing of the product of their inputs m_1 and m_2, respectively (in this case u_i and v_j).

This can be done with the following protocol. $\mathcal{P}_1$ encrypts his input under his public key pk and obtains a ciphertext $c_1 = \text{Enc}_{pk}(m_1; r_1)$, which he sends to $\mathcal{P}_2$. Upon receiving c_1, $\mathcal{P}_2$ computes a ciphertext $c_x = \text{Enc}_{pk}(x; r_x)$ of a random plaintext x and computes $c_2 = m_2 \cdot c_1 + c_x$, sends it to $\mathcal{P}_1$, and outputs $-x$ as his share. If the encryption scheme has certain homomorphic properties, then $c_2 = \text{Enc}_{pk}(m_1 m_2 + x)$. $\mathcal{P}_1$ decrypts c_2 and outputs $m_1 m_2 + x$ as his share, thus obtaining an additive sharing of $m_1 m_2$.

However, when players are malicious, $\mathcal{P}_2$ needs to ensure that c_1 is a valid ciphertext and $\mathcal{P}_1$ needs to ensure that $\mathcal{P}_2$ performed the multiplication step correctly. This can be done by having $\mathcal{P}_1$ and $\mathcal{P}_2$ provide zero-knowledge proofs that they performed their respective operations correctly: $\mathcal{P}_1$ sends a *proof of plaintext knowledge*, proving that there exist m_1, r_1 such that $c_1 = \text{Enc}_{pk}(m_1; r_1)$, and $\mathcal{P}_2$ sends a *proof of correct multiplication*, proving that there exist m_2, x, r_x such that $c_2 = m_2 \cdot c_1 + \text{Enc}_{pk}(x; r_x)$.

Unfortunately, these zero-knowledge proofs can incur a large communication cost, which increases the overall communication complexity of the MPC protocol in which they are used. A key observation is that even though many triples need to be created, they can be created simultaneously. This leads to the question of whether we can lower the *amortized* communication complexity of each proof, thus lowering the *total* communcation cost of all proofs. In this work, we answer this question affirmatively when the encryption scheme used is the Regev encryption scheme [29], whose security is based on the hardness of the Learning with Errors (LWE) problem.

Related Work. Bendlin et al. [8], Bendlin and Damgård [7], and Asharov et al. [2,1] give constructions of proofs of plaintext knowledge. The work of [8] shows proofs of plaintext knowledge for any "semi-homomorphic" encryption scheme, an example of which is the Regev scheme. When applied to this scheme, the communication cost of *each* proof is linear in the size of the public key (roughly quadratic in the lattice dimension, ignoring logarithmic factors). The works of [7] and [2,1] show proofs of plaintext knowledge specifically for the Regev scheme, but here again, the communication cost of each proof is linear in the size of the public key. Similarly, [8] shows proofs of correct multiplication which, when applied to the Regev encryption scheme, have communication complexity linear in the public key size per proof.

Unfortunately, the protocol of [7] only works for message space $\{0,1\}$ and randomness in $\{0,1\}^m$. Furthermore, the proofs of [8] and [2,1] suffer from the following weakness. To guarantee zero-knowledge, an honest prover must choose the message and randomness from a sufficiently small range. But in order to guarantee soundness against a cheating prover, we can only guarantee that if the verifier accepts then the message and randomness come from a much larger interval. Thus, there is a gap between the size of the witness of an honest prover and the size of which an accepting verifier will be convinced. Such a gap, which turns out to be *super-polynomial* in the security parameter, is undesirable.

Our Results and Techniques. We improve upon these results by showing proofs of plaintext knowledge and correct multiplication where the cost of $O(n)$ proofs, where n is the lattice dimension, is linear in the public key size. Thus, we improve the amortized cost of each proof by a linear factor in the lattice dimension. Furthermore, our protocol does not suffer from the weakness of [8] and [2,1]; there is no gap between the size of the witness of an honest prover and the size of which an accepting verifier is convinced. The message space in our schemes can be $\mathbb{Z}_p$ and the probability distribution for the randomness can be the discrete Gaussian.[1]

Our proof system uses the "MPC-in-the-head" technique of Ishai et al. [22], who show how to construct zero-knowlege proofs from MPC protocols. The basic idea is as follows. For an NP relation $R(x, w)$ with statement x and witness w, the prover runs an MPC protocol for the function $f_x(w) = R(x, w)$ "in his head" and commits to the view of each of the players. The verifier then outputs a subset T of the players as challenge, and the prover opens the commitments to the views of the players in T. If the views are consistent, the verifier accepts.

This is the same technique that was used in [7] yet we improve upon it. First, we also show how to obtain proofs of correct multiplication. But more importantly, we expand the proofs to allow the message space to be $\mathbb{Z}_p$ (rather than bits), and allow the randomness distribution to be the discrete Gaussian (rather than bit-vectors). To achieve this, we show a protocol that allows a dealer

---

[1] Technically, we'll need the Regev scheme to have perfect correctness, so the randomness distribution will be a "truncated" discrete Gaussian that is statistically close to the discrete Gaussian, where values output according to the distribution are guaranteed to be small (as opposed to small with high probability).

to prove that the secret that he secret-shared among N players is bounded by some publicly known bound B. The intuition behind this proof is as follows. Let $[s]$ denote the sharing of secret s. The dealer distributes a sharing of B, $[B]$, and the players compute sharings $[B - s]$ and $[B + s]$ by locally adding their corresponding shares. We know that $-B < s < B$ if and only if both $B - s$ and $B + s$ are positive, so the problem of proving that s is bounded by B reduces to proving that a secret s' that has been secret shared among N players is positive.

For this, we use Lagrange's Theorem that states that any positive integer can be written as the sum of four squares (see, e.g. [16]), and moreover, that these four squares can be computed efficiently [28,24] (a similar technique was used by Boudot [9]). The dealer computes u, v, w, y such that $s' = u^2 + v^2 + w^2 + y^2$, and distributes sharings $[u], [v], [w], [y]$. The players can then locally compute shares $[u^2 + v^2 + w^2 + y^2 - s'] = [0]$, and verify that these final shares reconstruct to 0.

However, we must ensure that the values u, v, w, y are all smaller than $\sqrt{q/8}$. Otherwise we can have overflow modulo q when we square and add the four squares, which would mean that we can no longer guarantee that the sum of the four squares is positive. For this, we use techniques from Cramer and Damgård [13]. The same techniques were used in [8], yet the key difference is that we use them to bound the numbers to be squared (and thus the bound can be loose), whereas in [8] they were used to bound the secrets themselves (thus leading to the gap discussed above). The use of this technique requires our modulus q to be super-polynomial in the security parameter λ (as was also the case in [7,8,2,1]). See Section 3 for more details.

Other Applications. Recently, Brakerski et al. showed that a variant of the Regev scheme is fully homomorphic [11,10]. The zero-knowledge PoPKs shown in this work can be used to prove that a ciphertext encrypted under this Regev-based FHE scheme is well-formed.

Presentation. In Section 2, we review some background needed for our constructions. This includes the IKOS construction (Section 2.2), packed secret sharing (Section 2.3), and a protocol for verifying the consistency of secret shares (Section 2.4). In Section 3, we show a protocol that allows parties to verify that a secret that is shared among them is numerically small. In Section 4 and Section 5 we show our protocols for proofs of plaintext knowledge and proofs of correct multiplication, respectively. Due to lack of space, we defer all proofs to the full version.

2 Preliminaries

2.1 Notation

The natural security parameter in this work is λ. We let $\mathbb{Z}_q = \{-q/2, \ldots, q/2\}$ and use $a \mod q$ to denote the mapping of a into the interval $(-q/2, q/2]$. We use $[n]$ to denote the set $\{1, \ldots, n\} \subset \mathbb{Z}$.

We use boldface lower-case letters to represent vectors, such as $\mathbf{u} = (u_1, \ldots, u_n) \in \mathbb{Z}_q^n$. Throughout what follows, *vectors will be assumed to be column vectors, unless stated otherwise.* We use subscripts to denote coordinates on a vector, e.g. u_i is the ith coordinate of vector $\mathbf{u}$. This is to differentiate between coordinates of a vector and elements in a sequence. For the latter case, we use superscripts: $m^{(i)}$ is the ith element of sequence $m^{(1)}, \ldots, m^{(k)}$. We will also sometimes use the notation $(u_i)_{i \in [n]}$ to denote the vector $(u_1, \ldots, u_n)$. We use boldface upper-case letters to represent matrices, such as $\mathbf{A} \in \mathbb{Z}_q^{n \times m}$. For a vector $\mathbf{x} = (x_1, \ldots, x_n)$ and a scalar a, we let $a\mathbf{x} = (ax_1, \ldots, ax_n)$.

For a distribution χ, we denote $x \leftarrow \chi$ to be the experiment of choosing x according to χ. If S is a set, then we use $x \leftarrow S$ to denote the experiment of choosing x from the uniform distribution on S. For a randomized function f, we write $f(x\,;r)$ to denote the unique output of f on input x with random coins r. Denote $\mathbb{T} = \mathbb{R}/\mathbb{Z}$ as the group of all reals in $[0, 1)$ with addition modulo 1. For $\alpha \in \mathbb{R}^+$, Ψ_α is defined to be the distribution on $\mathbb{T}$ of a normal variable with mean 0 and standard deviation $\alpha/\sqrt{2\pi}$, reduced modulo 1. For any probability distribution ϕ over $\mathbb{T}$ and integer $q \in \mathbb{Z}^+$, its *discretization* $\bar{\phi}$ is the discrete distribution over $\mathbb{Z}_q$ of the random variable $\lfloor q \cdot X_\phi \rceil \bmod q$, where $X_\phi \leftarrow \phi$.

We use lower case π to denote MPC protocols, such as π_f, and use upper case Π to denote zero-knowledge proof protocols, such as Π_R. We use greek letters to represent shares from a secret sharing. For example, $\boldsymbol{\alpha} = (\alpha^{(1)}, \alpha^{(2)}, \ldots, \alpha^{(N)})$ denotes the shares $\alpha^{(i)}$ of each of the N share holders.

2.2 Overview of IKOS Construction

Let $R(x, w)$ be a NP-relation. Consider the following N-player functionality f. The public statement x is known to all players $\mathcal{P}_1, \ldots, \mathcal{P}_N$. The functionality takes the entire input w from a special player $\mathcal{I}$ called the "input client", and outputs $R(x, w)$ to all N players. Ishai et al. [22] show how to construct a zero-knowledge proof protocol for NP-relation R from a MPC protocol π_f for the functionality f described above. We give a high-level idea of the construction. The prover runs the MPC protocol π_f "in his head" and commits to the views $V_1, \ldots, V_N$ of the N players. The verifier then chooses a subset $T \subset [N]$, and the prover opens his commitments to views $\{V_i\}_{i \in T}$. The verifier accepts iff the commitment openings are successful, the revealed views are consistent, and the output in each view is 1.

We show the formal statement of the result in Theorem 1, but first recall the security properties that the underlying MPC protocol will need to satisfy in the construction. The following definitions are taken almost verbatim from [22].

Definition 1 (Correctness). *We say that a protocol π realizes functionality f with* perfect correctness *if for all inputs (x, w), the probability that the output of some player is different from the output of f is 0, where the probability is taken over the random inputs $r_1, \ldots, r_N$.*

Definition 2 ((Statistical) t-Privacy). *Let $t \in [N]$. We say a protocol π realizes functionality f with* statistical t-privacy *if there exists a PPT simulator* $\mathtt{Sim}$ *such that for all inputs (x, w) and all sets of corrupted players $T \subset [N]$ with*

$|T| \leq t$, the joint view $(\text{VIEW}(P_i))_{i \in T}$ of players in T is distributed stastistically close to $\text{Sim}(T, x, R_T(x, w))$.

Definition 3 (t-Robustness). *Let* $t \in [N]$. *We say a protocol* π *realizes functionality* f *with* perfect t-robustness *if it is perfectly correct in the presence of a semi-honest adversary, and for any computationally unbounded malicious adversary corrupting* $\mathcal{I}$ *and a set* T *of at most* t *players, for all inputs* x, *it holds that if there does not exist* w *such that* $f(x, w) = 1$, *then the probability that an uncorrupted player* $P_i \notin T$ *outputs 1 is 0.*

Theorem 1 ([22]). *Let* f *be the* N-player functionality with input client $\mathcal{I}$ *described above. Suppose that* π_f *is a protocol that realizes* f *with perfect* t-robustness (in the malicious model) and statistical t-privacy (in the semi-honest model), where $t = \Omega(\lambda)$, and $N = ct$ for some constant $c > 1$. Given π_f and an unconditionally-binding commitment scheme, it is possible to construct a computational honest-verifier zero-knowledge proof protocol* $\Pi_{R, \mathcal{I}, t}$ *for the NP-relation* R, *with negligible (in* λ) *soundness error.*

One of the nice properties about the [22] construction is that we get *broadcast for free* because the Prover can simply send the broadcasted messages directly to the Verifier. Therefore, the communication cost of broadcasting a message is simply the size of the message. We also get *coin-flipping among the players for free* because the (honest) Verifier can simply provide the random value. Therefore, the communication cost of coin-flipping for a value is simply the size of the value. We will use these two facts in our constructions. Also, as observed by [7], if we use a commitment scheme that allows us to commit to strings with only a constant additive length increase such as those implicit in [27], then the zero-knowledge proof protocol $\Pi_{R, \mathcal{I}, t}$ (asymptotically) conserves the communication complexity of the underlying MPC protocol π_f.

Finally, using general zero-knowledge techniques, it is possible to convert the honest-verifier zero-knowledge proof protocol $\Pi_{R, \mathcal{I}, t}$ obtained from Theorem 1 into a full zero-knowledge protocol, while (asymptotically) preserving the communication complexity of the protocol. One such technique is described in [22].

2.3 Packed Secret Sharing

We will use the packed secret sharing technique of Franklin and Yung [17]. Similar to Shamir secret sharing over $\mathbb{Z}_q$ [30], packed secret sharing allows a dealer to share a vector of k values $\mathbf{x} = (x_1, x_2, \ldots, x_k)$ using a single random polynomial of degree at most d. To guarantee security against at most t corrupted players, we must have $d \geq t + k - 1$. The idea is to chose a random polynomial $P(\cdot)$ of degree at most d, subject to the condition $P(-j + 1) = x_j$ for $j \in [k]$. The share of player i is, as usual, the value $\alpha_i = P(i)$.

We use $[\mathbf{x}]_d$ to denote a packed secret-sharing $\boldsymbol{\alpha} = (\alpha_1, \ldots, \alpha_N) \in \mathbb{Z}_q^N$ for N players of the block $\mathbf{x}$ using a polynomial of degree at most d. We call $[\mathbf{x}]_d$ a d-sharing of $\mathbf{x}$. We say $\mathbf{x}$ is *correctly shared* if every honest player $\mathcal{P}_i$ is holding a share α_i of $\mathbf{x}$, such that there exists a degree at most d polynomial $P(\cdot)$ with

$P(i) = \alpha_i$ for $i \in N$, and $P(-j+1) = x_j$ for $j \in [k]$. Any (perhaps incomplete) set of shares is called d-*consistent* if these shares lie on a polynomial of degree at most d.

Let $\mathbf{Z} \in \mathbb{Z}_q^{m \times k}$ be a matrix of secrets. Suppose we have d-sharings of the rows of $\mathbf{Z}$: $[\mathbf{Z}_1]_d, \ldots, [\mathbf{Z}_m]_d \in \mathbb{Z}_q^{1 \times N}$. We define $\boldsymbol{\Psi} \in \mathbb{Z}_q^{m \times N}$, called a d-*share matrix* of $\mathbf{Z}$, to be a matrix

$$\boldsymbol{\Psi} = \begin{bmatrix} [\mathbf{Z}_1]_d \\ \vdots \\ [\mathbf{Z}_m]_d \end{bmatrix} \in \mathbb{Z}_q^{m \times N}$$

Note that the shares held by $\mathcal{P}_i$ are precisely the entries in the ith column vector of $\boldsymbol{\Psi}$, denoted by $\boldsymbol{\psi}^{(i)}$.

For any function $f : \mathbb{Z}_q^{m \times 1} \to \mathbb{Z}_q^{m' \times 1}$, we abuse notation and write

$$f(\boldsymbol{\Psi}) = f \begin{pmatrix} [\mathbf{Z}_1]_d \\ \vdots \\ [\mathbf{Z}_m]_d \end{pmatrix} = \begin{bmatrix} [\mathbf{Y}_1]_{d'} \\ \vdots \\ [\mathbf{Y}_{m'}]_{d'} \end{bmatrix},$$

to signify that each player $\mathcal{P}_i$ locally applies f to his shares of all $[\mathbf{Z}_j]_d$'s to obtain his share of each $[\mathbf{Y}_j]_{d'}$. In other words, if $\boldsymbol{\Psi}$ is the d-share matrix of $\mathbf{Z}$ then each player locally computes $f(\boldsymbol{\psi}^{(i)}) = \boldsymbol{\phi}^{(i)}$, where $\boldsymbol{\Phi} = [\boldsymbol{\phi}^{(1)}, \ldots, \boldsymbol{\phi}^{(N)}] \in \mathbb{Z}_q^{m' \times N}$ is the d'-share matrix of $\mathbf{Y}$ containing the $\mathbf{Y}_j$'s as rows.

It is easy to see that if $f(\mathbf{x})$ is a linear function and we define f_i to be f with its output restricted to the ith coordinate (i.e. $f(\mathbf{x}) = (f_1(\mathbf{x}), \ldots, f_{m'}(\mathbf{x}))^{\top}$), then

$$f \begin{pmatrix} [\mathbf{Z}_1]_d \\ \vdots \\ [\mathbf{Z}_m]_d \end{pmatrix} = \begin{bmatrix} [f_1(\mathbf{z}^{(1)}) , \cdots , f_1(\mathbf{z}^{(k)})]_d \\ \vdots \\ [f_{m'}(\mathbf{z}^{(1)}) , \cdots , f_{m'}(\mathbf{z}^{(k)})]_d \end{bmatrix}$$

Note that if f is a linear function, then the sharings obtained as a result of applying f are also d-sharings. In particular, if each player $\mathcal{P}_i$ multiplies his share vector $\boldsymbol{\psi}^{(i)}$ by a matrix $\mathbf{M} \in \mathbb{Z}_q^{m' \times m}$, the player obtains a $(m' \times 1)$-vector representing his corresponding shares of:

$$\mathbf{M}\boldsymbol{\Psi} = \begin{bmatrix} [\mathbf{M}_1 \mathbf{z}^{(1)} , \cdots , \mathbf{M}_1 \mathbf{z}^{(k)}]_d \\ \vdots \\ [\mathbf{M}_{m'} \mathbf{z}^{(1)} , \cdots , \mathbf{M}_{m'} \mathbf{z}^{(k)}]_d \end{bmatrix} = \begin{bmatrix} [(\mathbf{M}_1 \mathbf{z}^{(j)})_{j \in [k]}]_d \\ \vdots \\ [(\mathbf{M}_{m'} \mathbf{z}^{(j)})_{j \in [k]}]_d \end{bmatrix} = \begin{bmatrix} [(\mathbf{MZ})_1]_d \\ \vdots \\ [(\mathbf{MZ})_{m'}]_d \end{bmatrix},$$

where $(\mathbf{MZ})_i$ is the ith row of the matrix $\mathbf{MZ}$.

Parameters. We discuss requirements on the parameters of the scheme. We let $N = c_1 t$ for $c_1 > 2$, satisfying the requirements of the IKOS construction. In order to guarantee privacy of the secret shares, we must have $d \geq t + k - 1$. We will sometimes use $(d/2)$-shares, so we assume $d/2 \geq t + k - 1$. Furthermore, we must have enough honest players so that their shares alone can determine a polynomial of degree d (in case corrupt players do not send their shares for reconstruction). We therefore need $N - t \geq d \geq d/2 \geq t + k - 1$. For our choice of N this yields $k \leq (c_1 - 2)t + 1$. Thus, we assume $k = \Theta(t)$. Also, in order to have enough evaluation points, we must have $q > k + N$. Henceforth, we will use this choice of parameters.

2.4 Verifying Consistency of Shares

We now describe a protocol that can be used by N parties to check that their shares are d-consistent. Security is guaranteed if at most $t < N/2$ parties are corrupted. Players check $N - 2t$ sets of shares at a time. More formally, let $\mathbf{Z} \in \mathbb{Z}_q^{(N-2t)\times k}$ be a matrix of secrets, and suppose d-shares $[\mathbf{Z}_1]_d, \ldots [\mathbf{Z}_{N-2t}]_d$ of the rows of $\mathbf{Z}$ are distributed among the N players. The players want to verify that each sharing is d-consistent without revealing their individual shares. Beerliová-Trubíniová and Hirt [4] describe a protocol in which the N parties can perform this check when they hold N sharings (as opposed to $N - 2t$, as described here) and sharing $[\mathbf{Z}_i]_d$ was created by player $\mathcal{P}_i$. Bendlin and Damgård [7] extend this protocol to the case when all the shares were prepared by a (possibly corrupt) input client $\mathcal{I}$. We describe the protocol of [7] in Figure 1. In the protocol, all players receive as common input a *hyper-invertible* matrix $\mathbf{M} \in \mathbb{Z}_q^{N \times (N-t)}$ for $q > 2N$. Informally, a hyper-invertible matrix is a matrix such that every square submatrix of $\mathbf{M}$ is invertible. Beerliová-Trubíniová and Hirt [4] show how such matrices can be constructed.

Lemma 1. *The protocol π_{CHECK} described in Figure 1 allows N players, at most t of which are corrupted, to verify with zero error probability that $(N - 2t)$ pack-sharings, each of $k = \Theta(t)$ secrets in $\mathbb{Z}_q$, are d-consistent (for $d \geq t + k - 1$). It is t-private in the presence of a semi-honest adversary, t-robust in the presence of a malicious adversary, and has communication complexity $N(N + t)\log q$.*

2.5 Regev Encryption Scheme

Before presenting the Regev encryption scheme [29], we first introduce the hardness assumption on which its security is based. For positive integers $n = n(\lambda)$ and $q = q(\lambda) \geq 2$, a vector $\mathbf{s} \in \mathbb{Z}_q^n$, and a probability distribution χ on $\mathbb{Z}_q$, let $A_{\mathbf{s},\chi}$ be the distribution obtained by choosing $\mathbf{a} \leftarrow \mathbb{Z}_q^n$ and $x \leftarrow \chi$, and outputting $(\mathbf{a}, \langle \mathbf{a}, \mathbf{s} \rangle + x) \in \mathbb{Z}_q^n \times \mathbb{Z}_q$.

Learning with Errors (LWE$_{n,q,\chi}$ and dLWE$_{n,q,\chi}$). The Learning with Errors problem LWE$_{n,q,\chi}$ is defined as follows. Given $m = poly(n)$ samples chosen according to $A_{\mathbf{s},\chi}$ for *uniformly chosen* $\mathbf{s} \in \mathbb{Z}_q^n$, output $\mathbf{s}$ with noticeable probability. The Decisional Learning with Errors problem dLWE$_{n,q,\chi}$ is to distinguish (with non-negligible advantage) $m = poly(n)$ samples chosen according to $A_{\mathbf{s},\chi}$ for *uniformly chosen* $\mathbf{s} \in \mathbb{Z}_q^n$, from m samples chosen uniformly at random from

---

Protocol π_{Check} between parties $(\mathcal{P}_1, \ldots, \mathcal{P}_N)$ to verify d-consistency of shares.

Common input: hyper-invertible matrix $\mathbf{M} \in \mathbb{Z}_q^{N \times (N-t)}$
Input to $\mathcal{P}_i$: corresponding shares of $[\mathbf{Z}_1]_d, \ldots, [\mathbf{Z}_{(N-2t)}]_d$.

1. Input client $\mathcal{I}$ chooses and d-shares random vectors in $\mathbb{Z}_q^{1 \times k}$. Let $[\mathbf{Z}_{N-2t+1}]_d, \ldots [\mathbf{Z}_{N-t}]_d$ be the resulting shares. Augment matrix $\mathbf{Z}$ with rows $\mathbf{Z}_{N-2t+1}, \ldots, \mathbf{Z}_{N-t}$ to obtain matrix $\mathbf{Z}' \in \mathbb{Z}_q^{(N-t) \times k}$. Let $\boldsymbol{\Psi} \in \mathbb{Z}_q^{(N-t) \times N}$ be the d-share matrix of $\mathbf{Z}'$.

2. Players locally compute:

$$
\boldsymbol{\Phi} = \mathbf{M}\boldsymbol{\Psi} = \begin{bmatrix} [(\mathbf{M}\mathbf{Z}')_1]_d \\ \vdots \\ [(\mathbf{M}\mathbf{Z}')_N]_d \end{bmatrix} \in \mathbb{Z}_q^{N \times N}
$$

3. The players reconstruct the resulting shares, each towards a different player: player $\mathcal{P}_i$ receives $\boldsymbol{\Phi}_i$. Each player verifies that the shares he receives are d-consistent and broadcasts "ABORT" if he finds a fault, and otherwise broadcasts "OK".

4. If all players broadcast "OK" then the players conclude that the initial shares were d-consistent.

Fig. 1. Protocol π_{CHECK} to verify consistency of shares

$\mathbb{Z}_q^n \times \mathbb{Z}_q$. In other words, if $\text{dLWE}_{n,q,\chi}$ is hard then $A_{\mathbf{s},\chi}$ is pseudorandom. We will use $\chi = \bar{\Psi}_\alpha$ and in this case, we write $\text{LWE}_{n,q,\alpha}$ to mean $\text{LWE}_{n,q,\bar{\Psi}_\alpha}$.

Discrete Gaussian Distribution. We present an elementary fact that shows that the discrete Gaussian distribution with standard deviation r outputs an element x with with $||x|| \leq r\sqrt{n}$ with high probability.

Lemma 2 (see [25], Theorem 4.4). *Let $n \in \mathbb{N}$. For any real number $r > \omega(\sqrt{\log n})$, we have $\Pr_{\mathbf{x} \leftarrow D_{\mathbb{Z}^n, r}}[||\mathbf{x}|| > r\sqrt{n}] \leq 2^{-n+1}$.*

Using Lemma 2 together with the fact that for all $\mathbf{x} \in \mathbb{R}^n$, $||\mathbf{x}||_\infty \geq ||\mathbf{x}||/\sqrt{n}$ we arrive at the following bound.

Lemma 3. *Let $n \in \mathbb{N}$. For any real number $r > \omega(\sqrt{\log n})$, we have $\Pr_{\mathbf{x} \leftarrow D_{\mathbb{Z}^n, r}}[||\mathbf{x}||_\infty > r] \leq 2^{-n+1}$.*

This allows us to define a *truncated* Gaussian distribution that always outputs (with probability 1) elements with ℓ_∞ norm less than r. Simply define the truncated Gaussian $\overline{D}_{\mathbb{Z}^n, r}$ over $\mathbb{Z}^n$ with standard deviation r to sample a vector according to the discrete Gaussian $D_{\mathbb{Z}^n, r}$ and repeat the sampling if the vector has ℓ_∞ norm greater than r. We will use the truncated discrete Gaussian in our schemes to ensure that samples are bounded by r in each coordinate (and can thus ensure perfect correctness), but state security in terms of the discrete

Gaussian. Since the distributions are statistically close, all results stated using the discrete Gaussian also hold when using the truncated distribution.

We present a generalized version of the Regev encryption scheme [29] (with the modifications of [18]), using the truncated discrete Gaussian (as above). The scheme is parametrized by integers $n = n(\lambda), m = m(\lambda) > n, q = q(\lambda), r = r(\lambda)$, and $p = p(\lambda) < q$. The message space is $\mathcal{M} = \mathbb{Z}_p$, the ciphertext space is $\mathcal{C} = (\mathbb{Z}_q^n, \mathbb{Z}_q)$. All operations are performed over $\mathbb{Z}_q$.

- KeyGen(1^n): Output $sk = \mathbf{s}, pk = (\mathbf{A}, \mathbf{b})$, where $\mathbf{s} \leftarrow \mathbb{Z}_q^n$, $\mathbf{A} \leftarrow \mathbb{Z}_q^{n \times m}$, $\mathbf{x} \leftarrow \chi^m$, $\mathbf{b} = \mathbf{A}^\top \mathbf{s} + \mathbf{x} \in \mathbb{Z}_q^m$.
- Enc$_{pk}(m)$: Output $(\mathbf{u}, c)$, where $\mathbf{r} \leftarrow \overline{D}_{\mathbb{Z}^m, r}$, $\mathbf{u} = \mathbf{A}\mathbf{r} \in \mathbb{Z}_q^{n \times 1}$, $c = \mathbf{b}^\top \mathbf{r} + m \cdot \lfloor q/p \rfloor \in \mathbb{Z}_q$.
- Dec$_{sk}(\mathbf{u}, c)$: Output $m = \lfloor (c - \mathbf{s}^\top \mathbf{u}) \cdot p/q \rceil$.

Theorem 2 ([29,18]). *Let $q \geq 5prm, \alpha \leq 1/(p \cdot r \sqrt{m} \cdot \omega(\sqrt{\log \lambda})), \chi = \bar{\Psi}_\alpha, m \geq 2(n+1) \log q + \omega(\log \lambda)$. With this choice of parameters, the Regev encryption scheme is correct and IND-CPA-secure, assuming $LWE_{n,q,\chi}$ is hard.*

Parameters and Worst-case Guarantees. Our construction requires the modulus q to be super-polynomial in the security parameter λ. More specifically, we require $\sqrt{q/8} > 2^{\omega(\log \lambda)} \cdot m \cdot \max(p/2, r)$. We can use any choice of parameters that satisfies this constraint and keeps the cryptosystem secure.

One option is to let the dimension of the lattice be our security parameter, ie. $n = \lambda$ and set our modulus q to be exponential in the lattice dimension n. Peikert [26] showed that for such a large q, $LWE_{n,q,\alpha}$ is as hard as GapSVP$_{\tilde{O}(n/\alpha)}$ if q is a product of primes, each of polynomial size. The works of [7,8] use this choice of parameters.

Another possible choice is to let $n = \lambda^{1/\epsilon}$ for some $\epsilon \in (0, 1)$ (e.g. $n = \lambda^2$), $p, r, m = \text{poly}(\lambda)$ and let $q = 2^{n^\epsilon}$ be subexponential in the lattice dimension n. In this case, we can rely on Regev's quantum reduction [29] to GapSVP$_{\tilde{O}(n/\alpha)}$ or Peikert's classical reduction [26] to GapSVP$_{\zeta,\gamma}$ where $\gamma(n) \geq n/(\alpha\sqrt{\log n})$, $\zeta(n) \geq \gamma(n)$ and $q \geq \zeta \cdot \omega(\sqrt{\log n/n})$. The work of [2,1] uses this choice of parameters.

3 Verifying that Secrets are Numerically Small

At the heart of our constructions of proofs of plaintext knowledge and correct multiplication, we will use a protocol that allows a dealer (in our case the input client $\mathcal{I}$) to prove to the players that the secret that he secret-shared among them is bounded by some publicly known bound B. Formally, let $\mathbf{R} \in \mathbb{Z}_q^{m \times k}$ be a matrix of secrets. And suppose that a dealer has distributed d-sharings of the rows of $\mathbf{R}$: $[\mathbf{R}_1]_d, \ldots, [\mathbf{R}_m]_d$ between N players. We show a protocol π_{VERSM} that allows the dealer to prove to each player $\mathcal{P}_i$, without revealing $\mathbf{R}$, that all secrets in $\mathbf{R}$ are smaller than $B \ll q/2$.

We first have the dealer compute and distribute a sharing $[\mathbf{b}]_d$ of $\mathbf{b} = (B, \ldots, B) \in \mathbb{Z}_q^k$. Players can then compute

$$\begin{bmatrix} [\mathbf{b}]_d \\ \vdots \\ [\mathbf{b}]_d \end{bmatrix} - \begin{bmatrix} [\mathbf{R}_1]_d \\ \vdots \\ [\mathbf{R}_m]_d \end{bmatrix} = \begin{bmatrix} [\mathbf{b} - \mathbf{R}_1]_d \\ \vdots \\ [\mathbf{b} - \mathbf{R}_m]_d \end{bmatrix} \quad \text{and} \quad \begin{bmatrix} [\mathbf{b}]_d \\ \vdots \\ [\mathbf{b}]_d \end{bmatrix} + \begin{bmatrix} [\mathbf{R}_1]_d \\ \vdots \\ [\mathbf{R}_m]_d \end{bmatrix} = \begin{bmatrix} [\mathbf{b} + \mathbf{R}_1]_d \\ \vdots \\ [\mathbf{b} + \mathbf{R}_m]_d \end{bmatrix}$$

Proving that each secret is bounded by B (and thus lies between $-B$ and B) reduces to proving that all the secrets that are pack-shared by each $[\mathbf{b} - \mathbf{R}_i]_d$ and $[\mathbf{b} + \mathbf{R}_i]_d$ for $i \in [m]$, are positive. We thus show a subroutine, described in Figure 3 that allows a dealer to prove that secrets that are pack-shared among players are positive. To do this, we follow an idea of Boudot [9] and use Lagrange's Four-Square Theorem, which states that *every positive number can be written as the sum of four squares* (see e.g. [16]). Moreover, these four squares can be efficiently computed [28,24]. Suppose the dealer has pack-shared a secret vector $\mathbf{z} \in \mathbb{Z}_q^{1 \times k}$. For each coordinate z_j for $j \in [k]$, the dealer finds the four numbers u_j, v_j, w_j, y_j such that $z_j = u_j^2 + v_j^2 + w_j^2 + y_j^2$. We let $\widetilde{\mathbf{u}}, \widetilde{\mathbf{v}}, \widetilde{\mathbf{w}}, \widetilde{\mathbf{y}}$ be the vectors with u_j, v_j, w_j, y_j as the jth coordinate, respectively. The dealer $(d/2)$-shares each of these vectors $[\widetilde{\mathbf{u}}]_{d/2}, [\widetilde{\mathbf{v}}]_{d/2}, [\widetilde{\mathbf{w}}]_{d/2}, [\widetilde{\mathbf{y}}_i]_{d/2}$. Similarly, we let $\mathbf{u}, \mathbf{v}, \mathbf{w}, \mathbf{y}$ be the vectors with $u_j^2, v_j^2, w_j^2, y_j^2$ as the jth coordinate, respectively. Players can locally compute sharings $[\mathbf{u}]_d, [\mathbf{v}]_d, [\mathbf{w}]_d, [\mathbf{y}]_d$ by squaring their corresponding shares of $[\widetilde{\mathbf{u}}]_{d/2}, [\widetilde{\mathbf{v}}]_{d/2}, [\widetilde{\mathbf{w}}]_{d/2}, [\widetilde{\mathbf{y}}_i]_{d/2}$. Each player then computes,

$$[\mathbf{z}]_d - [\mathbf{u}]_d - [\mathbf{v}]_d - [\mathbf{w}]_d - [\mathbf{y}]_d = [\mathbf{z} - \mathbf{u} - \mathbf{v} - \mathbf{w} - \mathbf{y}]_d = [\mathbf{0}]_d$$

and together they check that the result is indeed a pack-sharing of the vector $\mathbf{0} \in \mathbb{Z}^k$.

However, suppose that a cheating dealer chooses $|u_j| > \sqrt{q/2}$. Then $|u_j^2| > q$ and we have wrap-around modulo q, which means that the cheating dealer could convince the players that a secret z_j is positive, without this being true. To ensure this does not happen, we have the dealer prove that each of u_j, v_j, w_j, y_j is bounded by some bound B', which although larger than B, is certainly much smaller than $\sqrt{q/2}$ (in fact, we will need $B' < \sqrt{q/8}$ so that we don't have overflow when adding the four squares).

Our protocol for verifying that numbers are bounded by B' uses techniques from Cramer and Damgård [13]. Players check τ shares at a time, where τ should be thought of as the "local security parameter" for the protocol π_{VERBND}. The players compute a linear combination of their shares (with some noise added) and reconstruct the result, such that if the secrets resulting from this reconstruction are "not too big" then the original secrets (i.e. the entries in $\mathbf{R}$) are also small. To ensure that the reconstructed result does not reveal $\mathbf{R}$, we let the added noise be in an interval that is a factor of 2^τ larger than the entries in $\mathbf{R}$. To guarantee that π_{VERBND} has statistical (in λ) t-privacy, we set $\tau = \omega(\log \lambda)$. The final bound that we are able to prove is $B' = 2^{2\tau+1}mB$. We will thus need to ensure that $\sqrt{q/8} > 2^{2\tau+1}mB$.

We give full descriptions of the protocol π_{VERSM} in Figure 2, of the subroutine to verify that secrets are positive in Figure 3, and the subroutine to verify that numbers are bounded by B' in Figure 4.

Protocol π_{VERSM} between parties $(\mathcal{P}_1, \ldots, \mathcal{P}_N)$ and input client $\mathcal{I}$.

Common input: bound B
Input to $\mathcal{I}$: $\mathbf{R} \in \mathbb{Z}_q^{m \times k}$.
Input to $\mathcal{P}_i$: Corresponding shares of $[\mathbf{R}_1]_d, \ldots, [\mathbf{R}_m]_d$.

1. $\mathcal{I}$ prepares a d-sharing of $\mathbf{b} = (B, \ldots, B) \in \mathbb{Z}_q^k$: $[\mathbf{b}]_d$. $\mathcal{I}$ gives each player its corresponding shares.
2. Players run the subroutine π_{VERPOS} (see Figure 3) with

$$
\begin{bmatrix} [\mathbf{b}]_d \\ \vdots \\ [\mathbf{b}]_d \end{bmatrix} - \begin{bmatrix} [\mathbf{R}_1]_d \\ \vdots \\ [\mathbf{R}_m]_d \end{bmatrix} = \begin{bmatrix} [\mathbf{b} - \mathbf{R}_1]_d \\ \vdots \\ [\mathbf{b} - \mathbf{R}_m]_d \end{bmatrix} \text{ and } \begin{bmatrix} [\mathbf{b}]_d \\ \vdots \\ [\mathbf{b}]_d \end{bmatrix} + \begin{bmatrix} [\mathbf{R}_1]_d \\ \vdots \\ [\mathbf{R}_m]_d \end{bmatrix} = \begin{bmatrix} [\mathbf{b} + \mathbf{R}_1]_d \\ \vdots \\ [\mathbf{b} + \mathbf{R}_m]_d \end{bmatrix}
$$

Fig. 2. Protocol π_{VERSM} to verify that secrets are numerically small

---

Subroutine π_{VERPOS} between parties $(\mathcal{P}_1, \ldots, \mathcal{P}_N)$ and input client $\mathcal{I}$, to verify that secrets are positive.

Input to $\mathcal{I}$: $\mathbf{Z} \in \mathbb{Z}_q^{m \times k}$.
Input to $\mathcal{P}_i$: Corresponding shares of $[\mathbf{Z}_1]_d, \ldots, [\mathbf{Z}_m]_d$.

1. For each entry $z_i^{(j)}$ of $\mathbf{Z}$ (for $i \in [m], j \in [k]$), the dealer finds the four numbers $u_{ij}, v_{ij}, w_{ij}, y_{ij}$ such that $z_i^{(j)} = u_{ij}^2 + v_{ij}^2 + w_{ij}^2 + y_{ij}^2$. Define $\widetilde{\mathbf{U}}, \widetilde{\mathbf{V}}, \widetilde{\mathbf{W}}, \widetilde{\mathbf{Y}}$ to be the matrices with $u_{ij}, v_{ij}, w_{ij}, y_{ij}$ as the (i,j)th entry, respectively. Similarly, define $\mathbf{U}, \mathbf{V}, \mathbf{W}, \mathbf{Y}$ to be the matrices with $u_{ij}^2, v_{ij}^2, w_{ij}^2, y_{ij}^2$ as the (i,j)th entry, respectively.
2. $\mathcal{I}$ computes and distributes $(d/2)$-sharings of the rows of $\widetilde{\mathbf{U}}, \widetilde{\mathbf{V}}, \widetilde{\mathbf{W}}, \widetilde{\mathbf{Y}}$: $[\widetilde{\mathbf{U}}_i]_{d/2}, [\widetilde{\mathbf{V}}_i]_{d/2}, [\widetilde{\mathbf{W}}_i]_{d/2}, [\widetilde{\mathbf{Y}}_i]_{d/2}$, for $i \in [m]$.
3. Players run protocol π_{CHECK} from Section 2.4 with the shares $[\widetilde{\mathbf{U}}_i]_{d/2}, [\widetilde{\mathbf{V}}_i]_{d/2}, [\widetilde{\mathbf{W}}_i]_{d/2}, [\widetilde{\mathbf{Y}}_i]_{d/2}$, for $i \in [m]$ (a total of $4m/(N-t)$ times) to verify that these shares are $d/2$-consistent.
4. $\mathcal{I}$ and the players run the subroutine π_{VERBND} (see Figure 4) with the shares $[\widetilde{\mathbf{U}}_i]_{d/2}, [\widetilde{\mathbf{V}}_i]_{d/2}, [\widetilde{\mathbf{W}}_i]_{d/2}, [\widetilde{\mathbf{Y}}_i]_{d/2}$, for $i \in [m]$ (a total of $4m/\tau$ times), to verify that each of the $u_{ij}, v_{ij}, w_{ij}, y_{ij}$ is bounded by $B' < \sqrt{q/8}$.
5. For each row $i \in [m]$, players locally compute d-sharings $[\mathbf{U}_i]_d, [\mathbf{V}_i]_d, [\mathbf{W}_i]_d, [\mathbf{Y}_i]_d$ by squaring their corresponding shares of $[\widetilde{\mathbf{U}}_i]_{d/2}, [\widetilde{\mathbf{V}}_i]_{d/2}, [\widetilde{\mathbf{W}}_i]_{d/2}, [\widetilde{\mathbf{Y}}_i]_{d/2}$.
6. For each row $i \in [m]$, players locally compute

$$
[\mathbf{Z}_i]_d - [\mathbf{U}_i]_d - [\mathbf{V}_i]_d - [\mathbf{W}_i]_d - [\mathbf{Y}_i]_d = [\mathbf{Z}_i - \mathbf{U}_i - \mathbf{V}_i - \mathbf{W}_i - \mathbf{Y}_i]_d
$$

and check that the result is a pack-sharing of the vector $\mathbf{0} \in \mathbb{Z}^{1 \times k}$.

Fig. 3. Subroutine π_{VERPOS} to verify that secrets are positive

---

Subroutine π_{VERBND} **between parties** $(\mathcal{P}_1, \ldots, \mathcal{P}_N)$ **and input client** $\mathcal{I}$, **to verify that numbers are bounded by** $B' = 2^{2\tau+1} mB$.

Common input: bound B
Input to $\mathcal{I}$: $\mathbf{Z}' \in \mathbb{Z}_q^{\tau \times k}$.
Input to $\mathcal{P}_i$: Corresponding shares of $[\mathbf{Z}'_1]_d, \ldots, [\mathbf{Z}'_\tau]_d$ (that are known to be d-consistent).

1. $\mathcal{I}$ chooses $\mathbf{X} \leftarrow [-2^\tau mB, 2^\tau mB]^{(2\tau-1) \times k}$, and prepares d-sharings of the rows of $\mathbf{X}$: $[\mathbf{X}_1]_d, \ldots, [\mathbf{X}_{2\tau-1}]_d$. $\mathcal{I}$ gives each player its corresponding shares.
2. Players $\mathcal{P}_1, \ldots, \mathcal{P}_N$ coin-flip for a random vector $\mathbf{e} \in \{0,1\}^{\tau \times 1}$.
3. Define matrix $\mathbf{M}_{\mathbf{e}}$ to be the $(2\tau - 1) \times \tau$ matrix with its (i,j)-th entry defined by $m_{\mathbf{e},i}^{(j)} = e_{i-j+1}$ for $1 \le i - j + 1 \le \lambda$. Each player locally computes

$$
\begin{bmatrix} [(\mathbf{M}_{\mathbf{e}}\mathbf{Z}')_1]_{d'} \\ \vdots \\ [(\mathbf{M}_{\mathbf{e}}\mathbf{Z}')_{2\tau-1}]_{d'} \end{bmatrix} + \begin{bmatrix} [\mathbf{X}_1]_{d'} \\ \vdots \\ [\mathbf{X}_{2\tau-1}]_{d'} \end{bmatrix} = \begin{bmatrix} [(\mathbf{M}_{\mathbf{e}}\mathbf{Z}' + \mathbf{X})_1]_{d'} \\ \vdots \\ [(\mathbf{M}_{\mathbf{e}}\mathbf{Z}' + \mathbf{X})_{2\tau-1}]_{d'} \end{bmatrix}
$$

4. Players reconstruct $\mathbf{M}_{\mathbf{e}}\mathbf{Z}' + \mathbf{X}$ row by row and check that all its entries are bounded by $2^{2\tau+1} mB$.

Fig. 4. Subroutine π_{VERBND} to verify that numbers are bounded by $B' = 2^{2\tau+1} mB < \sqrt{q/8}$.

We set $N = \Theta(t)$ as is required for the IKOS construction and for privacy (see Section 2.3), and analyze the communication complexity of the π_{VERSM} protocol. Each share has size at most $\log q$. Each execution of π_{VERBND} has communication cost $O(\tau N \log q)$: sharing the $\mathbf{X}_i$'s has communication cost $(2\tau - 1)N \log q$, the coin-flipping of $\mathbf{e}$ has communication cost τ since we'll use this MPC protocol inside the IKOS construction, and reconstructing $\mathbf{M}_{\mathbf{e}}\mathbf{Z}' + \mathbf{X}$ has communication cost $(2\tau - 1)N \log q$. The subroutine π_{VERPOS} (Figure 3) has communication complexity $O(mN \log q)$: sharing of the rows of $\mathbf{U}, \mathbf{V}, \mathbf{W}, \mathbf{Y}$ has cost $4mN \log q$, the total cost of running π_{CHECK} is $(N(N + t) \log q) \cdot 4m/(N - 2t) = O(mN \log q)$, the total cost of running π_{VERBND} is $O(\tau N \log q) \cdot 4m/\tau = O(mN \log q)$, and the final reconstruction has cost $mN \log q$. Finally, the communication complexity of protocol π_{VERSM} is $O(mN \log q)$: sharing $\mathbf{b}$ has communication cost $N \log q$, and we run the subroutine π_{VERPOS} twice.

Lemma 4. *Let n, m, r, q, N, t, k be as in Theorem 2 and Section 2.3, and let B be some publicly-known bound. If $\tau = \omega(\log \lambda)$ and $\sqrt{q/8} > 2^{2\tau+1} mB$ then the protocol π_{VERSM} described in Figure 2 allows N players to verify, with negligible error probability in λ, that all entries in a secret matrix $\mathbf{R} \in \mathbb{Z}_q^{m \times k}$ are bounded by B. It has statistical t-privacy in the presence of a semi-honest adversary, perfect t-robustness in the presence of a malicious adversary, and communication complexity $O(mN \log q)$.*

4   Proofs of Plaintext Knowledge

We wish to show a zero-knowledge proof protocol that allows a prover to prove that he knows the plaintexts of k different ciphertexts, each encrypted under the same public key. We show how to do this for the Regev encryption scheme described in Section 2.5. More formally, we show a zero-knowlege proof protocol for the following relation:

$$R_{\text{PoPK}} = \{ \ (x, w) \ \mid \ x = ((\mathbf{A}, \mathbf{b}), (\mathbf{u}^{(1)}, c^{(1)}), \dots, (\mathbf{u}^{(k)}, c^{(k)})),$$

$$w = ((m^{(1)}, \mathbf{r}^{(1)}), \dots, (m^{(k)}, \mathbf{r}^{(k)})) \quad \text{s.t.}$$

$$\forall \ j \in [k] : (\mathbf{u}^{(j)}, c^{(j)}) = \text{Enc}_{(\mathbf{A}, \mathbf{b})}(m^{(j)}; \mathbf{r}^{(j)})$$

$$\text{and} \ |m^{(j)}| \le p/2 \ , \ \|\mathbf{r}^{(j)}\|_\infty < r \ \}$$

We create protocol Π_{PoPK} for relation R_{PoPK} using the "MPC-in-the-head" technique of [22] described in Section 2.2. We let f_{PoPK} be the N-party functionality that takes the entire input w from $\mathcal{I}$ and outputs $R_{\text{PoPK}}(x, w)$ to all N players. In Figure 5, we show our construction of a t-robust and t-private N-party protocol, π_{PoPK}, realizing functionality f_{PoPK}. The idea is to have $\mathcal{I}$ pack secret-share the messages, as well as pack secret-share each coordinate of the randomness vectors. The players then locally run the encryption algorithm on their shares, reconstruct the resulting shares, and check that the reconstructed secrets are indeed the claimed ciphertexts. The input client $\mathcal{I}$ also needs to prove that the messages and randomness come from the correct spaces. For example, he would need to show that the magnitude of each message is less than $p/2$ (since the message space is $\mathbb{Z}_p$), and that each coordinate of each randomness vector is at most r (since we are using the truncated Gaussian distribution described in Section 2.5). For this, we will use the protocol π_{VERSM} described in Section 3.

We set $t = \Theta(k)$ and $N = \Theta(t)$ as is required for the IKOS construction and for privacy (see Section 2.3), and analyze the communication complexity of our protocol π_{PoPK} (see Figure 5). Since each share has size $\log q$, step 1 has communication cost $(m+1)N \log q = O(mk \log q)$. We run π_{CHECK} $m + 1/(N - 2t) = O(m/k)$ times, so step 2 has communication cost $N(N + t) \log q(m/k) = O(mk \log q)$ The reconstruction in step 3 has cost $2nN \log q$ and running protocol π_{VERSM} has cost $2mN \log q$ so the total cost of step 3 and of π_{PoPK} is $O(mk \log q)$.

Our techniques are similar to those of Bendlin and Damgård [7]. However, our protocol π_{VERSM} for proving that a secret is small (see Section 3) allows us to prove soundness for message space $\mathbb{Z}_p$ and randomness sampled from the discrete Gaussian, whereas the construction of [7] only worked for bit messages and bit-vector randomness. Finally, our use of packed secret sharing allows us to achieve a better amortized communication complexity. The protocol of [7] has complexity $O(nm \log q)$ per proof, whereas we achieve an amortized complexity of $O(m \log q)$ per proof.

Lemma 5. *Let n, m, r, p, q, N, t, k be as in Lemma 4 with $B = \max(p/2, r)$. The protocol π_{PoPK} described in Figure 5 realizes f_{PoPK} with statistical t-privacy in the presence of a semi-honest adversary and perfect t-robustness in the presence of a malicious adversary, and has communication complexity $O(mk \log q)$.*

Protocol π_{PoPK} between parties $(\mathcal{P}_1, \ldots, \mathcal{P}_N)$ and input client $\mathcal{I}$.

Common input: $p, q, R, x = ((\mathbf{A}, \mathbf{b}), (\mathbf{u}^{(1)}, c^{(1)}), \ldots, (\mathbf{u}^{(k)}, c^{(k)}))$
Input to $\mathcal{I}$: $w = ((m^{(1)}, \mathbf{r}^{(1)}), \ldots, (m^{(k)}, \mathbf{r}^{(k)}))$

1. Input client $\mathcal{I}$ prepares and distributes among the N players, d-shares over $\mathbb{Z}_q$ of the messages and randomness vectors, with $d = k + t - 1$. The ith coordinates of all randomness vectors are pack-shared to produce a single set of shares $\boldsymbol{\rho}_i$. More formally: define matrices $\mathbf{R} = [\mathbf{r}^{(1)} \; ; \; \mathbf{r}^{(2)} \; ; \; \ldots \; ; \; \mathbf{r}^{(k)}] \in \mathbb{Z}_q^{m \times k}$, $\mathbf{m} = [m^{(1)} \; ; \; \ldots \; ; \; m^{(k)}] \in \mathbb{Z}_p^{1 \times k}$, $\mathbf{U} = [\mathbf{u}^{(1)} \; ; \; \mathbf{u}^{(2)} \; ; \; \ldots \; ; \; \mathbf{u}^{(k)}] \in \mathbb{Z}_q^{n \times k}$, and $\mathbf{c} = (c^{(1)} \; ; \; \ldots \; ; \; c^{(k)}) \in \mathbb{Z}_q^{1 \times k}$. $\mathcal{I}$ prepares and distributes d-shares $[\mathbf{m}]_d, [\mathbf{R}_1]_d, \ldots, [\mathbf{R}_m]_d$.

2. Players run protocol π_{CHECK} from Section 2.4 (possibly several times) to verify that their shares are d-consistent.

3. Players "emulate" encryption by running the encryption algorithm on their local shares. More formally:

   - For $\ell \in [n]$, players locally compute $\left[\left(\mathbf{A}_\ell \mathbf{r}^{(j)} \right)_{j \in k} \right]_d$, and check that the result is a pack-sharing of $\mathbf{U}_\ell$.

   - Similarly, players locally compute

   $$\left[\left(\mathbf{br}^{(j)} \right)_{j \in k} \right]_d + \left\lfloor \frac{q}{p} \right\rfloor [\mathbf{m}]_d = \left[\left(\mathbf{br}^{(j)} + \left\lfloor \frac{q}{p} \right\rfloor m^{(j)} \right)_{j \in k} \right]_d$$

   Players check that the result is a pack-sharing of $\mathbf{c}$.

   - Players use π_{VERSM} from Section 3 to check that $|m^{(j)}| \leq p/2$ and $||\mathbf{r}^{(j)}||_\infty < r$ for all $j \in [k]$.

Fig. 5. MPC protocol π_{PoPK} that realizes f_{PoPK}

Putting together Lemma 5 with Theorem 1 yields the following theorem.

Theorem 3. *Let n, m, r, p, q be as in Lemma 4 with $B = \max(p/2, r)$. Given an unconditionally-binding commitment scheme, it is possible to construct a computational zero-knowledge proof protocol Π_{PoPK} for relation R_{PoPK} with negligible (in λ) soundness error and amortized communication complexity $O(m \log q)$ per proof.*

5   Proofs of Correct Multiplication

In this section we show proofs for correct multiplication for the Regev encryption scheme. In our protocol, the prover performs k proofs at a time, all under the same public key. More formally, we give a zero-knowledge proof protocol for the following relation:

Protocol π_{PoCM} between parties $(\mathcal{P}_1, \ldots, \mathcal{P}_N)$ and input client $\mathcal{I}$.

Common input: $p, q, R, x = ((\mathbf{A}, \mathbf{b}), (\mathbf{u}^{(1)}, c^{(1)}, \mathbf{v}^{(1)}, e^{(1)}), \ldots, (\mathbf{u}^{(k)}, c^{(k)}, \mathbf{v}^{(k)}, e^{(k)}))$
Input to $\mathcal{I}$: $w = ((m^{(1)}, \mathbf{r}^{(1)}, x^{(1)}), \ldots, (m^{(k)}, \mathbf{r}^{(k)}, x^{(k)}))$

1. Input client $\mathcal{I}$ prepares and distributes among the N players, d-shares over $\mathbb{Z}_q$
   of the messages and randomness vectors, with $d = k + t - 1$. The ith coordi-
   nates of all randomness vectors are packed shared to produce a single set of
   shares.. More formally: define matrices $\mathbf{R} = [\mathbf{r}^{(1)} \; ; \; \mathbf{r}^{(2)} \; ; \; \ldots \; ; \; \mathbf{r}^{(k)}] \in \mathbb{Z}_q^{m \times k}$,
   $\mathbf{m} = [m^{(1)} \; ; \; \ldots \; ; \; m^{(k)}] \in \mathbb{Z}_p^{1 \times k}, \mathbf{x} = [x^{(1)} \; ; \; \ldots \; ; \; x^{(k)}] \in \mathbb{Z}_q^{1 \times k}, \mathbf{U} =$
   $[\mathbf{u}^{(1)} \; ; \; \mathbf{u}^{(2)} \; ; \; \ldots \; ; \; \mathbf{u}^{(k)}] \in \mathbb{Z}_q^{n \times k}, \mathbf{c} = (c^{(1)}, \ldots, c^{(k)}) \in \mathbb{Z}_q^{1 \times k}, \mathbf{V} =$
   $[\mathbf{v}^{(1)} \; ; \; \mathbf{v}^{(2)} \; ; \; \ldots \; ; \; \mathbf{v}^{(k)}] \in \mathbb{Z}_q^{n \times k}$, and $\mathbf{e} = (e^{(1)} \; ; \; \ldots \; ; \; e^{(k)}) \in \mathbb{Z}_q^{1 \times k}$. $\mathcal{I}$
   prepares and distributes $(d/2)$-share $[\mathbf{m}]_d$ and d-shares $[\mathbf{x}]_d, [\mathbf{R}_1]_d, \ldots, [\mathbf{R}_m]_d$.
   $\mathcal{I}$ also prepares and *broadcasts* $(d/2)$-shares$[\mathbf{c}]_{d/2}, [\mathbf{U}_1]_{d/2}, \ldots, [\mathbf{U}_n]_{d/2}$.

2. Players run protocol π_{CHECK} from Section 2.4 (possibly several times) to verify
   that shares $[\mathbf{x}]_d, [\mathbf{R}_1]_d, \ldots, [\mathbf{R}_m]_d$ are d-consistent, and share $[\mathbf{m}]_d$ is $(d/2)$-
   consistent. They also check locally that $\mathbf{c}, \mathbf{U}_1, \ldots, \mathbf{U}_m$ are correctly shared.

3. Players "emulate" correct computation of each $(\mathbf{v}^{(i)}, c^{(i)})$. More formally:

   - For $\ell \in [n]$, players locally compute $\left[\left(\mathbf{A}_\ell \mathbf{r}^{(j)}\right)_{j \in k}\right]_d$. They also locally

     compute $\left[\left(\mathbf{b}\mathbf{r}^{(j)} + \left\lfloor \frac{q}{p} \right\rfloor x^{(j)}\right)_{j \in k}\right]_d$.

   - For $\ell \in [n]$, players locally compute

     $$[\mathbf{m}]_{d/2} [\mathbf{U}_\ell]_{d/2} + \left[\left(\mathbf{A}_\ell \mathbf{r}^{(j)}\right)_{j \in k}\right]_d = \left[\left(u_\ell^{(j)} m^{(j)} + \mathbf{A}_\ell \mathbf{r}^{(j)}\right)_{j \in k}\right]_d$$

     Players check that the result is a pack-sharing of $\mathbf{V}_\ell$.

   - Players locally compute

     $$[\mathbf{m}]_{d/2} [\mathbf{c}]_{d/2} + \left[\left(\mathbf{b}\mathbf{r}^{(j)} + \left\lfloor \frac{q}{p} \right\rfloor x^{(j)}\right)_{j \in k}\right]_d$$

     $$= \left[\left(c^{(j)} m^{(j)} + \mathbf{b}\mathbf{r}^{(j)} + \left\lfloor \frac{q}{p} \right\rfloor x^{(j)}\right)_{j \in k}\right]_d$$

     Players check that the result is a pack-sharing of $\mathbf{e}$..

   - Players use π_{VERSM} from Section 3 to check that $|m^{(j)}| \leq p/2, |x^{(j)}| \leq p/2$
     and $||\mathbf{r}^{(j)}||_\infty < r$ for all $j \in [k]$.

Fig. 6. MPC protocol π_{PoCM} that realizes f_{PoCM}

$$R_{\text{PoCM}} = \{ (x, w) \mid x = ((\mathbf{A}, \mathbf{b}), (\mathbf{u}^{(1)}, c^{(1)}, \mathbf{v}^{(1)}, e^{(1)}), \ldots, (\mathbf{u}^{(k)}, c^{(k)}, \mathbf{v}^{(k)}, e^{(k)})),$$
$$w = ((m^{(1)}, \mathbf{r}^{(1)}, x^{(1)}), \ldots, (m^{(k)}, \mathbf{r}^{(k)}, x^{(k)})) \quad \text{s.t.}$$
$$\forall j \in [k]: (\mathbf{v}^{(j)}, e^{(j)}) = m^{(j)}(\mathbf{u}^{(j)}, c^{(j)}) + \text{Enc}_{(\mathbf{A}, \mathbf{b})}(x^{(j)}; \mathbf{r}^{(j)})$$
$$\text{and } |m^{(j)}| \leq p/2, |x^{(j)}| \leq p/2, ||\mathbf{r}^{(j)}||_\infty < r \}$$

As in Section 4, we create protocol Π_{PoCM} for relation R_{PoCM} using the "MPC-in-the-head" technique of [22], described in Section 2.2. We let f_{PoCM} be the N-party functionality that takes the entire input w from $\mathcal{I}$ and outputs $R_{\mathrm{PoCM}}(x, w)$ to all N players. In Figure 6, we show our construction of a t-robust and t-private N-party protocol, π_{PoCM}, realizing functionality f_{PoCM}. Again, the idea is to have $\mathcal{I}$ pack secret-share the messages, as well as pack secret-share each coordinate of the randomness vectors. The players then locally emulate the encryption of the random message and perform the multiplication, then reconstruct the resulting shares, and check that the reconstructed secrets are indeed the claimed ciphertexts. As before, the input client $\mathcal{I}$ also needs to prove that the messages and randomness come from the correct spaces. We again use the protocol π_{VERSM} described in Section 3 for this purpose.

We set $t = \theta(k)$ and $N = \theta(t)$ as is required for the IKOS construction and for privacy (see Section 2.3), and analyze the communication complexity of π_{PoCM} described in Figure 6. Since each share has size $\log q$, step 1 has communication cost $2(m + 1)N \log q = O(mk \log q)$. We run π_{CHECK} $m + 1/(N - 2t) = O(m/k)$ times, so step 2 has communication cost $N(N + t) \log q(m/k) = O(mk \log q)$. The reconstruction in step 3 has cost $2nN \log q$ and running protocol π_{VERSM} has cost $2mN \log q$ so the total cost of step 3 and of π_{PoPK} is $O(mk \log q)$.

Lemma 6. *Let n, m, r, p, q, N, t, k be as in Lemma 4 with $B = \max(p/2, r)$. The protocol π_{PoCM} described in Figure 6 realizes f_{PoCM} with statistical t-privacy in the presence of a semi-honest adversary and perfect t-robustness in the presence of a malicious adversary, and has communication complexity $O(mk \log q)$.*

Putting Lemma 6 together with Theorem 1 yields the following theorem.

Theorem 4. *Let n, m, r, p, q be as in Lemma 4 with $B = \max(p/2, r)$. Given an unconditionally-binding commitment scheme, it is possible to construct a computational zero-knowledge proof protocol Π_{PoCM} for relation R_{PoCM} with negligible (in λ) soundness error and amortized communication complexity $O(m \log q)$ per proof.*

References

1. Asharov, G., Jain, A., López-Alt, A., Tromer, E., Vaikuntanathan, V., Wichs, D.: Multiparty Computation with Low Communication, Computation and Interaction via Threshold FHE. In: Pointcheval, D., Johansson, T. (eds.) EUROCRYPT 2012. LNCS, vol. 7237, pp. 483–501. Springer, Heidelberg (2012)
2. Asharov, G., Jain, A., Wichs, D.: Multiparty computation with low communication, computation and interaction via threshold fhe. Cryptology ePrint Archive: Report 2011/613 (2011)
3. Beaver, D.: Efficient Multiparty Protocols Using Circuit Randomization. In: Feigenbaum, J. (ed.) CRYPTO 1991. LNCS, vol. 576, pp. 420–432. Springer, Heidelberg (1992)
4. Beerliová-Trubíniová, Z., Hirt, M.: Perfectly-Secure MPC with Linear Communication Complexity. In: Canetti, R. (ed.) TCC 2008. LNCS, vol. 4948, pp. 213–230. Springer, Heidelberg (2008)

5. Beerliová-Trubíniová, Z., Hirt, M., Nielsen, J.B.: On the theoretical gap between synchronous and asynchronous mpc protocols. In: Richa, A.W., Guerraoui, R. (eds.) PODC, pp. 211–218. ACM (2010)
6. Ben-Or, M., Goldwasser, S., Wigderson, A.: Completeness theorems for noncryptographic fault-tolerant distributed computation (extended abstract). In: STOC, pp. 1–10 (1988)
7. Bendlin, R., Damgård, I.: Threshold Decryption and Zero-Knowledge Proofs for Lattice-Based Cryptosystems. In: Micciancio, D. (ed.) TCC 2010. LNCS, vol. 5978, pp. 201–218. Springer, Heidelberg (2010)
8. Bendlin, R., Damgård, I., Orlandi, C., Zakarias, S.: Semi-homomorphic Encryption and Multiparty Computation. In: Paterson, K.G. (ed.) EUROCRYPT 2011. LNCS, vol. 6632, pp. 169–188. Springer, Heidelberg (2011)
9. Boudot, F.: Efficient Proofs that a Committed Number Lies in an Interval. In: Preneel, B. (ed.) EUROCRYPT 2000. LNCS, vol. 1807, pp. 431–444. Springer, Heidelberg (2000)
10. Brakerski, Z., Gentry, C., Vaikuntanathan, V.: (Leveled) fully homomorphic encryption without bootstrapping. In: Goldwasser, S. (ed.) ITCS, pp. 309–325. ACM (2012)
11. Brakerski, Z., Vaikuntanathan, V.: Efficient fully homomorphic encryption from (standard) lwe. In: Ostrovsky, R. (ed.) FOCS, pp. 97–106. IEEE (2011)
12. Chaum, D., Crépeau, C., Damgård, I.: Multiparty unconditionally secure protocols (extended abstract). In: STOC, pp. 11–19 (1988)
13. Cramer, R., Damgård, I.: On the Amortized Complexity of Zero-Knowledge Protocols. In: Halevi, S. (ed.) CRYPTO 2009. LNCS, vol. 5677, pp. 177–191. Springer, Heidelberg (2009)
14. Damgård, I., Orlandi, C.: Multiparty Computation for Dishonest Majority: From Passive to Active Security at Low Cost. In: Rabin, T. (ed.) CRYPTO 2010. LNCS, vol. 6223, pp. 558–576. Springer, Heidelberg (2010)
15. Damgård, I., Pastro, V., Smart, N.P., Zakarias, S.: Multiparty computation from somewhat homomorphic encryption. IACR Cryptology ePrint Archive, 2011:535 (2011)
16. Fine, B., Rosenberger, G.: Number Theory: An Introduction via the Distribution of Primes. Birkhäuser (2006)
17. Franklin, M.K., Yung, M.: Communication complexity of secure computation (extended abstract). In: STOC, pp. 699–710. ACM (1992)
18. Gentry, C., Peikert, C., Vaikuntanathan, V.: Trapdoors for hard lattices and new cryptographic constructions. In: Dwork, C. (ed.) STOC, pp. 197–206. ACM (2008)
19. Goldreich, O., Micali, S., Wigderson, A.: How to play any mental game or a completeness theorem for protocols with honest majority. In: STOC, pp. 218–229 (1987)
20. Hirt, M., Maurer, U.M.: Robustness for Free in Unconditional Multi-party Computation. In: Kilian, J. (ed.) CRYPTO 2001. LNCS, vol. 2139, pp. 101–118. Springer, Heidelberg (2001)
21. Hirt, M., Nielsen, J.B., Przydatek, B.: Asynchronous Multi-Party Computation with Quadratic Communication. In: Aceto, L., Damgård, I., Goldberg, L.A., Halldórsson, M.M., Ingólfsdóttir, A., Walukiewicz, I. (eds.) ICALP 2008, Part II. LNCS, vol. 5126, pp. 473–485. Springer, Heidelberg (2008)
22. Ishai, Y., Kushilevitz, E., Ostrovsky, R., Sahai, A.: Zero-knowledge from secure multiparty computation. In: Johnson, D.S., Feige, U. (eds.) STOC, pp. 21–30. ACM (2007)

23. Katz, J., Koo, C.-Y.: Round-Efficient Secure Computation in Point-to-Point Networks. In: Naor, M. (ed.) EUROCRYPT 2007. LNCS, vol. 4515, pp. 311–328. Springer, Heidelberg (2007)
24. Lipmaa, H.: On Diophantine Complexity and Statistical Zero-Knowledge Arguments. In: Laih, C.-S. (ed.) ASIACRYPT 2003. LNCS, vol. 2894, pp. 398–415. Springer, Heidelberg (2003)
25. Micciancio, D., Regev, O.: Worst-case to average-case reductions based on gaussian measures. SIAM J. Comput. 37(1), 267–302 (2007)
26. Peikert, C.: Public-key cryptosystems from the worst-case shortest vector problem: extended abstract. In: Mitzenmacher, M. (ed.) STOC, pp. 333–342. ACM (2009)
27. Peikert, C., Vaikuntanathan, V., Waters, B.: A Framework for Efficient and Composable Oblivious Transfer. In: Wagner, D. (ed.) CRYPTO 2008. LNCS, vol. 5157, pp. 554–571. Springer, Heidelberg (2008)
28. Rabin, M.O., Shallit, J.O.: Randomized algorithms in number theory. Communications on Pure and Applied Mathematics 39(S1), S239–S259 (1986)
29. Regev, O.: On lattices, learning with errors, random linear codes, and cryptography. In: Gabow, H.N., Fagin, R. (eds.) STOC, pp. 84–93. ACM (2005)
30. Shamir, A.: How to share a secret. Commun. ACM 22(11), 612–613 (1979)
31. Yao, A.C.-C.: Protocols for secure computations (extended abstract). In: FOCS, pp. 160–164 (1982)

Fully Anonymous Attribute
Tokens from Lattices

Jan Camenisch, Gregory Neven, and Markus Rückert

IBM Research – Zurich
{jca,nev}@zurich.ibm.com
markus.rueckert@cased.de

Abstract. Anonymous authentication schemes such as group signatures and anonymous credentials are important privacy-protecting tools in electronic communications. The only currently known scheme based on assumptions that resist quantum attacks is the group signature scheme by Gordon et al. (ASIACRYPT 2010). We present a generalization of group signatures called *anonymous attribute tokens* where users are issued attribute-containing credentials that they can use to anonymously sign messages and generate tokens revealing only a subset of their attributes. We present two lattice-based constructions of this new primitive, one with and one without opening capabilities for the group manager. The latter construction directly yields as a special case the first lattice-based group signature scheme offering full anonymity (in the random oracle model), as opposed to the practically less relevant notion of chosen-plaintext anonymity offered by the scheme of Gordon et al. We also extend our scheme to protect users from framing attacks by the group manager, where the latter creates tokens or signatures in the name of honest users. Our constructions involve new lattice-based tools for aggregating signatures and verifiable CCA2-secure encryption.

Keywords: Anonymous attribute tokens, group signatures, lattices, post-quantum cryptography.

1 Introduction

We all increasingly use electronic services in our daily lives. To do so, we currently have no choice but to provide plenty of personal information for authorization, billing purposes, or as part of the terms and conditions of service providers. Dispersing all these personal information erodes our privacy and puts us at risk of abuse of this information by criminals. Therefore, these services and their authentication mechanisms should be built in a way that minimizes the disclosed personal information. For instance, to access a resource, users should not need to identify themselves but rather only to prove to the resource provider that they possess the necessary attributes (e.g., rights or properties) which are required for the access. In fact, in Europe it is widely acknowledged that to secure the future digital infrastructure one must employ this kind of attribute-based access

I. Visconti and R. De Prisco (Eds.): SCN 2012, LNCS 7485, pp. 57–75, 2012.
© Springer-Verlag Berlin Heidelberg 2012

control and use so-called attribute-based credentials or minimal disclose tokens (see, e.g., [RIS10, IA11]).

The cryptographic research literature has put forth a large body of protocols that allow for privacy-friendly access control. For instance, group signature [CvH91] and identity escrow [KP98] schemes allow a user to prove that she has authorization (i.e., is member of a group of people who all share the same property) without revealing her identity. Nevertheless, in case of abuse of this anonymity, group signature and identity escrow schemes allow a designated party to lift the anonymity and to identify the abusing user. The generalization of these schemes are anonymous credentials or pseudonym systems [Cha81, Bra99, CL01b, LRSW99]. Such schemes feature a *plurality* of organizations who assign *attributes* to users by issuing attribute-containing credentials. Users are known to the different issuers under different pseudonyms. Later, when users need to authenticate somewhere, they can do so in the most privacy-protecting manner, i.e., users can just prove that they possess credentials asserting them the attributes required by the authentication policy.

It is well known that the cryptographic assumptions underlying all known realizations of these privacy-protecting schemes can be broken with quantum computers. The only exception to this is the group signature scheme by Gordon, Katz, and Vaikuntanathan [GKV10]. Their scheme works on ordinary computers but is based on the hardness of lattice problems, which are believed to be immune to quantum computers. While so far only small quantum computers breaking toy keys could be built, it seems very plausible that in just a few years computers breaking currently used keys can be built [Los10]. Even if quantum computers are not considered an immediate threat, the hardness of lattice problems against sub-exponential time adversaries and their provable worst-case to average-case relation makes it desirable to build cryptographic schemes from these problems.

In this paper we provide a number of new schemes for privacy-protecting authentication with security based on lattice problems in the random-oracle model. In particular, as our first contribution, we define and present an *anonymous attribute token scheme without opening* (AAT–O). Here, a user can obtain a credential from a group manager or issuer, the credential containing the attributes that the manager wants to assert to the user. Later, the user can anonymously authenticate to a verifier by generating an authentication token from her credential, the token revealing only a subset of the attributes that are contained in the credential. Such authentication tokens are anonymous, i.e., a token containing a set of attributes could originate from any user who has been asserted a superset of these attributes. Minimal disclosure tokens as implemented by Microsoft's U-Prove [BP10] are an example of an AAT–O scheme.

As our second and main contribution, we extend our scheme to an *anonymous attribute token scheme with opening* (AAT+O), where the group manager additionally has the power to reveal the identity of the user who generated a given token. Group signatures can be seen as special case of AAT+O schemes where the manager issues to all users a credential without attributes (or a single attribute with a fixed value). Our scheme provides anonymity to honest users in the presence of adversaries with adaptive access to the opening functionality. This is a major improvement over the group signature scheme of Gordon et al., who provide a much weaker form of anonymity. In their model, anonymity may break down for *all* users in the system as soon as a *single* signature (or token in our terminology) is opened, even for users who never misbehaved and never had their tokens opened. Hence, their scheme can only be used as long as no signature (token) is opened—an event that users are typically not even aware of. This is a severe limitation that we overcome.

We furthermore show how our AAT–O and AAT+O schemes can be combined to obtain a new AAT+O scheme that protects users from *framing* by a dishonest group manager. That is, in this resulting third scheme, no one except the user herself can produce tokens that when opened will be attributed to the user. This is a further property that the Gordon et al. group signature scheme does not provide and which we believe is rather important when one wants to have accountability. Group signatures obtained from our AAT+O schemes do not only provide better security compared to the Gordon et al. scheme, but also offer other advantages: the manager's public and secret key are independent of the number of users (versus linear in their scheme[1]) and users can join dynamically (in theirs, all the users' keys need to be generated at setup time). Thus, while our main focus is on anonymous attribute token schemes, we present as a corollary the first lattice-based, non-frameable group signature scheme with full anonymity.

As an aside, to construct our scheme, we improve upon known tools and introduce a number of new building blocks, which we believe are of interest in their own right. We provide a verifiable encryption proof protocol for the CCA2-secure encryption scheme of Peikert [Pei09] and introduce and construct single-signer aggregate signatures as a restricted, but useful, form of aggregate signatures [BGLS03].

Related Work. We do not claim anonymous attribute tokens to be a new primitive: the U-Prove scheme [BP10] and the signature scheme with its proof protocols by Camenisch and Lysyanskaya [CL04] actually realize instantiations of it based on the discrete logarithm assumption and the strong RSA assumption, respectively. Nevertheless, to the best of our knowledge, an anonymous attribute token scheme (with or without opening) has never been formally defined. As we have pointed out already, group signature schemes can be seen as a special case of AAT+O schemes.

Several group signature schemes have been proposed in the literature. Most of these are based on strong RSA [ACJT00, AST02, CL01a] or on bilinear maps [BBS04, BS04, CL04, DP06, BCN+10]. The scheme due to Gordon et al. [GKV10] is the only based on assumptions that resist attacks by quantum computers.

---

[1] Note that secret keys can always be made of constant length by storing the random seed used to generate the key instead of the key itself. Likewise, one can always publish the hash of the public key instead of the public key itself. The first trick involves re-generating keys, which is particularly costly in lattice-based schemes that use trapdoors. The latter trick comes at the cost of having to attach the full public key to each signature or token.

Attribute-based signatures [MPR11] are a related primitive where signatures cannot be opened and where the signer can prove any predicate over the attributes that can be expressed as a monotone span program, which includes circuits of threshold gates. Attribute-based group signatures [Kha07] are a similar primitive where signatures can be opened by a dedicated authority, and is thereby closely related to our notion of AAT+O schemes. Unfortunately, however, the security notions proposed in [Kha07] are flawed.[2]

Ring signatures [ST01] are another privacy-enabling primitive which can be seen as an ad-hoc group signature scheme without a central group manager and without the possibility for opening. Ring signatures can also be constructed from our AAT–O scheme, as we shall point out later. Mesh signatures [Boy07] are a generalization of ring signatures to monotone access structures where each user can (be claimed to) sign a different message. Single-attribute AAT–O schemes are easily obtained from mesh signatures; multi-attribute schemes involve a combinatorial blowup of the credential size in the number of attributes. Similarly, mesh signatures with opening [BD08] can be used to build AAT+O schemes.

The most general privacy-enabling primitive are probably anonymous credential systems with additional features such as proving predicates over attributes, cryptographic pseudonyms, and partially blind issuing protocols to protect users against framing attacks by malicious issuers. While they are quite close to anonymous attribute token schemes, we leave it as an open problem to construct a full-fledged anonymous credential system based on lattices.

Organization of the Paper. We define anonymous attribute token schemes in Section 3. Then, we introduce, analyze, and discuss the building blocks for our constructions in Section 4, followed by our first construction in Section 4.2. Based on these results, we describe the full-blown scheme with opening and how to achieve group signatures and restricted anonymous credential systems in the full paper [CNR12].

2   Preliminaries

The statement $x \leftarrow_\$ X$ means that x is chosen uniformly at random from the finite set X. A function is negligible if it vanishes faster than $1/p(n)$ for any polynomial p. All logarithms are base 2 and we identify $\{1, \ldots, k\}$ with $[k]$ and $(x_i)_{i=a}^{b}$ with $(x_a, \ldots, x_b)$. Furthermore, $[a, b]_{\mathbb{Z}} := [a, b] \cap \mathbb{Z}$. Instead of $a \equiv b \pmod{q}$, we simply write $a \equiv b$. When we write "$\|$", we mean the concatenation of strings or matrix columns. The concatenation of two vectors $\mathbf{x}, \mathbf{y}$ is denoted $[\mathbf{x}, \mathbf{y}]$. The notation $\#S$ denotes the cardinality of a finite set S.

---

[2] The "selective-policy" anonymity notion of [Kha07] allows linkability of signatures when a signer signs the same message with the same set of revealed attributes twice. The traceability notion merely implies that any valid signature will open to some user. There is no guarantee that it opens to the actual signer behind the signature, however, nor does the notion offer any protection against users claiming attributes that they do not possess.

In this work, we only require full-rank lattices. A lattice in $\mathbb{R}^n$ is a discrete subgroup $\Lambda = \{\sum_{i=1}^{n} x_i \, \mathbf{b}_i \mid x_i \in \mathbb{Z}\}$, typically represented by a matrix $\mathbf{B} = [\mathbf{b}_1, \ldots, \mathbf{b}_n] \in \mathbb{Z}^{n \times n}$ of $\mathbb{R}$-linearly independent vectors. The matrix $\mathbf{B}$ is a basis of the lattice Λ and we write $\Lambda = \Lambda(\mathbf{B})$. The number of linearly independent vectors in $\mathbf{B}$ is the dimension $\dim(\Lambda)$. For a lattice $\Lambda(\mathbf{B})$ with $\mathbf{B} \in \mathbb{Z}^{n \times n}$ define the (full-rank) dual lattice as the set of all $\mathbf{x} \in \mathbb{R}^n$ with $\langle \mathbf{x}, \mathbf{y} \rangle \in \mathbb{Z}$ for all $\mathbf{y} \in \Lambda(\mathbf{B})$. The Gram-Schmidt orthogonalization (GSO) $\tilde{\mathbf{B}} = [\tilde{\mathbf{b}}_1 \| \ldots \| \tilde{\mathbf{b}}_n]$ of the columns of $\mathbf{B}$ is recursively computed by letting $\tilde{\mathbf{b}}_{i+1}$ be the orthogonal projection of $\mathbf{b}_{i+1}$ onto $span(\tilde{\mathbf{b}}_1, \ldots, \tilde{\mathbf{b}}_i)^{\perp}$. The length of $\mathbf{B}$ is defined as $\|\mathbf{B}\| := \max_{i \in [n]}(\|\mathbf{b}_i\|_2)$.

One of the main computational problems in lattices is the approximate shortest vector problem (SVP). Given a basis $\mathbf{B}$ of Λ and an approximation factor $\gamma \geq 1$, the task is to find a non-zero vector $\mathbf{v} \in \Lambda$ with length at most γ times the length of a shortest vector in Λ. A related problem is the approximate shortest independent vector problem (SIVP), where one is supposed to find a set $\{\mathbf{v}_1, \ldots, \mathbf{v}_n\}$ of linearly independent vectors in Λ such that $\max_i \|\mathbf{v}_i\|_2 \leq \gamma \lambda_n$. Here, λ_n denotes the n-th successive minimum of Λ, which is the smallest radius of a sphere that contains n linearly independent lattice vectors. For polynomial (in the dimension) approximation factors, which are relevant for cryptography, the best known algorithms require exponential space $\times$ time, e.g., [MV10].

In cryptography, we use lattices of a special form, which we call q-*ary lattices*: for $q \in \mathbb{N}$, $\mathbf{A} \in \mathbb{Z}_q^{n \times m}$, we define $\Lambda_q^{\perp}(\mathbf{A}) := \{\mathbf{v} \in \mathbb{Z}^m : \mathbf{A}\mathbf{v} \equiv \mathbf{0}\}$. Its, up to scaling, dual lattice $\Lambda_q(\mathbf{A})$ is defined as $\{\mathbf{w} \in \mathbb{Z}^m : \exists \mathbf{e} \in \mathbb{Z}^n \text{ s.t. } \mathbf{A}^t \mathbf{e} \equiv \mathbf{w}\}$. The main computational problem in $\Lambda_q^{\perp}(\mathbf{A})$ is the following "short integer solution" (SIS) problem: given n, m, q, uniformly random $\mathbf{A}$, and a norm bound $1 \leq \nu < q$, find $\mathbf{v} \in \Lambda_q^{\perp}(\mathbf{A})$ with $0 < \|\mathbf{v}\|_2 \leq \nu$. The SIS problem was introduced and analyzed by Ajtai [Ajt96] but there are numerous improvements to the analysis [MR07, GPV08]. We will also use the (equivalent) inhomogeneous problem ISIS, where the task is to find a short vector $\mathbf{x}$ that solves $\mathbf{A}\mathbf{x} \equiv \mathbf{y}$ given $\mathbf{y}$. For $\nu \leq \mathsf{poly}(n)$, prime $q \geq \nu g(n)$ for $g(n) = \omega(\sqrt{n \log(n)})$, and $m \geq 2n \log(q)$, the average-case $\mathsf{SIS}(n, m, q, \nu)$ is at least as hard as SIVP with $\gamma = \nu \tilde{\mathcal{O}}(\sqrt{n})$ in the worst case. For $\Lambda_q(\mathbf{A})$, we consider the following "learning with errors" (LWE) problem: given $n, m, q, \mathbf{A}$, and m "noisy" inner products $\mathbf{b} \equiv \mathbf{A}^t \mathbf{s} + \mathbf{e} \bmod q$, where $\mathbf{e}$ is chosen from a certain error distribution Ψ over $\mathbb{Z}^m$. The task is to recover $\mathbf{s} \in \mathbb{Z}_q^n$. This search version of LWE is at least as hard as solving the decision problem, i.e., distinguish $(\mathbf{A}, \mathbf{b})$ from uniform. The *standard* error distribution is a spherical discretized normal distribution Ψ_α^m with width parameter to $\alpha = \alpha(n) \in (0, 1)$. For prime $q > 2\sqrt{n}/\alpha$ and $m \leq \mathsf{poly}(n)$, these problems are, on the average, at least as hard as SIVP with $\gamma = \tilde{\mathcal{O}}(n/\alpha)$ in the worst case [Reg09] under a quantum reduction. A similar classical reduction can be found in [Pei09] at the expense of more constraints. We will use a different, true discrete Gaussian error distribution as defined below.

Gentry et al. [GPV08] define a special family of one-way trapdoor functions called a *preimage samplable functions*. For parameters $n \in \mathbb{N}$, $q = q(n) = \mathsf{poly}(n)$, $m = m(n) = \Omega(n \log(q))$, $\tilde{L} = \tilde{L}(n) = \mathcal{O}(n \log(n))$, $\rho(n) = \omega(\sqrt{\log(n)})$, and $\eta \geq \tilde{L}\rho(m)$ this family of one-way trapdoor functions is defined as follows.

- GPVGen(1^n) generates a matrix $\mathbf{A} \in \mathbb{Z}_q^{n \times m}$, distributed statistically close to uniform, and a secret trapdoor $\mathbf{T} \in \mathbb{Z}^{m \times m}$ such that $\mathbf{AT} \equiv \mathbf{0}$ and $\left\| \tilde{\mathbf{T}} \right\| \leq \tilde{L}$.
- The one-way function associated to $\mathbf{A}$ is $f_{\mathbf{A}} : \mathbb{Z}^m \to \mathbb{Z}_q^n : \mathbf{x} \mapsto \mathbf{Ax} \pmod q$.
- GPVInvert($\mathbf{A}, \mathbf{T}, \mathbf{y}, \eta$) samples elements from $f_{\mathbf{A}}^{-1}(\mathbf{y})$ so that $(\mathbf{x}, \mathbf{Ax} \pmod q)$ as well as (GPVInvert($\mathbf{A}, \mathbf{T}, \mathbf{y}, \eta$), $\mathbf{y}$) are statistically close for $\mathbf{x} \sim D_{\mathbb{Z}^m, \eta}$ and $\mathbf{y} \leftarrow_\$ \mathbb{Z}_q^n$ for a certain distribution D, defined below.
- The samples $\mathbf{x}$ returned by GPVInvert have a conditional min-entropy of $\omega(\log(n))$, conditioned on $\mathbf{Ax} \equiv \mathbf{y}$ and $\|\mathbf{x}\|_2 \leq \eta\sqrt{m}$ (or, $\|\mathbf{x}\|_\infty \leq \eta\rho(m)$). Refer to [GPV08, AP09, Pei10] for further details.

Let Λ be a lattice. We define the distribution $D_{\Lambda, \eta, \mathbf{c}}$ with parameter η as in [GPV08]: for all $\mathbf{x} \in \Lambda + \mathbf{c}$, it is $D_{\Lambda, \eta, \mathbf{c}}(\mathbf{x}) = \frac{D_\eta(\mathbf{x})}{\sum_{\mathbf{y} \in \Lambda + \mathbf{c}} D_\eta(\mathbf{y})}$ for $D_\eta(\mathbf{x}) = 1/\eta^m \exp(-\pi\|\mathbf{x}\|^2/\eta^2)$. For $\mathbf{c} = \mathbf{0}$, we write $D_{\Lambda, \eta}$. Note that, as in [GKV10], this distribution will serve as an error distribution for LWE later.

Theorem 1 ([GPV08]). *The family is collision-resistant if* $\mathsf{SIS}(n, m, q, 2\eta\sqrt{m})$ *is hard.*

The GPV signature scheme [GPV08] is essentially a full-domain hash scheme [BR93] based on this one-way function. It uses $\mathbf{A}$ as a public key and the trapdoor $\mathbf{T}$ as the signing key. A signature on message M is a vector $\boldsymbol{\sigma}$ such that $\mathbf{A}\boldsymbol{\sigma} \equiv \mathsf{H}(M)$ and $\|\boldsymbol{\sigma}\|_2 \leq \eta\sqrt{m}$ which can be computed using the probabilistic GPVInvert algorithm.[3] Signing is stateful, i.e., when the same message is signed twice, the same signature is returned.

3   Syntax and Security of Anonymous Attribute Tokens

An anonymous attribute token (AAT) scheme can be seen as an extension of group signatures or as a simplification of anonymous credentials where the issuer can assign a list of attributes to a user's signing key. When authenticating to a verifier, the user can selectively reveal some of these attributes in a token and convince the verifier that she has a valid credential (i.e., signing key with attributes) certifying the claimed attribute values, without revealing any information about the non-revealed attributes and without making her tokens linkable – that is, more linkable than directly implied by the revealed attributes. We define and design two kind of schemes: AAT without opening (AAT–O) where anonymity is absolute, i.e., opening tokens is impossible, even for the issuer; and AAT with opening (AAT+O), where the manager can uncover the user who created a given token. Minimal disclosure tokens as implemented by Microsoft's U-Prove [BP10] are an example of an AAT–O scheme.

---

[3] With negligible probability, GPVInvert returns $\sigma = \mathbf{0}$ or $\|\sigma\|_2 > \eta\sqrt{m}$. In this case, the algorithm starts over.

Our syntax and security definitions take inspiration from those for group signatures as put forward by Bellare et al. [BMW03], but we add support for dynamic issuing of credentials. We first lay out the definitions for the setting with opening (AAT+O), and then explain the differences to the AAT–O setting. We note that an AAT+O scheme does *not* trivially yield an AAT–O scheme, because in the former the manager can always open tokens, while the latter requires that even the manager cannot link tokens. The inverse relation does not hold either due to the lack of an opening algorithm in AAT–O schemes.

Syntax of AAT+O Schemes. An AAT+O scheme is parameterized by security parameter n, maximum number of users $u_{\max}$, and maximum number of attributes per credential ℓ_{max}, and is defined by the following algorithms.

- The manager runs MKeyGen on 1^n, $u_{\max}$ to generate his public key mpk and corresponding secret key msk.
- When a user with index u requests a credential for an ordered list of attribute values $(a_i)_{i=1}^{\ell}$, with $\ell \leq \ell_{max}$, the manager runs Issue on input msk, u, and $(a_i)_{i=1}^{\ell}$ to generate a credential $cred$.
- A user generates an authentication token τ revealing a subset of attribute values $(a_i)_{i \in R}$ for $R \subseteq [\ell]$ and authenticating a message M by running the GenToken algorithm on input mpk, $cred$, $(a_i)_{i=1}^{\ell}$, R, and M. The message M can be any string; in practice, it could encode authentication context information such as the identity of the verifier, a timestamp, a session identifier, or a random nonce.
- To verify a token, the verifier runs the VToken algorithm on input mpk, the token τ, the set R, the revealed attribute values $(a_i)_{i \in R}$, and the message M. It outputs 1 or 0, indicating the validity of τ.
- Using the Open algorithm on input msk, a token τ, a set R, the revealed attributes $(a_i)_{i \in R}$, and a message M, the manager recovers the index u of the user that generated the token.

Correctness is defined in the straightforward way that any honestly generated token will be accepted. Security consists of *anonymity*, requiring that tokens generated by the same user cannot be linked, and *traceability*, requiring that no adversary can produce a token that cannot be opened or that, when opened, falsely incriminates an honest user.

Anonymity of AAT+O Schemes. We consider *full anonymity* here, in other works (e.g., [BBS04]) often referred to as CCA2-anonymity, where the adversary has access to an opening oracle. The adversary $\mathcal{A}$ is given the manager's public key mpk as input. It has access to an *initialization oracle*, an *issuing oracle*, and an *opening oracle*, which offer the following functionalities.

- The initialization oracle, on input user index u and attribute values $(a_i)_{i=1}^{\ell}$, generates a credential $cred_u \leftarrow_\$ \mathsf{Issue}(isk, u, (a_i)_{i=1}^{\ell})$. The oracle does not generate any direct output to $\mathcal{A}$, but stores $cred_u$ locally, outside $\mathcal{A}$'s view. It can only be queried once for each user u. Once user u has been initialized, the adversary can query the issuing and token generation oracles for u.

- The issuing oracle, on input a user index u, returns $cred_u$ if a credential for u was previously initialized, or $\perp$ otherwise.
- The opening oracle, on input token τ, attribute indices $R \subseteq [\ell]$, attribute values $(a_i)_{i \in R}$ and message M, returns $u \leftarrow \mathsf{Open}(msk, \tau, R, (a_i)_{i \in R}, M)$.

At the end of the first phase, $\mathcal{A}$ outputs user indices $u_0, u_1 \in [u_{\max}]$, a set $R \subseteq [\ell]$, and a message M. Let $(a_{i,0})_{i=1}^{\ell_0}$ and $(a_{i,1})_{i=1}^{\ell_1}$ be the attributes with which u_0 and u_1 were associated by the initialization oracle, respectively. If one of u_0 or u_1 has not been initialized, or if $a_{i,0} \neq a_{i,1}$ from some $i \in R$, then $\mathcal{A}$ loses the game. Otherwise, the challenger chooses a random bit b, generates a token $\tau^* \leftarrow_\$ \mathsf{GenToken}(ipk, opk, cred_{u_b}, (a_{i,b})_{i=1}^{\ell_b}, R, M)$ and hands it to $\mathcal{A}$. The latter is allowed to make any additional oracle queries except submitting τ^* to the opening oracle. Eventually it outputs a bit b' and wins the game if $b' = b$.

Note that an even stronger anonymity notion would be obtained by considering an adversarially generated manager public key mpk. We leave the construction of a scheme satisfying this stronger notion as an open problem.

Traceability of AAT+O Schemes. The adversary $\mathcal{A}$ is given as input the manager's public key mpk. Apart from the initialization, issuing, and opening oracles described above, it has access to a *token generation oracle* offering the following functionality.

- The token generation oracle, on input user index u, attribute indices $R \subseteq [\ell]$, and message M, returns a token $\tau \leftarrow_\$ \mathsf{GenToken}(mpk, cred_u, (a_i)_{i=1}^\ell, R, M)$ and returns τ to the adversary if a credential for u was previously initialized, or returns $\perp$ otherwise.

At the end of the game, $\mathcal{A}$ outputs τ^*, R^*, $(a_i^*)_{i \in R^*}$, and M^*. Let $u^* \leftarrow \mathsf{Open}(msk, \tau^*, R^*, (a_i^*)_{i \in R^*}, M^*)$ be the index of the user to whom the token is attributed by the opening algorithm. The adversary wins the game if $\mathsf{VToken}(mpk, ipk, R^*, (a_i^*)_{i \in R^*}, M^*) = 1$ and either

- $\mathcal{A}$ initialized u^* with attributes $(a_i)_{i=1}^\ell$ where $a_i \neq a_i^*$ for some $i \in R^*$, or
- $\mathcal{A}$ never queried the issuing oracle on u^* and never queried a token by u^* on M^* and R^*.

Syntax and Security of AAT–O Schemes. An AAT–O scheme does not have an Open algorithm. It does, however, have an additional VCred algorithm that a user runs, upon receiving a credential $cred$, on input mpk, $cred$, $(a_i)_{i=1}^\ell$, to check whether $cred$ is a well-formed credential. The algorithm returns 1 in case it is well-formed, or 0 if not.

We define a stronger anonymity notion for AAT–O than for AAT+O. The adversary $\mathcal{A}$ is given the manager's keys mpk and msk as input. At the end of the first phase, $\mathcal{A}$ outputs user indices $u_0, u_1 \in [u_{\max}]$, credentials $cred_{u_0}, cred_{u_1}$, lists of attribute values $(a_{i,0})_{i=1}^{\ell_0}, (a_{i,1})_{i=1}^{\ell_1}$, a set $R \subseteq [\min(\ell_0, \ell_1)]$, and a message M. If $\mathsf{VCred}(mpk, cred_b, (a_{i,b})_{i=1}^{\ell_b}) = 0$ for either of $b \in \{0, 1\}$ or if $a_{i,0} \neq a_{i,1}$ from some $i \in R$, then $\mathcal{A}$ loses the game. Otherwise, the challenger chooses a random bit b, generates a token $\tau^* \leftarrow_\$ \mathsf{GenToken}(mpk, cred_{u_b}, (a_{i,b})_{i=1}^{\ell_b}, R, M)$ and hands it to $\mathcal{A}$. The latter outputs a bit b' and wins the game if $b' = b$.

The traceability notion for AAT+O is replaced with the notion of *unforgeability* for AAT–O. In the unforgeability experiment, the adversary is given mpk as input. It has access to the same initialization, issuing, and token generation oracles as in the traceability game above. The adversary wins the game if $\mathsf{VToken}(mpk, \tau^*, R^*, (a_i^*)_{i \in R^*}, M^*) = 1$ and if for *all* users u initialized with attributes $(a_i)_{i=1}^{\ell}$ such that $a_i = a_i^*$ for all $i \in R^*$, $\mathcal{A}$ never queried the issuing oracle on u and never queried a token for u, M^*, R^*.

4 An Anonymous Attribute Token Scheme without Opening

Our anonymous attribute token schemes build upon techniques in the GKV group signature scheme by Gordon et al. [GKV10]. We briefly recall their scheme and explain the fundamental differences in the way we issue credentials (signing keys) and generate tokens (signatures). In the GKV scheme, each user u is assigned a matrix $\mathbf{A}_u$ as public key and a corresponding trapdoor matrix $\mathbf{T}_u$ as signing key. To group-sign a message M, user u first uses $\mathbf{T}_u$ to compute a GPV signature [GPV08] $\boldsymbol{\sigma}_u$ on M, this GPV-signature being a *short* vector such that $\mathbf{A}_u \boldsymbol{\sigma}_u \equiv \mathsf{H}(M)$, where H is a hash function. She generates a "fake" GPV-signature $\boldsymbol{\sigma}_v$ for all other users $v \neq u$ through Gaussian elimination, i.e., $\boldsymbol{\sigma}_v$ will be a *long* vector such that $\mathbf{A}_v \boldsymbol{\sigma}_v \equiv \mathsf{H}(M)$. She subsequently encrypts each of these signatures using a variant of the Regev encryption scheme [Reg09] to obtain ciphertexts $\boldsymbol{\tau}_v = \mathbf{B}_v \mathbf{s} + \boldsymbol{\sigma}_v$ for $v = 1, \ldots, u_{\max}$, where $\mathbf{B}_v$ are matrices such that $\mathbf{A}_v \mathbf{B}_v^t \equiv 0$ and which are included in the group's public key. The encrypted GPV-signatures can still be verified by checking whether or not $\mathbf{A}_v \boldsymbol{\tau}_v \equiv \mathsf{H}(M)$ holds. The group signature contains the vectors $\boldsymbol{\tau}_1, \ldots, \boldsymbol{\tau}_{u_{\max}}$ plus a non-interactive witness-indistinguishable proof [MV03] that at least one of the encrypted GPV-signatures is actually short. Group signatures can be opened by decrypting $\boldsymbol{\tau}_v$ using a trapdoor $\mathbf{S}_v$ associated to $\mathbf{B}_v$ and checking which of the signatures $\boldsymbol{\sigma}_v$ is short.

Our AAT–O scheme uses only a single pair of matrices $\mathbf{A}, \mathbf{B}$ for the entire group, as opposed to a pair of matrices for each user. Only the manager knows the trapdoor $\mathbf{T}$ corresponding to $\mathbf{A}$. To prevent anyone, including the manager, from knowing a trapdoor corresponding to $\mathbf{B}$, the latter matrix is determined by a common reference string. The credential of a user u is a list of GPV signatures $\boldsymbol{\sigma}_{u,i}$ such that $\mathbf{A} \boldsymbol{\sigma}_{u,i} \equiv \mathsf{H}(u\|i\|a_i)$. A first idea to create a token for attribute a_i and message M could be to encrypt $\boldsymbol{\sigma}_{u,i}$ as in the GKV scheme and include M as an argument to the random oracle in the non-interactive proof that one of the ciphertexts $\boldsymbol{\tau}_v$ encrypts a short vector.

The problem with this approach, however, is that two signatures by the same user u can be linked by checking whether $\boldsymbol{\tau}_u - \boldsymbol{\tau}'_u$ is a lattice point. This can be fixed by re-randomizing the GPV signatures, for both real and fake ones, with a small short random $\mathbf{x} \sim D_{\mathbb{Z}^{m+n}, \eta}$. To enable verifiability, we compute

$\mathbf{y} \leftarrow \mathbf{A}\mathbf{x} \bmod q$ and append a non-interactive witness-indistinguishable proof of knowledge of a short vector $\mathbf{x}'$ such that $\mathbf{A}\mathbf{x}' \equiv \mathbf{y}$. This proof is the Fiat-Shamir transformation of a generalization of Lyubashevsky's identification scheme [Lyu08], where the message M is included as an argument in the hash.

This approach of treating each attribute separately has the obvious disadvantage that it blows up the signature size with a factor of $\#R \leq \ell$. We can obtain shorter tokens by observing that GPV signatures support a limited form of aggregation [BGLS03]. Namely, the GPV signatures $\boldsymbol{\sigma}_{u,i}$ for $i \in R$ can be summed up to form an aggregate signature $\boldsymbol{\alpha}_u \leftarrow \sum_{i \in R} \boldsymbol{\sigma}_{u,i}$. The aggregate satisfies $\mathbf{A}\boldsymbol{\alpha}_u \equiv \sum_{i \in R} \mathsf{H}(u\|i\|a_i)$ and is still "somewhat" short. Enabling such aggregation in Section 4.1.4 comes at the price of having to choose slightly larger security parameters, but only by a factor of $\log(\#R)$.

4.1   Cryptographic Ingredients

4.1.1   Sampling Orthogonal Lattices with Trapdoors Revisited

Gordon et al. [GKV10] present an algorithm that, given a matrix $\mathbf{B} \in \mathbb{Z}_q^{n \times (m+n)}$, samples a matrix $\mathbf{A} \in \mathbb{Z}_q^{n \times (m+n)}$ and an associated trapdoor $\mathbf{T} \in \mathbb{Z}^{n \times (m+n)}$ such that $\mathbf{A}\mathbf{B}^t \equiv \mathbf{0}$. We give a construction method based on [GKV10] that is more efficient and allows for better (i.e., shorter) trapdoors.

Proposition 1. *There exists a probabilistic polynomial-time (PPT) algorithm* OrthoSamp *that, on input* $\mathbf{B} = \mathbf{B}_1\|\mathbf{B}_2 \in \mathbb{Z}_q^{n \times (m+n)}$ *with* $\mathbf{B}_2 \in (\mathbb{Z}_q^{n \times n})^*$, *outputs a pair* $(\mathbf{A}, \mathbf{T}) \in \mathbb{Z}_q^{n \times (m+n)} \times \mathbb{Z}^{n \times (m+n)}$ *such that (1)* $\mathbf{A}\mathbf{B}^t \equiv \mathbf{0}$; *(2)* $\mathbf{A}$ *is distributed statistically close to uniform (conditioned on* $\mathbf{A}\mathbf{B}^t \equiv \mathbf{0}$*); (3)* $\mathbf{A}\mathbf{T} \equiv \mathbf{0}$; *and (4)* $\left\|\tilde{\mathbf{T}}\right\| \leq \tilde{L}$.

From [CHKP10], we adopt the notion of extending a lattices basis to a larger dimension. The corresponding algorithm ExtBasis takes as input a matrix $\mathbf{A}_1$, a basis $\mathbf{T}_1$ of $\Lambda_q^{\perp}(\mathbf{A}_1)$, and an extension $\mathbf{A}_2$. It picks a uniformly random $\mathbf{V} \in \mathbb{Z}_q^{m \times n}$ such that $\mathbf{A}_1 \mathbf{V} \equiv -\mathbf{A}_2$. Its output is a basis $\mathbf{T} = \left(\begin{array}{c|c} \mathbf{T}_1 & \mathbf{V} \\ \hline \mathbf{0} & \mathbf{I}_n \end{array}\right)$ of $\Lambda_q(\mathbf{A})$ for $\mathbf{A} = \mathbf{A}_1\|\mathbf{A}_2$ with $\left\|\tilde{\mathbf{T}}\right\| \leq \left\|\tilde{\mathbf{T}}_1\right\| \leq \tilde{L}$.

Proof. First, generate $(\mathbf{A}_1, \mathbf{T}_1) \leftarrow \mathsf{GPVGen}(1^n)$. Then, set $\mathbf{A}_2 \leftarrow -\mathbf{A}_1\mathbf{B}_1^t(\mathbf{B}_2^{-1})^t = [\mathbf{a}_1^{(2)}, \ldots, \mathbf{a}_n^{(2)}]$ and compute the basis $\mathbf{T} \leftarrow \mathsf{ExtBasis}(\mathbf{A}_1, \mathbf{T}_1, \mathbf{A}_2)$. Output $\mathbf{A} = \mathbf{A}_1\|\mathbf{A}_2$ and $\mathbf{T}$. The output satisfies (1) because $\mathbf{A}\mathbf{B}^t \equiv \mathbf{A}_1\mathbf{B}_1^t + \mathbf{A}_2\mathbf{B}_2^t \equiv \mathbf{A}_1\mathbf{B}_1^t - \mathbf{A}_1\mathbf{B}_1^t(\mathbf{B}_2^{-1})^t\mathbf{B}_2^t \equiv \mathbf{0}$. It satisfies (2) because the output $\mathbf{A}_1$ of GPVGen is distributed statistically close to uniform. It satisfies (3) because $\mathbf{A}\mathbf{T} \equiv \mathbf{A}_1\mathbf{T}_1\|(\mathbf{A}_1\mathbf{V} + \mathbf{A}_2) \equiv \mathbf{0}$. Finally, to see that it satisfies (4), recall that $\mathbf{T}_1$ is a basis of $\mathbb{R}^m$. Thus, after GSO, we have $\tilde{\mathbf{T}} = \left(\begin{array}{c|c} \tilde{\mathbf{T}}_1 & \mathbf{0} \\ \hline \mathbf{0} & \mathbf{I}_n \end{array}\right)$ and, as a consequence, $\left\|\tilde{\mathbf{T}}\right\| = \left\|\tilde{\mathbf{T}}_1\right\| \leq \tilde{L}$. $\square$

Notice that essentially the same procedure can be used to compute an orthogonal $\mathbf{A}$ such that $\mathbf{A}\mathbf{B}^t \equiv \mathbf{0}$ without a trapdoor for $\Lambda_q^\perp(\mathbf{A})$. Just sample a uniformly random matrix $\mathbf{A}_1$ in the first step and omit all subsequent steps that involve the trapdoor $\mathbf{T}_1$.

In our security proofs, we will require that a pair $(\mathbf{A}, \mathbf{T_A}, \mathbf{B}, \mathbf{T_B})$ does not reveal in which order they were generated by OrthoSamp as stated by the following proposition. We refer to the full paper for the proof.

Proposition 2. *Let* $\mathbf{A}, \mathbf{T_A}, \mathbf{B}, \mathbf{T_B}$ *be random variables where* $(\mathbf{B}_1, \mathbf{T}_{\mathbf{B}_1}) \leftarrow$ GPVGen(1^n)*;* $\mathbf{B}_2 \leftarrow_\$ (\mathbb{Z}_q^{n \times n})^*$*;* $\mathbf{T_B} \leftarrow$ ExtBasis$(\mathbf{B}_1, \mathbf{T}_{\mathbf{B}_1}, \mathbf{B}_2)$*; and* $(\mathbf{A}, \mathbf{T_A}) \leftarrow$ OrthoSamp$(\mathbf{B})$*. Then, the distributions* $X_1 = (\mathbf{A}, \mathbf{T_A}, \mathbf{B}, \mathbf{T_B})$ *and* $X_2 = (\mathbf{B}, \mathbf{T_B}, \mathbf{A}, \mathbf{T_A})$ *are statistically indistinguishable.*

Observe that we have applied a simplification to the above proposition, where we choose $\mathbf{B}_2$ directly from the set of invertible matrices. Whenever the proposition is applied in our schemes, this property can be easily ensured by repeating the sampling procedure a small number of times. For our parameters, a good approximation of the ratio $\left|(\mathbb{Z}_q^{n \times n})^*\right| / \left|\mathbb{Z}_q^{n \times n}\right|$ is $e^{-1/(q-1)}$ and a lower bound is $(1 - 1/q)^n$. Since the choice of q is mainly governed by the worst-case to average-case reduction for SIS, demanding that $q \gg \nu$ for SIS(n, m, q, ν), it will exceed $\eta\sqrt{m + n} = \Omega(n^{1.5} \log^{1.5}(n))$ in all our schemes. Hence, the fraction of invertible matrices over $\mathbb{Z}_q^{n \times n}$ is very close to 1.

All in all, our method differs from the corresponding lemma of [GKV10] in that we always use GPVGen in dimension m instead of sampling a trapdoor in dimension $m + n$ (as in [GKV10]) directly. Instead, we explicitly control how the trapdoor is extended to the super lattice. Hence, we have more control over the "shape" of the $(m+n)$-dimensional input trapdoor to OrthoSamp, resulting in efficiency advantages and a better-quality trapdoor $\mathbf{T}$. See the full version [CNR12] for details.

Efficient Sampling with Orthogonal Trapdoors. We apply a slight, well-known improvement to GPVInvert whenever we apply it in dimension $m + n$, i.e., whenever we call GPVInvert$(\mathbf{A}, \mathbf{T}, \mathbf{t}, \eta)$ for $(\mathbf{A}, \mathbf{T})$ being output by OrthoSamp. Instead of sampling directly using $\mathbf{T}$, we use the upper-left part $\mathbf{T}_1$ of $\mathbf{T}$ and the following algorithm: 1. Sample $\mathbf{x}_2 \sim D_{\mathbb{Z}^n, \eta}$; 2. Call $\mathbf{x}_1 \leftarrow$ GPVInvert$(\mathbf{A}_1, \mathbf{T}_1, \mathbf{t} - \mathbf{A}_2\mathbf{x}_2, \eta)$; 3. Output $\mathbf{x}_1 \| \mathbf{x}_2$. The result has norm at most $\eta\sqrt{m + n}$.

4.1.2 Verifiable Encryption of GPV Signatures

As mentioned in the construction sketch, we will "encrypt" GPV signatures with a variant of the "dual" encryption scheme [GPV08]. To this end, we define the following family of one-way trapdoor functions based on the LWE problem. For ease of exposition, we will slightly abuse the terms *encryption* for this trapdoor one-way function and *ciphertext* for an image under this trapdoor in the subsequent sections. Fix a truncated error distribution Ψ over $\mathbb{Z}^m$ with support D_Ψ. Other parameters are the same as for GPV signatures.

- Keys are generated using GPVGen(1^n), yielding a public key $\mathbf{B}$ and corresponding trapdoor $\mathbf{S}$.

- The one-way function associated to $\mathbf{B}$ is $g_{\mathbf{B}} : \mathbb{Z}_q^n \times \mathbb{Z}^m \to \mathbb{Z}_q^m : (\mathbf{s}, \mathbf{e}) \mapsto \mathbf{B}^t \mathbf{s} + \mathbf{e} \bmod q$.
- LWEInvert$(\mathbf{B}, \mathbf{S}, \boldsymbol{\tau})$ uses $\mathbf{S}$ to find a vector $\mathbf{B}^t \mathbf{s}'$ that is close to $\boldsymbol{\tau}$. Then, it computes $\mathbf{e}' \leftarrow \boldsymbol{\tau} - \mathbf{B}^t \mathbf{s}'$ and returns $(\mathbf{s}', \mathbf{e}')$.

Note that we modified LWEInvert() as to output $(\mathbf{s}', \mathbf{e}')$ instead of just $\mathbf{s}'$ as defined by Peikert [Pei09]. We will use $\Psi = \sum_{i=1}^{\ell} D_{\mathbb{Z}^m, \eta} = D_{\mathbb{Z}^m, \sqrt{\ell}\eta}$ and $D_{\Psi} = \{\mathbf{v} \in \mathbb{Z}^m : \|\mathbf{v}\|_2 \leq \eta\sqrt{m}\}$. Correctness follows from [Pei09] with $q(n) \geq \tilde{L}^2 \rho^2(m)$, security as a one-way function follows from [Reg09, Pei09, GKV10].

Theorem 2 ([GKV10]). *The family is one-way if* $g_{\mathbf{B}}(\mathbf{s}, \mathbf{e})$ *is indistinguishable from uniform for* $\mathbf{s} \leftarrow_\$ \mathbb{Z}_q^n$ *and* $\mathbf{e} \sim \Psi$. *It is hard to distinguish from uniform for* Ψ *if decision* LWE *is hard with the standard noise distribution* $\Psi_{\sqrt{\ell}\eta/(q\sqrt{2})}^m$.

Also note that if matrices $\mathbf{B}, \mathbf{A}, \mathbf{S}$ are generated via the GPVGen and OrthoSamp and $\boldsymbol{\sigma}$ is a GPV signature such that $\mathbf{A}\boldsymbol{\sigma} \equiv H(M)$, then the "encrypted" signature $\boldsymbol{\tau} \leftarrow \mathbf{B}^t \mathbf{s} + \boldsymbol{\sigma} \bmod q$ can still be verified by checking that $\mathbf{A}\boldsymbol{\tau} \equiv H(M)$. However, we need to ensure that the "noise" $\boldsymbol{\sigma}$ is small, which is why we require the following witness-indistinguishable proof of membership (WIPoM) system for bounded-distance decodeability (BDD).

4.1.3 Efficient Proofs for Lattice Problems

As mentioned in the construction sketch, we need two non-interactive proofs for our scheme: a proof that at least one of a number of ciphertexts encrypts a short vector, and a proof of knowledge of $\mathbf{x}$ such that $\mathbf{A}\mathbf{x} \equiv \mathbf{y}$.

WIPoM for BDD. We use a variant $\mathcal{L}_{\mathsf{BDD}}(\gamma, \beta) := \{\mathcal{L}_{\mathsf{BDD}}^{\mathsf{YES}}(\gamma, \beta), \mathcal{L}_{\mathsf{BDD}}^{\mathsf{NO}}(\gamma, \beta)\}$ of the γ-GapCVP language [Reg10] for lattices $\Lambda_q(\mathbf{B})$. The "YES" and "NO" instances for words $(\mathbf{B}, \boldsymbol{\tau}) \in \mathbb{Z}_q^{n \times m} \times \mathbb{Z}_q^m$ are defined as:

$$\mathcal{L}_{\mathsf{BDD}}^{\mathsf{YES}}(\gamma, \beta) := \{(\mathbf{B}, \boldsymbol{\tau}) | \exists \mathbf{s} \in \mathbb{Z}_q^n : \|\boldsymbol{\tau} - \mathbf{B}^t \mathbf{s} \bmod q\|_2 \leq \beta\}$$

$$\text{and} \quad \mathcal{L}_{\mathsf{BDD}}^{\mathsf{NO}}(\gamma, \beta) := \{(\mathbf{B}, \boldsymbol{\tau}) | \forall \mathbf{s} \in \mathbb{Z}_q^n : \|\boldsymbol{\tau} - \mathbf{B}^t \mathbf{s} \bmod q\|_2 > \gamma\beta\}.$$

The norms above are computed by taking the absolute smallest representative modulo q of the coordinates, i.e., integers in the interval $[\frac{1-q}{2}, \frac{q-1}{2}]$. Using standard techniques [CDS94, MV03, SCPY08] (see the full version [CNR12]), one can efficiently convert the k-bit parallelized version of Micciancio-Vadhan's proof of membership $(\mathcal{P}_{\mathsf{BDD}}, \mathcal{V}_{\mathsf{BDD}})$ [MV03] into a sound WIPoM $(\mathcal{P}_{\mathsf{V-pBDD}}, \mathcal{V}_{\mathsf{V-pBDD}})$ for the OR-combination of such statements:

$$\mathcal{L}_{\mathsf{V-BDD}}^{\mathsf{YES}}(\gamma, \beta, u_{\max}) := \{((\mathbf{B}, \boldsymbol{\tau}_v))_{v=1}^{u_{\max}} | \exists v \in [u_{\max}] \exists \mathbf{s}_v \in \mathbb{Z}_q^n : \|\boldsymbol{\tau}_v - \mathbf{B}^t \mathbf{s}_v\|_2 \leq \beta\}.$$

The "NO" instance is defined analogously. The resulting prover $\mathcal{P}_{\mathsf{V-pBDD}}$ generates simulated transcripts   for all $v \neq u$ and runs the real prover $\mathcal{P}_{\mathsf{pBDD}}((\mathbf{B}, \boldsymbol{\tau}_u), \mathbf{s}_u)$ to obtain the transcript for user u, using as a challenge the

XOR of the given challenge of the $\mathcal{P}_{\text{V-pBDD}}$ proof and the simulated challenges for $v \neq u$. This proof system is also statistical honest-verifier zero-knowledge. We will use the non-interactive variant of the proof system using the Fiat-Shamir transformation [FS86] where the challenge ch_V is generated through a random oracle.

Signatures from ISIS. In addition, our constructions will require a signature scheme based on a generalized version of the witness-indistinguishable identification scheme due to Lyubashevsky [Lyu08]. The main difference to [Lyu08] is that we require an entirely different distribution of secret keys to make the scheme applicable in our context.

The secret key is a short vector $\mathbf{x} \sim D_{\mathbb{Z}^{m+n},\eta}$, while the public key consists of a matrix $\mathbf{A} \leftarrow_\$ \mathbb{Z}^{n \times (m+n)}$ and the vector $\mathbf{y} \leftarrow \mathbf{A}\mathbf{x} \bmod q$. It follows a typical three-move structure where the prover first generates a commitment and state $(cmt_\text{ISIS}, st) \leftarrow_\$ \text{Comm}_\text{ISIS}(\mathbf{A})$. The verifier sends a challenge $ch_\text{ISIS} \leftarrow_\$ \{0,1\}^t$, upon which the prover sends the response $rsp_\text{ISIS} \leftarrow_\$ \text{Resp}_\text{ISIS}(\mathbf{x}, st, ch_\text{ISIS})$. The verifier accepts iff $\text{Verify}_\text{ISIS}(\mathbf{A}, \mathbf{y}, cmt_\text{ISIS}, ch_\text{ISIS}, rsp_\text{ISIS}) = 1$. The identification scheme has been shown statistically witness-indistinguishable and secure under active attack assuming that the ISIS problem related to $\mathbf{A}, \mathbf{y}$ is hard [Lyu08, Theorem 13]. We will turn the identification scheme into a signature scheme using the Fiat-Shamir transformation.

4.1.4 Single-Signer Aggregate Signatures

To make the token length logarithmic[4] instead of linear the number of attributes, we observe that GPV signatures support a restricted form of aggregation [BGLS03] where up to ℓ_{max} signatures by the same signer can be compressed to the size of a single signature. Namely, given $\ell \leq \ell_{max}$ signatures $(\sigma_i)_{i=1}^\ell$, the aggregate $\alpha \leftarrow \sum_{i=1}^\ell \sigma_i$ can be verified by checking that $\ell \leq \ell_{max}$, that $0 < \|\alpha\|_2 \leq \ell\eta\sqrt{m}$, and that $\mathbf{A}\alpha \equiv \sum_{i=1}^\ell \mathsf{H}(M_i)$.

Because of the similarity in structure between GPV signatures and the above single-signer aggregate scheme, the latter inherits the mechanisms to verifiably encrypt aggregate signatures from Section 4.1.2.

Theorem 3. *The above single-signer aggregate signature scheme is existentially unforgeable in the random oracle model if the $\mathsf{SIS}(n, m, q, 2\ell_{max}\eta\sqrt{m})$ problem is hard.*

4.2 Scheme and Security

In the following, we describe an anonymous attribute token scheme AAT–O = (IKeyGen, Issue, GenToken, VToken) with security parameter n based on hard lattice problems. The scheme uses random oracles $\mathsf{H} : \{0,1\}^* \rightarrow \mathbb{Z}_q^{m+n}$, $\mathsf{F} :$

---

[4] While an aggregate signature may seem constant in length, the security parameter actually needs to grow logarithmically in ℓ_{max} for security.

$\{0,1\}^* \to \{0,1\}^k$, and $G : \{0,1\}^* \to \{0,1\}^t$, as well as a uniformly distributed common reference string $\mathbf{B} \in \mathbb{Z}_q^{n \times (m+n)}$ that is a valid input to OrthoSamp.

MKeyGen($1^n, u_{\max}$): The manager runs $(\mathbf{A}, \mathbf{T}) \leftarrow$ OrthoSamp($\mathbf{B}$) and sets mpk $\leftarrow \mathbf{A}$ and $msk \leftarrow (\mathbf{A}, \mathbf{T})$.

Issue($msk, u, (a_i)_{i=1}^\ell$): For all $i \in [\ell]$, the manager computes $\boldsymbol{\sigma}_{u,i} \leftarrow$ GPVInvert($\mathbf{A}$, $\mathbf{T}, H(u\|i\|a_i), \eta$) and returns $cred = (u, (\boldsymbol{\sigma}_{u,i})_{i=1}^\ell)$.

VCred($mpk, cred, (a_i)_{i=1}^\ell$): The user parses $cred = (u, (\boldsymbol{\sigma}_i)_{i=1}^\ell)$ and outputs 1 iff $\mathbf{A}\boldsymbol{\sigma}_{u,i} \equiv H(u\|i\|a_i)$ and $\|\boldsymbol{\sigma}_{u,i}\|_2 \leq \eta\sqrt{m+n}$ for all $i \in [\ell]$.

GenToken($mpk, cred, (a_i)_{i=1}^\ell, R, M$): Let $cred = (u, (\boldsymbol{\sigma}_{u,i})_{i=1}^\ell)$. The user first chooses a random $\mathbf{x} \sim D_{\mathbb{Z}^{m+n}, \eta}$, computes $\mathbf{y} \leftarrow \mathbf{A}\mathbf{x} \bmod q$, and creates a signature $(ch_{\mathsf{ISIS}}, rsp_{\mathsf{ISIS}})$ by running $(cmt_{\mathsf{ISIS}}, st) \leftarrow_\$ \mathsf{Comm}_{\mathsf{ISIS}}(\mathbf{A})$, setting $ch_{\mathsf{ISIS}} \leftarrow G(\mathbf{y}\|cmt_{\mathsf{ISIS}}\|M)$, and computing $rsp_{\mathsf{ISIS}} \leftarrow \mathsf{Resp}_{\mathsf{ISIS}}(\mathbf{x}, st, ch_{\mathsf{ISIS}})$. In the unlikely event that $\mathsf{Verify}_{\mathsf{ISIS}}(\mathbf{A}, \mathbf{y}, cmt_{\mathsf{ISIS}}, ch_{\mathsf{ISIS}}, rsp_{\mathsf{ISIS}}) = 0$, she simply repeats these steps.

For all $v \in [u_{\max}] \setminus \{u\}$, she picks a uniformly random $\tilde{\boldsymbol{\alpha}}_v$ such that $\mathbf{A}\tilde{\boldsymbol{\alpha}}_v \equiv \sum_{i \in R} H(v\|i\|a_i)$ using Gauss elimination, chooses $\mathbf{s}_v \leftarrow_\$ \mathbb{Z}_q^n$ and computes $\boldsymbol{\tau}_v \leftarrow \mathbf{B}^t \mathbf{s}_v + \tilde{\boldsymbol{\alpha}}_v + \mathbf{x} \bmod q$. For her own index u, she chooses $\mathbf{s}_u \leftarrow_\$ \mathbb{Z}_q^n$ and computes $\boldsymbol{\tau}_u \leftarrow \mathbf{B}^t \mathbf{s}_u + \boldsymbol{\alpha}_u + \mathbf{x} \bmod q$, where $\boldsymbol{\alpha}_u \leftarrow \sum_{i \in R} \boldsymbol{\sigma}_{u,i}$. She generates a non-interactive proof $(cmt_\vee, rsp_\vee) \leftarrow \mathcal{P}_{\vee\text{-pBDD}}(((\mathbf{B}, \boldsymbol{\tau}_v))_{v=1}^{u_{\max}}, u, \mathbf{s}_u)$ using as challenge $ch_\vee = F(\mathbf{B}\|(\boldsymbol{\tau}_v)_{v=1}^{u_{\max}}\|cmt_\vee\|(a_i)_{i=1}^\ell\|R\|M)$. Finally, the resulting token becomes $\tau \leftarrow (\boldsymbol{\tau}_1, \ldots, \boldsymbol{\tau}_{u_{\max}}, \mathbf{y}, cmt_{\mathsf{ISIS}}, rsp_{\mathsf{ISIS}}, cmt_\vee, rsp_\vee)$.

VToken($mpk, \tau, R, (a_i)_{i \in R}, M$): The verifier accepts a token if $\mathsf{Verify}_{\mathsf{ISIS}}(\mathbf{A}, \mathbf{y}, cmt_{\mathsf{ISIS}}, G(\mathbf{y}\|cmt_{\mathsf{ISIS}}\|M), rsp_{\mathsf{ISIS}}) = 1$, if $\mathbf{A}\boldsymbol{\tau}_v \equiv \sum_{i \in R} H(v\|i\|a_i) + \mathbf{y}$ for all $v \in [u_{\max}]$, and if $\mathcal{V}_{\vee\text{-pBDD}}$ accepts the proof $(cmt_\vee, rsp_\vee)$ for statement $((\mathbf{B}, \boldsymbol{\tau}_v))_{v=1}^{u_{\max}}$ and challenge $ch_\vee = F(\mathbf{B}\|(\boldsymbol{\tau}_v)_{v=1}^{u_{\max}}\|cmt_\vee\|(a_i)_{i=1}^\ell\|R\|M)$. Otherwise, the verifier rejects the token.

Theorem 4. *The above anonymous attribute token scheme is anonymous in the random oracle model if* LWE *is hard for* $\Psi = D_{\mathbb{Z}^{m+n}, \eta}$.

Theorem 5. *The above anonymous attribute token scheme is unforgeable in the random oracle model if* SIS$(n, m+n, q, (2\ell_{max}+1)\eta\sqrt{m+n} + \tilde{\mathcal{O}}(n^{1.5}))$ *is hard and the decision* LWE *problem with noise distribution* Ψ *is hard.*

See the full version for the full-blown scheme with opening and for extended results on group signatures, ring signature, and for achieving non-frameability. In short, to add opening functionality to our AAT–O scheme, we generate the matrix $\mathbf{B}$ with an embedded trapdoor $\mathbf{S}$ using OrthoSamp, as done in [GKV10]. To achieve full anonymity, however, we need to be able to respond to opening queries. For this purpose, we borrow techniques from Rosen and Segev [RS09] and Peikert [Pei09] to obtain CCA-security for the LWE encryption scheme by using "correlated" ciphertexts. One problem is that the verifier needs a way to check that the included ciphertexts are valid, i.e., correctly correlated, without having the trapdoor $\mathbf{S}$. We solve this problem by a clever use of the $\mathcal{P}_{\vee\text{-pBDD}}$ proof system so that it simultaneously proves that a ciphertext contains a short vector and is correctly correlated.

5   An Anonymous Attribute Token Scheme with Opening

We add opening functionality to our AAT–O scheme by generating the matrix $\mathbf{B}$ with an embedded trapdoor $\mathbf{S}$ using OrthoSamp, as done in [GKV10]. To achieve full anonymity, however, we borrow techniques from Rosen and Segev [RS09] and Peikert [Pei09] to obtain CCA-security for the LWE encryption scheme using "correlated" ciphertexts. We then use the $\mathcal{P}_{\text{V-pBDD}}$ proof system to convince the verifier that the ciphertexts contain a short vector and are correctly correlated.

Details of the scheme can be found in the full version [CNR12], we only give a sketch here. Following [RS09, Pei09], define the family of correlated trapdoor one-way functions CTLWE with parameters $n, m, \kappa \in \mathbb{N}$ and with public key $(\mathbf{B}_0, \ldots, \mathbf{B}_\kappa)$ and trapdoor $\mathbf{S}_0$ so that $\mathbf{B}_0 \mathbf{S}_0 \equiv \mathbf{0}$. The one-way function is $g(\mathbf{s}, \mathbf{e}_0, \ldots, \mathbf{e}_\kappa) = (\mathbf{B}_0^t \mathbf{s} + \mathbf{e}_0 \bmod q, \ldots, \mathbf{B}_0^t \mathbf{s} + \mathbf{e}_\kappa \bmod q)$. Inversion is done by computing $(\mathbf{s}', \mathbf{e}'_0) \leftarrow \text{LWEInvert}(\mathbf{B}_0, \mathbf{S}_0, \mathbf{b}_0)$ and checking that $\|\mathbf{e}'_i\|_2 \leq \eta \sqrt{m}$ for all $i \in \{0, \ldots, \kappa\}$ where $\mathbf{e}'_i = \mathbf{b}_i - \mathbf{B}_i^t \mathbf{s}' \bmod q$. We also rely on a one-time signature scheme $\mathcal{OTS} = (\text{OTKeygen}, \text{OTSign}, \text{OTVerify})$ with verification key length κ.

The manager's keys are $mpk \leftarrow (\mathbf{A}, \mathbf{B}_0, \mathbf{B}_{1,0}, \mathbf{B}_{1,1}, \ldots, \mathbf{B}_{\kappa,0}, \mathbf{B}_{\kappa,1})$ and $msk \leftarrow (\mathbf{T}, \mathbf{S}_0, mpk)$ where $(\mathbf{A}, \mathbf{T}) \leftarrow \text{OrthoSamp}(\mathbf{B}_0)$, where $(\mathbf{B}_0, \mathbf{B}_{1,0} \ldots, \mathbf{B}_{\kappa,0})$ define a correlated one-way function with trapdoor $\mathbf{S}_0$, and where $\mathbf{B}_{1,1}, \ldots, \mathbf{B}_{\kappa,1}$ are random. A user's credential contains short vectors $(\boldsymbol{\sigma}_{u,i})_{i=1}^{\ell}$ such that $\mathbf{A} \boldsymbol{\sigma}_{u,i} \equiv H(u\|i\|a_i)$ computed using $\mathbf{T}$. To generate a token for attributes indices R and message M, the user u:

- chooses $\mathbf{x}_0 \sim D_{\mathbb{Z}^{m+n}, \eta}$, computes $\mathbf{y}_0 \leftarrow \mathbf{A}\mathbf{x}_0 \bmod q$, and creates a signature σ_{ISIS} using $G(\mathbf{y}_0 \| cmt_{\text{ISIS}} \| M)$ as challenge;
- computes $\boldsymbol{\rho}_u \leftarrow \sum_{i \in R} \boldsymbol{\sigma}_{u,i} + \mathbf{x}_0 \bmod q$, chooses $\mathbf{s}_u \leftarrow_\$ \mathbb{Z}_q^n$ and computes $\boldsymbol{\tau}_{u,0} \leftarrow \mathbf{B}_0^t \mathbf{s}_u + \boldsymbol{\rho}_u \bmod q$;
- for all $v \in [u_{\max}] \setminus \{u\}$, computes $\tilde{\boldsymbol{\alpha}}_v$ such that $\mathbf{A}\tilde{\boldsymbol{\alpha}}_v \equiv \sum_{i \in R} H(v\|i\|a_i)$, computes $\boldsymbol{\rho}_v \leftarrow \tilde{\boldsymbol{\alpha}}_v + \mathbf{x}_0 \bmod q$, chooses $\mathbf{s}_v \leftarrow_\$ \mathbb{Z}_q^n$ and computes $\boldsymbol{\tau}_{v,0} \leftarrow \mathbf{B}_0^t \mathbf{s}_v + \boldsymbol{\rho}_v \bmod q$;
- generates a signature key pair $(otvk, otsk) \leftarrow \text{OTKeygen}(1^n)$, and for all $v \in [u_{\max}]$ and $i \in [\kappa]$, chooses $\mathbf{x}_{v,i} \sim D_{\mathbb{Z}^{m+n}, \eta}$ and computes $\boldsymbol{\tau}_{v,i} \leftarrow \mathbf{B}_{i,otvk_i}^t \mathbf{s}_v + \mathbf{x}_{v,i} \bmod q$.

Let $\mathbf{B}_{otvk} = [\mathbf{B}_0 \| \mathbf{B}_{1,otvk_1} \| \ldots \| \mathbf{B}_{\kappa,otvk_\kappa}]$, and for all $v \in [u_{\max}]$, let $\mathbf{x}_v = [\boldsymbol{\rho}_v, \mathbf{x}_{v,1}, \ldots, \mathbf{x}_{v,\kappa}]$ and $\boldsymbol{\tau}_v = [\boldsymbol{\tau}_{v,0}, \ldots, \boldsymbol{\tau}_{v,\kappa}]$. Then for all $v \in [u_{\max}]$ we have that $\boldsymbol{\tau}_v \equiv \mathbf{B}_{otvk}^t \mathbf{s}_v + \mathbf{x}_v$, and for user u we have that $\|\mathbf{x}_u\|_2 \leq (\#R + \kappa + 1)\eta \sqrt{m+n}$. The user can therefore create a non-interactive proof $\pi_{\text{V-pBDD}}$ using $\mathcal{P}_{\text{V-pBDD}}$ to simultaneously prove that one of the vectors $\boldsymbol{\tau}_v$ encrypts a short vector $\boldsymbol{\alpha}_v$ and that all ciphertexts $\boldsymbol{\tau}_v$ are well-formed, i.e., that all components $\boldsymbol{\tau}_{v,i}$ are underlain by the same vector $\mathbf{s}_v$. The token contains vectors $\boldsymbol{\tau}_1, \ldots, \boldsymbol{\tau}_{u_{\max}}, \mathbf{y}_0$, non-interactive proofs σ_{ISIS} and $\pi_{\text{V-pBDD}}$, the one-time verification key $otvk$, and a one-time signature on everything.

The verifier checks that σ_{ISIS} and $\pi_{\vee\text{-pBDD}}$ are correct, that for all $v \in [u_{\max}]$ $\mathbf{A}\tau_{v,0} \equiv \sum_{i \in R} \mathsf{H}(v\|i\|a_i) + \mathbf{y}_0$, and verifies the one-time signature. Opening is done by inverting τ_v w.r.t. $\mathbf{B}_{otvk}$ and for $v = 1, \ldots, u_{\max}$ and returning the first v where the inversion successfully yields $(\mathbf{s}'_v, \boldsymbol{\rho}'_v)$ with $\boldsymbol{\rho}'_v \leq (\#R + 1)\eta\sqrt{m+n}$.

Theorem 6. *The AAT+O scheme sketched above is anonymous in the random oracle model if* LWE *is hard for* $\Psi = D_{\mathbb{Z}^{m+n},\eta}$ *and if* $\mathcal{OTS}$ *is existentially unforgeable under one-time chosen-message attack. It is traceable in the random oracle model if* SIS$(n, m+n, q, (2\ell_{max}+1)\eta\sqrt{m+n} + \widetilde{\mathcal{O}}(n^{1.5}))$ *is hard and the decision* LWE *problem with noise distribution* Ψ *is hard.*

6   Further Extensions and Conclusion

Non-frameability [BSZ05] ensures that the group manager cannot frame users by generating tokens on their behalf and falsely hold the users responsible for these tokens. One can obtain non-frameabilty for our construction by running a AAT+O and a AAT–O scheme in parallel, and merging both schemes so that a token is only accepted if it contains a valid token for both schemes. The AAT–O scheme ensures that users cannot be framed, while the AAT+O scheme ensures that tokens can be opened. We refer to the full version [CNR12] for more details.

As mentioned earlier, a group signature scheme can be seen as a special case of a AAT+O scheme, so our AAT+O scheme directly implies the first lattice-based group signature scheme that enjoys full anonymity, i.e., against an adversary with access to an opening oracle, as is standard for group signatures [BMW03]. Our scheme also has constant-size manager keys (versus linear in the number of group members GKV).

Our results and the above extensions bring us a step closer to a full-fledged lattice-based anonymous credential systems, but building such a system and reducing the signature/token size remain challenging open problems.

Acknowledgements. This work was supported in part by the European Commission through the ICT Programme under Contract ICT-2007-216676 ECRYPT II. The first and second authors were supported in party by EC Grant Agreement 257782 ABC4Trust. The third author work was supported by CASED (www.cased.de).

References

[ACJT00]   Ateniese, G., Camenisch, J., Joye, M., Tsudik, G.: A Practical and Provably Secure Coalition-Resistant Group Signature Scheme. In: Bellare, M. (ed.) CRYPTO 2000. LNCS, vol. 1880, pp. 255–270. Springer, Heidelberg (2000)

[Ajt96]   Ajtai, M.: Generating hard instances of lattice problems (extended abstract). In: STOC 1996. ACM (1996)

[AP09]   Alwen, J., Peikert, C.: Generating shorter bases for hard random lattices. In: STACS 2009. Dagstuhl Seminar Proceedings, vol. 09001, Schloss Dagstuhl (2009)

[AST02]   Ateniese, G., Song, D., Tsudik, G.: Quasi-Efficient Revocation in Group Signatures. In: Blaze, M. (ed.) FC 2002. LNCS, vol. 2357, pp. 183–197. Springer, Heidelberg (2003)

[Bab86]   Babai, L.: On Lovász' lattice reduction and the nearest lattice point problem. Combinatorica 6(1), 1–13 (1986)

[BBS04]   Boneh, D., Boyen, X., Shacham, H.: Short Group Signatures. In: Franklin, M. (ed.) CRYPTO 2004. LNCS, vol. 3152, pp. 41–55. Springer, Heidelberg (2004)

[BCN+10]   Bichsel, P., Camenisch, J., Neven, G., Smart, N.P., Warinschi, B.: Get Shorty via Group Signatures without Encryption. In: Garay, J.A., De Prisco, R. (eds.) SCN 2010. LNCS, vol. 6280, pp. 381–398. Springer, Heidelberg (2010)

[BD08]   Boyen, X., Delerablée, C.: Expressive Subgroup Signatures. In: Ostrovsky, R., De Prisco, R., Visconti, I. (eds.) SCN 2008. LNCS, vol. 5229, pp. 185–200. Springer, Heidelberg (2008)

[BGLS03]   Boneh, D., Gentry, C., Lynn, B., Shacham, H.: Aggregate and Verifiably Encrypted Signatures from Bilinear Maps. In: Biham, E. (ed.) EUROCRYPT 2003. LNCS, vol. 2656, pp. 416–432. Springer, Heidelberg (2003)

[BMW03]   Bellare, M., Micciancio, D., Warinschi, B.: Foundations of Group Signatures: Formal Definitions, Simplified Requirements, and a Construction Based on General Assumptions. In: Biham, E. (ed.) EUROCRYPT 2003. LNCS, vol. 2656, pp. 614–629. Springer, Heidelberg (2003)

[Boy07]   Boyen, X.: Mesh Signatures. In: Naor, M. (ed.) EUROCRYPT 2007. LNCS, vol. 4515, pp. 210–227. Springer, Heidelberg (2007)

[BP10]   Brands, S., Paquin, C.: U-Prove cryptographic specification v1.0 (2010), http://connect.microsoft.com/site642/Downloads/ DownloadDetails.aspx?DownloadID=26953

[BR93]   Bellare, M., Rogaway, P.: Random oracles are practical: A paradigm for designing efficient protocols. In: CCS 1993. ACM (1993)

[Bra99]   Brands, S.: Rethinking Public Key Infrastructure and Digital Certificates— Building in Privacy. PhD thesis, Eindhoven Institute of Technology (1999)

[BS04]   Boneh, D., Shacham, H.: Group signatures with verifier-local revocation. In: CCS 2004. ACM (2004)

[BSZ05]   Bellare, M., Shi, H., Zhang, C.: Foundations of Group Signatures: The Case of Dynamic Groups. In: Menezes, A. (ed.) CT-RSA 2005. LNCS, vol. 3376, pp. 136–153. Springer, Heidelberg (2005)

[CDS94]   Cramer, R., Damgård, I., Schoenmakers, B.: Proof of Partial Knowledge and Simplified Design of Witness Hiding Protocols. In: Desmedt, Y.G. (ed.) CRYPTO 1994. LNCS, vol. 839, pp. 174–187. Springer, Heidelberg (1994)

[Cha81]   Chaum, D.: Untraceable electronic mail, return addresses, and digital pseudonyms. Communications of the ACM 24(2), 84–88 (1981)

[CHKP10]   Cash, D., Hofheinz, D., Kiltz, E., Peikert, C.: Bonsai Trees, or How to Delegate a Lattice Basis. In: Gilbert, H. (ed.) EUROCRYPT 2010. LNCS, vol. 6110, pp. 523–552. Springer, Heidelberg (2010)

[CL01a]   Camenisch, J., Lysyanskaya, A.: Dynamic Accumulators and Application to Efficient Revocation of Anonymous Credentials. In: Yung, M. (ed.) CRYPTO 2002. LNCS, vol. 2442, pp. 61–76. Springer, Heidelberg (2002)

[CL01b]   Camenisch, J., Lysyanskaya, A.: An Efficient System for Non-transferable Anonymous Credentials with Optional Anonymity Revocation. In: Pfitzmann, B. (ed.) EUROCRYPT 2001. LNCS, vol. 2045, pp. 93–118. Springer, Heidelberg (2001)

[CL04]   Camenisch, J., Lysyanskaya, A.: Signature schemes and anonymous credentials from bilinear maps. In: Franklin, M. (ed.) CRYPTO 2004. LNCS, vol. 3152, pp. 56–72. Springer, Heidelberg (2004)

[CNR12]   Camenisch, J., Neven, G., Rückert, M.: Fully anonymous attribute tokens from lattices. Cryptology ePrint Archive, Report 2012/356 (2012)

[CvH91]   Chaum, D., van Heyst, E.: Group Signatures. In: Davies, D.W. (ed.) EUROCRYPT 1991. LNCS, vol. 547, pp. 257–265. Springer, Heidelberg (1991)

[DP06]   Delerablée, C., Pointcheval, D.: Dynamic Fully Anonymous Short Group Signatures. In: Nguyên, P.Q. (ed.) VIETCRYPT 2006. LNCS, vol. 4341, pp. 193–210. Springer, Heidelberg (2006)

[FS86]   Fiat, A., Shamir, A.: How to Prove Yourself: Practical Solutions to Identification and Signature Problems. In: Odlyzko, A.M. (ed.) CRYPTO 1986. LNCS, vol. 263, pp. 186–194. Springer, Heidelberg (1987)

[GKV10]   Dov Gordon, S., Katz, J., Vaikuntanathan, V.: A Group Signature Scheme from Lattice Assumptions. In: Abe, M. (ed.) ASIACRYPT 2010. LNCS, vol. 6477, pp. 395–412. Springer, Heidelberg (2010)

[GPV08]   Gentry, C., Peikert, C., Vaikuntanathan, V.: Trapdoors for hard lattices and new cryptographic constructions. In: STOC 2008, ACM (2008)

[IA11]   Danish National IT and Telecom Agency. New digital security models (2011), http://digitaliser.dk/resource/896495

[Kha07]   Khader, D.: Attribute based group signatures. Cryptology ePrint Archive, Report 2007/159, version 20080112:115123 (2007)

[Kle00]   Klein, P.N.: Finding the closest lattice vector when it's unusually close. In: SODA 2000. ACM/SIAM (2000)

[KP98]   Kilian, J., Petrank, E.: Identity Escrow. In: Krawczyk, H. (ed.) CRYPTO 1998. LNCS, vol. 1462, pp. 169–185. Springer, Heidelberg (1998)

[Los10]   Loss, D.: Personal communication (2010)

[LRSW99]   Lysyanskaya, A., Rivest, R.L., Sahai, A., Wolf, S.: Pseudonym Systems (Extended Abstract). In: Heys, H.M., Adams, C.M. (eds.) SAC 1999. LNCS, vol. 1758, pp. 184–199. Springer, Heidelberg (2000)

[Lyu08]   Lyubashevsky, V.: Lattice-Based Identification Schemes Secure Under Active Attacks. In: Cramer, R. (ed.) PKC 2008. LNCS, vol. 4939, pp. 162–179. Springer, Heidelberg (2008)

[MG02]   Micciancio, D., Goldwasser, S.: Complexity of Lattice Problems: a cryptographic perspective. The Kluwer International Series in Engineering and Computer Science, vol. 671. Kluwer Academic Publishers (2002)

[MPR11]   Maji, H.K., Prabhakaran, M., Rosulek, M.: Attribute-Based Signatures. In: Kiayias, A. (ed.) CT-RSA 2011. LNCS, vol. 6558, pp. 376–392. Springer, Heidelberg (2011)

[MR07]   Micciancio, D., Regev, O.: Worst-case to average-case reductions based on gaussian measures. SIAM J. Comput. 37(1), 267–302 (2007)

[MV03]   Micciancio, D., Vadhan, S.P.: Statistical Zero-Knowledge Proofs with Efficient Provers: Lattice Problems and More. In: Boneh, D. (ed.) CRYPTO 2003. LNCS, vol. 2729, pp. 282–298. Springer, Heidelberg (2003)

[MV10]   Micciancio, D., Voulgaris, P.: A deterministic single exponential time al-
            gorithm for most lattice problems based on voronoi cell computations. In:
            STOC 2010. ACM (2010)
[Pei09]   Peikert, C.: Public-key cryptosystems from the worst-case shortest vector
            problem: extended abstract. In: STOC 2009. ACM (2009)
[Pei10]   Peikert, C.: An Efficient and Parallel Gaussian Sampler for Lattices. In:
            Rabin, T. (ed.) CRYPTO 2010. LNCS, vol. 6223, pp. 80–97. Springer,
            Heidelberg (2010)
[Reg09]   Regev, O.: On lattices, learning with errors, random linear codes, and
            cryptography. J. ACM 56(6) (2009)
[Reg10]   Regev, O.: On the complexity of lattice problems with polynomial ap-
            proximation factors. In: The LLL Algorithm, Information Security and
            Cryptography. Springer (2010)
[RIS10]   RISEPTIS. Trust in the information society - a report of the advisory
            board (2010),
            http://www.think-trust.eu/general/news/finalreport.html
[RS09]   Rosen, A., Segev, G.: Chosen-Ciphertext Security via Correlated Products.
            In: Reingold, O. (ed.) TCC 2009. LNCS, vol. 5444, pp. 419–436. Springer,
            Heidelberg (2009)
[SCPY08]   De Santis, A., Di Crescenzo, G., Persiano, G., Yung, M.: On monotone
            formula composition of perfect zero-knowledge languages. SIAM J. Com-
            put. 38(4), 1300–1329 (2008)
[ST01]   Shamir, A., Tauman, Y.: Improved Online/Offline Signature Schemes. In:
            Kilian, J. (ed.) CRYPTO 2001. LNCS, vol. 2139, pp. 355–367. Springer,
            Heidelberg (2001)

Efficient Structure-Preserving Signature Scheme from Standard Assumptions

Jan Camenisch[1], Maria Dubovitskaya[1,2], and Kristiyan Haralambiev[1]

[1] IBM Research – Zurich, Switzerland
[2] Department of Computer Science, ETH Zurich, Switzerland

Abstract. We present an efficient signature scheme that facilitates Groth-Sahai proofs [25] of knowledge of a message, a verification key, and a valid signature on the message, without the need to reveal any of them. Such schemes are called structure-preserving. More precisely, the structure-preserving property of the signature scheme requires that verification keys, messages, and signatures are group elements and the verification predicate is a conjunction of pairing product equations. Our structure-preserving signature scheme supports multiple messages and is proven secure under the DLIN assumption. The signature consists of $53 + 6n$ group elements, where n is the number of messages signed, and to the best of our knowledge is the most efficient one secure under a standard assumption.

We build the scheme from a CCA-2 secure structure-preserving encryption scheme which supports labels, non-interactive zero-knowledge (NIZK) proofs, and a suitable hard relation. We provide a concrete realization using the encryption scheme by Camenisch et al. [12], Groth-Sahai (GS) NIZK proofs, and an instance of the computational Diffie-Hellman (CDH) problem [17]. To optimize the scheme and achieve better efficiency, we also revisit the Camenisch et al. structure-preserving encryption scheme and GS NIZK proofs, and present a new technique for doing more efficient proofs for mixed types of equations, namely, for multi-exponentiation and pairing product equations, using pairing randomization techniques.

Together with non-interactive zero-knowledge proofs, our scheme can be used as a building block for constructing efficient pairing-based cryptographic protocols that can be proven secure without assuming random oracles, such as anonymous credential systems [4], oblivious transfer [23,11], e-cash schemes [13], range and set membership proofs [9], blind signatures [20,3], group signatures [5].

Keywords: digital signatures, structure-preserving, decisional linear assumption.

1 Introduction

Pairings are a very powerful tool for constructing cryptographic protocols and pairing-based cryptography has been tremendously developed over the last 10 years. Thereby numerous new cryptographic assumptions have been introduced.

I. Visconti and R. De Prisco (Eds.): SCN 2012, LNCS 7485, pp. 76–94, 2012.
© Springer-Verlag Berlin Heidelberg 2012

Besides pairing-based variants of standard assumptions such as the Bilinear Diffie-Hellman (BDH) [8] and Decisional Linear (DLIN) [7] assumption, the new assumptions include quite a few so-called "q-type" [6] assumptions, for which the size of the instance of the assumption grows linearly with the number of the attacker's queries, as well as interactive assumptions - which are even stronger than "q-type" ones as they are not falsifiable [27].

The "q-type" assumptions say that given q solutions to the underlying problem, one cannot come up with a new solution. In the security proof of a signature scheme secure under a "q-type" assumption, these solutions allow one to sign q messages and then to create a new solution out the adversary's forgery. Thus, the size of the instance of the assumption problem is linked to the security parameter of the signature scheme; furthermore, the security of the signature scheme is directly derived from the "q-type" assumption itself. This is unfortunate, and it is preferable to construct signature schemes that rely on weaker and well-established assumptions.

When constructing complex cryptographic protocols, the goal is not only to satisfy strong security requirements, but also to remain efficient. Generalized Schnorr protocols [14] or Groth-Sahai (GS) proofs [25] allow one to do zero-knowledge proofs efficiently, but require staying within the structure of algebraic groups. In particular, to get efficient non-interactive zero knowledge proofs (NIZK) without assuming random oracles, Groth-Sahai proofs [25] seem to be the only choice. However, these proofs of knowledge can only be realized for witnesses made up entirely of group elements (and no exponents). This implies that messages and signatures have to consist only of group elements, and proscribes the use of hash-functions as the signature verification have to use only group operations. Such schemes are called structure-preserving. More formally, a signature scheme is called structure-preserving ([1]) if its verification keys, messages, and signatures are group elements and the verification predicate is a conjunction of pairing product equations. This also allows one to sign the verification keys and signatures themselves.

All current structure preserving signature schemes were either proven secure based on complex "q-type" assumptions or if secure under standard assumptions, are not practical due to the large constant factor ([24]). So, constructing an efficient structure preserving signature scheme based on simple assumptions still remains an open problem.

1.1 Our Contribution

We look into the problem of constructing structure-preserving signature schemes under simple assumptions and analyze the techniques of creating such schemes from encryption schemes, non-interactive zero-knowledge proofs, and hard computational problems. We provide an efficient structure-preserving signature scheme secure under a simple assumption (i.e., the standard DLIN assumption). Our signature scheme supports multiple messages, and the signatures consist of $53 + 6n$ group elements, where n is the number of group elements to sign.

Our scheme is built from a structure-preserving encryption scheme which supports labels that are also group elements, non-interactive zero-knowledge proofs (NIZK), and a hard relation or publicly verifiable random function. We follow an approach that is similar to ones from [24,26,18]. We present a scheme that works as follows. The verification key contains the public parameters for the NIZK proofs, the public key for the encryption scheme, and the public value of a hard relation. The signing key consists of the verification key and a witness for the hard relation. Instead of encrypting both the message m and a witness of the hard relation, like in [24], or binding m and the ciphertext inside the zero-knowledge proof, like in [26], we make use of labels and their non-malleability and encrypt only a witness of the hard relation under a label m, which results in a more efficient construction. So a witness for the public value of the hard relation is encrypted under multiple labels $m_1, \ldots, m_n$ (the messages to be signed), and a NIZK proof is created that 1) the encryption is valid and 2) indeed a witness for the public value of the hard relation is encrypted. The signature consists of the ciphertext and the NIZK proof. The verification of a signature is done by verifying the NIZK proof.

To optimize our scheme, we also revisit techniques for combining structure-pre-serving encryption with NIZK proofs and present a new technique for doing efficient proofs for mixed types of equations, namely for multi-exponentiation and pairing product equations, using pairing randomization techniques. We believe this new technique to be of interest for other applications of GS-proofs as well.

1.2   Related Work

Groth [24], who initiated the research on structure-preserving signature schemes, suggested a scheme secure under the DLIN assumption, but the scheme is not practical due to its large constant factor. Green and Hohenberger [22] presented a structure-preserving signature scheme that provides security against random message attacks under a q-Hidden LRSW assumption. Fuchsbauer [21] presented an efficient scheme based on the Double Hidden Strong Diffie-Hellman Assumption (DHSDH). However, the messages must have a particular structure.

Cathalo, Libert and Yung [15] provided a scheme based on a combination of the q-Hidden Strong Diffie-Hellman Assumption (HSDH), the Flexible Diffie-Hellman Assumption, and the DLIN assumption. Their signature consists of $9n + 4$ group elements, where n is a number of group elements signed and it was left as an open problem to construct constant-size signatures. Abe et al. [1] proposed the first constant-size structure-preserving signature scheme for messages of general bilinear group elements. A signature consists only of 7 group elements regardless of the size of the message. However it is proven unforgeable against adaptive chosen message attacks based on a novel non-interactive "q-type" assumption called the Simultaneous Flexible Pairing Assumption (SFP). While all these works provide interesting constructions, their security proofs rely on "q-type" assumptions.

In a different line of work, Abe et al. [2] established lower bounds on the complexity of structure-preserving signatures, i.e. the signature size must be at least 3 group elements, and gave a scheme matching those bounds. However, the security proof of the construction relies on interactive assumptions which are even stronger than "q-type" and are not falsifiable [27]. A variant of their scheme which increases the signature size with 1 or 3 group elements (depending whether the message contains elements from both base groups) is shown secure under a "q-type" assumption.

Finally, Chase and Kohlweiss [16] presented a framework for creating a structure-preserving signature scheme from a stateful signature, F-unforgeable under weak chosen message attacks, and efficient non-interactive zero-knowledge proofs. Their scheme is proven secure under the well established DLIN assumption, but the size of a signature is still $100 + 24n + 9x$, where n is the number of group elements signed and $N = 2^x$ is an upper bound on the number of signatures generated per key pair.

Below we provide a table (Table 1), in which we compare our work with other structure-preserving signature schemes both in terms of the assumption used and the size of a signature. One can see that our scheme is the most efficient one from those that rely on the standard, not "q-type", DLIN assumption.

Table 1. Comparison of the structure-preserving signature schemes. (n is the number of group elements signed and $N = 2^x$ is an upper bound on the number of signatures generated per key pair, s - bit-length of the message signed).

Paper	Assumption	Size of the signature (gr el.)	Size of the vk (gr el.)
[22]	q-type: Hidden LRSW	5 (single msg)	5
[1]	q-type: SFP	7	$12 + 2n$
[15]	q-type: HSDH	$9n + 4$	$13 + n$
[24]	DLIN	$O(n)$	$O(n)$
[16]	DLIN	$100 + 24n + 9x$	$17 + s$
This work	DLIN	$53 + 6n$	$25 + 2n$

The paper is organized as follows: first we give definitions in Section 2, then in Section 3 we describe the building blocks of our scheme, then we revisit NIZK proofs for structure-preserving encryption schemes and provide a new technique to improve the efficiency of these proofs in Section 4; finally, we present our construction in Section 5 and prove it secure in Section 6.

2   Definitions

Let $\mathsf{Pg}(1^\kappa)$ be a bilinear group generator that on input 1^κ outputs descriptions of multiplicative groups $\mathbb{G}, \mathbb{G}_T$ of prime order p. Let $\mathbb{G}^* = \mathbb{G}_1 \setminus \{1\}$ and let $g \in \mathbb{G}_1^*$. The generated groups are such that there exists an admissible bilinear map $e : \mathbb{G} \times \mathbb{G} \to \mathbb{G}_T$, meaning that (1) for all $a, b \in \mathbb{Z}_p$ it holds that $e(g^a, g^b) = e(g, g)^{ab}$; (2) $e(g, g) \neq 1$; and (3) the bilinear map is efficiently computable.

We refer to the output of the pairing group generator $\mathcal{G} = (p, \mathbb{G}, \mathbb{G}_T, e, g)$ as the group parameters.

2.1   Signature Scheme

Definition 1. *(Digital Signature Scheme). A digital signature scheme* Sig *is a set of algorithms* Sig = (Sig.KeyGen, Sig.Sign, Sig.Verify)*:*

• Sig.KeyGen$(1^\kappa) \xrightarrow{\$} (sk, vk)$ *is a probabilistic algorithm that takes as input a security parameter and outputs a verification key vk and a corresponding secret key sk. Message space M is associated with vk.*

• Sig.Sign$(sk, m) \xrightarrow{\$} \sigma$ *is a (possibly probabilistic) algorithm that takes as input a private key sk and a message m and outputs a signature σ.*

• Sig.Verify$(vk, m, \sigma) \rightarrow 1/0$ *is a deterministic algorithm that takes as input a public key pk, a message m and a signature σ and outputs 1 for acceptance or 0 for rejection according to the input.*

We define structure preserving signatures formally as follows [2]:

Definition 2. *(Structure-preserving Signature Scheme). A signature scheme* Sig *over a bilinear group generated by* Pg(1^κ)*, that outputs system parameters $(p, \mathbb{G}, \mathbb{G}_T, e, g)$, is said to be structure preserving if: (1) the verification key vk consists of the group parameters and group elements in $\mathbb{G}$; (2) the messages and the signatures consist of group elements in $\mathbb{G}$, and (3) the verification algorithm evaluates membership in $\mathbb{G}$ and pairing product equations of the form $\prod_i \prod_j e(y_i, y_j)^{a_{ij}} = 1_{\mathbb{G}_T}$, where $a_{11}, a_{12}, \ldots \in \mathbb{Z}_p$ are constants, $y_1, y_2, \ldots \in \mathbb{G}$ are group elements appearing in the group parameters, verification key, messages, and signatures.*

Some works, for example, [2], allow to relax the definition of structure-preserving signatures so that arbitrary target group elements could be included in the signature and verification key and appear in the verification equations. However, this is useful only when witness-indistinguishable proofs are sufficient, as Groth-Sahai proofs [25] are zero-knowledge when the verification equations contain group elements only from the base group.

We use the standard notion of existential unforgeability against adaptive chosen message attacks formally defined as follows.

Definition 3. *(Existential unforgeability against adaptive chosen message attacks (EUF-CMA)). A signature scheme* Sig *is (t, q, ϵ)-existentially unforgeable against adaptive chosen message attacks, if any adversary with runtime t after making at most q signing queries wins with a probability $\mathcal{P}$ at most ϵ the following game:*

Step 1. Sig.KeyGen$(1^\kappa) \xrightarrow{\$} (sk, vk)$*. Adversary $\mathcal{A}$ is given a verification key vk.*

Step 2. Adversary adaptively queries the signing oracle $\mathcal{O}_{sig}$ q times with a message m_i, and obtains signatures $\sigma_i =$ Sig.Sign(sk, m_i), $1 \leq i \leq q$.

Step 3. Adversary outputs a forgery (m^*, σ^*) and halts.

$\mathcal{A}$ wins if Sig.Verify$(vk, m^*, \sigma^*) = 1$ *and $m^* \notin \{m_1, \ldots, m_q\}$.*

2.2 Encryption Scheme

Definition 4. *(Encryption Scheme with Labels). An encryption scheme* Enc *with labels is a set of algorithms* Enc = (Enc.KeyGen, Enc.Encrypt, Enc.Decrypt):

- Enc.KeyGen$(1^\kappa) \xrightarrow{\$} (sk, pk)$ *is a probabilistic algorithm that takes as input a security parameter and outputs a public key pk and a corresponding secret key sk.*
- Enc.Encrypt$^\ell(pk, m) \xrightarrow{\$} C$ *is a probabilistic algorithm that takes as input a public key pk, a label ℓ, which consists of public data non-malleably attached to a ciphertext, and a message m and outputs a ciphertext C.*
- Enc.Decrypt$^\ell(sk, C) \to m/\bot$ *is a deterministic algorithm that takes as input a secret key sk, a label ℓ, and a ciphertext C and outputs a message m, or $\bot$, if the ciphertext is invalid.*

Definition 5. *(Structure-preserving Encryption Scheme). A structure-preserving encryption scheme has public keys, messages, and ciphertexts that consist entirely of group elements. Moreover, the encryption and decription algorithm perform only group and bilinear map operations.*

We refer to [19] for a formal definition of Security against adaptive Chosen Ciphertext Attack for an encryption scheme.

2.3 Non-Interactive Zero-Knowledge (NIZK) Proofs

Let $\mathcal{R}$ be an NP relation on pairs (X, Y), with a corresponding language $\mathcal{L}_\mathcal{R} = \{Y | \exists X \text{ s.t. } (X, Y) \in \mathcal{R}\}$.

Definition 6. *(Non-Interactive Zero-Knowledge (NIZK) proofs). A Non-Interactive Ze-ro-Knowledge proof system* NIZK *for a relation $\mathcal{R}$ on (X, Y) is a set of algorithms:* NIZK = (NIZK.Setup, NIZK.Prove, NIZK.Verify, NIZK.SetupSim, NIZK.Sim):

- NIZK.Setup$(1^\kappa) \xrightarrow{\$} (CRS)$ *is a randomized algorithm that takes as input a security parameter and outputs a common reference string CRS.*
- NIZK.Prove$(CRS, Y, X) \xrightarrow{\$} \pi$ *is a randomized algorithm that takes as input a common reference string CRS, and outputs a proof that $\mathcal{R}$ holds.*
- NIZK.Verify$(\pi, Y) \to 0/1$ *is a verification algorithm that verifies whether proof π that $(X, Y) \in \mathcal{R}$.*
- NIZK.SetupSim$(1^\kappa) \xrightarrow{\$} (CRS^{sim}, td)$ *is a randomized algorithm that takes as input a security parameter and outputs a simulated common reference string CRS^{sim} and a corresponding trapdoor key td.*
- NIZK.Sim$(CRS^{sim}, Y, td) \xrightarrow{\$} \pi^{sim}$ *is a randomized algorithm that takes as input a simulated common reference string CRS^{sim} with a trapdoor td and a statement, but no witness, and outputs a simulated proof π for which* NIZK.Verify(CRS^{sim}, Y, π) *accepts.*

We refer to [25] for the security definitions of NIZK proofs (correctness, soundness, zero-knowledge).

3 Preliminaries

3.1 Assumptions

Definition 7. *(Decisional Linear Assumption). We say that the DLIN problem in $\mathbb{G}$ of prime order p is hard, if for all algorithms A, with running time polynomial in κ, the following advantage* $\mathbf{Adv}_{\mathbb{G}}^{\mathrm{DLIN}}(\kappa) =$

$$\Pr\left[\mathsf{A}(g_1, g_2, g_3, g_1^r, g_2^s, g_3^{r+s}) = 1\right] - \Pr\left[\mathsf{A}(g_1, g_2, g_3, g_1^r, g_2^s, g_3^t) = 1\right]$$

is a negligible function in κ, where $g_1, g_2, g_3 \overset{\$}{\leftarrow} \mathbb{G}^*$ and $r, s, t \overset{\$}{\leftarrow} \mathbb{Z}_p$.

Definition 8. *(Computational Diffie-Hellman Assumption). We say that the CDH problem in $\mathbb{G}$ of prime order p is hard, if for all algorithms A, with running time polynomial in κ, the following advantage*

$$\mathbf{Adv}_{\mathbb{G}}^{\mathrm{CDH}}(\kappa) = \Pr\left[\mathsf{A}(g, g^a, g^b) = g^{ab}\right]$$

is a negligible function in κ, where $g \overset{\$}{\leftarrow} \mathbb{G}^*$ and $a, b \overset{\$}{\leftarrow} \mathbb{Z}_p$.

The hardness of the CDH problem is implied by DLIN.

3.2 One-Side Pairing Randomization Technique

Abe et al. [1] introduced techniques to randomize elements in a pairing without changing their value in $\mathbb{G}_T$. One of these useful techniques is called one-side randomization and allows one to replace an element from the target group by a set of elements from the source groups. We use this technique in our scheme and provide the details below.

RandOneSide($\{g_i, f_i\}_{i=1}^k$) $\rightarrow \{f_i'\}_{i=1}^k$. Let g_i be an element in $\mathbb{G}_1^*$ of symmetric setting $\mathcal{G} = (p, \mathbb{G}, \mathbb{G}_T, e, g)$. A pairing product $A = e(g_1, f_1)\, e(g_2, f_2) \ldots e(g_k, f_k)$ is randomized into $A = e(g_1, f_1')\, e(g_2, f_2') \ldots e(g_k, f_k')$ as follows.

Let $(t_1, \ldots, t_{k-1}) \leftarrow \mathbb{Z}_p^{k-1}$. First, multiply $1 = e(g_1, g_2^{t_1})\, e(g_2, g_1^{-t_1})$ to both sides of the formula. We thus obtain

$$A = e(g_1, f_1 g_2^{t_1})\, e(g_2, f_2 g_1^{-t_1})\, e(g_3, f_3) \ldots e(g_k, f_k).$$

Next multiply $1 = e(g_2, g_3^{t_2})\, e(g_3, g_2^{-t_2})$. We thus have

$$A = e(g_1, f_1 g_2^{t_1})\, e(g_2, f_2 g_1^{-t_1} g_3^{t_2})\, e(g_3, f_3 g_2^{-t_2}) \ldots e(g_k, f_k).$$

This continues until t_{k-1} and we eventually have $A = e(g_1, f_1') \ldots e(g_k, f_k')$. Observe that every f_i' for $i = 1, \ldots, k-1$ distributes uniformly in $\mathbb{G}$ due to the uniform multiplicative factor $g_{i+1}^{t_i}$. In the k-th pairing, f_k' follows the distribution determined by A and the preceding $k-1$ pairings. Thus $(f_1', \ldots, f_k')$ is uniform over $\mathbb{G}^k$ under constraint of being evaluated to A when paired entry-wise with $g_1, \ldots g_k$.

3.3 Camenisch et al. Structure-Preserving CCA-2 Encryption Scheme

To build our signature scheme we make use of a structure-preserving encryption scheme proposed by Camenisch et al. [12] which supports labels. The scheme works in a symmetric setting $\mathcal{G} = (p, \mathbb{G}, \mathbb{G}_T, e, g)$, both the message and the label(s) are in $\mathbb{G}$. The scheme consists of the key generation (Enc.KeyGen), encryption (Enc.Encrypt), and decryption (Enc.Decrypt) algorithms, and works as follows:

- Enc.KeyGen$(1^\kappa) \xrightarrow{\$} (sk, pk)$:

  Pick $g_1, g_2, g_3 \leftarrow \mathbb{G}, x_1, x_2, x_3 \xleftarrow{\$} \mathbb{Z}_p$; $\boldsymbol{y}_0, \ldots, \boldsymbol{y}_5 \xleftarrow{\$} \mathbb{Z}_p^3$.
  Compute $h_1 = g_1^{x_1} g_3^{x_3}, h_2 = g_2^{x_2} g_3^{x_3}, \{f_{i,1} = g_1^{y_{i,1}} g_3^{y_{i,3}}, f_{i,2} = g_2^{y_{i,2}} g_3^{y_{i,3}}\}_{i=0}^5$.
  Return $sk = (\boldsymbol{x}, \{\boldsymbol{y}_i\}_{i=0}^5)$; $pk = (g_1, g_2, g_3, h_1, h_2, \{f_{i,1}, f_{i,2}\}_{i=0}^5)$.

- Enc.Encrypt$^\ell(pk, m) \xrightarrow{\$} C$:

  Pick $r, s \xleftarrow{\$} \mathbb{Z}_p$. Compute $u_1 = g_1^r, u_2 = g_2^s, u_3 = g_3^{r+s}, c = mh_1^r h_2^s$,
  $$V = \prod_{i=0}^3 e(f_{i,1}^r f_{i,2}^s, u_i) e(f_{4,1}^r f_{4,2}^s, c) e(f_{5,1}^r f_{5,2}^s, \ell).$$
  Return $C = (u_1, u_2, u_3, c, V)$.

- Enc.Decrypt$^\ell(sk, C) \xrightarrow{\$} m/\bot$:

  Parse C as (u_1, u_2, u_3, c, V).
  If $V = \prod_{i=0}^3 e(u_1^{y_{i,1}} u_2^{y_{i,2}} u_3^{y_{i,3}}, u_i) e(u_1^{y_{4,1}} u_2^{y_{4,2}} u_3^{y_{4,3}}, c) e(u_1^{y_{5,1}} u_2^{y_{5,2}} u_3^{y_{5,3}}, \ell)$
      return $m = c \cdot (u_1^{x_1} u_2^{x_2} u_3^{x_3})^{-1}$;
  else return $\bot$.

Theorem 1. *The above scheme is CCA-2 secure if the DLIN assumption holds in $\mathbb{G}$.*

We refer to [12] for the security proof.

3.4 Non-Interactive Zero-Knowledge Proofs

Notation. We start with the descriptions of the basic algorithms of an instantiation of the Groth-Sahai proof system [25] for multi-exponentiation equations:

$$\texttt{stmnt} = \mathsf{GS}\Big\{(x_1, \ldots, x_K) \; : \; \bigwedge_{i=1}^M y_i = \prod_{j=1}^\ell g_j^{x_{\mu_i(j)}}\Big\},$$

the proof system where the y_i's and g_j's are public group elements of $\mathbb{G}$ (cf. [10]), $\mu_i()$ is a map $\{1, \ldots, \ell\} \to \{1, \ldots, K\}$, $i = 1, \ldots, M$ and $j = 1, \ldots, \ell$. We define X as $(x_{\mu_i(j)})$, and Y as $((y_i), (g_{ij}))$.

A trusted third party generates the common public reference string by running $CRS \xleftarrow{\$} \mathsf{GS.Setup}(1^\kappa)$. A prover generates a proof as $\pi \xleftarrow{\$} \mathsf{GS.Prove}(CRS, Y, X)$ and a verifier checks it via $b \leftarrow \mathsf{GS.Verify}(CRS, Y, \pi)$, where $b = 1$ if π is true w.r.t. $\mathcal{R}(X, Y)$, and $b = 0$ otherwise.

Multi-exponentiation Equations for DLIN Instantiation. We now present these algorithms in detail, based on the DLIN assumption in the group setting $\mathcal{G} = (p, \mathbb{G}, \mathbb{G}_T, e, g)$. For ease of notation, we will denote by $\{y_i\}$, $\{g_{ij}\}$, and $\{x_{\mu_i(j)}\}$ the lists $(y_1, \ldots, y_M)$, $((g_{11}, \ldots, g_{1\ell}), \ldots, (g_{M1}, \ldots, g_{M\ell}))$, and $((x_{\mu_1(1)}, \ldots, x_{\mu_1(\ell)}), \ldots, (x_{\mu_M(1)}, \ldots, x_{\mu_M(\ell)}))$, respectively, whenever the indicies are clear from the context.

- GS.Setup$(1^\kappa) \xrightarrow{\$} CRS$:

  1. Generate $\mathcal{G} = (p, \mathbb{G}, \mathbb{G}_T, e, g) \xleftarrow{\$} \mathsf{Pg}(1^\kappa)$.
  2. Pick $\chi_1, \chi_2, \chi_3, \gamma_1, \gamma_2, \gamma_3 \xleftarrow{\$} \mathbb{G}^6$.
  Return $CRS = (\mathcal{G}, \chi_1, \chi_2, \chi_3, \gamma_1, \gamma_2, \gamma_3)$.

- GS.Prove$(CRS, (\{y_i\}, \{g_{ij}\}), \{x_{\mu_i(j)}\}) \xrightarrow{\$} \pi$:
  For all $i = 1 \ldots M$ and $j = 1, \ldots, \ell$:

  1. Pick $r'_{\mu_i(j)}, r''_{\mu_i(j)} \xleftarrow{\$} \mathbb{Z}_p$.
  2. For each $x_{\mu_i(j)}$ in $\{x_{\mu_i(j)}\}$ compute the set of commitments:
  $$C_{ij} \leftarrow (\gamma_1^{x_{\mu_i(j)}} \chi_1^{r'_{\mu_i(j)}}, \gamma_2^{x_{\mu_i(j)}} \chi_2^{r''_{\mu_i(j)}}, \gamma_3^{x_{\mu_i(j)}} \chi_3^{r'_{\mu_i(j)}+r''_{\mu_i(j)}}).$$
  3. For each y_i in $\{y_i\}$ compute $p'_i = \prod_{j=1}^\ell g_{ij}^{r'_{\mu_i(j)}}$; $p''_i = \prod_{j=1}^\ell g_{ij}^{r''_{\mu_i(j)}}$.
  Return $\pi \leftarrow \{p'_i, p''_i, \{C_{ij}\}_{j=1}^\ell\}_{i=1}^M$.

- GS.Verify$(CRS, (\{y_i\}, \{g_{ij}\}), \pi) \rightarrow b$:
  If all equations hold:
  $$\bigwedge_{i=1}^M \left(\prod_{j=1}^\ell e(C_{ij}, g_{ij}) = e((\gamma_1, \gamma_2, \gamma_3), y_i) e((\chi_1, 1, \chi_3), p'_i) e((1, \chi_2, \chi_3), p''_i) \right),$$
  then return $b \leftarrow 1$, else return $b \leftarrow 0$.

- GS.SetupSim$(1^\kappa) \xrightarrow{\$} (CRS^{sim}, td)$:

  1. Generate $\mathcal{G} = (p, \mathbb{G}, \mathbb{G}_T, e, g) \xleftarrow{\$} \mathsf{Pg}(1^\kappa)$;
  2. Pick $\chi_1, \chi_2, \chi_3 \xleftarrow{\$} \mathbb{G}^3, \alpha, \beta \xleftarrow{\$} \mathbb{Z}_p$.
  3. Compute $\gamma_1 = \chi_1^\alpha, \gamma_2 = \chi_2^\beta, \gamma_3 = \chi_3^{\alpha+\beta}$.
  Return a simulated CRS and a trapdoor:
  $(CRS, td) = (\{\mathcal{G}, \chi_1, \chi_2, \chi_3, \gamma_1, \gamma_2, \gamma_3\}, \{\alpha, \beta\})$.

- GS.Sim$(CRS^{sim}, (\{y_i\}, \{g_{ij}\}), td) \xrightarrow{\$} \pi^{sim}$:
  For all $i = 1 \ldots M$ and $j = 1, \ldots, \ell$:

  1. Pick $r_{\mu_i(j)} \xleftarrow{\$} \mathbb{Z}_p$.
  2. For each $x_{\mu_i(j)}$ in $\{x_{\mu_i(j)}\}$ compute the set of commitments:
  $$C_{ij} \leftarrow (\chi_1^{r'_{\mu_i(j)}}, \chi_2^{r''_{\mu_i(j)}}, \chi_3^{r'_{\mu_i(j)}+r''_{\mu_i(j)}}).$$
  3. For each y_i in $\{y_i\}$ compute $p'_i = y_i^{-\alpha} \prod_{j=1}^\ell g_{ij}^{r'_{\mu_i(j)}}$; $p''_i = y_i^{-\beta} \prod_{j=1}^\ell g_{ij}^{r''_{\mu_i(j)}}$.
  Return $\pi^{sim} \leftarrow \{p'_i, p''_i, \{C_{ij}\}_{j=1}^\ell\}_{i=1}^M$.

Theorem 2. *The above NIZKGS is a NIZK proof system with perfect correctness, perfect soundness and composable zero-knowledge for satisfiability of a set of equations over a bilinear group where the DLIN problem is hard.*

We refer to [25] and [10] for the detailed security definitions and proofs.

4   Combining Camenisch et al. Structure-Preserving Encryption and Groth-Sahai Proofs

The encryption scheme from [12] described in Section 3.3 is the first efficient CCA-secure scheme that stays within the structure of the algebraic groups. But to say that it is structure-preserving, we need to be able to combine it with NIZK proofs.

Examining the encryption equations more closely:

$$r, s \xleftarrow{\$} \mathbb{Z}_p \,;\, u_1 = g_1^r, \quad u_2 = g_2^s, \quad u_3 = g_3^{r+s}, \quad c = mh_1^r h_2^s,$$

$$V = \prod_{i=0}^{3} e(f_{i,1}^r f_{i,2}^s, u_i) e(f_{4,1}^r f_{4,2}^s, c) e(f_{5,1}^r f_{5,2}^s, \ell),$$

we notice that the last one needs further discussion. Although it is a pairing product equation, if one wants to prove correctness of encryption, e.g. when proving another statement about the plaintext, the witness consists of scalars (r, s) rather than group elements. But only the latter ones are compatible with Groth-Sahai proofs, i.e. pairing product equations should contain no exponents as part of the witness. Given that the authors of [12] do not provide any details how to address this, we take the time to discuss this here.

So, to be able to prove a statement about the last equation and its scalar witnesses one would have to introduce new variables $\{w_i = f_{i,1}^r f_{i2}^s\}_{i=0}^5$, commit to $\{w_i\}_{i=0}^5$ in order to use them as witnesses for the pairing product equation, and also produce proofs that these commitments were computed correctly. Moreover, if zero-knowledge proofs are needed, V has to be replaced by a product of pairing equations, for which the authors suggest the above-described one-sided randomization technique, that yields

$$V = \prod_{i=0}^{3} e(f_i', u_i) e(f_4', c) e(f_5', \ell) \quad = \quad \prod_{i=0}^{3} e(f_{i,1}^r f_{i,2}^s, u_i) e(f_{4,1}^r f_{4,2}^s, c) e(f_{5,1}^r f_{5,2}^s, \ell),$$

and the ciphertext being $(u_1, u_2, u_3, c, \{f_i'\}_{i=0}^5)$. Note that $f_i' \neq f_{i,1}^r f_{i,2}^s$ as the $\{f_i'\}_{i=0}^5$ is the output of the one-side randomization which is oblivious to r and s. While all these equations would be compatible with Groth-Sahai proofs, they seem rather inefficient - the size of such proof would be more than 100 group elements if one assumes one label.

Instead of looking at the randomization trick and the encryption scheme in isolation, we propose to combine them. This results into significantly more efficient proofs.

In the following let $\{f_i = f_{i,1}^r f_{i,2}^s\}_{i=0}^5, u_0 = g, u_4 = c, u_5 = \ell$. Also, let $\{f_i'\}_{i=0}^5 \leftarrow \mathsf{RandOneSide}(\{u_i, f_i\}_{i=0}^5)$. As mentioned earlier, the ciphertext is $(u_1, u_2, u_3, c, \{f_i'\}_{i=0}^5)$, where the elements $\{f_i'\}_{i=0}^5$ are computed as follows: $t_0, \ldots, t_4 \xleftarrow{\$} \mathbb{Z}_p,$

$$f_0' = f_{0,1}^r f_{0,2}^s u_1^{t_0} \; ; \qquad f_1' = f_{1,1}^r f_{1,2}^s u_0^{-t_0} u_2^{t_1} \; ; \qquad f_2' = f_{2,1}^r f_{2,2}^s u_1^{-t_1} u_3^{t_2} \; ;$$

$$f_3' = f_{3,1}^r f_{3,2}^s u_2^{-t_2} u_4^{t_3} \; ; \qquad f_4' = f_{4,1}^r f_{4,2}^s u_3^{-t_3} u_5^{t_4} \; ; \qquad f_5' = f_{5,1}^r f_{5,2}^s u_4^{-t_4} .$$

Now to prove that the ciphertext is correctly formed, we need to generate a proof only for multi-exponentiation equations, namely:

$$u_1 = g_1^r, \quad u_2 = g_2^s \; ; \quad u_3 = g_3^{r+s} \; ; \quad c = m h_1^r h_2^s \; ;$$

$$v_0 = f_{0,1}^r f_{0,2}^s u_1^{t_0} \; ; \; f_1' = f_{1,1}^r f_{1,2}^s u_0^{-t_0} u_2^{t_1} \; ; \; f_2' = f_{2,1}^r f_{2,2}^s u_1^{-t_1} u_3^{t_2} \; ;$$

$$f_3' = f_{3,1}^r f_{3,2}^s u_2^{-t_2} c^{t_3} \; ; \; f_4' = f_{4,1}^r f_{4,2}^s u_3^{-t_3} \ell^{t_4} \; ; \; f_5' = f_{5,1}^r f_{5,2}^s c^{-t_4} .$$

The new proof now costs only 41 group elements, so one can see that this trick sufficiently reduces the size of the proof. We believe this new technique to be of interest for other applications of GS-proofs as well.

5   Our Construction

First we describe the main idea for creating a structure-preserving signature scheme from encryption schemes, NIZK proofs, one-time signatures and hard relations. Then we give a construction, analyze its efficiency and prove it secure.

5.1   Main Idea

We build our scheme from a CCA2-secure structure-preserving encryption scheme, which supports labels that are also group elements, non-interactive zero-knowledge proofs (NIZK), and a hard relation or publicly verifiable random function. The scheme works as follows. The signing key contains a public key of the encryption scheme and a witness for a hard problem. The verification key contains public parameters for the NIZK proofs, a public key for the encryption scheme, and a public value of a hard relation. To sign a message m, the signer encrypts the witness with the label m and produces a proof that the plaintext is a witness for the hard problem. To verify a signature, one checks the validity of the zero-knowledge proof. Intuitively, the construction is secure because the encryption is non-malleable and the proofs are zero-knowledge, hence queried signatures cannot be modified and reveal no information about the witness, and only the signer has the witness required to produce a new signature.

Similar approaches were presented in [24] for a structure preserving signature, and in the context of leakage-resilient signatures in [26,18]. The actual construction of [24] uses a relaxation of the CCA notion of security, i.e. RCCA, and it encrypts the message together with a witness for the hard problem instead of using labels. While the signatures are of constant size, the constant is rather big, hence the scheme is inefficient. The scheme of [26] used a CPA-secure encryption scheme and simulation-sound NIZK proofs, treating m as a label for the proof statement. As pointed out in [18], both CCA2 + NIZK and CPA + simulation-sound NIZK can be viewed as variants of specific simulation-extractable NIZK proofs, which yields a scheme generalizing both constructions. However, the previous instantiations of this scheme are not structure-preserving as they require hash functions or use the bit representation of group elements.

As discussed in Section 4, a structure-preserving encryption scheme secure under DLIN assumption was recently introduced. Therefore, we revisit the approach of creating a structure-preserving signature scheme and provide an efficient construction proven secure under the DLIN assumption. Furthermore, when instantiating it with Camenisch et al. encryption scheme, we present a new technique for combining structure-preserving encryption with NIZK proofs using pairing randomization techniques. To the best of our knowledge the proposed scheme is the most efficient structure-preserving signature scheme secure under a standard assumption.

5.2 Efficient Structure-Preserving Signature Scheme from the Decisional Linear Assumption

We apply our approach described above in the symmetric setting. The building blocks we use are efficient structure-preserving CCA secure encryption scheme with labels by [12], Groth-Sahai NIZK proofs [25] and the computational Diffie-Hellman problem [17]. We consider the case where a label m is a single group element, but we show how to extend the scheme to support messages being vectors of group elements. The scheme consists of the key generation (Sig.KeyGen), signing (Sig.Sign), and verification (Sig.Verify) algorithms and is presented on Figure 1.

5.3 Signing Multiple Messages

Our scheme can also support multiple messages or messages that consist of multiple group elements. To sign multiple messages $m_1, \ldots, m_n$ one needs to encrypt the challenge under a set of labels $m_1, \ldots, m_n$: in this case

$V = \prod_{i=0}^{3} e(f_{i,1}^r f_{i,2}^s, u_i) e(f_{4,1}^r f_{4,2}^s, c) e(f_{5,1}^r f_{5,2}^s, m_1) \cdot \ldots \cdot e(f_{(n+4),1}^r f_{(n+4),2}^s, m_n)$.

Public key will also contain $f_{i,1}, f_{i,2}$ for $i = 6, \ldots, n+4$, and the proof will be extended to prove statements about $\{f_i' = f_{i,1}^r f_{i,2}^s\}_{i=6}^{n+4}$.

The size of the verification key is $25 + 2n$ group elements, and the signature consists of $53 + 6n$ group elements, where n is the number of elements to sign. The proof optimization technique from Section 4 reduces almost twice the size of a signature.

6   Security Proofs

6.1   Correctness

Correctness follows from the correctness of the encryption scheme and Groth-Sahai proofs.

- Sig.KeyGen$(1^\kappa) \xrightarrow{\$} (sgk, vk)$:

  1. Generate CRS for GS proofs GS.Setup$(1^\kappa) \to CRS$:
  $CRS = (\mathcal{G}, \gamma_1, \gamma_2, \gamma_3, \chi_1, \chi_2, \chi_3)$.

  2. Generate keys for encryption Enc.KeyGen$(1^\kappa) \to (sk_e, pk_e)$:
  $g_1, g_2, g_3 \leftarrow \mathbb{G}, \boldsymbol{x} \xleftarrow{\$} \mathbb{Z}_p^3$; $h_1 = g_1^{x_1} g_3^{x_3}, h_2 = g_2^{x_2} g_3^{x_3}$.
  $\boldsymbol{y}_0, \ldots, \boldsymbol{y}_5 \xleftarrow{\$} \mathbb{Z}_p^3$; for i=0, ..., 5: $f_{i,1} = g_1^{y_{i,1}} g_3^{y_{i,3}}, f_{i,2} = g_2^{y_{i,2}} g_3^{y_{i,3}}$.
  $sk_e = (\boldsymbol{x}, \{\boldsymbol{y}_i\}_{i=0}^5)$; $pk_e = (g_1, g_2, g_3, h_1, h_2, \{f_{i,1}, f_{i,2}\}_{i=0}^5)$.

  3. Generate an instantiation of CDH challenge ch:
  $x \xleftarrow{\$} \mathbb{Z}_p, g_s, u_s \xleftarrow{\$} \mathbb{G}$; $h_s = g_s^x$; $ch = (g_s, u_s, h_s)$.

  Return signing and verification keys (sgk, vk):
  $sgk = (x, vk)$; $vk = (CRS, ch, pk_e)$.

- Sig.Sign$(sgk, m) \xrightarrow{\$} \sigma$:

  1. Parse sgk as (x, CRS, ch, pk_e).
  2. Compute $y = u_s^x$.
  3. Encrypt y with the label m Enc.Encrypt$^m(pk_e, y) \to E$:
  $r, s \xleftarrow{\$} \mathbb{Z}_p$; $u_1 = g_1^r$, $u_2 = g_2^s$, $u_3 = g_3^{r+s}$, $c = u_s^x h_1^r h_2^s$;
  For $i = 0 \ldots 5$: $t_i \xleftarrow{\$} \mathbb{Z}_p$;
  $f_0' = f_{0,1}^r f_{0,2}^s u_1^{t_0}$; $f_1' = f_{1,1}^r f_{1,2}^s g^{-t_0} u_2^{t_1}$; $f_2' = f_{2,1}^r f_{2,2}^s u_1^{-t_1} u_3^{t_2}$;
  $f_3' = f_{3,1}^r f_{3,2}^s u_2^{-t_2} c^{t_3}$; $f_4' = f_{4,1}^r f_{4,2}^s u_3^{-t_3} m^{t_4}$; $f_5' = f_{5,1}^r f_{5,2}^s c^{-t_4}$.
  $E = (u_1, u_2, u_3, c, f_0', \ldots, f_5')$.

  4. Generate GS proof that E is correct: GS.Prove$(CRS, Y, X) \to \pi(E)$:
  Prove the statement that the following multi-exponentiation equations hold:
  $$GS\{(x, r, s, t_0, \ldots, t_5): u_1 = g_1^r \wedge u_2 = g_2^s \wedge u_3 = g_3^{r+s} \wedge c = u_s^x h_1^r h_2^s \wedge$$
  $$f_0' = f_{0,1}^r f_{0,2}^s u_1^{t_0} \wedge f_1' = f_{1,1}^r f_{1,2}^s u_0^{-t_0} u_2^{t_1} \wedge f_2' = f_{2,1}^r f_{2,2}^s u_1^{-t_1} u_3^{t_2} \wedge$$
  $$f_3' = f_{3,1}^r f_{3,2}^s u_2^{-t_2} c^{t_3} \wedge f_4' = f_{4,1}^r f_{4,2}^s u_3^{-t_3} m^{t_4} \wedge f_5' = f_{5,1}^r f_{5,2}^s c^{-t_4} \wedge h_s = g_s^x\}.$$
  Here Y contains elements from the ciphertext E and the verification key vk:
  $Y = (\{u_1, u_2, u_3, c, f_0', f_1', f_2', f_3', f_4', f_5', h_s\}; \{(g_1), (g_2), (g_3, g_3), (u_s, h_1, h_2),$
       $(f_{0,1}, f_{0,2}, u_1), (f_{1,1}, f_{1,2}, u_0, u_2), (f_{2,1}, f_{2,2}, u_1, u_3), (f_{3,1}, f_{3,2}, u_2, c),$
       $(f_{4,1}, f_{4,2}, u_3, m), (f_{5,1}, f_{5,2}, c), (g_s)\})$;
  and X - elements from the signing key sgk:
  $X = \{(r), (s), (r, s), (x, r, s), (r, s, t_0), (r, s, -t_0, t_1), (r, s, -t_1, t_2),$
       $(r, s, -t_2, t_3), (r, s, -t_3, t_4), (r, s, -t_4), (x)\}$.
  Return the signature $\sigma \stackrel{def}{=} \{E, \pi(E)\}$.

- Sig.Verify$(vk; m; \sigma) \to 1/0$:

  1. Parse σ as (E, π), parse E as $(u_1, u_2, u_3, c, f_0', \ldots, f_5')$;
  2. Compute $b \leftarrow$ GS.Verify(CRS, Y, π), where Y is derived from (E, vk):
  $Y = (\{u_1, u_2, u_3, c, f_0', f_1', f_2', f_3', f_4', f_5', h_s\}; \{(g_1), (g_2), (g_3, g_3), (u_s, h_1, h_2),$
       $(f_{0,1}, f_{0,2}, u_1), (f_{1,1}, f_{1,2}, u_0, u_2), (f_{2,1}, f_{2,2}, u_1, u_3), (f_{3,1}, f_{3,2}, u_2, c),$
       $(f_{4,1}, f_{4,2}, u_3, m), (f_{5,1}, f_{5,2}, c), (g_s)\})$;
  Return b.

Fig. 1. Structure-preserving signature scheme secure under DLIN assumption

6.2 Unforgeability

Theorem 3. *The digital signature scheme* Sig *described in Section 5 is unforgeable against adaptive chosen message attacks, if the DLIN assumption holds.*

Proof. We consider an adaptive chosen message attack described in Section 2, where the polynomial time adversary $\mathcal{A}_{sig}$, given a verification key vk, adaptively queries the signing oracle $\mathcal{O}_{sig}$ q times with messages m_i, and obtains signatures $\sigma_i = \text{Sig.Sign}(sk, m_i)$, where $1 \leq i \leq q$. We show that any such adversary $\mathcal{A}_{sig}$ has only negligible probability $\mathcal{P}$ of producing a valid signature σ^* on a fresh message m^* that was not queried before.

The proof is through a sequence of games. We define the success probability of $\mathcal{A}_{sig}$ to produce a successful forgery in Game-i as $\mathcal{P}_i$. Game-0 is the real attack game ($\mathcal{P}_0 = \mathcal{P}$), and in Game-4 the adversary only sees encryptions of 1 instead of the encryption of a solution to the CDH problem. Thus from an adversary how wins Game-4, we can construct an algorithm to break the CDH assumption, thus $\mathcal{P}_4 = negl$.

Now we show that $|\mathcal{P}_4 - \mathcal{P}_0|$ is negligible, i.e., $\mathcal{P}_4 = \mathcal{P} + negl$. This means that $\mathcal{P} = negl$, i.e., no adversary $\mathcal{A}_{sig}$ can forge a signature with non-negligible probability.

Game-0. *We define Game-0 as the original attack game described above. More formally, the keys are generated using* Sig.KeyGen *algorithm: $(sgk, vk) \xleftarrow{\$} \text{Sig.KeyGen}(1^\kappa)$. The signature on a message m_i is computed as $\sigma_i \leftarrow \text{Sig.Sign}(sgk, m_i), i = 1, \ldots, q$. The adversary's forgery is $\sigma^* = (E^*, \pi^*)$. The forgery is successful, if* Sig.Verify$(\sigma^*, m^*) = 1$ *and $m^* \notin \{m_1, \ldots, m_q\}$.*
As this is the real attack game, the success probability of the adversary in this game $\mathcal{P}_0 = \mathcal{P}$.

Game-1. *Game-1 is the same as Game-0, except that during the key generation the challenger keeps the secret key for encryption scheme as part of the signing key $(sgk = (sgk, sk_e))$. After the adversary produces a forgery $\sigma^* = (E^*, \pi^*)$, the ciphertext E^* is decrypted under the label m^* using sk_e: $y' \leftarrow \text{Enc.Decrypt}^{m^*}(sk_e, E^*)$ and the following condition is checked: $e(y', g_s) = e(u_s, h_s)$. The adversary wins Game-1 when this condition is not satisfied.*
The forgery is successful, if GS.Verify$(CRS, (E^*, vk), \pi) = 1$, $m^* \notin \{m_1, \ldots, m_q\}$, and $e(y', g_s) = e(u_s, h_s)$. In this case the adversary may have less advantage of winning Game-1 compare to Game-0 only if the decryption did not work correctly, or the proofs were proofs of a false statement.

From the correctness of the encryption scheme follows, that, if the adversary has a non-negligible advantage in winning Game-1 compare to Game-0 by generating a proof of a false statement, then one can use it to break the soundness of the NIZK proofs: $|\mathcal{P}_1 - \mathcal{P}_0| \leq \mathcal{P}_{Snds(NIZK)}$. By the perfect soundness of GS proofs described in [25] and Section 3.4, $\mathcal{P}_1 = \mathcal{P}_0$.

Game-2. *Game-2 is the same as the previous one, except that now the real CRS in key generation is replaced by a simulated CRS^{sim} with a trapdoor, and GS proofs are simulated using zero-knowledge simulator, described in Section 3.4.*

By the zero-knowledge property of the GS proofs, described in [25] and Section 3.4, the adversary cannot distinguish between this game and the previous one if the DLIN assumption holds, so he must still produce a successful forgery with probability only negligibly different from one in the previous game, i.e., $|\mathcal{P}_2 - \mathcal{P}_1| \leq \mathcal{P}_{ZK(NIZK)} = \mathcal{P}_{DLIN}$.

Game-3. *Game-3 is the same as Game-2 except that* $\sigma_i = (E_i, \pi_i)$ *contains an encryption of 1 under the label* m_i *instead of* $y = u_s^x$.

To prove that it will only negligibly change the success probability of the adversary we use a hybrid argument. In the Hybrid-3.0 the adversary sees only ciphertexts with $y = u_s^x$, and in the Hybrid-3.q - only encryptions of 1, where $q(\kappa)$ is a polynomial number of queries.
It is easy to see that Hybrid-3.0 is the same as Game-2, so we have $\mathcal{P}_{3.0} = \mathcal{P}_2$.

Hybrid-3.k. *When the adversary makes the* i^{th} *query, the signatures are computed in the following way:*

- *for all* $i < k$ *1 is encrypted under the label* m_i;
- *for* $i \geq k$ *y is encrypted under the label* m_i.

Now we show that if the adversary $\mathcal{A}_{sig}$ can distinguish between Hybrid-k and Hybrid-$k + 1$ then we can use it to break CCA-2 security of the encryption scheme, i.e., to construct an adversary $\mathcal{A}_{CCA2}$ who plays the CCA-2 game and also represents a challenger with $\mathcal{A}_{sig}$ in adaptive chosen message attack, and, after $\mathcal{A}_{sig}$ produces a successful forgery, wins the CCA-2 game.

After receiving pk_e from the CCA-2 challenger, $\mathcal{A}_{CCA2}$ proceeds as follows:

Sig.KeyGen$(1^\kappa) \xrightarrow{\$} (sgk, vk)$:
    1. Generate simulated CRS and a trapdoor for GS proofs:
        $(CRS^{sim}, td) \xleftarrow{\$} \mathsf{GS.SetupSim}(1^\kappa)$;
    2. Generate keys for signing (CDH challenge):
        $x \xleftarrow{\$} \mathbb{Z}_p, g_s, u_s \xleftarrow{\$} \mathbb{G}$; $h_s = g_s^x$; $ch = (g_s, u_s, h_s)$;
    Output signing and verification keys:
        $sgk \leftarrow (x, vk, td)$; $vk \leftarrow (CRS^{sim}, ch, pk_e)$.

Sig.Sign$(sgk, m_i) \xrightarrow{\$} \sigma_i$:
    For the queries $1, \ldots, k - 1$ the signature is generated as follows:
    1. Parse sgk as $(x, CRS^{sim}, ch, pk_e, td)$.
    2. Encrypt 1 with label m_i:
        $E_i = \mathsf{Enc.Encrypt}^{m_i}(pk_e, 1) = (u_1, u_2, u_3, c, f_0', \ldots, f_5')$.

  3. Simulate GS proof that E_i was formed correctly:
  $$\pi(E_i) = \text{GS.Sim}(CRS^{sim}, (E_i, vk), td).$$
  Output $\sigma_i = (E_i, \pi(E_i))$.
For the queries $k, \ldots, q$ the signature is generated as follows:
  1. Parse sgk as $(x, CRS^{sim}, ch, pk_e, td)$.
  2. Compute $y = u_s^x$.
  3. Encrypt y with label m_i:
  $$E_i = \text{Enc.Encrypt}^{m_i}(pk_e, y) = (u_1, u_2, u_3, c, f_0', \ldots, f_5').$$
  4. Generate GS proof that E_i was formed correctly:
  $$\pi(E_i) = \text{GS.Prove}(CRS^{sim}, (E_i, vk), (sgk)).$$
  Output $\sigma_i = (E_i, \pi(E_i))$.

For the query m_k we define two challenge messages $M_0 = 1, M_1 = y = u_s^x$ for $\mathcal{A}_{CCA2}$.

When $\mathcal{A}_{CCA2}$ receives a challenge encryption $E' = \text{Enc.Encrypt}^{m_k}(pk_e, M_b)$ of one of these messages under the label m_k, its goal is to break CCA-2 security by distinguishing which one it received. It answers query k by simulating the proof and returning the challenge ciphertext E' together with the simulated proof. Namely, it does the following:

Sig.Sign$(sgk, m_i) \overset{\$}{\to} \sigma_i$:

  1. Parse sgk as $(x, CRS^{sim}, ch, pk_e, td)$.
  2. Compute $y = u_s^x$.
  3. Encrypt: $E' = (u_1, u_2, u_3, c, f_0', \ldots, f_5')$.
  4. Simulate GS proof that E' was formed correctly:
  $$\pi(E') = \text{GS.Prove}(CRS^{sim}, (E', vk), td).$$
  Output $\sigma_i = (E', \pi(E'))$.

If the challenge encryption has the plaintext 1, then this corresponds exactly to the Hybrid-k, while if the challenge encryption has plaintext u_s^x, then it corresponds exactly to the Hybrid-$k + 1$.

The adversary $\mathcal{A}_{sig}$ now produces a forged signature (E^*, π^*) on message m^* that was not queried before.

$\mathcal{A}_{CCA2}$ sends (m^*, E^*) to the decryption oracle. Note, that $\mathcal{A}_{CCA2}$ is not allowed to submit a pair label-ciphertext equal to the challenge pair $((m^*, E^*) = (m_k, E'))$. If this was the case or the ciphertext was formed incorrectly then the decryption oracle will return $\perp$.

In case the received M^* is equal u_s^x $\mathcal{A}_{CCA2}$ outputs 1, else it outputs 0. In case of receiving $\perp$ it outputs 0 as well. By definition, to be successful $\mathcal{A}_{sig}$ had to produce a ciphertext for u_s^x with a fresh label m^* (i.e., it is never successful if the answer is ε or $\perp$).

Therefore, if $\mathcal{A}_{sig}$ has more than negligible difference in success probability in respectively Hybrid-3.i and Hybrid-3.$(i + 1)$, then $\mathcal{A}_{CCA2}$ can break the CCA-2 security of the encryption scheme. By the CCA-2 security of the encryption scheme under DLIN assumption (see Section 3), the success probability of the $\mathcal{A}_{sig}$ changes negligibly, i.e. $\mathcal{P}_{3.k} - \mathcal{P}_{3.k+1} \leq \mathcal{P}_{CCA2} \leq \mathcal{P}_{DLIN}$ is negligible.

Summing up all hybrids we have that $|\mathcal{P}_{3.q} - \mathcal{P}_{3.0}| \leq q \cdot \mathcal{P}_{DLIN}$.

Game-4. *Now the adversary sees only an encryption of 1 under the label m_i on the i-th query, for $i = 1, \ldots, q$, yet to be successful it has to produce an encryption of $y = u_s^x$ under the label m^* such that $e(y, g_s) = e(u_s, h_s)$.*

We show how to construct an algorithm $\mathcal{A}_{CDH}$ that plays a challenger with $\mathcal{A}_{sig}$ in adaptive chosen message attack game, and, after $\mathcal{A}_{sig}$ produces a successful forgery, solves CDH problem.

Since the adversary sees the same the distribution as in Game-3.q, $\mathcal{P}_4 = \mathcal{P}_{3.q}$.

First $\mathcal{A}_{CDH}(\mathcal{A}_{sig})$ gets an input g_s, g_s^a, g_s^b and plays a role of a challenger in the adaptive chosen message attack game with an adversary $\mathcal{A}_{sig}$. It embeds the received input in a verification key and simulates the signature scheme as follows:

Sig.KeyGen$(1^\kappa) \xrightarrow{\$} (sgk, vk)$:

1. Generate simulated CRS and a trapdoor for GS proofs:
   $(CRS^{sim}, td) \xleftarrow{\$}$ GS.SetupSim(1^κ).
2. Incorporate the received CDH challenge: $ch \leftarrow (g_s, h_s = g_s^a, u_s = g_s^b)$.
   Output signing and verification keys:
   $sgk \leftarrow (x, vk, td)$; $vk \leftarrow (CRS^{sim}, ch, pk_e)$.

Sig.Sign$(sgk, m_i) \xrightarrow{\$} \sigma_i$:

1. Parse sgk as (x, CRS, ch, pk_e, td) ;
2. Encrypt 1 with label m_i:
   $E_i = $ Enc.Encrypt$^{m_i}(pk_e, 1) = (u_1, u_2, u_3, c, f'_0, \ldots, f'_5)$;
3. Simulate GS proof that E_i was formed correctly:
   $\pi(E_i) = $ GS.Sim$(CRS^{sim}, (E_i, vk), td)$;
   Output $\sigma_i = (E_i, \pi(E_i))$.

Sig.Verify$(vk, m^*, \sigma^*) \rightarrow 1/0$:

1. Parse σ^* as (E^*, π^*), parse E^* as $(u_1, u_2, u_3, c, f'_0, \ldots, f'_5)$.
2. Verify GS proofs: $b \leftarrow$ GS.Verify$(CRS^{sim}, (E^*, vk), \pi^*)$.
3. Decrypt $y' \leftarrow$ Enc.Decrypt$^{m^*}(sk_e, E^*)$.
4. Check if $(e(y', g_s) = e(u_s, h_s)) \wedge (m^* \notin \{m_1, \ldots, m_q\})$.

If $b = 1$ and equations (4) hold, output y' to the CDH challenger.

Since in order to win the Game-4 it needs to solve the CDH problem, the adversary has a negligible success probability in Game-4: $\mathcal{P}_4 \leq \mathcal{P}_{CDH}$.

Summing up, we have that $\mathcal{P} \leq \mathcal{P}_{CDH} + q \cdot \mathcal{P}_{DLIN} + \mathcal{P}_{DLIN} = negl$.

Acknowledgements. The research leading to these results has received funding from the European Community's Seventh Framework Programme (FP7/2007-2013) as part of the "ICT Trust and Security Research", under grant agreements n°257782 for the project ABC4Trust and n°216676 for the project Ecrypt II.

References

1. Abe, M., Fuchsbauer, G., Groth, J., Haralambiev, K., Ohkubo, M.: Structure-Preserving Signatures and Commitments to Group Elements. In: Rabin, T. (ed.) CRYPTO 2010. LNCS, vol. 6223, pp. 209–236. Springer, Heidelberg (2010)
2. Abe, M., Groth, J., Haralambiev, K., Ohkubo, M.: Optimal Structure-Preserving Signatures in Asymmetric Bilinear Groups. In: Rogaway, P. (ed.) CRYPTO 2011. LNCS, vol. 6841, pp. 649–666. Springer, Heidelberg (2011)
3. Abe, M., Ohkubo, M.: A Framework for Universally Composable Non-committing Blind Signatures. In: Matsui, M. (ed.) ASIACRYPT 2009. LNCS, vol. 5912, pp. 435–450. Springer, Heidelberg (2009)
4. Belenkiy, M., Chase, M., Kohlweiss, M., Lysyanskaya, A.: P-signatures and Noninteractive Anonymous Credentials. In: Canetti, R. (ed.) TCC 2008. LNCS, vol. 4948, pp. 356–374. Springer, Heidelberg (2008)
5. Bellare, M., Micciancio, D., Warinschi, B.: Foundations of Group Signatures: Formal Definitions, Simplified Requirements, and a Construction Based on General Assumptions. In: Biham, E. (ed.) EUROCRYPT 2003. LNCS, vol. 2656, pp. 614–629. Springer, Heidelberg (2003)
6. Boneh, D., Boyen, X.: Short signatures without random oracles and the SDH assumption in bilinear groups. Journal of Cryptology 21(2), 149–177 (2008)
7. Boneh, D., Boyen, X., Shacham, H.: Short Group Signatures. In: Franklin, M. (ed.) CRYPTO 2004. LNCS, vol. 3152, pp. 41–55. Springer, Heidelberg (2004)
8. Boneh, D., Franklin, M.: Identity-Based Encryption from the Weil Pairing. In: Kilian, J. (ed.) CRYPTO 2001. LNCS, vol. 2139, pp. 213–229. Springer, Heidelberg (2001)
9. Camenisch, J., Chaabouni, R., Shelat, A.: Efficient Protocols for Set Membership and Range Proofs. In: Pieprzyk, J. (ed.) ASIACRYPT 2008. LNCS, vol. 5350, pp. 234–252. Springer, Heidelberg (2008)
10. Camenisch, J., Chandran, N., Shoup, V.: A Public Key Encryption Scheme Secure against Key Dependent Chosen Plaintext and Adaptive Chosen Ciphertext Attacks. In: Joux, A. (ed.) EUROCRYPT 2009. LNCS, vol. 5479, pp. 351–368. Springer, Heidelberg (2009)
11. Camenisch, J., Dubovitskaya, M., Neven, G., Zaverucha, G.M.: Oblivious Transfer with Hidden Access Control Policies. In: Catalano, D., Fazio, N., Gennaro, R., Nicolosi, A. (eds.) PKC 2011. LNCS, vol. 6571, pp. 192–209. Springer, Heidelberg (2011)
12. Camenisch, J., Haralambiev, K., Kohlweiss, M., Lapon, J., Naessens, V.: Structure Preserving CCA Secure Encryption and Applications. In: Lee, D.H. (ed.) ASIACRYPT 2011. LNCS, vol. 7073, pp. 89–106. Springer, Heidelberg (2011)
13. Camenisch, J., Hohenberger, S., Lysyanskaya, A.: Compact E-Cash. In: Cramer, R. (ed.) EUROCRYPT 2005. LNCS, vol. 3494, pp. 302–321. Springer, Heidelberg (2005)
14. Camenisch, J., Kiayias, A., Yung, M.: On the Portability of Generalized Schnorr Proofs. In: Joux, A. (ed.) EUROCRYPT 2009. LNCS, vol. 5479, pp. 425–442. Springer, Heidelberg (2009)
15. Cathalo, J., Libert, B., Yung, M.: Group Encryption: Non-interactive Realization in the Standard Model. In: Matsui, M. (ed.) ASIACRYPT 2009. LNCS, vol. 5912, pp. 179–196. Springer, Heidelberg (2009)
16. Chase, M., Kohlweiss, M.: A domain transformation for structure-preserving signatures on group elements. Cryptology ePrint Archive, Report 2011/342 (2011), http://eprint.iacr.org/

17. Diffie, W., Hellman, M.E.: New directions in cryptography. IEEE Transactions on Information Theory 22(6), 644–654 (1976)
18. Dodis, Y., Haralambiev, K., López-Alt, A., Wichs, D.: Efficient Public-Key Cryptography in the Presence of Key Leakage. In: Abe, M. (ed.) ASIACRYPT 2010. LNCS, vol. 6477, pp. 613–631. Springer, Heidelberg (2010)
19. Dolev, D., Dwork, C., Naor, M.: Non-malleable cryptography. In: 23rd ACM STOC, pp. 542–552. ACM Press (1991)
20. Fischlin, M.: Round-Optimal Composable Blind Signatures in the Common Reference String Model. In: Dwork, C. (ed.) CRYPTO 2006. LNCS, vol. 4117, pp. 60–77. Springer, Heidelberg (2006)
21. Fuchsbauer, G.: Automorphic signatures in bilinear groups and an application to round-optimal blind signatures. Cryptology ePrint Archive, Report 2009/320 (2009), http://eprint.iacr.org/
22. Green, M., Hohenberger, S.: Universally Composable Adaptive Oblivious Transfer. In: Pieprzyk, J. (ed.) ASIACRYPT 2008. LNCS, vol. 5350, pp. 179–197. Springer, Heidelberg (2008)
23. Green, M., Hohenberger, S.: Practical adaptive oblivious transfer from simple assumptions. Cryptology ePrint Archive, Report 2010/109 (2010), http://eprint.iacr.org/
24. Groth, J.: Simulation-Sound NIZK Proofs for a Practical Language and Constant Size Group Signatures. In: Lai, X., Chen, K. (eds.) ASIACRYPT 2006. LNCS, vol. 4284, pp. 444–459. Springer, Heidelberg (2006)
25. Groth, J., Sahai, A.: Efficient Non-interactive Proof Systems for Bilinear Groups. In: Smart, N.P. (ed.) EUROCRYPT 2008. LNCS, vol. 4965, pp. 415–432. Springer, Heidelberg (2008)
26. Katz, J., Vaikuntanathan, V.: Signature Schemes with Bounded Leakage Resilience. In: Matsui, M. (ed.) ASIACRYPT 2009. LNCS, vol. 5912, pp. 703–720. Springer, Heidelberg (2009)
27. Naor, M.: On Cryptographic Assumptions and Challenges. In: Boneh, D. (ed.) CRYPTO 2003. LNCS, vol. 2729, pp. 96–109. Springer, Heidelberg (2003)

Compact Round-Optimal Partially-Blind Signatures

Olivier Blazy, David Pointcheval, and Damien Vergnaud

ENS, Paris, France*
{olivier.blazy,david.pointcheval,damien.vergnaud}@ens.fr

Abstract. Partially-blind signatures find many applications in the area of anonymity, such as in e-cash or e-voting systems. They extend classical blind signatures, with a signed message composed of two parts: a public one (common to the user and the signer) and a private one (chosen by the user, and blindly signed). The signer cannot link later the message-signature to the initial interaction with the user, among other signatures on messages with the same public part.

This paper presents a one-round partially-blind signature which achieves perfect blindness in the standard model using a Common Reference String, under classical assumptions: CDH and DLin assumptions in symmetric groups, and similar ones in asymmetric groups. This scheme is more efficient than the previous ones: reduced round complexity and communication complexity, but still weaker complexity assumptions. A great advantage is also to end up with a standard Waters signature, which is quite short.

In addition, in all the previous schemes, the public part required a prior agreement between the parties on the public part of the message before running the blind signature protocol. Our protocol does not require such pre-processing: the public part can be chosen by the signer only.

Our scheme even allows multiple messages provided from independent sources to be blindly signed. These messages can either be concatenated or aggregated by the signer, without learning any information about them, before returning the blind signature to the recipient. For the aggregation (addition of the messages), we provide a new result, of independent interest, about the Waters hash function over non binary-alphabets.

1 Introduction

Blind signatures were proposed by Chaum in 1982 [9]: they are an interactive signature scheme between a user and a signer, in a way that the signed message, and even the resulting signature, are unknown to the signer, this is the *blindness* property. More precisely, if the signer runs several executions of the protocol that led to several message-signature pairs, he cannot link back any pair to a specific execution: the view of the signer is unlinkable to the resulting message-signature pair. This unlinkability can either be computational, we

---

* CNRS – UMR 8548 and INRIA – EPI Cascade, Université Paris Diderot.

then talk about *computational blindness*, or perfect, we then talk about *perfect blindness*. In addition, they guarantee some kind of unforgeability for the signer, which has been formalized in [18] to cope with e-cash properties: the user cannot produce more message-signature pairs (coins) than the number of interactions (withdrawals).

There have been several highly interactive schemes (like [17]), but Fischlin [11] gave a generic construction of *round-optimal* blind signatures. Recent schemes have instantiated this construction, the user obtains an actual signature on the message, of which he proves knowledge [1, 12] or can simply randomize it to make it unlinkable [4, 5]. In the latter case, the blind signature has the same format as the underlying signatures and, in addition to being round-optimal, is thus short. Our construction, like this last one produced a simple (randomized) Waters signature on the message m so two group elements and a scalar m under basic assumptions DLin, where [1] uses less standard assumption SXDH and ADH-CDH, and around 38 elements in $\mathbb{G}_1$ and 34 in $\mathbb{G}_2$ for the final signature because of the required proofs of knowledge. [13] presented a round-optimal blind signature without CRS but less efficient than the construction relying on the Common Reference String.

A loophole in standard blind signatures was detailed by Abe and Okamoto [3]: the signer has no control over the signed messages (except in some sense the unforgeability which limits their number). In e-cash schemes, we want the bank to sign a coin (a random, and thus unknown, serial number), but with a specific expiration date. Partially-Blind Signatures proposed by Abe and Fujisaki [2] solve this problem, by allowing the user and the signer to agree on a predetermined piece of information which must be included in the final signed message.

Recently, in [19], Seo and Cheon presented a construction leading to (Partially) Blind-Signatures in the standard model. However their construction relies on a trick consisting in starting from prime order groups $\mathbb{G}_1, \mathbb{G}_2, \mathbb{G}_3$ and considering group elements in $\mathcal{G} = \mathbb{G}_1 \oplus \mathbb{G}_2 \oplus \mathbb{G}_3$. While their approach provides nice theoretical tools, the resulting signatures lies in $\mathcal{G}^2$ and are therefore three times longer than our proposal.

Our Contributions. In this paper, we go one step further, improving [4] in several directions. We first present a blind signature scheme with perfect blindness, using the perfectly hiding instantiation of Groth-Sahai commitments [14]. We also widen the model of partially-blind signatures to supplement the predetermined communication with an on-the-fly public information generated by the signer: the signer can simply include it during the signing process, even if the user does not want this extra information. In the latter case, the user can simply discard the signature and start anew. We call this new primitive *signer-friendly partially-blind signatures*. This new notion allows to skip the prior agreement and allow the public information to be set on-the fly. Of course this new notion does not forbid any kind of prior agreement on the public part, it just strengthens the existing notion.

It is now possible to get rid of the prior agreement on the common piece of information in the signed message and our instantiation allows the signer to do so in a round-optimal way. These two constructions being compatible, we can present a round-optimal partially-blind signature with perfect blindness. Our protocol does not need any pre-processing for the public part of the message. Basically both the user and the signer can choose a piece of the public part, but instead of having a computational overhead for the agreement both can simply choose during the 2 flows interaction what they want. The signer can always refuse to sign something where the user's public information doesn't suit him and the user can always choose not to exploit an uninteresting signature, so a protocol should avoid to waste communication costs when one can manage without any security loss to stay in a two-flows protocol.

Eventually, discarding the perfect blindness, we take advantage of this asynchronous property (the user and the signer can independently choose their inputs) and we consider the new context where the message to be signed comes from several independent sources that cannot communicate together. We first present a way to obtain a signature on the concatenation of the input messages. We also present a shorter instantiation which gives a signature on the sum of the input messages. Such a sum can be useful when working on ballots, sensor information, etc. Since we still apply the Waters signature, this led us to consider the Waters function programmability over a non-binary alphabet, in a similar way as it was done in [15] for the binary alphabet. We prove a negative result on the $(2, 1)$-programmability, but a nice positive one on the $(1, poly)$-programmability, which is of independent interest.

Instantiations. We give several instantiations of our different blind signatures, all of which are based on weak assumptions. Our constructions mainly use the two following building blocks, from which they inherit their security: Groth-Sahai proofs for languages over pairing-friendly groups [14] and Waters signatures derived from the scheme in [20] and used in [8]. Since verification of the revisited Waters signatures [4] is a statement of the language for Groth-Sahai proofs, these two building blocks combine smoothly. The first instantiations are in symmetric pairing-friendly elliptic curves and additionally use linear commitments [7]. Both unforgeability and semantic security of these constructions rely solely on the decision linear assumption (DLin). The blindness property is easily achieved granted the homomorphic property of the Waters signature. An instantiation with improved efficiency, in *asymmetric* bilinear groups, using the SXDH variant of Groth-Sahai proofs and commitments is drafted in the full version [6]. This setting requires an asymmetric Waters signature scheme secure under a slightly stronger assumption, called CDH^+, where some additional elements in the second group are given to the adversary.

Applications. Our blind signature schemes find various kinds of applications:

E-voting. The security of several e-voting protocols relies on the fact that each ballot is certified by an election authority. Since this authority should not learn the voter's choice, a blind signature scheme (or even partially-blind, if the authority wants to specify the election in the ballot) is usually used to achieve this property. In order to achieve privacy of the ballot in an information-theoretic sense, it is necessary to use a signature scheme that achieves perfect blindness. Our scheme is the first to achieve this property in the standard model and under classical complexity assumptions.

E-cash. As mentioned above, partially-blind signatures played an important role in many electronic commerce applications. In e-cash systems, for instance, the bank issuing coins must ensure that the message contains accurate information such as the face value of the e-cash without seeing it and moreover in order to prevent double-spending, the bank's database has to record all spent coins. Partially-blind signatures can cope with these problems, since the bank can explicitly include some information such as the expiration date and the face value in the coin. Thanks to our proposal, the coin issuing protocol can be done without prior agreement between the bank and the client.

Data aggregation in networks. A *wireless (ad hoc) sensor network* (WSN) consists of many sensor nodes that are deployed for sensing the environment and collecting data from it. Since transmitting and receiving data are the most energy consuming operations, data aggregation has been put forward as an essential paradigm in these networks. The idea is to combine the data coming from different sources – minimizing the number of transmissions and thus saving energy. In this setting, a WSN consists usually of three types of nodes:

- *sensor nodes* that are small devices equipped with one or more sensors, a processor and a radio transceiver for wireless communication.
- *aggregation nodes* (or aggregators) performing the data aggregation (*e.g.* average, sum, minimum or maximum of data).
- *base stations* responsible for querying the nodes and gathering the data collected by them.

WSNs are at high security risk and two important security goals when doing in-network data aggregation are *data confidentiality* and *data integrity*. When homomorphic encryption is used for data aggregation, end-to-end encryption allows aggregation of the encrypted data so that the aggregators do not need to decrypt and get access to the data and thus provides end-to-end data confidentiality. Achieving data integrity is a harder problem and usually we do not consider the attack where a sensor node reports a false reading value (the impact of such an attack being usually limited). The main security flaw is a *data pollution attack* in which an attacker tampers with the intermediate aggregation result at an aggregation node. The purpose of the attack is to make the base station receive the wrong aggregation result, and thus make the improper or wrong decisions.

   While in most conventional data aggregation protocols, data integrity and privacy are not preserved at the same time, our multi-source blind signature primitive permits to achieve data confidentiality and to prevent data pollution attacks simultaneously by using the following simple protocol:

1. Data aggregation is initiated by a base station, which broadcasts a query to the whole network.

2. Upon receiving the query, sensor nodes report encrypted values of their readings (for the base station public key) to their aggregators.
3. The aggregators check the validity of the received values, perform data aggregation via the homomorphic properties of the encryption scheme, (blindly) sign the result and route the aggregated results back to the base station.
4. The base station decrypts the aggregated data and the signature which proves the validity of the gathered information to the base station (but also to any other third party).

2   Definition

This section presents the global framework and the security model for partially-blind signature schemes. A reminder of standard definition and security notions on Blind Signature can be found in the full version [6].

Blind signatures introduced a nice feature, however it may be undesirable that requesters can ask the signer to blindly sign any message. For example, in an e-cash scheme, some expiration date information should be embedded in the e-coin, to avoid the bank's database an uncontrolled growth when storing information for double-spending checking. Partially-blind signatures are thus a natural extension of blind signatures: instead of signing an unknown message, the signer signs a message which contains a shared piece of information in addition to the hidden part. This piece is called info and, in the standard definition, is expected to have been defined before the execution of the protocol. But since our schemes will not require the public part to be agreed on by the two players before the protocol execution (as opposed to all the previous schemes from the literature), we extend the usual partially-blind signature scheme with two public parts in the message, in addition to the hidden part: $\text{info} = \text{info}_c \| \text{info}_s$, where info_c is the common public part with prior agreement, and info_s is set on-the-fly by the signer. This provides a more flexible scheme, and this definition generalizes all the above ones. If $\text{info}_s = \bot$, we are in the regular case of partially blind signature, whereas in case of regular blind signature both parts are empty $\bot$.

Definition 1 (Partially-Blind Signature Scheme). *A $\mathcal{PBS}$ scheme is defined by 4 algorithms or protocols* (Setup$_{\mathcal{PBS}}$, KeyGen$_{\mathcal{PBS}}$, $\langle \mathcal{S}, \mathcal{U} \rangle$, Verif$_{\mathcal{PBS}}$) *where*

- Setup$_{\mathcal{PBS}}(1^\lambda)$ *generates the global parameters* param$_{pbs}$ *of the system;*
- KeyGen$_{\mathcal{PBS}}$(param$_{pbs}$) *generates a pair of keys* (pk$_{\mathcal{PBS}}$, sk$_{\mathcal{PBS}}$);
- *Signature Issuing: this is an interactive protocol between* $\mathcal{S}(\text{sk}_{\mathcal{PBS}}, \text{info} = \text{info}_c \| \text{info}_s)$ *and* $\mathcal{U}(\text{pk}_{\mathcal{PBS}}, m, \text{info})$, *for a message* $m \in \{0,1\}^n$ *and shared information* info. *It generates an output* σ *for the user:*
  $\sigma \leftarrow \langle \mathcal{S}(\text{sk}_{\mathcal{PBS}}, \text{info}), \mathcal{U}(\text{pk}_{\mathcal{PBS}}, m, \text{info}) \rangle$.
- Verif$_{\mathcal{PBS}}$(pk$_{\mathcal{PBS}}$, m, info, σ) *outputs 1 if the signature* σ *is valid with respect to the message* $m \| \text{info}$ *and* pk$_{\mathcal{PBS}}$, *0 otherwise.*

Quick Note on Security: The security requirements are a direct extension of the classical ones: for unforgeability, we consider $m\|$info instead of m, and for the blindness, we condition the unlinkability between signatures with the same public part info. Without the latter restriction, anyone can simply distinguish which message was signed by comparing the public information. The unforgeability is strengthened by considering also the public information so that the signer can be sure that the user won't be able to exploit his signature in another context.

Definition 2 (Signer-Friendly Partially-Blind Signature Scheme). *A signer-friendly partially-blind signature scheme* $\mathcal{PBS}$ *is defined by 4 algorithms or protocols* $(\text{Setup}_{\mathcal{PBS}}, \text{KeyGen}_{\mathcal{PBS}}, \langle\mathcal{S},\mathcal{U}\rangle, \text{Verif}_{\mathcal{PBS}})$ *where*

- $\text{Setup}(1^\lambda)$ *generates the global parameters* param_{pbs} *of the system;*
- $\text{KeyGen}(\text{param}_{pbs})$ *generates a pair of keys* $(\text{pk}_{\mathcal{PBS}}, \text{sk}_{\mathcal{PBS}})$;
- *Signature Issuing: this is an interactive protocol between* $\mathcal{S}(\text{sk}_{\mathcal{PBS}}, \text{info}_c, \text{info}_s)$ *and* $\mathcal{U}(\text{pk}_{\mathcal{PBS}}, m, \text{info}_c)$, *for a message* $m \in \{0,1\}^n$, *signer information* info_s *and common information* info_c. *It generates an output* σ *for the user:* $\sigma \leftarrow \langle \mathcal{S}(\text{sk}_{\mathcal{PBS}}, \text{info}_c, \text{info}_s), \mathcal{U}(\text{pk}_{\mathcal{PBS}}, m, \text{info}_c)\rangle$.
- $\text{Verif}(\text{pk}_{\mathcal{PBS}}, m, \text{info}_c, \text{info}_s, \sigma)$ *outputs 1 if the signature* σ *is valid with respect to the message* $m\|\text{info}_c\|\text{info}_s$ *and* $\text{pk}_{\mathcal{PBS}}$, *0 otherwise.*

One notes that $\text{info}_c = \text{info}$ and $\text{info}_s = \perp$ lead to a standard partially-blind signature; whereas the case $\text{info}_c = \text{info}_s = \perp$ is the standard blind signature.

The signer always has the last word in the process, and so if he does not want to sign a specific info, he will simply abort the protocol several times until the shared part suits his will. So, in the following, we decided that it was wiser to let him choose this input. If the user wants a specific word in the final message he can always add it to the blinded message. Intuitively this strengthens the unforgeability notion as the adversary (the user in this case) won't be able to chose the whole message to be signed because of info_s. This is ensured in the security game, because the adversary should outputs valid signatures, therefore they should be done with the chosen info_s. For the blindness property, the adversary should guess on signatures with the same public $\text{info}_c\|\text{info}_s$ component, if it is not the case we answer with a blind-signature $\perp$.

The complete security games can be found in the full version [6].

3   Partially-Blind Signature

Our constructions will combine Groth-Sahai Linear Commitments [14] and the Waters signature [20] as follows: given a commitment on the "Waters hash" $\mathcal{F}(M)$ (and some additional values proving we know the message M and the randomness used), a pre-agreed shared information info_c, the signer can make a partially-blind signature on M, info_c and an extra piece of public information info_s. This construction makes use of a symmetric pairing, but we extend it to asymmetric pairings in the full version [6].

3.1 Assumptions

We rely on classical assumptions only: CDH for the unforgeability of signatures and DLin for the blindness property (when not perfect), and also for soundness of the proofs:

Definition 3 (The Computational Diffie-Hellman problem (CDH)). *The* CDH *assumption, in a cyclic group* $\mathbb{G}$ *of prime order* p, *states that for a generator* $g \in \mathbb{G}$ *and random* $a, b \in \mathbb{Z}_p$, *given* (g, g^a, g^b) *it is hard to compute* g^{ab}.

Definition 4 (Decision Linear Assumption (DLin)). *The* DLin *assumption, in a cyclic group* $\mathbb{G}$ *of prime order* p, *states that given* $(g, g^x, g^y, g^{xa}, g^{yb}, g^c)$ *for random* $a, b, x, y \in \mathbb{Z}_p$, *it is hard to determine whether* $c = a + b$ *or a random value. When* $(g, u = g^x, v = g^y)$ *is fixed, a tuple* (u^a, v^b, g^{a+b}) *is called a linear tuple w.r.t.* (u, v, g), *whereas a tuple* (u^a, v^b, g^c) *for a random and independent* c *is called a random tuple.*

One can easily see that if an adversary is able to solve a CDH challenge, then he can easily solve a DLin one. So the DLin assumption implies the CDH assumption. Some reminders on Groth-Sahai Commitments and Waters function can be found in the full version [6] as those are the main building blocks of our construction.

3.2 Partially-Blind Signature with Perfect Blindness

With those building blocks, we design a partially-blind signature scheme, which basically consists in committing the message to be signed. And granted the random coins of the commitment, the user can unblind the signature sent by the signer. Eventually, using the randomizability of the Waters signature, the user breaks all the links that could remain between the message-signature pair and the transaction. Our protocol proceeds as follows, on a commitment of $F = \mathcal{F}(M)$, a public common message info_c, and a public message info_s chosen by the signer. It is split into five steps, that correspond to an optimal 2-flow protocol: $\mathsf{Blind}_{\mathcal{BS}}$, which is first run by the user, $\mathsf{Sign}_{\mathcal{BS}}$, which is thereafter run by the signer, and $\mathsf{Verif}_{\mathcal{BS}}$, $\mathsf{Unblind}_{\mathcal{BS}}$, $\mathsf{Random}_{\mathcal{BS}}$ that are eventually successively run by the user to generate the final signature. We thus have $\mathcal{U} = (\mathsf{Blind}_{\mathcal{BS}}; \mathsf{Verif}_{\mathcal{BS}}, \mathsf{Unblind}_{\mathcal{BS}}, \mathsf{Random}_{\mathcal{BS}})$ and $\mathcal{S} = \mathsf{Sign}_{\mathcal{BS}}$:

- $\mathsf{Setup}_{\mathcal{BS}}(1^\lambda)$ first chooses a bilinear group $(p, \mathbb{G}, \mathbb{G}_T, e, g)$. We need an additional vector $\boldsymbol{u} = (u_0, \ldots, u_k) \xleftarrow{\$} \mathbb{G}^{k+1}$ which defines the Waters function $\mathcal{F}$ (where k is the global length of $M \| \mathsf{info}_c \| \mathsf{info}_s$), a generator $h \xleftarrow{\$} \mathbb{G}$, and a tuple of Groth-Sahai parameters $(\mathbf{u}_1, \mathbf{u}_2, \mathbf{u}_3)$ in the perfectly hiding setting: $\mathsf{param}_{bs} = (p, \mathbb{G}, \mathbb{G}_T, e, g, h, \mathcal{F}, \mathbf{u}_1, \mathbf{u}_2, \mathbf{u}_3)$;
- $\mathsf{KeyGen}_{\mathcal{BS}}(\mathsf{param}_{bs})$ chooses a random scalar $x \xleftarrow{\$} \mathbb{Z}_p$, which defines the public key as $\mathsf{pk}_{\mathcal{BS}} = Y = g^x$, and the secret key as $\mathsf{sk}_{\mathcal{BS}} = Z = h^x$;
- Signature Issuing $(\mathcal{S}(\mathsf{sk}_{\mathcal{BS}}, \mathsf{info}_c, \mathsf{info}_s), \mathcal{U}(\mathsf{pk}_{\mathcal{BS}}, M, \mathsf{info}_c))$, which is split in several steps:

- $\mathsf{Blind}_{\mathcal{BS}}(M, \mathsf{pk}_{\mathcal{BS}}; (r_1, r_2, r_3))$: For a message $M \in \{0,1\}^\ell$ and random scalars $(r_1, r_2, r_3) \xleftarrow{\$} \mathbb{Z}_p$, define the commitment as $c = (c_1 = u_{1,1}^{r_1} u_{3,1}^{r_3}, c_2 = u_{2,2}^{r_2} u_{3,2}^{r_3}, c_3 = g^{r_1+r_2} u_{3,3}^{r_3} \cdot \mathcal{F}(M))$ and compute $Y_{1,2} = Y^{r_1+r_2}, Y_3 = Y^{r_3}$. One also generates additional proofs of validity of the commitment:
  * A proof Π_M of knowledge of M in c, the encrypted $\mathcal{F}(M)$, which consists of a bit-by-bit commitment $C_M = (\mathcal{C}'(M_1), \ldots, \mathcal{C}'(M_\ell))$ and proofs that each committed value is a bit, and a proof that c_3 is well-formed. Π_M is therefore composed of $9\ell + 3$ group elements.
  * A proof Π_r containing the commitments $C_r = (\mathcal{C}(Y_{1,2}), \mathcal{C}(Y_3))$ and proofs asserting that they are correctly generated. It requires 9 additional group elements.

  Π thus consists of $9\ell + 12$ group elements, where ℓ is the bit-length of the message M

- $\mathsf{Sign}_{\mathcal{BS}}(\mathsf{sk}_{\mathcal{BS}}, (c, \Pi), \mathsf{info}_c, \mathsf{info}_s; s)$: To sign the commitment c, one first checks if the proof Π is valid. It then appends the public message $\mathsf{info} = \mathsf{info}_c \| \mathsf{info}_s$ to c_3 to create $c_3' = c_3 \cdot \prod u_{i+\ell}^{\mathsf{info}_i}$, which thus becomes a commitment of the Waters function evaluation on $M \| \mathsf{info}_c \| \mathsf{info}_s$ of global length k. It eventually outputs $\sigma = (Z \cdot c_3'^{s}, u_{3,3}^s, g^s)$ together with the additional public information info_s, for a random scalar $s \in \mathbb{Z}_p$.

- $\mathsf{Verif}(\mathsf{pk}_{\mathcal{BS}}, (c, \mathsf{info}_c, \mathsf{info}_s), \sigma = (\sigma_1, \sigma_2, \sigma_3))$: In order to check the validity of the signature, one first computes c_3' as above, and then checks whether the following pairing equations are verified: $e(\sigma_1, g) = e(h, \mathsf{pk}_{\mathcal{BS}}) \cdot e(c_3', \sigma_3)$ and $e(\sigma_2, g) = e(u_{3,3}, \sigma_3)$. If it is not the case, then this is not a valid signature on the original ciphertext, and the blind signature is set as $\Sigma = \perp$.

- $\mathsf{Unblind}_{\mathcal{BS}}((r_1, r_2, r_3), \mathsf{pk}_{\mathcal{BS}}, (c, \mathsf{info}_c, \mathsf{info}_s), \sigma)$: If the previous tests are positive, one can use the random coins r_1, r_2, r_3 to get back a valid signature on $M \| \mathsf{info}_c \| \mathsf{info}_s$: $\sigma' = (\sigma_1' = \sigma_1/(\sigma_3^{r_1+r_2} \sigma_2^{r_3}), \sigma_2' = \sigma_3)$, which is a valid Waters signature.

- $\mathsf{Random}_{\mathcal{BS}}(\mathsf{pk}_{\mathcal{BS}}, (c, \mathsf{info}_c, \mathsf{info}_s), \sigma'; s')$: The latter can eventually be rerandomized to get $\Sigma = (\sigma_1' \cdot \mathcal{F}(M \| \mathsf{info}_c \| \mathsf{info}_s)^{s'}, \sigma_2' \cdot g^{s'})$.

One can note that Σ is a random Waters signature on $M \| \mathsf{info}_c \| \mathsf{info}_s$, where we denote $F = \mathcal{F}(M \| \mathsf{info}_c \| \mathsf{info}_s)$:

$$\begin{aligned}
\Sigma &= (\sigma_1' \cdot F^{s'}, \sigma_2' \cdot g^{s'}) = (F^{s'} \cdot \sigma_1/(\sigma_3^{r_1+r_2} \sigma_2^{r_3}), g^{s'} \cdot \sigma_3) \\
&= (F^{s'} \cdot Z \cdot c_3'^{s}/(g^{s(r_1+r_2)} u_{3,3}^{sr_3}), g^{s+s'}) \\
&= (F^{s'} \cdot Z \cdot g^{s(r_1+r_2)} u_{3,3}^{sr_3} \cdot F^s/(g^{s(r_1+r_2)} u_{3,3}^{sr_3}), g^{s+s'}) = (M^{s+s'} \cdot Z, g^{s+s'})
\end{aligned}$$

- $\mathsf{Verif}_{\mathcal{BS}}(\mathsf{pk}_{\mathcal{BS}}, (M, \mathsf{info}_c, \mathsf{info}_s), \Sigma = (\Sigma_1, \Sigma_2))$: One checks whether the following pairing equations holds (Waters signature): $e(\Sigma_1, g) = e(h, \mathsf{pk}_{\mathcal{BS}}) \cdot e(\mathcal{F}(M \| \mathsf{info}_c \| \mathsf{info}_s), \Sigma_2)$.

Theorem 5. *This signer-friendly partially-blind signature scheme is unforgeable under the* CDH *assumption in* $\mathbb{G}$.

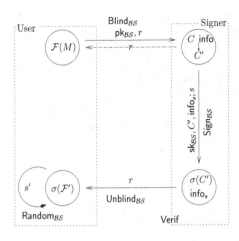

A message M can be hidden using random coins r (Blind$_{\mathcal{BS}}$).

The signer can adapt this commitment and concatenate a public message info$_s$ into the original commitment, with also the common public information info$_s$, creating a commitment C' on $F = \mathcal{F}(M\|\text{info}_c\|\text{info}_s)$.

A signature on the plaintext can be obtained using the randomness r (for Unblind$_{\mathcal{BS}}$); the result is the same as a direct signature on $M\|\text{info}_c\|\text{info}_s$ by the signer.

Randomizing this signature is easy, and prevents the signer to actually know which ciphertext was the one involved.

Fig. 1. Partially-Blind Signatures with Perfect Blindness

Proof. Let us denote $\mathcal{PBS}$ our above partially-blind signature (but omit it in the subscripts for clarity). Let us assume there is an adversary $\mathcal{A}$ against the unforgeability that succeeds within probability ϵ, we will build an adversary $\mathcal{B}$ against the CDH problem.

DLin *Assumption.* The unforgeability means that after q_s interactions with the signer, the adversary manages to output $q_s + 1$ valid message-signature pairs on distinct messages. If the adversary $\mathcal{A}$ can do that with probability ϵ with the above commitment scheme using a perfectly hiding setting, under the DLin assumption, $\mathcal{A}$ can also generate q_s+1 valid message-signature pairs in a perfectly binding setting, with not too small probability ϵ'.

Signer Simulation. Let us thus now consider the above blind signature scheme with a commitment scheme using a perfectly binding setting (named $\mathcal{PBS}'$), and our simulator $\mathcal{B}$ can extract values from the commitments since it knows ν and μ. We thus now assume that $\mathcal{A}$ is able to break the unforgeability of $\mathcal{PBS}'$ with probability ϵ' after q_s interactions with the signer. And we build an adversary $\mathcal{B}$ against the CDH problem: Let $(A = g^a, B = g^b)$ be a CDH-instance in a bilinear group $(p, \mathbb{G}, \mathbb{G}_T, e, g)$.

We now generate the global parameters using this instance: for simulating Setup$_{\mathcal{BS}}$/KeyGen$_{\mathcal{BS}}$, $\mathcal{B}$ picks a random position $j \overset{\$}{\leftarrow} \{0,\ldots,k\}$, chooses random indexes $y_0, y_1, \ldots, y_k \overset{\$}{\leftarrow} \{0,\ldots,2q_s - 1\}$, and random scalars $z_0, z_1, \ldots, z_k \overset{\$}{\leftarrow} \mathbb{Z}_p$. One defines $Y = A = g^a$, $h = B = g^b$, $u_0 = h^{y_0 - 2jq_s}g^{z_0}$, and $u_i = h^{y_i}g^{z_i}$ for $i = 1,\ldots,k$. $\mathcal{B}$ also picks two random scalars ν, μ, and generates the Groth-Sahai parameters $(\mathbf{u}_1, \mathbf{u}_2, \mathbf{u}_3)$ in the perfectly binding setting, and thus with $(\mathbf{u}_1 = (u_{1,1} = g^{x_1}, 1, g), \mathbf{u}_2 = (1, u_{2,2} = g^{x_2}, g), \mathbf{u}_3 = \mathbf{u}_1^\nu \odot \mathbf{u}_2^\mu)$, for two random scalars x_1, x_2. Note that $u_{3,3} = g^{\nu+\mu}$. It outputs param$_{bs} =$

$(p, \mathbb{G}, \mathbb{G}_T, e, g, h, \mathcal{F}, \mathbf{u}_1, \mathbf{u}_2, \mathbf{u}_3)$; one can note that the signing key is implicitly defined as $Z = h^a = B^a = g^{ab}$, and is thus the expected Diffie-Hellman value.

To answer a signing query on ciphertext $c = (c_1, c_2, c_3)$, with the additional proofs, one first checks the proof Π. From the proof Π and the commitment secret parameters x_1, x_2, $\mathcal{B}$ can extract M from the bit-by-bit commitments in Π_M, and $Y_{1,2} = Y^{r_1 + r_2}$, $Y_3 = Y^{r_3}$, from Π_r, where $c_1 = u_{1,1}^{r_1} u_{3,1}^{r_3}$ and $c_2 = u_{2,2}^{r_2} u_{3,2}^{r_3}$. Furthermore, we can compute $c_3' = g^{r_1 + r_2} u_{3,3}^{r_3} \cdot F$, where we denote $M' = M \| \mathsf{info}_c \| \mathsf{info}_s$ and $F = \mathcal{F}(M \| \mathsf{info}_c \| \mathsf{info}_s)$. $\mathcal{B}$ defines

$$H = -2jq_s + y_0 + \sum_i y_i M_i', \quad J = z_0 + \sum_i z_i M_i' \quad : \quad F = h^H g^J.$$

If $H \equiv 0 \pmod{p}$ then $\mathcal{B}$ aborts, otherwise it sets

$$\sigma = (Y^{-J/H}(Y_{1,2}Y_3^{\nu+\mu})^{-1/H}(F(c_1^{1/x_1} c_2^{1/x_2}))^s, (Y^{-1/H} g^s)^{\nu+\mu}, Y^{-1/H} g^s).$$

Defining $\tilde{s} = s - a/H$, we have

$$\sigma_1 = Y^{-J/H}(Y_{1,2}Y_3^{\nu+\mu})^{-1/H}(h^H g^J(c_1^{1/x_1} c_2^{1/x_2}))^s = Z \cdot (c_3')^{\tilde{s}}$$
$$\sigma_3 = Y^{-1/H} g^s = Y^{-1/H} g^{\tilde{s}+a/H} = g^{\tilde{s}}$$
$$\sigma_2 = (\sigma_3)^{\nu+\mu} = g^{(\nu+\mu)\tilde{s}} = u_{3,3}^{\tilde{s}}$$

It thus exactly looks like a real signature sent by the signer.

Diffie-Hellman Extraction. After at most q_s signing queries $\mathcal{A}$ outputs $q_s + 1$ valid Waters signatures. Since there are more than the number of signing queries, there is a least one message M^* that is different from all the messages $M \| \mathsf{info}_c \| \mathsf{info}_s$ involved in the signing queries. We define

$$H^* = -2jq_s + y_0 + \sum_i y_i M_i^*, \quad J^* = z_0 + \sum_i z_i M_i^* \quad : \quad \mathcal{F}(M^*) = h^{H^*} g^{J^*}.$$

If $H^* \not\equiv 0 \pmod{p}$ then $\mathcal{B}$ abort, otherwise, for some s^*, $\sigma^* = (h^a \mathcal{F}(M^*)^{s^*}, g^{s^*}) = (h^a g^{s^* J^*}, g^{s^*})$. Then, $\sigma_1^*/(\sigma_2^*)^{J^*} = h^a = g^{ab}$: one has solved the CDH problem.

Success Probability. (Based on [15]) The Waters hash function is $(1, q_s)$-programmable (*i.e.*, we can find with non negligible probability a case where q_s intermediate hashes are not null, and the last one is), therefore the previous simulation succeeds with non negligible probability ($\Theta(\epsilon/q_s\sqrt{k})$), and so $\mathcal{B}$ breaks CDH.   □

Theorem 6. *This signer-friendly partially-blind signature scheme achieves perfect blindness.*

Proof. The transcript sent to the signer contains a commitment on the message to be signed, but in a perfectly hiding setting: no information leaks about M. The additional proofs are perfectly witness-indistinguishable and thus do not provide any additional information about M. This is due to the fact that in the Groth Sahai framework in the perfectly hiding setting, for any message M, committed with randomness r and a message M', one can find random r' such that $c(M, r) = c(M', r')$. Granted the randomizability of the Waters signature, the final output signature is a random signature on $M\|\mathsf{info}_c\|\mathsf{info}_s$, on which no information leaked, and so the resulting signature is perfectly independent from the transcript seen by the signer, and any adversary.   □

4 Multi-source Blind Signature

4.1 Concatenation

The previous constructions lead to a good way to allow a user to obtain a signature on a plaintext without revealing it to the signer. But what happens when the original message is in fact coming from various users? We now present a new way to obtain a blind signature without requiring multiple users to combine their messages, providing once again a round-optimal way to achieve our goal.

We thus consider a variation of our blind signature scheme. In the Setup phase we no longer create perfectly hiding Groth-Sahai generators, but perfectly binding parameters, so we do not need to compute $u_{3,3}^s$ to run Unblind, since it will be performed with the decryption key and not the random coins. In addition, in this scenario, we do not consider a unique user providing a ciphertext, but several users. As a consequence, the signer will have to produce a signature on a multi-source message, provided as ciphertexts. The signature and the messages will actually be encrypted under a third-party key. The third-party only will be able to extract the message and the signature.

Basically the instantiation is similar to the previous ones in the perfectly binding setting. For the sake of clarity, we remove the partially-blind part, but of course it could be adapted in the same way.

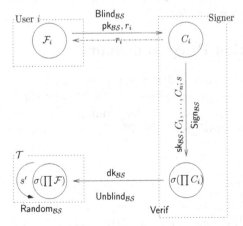

Several messages M_i can be hidden using random coins r_i (Blind$_{\mathcal{BS}}$) by different users.

The signer can adapt these commitments and concatenate the messages inside them, creating a commitment on $\mathcal{F} = \prod \mathcal{F}_i$.

A signature on the plaintext can be obtained by the tallier using the decryption key dk$_{\mathcal{BS}}$ (for Unblind$_{\mathcal{BS}}$); the result is the same as a direct signature on $\|M_i$ by the signer.

Randomizing this signature is easy, and prevent the signer from knowing which ciphertexts were involved.

Fig. 2. Multi-Source Blind Signature on Concatenation

A full instantiation of such protocol and its security analysis can be found in the full version [6]. One can see that it can be efficiently instantiated under DLin assumption.

4.2 Addition

The previous scheme presents a way to combine multiple blind messages into one in order to sign it. However it requires a huge number of generators and the final unblinded signature gives a lot of information on the repartition of the original messages, since they are simply concatenated. We now want to improve the previous scheme to drastically reduce the public key size, and the information leaked about the individual messages when one would like a signature on some computation on these messages, such as the addition or the mean. Instead of signing the concatenation of the messages, we now allow the users to use the same generators, and thus the messages will add together instead of concatenating.

The resulting algorithm is the same as before except during the Setup phase where $\boldsymbol{u} = (u_0, \ldots, u_k) \overset{\$}{\leftarrow} \mathbb{G}^{k+1}$. We then proceed as before considering $\mathcal{F}(M_i) = \prod_\ell u_\ell^{m_{i,\ell}}$. The Unblind algorithm now returns a valid signature on the sum of the messages. The various Groth-Sahai proofs help to ensure that the messages given to the Waters hash function are of reasonable size.

With this construction, the exponents in the Waters hash function are not longer bits but belong to a larger alphabet (*e.g.* $\{0, \ldots, t\}$ if t users sign only bit strings). Following the work done in [15], we will show in the next section that over a non-binary alphabet the Waters function remains $(1, poly)$-programmable as long as the size of the alphabet a polynomial in the security parameter. This result readily implies the security of the multi-source blind signature scheme for addition:

Theorem 7. *This multi-source blind signature scheme for addition is blind and unforgeable under the* DLin *assumption as long the alphabet size and the number of sources are polynomial in the security parameter.*

5   Non-binary Waters Function Programmability

In this section, we prove that for a polynomial-size alphabet, the Waters function remains programmable. We recall some notations introduced in [15] and show our result which can be seen as an improvement over the result presented by Naccache [16] where he considered a variant of Waters identity-based encryption [20] with shorter public parameters.

5.1   Definitions

Let us recall some basic definitions. A family of cyclic groups $G = (\mathbb{G}_\lambda)_{\lambda \in \mathbb{N}}$, indexed by a security parameter λ, is called a *group family*. A *group hash function* H for G, an alphabet $\Sigma = \Sigma(\lambda)$ and an input length $\ell = \ell(\lambda)$ is a pair of probabilistic polynomial-time algorithms (PHF.Gen, PHF.Eval) such that:

- PHF.Gen takes as input a security parameter λ and outputs a key κ.
- PHF.Eval takes as input a key κ output by PHF.Gen and a string $X \in \Sigma^\ell$ and outputs an element of $\mathbb{G}_\lambda$.

Definition 8 (*cf.* [15]). *A group hash function* (PHF.Gen, PHF.Eval) *is* (m, n, δ)-*programmable, if there exist two PPT algorithms* (PHF.TrapGen, PHF.TrapEval) *such that*

- **Syntactics:** *For* $g, h \in \mathbb{G}$, PHF.TrapGen$(1^\lambda, g, h)$ *generates a key* κ' *and a trapdoor* t *such that* PHF.TrapEval(t, X) *produces integers* a_X, b_X *for any* $X \in \Sigma^\ell$
- **Correctness:** *For all generators* $g, h \in \mathbb{G}$, *all* $(\kappa', t) \leftarrow$ PHF.TrapGen$(1^\lambda, g, h)$ *and all* $X \in \Sigma^\ell$, $H_{\kappa'}(X) := $ PHF.Eval(κ', X) *satisfies* $H_{\kappa'}(X) = g^{a_X} h^{b_X}$ *where* $(a_X, b_X) := $ PHF.TrapEval(t, X).
- **Statistically close trapdoor keys:** *For all generators* $g, h \in \mathbb{G}^2$, *the functions* PHF.Gen(1^λ) *and* PHF.TrapGen$(1^\lambda, g, h)$ *output keys* κ *and* κ' *statistically close.*
- **Well-distributed logarithms:** *For all generators* $g, h \in \mathbb{G}$, *all* (κ', t) *output by* PHF.TrapGen$(1^\lambda, g, h)$ *and all bit-strings* $(X_i)_{1,\ldots,m}, (Z_i)_{1,\ldots,n} \in \Sigma^\ell$ *such that* $\forall i, j, X_i \neq Z_j$, *we have* $\Pr[a_{X_1} = \ldots, a_{X_m} = 0 \wedge a_{Z_1} \cdot \ldots \cdot a_{Z_n} \neq 0] \geq \delta$, *where the probability is taken over the random coins used by* PHF.TrapGen *and* $(a_{X_i}, b_{X_i}) := $ PHF.TrapEval(t, X_i) *and* $(a_{Z_i}, b_{Z_i}) := $ PHF.TrapEval(t, Z_i).

5.2 Instantiation with Waters function

Let us consider the Waters function presented in [20].

Definition 9 (Multi-generator PHF). *Let* $G = (\mathbb{G}_\lambda)$ *be a group family, and* $\ell = \ell(\lambda)$ *a polynomial. We define* $\mathcal{F} = $ (PHF.Gen, PHF.Eval) *as the following group hash function:*

- PHF.Gen(1^λ) *outputs* $\kappa = (h_0, \ldots, h_\ell) \overset{\$}{\leftarrow} \mathbb{G}^{\ell+1}$;
- PHF.Eval(κ, X) *parses* κ *and* $X = (x_1, \ldots, x_\ell) \in \{0, 1\}^\ell$ *and outputs* $\mathcal{F}_\kappa(X) = h_0 \prod_{i=1}^\ell h_i^{x_i}$.

This function was shown to be $(1, q, \delta)$-programmable with a $\delta = O(1/(q\sqrt{\ell}))$ and $(2, 1, \delta)$-programmable with a $\delta = O(1/\ell)$ (*cf.* [15]). However this definition requires to generate and store $n+1$ group generators where n is the bit-length of the messages one wants to hash. We consider a more general case where instead of hashing bit-per-bit we decide to hash blocks of bits.

Definition 10 (Improved Multi-generator PHF). *Let* $G = (\mathbb{G}_\lambda)$ *be a group family,* $\Sigma = \{0, \ldots, \tau\}$ *a finite alphabet and* $\ell = \ell(\lambda)$ *a polynomial. We define* $\mathcal{F} = $ (PHF.Gen, PHF.Eval) *as the following group hash function:*

- PHF.Gen(1^λ) *returns* $\kappa = (h_0, \ldots, h_\ell) \overset{\$}{\leftarrow} \mathbb{G}^{\ell+1}$;
- PHF.Eval(κ, X) *parses* κ *and* $X = (x_1, \ldots, x_\ell) \in \Sigma^\ell$ *and returns* $\mathcal{F}^+{}_\kappa(X) = h_0 \prod_{i=1}^\ell h_i^{x_i}$.

Using a larger alphabet allows to hash from a larger domain with a smaller hash key, but it comes at a price since one can easily prove that the function is no longer $(2,1)$-programmable (*i.e.*, no longer $(2,1,\delta)$ programmable for a non-negligible δ):

Theorem 11 ((2,1)-Programmability). *For any group family G with known order and $\tau > 1$, the function $\mathcal{F}^+$ is not a $(2,1)$-programmable hash function if the discrete logarithm problem is hard in G.*

Proof. Consider a discrete logarithm challenge (g, h) in a group $\mathbb{G}_\lambda$ and suppose by contradiction that the function $\mathcal{F}^+$ is $(2,1)$-programmable with $\tau \geq 2$ (*i.e.*, we suppose that there exist two probabilistic polynomial-time algorithms $(\mathsf{PHF.TrapGen}, \mathsf{PHF.TrapEval})$ satisfying the definition 8 for a non-negligible δ).

For any hash key κ' and trapdoor t generated by $\mathsf{PHF.TrapGen}(1^\lambda, g, h)$, we can consider the messages $X_1 = (2, 0), X_2 = (1, 1), Z = (0, 2)$ and with non-negligible probability over the random coins used by $\mathsf{PHF.TrapGen}$ we have $a_{X_1} = a_{X_2} = 0$ and $a_Z \neq 0$ where $(a_{X_1}, b_{X_1}) := \mathsf{PHF.TrapEval}(t, X_1)$, $(a_{X_2}, b_{X_2}) := \mathsf{PHF.TrapEval}(t, X_2)$ and $(a_Z, b_Z) := \mathsf{PHF.TrapEval}(t, Z)$. By the correctness property, we have $g^{a_Z} h^{b_Z} = h_0 h_2^2 = h^{2b_{X_2}} / h^{b_{X_1}}$ and we can extract the discrete logarithm of g in base h as follows:

$$\log_h(g) = \frac{2b_{X_2} - b_{X_1} - b_Z}{a_Z} \quad \mathrm{mod}\ |\mathbb{G}_\lambda|. \qquad \square$$

However we still have the interesting property:

Theorem 12 ((1,poly)-Programmability). *For any polynomial q and a group family G with groups of known order, the function $\mathcal{F}^+$ is a $(1, q, \delta)$-programmable hash function with a $\delta = \Omega(1/\tau q\sqrt{\ell})$.*

Remark 13. This theorem improves the result presented by Naccache in [16] where the lower bound on the $(1, q, \delta)$-programmability was only $\delta = \Omega(1/\tau q\ell)$.

Remark 14. In order to be able to sign all messages in a set $\mathcal{M}$, we have to consider parameters τ and ℓ such that $\tau^\ell \geq \#\mathcal{M}$, but the security is proved only if the value δ is non-negligible (*i.e.* if $\ell = \lambda^{O(1)}$ and $\tau = \lambda^{O(1)}$). In particular if $\mathcal{M}$ is of polynomial size in λ (which is the case in our WSN application with data aggregation), one can use $\tau = \#\mathcal{M}$ and $\ell = 1$ (namely, the Boneh-Boyen hash function), and therefore get data confidentiality.

Proof. Let us first introduce some notations. Let $n \in \mathbb{N}^*$, let A_j be independent and uniform random variables in $\{-1, 0, 1\}$ (for $j \in \{1, \ldots, n\}$). If we denote $2\sigma_j^2$ their quadratic moment, we have $2\sigma_j^2 = 2/3$ and $\sigma_j = \sqrt{1/3}$. We note $s_n^2 = \sum_{j=1}^n \sigma_j^2 = n/3$.

The Local Central Limit Theorem. Our analysis relies on a classical result on random walks, called the *Local Central Limit Theorem*. It basically provides an approximation of $\Pr[\sum A_j = a]$ for independent random variables A_j. This is a version of the Central Limit Theorem in which the conclusion is strengthened from convergence of the law to locally uniform pointwise convergence of the densities. It is worded as follows in [10, *Theorem 1.1*], where ϕ and Φ are the standard normal density and distribution functions:

Theorem 15. *Let A_j be independent, integer-valued random variables where A_j has probability mass function f_j (for $j \in \mathbb{N}^*$). For each $j, n \in \mathbb{N}^*$, let $q(f_j) = \sum_k \min(f_j(k), f_j(k+1))$ and $Q_n = \sum_{j=1}^n q(f_j)$. Denote $S_n = A_1 + \cdots + A_n$. Suppose that there are sequences of numbers $(\alpha_n), (\beta_n)$ such that*

1. $\lim_{n \to \infty} \Pr[(S_n - \alpha_n)/\beta_n) < t] = \Phi(t), -\infty < t < \infty,$
2. $\beta_n \to \infty,$
3. *and* $\limsup \beta_n^2/Q_n < \infty,$

then $\sup_k |\beta_n \Pr[S_n = k] - \phi((k - \alpha_n)/\beta_n)| \to 0$ *as* $n \to \infty$[1].

While those notations may seem a little overwhelming, this can be easily explained in our case. With $A_j \in \{-1, 0, 1\}$ with probability $1/3$ for each value.

1. It requires the variables to verify the Lindeberg-Feller theorem. However as long as the variables verify the Lindeberg's condition[2], this is true for $\beta_n = s_n$ and $\alpha_n = 0$.
2. In our application, $\beta_n = s_n = \sqrt{n/3}$, so again we comply with the condition.
3. Since $f_j(k)$ is simply the probability that A_j equals k, then $q(f_j) = 2/3$. This leads to $Q_n = 2n/3$. As a consequence, $\beta_n^2/Q_n = 1/2$.

So we have: $\sup_k |\beta_n \Pr[S_n = k] - \phi((k - \alpha_n)/\beta_n)| \to 0$, that is, in our case

$$\sup_k |\sqrt{n/3} \Pr[S_n = k] - \phi(k/\sqrt{n/3})| \to 0.$$

We solely focus on the case $k = 0$: since $\phi(0) = 1/\sqrt{2\pi}$, $\Pr[S_n = 0] = \Theta(1/\sqrt{n})$. In addition, it is clear that $\Pr[S_n = k] \leq \Pr[S_n = 0]$ for any $k \neq 0$ (*c.f.* [15]).

Lemma 16. *Let $(A_{ij})_{[1,n] \times [1,J]}$ be independent, integer-valued random variables in $\{-1, 0, 1\}$, then $\forall X \in [1, \tau]^n$, $\Pr[\sum_{i=1}^n \sum_{j=1}^J X_i A_{ij} = 0] = \Omega(1/\tau\sqrt{nJ})$, where the probability distribution is over the A_{ij}.*

This lemma will be useful to prove the lower bound in the following, we only consider word with no null coefficient X_i, if a X_i is null, we simply work with a shorter random walk of length $J \cdot (n - 1)$ instead of Jn.

Proof. Let us denote d_{ij}, the random variable defined as $X_i A_{ij}$: they are independent, integer-valued random variables. As above, $s_n^2 = \sum_{i=1}^n \sum_{j=1}^J \sigma_j^2 = \sum_{i=1}^n JX_i^2/3$. So $nJ/3 \leq s_n^2 \leq n\tau^2 J/3$.

---

[1] The so-called Berry-Esseen theorem gives the rate of convergence of this supremum.
[2] Lindeberg's condition is a sufficient criteria of the Lindeberg-Feller theorem, for variables with a null expected value it requires that $\forall \epsilon > 0, \lim_{n \to \infty} 1/s_n^2 \sum_{j=1}^n E[A_j^2 \cdot 1_{\{|A_j| > \epsilon s_n\}}] \to 0$. In our case, as soon as $n > 3/\epsilon^2$, we have $|A_j| \leq 1 \leq \epsilon\sqrt{n/3} \leq \epsilon s_n$, so the sum is null. ($1_{\{|A_j| > \epsilon s_n\}}$ is the indicator function of variables greater that ϵs_n)

1. The Lindeberg's condition is verified. As soon as $n > 3\tau/J\epsilon^2$ we have $\epsilon s_n > \tau$ and so $|d_{ij}| < s_n$, and so once again the sum is null.
2. $s_n \to \infty$.
3. Each $d_{ij} \in \{-X_i, 0, X_i\}$ with probability $1/3$ for each value, so $q(f_{ij}) = 2/3$ and $Q_n = \sum_{i,j} q(f_{ij}) = 2nJ/3$. So $\beta_n^2/Q_n \leq (n\tau J/3)/(2nJ/3) \leq \tau/2 < \infty$.

Then we can apply the Local Central Limit Theorem to the d_{ij}'s, and conclude:
$\Pr[\sum_{i=1}^n \sum_{j=1}^J X_i A_{ij} = 0] = \Theta(1/s_n) = \Theta(1/\tau\sqrt{(nJ)})$.   □

In the following, we will denote $a(X) = \sum_{i=1}^n a_i X_i$, where $X \in \{0, \ldots, \tau\}^n$. The probabilities will be over the a_{ij}'s variables while X and Y are assumed to be chosen by the adversary. Our goal is to show that even for bad choices of X and Y, a random draw of a_{ij}'s provides enough freedom.

Let $J = J(\lambda)$ be a positive function. We define the following two probabilistic polynomial-time algorithms (PHF.TrapGen, PHF.TrapEval):

- PHF.TrapGen($1^\lambda, g, h$): which chooses some independent and uniform elements $(a_{ij})_{(0,\ldots,\ell),(1,\ldots,J)}$ in $\{-1, 0, 1\}$, and random group exponents $(b_i)_{(0,\ldots,\ell)}$. It sets $a_i = \sum_{j=1}^J a_{ij}$ and $h_i = g^{a_i} h^{b_i}$ for $i \in \{0, \ldots, \ell\}$. It then outputs the hash key $\kappa = (h_0, \ldots, h_\ell)$ and the trapdoor $t = (a_0, b_0, \ldots, a_\ell, b_\ell)$.
- PHF.TrapEval(t, X): which parses $X = (X_1, \ldots, X_\ell) \in \Sigma^\ell = \{0, \ldots, \tau\}^\ell$ and outputs $a_X = a_0 + \sum a_i X_i$ and $b_X = b_0 + \sum b_i X_i$.

As this definition verifies readily the syntactic and correctness requirements, we only have to prove the two other ones. We stress the importance of the hardwired 1 in front of a_0 this allows us to consider multisets $X' = 1 :: X$ and $Y' = 1 :: Y$, and so there is no k such that $X' = kY'$. And we also stress that $a_i = \sum_{j=1}^J a_{ij}$ is already a random walk of length J (described by the a_{ij}), on which we can apply the Local Central Limit Theorem and so $\Pr[a_i = 0] = \Theta(1/\sqrt{J})$. By noticing that summing independent random walks is equivalent to a longer one and applying the Local Central Limit Theorem, we have:

$$\Theta(1/\tau\sqrt{(\ell+1)J}) \leq \Pr[a(X') = 0] \leq \Theta(1/\sqrt{J}).$$

To explain further the two bounds:

- For the upper bound: we consider X fixed, and note $t = \sum_{i=1}^\ell a_i X_i$, by construction a_i are independent, so a_0 is independent from t then
$$\Pr[a(X') = 0] = \Pr[a_0 = -t] \leq \Pr[a_0 = 0] \leq \Theta(1/\sqrt{J})$$
using the above remark that a random walk is more likely to reach 0 than any other value, and a_0 is a random walk of length J.
- For the lower bound, we proceed by recurrence on ℓ, to show
$$H_\ell : \Theta(1/\tau\sqrt{(\ell+1)J}) \leq \Pr[a(X') = 0] \quad (\text{where } X' \in 1 :: [\![0, \tau]\!]^\ell).$$

For $\ell = 0$, we consider $X' = 1$, we have a random walk of length J, so $\Theta(1/\tau\sqrt{J}) \leq \Theta(1/\sqrt{J}) \leq \Pr[a(X') = 0]$. We note $X_0 = 1$ for the hardwired 1 in X'. Let us suppose the property true at rank k, let us prove it at rank $k + 1$:

- If $\exists i_0, X_{i_0} = 0$ then we can consider a random walk of length k and apply the previous step, and conclude because $\Theta(1/\tau\sqrt{(k+1)J}) \leq \Theta(1/\tau\sqrt{kJ})$
- Else, one can apply Lemma 16 to conclude.

Therefore, $\forall \ell, \forall X' \in 1 :: [0,\tau]^\ell, \Theta(1/\tau\sqrt{(\ell+1)J}) \leq \Pr[a(X') = 0]$.

We can now deduce that $\forall X, Y \in [0,\tau]^\ell$ with $X \neq Y$: $\Pr[a(Y') = 0|a(X') = 0] \leq \Theta(1/\sqrt{J})$. This can easily be seen by noting i_0 the first index where $Y_i \neq X_i$. We will note $\bar{X}' = X' - X_{i_0}$, in the following we will use the fact that $a(X') = 0 \Leftrightarrow a(\bar{X}') = -a_{i_0}X_{i_0}.$[3]

$$\Pr[a(Y') = 0|a(X') = 0] \leq \Pr[a(Y') = a(X')|a(X') = 0]$$
$$\leq \Pr[Y_{i_0}a_{i_0} + a(\bar{Y}') = X_{i_0}a_{i_0} + a(\bar{X}')|a(X') = 0]$$
$$\leq \max_t \Pr[(Y_{i_0} - X_{i_0})a_{i_0} = t|a(\bar{X}') = -X_{i_0}a_{i_0}] \quad (1)$$
$$\leq \max_{s,t'} \Pr[a_{i_0} = t'|a(\bar{X}') = s] \quad (2)$$
$$\leq \max_{t'} \Pr[a_{i_0} = t'] \quad (3)$$
$$\leq \Pr[a_{i_0} = 0] \leq \Theta(1/\sqrt{J})$$

(1) we start with $(Y_{i_0} - X_{i_0})a_{i_0} = a(\bar{X}') - a(\bar{Y}')$, and then consider the maximum probability for all values $a(\bar{X}') - a(\bar{Y}')$.
(2) We consider the maximum probability for all values of $-X_{i_0}a_{i_0}$.
(3) a_{i_0} and $a(\bar{X}')$ are independent.

Hence, for all $X_1, Y_1, \ldots, Y_q$, we have

$$\Pr[a_{X_1} = 0 \wedge a_{Y_1}, \ldots, a_{Y_q} \neq 0] = \Pr[a_{X_1} = 0]\Pr[a_{Y_1}, \ldots, a_{Y_q} \neq 0|a_{X_1} = 0]$$
$$\geq \Theta(1/\tau\sqrt{\ell J})\left(1 - \sum_{i=1}^{q}\Pr[a_{Y_i} = 0|a_{X_1} = 0]\right)$$
$$\geq \Theta(1/\tau\sqrt{\ell+1 J})(1 - q\Theta(1/\sqrt{J})).$$

Now we set $J = q^2$, to obtain the result. In that case the experiment success is lower-bounded by something linear in $1/(q\tau\sqrt{\ell+1})$. $\qquad\square$

Acknowledgments. This work was supported by the European Commission through the ICT Program under Contract ICT-2007-216676 ECRYPT II.

References

1. Abe, M., Fuchsbauer, G., Groth, J., Haralambiev, K., Ohkubo, M.: Structure-Preserving Signatures and Commitments to Group Elements. In: Rabin, T. (ed.) CRYPTO 2010. LNCS, vol. 6223, pp. 209–236. Springer, Heidelberg (2010)
2. Abe, M., Fujisaki, E.: How to Date Blind Signatures. In: Kim, K., Matsumoto, T. (eds.) ASIACRYPT 1996. LNCS, vol. 1163, pp. 244–251. Springer, Heidelberg (1996)

---

[3] $X \neq Y$ so i_0 exists, and thanks to the hardwired 1 we do not have to worry about Y' being a multiple of X'

3. Abe, M., Okamoto, T.: Provably Secure Partially Blind Signatures. In: Bellare, M. (ed.) CRYPTO 2000. LNCS, vol. 1880, pp. 271–286. Springer, Heidelberg (2000)
4. Blazy, O., Fuchsbauer, G., Pointcheval, D., Vergnaud, D.: Signatures on Randomizable Ciphertexts. In: Catalano, D., Fazio, N., Gennaro, R., Nicolosi, A. (eds.) PKC 2011. LNCS, vol. 6571, pp. 403–422. Springer, Heidelberg (2011)
5. Blazy, O., Pointcheval, D., Vergnaud, D.: Round-Optimal Privacy-Preserving Protocols with Smooth Projective Hash Functions. In: Cramer, R. (ed.) TCC 2012. LNCS, vol. 7194, pp. 94–111. Springer, Heidelberg (2012)
6. Blazy, O., Pointcheval, D., Vergnaud, D.: Compact Round-Optimal Partially-Blind Signatures. In: Visconti, I., De Prisco, R. (eds.) SCN 2012, vol. 7485, pp. 93–110. Springer, Heidelberg (2012)
7. Boneh, D., Boyen, X., Shacham, H.: Short Group Signatures. In: Franklin, M. (ed.) CRYPTO 2004. LNCS, vol. 3152, pp. 41–55. Springer, Heidelberg (2004)
8. Boyen, X., Waters, B.: Compact Group Signatures Without Random Oracles. In: Vaudenay, S. (ed.) EUROCRYPT 2006. LNCS, vol. 4004, pp. 427–444. Springer, Heidelberg (2006)
9. Chaum, D.: Blind signatures for untraceable payments. In: CRYPTO 1982, pp. 199–203. Plenum Press, New York (1983)
10. Davis, B., McDonald, D.: An elementary proof of the local central limit theorem. Journal of Theoretical Probability 8(3) (July 1995)
11. Fischlin, M.: Round-Optimal Composable Blind Signatures in the Common Reference String Model. In: Dwork, C. (ed.) CRYPTO 2006. LNCS, vol. 4117, pp. 60–77. Springer, Heidelberg (2006)
12. Fuchsbauer, G.: Commuting signatures and verifiable encryption and an application to non-interactively delegatable credentials. Cryptology ePrint Archive, Report 2010/233 (2010)
13. Garg, S., Rao, V., Sahai, A., Schröder, D., Unruh, D.: Round Optimal Blind Signatures. In: Rogaway, P. (ed.) CRYPTO 2011. LNCS, vol. 6841, pp. 630–648. Springer, Heidelberg (2011)
14. Groth, J., Sahai, A.: Efficient Non-interactive Proof Systems for Bilinear Groups. In: Smart, N.P. (ed.) EUROCRYPT 2008. LNCS, vol. 4965, pp. 415–432. Springer, Heidelberg (2008)
15. Hofheinz, D., Kiltz, E.: Programmable Hash Functions and Their Applications. In: Wagner, D. (ed.) CRYPTO 2008. LNCS, vol. 5157, pp. 21–38. Springer, Heidelberg (2008)
16. Naccache, D.: Secure and practical identity-based encryption. Cryptology ePrint Archive, Report 2005/369 (2005)
17. Okamoto, T.: Efficient Blind and Partially Blind Signatures Without Random Oracles. In: Halevi, S., Rabin, T. (eds.) TCC 2006. LNCS, vol. 3876, pp. 80–99. Springer, Heidelberg (2006)
18. Pointcheval, D., Stern, J.: Security arguments for digital signatures and blind signatures. Journal of Cryptology 13(3), 361–396 (2000)
19. Seo, J.H., Cheon, J.H.: Beyond the Limitation of Prime-Order Bilinear Groups, and Round Optimal Blind Signatures. In: Cramer, R. (ed.) TCC 2012. LNCS, vol. 7194, pp. 133–150. Springer, Heidelberg (2012)
20. Waters, B.: Efficient Identity-Based Encryption Without Random Oracles. In: Cramer, R. (ed.) EUROCRYPT 2005. LNCS, vol. 3494, pp. 114–127. Springer, Heidelberg (2005)

History-Free Sequential Aggregate Signatures

Marc Fischlin[1], Anja Lehmann[2], and Dominique Schröder[3]

[1] Darmstadt University of Technology, Germany
[2] IBM Research Zurich, Switzerland
[3] University of Maryland, USA & Saarland University, Germany

Abstract. Aggregation schemes allow to combine several cryptographic values like message authentication codes or signatures into a shorter value such that, despite compression, some notion of unforgeability is preserved. Recently, Eikemeier et al. (SCN 2010) considered the notion of *history-free* sequential aggregation for message authentication codes, where the sequentially-executed aggregation algorithm does not need to receive the previous messages in the sequence as input. Here we discuss the idea for signatures where the new aggregate does not rely on the previous messages and public keys either, thus inhibiting the costly verifications in each aggregation step as in previous schemes by Lysyanskaya et al. (Eurocrypt 2004) and Neven (Eurocrypt 2008). Analogously to MACs we argue about new security definitions for such schemes and compare them to previous notions for history-dependent schemes. We finally give a construction based on the BLS signature scheme which satisfies our notion.

1 Introduction

Aggregate signature schemes [6] allow to combine multiple signatures from different senders for possibly different messages, such that the aggregate has roughly the same size as a single signature. This helps to reduce the communication overhead in settings where authenticated information is forwarded from one party to another, such as the S-BGP routing protocol or certificate chains [6,13,3,5]. As in the case of regular signature schemes, the validity of aggregates can be publicly verified given all messages and public keys.

The original proposal of Boneh at al. [6] supports aggregation of the data independently of the order of the parties and, furthermore, the aggregating algorithm only relies on the aggregates and public data. In contrast, most other solutions today like [14,13,5,3,16,17] are *sequential* aggregate schemes where each party derives the next aggregate by taking the private key, the previous aggregate, and all the previous messages together with the corresponding keys in the sequence into account. For instance, in all[1] known sequential signature schemes the aggregation algorithm first checks with the public keys that the current aggregate

---

[1] With the exception of the recent work by Brogle et al. [8], discussed at the end of the introduction.

I. Visconti and R. De Prisco (Eds.): SCN 2012, LNCS 7485, pp. 113–130, 2012.
© Springer-Verlag Berlin Heidelberg 2012

is a valid signature for the preceding message sequence. Often, they also incorporate these messages in the computation of the new aggregate. Thus, so far, the aggregation in sequential signature schemes seems to be much more expensive than in the non-sequential setting, which might render sequential schemes impractical for resource-constraint devices. Another issue, pointed out in [8], is that the verification requires also obtaining and checking the public keys of the users in the sequence.

1.1 History-Free Sequential Aggregation

Recently, Eikemeier et al. [10] introduced the notion of *history-freeness* in the context of aggregate MACs, which aims to preserve the "lightweight" aggregation approach from general aggregate schemes also in the sequential setting. More precisely, in a history-free MAC a new aggregate is derived only from the aggregate-so-far and the local message, but does not rely on (explicit) access to the previous messages. Note that, strictly speaking, the aggregate-so-far certainly contains some information about the previous messages; this information, however, is limited due to the size restriction for aggregates.

In this work we adopt the notion of history-freeness to the case of sequential aggregate *signatures*, only allowing the aggregate-so-far, the local message, and signing key to enter the computation, but not the previous messages and public keys in the sequence. For signatures this property is especially worthwhile, because it means that the costly signature verifications for each aggregation step are suppressed. In fact, since the security of previous schemes strongly relies on such checks, omitting them indicates the hardness of finding history-free schemes. Eikemeier et al. [10] achieve this, to some extent, for the case of MACs by using an underlying pseudorandom permutation to encrypt parts of the data. This is usually not an admissible strategy for the case of signatures.

At first, history-free sequential aggregation might seem to be the second best solution compared to non-ordered aggregation (with history-free aggregation quasi built in). However, sequential aggregation is required for many applications such as for authenticating routing information or for certificate chains, and in these applications the verifiability of the order of signing steps is usually important, whereas general aggregate schemes do not allow this. Following the terminology for multi-signatures [5] we call such schemes ordered sequential-aggregate schemes. We also remark that all known sequential aggregate schemes are ordered, except for the one by Lu et al. [13], and that we usually consider history-freeness only in connection with such ordered schemes.

1.2 New Security Models

Introducing the idea of history-freeness affects known security definitions for sequential signature schemes. Since the history of previously signed messages is not available to the aggregation algorithm, an adversary can now initiate aggregation chains "from the middle", without specifying how the initial message sequence looks like. The starting aggregate for such a truncated iteration does not even need to be valid, as checking the validity of the aggregate with respect to the preceding message sequence is impossible for the aggregation algorithm.

Our security notions for history-free schemes, adopted from the work by Eikemeier et al. [10], follow the well-known approach for (regular and aggregate) signatures that an adversary can request data via oracles and is supposed to eventually output a valid but non-trivial forgery. In the original LMRS security model for sequential aggregation with full information about preceding messages [14], the adversary is considered to win if it produces a valid aggregate for a non-trivial sequence, where trivial sequences are previously queried sequences and, since appending some iterations for controlled parties is easy for the adversary, such extended sequences thereof.

Specifying the trivial combinations in our history-free model is more delicate because the adversary now gets to query partial chains and can potentially glue several of these data together. We resolve this by following the approach of Eikemeier et al., that is, by defining a transitive closure of trivial sequences, consisting of matching combinations of (possibly many) previously seen aggregates and contributions by corrupt parties. We define two versions of this closure, depending on whether intermediate values of partial chains are available to the adversary or not, yielding two security notions (one being stronger and implying the other). Intuitively, due to the additional adversarial power, one would expect our new security models to be weaker than the original ones for sequential aggregation. Interestingly, though, both our security notions for history-freeness are strictly stronger than the security model for sequential aggregation due to Lu et al. [13], but incomparable to the one of Lysyanskaya et al. [14], as we show in Section 3.3. Even more remarkably, by slightly relaxing the requirement for history-freeness, we can easily achieve the [14] security property (on top of our aggregation-unforgeability notion) if we simply prepend the hash value of all previous public keys and messages in the sequence to the message to be signed next. By this we get a strongly secure sequential aggregate signature which does not need verification of all preceding signatures!

We also briefly revisit the case of non-ordered aggregates. Here, adapting the idea of the closure yields strictly stronger security guarantees than in previous definitions for non-sequential schemes. Our models, both for sequential and for non-ordered schemes, reflect the resistance of aggregate schemes against "mix-and-match" attacks, where an attacker is already considered successful if it can recombine learned aggregates into a "fresh" aggregate that it has not seen before, or is able to remove parts of the aggregates. This is opposed to the common approach of reducing the unforgeability of aggregation schemes to the unforgeability of individual messages, where combining aggregates or removing a party's contribution are not deemed to be successful attacks (because they do not forge an individual signature). This is discussed for the symmetric setting in more detail in [10]. Yet, we are not aware if that high security standard can be achieved for aggregate signatures. Nonetheless, as a side effect of our approach, we point out that the scheme by Boneh et al. [6] allows attacks which are not covered by their security models. The discussion appears in Section 5.

1.3 Building History-Free Schemes

We finally provide a solution meeting our requirements in Section 4. We give a construction based on the signature scheme of Boneh et al. [7], which has already been successfully transformed into the BGLS scheme for non-sequential aggregation [6]. By this we derive a scheme for history-free sequential aggregation. Observe again that the resulting scheme also comes with the verifiability of the aggregation order.

Our construction chains the aggregates with the help of a collision-resistant hash function, i.e., instead of signing only the local message, we first compute the hash value of this message together with the previous aggregate.[2] Hence, instead of verifying a chain of signatures our aggregation algorithm only needs to compute bilinear mappings. The aggregates of our scheme are slightly larger than the ones of the original BGLS scheme and the construction satisfies our weaker security notion.

1.4 Concurrent Work

Recently, Brogle et al. [8] proposed a notion of sequential aggregate signatures with so-called lazy verification, resembling the idea of history-freeness as defined in [10] and also used here closely. They designed and implemented a history-free scheme based on trapdoor permutations, with a special focus on the BGPsec protocol [12]. Their security model, albeit appropriate for the BGPsec case, is a relaxation of the LMRS model which is implied by (even the weaker version of) our security notion. The reason is roughly that this relaxation merely demands that the message in the forgery has not been signed by the honest user before, implying that it cannot be in the closure and therefore also constitutes a breach of security in our model. We note that the relaxed LMRS notion does not cover the class of mix-and-match attacks discussed in [10] and here. The construction in [8] produces signatures proportional to the number of signers and explicitly relies on the random oracle model. In contrast, our scheme generates signatures of size independent of the number of signers, only implicitly relies on the random oracle model through the currently best proof for the underlying BLS signature scheme in the random oracle model. Our solution comes with stronger unforgeability guarantees (under reasonable cryptographic assumptions).

2 Preliminaries

2.1 Sequential Aggregate Signature Schemes

An aggregate signature [6] is a single signature of different signers on different messages such that this aggregate has roughly the same size as an ordinary

---

[2] The tricky part here is that we do not use the aggregate as it is, but first apply the underlying bilinear mapping to it, before giving it to the hash function. This is necessary to allow verification of aggregates without seeing individual signatures and relies on specific properties of the BLS scheme.

signature. In the sequential case the aggregation algorithm gets as input a sequence of public keys $\mathbf{pk} = (pk_1, \ldots, pk_i)$ and messages $\mathbf{M} = (M_1, \ldots, M_i)$, an aggregate σ' for this sequence, a message M and the secret signing key sk (with corresponding public key pk). It returns the new aggregate σ for the sequence $\mathbf{pk}\|pk := (pk_1, \ldots, pk_i, pk)$ and $\mathbf{M}\|M := (M_1, \ldots, M_i, M)$. More formally:

Definition 1 (Sequential Aggregate Signature Scheme). *A sequential aggregate signature scheme is a tuple of efficient algorithms* SAS = (SeqKg, SeqAgg, SeqAggVf), *where*

Key Generation. SeqKg(1^n) *generates a key pair* (sk, pk) *where* pk *is recoverable from* sk.

Signature Aggregation. *The aggregation algorithm* SeqAgg$(sk, M, \sigma', \mathbf{M}, \mathbf{pk})$ *takes as input a secret key* sk, *a message* $M \in \{0,1\}^*$, *an aggregate* σ' *and sequences* $\mathbf{M} = (M_1, \ldots, M_i)$ *of messages and* $\mathbf{pk} = (pk_1, \ldots, pk_i)$ *of public keys and computes the aggregate* σ *for message sequence* $\mathbf{M}\|M = (M_1, \ldots, M_i, M)$ *and key sequence* $\mathbf{pk}\|pk = (pk_1, \ldots, pk_i, pk)$. *(We assume that there is a special "starting" symbol* $\sigma_0 = \emptyset$ *for the empty aggregate, different from all other possible aggregates.)*

Aggregate Verification. *The algorithm* SeqAggVf$(\mathbf{pk}, \mathbf{M}, \sigma)$ *takes as input a sequence of public keys* $\mathbf{pk} = (pk_1, \ldots, pk_i)$, *a sequence of messages* $\mathbf{M} = (M_1, \ldots, M_i)$ *as well as an aggregate* σ. *It returns a bit.*

The scheme is complete if for any sequence of key pairs $(sk, pk), (sk_1, pk_1), \ldots \leftarrow$ SeqKg(1^n), *for any sequence* $\mathbf{M}$ *of messages, any* $M \in \{0,1\}^*$, *for any* $\sigma \leftarrow$ SeqAgg$(sk, M, \sigma', \mathbf{M}, \mathbf{pk})$ *with* SeqAggVf$(\mathbf{pk}, \mathbf{M}, \sigma') = 1$ *or* $\sigma' = \emptyset$, *we have* SeqAggVf$(\mathbf{pk}\|pk, \mathbf{M}\|M, \sigma) = 1$.

Note that we do not define "pure" signing and verification algorithms but only the aggregate counterparts. We can specify such algorithms in a straightforward way via the aggregation algorithm run on the starting aggregate σ_0. In fact, this is often how, vice versa, the aggregation algorithm works on this empty sequence. Second, we do not put any formal restriction on the size of aggregates, in the sense that aggregates must be smaller than individual signatures. Such restrictions can be always met by first "inflating" regular signatures artificially. We thus leave it to common sense to exclude such trivial examples. Finally, throughout the paper we assume that public keys of parties are unique, say, they include the identity and a sequence number as common in certificates.

2.2 LMRS Security of Sequential Aggregate Schemes

Lysyanskaya et al. [14] propose a security model for sequential aggregate signature schemes based on the chosen-key model of [4,6]. The adversary gets as input a challenge public key pk_c and has access to a sequential aggregate signing oracle SeqAgg$(sk_c, \cdots)$ which takes a message M, an aggregate σ' and sequences $\mathbf{M}$ and $\mathbf{pk}$ as input and returns the new aggregate σ. The adversary wins if it manages to output a valid sequential aggregate signature for a sequence $\mathbf{M}^* = (M_1^*, \ldots, M_i^*)$

under public keys $\mathbf{pk}^* = (pk_1^*, \ldots, pk_i^*)$ and $\mathbf{pk}^*$ contains the challenge key pk_c and the sequence $(M_1^*, \ldots, M_{i_c}^*)$ with $(pk_1^*, \ldots, pk_{i_c}^*)$ has never been queried to oracle SeqAgg, where i_c denotes the index of pk_c in $\mathbf{pk}^*$.

For the sake of distinctiveness with the unforgeability notion for regular signature schemes we call schemes being immune against such adversaries *sequentially unforgeable*:

Definition 2. *A sequential aggregate signature scheme* SAS $=$ (SeqKg, SeqAgg, SeqAggVf) *is* sequentially unforgeable *if for any efficient algorithm* $\mathcal{A}$ *the probability that the experiment* SeqForge$_{\mathcal{A}}^{\mathsf{SAS}}$ *evaluates to 1 is negligible (as a function of n), where*

Experiment SeqForge$_{\mathcal{A}}^{\mathsf{SAS}}(n)$
    $(sk_c, pk_c), \leftarrow \mathsf{SeqKg}(1^n)$
    $(\mathbf{pk}^*, \mathbf{M}^*, \sigma^*) \leftarrow \mathcal{A}^{\mathsf{SeqAgg}(sk_c, \cdots)}(pk_c)$
    Let i_c be the index of pk_c in $\mathbf{pk}^* = (pk_1^*, \ldots, pk_\ell^*)$ *and* $\mathbf{M}^* = (M_1^*, \ldots, M_\ell^*)$.
    Return 1 iff $\mathsf{SeqAggVf}(\mathbf{pk}^*, \mathbf{M}^*, \sigma^*) = 1$
      and $pk_c \in \mathbf{pk}^*$ and $pk_i \neq pk_j$ for $1 \leq i < j \leq \ell$ and
      $\mathcal{A}$ *never queried* $\mathsf{SeqAgg}(sk_c, \cdots)$ *about* $(M_1^*, \ldots, M_{i_c}^*)$, $(pk_1^*, \ldots, pk_{i_c}^*)$.

3   Security of History-Free Sequential Signatures

3.1   History-Freeness

So far, sequential aggregate schemes usually include the previous messages and public keys when deriving the new aggregate. This is a crucial disadvantage compared to the "lightweight" aggregation in non-sequential schemes, where the aggregation only depends on the previous signatures. To circumvent this issue we now apply the recently proposed notion of history-freeness [10] which restricts the input for the aggregation algorithm to the aggregate-so-far and the local message, i.e., the aggregation does not get access to the previous messages and keys. More formally:

Definition 3 (History-Freeness). *A sequential aggregate signature scheme* SAS $=$ (SeqKg, SeqAgg, SeqAggVf) *is called* history-free *if there exists an efficient algorithm* SeqAgg$_{hf}$ *such that* $\mathsf{SeqAgg}_{hf}(\cdot, \cdot, \cdot) = \mathsf{SeqAgg}(\cdot, \cdot, \cdot, \mathbf{M}, \mathbf{pk})$ *for all* $\mathbf{M}, \mathbf{pk}$.

To save on notation we will often identify SeqAgg$_{hf}$ with SeqAgg and simply omit $\mathbf{M}, \mathbf{pk}$ from the input of SeqAgg.

Note that history-free sequential signature schemes are not the same as non-sequential aggregate signatures as defined by Boneh et al. [6]. As mentioned in the introduction, the security requirement for (history-free) sequential schemes often allows to check the order of the signers, in contrast to non-sequential schemes.

3.2   Security Model

When considering history-free signature schemes the LMRS security model for
sequential schemes [14] does not fully reflect the new conditions of the adversary
and the desired security guarantees. This stems from the fact that in the history-
free setting the previously signed messages are not available to the aggregation
algorithm, which allows an adversary to trigger new aggregation chains "from
the middle" without knowing the previous message sequence. To capture those
attacks we modify the aggregation oracle such that it returns aggregates for
sequences of messages, starting now with an arbitrary aggregate-so-far. Thus,
we also incorporate some ideas of the *aggregation-unforgeability* notion [10] into
our new model.

Aggregation-unforgeability here demands that the adversary cannot output a
valid chain, unless its a trivial combination of previous aggregation queries and
values by corrupt parties. An example of such a trivial combination is depicted
in Figure 1, where the adversary computes the final value by simply iterating
through the sequence with the help of the aggregation oracle and local computations by corrupt players. Note that each aggregation query is for a sequence
of honest parties and this requires several public keys.

Attack Scenario. As in the aggregation-unforgeability model of Eikemeier et al.
for aggregated MACs, we also grant the adversary in our model an aggregation
oracle returning aggregates for (ordered) *sets* of messages. To allow reasonable
aggregation queries we hand the adversary now t genuine public keys $pk_1, \ldots, pk_t$
of initially honest parties as in [15], instead of considering a single challenge key
as in the chosen-key model [4,6].

The adversary's attack is divided into two phases. In the first phase, the
adversary has access to a corruption and a key-setting oracle, both initialized
with the t key pairs $((sk_1, pk_1) \ldots, (sk_t, pk_t))$. By querying the corruption oracle
the adversary can obtain at most $t - 1$ secret keys of his choice. We denote by
Q_{Cor} the set of corrupted keys. To model rogue-key attacks we also provide an
oracle SetKey which allows the adversary to change the public key of a previously
corrupted party, i.e., on input pk, pk^* the oracle replaces the public key pk of a
corrupt party by pk^*. Recall that we assume that public keys must be unique.
Any modifications of corrupted keys are captured by the set Q_{Cor} as well.

The adversary starts the second phase by interacting with the sequential
aggregate signature oracle OSeqAgg but is denied access to the corruption or
key-setting oracle in this phase (reflecting static corruptions[3]). On input of
an aggregate-so-far σ', a sequence of new messages $\mathbf{M}$ for public keys $\mathbf{pk}$ the
OSeqAgg oracle checks whether all public keys in $\mathbf{pk}$ are distinct and belong to
honest parties. If an invalid public key appears OSeqAgg answers $\perp$, otherwise
it responds with a new valid aggregate σ derived by running the aggregation
algorithm stepwise for all input data. We remark that the aggregation oracle

---

[3] We observe that the standard strategy to lift security against static corruptions to
security against adaptive corruptions by guessing the right "target" key in advance
does not work in our setting, as our security notion relies on multiple honest users.

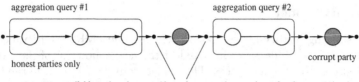

Fig. 1. Example of a trivial combination of replies to aggregation queries and local computations by corrupt parties

only aggregates for honest parties, i.e., where the corresponding keys were neither corrupted nor modified; for corrupt players the adversary, holding the secret key, must add the values herself.

Eventually the adversary $\mathcal{A}$ halts, outputting a tuple $(\mathbf{pk}^*, \mathbf{M}^*, \sigma^*)$. The forgery must be valid according to our definition of history-free sequential aggregate signature schemes. In addition, the signature must be non-trivial which is quantified by defining the closure of all query/answer pairs of $\mathcal{A}$. Here, we denote by Q_{Seq} the set of all query/answer tuples $((\sigma', \mathbf{M}, \mathbf{pk}), \sigma)$ that occur in $\mathcal{A}$'s interaction with the OSeqAgg oracle. Recall that Q_{Cor} denote the sets of all keys that were corrupted and possibly modified by the adversary. The closure contains all admissible combinations of aggregated data for the queried sequences together with all possible values by corrupted parties.

Closure. For history-free sequential aggregate signatures, defining the closure is more complex as in the general case that we discuss in Section 5. Here, an adversary can query partial chains and later possibly combine several of them by using corrupted keys or chains with matching starting/end points. Thus, we define the closure recursively through a function $\mathsf{Trivial}_{Q_{\mathsf{Seq}}, Q_{\mathsf{Cor}}}$ which, for parameters $(\mathbf{pk}, \mathbf{M}, \sigma)$ describes all sequences that can be derived trivially starting from message sequence $\mathbf{M}$ and aggregate-so-far σ, i.e., where one can append (recursively expanded) trivial sequences via aggregation queries or local computations by corrupt players. For example, if we have an aggregation query $(\sigma_0, \mathbf{pk}, \mathbf{M})$ with answer σ in Q_{Seq} and another query $(\sigma, \mathbf{pk}', \mathbf{M}')$ with the answer from the first query as the starting aggregate, then the sequence $(\mathbf{pk}\|\mathbf{pk}', \mathbf{M}\|\mathbf{M}')$ is in the trivial set. So is any extension of this sequence for corrupt players. We note that, if the final aggregate of a chain and the starting aggregate do not match, then the combined sequence is not in the closure, neither are subsequences of previous queries (unless either sequence appears in another query).

The closure is then defined to contain all trivial sequences starting from the information available to the adversary at the beginning, namely, the empty message sequence, the starting key $pk_0 = \emptyset$ and the starting tag $\sigma_0 = \emptyset$. Note that the closure here is now a set of tuples where each tuple represents a sequential aggregation.

Definition 4 (Sequential Closure of $\mathcal{A}$'s queries). *Let Q_{Cor} and Q_{Seq} be the sets corresponding to the different oracle responses and let $\mathsf{Trivial}_{Q_{\mathsf{Seq}}, Q_{\mathsf{Cor}}}$ be a recursive function of trivial combinations defined as*

$\mathsf{Trivial}_{Q_{\mathsf{Seq}}, Q_{\mathsf{Cor}}}(\mathbf{pk}, \mathbf{M}, \sigma)$

$$:= \quad \{(\mathbf{pk}, \mathbf{M})\} \cup \bigcup_{((\sigma, \overline{\mathbf{M}}, \overline{\mathbf{pk}}), \overline{\sigma}) \in Q_{\mathsf{Seq}}} \mathsf{Trivial}_{Q_{\mathsf{Seq}}, Q_{\mathsf{Cor}}}(\mathbf{pk} \| \overline{\mathbf{pk}}, \mathbf{M} \| \overline{\mathbf{M}}, \overline{\sigma})$$

$$\cup \bigcup_{\substack{\forall \overline{M}, \overline{\sigma} \\ \wedge pk_i \in Q_{\mathsf{Cor}}}} \mathsf{Trivial}_{Q_{\mathsf{Seq}}, Q_{\mathsf{Cor}}}(\mathbf{pk} \| pk_i, \mathbf{M} \| \overline{M}, \overline{\sigma}).$$

The closure Closure *of $\mathcal{A}$'s queries Q_{Seq} and Q_{Cor} is then defined by recursively generating the trivial combinations starting from the empty tuple as described above:*

$$\mathsf{Closure}(Q_{\mathsf{Seq}}, Q_{\mathsf{Cor}}) := \mathsf{Trivial}_{Q_{\mathsf{Seq}}, Q_{\mathsf{Cor}}}(\emptyset, \emptyset, \emptyset).$$

As an example consider an attack on a regular (non-aggregate) signature scheme, with a single honest party and no corrupt players. Then the closure contains all queries to the signing oracle and renders these values as trivial. Note that we do not treat the case of concatenating answers for the same public key in any special way.

A more important example are the mix-and-match attacks in which the adversary sees several aggregation chains (of honest parties) but is able to combine them into a new sequence. This new sequence would then be not in the closure and thus constitute a legitimate forgery attempt. In other words, any secure scheme according to our notion must prevent such mix-and-match attacks.

Aggregation Unforgeability. With the definition of the sequential closure, we propose the following security model for history-free sequential aggregate signatures.

Definition 5 (Aggregation Unforgeability). *A history-free sequential aggregate signature scheme* SAS = (SeqKg, SeqAgg, SeqAggVf) *is aggregation-unforgeable if for any efficient algorithm $\mathcal{A}$ (working in modes* CORRUPT, FORGE*) the probability that the experiment* $\mathsf{SeqForge}_{\mathcal{A}}^{\mathsf{SAS}}$ *evaluates to 1 is negligible (as a function of n), where*

Experiment $\mathsf{SeqForge}_{\mathcal{A}}^{\mathsf{SAS}}(n)$
  $(sk_1, pk_1), \ldots, (sk_t, pk_t) \leftarrow \mathsf{SeqKg}(1^n)$
  $\mathbf{K}' \leftarrow ((sk_1, pk_1), \ldots, (sk_t, pk_t))$
  $\mathsf{st} \leftarrow \mathcal{A}^{\mathsf{Corrupt}(\mathbf{K}', \cdot), \mathsf{SetKey}(\mathbf{K}', \cdot, \cdot)}(\mathrm{CORRUPT}, pk_1, \ldots, pk_t)$
    // it is understood that $\mathcal{A}$ keeps state st
  Let $\mathbf{K}$ *be the set of the updated keys of all parties*
  $(\mathbf{pk}^*, \mathbf{M}^*, \sigma^*) \leftarrow \mathcal{A}^{\mathsf{OSeqAgg}(\mathbf{K}, \cdots)}(\mathrm{FORGE}, \mathsf{st})$
  Return 1 iff $pk_i \neq pk_j$ *for all* $i \neq j$ *and* $\mathsf{SeqAggVf}(\mathbf{pk}^*, \mathbf{M}^*, \sigma^*) = 1$ *and*
    $(\mathbf{pk}^*, \mathbf{M}^*) \notin \mathsf{Closure}(Q_{\mathsf{Seq}}, Q_{\mathsf{Cor}})$.

Relaxed Security Notion. Our definition is very demanding in the sense that prefixes of aggregation sequences are considered to be non-trivial. In particular, this means that intermediate values in such a chain cannot be available to the

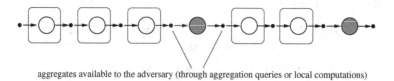

aggregates available to the adversary (through aggregation queries or local computations)

Fig. 2. Relaxed Security Notion: In comparison to the stronger notion (Figure 1) the adversary can only make aggregation queries of length 1. The closure potentially allows more combinations now and thus rules out more sequences as trivial.

adversary, or else successful attacks according to our model are straightforward. This model corresponds to the case that the forwarded data between honest parties are for instance encrypted.

Regarding existing sequential aggregate signature schemes like [14], all intermediate signatures that appeared in the computation of the final aggregate can be re-obtained by simply verifying the aggregate signature, since the verification algorithm "peels off" the aggregate. Thus, we also propose a relaxed definition of history-free unforgeability that takes the possibility of obtaining the *intermediate* signatures into account, inciting the name *mezzo aggregation unforgeability.*

We also remark that a simple approach like having the first party in a sequence create some unique identifier or nonce, which is used by all subsequent players, usually does not facilitate the design of schemes because the adversary can always put a corrupt player upfront. Similarly to the case of non-ordered aggregation we can have a solution with counters or time stamps but this again requires synchronization between the parties.

We can easily cast the weaker notion in our model by allowing only aggregation queries for sequences of length one, i.e., where the adversary has to compute longer chains itself by iterating through the sequence manually. Clearly, this adversary is a special case of our adversary above and the security guarantee is therefore weaker (in other words, the closure now contains more trivial elements). It is also very easy to prove this formally by considering a scheme where the new aggregate contains the previous aggregate. For the stronger notion this allows to obtain a valid aggregate of a prefix easily, whereas for the weaker notion the extra aggregate is already been input by the adversary and thus provides no additional information. The difference between the models is depicted in Figure 2.

Definition 6 (Mezzo Aggregation Unforgeability). *A history-free sequential aggregate signature scheme* $\mathsf{SAS} = (\mathsf{SeqKg}, \mathsf{SeqAgg}, \mathsf{SeqAggVf})$ *is* mezzo aggregation-unforgeable *if it is aggregation-unforgeable for any efficient algorithm* $\mathcal{A}$ *that only calls oracle* $\mathsf{OSeqAgg}$ *for sequences of length one.*

We note that mix-and-match attacks are still ruled out by the above definition. For this observe that any "manually iterated" sequence can only interfere with other sequences if intermediate signatures collide. Such collisions are, however,

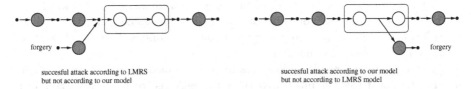

succesful attack according to LMRS
but not according to our model

succesful attack according to our model
but not according to LMRS model

Fig. 3. Comparison of the LMRS security model and our (strong) model: Prepending any values by corrupt parties is not considered a successful attack in our model (left part), whereas branching into a different sequence from some intermediate value is not considered a successful attack in the LMRS model (right part)

unlikely and can only happen with negligible probability. Else, such collisions would easily allow to forge individual signatures of honest parties and would constitute a successful forgery in the above sense.

3.3   Relationship to the **LMRS**-Model

It is easy to see that our security model is strictly stronger than the one by Lu et al. [13] because successful attacks according to their definition involve individual forgeries for fresh messages against a single challenge key (which thus cannot belong to our closure). At the same time their approach does not allow to verify the order of aggregation steps, whereas changing the order constitutes a successful attack according to our definition. We therefore focus on the comparison to the LMRS-model.

On one hand our model gives the adversary more power than in the LMRS-model for secure sequential aggregation, because it does not need to specify the starting message sequence for aggregation queries. On the other hand we allow the adversary less freedom when it comes to values of corrupt players in the forgery attempt. Hence, the possibilities in the attack are somewhat compensated for and this makes the models incomparable, as we show by the following separating examples.

The ideas of the separating examples are given in Figure 3. The left part of the figure shows an attack which is defined as trivial in our model but constitutes a break in the LMRS model. Indeed, it seems that in the history-free setting the adversary can always find "bad" keys for corrupt parties which enable collisions on the intermediate values. Since the information about the starting sequence then does not enter the further computations preventing such attacks in our setting seems impossible. The right side shows a successful attack in our model which takes advantage of a prefix of an aggregation subsequence; this is by definition not a successful attack in the LMRS model. A similar separation holds for our relaxed notion. We discuss these cases in more detail in the full version.

We briefly discuss how to add the LMRS security property to our (mezzo) aggregation unforgeability, if now all preceding public keys **pk** and messages **M** in a sequence are known. The idea is to use a collision-resistant hash function

h and, for each signature creation, to prepend the hash value $c = h(\mathbf{pk}, \mathbf{M})$ to the message to be signed. For verification one does the same. Note that, while this is formally not a history-free scheme anymore, signing still does not require verification of preceding signatures.

Aggregation unforgeability still holds in the modified scheme if we consider each hash value to be an integral part of the message to be signed. But the collision resistance of the hash function h now also ensures LMRS security, because we can assume that all hash values of sequences are unique. This implies that in an LMRS forgery attempt the message with the prepended hash value has not been signed by the honest user in question (either the prefix is new and thus the hash value, or the message in combination with this sequence is). This means that the forgery sequence is not in the closure and would thus constitute a breach of (mezzo) aggregation unforgeability.

4   Construction

We derive a history-free sequential aggregate signature scheme based on the BLS signature scheme that is secure in the random oracle model [7]. This scheme has already been successfully applied to derive the non-sequential BGLS aggregate signature scheme [6]. Below we assume that we have an efficient, non-degenerate bilinear map $\mathbf{e} : \mathbb{G}_1 \times \mathbb{G}_2 \to \mathbb{G}_3$ for system-wide available groups, where g_1 is a generator of $\mathbb{G}_1$ and g_2 is a generator of $\mathbb{G}_2$. We assume that $\mathbf{e}(\cdot, g_2)$ is one-to-one. Also, let $H : \{0,1\}^* \mapsto \mathbb{G}_1$ be a public hash function.

In the BLS signature scheme the key generation algorithm $\mathsf{Kg}(1^n)$ picks an element $x \leftarrow \mathbb{Z}_p$ at random and computes $v \leftarrow g_2^x$. It returns $(pk, sk) \leftarrow (v, x)$. The signing algorithm $\mathsf{Sign}(x, M)$ takes as input a message $M \in \{0,1\}^*$ and a secret key x. It computes $\sigma \leftarrow H(M)^x$ and returns the signature $\sigma \in \mathbb{G}_1$. The verification algorithm $\mathsf{Vf}(v, M, \sigma)$ outputs 1 iff $\mathbf{e}(\sigma, g_2) = \mathbf{e}(H(M), v)$.

4.1   Construction Based on BLS Signatures

The idea of our construction is as follows. We let the signer build a link between all previous all signatures by linking them through a hash chain. That is, in each aggregation step the signer receives the aggregate-so-far (σ', pk', c', s'), consisting of an aggregate σ', the public key pk' of the preceding signer, a hash chain value c' and the non-aggregated signature s' of the preceding party. The signer first checks that s' is a valid signature under pk' for c' and, if so, it extends the hash chain via $c \leftarrow h(\mathbf{e}(\sigma', g_2), M, pk', c')$ for its message M. Note that using the value under the bilinear mapping instead of σ' is necessary for the verification the whole sequence without knowing the individual aggregates and is a specific property of the BLS scheme. The signer next computes a non-aggregated signature s for c and aggregates s to σ' to derive σ, and finally forwards (σ, pk, c, s) to the next signer.

Construction 1. *Let* DS $=$ (Kg, Sig, Vf) *be the* BLS *signature scheme and* h : $\{0,1\}^* \mapsto \{0,1\}^n$ *be a hash function. Define the following efficient algorithms:*

Key Generation. *The key generation algorithm is identical to* Kg.

Sequential Signature Aggregation. *Algorithm* SeqAgg *gets as input a pair of keys* $(sk, pk) = (x, v)$, *a message* $M \in \{0,1\}^*$, *and a sequential aggregate signature* (σ', pk', c', s'). *The algorithm sets* $c \leftarrow h(\mathbf{e}(\sigma', g_2), M, pk', c')$, *where* $\mathbf{e}(\emptyset, g_2) = 1$ *by definition, checks that* Vf$(pk', c', s') = 1$ *or that* $pk', c', s' = \emptyset$ *are the starting symbols, and stops if not. Else it computes the signature* $s = H(c)^x \leftarrow$ Sig(sk, c) *on* c *and the value* $\sigma \leftarrow \sigma' \cdot s$. *It outputs the sequential aggregate signature* (σ, pk, c, s).

Aggregate Verification. *The input of algorithm* SeqAggVf$(\mathbf{pk}, \mathbf{M}, \sigma)$ *is a sequence of public keys* $\mathbf{pk} = (pk_1, \ldots, pk_\ell)$, *a sequence of messages* $\mathbf{M} = (M_1, \ldots, M_\ell)$ *as well as an aggregate* σ *(with* pk, c, s*). It parses* $pk_i = g_2^{x_i}$, *sets*

$$c_0 \leftarrow \emptyset \quad and \quad pk_0 \leftarrow \emptyset \quad and \quad c_i \leftarrow h\Big(\prod_{j=0}^{i-1} \mathbf{e}(H(c_j), pk_j), M_i, pk_{i-1}, c_{i-1} \Big)$$

for $i = 1, \ldots, \ell$, *where* $\mathbf{e}(H(\emptyset), pk_j) = 1$ *by definition, and outputs 1 if*

$$\mathbf{e}(\sigma, g_2) = \prod_{i=1}^{\ell} \mathbf{e}(H(c_i), g_2^{x_i}).$$

Completeness follows inductively, as for honest parties each intermediate aggregate σ_i is a valid signature for $c_1, \ldots, c_i$ and therefore the next output also satisfies $\mathbf{e}(\sigma_i, g_2) = \mathbf{e}(H(c_j), g_2^{x_i})$.

4.2   Security

Our security proof basically follows by reduction to the security to the BLS signature scheme and the collision resistance of h. We note that we do not explicitly rely on the random oracle model, only implicitly through the (currently best) security proof for the BLS scheme. Instead, we could give a straight reduction to the co-Diffie-Hellman problem [7], but then we would need to program the random oracle. The main idea of the proof is that we either break the underlying BLS scheme (in case $\mathbf{C}^*$ computed in the verification of the adversary's forgery attempt contains a new value c_i^*), or that the adversary has to forge a (regular) signature for an honest party or to find a collision for h (if all values in $\mathbf{C}^*$ have appeared during the attack).

Theorem 2. *Let* h *be a collision-resistant hash function. If the* BLS *signature scheme is unforgeable, then the scheme defined in Construction 1 is a history-free, mezzo aggregation-unforgeable sequential aggregate signature scheme.*

Proof. We prove this theorem assuming towards contradiction that there exists an adversary $\mathcal{A}$ breaking aggregation-unforgeability with non-negligible probability $\epsilon(n)$. Assume that this adversary eventually outputs a valid forgery $\mathbf{M}^*$, pk^* and σ^*. Let $\mathbf{C}^* = (c_1^*, \ldots, c_\ell^*)$ denote the values derived during the verification, and assume that the sequence $\mathbf{M}^*$ does not belong to the closure.

If the probability that the adversary $\mathcal{A}$ succeeds and there is some c_i^* for an honest party which has never been queried to an aggregation query for this party, then we can break the underlying aggregate signature scheme. To this end we construct an algorithm $\mathcal{B}$ (receiving a challenge key and having access to a signature oracle for this key) as follows:

Setup. Algorithm $\mathcal{B}$ gets as input a public key pk_c, it picks $t - 1$ key pairs $(sk_i, pk_i) \leftarrow \mathsf{SeqKg}(1^n)$ and inserts the key pk_c at a random position, $\mathbf{pk} \leftarrow (pk_1, \ldots, pk_{j-1}, pk_c, pk_{j+1} \ldots, pk_t)$. $\mathcal{B}$ simulates $\mathcal{A}$ in a black-box way on input $\mathbf{pk}$ (if we assume H to be a random oracle then $\mathcal{B}$ grants $\mathcal{A}$ direct access to H).

Key Oracles. During the simulation, $\mathcal{A}$ is allowed to corrupt keys and to change them. If $\mathcal{A}$ invokes the corruption oracle $\mathsf{Corrupt}(\mathbf{sk}, \cdot)$ on input pk, then $\mathcal{B}$ returns sk_i if $pk_i = pk$, for some $i \in \{1, \ldots, t\} \setminus j$, and otherwise failed. In the case that $\mathcal{A}$ wishes to substitute a certain public key $pk \in \mathbf{pk}$ and queries its key-modification oracle $\mathsf{SetKey}(\mathbf{sk}, \cdot)$ about a pair (pk, pk'), then $\mathcal{B}$ sets $pk_i = pk'$ if $pk_i = pk$ for an index $i \in \{1, \ldots, t\} \setminus j$. It returns succ if such a public key exists and substitution succeeded, otherwise failed.

Aggregate Signing. Whenever $\mathcal{A}$ asks the aggregate signing oracle SeqAgg to build a new sequential aggregate signature for an aggregate-so-far σ', a message M, and a public key pk, algorithm $\mathcal{B}$ answers this query in the following way. It first checks if the public key pk has never been corrupted nor substituted (if so, it returns $\perp$). Adversary $\mathcal{B}$ either computes the aggregate invoking its external signing oracle (in the case where $pk = pk_c$), or else by executing the signing algorithm itself (for the corresponding secret key sk). In both cases all other steps of the aggregation algorithm besides the signing step can be computed easily. $\mathcal{B}$ outputs the full aggregate to $\mathcal{A}$.

Output. At the end of the simulation $\mathcal{A}$ outputs a tuple $(\mathbf{M}^*, \mathbf{pk}^*, \sigma^*)$. Algorithm $\mathcal{B}$ computes $\mathbf{C}^*$ as in the description of the verification procedure and returns these values together with $\mathbf{pk}^*$ and σ^*. Algorithm $\mathcal{B}$ checks if $pk_c \in \mathbf{pk}^*$ and, if so, computes the values c_i^* as for verification, and outputs c_c^* together with $\sigma^* \cdot \prod_{i \neq c} H(c_i)^{-x_i}$ as the signature (for the known secret keys x_i belonging to the other parties in $\mathbf{pk}^*$).

For the analysis note that, in the case that some new c_i^* for some honest party is in $\mathbf{C}^*$ our algorithm $\mathcal{B}$ loses only a factor $1/t$ for guessing the right public key. But then, for a valid forgery of $\mathcal{A}$ we have $\mathbf{e}(\sigma^*, g_2) = \prod_{i=1}^{\ell} \mathbf{e}(H(c_i^*), g_2^{x_i})$. Dividing out $\prod_{i \neq c} H(c_i^*)^{x_i}$ of σ^* yields $\mathbf{e}(\sigma^* \cdot \prod_{i \neq c} H(c_i^*)^{-x_i}, g_2) = \mathbf{e}(H(c_c^*), pk_c)$ and therefore a valid forgery for the BLS scheme under public key pk_c. Hence, this case of $\mathcal{A}$ winning cannot have non-negligible probability.

Next assume that all the c_i^*'s of honest parties have appeared in aggregation requests before (and are answered without failure), but $\mathcal{A}$ still wins. In the forgery attempt consider the leftmost honest party at position i such that the leading sequence $(M_1^*, \ldots, M_i^*)$ of $\mathbf{M}^*$ does not lie in the closure. Since we assume that c_i^* has appeared in some aggregation query to party i before, we must have a query $(\sigma', pk', c'), M$ with

$$h(\mathbf{e}(\sigma', g_2), M, pk', c') = c_i^* = h(\prod_{j<i} \mathbf{e}(H(c_j^*), pk_j), M_i^*, pk_{i-1}, c_{i-1}).$$

By the collision-resistance of h we conclude that $M = M_i^*$, $pk' = pk_{i-1}$ and $c' = c_{i-1}^*$ and $\mathbf{e}(\sigma', g_2) = \prod_{j<i} \mathbf{e}(H(c_j^*), pk_j)$. By assumption, the leading sequence $(M_1^*, \ldots, M_i^*)$ is not in the closure. There are three cases:

- Our "target" party at position i is the first one in the sequence $(M_1^*, \ldots, M_i^*)$, i.e., $i = 1$. Since it then only computes an aggregate if $\sigma', pk', c' = \emptyset$ we derive the contradiction that the sequence is in fact in the closure, due to the aggregation query $(\sigma', pk', c'), M = M_i^*$ yielding c_i^*. This, however, contradicts our assumption.
- Assume that there is a corrupt party at position $i-1$ in the forgery sequence. Then, by construction and since party i is the leftmost with the sequence $(M_1^*, \ldots, M_i^*)$ not being in the closure, the sequence including the corrupt party must be in the closure (all subsequences must already be in the closure by assumption). But then the query triggering the appearance of c_i^* again makes $(M_1^*, \ldots, M_i^*)$ per definition also part of the closure. This is so since corrupt parties can "link" any trivial sequences.
- The final case is if there is an honest party at position $i - 1$. Note that our party at i only returns an aggregate if the signature s' is a valid signature for the incoming value $c' = c_i^*$ under the same key $pk' = pk_{i-1}$ of the honest party at position $i - 1$. We conclude again that the adversary needs to make the honest party at some step sign c_i^* (or needs to forge a signature for honest party at $i - 1$, which would again contradict the security of the BLS signature scheme). However, by the collision resistance of h and noting that the function $\mathbf{e}(\cdot, g_2)$ is one-to-one, it follows that this requires the same input $(\sigma'', pk'', c''), M'$ to the party at position $i - 1$ as on the "closure path". Furthermore, the valid signatures s'' for c'' and s' for c' are unique, and it therefore follows again that the closure extends to the party at position i, contradicting again our assumption.

This shows that the adversary can win in this case with negligible probability only, and concludes the proof.   □

We again note that, following the discussion in Section 3.3, we can easily get a (non history-free) signature scheme which is simultaneously also LMRS secure without the verification of signatures in the sequence, This is achieved by inserting the sequence of messages and public keys into the evaluation of the hash function h.

5 Security of Non-sequential Aggregation Schemes

The common security model for non-sequential aggregate signatures of Boneh et al. [6] only considers limited attacks (akin to our weaker security notion), even though stronger notions may be desirable for some applications (similar to our strong notion). For the case of symmetric authentication this was already discussed in [10] by presenting an attack against an aggregate MAC scheme, that was outside of the previous security model. Here we show that a similar argumentation holds for aggregate signatures as well.

Mix-and-Match Attacks. We first recall the example of an "mix-and-match" attack that was given for aggregate MACs by Eikemeier et al. From an abstract point of view, the attack uses three aggregates for message sets $\{M_1, M_2\}$, $\{M_3, M_2\}$ and $\{M_1, M_4\}$ to derive a valid aggregate for a fourth pair $\{M_3, M_4\}$. The attack is not considered a security breach according to the model by [6]. Roughly, the shortcoming is due to the definition of "trivial" attacks: an adversary is usually not considered to succeed if the messages in the forgery have been authenticated *individually* during the attack. In the example above this means that *any* combination of the messages M_1, M_2, M_3, M_4 cannot be used for a successful forgery, although only three of these combinations have actually appeared before. Ideally, however, an aggregation scheme should be considered insecure if an adversary is able to transform several aggregates into a *new combination* that has not been authenticated before.

More concretely, recall that an aggregate in the scheme by Boneh et al. is of the form $\sigma = \prod \sigma_i$ for regular BLS signatures $\sigma_i = H(M_i)^{x_i}$ for random oracle H, message M_i and secret key x_i. The public key is given by g^{x_i} and verification is performed with the help of the pairing operation. Given the replies

$$\sigma_1 = H(M_1)^{x_1} \cdot H(M_2)^{x_2}, \quad \sigma_2 = H(M_3)^{x_1} \cdot H(M_2)^{x_2}, \quad \sigma_3 = H(M_1)^{x_1} \cdot H(M_4)^{x_2}$$

to three aggregation queries for message sets $\{M_1, M_2\}$, $\{M_3, M_2\}$ and $\{M_1, M_4\}$, the adversary is able to compute a valid aggregate

$$\sigma^* = \sigma_1^{-1} \cdot \sigma_2 \cdot \sigma_3 = H(M_3)^{x_1} \cdot H(M_4)^{x_2}$$

for the set $\{M_3, M_4\}$. According to the definition of [6] this, however, does not constitute a security breach.

Relation to Boneh's et al. Aggregate Extraction Problem. Our mix-and-match attack on the scheme of Boneh et al. [6] benefits from the fact that we can remove some signatures from the aggregate. Interestingly, the authors in [6] already address the question whether it is possible to extract any subset of (unknown) signatures from the aggregate or not. This problem is called aggregate-extraction-problem. Extracting even a single (unknown) signature from such an aggregate is equivalent to solving the computational Diffie-Hellman problem, as subsequently shown by Coron and Naccache [9]. Thus, in a sense, our result can also be seen as a generalization of the aggregate extraction problem with respect to the BGLS aggregate signature scheme, to a more general context where we not only consider the extraction of single signatures, but also the *(re-)combination* of aggregates (as discussed above).

Defining Stronger Aggregation Unforgeability. To derive a stronger security notion Eikemeier et al. adapt their notion and attack model for the sequential case, except that the aggregation oracle now takes *unordered* sets of messages and public keys. The definition of the closure for our signature case simplifies and is then given by

$$\mathsf{Closure}(Q_{\mathsf{Agg}}, Q_{\mathsf{Cor}}) =$$

$$\left\{ \bigcup_{M_A \in A} M_A \cup M_C \,\middle|\, A \subseteq Q_{\mathsf{Agg}}, M_C \subseteq \bigcup_{pk^* \in Q_{\mathsf{Cor}}} \{(pk^*, M) \mid M \in \{0,1\}^*\} \right\}.$$

We remark again that it is unknown whether this notion can indeed be satisfied.

Synchronized Aggregate Signatures. A line of research studies aggregate signatures where signers share a synchronized clock [11,2,1], showing that efficient constructions under well known computational assumptions are possible in this model, even for unordered aggregation. Following this line, Eikemeier et al. [10] discuss how to derive MAC schemes secure according to a relaxed notion similar to the one above, and their ideas transfer to signatures as well. However, their solution still does not cover deletion attacks. Furthermore, it is of course preferable to avoid such synchronization assumptions.

Acknowledgments. We thank Leo Reyzin for discussions and clarifications about [8], especially about the (un)suitability of different security notions for the secure routing problem.

This work was supported by the Emmy Noether Program Fi 940/2-1 and the Heisenberg Program Fi 940/3-1 of the German Research Foundation (DFG) and by CASED (www.cased.de). This work was partially supported by the US Army Research Laboratory and the UK Ministry of Defense under Agreement Number W911NF-06-3-0001. The views and conclusions contained in this document are those of the authors and should not be interpreted as representing the official policies, either expressed or implied, of the US Army Research Laboratory, the US Government, the UK Ministry of Defense, or the UK Government. The US and UK Governments are authorized to reproduce and distribute reprints for Government purposes, notwithstanding any copyright notation herein. This work was also supported by the German Ministry for Education and Research (BMBF) through funding for the Center for IT-Security, Privacy and Accountability (CISPA — www.cispa-security.de). Part of the work of the second and third author done while being at Darmstadt University.

References

1. Ahn, J.H., Green, M., Hohenberger, S.: Synchronized aggregate signatures: New definitions, constructions and applications. In: Annual Conference on Computer and Communications Security (CCS), pp. 473–484. ACM Press (2010)
2. Bagherzandi, A., Jarecki, S.: Identity-Based Aggregate and Multi-Signature Schemes Based on RSA. In: Nguyen, P.Q., Pointcheval, D. (eds.) PKC 2010. LNCS, vol. 6056, pp. 480–498. Springer, Heidelberg (2010)
3. Bellare, M., Namprempre, C., Neven, G.: Unrestricted Aggregate Signatures. In: Arge, L., Cachin, C., Jurdziński, T., Tarlecki, A. (eds.) ICALP 2007. LNCS, vol. 4596, pp. 411–422. Springer, Heidelberg (2007)
4. Boldyreva, A.: Threshold Signatures, Multisignatures and Blind Signatures Based on the Gap-Diffie-Hellman-Group Signature Scheme. In: Desmedt, Y.G. (ed.) PKC 2003. LNCS, vol. 2567, pp. 31–46. Springer, Heidelberg (2002)
5. Boldyreva, A., Gentry, C., O'Neill, A., Yum, D.H.: New multiparty signature schemes for network routing applications. ACM Trans. Inf. Syst. Secur. 12(1) (2008)
6. Boneh, D., Gentry, C., Lynn, B., Shacham, H.: Aggregate and Verifiably Encrypted Signatures From Bilinear Maps. In: Biham, E. (ed.) EUROCRYPT 2003. LNCS, vol. 2656, pp. 416–432. Springer, Heidelberg (2003)
7. Boneh, D., Lynn, B., Shacham, H.: Short signatures from the Weil pairing. Journal of Cryptology 17(4), 297–319 (2004)
8. Brogle, K., Goldberg, S., Reyzin, L.: Sequential aggregate signatures with lazy verification. Cryptology ePrint Archive: Report 2011/222 (2011), http://eprint.iacr.org/2011/2221
9. Coron, J.-S., Naccache, D.: Boneh et al.'s k-Element Aggregate Extraction Assumption Is Equivalent to the Diffie-Hellman Assumption. In: Laih, C.-S. (ed.) ASIACRYPT 2003. LNCS, vol. 2894, pp. 392–397. Springer, Heidelberg (2003)
10. Eikemeier, O., Fischlin, M., Götzmann, J.-F., Lehmann, A., Schröder, D., Schröder, P., Wagner, D.: History-Free Aggregate Message Authentication Codes. In: Garay, J.A., De Prisco, R. (eds.) SCN 2010. LNCS, vol. 6280, pp. 309–328. Springer, Heidelberg (2010)
11. Gentry, C., Ramzan, Z.: Identity-Based Aggregate Signatures. In: Yung, M., Dodis, Y., Kiayias, A., Malkin, T. (eds.) PKC 2006. LNCS, vol. 3958, pp. 257–273. Springer, Heidelberg (2006)
12. Lepinski, M.: BGPSec protocol specification. IETF Internet-Draft (2011)
13. Lu, S., Ostrovsky, R., Sahai, A., Shacham, H., Waters, B.: Sequential Aggregate Signatures and Multisignatures Without Random Oracles. In: Vaudenay, S. (ed.) EUROCRYPT 2006. LNCS, vol. 4004, pp. 465–485. Springer, Heidelberg (2006)
14. Lysyanskaya, A., Micali, S., Reyzin, L., Shacham, H.: Sequential Aggregate Signatures from Trapdoor Permutations. In: Cachin, C., Camenisch, J.L. (eds.) EUROCRYPT 2004. LNCS, vol. 3027, pp. 74–90. Springer, Heidelberg (2004)
15. Micali, S., Ohta, K., Reyzin, L.: Accountable-subgroup multisignatures: extended abstract. In: Annual Conference on Computer and Communications Security (CCS), pp. 245–254. ACM Press (2001)
16. Neven, G.: Efficient Sequential Aggregate Signed Data. In: Smart, N.P. (ed.) EUROCRYPT 2008. LNCS, vol. 4965, pp. 52–69. Springer, Heidelberg (2008)
17. Schröder, D.: How to Aggregate the CL Signature Scheme. In: Atluri, V., Diaz, C. (eds.) ESORICS 2011. LNCS, vol. 6879, pp. 298–314. Springer, Heidelberg (2011)

A New Hash-and-Sign Approach
and Structure-Preserving Signatures from DLIN

Melissa Chase and Markulf Kohlweiss

Microsoft Research
{melissac,markulf}@microsoft.com

Abstract. Suppose we have a signature scheme for signing elements of message space $\mathcal{M}_1$, but we need to sign messages from $\mathcal{M}_2$. The traditional approach of applying a collision resistant hash function from $\mathcal{M}_1$ to $\mathcal{M}_2$ can be inconvenient when the signature scheme is used within more complex protocols, for example if we want to prove knowledge of a signature. Here, we present an alternative approach in which we can combine a signature for $\mathcal{M}_1$, a pairwise independent hash function with key space $\mathcal{M}_1$ and message space $\mathcal{M}_2$, and a non-interactive zero knowledge proof system to obtain a signature scheme for message space $\mathcal{M}_2$. This transform also removes any dependence on state in the signature for $\mathcal{M}_1$.

As a result of our transformation we obtain a new signature scheme for signing a vector of group elements that is based only on the decisional linear assumption (DLIN). Moreover, the public keys and signatures of our scheme consist of group elements only, and a signature is verified by evaluating a set of pairing-product equations, so the result is a structure-preserving signature. In combination with the Groth-Sahai proof system, such a signature scheme is an ideal building block for many privacy-enhancing protocols.

1 Introduction

The Hash and Sign Approach. In most settings it is straightforward to sign elements of any message space. We simply view the message as a binary string and apply a collision resistant hash function to map it into the desired range (usually $\mathbb{Z}_p$ or $\mathbb{Z}_n$) at which point it can be signed using constructions based on number theoretic primitives. However, in some applications there is also a disadvantage to this approach. In particular, it seems to be much more difficult to build efficient protocols for dealing with signatures on hidden messages, e.g. for proving knowledge of a signature on a hidden message, or issuing a signature given only the commitment to the message (as in blind signatures).

Such protocols are essential in numerous privacy-enhancing applications such as group signatures [ACJT00], anonymous credentials [CL01, BCL04], compact e-cash [CHL05, CHL06, CLM07], range proofs [CCS08], oblivious database access [CGH09], and others [CHK+06, TS06, CGH06]. One of the key elements in all of these protocols is the ability to prove that certain hidden values have been

I. Visconti and R. De Prisco (Eds.): SCN 2012, LNCS 7485, pp. 131–148, 2012.
© Springer-Verlag Berlin Heidelberg 2012

signed without revealing the signature nor all of the certified values. Similarly, one might want to jointly compute a signature without revealing the key or all the certified values.

While such protocols are extremely useful, there are relatively few known efficient constructions. Of course one could construct these protocols based on general commitment schemes, two party computation, and proofs of knowledge. However, these general building blocks are extremely inefficient. A far more practical approach is to consider particular languages for which we can generate efficient proofs and efficient protocols using Σ-protocols [CDS94, Cra97, Dam02] or the recent proof system of Groth and Sahai [GS08]. These protocols rely on the structure of the underlying groups to generate efficient proofs for large classes of statements.

This is where hash functions cease to be useful as universal domain extenders for digital signatures. If the original message must be first hashed and then signed, then a proof that a committed message has been signed must not only prove knowledge of a valid signature on the resulting hash, but must also prove that the pre-image of this value is contained in the given commitment. For most modern hash functions it is completely unclear how to do this efficiently.

On the other hand, pairwise-independent hash functions often have very simple, algebraic constructions that make them much better suited for proofs and multi-party computation. (For example, for a group G of prime order p, the simple function $H_{a,b}(x) = g^a x^b$ for key $(a,b) \in \mathbb{Z}_p^2$ can be shown to be a family of pairwise independent functions from G to G.) Thus, we consider an alternative approach, in which we can use pairwise-independent hash functions (together with NIZK proofs) to change the message spaces allowed by a given signature scheme.

Structure Preserving Signatures. The known efficient signature schemes used in the above applications, which are sometimes referred to as CL-signatures [CL02], focus on signing elements of $\mathbb{Z}_p$ or $\mathbb{Z}_n$, where no hashing is necessary, so one can directly construct efficient proof systems or multi-party protocols. However, these schemes do have significant limitations. First, the resulting proof systems must be either interactive or in the random oracle model, which means, among other things, that it will be impossible to give a proof of knowledge of a proof that a message has been signed. This is unfortunate, since such an approach seems to be the key to allowing delegation in anonymous scenarios [CG08, CL06, FP08]. Furthermore, in many cases we need to prove knowledge of a signature on a public key, a ciphertext, a commitment, or another signature. This can be difficult since these values are often group elements and thus not elements of the original message space. An additional disadvantage is that the known efficient constructions of CL-signatures require significantly stronger assumptions than traditional signature schemes.

Because of these limitations, there have been a number of efforts in recent years to look for alternate constructions. Many of these efforts have focused on constructions in bilinear groups because of their rich mathematical structure. In this setting public keys, ciphertexts, and signatures are usually group elements, and so the ideal scheme would be one whose message space consists of the elements of the bilinear group. Furthermore, if the signatures are made up of group elements and the signature verification is done using the bilinear pairing, then the proof system of Groth and Sahai [GS08] allows for simple, efficient proofs. Abe et al. [AHO10] formalized these requirements (that messages, signatures, and public keys be group elements and verification proceed via a product of pairings) as *structure-preserving signatures* (SPS).[1]

Even before the term was coined, several early protocols made use of adhoc structure-preserving signature schemes but relied on very strong assumptions [AWSM07, ASM08, GH08]. Recently there have been a series of constructions for structure-prserving signature schemes [CLY09, AHO10, AGHO11]. However, all known efficient schemes are based on so-called "q-type" or interactive assumptions that are primarily justified based on the Generic Group model.[2] Thus, we ask whether it is possible to construct structure preserving signatures for bilinear group elements based on weaker assumptions. Ideally we would like to be able to base privacy-protecting cryptography on the same assumptions as conventional pairing-based cryptography.

One partial result in this direction is the scheme by Groth [Gro06], which satisfies the standard notion of EUF-CMA security and is based on the decisional linear assumption(DLIN). DLIN is one of the weakest assumptions used in the pairing-based setting, and is also one of the assumptions underlying the Groth-Sahai proof system, so it seems a fairly natural choice. However, while asymptotically efficient, a signature in Groth's scheme requires as confirmed by the author himself [Gro07] "thousands if not millions of group elements" per signature, so it is mainly of theoretical interest.

We focus on achieving reasonably *efficient* constructions based on the DLIN assumption. Protocols based on our primitives are within an order of magnitude or two of the efficiency of the efficient protocols mentioned above.

Our Results. First, we give a general approach for constructing a signature scheme for a message space $\mathcal{M}_1$ from a signature scheme for message space $\mathcal{M}_2$, a NIZK proof system, and a pairwise independent hash function with message space $\mathcal{M}_2$, key space $\mathcal{M}_1$, and any exponential sized range.

Then, as an application, we construct the first practical structure preserving signature scheme secure under the DLIN assumption. To do this, we use the above transformation to transform a signature for signing elements of $\mathbb{Z}_p$ (with certain additional properties) into a structure preserving signature scheme.

Signature schemes for signing elements of $\mathbb{Z}_p$ seem to be simpler to construct, and there are a number of constructions based on various hardness assumptions [BCKL08, BCKL09, Fuc09]. Thus, this already generates a range of structure preserving signatures schemes. However, all of these possible underlying

---

[1] For details on applications of SPS, we refer to [AFG+10] and to the full version [CK11].

[2] The parameter q influences the instance size of the assumption and depends on the number of signatures an adversary is allowed to see.

signature constructions are based on fairly strong q-type assumptions, and thus they don't help us to achieve our final goal.

Instead, we construct a new DLIN based signature scheme with the necessary properties based on the scheme of Hohenberger and Waters (HW) [HW09a]. Combining this with our transformation yields our final result: a structure preserving signature scheme whose security is based on the DLIN assumption, which is among the weakest assumptions used in the bilinear group setting.[3]

2   Preliminaries

In this section, we first describe the building blocks that we will use in our generic construction, and then summarize the assumptions that we will need for our application to structure-preserving signatures.

2.1   Weak F-Unforgeable Signature Schemes

Our construction will require a signatures scheme unforgeable under a *weak chosen message attack* (Weak CMA) for signing elements of some messages space $\mathcal{K}$. In a weak chosen message attack, the adversary is required to make all of his signature queries at once, before seeing the public key or any signatures. In fact, we will see later that this signature scheme will only be used to sign random messages, thus security under weak chosen message attacks will suffice. In our SPS application, we will also require that the signature scheme be F-unforgeable for an appropriate bijection F. Intuitively, F-unforgeability guarantees that it is hard for the adversary to produce $F(m)$ and a signature on m for an m that wasn't signed. In our SPS application this is important because when the message space is $\mathbb{Z}_p$, known pairing based proof systems only allow one to efficiently prove knowledge of some function of the message (e.g. g^m). We now formally define these notions:

Definition 1 (Unforgeability under Weak Chosen Message Attacks).
A weak chosen message attack (Weak CMA) [BB04, HW09b] requires that the adversary submits all signature queries before seeing the public key. A signature scheme is unforgeable under weak chosen message attacks if for all $\mathcal{A}_1$, $\mathcal{A}_2$ there exists a negligible function ν such that

$$\Pr[(m_1, \ldots, m_Q, state) \leftarrow \mathcal{A}_1(1^\lambda); (sk, pk) \leftarrow \mathsf{SigKg}(1^\lambda);$$
$$\sigma^{(i)} = \mathsf{Sign}(sk, m_i) \text{ for } i = 1, \ldots, Q;$$
$$(\tilde{\sigma}, \tilde{m}) \leftarrow \mathcal{A}_2(state, pk, \sigma^{(1)}, \ldots, \sigma^{(Q)}):$$
$$\tilde{m} \notin \{m_1, \ldots, m_Q\} \wedge \mathsf{SigVerify}(pk, \tilde{m}, \tilde{\sigma}) = \mathsf{accept}] = \nu(\lambda).$$

---

[3] Alternatively if we use a different instantiation of GS proofs, we can also prove our scheme secure based on the SXDH assumption and an additional computational assumption that is implied by DLIN in the asymmetric pairing setting.

For a bijection F, the Weak CMA F-unforgeability game is the same with the exception that instead of $\tilde{m}$, $\mathcal{A}_1$ only has to output $\tilde{f}$, such that $F^{-1}(\tilde{f}) \notin \{m_1, \ldots, m_Q\} \wedge \mathsf{SigVerify}(pk, F^{-1}(\tilde{f}), \tilde{\sigma}) = \mathsf{accept}$.

2.2 Pairwise Independent Hash Functions

The second ingredient will be a family of pairwise independent hash functions. This will be a family of functions parameterized by a "key" $k \in \mathcal{K}$. Intuitively, pairwise independence means that knowing the result of a random hash function on any one input gives no information about the result of that function on any other point. More formally:

Definition 2. A family of hash-functions $\{H_k\}_{k \in \mathcal{K}}$, where $H_k : \mathcal{M} \to \mathcal{R}$ is called pairwise independent if $\forall x \neq y \in \mathcal{M}$ and $\forall a, b \in \mathcal{R}$, the probability
$$Pr[k \leftarrow \mathcal{K} : H_k(x) = a \wedge H_k(y) = b] = \frac{1}{|\mathcal{R}|^2} \ .$$

2.3 Non-Interactive Zero-Knowledge Proofs

The final tool we need is a non-interactive zero-knowledge (NIZK) proof of knowledge system. A NIZK proof system consists of three algorithms PKSetup, PKProve, and PKVerify. PKSetup(1^k) is run by a trusted party and generates parameters crs (sometimes refered to as a common reference string) which are given to both the prover and the verifier. The prover runs PKProve(crs, x, w) to prove statement x with witness w which generates a proof π. The verifier runs PKVerify(crs, x, π) to verify the proof. Informally, zero knowledge means that there should exist a simulator (PKSimSetup, PKSimProve) that generates simulated parameters and simulated proofs that are indistinguishable from those produced by the prover (PKSetup, PKProve); a proof system is a proof of knowledge if there exists an extractor algorithm PKExtract that can extract a valid witness from any adversarially generated proof that is accepted by PKVerify.

We use the notation $\pi \leftarrow \mathsf{NIZKPK}\{(f(w)) : R_L(x, w)\}$ to indicate that π is a proof for statement x with witness w satisfying relation R_L and that from π we can extract $f(w)$.

2.4 Assumptions

Our concrete constructions will use bilinear groups groups $\mathbb{G}, \mathbb{G}_T$ of prime order p with a map e such that for any $g \in \mathbb{G}$, and any $a, b \in Z_p$, it must hold that $e(g^a, g^b) = e(g, g)^{ab}$, and if g is a generator for $\mathbb{G}$, then $e(g, g)$ must be a generator for $\mathbb{G}_T$. We rely on the following assumptions:

Definition 3 (Decision Linear (DLIN) [BBS04]).

Given $g, g^a, g^b, g^{ac}, g^{bd}, Z \in \mathbb{G}$, for random exponents $a, b, c, d \in \mathbb{Z}_p$, decide whether $Z = g^{c+d}$ or a random element in $\mathbb{G}$. The Decision Linear assumption holds if all p.p.t. algorithms have negligible (with respect to the bit length of p) advantage in solving the above problem.

Definition 4 (External Diffie-Hellman (XDH)).
The XDH assumption requires that the DDH assumption holds for a group with a bilinear map. By necessity this can only be the case for an asymmetric bilinear map $e : \mathbb{G}_1 \times \mathbb{G}_2 \to \mathbb{G}_T$. Moreover, w.l.o.g., say that DDH should hold for $\mathbb{G}_1$, there must not exist efficiently computable homomorphisms that map elements of $\mathbb{G}_1$ to elements of $\mathbb{G}_2$. If homomorphisms in both directions are excluded, and if DDH is also required to hold for $\mathbb{G}_2$, the combined assumption is called **Symmetric XDH (SXDH)** *assumption.*

We also introduce a new assumption which we show is implied by DLIN:

Assumption 1 (Randomized Computational Diffie-Hellman (RCDH)).
Let $\mathbb{G}$ be a group of prime order $p \in \Theta(2^k)$. For all p.p.t. adversaries $\mathcal{A}$, the following probability is negligible in k:

$$\Pr[g, \hat{g} \leftarrow \mathbb{G}; a, b \leftarrow \mathbb{Z}_p; (R_1, R_2, R_3) \leftarrow \mathcal{A}(g, \hat{g}, g^a, g^b) :$$
$$\exists r \in \mathbb{Z}_p \text{ such that } R_1 = g^r, R_2 = \hat{g}^r, R_3 = g^{abr}]$$

Theorem 1. *In groups with a symmetric bilinear pairing RCDH is implied by DLIN.* The proof can be found in the full version [CK11].

3   A New Hash-and-Sign Approach

Our main result is to show how to construct a signature scheme for signing elements of a message space $\mathcal{M}$ based on an efficient NIZK proof of knowledge system, a signature scheme for signing message space $\mathcal{K}$ and a family of pairwise independent hash functions $\{H_k\} : \mathcal{M} \to \mathcal{R}$ with key space $\mathcal{K}$ and exponential sized range.

The basic idea is that, instead of hashing messages and signing the hash, we certify the key k of a pairwise independent hash function and append the output of the hash $h = H_k(M)$ to the certificate. Each hash-function key k is used exactly once, and by the pairwise independence of H_k the hash value h does not help an attacker to find the hash (under the same key) of any other message. Then, for the certification of k we make use of the signature scheme for $\mathcal{K}$ and the zero-knowledge proof of knowledge protocol. This allows us to guarantee that the adversary cannot learn any useful knowledge from the certification process about k and thus even given many signatures, he is not able to guess a hash value h' for any message M' different from M.

3.1   A Stateless Signature Scheme for Message Space $\mathcal{M}$

Let $\mathsf{Sig}_\mathcal{K} = (\mathsf{Kg}_\mathcal{K}, \mathsf{Sign}_\mathcal{K}, \mathsf{Verify}_\mathcal{K})$ be a (potentially stateful) Weak CMA F-unforgeable signature scheme on message space $\mathcal{K}$ for some bijection F. (Note that a stateless signature scheme would suffice - the construction would then simply not use the state s.) Let $\{h_k\}_{\mathcal{K}(\lambda)} : \mathcal{M} \to \mathcal{R}$ be a pairwise independent hash function.[4] Let $\mathsf{Setup}, \mathsf{Prove}, \mathsf{VerifyProof}$ be a non-interactive zero knowledge

---

[4] We will omit the security parameter λ and simply write $\mathcal{K}$ when it is clear from context.

proof of knowledge system. We construct a signature scheme with message space $\mathcal{M}$ as follows:

SigKg(1^λ): Run $\mathsf{Kg}_\mathcal{K}(1^\lambda)$ to generate a key pair $(pk_\mathcal{K}, sk_\mathcal{K})$. Generate the common reference string crs for a NIZKPK proof system. Output $pk = (pk_\mathcal{K}, crs)$ and $sk = (sk_\mathcal{K}, crs)$.

Sign(sk, M): Parse $sk = (sk_\mathcal{K}, crs)$. Choose random key $k \leftarrow \mathcal{K}$. Compute the signature $\sigma_\mathcal{K} \leftarrow \mathsf{Sign}_\mathcal{K}^{s=0}(sk_\mathcal{K}, k)$ and the hash value $h = H_k(M)$. Finally, construct a proof of knowledge of $F(k)$ and the corresponding signature, i.e.:

$$\pi \in \mathsf{NIZKPK}\{(f, \sigma_\mathcal{K}) : \{\exists k \in \mathcal{K} \text{ s.t. } f = F(k) \wedge$$
$$\mathsf{Verify}_\mathcal{K}(pk_\mathcal{K}, k, \sigma_\mathcal{K}) = 1 \wedge h = H_k(M)\}\}$$

Output $\sigma = (h, \pi)$.

Note that we write $\mathsf{Sign}_\mathcal{K}^{s=0}$ to indicate that in case of a stateful signature we reset the state to the initial state after each signing operation. We will see below that as the signature is always used inside of a NIZKPK this does not impact security.

SigVerify(pk, M, σ): Parse $pk = (pk_\mathcal{K}, crs)$ and $\sigma = (h, \pi)$. Verify the proof π w.r.t. crs and $pk_\mathcal{K}, h, M$.

3.2 Unforgeability of the Signature Scheme

We now prove our main result:

Theorem 2. *Given a (potentially stateful) Weak CMA F-unforgeable signature scheme* ($\mathsf{Kg}_\mathcal{K}, \mathsf{Sign}_\mathcal{K}^s, \mathsf{Verify}_\mathcal{K}$), *a secure NIZKPK proof system* (Setup, Prove, VerifyProof), *and a pairwise independent hash function family* $\{H_k\}_{k \in \mathcal{K}(\lambda)}$ *whose range is exponential in* λ, *the resulting construction* (SigKg, Sign, SigVerify) *is a stateless CMA unforgeable signature scheme.*

Proof. We formally prove the security of the transformation using a sequence of games. For simplicity, we will assume that the proof system has perfect soundness and perfect extraction, but this can be relaxed to allow for a negligible error. Let $p_i(\lambda)$ be the probability that the adversary succeeds in **Game i**. We let **Game 1** be the EUF-CMA game for the signature scheme described above. We will show via a series of hybrid games that the success probability in this game must be negligible.

Game 1: EUF-CMA. This is the original EUF-CMA game for the signature scheme described above, i.e. signing queries are answered using Sign and the adversary succeeds if it can make SigVerify accept for a message vector that was never signed before.

The adversary succeeds with probability $p_1(\lambda)$.

Game 2: Implement State Updates. This game proceeds just as the EUF-CMA game except that Sign uses calls to $\mathsf{Sign}_\mathcal{K}^s$ instead of calls to $\mathsf{Sign}_\mathcal{K}^{s=0}$. This means that the state is no longer reset. Let $p_2(\lambda)$ be the probability that the adversary succeeds in this game.

Lemma 1. $\Delta_1(\lambda) = |p_2(\lambda) - p_1(\lambda)|$ *is negligible by computational witness indistinguishability property of the proof system.*

Proof. Note first that a proof system that is zero-knowledge is also witness indistinguishable. Clearly, both the signatures generated by $\mathsf{Sign}_{\mathcal{K}}{}^{s=0}$ and by $\mathsf{Sign}_{\mathcal{K}}{}^{s}$ correspond to valid witnesses for the NIZKPK in the signing algorithm. We first construct a sequence of hybrid games. In each hybrid an additional call to $\mathsf{Sign}_{\mathcal{K}}{}^{s=0}$ is replaced by $\mathsf{Sign}_{\mathcal{K}}{}^{s}$. Given an adversary $\mathcal{A}$ that has a non-negligible success difference between any of these hybrids, we can build an algorithm $\mathcal{B}$ that breaks the witness indistinguishability property of the proof system. $\mathcal{B}$ computes two witnesses w_0 and w_1 that are based on $\mathsf{Sign}_{\mathcal{K}}{}^{s=0}$ and $\mathsf{Sign}_{\mathcal{K}}{}^{s}$ respectively. $\mathcal{B}$ outputs w_0 and w_1 to the witness indistinguishability challenge game and uses the resulting proof π to respond to the ith signature query. Depending on the bit flipped by the challenge game, $\mathcal{A}$ will interact with one of the two hybrids. If $\mathcal{A}$ succeeds in producing a forgery, $\mathcal{B}$ outputs 1, otherwise 0. It follows that since $\mathcal{A}$ can make at most a polynomial number of queries, $\Delta_1(\lambda)$ is negligible □

Game 3: Reusing k. This game will proceed just as **Game 2** except that once the adversary outputs his forgery, $\tilde{M}, \tilde{\sigma} = (\tilde{h}, \tilde{\pi})$, we will extracts $\tilde{f}$ from $\tilde{\pi}$, and compare it against the values used to answer the adversary's queries. The adversary succeeds in this game if and only if the signature verifies, the message is new, and the value $\tilde{f}$ corresponds to $F(k)$ for some k used to answer a previous query. Let $p_3(\lambda)$ be the probability that the adversary succeeds in this game.

Lemma 2. $\Delta_2(\lambda) = |p_3(\lambda) - p_2(\lambda)|$ *is negligible by the F-unforgeability of the signature scheme.*

Proof. The two games differ only in the event **Bad** that $\mathcal{A}$ outputs a forgery from which a value $\tilde{f}$ can be extracted that does not correspond to previous signature queries. We give a reduction to show that an attacker for which this event has non-negligible probability can be used to construct an algorithm $\mathcal{B}$ that breaks the security of the underlying Weak CMA F-unforgeable signature scheme.

Let Q correspond to the maximum number of signing queries made by $\mathcal{A}$. $\mathcal{B}$ publishes Q random values $k_1 \ldots k_Q \in \mathcal{K}$ to the Weak F-unforgeability CMA challenger and receives Q signatures in return. It sets up the proof system by providing extraction parameters, and uses these signatures to answer the signing queries of $\mathcal{A}$. $\mathcal{B}$ extracts $\tilde{\sigma}_{\mathcal{K}}$ and $\tilde{f} \notin \{F(k_1), \ldots, F(k_Q)\}$ from $\tilde{\pi}$ and outputs it as a forgery. By perfect extraction, we are guaranteed that $\tilde{\sigma}_{\mathcal{K}}$ is a valid signature on $F^{-1}(f)$, so if $\mathcal{A}$ is successful in producing event **Bad**, then $\tilde{f}, \tilde{\sigma}_{\mathcal{K}}$ exactly matches the definition of a valid Weak CMA F-forgery. Consequently we conclude that $\Delta_2(\lambda) \leq Pr[\textbf{Bad}]$. □

Game 4: Check h. This game will proceed as in **Game 2** except that once the adversary outputs his forgery, $M, \sigma = (h, \pi)$, we let $K = (k_1, \ldots, k_Q)$ be the set of hash keys used to answer the adversary's queries. Then we verify whether $h = H_{k_i}(M)$ for any $i \in 1 \dots Q$. The adversary succeeds if and only if the signature verifies, the message is new, and this check succeeds (i.e. there is such a value). Let $p_4(\lambda)$ be the probability that the adversary succeeds in this game.

Lemma 3. $p_3(\lambda) \leq p_4(\lambda) + \Delta_3(\lambda)$ *for negligible $\Delta_3(\lambda)$ by the soundness of the proof system.*

Proof. If h is computed correctly with the hash key k corresponding to the value $\tilde{f} = F(k)$ extracted from the proof, **Game 4** will be successful in all cases in which **Game 3** is successful. Thus, this follows directly from the perfect extraction of the proof system.   □

Game 5: Simulate Proofs. In this game, when the public parameters are generated, the challenger will run SimSetup to generate parameters crs, and trapdoor sim. When responding to signature queries, the challenger chooses random $k \leftarrow \mathcal{K}$ and forms h as in the real signing protocol, but generates the proof using SimProve. As above, we judge the adversary's success by verifying the proof and checking the h component of the signature against the set of hash keys $\{k_1, \dots, k_Q\}$ used in previous queries. Let $p_5(\lambda)$ be the probability that the adversary succeeds in this game.

Lemma 4. $\Delta_4(\lambda) = |p_5(\lambda) - p_4(\lambda)|$ *is negligible by the zero-knowledge property of the proof system.*

Proof. An attacker with non-negligible $\Delta_4(\lambda)$ can be used to break the zero-knowledge property of the proof system. We use the standard definition of multi-theorem zero-knowledge. Given an attacker $\mathcal{A}$ with non-negligible $\Delta_4(\lambda)$, we construct an algorithm $\mathcal{B}$ that can distinguish whether, when interacting with a multi-theorem zero-knowledge challenge game, it is given real proofs or simulated proofs. $\mathcal{B}$ sets up the public key using the parameters received from the challenge game; to generate each signature, it chooses random $k \leftarrow \mathcal{K}$, generates $h, \sigma_{\mathcal{K}}$ as in the signing algorithm, and generate the zero-knowledge proof using an oracle query. If $\mathcal{A}$ succeeds in producing h which does not correspond to any of the hash keys $k_1, \dots, k_Q$ together with a proof π that verifies, then $\mathcal{B}$ outputs 1. If $|p_5(\lambda) - p_4(\lambda)|$ is non-negligible, then $\mathcal{B}$ will succeed in the zero knowledge game with non-negligible advantage.   □

Lemma 5. $p_5(\lambda)$ *is negligible when h is computed by a pairwise-independent hash function whose range $\mathcal{R}$ is exponential in λ.*

Proof. Suppose we know h and M for some unknown hash key k. Then for any other $h' \in \mathcal{R}$, $M' \in \mathcal{M}$, the probability (taken over possible values of $k \in \mathcal{K}$) that $h' = H_k(M')$ is $1/|\mathcal{R}|$ by pairwise independence. Thus, for any key k used by the signer, the probability of $\mathcal{A}$ producing a correct pair h', M' for that tuple is at most $1/|\mathcal{R}|$. Taking a union bound over all tuples used gives $q/|\mathcal{R}|$ where q is the total number of queries made by $\mathcal{A}$. This will be negligible since q is polynomial and $|\mathcal{R}|$ is exponential in λ.

By the triangle inequality $p_1(\lambda) \le \Delta_1(\lambda) + \Delta_2(\lambda) + \Delta_3(\lambda) + \Delta_4(\lambda) + p_5(k)$ is negligible as desired. □

4   Structure-Preserving Signatures from DLIN

Here we show that we can instantiate the building blocks described in the previous section based on DLIN, to construct a structure-preserving signature scheme. (In fact, we will describe a structure preserving scheme which allows us to sign vectors of ℓ group elements at once.)

First, we will review the Groth-Sahai NIZK proof system [GS08], which gives efficient proofs that are compatible with many pairing based schemes. Then we briefly present the pairwise-independent hash function we use, and how it can be used with Groth-Sahai. Finally, we will construct a new signature scheme for elements in $\mathbb{Z}_p^{\ell+1}$ which is both secure under DLIN and compatible with the Groth-Sahai proof system. Putting all of these together using the generic construction in Section 3 gives a secure signature scheme. Finally, since the hash function produces elements in the bilinear group $\mathbb{G}$, and Groth-Sahai proofs are composed of elements in $\mathbb{G}$ and can be verified with pairing product equations, the result is a structure preserving signature scheme.

4.1   NIZK Proofs Based on DLIN: The Groth-Sahai Proof System

Groth and Sahai [GS08] (in an extension of the results of [GOS06b] and [GOS06a]) showed how to construct non-interactive proof systems under the sub-group hiding, decisional linear, and external Diffie-Hellman assumptions that allow one to directly prove the pairing product equations common in pairing-based cryptography.

Groth-Sahai Proofs. The Groth-Sahai proof system allows to generate non-interactive zero-knowledge proofs of knowledge of values satisfying pairing product equations. We denote a proof π that proves knowledge of secret values $x_1, \ldots, x_N$ that fulfill a pairing product equation with constants $\{a_i\}_{i=1..N} \in \mathbb{G}, t \in \mathbb{G}_T$ and $\{\gamma_{i,j}\}_{i=1..N, j=1..N}$ by

$$\pi \leftarrow \mathsf{NIZKPK}\{(x_1, \ldots, x_N) : \prod_{i=1}^{N} e(a_i, x_i) \prod_{i=1}^{N} \prod_{j=1}^{N} e(x_i, x_j)^{\gamma_{i,j}} = t\} .$$

In a nutshell, Groth-Sahai proofs work by committing to all secret elements using either Linear [BBS04] or ElGamal [EG85] commitments (depending on the assumption used). The homomorphic properties of these commitments allow one to evaluate the pairing product equation in the committed domain. In addition, a Groth-Sahai proof contains a constant number of group elements that allow a verifier to check that the result of this computation corresponds to t. The verification algorithm only consists of pairings between the group elements of the commitments and these additional proof elements. Linear and ElGamal commitments are extractable. Given a setup with an extraction trapdoor, we can extract the committed value x_i from a proof, but not the opening $open_i$. This means that given a Groth-Sahai proof for a pairing product equation we can extract all the elements of $\mathbb{G}$ that make up the witness.

4.2 Pairwise Independent Hash Functions

We will need a pairwise independent family of hash-functions $\{H_k\}$, where $H_k :$ $\mathbb{G}^\ell \to \mathbb{G}$ with $\mathcal{M} = \mathbb{G}^\ell$ and $k \in \mathbb{Z}_p^{\ell+1}$. The function we propose is computed as

$$H_k(M_1, \ldots, M_\ell) = g^{k_0} \prod_{i=1..\ell} M_i^{k_i},$$

where $k = (k_0, \ldots, k_\ell)$. We show that this function family is indeed pairwise independent:

Theorem 3. *The above function family is pairwise independent.*

Proof. Let us express the probability
$$Pr[k \leftarrow \mathcal{K} : H_k(x) = a \wedge H_k(y) = b] =$$
$$\frac{|\{k_0, \ldots, k_\ell \mid g^{k_0} \prod_{i=1..\ell} x_i^{k_i} = a \wedge g^{k_0} \prod_{i=1..\ell} y_i^{k_i} = b\}|}{|\mathbb{Z}_p|^{\ell+1}}.$$

We have to show that the numerator equals $|\mathbb{Z}_p|^{\ell-1}$. This can be seen by looking at $g^{k_0} \prod_{i=1..\ell} x_i^{k_i} = a$ and $g^{k_0} \prod_{i=1..\ell} y_i^{k_i} = b$ as independent linear equations over the variables $k_0, \ldots, k_\ell$ (independence follows from $x \neq y$). As there are $\ell + 1$ variables and 2 equations, the solution set has $\ell - 1$ dimensions and thus has size $|\mathbb{Z}_p|^{\ell-1}$.

Finally, we observe that, given $g^{k_0}, \ldots, g^{k_\ell}$, we can easily use a pairing product equation to verify that h is correctly computed: for key $k = k_0, \ldots, k_\ell$ and message $M = M_1, \ldots, M_\ell$, it will be the case that $h = H_k(M)$ iff $e(h, g) = e(g, g^{k_0}) \prod_{i=1}^{\ell} e(M_i, g^{k_i})$. Thus, we can use the Groth-Sahai proof system to prove knowledge of $g^{k_0}, \ldots, g^{k_1}$ and $M_1, \ldots, M_k$ such that h is correct.

4.3 A Signature Scheme for Elements of Z_p

We will base our exponent-signature scheme $\mathsf{Sig}_{n \cdot exp}$ on the Hohenberger and Waters [HW09a] stateful signature scheme which was proved secure under the CDH assumption. In that scheme, each signature is indexed by a unique index s that is initialized to 0, and increased before each signing. A signature with message m, secret key a, public bases u, v, d, w, z, and randomness t, r consists of two group elements $\sigma_1 = (u^m v^r d)^a (w^{\lceil \lg(s) \rceil} z^s h)^t$ and $\sigma_2 = g^t$, and the two exponents $r, s \in \mathbb{Z}_p$. We adapt their scheme to obtain a stateful signature that is F-unforgeable under weak chosen message attacks (Weak CMA F-unforgeable) under the Randomized Computational Diffie-Hellman (RCDH) assumption, a new assumption which is implied by the DLIN assumption. We also show how to reuse the state to sign multiple message blocks. Interestingly, when we apply the transformation presented in Section 3, the result will be a fully secure, stateless signature scheme for signing group elements.

Simplifying the Hohenberger and Waters scheme. Recall that in the HW scheme, signatures include elements $\sigma_1 = (u^m v^r d)^a (w^{\lceil \lg(s) \rceil} z^s h)^t$ and $\sigma_2 = g^t$, and the two exponents $r, s \in \mathbb{Z}_p$. When building a zero-knowledge proof of knowledge of signature possession, we must prove that the signature is well formed, which in this case requires proving the correspondence between $\lceil \lg(s) \rceil$ and s. This typically involves two steps: 1) proving that a commitment contains the value $2^{\lceil \lg(s) \rceil}$, and 2) proving that this value is bigger than s. The range proof technique by [Bou00] for interactively proving the latter relation for large s uses hidden order groups and is based on the Strong RSA assumption. To obtain a scheme that is based purely on CDH, one has to use alternative range proof techniques, e.g. [BCDvdG87]. While such proofs can be efficiently computed ([Bou00] estimates a proof size of 27.5 kB), we are primarily interested in non-interactive proofs based on the Groth-Sahai proof system.

As pointed out in [HW09a], instead of signing $\lg(s)$ as part of σ_1 one can also sign s using a signature scheme that is already CMA secure under the CDH assumption, e.g. by employing the Waters signature [Wat05]. While this approach may be slightly circular, it gives us a performance advantage, as the expected number of signatures is usually much smaller than the size of the message space $\mathbb{Z}_p$.[5] Moreover, as we will see, when many messages are signed with related state (e.g. when we sign multiple message blocks at once), we need only sign a single state value, thus resulting in greater advantage.

Finally, we note that for our transformation we only require a weak signature scheme; thus we can simplify the resulting signature scheme further by replacing the Chameleon hash $u^m v^r$ with u^m itself.[6]

Our Construction. Let $\mathbb{G}$ be a symmetric bilinear group with pairing operation $e : \mathbb{G} \times \mathbb{G} \to \mathbb{G}_T$. Let $g, \hat{g}$ be random generators for $\mathbb{G}$. The resulting signature scheme is as follows:

$\mathsf{SigKg}_{exp}(1^\lambda)$ runs the Waters key generation to generate (pk_w, sk_w), chooses random $a \leftarrow \mathbb{Z}_p$ and $u, d, z, h \leftarrow \mathbb{G}$, and outputs secret key $sk = (a, sk_w)$ and a public key $pk = (g, \hat{g}, g^a, u, d, z, h, pk_w)$. (The initial value of s is 0.)

$\mathsf{Sign}_{exp}^s(sk, m)$ is a stateful signature algorithm which first increases the state s. To sign a message m, it computes $\sigma_1 = (u^m d)^a (z^s h)^t$, $\sigma_2 = g^t$, and a Waters signature σ_3 on s. The algorithm outputs $\sigma = (\sigma_1, \sigma_2, \sigma_3, s)$.

---

[5] The Waters signature operates bit-by-bit on it's message, and directly proving knowledge of a valid Waters signature has cost proportional to the bit-length of the message. Thus, proving correctness of our resulting signature will thus have cost proportional to the bit-length of the maximum possible value of s rather than the bit length of the message.

[6] We note that, as part of their result, Hohenberger and Waters [HW09b] give a generic transformation from Weak CMA security to CMA security based on Chameleon hashes. Weak CMA F-unforgeable signatures are, however, sufficient to obtain a CMA secure signature scheme for signing group elements via our transform.

$\mathsf{SigVerify}_{exp}(pk, m, \sigma)$ parses σ as $(\sigma_1, \sigma_2, \sigma_3, i)$ and checks that signature σ_3 on i is valid. Then it uses the bilinear map to check $e(\sigma_1, g) = e(u^m d, g^a) e(\sigma_2, z^i h)$.

Note: We write $\mathsf{Sign}^s_{exp}(sk, m)$ to indicate that we run the signing algorithm on state s.

Security of Our Construction. We show that this signature scheme is unforgeable under weak chosen message attacks, and moreover, that it is F-unforgeable under such attacks for a simple function F that maps exponents to group elements. (Recall that F-unforgeability means that it is impossible to produce $F(m)$ and a forged signature on m. This allows us to prove a contradiction even when we can extract only $F(m)$ and not m as is the case when we use the Groth-Sahai proof system.)

Theorem 4. *Our* $(\mathsf{SigKg}_{exp}, \mathsf{Sign}^s_{exp}, \mathsf{SigVerify}_{exp})$ *signature scheme is unforgeable under weak chosen message attacks under the CDH assumption. The proof is omitted. It follows very closely the proof of F-unforgeability presented below.*

Theorem 5. *Let $F(m) = (g^m, \hat{g}^m)$. Our* $(\mathsf{SigKg}_{exp}, \mathsf{Sign}^s_{exp}, \mathsf{SigVerify}_{exp})$ *signature scheme is Weak CMA F-unforgeable under the RCDH assumption. Since RCDH is implied by DLIN, this means the signature is secure under DLIN.*

Proof. A successful adversary $\mathcal{A}$ outputs a forgery $\tilde{\sigma} = (\tilde{\sigma}_1, \tilde{\sigma}_2, \tilde{\sigma}_3, \tilde{i})$. If the signature on index $\tilde{i}$ was never created, we break the signature scheme that is used to sign the index s. Thus we concentrate on the case where the adversary reuses one of the s values from the signing queries as $\tilde{i}$. The first step in a reduction to RCDH will be to guess this $\tilde{i}$. (Here we have at most a polynomial loss in the tightness of the reduction.)

Setup: As we consider a weakly secure signature scheme, the game starts with the adversary outputting polynomially many messages $m_1, \ldots, m_Q, Q \le poly(\lambda)$. The reduction chooses a random index i^*, $1 \le i^* \le Q$. Given (g, g^a, g^b) as specified in the RCDH assumption, the parameters are set up as follows. Choose random $y_d \in \mathbb{Z}_p$ and set $u = g^b$, $d = g^{-bm_{i^*}} g^{y_d}$, then choose random $x_z, x_h \in \mathbb{Z}_p$, and set $z = g^b g^{x_z}$, $h = g^{-bi^*} g^{x_h}$. The reduction outputs $pk = (g, g^a, u, d, z, h)$.

Sign: The adversary is now given signatures on messages $m_1, \ldots, m_Q, Q \le poly(\lambda)$, that are computed as follows:

For $s = i^*$, choose random t and form $\sigma_1 = (g^a)^{y_d} (z^s h)^t$, $\sigma_2 = g^t$. Note that this results in a correctly distributed signature as

$$(g^a)^{y_d} (z^s h)^t =$$
$$((g^{ab})^{m_{i^*} - m_{i^*}})(g^a)^{y_d} (z^s h)^t =$$
$$((g^b)^{m_{i^*}} (g^{-bm_{i^*}} g^{y_d}))^a (z^s h)^t = (u^{m_{i^*}} d)^a (z^s h)^t .$$

For $s \ne i^*$, choose random t' and implicitly let $t = t' - a(m_s - m_{i^*})/(s - i^*)$. Form $\sigma_1 = (g^a)^{y_d} T^{x_z s + x_h} (g^b)^{t'(s-i^*)}$ and $\sigma_2 = T$ for $T = g^{t'}/(g^a)^{(m_s - m_{i^*})/(s-i^*)}$.

Then $T = g^{t'-a(m_s-m_{i*})/(s-i^*)} = g^t$ and

$$(g^a)^{y_d} T^{x_z s + x_h} (g^b)^{t'(s-i^*)} =$$
$$(g^{y_d})^a (g^{x_z s} g^{x_h})^t (g^b)^{t'(s-i^*)} =$$
$$(u^{m_s} d)^a (g^{x_z s} g^{x_h})^t (g^b)^{t'(s-i^*)} (g^{-ab})^{(m_s-m_{i*})} =$$
$$(u^{m_s} d)^a (g^{x_z s} g^{x_h})^t (g^{b(s-i^*)})^t =$$
$$(u^{m_s} d)^a (g^{(b+x_z)s} g^{-bi^* + x_h})^t = (u^{m_s} d)^a (z^s h)^t .$$

Response: Eventually the adversary responds with a forgery $\tilde{\sigma} = (\tilde{\sigma}_1, \tilde{\sigma}_2, \tilde{\sigma}_3, \tilde{i})$, $g^{\tilde{m}}, \hat{g}^{\tilde{m}}$, such that $\tilde{m} \notin \{m_1, \ldots, m_Q\}$. If $\tilde{i} \neq i^*$ the reduction aborts. Otherwise it outputs $g^{\tilde{m}}/g^{m_{i*}}$, $\hat{g}^{\tilde{m}}/\hat{g}^{m_{i*}}$ and $\tilde{\sigma}_1/g^{a y_d} \tilde{\sigma}_2^{(x_z \tilde{i} - x_h)}$ as a RCDH triple.

Signing Multiple Message Blocks. For our transformation, we actually need to be able to sign vector of exponents, i.e. we need our signature scheme Sign_{exp} to have message space $\mathbb{Z}_p^n$ for $n > 1$. There is also an efficiency advantage to batching several messages together: We note that the Waters signature on the index s needs to be done only once. The indices of the individual signatures will be set to $n \cdot (s-1) + 1, \ldots, n \cdot (s-1) + n$.

Our multiple message block signature is as follows:

$\text{SigKg}_{exp}(1^\lambda)$ is unchanged.

$\text{Sign}_{n \cdot exp}^s(sk, m_1, \ldots, m_n)$. The signature algorithm increases the state s. To sign message m, it then computes $\sigma_{1,j} = (u^{m_j} d)^a (z^{n(s-1)+j} h)^{t_j}$, and $\sigma_{2,j} = g^{t_j}$, for $j = 1..n$ and $t_j \leftarrow \mathbb{Z}_p$. We also add a Waters signature σ_3 on s. The algorithm outputs $\sigma = (\{\sigma_{1,j}, \sigma_{2,j}\}_{j=1..n}, \sigma_3, s)$.

$\text{SigVerify}_{n \cdot exp}(pk, m_1, \ldots, m_n, \sigma)$. Parse σ as $(\{\sigma_{1,j}, \sigma_{2,j}\}_{j=1..n}, \sigma_3, i)$. The verification algorithm first checks that signature σ_3 on i is valid. It uses the bilinear map to verify $e(\sigma_{1,j}, g) = e(u^{m_j} d, g^a) e(\sigma_{2,j}, z^{n(i-1)+j} h)$, for $j = 1..n$.

Unforgeability and F-unforgeability under weak CMA attacks can be shown via a straightforward extension of the proof for the single message scheme. Note that the reduction now has to guess values i^* and j^*, where $1 \leq i^* \leq Q$ and $1 \leq j^* \leq n$ respectively. The RCDH challenge is embedded into message block j^* of signature query i^*.

Efficient Zero-Knowledge Proof of Knowledge. Except for the value s, the signature $\sigma = (\{\sigma_{1,j}, \sigma_{2,j}\}_{j=1..n}, \sigma_3, s)$ consists only of group elements. When employing the Groth-Sahai proof system, the Waters signature σ_3 is proved in a bit-by-bit fashion that allows us to extract s (see [FP09] for further details). It is thus possible to give proofs of knowledge for the above signature scheme using the pairing-product equation proofs in [GS08] in a straightforward way. If we combine this with the pairing-product equations described in Section 4.2, we can generate an efficient GS proof for the relation needed for our generic construction.

Table 1. Estimated size in group elements of a signature and a proof for different versions of our transform: ℓ is the number of group elements signed and $N = 2^x$ is an upper bound on the number of signatures generated per key pair

Instantiation	stateless signature
DLIN	$100 + 24\ell + 9x$
q-BB-HSDH + q-TDH + DLIN	$79 + 7\ell$
RCDH + SXDH	$77 + 18\ell + 6x$
q-BB-HSDH + q-TDH + SXDH	$61 + 6\ell$

4.4   Performance Analysis

For the performance analysis we instantiate our signatures and proofs with two signature schemes – the scheme based on RCDH described in Section 4.3 and one based on q-BB-HSDH and q-TDH described in [BCKL09].[7] We instantiate the Groth-Sahai proofs under DLIN and SXDH. Here ℓ is the number of signatures, and 2^x is the maximum number of signatures issued. Table 1 gives estimates for the size of a signature and a proof of signature possession (expressed in number of group elements). More details concerning the performance analysis can be found in the full version [CK11]. We note that while our signatures and proofs are still somewhat expensive, they are still within the realm of feasibility (and not much more expensive than the signature scheme used in [BCKL09] for example).

5   Conclusion and Open Problems

We construct a reasonably efficient signature scheme for signing group elements based on DLIN, one of the weakest decisional assumptions in the pairing setting (and the weakest one that was used to construct Groth-Sahai proofs). We show that such a signature scheme is an important building block for numerous cryptographic protocols. As our construction does not make use of "q-type" assumptions, it can be used for instantiations of protocols under weaker assumptions for which as of now only instantiations in the random oracle or generic group model were known.

Thus, we see a tradeoff between efficiency and security, and we argue that in many cases sacrificing an order of magnitude in efficiency for a significantly weaker (and non q-type) and more standard assumption may be a reasonable exchange. Furthermore, this result can be seen as evidence that schemes based on relatively weak assumptions can be practical, and as support for the argument that, while they are very important developments, we need not necessarily be satisfied with schemes based on the generic group model, but rather that we should continue looking for schemes which are *both* efficient *and* based on weak assumptions.

---

[7] For a discussion of other possible instantiations for the exponent signature scheme, see the full version [CK11].

References

[ACJT00]   Ateniese, G., Camenisch, J., Joye, M., Tsudik, G.: A Practical and Provably Secure Coalition-Resistant Group Signature Scheme. In: Bellare, M. (ed.) CRYPTO 2000. LNCS, vol. 1880, pp. 255–270. Springer, Heidelberg (2000)

[AFG+10]   Abe, M., Fuchsbauer, G., Groth, J., Haralambiev, K., Ohkubo, M.: Structure-Preserving Signatures and Commitments to Group Elements. In: Rabin, T. (ed.) CRYPTO 2010. LNCS, vol. 6223, pp. 209–236. Springer, Heidelberg (2010)

[AGHO11]   Abe, M., Groth, J., Haralambiev, K., Ohkubo, M.: Optimal Structure-Preserving Signatures in Asymmetric Bilinear Groups. In: Rogaway, P. (ed.) CRYPTO 2011. LNCS, vol. 6841, pp. 649–666. Springer, Heidelberg (2011)

[AHO10]   Abe, M., Haralambiev, K., Ohkubo, M.: Signing on elements in bilinear groups for modular protocol design, Cryptology ePrint Archive, Report 2010/133 (2010), http://eprint.iacr.org/

[ASM08]   Au, M.H., Susilo, W., Mu, Y.: Practical Anonymous Divisible E-Cash from Bounded Accumulators. In: Tsudik, G. (ed.) FC 2008. LNCS, vol. 5143, pp. 287–301. Springer, Heidelberg (2008)

[AWSM07]   Au, M.H., Wu, Q., Susilo, W., Mu, Y.: Compact E-Cash from Bounded Accumulator. In: Abe, M. (ed.) CT-RSA 2007. LNCS, vol. 4377, pp. 178–195. Springer, Heidelberg (2006)

[BB04]   Boneh, D., Boyen, X.: Short Signatures Without Random Oracles. In: Cachin, C., Camenisch, J. (eds.) EUROCRYPT 2004. LNCS, vol. 3027, pp. 56–73. Springer, Heidelberg (2004)

[BBS04]   Boneh, D., Boyen, X., Shacham, H.: Short Group Signatures. In: Franklin, M. (ed.) CRYPTO 2004. LNCS, vol. 3152, pp. 41–55. Springer, Heidelberg (2004)

[BCDvdG87] Brickell, E.F., Chaum, D., Damgård, I., van de Graaf, J.: Gradual and Verifiable Release of a Secret. In: Pomerance, C. (ed.) CRYPTO 1987. LNCS, vol. 293, pp. 156–166. Springer, Heidelberg (1988)

[BCKL08]   Belenkiy, M., Chase, M., Kohlweiss, M., Lysyanskaya, A.: P-signatures and Noninteractive Anonymous Credentials. In: Canetti, R. (ed.) TCC 2008. LNCS, vol. 4948, pp. 356–374. Springer, Heidelberg (2008)

[BCKL09]   Belenkiy, M., Chase, M., Kohlweiss, M., Lysyanskaya, A.: Compact E-Cash and Simulatable VRFs Revisited. In: Shacham, H., Waters, B. (eds.) Pairing 2009. LNCS, vol. 5671, pp. 114–131. Springer, Heidelberg (2009)

[BCL04]   Bangerter, E., Camenisch, J., Lysyanskaya, A.: A Cryptographic Framework for the Controlled Release of Certified Data. In: Christianson, B., Crispo, B., Malcolm, J.A., Roe, M. (eds.) Security Protocols 2004. LNCS, vol. 3957, pp. 20–42. Springer, Heidelberg (2006)

[Bou00]   Boudot, F.: Efficient Proofs that a Committed Number Lies in an Interval. In: Preneel, B. (ed.) EUROCRYPT 2000. LNCS, vol. 1807, pp. 431–444. Springer, Heidelberg (2000)

[CCS08]   Camenisch, J., Chaabouni, R., Shelat, A.: Efficient Protocols for Set Membership and Range Proofs. In: Pieprzyk, J. (ed.) ASIACRYPT 2008. LNCS, vol. 5350, pp. 234–252. Springer, Heidelberg (2008)

[CDS94]   Cramer, R., Damgård, I., Schoenmakers, B.: Proof of Partial Knowledge and Simplified Design of Witness Hiding Protocols. In: Desmedt, Y.G.

(ed.) CRYPTO 1994. LNCS, vol. 839, pp. 174–187. Springer, Heidelberg (1994)

[CG08]   Canard, S., Gouget, A.: Anonymity in transferable E-cash. In: Bellovin, S.M., Gennaro, R., Keromytis, A.D., Yung, M. (eds.) ACNS 2008. LNCS, vol. 5037, pp. 207–223. Springer, Heidelberg (2008)

[CGH06]   Canard, S., Gouget, A., Hufschmitt, E.: A Handy Multi-coupon System. In: Zhou, J., Yung, M., Bao, F. (eds.) ACNS 2006. LNCS, vol. 3989, pp. 66–81. Springer, Heidelberg (2006)

[CGH09]   Coull, S., Green, M., Hohenberger, S.: Controlling Access to an Oblivious Database Using Stateful Anonymous Credentials. In: Jarecki, S., Tsudik, G. (eds.) PKC 2009. LNCS, vol. 5443, pp. 501–520. Springer, Heidelberg (2009)

[CHK⁺06] Camenisch, J., Hohenberger, S., Kohlweiss, M., Lysyanskaya, A., Meyerovich, M.: How to win the clone wars: Efficient periodic n-times anonymous authentication. In: Juels, A., Wright, R.N., De Capitani, di Vimercati, S. (eds.) ACM CCS, pp. 201–210. ACM (2006)

[CHL05]   Camenisch, J., Hohenberger, S., Lysyanskaya, A.: Compact E-cash. In: Cramer, R. (ed.) EUROCRYPT 2005. LNCS, vol. 3494, pp. 302–321. Springer, Heidelberg (2005)

[CHL06]   Camenisch, J., Hohenberger, S., Lysyanskaya, A.: Balancing Accountability and Privacy Using E-Cash (Extended Abstract). In: De Prisco, R., Yung, M. (eds.) SCN 2006. LNCS, vol. 4116, pp. 141–155. Springer, Heidelberg (2006)

[CK11]   Chase, M., Kohlweiss, M.: A domain transformation for structure-preserving signatures on group elements. IACR Cryptology ePrint Archive, 342 (2011)

[CL01]   Camenisch, J., Lysyanskaya, A.: An Efficient System for Non-transferable Anonymous Credentials with Optional Anonymity Revocation. In: Pfitzmann, B. (ed.) EUROCRYPT 2001. LNCS, vol. 2045, pp. 93–118. Springer, Heidelberg (2001)

[CL02]   Camenisch, J., Lysyanskaya, A.: A Signature Scheme with Efficient Protocols. In: Cimato, S., Galdi, C., Persiano, G. (eds.) SCN 2002. LNCS, vol. 2576, pp. 268–289. Springer, Heidelberg (2003)

[CL06]   Chase, M., Lysyanskaya, A.: On Signatures of Knowledge. In: Dwork, C. (ed.) CRYPTO 2006. LNCS, vol. 4117, pp. 78–96. Springer, Heidelberg (2006)

[CLM07]   Camenisch, J., Lysyanskaya, A., Meyerovich, M.: Endorsed e-cash. In: IEEE Symposium on Security and Privacy, pp. 101–115. IEEE Computer Society (2007)

[CLY09]   Cathalo, J., Libert, B., Yung, M.: Group Encryption: Non-interactive Realization in the Standard Model. In: Matsui, M. (ed.) ASIACRYPT 2009. LNCS, vol. 5912, pp. 179–196. Springer, Heidelberg (2009)

[Cra97]   Cramer, R.: Modular design of secure yet practical cryptographic protocols, Ph.D. thesis, University of Amsterdam, Amsterdam (1997)

[Dam02]   Damgård, I.: On σ-protocols (2002),
          http://www.daimi.au.dk/~ivan/Sigma.ps

[EG85]   El Gamal, T.: A Public Key Cryptosystem and a Signature Scheme Based on Discrete Logarithms. In: Blakely, G.R., Chaum, D. (eds.) CRYPTO 1984. LNCS, vol. 196, pp. 10–18. Springer, Heidelberg (1985)

[FP08]   Fuchsbauer, G., Pointcheval, D.: Anonymous Proxy Signatures. In: Ostro-
           vsky, R., De Prisco, R., Visconti, I. (eds.) SCN 2008. LNCS, vol. 5229, pp.
           201–217. Springer, Heidelberg (2008)
[FP09]   Fuchsbauer, G., Pointcheval, D.: Proofs on Encrypted Values in Bilinear
           Groups and an Application to Anonymity of Signatures. In: Shacham, H.,
           Waters, B. (eds.) Pairing 2009. LNCS, vol. 5671, pp. 132–149. Springer,
           Heidelberg (2009)
[Fuc09]   Fuchsbauer, G.: Automorphic signatures in bilinear groups, Cryptology
           ePrint Archive, Report 2009/320 (2009), http://eprint.iacr.org/
[GH08]   Green, M., Hohenberger, S.: Universally Composable Adaptive Oblivious
           Transfer. In: Pieprzyk, J. (ed.) ASIACRYPT 2008. LNCS, vol. 5350, pp.
           179–197. Springer, Heidelberg (2008)
[GOS06a]   Groth, J., Ostrovsky, R., Sahai, A.: Non-interactive Zaps and New Tech-
           niques for NIZK. In: Dwork, C. (ed.) CRYPTO 2006. LNCS, vol. 4117,
           pp. 97–111. Springer, Heidelberg (2006)
[GOS06b]   Groth, J., Ostrovsky, R., Sahai, A.: Perfect Non-interactive Zero Knowl-
           edge for NP. In: Vaudenay, S. (ed.) EUROCRYPT 2006. LNCS, vol. 4004,
           pp. 339–358. Springer, Heidelberg (2006)
[Gro06]   Groth, J.: Simulation-Sound NIZK Proofs for a Practical Language and
           Constant Size Group Signatures. In: Lai, X., Chen, K. (eds.) ASIACRYPT
           2006. LNCS, vol. 4284, pp. 444–459. Springer, Heidelberg (2006)
[Gro07]   Groth, J.: Fully anonymous group signatures without random
           oracles, Cryptology ePrint Archive, Report 2007/186 (2007),
           http://eprint.iacr.org/
[GS08]   Groth, J., Sahai, A.: Efficient Non-interactive Proof Systems for Bilinear
           Groups. In: Smart, N.P. (ed.) EUROCRYPT 2008. LNCS, vol. 4965, pp.
           415–432. Springer, Heidelberg (2008)
[HW09a]   Hohenberger, S., Waters, B.: Realizing Hash-and-Sign Signatures under
           Standard Assumptions. In: Joux, A. (ed.) EUROCRYPT 2009. LNCS,
           vol. 5479, pp. 333–350. Springer, Heidelberg (2009)
[HW09b]   Hohenberger, S., Waters, B.: Short and Stateless Signatures from the RSA
           Assumption. In: Halevi, S. (ed.) CRYPTO 2009. LNCS, vol. 5677, pp. 654–
           670. Springer, Heidelberg (2009)
[TS06]   Teranishi, I., Sako, K.: k-Times Anonymous Authentication with a Con-
           stant Proving Cost. In: Yung, M., Dodis, Y., Kiayias, A., Malkin, T. (eds.)
           PKC 2006. LNCS, vol. 3958, pp. 525–542. Springer, Heidelberg (2006)
[Wat05]   Waters, B.: Efficient Identity-Based Encryption Without Random Oracles.
           In: Cramer, R. (ed.) EUROCRYPT 2005. LNCS, vol. 3494, pp. 114–127.
           Springer, Heidelberg (2005)

Blackbox Construction of a More Than Non-Malleable CCA1 Encryption Scheme from Plaintext Awareness

Steven Myers[1], Mona Sergi[2], and abhi shelat[2]

[1] Indiana University, Bloomington IN 47408, USA
[2] University of Virginia, Charlottesville VA 22904, USA

Abstract. We construct an NM-CCA1 encryption scheme from any CCA1 encryption scheme that is also plaintext aware and weakly simulatable. We believe this is the first construction of a NM-CCA1 scheme that follows strictly from encryption schemes with seemingly weaker or incomparable security definitions to NM-CCA1.

Previously, the statistical PA1 notion of plaintext awareness was only known to imply CCA1. Our result is therefore novel because unlike the case of CPA and CCA2, it is unknown whether a CCA1 scheme can be transformed into an NM-CCA1 scheme. Additionally, we show both the Damgård Elgamal Scheme (DEG) [Dam91] and the Cramer-Shoup Lite Scheme (CS-Lite) [CS03] are weakly simulatable under the DDH assumption. Since both are known to be statistical PA1 under the Diffie-Hellman Knowledge (DHK) assumption, they instantiate our scheme securely.

Next, in a partial response to a question posed by Matsuda and Matsuura [MM11], we define an extended version of the NM-CCA1, cNM-CCA1, in which the security definition is modified so that the adversary is permuted to ask a $c \geq 1$ number of parallel queries after receiving the challenge ciphertext. We extend our construction to yield a cNM-CCA1 scheme for any constant c. All of our constructions are black-box.

Keywords: Public-Key Encryption, Plaintext-Awareness, Non-Malleability.

1 Introduction

The standard security definition of an encryption scheme does not prevent an adversary who observes an encryption of the message m from producing an encryption of the message $f(m)$ for some function f (even though the value m remains private). The seminal work of Dolev, Dwork, and Naor [DDN03] addressed this security issue by introducing the area of non-malleable cryptographic primitives such as encryption schemes, commitment schemes, and zero-knowledge. Later, Pass, shelat and Vaikuntanathan [PSV06] strengthened the DDN definition and presented a construction from CPA to non-malleable CPA using non-blackbox use of the original encryption scheme. There have been many follow-up works that propose more efficient constructions of non-malleable primitives. A

I. Visconti and R. De Prisco (Eds.): SCN 2012, LNCS 7485, pp. 149–165, 2012.
© Springer-Verlag Berlin Heidelberg 2012

notable achievement in this line of research has been the construction of non-malleable primitives using only black-box access to the standard version of the same primitive [CDSMW08, PW09, Wee10]. In particular, [CDSMW08] show how non-malleable CPA encryption can be constructed from standard versions of encryption in a black-box manner.

However, the question of whether an NM-CCA1 encryption scheme can be constructed from a CCA1 encryption scheme has remained open. This blemish on our understanding of the theory of encryption has remained despite multiple advances including many novel techniques for constructing encryption schemes. In this work, we present a black-box construction of an NM-CCA1 encryption scheme for a subset of CCA1 encryption schemes, namely those which are also plaintext aware under multiple keys and weakly simulatable (we will formally define these concepts later). Intuitively, an encryption scheme is plaintext aware (called **sPA1** in [BP04]) if the only way that a p.p.t. adversary can produce a valid ciphertext is to apply the (randomized) encryption algorithm to the public key and a message [BP04]. Notice that this definition does not imply non-malleability since there is no guarantee of what an adversary can do *when given a valid ciphertext*. In fact, both encryption schemes from [BP04] are multiplicatively homomorphic. The weakly simulatable property in our construction is required for technical reasons and roughly corresponds to the ability to to sample ciphertexts and pseudo-ciphertexts with random coins used to generate them.

Note that there exist encryption schemes that satisfy security notions that "sit between" standard notions. One such example from Cramer et al. [CHH$^+$07] consists of a black-box construction of a q-bounded CCA2 encryption scheme which is not NM-CPA, but which satisfies a stronger security notion than CPA. In particular, as a generalization of NM-CPA, Matsuda and Matsuura [MM11] put forth the challenge of constructing encryption schemes that can handle more than one parallel query after revealing the challenge ciphertext. They write:

> Since any (unbounded) CCA secure PKE construction from IND-CPA secure ones must first be secure against adversaries who make two or more parallel decryption queries, we believe that overcoming this barrier of two parallel queries is worth tackling.

In this spirit, we define an extension over NM-CCA1, cNM-CCA1, that is defined identically to NM-CCA1 except that the adversary can make c adaptive parallel decryption queries after seeing the challenge ciphertext, where each parallel decryption query can request that a polynomial number of ciphertexts be decrypted (excluding the challenge ciphertext). (Note that NM-CCA1 is cNM-CCA1 where the parameter c is set to be one.) Then we show how to construct a cNM-CCA1 secure encryption scheme for an arbitrary constant c. Unfortunately, the size of the ciphertext in a cNM-CCA1 encryption scheme is polynomially bigger than the size of the ciphertext in a (c-1)NM-CCA1 encryption scheme and thus the parameter c must be a constant to obtain an efficient construction.

About Knowledge Extraction Assumptions. Our constructions rely on encryption schemes that are plaintext aware (**sPA1$_\ell$**) in the multi-key setup and are weakly simulatable. In Appendix A.1, we show that such encryption schemes exist under a suitable extension of the Diffie-Hellman Knowledge (DHK) assumption that was originally proposed by Damgård, and modified to permit interactive extractors by Bellare and Palacio [BP04]. Dent [Den06b] has since shown that it is secure in the generic group model. We understand that there are some critics of the DHK assumption, due to its strength and the fact that it is not efficiently falsifiable. However, it is not our goal to argue whether or not it is an assumption which should be used in deployable systems. Instead we note it is seemingly a weaker assumption than the Random Oracle model (which is known to be incorrect in full generality, cf. [CGH04]), under which it is relatively easy to show that simple IND-CPA secure encryption schemes imply CCA2 secure ones. In contradistinction, there are no security definitions that seem weaker or incomparable to NM-CCA1 that are known to imply schemes which are NM-CCA1. Similarly, the gap between NM-CCA1 and CCA2 is poorly understood.

Techniques. Similar to the nested encryption construction in [MS09], both our NM-CCA1 and cNM-CCA1 constructions are based on the notion of double encryption. We first encrypt the message under one key (we refer to this ciphertext as the "inner layer"), and encrypt the resulting inner layer ciphertext repetitively under an additional k keys, where k is the security parameter (we refer to these k keys as the "outer keys", and the ciphertexts they produce as the "outer layer"). During decryption, all the outer layer ciphertexts are decrypted, and it is verified they all encode the same inner layer value. This is combined with the well studied notion of non-duplicatable set selection (in this case of public-keys used to encrypt the outer-layer encryptions), such that anyone attempting to maul a ciphertext has to perform their own independent outer layer encryption. Intuitively, anyone that can encrypt to a consistent outer layer encryption under a new key must have knowledge of the underlying inner-layer, and thus a valid ciphertext is not mauled.

On a more technical level, there are several challenges that need to be overcome. The traditional technical difficulty in proving weaker public-key encryption security notions imply stronger security notions is in showing how to simulate the decryption oracle. When beginning with a **sPA1**-secure encryption primitive, we can easily simulate the initial decryption oracle in the NM-CCA1 security definition, which is present before the challenge ciphertext is presented, by using the extractor guaranteed by the **sPA1** security definition. However, we cannot simply use the extractor to simulate the decryption oracle after receiving the challenge ciphertext in the NM-CCA1 security experiment. This is because the plaintext aware security does not guarantee that an extractor could decrypt ciphertexts where the underlying randomness is not known to the party that created the ciphertext. Generally, a party that mauls a ciphertext as in the case of non-malleability will not have access to this underlying randomness. To overcome this problem, we make use of a weak notion of simulatability.

To summarize, our contribution is twofold. Firstly, our work shows the first black-box construction of a non-malleable CCA1 encryption scheme in the standard model that is not CCA2 secure. Secondly, for the first time, we show how to construct an encryption scheme that is not CCA2 secure but is secure against an adversary that can ask a bounded number of polynomial-parallel queries after receiving the challenge ciphertext, satisfying a natural extension to the notion of NM-CCA1 security. This might be of independent interest since the development of constructions that satisfy stronger notions than non-malleable CCA1 security but do not satisfy CCA2 security can provide insight in trying to understand the technical difficulties in understanding the larger relationship between CCA1 and CCA2.

2   Notations and Definitions

We use $[n]$ to denote the set $\{1, 2, \cdots, n\}$. We say a function $\mu : \mathbb{N} \to \mathbb{R}$ is negligible if for all polynomials p and all sufficiently large $n : \mu(n) \leq 1/p(n)$. Given two families of distributions $D_0 = \{D_{0,i}\}_{i \in \mathbb{N}}$ and $D_1 = \{D_{1,i}\}_{i \in \mathbb{N}}$, we denote that they are computationally indistinguishable by writing $D_0 \approx_c D_1$. For any vector v, we use $|v|$ to denote the number of elements in v.

Although non-malleability can be defined for any CPA, CCA1 or CCA2 secure encryption scheme (we use the standard definition for CPA/CCA1/CCA2 security),we only use and hence only define non-malleability for CCA1 secure encryption schemes. We use a definition similar to the non-malleability definition for CPA secure encryption schemes in [PSV06].

Definition 1 (NM-CCA1). *We say that $\boldsymbol{E} = (\mathsf{nmg}, \mathsf{nme}, \mathsf{nmd})$ is non-malleable CCA1 secure if for all p.p.t. adversaries and p.p.t. distinguishers $\mathcal{A}$ and $\mathcal{D}$ respectively and for all polynomials $p(\cdot)$, we have that $\{\mathsf{NME}_0(\boldsymbol{E}, \mathcal{A}, \mathcal{D}, k, p(k))\}_k \approx_c \{\mathsf{NME}_1(\boldsymbol{E}, \mathcal{A}, \mathcal{D}, k, p(k))\}_k$ where experiment NME is defined as follows:*

$\mathsf{NME}_b(\mathbf{E}, \mathcal{A}, \mathcal{D}, k, p(k))$
(1) $(\mathrm{NPK}, \mathrm{NSK}) \leftarrow \mathsf{nmg}(1^k)$
(2) $(m_0, m_1, S_1) \leftarrow \mathcal{A}_1^{\mathsf{nmd}_{\mathrm{NSK}}}(\mathrm{NPK})$ s.t. $|m_0| = |m_1|$
(3) $y \leftarrow \mathsf{nme}(\mathrm{NPK}, m_b)$
(4) $(\boldsymbol{c}, S_2) \leftarrow \mathcal{A}_2(y, S_1)$ where $|\boldsymbol{c}| = p(k)$
(5)   Output $\mathcal{D}(\boldsymbol{d}, S_2)$ where $d_i \leftarrow \mathsf{nmd}(\mathrm{NSK}, c_i)$ if $c_i \neq y$ and
        $d_i \leftarrow \perp$ if $c_i = y$

2.1   Plaintext Awareness for Multiple Key Setup

We present a slight generalization to the definition of **sPA1** by [BP04] in which multiple keys are permitted to be constructed and given to the ciphertext creator, and the extractor must be able to decrypt relative to all of the keys. Notice that the **sPA1** definition is a special case of **sPA1**$_\ell$ where $\ell(k) = 1$.

sPA1$_\ell$(E, C, C*, k)

(1)   Let $R[\mathbf{C}]$, $R[\mathbf{C}^*]$ be randomly chosen bit strings for $\mathbf{C}$ and $\mathbf{C}^*$.

(2) $((pk_i, sk_i))_{i \in [\ell(k)]} \leftarrow \mathsf{gen}(1^k)$

(3) $st \leftarrow ((pk_i)_{i \in [\ell(k)]}, R[C])$

(4) $\mathbf{C}^{\mathbf{C}^*(st,.)}\left((pk_i)_{i \in [\ell(k)]}\right)$

(5)   Let $Q = \{(q_i = (pk_{j_i}, c_i), m_i)\}$ be the set of queries $\mathbf{C}$ made to $\mathbf{C}^*$ until it halted and $\mathbf{C}^*$'s responses to them. Return $\wedge_{i=1}^{|Q|}(m_i = \mathsf{dec}_{sk_{j_i}}(c_i))$.

In the above experiment, $\mathbf{C}$ is a ciphertext creator, and $\mathbf{C}^*$ is a stateful p.p.t. algorithm called the *extractor* that takes as input the state information st and a ciphertext given by the ciphertext creator $\mathbf{C}$, and will return the decryption of that ciphertext and the updated state st. The state information st is initially set to the public key pk and the adversary $\mathbf{C}$'s random coins. It gets updated by $\mathbf{C}^*$ as $\mathbf{C}^*$ answers each query that the adversary $\mathbf{C}$ submits. The above experiment returns 1 if all the extractor's answers to queries are the true decryption of those queries under sk. Otherwise, the experiment returns 0.

Definition 2 (sPA1$_\ell$). *Let ℓ be a polynomial. Let $E = (\mathsf{gen}, \mathsf{enc}, \mathsf{dec})$ be an asymmetric encryption scheme. Let the ciphertext-creator adversary C and the extractor C^* be p.p.t. algorithms. For $k \in \mathbb{N}$, the sPA1-advantage of C relative to C^* is defined as:*

$$Adv^{sPA1_\ell}(E, C, C^*, k) = \Pr[sPA1_\ell(E, C, C^*, k) = 0]$$

The extractor C^* is a successful sPA1$_\ell$-extractor for the ciphertext-creator adversary C if for all $k \in \mathbb{N}$, the function $Adv^{sPA1_\ell}(E, C, C^*, k)$ is negligible. The encryption scheme E is called sPA1$_\ell$ multi-key secure if for any p.p.t. ciphertext creator there exists a successful sPA1$_\ell$-extractor.

We provide further discussion on the relationship between sPA1$_\ell$ security and sPA1 security in the full version of this paper. In Appendix A.1, we show that both the Damgård Elgamal encryption scheme (DEG) and the lite version of Cramer-Shoup encryption scheme (CS-lite) are sPA1$_\ell$ secure under a suitable generalization of the DHK1 assumption.

2.2   Weakly Simulatable Encryption Scheme

Dent in [Den06a] introduced the notion of simulatability for an encryption scheme. Intuitively, an encryption scheme is simulatable if no attacker can distinguish valid ciphertexts from some family of pseudo-ciphertexts (which will include both valid encryptions and invalid encryptions). This family of pseudo-ciphertexts must be efficiently and publicly computable (i.e. without access to any private knowledge, say related to the secret-key), and somewhat invertible (given a pseudo-ciphertext, one can find a random looking string that generates it). In Dent's definition, the attacker also has access to a decryption oracle to help it distinguish between pseudo-ciphertexts and legitimate ones, but it cannot query the decryption oracle on the challenges that it is trying to distinguish.

For our purposes, consider a restricted notion of simulatability where the attacker is not given access to the decryption oracle. If an encryption scheme satisfies this weaker notion of simulatability, we say it is weakly simulatable.

Definition 3. *(Weakly Simulatable Encryption Scheme) An asymmetric encryption scheme* (gen, enc, dec) *is weakly simulatable if there exist two poly-time algorithms* (f, f^{-1})*, where* f *is deterministic and* f^{-1} *is probabilistic, such that for all* $k \in \mathbb{N}$ *there exists the polynomial function* $p(.)$ *where* $l = p(k)$*, we have the following correctness properties:*

1. f *on inputs of public key* pk *(in the range of* gen*) and a random string* $r \in \{0,1\}^l$*, returns elements in* $\mathcal{C}$*, where* $\mathcal{C}$ *is the set of all possible "cipher text"-strings that can be submitted to the decryption oracle (notice that* $\mathcal{C}$ *might not be a valid ciphertext).*
2. f^{-1} *on input of a public key* pk *(in the range of* gen*) and an element* $C \in \mathcal{C}$*, outputs elements of* $\{0,1\}^l$*.*
3. $f(pk, f^{-1}(pk, C)) = C$ *for all* $C \in \mathcal{C}$*.*

And the following security properties. No polynomial time attacker $\mathcal{A}$ *has probability better than* $1/2 + \mu(k)$ *of winning in the following experiment, where* μ *is some negligible function.*

1. *The challenger generates a random key pair* $(pk, sk) \leftarrow$ gen(1^k)*, and chooses randomly* $b \in \{0,1\}$*.*
2. *The attacker* $\mathcal{A}$ *executes on the input* 1^k *and the public key* pk *outputs* $m \in \mathcal{M}$*. The challenger sends* $\mathcal{A}$ *the pair* $(f^{-1}(pk, c = \text{enc}_{pk}(m)), c)$ *if* $b = 0$*, or* $(r, f(pk, r))$ *for some randomly generated element* $r \in \{0,1\}^l$ *if* $b = 1$*. The attacker* $\mathcal{A}$ *terminates by outputting a guess* b' *for* b*.*
   $\mathcal{A}$ *wins if* $b = b'$ *and its advantage is defined in the usual way.*

In a scheme where you cannot distinguish legitimate ciphertexts from pseudo-ciphertexts that need not encode actual messages, CPA security is immediate. The converse need not hold, as ciphertexts might be hard to generate, and invalid ciphertexts might be easily distinguishable from illegitimate ones (for example, they might contain a zero-knowledge proof of validity). Notice that the weak simulatability notion is not equivalent to the Invertible Sampling notion introduced in [DN00] since the plaintext is not needed to compute the random looking string that generates the ciphertext.

Theorem 1. *If* E *is a weakly simulatable encryption scheme, then* E *is* CPA *secure.*

Proof. See the full version.   □

Following the ideas of Dent, in the full version, we show how DEG and CS-lite schemes can both be weakly simulatable when instantiated in proper groups.

2.3   A Note on PA1$^+$

Dent [Den06a] also investigated an augmented notion of plaintext awareness in which he provides the ciphertext creator access to an oracle that produces random bits, PA1$^+$. The extractor receives the answers to any queries generated by the creator, but only at the time these queries are issued. The point of this oracle in the context of a plaintext awareness definition is to model the fact that the extractor might not receive all of the random coins used by the creator *at the beginning* of the experiment. Much in the spirit of "adaptive soundness" and "adaptive zero-knowledge", this oracle requires the extractor to work even when it receives the random coins at the same time as the ciphertext creator. Therefore, the extractor potentially needs to be able to extract some ciphertexts independent of future randomness. This modification has implications when the notion of plaintext awareness is computational—as in the case of Dent's work. However, in our case, we require statistical plaintext awareness, and as we argue below, allowing access to such an oracle does not affect the **sPA1**$_\ell$ security.

We claim that any encryption scheme that is **sPA1**$_\ell$ secure is also **sPA1**$_\ell^+$ secure.

Definition 4. *Define the **sPA1**$_\ell^+$ experiment in a similar way to the **sPA1**$_\ell$ experiment. The only difference between the two is that during the **sPA1**$_\ell^+$ experiment, the ciphertext creator has access to a random oracle $\mathcal{O}$ that takes no input, but returns independent uniform random strings upon each access. Any time the creator access the oracle, the oracle's response is forwarded to both the creator and extractor.*

*If an encryption scheme would be deemed **sPA1**$_\ell$ secure, when we replace the **sPA1**$_\ell$ experiment in the definition with the modified **sPA1**$_\ell^+$ experiment, then the encryption scheme is said to be **sPA1**$_\ell^+$ secure.*

Lemma 1. *If an encryption scheme Π is **sPA1**$_\ell$ secure, then it is **sPA1**$_\ell^+$ secure.*

Proof. See the full version.   □

3   The Construction

Let $E = (\mathsf{gen}, \mathsf{enc}, \mathsf{dec})$ be any encryption scheme that is weakly simulatable and **sPA1**$_\ell$ secure. Then we construct the encryption scheme Π represented in Fig. 1 that is a non-malleable CCA1 encryption scheme. Let $\Sigma = (\mathsf{GenKey}, \mathsf{Sign}, \mathsf{Verify})$ be a strong one-time signature scheme,[1] such that on security parameter k the verification keys that are constructed have length k.

As a first step, we define an encryption scheme $E' = (\mathsf{gen}', \mathsf{enc}', \mathsf{dec}')$ in which one encrypts the encryption of a message k times with k independently chosen public keys. More specifically:

---

[1] A strong one-time signature is a one-time signature where it is not even possible for an adversary to find an alternate signature to an already signed message.

— gen$'(1^k)$: For $i \in [0, k]$, run $(pk_i, sk_i) \leftarrow$ gen(1^k). Set the public and secret keys as $pk \overset{def}{=} (pk_0, pk_1, \ldots, pk_k)$ and $sk \overset{def}{=} (sk_0, sk_1, \ldots, sk_k)$

— enc$'_{pk=pk_0,\ldots,pk_k}(m)$:   Output $[\text{enc}_{pk_1}(\text{enc}_{pk_0}(m; r_0); r_1), \ldots \text{enc}_{pk_k}$ $(\text{enc}_{pk_0}(m; r_0); r_k)]$ using independently chosen coins r_i.

— dec$'_{sk=sk_0,\ldots,sk_k}([c_1, c_2, \ldots, c_k])$: Compute $c'_i = \text{dec}_{sk_i}(c_i)$. If all c'_i are not equal, output $\perp$, else output $\text{dec}_{sk_0}(c'_1)$.

We are now ready to present our main construction Π defined in Fig. 1.

NMGEN(1^k)
  (1) $(pk_0, sk_0) \leftarrow$ gen(1^k); $(pk_i^b, sk_i^b) \leftarrow$ gen(1^k), $\forall i \in [k]$ and $b \in \{0, 1\}$
  (2)   Output   NPK $=$ $\{pk, pk_0\}$ and   NSK $=$ $\{sk, sk_0\}$ where $pk = \{(pk_i^0, pk_i^1)\}_{i \in [k]}$ and $sk = \{(sk_i^0, sk_i^1)\}_{i \in [k]}$

NMENC$(\text{NPK} = (pk, pk_0), m)$
  (1) $(\text{SigSK}, \text{SigVK}) \leftarrow$ GenKey(1^k)
  (2) $c \leftarrow$ enc$'_{pk_0, pk_1^{\text{SigVK}_1}, \ldots, pk_k^{\text{SigVK}_k}}(m)$
  (3) $\sigma \leftarrow$ Sign$_{\text{SigSK}}(c)$.
  (4)   Output $(c, \text{SigVK}, \sigma)$

NMDEC$(\text{NSK} = (sk, sk_0), C = (c, \text{SigVK}, \sigma)))$
  (1)   if Verify$_{\text{SigVK}}(\sigma, c) = 0$ then Output $\perp$
  (2)   Output dec$'_{sk_0, sk_1^{\text{SigVK}_1}, \ldots, sk_k^{\text{SigVK}_k}}(c_1)$

Fig. 1. The Non-malleable CCA1 Encryption Scheme Π

Lemma 2. *If* $E = (\text{gen}, \text{enc}, \text{dec})$ *is weakly simulatable, then* $E' = (\text{gen}', \text{enc}', \text{dec}')$ *is weakly simulatable as well.*

Proof. Via a standard hybrid argument.   □

Theorem 2. *If* $E = (\text{gen}, \text{enc}, \text{dec})$ *is an encryption scheme that is weakly simulatable and also* $sPA1_{\ell(k)=2k+1}$ *secure where* k *is the security parameter, then the encryption scheme* Π *as described in Fig. 1 is a non-malleable* CCA1 *encryption scheme.*

Proof. Recall that Lemma 1 shows that if E is $sPA1_\ell$ secure, then it is also $sPA1_\ell^+$ secure. In what follows, the $sPA1_\ell^+$ ciphertext creator adversaries always have access to an oracle $\mathcal{O}$ that produces random strings upon access.

To prove that Π is a non-malleable CCA1 encryption scheme, we need to show that for any p.p.t. adversary $\mathcal{A}$ and p.p.t. distinguisher $\mathcal{D}$ and for all polynomials $p(k)$,

$$\{\mathsf{NME}_0\,(\Pi,\mathcal{A},\mathcal{D},k,p\,(k))\}_{k\in\mathbb{N}} \approx_c \{\mathsf{NME}_1\,(\Pi,\mathcal{A},\mathcal{D},k,p\,(k))\}_{k\in\mathbb{N}}$$

We show this by a hybrid argument. Consider the following experiments:

Experiment $\mathsf{NME}_b^{(1)}(\Pi,\mathcal{A},\mathcal{D},k,p(k))$ modifies NME_b in two ways. First, instead of selecting vkSig* when the challenge ciphertext is encrypted, choose this value as the first step of the experiment. Second, when processing decryption queries during the experiment, replace Verify with Verify* as follows:

Verify* Let vkSig* be the verification key in the challenge ciphertext $(c^*,\sigma^*,\text{vkSig}^*)$. Upon receiving a decryption query on (c,σ,vkSig), output $\perp$ if either vkSig $=$ vkSig* or $\text{Verify}_{\text{vkSig}}(c,\sigma) = 0$.

Claim. For $b \in \{0,1\}$, $\{\mathsf{NME}_b\,(\Pi,\mathcal{A},\mathcal{D},k,p\,(k))\}_{k\in\mathbb{N}}\approx_c\{\mathsf{NME}_b^{(1)}\,(\Pi,\mathcal{A},\mathcal{D},$ $k,p\,(k))\}_{k\in\mathbb{N}}$

Proof. Follows using standard techniques from the security of the signature scheme.   □

Experiment $\mathsf{NME}_b^{(2)}(\Pi,\mathcal{A},\mathcal{D},k,p(k))$ modifies $\mathsf{NME}_b^{(1)}$ to use an extractor to decrypt the inner layer cipher text for the decryptions in the final parallel decryption query. Specifically, in $\mathsf{NME}_b^{(2)}$ the calls are submitted to NMDec* as described below. This is unlike $\mathsf{NME}_b^{(1)}$ where the final ciphertexts $d_1,...,d_{p(k)}$ are presented by A_2 for parallel decryption via calls to NMDec, :

NMDec$^*(d_i = \boldsymbol{C},\sigma,\mathbf{vkSig})$ If $0 = \text{Verify}_{\text{vkSig}}^*(\boldsymbol{C},\sigma)$ output $\perp$. For $i = 1\ldots k$, do $C_i' \leftarrow \text{dec}_{sk_i^{\text{vkSig}_i}}(C_i)$
If $\exists_j, C_1' \neq C_j'$, output $\perp$. Use the extractor $C_{\mathcal{A}}^*$ (defined in Lemma 3) to extract C_i', where i is the smallest value s.t. $\text{vkSig}_i \neq \text{vkSig}_i^*$, where vkSig* is the verification key of the challenge ciphertext. Return the extracted plaintext.

Lemma 3. *For $b \in \{0,1\}$, $\{\mathsf{NME}_b^{(1)}\,(\Pi,\mathcal{A},\mathcal{D},k,p\,(k))\}_{k\in\mathbb{N}}\approx_c\{\mathsf{NME}_b^{(2)}\,(\Pi,\mathcal{A},$ $\mathcal{D},k,p\,(k))\}_{k\in\mathbb{N}}$*

This lemma might, on first glance, seem to follow immediately because the whole purpose of the extractor is that it be able to simulate a decryption oracle. However, since the adversary has (i) seen the challenge ciphertext, (ii) it is not aware of the randomness used to produce this ciphertext, and (iii) created final parallel decryption queries potentially based on the challenge ciphertext, there is no a priori reason to believe the sPA1 extractor will "decrypt" properly. However, we are only extracting on the inner layers of ciphertexts, and the inner layer of the challenge ciphertext has been hidden by the encryptions on the outer layer. Further, the outer layer is weakly simulatable, so we can argue that these new ciphertexts issued for parallel decryption, described in point (iii) above, are not dependent on the randomness of the inner-layer of the challenge ciphertext. Therefore, the extractor will function correctly.

Proof. The experiments differ only if the extractor returns a result that is different from the of the decryption oracle. We define **badExtract** to capture this event, and show that it occurs with negligible probability. Assume (for contradiction) that there exists an adversary $\mathcal{A}$ which induces the event **badExtract** to occur with non-negligible probability. We show that **E** is not a weakly simulatable encryption scheme.

Note that the public- and secret-keys for Π are composed of $2k+1$ keys that are generated using the key generation algorithm for encryption scheme **E**. To encrypt a message m, we first generate a pair of signing keys, (vkSig, skSig), and then encrypt m with a fixed public key, pk_0, in the set of $2k+1$ public keys (we refer to this ciphertext as the inner layer). Then, we select a subset of size k out of the $2k$ remaining keys determined by the bits of vkSig, and encrypt the inner layer using fresh random coins for k times under those k keys (we refer to these k ciphertexts as the outer layer). We refer to the key used to encrypt the inner layer as the inner key, and the remaining $2k$ keys as the outer keys.

The technical difficulty in showing that **badExtract** does not occur in the $\mathsf{NME}_b{}^{(2)}\left(\Pi, \mathcal{A}, \mathcal{D}, k, p\left(k\right)\right)$ experiment is that by providing the challenge ciphertext, we actually provide the adversary with ciphertexts that are encrypted using k keys out of the $2k$ outer keys. We must argue that even in this case, there should be a way to extract the plaintext of the queries submitted by the adversary on the spots in the outer layer that are encrypted under a new key from the k keys used in the outer layer of the challenge ciphertext.

To do so, we first construct an $\mathsf{sPA1}_\ell^+$ ciphertext creator $\mathbf{C}_\mathcal{A}$ using the adversary $\mathcal{A}$. Since the encryption scheme **E** is $\mathsf{sPA1}_\ell^+$ secure, there exists an extractor for $\mathbf{C}_\mathcal{A}$ which we call $\mathbf{C}_\mathcal{A}^*$. Then we define a series of hybrids using $\mathbf{C}_\mathcal{A}$ and $\mathbf{C}_\mathcal{A}^*$, that are indistinguishable assuming **E** is weakly simulatable. The last hybrid in that series perfectly simulates the $\mathsf{NME}_b{}^{(2)}(\Pi, \mathcal{A}, \mathcal{D}, k, p(k))$ experiment for $\mathcal{A}$ up to the point when $\mathcal{A}$ returns the vector of the ciphertexts after receiving the challenge ciphertext. Based on the indistinguishability of the hybrids, we will argue that there exists an extractor that can decrypt the adversary's queries on the first spot i where $\mathrm{vkSig}_i \neq \mathrm{vkSig}_i^*$ with overwhelming probability. Notice that the extractor cannot be used to decrypt the outer layer on the spots where $\mathrm{vkSig}_i = \mathrm{vkSig}_i^*$, otherwise it could be argued that the encryption scheme **E** is indeed **PA2** secure (**PA2** security is defined in [BP04]) and hence **CCA2** secure.

First we construct an $\mathsf{sPA1}_\ell^+$ ciphertext creator $\mathbf{C}_\mathcal{A}$ from $\mathcal{A}$ where $\ell = 2k+1$. $\mathbf{C}_\mathcal{A}$ interacts with the $\mathsf{sPA1}_\ell^+$ experiment in "the outside" as follows:

- $\mathbf{C}_\mathcal{A}$ receives $2k+1$ public keys $\left(\{pk_i'\}_{i\in[0...2k]}\right)$ from the $\mathsf{sPA1}_\ell^+$ experiment. It generates a pair of signing keys $(\mathrm{vkSig}^*, \mathrm{skSig}^*) \leftarrow \mathsf{GenKey}(1^k)$ internally and sets $pk = \left(\{pk_i^\alpha\}_{i\in[0...2k],\alpha\in\{0,1\}}\right)$ as described (intuitively, $\mathbf{C}_\mathcal{A}$ arranges pk such that it can potentially sign a vector of ciphertexts that are supposed to be encrypted under the last k keys in $\boldsymbol{pk'}$, $(pk_{k+1}', \ldots, pk_{k+k}')$, to generate a valid ciphertext in the Π scheme):

$$\text{for } i \in [0\ldots k] \ \& \ \alpha \in \{0,1\}, pk_i^\alpha = \begin{cases} pk_0' & \text{if } i = 0 \\ pk_i' & \text{else if } \mathrm{vkSig}_i^* \neq \alpha \\ pk_{i+k}' & \text{otherwise} \end{cases}$$

$\mathbf{C}_{\mathcal{A}}$ runs $\mathcal{A}_1$ on the input of pk. Note that this rearrangement of keys is crucial to make the view of the adversary $\mathcal{A}$ on the arrangement of the keys identical to its view in a real $\mathsf{NME}_b^{(2)}(\Pi, \mathcal{A}, \mathcal{D}, k, p(k))$ experiment. To see this, consider the following example. The adversary $\mathcal{A}$ might abort whenever the keys used in the outer layer of the challenge ciphertext are the last k keys in pk. Such a coincidence occurs in the simulated $\mathsf{NME}_b^{(2)}(\Pi, \mathcal{A}, \mathcal{D}, k, p(k))$ experiment with probability 1 if $\mathbf{C}_{\mathcal{A}}$ sets pk to be the same as pk', while this coincidence occurs in a real $\mathsf{NME}_b^{(2)}(\Pi, \mathcal{A}, \mathcal{D}, k, p(k))$ experiment with negligible probability due to the security of the signature scheme.

- Whenever $\mathbf{C}_{\mathcal{A}}$ receives a query $(\{y_i\}_{i \in [k]}, \sigma, \mathsf{vkSig})$ from $\mathcal{A}_1$, it first checks if the signature is valid. If not, it returns $\bot$ as the answer to this query. Next, it checks whether $\mathsf{vkSig} = \mathsf{vkSig}^*$. If so, it aborts. Otherwise, $\mathbf{C}_{\mathcal{A}}$ submits y_i's one by one to the extractor. If all of the queries do not get decrypted to the same value, $\mathbf{C}_{\mathcal{A}}$ returns $\bot$ to $\mathcal{A}_1$ as the answer to that query. But if all of the queries get decrypted to the same value y_0, $\mathbf{C}_{\mathcal{A}}$ then submits y_0 (which is supposed to be an encryption under pk_0^0) to the extractor and returns the result to $\mathcal{A}_1$. Eventually $\mathcal{A}_1$ returns (m_0, m_1, St) and halts. $\mathbf{C}_{\mathcal{A}}$ outputs (m_0, m_1).

- $\mathbf{C}_{\mathcal{A}}$ accesses its oracle $\mathcal{O}$ and generates k blocks of random bits of length l, giving the vector $\boldsymbol{x} = (x_1, \ldots, x_k)$. Let $\boldsymbol{y} = \left(f(pk'_{k+1}, x_1), \ldots, f(pk'_{k+k}, x_k)\right)$. $\mathbf{C}_{\mathcal{A}}$ then computes $\sigma^* = \mathsf{Sign}(\boldsymbol{y}, \mathsf{skSig}^*)$, and runs $\mathcal{A}_2$ on the input $y^* = (\boldsymbol{y}, \sigma^*, \mathsf{vkSig}^*)$ and St.

- $\mathcal{A}_2$ returns a vector of ciphertexts $\boldsymbol{Y}$ and the state information S and halts. For all $j \in [|\boldsymbol{Y}|]$, $\mathbf{C}_{\mathcal{A}}$ does the following: on the query $Y_j = (\{y_i\}_{i \in [k]}, \sigma, \mathsf{vkSig})$, it first checks if the signature is valid. If not, it moves to the next query. Otherwise, it checks whether $\mathsf{vkSig} = \mathsf{vkSig}^*$. If so, it aborts. Otherwise, $\mathbf{C}_{\mathcal{A}}$ finds the first index i where $\mathsf{vkSig}_i \neq \mathsf{vkSig}_i^*$, and submits y_i to its extractor to be "decrypted" under $pk_i^{\mathsf{vkSig}_i}$. $\mathbf{C}_{\mathcal{A}}$ then submits the answer from the extractor (which is supposed to be an encryption under pk_0^0) again to the extractor to be "decrypted" under pk_0^0. Denote the result m'_j.
  $\mathbf{C}_{\mathcal{A}}$ returns $\{Y_j, m'_j\}_{j \in [|\boldsymbol{Y}|]}$ and the state information S, it halts.

Since $\mathbf{C}_{\mathcal{A}}$ is a $\mathsf{sPA1}_\ell^+$ ciphertext creator adversary, the $\mathsf{sPA1}_\ell^+$ security of $\mathbf{E}$ implies there exists an extractor $\mathbf{C}_{\mathcal{A}}^*$ whose answers to the decryption queries submitted by $\mathbf{C}_{\mathcal{A}}$ are indistinguishable from their true decryptions. We call the above interaction **Game 1**. Let $\Pr[W_i]$ be the probability of the adversary $\mathbf{C}_{\mathcal{A}}$ inducing the event **badExtract** in the **Game** i. The $\mathsf{sPA1}_\ell^+$ security implies that $\Pr[W_1]$ is bounded by $\mathbf{Adv}^{\mathsf{sPA1}_\ell^+}(\mathbf{E}, \mathbf{C}_{\mathcal{A}}, \mathbf{C}_{\mathcal{A}}^*, k)$ which is negligible in k. Hence:

$$\Pr[W_1] \leq \mathbf{Adv}^{\mathsf{sPA1}_\ell^+}(\mathbf{E}, \mathbf{C}_{\mathcal{A}}, \mathbf{C}_{\mathcal{A}}^*, k) \tag{1}$$

We will define another game, **Game 2**, which is identical to **Game 1** with the difference that instead of a fake ciphertext, $\mathcal{A}_2$ is fed with a real ciphertext as the challenge ciphertext. The aborting probability of $\mathcal{A}_2$ in **Game 1** and **Game 2** is negligibly close otherwise it can be argued that $\mathbf{E}$ is not weakly simulatable. In what follows, we only deal with the probability of inducing the event

badExtract. Also notice that **Game 2** simulates $\mathsf{NME}_b^{(2)}(\Pi, \mathcal{A}, \mathcal{D}, k, p(k))$ for the adversary $\mathcal{A}$ up to the point when the adversary $\mathcal{A}$ returns a vector of ciphertexts after seeing the challenge ciphertext. That is because $\mathbf{C}_\mathcal{A}$ only needs the vector of the ciphertext generated by $\mathcal{A}$ after revealing the challenge ciphertext to induce the event **badExtract** to occur. After receiving such a vector of ciphertexts, $\mathbf{C}_\mathcal{A}$ does not need to complete the simulation of the $\mathsf{NME}_b^{(2)}(\Pi, \mathcal{A}, \mathcal{D}, k, p(k))$ experiment for $\mathcal{A}$.

In **Game 2** we modify the oracle $\mathcal{O}$ as follows: when $\mathbf{C}_\mathcal{A}$ accesses the oracle $\mathcal{O}$ for the ith time, instead of $r \in \{0,1\}^l$, $\mathcal{O}$ returns $f^{-1}(pk'_{k+i}, \mathsf{enc}_{pk'_{k+i}}(m_d))$ where m_d is picked randomly out of the two messages returned by $\mathcal{A}$. During **Game 2**, the random bit d is fixed. We argue that such a change does not affect the advantage of $\mathbf{C}_\mathcal{A}$ in inducing the event **badExtract** as otherwise $\mathbf{E}$ is not weakly simulatable countering our assumption. Using $\mathbf{C}_\mathcal{A}$ and $\mathbf{C}^*_\mathcal{A}$, we build the attacker $\mathcal{B}$ that distinguishes $(r, f(., r))$ and $(f^{-1}(., c = \mathsf{enc}(.,.)), c)$ as follows:

1. The challenger samples k pairs of random keys $(pk_i, sk_i) \leftarrow \mathsf{gen}(1^k)$ for $1 \le i \le k$, and a random bit b.
2. The attacker $\mathcal{B}$ receives $\{pk_i\}_{i \in [k]}$. $\mathcal{B}$ then samples $k+1$ other random keys $(pk'_i, sk'_i) \leftarrow \mathsf{gen}(1^k)$ for $0 \le i \le k$. Let $\boldsymbol{pk''} = (pk'_0, pk'_1, \ldots, pk'_k, pk_1, pk_2, \ldots, pk_k)$. $\mathcal{B}$ samples random coins for $\mathbf{C}_\mathcal{A}$ and $\mathbf{C}^*_\mathcal{A}$ and sets $st \leftarrow (\boldsymbol{pk''}, R[\mathbf{C}_\mathcal{A}])$. $\mathcal{B}$ runs $\mathbf{C}_\mathcal{A}$ on the input $\boldsymbol{pk''}$, and $\mathbf{C}^*_\mathcal{A}$ on the input st. Eventually $\mathbf{C}_\mathcal{A}$ outputs (m_0, m_1). $\mathcal{B}$ randomly chooses $d \in \{0,1\}$ and outputs $c'_d = \mathsf{enc}_{pk'_0}(m_d)$. The challenger samples $r_i \in \{0,1\}^l$ for $1 \le i \le k$ and returns $\{(r_i, f(pk_i, r_i))\}_{i \in [k]}$ if $b = 0$, and $\{(f^{-1}(pk_i, c_i = \mathsf{enc}_{pk_i}(c'_d)), c_i)\}_{i \in [k]}$ if $b = 1$. Call the resulting vector (given by the challenger) $\boldsymbol{y}$. $\mathcal{B}$ then forwards $\{f^{-1}(pk_i, y_i)\}_{i \in [k]}$ to $\mathbf{C}_\mathcal{A}$ and $\mathbf{C}^*_\mathcal{A}$ when $\mathbf{C}_\mathcal{A}$ queries $\mathcal{O}$ for the ith time. After $\mathbf{C}_\mathcal{A}$ halts, the attacker $\mathcal{B}$ checks if all the queries made by $\mathbf{C}_\mathcal{A}$ to the extractor after outputting m_0 and m_1 were answered correctly. This is done by using the extractor using $\boldsymbol{sk'}$ (notice that $\mathbf{C}_\mathcal{A}$ was made in a way that after returning m_0 and m_1, it always only asks the extractor on the ciphertexts encrypted under $\boldsymbol{pk'}$ which are the first $k+1$ keys in $\boldsymbol{pk}$). If so it outputs $b' = 0$ otherwise $b' = 1$.

When $b = 0$, **Game 1** is being simulated, and when $b = 1$, **Game 2** is being simulated. Therefore:

$$\Pr[b' = b] = \Pr[b = 0] \cdot \Pr[b' = b | b = 0] + \Pr[b = 1] \cdot \Pr[b' = b | b = 1]$$

$$= \frac{1}{2} \cdot (1 - \Pr[W_1]) + \frac{1}{2} \cdot \Pr[W_2]$$

On the other hand, by Lemma 2, the advantage of the attacker $\mathcal{B}$ in guessing the bit b is negligible in k, and hence there exists a negligible function $\epsilon_1(.)$ such that $\Pr[b' = b] \le \frac{1}{2} + \epsilon_1(k)$. Therefore:

$$\Pr[b' = b] = \frac{1}{2} \cdot (1 - \Pr[W_1]) + \frac{1}{2} \cdot \Pr[W_2] \le \frac{1}{2} + \epsilon_1(k)$$

$$\implies \Pr[W_2] \le 2 \cdot \epsilon_1(k) + \Pr[W_1] \tag{2}$$

$$\implies \Pr[W_2] \le 2 \cdot \epsilon_1(k) + \mathbf{Adv}^{\mathbf{sPA1}_\ell^+} (\mathbf{E}, \mathbf{C}_\mathcal{A}, \mathbf{C}_\mathcal{A}^*, k) \tag{3}$$

Inequality (3) follows from Inequalities (1) and (2). Therefore $\Pr[W_2]$ is negligible. Since $\Pr[W_2]$ is the probability that the event **badExtract** occurs, we conclude that there is a negligible chance that **badExtract** occurs. Hence:

$$\{\mathsf{NME}_b{}^{(1)}\left(\Pi, \mathcal{A}, \mathcal{D}, k, p\left(k\right)\right)\}_{k \in \mathbb{N}} \approx_c \{\mathsf{NME}_b{}^{(2)}\left(\Pi, \mathcal{A}, \mathcal{D}, k, p\left(k\right)\right)\}_{k \in \mathbb{N}}$$

$\square$

Lemma 4. *For every p.p.t. adversary* $\mathcal{A} = (\mathcal{A}_1, \mathcal{A}_2)$, *there exists a p.p.t. adversary* $\mathcal{B}$ *such that for* $b \in \{0, 1\}$,

$$\{\mathsf{NME}_b{}^{(2)}\left(\Pi, \mathcal{A}, \mathcal{D}, k, p\left(k\right)\right)\}_{k \in \mathbb{N}} \equiv \{\mathsf{CPA}_b\left(\boldsymbol{E}, \mathcal{B}, k\right)\}_{k \in \mathbb{N}}$$

Proof. In the proof of Lemma 3, we showed how to construct the ciphertext creator $\mathbf{C}_\mathcal{A}$ that runs $\mathcal{A}$ internally and proved that there exists an extractor $\mathbf{C}_\mathcal{A}^*$ that can decrypt the queries submitted by $\mathbf{C}_\mathcal{A}$ with overwhelming probability.

We build the CPA adversary $\mathcal{B}$ that interacts with the CPA experiment. Having the algorithms for $\mathcal{A}$, $\mathbf{C}_\mathcal{A}$ and $\mathbf{C}_\mathcal{A}^*$, the CPA adversary $\mathcal{B}$ acts as follows: $\mathcal{B}$ receives the public key pk' from the CPA experiment, and generates $2k$ keys as $(pk_i'', sk_i'') \leftarrow \mathsf{gen}(1^k)$ for $i \in [2k]$. Let $\boldsymbol{pk} = \left(pk', \boldsymbol{pk}''\right)$. $\mathcal{B}$ runs $\mathbf{C}_\mathcal{A}$ (that simulates $\mathcal{A}$ internally) on $\boldsymbol{pk}$ and its random coins. Whenever $\mathbf{C}_\mathcal{A}$ asks a query, $\mathcal{B}$ runs $\mathbf{C}_\mathcal{A}^*$ to answer them ($\mathbf{C}_\mathcal{A}^*$ gets to know the random coins of $\mathbf{C}_\mathcal{A}$ and all of its input as described in the proof of Lemma 3). Eventually $\mathbf{C}_\mathcal{A}$ outputs (m_0, m_1). $\mathcal{B}$ outputs m_0 and m_1 to the CPA experiment, and receives a ciphertext y. Remember that $\mathbf{C}_\mathcal{A}$ now accesses the oracle $\mathcal{O}$ k times. Using fresh random coins for each encryption, $\mathcal{B}$ computes $C_i = \mathsf{enc}_{pk_{k+i}}(y)$ and sends $f^{-1}(pk_{k+i}, C_i)$ to $\mathbf{C}_\mathcal{A}$ (and $\mathbf{C}_\mathcal{A}^*$) on the ith access to $\mathcal{O}$. Eventually $\mathbf{C}_\mathcal{A}$ returns $\{Y_i, m_i'\}_{i \in [\|\boldsymbol{Y}\|]}$ and the state information S and halts. The only step left in determining the decryption of Y_i is to decrypt all the ciphertexts in the outer layer, and check that they all decrypt to the same value. $\mathcal{B}$ has the $2k$ secret keys for the outer layer, hence it can do the mentioned check. If the outer layer ciphertexts of Y_i do not decrypt to the same value, the decryption of Y_i is $\perp$, otherwise the decryption of Y_i is m_i'. After $\mathcal{B}$ decrypts all the Y_i, it submits the results along with the state information S to the distinguisher $\mathcal{D}$ and forwards $\mathcal{D}$'s output to the CPA experiment.

4   More Than Non-Malleable CCA1 Encryption Scheme

In the previous section, we showed how to build a non-malleable CCA1 encryption scheme from any encryption scheme that is weakly simulatable and $\mathbf{sPA1}_\ell$

Algorithm 1: DEG	**Algorithm 2:** CS-Lite
function $\mathcal{G}(1^k)$	function $\mathcal{G}(1^k)$
$\quad (p,q,g) \leftarrow G(1^k)$	$\quad (p,q,g_1) \leftarrow G(1^k); g_2 \leftarrow G_q\backslash\{1\}$
$\quad x_1 \leftarrow \mathbb{Z}_q; X_1 \leftarrow g^{x_1} \mod p.$	$\quad x_1 \leftarrow \mathbb{Z}_q; x_2 \leftarrow \mathbb{Z}_q; z \leftarrow \mathbb{Z}_q.$
$\quad x_2 \leftarrow \mathbb{Z}_q; X_2 \leftarrow g^{x_2} \mod p.$	$\quad X \leftarrow g_1^{x_1}.g_2^{x_2} \mod p; Z \leftarrow g_1^z \mod p.$
$\quad$ Return $(pk = (p,q,g,X_1,X_2),$	$\quad$ Return $(pk = (p,q,g_1,g_2,X,Z),$
$sk = (p,q,g,x_1,x_2))$	$sk = (p,q,g_1,g_2,x_1,x_2,z))$
function $\mathcal{E}(pk,M)$	function $\mathcal{E}(pk,M)$
$\quad y \leftarrow \mathbb{Z}_q; Y \leftarrow g^y \mod p.$	$\quad r \leftarrow \mathbb{Z}_q.$
$\quad W \leftarrow X_1^y; V \leftarrow X_2^y \mod p.$	$\quad R_1 \leftarrow g_1^r \mod p; R_2 \leftarrow g_2^r \mod p.$
$\quad U \leftarrow V \cdot M \mod p$	$\quad E \leftarrow Z^r \cdot M \mod p; V \leftarrow X^r \mod p$
$\quad$ Return $C = (Y,W,U)$	$\quad$ Return $C = (R_1,R_2,E,V)$
function $\mathcal{D}(sk,C)$	function $\mathcal{D}(sk,C)$
$\quad$ if $W \neq Y^{x_1} \mod p$ **then** Return $\bot$.	$\quad$ if $V \neq R_1^{x_1} \cdot R_2^{x_2} \mod p$ **then** Return $\bot$.
$\quad$ **else** Return $M \leftarrow U \cdot Y^{-x_2} \mod p$	$\quad$ **else** Return $M \leftarrow E \cdot R_1^{-z} \mod p$

secure. Define a parallel query as a query consisting of unbounded number of ciphertexts, none of which will be decrypted until all the ciphertexts in the query are submitted. In the NM-CCA1 game, the adversary is allowed to ask an unbounded number of queries before seeing the challenge ciphertext, and one parallel query afterwards. This compares with CCA2 secure encryption schemes, which are secure even if the adversary asks an unbounded number of queries before and after seeing the challenge ciphertext. The NM-CCA1 constructions seem to be much weaker primitives. However, between the extremes of the NM-CCA1 security and the CCA2 security, a range of security notions can be defined that distinguish themselves based on how many queries the adversary may ask after revealing the challenge ciphertext without sacrificing indistinguishability of ciphertexts.

Define cNM-CCA1 security identically to NM-CCA1 security except that the adversary can make $c \geq 1$ parallel queries after seeing the challenge ciphertext. We show how to extend our result to construct an encryption scheme that is cNM-CCA1 secure where c is a constant. The high level idea for constructing a cNM-CCA1 scheme is to add another c layers of encryption on top of the ciphertext from the previous section. Intuitively, with the first parallel query, the adversary can only ask queries that can help it to maul the first layer of encryption from the outside in the future. In other words, with the first parallel query, the adversary can gain no information about all the inner ciphertexts. Hence, to penetrate the innermost layer, the adversary has to ask at least c parallel queries. Notice also that this type of construction can only allow a constant c since each layer of encryption increases ciphertext size by a polynomial factor. For more details, see the full version.

References

[BP04]   Bellare, M., Palacio, A.: Towards Plaintext-Aware Public-Key Encryption Without Random Oracles. In: Lee, P.J. (ed.) ASIACRYPT 2004. LNCS, vol. 3329, pp. 48–62. Springer, Heidelberg (2004)

[CDSMW08] Choi, S.G., Dachman-Soled, D., Malkin, T., Wee, H.: Black-Box Construction of a Non-malleable Encryption Scheme from Any Semantically Secure One. In: Canetti, R. (ed.) TCC 2008. LNCS, vol. 4948, pp. 427–444. Springer, Heidelberg (2008)

[CGH04]   Canetti, R., Goldreich, O., Halevi, S.: The random oracle methodology, revisited. J. ACM 51(4), 557–594 (2004)

[CHH+07]   Cramer, R., Hanaoka, G., Hofheinz, D., Imai, H., Kiltz, E., Pass, R., Shelat, A., Vaikuntanathan, V.: Bounded CCA2-Secure Encryption. In: Kurosawa, K. (ed.) ASIACRYPT 2007. LNCS, vol. 4833, pp. 502–518. Springer, Heidelberg (2007)

[CS03]   Cramer, R., Shoup, V.: Design and analysis of practical public-key encryption schemes secure against adaptive chosen ciphertext attack. SIAM J. Comput. 33(1), 167–226 (2003)

[Dam91]   Damgård, I.: Towards Practical Public Key Systems Secure against Chosen Ciphertext Attacks. In: Feigenbaum, J. (ed.) CRYPTO 1991. LNCS, vol. 576, pp. 445–456. Springer, Heidelberg (1992)

[DDN03]   Dolev, D., Dwork, C., Naor, M.: Nonmalleable cryptography. SIREV: SIAM Review 45 (2003)

[Den06a]   Dent, A.W.: The Cramer-Shoup Encryption Scheme Is Plaintext Aware in the Standard Model. In: Vaudenay, S. (ed.) EUROCRYPT 2006. LNCS, vol. 4004, pp. 289–307. Springer, Heidelberg (2006)

[Den06b]   Dent, A.W.: The hardness of the DHK problem in the generic group model. IACR Cryptology ePrint Archive 2006, 156 (2006)

[DN00]   Damgård, I., Nielsen, J.B.: Improved Non-committing Encryption Schemes Based on a General Complexity Assumption. In: Bellare, M. (ed.) CRYPTO 2000. LNCS, vol. 1880, pp. 432–450. Springer, Heidelberg (2000)

[MM11]   Matsuda, T., Matsuura, K.: Parallel Decryption Queries in Bounded Chosen Ciphertext Attacks. In: Catalano, D., Fazio, N., Gennaro, R., Nicolosi, A. (eds.) PKC 2011. LNCS, vol. 6571, pp. 246–264. Springer, Heidelberg (2011)

[MS09]   Myers, S., Shelat, A.: Bit encryption is complete. In: FOCS, pp. 607–616 (2009)

[PSV06]   Pass, R., Shelat, A., Vaikuntanathan, V.: Construction of a Non-malleable Encryption Scheme from Any Semantically Secure One. In: Dwork, C. (ed.) CRYPTO 2006. LNCS, vol. 4117, pp. 271–289. Springer, Heidelberg (2006)

[PW09]   Pass, R., Wee, H.: Black-box constructions of two-party protocols from one-way functions. In: Reingold, O. (ed.) TCC 2009. LNCS, vol. 5444, pp. 403–418. Springer, Heidelberg (2009)

[Wee10]   Wee, H.: Black-box, round-efficient secure computation via non-malleability amplification. In: FOCS, pp. 531–540. IEEE Computer Society (2010)

A   Plaintext Awareness

A.1   sPA1$_\ell$ Secure Schemes

We argue that Cramer-Shoup Lite (CS-Lite) and Damgard's ElGammal (DEG) are sPA1$_\ell$ secure, based on a suitable modification of the Diffie-Hellman Knowledge definition originally proposed by Damgård, and modified to permit interactive extractors by Bellare and Palacio [BP04].

$DHK1_\ell(k)$
$(p_i, q_i, g_i)_{i \in \ell[k]} \leftarrow G(1^k); (a_i)_{i \in \ell[k]} \leftarrow \mathbb{Z}_q; A_i \leftarrow g_i^{a_i} \mod p$ for $i \in \ell[k]$
Let $R[H]$ and $R[H^*]$ be randomly selected strings for H and H^*.
$st \leftarrow ((p_i)_{i \in \ell[k]}, (q_i)_{i \in \ell[k]}, (g_i)_{i \in \ell[k]}, (A_i)_{i \in [\ell]}, R[H])$
while Simulate $H((p_i)_{i \in \ell[k]}, (q_i)_{i \in \ell[k]}, (g_i)_{i \in \ell[k]}, (A_i)_{i \in [\ell]}; R[H])$ **do**
    if H queries (i, B, W) **then**
        $(b, st) \leftarrow H^*((i, B, W), st; R[H^*])$
        if $W \equiv B^{a_i} \mod p$ and $B \not\equiv g_i^b \mod p$ **then** Return 1.
        else Return b.
Return 0.

We note that in the experiment, the change requires that the ciphertext creator be able to generate ciphertexts relative to a polynomial number of randomly chosen public-keys. It seems reasonable to conjecture that any extractor that could extract exponents with respect to single value $A = g^a$, could do so efficiently for many A_i.

We now argue that DEG is $\mathbf{sPA1}_\ell$ secure under the $DHK1_\ell$ definition.

Theorem 3. *For any polynomial ℓ, The DEG scheme is $\mathbf{sPA1}_\ell$ secure under the DHK_ℓ assumption.*

Proof. We build the DHK_ℓ adversary $\mathcal{B}$ that runs the $\mathbf{sPA1}_\ell$ adversary $\mathcal{A}$ internally and simulates the $\mathbf{sPA1}_\ell$ experiment for it. $\mathcal{B}$ receives $(p_i)_{i \in \ell[k]}, (q_i)_{i \in \ell[k]}, (g_i)_{i \in \ell[k]}, (A_i)_{i \in \ell[k]}$ and its random coins $R[H]$. For each $i \in [\ell]$, $\mathcal{B}$ samples $\hat{a}_i \leftarrow \mathbb{Z}_{q_i}$, computes $\hat{A}_i \leftarrow g_i^{\hat{a}_i} \mod p_i$ and sets $pk_i \leftarrow (q_i, g_i, A_i, \hat{A}_i)$. $\mathcal{B}$ then runs $\mathcal{A}$ on $(pk_i)_{i \in [\ell]}$ and the random coins $R[H]$ until $\mathcal{A}$ halts, answering to $\mathcal{A}$'s queries as follows: upon receiving the query $C = (i, Y, W, U)$ from $\mathcal{A}$, $\mathcal{B}$ submits (i, Y, W) to the DHK_ℓ extractor. The DHK_ℓ extractor returns the value b. If $b = 1$ then $\mathcal{B}$ returns $\perp$ as the decryption of C, otherwise $\mathcal{B}$ computes $M \leftarrow U.(\hat{A}_i^b)^{-1} \mod p_i$ and return the result to $\mathcal{A}$.

Trivially, the integration of algorithm of $\mathcal{B}$ and its extractor(which depends on the algorithm of $\mathcal{A}$ and $\mathcal{B}$) is a potential extractor for the $\mathbf{sPA1}_\ell$ ciphertext creator adversary $\mathcal{A}$.

$\square$

Theorem 4. *For any polynomial ℓ, The CS-Lite scheme is $\mathbf{sPA1}_\ell$ secure under the DHK_ℓ assumption.*

Proof. The proof is similar to the proof for Theorem 3. See the full version. $\square$

B   Weakly Simulatable Encryption Schemes

We argue that the Damgard ElGamal (DEG) scheme is weakly simulatable using an argument parallel to that of Dent[Den06a]. We remind the reader that the definition for DEG is given on page 162. It has previously been shown that DEG is **sPA1** secure.

We use the notion of a simulatable group given by Dent [Den06a].

Definition 5. *(Simulatable Group)* *[Den06a] A Group G is simulatable if there exist two polynomial turing machines (f, f^{-1}) such that:*

- *f is a deterministic turing machine that takes a random element $r \in \{0,1\}^l$ as input, and outputs elements of G.*
- *f^{-1} is a probabilistic turing machine that takes elements of $h \in G$ as input, and outputs elements of $\{0,1\}^l$.*
- *$f(f^{-1}(C)) = C$ for all $h \in G$.*
- *There exists no polynomial time attacker $\mathcal{A}$ that has a non-negligible advantage in winning the following game:*
    1. *The challenger randomly chooses a bit $b \in \{0,1\}$.*
    2. *The attacker $\mathcal{A}$ executes on the input 1^k. The attacker has access to an oracle $\mathcal{O}_f$ that takes no input, generates a random element $r \in \{0,1\}^l$, and returns r if $b = 0$, and $f^{-1}(f(r))$ if $b = 1$. The attacker terminates by outputting a guess b' for b.*
    The attacker wins if $b = b'$ and its advantage is defined in the usual way.
- *There exists no polynomial-time attacker $\mathcal{A}$ that has a non-negligible advantage in winning the following game:*
    1. *The challenger randomly chooses $b \in \{0,1\}$.*
    2. *The attacker $\mathcal{A}$ executes on the input 1^k. The attacker has access to an oracle $\mathcal{O}_f$ that takes no input. If $b = 0$, then the oracle generates a random $r \in \{0,1\}^l$ and returns $f(r)$. Otherwise the oracle generates a random $h \in G$ and returns h. The attacker terminates by outputting a guess b' for b.*
    The attacker wins if $b = b'$ and its advantage is defined in the usual way.

Dent showed that groups in which the DDH assumptions are believed to hold are simulatable.

Lemma 5. *[Den06a] If q and p are primes such that $p = 2q + 1$, and G is the subgroup of $\mathbb{Z}_p^*$ of order q, then G is simulatable.*

Using this fact we show that DEG is weakly simulatable.

Theorem 5. *The DEG encryption scheme is weakly simulatable if it is instantiated on a simulatable group G (for the definition for simulatable groups, see [Den06a]) on which the DDH problem is hard.*

Proof. See the full version. $\square$

Theorem 6. *The Cramer-Shoup lite encryption scheme is weakly simulatable if it is instantiated on a simulatable group G on which the DDH problem is hard.*

Proof. Similar to the proof of Theorem 5 which is presented in full version of the paper. $\square$

Decentralized Dynamic Broadcast Encryption

Duong Hieu Phan[1,2], David Pointcheval[2], and Mario Strefler[2]

[1] LAGA, University of Paris 8
[2] ENS / CNRS / INRIA
{phan,pointche,strefler}@di.ens.fr

Abstract. A broadcast encryption system generally involves three kinds of entities: the group manager that deals with the membership, the encryptor that encrypts the data to the registered users according to a specific policy (the target set), and the users that decrypt the data if they are authorized by the policy. Public-key broadcast encryption can be seen as removing this special role of encryptor, by allowing anybody to send encrypted data. In this paper, we go a step further in the decentralization process, by removing the group manager: the initial setup of the group, as well as the addition of further members to the system, do not require any central authority. Our construction makes black-box use of well-known primitives and can be considered as an extension to the subset-cover framework. It allows for efficient concrete instantiations, with parameter sizes that match those of the subset-cover constructions, while at the same time achieving the highest security level in the standard model under the DDH assumption.

1   Introduction

Broadcast encryption (BE), introduced by Fiat and Naor [18] in 1993, allows a sender to securely send private messages to a subset of users, the target set. In 2001, Naor, Naor, and Lotspiech (NNL [24]) introduced the subset-cover framework, where for any target set, the sender can find a partition of the user set, encrypt a session key using the keys associated to each subset in the partition, and finally encrypt the content using the session key. The ciphertext length of the subset-difference (SD) version of NNL depends linearly on the number of users in the revoked set, which was considered to be efficient enough for use in the AACS DRM standard [1]. We generalize the subset-cover framework of NNL to deal with both public-key encryption and dynamic changes of the registered user sets. We furthermore remove the need for trusted authorities by eliminating the group manager, who typically interacts with users to distribute keys at the setup phase or when users join the system. Our approach makes use of group key exchange with subgroup keys [2,23], a primitive that simultaneously distributes different keys to certain subsets of the user group and applies well to the subset-cover framework if one can assign keys for the subgroups involved in the subset cover.

We first instantiate our construction with the Diffie-Hellman key agreement for the key generation and the ElGamal encryption for the public-key encryption, which leads to quite an efficient scheme. The complete-subtree (CS) tree

I. Visconti and R. De Prisco (Eds.): SCN 2012, LNCS 7485, pp. 166–183, 2012.
© Springer-Verlag Berlin Heidelberg 2012

construction resembles the tree-based group key agreement in [21], with the exception that we also create key pairs for internal nodes, and we go beyond their scheme in our construction of SD trees. We then show how our scheme can be extended to achieve the strongest security notion by using Cramer-Shoup encryption, which allows adaptive corruptions and chosen-ciphertext attacks, in the standard model, under the DDH assumption. In addition, we consider various criteria of efficiency: ciphertext size, private part and public part of the decryption keys, number of rounds for the key generation, etc. Thanks to the modularity of our approach, we can use any appropriate group key exchange with subgroup keys: our initial technique iteratively uses the two-party Diffie-Hellman key exchange in a binary tree, which requires a logarithmic number of rounds; we can replace it by logarithmically many parallel executions of the Burmester-Desmedt group key exchange protocol [8], which reduces the number of rounds to two. Besides allowing members to join the system, we also sketch how groups could merge at low cost, and how to permanently revoke some users, but we cannot elaborate on this due to space constraints. Our scheme thus achieves a maximum of functionality and security under minimal assumptions, while still being reasonably efficient.

Related Work. Dodis and Fazio [14] already constructed a public-key version of the subset-cover framework using IBE for the Complete-Subtree (CS) structure and HIBE of depth $\log N$ for the Subset-Difference (SD) structure. They retain the same efficiency, using (H)IBE keys instead of symmetric keys, and achieve generalized CCA security. In the same year, Dodis and Fazio presented a dynamic, IND-CCA-secure BE scheme [15], where the adversary may corrupt users before the challenge phase. IND-CPA-security under adaptive corruption was first achieved by Boneh and Waters [7], who presented a fully-collusion resistant trace-and-revoke scheme. More recently, Gentry and Waters [19] described another adaptively IND-CPA-secure scheme. For both schemes, there is no obvious way to make them IND-CCA-secure in the standard model.

Delerablée [11] constructed selectively IND-CPA-secure ID-based BE, which allows adding users after the setup. The only existing dynamic BE scheme was developed by Delerablée, Paillier, and Pointcheval [12]. However, their scheme does not provide forward-secrecy, i. e. a new user can decrypt all ciphertexts sent before he joined. Because our scheme provides forward-secrecy, we have to relax their definition of "dynamic". Forward-security has been considered by Yao, Fazio, Dodis, and Lysyanskaya [30], first for HIBE and then by extension for BE. Their notion of forward-security refers to security of ciphertexts against later corruption of users, which means that user keys must evolve so that previously sent messages remain secure. This is distinct from our notion of forward-secrecy, where we only require that newly joined users cannot decrypt previously sent ciphertexts. However, when a user gets corrupted, messages this user received prior to corruption can be read by the adversary, since the adversary gets the same power as the user. The scheme in [30] is IND-CCA-secure, but the adversary is more restricted in corrupting users after the challenge phase than in our setting.

Broadcast encryption without a central authority replaces the traditional setup with a group key exchange process that can be an interactive protocol. It was proposed under the name "contributory broadcast encryption" (CBE) in [29], along with a semi-adaptively IND-CPA-secure scheme that is not dynamic. A possible application of this could be communication in a social network, where some private information is meant to be read only be a subset of a user's acquaintances, and the network is either peer-to-peer or the service provider is not trusted. The first steps toward subgroup key exchange were done by Manulis [23], who extended a group key exchange (GKE) protocol to allow any two users to compute a common key after the initial phase in which the group key is computed. Following this work, Abdalla et al. [2] generalized this approach to allow the computation of session keys for arbitrary subsets. We use such a group key exchange protocol with subgroup keys to derive asymmetric encryption keys for subsets. Something similar has been done under the name of "asymmetric group key agreement" (ASGKA) [28]. In [28], ASGKA is defined in a way that guarantees only that the keys held by the participants are good for use with a specific encryption scheme. We want to generalize this requirement so that at the end of the protocol run, each user has some randomness, which can thereafter be used for any key generation, and namely to generate key pairs for any key encapsulation mechanism. Since this randomness is shared between various subgroups, we call the scheme we use for the setup "subgroup key exchange" (SKE). Kurnio, Safavi-Naini, and Wang [22] explicitly consider sponsorship of group candidates by existing members. In our scheme, because of the tree structure, each user can act as a sponsor, and only one sponsor is required for a candidate to join the user set.

Contributions and Organization. In section 2, we define decentralized dynamic broadcast encryption and subgroup key exchange, a building block we use in our construction that may be of independent interest. We extend the security notions of adaptive IND-CPA and IND-CCA from [26] to our case. We describe a black-box construction of decentralized dynamic broadcast encryption using the subset-cover framework in section 3 and prove the security of the construction, assuming that the building blocks are secure. In section 4, we construct a subgroup key exchange protocol based on any secure two-party key exchange protocol. We give two concrete instantiations using our methodology in section 5, that provide keys for subgroups in the CS and SD structures. Combined with the Cramer-Shoup encryption scheme, this gives us a decentralized dynamic broadcast encryption schemes which additionally achieves the highest security level (fully adaptive IND-CCA-security) in the standard model under the DDH-assumption.

2   Definitions

In the following, we describe some generic constructions for broadcast encryption that make use of standard definitions of well-known primitives. We briefly review the notations here, but provide full definitions in the full version [25].

A public-key encryption scheme is defined by a tuple of four algorithms $\mathcal{PKE} = (\mathsf{Setup}, \mathsf{KeyGen}, \mathsf{Encrypt}, \mathsf{Decrypt})$. A two-party key exchange protocol is a tuple of two algorithms/protocols $\mathcal{KE} = (\mathsf{Setup}, \mathsf{CommonKey})$. Note that CommonKey is an interactive protocol, but we expect it to be one-round only for the efficiency of our constructions. A message authentication code is a tuple of three algorithms $\mathcal{MAC} = (\mathsf{KeyGen}, \mathsf{GenMac}, \mathsf{VerifMac})$. A pseudo-random generator is a function $\mathcal{F} : X \to Y$ with $|X| \leq |Y|$.

2.1 Decentralized Broadcast Encryption

Let us start with the main protocol we want to build: a broadcast encryption scheme, which aims at encrypting a message for a group of users, with a fine-grained selection of the target group. As in [18], broadcast encryption generally involves a group manager, that deals with the membership of the users, and an encryptor that specifies the target group (a subgroup of the registered members) for a ciphertext. The encryptor is either a specific person in case of secret-key broadcast encryption, or anybody in case of public-key broadcast encryption. The group manager is either involved once only, at the setup phase, in static schemes, or at any time a new member wants to join the system, in dynamic schemes [12]. The latter dynamic situation is the most realistic, but makes the group manager quite sensitive, for both security and availability. Our goal is to get rid of such a centralized system.

We thus extend the dynamic broadcast encryption setting [12] so that the membership management can be decentralized. At the same time, we would like to keep everything as small as possible.

1. The ciphertext size should be as small as possible: the ciphertext has to contain the target group structure, and so cannot be smaller than the representation of this structure, which can either be encoded on N bits, where N is the total number of users, and each bit tells whether a user is in the target group or not, or on $r \log N$ bits (resp. $s \log N$ bits), where r (resp. s) is the number of revoked users (resp. included users) among the N registered users. This is sometimes considered independently from the ciphertext, in the header, but anyway both the target set and the encrypted data have to be sent. Our goal is to make the global length as small as possible.

2. When a new user joins the system, it should have minimal impact on other users' secret information and the public information: no impact at all on the keys as in [12] is of course optimal, but when one wants to achieve forward secrecy, it is not possible: some of the keys have to be modified. We will try to keep the impact as small as possible too.

Since we want to avoid any centralized group manager, we will also focus on public-key broadcast encryption, in which a public key is enough to target any subgroup at the encryption time. In addition, instead of encrypting a message, our schemes will generate an encapsulation (or key header) and session keys to be used with any symmetric encryption scheme [27].

Definition 1 (Decentralized Dynamic Broadcast Encapsulation). *A decentralized dynamic broadcast encapsulation scheme is a tuple of five algorithms or protocols* $\mathcal{DBE} = (\mathsf{Setup}, \mathsf{KeyGen}, \mathsf{Join}, \mathsf{Encaps}, \mathsf{Decaps})$:

- $\mathsf{Setup}(1^k)$, *where k is the security parameter, generates the global parameters* param *of the system.*
- $\mathsf{KeyGen}(\mathrm{param}, U)$ *is an interactive protocol between the users in the set U. After the protocol run, it returns the public encryption key* EK *and a list Reg of the registered users with additional public information. Each user $u \in U$ eventually gets a secret decryption key* dk_u.
- $\mathsf{Join}(v, \{u(\mathsf{dk}_u)\}_{u \in U}, \mathrm{Reg}, \mathsf{EK})$ *is an interactive protocol run between a user v and the set of users U, described in Reg. Each user takes as input his secret key and/or some random coins, the list Reg, and the encryption key* EK. *After the protocol, Reg and EK are updated, and each user (including v) has a secret decryption key.*
- $\mathsf{Encaps}(\mathsf{EK}, \mathrm{Reg}, S)$ *takes as input the encryption key* EK, *the user register Reg, and a target set S. It outputs a key header H and a session key $K \in \{0,1\}^k$.*
- $\mathsf{Decaps}(\mathsf{dk}_u, S, H)$ *takes as input the target set S and a user decryption key* dk_u *together with a key header H. If* dk_u *corresponds to a recipient user, it outputs the session key K, else it outputs the error symbol $\perp$.*

The correctness requirement is that for all N, any target set $S \subset U_N = [1, N]$ and for any $u \in U_N$, if $u \in S$ then the decapsulation algorithm gives back the key. A decentralized scheme requires that no authority is involved in the KeyGen and Join protocols.

Security Notions. A general overview of the security notions for broadcast encryption has been done in [26]. We extend the strongest one to the decentralized setting. The adversary is still given unlimited access to the Join oracle (dynamic), the Corrupt oracle (adaptive) and Decaps oracle (chosen-ciphertext security). For the group key generation, the definition from [26] models passive adversaries only, since they only receive the public keys. Since in our case this group key generation may be an interactive protocol, we make it more explicit with a Execute-oracle that outputs the public transcript of the full run of this protocol. The security game for DBE is presented in figure 1: the restriction for the adversary is not to ask for the decapsulation of the challenge ciphertext (which includes the target set S) nor corrupt any user in the target set.

The adversary can ask once the generation of the group structure with a single call to Execute on a group U of its choice, from which it gets the transcript τ, the encryption key EK and the register Reg. It can thereafter make as many calls it wants to Join, to add a user to the structure Reg, which updates EK. The adversary also gets the transcript τ of this interactive protocol. At any time, the adversary can also corrupt a user with a key pair, calling Cor and getting back all the secret information of the user, and decapsulate a ciphertext H, calling Dec in the name of a user u.

$\mathrm{Exp}_{\mathcal{DBE},\mathcal{A}}^{\mathrm{ind-acca}-b}(k)$
    $\mathcal{Q}_C \leftarrow \emptyset;\ \mathcal{Q}_D \leftarrow \emptyset;$
    param $\leftarrow$ Setup(1^k);
    $(st, U) \leftarrow \mathcal{A}(\mathrm{SETUP}; \mathrm{param});$
    $(\mathsf{EK}, Reg, \tau) \leftarrow \mathsf{Execute}(U);$
    $(st, S) \leftarrow \mathcal{A}^{\mathsf{Join}(\cdot),\mathsf{Cor}(\cdot),\mathsf{Dec}(\cdot,\cdot,\cdot)}(st; \mathsf{EK}, Reg, \tau);$
    $(H, K) \leftarrow \mathsf{Encaps}(\mathsf{EK}, Reg, S);$
    $K_b \leftarrow K;\ K_{1-b} \stackrel{\$}{\leftarrow} \mathcal{K};$
    $b' \leftarrow \mathcal{A}^{\mathsf{Join}(\cdot),\mathsf{Cor}(\cdot),\mathsf{Dec}(\cdot,\cdot,\cdot)}(st; H, K_0, K_1);$
    if $\exists i \in S, (i, S, H) \in \mathcal{Q}_D$ or $i \in \mathcal{Q}_C;$
    then return 0
    else return $b';$

$\mathsf{Execute}(U)$
    $(\mathsf{EK}, Reg) \leftarrow \mathsf{KeyGen}(\mathrm{param}, U);$
    return $\mathsf{EK}, Reg, \tau;$

$\mathsf{Join}(v)$
    $(\mathsf{EK}, Reg) \leftarrow \mathsf{Join}(v, U, Reg, \mathsf{EK});$
    return $\mathsf{EK}, Reg, \tau;$

$\mathsf{Cor}(u)$
    $\mathcal{Q}_C \leftarrow \mathcal{Q}_C \cup \{u\};$ return $dk_u;$

$\mathsf{Dec}(u, S, H)$
    $\mathcal{Q}_D \leftarrow \mathcal{Q}_D \cup \{(u, S, H)\};$
    $K \leftarrow \mathsf{Decaps}(dk_u, S, H);$
    return $K;$

Fig. 1. $\mathcal{DBE}$: Key Indistinguishability (IND-ACCA)

The main security goal of an encryption scheme (or an encapsulation scheme) is the indistinguishability of a challenge ciphertext: at some point, the adversary thus gets a challenge (H, K_0, K_1), where H encapsulates either K_0 or K_1 for a target set S chosen by the adversary. It has to guess which key is actually encapsulated. Of course, there are the natural restrictions, which are controlled granted the lists $\mathcal{Q}_C$ and $\mathcal{Q}_D$:

- (S, H) has not been asked to the decapsulation oracle for a user u in S
- none of the users in S have been corrupted

A dynamic broadcast encapsulation scheme is $(t, N, q_C, q_D, \varepsilon)$-IND-ACCA-secure (security against adaptive corruption and chosen-ciphertext attacks) if in the security game presented in figure 1, the advantage $\mathrm{Adv}_{\mathcal{DBE}}^{\mathrm{ind-acca}}(k, t, N, q_C, q_D)$, of any t-time adversary $\mathcal{A}$ creating at most N users (Join oracle), corrupting at most q_C of them (Cor oracle), and asking for at most q_D decapsulation queries (Dec oracle), is bounded by ε.

$$\mathrm{Adv}_{\mathcal{DBE}}^{\mathrm{ind-acca}}(k, t, N, q_C, q_D)$$
$$= \max_{\mathcal{A}}\{\Pr[\mathrm{Exp}_{\mathcal{DBE},\mathcal{A}}^{\mathrm{ind-acca}-1}(k) = 1] - \Pr[\mathrm{Exp}_{\mathcal{DBE},\mathcal{A}}^{\mathrm{ind-acca}-0}(k) = 1]\}.$$

This definition includes IND-ACPA (for adaptive chosen-plaintext attacks) when $q_D = 0$.

Remark 2 (Forward-secrecy). This definition includes forward-secrecy against new users, i.e. a new user cannot decrypt ciphertexts that were created before he joined. For a definition without forward secrecy, the adversary is prohibited from corrupting users that joined after the challenge phase.

2.2   Subgroup Key Exchange

The novelty of our definition is the decentralized key generation procedure, that should also generate keys for certain subgroups in order to be able to broadcast to any target set. This is thus in the same vein as the notion of group key exchange with on-demand computation of subgroup keys (GKE+S) from [2], that allows some subgroups of users to run a protocol to establish keys between them. But we extend this definition by allowing for keys of some subgroups to be computed during the first protocol run that establishes the global key, without any additional interaction.

Since we want to remain independent of the encryption scheme to be used with the session key, we require that for each subgroup a proto-key is computed, whose entropy can be used as input to a PKE key-pair generation, or to generate a symmetric encryption key.

Definition 3 (Dynamic $\mathcal{S}$-Subgroup Key Exchange Protocol). *For a collection $\mathcal{S} : \mathbb{N} \to \mathcal{P}(\mathbb{N})$ of subsets of the user set, where for any N, $\mathcal{S}(N) \in \mathcal{P}(N)$, a dynamic $\mathcal{S}$-subgroup key exchange protocol $\mathcal{SKE}$ is a tuple of three algorithms and interactive protocols:*

- *Setup(1^k), where k is the security parameter, generates the global parameters param of the system;*
- *KeyGen(param, U) is an interactive protocol run between all users in U. It outputs a register Reg that contains a description of U and the subsets for which keys were established according to $\mathcal{S}$, and for each user $u \in U$ a secret usk_u that contains the proto-keys pt_S for all the sub-groups S containing u.*
- *Join(v, U, Reg) is an interactive protocol run between user v and the group of users U. It outputs an updated register Reg and for user v and some of the users in U a new secret usk_u that contains the proto-keys pt_S of all the subgroups S they are part of.*

We require that all the users $u \in U$ that run KeyGen(param, U) receive the same register Reg and compute matching proto-keys for the subsets they have in common. The same is required of Join.

For the security definition, we extend the definition given in [2], which seems to be most applicable to our case. Since the protocol is dynamic, the user set can change over time. As in the previous section, we stick to passive adversaries. This is a way of modularizing protocol construction, as passively secure protocols can be made secure against active adversaries using constructions such as [20], with additional authentication mechanisms.

The adversary can ask once the generation of the group structure with a unique call to Execute, at time $t = 0$, on a group U of its choice from which it gets the transcript τ and the register *Reg*. It can thereafter make as many calls as it wants to Join, to add a user to the structure *Reg*. Each query increases the time index t. The adversary also gets the transcripts τ of these interactive protocols.

$\mathrm{Exp}_{\mathcal{SKE},\mathcal{A}}^{\mathrm{ind}-b}(k)$

   $Reg \leftarrow \emptyset; \mathcal{Q}_T \leftarrow \emptyset;$

   $\mathsf{param} \leftarrow \mathsf{Setup}(1^k);$

   $(st, U) \leftarrow \mathcal{A}(\mathsf{param});$

   $(\mathsf{EK}, Reg, \tau) \leftarrow \mathsf{Execute}(U);$

   $b' \leftarrow \mathcal{A}^{\mathsf{Join}(\cdot),\mathsf{OTest}(\cdot,\cdot)}(st; \mathsf{EK}, Reg, \tau);$

   $\mathbf{return}\ b';$

$\mathsf{OTest}(t, S)$

   $\mathbf{if}\ \exists(t', K) \wedge t \equiv_S t' \wedge (t', S, K) \in \mathcal{Q}_T$

    $\mathbf{then\ return}\ K;$

   $\mathbf{else\ if}\ b = 0\ \mathbf{then}\ K \leftarrow \mathsf{pt}_S(t);$

    $\mathbf{else}\ K \xleftarrow{\$} \mathcal{K};$

   $\mathcal{Q}_T \leftarrow \mathcal{Q}_T \cup \{(t, S, K)\};$

   $\mathbf{return}\ K;$

$\mathsf{Execute}(U)$

   $t \leftarrow 0;$

   $Reg \leftarrow \mathsf{KeyGen}(\mathsf{param}, U);$

   $\mathbf{return}\ Reg, \tau;$

$\mathsf{Join}(v)$

   $t \leftarrow t + 1;$

   $Reg \leftarrow \mathsf{Join}(v, U, Reg);$

   $\mathbf{return}\ Reg, \tau;$

Fig. 2. $\mathcal{SKE}$: Key Indistinguishability (IND)

The main security goal of key exchange is the indistinguishability of the keys, and their independence. Hence, we use the stronger notion proposed in [3], similar to the Real-or-Random [5] for encryption. The adversary has access to many $\mathsf{OTest}(t, S)$ queries, that are either answered by the real keys or by truly random and independent keys. Note that according to the protocol, some keys may remain unchanged even when the time period evolves. We even hope to have as many keys as possible that do not evolve, since we want that not too many users are impacted by a new member in the system. We thus say that two pairs (t_1, S) and (t_2, S) are equivalent (denoted by $t_1 \equiv_S t_2$) if S is unchanged between the time periods and therefore they should have the same key. For such equivalent pairs, the same random key is output. We do not provide direct access to a $\mathsf{OReveal}$ oracle, which returns the secret key of a user, because as explained in [3], having access to many OTest queries annihilates the advantage provided by $\mathsf{OReveal}$ queries.

A subgroup key exchange scheme is said to be (t, N, q_T, ε)-IND-secure if, in the security game presented in figure 2, the advantage $\mathrm{Adv}_{\mathcal{SKE}}^{\mathsf{ind}}(k, t, N, q_T)$ of any t-time adversary $\mathcal{A}$ creating at most N users (the final size of the set U), testing at most q_T keys is bounded by ε.

$$\mathrm{Adv}_{\mathcal{SKE}}^{\mathsf{ind}}(k, t, N, q_T) = \max_{\mathcal{A}}\{\Pr[\mathrm{Exp}_{\mathcal{SKE},\mathcal{A}}^{\mathsf{ind}-1}(k) = 1] - \Pr[\mathrm{Exp}_{\mathcal{SKE},\mathcal{A}}^{\mathsf{ind}-0}(k) = 1]\}.$$

3 Generic Decentralized Broadcast Encryption

As already remarked, in the first definition of dynamic broadcast encryption schemes [12], it is required that the existing users are not affected by a join: their decryption keys should not be modified. Only the encryption key could be modified. This constraint is actually achieved by their scheme, but this is possible because the scheme is not forward-secure: a new user can decrypt all ciphertexts that were sent before he joined (since he cannot be in any revoked set).

To achieve forward-secrecy, we have to relax their definition and allow updates of the user decryption keys. Namely, updates of the decryption keys are necessary for forward-secrecy in the subset-cover framework [24], because some keys are shared by several users. With an appropriate subset-cover structure, it can reach asymptotically optimal overall ciphertext size. On the other hand, the naive scheme, where each user has a single key specific to him, can be made dynamic without decryption key updates, but has ciphertexts whose length is linear in the number of users. As soon as keys are shared between users, forward-secrecy makes it necessary to update these shared keys. Hence our relaxation of the model. However, we require these updates of existing keys to be made via public channels.

3.1   Generic Public-Key Subset Cover

A subset-cover structure $\mathcal{SC} = \{S_i\}_{i \in I}$ is a set of subsets S_i of a user set U such that for any subset $S \subset U$ there is a subset $\mathcal{L} \subset I$ such that S can be *partitioned* as $S = \bigcup_{i \in \mathcal{L}} S_i$. In particular, this implies that for all users $u \in U$, $\{u\} \in \mathcal{SC}$. In [24], a secret key is assigned to each set S_i, so a message can be encrypted to any subset $S \subset U$ by finding the cover $\mathcal{L}$ of S. Then a session key is encrypted under all the keys associated to the selected subsets. All the other users are then implicitly revoked, since they cannot decrypt the session key. Because of the partition property, a user in S is in one subset S_i only. Efficiency will thereafter depend on the subset-cover structure.

We extend this framework in three directions:

1. First, we transfer this approach to the public-key world. Each S_i is assigned a key pair of some PKE scheme by some key assignment procedure. This means that the assignment of keys to the subsets depends on the PKE scheme used as well as the assignment procedure. For example, for a subset-cover structure $\mathcal{SC}$ and a PKE $\mathcal{PKE}$, we can use the key assignment that assigns each subset with a key pair drawn independently at random by the trusted center.
2. Second, we replace the trusted center by an interactive protocol, a subgroup key exchange.
3. Third, we allow for the addition of users, hence using a *dynamic subgroup key exchange* to generate the keys for a dynamic subset-cover structure.

We first deal with a dynamic subset-cover structure, assuming a subgroup key exchange as a black box. Thereafter, we will consider concrete structures and efficient subgroup key exchanges.

3.2   Dynamic Subset-Cover

We define a dynamic subset-cover as a sequence of subset-covers $\{\mathcal{SC}_i\}$ for $i \geq 0$ users, where each $\mathcal{SC}_i$ contains subsets S_j. These subsets never change, so instead of adding a user to a subset, we remove the old one and add a new one. This also means that the same subset S_j can occur in different time periods (the time period changes each time a new user joins). We start with $\mathcal{SC}_0 = \emptyset$ and an empty user set $U_0 = \emptyset$, and then have $U_{n+1} = U_n \cup \{u_{n+1}\}$. From the definition, it is clear that $|U_n| = n$, and w.l.o.g. $U_n = [1, n]$.

For subset-cover based dynamic broadcast encryption, we will have to generate the keys for all the subsets that are involved in $\mathcal{SC}_n$. The following property will optimize efficiency, in the sense that a minimal number of existing users will be impacted by a new member.

Definition 4 (Splitting Property). *We say that a dynamic subset cover $\mathcal{SC}$ has the* splitting property, *if the subset cover at time $n+1$ is composed of subsets that either were part of the subset cover at time n, or contain the new user. $\mathcal{SC}_{n+1} = \mathcal{SC}'_{n+1} \cup \mathcal{SC}''_{n+1}$, where $\mathcal{SC}'_{n+1} \subset \mathcal{SC}_n$ and $S_i \in \mathcal{SC}''_{n+1} \Rightarrow u_{n+1} \in S_i$.*

With this property, if a subset changes, it is either removed, or it contains u_{n+1}. Then only sets with the new user need new key generation, which is a minimal requirement anyway.

3.3   SC-Based Decentralized Dynamic Broadcast Encryption

We first assume we have a dynamic subgroup key exchange $\mathcal{SKE}$ that is compatible with our dynamic subset-cover structure. It means that for any n, the subgroup key exchange provides keys for all the subsets S in $\mathcal{SC}_n$. We will later instantiate such a dynamic subgroup key exchange for some dynamic subset-cover structures.

Let us recall that the SC-based broadcast encryption [24] consists in encrypting the same message under the keys of all the subsets that cover the target set. Since one of our goals is to achieve the highest security level, adaptive chosen-ciphertext security, any modification of the description of the target set or one of the ciphertexts in the list should make the global ciphertext invalid, otherwise the scheme is somewhat malleable, and thus insecure against chosen-ciphertext attacks. We will add a MAC to bind the target header and the ciphertexts together. A similar approach has been used by [6, 16]. Instead of a master secret key, our scheme needs only a public register Reg to keep track of the users currently enrolled in the system and their public keys.

We first present in details our construction, and then state the security of the construction. It is important to remember that the subgroup key exchange scheme is only assumed to be passively secure, meaning that the protocol requires authenticated channels. This can be achieved in several ways that we will not discuss here. Because the subset cover is a fixed part of the protocol and defines the subsets for each number of users, and we assume that the number of users in the system is always known, the number of a new user and the subsets he belongs to can be computed deterministically by all users. Meta-issues like trust between users and how they should agree on which users to allow into the group are beyond the scope of this paper.

Definition 5 (dBE). *Let $\mathcal{PKE}$ be a PKE, $\mathcal{MAC}$ a MAC, $\mathcal{F} : \mathcal{K} \to \mathcal{R}$ a pseudo-random generator, $\mathcal{SC}$ a dynamic subset-cover, and $\mathcal{SKE}$ a dynamic subgroup key exchange compatible with $\mathcal{SC}$ with keys in $\mathcal{K}$. Our Broadcast Encryption Scheme is defined as follows.*

- Setup(1^k):
    1. *Run $\mathcal{PKE}$.Setup(1^k) to get param$_{\mathcal{PKE}}$;*
    2. *Run $\mathcal{SKE}$.Setup(1^k) to get param$_{\mathcal{SKE}}$;*
    3. *Publish param $= ($param$_{\mathcal{PKE}},$ param$_{\mathcal{SKE}})$.*
- KeyGen(param, U_n), *for some integer n:*
    1. *Run $\mathcal{SKE}$.KeyGen(param$_{\mathcal{SKE}}, U_n$) to get Reg; Each user $u \in U_n$ gets as output of the protocol the proto-keys pt$_S$ for all subsets S he belongs to according to $\mathcal{SC}$. The decryption key dk$_u$ consists of all these pt$_S$.*
    2. *He computes (dk$_S$, ek$_S$) $\leftarrow \mathcal{PKE}$.KeyGen(param$_{\mathcal{PKE}}$; $\mathcal{F}$(pt$_S$)), where we use the PRG to generate from the proto-key the random coins of the key generation algorithm;*
    3. *All the encryption keys ek$_S$ are published as EK;*
    4. *The decryption keys dk$_S$ can be either stored in dk$_u$ for users $u \in S$, or deleted since they can be recomputed;*
- Join(v, {$u($dk$_u)$}$_{u \in U_n}$, Reg, EK):
    1. *Run $\mathcal{SKE}$.Join(v, {$u($dk$_u)$}$_{u \in U_n}$, Reg) to get the new Reg;*
    2. *Each user u does as above to compute dk$_S$, ek$_S$ and dk$_u$. Note that granted the splitting properties, only dk$_S$, and thus ek$_S$, for S that contain v are affected;*
- Encaps(EK, Reg, S):
    1. *From the target set S, generate the partition $\mathcal{L}$ with $S = \cup_{\mathcal{L}} S_i$;*
    2. *Generate a session key $\mathcal{K}_e$ and a MAC key $\mathcal{K}_m$;*
    3. *For each subset $i \in \mathcal{L}$, generate $c_i = \mathcal{PKE}$.Encrypt(ek$_{S_i}$, $\mathcal{K}_e || \mathcal{K}_m$);*
    4. *Compute $\sigma = \mathcal{MAC}$.GenMac($\mathcal{K}_m$, $S || (c_i)_{i \in \mathcal{L}}$);*
    5. *Output $\mathcal{K}_e$ and $H = ((c_i)_{i \in \mathcal{L}}, \sigma)$.*
- Decaps(dk$_u$, S, H):
    1. *If $u \in S$, then there is a unique i such that $u \in S_i$, and then dk$_u$ allows to derive dk $=$ dk$_{S_i}$;*
    2. *Extract $\mathcal{K}_e || \mathcal{K}_m = \mathcal{PKE}$.Decrypt(dk, c_i);*
    3. *Check if σ is a valid MAC under key $\mathcal{K}_m$;*
    4. *In case of validity, output $\mathcal{K}_e$, otherwise output $\perp$.*

The scheme is a correct dynamic broadcast encryption scheme, because of the correctness of the basic primitives $\mathcal{PKE}$, $\mathcal{MAC}$ and $\mathcal{F}$, but also $\mathcal{SKE}$.

Theorem 6. *Let us consider the scheme $\mathcal{BE}^{\mathcal{PKE},\mathcal{MAC},\mathcal{F},\mathcal{SKE}}$ from definition 5. We define L_N to be the total number of distinct subsets over all time periods and ℓ_N to be the maximal number of subsets necessary to cover any authorized target set S in $\mathcal{SC}_i$ for any i. If $\mathcal{PKE}$ is an IND-CCA-secure PKE, $\mathcal{MAC}$ is a SUF-CMA-secure MAC, $\mathcal{SKE}$ is a IND-secure SKE, and $\mathcal{F}$ is a pseudo-random generator, then this scheme is a forward-secure IND-ACCA-secure BE scheme:*

$$\mathrm{Adv}_{\mathcal{DBE}}^{\mathsf{ind-acca}}(k, t, N, q_C, q_D) \leq 2\mathrm{Adv}_{\mathcal{SKE}}^{\mathsf{ind}}(k, t, L_N, L_N) + 3\ell_N L_N \mathrm{Adv}_{\mathcal{PKE}}^{\mathsf{ind-cca}}(k, t, q_D)$$
$$+ 2L_N \mathrm{Adv}_{\mathcal{F}}^{\mathsf{prg}}(k, t) + 2\mathrm{Succ}_{\mathcal{MAC}}^{\mathsf{suf-cma}}(k, t, 1, q_D).$$

The variables L_N and ℓ_N depend on the type of subset cover used in the scheme. For CS, L_N is less than $N \log N$ (since at most $\log N$ sets change in each of the at most N steps), and ℓ_N is $r \log \frac{N}{r}$, which is bounded by $N/2$ (the worst-case ciphertext length). For SD, we have $L_N \leq N \log^2 N$ and $\ell_N = 2r - 1$. The complete security proof can be found in the full version [25].

4   Tree-Based Subgroup Key Exchange

In this section, we define two subgroup key exchange protocols compatible with the efficient tree-based methods defined in [24]. The tree-based methods are special cases in the subset-cover framework, where the users are organized as leaves in a binary tree, and the subsets S_i can be described in terms of subtrees of this tree.

Complete Subtree. We first review the static complete subtree (CS) structure for N users $\{u_0, \ldots, u_{N-1}\}$. For simplicity, we assume $N = 2^d$, but the description can be generalized to any N. All the users are leaves of the tree, and can be seen as singletons $S_{2^d+i} = \{u_i\}$, for $i = 0, \ldots, 2^d - 1$. Then, for $i = 2^d - 1$ to 1, $S_i = S_{2i} \cup S_{2i+1}$ which contains all the leaves below the node with index i.

Subset Difference. The subset difference (SD) method uses subsets $S_{i,j} = S_i \setminus S_j$, where S_i, S_j are defined as in the CS method, and S_j is a subtree of S_i. All sets S_i from the CS tree are also contained in the SD method, because $S_i = S_{\mathrm{parent}(i),\mathrm{sibling}(i)}$; S_0 is included as a special set.

4.1   Static Tree Construction

Let us show how such subset-cover structures naturally give rise to subgroup key exchange protocols. The main tools for our construction of the subgroup key exchange are two primitives: a 2-party key exchange protocol $\mathcal{KE}$ that outputs keys in $\mathcal{K_{KE}}$ and a pseudo-random generator $\mathcal{G} : \mathcal{K_{KE}} \to \mathcal{K} \times \mathcal{R_{KE}}$.

Two users start from random coins in $\mathcal{R_{KE}}$, and run a key exchange protocol $\mathcal{KE}$.CommonKey in order to derive a secret value ck for the subset represented by the node in the tree that is their parent. This common key ck is used as the seed for the PRG $\mathcal{G}$ to derive the two secret keys, the proto-key $\mathsf{pt} \in \mathcal{K}$ and the random coins $r \in R_{\mathcal{KE}}$ for the next key exchange at the level above. Internal nodes thus involve "virtual" users. In summary, the tree is constructed by executing $\mathcal{KE}$.CommonKey, then computing $\mathcal{G}$, at each level from the bottom up. We derive generic instantiations of the complete subtree (CS) and subset difference (SD) methods on binary trees described in [24].

CS Tree. We define the neighbour of user u with identifier i to be the user u' with identifier $i + 1$ if $i \equiv 0 \mod 2$, $i - 1$ else and its parent to be the user w with identifier $\lfloor i/2 \rfloor$. At round r, each (virtual) user u created in round $r-1$ has a uniquely defined neighbour u' and a parent w. If he does not, the protocol run is completed: we are either at the root of the tree, or the tree is not complete. The users u and u' have random coins r_u and $r_{u'}$, which they use to run the $\mathcal{KE}$ protocol, resulting in a common key ck_w. From this common key, they derive the proto-key of node w and the randomness for the virtual user w to participate in the next round of key exchanges. The user with the smaller identifier then plays the role of the virtual user w in the next round. As a consequence, for N users, there are $\log N$ rounds. Round r involves $N/2^{r-1}$ (virtual) users.

- KeyGen(U_n): In round r, for $r = 1, \ldots, \log n$, the users u, u' with parent w at level $(\log n - r)$ proceed as follows:
    1. $\mathsf{ck}_w \leftarrow \mathcal{KE}.\mathsf{CommonKey}(u, u')$;
    2. $(\mathsf{pt}_w, r_w) \leftarrow \mathcal{G}(\mathsf{ck}_w)$;
    3. If $u < u'$, set $u \stackrel{\text{def}}{=} w$;

A similar construction is possible for the more efficient SD scheme. Due to lack of space, we present this construction in the full version [25].

4.2   Dynamic Tree Construction

Dynamic CS. We define a join procedure for the CS tree described above. We go from $\mathcal{SC}_n$ to $\mathcal{SC}_{n+1}$ by taking the leaf u' with the lowest distance to the root, and if there are several with that property, the one with the lowest index. We then replace it with an inner node w, to which we append both the leaf u' and the new user v. We note that the user identifiers will not be in the same order as the node numbers in the tree. Then we replace the subsets S_j where j is an ancestor of the new user with the new subsets. This ensures that our dynamic CS scheme is forward-secure and has the splitting property of definition 4. The CS key assignment is done as follows.

First the new user v derives a common key c_w with its sibling u'. From this common key, he derives the proto-key of node w and the randomness for the virtual user w to participate in the next round of key exchanges. The user with the smaller identifier then plays the role of w in the next round. This procedure is repeated until the keys of all ancestors of v are recomputed.

- Join(v, U_n) In the first round, set $u \stackrel{\text{def}}{=} v$. In round r, for $r = 1, \ldots, \log(n+1)$, the user u with neighbour u' and parent w at level $(\log(n+1) - r)$ proceeds as follows:
    1. $\mathsf{ck}_w \leftarrow \mathcal{KE}.\mathsf{CommonKey}(u, u')$;
    2. $(\mathsf{pt}_w, r_w) \leftarrow \mathcal{G}(\mathsf{ck}_w)$;
    3. set $u \stackrel{\text{def}}{=} w$, $u' \stackrel{\text{def}}{=} neighbour(w)$, $w \stackrel{\text{def}}{=} parent(w)$;

A similar construction is possible for the more efficient SD scheme. Due to lack of space, we present this construction in the full version [25]. We state exactly the security of the dynamic CS construction. Because of the similarities in the construction, a similar result can be obtained for SD.

Theorem 7. *Let $\mathcal{KE}$ be an IND-secure KE scheme with session keys in $\mathcal{K}_{\mathcal{KE}}$, and $\mathcal{G} : \mathcal{K}_{\mathcal{KE}} \to \mathcal{K} \times \mathcal{R}_{\mathcal{KE}}$ be a PRG. Then our dynamic CS construction of a $\mathcal{SKE}$ is IND-secure and*

$$\mathrm{Adv}^{\mathrm{ind}}_{\mathcal{SKE}}(k, t, N, q_T) \leq (N \log N)\left(\mathrm{Adv}^{\mathrm{ind}}_{\mathcal{KE}}(k, t) + \mathrm{Adv}^{\mathrm{prg}}_{\mathcal{G}}(k, t)\right).$$

The full proof can be found in the full version [25].

4.3 Efficiency Properties

One of the main advantages of the NNL constructions [24] is the efficient revocation with small ciphertext lengths ($\mathcal{O}(r \log N/r)$ for CS, $\mathcal{O}(2r - 1)$ for SD) which is immediately inherited in our public-key scheme. The decryption key is the same length for CS, where each user has to store $\log N$ keys only, and longer ($\mathcal{O}(N \log N)$ for SD), where we cannot use the same key derivation.

In our scheme, for many instantiations of the 2-party key exchange, the private part of the decryption key can even be constant-size: each user keeps his secret random coins r_i, which is enough to iteratively generate all the private information from the public transcript of the key exchange protocols (stored in *Reg* or in the public key). Then, granted the key exchange scheme and $\log N$ public keys, each user can iteratively compute the decryption keys along the path to the root of the tree, and it is in this sense that the user random coins "contain" the keys used to decrypt, as required by the decapsulation algorithm.

Permanent Revocation. Because the length of the ciphertext for SC schemes depends on the number of revoked users, it is desirable to be able to completely remove users from a group. To permanently remove a user at leaf $2i$, we remove it and its sibling leaf $2i + 1$ and simply move the user at $2i + 1$ to be at node i which becomes a leaf. The keys of the user now at i remain the same as his own key before (at node $2i + 1$) and we thus have to update the keys of all subsets in which the revoked user was a member. Concerning the security, it is easy to see that the user $2i$, not having the key of the user $2i + 1$, can not learn anything about the updated keys, and this ensures the forward secrecy.

The only problem we face is that we need to keep the tree balanced. Fortunately, our constructions allow a re-organization of the tree in a very efficient manner. Indeed, the tree could be maintained to be an AVL tree at low cost [4]. Whenever a user leaves the system and makes the tree unbalanced, by using $\log N$ rotations, we can re-balance the tree. Note that a rotation needs $\log N$ update operations at worst, so the total cost for a re-balancing is just $\log^2 N$ update operations at worst.

Merging Groups. Instead of joining a single user, we can also efficiently merge two existing groups by executing the key exchange protocol for their root nodes. This will allow every user in the two groups to compute the keys of the new root node.

5   Concrete Instantiations

We now give two instantiations of our scheme. The first one is probably the simplest possible case, and achieves IND-ACPA-security under the DDH-assumption. We use the Diffie-Hellman protocol [13] as our KE (where the users publish g^x and g^y from their random coins x and y, and get g^{xy} as common key) and El-Gamal [17] as the PKE where $\mathsf{ek} = g^{\mathsf{dk}}$, for a random scalar dk. A similar idea can be found in [21], where the authors use a group key exchange protocol on a DH-tree. Because the random coin spaces of both protocols are identical, when we run both in the same group G of order q (scalars in $\mathbb{Z}_q$), if we only want to prove IND-ACPA-security, we can identify dk with the random coins for the key exchange, and thus ek is part of the transcript of the key exchange protocol, leaving us with a single key pair for both schemes. There are several alternatives for the PRG, the simplest one being a hash function modeled by a random oracle, to extract $\mathsf{dk} \in \mathbb{Z}_q$ from the proto-key $\mathsf{pt} \in G$. But we can avoid it, and even any computational assumption, by using a deterministic randomness extractor, as described in [9, Th. 7], that is a bijection and thus a perfect generator:

Definition 8. *If $p = 2q + 1$, and G is defined as the sub-group of the squares in $\mathbb{Z}_p^*$, then $\mathrm{ord}(G) = q$ and f is a bijection from G onto $\mathbb{Z}_q$: $f(x) = x$ (if $x \leq q$) or $p - x$ (if $x > q$).*

The second instantiation is more involved. To achieve IND-ACCA-security, we use Cramer-Shoup encryption [10] as our PKE. Because the keys in Cramer-Shoup are larger, our KE is a 3-to-8 parallel Diffie-Hellman, where we use public and private keys consisting of three elements each to generate a shared key consisting of eight elements, which allows us to generate additional pseudo-randomness in each step. Our PRG is an embedding function $G^8 \rightarrow \mathbb{Z}_q^3 \times \mathbb{Z}_q^5$ that applies the above function f to all components. The first part in $\mathbb{Z}_q^3$ will be used again as random coins for the key exchange, whereas the second part in $\mathbb{Z}_q^5$ leads to the Cramer-Shoup decryption key. To counter malleability of our scheme, we also need a SUF-CMA-secure MAC scheme. As the first scheme, this one relies only on the DDH assumption.

When using the Cramer-Shoup PKE, the decryption key of node i is the tuple $\mathsf{dk}_i = (v_i, w_i, x_i, y_i, z_i)$, the corresponding encryption key ek_i is $(X_i, Y_i, H_i) = (g^{x_i} h^{v_i}, g^{y_i} h^{w_i}, g^{z_i})$. We need to generate more pseudo-randomness than before, so we define a new key exchange that is essentially a parallel Diffie-Hellman.

Definition 9 (3-8-DHKE). *We define a modified Diffie-Hellman key exchange scheme.*

- *User i draws $a_i, b_i, c_i \xleftarrow{\$} \mathbb{Z}_q$, and sends $(A_i, B_i, C_i) = (g^{a_i}, g^{b_i}, g^{c_i})$;*
- *User j draws $a_j, b_j, c_j \xleftarrow{\$} \mathbb{Z}_q$, and sends $(A_j, B_j, C_j) = (g^{a_j}, g^{b_j}, g^{c_j})$;*
- *Then $\mathsf{ck} = (A_i^{a_j}, A_i^{b_j}, A_i^{c_j}, B_i^{a_j}, B_i^{b_j}, B_i^{c_j}, C_i^{a_j}, C_i^{b_j})$.*

This easily defines the CommonKey protocol. Its key indistinguishability follows from the following theorem.

Theorem 10 (3-8-DDH). *Under the DDH assumption, it is infeasible to distinguish the 14-tuple*
$(g^a, g^b, g^c, g^{a'}, g^{b'}, g^{c'}, g^{aa'}, g^{ab'}, g^{ac'}, g^{ba'}, g^{bb'}, g^{bc'}, g^{ca'}, g^{cb'})$ *from a random 14-tuple even when given* g*, and* $\mathrm{Adv}^{3-8-ddh}(k,t) \leq 8 \cdot \mathrm{Adv}^{ddh}(k, t+11\tau_{exp})$*, where* τ_{exp} *is the time for an exponentiation.*

Proof. We define tuple T_0 to be the tuple as defined above, T_i as the same tuple with all "combined" elements up to the i-th one replaced by a random element. T_8 is therefore a tuple of 14 random elements. Given a distinguisher $\mathcal{A}$ between T_i and T_{i+1}, we construct a solver $\mathcal{B}$ for DDH as follows. Let $(X, Y, Z) = (g^x, g^y, g^z)$ be a DDH challenge tuple. Let $g^{de'}$ be the $i+1$-st combined element. $\mathcal{B}$ chooses a tuple T_i and replaces g^d with X, $g^{e'}$ with Y, and $g^{de'}$ with Y. All other combined elements can be constructed because at least one exponent is known, which takes 11 exponentiations ($11\tau_{exp}$) time. If $z = xy$, $T' = T_i$, else $T' = T_{i+1}$ and the theorem follows.

As a PRG we use the PRG of definition 8 on each component of the common key. This gives us all the components we need to construct an IND-ACCA-secure BE scheme, whose security is based only on the DDH-assumption. (The DDH-assumption implies the existence of OWF, which is sufficient for MACs.)

Constant-Round Key Generation. While this construction achieves constant-size secrets for the users and requires very little interaction during the Join-procedure, it requires a logarithmic number of rounds for the subgroup key exchange protocol to complete. The Burmester-Desmedt group key exchange protocol [8] is, like the above scheme, passively secure in the standard model under the DDH assumption [20]. It requires only two rounds, and several instances could be run in parallel to compute keys for all subsets in two rounds. This would however require interaction between all the users each time a new users wants to join.

Acknowledgments. This work was supported by the French ANR-09-VERS-016 BEST Project and the European Commission through the ICT Programme under Contract ICT-2007-216676 ECRYPT II.

References

1. AACS Consortium. Advanced Access Content System (AACS) - introduction and common cryptographic elements book. Revision 0.951 (September 2009), http://www.aacsla.com/specifications/
2. Abdalla, M., Chevalier, C., Manulis, M., Pointcheval, D.: Flexible Group Key Exchange with On-demand Computation of Subgroup Keys. In: Bernstein, D.J., Lange, T. (eds.) AFRICACRYPT 2010. LNCS, vol. 6055, pp. 351–368. Springer, Heidelberg (2010)
3. Abdalla, M., Fouque, P.-A., Pointcheval, D.: Password-Based Authenticated Key Exchange in the Three-Party Setting. In: Vaudenay, S. (ed.) PKC 2005. LNCS, vol. 3386, pp. 65–84. Springer, Heidelberg (2005)

4. Adelson-Velskii, G., Landis, E.M.: An algorithm for the organization of information. Proceedings of the USSR Academy of Sciences 146, 263–266 (1962)
5. Bellare, M., Desai, A., Jokipii, E., Rogaway, P.: A concrete security treatment of
   symmetric encryption. In: FOCS 1997, pp. 394–403. IEEE Computer Society Press
   (October 1997)
6. Boneh, D., Katz, J.: Improved Efficiency for CCA-Secure Cryptosystems Built
   Using Identity-Based Encryption. In: Menezes, A.J. (ed.) CT-RSA 2005. LNCS,
   vol. 3376, pp. 87–103. Springer, Heidelberg (2005)
7. Boneh, D., Waters, B.: A fully collusion resistant broadcast, trace, and revoke system. In: ACM CCS, pp. 211–220. ACM (2006), Full version available at Cryptology
   ePrint Archive http://eprint.iacr.org/2006/298
8. Burmester, M., Desmedt, Y.: A secure and scalable group key exchange system.
   Inf. Proc. Letters 94(3), 137–143 (2005)
9. Chevassut, O., Fouque, P.-A., Gaudry, P., Pointcheval, D.: The Twist-AUgmented
   Technique for Key Exchange. In: Yung, M., Dodis, Y., Kiayias, A., Malkin, T.
   (eds.) PKC 2006. LNCS, vol. 3958, pp. 410–426. Springer, Heidelberg (2006),
   http://eprint.iacr.org/2005/061
10. Cramer, R., Shoup, V.: A Practical Public Key Cryptosystem Provably Secure
    against Adaptive Chosen Ciphertext Attack. In: Krawczyk, H. (ed.) CRYPTO 1998.
    LNCS, vol. 1462, pp. 13–25. Springer, Heidelberg (1998)
11. Delerablée, C.: Identity-Based Broadcast Encryption with Constant Size Ci-
    phertexts and Private Keys. In: Kurosawa, K. (ed.) ASIACRYPT 2007. LNCS,
    vol. 4833, pp. 200–215. Springer, Heidelberg (2007)
12. Delerablée, C., Paillier, P., Pointcheval, D.: Fully Collusion Secure Dynamic Broad-
    cast Encryption with Constant-Size Ciphertexts or Decryption Keys. In: Takagi,
    T., Okamoto, T., Okamoto, E., Okamoto, T. (eds.) Pairing 2007. LNCS, vol. 4575,
    pp. 39–59. Springer, Heidelberg (2007)
13. Diffie, W., Hellman, M.: New directions in cryptography. IEEE Trans. on Info.
    Theory 22(6), 644–654 (1976)
14. Dodis, Y., Fazio, N.: Public Key Broadcast Encryption for Stateless Receivers. In:
    Feigenbaum, J. (ed.) DRM 2002. LNCS, vol. 2696, pp. 61–80. Springer, Heidelberg
    (2003)
15. Dodis, Y., Fazio, N.: Public key trace and revoke scheme secure against adaptive
    chosen ciphertext attack. In: Desmedt, Y.G. (ed.) PKC 2003. LNCS, vol. 2567,
    pp. 100–115. Springer, Heidelberg (2002), http://eprint.iacr.org/2003/095
16. Dodis, Y., Katz, J.: Chosen-Ciphertext Security of Multiple Encryption. In: Kilian,
    J. (ed.) TCC 2005. LNCS, vol. 3378, pp. 188–209. Springer, Heidelberg (2005)
17. ElGamal, T.: A public key cryptosystem and a signature scheme based on discrete
    logarithms. IEEE Transactions on Information Theory 31, 469–472 (1985)
18. Fiat, A., Naor, M.: Broadcast Encryption. In: Stinson, D.R. (ed.) CRYPTO 1993.
    LNCS, vol. 773, pp. 480–491. Springer, Heidelberg (1994)
19. Gentry, C., Waters, B.: Adaptive Security in Broadcast Encryption Systems (with
    Short Ciphertexts). In: Joux, A. (ed.) EUROCRYPT 2009. LNCS, vol. 5479,
    pp. 171–188. Springer, Heidelberg (2009), http://eprint.iacr.org/2008/268
20. Katz, J., Yung, M.: Scalable protocols for authenticated group key exchange. Jour-
    nal of Cryptology 20(1), 85–113 (2007)
21. Kim, Y., Perrig, A., Tsudik, G.: Tree-based group key agreement. ACM Trans. on
    Inf. Systems Security 7(1), 60–96 (2004)
22. Kurnio, H., Safavi-Naini, R., Wang, H.: A Group Key Distribution Scheme with
    Decentralised User Join. In: Cimato, S., Galdi, C., Persiano, G. (eds.) SCN 2002.
    LNCS, vol. 2576, pp. 146–163. Springer, Heidelberg (2003)

23. Manulis, M.: Group Key Exchange Enabling On-Demand Derivation of Peer-to-Peer Keys. In: Abdalla, M., Pointcheval, D., Fouque, P.-A., Vergnaud, D. (eds.) ACNS 2009. LNCS, vol. 5536, pp. 1–19. Springer, Heidelberg (2009), http://www.manulis.eu/pub.html

24. Naor, D., Naor, M., Lotspiech, J.: Revocation and Tracing Schemes for Stateless Receivers. In: Kilian, J. (ed.) CRYPTO 2001. LNCS, vol. 2139, pp. 41–62. Springer, Heidelberg (2001); Full version available at Cryptology ePrint Archive at http://www.cs.brown.edu/~anna/research.html

25. Phan, D.H., Pointcheval, D., Strefler, M.: Decentralized dynamic broadcast encryption. Cryptology ePrint Archive, Report 2011/463 (2011), http://eprint.iacr.org/

26. Phan, D.H., Pointcheval, D., Strefler, M.: Security Notions for Broadcast Encryption. In: Lopez, J., Tsudik, G. (eds.) ACNS 2011. LNCS, vol. 6715, pp. 377–394. Springer, Heidelberg (2011)

27. Shoup, V.: Using Hash Functions as a Hedge against Chosen Ciphertext Attack. In: Preneel, B. (ed.) EUROCRYPT 2000. LNCS, vol. 1807, pp. 275–288. Springer, Heidelberg (2000)

28. Wu, Q., Mu, Y., Susilo, W., Qin, B., Domingo-Ferrer, J.: Asymmetric Group Key Agreement. In: Joux, A. (ed.) EUROCRYPT 2009. LNCS, vol. 5479, pp. 153–170. Springer, Heidelberg (2009)

29. Wu, Q., Qin, B., Zhang, L., Domingo-Ferrer, J., Farràs, O.: Bridging Broadcast Encryption and Group Key Agreement. In: Lee, D.H., Wang, X. (eds.) ASIACRYPT 2011. LNCS, vol. 7073, pp. 143–160. Springer, Heidelberg (2011)

30. Yao, D., Fazio, N., Dodis, Y., Lysyanskaya, A.: Id-based encryption for complex hierarchies with applications to forward security and broadcast encryption. In: ACM CCS 2004, ACM (2004), http://www.cs.brown.edu/~anna/research.html

Time-Specific Encryption
from Forward-Secure Encryption

Kohei Kasamatsu[1], Takahiro Matsuda[2,*], Keita Emura[3],
Nuttapong Attrapadung[2], Goichiro Hanaoka[2], and Hideki Imai[1]

[1] Chuo University, Japan
{kasamatsu-kohei,h-imai}@imailab.sakura.ne.jp
[2] National Institute of Advanced Industrial Science and Technology, Japan
{t-matsuda,n.attrapadung,hanaoka-goichiro}@aist.go.jp
[3] National Institute of Information and Communications Technology, Japan
k-emura@nict.go.jp

Abstract. Paterson and Quaglia (SCN 2010) proposed the concept of
time-specific encryption (TSE) and its efficient constructions. TSE is a
type of public key encryption with additional functionality where an encryptor can specify a suitable time interval, meaning that the ciphertexts
may only be decrypted within this time interval. In this work, we propose
a new methodology for designing efficient TSE scheme by using forward-
secure encryption (FSE), and based on this methodology, we present a
specific TSE scheme using Boneh-Boyen-Goh FSE, and a generic construction from any FSE. Our proposed TSE schemes are practical in *all*
aspects with regard to computational costs and data sizes. The sizes of
the ciphertext and the public parameter in our schemes are significantly
smaller than those in previous schemes in an asymptotic sense.

1 Introduction

In SCN 2010, Paterson and Quaglia proposed the concept of time-specific encryption (TSE), and showed its efficient constructions [22]. TSE is a class of
public key encryption (PKE) with additional functionality where an encryptor can specify a suitable time interval such that the ciphertexts may only be
decrypted within this time interval. Such an encryption scheme is useful in applications where it is necessary to ensure that the receiver can recover the plaintext
within only a specific time interval, e.g. in electronic sealed-bid auctions.

In this paper, we propose a novel methodology for the construction of TSE
schemes, and provide practical constructions based on our methodology. We
show that forward-secure encryption (FSE) [1,7] is a powerful building block
for designing efficient TSE schemes compared to the previous methodologies
[22], which were based on identity-based encryption (IBE) [24,5] and broadcast
encryption (BE) [15,6]. Based on our methodology, new TSE schemes can be
obtained that are practical in terms of computational costs and data sizes.

In the remaining parts of this section, we provide a review of TSE and discuss
our results in detail.

---

* The second author is supported by a JSPS Fellowship for Young Scientists.

I. Visconti and R. De Prisco (Eds.): SCN 2012, LNCS 7485, pp. 184–204, 2012.
© Springer-Verlag Berlin Heidelberg 2012

1.1   Time-Specific Encryption

In a typical scenario where TSE is used, a semi-trusted agent called a *time-server* publishes a global system parameter and periodically issues a time instant key (TIK) that is used by each receiver to decrypt a ciphertext. In TSE, a sender can specify any interval (decryption time interval, DTI) $[t_L, t_R]$ when encrypting a plaintext M to form a ciphertext c, where t_L and t_R denote the start and end points of the DTI, respectively, and a receiver can decrypt the ciphertext if the receiver is in possession of the TIK SK_t for some t with $t \in [t_L, t_R]$. This functionality seems to be a natural extension of that of timed-release encryption (TRE) [20,8,9,12,19], but interestingly, it is not easy to construct TSE by straightforward modifications of existing TRE schemes.

Paterson and Quaglia presented elegant methods to efficiently achieve the required functionality of TSE [22]. Specifically, they proposed two generic constructions of TSE where one is based on IBE, and the other is based on BE, and instantiations of these schemes can yield significantly higher efficiencies than those using straightforward modification of existing TRE. However, as shown in Table 1 (in Sect. 5), these schemes are still not very efficient in some aspects, and it is thus necessary to explore other solutions which can overcome their (potential) shortcomings. In particular, if we assume that the lifetime of the global system parameter is divided into T time periods, then the size of a ciphertext in the generic construction from IBE may be linear in T, and the size of the global system parameter in the construction from BE may also be linear in T. Because T is generally a large value, this could be problematic in certain situations.

1.2   Our Contribution

In this work, we propose a new methodology for designing efficient TSE scheme by using FSE. We consider this approach to be more promising than the previous methods because of the similarity between the functionalities of TSE and FSE. In fact, we can immediately produce a TSE scheme that allows only restricted DTIs with $t_L = 0$ by directly using FSE as it is. Based on this observation, we give a specific (i.e. not generic) construction of TSE from an existing FSE scheme[1] by Boneh, Boyen, and Goh [4], and a generic construction that can be used with any FSE scheme. Remarkably, these schemes can yield sufficiently high efficiency in all aspects in terms of computational cost and data size, and in particular, with regard to the evaluation items given in Table 1 (in Sect. 5), the complexities of our proposed schemes are all at most poly-logarithmic in T, and are thus significantly smaller than $O(T)$ in the asymptotic sense. Also, our specific construction is more efficient than the best-known instantiation from our generic construction in all aspects (except for the computational cost for decryption). However, our generic construction is still advantageous in the sense that when a new construction is discovered, this then automatically results in a

---

[1] This FSE scheme is obtained from the hierarchical IBE (HIBE) scheme in [4] via the "HIBE-to-FSE" transformation by Canetti, Halevi, and Katz [7]. See Sect. 2.2.

new TSE scheme via our generic construction, and this scheme may potentially be more efficient than our specific construction.

Here, we give an overview of our basic ideas for construction of our proposed schemes. As noted above, from FSE, we can immediately derive a TSE scheme for restricted DTIs with $t_L = 0$. This is based on the following observation: in FSE, a decryption key is updated periodically, while the corresponding encryption key is fixed, and more specifically, a decryption key for one particular time period can be derived from another decryption key for any previous time period, but *not vise versa*. Therefore, if a decryption key for one time period is publicized, then all other decryption keys for subsequent time periods can be generated from it. *This exactly describes a TSE scheme for restricted DTIs with $t_L = 0$.* Similarly to this construction, we can also derive another TSE scheme for restricted DTIs with $t_R = T - 1$, and it seems that we can also obtain full-fledged TSE by considering multiple encryptions [27,13] of these two restrictive TSE schemes. However, unfortunately, this idea does not immediately work. Because, in this (insecure) TSE scheme, a decryption key for each time period consists of the two independent decryption keys of the two underlying restrictive TSE schemes, a malicious user can thus illegally generate decryption keys for various time periods by combining these components (i.e. the decryption keys of the underlying restrictive TSE schemes) in multiple decryption keys. In our proposed schemes, we overcome this technical hurdle by introducing the following ideas: (1) in our specific construction, the two decryption keys of the underlying restrictive TSE schemes are connected in an inseparable manner (by using the algebraic property of the FSE scheme in [4]), meaning that it consequently becomes impossible to generate an illegal decryption key from the components of multiple decryption keys for the different time periods; and (2) in our generic construction, we set up many underlying restrictive TSE schemes (rather than using only two underlying schemes), and avoid the above attack by using a combinatorial method proposed by Attrapadung et al. [2]. Because our specific construction requires only two underlying restrictive TSE schemes, it is more efficient than our generic construction, which requires many underlying schemes. However, our generic construction does not depend on the algebraic property of the underlying scheme and therefore can be constructed from any FSE scheme.

1.3   Related Works

TSE was introduced as an extension of TRE, and thus we briefly describe TRE here. TRE is a type of encryption system introduced by May [20] in 1993. In TRE, a message can be encrypted in such a way that it cannot be decrypted (even by a legitimate receiver who owns the decryption key for the ciphertext) until the time (called the release-time) that was specified by the encryptor. TRE can therefore be interpreted as TSE in which we can only use the most restricted type of DTI $[t_L, t_R]$ with $t_L = t_R$. Many practical applications and situations where TRE schemes can be used have been considered, including sealed-bid auctions, electronic voting, content predelivery systems, and on-line examinations.

There are mainly two major approaches for realizing TRE. One approach is the use of *time-lock puzzles* [23]. In this approach, a sender generates a ciphertext which cannot be completely decrypted until the release-time in a receiver's environment, even if the receiver continues computing to decrypt the ciphertext after it is received. This imposes a heavy computational cost on the receiver, and it is difficult to precisely estimate the required time at which the receiver recovers a message. (This approach is also unsuitable for TSE.)

The other approach uses a semi-trusted agent, called the *time-server*, which periodically generates the time specific information needed to encrypt a message and/or decrypt a ciphertext. Earlier TRE schemes [20,23] adopted a model in which the time-server and the system users needed to interact.

Chan et al. [9] and Cheon et al. [10] proposed TRE schemes in which no interaction between the time-server and users was required. Most of the TRE schemes [8,18,11,21,12,19,14] that were proposed after these schemes [9,10], and the TSE schemes of Paterson and Quaglia [22], follow this approach.

It should be noted that most of the previous TRE schemes that adopted the time-server model of [9,10] are in fact *public-key* (or *identity-based*) TRE schemes, which consider confidentiality against the time-server. In the model, each receiver has its own secret key along with its corresponding public information (either a public key or an identity), and when encrypting a message, the encryptor specifies not only release time but also a receiver's public information to generate a receiver-specific ciphertext. We can also consider a "plain" version of TRE in the time-server model in which each ciphertext is not specific to any receiver and the ciphertext can be decrypted by anyone who receives the time-specific information from the time-server. (In this model, the confidentiality against the time-server is not considered.) This plain TRE can be realized easily from any IBE by regarding an identity as a time. Indeed, most of the previous public key TRE schemes mentioned above were realized by combining an IBE-like primitive with a PKE-like primitive. The difference between these settings (i.e. the "public key" setting and the "plain" setting) were explicitly considered for TSE by Paterson and Quaglia [22]. For a more detailed explanation, see Sect. 2.1.

2 Preliminaries

In this section, we formally introduce the definition of TSE, FSE, and bilinear groups, and describe the decisional ℓ-weak Bilinear Diffie-Hellman Inversion (ℓ-wBDHI) assumption.

Notation. Throughout this paper, we will consider time as a discrete set of time periods, regarding these as integers between 0 and $T - 1$, where T represents the number of time periods supported by the system. We denote by $[t_L, t_R]$, where $t_L \leq t_R$, the interval containing all time periods from t_L to t_R inclusive. "$x \xleftarrow{U} y$" denotes that x is chosen uniformly at random from y. $x \leftarrow y$ denotes x is output from y if y is an algorithm, or y is assigned to x otherwise. "PPT" denotes *probabilistic polynomial time*. We say that a function $f(k)$ is negligible (in k) if $f(k) < 1/p(k)$ for any positive polynomial $p(k)$ and all sufficiently large k.

2.1   Time-Specific Encryption

As explained in the introduction, a TSE scheme is an extension of a TRE scheme which supports decryption of ciphertexts with respect to DTI. Paterson et al. [22] defined several settings for TSE, namely, plain TSE, public-key TSE, and identity-based TSE. In the plain TSE setting, a ciphertext is not specified to any user and any entity who obtains a TIK corresponding to the DTI of the ciphertext can decrypt the ciphertext. The plain setting is mainly introduced in order to be used as building blocks for TSE schemes for the other two settings (though a plain TSE scheme itself might have some interesting applications). In public-key and identity-based TSE settings, on the other hand, each user (receiver) has its own secret key and either a public-key or an identity, and a ciphertext is made specific to a particular receiver using these public information. Correspondingly, to decrypt a ciphertext, not only a TIK but also the receiver's secret key is now required. TSE schemes in the latter two settings provide confidentiality even against a curious time-server. In this paper, we will only consider the plain setting, which is because public-key (resp. identity-based) TSE scheme with desirable security can be generically obtained by appropriately combining a plain TSE scheme with a chosen-ciphertext secure PKE (resp. IBE) scheme with the previously known methods for TRE schemes [10,21,19]. From here on, when we just write "TSE", we always mean "plain TSE".

A TSE scheme is defined by the four algorithms (TSE.Setup, TSE.Ext, TSE.Enc, TSE.Dec), which has the associated message space MSP. The four algorithms are as follows: The setup algorithm TSE.Setup($1^k, T$) takes a security parameter 1^k and $T \in \mathbb{N}$ as input, and outputs a master public key MPK and a master secret key MSK, where the TSE system supports time space $\mathsf{T} = [0, T-1]$. The key extraction algorithm TSE.Ext(MPK, MSK, t) takes MPK, MSK, and a time $t \in \mathsf{T}$ as input, and outputs a TIK SK_t. The encryption algorithm TSE.Enc($MPK, [t_L, t_R], M$) takes MPK, a DTI $[t_L, t_R] \subseteq \mathsf{T}$, and a message $M \in MSP$ as input, and outputs a ciphertext C. The decryption algorithm TSE.Dec(MPK, SK_t, C) takes MPK, SK_t, and C as input, outputs either a message M or the failure symbol $\perp$. We require, for all $k \in \mathbb{N}$, all $T \in \mathbb{N}$, all integers t_L, t_R, and t satisfying $0 \leq t_L \leq t \leq t_R \leq T-1$, all $(MPK, MSK) \leftarrow$ TSE.Setup($1^k, T$), and all messages $M \in MSP$, that TSE.Dec(TSE.Ext(MSK, t), TSE.Enc($MPK, [t_L, t_R], M$)) $= M$.

Security. We review the security definition for a TSE scheme by Paterson et al. [22]. This security requires that an adversary cannot gain any useful information from a ciphertext under a DTI $[t_L, t_R]$, if the adversary has no TIKs SK_t for $t \in [t_L, t_R]$.

Formally, we say that a TSE scheme is IND-CPA secure if any PPT adversary $\mathcal{A}$ has at most negligible advantage (in the security parameter k) in

the following game between a challenger $\mathcal{C}$ and $\mathcal{A}$ for any polynomial T: $\mathcal{C}$ runs
$\mathsf{TSE.Setup}(1^k, T)$ to generate a master public/secret key pair (MPK, MSP), and
gives MPK to $\mathcal{A}$. $\mathcal{A}$ can adaptively issue TIK extraction queries $t_1, t_2, \ldots$. For
each TIK extraction query t_i, $\mathcal{C}$ responds by running $\mathsf{TSE.Ext}(MPK, MSK, t_i)$
to generate a TIK SK_{t_i} corresponding to t_i, and then returns SK_{t_i} to $\mathcal{A}$.
At some point $\mathcal{A}$ selects two challenge messages $M_0, M_1 \in MSP$ and the
challenge DTI $[t_L, t_R] \subseteq T$ with the restriction that $t_i \notin [t_L, t_R]$ for all of
the previous TIK extraction queries t_i that $\mathcal{A}$ made before the challenge. $\mathcal{A}$
then sends $(M_0, M_1, [t_L, t_R])$ to $\mathcal{C}$. $\mathcal{C}$ chooses a random bit b and computes
$C^* \leftarrow \mathsf{TSE.Enc}(MPK, [t_L, t_R], M_b)$, and returns C^* to $\mathcal{A}$. $\mathcal{A}$ can continue to make
TIK extraction queries t_i under the restriction $t_i \notin [t_L, t_R]$, and $\mathcal{C}$ responds to
those as before. Finally, $\mathcal{A}$ outputs its guess $b' \in \{0, 1\}$ for b. The adversary $\mathcal{A}$'s
advantage in the above game is defined as $Adv_{TSE, \mathcal{A}}^{CPA}(k) = |\Pr[b' = b] - \frac{1}{2}|$.

2.2   Forward-Secure Encryption

An FSE scheme has the property that the threat of key exposure is confined to
some span by updating the secret key at each time unit. This scheme realizes the
property by using the functionality that a receiver can update the previous secret
key d_{t-1} to the next secret key d_t without interacting with any outside entity.
We provide a formal definition of FSE by following [7] but slightly customized
for our purpose.

An FSE scheme is defined by the four algorithms $(\mathsf{FSE.Gen}, \mathsf{FSE.Upd}, \mathsf{FSE.Enc}, \mathsf{FSE.Dec})$, which has the associated message space MSP. The key generation algorithm $\mathsf{FSE.Gen}(1^k, N)$ takes a security parameter 1^k and the total number of
time periods N as input, and outputs a public key pk and an initial secret key d_0.
The key update algorithm $\mathsf{FSE.Upd}(pk, i, j, d_i)$ takes pk, an index $i < N$ of a previous time period, an index $j > i$ for the current time period, and a secret key d_i
(corresponding to the period i) as input, and outputs a secret key d_j for the time
period j. The encryption algorithm $\mathsf{FSE.Enc}(pk, i, M)$ takes pk, $i < N$, and a message $M \in MSP$ as input, and outputs a ciphertext c. The decryption algorithm
$\mathsf{FSE.Dec}(pk, d_{i'}, c)$ takes pk, $d_{i'}$, and c as input, and outputs either M or a failure
symbol $\perp$. We require, for all $k \in \mathbb{N}$, all $N \in \mathbb{N}$, all $(pk, d_0) \leftarrow \mathsf{FSE.Gen}(1^k, N)$, all
indices $i \in [0, N - 1]$ (for specifying time periods), and all messages $M \in MSP$,
that $\mathsf{FSE.Dec}(pk, \mathsf{FSE.Upd}(pk, 0, i, d_0), \mathsf{FSE.Enc}(pk, i, M)) = M$.

We note that Canetti et al. [7] defined only the "sequential update" algorithm.
That is, in their syntax, the key update algorithm only allows an update from a
secret key d_i for the time period i to a key d_{i+1} for the next time period. However,
for the sake of simplicity, we use the syntax in which the update algorithm allows
the "direct update", so that $\mathsf{FSE.Upd}$ takes a key d_i for the time period i as input
and outputs the secret key d_j as long as $i < j$. It is straightforward to see that the
direct update functionality can be generally achieved by the sequential update
algorithm of [7]. In addition, there are FSE schemes which support efficient
direct update algorithm (compared to running "sequential update algorithms
many times), such as the FSE scheme instantiated with the HIBE scheme by
Boneh et al. [4] via the HIBE-to-FSE transformation shown in [7].

Security. We say that an FSE scheme is IND-CPA secure if any PPT algorithm $\mathcal{A}$ has at most negligible advantage (in the security parameter k) in the following game between a challenger $\mathcal{C}$ and $\mathcal{A}$ for any polynomial N: At the beginning of the game $\mathcal{A}(1^k, N)$ outputs the challenge time period j^*. $\mathcal{C}$ runs FSE.Gen$(1^k, N)$ to generate a pair of a public key pk and an initial secret key d_0, runs $d_{j^*+1} \leftarrow$ FSE.Upd$(pk, 0, j^* + 1, d_0)$, and then gives pk and d_{j^*+1} to $\mathcal{A}$. $\mathcal{A}$ selects two challenge messages $m_0, m_1 \in MSP$, and sends m_0, m_1 to $\mathcal{C}$. $\mathcal{C}$ chooses a random bit b, computes $c^* =$ FSE.Enc(pk, j^*, m_b), and returns c^* to $\mathcal{A}$. Finally $\mathcal{A}$ outputs its guess $b' \in \{0, 1\}$ for b. The adversary $\mathcal{A}$'s advantage in the above game is defined as $Adv^{CPA}_{FSE, \mathcal{A}}(k) = |\Pr[b' = b] - \frac{1}{2}|$.

Note that in the above security game, the adversary is required to commit to the time period to be attacked at the beginning of the game. While this definition is weaker than the definition of [7], it suffices for our construction of a TSE scheme from any FSE scheme that we will show in the following sections.

Transformations from Hierarchical IBE. There is a trivial construction of an FSE scheme that supports N time periods from a hierarchical IBE (HIBE) scheme that supports hierarchy with depth N, by interpreting a time period i in FSE as a "chain" $(1, \ldots, i)$ of identities in HIBE. More specifically, for a secret key for the time period t in FSE, we use a decryption key for the identity-vector $(1, \cdots, i)$ in HIBE. To update a secret key for time period j to time period $j > i$, one can run the derivation algorithm of the HIBE scheme to obtain a decryption key for the identity-vector $(1, \cdots, j)$.

Another more sophisticated HIBE-to-FSE transformation is the binary tree-based construction due to Canetti, Halevi, and Katz [7]. This construction has the advantage in that to instantiate an FSE scheme with N time periods, a building block HIBE only needs to support a hierarchy with depth $\log N$.

The common feature of these HIBE-to-FSE transformations is that multiple instances of FSE can virtually be instantiated so that they all share the same public parameters, by regarding the top-level identities as the indices for specifying an independent HIBE scheme, and then applying the HIBE-to-FSE transformations to each HIBE scheme instantiated in the second (and lower) level identity space. This trick will be used in our constructions of TSE.

Concrete Instantiation from the Boneh-Boyen-Goh HIBE Scheme [4]. In Fig. 1, we review the instantiation of an FSE scheme, which we call the *basic BBG-FSE* scheme, using the HIBE scheme by Boneh, Boyen, Goh (BBG HIBE) [4] via the "chain"-style transformation explained above.

Looking ahead, the basic version of our TSE scheme in Sect. 3.2 is obtained from the above basic BBG-FSE scheme, and our full TSE scheme in Appendix A is based on the FSE scheme obtained from the HIBE-to-FSE transformation due to Canetti et al. [7] (we call this FSE scheme *full BBG-FSE*).

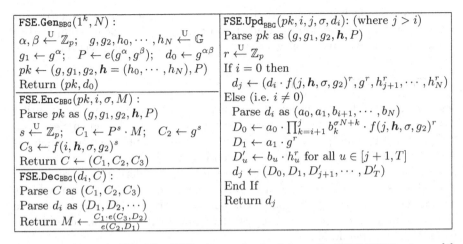

Fig. 1. Basic BBG-FSE: The FSE scheme obtained from the BBG HIBE scheme [4], where $f(i, \boldsymbol{h} = (h_0, \cdots, h_N), \sigma, b) = h_0^{2N+1} \cdot \prod_{k=1}^{i} h_k^{\sigma N+k} \cdot b$

For notational convenience, in Fig. 1, we describe the scheme so that the encryption and update algorithms take an additional input $\sigma \in \{0, 1\}$. This bit σ is used to instantiate two BBG-FSE schemes with N time periods under the same public parameter: the first scheme uses the "ordinary" interval $[0, N-1]$, and the second scheme uses the "shifted" interval $[N, 2N-1]$.

2.3 Decisional ℓ-wBDHI Assumption

We first recall bilinear groups. Let $\mathbb{G}$ and $\mathbb{G}_T$ be groups of order p for some large prime p (we assume that the size of p is implicitly determined by the security parameter k), and let $e : \mathbb{G} \times \mathbb{G} \to \mathbb{G}_T$ be an efficiently computable mapping. We call a tuple $(\mathbb{G}, \mathbb{G}_T, e)$ *bilinear groups*, and e a *bilinear map*, if the following two conditions hold: (Bilinear:) for all generators $(g, h) \in \mathbb{G} \times \mathbb{G}$ and $a, b \in \mathbb{Z}_p$, we have $e(g^a, h^b) = e(g, h)^{ab}$. (Non-degenerate:) for all generators $g, h \in \mathbb{G}$, we have $e(g, h) \neq 1$.

Now we recall the decisional ℓ-wBDHI assumption (which is defined via the so-called decisional ℓ-wBDHI* problem [4, Sect. 2.3]). Let $\ell \in \mathbb{N}$. We say that the decisional ℓ-wBDHI assumption holds in $(\mathbb{G}, \mathbb{G}_T, e)$ if for any PPT algorithm $\mathcal{A}$ the following difference is negligible in the security parameter k:

$$| \Pr[\mathcal{A}(g, h, y_1, \cdots, y_\ell, e(g, h)^{\alpha^{\ell+1}}) = 0] - \Pr[\mathcal{A}(g, h, y_1, \cdots, y_\ell, W) = 0]|$$

where $g, h \xleftarrow{\text{U}} \mathbb{G}$, $\alpha \xleftarrow{\text{U}} \mathbb{Z}_p$, $y_i \leftarrow g^{(\alpha^i)}$, and $W \xleftarrow{\text{U}} \mathbb{G}_T$.

3 Concrete Construction from Specific FSE

In this section, we present our proposed TSE scheme based on a specific FSE scheme obtained from the BBG HIBE scheme. Although the construction strongly depends on the algebraic structure of the underlying BBG-FSE scheme (thus it is not a generic construction), it leads to an efficient TSE scheme compared to TSE schemes derived from our generic construction in the next section.

3.1   The Idea of Our Construction

Before going into the description of the scheme, we give an intuitive explanation of our strategy behind the proposed construction. As explained in Sect. 1.2, TSE obtained by multiple encryption of two restrictive TSE schemes (which are derived from FSE) is insecure. In this insecure TSE scheme, a TIK for each time period consists of two independent decryption keys of underlying two restrictive TSE schemes. A malicious user can illegally generate decryption keys for various time period by combining components in multiple decryption keys. Here, observe that such an attack is possible because these two restrictive TSE schemes are instantiated independently.

Our idea for the proposed construction is to "connect" the secret keys from the underlying two restrictive TSE schemes in an "inseparable" manner by using the specific algebraic structure of the BBG-FSE scheme. Specifically, we divide the master secret key information $d_0 = g^{\alpha\beta}$ of the BBG-FSE scheme into two shares $g^{\alpha\beta+\xi}$ and $g^{-\xi}$ in the 2-out-of-2 secret-sharing manner using a "blinding factor" ξ. This blinding factor ξ is a randomness generated for each execution of a TIK extraction algorithm. Intuitively, this ξ connects the secret keys from the underlying restrictive TSE schemes, and thus an adversary cannot come up with an illegal "virtual" TIK as above by combining multiple TIKs for time periods that do not include the DTI. In order to make the decryption by the above TIK possible, we appropriately modify the encryption algorithm so that the underlying BBG-FSE-based TSE schemes (one with DTI for $t_L = 0$ and the other with DTI for $t_R = T - 1$) use a common randomness s. Such use of a common randomness is possible again due to the algebraic structure of the BBG-FSE scheme.

For the sake of simplicity, in this section we only give the basic version of our proposed construction whose public parameter size and TIK size are $O(T)$ and whose ciphertext size is constant. Our full TSE scheme, in which the public parameter size is $O(\log T)$ and TIKs size is $O(\log^2 T)$ by using binary tree structures inspired by the HIBE-to-FSE transformation of Canetti et al. [7], is given in Appendix A. We stress that those proposed schemes share the same idea as explained above, and we believe that the basic version of our proposed scheme is helpful for understanding the full construction.

3.2   Basic Construction

Here, we give the basic version of our proposed TSE scheme. Let $(\mathbb{G}, \mathbb{G}_T, e)$ be bilinear groups, and let $T \in \mathbb{N}$ be the number of time periods. Then we construct the basic version of our TSE scheme as in Fig. 2.

As mentioned in Sect. 3.1, we combine two basic BBG-FSE schemes (from Fig. 1) in which one of the schemes is regarded as a TSE scheme which allows

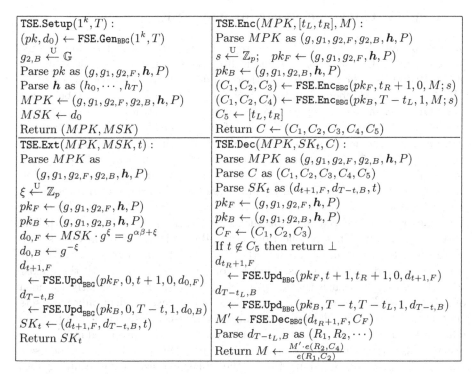

Fig. 2. The basic version of the proposed TSE scheme based on the BBG-FSE scheme

only DTIs with $t_R = T - 1$, by introducing a blinding factor ξ in order to construct a TSE scheme. More specifically, we set the initial key $d_{0,F}$ of the TSE scheme for restricted DTIs with $t_L = 0$ as $g^{\alpha\beta+\xi}$ which includes the blind factor g^{ξ}, and the initial key $d_{0,B}$ of the TSE scheme for restricted DTIs with $t_R = T - 1$ as $g^{-\xi}$ which will remove the blinding factor, by using the above mentioned method.

We would like the reader to notice that in Fig. 2, the scheme is described at the cost of efficiency, so that it is easy to see that two basic BBG-FSE schemes are combined by the blinding factor ξ as we explained above. For example, in the encryption scheme, the ciphertext components C_1 and C_2 are computed twice by running $\mathsf{FSE.Enc_{BBG}}$ from common randomness s. However, in practice, only C_4 needs to be computed in the second execution of $\mathsf{FSE.Enc_{BBG}}$, which can be done without calculating C_1 and C_2.

The security is guaranteed by the following theorem (the proof is given in the full version of this paper).

Theorem 1. *If the decisional* $(T + 1)$-*wBDHI assumption holds in* $(\mathbb{G}, \mathbb{G}_T, e)$, *then the TSE scheme (which supports T time periods) constructed as in Fig. 2 is IND-CPA secure.*

4   Generic Construction from Any FSE

In Sect. 3 (and in Appendix A), we proposed an efficient construction of TSE based on the BBG-FSE scheme, where it directly exploits the algebraic structure of the BBG-FSE scheme. In this section, we describe a generic construction of TSE from any FSE scheme in a black-box manner; nevertheless, it can be shown to be far more efficient compared to trivial generic constructions.

The intuition for our construction is as follows. Recall that we have observed that any FSE scheme already implies a TSE scheme with restricted interval types of the form $[A, *] \subseteq [A, B]$, where $*$ denotes arbitrary value where the encryptor would specify, and A, B are a-priori fixed values. By taking the key derivation in the backward manner, FSE also implies another TSE scheme with restricted interval types of the form $[*, D] \subseteq [C, D]$, where C, D are fixed. Our purpose is to construct a TSE scheme that allows any intervals $[*, *] \subseteq [0, T - 1]$. The idea is then to pre-define a collections S of allowed intervals to only consist of these restricted types in such a way that for any interval we can "cover" it by using these predefined intervals. That is, for any $[x, y] \subseteq [0, T - 1]$, there exist some $S_1, \dots, S_j \in S$ such that $[x, y] = S_1 \cup \cdots \cup S_j$. This is exactly the idea of subset-cover broadcast encryption, albeit in our case we deal only with sets that are intervals. We will therefore utilize a subset-cover system which permits efficient covering for interval sets. The subset-cover system proposed in [2] allows exactly this: for any interval, we can cover by using at most two predefined sets (*i.e.*, $j \leq 2$ in the above union). Hence, the ciphertext size of the resulting TSE will be only at most twice of that of FSE. In the following subsection, we first capture TSE schemes that allow restricted types of the form $[A, *]$ and $[*, D]$ as future TSE and past TSE, respectively.

4.1   Future TSE and Past TSE

In this subsection, we introduce two special classes of TSE, which we call *future time-specific encryption* (FTSE) and *past time-specific encryption* (PTSE), that we will use as "intermediate" building blocks for our generic construction of a TSE scheme from an FSE scheme. Using FTSE and PTSE, the description of our generic construction can be simplified. We also show how to generically construct these schemes from an FSE scheme.

FTSE (resp. PTSE) is a special class of a TSE scheme in which any ciphertext for time t' can be decrypted by using a TIK for time t as long as $t' \geq t$ (resp. $t' \leq t$). FTSE (resp. PTSE) can be viewed as a TSE scheme whose starting time t_L (resp. closing time t_R) of a DTI is always fixed to be 0 (resp. $T - 1$). An FTSE scheme (resp. a PTSE scheme) consists of the four algorithms (FTSE.Setup, FTSE.Ext, FTSE.Enc, FTSE.Dec) (resp. (PTSE.Setup, PTSE.Ext, PTSE. Enc, PTSE.Dec)) that are defined in the same way as those for a TSE scheme, with the following exceptions: Since the starting time t_L (resp. the closing time t_R) of a DTI is always fixed to be 0 (resp. $T - 1$), the encryption algorithm FTSE.Enc (resp. PTSE.Enc) does not need to take t_L (resp. t_R) as an input, and thus we denote by "$c \leftarrow$ FTSE.Enc(mpk, t_R, M)" (resp. "$c \leftarrow$ PTSE.Enc(mpk, t_L, M)") the process of generating a ciphertext c of a plaintext M that can be decrypted using a TIK generated by FTSE.Ext(msk, t) (resp. PTSE.Ext(msk, t)) with $t \in [0, t_R]$ (resp. $t \in [t_L, T - 1]$). Furthermore, in order to stress that a TIK for time t generated by the extraction algorithm can be used to decrypt all ciphertexts corresponding to time later than t (resp. time t or earlier), a TIK generated by FTSE.Ext(msk, t) (resp. PTSE.Ext(msk, t)) is denoted by "$sk_{\geq t}$" (resp. "$sk_{\leq t}$").

Correctness. As a correctness requirement of an FTSE scheme, we require that for all $k \in \mathbb{N}$, $T \in \mathbb{N}$, all $(mpk, msk) \leftarrow$ FTSE.Setup($1^k, T$), all integers t and t_R such that $0 \leq t \leq t_R \leq T - 1$, and all plaintexts M, it holds that FTSE.Dec(FTSE.Ext(msk, t), FTSE.Enc(mpk, t_R, M)) = M.

In a similar way, as a correctness requirement of a PTSE scheme, we require that for all $k \in \mathbb{N}$, $T \in \mathbb{N}$, all $(mpk, msk) \leftarrow$ PTSE.Setup($1^k, T$), all integers t and t_L satisfying $0 \leq t_L \leq t \leq T - 1$, and all plaintexts M, it holds that PTSE.Dec(PTSE.Ext(msk, t), PTSE.Enc(mpk, t_L, M)) = M.

Security Definitions. IND-CPA security of an FTSE scheme and that of a PTSE scheme is defined analogously to that of a TSE scheme.

Generic Constructions. We can construct an FTSE scheme by using an FSE scheme (FSE.Gen, FSE.Upd, FSE.Enc, FSE.Dec) as shown in Fig. 3. Since the following theorem is straightforward from the security and the functionality of an FSE scheme, we omit the proof.

Theorem 2. *If the building block FSE scheme is IND-CPA secure, then the FTSE scheme constructed as in Fig. 3 is IND-CPA secure.*

We can also easily obtain a PTSE scheme from an FTSE scheme by "reversing" the role of time in FTSE, i.e., regarding a time t in an FTSE scheme as a time $T - t - 1$ for a PTSE scheme. This means that we also have a generic construction of a PTSE scheme from an FSE scheme. More specifically, we identity a TIK $sk_{\leq t}$ with a TIK $sk_{\geq T - t - 1}$ of an FTSE scheme. Furthermore, PTSE.Enc(mpk, t', M) internally runs FTSE.Enc($mpk, T - t' - 1, M$). Since the construction we explain here is fairly intuitive and straightforward, we omit the detailed description of the construction.

4.2   Generic Construction

Here, we show our generic construction of a TSE scheme from an FSE scheme.

Notation for Binary Trees. Let $\lambda \in \mathbb{N}$, and let $T = 2^\lambda$. Our generic construction uses a binary tree as its internal structure, and we introduce several notation regarding them. Consider the complete binary tree with $2^{\lambda+1} - 1$ nodes. We number all the internal nodes (i.e. nodes that are not leaves) from the root in the breast first order (from left to right in numerical order), with the root node being 1. Furthermore, we also put 0 to the root node for convenience (and thus the root node has indices 0 and 1 at the same time). We will later put numbers

FTSE.Setup$(1^k, T)$:	FTSE.Ext(msk, t) :
$\quad (pk, d_0) \leftarrow$ FSE.Gen$(1^k, T)$	$\quad d_t \leftarrow$ FSE.Upd$(pk, 0, t, msk)$
$\quad$ Return $(mpk, msk) \leftarrow (pk, d_0)$	$\quad$ Return $sk_{\geq t} \leftarrow (t, d_t)$
FTSE.Enc(mpk, t_R, M) :	FTSE.Dec$(sk_{\geq t}, C)$:
$\quad c \leftarrow$ FSE.Enc(mpk, t_R, M)	$\quad$ Parse $sk_{\geq t}$ as (t, d_t) and C as (t_R, c)
$\quad$ Return $C \leftarrow (t_R, c)$	$\quad$ If $t_R < t$ then return $\perp$
	$\quad d_{t_R} \leftarrow$ FSE.Upd(pk, t, t_R, d_t)
	$\quad$ Return FSE.Dec(d_{t_R}, c)

Fig. 3. Generic construction of FTSE from FSE

also for leaves, and thus in order not to mix up with them, we denote by INT the set of indices for the internal nodes. Namely, $\text{INT} = \{0, 1, \ldots, 2^\lambda - 1\}$.

Let LEFT and RIGHT be subsets of INT defined as follows: $0 \in$ LEFT, $1 \in$ RIGHT, and for any remaining node $v \in \text{INT} \backslash \{0, 1\}$, if v is the left node of its parent node, then $v \in$ LEFT, otherwise $v \in$ RIGHT.

We next number the leaves from left to right in numerical order, with the leftmost node being 0 (and thus the rightmost being $T - 1$). For $v \in$ INT, let ℓ_v (resp. r_v) be the index of the leftmost (resp. rightmost) leaf node that is a descendant of v. That is, we have $\ell_v = (v \mod 2^{\text{depth}(v)}) \cdot 2^{\lambda - \text{depth}(v)}$ and $r_v = \ell_v + 2^{\lambda - \text{depth}(v)} - 1$, where $\text{depth}(v)$ is defined as the "depth of the node with the root node being depth 0".

For $v \in$ INT, we define the corresponding set S_v of indices of leaves by:

$$S_v = \begin{cases} (0 \leftharpoonup (2^\lambda - 1)) & \text{If } v = 0 \\ ((\ell_v + 1) \leftharpoonup r_v) & \text{If } v \in \text{LEFT} \backslash \{0\} \\ (\ell_v \rightharpoonup (r_v - 1)) & \text{If } v \in \text{RIGHT} \end{cases}$$

where we use the followng notations: $(i \rightharpoonup j) := \{i, i+1, \ldots, j\}$, $(i \leftharpoonup j) := \{j, j-1, \ldots, i\}$, $(i \rightharpoonup i) := \{i\}$, and $(i \leftharpoonup i) := \{i\}$.

Finally, for $v \in$ INT, we let $\widetilde{\ell}_v$ and $\widetilde{r}_v$ be the smallest index and the largest index in the set S_v, respectively.

Generic Construction. For simplicity, our TSE scheme is parameterized by an integer $\lambda \in \mathbb{N}$ and supports the total number of time periods $T = 2^\lambda$. Let (FTSE.Setup, FTSE.Ext, FTSE.Enc, FTSE.Dec) be an FTSE scheme and let (PTSE.Setup, PTSE.Ext, PTSE.Enc, PTSE.Dec) be a PTSE scheme. Using these as building blocks, we construct a TSE scheme as in Fig. 4. In the construction, we use the following notations: For each DTI $[t_L, t_R]$, we define the corresponding left-index $v_L \in$ LEFT and the right-index $v_R \in$ RIGHT, that determine which instance(s) of the building block FTSE and/or PTSE schemes are used to encrypt a message, by:

$$v_L = \min\{v \in \text{LEFT} : \widetilde{r}_v \in [t_L, t_R]\}$$

$$v_R = \min\{v \in \text{RIGHT} : \widetilde{\ell}_v \in [t_L, t_R]\}$$

TSE.Setup$(1^k, T)$:	TSE.Ext(MSK, t) :
For $v \in$ LEFT:	Let NODES$(t) = \{v \in$ INT $: t \in S_v\}$
$\quad (mpk_v, msk_v) \leftarrow$ PTSE.Setup$(1^k, |S_v|)$	For $v \in$ LEFT $\cap$ NODES(t):
For $v \in$ RIGHT:	$\quad sk^{(v)}_{\leq t - \widetilde{\ell}_v} \leftarrow$ PTSE.Ext$(msk_v, t - \widetilde{\ell}_v)$
$\quad (mpk_v, msk_v) \leftarrow$ FTSE.Setup$(1^k, |S_v|)$	$SK_{t,L} \leftarrow \{sk^{(v)}_{\leq t - \widetilde{\ell}_v}\}_{v \in \text{LEFT} \cap \text{NODES}(t)}$
$MPK \leftarrow \{mpk_v\}_{v \in \text{INT}}$	For $v \in$ RIGHT $\cap$ NODES(t):
$MSK \leftarrow \{msk_v\}_{v \in \text{INT}}$	$\quad sk^{(v)}_{\geq t - \widetilde{\ell}_v} \leftarrow$ FTSE.Ext$(msk_v, t - \widetilde{\ell}_v)$
Return (MPK, MSK)	$SK_{t,R} \leftarrow \{sk^{(v)}_{\geq t - \widetilde{\ell}_v}\}_{v \in \text{RIGHT} \cap \text{NODES}(t)}$
TSE.Enc$(MPK, [t_L, t_R], M)$:	$SK_t \leftarrow (t, SK_{t,L}, SK_{t,R})$
$v_L \leftarrow \min\{v \in$ LEFT $: \widetilde{r}_v \in [t_L, t_R]\}$	Return SK_t
$v_R \leftarrow \min\{v \in$ RIGHT $: \widetilde{\ell}_v \in [t_L, t_R]\}$	TSE.Dec(SK_t, C) :
If depth$(v_L) =$ depth(v_R) then	Parse SK_t as $(t, SK_{t,L}, SK_{t,R})$
$\quad$ If $v_L = 0$ then	Let NODES$(t) = \{v \in$ INT $: t \in S_v\}$
$\quad\quad c_L \leftarrow$ PTSE.Enc$(mpk_{v_L}, t_L - \widetilde{\ell}_{v_L}, M)$	Parse $SK_{t,L}$ as $\{sk^{(v)}_{\leq t - \widetilde{\ell}_v}\}_{v \in \text{LEFT} \cap \text{NODES}(t)}$
$\quad\quad c_R \leftarrow \emptyset$	Parse $SK_{t,R}$ as $\{sk^{(v)}_{\geq t - \widetilde{\ell}_v}\}_{v \in \text{RIGHT} \cap \text{NODES}(t)}$
$\quad$ Else (i.e. $v_L \neq 0$) then	Parse C as $([t_L, t_R], c_L, c_R)$
$\quad\quad c_L \leftarrow$ PTSE.Enc$(mpk_{v_L}, t_L - \widetilde{\ell}_{v_L}, M)$	If parsing fails or $t \notin [t_L, t_R]$
$\quad\quad c_R \leftarrow$ FTSE.Enc$(mpk_{v_R}, t_R - \widetilde{\ell}_{v_R}, M)$	$\quad$ then return $\perp$
$\quad$ End If	$v_L \leftarrow \min\{v \in$ LEFT $: \widetilde{r}_v \in [t_L, t_R]\}$
Else If depth$(v_L) <$ depth(v_R) then	$v_R \leftarrow \min\{v \in$ RIGHT $: \widetilde{\ell}_v \in [t_L, t_R]\}$
$\quad c_L \leftarrow$ PTSE.Enc$(mpk_{v_L}, t_L - \widetilde{\ell}_{v_L}, M)$	$v \leftarrow \min(\text{NODES}(t) \cap \{v_L, v_R\})$
$\quad c_R \leftarrow \emptyset$	If $v = \emptyset$ then return $\perp$
Else (i.e. depth$(v_L) >$ depth(v_R))	If $v \in$ LEFT then
$\quad c_L \leftarrow \emptyset$	$\quad$ return PTSE.Dec$(sk^{(v)}_{\leq t - \widetilde{\ell}_v}, c_L)$
$\quad c_R \leftarrow$ FTSE.Enc$(mpk_{v_R}, t_R - \widetilde{\ell}_{v_R}, M)$	Else (i.e. $v \in$ RIGHT)
End If	$\quad$ return FTSE.Dec$(sk^{(v)}_{\geq t - \widetilde{\ell}_v}, c_R)$
Return $C \leftarrow ([t_L, t_R], c_L, c_R)$	End If

Fig. 4. Generic construction of TSE from FTSE and PTSE

Furthermore, for each $t \in [0, T-1]$, we define the set NODES(t) of internal nodes that determines which instance(s) of the building block FTSE and PTSE schemes are used to generate a TIK (for a TSE) in the extraction algorithm, by:

$$\text{NODES}(t) = \{v \in \text{INT} : t \in S_v\}$$

Our scheme is IND-CPA secure assuming that the underlying FTSE and PTSE schemes are both IND-CPA secure (the proof is given in the full version). Since Fig. 4 might look slightly complicated, in Appendix B we show the instantiation of our TSE scheme in case $T = 2^3$ (see also Fig. 5 there).

Theorem 3. *If the FTSE scheme and the PTSE scheme are both IND-CPA secure, then the proposed TSE scheme constructed as in Fig. 4 is IND-CPA secure.*

Table 1. Efficiency comparison for TSE schemes. T is the size of the time space. $|g|$ denotes the length of a group element. $|g_T|$ denotes the length of an element in $\mathbb{G}_T$. For $[a, b, c]$, a denotes the number of pairings, b denotes the number of exponentiations, c denotes the number of multiplications.

	Public Param. Size	Ciphertext Overhead	TIK Size	Encryption Cost	Decryption Cost
Ours in Appendix A	$O(\log T)\,|g| + |g_T|$	$3|g|$	$O(\log^2 T)|g| + |\mathbb{Z}_p|$	$[0, O(\log T), O(\log T)]$	$[3, O(\log T), O(\log T)]$
Ours §4 ([4]+[7]+§4.3)	$O(\log T)\,|g| + |g_T|$	$4|g|$	$O(\log^3 T)|g| + |\mathbb{Z}_p|$	$[0, O(\log T), O(\log T)]$	$[2, O(\log T), O(\log T)]$
PQ-IBE [22] + Waters [25]	$4|g| + |g_T|$	$O(T)|g|$	$O(\log T)|g| + |\mathbb{Z}_p|$	$[0, O(T), O(T)]$	$[2, 0, 2]$
PQ-IBE [22] + Gentry [16]	$3|g| + |g_T|$	$O(T)|g| + O(T)|g_T|$	$O(\log T)|g| + O(\log T)|\mathbb{Z}_p|$	$[0, O(T), O(T)]$	$[1, 0, 2]$
PQ-BE [22] + GW [17]	$O(T)|g| + |g_T|$	$8|g| + 2|t_T|$	$|g| + |\mathbb{Z}_p|$	$[0, 5, O(T)]$ $[0, 5, O(T)]$	$[2, 3, O(T)]$ $[2, 3, O(T)]$
PQ-BE [22] + BGW1 [6]	$O(T)|g| + |g_T|$	$2|g|$	$|g| + |\mathbb{Z}_p|$	$[0, 2, O(T)]$ $[0, 2, O(T)]$	$[2, 0, O(T)]$ $[2, 0, O(T)]$
PQ-BE [22] + BGW2 [6]	$O(\sqrt{T})|g| + |g_T|$	$O(\sqrt{T})|g|$	$|g| + |\mathbb{Z}_p|$	$[0, O(\sqrt{T}), O(T)]$	$[2, 0, O(\sqrt{T})]$
PQ-BE [22] + Waters [26]	$O(T)|g| + |g_T|$	$8|g|$	$O(T)|g| + |\mathbb{Z}_p|$	$[0, 12, O(T)]$ $[0, 12, O(T)]$	$[9, 0, O(T)]$ $[9, 0, O(T)]$

4.3 Extension Using HIBE

The proposed generic construction shown in Sect. 4.2 uses T independent instances of the underlying FSE scheme (assuming that the building block FTSE and PTSE schemes are instantiated with an FSE scheme), and thus the size of the master public key MPK grows linearly in the total number of time periods T. However, if the underlying FSE scheme is furthermore instantiated from an HIBE scheme, we can use the trick of sharing the public parameter (by using the first-level identities for indices for each "independent" FSE scheme) explained in the second last paragraph in Sect. 2.2. In this case, the size of the master public key of the constructed TSE scheme does not depend on the size of the time space $|T|$, but becomes identical to that of the underlying HIBE scheme. Using this trick with the full BBG-FSE (obtained via the HIBE-to-FSE transformation of [7]), we still obtain a TSE scheme whose parameter size and computational costs are all polylogarithmic in the number of time periods T.

5 Comparison

Table 1 shows an efficiency comparison among TSE schemes. We compare our scheme in Appendix A and an instantiation obtained from our generic construction in Sect. 4 in which the full BBG-FSE scheme is used together with the extension explained in Sect. 4.3, with the existing TSE schemes. Here, for the existing TSE schemes, we choose the concrete instantiations of TSE schemes obtained from the generic construction from IBE schemes (denoted "PQ-IBE") and the generic construction from BE schemes (denoted "PQ-BE") both proposed by Paterson and Quaglia [22]. For concrete IBE schemes, we choose the schemes by Waters [25] and by Gentry [16], and for concrete BE schemes we choose the schemes by Boneh, Gentry, and Waters [6] (BGW1 was proposed in Sect. 3.1 of [6], and BGW2 was proposed in Sect. 3.2 of [6]), by Boneh and Gentry [17], and Waters [26].

As seen in Table 1, our schemes yield both better computational cost for encryption and short ciphertext length than those of the PQ-IBE schemes. In particular, our schemes have constant ciphertext overhead, while the PQ-IBE schemes have the ciphertext overhead of $O(T)$ group elements. Compared to the PQ-BE schemes, our schemes are superior in the size of public parameter, i.e. our schemes have the public parameter size of $O(\log T)$, while the PQ-BE schemes have the public parameter size of $O(T)$. Comparing the scheme in Appendix A and the instantiation from the generic construction in Sect. 4, the former scheme has shorter TIK size, i.e. the scheme in Appendix A has the TIK size of $O(\log^2 T)$ and the scheme in Sect. 4 has the TIK size of $O(\log^3 T)$. Furthermore, most notably, both of our schemes have at most poly-logarithmic size/cost in all measures in the table, which has not been achieved by any of the existing TSE schemes. Therefore, we see that our schemes have a feature which has not been achieved by all of the previous TSE schemes, and due to our results, a system designer can choose the parameters regarding TSE schemes that he/she wants to optimize more flexibly. We believe that our results will potentially broaden the applicability of TSE.

Lastly, we remark that both of our TSE schemes in Table 1 have the reduction costs of at least $O(T^2)$, while the PQ-IBE scheme instantiated with Gentry's IBE scheme [16] and the PQ-BE scheme instantiated with the Gentry-Waters BE scheme [17] have tight security reductions to their underlying hardness assumptions. However, all the TSE schemes mentioned here require non-static ℓ-type assumptions (e.g. the decisional ℓ-wBDHI in our case). It would be interesting to clarify whether it is possible to construct a TSE scheme whose security can be tightly reduced to more standard "static" assumptions such as decisional linear (DLIN) and decisional bilinear Diffie-Hellman (DBDH), and whose efficiency (parameter sizes and computational costs) is comparable to our schemes.

References

1. Anderson, R.: Two remarks on public key cryptology. Invited Lecture, ACM CCS 1997 (1997), http://www.cyphernet.org/cyphernomicon/chapter14/14.5.html
2. Attrapadung, N., Imai, H.: Graph-Decomposition-Based Frameworks for Subset-Cover Broadcast Encryption and Efficient Instantiations. In: Roy, B. (ed.) ASIACRYPT 2005. LNCS, vol. 3788, pp. 100–120. Springer, Heidelberg (2005)
3. Boneh, D., Boyen, X., Goh, E.-J.: Hierarchical Identity Based Encryption with Constant Size Ciphertext. In: Cramer, R. (ed.) EUROCRYPT 2005. LNCS, vol. 3494, pp. 440–456. Springer, Heidelberg (2005)
4. Boneh, D., Boyen, X., Goh, E.J.: Hierarchical identity based encryption with constant size ciphertext. Full version of [3]. Cryptology ePrint Archive: Report 2005/015 (2005)

5. Boneh, D., Franklin, M.: Identity-Based Encryption from the Weil Pairing. In: Kilian, J. (ed.) CRYPTO 2001. LNCS, vol. 2139, pp. 213–229. Springer, Heidelberg (2001)
6. Boneh, D., Gentry, C., Waters, B.: Collusion Resistant Broadcast Encryption with Short Ciphertexts and Private Keys. In: Shoup, V. (ed.) CRYPTO 2005. LNCS, vol. 3621, pp. 258–275. Springer, Heidelberg (2005)
7. Canetti, R., Halevi, S., Katz, J.: A Forward-secure Public-key Encryption Scheme. In: Biham, E. (ed.) EUROCRYPT 2003. LNCS, vol. 2656, pp. 646–646. Springer, Heidelberg (2003)
8. Cathalo, J., Libert, B., Quisquater, J.J.: Efficient and Non-interactive Timed-Release Encryption. In: Qing, S., Mao, W., López, J., Wang, G. (eds.) ICICS 2005. LNCS, vol. 3783, pp. 291–303. Springer, Heidelberg (2005)
9. Chan, A.C.F., Blake, I.F.: Scalable, server-passive, user-anonymous timed release cryptography. In: Proceedings. 25th IEEE International Conference on ICDCS 2005, pp. 504–513. IEEE (2005)
10. Cheon, J.H., Hopper, N., Kim, Y., Osipkov, I.: Provably secure timed-release public key encryption. ACM Trans. Inf. Syst. Secure. 11(2) (2008)
11. Chow, S., Roth, V., Rieffel, E.: General Certificateless Encryption and Timed-Release Encryption. In: Ostrovsky, R., De Prisco, R., Visconti, I. (eds.) SCN 2008. LNCS, vol. 5229, pp. 126–143. Springer, Heidelberg (2008)
12. Dent, A., Tang, Q.: Revisiting the Security Model for Timed-Release Encryption with Pre-open Capability. In: Garay, J.A., Lenstra, A.K., Mambo, M., Peralta, R. (eds.) ISC 2007. LNCS, vol. 4779, pp. 158–174. Springer, Heidelberg (2007)
13. Dodis, Y., Katz, J.: Chosen-Ciphertext Security of Multiple Encryption. In: Kilian, J. (ed.) TCC 2005. LNCS, vol. 3378, pp. 188–209. Springer, Heidelberg (2005)
14. Emura, K., Miyaji, A., Omote, K.: Adaptive Secure-Channel Free Public-Key Encryption with Keyword Search Implies Timed Release Encryption. In: Lai, X., Zhou, J., Li, H. (eds.) ISC 2011. LNCS, vol. 7001, pp. 102–118. Springer, Heidelberg (2011)
15. Fiat, A., Naor, M.: Broadcast Encryption. In: Stinson, D.R. (ed.) CRYPTO 1993. LNCS, vol. 773, pp. 480–491. Springer, Heidelberg (1994)
16. Gentry, C.: Practical Identity-Based Encryption Without Random Oracles. In: Vaudenay, S. (ed.) EUROCRYPT 2006. LNCS, vol. 4004, pp. 445–464. Springer, Heidelberg (2006)
17. Gentry, C., Waters, B.: Adaptive Security in Broadcast Encryption Systems (with Short Ciphertexts). In: Joux, A. (ed.) EUROCRYPT 2009. LNCS, vol. 5479, pp. 171–188. Springer, Heidelberg (2009)
18. Hwang, Y., Yum, D., Lee, P.: Timed-Release Encryption with Pre-open Capability and Its Application to Certified E-mail System. In: Zhou, J., López, J., Deng, R.H., Bao, F. (eds.) ISC 2005. LNCS, vol. 3650, pp. 344–358. Springer, Heidelberg (2005)
19. Matsuda, T., Nakai, Y., Matsuura, K.: Efficient Generic Constructions of Timed-Release Encryption with Pre-open Capability. In: Joye, M., Miyaji, A., Otsuka, A. (eds.) Pairing 2010. LNCS, vol. 6487, pp. 225–245. Springer, Heidelberg (2010)
20. May, T.: Time-release crypto (1993) (manuscript),
http://www.cyphernet.org/cyphernomicon/chapter14/14.5.html
21. Nakai, Y., Matsuda, T., Kitada, W., Matsuura, K.: A Generic Construction of Timed-Release Encryption with Pre-open Capability. In: Takagi, T., Mambo, M. (eds.) IWSEC 2009. LNCS, vol. 5824, pp. 53–70. Springer, Heidelberg (2009)
22. Paterson, K., Quaglia, E.: Time-Specific Encryption. In: Garay, J.A., De Prisco, R. (eds.) SCN 2010. LNCS, vol. 6280, pp. 1–16. Springer, Heidelberg (2010)
23. Rivest, R.L., Shamir, A., Wagner, D.A.: Time-lock puzzles and timed-release crypto. Technical Report MIT/LCS/TR-684 (1996)

24. Shamir, A.: Identity-Based Cryptosystems and Signature Schemes. In: Blakely, G.R., Chaum, D. (eds.) CRYPTO 1984. LNCS, vol. 196, pp. 47–53. Springer, Heidelberg (1985)
25. Waters, B.: Efficient identity-based encryption without random oracles. In: Cramer, R. (ed.) EUROCRYPT 2005. LNCS, vol. 3494, pp. 114–127. Springer, Heidelberg (2005)
26. Waters, B.: Dual System Encryption: Realizing Fully Secure IBE and HIBE under Simple Assumptions. In: Halevi, S. (ed.) CRYPTO 2009. LNCS, vol. 5677, pp. 619–636. Springer, Heidelberg (2009)
27. Zhang, R., Hanaoka, G., Shikata, J., Imai, H.: On the Security of Multiple Encryption or CCA-security+CCA-security=CCA-security? In: Bao, F., Deng, R., Zhou, J. (eds.) PKC 2004. LNCS, vol. 2947, pp. 360–374. Springer, Heidelberg (2004)

A   Main Concrete Construction

Here, we describe the full TSE scheme obtained by using the binary tree structures for the basic version of our scheme presented in Sect. 3. As noted earlier, this construction is obtained by applying the technique from the HIBE-to-FSE transformation by Canetti et al. [7] to the basic version of the proposed scheme for reducing the sizes of the public parameter and TIKs.

Let $\ell \in \mathbb{N}$. Consider two complete binary trees B_1 and B_2 with $T = 2^\ell - 1$ nodes, where T will be the number of time periods supported by the proposed TSE construction. The nodes in those binary trees are numbered according to a pre-order traversal in an incremental order, with the root node of B_1 being 1 and that of B_2 being $T + 1$. Then, consider the binary tree B with $2T + 1$ nodes in which the children of the root nodes are the root nodes of B_1 and B_2, with B_1 being left. (That is, B has B_1 and B_2 as sub trees.) For convenience, we put the number $2T + 1$ to the root node of B. Intuitively, each subtree in B will correspond to one instantiation of FSE obtained via the HIBE-to-FSE transformation of Canetti et al. [7] to the BBG HIBE scheme (and will also correspond to one chain in our basic construction shown in Sect. 3.2).

We need to introduce vectors "TV_t" and sets "TVSet_t" (for $t \in [1, 2T]$). TV_t is the vector consisting of the indices corresponding to the nodes included in the path from the node t to the root node (of B). For $t \in [1, 2T]$, the set TVSet_t defined as follows: $\mathsf{TVSet}_1 = \{TV_1\}$, $\mathsf{TVSet}_{T+1} = \{TV_{T+1}\}$. Recursively, for $t \in [1, 2T] \setminus \{1, T+1\}$, TVSet_{t+1} is defined depending on TVSet_t as follows: Let $s = \min\{u : TV_u \in \mathsf{TVSet}_t\}$. If TV_s is a leaf node, then TVSet_{t+1} is obtained by removing the vector TV_s from the set TVSet_t. Otherwise, let s_F (resp. s_B) be the index of the left (resp. right) node of the node s. TVSet_{t+1} is the set obtained by removing TV_s from and adding TV_{s_F} and TV_{s_B} to the set TVSet_t.

Let $(\mathbb{G}, \mathbb{G}_T, e)$ be bilinear maps, and let $T = 2^\ell - 1$ be a polynomial that indicates the number of time periods. Using the above notations, We describe our TSE scheme in the following:

TSE.Setup$(1^k, T = 2^\ell - 1)$: Pick $\alpha, \beta \xleftarrow{U} \mathbb{Z}_p$, $g_{2,F}, g_{2,B}, h_0, \cdots, h_\ell \xleftarrow{U} \mathbb{G}$. Then compute $MSK \leftarrow g^{\alpha\beta}$ and

$$MPK \leftarrow (g, g_1 \leftarrow g^\alpha, g_{2,F}, g_{2,B}, h_0, \cdots, h_\ell, P \leftarrow e(g^\alpha, g^\beta)),$$

and return (MPK, MSK).

TSE.Ext(MSK, t): Firstly, pick $\xi \xleftarrow{U} \mathbb{Z}_p$.

For each $TV = (J_0, J_1, \cdots, J_m) \in \mathsf{TVSet}_{t+1}$: pick $r_F \xleftarrow{U} \mathbb{Z}_p$, and compute

$$d_{TV} \leftarrow (g^{\alpha\beta+\xi} \cdot (\prod_{i=0}^{m} h_i^{J_i} \cdot g_{2,F})^{r_F}, g^{r_F}, h_{m+1}^{r_F}, \cdots, h_\ell^{r_F}).$$

For each $TV' = (K_0, K_1, \cdots, K_n) \in \mathsf{TVSet}_{2T-t}$: pick $r_B \xleftarrow{U} \mathbb{Z}_p$, and compute

$$d_{TV'} \leftarrow (g^{-\xi} \cdot (\prod_{i=0}^{n} h_i^{K_i} \cdot g_{2,B})^{r_B}, g^{r_B}, h_{n+1}^{r_B}, \cdots, h_\ell^{r_B}).$$

Finally, set $SK_{t,L} \leftarrow \{d_{TV}\}_{TV \in \mathsf{TVSet}_{t+1}}$ and $SK_{t,R} \leftarrow \{d_{TV'}\}_{TV' \in \mathsf{TVSet}_{2T-t}}$, and return $SK_t = (t, SK_{t,L}, SK_{t,R})$.

TSE.Enc$(MPK, [t_L, t_R], M)$: Let $TV_{t_R+1} = (J_0, J_1, \cdots, J_m)$ and $TV_{2T-t_L} = (K_0, K_1, \cdots, K_n)$. Pick $s \xleftarrow{U} \mathbb{Z}_p$, compute

$$(C_1, C_2, C_3, C_4) \leftarrow (P^s \cdot M, g^s, (\prod_{i=0}^{m} h_i^{J_i} \cdot g_{2,F})^s, (\prod_{i=0}^{n} h_i^{K_i} \cdot g_{2,B})^s)$$

and return $C = (C_1, C_2, C_3, C_4, [t_L, t_R])$.

TSE.Dec(SK_t, C): Let $SK_t = (t, SK_{t,L}, SK_{t,R})$ and $C = (C_1, C_2, C_3, C_4, C_5)$. If $t \notin C_5$, then return $\perp$. Otherwise, retrieve $d_{TV_{t_R+1}} = (L_1, L_2, \cdots)$ and $d_{TV_{2T-t_L}} = (R_1, R_2, \cdots)$ from $SK_{t,L}$ and $SK_{t,R}$, respectively. Compute

$$M = \frac{C_1 \cdot e(L_2, C_3) \cdot e(R_2, C_4)}{e(L_1 \cdot R_1, C_2)}$$

and return M.

The security is guaranteed by the following (the proof is given in the full version).

Theorem 4. *If the decisional $(\ell + 1)$-wBDHI assumption holds in $(\mathbb{G}, \mathbb{G}_T, e)$, then the above TSE scheme (with $T = 2^\ell - 1$ time periods) is IND-CPA secure.*

B   Toy Example of Our Generic Construction

In order to better understand our generic construction in Sect. 4.2, here we describe a toy example of our generic construction in which $T = 2^3$. See also Fig. 5 for the illustration that represents the "directions" (or, "realms" in other words) that the secret keys from the underlying FTSE and PTSE schemes can cover. Note that in this example, LEFT $= \{0, 2, 4, 6\}$, and RIGHT $= \{1, 3, 5, 7\}$.

t	0	1	2	3	4	5	6	7	

$$sk_{\le0}^0 \longleftarrow sk_{\le1}^0 \longleftarrow sk_{\le2}^0 \longleftarrow sk_{\le3}^0 \longleftarrow sk_{\le4}^0 \longleftarrow sk_{\le5}^0 \longleftarrow sk_{\le6}^0 \longleftarrow sk_{\le7}^0 \; PTSE_0$$

$$FTSE_1 \; sk_{\ge0}^1 \longrightarrow sk_{\ge1}^1 \longrightarrow sk_{\ge2}^1 \longrightarrow sk_{\ge3}^1 \longrightarrow sk_{\ge4}^1 \longrightarrow sk_{\ge5}^1 \longrightarrow sk_{\ge6}^1$$

$$PTSE_2 \qquad sk_{\le0}^2 \longleftarrow sk_{\le1}^2 \longleftarrow sk_{\le2}^2 \qquad sk_{\ge0}^3 \longrightarrow sk_{\ge1}^3 \longrightarrow sk_{\ge2}^3 \qquad FTSE_3$$

$$PTSE_4 \qquad | \qquad | \quad FTSE_5 \;\; PTSE_6 \quad | \qquad | \qquad FTSE_7$$

$$sk_{\le0}^4 \qquad sk_{\ge0}^5 \qquad\qquad\qquad sk_{\ge0}^6 \quad sk_{\ge0}^7$$

Fig. 5. Illustration for our generic construction in case $T = 2^3$

TSE.Setup($1^k, T$): Run the setup algorithms of the underlying FTSE and PTSE schemes as follows:

$(mpk_0, msk_0) \leftarrow$ PTSE.Setup($1^k, 8$); $(mpk_1, msk_1) \leftarrow$ FTSE.Setup($1^k, 7$)
$(mpk_2, msk_2) \leftarrow$ PTSE.Setup($1^k, 3$); $(mpk_3, msk_3) \leftarrow$ FTSE.Setup($1^k, 3$)
$(mpk_4, msk_4) \leftarrow$ PTSE.Setup($1^k, 1$); $(mpk_5, msk_5) \leftarrow$ FTSE.Setup($1^k, 1$)
$(mpk_6, msk_6) \leftarrow$ PTSE.Setup($1^k, 1$); $(mpk_7, msk_7) \leftarrow$ FTSE.Setup($1^k, 1$)
$MPK \leftarrow (mpk_0, mpk_1, \ldots, mpk_7)$; $MSK \leftarrow (msk_0, msk_1, \ldots, msk_7)$
Return (MPK, MSK).

TSE.Ext(msk, t): The algorithm sets the TIK SK_t corresponding to the column of the time t in Fig. 5 to the secret keys of FTSE and PTSE. For example,

– $SK_0 = (0, SK_{0,L}, SK_{0,R})$ where $SK_{0,L} = sk_{\le0}^{(0)}$ and $SK_{0,R} = sk_{\ge0}^{(1)}$.
– $SK_1 = (1, SK_{1,L}, SK_{1,R})$ where $SK_{1,L} = (sk_{\le1}^{(0)}, sk_{\le0}^{(2)}, sk_{\le0}^{(4)})$, and $SK_{1,R} = sk_{\ge1}^{(1)}$.
– $SK_4 = (4, SK_{4,L}, SK_{4,R})$ where $SK_{4,L} = sk_{\le4}^{(0)}$ and $SK_{4,R} = (sk_{\ge4}^{(1)}, sk_{\ge0}^{(3)})$

Note that NODES(0) = $\{0, 1\}$, NODES(1) = $\{0, 1, 2, 4\}$, and NODES(4) = $\{0, 1, 3\}$.

TSE.Enc($mpk, [t_L, t_R], M$): We exemplify the cases in which $[t_L, t_R] = [4, 7]$, $[4, 5]$, and $[2, 6]$ in the following:

– $C = ([4, 7], c_L, c_R)$, where $c_L \leftarrow$ PTSE.Enc($mpk_0, 4, M$) and $c_R \leftarrow \emptyset$. Note that $v_L = \min\{v \in$ LEFT $: \widetilde{r}_v \in [4, 7]\} = 0$ and thus depth(v_L) = 0, while $v_R = \min\{v \in$ RIGHT $: \widetilde{\ell}_v \in [4, 7]\} = 3$ and thus depth(v_R) = 1.
– $C = ([4, 5], c_L, c_R)$, where $c_L \leftarrow \emptyset$ and $c_R \leftarrow$ FTSE.Enc($mpk_3, 1, M$). Note that $v_L = \min\{v \in$ LEFT $: \widetilde{r}_v \in [4, 5]\} = 6$ and thus depth(v_L) = 2, while $v_R = \min\{v \in$ RIGHT $: \widetilde{\ell}_v \in [4, 5]\} = 3$ and thus depth(v_R) = 1.
– $C = ([2, 6], c_L, c_R)$, where $c_L \leftarrow$ PTSE.Enc($mpk_2, 1, M$) and $c_R \leftarrow$ FTSE.Enc($mpk_3, 2, M$). Note that, $v_L = \min\{v \in$ LEFT $: \widetilde{r}_v \in [2, 6]\} = 2$ and thus depth(v_L) = 1, while $v_R = \min\{v \in$ RIGHT $: \widetilde{\ell}_v \in [2, 6]\} = 3$ and thus depth(v_R) = 1.

TSE.Dec(SK_t, C): Using $SK_4 = (4, SK_{4,L}, SK_{4,R})$, we can decrypt the above (correctly generated) ciphertexts:

- If DTI is $[4, 7]$, run $M \leftarrow$ FTSE.Dec($sk_{\leq 4}^{(0)}, c_L$). Note that in this case, $\min(\text{NODES}(4) \cap \{v_L, v_R\}) = 0 \in \text{LEFT}$.
- If DTI is $[4, 5]$ or $[2, 6]$, run $M \leftarrow$ PTSE.Dec($sk_{\geq 0}^{(3)}, c_R$). Note that in both cases, $\min(\text{NODES}(4) \cap \{v_L, v_R\}) = 3 \in \text{RIGHT}$.

Improved Secure Two-Party Computation
via Information-Theoretic Garbled Circuits

Vladimir Kolesnikov[1] and Ranjit Kumaresan[2,*]

[1] Bell Labs, Murray Hill, NJ 07974, USA
kolesnikov@research.bell-labs.com
[2] University of Maryland, College Park, MD 20740, USA
ranjit@cs.umd.edu

Abstract. We optimize the communication (and, indirectly, computation) complexity of two-party secure function evaluation (SFE). We propose a new approach, which relies on the *information-theoretic* (IT) Garbled Circuit (GC), which is more efficient than Yao's GC on shallow circuits. When evaluating a large circuit, we "slice" it into thin layers and evaluate them with IT GC. Motivated by the client-server setting, we propose two variants of our construction: one for semi-honest model (relatively straightforward), and one secure against a semi-honest server and covert client (more technically involved). One of our new building blocks, String-selection Oblivious Transfer (SOT), may be of independent interest.

Our approach offers asymptotic improvement over the state-of-the-art GC, both in communication and computation, by a factor $\log \kappa$, where κ is a security parameter. In practical terms, already for today's $\kappa \in \{128, 256\}$ our (unoptimized) algorithm offers approximately a factor 2 communication improvement in the semi-honest model, and is only a factor ≈ 1.5 more costly in setting with covert client.

1 Introduction

We propose efficiency improvements of two-party Secure Function Evaluation (SFE). SFE allows two parties to evaluate any function on their respective inputs x and y, while maintaining privacy of both x and y. SFE is justifiably a subject of an immense amount of research. Efficient SFE algorithms enable a variety of electronic transactions, previously impossible due to mutual mistrust of participants. Examples include auctions, contract signing, set intersection, etc. As computation and communication resources have increased, SFE of many useful functions has become practical for common use.

Still, SFE of most of today's functions of interest is either completely out of reach of practicality, or carries costs sufficient to deter would-be adopters, who instead choose stronger trust models, entice users to give up their privacy with incentives, or use similar crypto-workarounds. We believe that truly practical efficiency is required for SFE to see use in real-life applications.

* Work partly done while the author was visiting Bell Labs. Work partly supported by NSF grants #0830464 and #1111599.

I. Visconti and R. De Prisco (Eds.): SCN 2012, LNCS 7485, pp. 205–221, 2012.
© Springer-Verlag Berlin Heidelberg 2012

On the Cost of SFE Rounds. This work is mainly motivated by the client-server setting, and its specific scalability and performance issues. We argue that in this setting, the number of communication rounds in SFE often plays an insignificant role in practice.

Of course, additional rounds may cause somewhat increased *latency* of an individual computation – a possible inconvenience to the user of interactive applications. However, many SFE protocols allow for a significant precomputation and also for streaming, where message transmission may begin (and even a response may be received) before the sender completes the computation of the message. Thus, even in the peer-to-peer setting round-related latency need not be a wasted time. And this is certainly true in the client-server environment, where the idle server can always busy itself with the next client.

Further, in the server environment, where computation and communication resources are provisioned as close to demand as possible, we are particularly interested in *throughput* (rather than latency) of the total computation.

1.1   Our Setting

As justified above, we aim to optimize computation and, mainly, communication of two-party SFE, without particular worry about round complexity. Further, our main algorithm is in an asymmetric setting: one player (presumably, server) is semi-honest, while the other (presumably, client), is covert [4]. This is in line with our goal of achieving maximal performance, while providing appropriate security guarantees. We argue that it is reasonable that a server (a business) would not deviate from a prescribed protocol for fear of lawsuits and bad publicity, and the client – for fear of being caught with probability guaranteed by the covert-secure protocol. While we also give a simpler protocol in the semi-honest model, the hybrid protocol (semi-honest server and covert client) is our main focus.

Finally, we remark that we are interested in the scalable client-server setting, since we believe it to be the setting most likely to pioneer practical use of SFE.

For simplicity, we present our protocols in the Random Oracle (RO) model. We stress that we can weaken this assumption to correlation-robust hash functions, sufficient for OT extension [14,13] (cf. Observation 5). Further, as shown by [2], OT extension can be obtained from semantically encryption secure against related key attacks (RKA).

1.2   Our Contributions, Outline of the Work, and Results

We optimize computation and communication complexity of two-party SFE for the important practical settings of semi-honest server and semi-honest or covert client. Our Garbled-Circuit (GC)-like protocol, built on consecutive secure evaluation of "slices" of the original circuit, takes advantage of the high efficiency of underlying information-theoretic (IT) GC-variant of Kolesnikov [19].

The main technical challenge with this approach is efficient wire key translation between the circuit slices, secure against covert GC evaluator. Natural but expensive use of committed OT [8,18] would negate IT GC performance gain.

Instead, we introduce and efficiently implement a new OT variant of independent interest, which we call String-selection OT (SOT). Here, the receiver submits a selection string (instead of just one bit); he obtains corresponding OT output only if he submitted one of the two sender-specified (presumably secret) strings. Our second contribution is a construction of SFE slice-evaluation protocol, which also has several subtleties in the covert-client setting.

We start with presenting detailed overview of our entire solution in Section 1.4, and cover preliminaries in Section 2. In Section 3.1, we define SOT and build SFE protocol secure against covert client $\mathcal{C}$, assuming a SOT protocol in the same model. Next, in Section 3.2 we present an efficient SOT protocol, based on OT extension [14,13]. Our SOT protocol is actually secure against a malicious $\mathcal{C}$, since we are able to get this advantage at comparable cost to that with a covert $\mathcal{C}$. In Section 3.1 we remark on shortcuts our SFE protocol could take when both server $\mathcal{S}$ and client $\mathcal{C}$ are semi-honest.

Finally, in Section 4, we calculate the costs of our protocol, and compare them with that of state-of-the-art Yao GC protocols, such as [32]. We achieve asymptotic log factor improvement in security parameter κ in communication and computation in both covert and semi-honest $\mathcal{C}$ settings. In practical terms, for today's $\kappa \in \{128, 256\}$ we offer approximately a factor 2 communication improvement in the semi-honest model, and are a factor ≈ 1.5 more costly in setting with covert client. We note that our protocols can be further optimized, resulting in even better concrete performance, while GC protocols we are comparing with have been highly fine-tuned for performance.

1.3   Related Work

We survey efficient state-of-the-art SFE, and discuss how it relates to our work.

Most relevant to us is a comparatively small body of work that provides improvements to the SFE core techniques that address the semi-honest model. We mention, but do not discuss in detail here the works that specifically concentrate on the malicious setting, such as [22,16,31,24,33,30,6,9]. This is because their improvement techniques cannot be transferred into the semi-honest world, and, further, malicious-secure protocols are much more costly than the protocols we are considering. To securely evaluate circuits of size c, even the most efficient protocols in this setting (e.g., [30]) incur a multiplicative overhead of $O(\kappa/\log c)$ over protocols in the semi-honest setting. In fact, to match the scale of circuits that are computable efficiently in the semi-honest setting, researchers have appealed to the power of parallelization [21] in the construction of malicious-secure protocols. However, it is conceivable that improvement techniques for malicious-secure protocols can be transferred to protocols in the covert setting. We stress that state-of-the-art malicious-secure protocols build on top of either semi-honest Yao garbled circuit protocol, or semi-honest GMW protocol, and consequently, their complexity is at least as high as these semi-honest protocols. On the other hand, our protocols (including our construction in the covert setting) asymptotically outperform state-of-the-art SFE protocols in the semi-honest setting.

After Yao's original GC work [34], we are aware of few improvements to the core algorithm. Naor et al. [29] mentioned that it was possible to reduce the number of entries (each of size security parameter κ) in the GC garbled table to 3 from 4. Kolesnikov [19] introduced the GESS construction, which can be viewed as information-theoretic (IT) GC, and is much more efficient than standard GC on shallow circuits. Using a GESS block in GC, Kolesnikov and Schneider [20] showed how to get XOR gates "for free" in GC. Finally, Pinkas et al. [32] showed how to reduce the garbled table size to 3 entries, while preserving the free-XOR compatibility, or to two entries, but disallowing free-XOR technique.

Aside from the cost of OT, GMW [12], a non-constant-round SFE protocol like ours, is very communication-efficient. However, using today's best two-party OT [14], GMW's communication cost, 4κ per gate, is slightly worse than GC. Further, GMW is not secure against covert client.

In this work, we are building on [19], and demonstrate communication cost improvement over [32], as a trade-off with round complexity. Our costs are correspondingly better than that of GMW, and we need fewer rounds than GMW. We also point out that the "slicing" technique is also used in [5] mainly as a method to reduce rounds in multi-party secure computation with an honest majority.

We note the theoretical work of Naor and Nissim [27], which uses indexing to perform SFE of branching programs (BP), and achieves costs polynomial in the communication complexity of the *insecurely* computed function. We note that, firstly, [27] is not performance-optimized. However, more importantly, BP function representation often carries dramatic overhead (exponential for integer multiplication), as compared to circuits.

Finally, we mention recent efficiency improvements in secure computation [3,26,25,11] based on fully homomorphic encryption [10], and note that these solutions are still orders of magnitude less efficient than symmetric-key-based approaches we consider.

1.4 Overview of Our Solution

As discussed and justified above, our main goal is communication and computational complexity reduction of the solution. We allow ourselves additional communication rounds.

Our main idea is to build on the information-theoretic version of GC of Kolesnikov [19], which, due to its avoidance of encryption, is *more efficient* than computational GC for small-depth circuits. We capitalize on this by "slicing" our original circuit C into a sequence of shallow circuits $C_1, \ldots, C_\ell$, which we then evaluate and obtain corresponding efficiency improvement. There are several technical problems that need to be solved.

First, recall that Kolesnikov's scheme, GESS, does not require generation or sending of garbled tables. It does use wire keys, which may start with 1-bit-long strings for output wires, and grow in size approximately quadratically with the depth d of the fan-out-one circuit. For generic fan-out-2 circuits, thus, total length of wire keys at depth d is up to $O(2^d d^2)$.

The first problem is allowing for piece-wise secure circuit evaluation, given the circuit's slicing. In the semi-honest model, this can be achieved as follows. Consider any slicing of C, where some wire w_j of C is an output wire of C_i, and is an input wire of C_{i+1}. Now, when a slice C_i is evaluated, C_i's 1-bit wire key for w_j is computed by the evaluator, and then used, via OT, to obtain the wire key for the corresponding input wire of C_{i+1}. This process repeats until C's output wire keys are computed by the evaluator. In order to prevent the evaluator from learning the intermediate wire values of C, the 1-bit wire keys of slices' output wires are randomly assigned to wire values.

While secure against passive adversaries, above construction is easily compromised by an active evaluator. Indeed, he can influence the output of the computation simply by flipping the 1-bit key of w_j before using it in OT, which will result in flipping the underlying bit on that wire.

To efficiently resolve this problem and achieve covert security against the evaluator, we introduce String-selection OT (SOT), a variant of 1-out-of-2 OT, where the receiver submits a selection string (instead of a selection bit). Naturally, in SOT, receiver obtains OT output corresponding to his selection string; submission of a string not expected by the sender S results in error output. In our construction, we will use multi-bit wire keys on output wires of each slice; client C will submit them to SOT to obtain input wire keys for next slice. Now, a cheating C wishing to flip a wire value must guess, in the on-line fashion, the multi-bit wire key corresponding to the opposite wire value. We will show that this results in covert security against the evaluator.

Efficient OT is a critical component in our construction. Another technical contribution of this paper is an efficient SOT protocol for arbitrary-length selection strings, secure against malicious C.

Finally, we evaluate and compare efficiency of our approach to previous solutions.

2 Preliminaries and Notation

2.1 Garbled Circuits (GC)

Yao's Garbled Circuit approach [34], excellently presented in [23], is the most efficient method for one-round secure evaluation of a boolean circuit C. We summarize its ideas in the following. The circuit *constructor* (server S) creates a *garbled circuit* $\widetilde{C}$: for each wire w_i of the circuit, he randomly chooses two garblings $\widetilde{w}_i^0, \widetilde{w}_i^1$, where $\widetilde{w}_i^j$ is the *garbled value* of w_i's value j. (Note: $\widetilde{w}_i^j$ does not reveal j.) Further, for each gate G_i, S creates a *garbled table* $\widetilde{T}_i$ with the following property: given a set of garbled values of G_i's inputs, $\widetilde{T}_i$ allows to recover the garbled value of the corresponding G_i's output, but nothing else. S sends these garbled tables, called *garbled circuit* $\widetilde{C}$ to the *evaluator* (client C). Additionally, C obliviously obtains the *garbled inputs* $\widetilde{w}_i$ corresponding to inputs of both parties: the garbled inputs $\widetilde{x}$ corresponding to the inputs x of S are sent directly and $\widetilde{y}$ are obtained with a parallel 1-out-of-2 oblivious transfer (OT) protocol [28,1,23]. Now, $\mathcal{C}$ can evaluate the garbled circuit $\widetilde{C}$ on the garbled inputs to obtain the *garbled outputs* by evaluating $\widetilde{C}$ gate by gate, using the garbled tables $\widetilde{T}_i$. Finally, $\mathcal{C}$ determines the plain values corresponding to the obtained garbled output values using an output translation table received from $\mathcal{S}$. Correctness of GC follows from the way garbled tables $\widetilde{T}_i$ are constructed.

2.2 GESS: Efficient Information-Theoretic GC for Shallow Circuits

We review the Gate Evaluation Secret Sharing (GESS) scheme of Kolesnikov [19], which is the most efficient information-theoretic analog of GC. Because encryption there is done with bitwise XOR and bit shufflings, rather than with standard primitives such as AES, GESS is significantly more efficient than standard GC, both in computation and communication, for shallow circuits.

At a high level, GESS is a secret sharing scheme, designed to match with the gate function g, as follows. The output wire keys are the secrets, from which the *constructor* produces four secret shares, one for each of the wire keys of the two input wires. GESS guarantees that a combination of shares, corresponding to any of the four possible gate inputs, reconstructs the corresponding key of the output wire. This secret sharing can be applied recursively, enabling reduction of SFE to OT (to transfer the wire secrets on the input wires). One result of [19] is the SFE protocol for a boolean formula F of communication complexity $\approx \sum d_i^2$, where d_i is the depth of the i-th leaf of F. This improvement (prior best construction – [17] combined with [7] – cost $\approx \sum 2^{\theta(\sqrt{d_i})}$) will allow us to outperform the standard GC by evaluating thin slices of the circuit. We note that other IT GC variants (e.g., [15]) could also be used in our work, with corresponding performance disadvantage.

2.3 Covert Security

In this work, we consider a semi-honest server, and a stronger client-adversary who may deviate from the protocol specification in an attempt to cheat. While cheating attempts may be successful, the covert model [4] guarantees that any attempted cheating is caught with a certain minimal probability.

Aumann and Lindell [4] give three formalizations of this notion; we consider their strongest definition, the strong explicit-cheat formulation. Informally, this variant of the covert-security definition guarantees that, if caught, the adversary does not learn the honest player's input. If not caught, the adversary may succeed either in learning the honest player's input or influencing the computation (or both). The definition is given in the standard ideal-real paradigm. Intuitively, the difference with the malicious model is that covert ideal world allows the cheat request: if successful (based on the coin flip by a trusted party), the adversary is allowed to win, if not, honest players are informed of cheat attempt.

We refer the reader to [4] for details and formal definitions.

2.4 Notation

Let κ be the computational security parameter.

Our SFE protocol is given a circuit C which represents a function f that a server $\mathcal{S}$ (with input x) and a client $\mathcal{C}$ (with input y) wish to compute. Let d denote the depth of C. Our protocol proceeds by dividing the circuit C into horizontal slices. Let ℓ denote the number of such slices, and let $C_1, \ldots, C_\ell$ denote these ℓ slices of C. We let d' denote the depth of each slice C_i.

In circuit slice C_i, we let $u_{i,j}$ (resp. $v_{i,j}$) denote the j-th input (resp. output) wire. For a wire $u_{i,j}$ (resp. $v_{i,j}$), we refer to the garbled values corresponding to 0 and 1 by $\tilde{u}_{i,j}^0, \tilde{u}_{i,j}^1$ (resp. $\tilde{v}_{i,j}^0, \tilde{v}_{i,j}^1$) respectively. In our protocol, let k (resp. k') denote the length of input (resp. output) wire garblings (k' will be related to the covert deterrent factor as $\epsilon = 1 - \frac{1}{2^{k'}-1}$). While evaluating the garbled circuit, $\mathcal{C}$ will possess only one of two garbled values for each wire in the circuit. We let $\tilde{u}_{i,j}'$ (resp. $\tilde{v}_{i,j}'$) denote the garbled value on wire $u_{i,j}$ (resp. $v_{i,j}$) that is possessed by $\mathcal{C}$.

In Section 3, we introduce the primitive $\text{SOT}_{k,k'}$ which requires a receiver $\mathcal{R}$, with input a k'-bit selection string, to select one of two k-bit strings held by sender $\mathcal{S}$. Our protocol for $\text{SOT}_{k,k'}$ uses calls to the standard 1-out-of-2 OT primitive (where receiver $\mathcal{R}$, with input a selection bit, selects one of two k-bit strings held by sender $\mathcal{S}$).

3 Our Protocol for Secure Two-Party Computation

We describe our protocol for secure two-party computation against a semi-honest server and a covert receiver in a hybrid model with ideal access to String-selection OT (SOT), defined below:

Definition 1. *String-selection OT,* $\text{SOT}_{k,k'}$, *is the following functionality:*

Inputs: $\mathcal{S}$ *holds two pairs* $(x_0, r_0), (x_1, r_1)$, *where each* x_0, x_1 *are* k-bit strings, *and* r_0, r_1 *are* k'-bit strings (with $r_0 \neq r_1$). $\mathcal{R}$ *holds* k'-bit selection string r.

Outputs: *If* $r = r_i$ *for some* $i \in \{0,1\}$, *then* $\mathcal{R}$ *outputs* x_i, *and* $\mathcal{S}$ *outputs empty string* λ. *Otherwise,* $\mathcal{R}$ *and* $\mathcal{S}$ *both output error symbol* $\perp$.

3.1 Our Protocol

We now present our protocol for securely computing a function f, represented by a circuit C, where semi-honest $\mathcal{S}$ has input x and covert $\mathcal{C}$ has input y.

Our protocol uses OT, the standard 1-out-of-2 OT protocol, and $\text{SOT}_{k,k'}$, a SOT protocol, as defined in Definition 1. Assume both OT and $\text{SOT}_{k,k'}$ are secure against a semi-honest sender and a covert receiver with deterrent ϵ (the required value of ϵ will depend on the parameters of the SFE protocol and is stated in the security theorems below). We prove security in the strongest covert formulation of [4], the strong explicit cheat formulation.

We evaluate C slice-by-slice. Further, each slice is viewed as a fan-out-1 circuit, as needed for the GESS scheme. We will discuss slicing the circuit with the view for performance, and the corresponding calculations in the full version of this paper.

Protocol 1. *1.* CIRCUIT PREPARATION:

(a) Slicing. *Given d, d', server S divides circuit C of depth d into horizontal sub-circuit layers, or slices, $C_1, \ldots, C_\ell$ of depth d'.*

(b) Preparing each slice. *In this step, S randomly generates the output secrets of the slice, and, applying the GESS sharing scheme, obtains corresponding input secrets, as follows.*

Denote by $u_{i,j}$ the input wires and by $v_{i,j}$ the output wires of the slice C_i. For each wire $v_{i,j}$, S picks two random garblings $\tilde{v}_{i,j}^0, \tilde{v}_{i,j}^1$ of length $k' \geq 1$ (conditioned on $\tilde{v}_{i,j}^0 \neq \tilde{v}_{i,j}^1$). S then (information-theoretically) computes the GESS garblings for each input wire in the subcircuit, as described in [19]. Let k be the maximal length of the garblings $\tilde{u}_{i,j}^0, \tilde{u}_{i,j}^1$ of the input wires $u_{i,j}$. Recall, GESS does not use garbled tables.

2. CIRCUIT EVALUATION:

For $1 \leq i \leq \ell$, in round i do:

(a) Oblivious transfer of keys.

 i. *For the top slice (the sub-circuit C_1), do the standard SFE garblings transfer:*

 For each client input wire $u_{1,j}$ (representing the bits of C's input y), S and C execute a 1-out-of-2 OT protocol, where S plays the role of a sender, with inputs $\tilde{u}_{1,j}^0, \tilde{u}_{1,j}^1$, and C plays the role of the receiver, directly using his inputs for OT.

 For each server input wire $u_{1,j}$ (representing the bits of S's input x), S sends to C one of $\tilde{u}_{1,j}^0, \tilde{u}_{1,j}^1$, corresponding to its input bits.

 ii. *For slices $C_i, i \neq 1$, transfer next slice's input keys based on the current output keys:*

 For each input wire $u_{i,j}$ of the slice C_i, S uniformly at random chooses a string $r_{i,j}$ of length k (this will mask the transferred secrets[1]). S then acts as sender in $\mathrm{SOT}_{k,k'}$ with input $((\tilde{u}_{i,j}^0 \oplus r_{i,j}, \tilde{v}_{i-1,j}^0), (\tilde{u}_{i,j}^1 \oplus r_{i,j}, \tilde{v}_{i-1,j}^1))$, and C acts as receiver with input $\tilde{v}_{i-1,j}'$ (this is the output wire secret of the one-above slice C_{i-1}, which C obtains by executing Step 2b described next). Let C obtain $\tilde{u}_{i,j}' \oplus r_{i,j}$ as the output from $\mathrm{SOT}_{k,k'}$.

 Once all $\mathrm{SOT}_{k,k'}$ have been completed, S sends all $r_{i,j}$ to C, who then computes all $\tilde{u}_{i,j}'$.

(b) Evaluating the slice. *C evaluates the GESS sub-circuit C_i, using garbled input values $\tilde{u}_{i,j}'$ to obtain the output values $\tilde{v}_{i,j}'$.*

3. Output of the computation. *Recall, w.l.o.g., only C receives the output. S now sends the output translation tables to C. For each output wire of C, C outputs the bit corresponding to the wire secret obtained in evaluation of the last slice C_ℓ.*

Observation 1. *We note that technically the reason for sending masked wire values via $\mathrm{SOT}_{k,k'}$ in Step 2(a)ii is to facilitate the simulation proof, as follows. When simulating covert C^* without the knowledge of the input, the simulator*

---

[1] The reason for the masking is to enable simulation of C. See Observation 1 for details.

Sim_C's messages to C^* "commit" Sim_C to certain randomized representation of players' inputs. When, in SOT of the i-th slice C_i, a covert C^* successfully cheats, he will be given both wire keys for some wire of C_i. Without the masking, this knowledge, combined with the knowledge of the gate function and a key on a sibling wire, allows C^* to infer the wire value encrypted by the simulation, which might differ from the expected value. We use the mask to hide the encrypted value even when both wire keys are revealed. Mask can be selected to "decommit" transcript seen by C^* to either wire value.

Observation 2. We note that in the semi-honest-C case the above protocol can be simplified and made more efficient. In particular, k' is set to 1, in Step 2(a)ii, it is sufficient to use OT (vs. SOT), and offset strings $r_{i,j}$ are not needed.

We prove security of Protocol 1 against a semi-honest server S and a *covert* client C.

Theorem 3. Let OT be a 1-out-of-2 OT, and $SOT_{k,k'}$ be a string-selection OT (cf. Definition 1), both secure against semi-honest sender. Then Protocol 1 is secure against a semi-honest server S.

Further, let k' be a parameter upper-bounded by $\mathrm{poly}(n)$, and set $\epsilon = 1 - \frac{1}{2^{k'}-1}$. Let f be any probabilistic polynomial-time function. Assume that the underlying OT and SOT protocols are secure in the presence of covert receiver with ϵ-deterrent, in the strong explicit cheat formulation of covert security. Then, Protocol 1 securely computes f in the presence of covert client C with ϵ-deterrent, in the strong explicit cheat formulation.

We note that the deterrent $\epsilon = 1 - \frac{1}{2^{k'}-1}$ reflects the probability of C incorrectly guessing the selection string unknown to him from the set of all strings of size k'. In particular, setting $k' = 2$ results in $\epsilon = 2/3$.

Proof. **Security against semi-honest S.** Given input x, the semi-honest S^* is simulated as follows. Sim_S chooses a random input y' for C and plays honest C interacting with S^*. He then outputs whatever S^* outputs.

It is easy to see that S^* does not receive any messages – all protocol messages related to C's input are delivered inside OT and $SOT_{k,k'}$, the protocols that do not return output to S^* (other than possible error symbols, which will never be output in this simulation, since it presumes that C is acting honestly, and S^* is semi-honest). Hence, this is a perfect simulation (however, the function calls to underlying OT and SOT primitives will not be perfectly simulated).

The proof of security in the client-corruption case is somewhat more complex.

Security against Covert C. This part of the proof is somewhat more involved. We present the simulator Sim_C of a covert attacker C^*, and argue that it produces a good simulation.

Sim_C starts C^* and interacts with it, sending C^* messages it expects to receive, and playing the role of the trusted party for the OT and $SOT_{k,k'}$ oracle calls that C^* may make, where C^* plays the role of the receiver. Unless terminating early (e.g. due to simulating abort), Sim_C will first simulate processing the top slice C_1, then all internal slices (using same procedure for each internal slice), and then the last, output slice C_ℓ.

For each output wire of each slice C_i, Sim_C samples two random strings of length k' (with the restriction that these two strings are different per wire). Based on these, Sim_C computes C_i's input wire garblings by applying the GESS algorithm.

For the top slice C_1, Sim_C plays the role of OT trusted party, where $\mathcal{C}^*$ is the receiver, and receives OT input from $\mathcal{C}^*$.

1. If the input is abort or corrupted, then Sim_C sends abort or corrupted (respectively) to the trusted party computing f, simulates $\mathcal{C}$ aborting and halts (outputting whatever $\mathcal{C}^*$ outputs).
2. If the input is cheat, then Sim_C sends cheat to the trusted party. If it receives back corrupted, then it hands $\mathcal{C}^*$ the message corrupted as if it received it from the trusted party, simulates $\mathcal{C}$ aborting and halts (outputting whatever $\mathcal{C}^*$ outputs). If it receives back undetected (and thus $\mathcal{S}$'s input x as well), then Sim_C works as follows. First, it hands $\mathcal{C}^*$ the string undetected together with all the input wire keys that were part of server's input in the OT ($\mathcal{C}^*$ expects to receive OT inputs in this case). Next, Sim_C uses the input x of $\mathcal{S}$ that it received in order to perfectly emulate $\mathcal{S}$ in the rest of the execution. This is easily done, since so far Sim_C had not delivered to $\mathcal{C}^*$ any messages "from $\mathcal{S}$" that depended on $\mathcal{S}$'s input.
3. If the input is a representation of $\mathcal{C}^*$'s input to OT, then Sim_C hands $\mathcal{C}^*$ the input wire garbling keys that are "chosen" by the $\mathcal{C}^*$'s OT input, and proceeds with the simulation below.

Sim_C now also sends $\mathcal{C}^*$ the wire secrets corresponding to a random input of $\mathcal{S}$. Now, presumably, $\mathcal{C}^*$ will evaluate the slice and use the output wire secrets in $\mathrm{SOT}_{k,k'}$ oracles.

For all internal slices $C_2, ..., C_{\ell-1}$ Sim_C plays $\mathrm{SOT}_{k,k'}$ trusted party, where $\mathcal{C}^*$ is the receiver, and receives $\mathrm{SOT}_{k,k'}$ input from $\mathcal{C}^*$.

1. If the input is abort or corrupted, then Sim_C sends abort or corrupted (respectively) to the trusted party computing f, simulates $\mathcal{C}$ aborting and halts (outputting whatever $\mathcal{C}^*$ outputs).
2. If the input is cheat, then Sim_C sends cheat to the trusted party.
   If it receives back corrupted, then it hands $\mathcal{C}^*$ the message corrupted as if it received it from the trusted party, simulates $\mathcal{C}$ aborting and halts (outputting whatever $\mathcal{C}^*$ outputs).
   If it receives back undetected (and thus $\mathcal{S}$'s input x as well), then Sim_C works as follows. First, it hands $\mathcal{C}^*$ the string undetected together with all the masked input wire keys $\tilde{u}_{i,j}^0 \oplus r_{i,j}, \tilde{u}_{i,j}^1 \oplus r_{i,j}$ and the corresponding selection-string keys $\tilde{v}_{i-1,j}^0, \tilde{v}_{i-1,j}^1$ that were part of sender's input in current $\mathrm{SOT}_{k,k'}$ ($\mathcal{C}^*$ expects to receive SOT inputs in this case). These input wire keys were generated by Sim_C by running GESS wire key generation for the current slice, the selection-string keys are the output keys from preceding slice, and the wire-key to selection-string correspondence is set at random at this time (we will reconcile it when needed later).

Next, Sim_C uses the input x of S that it just received and the input y of C^* that it received in OT in slice C_1, to perfectly emulate S in the rest of the execution. We note that Sim_C had already sent messages to C^* which should depend on S's input, which we now need to reconcile with the real input x received. First, we observe that the view of C^* of the prior slices' evaluation is consistent with any input of S, since C^* is never given both secrets on any wire. (C^* only sees both secrets on the immediately preceding slice's output wires since Sim_C gave him both string-selection keys for current slice. However, this is allowed in the underlying GESS scheme, and hence is also consistent with any input of S.) At the same time, both $\mathrm{SOT}_{k,k'}$ secrets are revealed to C^* in the current slice, and C^* can obtain both wire encodings for each of the slice's input wires, which, in turn, may reveal correspondence between wire values and encodings (cf. Observation 1). Since C^*'s $\mathrm{SOT}_{k,k'}$ selection string determines the "active" $\mathrm{SOT}_{k,k'}$ value, which is offset by $r_{i,j}$ into the "active" wire encoding, we now have to be careful that it is consistent with the players' input into the function. This reconciliation is easily achieved by appropriately setting the simulated offset string $r'_{i,j}$ for each wire j. The simulated $r'_{i,j}$ is selected so that the "active" (resp. "inactive") encoding corresponding to the function's inputs x and y is obtained by XORing $r'_{i,j}$ with the "active" (resp. "inactive") string-selection OT value. In other words, for each wire where Sim_C chose incorrect wire-key to selection-string correspondence, this correspondence is flipped by choosing the right offset $r'_{i,j}$. This flipping selection is computed as follows: for GESS input keys $\tilde{u}_0, \tilde{u}_1$, offset r (and $\mathrm{SOT}_{k,k'}$ inputs $\tilde{u}_0 \oplus r, \tilde{u}_1 \oplus r$) the correspondence is reversed by applying offset $r' = \tilde{u}_0 \oplus \tilde{u}_1 \oplus r$.
Sim_C simulates the rest of the interaction simply by playing the honest S.

3. If the input is a representation of C^*'s input to $\mathrm{SOT}_{k,k'}$ then Sim_C proceeds as follows. We stress that Sim_C knows exactly the garblings of the input wires of C_{i-1} sent to C^* (and hence the garblings of the output wires of C_{i-1} that C^* should reconstruct and use as inputs to $\mathrm{SOT}_{k,k'}$ oracles for slice C_i).
   (a) If C^* submits $\mathrm{SOT}_{k,k'}$ inputs as expected, then Sim_C sends C^* the corresponding garblings of the C_i input wires.
   (b) Otherwise, we deal with the cheating attempt by C^*. Sim_C then sends cheat to the trusted party. By the definition of the ideal model, with probability $1 - \epsilon = \frac{1}{2^{k'}-1}$ Sim_C receives back the message undetected together with S's input x, and with probability $\epsilon = 1 - \frac{1}{2^{k'}-1}$ it receives the message corrupted.

   If it receives back corrupted, then it simulates S aborting due to detected cheating and outputs whatever C^* outputs.

   If it receives back undetected, then it receives S's input, simulates honest S, and outputs whatever C^* outputs. We stress that the C^*'s view of execution so far is independent of S's input, since C^* never receives more than one wire-key per wire. (The only exception to this is the information inferred by C^* based on the fact that he was undetected in attempting to submit another string to string-selection OT. Specifically, this gives C^* the knowledge of both wire keys on one of the output wires of the preceding slice (importantly, he will not learn both input garblings of the corresponding input wire of the current slice). This information is allowed in the GESS protocol, and will not allow to correlate wire keys.) Therefore, the simulation goes through in this case.

To simulate the output slice C_ℓ, Sim_C first performs the simulation steps of an internal slice described above. Upon completion, he additionally has to reconcile the view with the output of the function. If after the $\mathrm{SOT}_{k,k'}$ step C^* still has not attempted to cheat, Sim_C provides to the trusted party the input that was provided by C^* in the OT of slice C_1, and gets back the output of the computation. Now Sim_C simply provides C^* the output translation tables with the mapping of the output values, which would map to the output received from the trusted party.

3.2   A Protocol for $\mathrm{SOT}_{k,k'}$

In this section, we introduce an efficient string-selection OT protocol, secure against semi-honest sender and malicious receiver, which works for selection strings of arbitrary length k'. We build it from k' standard 1-out-of-2 OTs. We note that, while Protocol 1 requires only covert-C security, we provide a stronger building block (at no or very little extra cost).

The intuition behind our construction is as follows. We will split each of the two secrets x_0, x_1 into k' random shares x_i^j (i.e. $2k'$ total shares), with the restriction that the sets of x_i^j, indexed by each of the two selection strings, reconstructs the corresponding secret. Then, in the semi-honest model, performing k' standard OTs allows receiver to reconstruct one of the two secrets, corresponding to his selection string.

To protect against malicious or covert receiver, we, firstly, assume that underlying OTs are secure against such receiver. Further, we allow the sender to confirm that the receiver indeed received one of the two secrets, as follows. Denote by h_0 (resp. h_1) the hash of the vector of secret shares corresponding to the secret x_0 (resp. x_1). To confirm that receiver obtained shares to reconstruct at least one of x_0, x_1, the sender will send $h_0 \oplus h_1$ to $\mathcal{R}$, and expect to receive both h_0 and h_1 back (actually, it is sufficient to receive just one of h_0, h_1 selected by $\mathcal{R}$ at random).

The above check introduces a subtle vulnerability: the value $h_0 \oplus h_1$ leaks information if selection strings differ in a single position. Indeed, then there is only one secret share unknown to malicious $\mathcal{R}$, and secrets' values can be verified by checking against received $h_0 \oplus h_1$. (If we restricted the selection strings to differ in at least two positions, this approach can be made to work. However, such restriction is less natural.) As a result, we now can not transfer the $\mathrm{SOT}_{k,k'}$ secrets directly. To address this, we transfer $\mathrm{SOT}_{k,k'}$ secrets by encrypting each with a random key, and then OT-transferring one of the two keys as above, which is secure for OT of long random secrets.

Our Protocol. Let sender $\mathcal{S}$ have input $(x_0, r_0), (x_1, r_1)$ with $|x_0| = |x_1| = k$, and $|r_0| = |r_1| = k'$. Let receiver $\mathcal{R}$ have input $r \in \{r_0, r_1\}$. Let κ be a security parameter, OT be a standard 1-out-of-2 OT, and $H : \{0,1\}^* \rightarrow \{0,1\}^\kappa$ be a random oracle.

Protocol 2. STRING-SELECTION OT

1. Let $r_0 = r_{01}, r_{02}, ..., r_{0k'}$, and $r_1 = r_{11}, r_{12}, ..., r_{1k'}$, where r_{ij} are bits. $\mathcal{S}$ chooses $s_i^j \in_R \{0,1\}^\kappa$, for $i \in \{0,1\}, j \in \{1,...,k'\}$. $\mathcal{S}$ sets keys $s_0 = \bigoplus_j s_j^{r_{0j}}$, and $s_1 = \bigoplus_j s_j^{r_{1j}}$.
2. $\mathcal{S}$ and $\mathcal{R}$ participate in k' OTs as follows. For $j = 1$ to k':
   (a) $\mathcal{S}$ with input (s_j^0, s_j^1), and $\mathcal{R}$ with input r_j, where r_j is the j-th bit of $\mathcal{R}$'s selection string r, send their inputs to OT. $\mathcal{R}$ receives $s_j^{r_j}$.
3. $\mathcal{S}$ computes hashes of shares corresponding to the two secrets/selection strings: $h_0 = H(s_1^{r_{01}}, s_2^{r_{02}}, ..., s_{k'}^{r_{0k'}})$, and $h_1 = H(s_1^{r_{11}}, s_2^{r_{12}}, ..., s_{k'}^{r_{1k'}})$. $\mathcal{S}$ then sends $h = h_0 \oplus h_1$ to $\mathcal{R}$.
4. $\mathcal{R}$ computes $h_\mathcal{R} = H(s_1^{r_1}, ..., s_{k'}^{r_{k'}})$ and sends to $\mathcal{S}$ either $h_\mathcal{R}$ or $h \oplus h_\mathcal{R}$, equiprobably.
5. $\mathcal{S}$ checks that the hash received from $\mathcal{R}$ is equal to either h_0 or h_1. If so, it sends, in random order, $H(s_0) \oplus x_0, H(s_1) \oplus x_1$ and terminates with output λ; if not, $\mathcal{S}$ sends $\perp$ to $\mathcal{R}$ and outputs failure symbol $\perp$.
6. $\mathcal{R}$ computes key $s_r = \bigoplus_j s_j^{r_j}$ and recovers the secret by canceling out $H(s_r)$.

For readability, we omitted simple technical details, such as adding redundancy to x_i which allows $\mathcal{R}$ to identify the recovered secret. We also slightly abuse notation and consider the output length of H sufficiently stretched when we use it to mask secrets x_i.

Theorem 4. *Assume that the underlying OT is secure in the presence of semi-honest sender and malicious receiver. When $k' > 1$, Protocol 2 is a secure SOT protocol in the presence of semi-honest sender and malicious receiver.*

Proof. (sketch) **Security against semi-honest $\mathcal{S}$.** We start with showing that the protocol is secure against the semi-honest sender $\mathcal{S}$. The information received by $\mathcal{S}$ are transcripts of the underlying OTs, and the hash of one of the two shares sequences. Neither leaks information. Firstly, OT's are secure against semi-honest $\mathcal{S}$. Further, an honest receiver uses $r \in \{r_0, r_1\}$ selection string, hence the hash sent to $\mathcal{S}$ will in fact be of one of the two sequences corresponding to the selection strings. The simulator Sim_S follows naturally.

Security against Malicious Receiver $\mathcal{R}$. We present the simulator Sim_R of a malicious $\mathcal{R}^*$, and argue that it produces a good simulation.

Sim_R starts $\mathcal{R}^*$ and interacts with it, sending it messages it expects to receive, and playing the role of the trusted party for the OT oracle calls that $\mathcal{R}^*$ makes, in which $\mathcal{R}^*$ plays the role of the receiver.

Sim_R starts by playing OT trusted party k' times, where $\mathcal{R}^*$ is the receiver; as such, Sim_R receives all k' OT selection bits from $\mathcal{R}^*$ and each time uses a random string s_j' to hand to $\mathcal{R}^*$ as his OT output. If any of the underlying OT's input is abort, then Sim_R sends abort to the trusted party computing $\mathrm{SOT}_{k,k'}$ and halts, outputting whatever $\mathcal{R}^*$ outputs.

Sim_R then sends a random κ-bit string h' to $\mathcal{R}^*$, simulating the message of Step 3. Sim_R then receives a hash value from $\mathcal{R}^*$ as Step 4 message. If this value was *not* computed correctly from the simulated OT strings s'_j and hash h', then Sim_R sends abort to the trusted party, and terminates outputting whatever $\mathcal{R}^*$ outputs. Otherwise, Sim_R feeds $\mathcal{R}^*$'s selection bits to the trusted party of $SOT_{k,k'}$. Sim_R gets back from the trusted party either:

- string x', one of $\mathcal{S}$'s secrets. In this case, $\mathcal{R}^*$ submitted a valid selection string, and we simulate successful completion. Sim_R sends, in random order, $x' \oplus H(\oplus_j s'_j)$ and a random string of equal length, and then terminates outputting whatever $\mathcal{R}^*$ outputs.
- $\perp$. In this case, $\mathcal{R}^*$ did not submit a valid selection string, and we simulate abnormal termination. Sim_R sends $\perp$ to $\mathcal{R}^*$ and terminates outputting whatever $\mathcal{R}^*$ outputs.

We now argue that Sim_R produces view indistinguishable from the real execution. We first note that Sim_R's interaction with $\mathcal{R}^*$ is indistinguishable from that of honest $\mathcal{S}$. Indeed, OT secrets delivered to $\mathcal{R}^*$ are distributed identically to real execution. Further, since non-selected OT secrets remain hidden, the string h' sent is also indistinguishable from real execution. Finally, the simulation of Step 5 is indistinguishable from real, since it is infeasible to search for a preimage of H to check whether it satisfies both simulation of Steps 3 and 5.

Observation 5. *We stress that our use of RO H is not inherent in Protocol 2, and a PRFG or certain encryption can be appropriately used instead. Hence we can remove the RO assumption, and assume correlation-robust hash functions or RKA-secure encryption sufficient for OT extension [14,13,2].*

4   Performance Analysis

For the lack of space, we present all calculations in the full version of this paper. Here we summarize the results.

Consider a fan-out 2 circuit C with c gates. To simplify our cost calculation and w.l.o.g., we assume C is a rectangular circuit of constant width, where each gate has fan-out 2. Let C be divided into ℓ slices, each of depth d'. Let k (resp. k') be key length on input (resp. output) wires of each slice. k' is effectively the covert deterrent parameter, and k grows as $O(2^{d'})$ due to fan-out 2.

Then communication cost (measured in bits) of GC [32] is $cost(Yao) = 2\kappa c$, and of GMW is $cost(GMW) = 4c + 4\kappa c$. Our costs are $O(\kappa c/\log \kappa)$ in the semi-honest model, and $O(k'\kappa c/\log(\kappa/k'))$ in the covert-client setting, with small constants. Intuitively, in the semi-honest model, our gain of $\log \kappa$ comes from the fact that for slice of depth $d' \approx \log \kappa$, the total size of GESS wire secrets to be transferred by OT is approximately equal to the total GC wire secrets length of a single layer of GC. Same intuition applies to the covert-client case. The computation costs (the number of hash function evaluations) of all protocols, including ours is proportional to the communication cost; hence our asymptotic improvements translate into computation as well.

In concrete terms, we get up to factor 2 improvement in the semi-honest model for today's typical parameters. Setting $d' = 3$ and $\kappa = 256$, our cost is $\approx 208c$, as compared to $\approx 512c$ of [32]. In the setting with covert client ($k' = 2$, deterrent $2/3$), our protocol has cost $\approx 818c$, at less than factor 2 disadvantage; it surpasses [32] for $\kappa \approx 4800$.

Finally, while the GC protocol has been highly fine-tuned for performance, we note that our protocols have room for optimization, resulting in even better concrete advantage.

Acknowledgments. The authors would like to thank the anonymous reviewers of SCN 2012.

References

1. Aiello, W., Ishai, Y., Reingold, O.: Priced Oblivious Transfer: How to Sell Digital Goods. In: Pfitzmann, B. (ed.) EUROCRYPT 2001. LNCS, vol. 2045, pp. 119–135. Springer, Heidelberg (2001)

2. Applebaum, B., Harnik, D., Ishai, Y.: Semantic security under related-key attacks and applications. In: Chazelle, B. (ed.) ICS, pp. 45–60. Tsinghua University Press (2011)

3. Asharov, G., Jain, A., López-Alt, A., Tromer, E., Vaikuntanathan, V., Wichs, D.: Multiparty Computation with Low Communication, Computation and Interaction via Threshold FHE. In: Pointcheval, D., Johansson, T. (eds.) EUROCRYPT 2012. LNCS, vol. 7237, pp. 483–501. Springer, Heidelberg (2012)

4. Aumann, Y., Lindell, Y.: Security Against Covert Adversaries: Efficient Protocols for Realistic Adversaries. In: Vadhan, S.P. (ed.) TCC 2007. LNCS, vol. 4392, pp. 137–156. Springer, Heidelberg (2007)

5. Bar-Ilan, J., Beaver, D.: Non-cryptographic fault-tolerant computing in constant number of rounds of interaction. In: 8th ACM Symposium Annual on Principles of Distributed Computing, pp. 201–209. ACM Press (1989)

6. Bendlin, R., Damgård, I., Orlandi, C., Zakarias, S.: Semi-homomorphic Encryption and Multiparty Computation. In: Paterson, K.G. (ed.) EUROCRYPT 2011. LNCS, vol. 6632, pp. 169–188. Springer, Heidelberg (2011)

7. Cleve, R.: Towards optimal simulations of formulas by bounded-width programs. In: Proceedings of the Twenty-Second Annual ACM Symposium on Theory of Computing, STOC 1990, pp. 271–277. ACM, New York (1990)

8. Crépeau, C.: Verifiable Disclose for Secrets and Applications (Abstract). In: Quisquater, J.-J., Vandewalle, J. (eds.) EUROCRYPT 1989. LNCS, vol. 434, pp. 150–154. Springer, Heidelberg (1990)

9. Damgard, I., Pastro, V., Smart, N., and Zakarias, S. Multi-party computation from somewhat homomorphic encryption. Cryptology ePrint Archive, Report 2011/535 (2011), http://eprint.iacr.org/

10. Gentry, C.: Fully homomorphic encryption using ideal lattices. In: Mitzenmacher, M. (ed.) 41st Annual ACM Symposium on Theory of Computing, pp. 169–178. ACM Press (May/June 2009)

11. Gentry, C., Halevi, S., Smart, N.: Homomorphic evaluation of the aes circuit. Cryptology ePrint Archive, Report 2012/099 (2012), http://eprint.iacr.org/

12. Goldreich, O., Micali, S., Wigderson, A.: How to play any mental game, or a completeness theorem for protocols with honest majority. In: Aho, A. (ed.) 19th Annual ACM Symposium on Theory of Computing, pp. 218–229. ACM Press (May 1987)

13. Harnik, D., Ishai, Y., Kushilevitz, E., Nielsen, J.B.: OT-Combiners via Secure Computation. In: Canetti, R. (ed.) TCC 2008. LNCS, vol. 4948, pp. 393–411. Springer, Heidelberg (2008)

14. Ishai, Y., Kilian, J., Nissim, K., Petrank, E.: Extending Oblivious Transfers Efficiently. In: Boneh, D. (ed.) CRYPTO 2003. LNCS, vol. 2729, pp. 145–161. Springer, Heidelberg (2003)

15. Ishai, Y., Kushilevitz, E.: Randomizing polynomials: A new representation with applications to round-efficient secure computation. In: 41st Annual Symposium on Foundations of Computer Science, pp. 294–304. IEEE Computer Society Press (November 2000)

16. Jarecki, S., Shmatikov, V.: Efficient Two-Party Secure Computation on Committed Inputs. In: Naor, M. (ed.) EUROCRYPT 2007. LNCS, vol. 4515, pp. 97–114. Springer, Heidelberg (2007)

17. Kilian, J.: Founding cryptography on oblivious transfer. In: STOC, pp. 20–31 (1988)

18. Kiraz, M.S., Schoenmakers, B.: An Efficient Protocol for Fair Secure Two-Party Computation. In: Malkin, T. (ed.) CT-RSA 2008. LNCS, vol. 4964, pp. 88–105. Springer, Heidelberg (2008)

19. Kolesnikov, V.: Gate Evaluation Secret Sharing and Secure One-Round Two-Party Computation. In: Roy, B. (ed.) ASIACRYPT 2005. LNCS, vol. 3788, pp. 136–155. Springer, Heidelberg (2005)

20. Kolesnikov, V., Schneider, T.: Improved garbled circuit: Free XOR gates and applications. In: Aceto, L., Damgård, I., Goldberg, L.A., Halldórsson, M.M., Ingólfsdóttir, A., Walukiewicz, I. (eds.) ICALP 2008, Part II. LNCS, vol. 5126, pp. 486–498. Springer, Heidelberg (2008)

21. Kreuter, B., Shelat, A., Hao Shen, C.: Towards billion-gate secure computation with malicious adversaries. Cryptology ePrint Archive, Report 2012/179 (2012), http://eprint.iacr.org/

22. Lindell, Y., Pinkas, B.: An Efficient Protocol for Secure Two-Party Computation in the Presence of Malicious Adversaries. In: Naor, M. (ed.) EUROCRYPT 2007. LNCS, vol. 4515, pp. 52–78. Springer, Heidelberg (2007)

23. Lindell, Y., Pinkas, B.: A proof of security of Yao's protocol for two-party computation. Journal of Cryptology 22(2), 161–188 (2009)

24. Lindell, Y., Pinkas, B.: Secure Two-Party Computation via Cut-and-Choose Oblivious Transfer. In: Ishai, Y. (ed.) TCC 2011. LNCS, vol. 6597, pp. 329–346. Springer, Heidelberg (2011)

25. Lopez-Alt, A., Tromer, E., Vaikuntanathan, V.: On-the-fly multiparty computation on the cloud via multikey fully homomorphic encryption. In: 44th Annual ACM Symposium on Theory of Computing. ACM Press (2012)

26. Myers, S., Sergi, M., Shelat, A.: Threshold fully homomorphic encryption and secure computation. Cryptology ePrint Archive, Report 2011/454 (2011), http://eprint.iacr.org/

27. Naor, M., Nissim, K.: Communication preserving protocols for secure function evaluation. In: 33rd Annual ACM Symposium on Theory of Computing, pp. 590–599. ACM Press (July 2001)

28. Naor, M., Pinkas, B.: Efficient oblivious transfer protocols. In: 12th Annual ACM-SIAM Symposium on Discrete Algorithms, pp. 448–457. ACM-SIAM (January 2001)

29. Naor, M., Pinkas, B., Sumner, R.: Privacy preserving auctions and mechanism design. In: ACM Conference on Electronic Commerce, pp. 129–139 (1999)
30. Nielsen, J. B., Nordholt, P. S., Orlandi, C., Burra, S. S.: A new approach to practical active-secure two-party computation. Cryptology ePrint Archive, Report 2011/091 (2011), http://eprint.iacr.org/
31. Nielsen, J.B., Orlandi, C.: LEGO for Two-Party Secure Computation. In: Reingold, O. (ed.) TCC 2009. LNCS, vol. 5444, pp. 368–386. Springer, Heidelberg (2009)
32. Pinkas, B., Schneider, T., Smart, N.P., Williams, S.C.: Secure Two-Party Computation Is Practical. In: Matsui, M. (ed.) ASIACRYPT 2009. LNCS, vol. 5912, pp. 250–267. Springer, Heidelberg (2009)
33. Shelat, A., Shen, C.-H.: Two-Output Secure Computation with Malicious Adversaries. In: Paterson, K.G. (ed.) EUROCRYPT 2011. LNCS, vol. 6632, pp. 386–405. Springer, Heidelberg (2011)
34. Yao, A.C.-C.: How to generate and exchange secrets (extended abstract). In: FOCS, pp. 162–167 (1986)

5PM: Secure Pattern Matching

Joshua Baron[1], Karim El Defrawy[2], Kirill Minkovich[2],
Rafail Ostrovsky[1], and Eric Tressler[2]

[1] UCLA, Los Angeles, CA, USA 90095
[2] HRL Laboratories, LLC, Malibu, CA, USA, 90265
jwbaron@math.ucla.edu, {kmeldefrawy,kminkovich,eptressler}@hrl.com,
rafail@cs.ucla.edu

Abstract. In this paper we consider the problem of secure pattern matching that allows single character wildcards and substring matching in the malicious (stand-alone) setting. Our protocol, called 5PM, is executed between two parties: Server, holding a text of length n, and Client, holding a pattern of length m to be matched against the text, where our notion of matching is more general and includes non-binary alphabets, non-binary Hamming distance and non-binary substring matching.

5PM is the first protocol with communication complexity sub-linear in circuit size to compute non-binary substring matching in the malicious model (general MPC has communication complexity which is at least linear in the circuit size). 5PM is also the first sublinear protocol to compute non-binary Hamming distance in the malicious model. Additionally, in the honest-but-curious (semi-honest) model, 5PM is asymptotically more efficient than the best known scheme when amortized for applications that require single charcter wildcards or substring pattern matching. 5PM in the malicious model requires $O((m+n)k^2)$ bandwidth and $O(m+n)$ encryptions, where m is the pattern length and n is the text length. Further, 5PM can hide pattern size with no asymptotic additional costs in either computation or bandwidth. Finally, 5PM requires only 2 rounds of communication in the honest-but-curious model and 8 rounds in the malicious model. Our techniques reduce pattern matching and generalized Hamming distance problem to a novel linear algebra formulation that allows for generic solutions based on any additively homomorphic encryption. We believe our efficient algebraic techniques are of independent interest.

Keywords: Secure pattern matching, wildcard pattern matching, substring pattern matching, non-binary Hamming distance, secure two-party computation, malicious adversary, full simulation, homomorphic encryption, threshold encryption.

1 Introduction

Pattern matching[1] is fundamental to computer science. It is used in many areas, including text processing, database search [1], networking and security applications

---

[1] The full version of this paper can be found at
http://www.ics.uci.edu/~keldefra/papers/5pm_scn12.pdf

I. Visconti and R. De Prisco (Eds.): SCN 2012, LNCS 7485, pp. 222–240, 2012.
© Springer-Verlag Berlin Heidelberg 2012

[2] and recently in the context of bioinformatics and DNA analysis [3,4,5]. It is a problem that has been extensively studied, resulting in several efficient (although insecure) techniques to solve its many variations, e.g,[6,7,8,9]. The most common interpretation of the pattern matching problem is the following: given a finite alphabet Σ, a text $T \in \Sigma^n$ and a pattern $p \in \Sigma^m$, the *exact pattern matching decision problem* requires one to decide whether or not a pattern appears in the text. The *exact pattern matching search problem* requires finding all indices i of T (if any) where p occurs as a substring starting at position i. If we denote by T_i the ith character of T, the output should be the set of matching positions $MP := \{i \mid p \text{ matches } T \text{ beginning at } T_i\}$. The following generalizations of the exact matching problem are often encountered, where the output in all cases is the set MP:

- *Pattern matching with single character wildcards[2]:* There is a special character " $*$ " $\notin \Sigma$ that matches any single character of the alphabet, where $p \in \{\Sigma \cup \{*\}\}^m$ and $T \in \Sigma^n$. Using such a "wildcard" character allows one pattern to be specified that could match several sequences of characters. For example the pattern "$TA*$" , would match any of the following character sequence in a text[3]: $TAA, TAC, TAG,$ and TAT.
- *Substring pattern matching:* Fix some $l \leq m$; a match for p is found whenever there exists in T an m-length string that differs in l characters from p (i.e., has Hamming distance l from p). For example, the pattern "TAC" has $m = 3$. If $l = 1$, then any of the following words would match: $*AC, T*C,$ or $TA*$; note that this is an example of non-binary substring matching.

A secure version of pattern matching has many applications. For example, secure pattern matching can help secure databases containing medical information, such as DNA records, while still allowing one to perform pattern matching operations on such data. The need for privacy-preserving DNA matching has been highlighted in recent papers [10,11,12]. In addition to the case of DNA matching, where substring matching may be particularly useful, Hamming distance-based approximate matching has also been demonstrated in the case of secure facial recognition [3]. We note that both of these settings require computation over non-binary alphabets.

1.1 Our Contributions

This paper presents a new protocol for arbitrary alphabets, **5**ecure **P**attern **M**atching (or 5PM), that addresses, in addition to exact matching, more expressive search queries including single character wildcards and substring pattern matching, in addition to providing the ability to hide pattern length.

5PM is the first protocol with communication complexity sub-linear in circuit size (as opposed to general MPC, which has communication complexity linear in

---

[2] Such wildcards are also called "do not cares" and "mismatches" in the literature.
[3] Here and throughout, we use the DNA alphabet ($\Sigma = \{A, C, G, T\}$) for examples.

circuit size) to securely compute non-binary substring matching in the malicious model and is also the first non-general MPC protocol to compute non-binary Hamming distance in the malicious model. In addition, our extension of Hamming distance computation to substring matching has minimal overhead; our protocol makes a single computation pass per text element, even for multiple Hamming distance values, and therefore is able to securely compute non-binary substring matching efficiently (see Table 2 for details).

5PM performs exact, single character wildcard, and substring pattern matching in the honest-but-curious and malicious (static corruption) models. Our malicious model protocol requires $O((m+n)k^2)$ bandwidth complexity. Further, our protocol can be specified to require 2 (one-way) rounds of communication in the semi-honest model and 8 (one-way) rounds of communication in the malicious model.

We construct our protocols by reducing the problems of Hamming distance and pattern matching, including single character wildcards and substring matching, to a sequence of linear operations. We then rely on the observation that such linear operations, such as the inner products and matrix multiplication, can be efficiently computed in the malicious model using additively homomorphic encryption schemes.

The security requirements (informally) dictate that the party holding the text learns nothing except the upper bound on the length of the pattern, while the party holding the pattern only learns either a binary (yes/no) answer for the decision problem or the matching positions (if any), and nothing else.

1.2 Comparison to Previous Work

Exact Matching. In the exact pattern matching setting, the algorithm of Freedman, Ishai, Pinkas and Reingold [13] achieves polylogarithmic overhead in m and n and polynomial overhead in the security parameters in the honest-but-curious setting. Using efficient arguments [17,18] with the modern probabilistically checkable proofs (PCP) of proximity [19], one can extend (at least asymptotically) their results to the malicious (static corruption) model. However, the protocol in [13] works only for exact matching and does not address more general problems including single character wildcards and substring matching, which is the main focus of our work. Other protocols that address secure exact matching (and not wildcard or substring matching) are [12,20,21,22,23,11]; of these, only [22] obtains (full) security in the malicious setting. We note that [23] is more efficient than [13] but only in the random oracle model; here, we are interested in standard security models.

Single Character Wildcards. Recently, Vergnaud [14] built on the work of Hazay and Toft [16] to construct an efficient secure pattern matching scheme for wildcard matching (over arbitrary alphabets) and binary substring matching (requiring t runs over the preliminary matching result to search for t different Hamming distance values, which is also required by 5PM) in the malicious adversary model. Unlike our work, neither [14] nor [16] are able to compute

Table 1. Comparison of previous protocol functionality, NB= Non-Binary HBC = Honest but Curious, M= Malicious, *=Can be extended

Protocol	NB Hamming Distance	Exact Matching	Wildcard Matching	NB Substring Matching	Security
[13]	No	Yes	No	No	HBC/M
[14]	No	Yes	Yes	No	HBC/M
[15]	Yes	No*	No*	No*	HBC
5PM	Yes	Yes	Yes	Yes	HBC/M

Table 2. Detailed comparison with [15] for non-binary substring matching in HBC model with Text length=n, Pattern length=m, Security Parameter=k

Protocol	Encryptions	Exponentiations	Multiplications	Bandwidth	Rounds
[15]	$O(n+m)$	$O(nm)$	$O(nm)$	$O((nm)k)$	$O(1)$
5PM	$O(n+m)$	$O(n+m)$	$O(nm)$	$O((n+m)k)$	2

Table 3. Detailed comparison with [14] and [16] for arbitrary alphabets and single character wildcards in malicious model with Text length=n, Pattern length=m, Security Parameter=k

Protocol	Encryptions	Exponentiations	Multiplications	Bandwidth	Rounds
[16]	$O(mn)$	$O(mn)$	$O(mn)$	$O(mnk^2)$	$O(1)$
[14]	$O(n+m)$	$O(n\log m)$	$O(nm)$	$O((n+m)k^2)$	$O(1)$
5PM	$O(n+m)$	$O(nm)$	$O(nm)$	$O((n+m)k^2)$	8

non-binary Hamming distance or non-binary substring matching; the reason is that their schemes are built on top of oblivious polynomial evaluations that can count non-binary character matches but cannot count individual non-binary character mismatches. More specifically, [14,16] take advantage of the fact that $(p_i - t_i)^2$ equals 0 if binary values p_i and t_i are equal and 1 if they are not equal; therefore, binary Hamming distance can essentially be computed by counting the number of 1s in the computation. However, when p_i and t_i are non-binary, it is unknown how to execute oblivious polynomial computations that output 0 when p_i and t_i equal and 1 (or some other fixed value) when they do not equal. Therefore [14,16] only discuss binary Hamming distance, which may not be suitable for applications such as DNA and secure biometric substring matching as the number of binary mismatches does not generally capture the number of non-binary character mismatches. [14] requires $O(m + n)$ encryptions, $O(n\log m)$ exponentiations, $O(nm)$ multiplications (of encrypted elements), and $O(n + m)$ bandwidth, all in a constant number of rounds. By contrast, 5PM has the same overhead except for $O(nm)$ exponentiations (see Table 3).

Non-binary Hamming Distance. Jarrous and Pinkas [15] gave the first construction of a secure protocol for computing non-binary Hamming distances. In order to count the non-binary mismatches, they leverage 1-out-of-2 oblivious transfers. 5PM can also compute non-binary Hamming distance even when the text and pattern have the same length (and where the output is not blinded to only reveal whether or not a pattern match occurred). We note that [15] can be used to implement exact and substring matching with additional tools to blind Hamming distance output (for instance, see [14]). [15], to compare 2 strings of length n, requires $O(n)$ 1-out-of-2 OTs, $O(n)$ multiplications of encryptions and $O(nk)$ bandwidth, while 5PM requires $O(n)$ exponentiations (which require less computation than OTs), $O(n^2)$ multiplications, and $O(nk)$ bandwidth. The advantage of 5PM over [15] is twofold: the first is that it is proven secure in the malicious model while [15] is not. The second advantage is that 5PM, in both the honest-but-curious and malicious models, amortizes well in the substring matching setting, while [15] does not amortize because it cannot reuse OT outputs to compute substring matching (see table 2).

Other Techniques. In the most general case, secure exact, approximate and single character wildcards pattern matching is an instance of general secure two-party computation techniques (for instance, [24,25,26,27]). All of these schemes have bandwidth and computational complexity at best linear in the circuit size. For instance, a naive implementation of Yao [24] requires bandwidth $O(mn)$ in the security parameter. In contrast, we aim for a protocol where circuit size is $O(mn)$ yet we achieve communication complexity of $O(m + n)$.

Finally, we observe that with the construction of fully homomorphic encryption (FHE) schemes [28], the following "folklore" construction can be executed for any pattern matching algorithm: Client encrypts its pattern using an FHE scheme and sends it to Server. Server applies the appropriate pattern matching circuit to the encrypted pattern (where the circuits output is a *yes/no* indicating whether a match exists or not), and sends the FHE circuit output to Client. Client decrypts to obtain the answer. Such a scheme requires $O(m)$ bandwidth, but since FHE schemes are not yet practical, we view the 5PM protocol outlined here as an efficient and practical solution to secure pattern matching with single character wildcards and substring matching.

2   Preliminaries

The rationale behind our secure 5PM protocol is based on a modification of an insecure pattern matching algorithm (IPM) [29] that can perform exact matching, exact matching with single character wildcards and substring matching within the same algorithm. In Section 3.1, we show how our modified algorithm can be reduced to basic linear operations whose secure and efficient evaluation allows us to obtain our 5PM protocol.

2.1   Insecure Pattern Matching (IPM) Algorithm

To illustrate how our modified algorithm works, we begin by describing how it performs exact matching; we then show how it handles single character wildcards and substring matching.

2.1.1 Exact Matching

IPM involves the following steps:

a. *Inputs*: An alphabet Σ, a text $T \in \Sigma^n$ and a pattern $p \in \Sigma^m$.

b. *Initialization*: For each character in Σ, the algorithm constructs a vector, here termed a **Character Delay Vector** (CDV), of length equal to the pattern length, m. These vectors are initialized with zeros. For example, if the pattern is: "$TACT$" over $\Sigma = \{A, C, G, T\}$, then the CDVs will be initialized to: $CDV(A) = [0,0,0,0]$, $CDV(C) = [0,0,0,0]$, $CDV(G) = [0,0,0,0]$ and $CDV(T) = [0,0,0,0]$.

c. *Pattern preprocessing*: For each pattern character p_i ($i \in \{1, ..., m\}$), a delay value, $d_{p_i}^r$, is computed to be the number of characters from p_i to the end of the pattern, i.e., $d_{p_i}^r = m - i$ for the rth occurrence of p_i in p. The $d_{p_i}^r$th position of $CDV(p_i)$ is set to 1. For example the CDVs of "$TACT$" would be:

$CDV(A) = [0,0,1,0]$ because $d_A^1 = 4 - 2 = 2$
$CDV(C) = [0,1,0,0]$ because $d_C^1 = 4 - 3 = 1$
$CDV(G) = [0,0,0,0]$ because $G \notin p$
$CDV(T) = [1,0,0,1]$ because $d_T^1 = 4 - 4 = 0$ and $d_T^2 = 4 - 1 = 3$

d. *Matching pass and comparison with pattern length*: A vector of length n called the **Activation Vector** (AV) is constructed and its elements are initialized with zeros. For each input text character T_j, $CDV(T_j)$ is added element-wise to the AV from position j to position $\min(n, j + m - 1)$. To determine if there was a pattern match in the text, after these operations the algorithm checks (when $j \geq m$) if $AV_j = m$. If so, then the match started at position $j - m + 1$. The value $j - m + 1$ is added to the set of matching positions (MP). Note that $n - AV_j$ is the non-binary Hamming distance of the pattern and the text staring at position $j - m + 1$.

The intuition behind the algorithm is that when an input text character matches a character in the pattern, the algorithm *optimistically* assumes that the following characters will correspond to the rest of the pattern characters. It then adds a 1 at the position in the activation vector several steps ahead, where it would expect the pattern to end (if the character appears in multiple positions in the pattern, it adds a 1 to all the corresponding positions where the pattern might end). If all subsequent characters are indeed characters in the pattern, then at the position where a pattern would end the number of added 1s will sum up to the pattern length; otherwise the sum will be strictly less than the pattern length. This algorithm does not incur false positives and always indicates when (and where) a pattern occurs if it exists, as shown in [29].

2.1.2 Single Character Wildcards, Pattern Hiding and Substring Matching

Single character wildcards can be handled in IPM by representing a single character wildcard with a special character, "$*$" which is not in the text alphabet. When "$*$" is encountered in the pattern preprocessing phase it is ignored, i.e., no 1s are added to any CDV. Additionally, at the last step when elements of the

AV are searched in the comparison phase, the threshold value being compared against will be $m - l$ instead of m, where l is the number of occurrences of "*" in the pattern. The intuition behind single character wildcards is that by reducing the threshold for each wildcard, the algorithm implicitly skips matching that position in the text, allowing that position of the pattern to correspond to any character. This operation does not incur any false positives for the same reason that the exact matching IPM algorithm does not: there, for each pattern p, there is only one encoding into CDVs and only one sequence of adding CDVs as one moves along the text that could add up to m. The same reasoning holds when "*" is present in p (except that the sequence adds to $m - l$).

We note that, using single character wildcards, one can always hide pattern length by setting p' as the concatenation of p and a string of $n - m$ wildcards, $*^{n-m}$, and using p' to execute pattern matching for p.

Substring matching, or matching text substrings of Hamming distance $m - l$ from the pattern, is handled similarly to single character wildcards; the threshold value being compared against in the AV is decreased to $m - l$. For further details, we refer the reader to [29].

2.2 Preliminary Cryptographic Tools

This section outlines preliminary cryptographic tools required for our protocols. For $x, y \in \mathbb{Z}_q^n$, we define the inner product of x and y over $\mathbb{Z}_q$, denoted $\langle x, y \rangle$, as $\sum x_i y_i \bmod q$.

Additively Homomorphic Encryption: We make use of additively homomorphic semantically secure encryption schemes.

For concreteness, we concentrate in the rest of the paper on the additively homomorphic ElGamal encryption scheme whose security depends on the Decisional Diffie-Hellman (DDH) computational hardness assumption. An additively homomorphic ElGamal encryption scheme [30] is instantiated by choosing a group of appropriate prime order q, $\mathbb{G}_q$, with generator g, and setting the secret-key to be $x \in \mathbb{Z}_q$ and the public-key to be $(g, h = g^x)$. To encrypt a message m one chooses a uniformly random $r \in \mathbb{Z}_q$ and computes $(g^r, g^m h^r)$. To decrypt a pair (α, β), one computes $\log_g \frac{\beta}{\alpha^x}$. It is important to note for additive ElGamal that the decryptor has to both decrypt and also compute a discrete logarithm to discover the message. However, our scheme only requires a determination of whether an encrypted value is of a 0 or not, which can accomplished without computing logarithms.

Threshold Encryption: The malicious model version of 5PM requires an additively homomorphic, semantically secure, threshold encryption scheme [31]. While we use threshold ElGamal, in practice, any scheme is acceptable if it satisfies the required properties and supports the needed zero-knowledge arguments. Threshold ElGamal in the two party case can be informally defined as follows [32]: party P_1 has share x_1 and party P_2 has share x_2. The parties jointly set the secret-key to be $x = x_1 + x_2$ (this can be performed without revealing x_1 and x_2, see subprotocol π_{encr} in Section 3.3). Without loss of generality, P_1 partially decrypts (α, β) by sending $(\alpha, \frac{\beta}{\alpha^{x_1}})$ to P_2, who fully decrypts (α, β)

by computing $\frac{\beta}{\alpha^{x_1}\alpha^{x_2}} = \frac{\beta}{\alpha^{x_1+x_2}}$. We denote the partial decryption algorithm for party P_i as D_{P_i}.

Commitment Schemes: For the malicious model protocol, we will make use of perfectly hiding, computationally binding commitment schemes (for further discussion, see [33]). The Pedersen commitment scheme [34] is a well-known example of such a commitment scheme; for a multiplicative group of prime order q, $\mathbb{G}_q$ and for fixed generators $g, h \in \mathbb{G}_q$, commitment to message s using randomness r is $g^s h^r = comm(g, h, r, s)$.

Zero-Knowledge Arguments of Knowledge: In order to construct a protocol that guarantees that each party behaves properly even in the malicious setting, we utilize efficient interactive zero-knowledge arguments of knowledge (ZK-AoKs) (for further discussion, see [35]).

2.3 Computing Linear Operations Using Additively Homomorphic Encryption Schemes

Our secure pattern matching protocol relies on the following observations about linear operations and additively homomorphic encryption schemes. In what follows, let E be the encryption algorithm for an additively homomorphic encryption scheme for key pair (pk, sk). Suppose the plaintext group G can be expressed as $\mathbb{Z}_n$ for some $n \in \mathbb{N}$; in particular, G is a ring. Let $M_{a,b}(G)$ denote the set of matrices of size $a \times b$ with entries in G.

2.3.1 Matrix Multiplication

Consider two matrices, A and B, where $A \in M_{k,l}(G)$ and $B \in M_{l,m}(G)$. Suppose that P_1 possesses pk, $E_{pk}(A)$, the entry-wise encryption of A , and also the unencrypted matrix B. Then P_1 can compute $E_{pk}(A \cdot B)$, the encryption of the multiplication of A and B under the same pk. Such an operation is possible because one can obtain an encryption of the inner product over G of an unencrypted vector $(x_1, ..., x_m)$ with an encrypted vector $(E(y_1), ..., E(y_m))$ by computing $\Pi E(y_i)^{x_i} = E(\sum x_i y_i)$.

2.3.2 Matrix Operators

Consider a matrix $A \in M_{k,l}(G)$. One can construct a $k \times (k + l - 1)$ matrix A' by initializing A' as a matrix with all 0s and then, for each row $1 \leq i \leq k$, setting $(A'(i,i), ..., A'(i, i + l - 1)) = (A(i, 1), ..., A(i, l))$. We denote such a function by $A' \leftarrow Stretch(A)$, and note that since this function is a linear operator, it can be computed using matrix multiplication. We observe that for any encryption scheme E, $E(Stretch(A)) = Stretch(E(A))$, when E is applied to each entry in A.

Consider a matrix $A \in M_{k,l}(G)$. We denote by $Cut(A, j)$ as the matrix $A' \in M_{k, l-2j+2}$ such that for $1 \leq a \leq k$, $1 \leq b \leq l - 2j + 2$, $A'(a, b) = A(a, b + j - 1)$. In particular, such a function outputs the middle $l - 2j + 2$ columns of $M_{k,l}$. We note that Cut is a simple projection operator and is also computable by matrix multiplication. We observe that for any encryption scheme E, $E(Cut(A, j)) = Cut(E(A), j)$.

Finally, consider a matrix $A \in M_{k,l}(G)$. We denote by $ColSum(A)$ the function that takes as input A and outputs a $1 \times l$ vector whose ith entry is the sum of all entries in the i column of A. In particular, $ColSum(A) = [1....1] \cdot A$. We observe that for any additively homomorphic encryption scheme E, $ColSum(E(A)) = E(ColSum(A))$.

Since we will be composing these functions, a shorthand for their composition will be convenient. For matrices $A \in M_{k,l}(G)$ and $B \in M_{l,m}(G)$, we denote the composition function $ColSum(Cut(Stretch(A \cdot B), j))$ by $PM_{5PM}(A, B, j)$.

2.3.3   Searching an Encrypted Vector, π_{VFind}

Suppose party P_1 possesses (pk, sk) for an additively homomorphic encryption algorithm E, and a single value $m \in G$ and P_2 possesses a vector of l distinct encryptions $E_{pk}(vec)$, where $vec = (x_1, \ldots, x_l) \in G^l$. Then P_1 can determine if $E(vec)$ contains an encryption of m while learning nothing else about vec, while P_2 cannot learn m, through the following protocol π_{VFind}:

1. P_1 computes $E(-m)$ from $-m$. P_1 sends $E(-m)$ to P_2.
2. P_2 computes $E(vec')$ by multiplying (via the group operation of the ciphertext space) $E(-m)$ to each encrypted entry in $E(vec)$. Note that an entry in $E(vec')$ will be an encryption of 0 if and only if one of the encryptions of $E(vec)$ was an encryption of m. P_2 computes $E(vec^r)$ from $E(vec')$ by exponentiating each encrypted entry of $E(vec')$ by an (independent) random exponent. P_2 sends $E(vec^r)$ to P_1.
3. P_1 decrypts $E(vec^r)$ to obtain vec^r; if a 0 exists at position i, the ith position of $E(vec)$ is $E(m)$.

Note that if P_2 wishes to hide the position of $E(m)$ from P_1, P_2 could randomly permute the positions of $E(vec^r)$ and send the permuted vector to P_1.

2.3.4   Efficiently Determining Equality of Two Matrices, π_{VecEQ}

Suppose parties P_1 and P_2 have agreed upon an additively homomorphic threshold encryption scheme E_{th}. Further, suppose P_1 and P_2, possess encrypted matrices $E_{th}(A) \in M_{k,l}(G')$ and $E_{th}(B) \in M_{k,l}(G')$, respectively, where the message space G' is the group $\mathbb{Z}_q$, for a prime q. Let D_{P_i} denote the partial decryption algorithm of party P_i. P_1 and P_2 wish to determine if their encrypted matrices are equal without exchanging their decryptions. They can do so by hashing their encrypted matrices to a single group element and exchanging the outcome of the hashes. More specifically, an affine hash function $\mathbb{Z}_q^{kl} \to \mathbb{Z}_q$ can be specified by letting P_1 and P_2 jointly compute a uniformly random pair $(a, b) \in \mathbb{Z}_q^{kl} \times \mathbb{Z}_q$ using standard commitment techniques and setting the hash to $hf(x) = \langle x, a \rangle + b$, where $\langle \cdot, \cdot \rangle$ is the inner product over $\mathbb{Z}_q$ (here, we consider the matrices as kl-length strings). Note that such a hash function can be computed on encrypted strings because the encryption scheme is additively homomorphic. Denote by $comm$ a (perfectly hiding, computationally binding) commitment scheme; in practice we use Pedersen commitments [34]. We denote the following subprotocol by π_{VecEQ}:

1. P_1 selects $(a_1, b_1) \in \mathbb{Z}_q^{kl} \times \mathbb{Z}_q$ uniformly at random and computes $E_{th}(b_1)$. P_1 computes and sends
   $comm(a_1), comm(E_{th}(b_1)), comm(E_{th}(A))$ to P_2.
2. P_2 selects $(a_2, b_2) \in \mathbb{Z}_q^{kl} \times \mathbb{Z}_q$ uniformly at random and computes $E_{th}(b_2)$. P_2 sends $a_2, E_{th}(b_2), E_{th}(B)$ to P_1.
3. P_1 sets $a = a_1 + a_2$, $E_{th}(b) = E_{th}(b_1 + b_2)$ and computes $z_1 = E_{th}(\langle a, A \rangle + b)$, $z_2 = E_{th}(\langle a, B \rangle + b)$. P_1 decommits to a_1, $E_{th}(b_1)$ and $E_{th}(A)$ to P_2 and sends $D_{P_1}(z_1)$, $D_{P_1}(z_2)$ to P_2.
4. P_2 aborts if it does not accept the decommitments, else P_2 sets $a = a_1 + a_2$, $E_{th}(b) = E_{th}(b_1 + b_2)$ and computes $z_1 = E_{th}(\langle a, A \rangle + b)$, $z_2 = E_{th}(\langle a, B \rangle + b)$. P_2 sends $D_{P_2}(z_1)$, $D_{P_2}(z_2)$, $D_{P_2}(D_{P_1}(z_1))$, and $D_{P_2}(D_{P_1}(z_2))$ to P_1.
5. P_1 aborts if $D_{P_2}(D_{P_1}(z_1)) \neq D_{P_2}(D_{P_1}(z_2))$, otherwise P_1 sends $D_{P_1}(D_{P_2}(z_1))$ and $D_{P_1}(D_{P_2}(z_2))$ to P_2.
6. P_2 aborts if $D_{P_1}(D_{P_2}(z_1)) \neq D_{P_1}(D_{P_2}(z_2))$.

The bandwidth complexity of π_{VecEQ} is dominated by the size of $E_{th}(A)$ (and $E_{th}(B)$). Only with probability $1/q$ will the decryptions equal each other when $A \neq B$ because the hash function is chosen uniformly at random. In the malicious case, arguments of consistency for correct partial decryptions will also be needed.

3   5PM Protocol

This section utilizes the above observations and cryptographic tools to construct the secure pattern matching protocol (5PM). We develop π_{5PM}^H for the honest-but-curious adversary model and π_{5PM}^M for the malicious (static corruption) adversary model.

3.1   Converting IPM to Linear Operations

For a fixed alphabet Σ, a text $T \in \Sigma^n$, and pattern $p \in (\Sigma \cup \{*\})^m$, IPM can be represented in terms of linear operations described in Section 2.3 as follows:

a. The text T can be transformed into an $n \times |\Sigma|$ matrix, M_T. The transformation is performed by applying a unary encoding of alphabet characters to T, i.e., $M_T(i, T_i) = 1, \forall i \in \{1, ..., n\}$; all other entries in M_T are 0. We denote the algorithm that computes M_T from T as $M_T \leftarrow Gen_{M_T}(T)$.
b. The CDVs of alphabet characters can be grouped into a $|\Sigma| \times m$ matrix, M_{CDV}. This step is equivalent to constructing CDVs for alphabet characters (steps b and c in Section 2.1.1). We denote the algorithm that compute M_{CDV} from p as $M_{CDV} \leftarrow Gen_{M_{CDV}}(p)$.
c. Multiply M_T by M_{CDV} to obtain an $n \times m$ matrix $M_{T(CDV)}$ that represents T row-wise in terms of CDVs, where the ith row is $CDV(T_i)$. In reality, since M_T and M_{CDV} are 0/1 matrices, multiplication is more computationally expensive than necessary, and vectors can simply be selected (as shown in IPM description in Section 2.1).
d. Compute $\overline{M}_{T(CDV)} = Stretch(M_{T(CDV)})$. This transformation, jointly with the previous step, constructs a matrix of CDVs where the ith row

contains only $CDV(T_i)$, which starts in the ith position in the ith row (sets up step d in Section 2.1.1).

e. Compute $AV = ColSum(Cut(\overline{M}_{T(CDV)}, m))$ to obtain the final activation vector AV of length $n - m + 1$. Entries in AV are checked to see if any are equal to the threshold value m, or $m - l$ for single character wildcards or substring matching (completes step d in Section 2.1.1).

A key observation is that if only one of M_T and M_{CDV} are encrypted, an encrypted activation vector, $E(AV)$ can be obtained by both parties as shown in Sections 2.3.1 and 2.3.2.

3.2 Honest-But-Curious (HBC) 5PM Protocol

We begin by describing the intuition behind required modifications to secure IPM in the HBC adversary model. We then describe details of the HBC protocol, π_{5PM}^H.

3.2.1 Protocol Intuition

For an additively homomorphic encryption scheme E, if Client sends Server $E(M_{CDV})$, by the reasoning of Sections 2.3 and 3.1, since the pattern matching operation can be reduced to a sequence of linear operations (namely matrix multiplication and the functions $Stretch$, Cut, and $ColSum$), Server can compute $E(AV)$, an encrypted activation vector, using only M_T and $E(M_{CDV})$. Since Client sends only $E(M_{CDV})$ and $E(m - l)$, Server learns nothing about Client's pattern due to semantic security of the encryption scheme.

Next, Client, for pattern matching threshold m (or $m - l$ in the single character wildcards/substring matching case) executes π_{VFind} specified in Section 2.3.3, where Client uses $E(AV)$, to discover whether (and where) a pattern exists. By the security of π_{VFind}, Server does not learn m and Client learns nothing about $E(AV)$ other than whether or not (and where, if the pattern matching locations are not hidden by Server) an encryption of m exists in $E(AV)$. In practice, Client sends $E(m)$ in the same (first) round as $E(M_{CDV})$, and Server's response to π_{VFind} occurs in the second round, concluding execution of the secure pattern matching protocol.

3.2.2 π_{5PM}^H Protocol Specification

Recall that, over a specified alphabet Σ, Server holds text $T \in \Sigma^n$ and Client holds a pattern $p \in (\Sigma \cup \{*\})^m$. The output of Server is an encrypted activation vector $E(AV)$ of length n. We refer the reader to Sections 3.1 and 2.3.2 for the notation used here. The protocol operation is as follows:

1. Client computes $(sk, pk) \leftarrow Key(1^k)$ using the key generation algorithm of an additively homomorphic encryption scheme, E.
2. Client computes $M_{CDV} \leftarrow Gen_{CDV}(p)$. In the case where Client wishes to hide the length of p, Client computes M_{CDV} for the pattern p' equal to the concatenation of p with $*^{n-m}$.
3. Client encrypts M_{CDV} entry-wise using public-key pk to obtain $E(M_{CDV})$.

4. Client sends $E(M_{CDV})$ and pk to Server. In addition, Client sends $E(-m)$ (or $E(-m+l)$ in the single character wildcards or substring matching cases).
5. Server computes $M_T \leftarrow Gen_T(T)$. Server computes $E(AV) = E(PM_{5PM}(M_T, M_{CDV}, m))$, which is computed as specified in Section 2.3.1 and Section 2.3.2.
6. Server executes round 2 of π_{VFind} (see Section 2.3.3) using $E(-m)$ and $E(AV)$. Server sends output of the subprotocol, denoted $E(AV_S^r)$, to Client.
7. Optional: Per π_{VFind}, Server randomly permutes $E(AV_S^r)$ to hide possible pattern match locations.
8. Client executes round 3 of π_{VFind} using $E(AV_S^r)$ to determine results of the pattern matching.

We note that π_{5PM}^H can perform substring matching for multiple substring lengths (such as for a Hamming distance bound) simultaneously by sending multiple $E(m-l)$ values at step 6 in the above specification. Then, for each value of l, Server constructs a distinct $E(AV)$ and sends Client a distinct corresponding $E(AV_S^r)$ indicating matching locations for that l value. In particular, π_{5PM}^H does not require multiple independent protocol executions to compute substring matching for a range of substring length values. In addition, π_{5PM}^H can simply compute the Hamming distance of the pattern with each consecutive m positions of the text by simply not executing π_{VFind} and sending the output of the protocol at step 5, and Client can decrypt to obtain all of the Hamming distance values between the pattern and the text.

Theorem 1. *Given an additively homomorphic semantically secure encryption scheme over a prime-order cyclic group (Key, E, D), π_{5PM}^H is secure in the HBC model.*

See the full version for a detailed security proof.

3.3 Malicious Model 5PM Protocol

In this section, we explain how to modify π_{5PM}^H to obtain a protocol, π_{5PM}^M, which is secure in the malicious (static corruption) model. We describe an instantiation of π_{5PM}^M based on additively homomorphic threshold ElGamal encryption (see Section 2.2) for concreteness; generalization to other encryption schemes follows provided they have efficient Σ protocols for the statements required here. First, we explain intuition behind π_{5PM}^M. Second, we give interactive zero-knowledge consistency arguments that will be required. Finally, we divide π_{5PM}^M into 6 subprotocols and describe their construction and how they are combined into the final protocol π_{5PM}^M. In the interest of clarity and space, we leave the exact protocol specification and security proof to the full version of this paper. Note that this protocol, as noted in Section 2.1.2, can be modified to both hide pattern length (by using, for pattern p, the pattern p' equal to to p concatenated with $*^{n-m}$) and also to match against multiple substring values without multiple executions of the entire protocol (i.e., by sending multiple $E(m-l)$ values and computing a new activation vector for each value).

3.3.1   Protocol Intuition

The 8 round protocol for the malicious model, π_{5PM}^{M}, consists of the following six subprotocols:

1. π_{encr}: initializes an additively homomorphic threshold encryption scheme.
2. $\pi_{S,AV}$: allows Server to construct an encrypted activation vector for Client's encrypted pattern and Server's text.
3. $\pi_{C,AV}$: allows Client to construct an encrypted activation vector for Client's pattern and Server's encrypted text.
4. π_{vec}: allows Client and Server to verify that their activation vectors are equal without revealing them.
5. π_{rand}: allows Server to send an encryption of its randomized activation vector to Client.
6. π_{ans}: demonstrates to Client where the pattern matches the text (if at all).

The intuition behind constructing π_{5PM}^{M} is as follows: in π_{5PM}^{H}, only Server performs the computation to obtain the activation vector, AV. In the malicious setting, Client has to verify that Server correctly computed AV. Since Server performs $O(nm)$ multiplications when computing AV in π_{5PM}^{H}, requiring a zero-knowledge argument for each multiplication therefore would require bandwidth of at least $O(nm)$. Such overhead is unacceptable if bandwidth $O(n + m)$ is desired.

We utilize a more bandwidth-efficient approach to ensure that a malicious Server has computed the correct AV: in π_{5PM}^{M}, both Client and Server perform secure pattern matching independently using the function PM_{5PM} where one of M_{CDV} and M_T are encrypted, and then compare their results. Each party computes an AV in parallel (see subprotocols $\pi_{C,AV}$ and $\pi_{S,AV}$, respectively, in Section 3.3.3) using an additively homomorphic threshold encryption scheme (instantiated using subprotocol π_{encr} in Section 3.3.3). To ensure that no cheating has occurred, Client and Server then check that each other's AV was computed correctly. Therefore, proving that Server has behaved honestly is reduced to proving that Client and Server have obtained the same result from matching p against T. To efficiently perform comparison of encrypted AVs, Client and Server check that their encrypted AVs are equal using subprotocol π_{VecEQ} described in Section 2.3.4 (in addition to some zero-knowledge arguments to demonstrate well-formedness). Only if hashed AV values match will Server provide Client with its decrypted (and blinded) AV (using the subprotocols π_{rand} and π_{ans} in Section 3.3.3). The comparison subprotocol is denoted by π_{vec} in Section 3.3.3.

Throughout, both Client and Server will have to use various arguments of consistency outlined in Section 3.3.2 to prove that they have not deviated from the protocol.

There is one additional technical difficulty that we have to overcome: in order to prove security we must provide simulators that simulate transcripts when interacting with adversarial parties (see full version for security definitions and simulator constructions). When constructing the Simulator for Client's view, Simulator receives the actual answer that it must provide to Client from the ideal functionality only at the last moment (if Client does not abort). Thus, the

Simulator must provide a final answer which is not consistent with the previous interactions, while the real Server must be unable to do so. To achieve this, we demonstrate that the Simulator can extract the knowledge of the exponent of some h^* specified by Client during the first subprotocol (π_{encr}); then, the final subprotocol (π_{ans}) utilizes a zero-knowledge argument of knowledge that demonstrates that either the final randomized AV is correct or that Server knows the discrete logarithm of h^*. Since a real Server cannot extract the discrete logarithm of h^* but the Simulator can by construction, this allows the Simulator to reveal the correct randomized AV even when it is inconsistent with the previous outputs of the conversation. We stress that we do not use NP-reductions and rather build highly efficient protocols to fit our needs.

3.3.2 Zero-Knowledge Arguments of Knowledge (ZK-AoKs) of Consistency

We first describe five required interactive arguments which we rely on to prove statements required for the π_{5PM}^M protocol. They are designed for use with the specified threshold ElGamal encryption scheme (Section 2.2). We apply a standard construction outlined in the full version of this paper to transform three-move arguments of knowledge and construct five-move ZK arguments of knowledge π_{DL}, π_{isBit}, π_{eqDL} and π_{fin}, respectively. All ZK-AoKs are executed between a prover P and a verifier V in five moves; we note that either Client or Server may execute the arguments of consistency as P while the other party will then execute as V. π_{DL} is the only ZK-AoK used on its own in π_{5PM}^M; it proves knowledge of a discrete logarithm of a public $h = g^x$. π_{isBIT} is a ZK-AoK that proves that an encryption is either of a 0 or of a 1, π_{eqDL} is a ZK-AoK that proves that two discrete logarithms are equal, and π_{fin} is a ZK-AoK that proves that *either* two discrete logarithms are equal *or* that P knows the discrete logarithm of a public $h = g^x$. The five required interactive arguments are:

1. **A$_{M01}$**, an *AoK of Consistency for Matrix formation 0/1*: P, for an $l \times u$ matrix of encryptions, $E(M)$, proves to V that each column of $E(M)$ contains encryptions of 0 and at most one 1.
2. **A$_{M1}$**, an *AoK of Consistency for Matrix formation 0/1-1*: P, for an $l \times u$ matrix of encryptions, $E(M)$, proves to V that each row of $E(M)$ contains encryptions of 0 and *exactly* one 1.
3. **A$_{PD}$**, an *AoK of Consistency for Partial Decryption*: P, for a vector of l encryptions, (x_i, y_i) and a vector of their l partial decryptions (x_i', y_i'), proves to V that the partial decryptions are correctly constructed.
4. **A$_{Rand}$**, an *AoK of Consistency for Randomization*: P, for a vector of l encryptions (x_i, y_i) and a vector of their exponentiations, $(x_i^{r_i}, y_i^{r_i})$, proves to V that P knows r_i for each i.
5. **A$_{FD}$**, an *AoK of Consistency for Final Decryption*: P, for a vector of l encryptions (x_i, y_i), their partial decryptions (x_i', y_i'), and some g^w, proves to V that either P has computed all the partial decryptions correctly *or* that possesses the discrete logarithm w of g^w.

3.3.3 π_{5PM}^M Protocol Outline

We provide the details of π_{5PM}^M by describing individual subprotocols that constitute it, π_{encr}, $\pi_{S,AV}$, $\pi_{C,AV}$, π_{vec}, π_{rand} and π_{ans}. These subprotocols utilize the interactive arguments described in Section 3.3.2 to prove various statements of consistency. We denote by $comm(s)$ as the (perfectly hiding, computationally binding) commitment of s, which using Pedersen commitments [34] is $g^s h^r = comm(g, h, r, s)$. For the exact protocol specification of π_{5PM}^M, including precisely how the subprotocols are interleaved so that π_{5PM}^M requires only 8 rounds, see the full version; we will however mention here during which global rounds (1 through 8) these subprotocols occur.

We remark that in our construction of ZK arguments of knowledge from Σ protocols, whenever a ZK subprotocol is required, the first two rounds of the five round protocol can be completed in parallel at the very beginning of the overall protocol π_{5PM}^M. Such "preprocessing" does not affect security. Further, knowledge extraction used in the security proofs is not affected by this preprocessing.

$\pi_{\mathbf{encr}}$ is a two party protocol executed between Client and Server that initializes an additively homomorphic threshold encryption scheme (e.g., ElGamal) and also sets up an independent "trapdoor" s^* alluded to in Section 3.3.1 and required for the simulator in the security proof. In the ElGamal case, for simplicity, we assume that Client and Server have already agreed on appropriate prime q such that $\log q = O(k)$, $\mathbb{G}_q$ and $g \in \mathbb{G}_q$. This subprotocol begins at the first global round and ends at global round 6. Client chooses its secret-key s_C and trapdoor s^*, and sets $h_1 \leftarrow g^{s_C}$, $h^* \leftarrow g^{s^*}$. Client sends h_1, h^* to Server. Client executes two parallel instantiations of π_{DL} proving knowledge of the discrete logs of h_1 and h^* (i.e., s_C and s^*). Then, Server chooses its secret-key s_S, sets $h_2 \leftarrow g^{s_S}$, and sends h_2 to Client and executes π_{DL} proving knowledge of the discrete logarithm of h_2 (i.e., s_S). Both parties set the public-key to be $h = h_1 h_2 = g^{s_C + s_S}$.

$\pi_{\mathbf{C,AV}}$ is a two party protocol executed between Client and Server which outputs to Client an encrypted activation vector $E(AV_C)$ corresponding to matching Client's p against Server's T. This subprotocol starts at global round 2 and ends at global round 6. First, Server constructs $M_T \leftarrow Gen_{M_T}(T)$ as specified in Section 3.1. Then, Server encrypts M_T and sends $E(M_T)$ to Client. Server also executes, for $E(M_T)$, A_{M1} to prove that $E(M_T)$ is formatted correctly (namely, that each row of $E(M_T)$ has one encryption of a 1 per row and encryptions of 0 everywhere else- therefore each row of $E(M_T)$ corresponds to the encoding of exactly one element of the alphabet Σ). Client then obtains $E(AV_C)$ by computing $E(PM_{5PM}(M_T, M_{CDV}, m))$ (see Section 2.3.2) and then multiplying each encryption by $E(-p_t)$ (where p_t is the pattern matching threshold), observing the function PM_{5PM} can be computed using encrypted $E(M_T)$.

$\pi_{\mathbf{S,AV}}$ is a two party protocol executed between Client and Server which outputs to Server an encrypted activation vector corresponding to matching Client's p against Server's T. This subprotocol starts at global round 3 and ends at global round 5, with ZK preprocessing occurring during global rounds 1 and 2. Client encrypts M_{CDV} and p_t and sends $E(M_{CDV})$ and $E(p_t)$ to

Server. Client also executes A_{M01} to prove that $E(M_{CDV})$ is formatted correctly (namely, $E(M_{CDV})$ consists of at most one encryption of 1 per column and consists of encryptions of 0 everywhere else, therefore ensuring that there is at most one character delay value per distance). Server computes $E(AV_S)$ by computing $E(PM_{5PM}(M_T, M_{CDV}, m))$ and then multiplying each encryption by $E(-p_t)$ (this slightly differs from Server's actions during π_{5PM}^H since the consistency proof of π_{vec} must also include subtraction of the pattern matching threshold p_t).

$\pi_{\mathbf{vec}}$ is a two party protocol executed between Client and Server that outputs to each party whether their respective encrypted activation vectors are equal (without revealing their values). This subprotocol begins at global round 3 and ends at global round 8, with ZK preprocessing occurring during global rounds 1, 2 and 3. Client computes $E(AV_C')$ by multiplying each element of AV_C with an encryption of 0; Server computes $E(AV_S')$ from $E(AV_S)$ similarly. Client and Server execute π_{VecEQ} (see Section 2.3.4) where Client has input $E(AV_C')$ and Server has input $E(AV_S')$. In addition, whenever a party sends the other a partial decryption, they execute A_{PD} to prove that the execution is well formed. Note that the probability that π_{VecEQ} will complete without abort for unequal vectors AV_S and AV_C is negligible ($\frac{1}{q}$).

$\pi_{\mathbf{rand}}$ is a two party protocol executed between Client and Server that outputs to Client an encrypted vector $E(AV_S^r)$ that contains randomizations of the values in non-matching (non-zero) positions in $E(AV_S')$. This subprotocol starts at global round 6 and ends at global round 8, with ZK preprocessing occurring during global rounds 2 and 3. Server computes $E(AV_S^r)$ from $E(AV_S')$ by exponentiating each encryption in $E(AV_S')$ by a random value. Server sends $E(AV_S^r)$ to Client and executes A_{rand} to prove that $E(AV_S^r)$ was obtained correctly from $E(AV_S')$.

$\pi_{\mathbf{ans}}$ is a two party protocol executed between Client and Server that outputs to Client the randomization, AV_S^r, of Server's activation vector AV_S. Note that AV_S^r will have a 0 wherever there is a match; every non-matching entry will contain a random element. Client is assumed to already know $E(AV_S^r)$. This subprotocol starts at global round 6 and ends at global round 8, with ZK preprocessing occurring during global rounds 2 and 3. We present a slightly modified version of the actual subprotocol used because this protocol in practice must be rearranged slightly to keep π_{5PM}^M at 8 rounds (see full version for details). Server sends $D_S(E(AV_S^r))$ to Client and executes A_{FD} to prove that either $D_S(E(AV_S^r))$ was obtained correctly or that Server knows s^* (for h^* sent by Client in the first round of π_{encr}). Client aborts if it does not accept A_{FD} and otherwise obtains AV_S^r by computing $D_C(D_S(E(AV_S^r)))$.

Protocol Efficiency and Security. Overall bandwidth of π_{5PM}^M is dominated by the $O(m|\Sigma|)$ encrypted values that Client sends to Server in $\pi_{S,AV}$ and $O(n|\Sigma|)$ encrypted values that Server sends to Client in $\pi_{C,AV}$ and π_{ans}. Since alphabet size, $|\Sigma|$, is constant, we obtain the desired bandwidth, including the ZK protocols, of $O((m+n)k^2)$ for security parameter k and total number of encryptions of $O(m+n)$. In particular, when Client hides pattern size, the corresponding pattern will have length n and therefore the bandwidth complexity is $O(nk^2)$. Computational complexity for Client is dominated by the subprotocol $\pi_{C,AV}$ where Client performs $O(mn)$ exponentiations of encrypted elements, and computational complexity for Server is dominated by subprotocols $\pi_{S,AV}$, where Server performs $O(mn)$ multiplications of encrypted elements, and π_{vec} and π_{ans}, where $O(nk)$ exponentiations are needed for the ZK protocols.

Theorem 2. *Assuming that the Decisional Diffie-Hellman (DDH) problem is hard, π_{5PM}^M is secure in the malicious (static corruption) model.*

See the full version for detailed security proofs.

4   Implementation Results

We implemented π_{5PM}^H in C++ using several additively homomorphic encryption schemes (including additive ElGamal) to show that the protocol is efficient in performing secure single character wildcards and substring pattern matching. For example, using fast-decryption Paillier [36], for $k = 1024$ and using the DNA alphabet, performing secure single character wildcards and substring pattern matching can be performed in 64 seconds for a pattern of 100 characters and a text of 100,000 characters.

We note that while π_{5PM}^H can easily be shown to have security that reduces to the semantic security of Paillier encryption, we will require Paillier-specific ZK-AoKs in order to use Paillier encryption in π_{5PM}^M.

Acknowledgments. The work of the first and fourth author is supported in part by NSF grants 0830803, 09165174, 1065276, 1118126 and 1136174, US-Israel BSF grant 2008411, OKAWA Foundation Research Award, IBM Faculty Research Award, Xerox Faculty Research Award, B. John Garrick Foundation Award, Teradata Research Award, and Lockheed-Martin Corporation Research Award. This material is based upon work supported by the Defense Advanced Research Projects Agency throug h the U.S. Office of Naval Research under Contract N00014-11-1-0392. The views expressed are those of the author and do not reflect the official policy or position of the Department of Defense or the U.S. Government.

References

1. Al-Khalifa, S., Jagadish, H.V., Patel, J.M., Wu, Y., Koudas, N., Srivastava, D.: Structural joins: A primitive for efficient xml query pattern matching. In: ICDE 2002, pp. 141–152 (2002)
2. Namjoshi, K., Narlikar, G.: Robust and fast pattern matching for intrusion detection. In: INFOCOM 2010, pp. 740–748. IEEE Press (2010)
3. Osadchy, M., Pinkas, B., Jarrous, A., Moskovich, B.: Scifi - a system for secure face identification. In: IEEE S&P 2010, pp. 239–254. IEEE Computer Society (2010)

4. Tumeo, A., Villa, O.: Accelerating dna analysis applications on gpu clusters. In: SASP 2010, pp. 71–76. IEEE Computer Society (2010)
5. Betel, D., Hogue, C.: Kangaroo - a pattern-matching program for biological sequences. BMC Bioinformatics 3(1), 20 (2002)
6. Tsai, T.H.: Average case analysis of the Boyer-Moore algorithm. Random Struct. Algorithms 28, 481–498 (2006)
7. Aho, A.V., Corasick, M.J.: Efficient string matching: an aid to bibliographic search. Commun. ACM 18(6), 333–340 (1975)
8. Knuth, D.E., Morris Jr., J.H., Pratt, V.R.: Fast pattern matching in strings. SIAM J. Comput. 6(2), 323–350 (1977)
9. Karp, R.M., Rabin, M.O.: Efficient randomized pattern-matching algorithms. IBM J. Res. Dev. 31, 249–260 (1987)
10. Baldi, P., Baronio, R., De Cristofaro, E., Gasti, P., Tsudik, G.: Countering gattaca: efficient and secure testing of fully-sequenced human genomes. In: CCS 2011, pp. 691–702. ACM (2011)
11. Katz, J., Malka, L.: Secure text processing with applications to private DNA matching. In: CCS 2010, pp. 485–492. ACM (2010)
12. Troncoso-Pastoriza, J.R., Katzenbeisser, S., Celik, M.: Privacy preserving error resilient DNA searching through oblivious automata. In: CCS 2007, pp. 519–528. ACM (2007)
13. Freedman, M.J., Ishai, Y., Pinkas, B., Reingold, O.: Keyword Search and Oblivious Pseudorandom Functions. In: Kilian, J. (ed.) TCC 2005. LNCS, vol. 3378, pp. 303–324. Springer, Heidelberg (2005)
14. Vergnaud, D.: Efficient and Secure Generalized Pattern Matching via Fast Fourier Transform. In: Nitaj, A., Pointcheval, D. (eds.) AFRICACRYPT 2011. LNCS, vol. 6737, pp. 41–58. Springer, Heidelberg (2011)
15. Jarrous, A., Pinkas, B.: Secure Hamming Distance Based Computation and Its Applications. In: Abdalla, M., Pointcheval, D., Fouque, P.-A., Vergnaud, D. (eds.) ACNS 2009. LNCS, vol. 5536, pp. 107–124. Springer, Heidelberg (2009)
16. Hazay, C., Toft, T.: Computationally Secure Pattern Matching in the Presence of Malicious Adversaries. In: Abe, M. (ed.) ASIACRYPT 2010. LNCS, vol. 6477, pp. 195–212. Springer, Heidelberg (2010)
17. Kilian, J.: A note on efficient zero-knowledge proofs and arguments (extended abstract). In: STOC 1992, pp. 723–732. ACM (1992)
18. Micali, S.: Cs proofs. In: FOCS 1994, pp. 436–453. IEEE Computer Society (1994)
19. Ben-Sasson, E., Goldreich, O., Harsha, P., Sudan, M., Vadhan, S.P.: Robust PCPs of proximity, shorter PCPs, and applications to coding. SIAM J. Comput. 36(4), 889–974 (2006)
20. Frikken, K.B.: Practical Private DNA String Searching and Matching through Efficient Oblivious Automata Evaluation. In: Gudes, E., Vaidya, J. (eds.) Data and Applications Security XXIII. LNCS, vol. 5645, pp. 81–94. Springer, Heidelberg (2009)
21. Hazay, C., Lindell, Y.: Efficient Protocols for Set Intersection and Pattern Matching with Security Against Malicious and Covert Adversaries. In: Canetti, R. (ed.) TCC 2008. LNCS, vol. 4948, pp. 155–175. Springer, Heidelberg (2008)
22. Gennaro, R., Hazay, C., Sorensen, J.S.: Text Search Protocols with Simulation Based Security. In: Nguyen, P.Q., Pointcheval, D. (eds.) PKC 2010. LNCS, vol. 6056, pp. 332–350. Springer, Heidelberg (2010)
23. Mohassel, P., Niksefat, S., Sadeghian, S., Sadeghiyan, B.: An efficient protocol for oblivious dfa evaluation and applications (2012)

24. Yao, A.C.C.: How to generate and exchange secrets. In: FOCS 1986, pp. 162–167. IEEE Computer Society (1986)
25. Goldreich, O., Micali, S., Wigderson, A.: How to play any mental game. In: STOC 1987, pp. 218–229. ACM (1987)
26. Ishai, Y., Prabhakaran, M., Sahai, A.: Founding Cryptography on Oblivious Transfer – Efficiently. In: Wagner, D. (ed.) CRYPTO 2008. LNCS, vol. 5157, pp. 572–591. Springer, Heidelberg (2008)
27. Damgård, I., Orlandi, C.: Multiparty Computation for Dishonest Majority: From Passive to Active Security at Low Cost. In: Rabin, T. (ed.) CRYPTO 2010. LNCS, vol. 6223, pp. 558–576. Springer, Heidelberg (2010)
28. Gentry, C.: Fully homomorphic encryption using ideal lattices. In: STOC 2009, pp. 169–178. ACM (2009)
29. Hoffmann, H., Howard, M.D., Daily, M.J.: Fast pattern matching with time-delay neural networks. In: IJCNN 2011, pp. 2424–2429 (2011)
30. Cramer, R., Gennaro, R., Schoenmakers, B.: A Secure and Optimally Efficient Multi-authority Election Scheme. In: Fumy, W. (ed.) EUROCRYPT 1997. LNCS, vol. 1233, pp. 103–118. Springer, Heidelberg (1997)
31. Desmedt, Y.G., Frankel, Y.: Threshold Cryptosystems. In: Brassard, G. (ed.) CRYPTO 1989. LNCS, vol. 435, pp. 307–315. Springer, Heidelberg (1990)
32. Brandt, F.: Efficient Cryptographic Protocol Design Based on Distributed El Gamal Encryption. In: Won, D., Kim, S. (eds.) ICISC 2005. LNCS, vol. 3935, pp. 32–47. Springer, Heidelberg (2006)
33. Goldreich, O.: Foundations of Cryptography: Basic Tools. Cambridge University Press, New York (2000)
34. Pedersen, T.P.: Non-interactive and Information-Theoretic Secure Verifiable Secret Sharing. In: Feigenbaum, J. (ed.) CRYPTO 1991. LNCS, vol. 576, pp. 129–140. Springer, Heidelberg (1992)
35. Damgård, I.: On Σ protocols, www.daimi.au.dk/~ivan/Sigma.pdf
36. Paillier, P.: Public-Key Cryptosystems Based on Composite Degree Residuosity Classes. In: Stern, J. (ed.) EUROCRYPT 1999. LNCS, vol. 1592, pp. 223–238. Springer, Heidelberg (1999)

Implementing AES via an Actively/Covertly Secure Dishonest-Majority MPC Protocol

Ivan Damgård[1], Marcel Keller[2], Enrique Larraia[2],
Christian Miles[2], and Nigel P. Smart[2]

[1] Department of Computer Science,
University of Aarhus,
IT-parken, Aabogade 34, DK-8200 Aarhus N,
Denmark
[2] Dept. Computer Science,
University of Bristol,
Woodland Road,
Bristol, BS8 1UB,
United Kingdom

Abstract. We describe an implementation of the protocol of Damgård, Pastro, Smart and Zakarias (SPDZ/Speedz) for multi-party computation in the presence of a dishonest majority of active adversaries. We present a number of modifications to the protocol; the first reduces the security to covert security, but produces significant performance enhancements; the second enables us to perform bit-wise operations in characteristic two fields. As a bench mark application we present the evaluation of the AES cipher, a now standard bench marking example for multi-party computation. We need examine two different implementation techniques, which are distinct from prior MPC work in this area due to the use of MACs within the SPDZ protocol. We then examine two implementation choices for the finite fields; one based on finite fields of size 2^8 and one based on embedding the AES field into a larger finite field of size 2^{40}.

1 Introduction

The invention of secure multi-party computation is one of the crowning achievements of theoretical cryptography, yet despite being invented around twenty-five years ago it has only recently been implemented and tested in practice. In the last few years a number of MPC "systems" have appeared [4,7,8,9,12,15,22], as well as experimental research results [13,16,21,25,26].

The work (both theoretical and practical) can be essentially divided into two camps. On one side we have techniques based on Yao circuits [28], which are mainly focused on two party computations, and on the other we have techniques based on secret sharing [6,11], which can be applied to more general numbers of players. This is rather a coarse divide as some techniques, such as that from [25], only apply in the two party case but it is based on secret sharing as opposed to Yao circuits. Following this coarse divide we can then divide work into those which consider only honest-but-curious adversaries and those which consider more general active adversaries.

I. Visconti and R. De Prisco (Eds.): SCN 2012, LNCS 7485, pp. 241–263, 2012.
© Springer-Verlag Berlin Heidelberg 2012

As in theory, it turns out that in practice obtaining active security is a much more challenging task; requiring more computational and communication resources. All prior implementation reports to our knowledge for active adversaries have either been in the two party setting, or have restricted themselves to the multi-party setting with honest majority. In the two party setting one can adopt specialist protocols, such as those based on Yao circuits, whilst the restriction to honest majority in the multi-party setting means that cheaper information theoretic constructions can be employed. Recently, Damgård et al [14] following on from work in [5], presented an actively secure protocol (dubbed "SPDZ" and pronounced "Speedz") in the multi-party setting which is secure in the presence of dishonest majority. The paper [14] contains some simple implementation results, and extrapolated estimates, but it does not report on a fully working implementation which computes a specific function.

Whilst active security is the "gold standard" of security, many applications can accept a weaker notion called covert security [1,2]. In this model a dishonest party deviating from the protocol will be detected with high probability; as opposed to the overwhelming probability required by active security. Due to the weaker requirements, covert security can often be achieved for less computational effort.

Our Contribution. As already remarked much progress has been made on implementation of MPC protocols in the last few years, but most of the "fast" implementations have been for simpler security models. For example prior work has focused on protocols for two party computation only, or honest-but-curious adversaries only, or for threshold adversaries only. In this work we extend the prior implementation work to the most complex setting namely covert and active security against a dishonest majority. In addition we examine more than four players; with some experiments being carried out with ten players. Thus our work shows that even such stringent security requirements and parameter settings are beginning to be within reach of practical application of MPC technology.

More concretely, we show how to simplify the SPDZ protocol so that it achieves covert security for a greatly improved computational performance, we present the first implementation results for the SPDZ protocol (in both the active and covert cases), and we describe an evaluation of the AES functionality with this protocol. Our protocol implementation is in the random oracle model, specifically the zero-knowledge proofs required by SPDZ are implemented using the Fiat–Shamir heuristic. We also simplify some other parts of the SPDZ protocol in the random oracle model (details are provided below), and present extensions to enable bit-wise operations in characteristic two fields.

Since the work of [26] it has become common to measure the performance of an MPC protocol with the time it takes to evaluate the AES functionality. This is for a number of reasons: Firstly AES provides a well understood function which is designed to be highly non-linear, secondly AES has a regular and highly mathematical structure which allows one to investigate various different optimization techniques in a single function, and thirdly "oblivious" evaluation of AES on its own is an interesting application which if one could make it fast enough could have practical application.

The paper is structured as follows. We start by covering details of prior work on using MPC to implement AES. In Section 3 we detail the basics of the SPDZ protocol and the minor changes we made to the presentation in [14]. Then in Section 4 we describe how we implemented the S-Box, this is the only non-linear component in AES and so it is the only part which requires interaction. Finally in Section 5 we present our implementation results.

2 Prior Work on Evaluating AES via MPC Protocols

As noted earlier the first MPC evaluation of the AES functionality was presented in [26]. This paper presented a protocol for the case of two parties, using Yao circuits as the basic building block. On their own Yao circuits only provide security against semi-honest adversaries, and in this case the authors obtained a run-time of 7 seconds to evaluate a single AES block (the model being that party A holds the key, and party B holds a message, with B wishing to obtain the encryption of their message under A's key). To obtain security against active adversaries a variant of the cut-and-choose methodology of Lindell and Pinkas [20] was used, this resulted in the run-time dropping to 19 minutes to evaluate an AES encryption.

In [15] Henecka et al again look at two-party computation based on Yao circuits, but restrict to the case of semi-honest adversaries only. They reduce the run time per block from the previous 7 seconds down to 3.3 seconds. Huang et al [16] improve this even further obtaining a time of 0.2 seconds per block for semi-honest adversaries.

In [25] the authors present a two party protocol, but instead of their protocol being based on Yao circuits they instead base it on OT extension in the Random Oracle Model, and a form of "secret sharing with MACs" (similar to the SPDZ protocol which we examine below). This enables the authors to obtain active security and to improve on the prior performance of other implementations. The run time for a single evaluation of the AES circuit is 64 seconds, however this drops to around 2.5 seconds when amortized over a number of encryption blocks.

The most recent result in the two party setting is [17], which returns to using Yao circuit based protocols. By use of clever engineering of the overall run-time design the authors are able to significantly improve the execution time for a single AES evaluation down to 1s in the case of active adversaries.

Moving to the case of more than two players, all prior implementation results have either been for three or four players; and have been in the semi-honest setting for the case of three players. Like our work, in this setting one utilizes secret sharing but prior work has been based on Shamir secret sharing, or specialised protocols; and in the case of active security has been based on Verifiable Secret Sharing.

The main paper which is related to our work is that of [13], so we now spend some time to explain the differences between our approach and that of [13]. In [13] the authors examine an AES implementation in the case of standard threshold-secret-sharing based MPC protocols. An implementation for one semi-honest adversary amongst three players and one active adversary amongst four players is described using the VIFF framework [12]. The VIFF framework works much like the SPDZ protocol, in that it utilizes Beaver's [3] method for MPC evaluation. In an Offline Phase "multiplication triples" are produced, and then in an Online Phase the function specific calculation is performed. The two key differences between the protocol in [13] and the use of SPDZ is that the method to produce the triples is different, and the method to ensure non-cheating adversaries during the evaluation of the circuit is also different. These differences are induced since [13] is interested in threshold adversary structures, whereas we are interested in the more challenging case of dishonest majority.

The protocol of [13] is however similar to our work in that it looks at the AES circuit as a circuit over the finite field $\mathbb{F}_{2^8}$, and not as an arbitrary binary circuit. The S-Box in AES is (usually) composed of two operations an inversion in the field $\mathbb{F}_{2^8}$ followed by a linear operation on the bits of the resulting element. In [13] the authors discuss various techniques for computing the inversion, and for the bitwise linear operation they utilize a trick of bit-decomposition of the shared value. This bit-decomposition is itself implemented using the technique of pseudorandom secret sharing (PRSS) of bits.

For MPC protocols based on Shamir secret sharing, obtaining a PRSS is relatively straight forward, indeed it is a local operation assuming some set-up. However, for protocols using secret sharing with MACs (as in our approach) it is unknown how to build a PRSS in such a clean way. Thus we produce such shared random bits by executing another stage in the Offline Phase of the SPDZ protocol. We also present a simplification of the technique in [13] to use such bit-decompositions to implement the S-Box. This approach does however assume that the Offline Phase somehow "knows" that the computed function will required shared random bits; which defeats the point of having a function independent Offline stage and also adds to the run time of the Offline stage. Thus we also present a distinct approach which utilizes a surprising algebraic formulation of the S-Box.

The implementation of [13] required less than 2 seconds per AES block (including key expansion) when computing with three players and at most one semi-honest adversary, and less than 7 seconds per AES block when computing with four players and at most one active adversary. These times include the time for the Offline Phase. If one is only interested in the Online Phase times, then the active adversary case can be executed in between three and four seconds per AES block.

More recent work has focused on the case of semi-honest adversaries and three players only. Two recent results [18,19] have used an additive secret sharing scheme and a novel multiplication protocol to perform semi-honest three party MPC in the presence of at most one adversary. In [18] the authors present an AES implementation using a novel implementation of the S-Box component via an MPC table-lookup procedure. They report being able to perform 67 AES block cipher evaluations per second. In [19] the authors report on an implementation of AES, using the Sharemind framework [7], in which they can accomplish over one thousand AES block cipher evaluations per second.

In summary Table 1 summarizes the different performance figures and security models for prior work on implementing AES using multi-party computation, with also a comparison with our own work. Like all network based protocols a significant time can be spent waiting for data, thus authors have found that executing many calculations in parallel (as in for example AES-CTR mode) can have significant performance enhancements. Thus for papers which report such results we give the improved amortized costs for multiple executions (or just the blocks-per-second count for a single execution if no improvement via amortization occurs). However, single execution costs are still important since this deals with the case of (for example) AES-CBC mode. In our implementation we found little gain in performing multiple AES evaluations in parallel.

Table 1. A comparison of different MPC implementations of AES. We only give the online-times for those protocols which have a pre-processing phase. We also note whether the implementation assumes a pre-expanded key or not.

Paper	Security	Total Number Parties	Max Number Adv.	Time for single AES Block	(Amortized) Blocks per Sec	Expanded Key	Notes
[26]	semi-honest	2	1	7.0s	0.1	N	Yao
[15]	semi-honest	2	1	3.3s	0.3	N	Yao
[16]	semi-honest	2	1	0.2s	5.0	Y	Yao
[13]	semi-honest	3	1	1.2s	0.9	N	Shamir
[18]	semi-honest	3	1	N/A	67	Y	Additive
[19]	semi-honest	3	1	1.0s	1893	Y	Additive
[26]	covert	2	1	95s	≈ 0	N	Yao
This work	covert	2	1	0.17s	10.3	Y	SPDZ
This work	covert	3	2	0.19s	9.6	Y	SPDZ
This work	covert	4	3	0.18s	9.2	Y	SPDZ
This work	covert	5	4	0.19s	7.4	Y	SPDZ
This work	covert	10	9	0.23s	5.2	Y	SPDZ
[26]	active	2	1	19m	≈ 0	N	Yao
[25]	active	2	1	4.0s	32	N	OT
[17]	active	2	1	1.0s	1.0	Y	Yao
[13]	active	4	1	2.1s	0.5	N	Shamir
This work	active	2	1	0.26s	5.0	Y	SPDZ
This work	active	3	2	0.29s	4.7	Y	SPDZ
This work	active	4	3	0.32s	4.6	Y	SPDZ
This work	active	5	4	0.34s	4.4	Y	SPDZ
This work	active	10	9	0.41s	3.6	Y	SPDZ

In interpreting the table one needs to note that Yao based experiments usually implement a different functionality. Namely, the circuit constructor is the player holding the key. Whether the key is expanded or not refers to whether the garbled circuit has this key hardwired in or not.

3   The SPDZ Protocol

We now give an overview of the SPDZ protocol, for more details see [14]. The reader should however note we make a number of minor alterations to the basic protocol, all of which are describe below. Some of these alterations are due to us working in the random oracle model (which enables us to simplify a number of sub-protocols), whilst some are simply a functional change in terms of how inputs to the parties are created and distributed. In addition we describe how to simplify the SPDZ protocol to the case of covert adversaries.

The SPDZ protocol, being based on the Beaver circuit randomization technique [3], comes in two phases. In the first phase a large number of random triples are produced, such that each party holds a share of the triple, and such that the underlying values in the triple satisfy a multiplicative relation. This phase is referred to as the "Offline Phase" since the triples do not depend on either the function to be evaluated (bar their number should exceed a constant multiple of the number of multiplication gates in the evaluated function), and the triples do not depend on the inputs to the function to be evaluated. In the second phase, called the "Online Phase" the triples are used to evaluate the function on the given input.

The key to understanding the SPDZ protocol is to note that all values are shared with respect to a non-standard secret sharing scheme, which incorporates a MAC value. To describe this secret sharing scheme we fix a finite field $\mathbb{F}_q$. The MAC keys are values $\alpha_j \in \mathbb{F}_q$ for $1 \leq j \leq n_{\mathsf{MAC}}$ such that player i holds the share $\alpha_{j,i} \in \mathbb{F}_q$ where

$$\alpha_j = \alpha_{j,1} + \cdots + \alpha_{j,n}.$$

The shared values are then given by the following sharing of a value $a \in \mathbb{F}_q$,

$$\langle a \rangle := (\delta, (a_1, \ldots, a_n), (\gamma_{j,1}, \ldots, \gamma_{j,n})_{j=1}^{n_{\mathsf{MAC}}}),$$

where a is the shared value, δ is public and we have the equalities

$$a = a_1 + \cdots + a_n,$$
$$\alpha_j \cdot (a + \delta) = \gamma_{j,1} + \cdots + \gamma_{j,n} \text{ for } 1 \leq j \leq n_{\mathsf{MAC}}.$$

Given this data representing a shared value a each player P_i holds the data $(\delta, a_i, \{\gamma_{j,i}\}_{j=1}^{n_{\mathsf{MAC}}})$. To ease notation we write $\gamma_{j,i}(a)$ to denote the share of the jth MAC on item a held by party i. Arithmetic in this representation is componentwise, more precisely we have

$$\langle a \rangle + \langle b \rangle = \langle a + b \rangle, \quad e \cdot \langle a \rangle = \langle e \cdot a \rangle \quad \text{and} \quad e + \langle a \rangle = \langle e + a \rangle,$$

where

$$e + \langle a \rangle = (\delta - e, (a_1 + e, a_2, \ldots, a_n), (\gamma_{j,1}, \ldots, \gamma_{j,n})_{j=1}^{n_{\mathsf{MAC}}}).$$

The simplicity of the above method for adding a constant value to $\langle a \rangle$ is the reason of the public value δ. In [14] the presentation is simplified to having only $n_{\mathsf{MAC}} = 1$, however the case of more general values of n_{MAC} is discussed. In our implementation having $n_{\mathsf{MAC}} > 1$ will be vital to ensure active security when dealing with small finite fields, thus we present the more general case above.

The SPDZ protocol can tolerate active adversaries and dishonest majority (ignoring the case where one of the dishonest players aborts) amongst a total of n parties. Thus we can assume that $n - 1$ of the parties are dishonest and will arbitrarily deviate from the protocol. The SPDZ protocol guarantees that if the protocol terminates then the honest parties know that their resulting output is correct, except with a negligible probability. For active adversaries we set this probability, to mirror the choice in [14], to 2^{-40}. For covert adversaries we adapt the protocol so that the probability that a cheating adversary will be detected is lower bounded by

$$\min\left\{1 - q^{-n_{\mathsf{MAC}}}, 1 - q^{-n_{\mathsf{SAC}}}, \frac{1}{2 \cdot (n - 1)}\right\},$$

where n_{MAC} and n_{SAC} are parameters to be discussed later and $\mathbb{F}_q$ is the finite field over which our triples are defined.

3.1   Offline Phase

The Offline Phase makes use of a somewhat homomorphic encryption (SHE) scheme, with a distributed decryption procedure, and zero-knowledge proofs. In our implementation we use the optimized non-interactive zero-knowledge proofs of knowledge (NIZKPoKs) derived from the Fiat–Shamir heuristic which are described in [14]. Thus our Offline Phase is only secure in the Random Oracle model.

The specific SHE scheme used is a variant of the BGV scheme [10] over the mth cyclotomic field. We thus have lattices of dimension $\phi(m)$, over a modulus of size Q. Each ciphertext consists of two (or three) polynomials modulo Q of degree less than $\phi(m)$. The underlying plaintext space can hold an element of $(\mathbb{F}_q)^\ell$.

The Offline Phase produces many triples of such sharings $\langle a \rangle, \langle b \rangle, \langle c \rangle$ such that $c = a \cdot b$, where these values are authenticated via a global set of n_{MAC} shared MAC keys as described above. The NIZKPoKs mentioned above have soundness error $1/2$, and so in [14], we "batch" together sec executions so as to reduce the soundness error to $2^{-\mathsf{sec}}$. This batching, combined with the vectoral plaintext space, means that a single execution of the Offline phase produces $\mathsf{sec} \cdot \ell$ triples.

We can trivially modify the Offline Phase so that it also outputs, for characteristic two fields, a set of shared random bits and their associated MACs. We can produce one such shared bit for roughly one third of the cost of one shared triple. As for the shared triples, each invocation of the method to produce shared random bits will produce $\mathsf{sec} \cdot \ell$ bits in one go.

The main cost of the Offline phase is in the production and verification of the zero-knowledge proofs. For n players, for each proof that a player needs to produce he will need to verify $n - 1$ proofs of the other players. For the case of covert adversaries we simplify the Offline Phase as follows. We do not batch together proofs, i.e. we take $\mathsf{sec} = 1$, which results in soundness error for each proof of $1/2$. In addition each player when it receives $n - 1$ proofs from all other players only verifies a random proof. This means that a cheating player will be detected with probability at least $1/(2 \cdot (n-1))$ in the Offline phase, as opposed to $1 - 2^{-40}$ when we use the standard actively secure Offline Phase.

3.2 Online Phase

Given that our Offline Phase is given in the Random Oracle Model we alter the Online Phase from [14] so that it too utilizes Random Oracles. This means we can present a more efficient Online Phase than that used in [14]. Our Online Phase makes use of three hash functions: The first one H_1 is used to ensure that broadcast has happened, for this hash function we require it is one which supports an API of standard hash functions consisting of Init, Update and Finalise methods. The second hash function H_2 is used to generate random values for checking the linear MAC equations and the triples. The third hash function H_3, which we model as a random oracle, is used to define a commitment scheme as follows: To commit to a value x, which we denote by $\mathsf{Commit}(x)$, one generates a random value $r \in \{0,1\}^{\mathsf{sec}}$, for some security parameter sec, and computes $\mathsf{comm} = H_3(x\|r)$. To open $\mathsf{Open}(\mathsf{comm}, x, r)$ one verifies that $\mathsf{comm} = H_3(x\|r)$ returning x if this is true, and $\bot$ if it is not.

The first change we make is in how we guarantee that consistent broadcast occurs. For the Online phase we assume that the point-to-point links between the parties are authenticated, but we need to guarantee that a dishonest party is not allowed to send different messages to different players when he is required to broadcast a single value to all players. This is done by modifying the notion of a "partial opening" from [14] and the notion of "broadcast". The "broadcasts" are ensured to be correct via the parties maintaining a hash of all values received. This is checked before the output is reconstructed; thus in the final broadcast to recover the output we utilize the re-transmit method from [14] to check consistency of the final broadcast.

In the original protocol "partial opening" just means a broadcast of the share of a value held by a party, but not the broadcast of the share of the MAC on that value. Thus only the value is opened, not the MAC on the value. However, we each ensure player maintains the running totals of the linear equations they will eventually check. In [14] these linear equations were of the form $\sum_k e^k a_k$, for some random agreed value e. This gives an error probability of T/q, where T is the number of partial openings in an execution of the Online Phase. For small values of q this is not effective, thus we replace the values e^k by the output of hash function H_2. In Figure 1 we describe our modified partial opening, and broadcast protocol, which maintains a hash value of all values broadcast; as well as a method for checking consistency.

Init(): We initialize the following data:
  1. Party i executes H_1.Init().
  2. Party i sets $\mathsf{cnt}_i = 0$.
  3. For $j = 1, \ldots, n_{\mathsf{MAC}}$
     (a) Party i sets $\hat{a}_{j,i} = 0$ and $\gamma_{j,i} = 0$.
  4. Party i generates a random value $\mathsf{seed}_i \in \{0,1\}^{\mathsf{sec}}$ and sends it to all other
     players.
Broadcast(v_i): We broadcast v_i and receive the equivalent broadcasts from other
  players:
  1. Party i sends v_i to each player.
  2. On receipt of $\{v_1, \ldots, v_n\} \setminus \{v_i\}$ execute H_1.Update($v_1 \| \ldots \| v_n$).
  3. Return $\{v_1 + \cdots + v_n\}$.
PartialOpen($\langle a \rangle$): Party i obtains the partial opening of the shared value and updates their partial sums:
  1. Execute $\{a_1, \ldots, a_n\} = $ Broadcast(a_i).
  2. $a = a_1 + \cdots + a_n$.
  3. $(e_1 \| \ldots \| e_{n_{\mathsf{MAC}}}) = H_2(0 \| \mathsf{seed}_1 \| \ldots \| \mathsf{seed}_n \| \mathsf{cnt}_i) \in \mathbb{F}_q$.
  4. $\mathsf{cnt}_i = \mathsf{cnt}_i + 1$
  5. For $j = 1, \ldots, n_{\mathsf{MAC}}$
     (a) $\hat{a}_{j,i} = \hat{a}_{j,i} + e_j \cdot (a + \delta_a)$.
     (b) $\gamma_{j,i} = \gamma_{j,i} + e_j \cdot \gamma_{j,i}(a)$.
  6. Return a.
Verify(): We check all broadcasts have been consistent:
  1. Party i computes $h_i = H_1$.Finalise() and sends h_i to each player.
  2. On receipt of h_j from player j, if $h_i \neq h_j$ then abort.

Fig. 1. Methods for Partial Opening and Broadcast for Party i

In the Online Phase the key issue is that the triples produced by the Offline
Phase may not satisfy the relation $c = a \cdot b$, nor may the MACs verify. This is
because we do not ensure that the dishonest parties were "well behaved" in the
Offline Phase. Thus these two properties must be checked. The Online Protocol
of [14] does this as follows: To check that $c = a \cdot b$ for the triples, we will use for
the MPC evaluation we "sacrifice" a set of n_{SAC} extra triples per evaluated triple.
For the sacrificing method in our implementation, we adopted the naïve method
of [14]. This results in consuming more triples, but is simpler computationally.
To check the MAC values a series of n_{MAC} linear equations are checked at the
end of the Online Phase.

Each triple sacrifice and MAC equation check can be made to hold by the
adversary with probability $1/q$. Thus to reduce this to something negligible we
sacrifice many triples, and utilize many MAC equations. But in the case of covert
adversaries we select $n_{\mathsf{MAC}} = n_{\mathsf{SAC}} = 1$, and so the probability of a cheating
adversary being detected is bounded from below by $1 - 1/q$.

Both of these checks require that the parties agree on some global random
values at different points in the protocol. In [14] these extra shared values are
determined in the Offline Phase, via a different form of secret sharing; with the
sharings being opened at the critical point in the Online protocol. The benefit

of this approach is that one obtains a protocol which is UC secure without the need for Random Oracles; however the down-side is that the Offline Phase becomes relatively complex. In our work we take the view that since Random Oracles have been used in the Offline Phase one might as well exploit them in the Online Phase. Thus these shared values are obtained via a Random Oracle based commitment scheme as we now describe.

The next alteration we make to the Online Phase of [14] is that we assume that the players shares of the input values are "magically distributed" to them. This can be justified in two ways. Firstly we are only interested in timing the main Offline and Online Protocol and the input distribution phase is just an added complication. Secondly, a key application scenario for MPC is when the players are computing a function on behalf of some client. In such a situation the players do not themselves have any input, it is the client which has input. In such a situation the players would obtain their respective input shares directly from the client; thus eliminating the need entirely for a special protocol to deal with obtaining the input shares.

Our final alteration is that we utilize a new online operation, in addition to local addition and multiplication, called BitDecomposition. We first note that we can given a sharing $\langle a \rangle$ of a finite field element $a \in \mathbb{F}_{2^k} = \mathbb{F}_2[X]/F(X)$, and a set of k randomly shared bits $\langle r_i \rangle$ for $i = 0, \ldots, k-1$. Suppose we write a as $\sum_{i=0}^{k-1} a_i \cdot X^i$, our goal is to produce $\langle a_i \rangle$. Firstly via a local operation we compute a sharing of $r = \sum r_i \cdot X^i$ by computing $\langle r \rangle = \sum \langle r_i \rangle \cdot X^i$. Then we produce a masked value of a, via $\langle c \rangle = \langle a \rangle + \langle r \rangle$. The value of $\langle c \rangle$ is then opened to reveal c and we compute the decomposition $c = \sum c_i \cdot X^i$. Then we can locally compute $\langle a_i \rangle = c_i + \langle r_i \rangle$. Note, if a is known to be in a subfield of $\mathbb{F}_{2^k}$, as it will be in one of our implementations for $k = 40$, we can utilize the embedding of the subfield into the larger field to reduce the number of shared random bits needed for this decomposition down to the degree of the subfield. We refer to Appendix A for more details.

Given these alterations to the Online Phase of [14] we present the modified protocol in Figure 2 of the Appendix.

4   S-Box Implementation

We present two distinct methodologies to implement the S-Box. The first requires the Offline Phase to only produce multiplication triples, and utilizes the algebraic properties of the S-Box. The second requires the Offline Phase to also produce sharings (and associated MACs) of random bits.

4.1   S-Box via Algebraic Operations

A key design criteria of any block cipher is that it should be highly non-linear. In addition it should be hard to write down a series of simple algebraic equations to describe the cipher. Since such equations could give rise to an attack via algebraic cryptanalysis. Indeed one reason for choosing AES as an example benchmark for

MPC protocols, is that being a block cipher it should be highly non-linear and hence a challenge for MPC protocols. However, as was soon realised after the standardization of AES the S-Box (the only non-linear component in the entire cipher) can be represented in a relatively clean algebraic manner.

Our algebraic method to implement the S-Box operation is based on the analysis of AES of Murphy and Robshaw [23]. In this work the authors demonstrate that actually AES can be described by (relatively simple) algebraic formulae over $\mathbb{F}_{2^8}$, in other words the transform between byte-wise and bit-wise operations in the standard representation of the AES S-Box is a bit of a MacGuffin.

Recall the AES S-Box consists of an inversion in $\mathbb{F}_{2^8}$ (which is indeed a highly non-linear function) followed by a linear operation over the bits of the result. This is usually explained that the mixture of the two operations in two distinct finite fields "breaks any algebraic structure". This was shown to be false in [23]. Indeed one can express the S-Box calculation via the following simple polynomial

$$\text{S-Box}(z) = \text{0x63} + \text{0x8F} \cdot z^{127} + \text{0xB5} \cdot z^{191} + \text{0x01} \cdot z^{223} + \text{0xF4} \cdot z^{239}$$
$$+ \text{0x25} \cdot z^{247} + \text{0xF9} \cdot z^{251} + \text{0x09} \cdot z^{253} + \text{0x05} \cdot z^{254}.$$

where (as is usual) operations are in the finite field defined by $\mathbb{F}_{2^8} = \mathbb{F}_2[x]/(x^8 + x^4 + x^3 + x + 1)$ and the notation 0x12 represents the element defined by the polynomial $x^4 + x$. That the operation can be defined by a polynomial of degree bounded by 255 is not surprising, since by interpolation any functions from $\mathbb{F}_{2^8}$ to $\mathbb{F}_{2^8}$ can be represented in such a way. What is surprising is that the polynomial is relatively sparse, however this can be easily shown from first principles.

Lemma 1. *The AES S-Box can be represented by a polynomial which has a non-zero coefficient for the term i if and only if $i \in \{0, 127, 191, 223, 239, 247, 251, 253, 254\}$.*

Proof. Recall the AES S-Box consists first of inversion $z \to z^{-1} = y$ followed by an $\mathbb{F}_2$ linear operation $\mathbf{w} = A \cdot \mathbf{y}^\mathsf{T} + \mathbf{b}$ on the bits of the result, where $\mathbf{y}$ are the bits in y. The bit matrix A and the bit vector $\mathbf{b}$ are fixed. The final result is obtained by forming the dot-product of the $(\mathbb{F}_2)^8$ vector $\mathbf{w}$ with the fixed vector $\mathbf{x} = (1, x, x^2, x^3, x^4, x^5, x^6, x^7) \in (\mathbb{F}_{2^8})^8$.

First note that inversion in $\mathbb{F}_{2^8}$ can be accomplished by computing $z^{-1} = z^{254}$, since $z^{255} = 1$ for all $z \neq 0$. The AES standard "defines" $0^{-1} = 0$, and so the formula of z^{254} can be applied even when $z = 0$ as well.

We then note that extracting the bits $\mathbf{y} = (y_0, \ldots, y_7) \in (\mathbb{F}_2)^8$ of an element $y = y_0 + y_1 \cdot x + \cdots + y_7 \cdot x^7$ can be obtained via a linear operation on the action of Frobenius on y. This follows since Frobenius acts as a linear map, and hence by applying Frobenius eight times we find eight linear equations linking the set $\{y_0, \ldots, y_7\}$ with the Frobenius actions on y. This in turn allows us to solve for the bits $\mathbf{y} = (y_0, \ldots, y_7)$. Thus there is matrix $B \in (\mathbb{F}_{2^8})^{8 \times 8}$ such that

$$\mathbf{y} = B \cdot (y, y^2, y^4, y^8, y^{16}, y^{32}, y^{64}, y^{128})^\mathsf{T}.$$

Hence, the output of the S-Box can be written as

$$S\text{-Box}(z) = \mathbf{x} \cdot (A \cdot \mathbf{y} + \mathbf{b}),$$
$$= \mathbf{x} \cdot (A \cdot B) \cdot (y, y^2, y^4, y^8, y^{16}, y^{32}, y^{64}, y^{128})^\mathsf{T} + \mathbf{x} \cdot \mathbf{b},$$
$$= \mathbf{s} \cdot (1, y, y^2, y^4, y^8, y^{16}, y^{32}, y^{64}, y^{128})^\mathsf{T}$$

where $\mathbf{s}$ is a fixed nine dimensional vector over $\mathbb{F}_{2^8}$. On replacing y with z^{254} in the above equation, using $z^{255} = 1$ for all $z \neq 0$, we obtain our result. With the result also following for $z = 0$ by inspection.

Finally to implement the S-Box we therefore need an efficient method to obtain from an shared input value z, the shared values of the elements $\{z^{127}, z^{191}, z^{223}, z^{239}, z^{247}, z^{251}, z^{253}, z^{254}\}$. This is equivalent to finding a short addition chain for the set $\{127, 191, 223, 239, 247, 251, 253, 254\}$. We found the shortest such addition chain consists of eighteen additions and is the chain

$$\{1, 2, 3, 6, 12, 15, 24, 48, 63, 64, 96, 127, 191, 223, 239, 247, 251, 253, 254\}.$$

Thus to evaluate a single S-Box requires eighteen MPC multiplication operations, as well as some local computation. Hence, to evaluate the entire AES cipher we require $18 \cdot 16 \cdot 10 = 2880$ MPC multiplications.

Looking ahead each multiplication operation will require interaction, and to reduce execution times we need to ensure that each player is kept "busy", i.e. is not left waiting for data to arrive. To do this we will interleave various different multiplications together; essentially exploiting the instruction level parallelism (ILP) within the basic AES algorithm. Clearly one can execute each of the 16 S-Box operations in a single round in parallel, thus obtaining an immediate 16-fold factor of ILP. However, further ILP can be exploited in the addition chain above as can be seen from its graphical realisation in Figure B. in the Appendix. We see that the addition chain can be executed in twelve parallel multiplication steps; thus the total number of rounds of multiplication need for the entire AES cipher will be $12 \cdot 10 = 120$.

4.2   S-Box via BitDecomposition

As explained in [13] the S-Box can be implemented if one has access to shared random bits, via the BitDecomposition operation. In our second implementation choice we extend this technique, and reduce even further the amount of interaction needed to compute the S-Box.

We use this BitDecomposition trick in two ways. The first way is to decompose an element in $\mathbb{F}_{2^8}$ into it's bit components, so as to apply the linear map of the S-Box. This part is exactly as described in [13]; except when we open the value of $\langle c \rangle$ we perform a partial opening, leaving the checking of the MACs until the end.

In our second application of BitDecomposition we use BitDecomposition to implement the operation $x \longrightarrow x^{254}$. This done as follows: We decompose x into it's constituent bits. Then the operations $x \longrightarrow x^2$, $x \longrightarrow x^4$ are all *linear operations*, and so can be performed locally. Finally the value of $x^{254} = x^{-1}$ is computed via the combination

$$x^{254} = \left(\left(x^2 \cdot x^4 \right) \cdot \left(x^8 \cdot x^{16} \right) \right) \cdot \left(\left(x^{32} \cdot x^{64} \right) \cdot x^{128} \right),$$

which requires a total of six multiplications. We could reduce this down to four multiplications by applying the Frobenius map to other elements [27]; but this will consume even more random bits per S-Box thus we settled for the above implementation which consumes 16 sharings of random bits per S-Box invocation.

5   Experimental Results

We implemented the SPDZ protocol over finite fields of characteristic two and used it to evaluate the AES function, with the S-Box implemented using both the algebraic formulation described earlier and the variant by BitDecomposition. As described earlier we examined the case of dealing with both covert adversaries and fully malicious (a.k.a. active) adversaries (with cheating probability of 2^{-40}). We note that the probability of 2^{-40} could be extended to smaller values, but we used 2^{-40} so as to be comparable with the theoretical run-time estimates given in [14]. For example to reduce the probability down to 2^{-80} would essentially require a doubling of the cost of both the Offline and Online stages.

The first decision one needs to take is as to what finite field one should work with. Since we are evaluating AES it is natural to pick the field

$$K_8 = \mathbb{F}_2[x]/(x^8 + x^4 + x^3 + x + 1).$$

Another choice, particularly suited to our active adversary cheating probability of 2^{-40}, would be to use the field

$$K_{40} = \mathbb{F}_2[y]/(y^{40} + y^{20} + y^{15} + y^{10} + 1).$$

Using this finite field has the advantage that, for active adversaries, we only need to keep one MAC share per data item, and only one triple per multiplication needs to be sacrificed. In addition the field K_8 lies in K_{40} via the embedding $x = y^5 + 1$. We also for means of comparison of the Offline phase implemented the Offline protocol over a finite field $\mathbb{F}_q$ with q a 64-bit prime.

We also experimented with various numbers of players, and different values of n_{MAC} and n_{SAC}. As explained in [14] all such variants lead to different basic parameters (m, Q, ℓ) of the underlying SHE scheme.

We now determine values of (m, Q, ℓ) for our SHE scheme given a specific finite field $\mathbb{F}_q$ (or in the case of q prime a rough size for q), a value for the sec (the number of NIZKPoKs we run in parallel in the Offline stage), and the number of players n. As a "lattice security parameter" we selected $\delta = 1.0052$ which corresponds to roughly 128 bits of symmetric security.

We require finite fields $\mathbb{F}_q$ of size $\mathbb{F}_{2^8}$ and $\mathbb{F}_{2^{40}}$, as well for comparison a finite field where q was a 64-bit prime. We also looked for parameters for $n \in \{2, 3, 4, 5, 10\}$ and sec $\in \{1, 40\}$. As in [14] we first search for rough estimate of the parameters (m, Q) which fit these needs:

char($\mathbb{F}_q$)	n	sec	$\phi(m) \geq$	$\log_2(Q)$
2	$2 \leq n \leq 10$	40	12300	370
2	$2 \leq n \leq 5$	1	8000	200
2	10	1	8000	210
$\approx 2^{64}$	$2 \leq n \leq 10$	40	16700	500
$\approx 2^{64}$	$2 \leq n \leq 5$	1	11000	330
$\approx 2^{64}$	10	1	11300	340

We then selected values for m as follows:

$\mathbb{F}_{2^8}$ and $\mathbb{F}_{2^{40}}$, sec $= 40$: We select $m = 17425$, which gives us $\phi(m) = 12800$. The polynomial $\Phi_m(X)$ factors modulo two into $\ell = 320$ factors each of degree 40. Thus these parameters can support both our finite fields $\mathbb{F}_{2^8}$ and $\mathbb{F}_{2^{40}}$.

$\mathbb{F}_{2^8}$, sec $= 1$: We select $m = 13107$, which gives us $\phi(m) = 8192$. The polynomial $\Phi_m(X)$ factors modulo two into $\ell = 512$ factors each of degree 16.

$\mathbb{F}_{2^{40}}$, sec $= 1$: We select $m = 13175$, which gives us $\phi(m) = 9600$. The polynomial $\Phi_m(X)$ factors modulo two into $\ell = 240$ factors each of degree 40.

$p \approx 2^{64}$, sec $= 40$: We select, as in [14], $p = 2^{64} + 4867$ and $m = 16729$ so that $\ell = \phi(m) = 16728$.

$p \approx 2^{64}$, sec $= 1$: We select, as in [14], $p = 2^{64} + 8947$ and $m = 11971$ so that $\ell = \phi(m) = 11970$.

Recall that one invocation of the Offline Phase produces sec $\cdot \ell$ triples; thus using the choices above we obtain the following summary table, where "# Trip/# Bits" denotes the number of triples/bits produced per invocation of the Offline Phase.

Field	Adversary Type	sec	$n_{\mathsf{MAC}} = n_{\mathsf{SAC}}$	# Trip/ # Bits
K_8	covert	1	1	512
K_8	active	40	5	12800
K_{40}	covert	1	1	240
K_{40}	active	40	1	12800

We ran the Offline phase on machines with Intel i5 CPU's running at 2.8 GHz. with 4 GB of RAM. The ping between machines over the local area network was approximately 0.3 ms. We obtained the executions time given in Table 2 and Table 3, for the two different finite field choices and covert/active security choices, and various numbers of players. We did not run an example with ten players and active adversaries since this took too long. We first ran the Offline Phase in each example to produce a minimum of 5000 triples. Clearly for some parameter sets a single run produced much more than 5000, whilst for others we required multiple runs so as to reach 5000 triples. These results are in Table 2. These runs are compatible with our algebraic S-Box formulation.

This table also presents the average time needed to produce each triple, plus also the amortized time to produce triples per AES invocation (in the case where one wants to evaluate the AES functionality many times). Recall to evaluate the AES functionality with our method requires $10 \cdot 16 \cdot 18 = 2880$ multiplications in total; thus the number of triples needed is $2880 \cdot (n_{\mathsf{SAC}} + 1)$, since each multiplication consumes $n_{\mathsf{SAC}} + 1$ triples. What is clear from the table is that if one is wishing to obtain security against covert adversaries then utilizing the field K_8 is preferable. However, for security against active adversaries the field K_{40} is to be preferred.

Table 2. Offline Run Time Examples For The Algebraic S-Box Method

		Covert Security			Active Security		
Field	Num. Parties	Total Time (h:m:s)	Time per Triple (seconds)	Offline time per AES blk (h:m:s)	Total Time (h:m:s)	Time per Triple (seconds)	Offline time per AES blk (h:m:s)
		No. Triples Produced: 5120			No. Triples Produced: 12800		
K_8	2	0:01:31	0.018	0:01:42	1:25:57	0.403	1:56:02
K_8	3	0:01:32	0.018	0:01:43	1:50:25	0.518	2:29:03
K_8	4	0:01:32	0.018	0:01:43	2:14:16	0.629	3:01:15
K_8	5	0:01:33	0.018	0:01:44	2:37:30	0.738	3:32:37
K_8	10	0:01:48	0.021	0:02:01	4:40:15	1.314	6:18:20
		No. Triples Produced: 5040			No. Triples Produced: 12800		
K_{40}	2	0:05:08	0.061	0:05:52	0:29:34	0.136	0:13:18
K_{40}	3	0:05:13	0.062	0:05:57	0:38:18	0.180	0:17:14
K_{40}	4	0:05:14	0.062	0:05:58	0:46:02	0.216	0:20:42
K_{40}	5	0:05:17	0.063	0:06:02	0:55:51	0.262	0:25:07
K_{40}	10	0:06:02	0.072	0:06:53	1:39:14	0.465	0:44:39

We then run an Offline phase tailored to our BitDecomposition S-Box formulation. Here we need to perform $10 \cdot 16 \cdot 6 = 960$ multiplications, and thus we require $960 \cdot (n_{\mathsf{SAC}} + 1)$ triples to evaluate a single block. But we also require $10 \cdot 16 \cdot 16 = 2560$ shared random bits so as to perform two eight bit, BitDecompositions per S-Box invocation. Thus in Table 3 we present run times for a second invocation of the Offline Phase in which we aimed to produce a minimum of 5000 triples and 6600 shared random bits (which is the correct ratio for covert security). Due to the inbalance between Triple and Bit production the "Offline Time per AES Block" column needs to be taken as rough estimate. Again we see that for covert security K_8 is preferable, and for active security K_{40} is preferable.

But, these run times do not seem comparable with the 13ms per triple estimated by the authors of [14] for the Offline Phase. However, this discrepancy can easily be explained. The run time estimates in [14] are given for arithmetic circuit evaluation over a finite field of prime characteristic of 64-bits. With the parameter choices in [14] this means one can select parameters for the SHE scheme which enable a 16000-fold SIMD parallelism. For our finite fields of degree two

Table 3. Offline Run Time Examples For The S-Box Via BitDecomposition

		Covert Security		Active Security	
		Total	Offline Time	Total	Offline Time
	Number	Time	per AES Block	Time	per AES Block
Field	Players	(h:m:s)	(h:m:s)	(h:m:s)	(h:m:s)
		No. Triples/Bits: 5120/6556		No. Triples/Bits: 12800/12800	
K_8	2	0:02:07	0:00:47	1:54:42	0:51:36
K_8	3	0:02:10	0:00:49	2:26:21	1:05:51
K_8	4	0:02:13	0:00:50	2:56:47	1:19:33
K_8	5	0:02:36	0:00:52	3:29:49	1:34:25
K_8	10	0:02:33	0:00:58	6:06:20	2:44:51
		No. Triples/Bits: 5040/6720		No. Triples/Bits: 12800/12800	
K_{40}	2	0:07:12	0:02:43	0:36:14	0:05:26
K_{40}	3	0:07:12	0:02:43	0:47:30	0:07:07
K_{40}	4	0:07:19	0:02:47	0:58:55	0:08:57
K_{40}	5	0:07:24	0:02:49	1:10:33	0:10:34
K_{40}	10	0:08:32	0:03:15	2:10:03	0:19:32

the amount of SIMD parallelism in the Offline Phase is much lower than this. To see the difference that using large prime characteristic fields makes to the Offline Phase we implemented it, using the parameters above to obtain the results in Table 4. As can be seen from the table we produce triples for prime fields of 64-bits in size around twice as fast as the estimates in [14] would predict.

Table 4. Offline Run Time Examples For $\mathbb{F}_p$ With $p \approx 2^{64}$

	Covert Security			Active Security		
	Total	Total	Time per	Total	Total	Time per
Number	Number	Time	Triple	Number	Time	Triple
Players	Triples	(h:m:s)	(seconds)	Triples	(h:m:s)	(seconds)
2	11970	0:00:27	0.002	669120	1:10:48	0.006
3	11970	0:00:27	0.002	669120	1:32:13	0.008
4	11970	0:00:28	0.002	669120	1:55:05	0.010
5	11970	0:00:29	0.002	669120	2:20:42	0.013
10	11970	0:00:31	0.002	669120	4:17:10	0.023

We now turn to the Online Phase; recall that this itself comes in two steps (and two variants). In the first step we evaluate the function itself (consuming the triples produced in the Offline Phase), whereas in the second step we check the MAC values and open the final result. In Table 5 we present the run-times to evaluate the AES functionality for the various parameter sets generated above using our algebraic formulation of the S-Box. These are average run-times from all the players, executed over 20 different runs. The Online Phase was run on the same machines as in the Offline Phase. In Table 6 we present the same times using the S-Box variant utilizing the BitDecomposition method.

Table 5. Online Phase Runtime Examples (all in seconds) – Algebraic S-Box

Field	Number Players	Covert Security			Active Security		
		Function Evaluation	Checking Step	Total Time	Function Evaluation	Checking Step	Total Time
K_8	2	0.284	0.017	0.301	1.319	0.031	1.350
K_8	3	0.307	0.062	0.369	1.381	0.035	1.416
K_8	4	0.316	0.027	0.343	1.422	0.028	1.450
K_8	5	0.344	0.034	0.378	1.461	0.018	1.479
K_8	10	0.444	0.010	0.454	1.659	0.023	1.682
K_{40}	2	0.449	0.012	0.461	0.460	0.021	0.481
K_{40}	3	0.486	0.022	0.498	0.475	0.025	0.500
K_{40}	4	0.490	0.042	0.532	0.486	0.055	0.541
K_{40}	5	0.508	0.037	0.544	0.510	0.026	0.536
K_{40}	10	0.765	0.021	0.786	0.672	0.017	0.689

Table 6. Online Phase Runtime Examples (all in seconds) – S-Box Via BitDecomposition

Field	Number Players	Covert Security			Active Security		
		Function Evaluation	Checking Step	Total Time	Function Evaluation	Checking Step	Total Time
K_8	2	0.156	0.009	0.165	0.569	0.011	0.580
K_8	3	0.178	0.008	0.186	0.616	0.019	0.635
K_8	4	0.169	0.015	0.184	0.620	0.015	0.635
K_8	5	0.173	0.019	0.192	0.727	0.019	0.746
K_8	10	0.211	0.015	0.226	0.722	0.044	0.766
K_{40}	2	0.260	0.006	0.266	0.256	0.004	0.260
K_{40}	3	0.303	0.009	0.312	0.279	0.011	0.290
K_{40}	4	0.303	0.010	0.313	0.287	0.029	0.316
K_{40}	5	0.319	0.022	0.341	0.319	0.016	0.335
K_{40}	10	0.399	0.016	0.415	0.387	0.027	0.414

The networking between players was implemented in a point-to-point fashion with each player acting as both a server and a client. We ensured that data was sent over the sockets as soon as it was ready by disabling Nagle's algorithm [24]. To complete the function evaluation each player first parses a program written in a specialised instruction language. This allows our implementation to take advantage of the instruction level parallelism as described above so as to schedule many multiplication operations to happen in parallel.

Again we see that if security against covert adversaries is the goal then using the field K_8 is to be preferred. However, for security against active adversaries the field K_{40} performs better. We also ran the Online Phase in a run which performed ten AES encryptions in parallel. This resulted in only a small improvement in time per AES block over executing just one AES encryption at a time, thus we do not present these figures. Improving the throughput for parallel execution is the subject of future research.

Overall, the two methods of AES evaluation are roughly comparable. The method via BitDecomposition being faster, and significantly faster when one also takes into account the associated cost of the Offline Phase. However, as remarked previously this method does not result in a generic Offline Phase; since the Offline Phase needs to "know" the expected ratio of Bits to Triples that it needs to produce for the actual function which will be evaluated in the Online Phase.

In summary we have presented the first experimental results for running MPC protocols with large numbers of players (10 as opposed to the four or less of prior work), and for a dishonest majority of active or covert adversaries (as opposed to threshold adversaries). It is expected that our reported execution times will fall as dramatically as those have done for two party MPC protocols in the last couple of years. Thus we can expect actively/covertly secure MPC protocols for dishonest majority to be within reach of some practical applications within a few years.

Acknowledgements. The first author acknowledges the support from the Danish National Research Foundation and The National Science Foundation of China (under the grant 61061130540) for the Sino-Danish Center for the Theory of Interactive Computation, within which [part of] this work was performed; and also from the CFEM research center (supported by the Danish Strategic Research Council) within which part of this work was performed.

The second, third and fifth author were partially supported by EPSRC via grant COED–EP/I03126X. The fifth author was also supported by the European Commission through the ICT Programme under Contract ICT-2007-216676 ECRYPT II and via an ERC Advanced Grant ERC-2010-AdG-267188-CRIPTO, the Defense Advanced Research Projects Agency (DARPA) and the Air Force Research Laboratory (AFRL) under agreement number FA8750-11-2-0079, and by a Royal Society Wolfson Merit Award. The US Government is authorized to reproduce and distribute reprints for Government purposes notwithstanding any copyright notation hereon. The views and conclusions contained herein are those of the authors and should not be interpreted as necessarily representing the official policies or endorsements, either expressed or implied, of DARPA, AFRL, the U.S. Government, the European Commission or EPSRC.

References

1. Aumann, Y., Lindell, Y.: Security Against Covert Adversaries: Efficient Protocols for Realistic Adversaries. In: Vadhan, S.P. (ed.) TCC 2007. LNCS, vol. 4392, pp. 137–156. Springer, Heidelberg (2007)
2. Aumann, Y., Lindell, Y.: Security against covert adversaries: Efficient protocols for realistic adversaries. J. Cryptology 23, 281–343 (2010)
3. Beaver, D.: Correlated pseudorandomness and the complexity of private computations. In: Symposium on Theory of Computing, STOC 1996, pp. 479–488. ACM (1996)

4. Ben-David, A., Nisan, N., Pinkas, B.: FairplayMP: a system for secure multi-party computation. In: Computer and Communications Security, CCS 2008, pp. 257–266. ACM (2008)

5. Bendlin, R., Damgård, I., Orlandi, C., Zakarias, S.: Semi-homomorphic Encryption and Multiparty Computation. In: Paterson, K.G. (ed.) EUROCRYPT 2011. LNCS, vol. 6632, pp. 169–188. Springer, Heidelberg (2011)

6. Ben-Or, M., Goldwasser, S., Wigderson, A.: Completeness theorems for non-cryptographic fault-tolerant distributed computation. In: Symposium on Theory of Computing, STOC 1988, pp. 1–10. ACM (1988)

7. Bogdanov, D., Laur, S., Willemson, J.: Sharemind: A Framework for Fast Privacy-Preserving Computations. In: Jajodia, S., Lopez, J. (eds.) ESORICS 2008. LNCS, vol. 5283, pp. 192–206. Springer, Heidelberg (2008)

8. Bogetoft, P., Christensen, D.L., Damgård, I., Geisler, M., Jakobsen, T., Krøigaard, M., Nielsen, J.D., Nielsen, J.B., Nielsen, K., Pagter, J., Schwartzbach, M., Toft, T.: Secure Multiparty Computation Goes Live. In: Dingledine, R., Golle, P. (eds.) FC 2009. LNCS, vol. 5628, pp. 325–343. Springer, Heidelberg (2009)

9. Bogetoft, P., Damgård, I., Jakobsen, T., Nielsen, K., Pagter, J.I., Toft, T.: A Practical Implementation of Secure Auctions Based on Multiparty Integer Computation. In: Di Crescenzo, G., Rubin, A. (eds.) FC 2006. LNCS, vol. 4107, pp. 142–147. Springer, Heidelberg (2006)

10. Brakerski, Z., Gentry, C., Vaikuntanathan, V.: Fully homomorphic encryption without bootstrapping. In: Innovations in Theoretical Computer Science, ITCS 2012, pp. 309–325. ACM (2012)

11. Chaum, D., Crepeau, C., Damgård, I.: Multiparty unconditionally secure protocols. In: Symposium on Theory of Computing – STOC 1988, pp. 11–19. ACM (1988)

12. Damgård, I., Geisler, M., Krøigaard, M., Nielsen, J.B.: Asynchronous Multi-party Computation: Theory and Implementation. In: Jarecki, S., Tsudik, G. (eds.) PKC 2009. LNCS, vol. 5443, pp. 160–179. Springer, Heidelberg (2009)

13. Damgård, I., Keller, M.: Secure Multiparty AES. In: Sion, R. (ed.) FC 2010. LNCS, vol. 6052, pp. 367–374. Springer, Heidelberg (2010)

14. Damgård, I., Pastro, V., Smart, N.P., Zakarias, S.: Multiparty Computation from Somewhat Homomorphic Encryption. In: Safavi-Naini, R. (ed.) CRYPTO 2012. LNCS, vol. 7417, pp. 643–662. Springer, Heidelberg (2012), http://eprint.iacr.org/2011/535

15. Henecka, W., Kögl, S., Sadeghi, A.-R., Schneider, T., Wehrenberg, I.: TASTY: Tool for automating secure two-party computations. In: Computer and Communications Security, CCS 2010, pp. 451–462. ACM (2010)

16. Huang, Y., Evans, D., Katz, J., Malka, L.: Faster secure two-party computation using garbled circuits. In: Proc. USENIX Security Symposium (2011)

17. Kreuter, B., Shelat, A., Shen, C.-H.: Towards billion-gate secure computation with malicious adversaries. IACR e-print 2012/179 (2012), http://eprint.iacr.org/2012/179

18. Launchbury, J., Adams-Moran, A., Diatchki, I.: Efficient lookup-table protocol in secure multiparty computation (2012) (manuscript)

19. Laur, S., Talviste, R., Willemson, J.: AES block cipher implementation and secure database join on the SHAREMIND secure multi-party computation framework (2012) (manuscript)

20. Lindell, Y., Pinkas, B.: An Efficient Protocol for Secure Two-Party Computation in the Presence of Malicious Adversaries. In: Naor, M. (ed.) EUROCRYPT 2007. LNCS, vol. 4515, pp. 52–78. Springer, Heidelberg (2007)

21. Lindell, Y., Pinkas, B., Smart, N.P.: Implementing Two-Party Computation Efficiently with Security Against Malicious Adversaries. In: Ostrovsky, R., De Prisco, R., Visconti, I. (eds.) SCN 2008. LNCS, vol. 5229, pp. 2–20. Springer, Heidelberg (2008)

22. Malkhi, D., Nisan, N., Pinkas, B., Sella, Y.: Fairplay — a secure two-party computation system. In: Proc. USENIX Security Symposium (2004)

23. Murphy, S., Robshaw, M.J.B.: Essential Algebraic Structure within the AES. In: Yung, M. (ed.) CRYPTO 2002. LNCS, vol. 2442, pp. 1–16. Springer, Heidelberg (2002)

24. Nagle, J.: Congestion control in IP/TCP internetworks. IETF RFC 896 (1984)

25. Nielsen, J.B., Nordholt, P.S., Orlandi, C., Sheshank Burra, S.: A new approach to practical active-secure two-party computation. IACR e-print 2011/91 (2011), http://eprint.iacr.org/2011/91

26. Pinkas, B., Schneider, T., Smart, N.P., Williams, S.C.: Secure Two-Party Computation Is Practical. In: Matsui, M. (ed.) ASIACRYPT 2009. LNCS, vol. 5912, pp. 250–267. Springer, Heidelberg (2009)

27. Rivain, M., Prouff, E.: Provably Secure Higher-Order Masking of AES. In: Mangard, S., Standaert, F.-X. (eds.) CHES 2010. LNCS, vol. 6225, pp. 413–427. Springer, Heidelberg (2010)

28. Yao, A.: Protocols for secure computation. In: Proc. Foundations of Computer Science – FoCS 1982, pp. 160–164. IEEE Press (1982)

A   Generalized BitDecomposition

In this section, we describe a generalized variant of BitDecomposition, which includes bit-decomposition in K_8 as a subfield of K_{40}.

Let $f : V \to W$ be a linear map between two vector spaces over $\mathbb{F}_2$. Then, $\langle r \rangle$ and $\langle f(r) \rangle$ for a random element $r \in V$ allows to securely compute $\langle f(x) \rangle$ for any $\langle x \rangle$ by computing and opening $\langle x + r \rangle$, and then computing $\langle f(x) \rangle = f(x + r) + \langle f(r) \rangle$.

For bit-decomposition in K_8, define $f : K_8 \to \mathbb{F}_2^8$ by

$$f\left(\sum_{i=0}^{7} a_i \cdot X^i \right) := (a_0, \ldots, a_7).$$

This function clearly is linear over $\mathbb{F}_2$. In the offline phase, it suffices to generate $\langle (r_0, \ldots, r_7) \rangle = (\langle r_0 \rangle, \ldots, \langle r_7 \rangle)$ for random bits $(r_0, \ldots, r_7)$ because $\langle r \rangle = \sum_{i=0}^{7} \langle r_i \rangle \cdot X^i$ can be computed locally. Note that $r_0, \ldots, r_7$ are understood as elements of K_8, like all variables in the protocol over K_8. Therefore, one has to make sure that they are in fact 0 or 1 and not another element of K_8. This is done by modifying the Offline Phase; in particular each party encrypts a random bit and proves that it is actually a bit. The homomorphic structure of the NIZKPoKs makes this straight-forward. As with the triples components, the secret bit is defined as the sum of all inputs, and the secret sharing with MAC is computed by multiplication via the homomorphic property of the ciphertexts and threshold decryption.

We now move to bit-decomposition for K_8 embedded in K_{40}. Let $\imath$ denote the embedding of K_8 in K_{40}. This embedding is a field homomorphism and thus a linear map between vector spaces over $\mathbb{F}_2$. The bit-decomposition for $\imath(K_8)$ is defined by $f : \imath(K_8) \to \mathbb{F}_2^8$,

$$f\Big(\imath\Big(\sum_{i=0}^{7} a_i \cdot X^i\Big)\Big) := (a_0, \ldots, a_7).$$

Again, f is linear over $\mathbb{F}_2$, and thus, the protocol explained above is applicable. Similarly to the case of K_8, it suffices to generate eight bits $(\langle r_0 \rangle, \ldots, \langle r_7 \rangle)$ in the offline phase. There is one peculiarity in this case: We defined f over $\imath(K_8) \subset K_{40}$, not K_{40}. That means, we assume that the input of f is an element of $\imath(K_8)$, not an arbitrary element. This is guaranteed in our application, but may not be true in general.

In general the function f can easily be extended to $f' : K_{40} \to \mathbb{F}_2^8$ by defining $f'(x) := f(p_{\imath(K_8)}(x))$ for $p_{\imath(K_8)}$ denoting the natural projection to $\imath(K_8)$. However, masking an arbitrary element $x \in K_{40}$ with a random element of $\imath(K_8)$ reveals $x - p_{\imath(K_8)}(x)$. Therefore, one has to mask x additionally with a random $r' \in K_{40}/\imath(K_8)$ before opening it, i.e., compute and open $\langle x + \imath(\sum_{i=0}^{7} r_i \cdot X^i) + r' \rangle$. As above, the homomorphic structure of the NIZKPoKs allow to generate $\langle r' \rangle$ with the same cost as a random element.

The above discussion re $\mathbb{F}_{2^8}$ and $\mathbb{F}_{2^{40}}$ can be extended to an arbitrary field $\mathbb{F}_{2^n}$ and a subfield $\mathbb{F}_{2^m}$ if required.

B   Figures

Online Protocol

Initialize: We assume i) the parties have already invoked the Offline Phase to obtain a sufficient number of multiplication triples $(\langle a \rangle, \langle b \rangle, \langle c \rangle)$; ii) each party holds its share of the global MAC keys $\alpha_{j,i}$; iii) that the parties have obtained (by some means) the $\langle \cdot \rangle$ sharing of the input values to the computation.

  1. The parties execute $\mathsf{Init}()$ to initialize their local copy of the hash function H_1, and the values seed_i, cnt_i, $\hat{a}_{j,i}$, and $\gamma_{j,i}$.

  2. The parties generate global random values $t_j \in \mathbb{F}_q$ for $j = 1, \ldots, n_{\mathsf{SAC}}$ by computing $(t_1 \| \ldots \| t_{n_{\mathsf{SAC}}}) = H_2(1 \| \mathsf{seed}_1 \| \ldots \| \mathsf{seed}_n)$.

The following steps are performed according to the circuit being evaluated.

Add: To add two representations $\langle x \rangle$, $\langle y \rangle$, the parties locally compute $\langle x \rangle + \langle y \rangle$.

Multiply: To multiply $\langle x \rangle$, $\langle y \rangle$ the parties do the following:

  1. They take $n_{\mathsf{SAC}} + 1$ triples $(\langle a \rangle, \langle b \rangle, \langle c \rangle), ((\langle f_i \rangle, \langle g_i \rangle, \langle h_i \rangle)_{i=1}^{n_{\mathsf{SAC}}}$ from the set of the available ones (and update this latter list by deleting these triples).

  2. For $j = 1, \ldots, n_{\mathsf{SAC}}$ player P_i computes

    (a) $\rho_j = \mathsf{PartialOpen}(t_j \cdot \langle a \rangle - \langle f_j \rangle)$.

    (b) $\sigma_j = \mathsf{PartialOpen}(\langle b \rangle - \langle g_j \rangle)$.

    (c) $\tau_j = \mathsf{PartialOpen}(t_j \cdot \langle c \rangle - \langle h_j \rangle - \sigma_j \cdot \langle f_j \rangle - \rho_j \cdot \langle g_j \rangle - \sigma_j \cdot \rho_j)$.

    (d) If $\tau_j \neq 0$ then abort.

  3. If no player has aborted the triple $(\langle a \rangle, \langle b \rangle, \langle c \rangle)$ is accepted, and the parties execute $\epsilon = \mathsf{PartialOpen}(\langle x \rangle - \langle a \rangle)$ and $\delta = \mathsf{PartialOpen}(\langle y \rangle - \langle b \rangle)$.

  4. The parties locally compute the answer $\langle z \rangle = \langle c \rangle + \epsilon \cdot \langle b \rangle + \delta \cdot \langle a \rangle + \epsilon \cdot \delta$

BitDecomposition: This produces the BitDecomposition of a shared value $\langle a \rangle$. We present a simplified protocol for when $q = 2^k$.

  1. $c = \mathsf{PartialOpen}\left(\langle a \rangle + \sum_{i=0}^{k-1} \langle r_i \rangle \cdot X^i\right)$.

  2. Write $c = \sum_{i=0}^{k-1} c_i \cdot X^i$.

  3. Output $\langle a_i \rangle = c_i + \langle r_i \rangle$.

Output: We enter this stage when the players have $\langle y \rangle$ for the output value y, but this value has not yet been opened. This output value is only correct if players have behaved honestly, which we now need to check. Let $a_1, \ldots, a_T$ be all values publicly opened so far, where $\langle a_k \rangle = (\delta_k, (a_{k,1}, \ldots, a_{k,n}), (\gamma_{j,1}(a_k), \ldots, \gamma_{j,n}(a_k))_{j=1}^{n_{\mathsf{MAC}}})$.

  1. Player P_i computes $(\mathsf{comm}_i, r_i) = \mathsf{Commit}(y_i \| (\gamma_{j,i}(y))_{j=1}^{n_{\mathsf{MAC}}})$.

  2. The players execute $\{\mathsf{comm}_1, \ldots, \mathsf{comm}_n\} = \mathsf{Broadcast}(\mathsf{comm}_i)$.

  3. For $j = 1, \ldots, n_{\mathsf{MAC}}$ the players execute

    (a) Player P_i computes $(\mathsf{comm}_{j,i}, r_{j,i}) \leftarrow \mathsf{Commit}(\gamma_{j,i})$.

    (b) Execute $\{\mathsf{comm}_{j,1}, \ldots, \mathsf{comm}_{j,n}\} = \mathsf{Broadcast}(\mathsf{comm}_{j,i})$.

    (c) Execute $\{\alpha_{j,1}, \ldots, \alpha_{j,n}\} = \mathsf{Broadcast}(\alpha_{j,i})$.

    (d) Player P_i computes $\alpha_j = \alpha_{j,1} + \cdots + \alpha_{j,n}$.

    (e) All players open $\mathsf{comm}_{j,i}$ to $\gamma_{j,i}$ (via a call to $\mathsf{Broadcast}$), the commitments are checked and if Open returns $\perp$ for a player then it aborts.

    (f) Each player verifies that $\alpha_j \cdot \hat{a}_{j,i} = \sum_i \gamma_{j,i}$ for his own values of $\hat{a}_{j,i}$.

  4. The players execute $\mathsf{Verify}()$ to confirm all broadcasts have been valid.

  5. To obtain the output value y, the commitments to $y_i, \gamma_{j,i}(y)$ are opened via each player transmitting to their openings to each player, and each player transmitting what it receives to each other to check consistency.

  6. Now, y is defined as $y := \sum_i y_i$ and each player checks that $\alpha_j \cdot (y + \delta_y) = \sum_i \gamma_{j,i}(y)$, for $j = 1, \ldots, n_{\mathsf{MAC}}$.

Fig. 2. The (slightly) modified SPDZ online phase

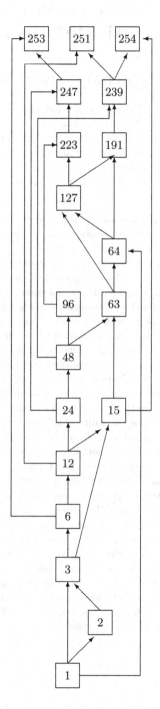

Fig. 3. Data flow graph of our addition chain

On the Centrality of Off-Line E-Cash to Concrete Partial Information Games

Seung Geol Choi[1], Dana Dachman-Soled[2], and Moti Yung[3]

[1] University of Maryland
sgchoi@cs.umd.edu
[2] Microsoft Research New England
dadachma@microsoft.com
[3] Google Inc. & Columbia University
moti@cs.columbia.edu

Abstract. Cryptography has developed numerous protocols for solving "partial information games" that are seemingly paradoxical. Some protocols are generic (e.g., secure multi-party computation) and others, due to the importance of the scenario they represent, are designed to solve a concrete problem directly. Designing efficient and secure protocols for (off-line) e-cash, e-voting, and e-auction are some of the most heavily researched concrete problems, representing various settings where privacy and correctness of the procedure is highly important.

In this work, we initiate the exploration of the relationships among e-cash, e-voting and e-auction in the universal composability (UC) framework, by considering general variants of the three problems. In particular, we first define ideal functionalities for e-cash, e-voting, and e-auction, and then give a construction of a protocol that UC-realizes the e-voting (resp., e-auction) functionality in the e-cash hybrid model. This (black-box) reducibility demonstrates the centrality of off-line e-cash and implies that designing a solution to e-cash may bear fruits in other areas. Constructing a solution to one protocol problem based on a second protocol problem has been traditional in cryptography, but typically has concentrated on building complex protocols on simple primitives (e.g., secure multi-party computation from Oblivious Transfer, signature from one-way functions, etc.). The novelty here is reducibility among mature protocols and using the ideal functionality as a design tool in realizing other ideal functionalities. We suggest this new approach, and we only consider the very basic general properties from the various primitives to demonstrate its viability. Namely, we only consider the basic coin e-cash model, the e-voting that is correct and private and relies on trusted registration, and e-auction relying on a trusted auctioneer. Naturally, relationships among protocols with further properties (i.e., extended functionalities), using the approach advocated herein, are left as open questions.

1 Introduction

1.1 Motivation

Research on the security and privacy of cryptographic protocols where parties share information (i.e., partial information games) is a major area of research in

I. Visconti and R. De Prisco (Eds.): SCN 2012, LNCS 7485, pp. 264–280, 2012.

cryptography. Many scenarios which seem paradoxical and unsolvable have been shown to be realizable, based on the power of information distribution and/or that of public-key cryptography.

While a good deal of research has been performed on constructing generic protocols (i.e., general secure multi-party computation) [Yao86, GMW87], there still exist important real life procedures that deserve special considerations: e-cash [Cha83, CFN88], e-voting [Cha81, CF85, BY86] and e-auction [FR96, NPS99]. Due to the great impact on the viability of cyberspace transactions that the successful deployment of these protocols brings about, they have attracted numerous researchers, and for decades, much work has been done on defining security and constructing secure protocols for these tasks. These specific partial information games share some basic configuration: Each of these games is structured so that players are either authorities (i.e., banks, talliers and auctioneers) or users. These fundamental similarities naturally beg the question:

> *What are the (black-box) relations among e-cash, e-voting and e-auction in the UC framework?*

This question is firstly of theoretical interest. Although, initiated in [IR89], a fairly complete picture of the black-box relations among most cryptographic primitives has been obtained, not much is known about the black-box relationship among *fairly complicated concrete protocols*. This direction of research may shed new light on understanding the definitions, security and complexity of these protocols.

Moreover, it is desirable to explore such relations in the modern *UC framework* introduced by Canetti [Can01]. Informally speaking, protocols secure in this framework remain secure even when executed concurrently with other arbitrary protocols running in some larger network, and can be used as subroutines of larger protocols in a modular fashion. The property is important considering that nowadays many protocols are executed concurrently with others on the Internet. We note that there are only a few results on the relationship among cryptographic primitives in the UC framework.

The question is also of practical interest. In practice, the simpler the system implementation is, the better. That is, if there is a significant black-box component that makes the implementation much simpler, there is no reason not to use it. Building a system from scratch, not employing available software in a black box manner, but using instead "smaller" black boxes (i.e., lower primitives such as one-way functions) potentially entails a lot of design and thus creates further sources for bugs in protocols or the need to embed the new protocol in a secure trusted systems component, which in turn lead to high costs (involved in resolving these issues). For example, if it is known that protocol-Y can be constructed from protocol-X, an optimized secure implementation (suitable for the setting) of protocol-X may lead to fairly simple deployment of a secure protocol-Y.

1.2   Our Results

Motivated by the above theoretical and practical considerations, we explore the relations among (off-line) e-cash, e-voting, and e-auction in the UC framework.

Concretely, we explore whether a secure protocol for e-voting (and for e-auction) can be constructed using a secure protocol for e-cash. This type of an investigation involves two tasks: defining security and achieving constructions in the UC framework.

Definition of Security. We first present ideal functionalities capturing the security of e-cash, e-voting, and e-auction; we concentrate in this work only on basic models with the most important security properties (generalizations to include further properties require extended functionalities and are left for future investigations). Intuitively, the e-cash functionality provides two important features of protection against double-spending and anonymity of honest spenders (we do not deal with extensions such as "fair cash" and "divisible cash"). The e-voting functionality provides protection against double-voting and unlinkability between voters and votes, i.e., correctness of voting and voter privacy. Again, it doesn't provide advanced properties like incoercibility [BT94, JCJ05].[1] The e-auction functionality provides secrecy of the bidding information until the end of the bidding procedure (once again, ignoring various added more advanced concerns like totally untrusted auctioneer, etc.).

E-Voting from E-Cash. We show a construction of a protocol that UC realizes the e-voting functionality in the e-cash hybrid model, under a certain restriction on the corruption pattern of the adversary. Due to the UC composition theorem [Can01], this implies that there exists a protocol π_{vote} UC-realizing the e-voting functionality with black-box access to π_{cash} UC-realizing the e-cash functionality.

We first notice similar security features between e-cash and e-voting. That is, if a voter casts a ballot more than once, his vote is rejected and possibly the identity of the double-voter is compromised (similarly to protection against double-spending in e-cash); on the other hand, voters and votes should be unlinkable (similarly to unlinkability between spenders and coins in e-cash). By utilizing these similarities (which are certainly known in the folklore) and by exploring more carefully the relationships and the needs of each problem, we were able to construct an e-voting protocol in the e-cash hybrid.

E-Auction from E-Cash. We also give a construction for e-auction (with a bound on the maximum bidding amount) in the e-cash hybrid. In the construction, there are two authorized agents, and it is assumed that at most one of them is semi-honestly corrupted. In the bidding stage, each bidder spends coins with the two authorities so that the bidding amount may be equal to the number of coins doubly-spent. Note that secrecy of the bidding amount is guaranteed since neither authority alone can determine the number of doubly-spent coins. Then, after the bidding stage ends, both authorities deposit their coins and count the number of doubly-spent coins for each bidder.

---

[1] In an e-voting scheme with incoercibility, it is infeasible for the adversary to determine if a coerced voter complies with the demands. We leave as an interesting open problem achieving incoercibile e-voting from e-cash.

1.3 Related Work

There have been a few results that provide an ideal functionality for e-cash [Tro05, Lin09] or e-voting [Gro04, dMPQ07]. The e-cash functionality in [Tro05] is not general enough in that the functionality contains a hash function and a tree structure inside. The e-cash functionality in [Lin09] does not deal with anonymous coins or detection of double-spending. The e-voting functionality in [Gro04] is different from ours in that it allows the adversary to prevent a voter from casting a vote while our functionality does not. The e-voting functionality in [dMPQ07] is parameterized with a post-processing function on the gathered ballots and can consider more general types of voting, e.g., outputting three most-favored candidates.

Maji, Prabhakaran, and Rosulek considered relations between cryptographic primitives in the UC framework [PR08, MPR09, MPR10a, MPR10b]. However, they have a different focus, and they rather retained more of a complexity theoretic perspectives (general feasibility) and explored which ideal functionality is complete.

1.4 Organization

In Section 2 we define ideal functionalities for e-cash, e-voting, and e-auction. Constructions of e-voting and e-auction in the e-cash hybrid are described in Section 3 and Section 4 respectively. We conclude in Section 5.

2 Ideal Functionalities

We present below the ideal functionalities for e-cash, e-voting and e-auction. We note that, although not explicitly stated in the description of the functionalities, the ideal adversary initially corrupts a subset of parties by sending a corrupt message for each party in the subset to the ideal functionality. Thus, the ideal functionality is always aware of the set of corrupted parties.

2.1 Ideal Functionality for E-Cash

We start with defining the ideal functionality $\mathcal{F}_{cash}$ for e-cash in Fig. 1. In the functionality, a user may open an account with his identity or a pseudonym *Nym* under the permission of the bank. Each coin is associated with a randomly generated serial number; when withdrawing w coins, a user is given w serial numbers, with which he can spend coins on other parties.

The functionality achieves *anonymity of honest spenders* in executing the command spend by directly notifying the serial number, but with no information about the corresponding spender, to the merchant. Note that the functionality stipulates that neither the bank nor the *merchant* should have any knowledge of who the spender is. We believe this modeling is reasonable; if merchants know the information about the spenders they may be able to sell it to the banks

---

Functionality $\mathcal{F}_{cash}$

- Upon receiving (setup, sid) from the prospective bank B:
  If there is already a party registered as the bank, ignore this message. Otherwise, record B as the bank. If there is no registered bank for this session sid, all the messages below are ignored.
- Upon receiving (open_account, sid, Nym, k) from U_i:
  If there is already an account for U_i, ignore the request. Otherwise, send (open_account, $sid, Nym, k, type$) to the bank, where $type$ is identity if $U_i = Nym$, or anonymous otherwise. Let (opened_account, sid, Nym, rep) be the reply from the bank. If $rep \neq \bot$, initialize an account for U_i tagged with Nym with initial balance k. Send (opened_account, sid, rep) to U_i.
- Upon receiving (withdraw, sid, w) from U_i:
  1. If there is no account for U_i or if the balance of account U_i is less than w, send (withdrawn, $sid, \bot$) to U_i and terminate.
  2. Decrease the balance of U_i by w, choose w random numbers ($serial_1, \ldots, serial_w$), and record the tuples ($withdrawn, U_i, serial_1, \ldots, serial_w$). Then, send (withdrawn, $sid, serial_1, \ldots, serial_w$) to U_i and (withdrawn, sid, Nym, w) to the bank B, where Nym is the tag for U_i.
- Upon receiving (spend, $sid, Nym, serial$) from U_i:
  1. If there is no such record as ($withdrawn, U_i, serial$), send (spent, $sid, \bot$) to U_i and terminate.
  2. Let U_j be the user whose account is tagged with Nym — if there no such user, send (spent, $sid, \bot$) to U_i and terminate. Record the tuple ($spent, U_i, U_j, serial$), send (spent, sid, Nym) to U_i, and send (spent, $sid, serial$) to U_j.
- Upon receiving (deposit, $sid, serial$) from U_j:
  1. If there is no record of a form ($spent, *, U_j, serial$) or if there is already a record ($deposited, *, U_j, serial$), then send (deposited, $sid, \bot$) to U_j and terminate.
  2. Let Nym be the tag for U_j. If there is already a record ($deposited, U_i, U_k, serial$) for some U_i and $U_k \neq U_j$, then record ($doubly\text{-}spent, serial, U_j$), send (deposited, $sid, doubly\text{-}spent$) to U_j, send (deposited, $sid, Nym, serial, doubly\text{-}spent$) to the bank, and terminate.
  3. Record ($deposited, U_i, U_j, serial$) where U_i is the spender of the coin (i.e., there is a record ($spent, U_i, U_j, serial$)). Increment the balance of U_j's account. Then send (deposited, $sid, serial$) to U_j and send (deposited, $sid, Nym, serial$) to the bank.
- Upon receiving (double_spender, $sid, serial$) from the bank B:
  If there is no such record as ($doubly\text{-}spent, serial, *$), send (double_spender, $sid, \bot$) to B. Otherwise, find the record ($deposited, U_i, U_j, serial$) for some U_i and U_j, and send (double_spender, sid, Nym_i, Nym_j) to B, where Nym_i and Nym_j are the tags for U_i and U_j respectively.
- Upon receiving (double_spenders, sid) from the bank B:
  Perform as above for $serial$ such that there is a record ($doubly\text{-}spent, serial, *$). Let S be the list of the tuples ($serial, Nym_i, Nym_j$), where Nym_i is the tag for a double spender, Nym_i is the tag on which the coin $serial$ is deposited. Send (double_spender, sid, S) to B.
- Upon receiving (balance, sid) from U_i:
  Let b be the balance of U_i. Send (balance, sid, b) to U_i.
- Upon receiving (balance, sid, Nym) from the bank B:
  Let b be the balance of the account with a tag Nym. Send (balance, sid, b) to B.

Fig. 1. Ideal Functionality for E-Cash

and other marketing organizations, which defeats the purpose Chaum [Cha83] originally tries to achieve. Indeed, this goes in line with a standard method to achieve a secure e-cash system, that is, executing an e-cash scheme through an anonymous channel [Cha81, SGR97, RR98, SL00, DMS04].

The functionality also provides *detecting the double-spender* of a coin in an off-line manner — detection occurs when the coin is deposited. Note that the power of the bank is restricted in that it only approves the account-opening requests, observes withdrawals and deposits, and detects double spenders. Further recall that we do not model more advanced properties of various e-cash schemes beyond the simple "basic coin" model.

2.2 Ideal Functionality For Basic E-Voting

Next, we define the ideal functionality $\mathcal{F}_{vote}$ for e-voting. The functionality assumes an authority that manages the voting procedure. Each party registers for voting, and then casts a vote for his favorite candidate.

At the tallying stage, the functionality allows corrupted candidates, not knowing the voting information of others, to decrease the number of votes they have received. Since it only allows them to give up the election, the functionality regards this case as legitimate. Note also that the voting information is kept secret even to the authority until the voting stage ends. As mentioned above, note that the functionality does not consider further advanced properties desired in various election scenarios, such as incoercibility [BT94, JCJ05].

2.3 Ideal Functionality for Basic E-Auction

Finally, we formulate the ideal functionality $\mathcal{F}_{auc}$ for e-auction in Fig. 3. The functionality assumes an authority that manages the auction process. Each party registers for auction, and then casts a bid. The authority does not know the bidding information until the bidding stage ends.

In our formulation, however, the authority will eventually see all the bidding information. As mentioned above, this is the basic case we deal with in this work. Obviously, more private auctions are suitable in many scenarios, yet considering that in many practical scenarios the authority ultimately sees the bids (e.g., Google AD Exchange), we believe our modeling is still a meaningful starting point.

3 E-Voting from E-Cash

We present an e-voting protocol that UC-realizes $\mathcal{F}_{vote}$ in the $\mathcal{F}_{cash}$ hybrid, with some restrictions on the corruption pattern of an adversary. In the protocol, we employ the similar security features between e-cash and e-voting. That is, if a voter casts a ballot more than once, his vote is rejected and possibly the identity of the double-voter is compromised (similarly to protection against double-spending in e-cash); on the other hand, voters and votes should be unlinkable (similarly to unlinkability between spenders and coins in e-cash).

Functionality $\mathcal{F}_{vote}$

Let A be the voting authority and $C_1, \ldots, C_k$ be the candidates.
- Upon receiving (register, sid) from V_i:

  If there is a record $(registered, V_i)$, ignore this message. Otherwise, record the tuple $(registered, V_i)$ and broadcast (registered, sid, V_i).

- Upon receiving (vote, sid, v) from V_i:

  If there is no such record as $(registered, V_i)$ or if $v \notin [k]$, then ignore this message. Otherwise, record the tuple $(voted, V_i, v)$.

- Upon receiving (tally, sid) from the authority A:

  1. Compute the tally result $R = (r_1, \ldots, r_k)$, where r_i is the tally for candidate C_i. In computing the tally results, ignore all tuples of the form $(voted, V_j, *)$ such that V_j appears more than once.
  2. For $1 \le i \le k$, if candidate C_i is corrupted, send message (tally, sid, r_i) to candidate C_i.
  3. Upon receiving a message of the form (tally, sid, r'_i) from each corrupted candidate C_i, compute $R_{final} = R - (r''_1, \ldots, r''_k)$, where $r''_i = r'_i$ if $0 \le r'_i \le r_i$, or $r''_i = 0$ otherwise, and broadcast (tally, sid, R_{final}).

Fig. 2. Ideal Functionality for E-Voting

We emphasize that the construction does not use any cryptographic tools or assumptions beyond $\mathcal{F}_{cash}$. Therefore, given a secure e-cash scheme, we can construct a secure e-voting scheme against an adversary with the specified corruption pattern.

Toy Construction. We start with a toy construction illustrating the basic idea of how to use an e-cash scheme, although with weak security.

> Some of the participants are designated as candidates. Each voter withdraws one coin from his bank account and spends his coin on the candidate of his choice. At the end of the election, each candidate deposits the coins that he receives, and broadcasts his balance as the result of the election.

In the above scheme, due to the anonymity of honest spenders of e-cash, the voting authority does not know the tallying information during the voting stage. However, the scheme is only secure against an adversary that corrupts voters maliciously and the authority semi-honestly but does not corrupt candidates. In particular, each candidate knows the exact number of votes in favor of himself.

3.1   Construction

Our final construction uses the following ideas to remove the trust trust that is placed in each of the candidates in the toy construction.

Functionality $\mathcal{F}_{auc}$

Let A be the auction authority.

- Upon receiving (register, sid) from party P_i:

  If there is a record $(registered, P_i)$, ignore this message. Otherwise, record the tuple $(registered, P_i)$ and broadcast (registered, sid, P_i).

- Upon receiving (bid, sid, P_i, v) from party P_i:

  If there is no such record as $(registered, P_i)$ or if there is a record of a form $(bid, P_i, *)$, then ignore this message. Otherwise, record the tuple (bid, P_i, v).

- Upon receiving (result, sid, A) from the auctioneer A:

  Send all the bidding information to A, that is, (result, $sid, \{(P_i, v_i)\}_{i=1}^n$), where n is the number of registered bidders and v_i is the bidding amount of P_i. Also, broadcast (result, $sid, \mathcal{P}$), where $\mathcal{P}$ is the set of highest bidders.

Fig. 3. Ideal Functionality for E-Auction

Two Authorities: The construction has two authorities: A registration authority B_1 and a tallying authority B_2.

Use of Detecting Double Spenders in E-Cash: The construction actively uses the feature of detection of double spenders in the e-cash scheme. In particular, let k be the number of candidates. Suppose a voter wants to cast a vote to the j-th candidate. Then, he withdraws k coins from the bank (i.e., the tallying authority B_2), spends each of the k coins to each candidate, and then *spends the j-th coin to the registration authority*. Each candidate deposits the coins that it received.

At the tallying stage, the registration authority deposits the coins that it has. Then the doubly spent coins are used to compute the tally result.

Use of Anonymous Spending in E-Cash: One security concern in the above description is that the identity of the voter is revealed, since the feature of detecting double spenders is used legitimately. To avoid this, each voter uses a pseudonym in spending coins. In particular, the registration authority plays a role of another bank, and the serial number of the coin with respect to the registration authority becomes a pseudonym of a voter. Since the serial number is generated at random, the pseudonym reveals no information of its owner's identity. The coins with respect to the tallying authority can now be safely used as explained above.

The description of the overall protocol π_{vote} is given in Figure 4.

Protocol π_{vote}

There are two distinguished parties — registration authority B_1 and tallying authority B_2. Both play the role of a bank in the e-cash scheme. Let $C_1, \ldots, C_k$ be the candidates.

- B_1 and B_2 send (setup, sid_1) and (setup, sid_2) to $\mathcal{F}_{cash}$ respectively. Each candidate C_i opens an account with balance 0 with respect to B_2.
- When V_i receives a message (register, sid) from the environment $\mathcal{Z}$:
  1. V_i sends (open_account, $sid_1, V_i, 1$) to $\mathcal{F}_{cash}$. Then B_1 in turn approve the open_account request via $\mathcal{F}_{cash}$, if V_i is a fresh, legitimate voter. Upon receiving (opened_account, sid_1, rep) from $\mathcal{F}_{cash}$, if $rep = \bot$, V_i terminates.
  2. V_i sends (withdraw, $sid_1, 1$) to $\mathcal{F}_{cash}$. Let (withdrawn, sid_1, s) be the reply from $\mathcal{F}_{cash}$. If $s = \bot$, V_i terminates; otherwise V_i sets $N_i = s$.
  3. V_i sends (spend, sid_1, B_2, N_i) to $\mathcal{F}_{cash}$. If the reply from $\mathcal{F}_{cash}$ is (spent, $sid_1, \bot$), V_i terminates.
  4. V_i sends (open_account, sid_2, N_i, k) to $\mathcal{F}_{cash}$. Then, B_2, upon receiving the (spent, sid_1, N_i) and (opened_account, sid_2, N_i, k, anonymous) from $\mathcal{F}_{cash}$, will send (deposit, sid_1, B_2, N_i) to $\mathcal{F}_{cash}$; if the response from $\mathcal{F}_{cash}$ is (deposited, sid_1, N_i), B_2 will send (open_account, sid_2, N_i, ok) to $\mathcal{F}_{cash}$; otherwise B_2 will send (open_account, $sid_2, N_i, \bot$).
- When V_i receives a message (vote, sid, v) from the environment $\mathcal{Z}$:
  1. V_i sends (withdraw, sid_2, k) to $\mathcal{F}_{cash}$. If $\mathcal{F}_{cash}$ responds with a message (withdrawn, $sid_2, serial_1, \ldots, serial_k$), then V_i records the values $serial_1, \ldots, serial_k$; otherwise, V_i terminates.
  2. For $1 \leq \ell \leq k$, V_i sends (spend, $sid_2, C_\ell, serial_\ell$) to $\mathcal{F}_{cash}$. If $\mathcal{F}_{cash}$ responds with a message (spent, $sid_2, \bot$) for any of the requests, V_i terminates.
  3. V_i sends (spend, $sid_2, B_1, serial_v$) to $\mathcal{F}_{cash}$. If $\mathcal{F}_{cash}$ responds with a message (spent, $sid_2, \bot$), V_i terminates.
  4. Now, each candidate C_ℓ, upon receiving a message (spent, sid_2, s) from $\mathcal{F}_{cash}$, sends a message (deposit, sid_2, s) to $\mathcal{F}_{cash}$.
- When B_1 receives a message (tally, sid) from $\mathcal{Z}$:
  1. B_1 sends a message (deposit, sid_2, s) to $\mathcal{F}_{cash}$ for each s of the coins that it has received; while B_1 is doing so, B_2 records the serial number s if B_2 receives (deposited, sid_2, B_1, s, doubly-spent) from $\mathcal{F}_{cash}$. B_1 sends (tally, sid) to B_2.
  2. For each recorded serial number s, B_2 sends (double_spender, sid_2, s) to $\mathcal{F}_{cash}$ and retrieves the corresponding pseudonym (i.e., the double spender) and the corresponding candidate. Using this list, B_2 computes the tally $R = (r_1, \ldots, r_k)$ and broadcasts (tally, sid, R). If a pseudonym appears more than once in the list, B_2 ignores all the votes given by the pseudonym.
  3. Each party outputs R.

Fig. 4. The Protocol for E-Voting in the $\mathcal{F}_{cash}$-Hybrid

3.2   Security

The authorities, once corrupted, are assumed to behave in a semi-honest manner. Also, we consider the case where at most one of the authorities is corrupted by the adversary. A more serious restriction is that the adversary is not allowed to corrupt the registration authority and candidates at the same time. If both the registration authority and a candidate have received a coin with the same serial number, it means that someone voted for the candidate. Therefore, such corruptions reveal to the adversary the number of votes casted for the corrupted voters before the tallying stage. We believe this restriction on the authorities is reasonable.

Theorem 1. *The protocol π_{vote} UC-realizes $\mathcal{F}_{vote}$ functionality against an adversary that corrupts voters and candidates maliciously and the authorities semi-honestly, with the restriction that it is not allowed to corrupt the registration authority and some candidates at the same time.*

Proof. We show that for every adversary $\mathcal{A}$, there exists a PPT $\mathcal{S}$ such that for every non-uniform PPT $\mathcal{Z}$ it holds that

$$\mathrm{EXEC}^{\mathcal{F}_{cash}}_{\pi_{vote}, \mathcal{A}, \mathcal{Z}} \approx \mathrm{IDEAL}_{\mathcal{F}_{vote}, \mathcal{S}, \mathcal{Z}}.$$

Fix $\mathcal{A}$. Wlog, we assume B_2 is semi-honestly corrupted; the proof is only easier when B_2 is not corrupted. We consider two cases according to whether B_1 is corrupted or not.

We will refer to the communication of $\mathcal{S}$ with $\mathcal{Z}$ and $\mathcal{F}_{vote}$ as external communication, and that with $\mathcal{A}$ as internal communication. For clarity, the message exchanges between the real adversary $\mathcal{A}$ (on behalf of a corrupted party P) and the simulator $\mathcal{S}$ (simulating ideal functionality $\mathcal{F}_{cash}$) are represented as exchanges between P and $\mathcal{S}$.

Roughly speaking, the simulator $\mathcal{S}$ simulates the functionality $\mathcal{F}_{cash}$ internally and tries to extract votes from corrupted voters.

Throughout the running of $\mathcal{S}$, it $\mathcal{S}$ forwards all the messages between $\mathcal{A}$ and $\mathcal{Z}$. Below, we describe how $\mathcal{S}$ handles other messages.

Case 1: B_1 Is Not Corrupted.   Let's first consider the case where B_1 is not corrupted. Then, the adversary may corrupt some candidates as well.

Handling register. $\mathcal{S}$ handles register messages as follows:

- $\mathcal{S}$, as $\mathcal{F}_{cash}$ and B_1 in the internal communication, handles the following messages exactly as $\mathcal{F}_{cash}$ and B_1 would do:
  - (setup, sid_2) from B_2.
  - (open_account, sid_1, V_i, bal) from a corrupted V_i.
  - (withdraw, sid_1, w) from a corrupted V_i.
  - (spend, $sid_1, B_2, serial$) from a corrupted V_i.
  - (deposit, $sid_1, serial$) from B_2.

- When S as $\mathcal{F}_{cash}$ receives (open_account, sid_2, $serial$, k) from a corrupted V_i:
  S does exactly what $\mathcal{F}_{cash}$ would do. In addition, when B_2 approves the request with (opened_account, sid_2, ok), then S, as the corrupted V_i in the external communication, sends (register, sid) to $\mathcal{F}_{vote}$.
- When S receives (registered, sid, V_j) externally from $\mathcal{F}_{vote}$ for an uncorrupted V_j:
  S does exactly what V_j will do in the internal communication. In particular, S handles virtual register, open_account, withdraw, and spend messages for V_j, as specified in the protocol.

Handling vote. S handles vote messages as follows:

- S as $\mathcal{F}_{cash}$ handles the following messages exactly as $\mathcal{F}_{cash}$ would do:
  - (withdraw, sid_2, k) from a corrupted V_i.
  - (spend, sid_2, B_1, s) from V_i.
  - (spend, sid_2, C_j, s) from V_i.
- When S as $\mathcal{F}_{cash}$ receives (deposit, sid_2, s) from a corrupted candidate C_j:
  S behaves exactly $\mathcal{F}_{cash}$ would. In addition, if the coin s has been successfully deposited and if the coin s has also been spent on B_1, find the spender V_i of the coins s using the recorded data, and S as the corrupted V_i (in the external communication), externally sends a message (vote, sid, v) to $\mathcal{F}_{vote}$.
- For each uncorrupted voter V_i, S simulates its behavior as specified in the protocol. The only exception is that V_i delays spending a coin on B_1 until the tally result comes out. This is because S cannot know which vote to cast on behalf of the honest party until it receives the final tally from the ideal voting functionality.
- For each uncorrupted candidate C_i, S simulates its behavior as specified in the protocol. In addition, if C_i has successfully deposited a coin s and if the coin s has also been spent on B_1, find the spender V_i of the coins s using the recorded data, and S as the corrupted V_i (in the external communication), externally sends a message (vote, sid, v) to $\mathcal{F}_{vote}$.

Handling tally. S handles tally messages as follows:

- When S, as a corrupted candidate C_i (in the external communication), externally receives (tally, sid, r_i) from $\mathcal{F}_{vote}$:
  1. Let m_i be the number of votes given by the corrupted voters to C_i, in the internal communication. This can be computed from the recorded data.
  2. Let $h_i = r_i - m_i$; that is, h_i is the number of votes from uncorrupted voters. S arbitrary generate a set H_i (disjoint with H_j for other candidate C_j) of uncorrupted voters of size h_i. On behalf of each uncorrupted voter V in H_i, S now handles a virtual message (spend, sid_2, B_1, s') from V, where s' is the coin that V has spent on C_i. Note that this simulation is good since $\mathcal{F}_{cash}$ guarantees that identities of spenders and serial numbers of coins are completely disassociated.

   3. Let h'_i be the number of coins belonging to H_i that C_i didn't deposit. $\mathcal{S}$, as the corrupted C_i (in the external communication), externally sends (tally, sid, h'_i) to $\mathcal{F}_{vote}$.

– Once $\mathcal{S}$ handles the tally messages from $\mathcal{F}_{vote}$ for all the corrupted candidates in the external communication, $\mathcal{S}$ as B_1 internally sends (tally, sid) to B_2.

– When $\mathcal{S}$ as $\mathcal{F}_{cash}$ receives a message (double_spender, sid_2, s) from B_2:
   $\mathcal{S}$ does exactly what $\mathcal{F}_{cash}$ would do.

Case 2: When B_1 Is Corrupted.   In this case, due the restriction on the corruption pattern of the adversary, the candidates are not to be corrupted.

Handling register. $\mathcal{S}$ handles register messages as follows:

– $\mathcal{S}$ as $\mathcal{F}_{cash}$ handles the following messages as $\mathcal{F}_{cash}$ would do:
   • setup messages from B_1 or B_2.
   • (open_account, sid_1, V_i, bal) from a corrupted V_i.
   • (withdraw, sid_1, w) from a corrupted V_i.
   • (spend, $sid_1, B_2, serial$) from a corrupted V_i.
   • (deposit, $sid_1, serial$) from B_2.

– When $\mathcal{S}$ as $\mathcal{F}_{cash}$ receives (open_account, $sid_2, serial, k$) from a corrupted V_i: $\mathcal{S}$ does exactly what $\mathcal{F}_{cash}$ would do. In addition, when B_2 approves the request with (opened_account, sid_2, ok), $\mathcal{S}$ as the corrupted V_i (in the external communication) externally sends (register, sid) to $\mathcal{F}_{vote}$.

– When $\mathcal{S}$ receives (registered, sid, V_j) from $\mathcal{F}_{vote}$:
$\mathcal{S}$ internally simulates what the uncorrupted V_j would do. In particular, $\mathcal{S}$ handles virtual register, open_account, withdraw, and spend messages for V_j, as specified in the protocol.

Handling vote. $\mathcal{S}$ handles vote messages as follows:

– $\mathcal{S}$ as $\mathcal{F}_{cash}$ handles the following messages as $\mathcal{F}_{cash}$ would do:
   • (withdraw, sid_2, k) from a corrupted V_i.
   • (spend, sid_2, B_1, s) from a corrupted V_i.
   • (spend, sid_2, C_j, s) from a corrupted V_i:

– For each uncorrupted voter V_i, $\mathcal{S}$ simulates its behavior as specified in the protocol, except the following:
   Let $s_1, \ldots, s_k$ be the coins that V_i has. V_i spends s_1 on B_1 and delays spending coins on candidates until the tally result comes out.

– For each uncorrupted candidate C_i, $\mathcal{S}$ simulates its behavior as specified in the protocol.

– If C_i, whether or not it is corrupted, has successfully deposited a coin s and if the coin s has also been spent on B_1, find the spender V_i of the coins s using the recorded data, and $\mathcal{S}$ as the corrupted V_i (in the external communication), externally sends a message (vote, sid, v) to $\mathcal{F}_{vote}$.

Handling tally. S handles tally messages as follows:

- When S, as $\mathcal{F}_{cash}$, starts to get deposit requests from B_1, S, as the corrupted registration authority (in the external communication) sends (tally, sid) to $\mathcal{F}_{vote}$. The deposit requests are handled as $\mathcal{F}_{cash}$ would do.
- Upon receiving (tally, sid, R_{final}) externally from $\mathcal{F}_{vote}$:
  1. Let $R_{final} = (r_1, \ldots, r_k)$. For each candidate C_i, let m_i be the number of votes given by corrupted voters to C_i in the internal communication. This can be computed from the recorded data. Let $h_i = r_i - m_i$; that is, h_i is the number of votes from uncorrupted voters. S arbitrary generate a set H_i (disjoint with H_j for other candidate C_j) of uncorrupted voters of size h_i. Now, each uncorrupted voter V in H_i spends coins on candidates. Let $s_1, \ldots, s_k$ be the coins that V has. V spends $(s_1, s_2, s_3, \ldots, s_k)$ on $(C_i, C_2, C_3, \ldots, C_{i-1}, C_1, C_{i+1}, \ldots C_k)$.
- When S as $\mathcal{F}_{cash}$ receives a message (double_spender, sid_2, s) from B_2:
  S does exactly what $\mathcal{F}_{cash}$ would do.

4   E-Auction from E-Cash

We construct a protocol π_{auc} for e-auction with a bound on the maximum bidding amount in the $\mathcal{F}_{cash}$-hybrid that UC-realizes the $\mathcal{F}_{auc}$ functionality in Fig. 5.

Overview of the Protocol.   In the protocol, there are two authorized agents A_1 and A_2, which will play the role of a bank in the e-cash scheme. We note that A_1 and A_2 are assumed to be semi-honest and are trusted not to collude (i.e., we allow at most one of them to be corrupted).

Let θ be the maximum bidding value. Each player withdraws 2θ coins from the first authority A_1 and spends θ coins on A_1 and A_2 respectively. The idea is that each party spends coin, using the feature of detecting the double spenders in $\mathcal{F}_{cash}$, so that the bidding amount may be equal to the number of coins doubly-spent. For example, party P with bidding amount k will spend the k coins (out of θ) on both A_1 and A_2. Then, after the bidding stage ends, A_1 and A_2 will deposit their coins and count the number of doubly-spent coins for each bidder.

Theorem 2. *The protocol π_{auc} UC-realizes $\mathcal{F}_{auc}$ functionality as long as at most one of A_1 and A_2 is semi-honestly corrupted.*

Proof. We show that for every adversary $\mathcal{A}$, there exists a PPT S such that for every non-uniform PPT $\mathcal{Z}$ it holds that

$$\mathrm{EXEC}^{\mathcal{F}_{cash}}_{\pi_{auc}, \mathcal{A}, \mathcal{Z}} \approx \mathrm{IDEAL}_{\mathcal{F}_{auc}, S, \mathcal{Z}}.$$

Fix $\mathcal{A}$. At the outset of the protocol, there are some bidders that are corrupted. We consider the case where A_1 is semi-honestly corrupted; the case where A_1 is not corrupted is only easier. We will refer to the communication of S with $\mathcal{Z}$ and $\mathcal{F}_{auc}$ as external communication, and that with $\mathcal{A}$ as internal communication.

Protocol π_{auc}

Let θ be the maximum bidding value and A_1 and A_2 be auction authorities.

- A_1 sends (setup, sid) to $\mathcal{F}_{cash}$. A_1 and A_2 open their accounts respectively.
- When P_i receives a message (register, sid) from the environment $\mathcal{Z}$:
  1. P_i sends (open_account, $sid, P_i, 2\theta$) to $\mathcal{F}_{cash}$. Then A_1 in turn will receive the open_account request from $\mathcal{F}_{cash}$ and, if P_i is legitimate, approve the request.
  2. Upon receiving (opened_account, sid, rep) from $\mathcal{F}_{cash}$, if $rep = \bot$, P_i terminates.
  3. P_i sends (withdraw, $sid_1, P_i, A_1, 2\theta$) to $\mathcal{F}_{cash}$. If $\mathcal{F}_{cash}$ responds with a message (withdrawn, sid_1, $serial_1$, ..., $serial_{2\theta}$), then P_i records the values $serial_1, \ldots, serial_{2\theta}$.
- When P_i receives a message (bid, sid, v) from the environment $\mathcal{Z}$:
  1. If P_i does not have a recorded $serial_1, \ldots, serial_{2\theta}$, it terminates.
  2. For $1 \le j \le \theta$, P_i sends a message (spend, $sid, P_i, A_1, serial_j$) to $\mathcal{F}_{cash}$. If $\mathcal{F}_{cash}$ responds with a message (spent, $sid, \bot$) to any of the requests, P_i terminates.
  3. For $\theta-v+1 \le j \le 2\theta-v$, P_i sends a message (spend, $sid, P_i, A_2, serial_j$) to $\mathcal{F}_{cash}$. If $\mathcal{F}_{cash}$ responds with a message (spent, $sid, \bot$) to any of the requests, P_i terminates.
- When A_1 receives a message (result, sid) from $\mathcal{Z}$:
  1. A_1 tells A_2 to deposit its coins. After A_2 has finished the deposit procedure, A_1 deposits all the coins. For each serial number $serial_j$ that has been doubly-spent, A_1 sends a message (double_spender, $sid, serial_j$) to $\mathcal{F}_{cash}$ and receives back the identity of the spender of coin $serial_j$. Now, using this information, A_1 determines the bidding amount of each participant P_k. A_1 broadcasts the message (result, $sid, \mathcal{P}$), where $\mathcal{P}$ is the set of parties whose bidding amount is the largest.

Fig. 5. Protocol for E-Auction in the $\mathcal{F}_{cash}$-hybrid

Roughly speaking, the simulator $\mathcal{S}$ simulates the functionality $\mathcal{F}_{cash}$ internally and tries to extract bids from corrupted bidders.

For clarity, message exchanges between the real adversary $\mathcal{A}$ (on bahalf of a corrupted party P) and the simulator $\mathcal{S}$ (simulating ideal functionality $\mathcal{F}_{cash}$) are represented as exchanges between P and $\mathcal{S}$.

Throughout the running of $\mathcal{S}$, it $\mathcal{S}$ forwards all the messages between $\mathcal{A}$ and $\mathcal{Z}$. Below, we describe how $\mathcal{S}$ handles other messages.

Handling register
The simulator $\mathcal{S}$ handles the register messages as follows:

- When $\mathcal{S}$ as $\mathcal{F}_{cash}$ receives (open_account, $sid_1, P_i, 2\theta$) from a corrupted bidder P_i:

  $\mathcal{S}$ does exactly what $\mathcal{F}_{cash}$ would do.

- When $\mathcal{S}$ as $\mathcal{F}_{cash}$ receives (withdraw, sid_1, P_i, w) from a corrupted P_i:
    $\mathcal{S}$ does exactly what $\mathcal{F}_{cash}$ would do. In addition, for a successful with-drawal, $\mathcal{S}$, as P_i in the external communication, sends (register, sid) externally to $\mathcal{F}_{auc}$.
- When $\mathcal{S}$ receives (registered, sid, P_j) externally from $\mathcal{F}_{auc}$ for an uncorrupted P_j:
    $\mathcal{S}$ does exactly what P_j will do in the internal communication. In particular, $\mathcal{S}$ as P_j sends (open_account, $sid_1, P_i, 2\theta$) to $\mathcal{F}_{cash}$ ($\mathcal{S}$ itself) and handles the virtual withdraw message (i.e., sends the message to $\mathcal{S}$ itself).

Handling bid
The simulator $\mathcal{S}$ handles the bid messages as follows:

- When $\mathcal{S}$ as $\mathcal{F}_{cash}$ receives (spend, $sid_1, P_i, A_j, serial$) where $j \in \{1,2\}$ from a corrupted P_i:
    $\mathcal{S}$ does exactly what $\mathcal{F}_{cash}$ would do:
- $\mathcal{S}$ handles virtual spend messages from the uncorrupted parties. That is, for each uncorrupted P_j, let $serial_1, \ldots, serial_{2\theta}$ be the serial numbers of the coins belonging to P_j. $\mathcal{S}$ as $\mathcal{F}_{cash}$ sends $\left\{ (\text{spent}, P_j, A_1, serial_i) \right\}_{i=1}^{\theta}$ to A_1, and it also sends $\left\{ (\text{spent}, P_j, A_2, serial_i) \right\}_{i=\theta+1}^{2\theta}$ to A_2.

Handling result
The simulator $\mathcal{S}$ handles the result messages as follows:

- When $\mathcal{S}$ as A_2 receives a message from the corrupted A_1 to deposit the coins:
    1. For each corrupted bidder P_i, $\mathcal{S}$ computes the number b of doubly-spent coins by P_i, and, as P_i in the external communication, sends (bid, sid, b) to $\mathcal{F}_{auc}$ externally.
    2. $\mathcal{S}$ as the corrupted A_1 (in the external communication) sends (result, sid, A_1) externally to $\mathcal{F}_{auc}$ and gets the results (result, $sid, \{(P_i, v_i)\}_{i=1}^{n}$). Now, $\mathcal{S}$ changes the serial numbers spent by uncorrupted parties P_j so that the number of doubly-spend coins by P_j are v_j. Then $\mathcal{S}$ handles the virtual deposit messages — i.e., sends (deposit, $sid, A_2, serial$) messages to itself — exactly as $\mathcal{F}_{cash}$ would do, using the recorded data.
- When $\mathcal{S}$ as $\mathcal{F}_{cash}$ receives deposit and double_spender messages from the corrupted A_1, $\mathcal{S}$ handles the messages exactly $\mathcal{F}_{cash}$ would do using the recorded data.

The only modification that $\mathcal{S}$ performs lies in the serial numbers of the uncorrupted parties spend on A_2. However, to the view of the adversary (in particular to A_1), this modification is invisible. Therefore, the simulation is perfect.

The case where A_1 is honest and A_2 is semi-honestly corrupted can be simulated in a similar fashion. In particular, the simulator extracts the bidding amount of corrupted bidders while simulating $\mathcal{F}_{cash}$. Then, upon receiving (result, $sid, \mathcal{P}$) from $\mathcal{F}_{auc}$, $\mathcal{S}$, as A_1 in the internal communication, internally broadcasts (result, $sid, \mathcal{P}$).

5   Conclusions

Our work reveals interesting relationships between some basic protocols that have been so far developed independently. Natural questions remain:

- Is it possible to eliminate the restriction on the corruption pattern of the adversary that the current constructions have or to show a separation when an arbitrary number of parties may be corrupt?
- It is also interesting to explore the remaining relationships among e-cash, e-voting, and e-auction, to consider extended functionalities (with extra properties) and explore relationships among them.
- Are there other "partial information protocols" that can be used as building blocks for other protocols or can be built on top of some known protocols?

References

[BT94]   Benaloh, J.C., Tuinstra, D.: Receipt-free secret-ballot elections (extended abstract). In: STOC, pp. 544–553 (1994)

[BY86]   Benaloh, J.C., Yung, M.: Distributing the power of a government to enhance the privacy of voters (extended abstract). In: PODC, pp. 52–62 (1986)

[Can01]   Canetti, R.: Universally composable security: A new paradigm for cryptographic protocols. In: FOCS, pp. 136–145 (2001)

[CF85]   Cohen, J.D., Fischer, M.J.: A robust and verifiable cryptographically secure election scheme (extended abstract). In: FOCS, pp. 372–382 (1985)

[CFN88]   Chaum, D., Fiat, A., Naor, M.: Untraceable Electronic Cash. In: Goldwasser, S. (ed.) CRYPTO 1988. LNCS, vol. 403, pp. 319–327. Springer, Heidelberg (1990)

[Cha81]   Chaum, D.: Untraceable electronic mail, return addresses, and digital pseudonyms. Commun. ACM 24(2), 84–88 (1981)

[Cha83]   Chaum, D.: Blind signature system. In: Advances in Cryptology, Proceedings of CRYPTO 1983, Santa Barbara, California, USA, August 21-24, p. 153. Plenum Press, New York (1983)

[dMPQ07]   de Marneffe, O., Pereira, O., Quisquater, J.-J.: Simulation-based analysis of e2e voting systems. In: Frontiers of Electronic Voting (2007)

[DMS04]   Dingledine, R., Mathewson, N., Syverson, P.F.: Tor: The second-generation onion router. In: Proc. of the 13th. USENIX Security Symposium (August 2004)

[FR96]   Franklin, M.K., Reiter, M.K.: The design and implementation of a secure auction service. IEEE Trans. Software Eng. 22(5), 302–312 (1996)

[GMW87]   Goldreich, O., Micali, S., Wigderson, A.: How to play any mental game or a completeness theorem for protocols with honest majority. In: STOC, pp. 218–229 (1987)

[Gro04]   Groth, J.: Evaluating Security of Voting Schemes in the Universal Composability Framework. In: Jakobsson, M., Yung, M., Zhou, J. (eds.) ACNS 2004. LNCS, vol. 3089, pp. 46–60. Springer, Heidelberg (2004)

[IR89]   Impagliazzo, R., Rudich, S.: Limits on the provable consequences of one-way permutations. In: STOC, pp. 44–61 (1989)

[JCJ05]   Juels, A., Catalano, D., Jakobsson, M.: Coercion-resistant electronic elections. In: WPES, pp. 61–70 (2005)

[Lin09]   Lindell, Y.: Legally enforceable fairness in secure two-party communication. Chicago J. Theor. Comput. Sci. (2009)

[MPR09]   Maji, H.K., Prabhakaran, M., Rosulek, M.: Complexity of Multi-party Computation Problems: The Case of 2-Party Symmetric Secure Function Evaluation. In: Reingold, O. (ed.) TCC 2009. LNCS, vol. 5444, pp. 256–273. Springer, Heidelberg (2009)

[MPR10a]   Maji, H.K., Prabhakaran, M., Rosulek, M.: Cryptographic complexity classes and computational intractability assumptions. In: ICS, pp. 266–289 (2010)

[MPR10b]   Maji, H.K., Prabhakaran, M., Rosulek, M.: A Zero-One Law for Cryptographic Complexity with Respect to Computational UC Security. In: Rabin, T. (ed.) CRYPTO 2010. LNCS, vol. 6223, pp. 595–612. Springer, Heidelberg (2010)

[NPS99]   Naor, M., Pinkas, B., Sumner, R.: Privacy preserving auctions and mechanism design. In: ACM Conference on Electronic Commerce, pp. 129–139 (1999)

[PR08]   Prabhakaran, M., Rosulek, M.: Cryptographic Complexity of Multi-Party Computation Problems: Classifications and Separations. In: Wagner, D. (ed.) CRYPTO 2008. LNCS, vol. 5157, pp. 262–279. Springer, Heidelberg (2008)

[RR98]   Reiter, M.K., Rubin, A.D.: Crowds: Anonymity for Web Transactions. ACM Transactions on Information and System Security 1(1), 66–92 (1998)

[SGR97]   Syverson, P.F., Goldschlag, D.M., Reed, M.G.: Anonymous connections and onion routing. In: IEEE Symposium on Security and Privacy, Oakland, California, pp. 44–54 (1997)

[SL00]   Shields, C., Levine, B.: A Protocol for Anonymous Communication over the Internet. In: Proc. 7th ACM Conference on Computer and Communication Security (November 2000)

[Tro05]   Trolin, M.: A Universally Composable Scheme for Electronic Cash. In: Maitra, S., Veni Madhavan, C.E., Venkatesan, R. (eds.) INDOCRYPT 2005. LNCS, vol. 3797, pp. 347–360. Springer, Heidelberg (2005)

[Yao86]   Yao, A.C.-C.: How to generate an exchange secrets. In: FOCS, pp. 162–167 (1986)

Universally Composable Security
with Local Adversaries

Ran Canetti* and Margarita Vald*

Boston University and Tel Aviv University

Abstract. The traditional approach to formalizing ideal-model based definitions of security for multi-party protocols models adversaries (both real and ideal) as centralized entities that control all parties that deviate from the protocol. While this centralized-adversary modeling suffices for capturing basic security properties such as secrecy of local inputs and correctness of outputs against coordinated attacks, it turns out to be inadequate for capturing security properties that involve restricting the sharing of information between separate adversarial entities. Indeed, to capture collusion-freeness and game-theoretic solution concepts, Alwen et al. [Crypto, 2012] propose a new ideal-model based definitional framework that involves a de-centralized adversary.

We propose an alternative framework to that of Alwen et al. We then observe that our framework allows capturing not only collusion-freeness and game-theoretic solution concepts, but also several other properties that involve the restriction of information flow among adversarial entities. These include some natural flavors of anonymity, deniability, timing separation, and information-confinement. We also demonstrate the inability of existing formalisms to capture these properties.

We then prove strong composition properties for the proposed framework, and use these properties to demonstrate the security, within the new framework, of two very different protocols for securely evaluating any function of the parties' inputs.

1 Introduction

Rigorously capturing the security properties of cryptographic protocols has proven to be a tricky endeavor. Over the years, the *trusted party* (or, simulation) paradigm has emerged as a useful and general definitional methodology. The basic idea, first coined in [GM84, GMR85, GMW87], is to say that a protocol "securely realizes" a given computational task if participating in the protocol "emulates" the process of interacting with an imaginary "trusted party" that securely receives parties' inputs and locally computes their outputs. Intuitively, this paradigm allows expressing and capturing many security properties. Moreover, it has an attractive potential "composability" property: any system using a

---

* Both authors are supported by the Check Point Institute for Information Security, Marie Curie grant PIRG03-GA-2008-230640, and ISF grant 0603805843.

I. Visconti and R. De Prisco (Eds.): SCN 2012, LNCS 7485, pp. 281–301, 2012.

trusted party $\mathcal{F}$ should behave the same way when we replace the trusted party with the realizing protocol.

Over the years, many security definitions were based on this intuitive idea, e.g., [GL90, MR91, Can00, DM00, PW00, Can01, PS04, CDPW07]. First, these definitions formulate an execution model; then they formalize the notion of emulating an ideal task with an "ideal world" attacker, called simulator. The security requirement is based on the inability of an external observer to distinguish an "ideal world" execution from a real one.

These formalisms differ in many ways; however, they have one major thing in common: they all model the attacker as a centralized entity, who can corrupt parties, coordinate their behavior and, intuitively, constitute an "evil coalition" against the protocol being executed. This seems to be an over-simplification of real life situations. Indeed, in real life, parties are often individuals who are not necessary controlled by the same entity or have anything in common. It would seem that letting the malicious parties coordinate their attacks should be a strengthening of the model; however, when this power is also given to the adversary in the ideal model (aka the simulator), the security guarantee can potentially be weakened. Therefore, a natural question to ask is whether it is justified to model the attacker as a centralized entity or does this modeling unduly limit its expressiveness?

Indeed, the existing formalisms do capture basic properties such as privacy of inputs, and correctness of outputs against coordinated attack. However, as has been observed in the past, there exist security concerns that are not naturally captured using the centralized adversary approach. Consider for instance the *collusion- freeness* concern: a protocol is *collusion-free* if even misbehaving protocol participants cannot use the protocol to exchange "disallowed" information without being detected. As pointed out by [ILM05], "centralized simulator" formalisms do not capture the inability of parties to collude. That is, with a centralized adversary, a protocol might allow collusions between corrupted parties even when it realizes an ideal task that is collusion-free.

An additional known limitation of standard security notions is cryptographic implementations of game-theoretic mechanisms. In contrast to cryptography, game theory considers rational players that behave according to their individual goals. In many realistic settings, the incentive structure depends on whom players can collaborate with and the cost of this collaboration. Security with a centralized adversary does not guarantee that the incentive structure with respect to collaboration is preserved when moving from the ideal protocol to the one that realizes it. Consequently, it does not correctly capture the incentive structure and does not suffice for preserving game-theoretic solution concepts that restrict the formation of coalitions.

A natural way to handle those concerns would be to strengthen the model by requiring that the simulation be "local" in some sense; that is, shattering the centralized simulator to many simulators, where each simulator has only some "local" information and is responsible to simulate adversarial behavior in only a "local" sense. However, requiring local simulators while allowing the adversary to be centralized results in an unrealistically strong security requirement that fails to admit many useful schemes that have practical security guarantees. Therefore, the next promising idea would be to restrict also the adversary to be local. This approach indeed appears in the works of [LMS05, ASV08, AKL+09, ILM11, MR11, AKMZ12]. In particular, [AKMZ12] gives general model with a composition theorem and application to game-theory. These works give different and incomparable definitions of collusion-freeness; a common aspect is that they all postulate an adversary/simulator for each *participant*, where a participant represents an entity that is identified via its party identifier and treated as a "single domain" (i.e., it is corrupt as a unit, either wholly or none at all). However, as we demonstrate below, there are a number of security concerns that cannot be naturally captured even by the above formalizations of local simulation.

Our Contributions. We provide an alternative formalization of the local simulators approach in a way that preserves its intuitive appeal and captures reality more tightly. In particular, we establish a general security notion that allows capturing the requirements of arbitrary tasks while preserving the local view of each individual component *and each communication link between components* in the system. This notion enables expressing variety of partitions of the system. Specifically, we refine the UC framework to deal with the locality of information available to clusters of components. The new formalism, called local UC (LUC), assigns a different adversary/simulator to each *ordered pair* of participants. Intuitively, the adversaries/simulators assigned to a pair of parties handle all the communication between the two parties. Informally,

If π is a *LUC-secure* protocol that implements a trusted party $\mathcal{F}$, then each *individual entity* participating in π affects each other entity in the system no more than it does so in the ideal execution with $\mathcal{F}$.

Note that this is conceptually different from the guarantees provided by the UC framework of [Can01] and the Collusion-Preserving framework of [AKMZ12] (referred as CP). In the UC framework, protocols that implement a trusted party are guaranteed to have similar effect on the external environment as in the ideal execution with $\mathcal{F}$. In the CP framework, the protocol is guaranteed to have the same effect as the trusted party *individually on each entity*. In the LUC framework, it is guaranteed that *each entity affects each other entity* in the same way as in the ideal execution.

We show that this refined granularity allows LUC to capture various security concerns that cannot be captured by previous frameworks. We address some flavors of anonymity, deniability, collusion-freeness, information-confinement, and preservation of incentive structure.

We also extend the UC composition theorem and the dummy adversary theorem to the new framework. We obtain strong composition results that enable "game theoretic composition", i.e., composition that preserves the power of coalitions (whatever they may be). Moreover, our strong composition also preserves deniability and confinement.

Next we present two protocols for secure function evaluation with LUC security. The protocols, called the Physical GMW and the Mediated SFE protocols, satisfy the new security definition. The protocols are very different from each other: The Physical GMW protocol, which is strongly inspired by [ILM05], models players sitting in a room equipped with machines and jointly computing a function. The Mediated SFE protocol is a simplified version of [AKL+09]. Like there, we use a semi-trusted mediator. That is, if the mediator is honest then the protocol is LUC secure. It is also UC secure in the standard sense even if the mediator is corrupted. It is interesting to note that although these two protocols have significantly different nature, they are both analyzable within our framework.

1.1 Our Contributions in More Details

The New Formalism. In a nutshell, the new modeling proceeds as follows. Recall that in the UC framework, the adversary is a centralized entity that not only controls the communication in the network, but also coordinates the corrupted parties' behavior. This centralization is also inherited by the simulator. As mentioned above, while this modeling captures privacy and correctness, which are "global" properties of the execution, it certainly does not capture rationality or locality of information. This implicitly means that only the situations where corrupted parties enjoy global view of the system are being fully captured.

A first attempt to bridge this gap might be to follow the formalisms of previous works [ASV08, AKMZ12, MR11] and consider one adversary per party. However, this modeling does not completely capture reality either. Consider for instance the following scenario: one of two parties A and B is having a conversation with a third party C. Later C is instructed to transfer this information to some honest but curious fourth party D without revealing whether the source was A or B. Clearly for the protocol to make intuitive sense, A and B need to assume that C is trusted, or "incorruptible". However, going back to the suggested model we notice that the adversary associated with C participates in all the conversations that C participates in, and can thus correlate the $C - D$ communication with the $A - C$ and $B - C$ communication without corrupting C at all, thereby harming the anonymity in a way that is not intended by the protocol (see more detailed account of this issue in Section 3). In other words, the suggested modeling does not distinguish between the "obviously insecure" protocol that allows C to be corrupted, and the "obviously secure" protocol that uses an incorruptible C. We conclude that having a single adversary per party does not faithfully model honest parties. This motivates us to look for a more refined model.

To adequately capture locality, we extend the UC model as follows: For each party identity (denoted PID) we consider an adversary for any PID it might communicate with. In other words, each pair of PIDs has a pair of adversaries, where each adversary is in a different side of the "potential communication line".

Each local adversary is in charge of a specific communication line and is aware only of the communication via this line.

Another feature of our modeling is that we let the environment directly control the communication, by letting the local adversaries communicate with each other only through the environment. This is an important definitional choice that is different from [AKMZ12]. In particular, this means that the centralized simulator no longer exists and, each local adversary is replaced with a local simulator in the ideal process, where the protocol is replaced by the trusted party. The trusted party may allow different subsets of simulators to communicate by forwarding messages between them. Therefore, the communication interface provided by the trusted party to the simulators represents partition of the system to clusters. The effect of this modeling is that the simulator for an entity can no longer rely on other parties' internal information or communication in which it was not present. This way, a proof of security relies only on each entity's local information, and potentially, represents independence of clusters defined by the trusted party.

To preserve meaningfulness, we allow the local adversaries to communicate across party identities only via the environment or with ideal functionalities. Aside from these modifications in the adversarial interface, the model is identical to the UC model.

Capturing security concerns. We discuss variety of security concerns that are captured by LUC security but not in other security notions:

Collusion-freeness. To provide initial evidence for the expressiveness of LUC, we consider any UC-secure protocol for multi-party computation (e.g. the [CLOS02] protocol). While this protocol UC realizes any ideal functionality (even ones that guarantee collusion freeness) in the presence of malicious adversaries, it allows individually corrupted parties to collude quite freely, even when the environment does not pass any information among parties. Indeed, this protocol does not LUC-realize any ideal functionality that guarantees collusion-freeness. This is so even in the presence of only semi-honest adversaries. The reason for the failure in the LUC model is the inability of the separate simulators to produce consistent views on adversaries' shared information (i.e., scheduling, committed values etc.) We note that this concern is captured by the definitions of [LMS05, ASV08, AKL+09, AKMZ12] as well.

Anonymity. We consider several flavors of anonymity such as existence-anonymity, timing-anonymity, and sender-anonymity. Specifically, we show UC and CP realizations of ideal functionalities that have these anonymity requirements by a protocol that does not have these properties. We'll then show that this realization is not LUC secure. Let us informally present the above flavors of anonymity: The first anonymity concern we present is existence-anonymity. Intuitively, we would like to have a "dropbox" that does not let the recipient know whether a new message was received, and thus hides information regarding the existence of the sender.

Consider the following one-time-dropbox functionality. The dropbox is a virtual box initialized with some random file. People can put files into ones dropbox. In addition, the owner can one time query the dropbox if any new file has been received; if there are any incoming files in the box, they would be delivered to the owner; else the default file would be delivered.

Indeed, whenever receiving a file from this dropbox, there is no certainty regarding the existence of a sender. Correspondingly, any protocol that LUC-realizes the dropbox functionality is guaranteed to provide anonymity regarding the existence of a sender. This is not so for standard UC security.

An additional anonymity concern that we consider is timing-anonymity. Timing-anonymity means hiding the time in which an action took place. For example consider the following email feature: whenever sending an email, the sender can delay the sending of the email by some amount of time (say, randomly chosen from some domain).

Indeed, upon receiving an email, the receiver does not know when this email was sent. This property can be captured via an ideal functionality in a straightforward way. Again, any protocol that LUC-realizes this functionality will provide anonymity regarding the time of sending. This is not so for standard UC security.

An additional anonymity property already mentioned here is sender-anonymity. The common way to achieve this anonymity property in practice is onion routing. In the work of [CL05] the onion-routing problem is defined in the UC framework; however, they only address a potential solution to the sender-anonymity concern rather than the concern itself. In contrast, we formalize the sender-anonymity property. We also show how UC security (and even CP security) fails to capture this property. Specifically, we define an ideal functionality and show a protocol that is clearly non-anonymous but still CP-realizes the functionality according to the definition of [AKMZ12]. This protocol is not LUC secure.

Deniability. It was pointed out in [CDPW07, DKSW09] that UC security does not guarantee deniability due to issues with modeling of the PKI. While these issues were resolved in the context of global setup and deniable authentication in the generalized UC framework, it turns out that the UC formalism does not capture another deniability flavor, called *bi-deniability* (the name is taken from [OPW11]): A protocol is *bi-deniable* if the protocol participants can "deny" before a judge having participated in the protocol by arguing that any "evidence" of their participation in the protocol could have been fabricated without their involvement, *even if there exists an external entity that has an access to parties' log files of the communication.* In the context of authentication, the judge is provided with "evidences" of sender's participation not only by the receiver but also by this external entity. Specifically, the sender can argue that any "evidence" of participation was fabricated by this external entity, even though this external entity cannot communicate with the receiver and only has an access to the communication log files of the sender. This notion is stronger than standard deniability, in which sender's log files are ideally hidden from the judge. To motivate bi-deniability consider a corporation that is obligated to store its communication log files. The log files are collected by an external law enforcement agency. Clearly, it would be desirable to ensure that even if these files are disclosed, the corporation can always deny their authenticity.

In this work, we give a simulation-based definition of bi-deniable authentication and prove its equivalence to LUC secure authentication. Moreover, due to the strong connection between bi-deniability and LUC security, we obtain that bi-deniability is preserved under composition. In addition, we show that UC framework fails to capture this flavor of deniability.

Confinement. Another important concern that seems hard to capture by the standard notions is the *information confinement* property, defined by [Lam73]. A protocol is said to enforce confinement if even misbehaving participants cannot leak secret information that they possess across predefined boundaries. [HKN05] presents a game based definition of confinement. Their definition introduces changes in the basic UC model, but still considers a centralized adversary. We show that the definition of [HKN05] is excessively strong and protocols that clearly enforce confinement fail to admit it. The root of the problem is the centralized adversary that enables information flow to unauthorized entities.

Intuitively, separate adversaries controlling different parts of the network or different groups of parties would indeed capture this requirement more tightly. We present a formal definition of confinement and show that LUC security implies it. Similarly to bi-deniability, we obtain composability with respect to confinement. In addition, we show the inability of UC to capture confinement. More specifically, we show that any UC functionality that enforces confinement is *super-ideal* in some well-defined sense. As before, this is not so for LUC functionalities.

Game-theoretic implications. As pointed out in [ILM05], standard security does not suffice for implementation of general equilibria due to collusion. In order to overcome this problem, new notions of mechanism implementation were defined in [ILM05, ILM08, ILM11]. However, these notions are specific to the problem at hand and are not suitable as general definitions of security. Alwen et al. [AKMZ12] translate their security notion to the game-theoretic setting and define a corresponding model of mediated games. In addition, they show that their security notion achieves preservation of incentive-structure for mediated games.

In this work, we show how protocols modeled in the LUC framework can be viewed as games. Moreover, we show that *any protocol* that LUC-securely realizes some ideal functionality preserves the incentive structure of the realized functionality. More concretely, for any LUC-secure protocol π there exists an efficient mapping between real world strategies and ideal world strategies that can be computed by each player in a local manner and achieves indistinguishable payoffs. This in particular implies that any Nash Equilibrium (NE) in the ideal-world game is mapped to a computational NE in the real-world game and no new equilibria are introduced. A more complete description of the game-theoretic implications provided by LUC security appears in [CV12].

Composition and Dummy Adversary. We demonstrate that LUC-security is preserved under composition. Due to the local nature of the model, this preservation applies not only to basic security concerns under composition, but rather to much more general security concerns such as deniability, confinement, and game-theoretic solution concepts. The obtained game-theoretic composition implies that Nash equilibrium is preserved under concurrent composition.

We also extend the dummy adversary notion to the local UC framework, and show its equivalence to the general LUC-security notion.

An interesting line for future research is to try to cast the LUC framework within the Abstract Cryptography framework [MR11]. In particular, such a work might provide a unified basis for the LUC, CP and UC frameworks.

LUC Secure Protocols

We sketch the two secure function evaluation protocols that we analyze in this work.

The Physical GMW Protocol. The GMW version we use is the protocol from [Gol04]. Still, our construction is strongly inspired by [ILM05]. We cast the protocol in the physical world by considering a set of players sitting in a room and jointly computing a function by evaluation the gates of its circuit. In order to properly compute the function, the players use the following physical machinery: boxes with serial number, and machines for addition, multiplication, duplication, and shuffle of boxed values. In more details, Let $P_1, ..., P_n$ be a set of parties in the room and let f be the function of interest. Next:

1. *Sharing the inputs:* Each player partitions its input to random shares, one share for each player and then, it publically sends those shares, in opaque boxes, to the players.
2. *Circuit emulation:* Proceeding by the order of wires, all players jointly and publically evaluate the circuit gates.
3. *Output reconstruction:* Each player publically hands the Boxes of the output shares to the appropriate parties. Lastly, each party privately opens the boxes and computes its output.

Theorem 1 (Informal statement). *Let f be a PPT function. Then, there exists a protocol that information-theoretically LUC-securely computes f with respect to adaptive adversaries.*

Throughout the process, everyone sees which operations are performed by each player. Still, the actual values inside the boxes remain secret.

In contrast with classic GMW protocol, here the byzantine case is not done by introducing ZK proofs; rather the primitives themselves are robust.

We achieve LUC-security for any number of corrupted parties. While the work of [ILM05] requires at least one honest party for the collusion-freeness to hold, we achieve LUC security (which implies collusion-freeness) even when all the parties are corrupted. In addition, this protocol meets the strong notion of *perfect implementation* defined by [ILM11], and therefore achieves privacy, strategy, and complexity equivalence.

The Mediated-SFE Protocol. We present here a high-level description of the mediated protocol, following [AKL+09].

Let $P_1, ..., P_n$, and mediator $\mathcal{M}$ be a set of parties and let π be a k-round protocol that UC-securely computes function f. (Inspired by [AKMZ12], we think of the protocol as running directly over unauthenticated communication channels.) The protocol π is compiled to a new LUC-secure protocol for computing f with a semi-trusted mediator, where all the communication is done through the mediator. Specifically, for each round of the protocol π does:

1. Each party and $\mathcal{M}$ runs two-party secure computation, which outputs to $\mathcal{M}$ the next round messages of this party in π.
2. $\mathcal{M}$ sends a commitment to the relevant messages to each party P_i.
3. In the last round of π, the mediator $\mathcal{M}$ and each party run secure two-party computation, where each party obtain its output.

Theorem 2 (Informal statement). *Given a (poly-time) function $f = (f_1, ..., f_n)$ and a protocol π that UC-securely computes f. Then there exists a protocol Π that LUC-securely computes f with respect to adaptive adversaries.*

When $\mathcal{M}$ is honest it separates the parties of π and makes them be independent of each other. When $\mathcal{M}$ is corrupted, the independence disappears. Still, we obtain standard UC security.

We strengthen the protocol to be immune to powerful adversaries that control the scheduling, gain information via leakage in the protocol, and are able to adaptively corrupt players. In contrast to [AKMZ12], we do not assume ideally secure channels between parties and the mediator.

Organization. Section 2 presents an overview of the LUC security definition and composition theorem. Section 3 presents the insufficiency of standard notions to capture interesting flavors of anonymity. Section 4 presents bi-deniability and shows its relationship to security notions. Section 5 presents confinement and states its relationship to various security notions.

2 LUC Security Definition and Composition Overview

The model of protocol execution is defined in terms of a system of ITMs as in [Can01]. At first, a set of party IDs is chosen. Then, we consider a pair of adversaries for all potentially communicating ITIs based on the chosen party IDs (the definition of ITI appears in [Can01]). In addition, jointly with the environment, these adversaries have complete control over the communication between ITIs which under their custody, as opposed to the UC framework, where a centralized adversary controls all the communication in the system. Formally, the technical difference from the UC framework is expressed in the control function, summarized below. The underlying computational model remains unchanged.

Let π be a protocol over a fixed set of parties. The model is parametrized by three ITMs: the protocol π to be executed, an environment $\mathcal{Z}$ and an adversary $\mathcal{A}$.

The initial ITM in the system is the environment $\mathcal{Z}$. The input of the initial ITM $\mathcal{Z}$ represent all the external inputs to the system, including the local inputs of all parties. As a first step, $\mathcal{Z}$ chooses a set $\mathcal{P}$ of party identities (PIDs) and session ID s. The first ITIs to be invoked by $\mathcal{Z}$ is the adversaries. An adversary with identity $id = ((i,j), \bot)$ where $i, j \in \mathcal{P}$, denoted $\mathcal{A}_{(i,j)}$, is invoke for each ordered pair $i, j \in \mathcal{P}$. The adversaries code is set to be $\mathcal{A}$. In addition, as the computation proceeds, $\mathcal{Z}$ can invoke any ITI, by passing inputs to it, subject to the restriction that all these ITIs have session ID s and PID $\in \mathcal{P}$. The code of these ITIs is set to be π. Consequently, all the ITIs invoked by $\mathcal{Z}$, except for the adversaries, are parties in a single instance of π. Other than that, $\mathcal{Z}$ cannot pass inputs to any ITI other than the adversaries or the parties invoked by $\mathcal{Z}$, nor can any ITI other than these pass outputs to $\mathcal{Z}$.

Each adversary $\mathcal{A}_{(i,j)}$ is allowed to send messages to any ITI in the system with PID= i where the sender identity of delivered messages must be PID=j. There need not be any correspondence between the messages sent by the parties and the messages delivered by the adversaries. The adversaries may not pass input to any party, nor can it pass output to any party other than $\mathcal{Z}$. It is important to notice that there is no direct communication between the adversaries and all their communication must go through the environment.

Adversaries may also *corrupt* parties. Corruption of a party (ITI) with identity id is modeled via a special (Corrupt, id, p) message delivered by $\mathcal{A}_{(i,j)}$ to that ITI, where p denotes potential additional parameters.

Any ITI other than $\mathcal{Z}$ and the adversaries, are allowed to pass inputs and outputs to any other ITI other than $\mathcal{Z}$ and the adversaries subject to the restriction that the recipient have the same PID as the sender. In addition, they can send messages to the adversaries where adversary's PID$_{(i,j)}$ requires sender's PID i and recipient's PID j. (These messages may indicate an identity of an intended recipient ITI; but the adversaries is not obliged to respect these indications.)

To summarize the above restrictions, for any ordered pair of PIDs (i,j), there is only one possible route for messages from the ITI with PID i to the ITI with PID j: a message m from the ITI with PID i is sent to the adversary $\mathcal{A}_{(i,j)}$, then it can only be outputted to $\mathcal{Z}$, then it is given to $\mathcal{A}_{(j,i)}$, then it is sent to the ITI with PID j.

The response of the party or sub-party to a (Corrupt) message is not defined in the general model; rather, it is left to the protocol. Here we specify one corruption model, namely that of Byzantine party corruption. We extend the known definition to fit multiple adversaries. Here, once a party or a sub-party receives a (Corrupt) message for the first time, it sends to that adversary its entire current local state. Also, in all future activations, a corrupted ITI merely forwards the incoming information to that adversary and follows instructions of all PID related adversaries.

All the restrictions above are enforced by the control function that is formally presented in [CV12]. Figure 1 presents a graphical depiction of the model.

Let LEXEC$_{\pi,\mathcal{A},\mathcal{Z}}$ denote the output distribution of $\mathcal{Z}$ in the execution above.

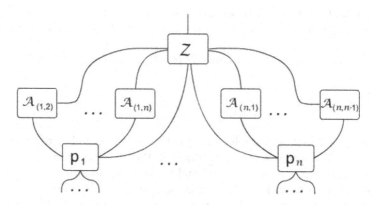

Fig. 1. The model of protocol execution. The environment $\mathcal{Z}$ writes the inputs and reads the subroutine outputs of the main parties running the protocol, while the adversaries, jointly with $\mathcal{Z}$, control the communication. In addition, $\mathcal{Z}$ may interact freely with all adversaries. The parties of π may have subroutines, to which $\mathcal{Z}$ has no direct access.

Now we present the general notion of emulating one protocol via another protocol. Informally, we say that a protocol π emulates protocol ϕ if no environment $\mathcal{Z}$ can tell whether it is participating in an execution of π or ϕ. That is, let A and B be binary distributions, then $A \approx B$ if the statistical distance between A and B is negligible.

Balanced Environments. In order to keep the notion of protocol emulation from being unnecessarily restrictive, we consider only environments where the amount of resources given to each adversary (namely, the length of the adversary's input) is at least some fixed polynomial fraction of the amount of resources given to the protocol. To be concrete, we consider only environments where, at any point in time during the execution, the overall length of the inputs given by $\mathcal{Z}$ to the parties of the main instance of π is at most k times the length of input to each adversary, where k is the security parameter in use. We call such environments Balanced environments.

Definition 1 (LUC-emulation). *Let π and ϕ be PPT protocols. We say that π LUC-emulates ϕ if for any PPT adversary $\mathcal{A}$ there exists an PPT adversary $\mathcal{S}$ such that for any balanced PPT environment $\mathcal{Z}$ we have:* LEXEC$_{\pi,\mathcal{A},\mathcal{Z}} \approx$ LEXEC$_{\phi,\mathcal{S},\mathcal{Z}}$

If $\mathcal{F}$ is an ideal functionality we say that π LUC-realizes $\mathcal{F}$.

Hybrid Protocols. As in the UC framework, we define hybrid protocols to be protocols where, in addition to communicating via the adversary in the usual way, the parties also make calls to instances of ideal functionalities. In other words, an $\mathcal{F}$-hybrid protocol π, denoted by $\pi^{\mathcal{F}}$, is a protocol that includes subroutine calls to $\mathcal{F}$.

Theorem 3 (Universal composition, informal statement). *Let* π, ρ, ϕ *be PPT protocols. If* ρ *LUC-emulates* ϕ *then protocol* π^ρ *LUC-emulates protocol* π^ϕ.

The formal composition theorem and its proof can be found in [CV12].

3   Anonymity

The timing, existence and sender anonymity were informally presented in the introduction. Recall that in the introduction, these concerns are presented via devices such as dropbox, email future, and trusted coordinator; but in fact these are cryptographic channels guaranteeing anonymity in the subject matter. We present ideal functionalities, which are the formalizations of these channels, and realization by non-trivial protocols that do not provide anonymity. The functionalities are defined in LUC, and the corresponding UC (and CP) functionalities are defined by replacing the multiple adversarial interfaces with an equivalent single adversarial interface. We remark that in absence of any formal definition, we can only show that these protocols do not satisfy our intuitive perception of anonymity. Here, we present the inability of the UC and CP to capture the intuitive idea of anonymity.

3.1   Existence-Anonymity

Here our goal is to model a sender-receiver channel, denoted by existence-anonymous channel that has a strong anonymity guarantee regarding the existence of a sender. The existence-channel always allows the receiver to retrieve a message. However, in absence of a sender this message will be some randomly chosen message. The LUC existence-anonymous channel $\mathcal{F}_{\overline{\text{EA}}}$ is formally presented in Figure 2.

Functionality $\mathcal{F}_{\overline{\text{EA}}}^D$

Functionality $\mathcal{F}_{\overline{\text{EA}}}^D$ runs with parties S, R, adversaries $\mathcal{S}_{(S,R)}$, $\mathcal{S}_{(R,S)}$, and parametrized on message distribution D. It proceeds as follows:

- Upon receiving an input (Send, sid, m) from party S do: verify that $sid = (S, R, sid')$, else ignore the input. Next, record m, and send output (Send, sid, m) to $\mathcal{S}_{(S,R)}$. Ignore any subsequent (Send, ...) inputs. Once $\mathcal{S}_{(S,R)}$ allows to forward the message, mark m as approved.
- Upon receiving an input (Output, sid) from party R do:
  1. if there is an approved message m then set OUT $= m$; else set OUT $\leftarrow D$.
  2. send output (OUT, sid) to $\mathcal{S}_{(R,S)}$; Once $\mathcal{S}_{(R,S)}$ allows to forward the message output (OUT, sid) to R and halt.

Fig. 2. The existence-anonymous channel functionality $\mathcal{F}_{\overline{\text{EA}}}$

Functionality $\mathcal{F}_{\overline{EB}}$

Functionality $\mathcal{F}_{\overline{EB}}$ runs with parties S, R, and adversaries $\mathcal{S}_{(S,R)}$, $\mathcal{S}_{(R,S)}$. Initialize $OUT = \perp$ and proceed as follows:

- Upon receiving an input (Send, sid, m) from party S do: verify that $sid = (S, R, sid')$, else ignore the input. Next, record m, and send output (Send, sid, m) to $\mathcal{S}_{(S,R)}$. Ignore any subsequent (Send, ...) inputs. Once $\mathcal{S}_{(S,R)}$ allows to forward the message, mark m as approved.
- Upon receiving an input (Output, sid) from party R and there is an approved message m do:
  1. set $OUT = m$, and output (OUT, sid) to $\mathcal{S}_{(R,S)}$; Once $\mathcal{S}_{(R,S)}$ allows to forward the message output (OUT, sid) to R and halt.

Fig. 3. The basic existence-channel functionality $\mathcal{F}_{\overline{EB}}$

The underlying communication model is a channel called $\mathcal{F}_{\overline{EB}}$ that is similar to authentication channel with a difference in the message delivery. More specifically, a message is delivered to the recipient upon recipient's request and only if there exists a message sent to him. It is important to note that $\mathcal{F}_{\overline{EB}}$ does not provide existence-anonymity since the recipient is guaranteed that any message received was sent by the sender. The LUC channel $\mathcal{F}_{\overline{EB}}$ is formally presented in Figure 3.

Claim. The functionality $\mathcal{F}_{\overline{EB}}$ UC-realizes $\mathcal{F}_{\overline{EA}}$ and does not LUC-realize $\mathcal{F}_{\overline{EA}}$.

3.2 Timing-Anonymity

Here, our goal is to define a channel that guarantees to the sender that no receiver, upon receiving a message from him, can tell when this message was sent. As mentioned in the introduction, we define a timing-anonymous channel, denoted by $\mathcal{F}_{\overline{TA}}$, that randomly delay a message in a way that the amount of the delay is unknown to the receiver. In particular, the message is delivered only after a certain delay. The LUC channel $\mathcal{F}_{\overline{TA}}$ is formally presented in Figure 4.

Now we formally define the underlying model. In order to capture time, we introduce a clock functionality $\mathcal{F}_{\text{clock}}$ that is observable by all participants. This clock is not directly observed by the environment, instead, it is indirectly advanced by the environment, by instructing the sender to advance the clock; this captures a setting in which the receiver's future actions are not affected by the amount of the delay. The formal description of $\mathcal{F}_{\text{clock}}$ presented in Figure 5. The second component is the authentication functionality $\mathcal{F}_{\text{auth}}$. The difference between the LUC and the UC authentication functionality is that the LUC functionality, denoted by $\mathcal{F}_{\overline{\text{auth}}}$, operates not only when a message is sent. That is, it allows the adversary associated with the sender to approve delivery even when

---

Functionality $\mathcal{F}_{\overline{\text{TA}}}$

Functionality $\mathcal{F}_{\overline{\text{TA}}}$ runs with parties S, R, and adversaries $\mathcal{S}_{(S,R)}$, $\mathcal{S}_{(R,S)}$. Let T be some finite set of natural numbers. The functionality proceeds as follows:

- Upon receiving an input (Send, sid, m) from party S do: verify that $sid = (S, R, sid')$, else ignore the input. Next, choose uniformly at random $N \leftarrow T$, set $k = N$, and record (k, m). Ignore any subsequent (Send, ...) inputs.
- Upon receiving an input (Advance, sid) from party S and $k > 0$ do:
  1. update $k = k - 1$ and output (Advance, sid) to adversary $\mathcal{S}_{(S,R)}$.
  2. if $k = 0$ output m to $\mathcal{S}_{(S,R)}$. Once $\mathcal{S}_{(S,R)}$ allows to forward the message output m to $\mathcal{S}_{(R,S)}$. Once also $\mathcal{S}_{(R,S)}$ allows to forward m output it to R.

1. Upon receiving (Corruptsend, sid, m') from $\mathcal{S}_{(S,R)}$, if S is corrupt and m has not been delivered to $\mathcal{S}_{(R,S)}$, then change the recorded message to m'.

Fig. 4. The timing-anonymous channel functionality $\mathcal{F}_{\overline{\text{TA}}}$

Functionality $\mathcal{F}_{\text{clock}}$

Functionality $\mathcal{F}_{\text{clock}}$ runs with parties S, R, and adversaries $\mathcal{S}_{(S,R)}$, $\mathcal{S}_{(R,S)}$. Initialize $T = 0$. Next:

- Upon receiving an input (Advance, sid) from party S do: in the first activation verify that $sid = (S, R, sid')$, else ignore the input. Next, set $T = T + 1$.
- Upon receiving an input (time, sid) from some party, output (time, sid, T).

Fig. 5. The clock functionality $\mathcal{F}_{\text{clock}}$

no message was sent; in this case $\mathcal{F}_{\overline{\text{auth}}}$ outputs $\bot$ to receiver's adversary and halts. We note that $\mathcal{F}_{\overline{\text{auth}}}$ seems as a natural relaxation of the UC authentication functionality. The LUC authentication functionality $\mathcal{F}_{\overline{\text{auth}}}$ is formally presented in Figure 6.

Claim. There exists a protocol π_{TA} that UC-realizes $\mathcal{F}_{\overline{\text{TA}}}$ and does not LUC-realize $\mathcal{F}_{\overline{\text{TA}}}$.

A protocol π_{TA} that UC-realizes $\mathcal{F}_{\overline{\text{TA}}}$ is:
Let T be some finite set of natural numbers.

1. INPUT: Having received input (Send, sid, m), S chooses uniformly at random $N \leftarrow T$, set $k = N$, and records (k, m).
2. ADVANCE: Having received input (Advance, sid), S forward it to $\mathcal{F}_{\text{clock}}$ and updates $k = k - 1$. Once $k = 0$ send m to $\mathcal{F}_{\overline{\text{auth}}}$ and halt.
3. OUTPUT: Having received (Send, sid, m) from $\mathcal{F}_{\overline{\text{auth}}}$, the receiver R outputs m.

Functionality $\mathcal{F}_{\overline{\text{auth}}}$

Functionality $\mathcal{F}_{\overline{\text{auth}}}$ runs with parties S, R, and adversaries $\mathcal{S}_{(S,R)}$, $\mathcal{S}_{(R,S)}$. It proceeds as follows:

1. Upon receiving an input (Send, sid, m) from party S, do: If $sid = (S, R, sid')$ for some R, then record m and output (Send, sid, m) to $\mathcal{S}_{(S,R)}$.
2. Upon receiving "approve" from $\mathcal{S}_{(S,R)}$, if m is recorded provide (Send, sid, m) to $\mathcal{S}_{(R,S)}$, and after $\mathcal{S}_{(R,S)}$ approves, output (Send, sid, m) to R and halt. Otherwise, provide (Send, sid, $\perp$) to $\mathcal{S}_{(R,S)}$ and halt. (Both adversaries control the channel delay.)
3. Upon receiving (Corruptsend, sid, m') from $\mathcal{S}_{(S,R)}$, if S is corrupt and m has not yet been delivered to $\mathcal{S}_{(R,S)}$, then output (Send, sid, m') to $\mathcal{S}_{(R,S)}$, and after $\mathcal{S}_{(R,S)}$ approves, output (Send, sid, m') to R and halt.

Fig. 6. The message authentication functionality $\mathcal{F}_{\overline{\text{auth}}}$

We note that π_{TA} does not provide timing anonymity since all participants in the protocol observe the clock. In particular, upon receiving a message, the receiver can retrieve the time by sending (time,sid) to $\mathcal{F}_{\text{clock}}$, and thus knows exactly when the message was sent.

3.3   Sender-Anonymity

The sender anonymity property is presented in the introduction via a trusted mediator that masks the identity of the sender. This mediator is similar to the two-anonymous channels of [NMO08]; however, their formalism is not applicable in our setting. The channel enables two senders and a *honest but curious* receiver to communicate anonymously in the following sense: both senders may send a message to the receiver but only one message is delivered. This sender-anonymous channel, denoted by $\mathcal{F}_{\overline{\text{SA}}}$, does not disclose the identity of the actual sender. The LUC formulation of $\mathcal{F}_{\overline{\text{SA}}}$ is presented in Figure 7.

Functionality $\mathcal{F}_{\overline{\text{SA}}}$

Functionality $\mathcal{F}_{\overline{\text{SA}}}$ running with parties S_1, S_2, R, and adversaries $\mathcal{S}_{(S_1,R)}$, $\mathcal{S}_{(S_2,R)}$, $\mathcal{S}_{(R,S_1)}$, $\mathcal{S}_{(R,S_2)}$. At first activation verify that $sid = (S_1, S_2, R, sid')$, else halt. Next, proceed as follows:

– Upon receiving an input (Send, sid, m_i) from party S_i do: record m_i and send output (Send, sid, m_i) to $\mathcal{S}_{(S_i,R)}$. Ignore any subsequent (Send, ...) inputs from S_i. Once $\mathcal{S}_{(S_i,R)}$ allows to forward the message, output (Send, sid, m_i) to $\mathcal{S}_{(R,S_i)}$. Once approved, output (Send, sid, m_i) to R and halt.

Fig. 7. The sender-anonymous channel functionality $\mathcal{F}_{\overline{\text{SA}}}$

Functionality $\mathcal{F}_{\overline{\text{SI}}}$

Functionality $\mathcal{F}_{\overline{\text{SI}}}$ running with parties S_1, S_2, R, and adversaries $\mathcal{S}_{(S_1,R)}$, $\mathcal{S}_{(S_2,R)}$, $\mathcal{S}_{(R,S_1)}$, $\mathcal{S}_{(R,S_2)}$. Initialize variable BLOCK = 0. At first activation verify that $sid = (S_1, S_2, R, sid')$, else halt. Next, proceed as follows:

- Upon receiving an input (Send, sid, m_1) from party S_1 do: record m_1, and send output (Send, sid, m_1) to $\mathcal{S}_{(S_1,R)}$. Ignore any subsequent (Send, ...) inputs from S_1. Once $\mathcal{S}_{(S_1,R)}$ allows to forward the message output (Send, sid, m_1) to $\mathcal{S}_{(R,S_1)}$. Once approved, if BLOCK = 0 output (Send, sid, m_1) to R and halt; else halt.
- Upon receiving an input (Send, sid, m_2) from party S_2 do: record m_2, and send output (Send, sid, m_2) to $\mathcal{S}_{(S_2,R)}$. Ignore any subsequent (Send, ...) inputs from S_2. Once $\mathcal{S}_{(S_2,R)}$ allows to forward the message output (Send, sid, m_2) to $\mathcal{S}_{(R,S_2)}$. Once approved set BLOCK = 1.

Fig. 8. The basic sender-channel functionality $\mathcal{F}_{\overline{\text{SI}}}$

The underlying communication channel, denoted by $\mathcal{F}_{\overline{\text{SI}}}$, is a two-sender one receiver channel that delivers only messages sent by the first sender S1. We note that $\mathcal{F}_{\overline{\text{SI}}}$ does not provide sender-anonymity. The formal description of $\mathcal{F}_{\overline{\text{SI}}}$ is presented in Figure 8.

Claim. The functionality $\mathcal{F}_{\overline{\text{SI}}}$ UC-realizes $\mathcal{F}_{\overline{\text{SA}}}$ and does not LUC-realize $\mathcal{F}_{\overline{\text{SA}}}$.

Sender-Anonymity in the CP Framework. We note that in the context of sender-anonymity, the CP model suffers from the same weakness as the UC model. That is, the above non sender-anonymous protocol is a CP-realization of the sender-anonymous channel $\mathcal{F}_{\overline{\text{SA}}}$.

4   Bi-deniability

Here, we formalize a notion of bi-deniable authentication and show that UC security does not capture this flavor of deniability. In fact, this is true also for GUC. Moreover, we define bi-deniability separately and show equivalence between bi-deniable authentication and LUC secure authentication.

4.1   Bi-deniable Authentication

Bi-deniability aims to capture the ability of a participant in a two party protocol to deny participation in a protocol execution even if its communication had been externally exposed. The actual definition has some similarities to the definition presented in [DKSW09] (see details in the full version [CV12]).

The relevant entities are the following: we have a sender S who is potentially communicating with a receiver R, a judge $\mathcal{J}$ who will eventually rule whether or not the transmission was attempted, two informants $\mathcal{I}_S$, $\mathcal{I}_R$ who witness the communication (represented as log files owned by $\mathcal{I}_S$, $\mathcal{I}_R$) between S and R and are trying to convince the judge, and two misinformants $\mathcal{M}_S$, $\mathcal{M}_R$ who did not witness any communication but still want to convince the judge that one occurred.

The idea of the bi-deniability definition is that no party should be accused of participating in a protocol, if any evidence presented to the judge (by the informants) based on witnessing the protocol execution can be also presented (by the misinformants) without any communication whatsoever. This idea is formalized via indistinguishability of experiments as follows: Let π be some two-party protocol.

Informant-Experiment. The inputs to parties are given by the judge, and any output produced by the parties is given to the judge. S and R run π in the presence of the informants $\mathcal{I}_S$, $\mathcal{I}_R$. The informants report to $\mathcal{J}$ regarding any observed communication and execute all $\mathcal{J}$'s instruction. The output distribution of the judge $\mathcal{J}$ in this basic informant-experiment is denoted by $\text{EXP}_{\pi,\mathcal{I}_S,\mathcal{I}_R,\mathcal{J}}$.

Misinformant-Experiment. The inputs to parties are also given to the mis-informants. S and R do not communicate except with $\mathcal{M}_S$, $\mathcal{M}_R$. The misinformant $\mathcal{M}_S$ can send a single (signal) message[1] to $\mathcal{M}_R$; in addition, they can freely communicate with $\mathcal{J}$. Any message received by the parties from their misinformant is outputted to the judge. The output distribution of the judge $\mathcal{J}$ in this basic misinformant-experiment is denoted by $\text{EXP}_{\mathcal{M}_S,\mathcal{M}_R,\mathcal{J}}$.

Definition 2 (Bi-deniability). *Let π be some PPT protocol and let the informants $\mathcal{I}_S,\mathcal{I}_R$ be as defined above. We say that π is bi-deniable if there exist PPT misinformants $\mathcal{M}_R$ and $\mathcal{M}_S$ such that for any PPT judge $\mathcal{J}$ we have: $\text{EXP}_{\pi,\mathcal{I}_S,\mathcal{I}_R,\mathcal{J}} \approx \text{EXP}_{\mathcal{M}_S,\mathcal{M}_R,\mathcal{J}}$.*

Theorem 4. *Let $\mathcal{F}_{\overline{\text{auth}}}$ be the LUC authentication functionality, and let $\mathcal{F}_{\text{auth}}$ be the UC authentication functionality of [Can01]. Then:*

1. $\mathcal{F}_{\overline{\text{auth}}}$ is bi-deniable.

2. Let π be some protocol. Then π LUC-realizes $\mathcal{F}_{\overline{\text{auth}}}$ if and only if π is bi-deniable.

3. $\mathcal{F}_{\text{auth}}$ is not bi-deniable.

5 Confinement

Recall that a protocol is said to enforce confinement if it prevents leakage of secret information to unauthorized processes in the network. This guarantee should hold even if all parties are faulty. In this section we present a definition of confinement and show that any LUC secure realization enforces confinement as long as the realized task does. In contrast to the other concerns, we will not show that UC security does not imply confinement but rather argue that

---

[1] Discussion regarding (signal) message appears in the full version [CV12].

any definition based on a centralized adversary does not enable proper separation between protocols that enforces confinement and the one that do not. In addition, we show that any UC functionality that enforces confinement is "super-ideal", in a well-defined sense.

5.1 Confinement with a Centralized Adversary

In the work of [HKN05] a definition of confinement is presented. Their definition considers the UC execution model with the following modifications: the UC environment is split into two environments $\mathcal{E}_{\mathcal{H}}$ and $\mathcal{E}_{\mathcal{L}}$, where $\mathcal{E}_{\mathcal{H}}$ interacts with the high-level processes and $\mathcal{E}_{\mathcal{L}}$ with the low-level processes. All processes have an I/O interface with the appropriate environment according to their classification. In addition, the high-level environment $\mathcal{E}_{\mathcal{H}}$ cannot give inputs either to the adversary or to the low-level environment $\mathcal{E}_{\mathcal{L}}$. [HKN05] define confinement as the following game: a random bit b is chosen by $\mathcal{E}_{\mathcal{H}}$, the parties run the protocol π, and eventually $\mathcal{E}_{\mathcal{L}}$ outputs its guess for b. We say that π enforce confinement for partition $\mathcal{H} : \mathcal{L}$ of the parties in π, if for any environments $\mathcal{E}_{\mathcal{H}}$, $\mathcal{E}_{\mathcal{L}}$ and adversary as above, $\mathcal{E}_{\mathcal{L}}$ succeeds in the confinement game with probability $\approx \frac{1}{2}$.

This definition enforces very strong requirements on the examined protocols[2], and as a consequence, many protocols that "obviously enforce confinement" do not satisfy this definition. We remark that this weakness is not unique to the [HKN05] definition, and any definition based on centralized adversary is subject to this weakness.

5.2 Definition of Confinement

Our definition follows the idea of [HKN05]. Like there, we consider split environments. More precisely, our definition consists of the same entities as in [HKN05] where the centralized adversary is split to multiple adversaries, an adversary for each pair of potentially communicating parties. We denote by $\mathcal{A}_{(i,j)}$ the adversary with identity $((i,j), \perp)$ and code $\mathcal{A}$.

The executed experiment for partition $\mathcal{H} : \mathcal{L}$ of the participating parties in π is the following: a random bit b is chosen by $\mathcal{E}_{\mathcal{H}}$, the parties run π, while the adversaries, jointly with $\mathcal{E}_{\mathcal{H}}$ and $\mathcal{E}_{\mathcal{L}}$ control the communication. The environments $\mathcal{E}_{\mathcal{H}}$ and $\mathcal{E}_{\mathcal{L}}$ write inputs and read the subroutine outputs of parties according to their classification. $\mathcal{E}_{\mathcal{L}}$ can also give inputs to $\mathcal{E}_{\mathcal{H}}$. In addition, $\mathcal{E}_{\mathcal{L}}$ can interact freely with all adversaries associated with $\mathcal{L}$, and all the adversaries associated with $\mathcal{H}$ can give outputs to $\mathcal{E}_{\mathcal{H}}$. The adversaries can communicate with the appropriate party and corrupt it. Eventually $\mathcal{E}_{\mathcal{L}}$ outputs its guess for b.

Let $\mathrm{CEXP}_{\pi,\mathcal{A},\mathcal{E}_{\mathcal{H}},\mathcal{E}_{\mathcal{L}}}^{\mathcal{H}:\mathcal{L}}$ denote the success indicator of $\mathcal{E}_{\mathcal{L}}$ in the above experiment.

Definition 3 (Confinement). *Let π be a PPT protocol and let $\mathcal{H} : \mathcal{L}$ be some partition of the parties in π. We say that π enforces $(\mathcal{H} : \mathcal{L})$-confinement if for*

---

[2] Shown in the full version [CV12].

any PPT adversary $\mathcal{A}$ and for any balanced PPT environments $\mathcal{E}_{\mathcal{H}}$ and $\mathcal{E}_{\mathcal{L}}$ we have: $\mathrm{CEXP}^{\mathcal{H}:\mathcal{L}}_{\pi,\mathcal{A},\mathcal{E}_{\mathcal{H}},\mathcal{E}_{\mathcal{L}}} \approx U_1$, where U_1 is the uniform distribution over $\{0,1\}$.

Theorem 5. *Let π, ϕ be protocols such that π LUC emulates ϕ. Then π enforce $(\mathcal{H} : \mathcal{L})$-confinement for all partitions $\mathcal{H} : \mathcal{L}$ of the parties in π for which ϕ enforce $(\mathcal{H} : \mathcal{L})$-confinement.*

5.3 Confinement with Respect to Super-Ideal Functionalities

Here, we show that any UC functionality that enforces confinement must be "super-ideal". That is, such functionalities do not provide the adversary with any information, even when a party is corrupted. We call such functionalities super-ideal since such functionalities essentially mandate communication channels which offer absolute physical security that hides even whether communication took place at all.

Definition 4 (Super-ideal, informal statement). *Let $\mathcal{F}$ be a n-party functionality and let $\mathcal{H} : \mathcal{L}$ be some partition of the parties. Then $\mathcal{F}$ is super-ideal with respect to a set of identities $\mathcal{H}$ if for any adversary associated with a party P_i for $i \in \mathcal{H}$ and for any two possible inputs the following holds: the adversary cannot tell, even with the assistance of the adversarial interface of $\mathcal{F}$, which one of the inputs was used by party P_i.*

Claim. Let $\mathcal{F}$ be a UC functionality and let $\mathcal{H} : \mathcal{L}$ be some partition for which $\mathcal{F}$ enforces $(\mathcal{H} : \mathcal{L})$-confinement. Then, $\mathcal{F}$ is super-ideal with respect to all parties in $\mathcal{H}$.

Acknowledgments. We thank Noam Livne, Vassilis Zikas, Ilia Gorelik, and Daniel Shahaf for helpful discussions.

References

[AKL+09]   Alwen, J., Katz, J., Lindell, Y., Persiano, G., Shelat, A., Visconti, I.: Collusion-Free Multiparty Computation in the Mediated Model. In: Halevi, S. (ed.) CRYPTO 2009. LNCS, vol. 5677, pp. 524–540. Springer, Heidelberg (2009)

[AKMZ12]   Alwen, J., Katz, J., Maurer, U., Zikas, V.: Collusion-Preserving Computation. In: Safavi-Naini, R. (ed.) CRYPTO 2012. LNCS, vol. 7417, pp. 124–143. Springer, Heidelberg (2012), http://eprint.iacr.org/2011/433.pdf

[ASV08]   Alwen, J., Shelat, A., Visconti, I.: Collusion-Free Protocols in the Mediated Model. In: Wagner, D. (ed.) CRYPTO 2008. LNCS, vol. 5157, pp. 497–514. Springer, Heidelberg (2008)

[CL05]   Camenisch, J., Lysyanskaya, A.: A Formal Treatment of Onion Routing. In: Shoup, V. (ed.) CRYPTO 2005. LNCS, vol. 3621, pp. 169–187. Springer, Heidelberg (2005)

[Can00]   Canetti, R.: Security and composition of multiparty cryptographic proto-
           cols. J. Cryptology 13(1), 143–202 (2000)
[Can01]   Canetti, R.: Universally Composable Security: A New Paradigm for
           Cryptographic Protocols. In: 42nd FOCS (2001); revised version (2005),
           eprint.iacr.org/2000/067
[CDPW07]   Canetti, R., Dodis, Y., Pass, R., Walfish, S.: Universally Composable Secu-
           rity with Global Setup. In: Vadhan, S.P. (ed.) TCC 2007. LNCS, vol. 4392,
           pp. 61–85. Springer, Heidelberg (2007)
[CLOS02]   Canetti, R., Lindell, Y., Ostrovsky, R., Sahai, A.: Universally composable
           two-party and multi-party secure computation. In: 34th STOC (2002)
[CV12]   Canetti, R., Vald, M.: Universally Composable Security With Local Ad-
           versaries. IACR Eprint (2012)
[DM00]   Dodis, Y., Micali, S.: Parallel Reducibility for Information-Theoretically
           Secure Computation. In: Bellare, M. (ed.) CRYPTO 2000. LNCS,
           vol. 1880, pp. 74–92. Springer, Heidelberg (2000)
[DKSW09]   Dodis, Y., Katz, J., Smith, A., Walfish, S.: Composability and On-Line
           Deniability of Authentication. In: Reingold, O. (ed.) TCC 2009. LNCS,
           vol. 5444, pp. 146–162. Springer, Heidelberg (2009)
[GL90]   Goldwasser, S., Levin, L.: Fair Computation of General Functions in
           Presence of Immoral Majority. In: Menezes, A.J., Vanstone, S.A. (eds.)
           CRYPTO 1990. LNCS, vol. 537, pp. 77–93. Springer, Heidelberg (1991)
[GM84]   Goldwasser, S., Micali, S.: Probabilistic encryption. JCSS 28(2), 270–299
           (1984)
[GMR85]   Goldwasser, S., Micali, S., Rackoff, C.: The Knowledge Complexity of In-
           teractive Proof-Systems. SIAM J. Comput. 18, 186–208 (1989); (also in
           STOC 1985, pp. 291-304)
[GMW87]   Goldreich, O., Micali, S., Wigderson, A.: How to Play any Mental Game.
           In: 19th Symposium on Theory of Computing (STOC), pp. 218–229. ACM
           (1987)
[Gol04]   Goldreich, O.: Foundations of Cryptography, vol. 2: Basic Applications.
           Cambridge University Press, Cambridge (2004)
[HKN05]   Halevi, S., Karger, P.A., Naor, D.: Enforcing confinement in distributed
           storage and a cryptographic model for access control. Cryptology Eprint
           Archive Report 2005/169 (2005)
[ILM05]   Izmalkov, S., Lepinski, M., Micali, S.: Rational Secure Computation and
           Ideal Mechanism Design. In: FOCS 2005: Proceedings of the 46th An-
           nual IEEE Symposium on Foundations of Computer Science, pp. 585–595.
           IEEE Computer Society, Washington, DC (2005)
[ILM08]   Izmalkov, S., Lepinski, M., Micali, S.: Verifiably Secure Devices. In:
           Canetti, R. (ed.) TCC 2008. LNCS, vol. 4948, pp. 273–301. Springer, Hei-
           delberg (2008)
[ILM11]   Izmalkov, S., Lepinski, M., Micali, S.: Perfect implementation. Games and
           Economic Behavior 71(1), 121–140 (2011)
[Lam73]   Lampson, B.W.: A note on the confinement problem. Communications of
           the ACM 16(10), 613–615 (1973)
[LMS05]   Lepinksi, M., Micali, S., Shelat, A.: Collusion-Free Protocols. In: STOC
           2005: Proceedings of the Thirty-Seventh Annual ACM Symposium on The-
           ory of Computing, pp. 543–552. ACM, New York (2005)
[MR11]   Maurer, U., Renner, R.: Abstract cryptography. In: Innovations in Com-
           puter Science. Tsinghua University Press (2011)

[MR91]   Micali, S., Rogaway, P.: Secure Computation. In: Feigenbaum, J. (ed.)
           CRYPTO 1991. LNCS, vol. 576, pp. 392–404. Springer, Heidelberg (1992)
[NMO08]   Nagao, W., Manabe, Y., Okamoto, T.: Relationship of Three Crypto-
           graphic Channels in the UC Framework. In: Baek, J., Bao, F., Chen, K.,
           Lai, X. (eds.) ProvSec 2008. LNCS, vol. 5324, pp. 268–282. Springer, Hei-
           delberg (2008)
[OPW11]   O'Neill, A., Peikert, C., Waters, B.: Bi-Deniable Public-Key Encryption.
           In: Rogaway, P. (ed.) CRYPTO 2011. LNCS, vol. 6841, pp. 525–542.
           Springer, Heidelberg (2011)
[PS04]   Prabhakaran, M., Sahai, A.: New notions of security: achieving universal
           composability without trusted setup. In: 36th STOC, pp. 242–251 (2004)
[PW00]   Pfitzmann, B., Waidner, M.: Composition and integrity preservation of
           secure reactive systems. In: 7th ACM Conf. on Computer and Communi-
           cation Security, pp. 245–254 (2000)

On the Strength Comparison
of the ECDLP and the IFP*

Masaya Yasuda, Takeshi Shimoyama, Jun Kogure, and Tetsuya Izu

Fujitsu Laboratories Ltd.
1-1, Kamikodanaka 4-chome, Nakahara-ku, Kawasaki, 211-8588, Japan
{myasuda,shimo,izu}@labs.fujitsu.com, kogure@jp.fujitsu.com

Abstract. At present, the RSA cryptosystem is most widely used in public key cryptography. On the other hand, elliptic curve cryptography (ECC) has recently received much attention since smaller ECC key sizes provide the same security level as RSA. Although there are a lot of previous works that analyze the security of ECC and RSA, the comparison of strengths varies depending on analysis. The aim of this paper is once again to compare the security strengths, considering state-of-the-art of theory and experiments. The security of RSA is closely related to the hardness of the integer factorization problem (IFP), while the security of ECC is closely related to the elliptic curve discrete logarithm problem (ECDLP). In this paper, we compare the computing power required to solve the ECDLP and the IFP, respectively, and estimate the sizes of the problems that provide the same level of security.

1   Introduction

After Rivest, Shamir, and Adleman proposed the RSA cryptosystem in 1977 [38], Koblitz and Miller independently proposed ECC in 1985 [20,28,32]. We can break RSA (resp. ECC) if we can solve the IFP (resp. the ECDLP). Currently, subexponential-time algorithm to solve the IFP are known. On the other hand, the best known algorithm to solve the ECDLP has fully exponential running time. This fact ensures that smaller ECC key sizes provide the same security level as RSA. The advantages of smaller key sizes are very important to use devices with limited processing capacity, storage or power supply, like smart cards. Hence ECC can be used more widely in the future, and it is important to compare the security strengths of ECC and RSA in order to embed ECC into information systems. In this paper, we estimate the computing power required to solve the ECDLP and the IFP in a year, respectively. Using special-purpose hardware for the ECDLP or the IFP is a theme of great interest and there are some previous works such as [18,22,42,43]. However, these platforms and architectures vary, and it is difficult to make an analysis on the cost performance. We focus on the hardness of the ECDLP and the IFP from the view point of software implementation.

---

* The preliminary version of this work was presented at SHARCS 2012 [50].

I. Visconti and R. De Prisco (Eds.): SCN 2012, LNCS 7485, pp. 302–325, 2012.
© Springer-Verlag Berlin Heidelberg 2012

Table 1. The comparable security strengths by NIST SP 800-57 [34]

Bits of security	Symmetric key algorithms	FFC (e.g., DSA, D-H)	IFP (e.g., RSA)	ECDLP (e.g., ECDSA)
80	2TDEA	$L = 1024, N = 160$	$k = 1024$	$f = 160 - 223$
112	3TDEA	$L = 2048, N = 224$	$k = 2048$	$f = 224 - 255$
128	AES-128	$L = 3072, N = 256$	$k = 3072$	$f = 256 - 383$
192	AES-192	$L = 7680, N = 384$	$k = 7680$	$f = 384 - 511$
256	AES-256	$L = 15360, N = 512$	$k = 15360$	$f = 512+$

L is the size of the public key and N is the size of the private key. The values of k and f are commonly considered as the key sizes.

Although a number of ways to solve the ECDLP are known, Pollard's rho method [36] is the fastest known algorithm for solving the ECDLP except special cases such as the supersingular and the anomalous cases [11,20,31,40,41,44]. To evaluate the hardness of the ECDLP, we estimate the complexity of the rho method. The rho method works by giving a pseudo-random sequence defined by an iteration function and then detecting a collision in the sequence (see [20] for details of the rho method). The complexity of the rho method is determined by the number of iterations before obtaining a collision and the processing performance of iterations. Since the number of iterations depends heavily on an iteration function, we first discuss the choice of iteration functions suitable for solving the ECDLP. Since the rho method is probabilistic, we next estimate the number of iterations required to solve the ECDLP with very high probability based on our experiments (we here consider 99% as the success probability). Based on the previously known methods, we implement elliptic curve operations with our software and estimate the processing performance of iterations. Furthermore, we consider three types in the ECDLP, namely, prime fields, binary fields, and Koblitz curves types.

On the other hand, it is known that the general number field sieve (GNFS) is the most efficient known algorithm for solving the IFP of large composite integers [29]. Similarly to the ECDLP side, we estimate the complexity of the GNFS for evaluating the hardness of the IFP. To evaluate the complexity of the GNFS, we use the result of CRYPTREC report 2006 [10] which is based on the papers [23,24]. This report gives the estimated computing power required to solve the IFP of composite integers of N-bit with $N = 768, 1024, 1536$ and 2048 by investigating the complexity of the sieving step based on extensive experiments. In [50], we estimated the computing power of the GNFS under the condition with limited memory size. In contrast, we estimate the computing power in the case with unlimited memory size.

Previously known estimations : We here summarize previously known results of the security evaluation of the ECDLP and the strength comparison of the ECDLP and the IFP: In Table 1, we show the comparable security strengths for the approved algorithms reported by NIST SP 800-57 [34, Table 2 in p. 63]. We also show the evaluation of solving the ECDLP reported by ANSI X9.62

Table 2. The evaluation of solving the ECDLP of order n by ANSI X9.62 [1]

bit sizes of n	$\sqrt{\pi n/4}$	MIPS year
160	2^{80}	8.5×10^{11}
186	2^{93}	7.0×10^{15}
234	2^{117}	1.2×10^{23}
354	2^{177}	1.3×10^{41}
426	2^{213}	9.2×10^{51}

Table 3. The comparison of security strengths of the ECDLP and the IFP with 80-bit security

Report	ECDLP	IFP
NIST [34]	160	1024
Lenstra-Verheul [30]	160	1300
RSA Labs. [39]	160	760
NESSIE [33]	160	1536
IETF [35]	-	1228
ECRYPT II [14]	160	1248

[1] in Table 2. For example, the data of Table 2 imply that we need to have a computer with 8.5×10^{11} MIPS to solve the ECDLP of 160-bit in a year. It needs 485 years to solve the ECDLP of 160-bit even if we use a 'Jaguar', which is one of the most powerful computers in the world and has 1.75×10^{15} FLOPS ($\approx 1.75 \times 10^9$ MIPS). Furthermore, we summarize results of the comparable security strengths of the ECDLP and the IFP given by certain organizations and researchers in Table 3.

Organization : In Section 2 (resp. Section 3), we estimate the hardness of the ECDLP (resp. the IFP) based on our own experiment and implementation results. In Section 4, we compare the computing power required to solve the ECDLP and the IFP, and calculate the bit sizes of the problems that provide the same level of security. Finally in Section 5, we conclude our work.

2   The Hardness of the ECDLP

To evaluate the hardness of the ECDLP, we estimate the complexity of the rho method.

2.1   Review of the Rho Method

To fix our notations, we review the rho method for the ECDLP due to [20].

Definition 1 (ECDLP). *Given an elliptic curve E defined over a finite field $\mathbb{F}_q$ with q elements, a point $S \in E(\mathbb{F}_q)$ of prime order n, and a point $T \in \langle S \rangle$, find the integer $k \in [0, n-1]$ with $T = kS$.*

Fix an iteration function $f : \langle S \rangle \to \langle S \rangle$ such that it is easy to compute $X' = f(X)$ and $c', d' \in [0, n-1]$ with $X' = c'S + d'T$ for given $X = cS + dT$. For a starting point $X_0 = c_0 S + d_0 T$ with randomly chosen $c_0, d_0 \in [0, n-1]$, we define a sequence $\{X_i\}_{i \geq 0}$ by $X_{i+1} = f(X_i)$ for $i \geq 0$. It follows from the property of the iteration function f that we can easily compute $c_i, d_i \in [0, n-1]$ with $X_i = c_i S + d_i T$. Since the set $\langle S \rangle$ is finite, the sequence will eventually meet a point that has occurred before, which is called a *collision*. A collision $X_i = X_j$ with $i \neq j$ gives the relation $c_i S + d_i T = c_j S + d_j T$. Since we have

$(c_i - c_j)S = (d_j - d_i)T = (d_j - d_i)kS$, we can compute the solution $k = (c_i - c_j) \cdot (d_j - d_i)^{-1} \bmod n$ of the ECDLP if $d_j \not\equiv d_i \bmod n$. This is the basic idea of the rho method for solving the ECDLP (see [20, pp. 157- 158] for details).

Since a collision gives the solution of the ECDLP with very high probability, the number of iterations before obtaining a collision is significant for the running time of the rho method. To solve the ECDLP efficiently, we take an iteration function f with the characteristic of a random function. If f is a random function, the expected number of iterations before obtaining a collision is approximately $\sqrt{\pi n/2} \approx 1.2533\sqrt{n}$ by the birthday paradox.

Improving the Rho Method

Parallelized rho method : Van Oorschot and Wiener [47] proposed a variant of the rho method that yields a factor M speed up when M processors are employed. The idea is to allow the sequences $\{X_i^{(j)}\}_{i \geq 0}$ generated by the processors to collide with one another, where j is the index of processors. More precisely, each processor randomly selects its own starting point $X_0^{(j)}$, but all processors use the same iteration function f to compute subsequent points $X_i^{(j)}$.

Collision detection : Floyd's cycle-finding algorithm [27] finds a collision in the sequence generated by a single processor. The following strategy enables efficient finding of a collision in the sequences generated by different processors. An easy testable *distinguishing property* of points is selected. For example, a point may be *distinguished* if the leading t bits of its x-coordinate are zero. Let $0 < \theta < 1$ be the proportion of points in the set $\langle S \rangle$ having this distinguishing property. Whenever a processor encounters a distinguished point, it transmits the point to a central server that stores it in a list. When the server receives the same distinguished point for the second time, it computes the desired logarithm and terminates all processors. The expected number of iterations per processor before obtaining a collision is $(\sqrt{\pi n/2})/M$, when M processors are employed. A subsequent distinguished point is expected after $1/\theta$ iterations. Hence the expected number of elliptic curve operations performed by each processor before observing a collision of distinguished points is $\frac{1}{M}\sqrt{\frac{\pi n}{2}} + \frac{1}{\theta}$. We note that the running time of $1/\theta$ iterations after a collision occurs is negligible for the total running time if we select θ such that $1/\theta$ is small enough compared to $\sqrt{n}$.

Speeding up the rho method using automorphisms : Wiener and Zuccherato [48] and Gallant, Lambert and Vanstone [17] show that we can speed up the rho method using automorphisms. Let $\psi : \langle S \rangle \to \langle S \rangle$ be a group automorphism of order r such that ψ can be computed very efficiently. We define an equivalence relation $\sim$ on the set $\langle S \rangle$ by $P \sim Q \iff P = \psi^j(Q)$ for some $j \in [0, r-1]$. We denote the set of equivalence classes by $\langle S \rangle / \sim$, and let $[P]$ denote the equivalence class containing a point P. The idea of the speed-up using the automorphism ψ is to modify an iteration function on $\langle S \rangle$ so that it is defined on $\langle S \rangle / \sim$. To achieve this, we can define an iteration function f on $\langle S \rangle / \sim$ by $f([P]) := [g(P)]$

for an iteration function g on $\langle S \rangle$. Since almost all equivalence classes have size r, then the collision search space has size approximately n/r. Hence the expected number of iterations of the rho method sped up by the automorphism ψ is $\sqrt{\frac{\pi n}{2r}}$, which is a speed-up by a factor of $\sqrt{r}$.

Any elliptic curve has the negation map $\psi(P) = -P$ of order 2 as an automorphism. Since the negation map can be computed efficiently, it is useful to use the speed-up of the rho method. Hence the expected number of iterations of the rho method sped up by the negation map is $\frac{\sqrt{\pi n}}{2}$, which is a speed-up by a factor of $\sqrt{2}$. Koblitz curves were first suggested for use in cryptography by Koblitz [28]. The defining equation for a Koblitz curves E is $y^2 + xy = x^3 + ax^2 + b$, where $a, b \in \mathbb{F}_2$ with $b \neq 0$. The *Frobenius map* $\phi : E(\mathbb{F}_{2^m}) \to E(\mathbb{F}_{2^m})$ is defined by $\phi : (x,y) \mapsto (x^2, y^2)$ and $\phi : \mathcal{O} \mapsto \mathcal{O}$, where $\mathcal{O}$ is the point of infinity of E. We note that the Frobenius map is a group automorphism of order m on the group $E(\mathbb{F}_{2^m})$ and can be computed efficiently since squaring in $\mathbb{F}_{2^m}$ is relatively inexpensive (see [20] for details). Using both the Frobenius and the negation maps, the rho method on Koblitz curves is sped up. The expected number of iterations of the rho method sped up by both the Frobenius and the negation maps is $\frac{1}{2}\sqrt{\frac{\pi n}{m}}$, which is a speed-up by a factor of $\sqrt{2m}$.

2.2   Discussion on the Rho Method for Solving the ECDLP

In this subsection, we first discuss the choice of iteration functions suitable for solving the ECDLP. We next estimate the number of iterations before obtaining a collision and the processing performance of iterations.

Choice of Suitable Iteration Functions: The complexity of the rho method heavily depends on choice of iteration functions. An iteration function f is most suitable for solving the ECDLP if f is a random function (see §2.1 for details). To analyze the randomness of iteration functions, we consider the value defined by

$$\delta(f) := \sharp\{\text{iterations with } f \text{ before obtaining a collision}\}/\text{Exp},$$

where 'Exp' denotes the expected number of iterations (see §2.1 for details). We see that f has enough randomness if $\delta(f)$ is very close to 1.

Prime and binary fields cases : A typical iteration function is as follows: Let $\{H_1, H_2, \ldots, H_L\}$ be a random partition of the set $\langle S \rangle$ into L sets of roughly the same size. We call L a *partition number*. We write $H(X) = j$ if $X \in H_j$. For $a_j, b_j \in_R [0, n-1], 1 \leq j \leq L$, set $M_j = a_j S + b_j T \in \langle S \rangle$. Then we define an iteration function by $f_{\text{TA}}(X) = X + M_j$, where $j = H(X)$. For given a point $X = cS + dT$, we can compute $X' = f_{\text{TA}}(X) = c'S + d'T$ with $c' = c + a_j \bmod n$ and $d' = d + b_j \bmod n$. This iteration function is called an *L-adding walk* proposed by Teske (see [45,46]). Teske investigated the randomness of some iteration functions and showed that f_{TA} has better randomness than the other iteration functions. In [46], Teske also analyzed the randomness of f_{TA} by experiments on the ECDLP over prime fields of $5 - 13$ digits and concluded that f_{TA} has enough randomness over prime fields if $L \geq 16$. Furthermore, from our experimental results for solving the ECDLP over prime and binary fields of 40 and 50-bits, we see that the average of $\delta(f_{TA})$ is very close to 1 over prime and binary fields if $L \geq 20$ (see Fig. 4). Hence we conclude that f_{TA} with $L \geq 20$ has enough randomness over prime and binary fields on average. In using the speed-up with the negation map, the iteration function f_{TA} can fall into short cycles not giving the solution, which are called *fruitless cycles* [16,17], and hence we have to deal with the fruitless cycles. Note that choosing larger L decreases the chance of hitting a fruitless cycle, and hence it helps us to reduce the frequency for checking fruitless cycles.

Koblitz curves case : Let E be a Koblitz curve and let $E/ \sim$ denote the set of equivalence classes defined by both the Frobenius and the negation maps. In [49], we proposed an iteration function on Koblitz curves, which is an extension of that proposed by Gallant, Lambert and Vanstone in [17] based on Teske's idea [45]: For $0 \leq s \leq m$, we define an iteration function on $E(\mathbb{F}_{2^m})$ given by

$$
g_s(X) = \begin{cases} 2X & \text{if } 0 \leq j \leq s, \\ X + \phi^j(X) & \text{otherwise,} \end{cases}
$$

with $j = \text{hash}_m(\mathcal{L}(X))$, where hash_m is a conventional hash function (in the computer science) with range $[0, m - 1]$ and $\mathcal{L}$ is a labeling function from $E/ \sim$ to some set of representatives. We then give an iteration function $f_{\text{GLV},s}$ on $E/ \sim$ defined by $f_{\text{GLV},s}([X]) = [g_s(X)]$ for $X \in E$. Note that $f_{\text{GLV},s}$ is well-defined on $E/ \sim$ and $f_{\text{GLV},s}$ with $s = 0$ is the same as the iteration function proposed by Gallant, Lambert and Vanstone. We give our experimental results on the average of $\delta(f_{\text{GLV},s})$ in Appendix A-2. From our experimental results, we see the following (see Table 12): The number of iterations with $f_{\text{GLV},s}$ increases as the parameter s becomes large on average. In particular, we see that $f_{\text{GLV},s}$ with $s = 0$, which was proposed by Gallant, Lambert and Vanstone, has enough randomness on average since the average of $\delta(f_{\text{GLV},s})$ with $s = 0$ is equal to 1.05.

Remark 1. For solving the ECC2K-130 which is one of the Certicom ECC challenges on Koblitz curves [13], the authors in [2,5,7] proposed new iteration function f on $E/ \sim$ as follows (see also [21] for the iteration used to solve the ECC2K-95 and the ECC2K-108):

$$
f([X]) = [g(X)], \ g(X) = X + \phi^j(X), \ j = ((\text{HW}(x)/2 \bmod 8) + 3), \quad (1)
$$

where $\text{HW}(x)$ is the Hamming weight of the x-coordinate of X. Although this function has the advantage of fast processing performance, this function might reduce the randomness due to using $\text{HW}(x)$ (see [7, Appendix B] for details). The authors analyzed the randomness of this function based on a refinement of the heuristic method given by Brent and Pollard [8]. Their analysis shows that we have $\delta(f) = 1.07$ on average. In order to estimate the number of iterations required to solve the ECDLP with very high probability, we used $f_{\text{GLV},s}$ with

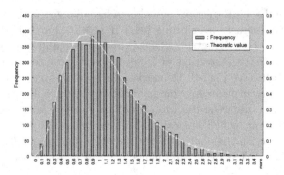

Fig. 1. Distribution of the frequencies of the number of iterations of the rho method for solving the ECDLP over prime field of 40-bit (we set $1 = \sqrt{\pi n/2}$ as the expected number of iterations)

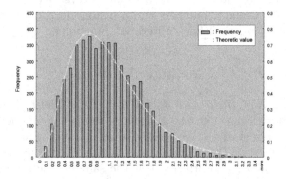

Fig. 2. Same as Fig. 1, but over binary field of 40-bit

$s = 0$ in our analysis. To investigate the randomness of this function in more detail is our future work.

The Number of Iterations of the Rho Method for the ECDLP: For simplicity, we denote $f_{\mathrm{GLV},s}$ with $s = 0$ by f_{GLV}. To estimate the number of iterations required to solve the ECDLP with very high probability, we consider f_{TA} with $L \geq 20$ (resp. f_{GLV}) as an iteration function for solving the ECDLP in prime and binary fields cases (resp. Koblitz curves case).

Prime and binary fields cases : In Fig. 1 and 2, we give our experimental results on the distribution of the frequencies of the number of iterations f_{TA} with $L = 20$. Data of Fig. 1 and 2 are obtained by solving the ECDLP over prime and binary fields of 40-bit for $10,000$ times with randomly chosen starting points (note that we did not use the speed-up with the negation map). As the numbers of iterations before obtaining a collision can be modeled as waiting times, it is reasonable to approximate the graph by Γ-distribution. The theoretic value in Fig. 1 and 2 is the curve of Γ-distribution, where we set shape parameter $k = 3.46$ and scale parameter $\theta = 0.317$ in the probability density function

$$f(x; k, \theta) = \frac{1}{\theta^k \Gamma(k)} x^{k-1} e^{-\frac{x}{\theta}}.$$

With this approximation, we see that we can solve the ECDLP with 99% probability if we compute iterations of the rho method by three times of Exp $= \sqrt{\pi n/2}$ in using f_{TA} with $L = 20$. We expect that the same result follows in using f_{TA} with $L \geq 20$ since the standard deviation of the number of iterations with f_{TA} is roughly the same if $L \geq 20$ (see Table 9 and 10 in Appendix A-1 for the standard deviation with f_{TA}).

Recently, Bernstein, Lange and Schwabe in [6] improved the rho method for obtaining the speed-up with the negation map and showed a speed-up very close to $\sqrt{2}$ on hardware with f_{TA}. To estimate the complexity of the rho method, we consider $\frac{3 \cdot \sqrt{\pi n}}{2}$ as the number of iterations for solving the ECDLP with 99% probability in using f_{TA} with $L \geq 20$.

Koblitz curves case : Since the standard deviation of the number of iterations with f_{TA} ($L = 20$) divided Exp (see Table 9 and 10 in Appendix A-1) is close to that with f_{GLV} (see Table 11 in Appendix A-2), we expect that the distribution of the frequencies of the number of iterations with f_{GLV} is approximated by the same Γ-distribution as Fig. 1 and 2. Hence we consider $\frac{3}{2} \cdot \sqrt{\frac{\pi n}{m}}$ as the number of iterations for solving the ECDLP with 99% probability in using f_{GLV}.

The Processing Performance of Iterations: We here estimate the processing performance of iterations f_{TA} with $L \geq 20$ and f_{GLV} by our implementation. Fix an integer number N and let $t(f)$ denote the processing performance of an iteration function f on an elliptic curve of N-bit.

Prime fields case : The authors in [6] implemented the L-adding walk f_{TA} for solving the ECDLP on the elliptic curve secp112r1 over prime field of 112-bit. They showed from their implementation that it needs 306.08 cycles per iteration for their software (CPU: Cell SPE 3GHz). They also reported that their software actually took 362 cycles per iteration. Based on their implementation method, we implement the addition operation on the same curve with our software. They implemented f_{TA} in a SIMD environment, while we use the normal registers for the addition operation. Let p denote the 112-bit prime number over which the curve secp112r1 is defined. Since p has the special form $p = (2^{128} - 3)/76439$, they used operations over the ring $R := \mathbb{Z}/(2^{128} - 3)\mathbb{Z}$ for the fast implementation. Since our software has the advantage of the fast processing performance of the 64-bit $\times$ 64-bit $\to$ 128-bit multiplication operation (the paper [19] shows that it needs about 4 clocks for this multiplication operation), we use the normal method for the multiplication over R, instead of the Karatsuba method used in [6]. In their implementation, they used the standard formulas for elliptic curve addition in affine coordinates with Montgomery's trick for batching the inversion in $A = 224$ independent iterations. It follows from [6, Section 3] that it needs $(1/A) \cdot (\mathbf{I} - 3\mathbf{M}) + 5\mathbf{M} + 1\mathbf{S} + 6\mathbf{b}$ for implementing the elliptic curve addition operation over prime fields, where $\mathbf{I}, \mathbf{M}, \mathbf{S}$ and $\mathbf{b}$ are the costs of the inversions, multiplications, squarings and subtractions over the field, respectively. Our implementation shows that we have the following (CPU: Intel Xeon X3460 2.8GHz 8GB memory, cf. [6, Section 5]):

- $5\mathbf{M} : 39.654 \times 5 = 198.27$ cycles (cf. $53.61 \times 5 = 268.05$ by using the Karatsuba method);
  - The authors in [6] reported that it needs 218.75 cycles for $5\mathbf{M}$ with their software, which costs more almost 20 cycles than our implementation. This difference is due to the property that our software has the much faster processing performance of the multiplication operation than their software (the CPU used in their implementation only has the 16-bit × 16-bit → 32-bit multiplication operation).
- $1\mathbf{S} : 37.94$ cycles;
- $6\mathbf{b} : 3.105 \times 6 = 18.63$ cycles;
- $(1/224) \cdot (\mathbf{I} - 3\mathbf{M})$: $(5676.65 - 39.654 \times 3)/224 = 24.81$ cycles.

By adding them up, we estimate that it needs 279.65 cycles per elliptic curve addition over R. Our software actually takes 270.05 per elliptic curve addition over R, about 3.5% less than the estimation. This is due to the efficiency of the inline implementation and the parallelized ALU operations.

Remark 2. According to [6, Section 5], we also need to estimate the cost of the 'canonicalization' operation for estimating the cost of f_{TA} on the curve secp112r1. Note that this operation is necessary to obtain the unique representation of $\mathbb{F}_p$ from an element of R. Since it follows from [6, Section 5] that the cost of this operation is almost half of that of the multiplication over R, we estimate that the cost of this operation is $39.654/2 \approx 19.83$ cycles. By adding it to our implementation result, we estimate that it needs $270.05 + 19.83 = 289.88$ cycles per iteration. The method in [6] is specialized for the curve secp112r1, in which p has the special form. Since the cost of the canonicalization operation is approximately equal to 8% of the total cost in the implementation of [6], we estimate the processing performance of f_{TA} only from the cost of an elliptic curve addition in the next paragraph, and consider 270.05 cycles per elliptic curve addition over R as the cost over prime fields of 128-bit.

There can be a loss in performance if we take so large L that the precomputed points do not fit in cache. Therefore we assume that we take L so that the precomputed points fit in cache and $t(f_{\mathrm{TA}})$ is not affected by the size of L. Moreover, since $t(f_{\mathrm{TA}})$ is approximately equal to the processing performance of a point addition on elliptic curves, we estimate that $t(f_{\mathrm{TA}})$ is proportional to the value $\left(\lceil \frac{N}{64} \rceil\right)^2$ due to the normal method for the multiplication over prime fields with 64-bit registers. We compare the efficiency of the normal method and the Karatsuba method for the multiplication: In the case $N = 256$, we estimate that $1\mathbf{M} = 39.61 \times (256/128)^2 = 158.62$ cycles with the normal method.

On the other hand, we estimate that $1\mathbf{M} = 53.61 \times (256/128)^{1.585} = 160.83$ cycles with the Karatsuba method. These estimations show that the normal method is better than the Karatsuba method if $N \leq 256$. From the above arguments, we estimate that we have

$$t(f_{\mathrm{TA}}) = \frac{270.05}{4} \times \left(\left\lceil \frac{N}{64} \right\rceil \right)^2 \text{ cycles } (64 \leq N \leq 256).$$

Binary fields case : The authors in [7] implemented the iteration function defined by (1) for solving the Certicom ECC2K-130 challenge. The challenge curve is given by the Koblitz curve $E : y^2 + xy = x^3 + 1$ over binary field of 131-bit (the polynomial basis representation is given by $\mathbb{F}_{2^{131}} = \mathbb{F}_2[z]/(F)$ with $F(z) = z^{131} + z^{13} + z^2 + z + 1$). Their implementation method is similar to that in [6], and they showed from their implementation that it needs 534 cycles per iteration for their software (CPU: Core 2 Extreme Q6850 3GHz). As in the case of prime fields, we implement the addition operation in polynomial-basis on the same curve E with our software based on their implementation method. Note that a Koblitz curve is one of the binary elliptic curves on which we can implement the addition operation effectively. In this case, we use the 128-bit MMX registers in a SIMD environment for effectively using the bitslice technique, which is the main part of their method. Furthermore, we use the Karatsuba method for the fast multiplication over $\mathbb{F}_{2^{131}}$ as in [7]. It follows from [7, Section 3] that it needs $(1/A) \cdot (\mathbf{I} - 3\mathbf{M}) + 5\mathbf{M} + 1\mathbf{S} + 7\mathbf{a}$ for the elliptic curve operation over binary fields, where $\mathbf{a}$ is the cost of the additions over the field. We set $A = 52$ as in [7]. Note that the larger A causes the delay of memory access since the data size is big compared to the prime field case due to the bitslice technique. Our implementation shows that we have the following (CPU: Intel Xeon E31275 3.4GHz 16GB memory):

- $5\mathbf{M}$: $76.288 \times 5 = 381.44$ cycles;
  - The authors in [7] reported that it needs 94 cycles per multiplication and hence $94 \times 5 = 470$ cycles for $5\mathbf{M}$ with their software. Their implementation costs more almost 90 cycles than our implementation. This seems to be mainly due to the fact that the CPU used in our implementation has three throughputs while the CPU used in their implementation has only two throughputs.
- $1\mathbf{S}$: 6.15 cycles;
- $7\mathbf{a}$: $1.814 \times 7 = 12.70$ cycles;
- $(1/52) \cdot (\mathbf{I} - 3\mathbf{M})$: $(1284.559 - 76.288 \times 3)/52 = 20.30$ cycles.

By adding them up, we estimate that it needs 420.59 cycles per elliptic curve addition over $\mathbb{F}_{2^{131}}$. Our software actually takes 388.48 cycles per elliptic curve addition, about 7.6% less than the estimation due to the same reason in the prime fields case.

In this case, we estimate that $t(f_{\mathrm{TA}})$ is proportional to the value $N^{1.585}$ due to the Karatsuba method with the bitslice technique (note that the bitslice

Table 4. The estimated cost of each Step in computing $g(X) = X + \phi^j(X)$

	Step 1	Step 2	Step 3	Step 4	Total
Cost	0.22	0.25	1.00	0.15	1.62

We consider the cost of a point addition on E in polynomial-basis as the standard value.

technique is not effected by the size of the registers). Therefore we estimate that we have

$$t(f_{\text{TA}}) = 388.48 \times (N/131)^{1.585} \text{ cycles.}$$

Our software actually takes 720.05 cycles over $\mathbb{F}_{2^{192}}$ and 1102.09 cycles over $\mathbb{F}_{2^{256}}$ for the elliptic curve operation on the Koblitz curve E. Since we have $t(f_{\text{TA}}) = 712.08$ cycles in the case $N = 192$ and $t(f_{\text{TA}}) = 1123.45$ cycles in the case $N = 256$, we see that our estimation $t(f_{\text{TA}})$ is very close to our implementation results.

Koblitz curves case : For simplicity, we denote g_s with $s = 0$ by g. In computing f_{GLV}, the cost of computing $g(X) = X + \phi^j(X)$ is dominant. In our implementation, we take a point $X \in E$ represented by normal-basis as input, get the index $j = \text{hash}_m(\mathcal{L}(X))$ by computing $m - 1$ elements $\phi^i(X)$ for $i = 1, \dots, m - 1$ and take $Y = \phi^j(X)$ in normal-basis (Step 1), transform normal-basis to polynomial-basis (Step 2), compute $X + Y$ in polynomial-basis (Step 3), transform bases again (Step 4) and finally output $g(X)$ represented by normal-basis. Note that it needs to map $g(X) \in E$ to $[g(X)] \in E/\sim$ in computing f_{GLV}, but the cost of this mapping is included in Step 1 of the next computation of g. In Table 4, we give the cost of each Step from our implementation. We estimate from Table 4 that $t(f_{\text{GLV}})$ is 1.62 times of the processing performance of a point addition on E over binary fields in polynomial-basis. Therefore we estimate that we have

$$t(f_{\text{GLV}}) = 1.62 \times 388.48 \times (N/131)^{1.585} \text{ cycles.}$$

As we said above, the authors in [7] implemented the iteration function defined by (1) over $\mathbb{F}_{2^{131}}$ and showed that it needs 534 cycles per iteration over $\mathbb{F}_{2^{131}}$. On the other hand, our estimation shows that it needs $1.62 \times 389.50 = 631$ cycles per iteration over $\mathbb{F}_{2^{131}}$. This delay is mainly due to the difference of the iteration function used for solving the ECDLP.

2.3   Estimation of the Complexity of the Rho Method

Since the running time due to the collision detection of distinguished points is negligible, we see that the complexity of the rho method with f for solving the ECDLP of N-bit is approximately equal to $\#\{\text{iterations}\} \times t(f)$. Hence we

Table 5. Estimation of the computing power T_{ECDLP} required to solve the ECDLP of N-bit in a year by using the rho method (FLOPS is the unit of T_{ECDLP})

Prime fields case		Binary fields case		Koblitz curves case	
N	$\log_{10} T_{\text{ECDLP}}$	N	$\log_{10} T_{\text{ECDLP}}$	N	$\log_{10} T_{\text{ECDLP}}$
112	12.21	112	12.27	117	12.22
113	12.37	113	12.42	118	12.38
124	14.02	124	14.14	129	14.08
133	15.73	134	15.70	139	15.62
153	18.74	154	18.81	159	18.69
160	19.79	160	19.74	166	19.76
168	21.00	168	20.97	174	20.99
195	25.31	196	25.29	202	25.27
224	29.67	224	29.60	231	29.70
247	33.14	247	33.13	254	33.21

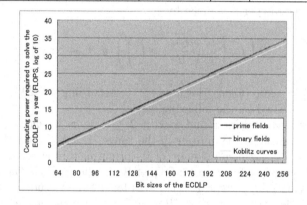

estimate the computing power T_{ECDLP} required to solve the ECDLP of N-bit in a year using the rho method as follows (FLOPS is the unit of T_{ECDLP}):

$$T_{\text{ECDLP}} = \begin{cases} 3 \cdot \sqrt{\pi 2^N}/2 \times \frac{270.05}{4} \cdot \left(\left\lceil \frac{N}{64} \right\rceil\right)^2 /Y & \text{(prime fields case, } 64 \leq N \leq 256), \\ 3 \cdot \sqrt{\pi 2^N}/2 \times 388.48 \cdot (N/131)^{1.585}/Y & \text{(binary fields case)}, \\ 3 \cdot \sqrt{\pi 2^N/N}/2 \times 1.62 \cdot 388.48 \cdot (N/131)^{1.585}/Y & \text{(Koblitz curves case)}. \end{cases}$$

We set $Y = 365 \cdot 24 \cdot 60 \cdot 60$ (seconds) and $n = 2^N$ as the order of the point S. In Table 5, we give T_{ECDLP} for each N.

Remark 3. In [5], Bernstein et al. measured the computing power to break the Certicom ECC2K-130 challenge based on their extensive experiments. This challenge is to solve the ECDLP on a Koblitz curve E over $\mathbb{F}_{2^{131}}$ with $\sharp E(\mathbb{F}_{2^m}) = 4n$ and $n \approx 2^{129}$. They showed that this challenge would be solved in two years on average using 534 GPUs (1.242 GHz NVIDIA GTX 295, 60 core). On the other hand, we extrapolate by our estimation formula that it needs $10^{14.086}$ FLOPS ≈ 1636 GPUs to solve the ECDLP of 129-bit in a year with 99% probability

(1 GPU=1.242 · 10^9 · 60 FLOPS). The difference is mainly due to the solving period (2 years vs 1 year), the success probability of the rho method (50% vs 99%) and the processing performance of iterations (1164 cycles [5] vs 631 cycles).

3   The Hardness of the IFP

To evaluate the hardness of the IFP, we estimate the complexity of the GNFS.

3.1   The GNFS and Its Complexity

The GNFS consists of four steps, namely, the polynomial selection step, the sieving or the relation finding step, the linear algebra step, and the square root step. Among these four steps, the sieving step is dominant procedure theoretically and experimentally. The conjectural complexity of the GNFS for factoring a composite large integer n is given by

$$O\left(L_n\left(\frac{1}{3}, \sqrt[3]{\frac{64}{9}} + o(1) \right) \right) \quad \text{as } n \to \infty \qquad (2)$$

where $L_n(s, c) = \exp(c(\log n)^s (\log \log n)^{1-s})$. According to [29,37], the above complexity is obtained by the following way:

For two positive integers x and z with $2 \le z < x$, let $\Phi(x, z)$ denote the probability that an arbitrary integer in the range $[1, x]$ is z-smooth. Note that a positive integer is *z-smooth* if none of its prime factors is greater than z. It is known that there is a function $\rho : \mathbb{R}_{>0} \to \mathbb{R}_{>0}$ called the *Dickman-de Bruijn function* satisfying $\lim_{x \to \infty} \Phi(x, x^{1/u}) = \rho(u)$ for $u \ge 1$. A crude but very useful estimation of ρ is $\rho(u) = u^{-u(1+o(1))}$ as $u \to \infty$. By using this result on ρ, Canfield, Erdös and Pomerance [9] showed that we have

$$\Phi(x, z) = u^{-u(1+o(1))} \text{ as } x \to \infty \qquad (3)$$

for $z \ge (\log x)^{1+\varepsilon}$ with $\varepsilon > 0$, where $u = \log x / \log z$. We see from the above estimation of $\Phi(x, z)$ that

$$\Phi(L_x(a, c), L_x(b, d)) = L_x(a - b, -c(a - b)/d + o(1)) \text{ as } x \to \infty. \qquad (4)$$

Note that the $o(1)$-value in the expression (4) is approximately equal to $-c(a - b)/d$ times of the $o(1)$-value of $\Phi(x, z)$ in the expression (3). In the GNFS for factoring a composite large integer n, we take a polynomial $f(X) = c_d X^d + c_{d-1} X^{d-1} + \cdots + c_0 \in \mathbb{Q}[X]$ of degree d and an integer M such that $f(M) \equiv 0 \bmod n$ and $M \approx n^{1/(d+1)}$. Note that d is determined by $d = \lfloor \lambda^{-1}(\log n / \log \log n)^{1/3} \rfloor$ and the most suitable value of λ will be determined in the next paragraph ($\lambda = \sqrt[3]{1/3}$). Fix a root θ of $f(X) = 0$ and let $K = \mathbb{Q}(\theta)$ denote the number field generated by θ. For a relation (a, b), the size of the algebraic norm $c_d N_{K/\mathbb{Q}}(a + b\theta) = (-b)^d f(-a/b) = c_d a^d + c_{d-1} a^{d-1}(-b) + \cdots + c_0(-b)^d$ is approximately equal to $n^{1/(d+1)} \cdot \max(a, b)^d$.

Table 6. The estimated computing power T required to solve the IFP of N-bit in a year by CRYPTREC report 2006 [10] (FLOPS is the unit of T)

N	768	1024	1536	2048
$\log_{10} T$	12.4026	15.6646	20.8987	25.2455

Take $L_n(1/3, 2\lambda^2)$ as both the upper bound B of the factor base and the sieving area of the relations (a, b). Then the size of $c_d N_{K/\mathbb{Q}}(a + b\theta)$ is approximately equal to

$$L_n(1/3, 2\lambda^2)^d \cdot n^{1/(d+1)}$$
$$= \exp(2\lambda(\log n)^{2/3}(\log\log n)^{1/3}) \cdot \exp(\lambda(\log n)^{2/3}(\log\log n)^{1/3})$$
$$= L_n(2/3, 3\lambda)$$

and the size of M is approximately equal to

$$n^{1/(d+1)} = \exp(\lambda(\log n)^{2/3}(\log\log n)^{1/3}) = L_n(2/3, \lambda).$$

We have the probability that both the above numbers become $B = L_n(1/3, 2\lambda^2)$-smooth is

$$\Phi(L_n(2/3, 3\lambda), B) \cdot \Phi(L_n(2/3, \lambda), B) = L_n(1/3, -2/(3\lambda) + o(1))$$

by the expression (4). Note that the $o(1)$-value in the above expression is approximately equal to $-2/(3\lambda)$ times of the $o(1)$-value of $\Phi(x, z)$. Since the number of relations should be more than that of the factor base, we have $L_n(1/3, -2/(3\lambda) + o(1)) \cdot L_n(1/3, 2\lambda^2)^2 \geq L_n(1/3, 2\lambda^2)$. We then have $\lambda^3 \geq 1/3$, which shows that $\sqrt[3]{1/3}$ is the most suitable value for λ. Set $\lambda = \sqrt[3]{1/3}$. Since we need more smooth relations than the number of the elements in the factor base, the complexity of the GNFS is given by

$$\underbrace{L_n(1/3, 2\lambda^2)}_{\sharp(\text{the factor base})} \cdot \underbrace{L_n(1/3, -2/(3\lambda) + o(1))^{-1}}_{(\text{probability of the smoothness})^{-1}} = L_n\left(\frac{1}{3}, \sqrt[3]{\frac{64}{9}} + o(1)\right),$$

which gives the conjectural complexity (2). Note that the $o(1)$-value of the above expression is approximately equal to $2/(3\lambda) \approx 0.9615$ times of the $o(1)$-value of $\Phi(x, z)$.

3.2   Estimation of the Complexity of the GNFS

Let T_{IFP} denote the computing power required to solve the IFP of N-bit in a year. By the complexity (2), we expect that we have

$$T_{\text{IFP}} = \ell \cdot L_{2^N}\left(\frac{1}{3}, \sqrt[3]{\frac{64}{9}} + o(1)\right) \tag{5}$$

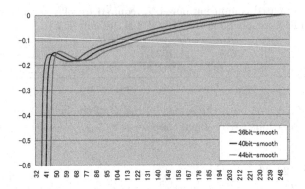

Fig. 3. Experimental result on the $o(1)$-value of $\Phi(x, z)$ with $z = 2^{36}, 2^{40}, 2^{44}$

for some $o(1)$ and ℓ. To evaluate the complexity of the GNFS for each N, we set $o(1)$ and ℓ as follows: CRYPTREC report 2006 [10, Figure 2.2] gives the estimated computing power required to solve the IFP of N-bit with $N = 768, 1024, 1536$ and 2048 under the condition with unlimited memory size, which we show in Table 6. The result [10] is based on the papers [23,24], and the data of Table 6 are estimated by evaluating the computing power of the sieving step by extensive experiments. To determine T_{IFP}, we set $o(1)$ and ℓ satisfying the condition that the complexity of T_{IFP} is very close to each data of Table 6. A computation shows that

$$o(1) = -0.1091 \text{ and } \ell = 10^{-11.9368} \tag{6}$$

satisfy the above condition. The constants (6) are determined by the following method: We first consider the relation of $o(1)$ and ℓ satisfying that T_{IFP} is equal to the data of Table 6 in the case $N = 1024$. By the binary search algorithm, we next determine $o(1)$ (and hence ℓ with the relation) so that T_{IFP} is equal to the data of Table 6 in the case $N = 2048$. Then T_{IFP} with the constants (6) is very close to the data of Table 6 in the cases $N = 768$ and 1536.

In Fig. 3, we give our experimental result on the $o(1)$-value of $\Phi(x, z)$ by computing $\Phi(x, z)$ with $2^{32} \leq x \leq 2^{256}$ and $z = 2^{36}, 2^{40}, 2^{44}$. From Fig. 3, we see that the $o(1)$-value of $\Phi(x, z)$ is included in the range $[-0.2, 0]$ if $x \geq 2^{64}$. As we explained in §3.1, the $o(1)$-value of T_{IFP} is approximately equal to 0.9615 times of the $o(1)$-value of $\Phi(x, z)$. Therefore we expect that the $o(1)$-value of T_{IFP} is included in the range $[-0.1923, 0]$ for large N. Since $o(1) = -0.1091$ is included in this range, we expect that the computing power T_{IFP} with the $o(1)$ and ℓ same as (6) is practically suitable for evaluating the complexity of the GNFS. In Table 7, we give the estimation of the computing power T_{IFP}.

4   Comparison of the ECDLP and the IFP

In our estimation, we make the following assumptions:

Table 7. The computing power T_{IFP} with the $o(1)$ and ℓ same as (6) (FLOPS is the unit of T_{IFP})

N	755	768	894	1024	1308	1413	1536	2048	2671	3241
$\log_{10} T_{\mathrm{IFP}}$	12.22	12.40	14.08	15.66	18.75	19.79	20.95	25.25	29.67	33.20

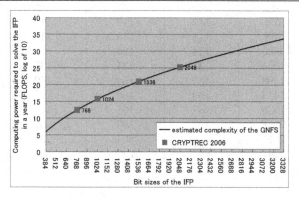

- ECDLP (THE RHO METHOD) SIDE : The processing performance of iterations scales proportionally to $(\lceil N/64 \rceil)^\alpha$ or N^α, where N is the bit size of the order of the ECDLP and α is a constant determined by the method for the multiplication over fields. We note that N is different from the bit size of fields in the cases of binary fields and the Koblitz curves. Table 5 and 8 are obtained when we use the normal method in the prime fields case (i.e., $(\lceil N/64 \rceil)^2$), and the Karatsuba method in the cases of binary and the Koblitz curves (i.e., $N^{1.585}$). The memory requirement of the rho method can be controlled by using the technique of distinguished points. Therefore the memory requirement of the rho method is negligible.
- IFP (THE GNFS) SIDE : The complexity of the GNFS is given by the computing power T_{IFP} with the $o(1)$ and ℓ same as (6). Although we in [50] assumed the limited memory size, we here assume that the memory requirement for executing the GNFS is unlimited (note that limited memory size would increase the complexity of the GNFS).

We then calculate the bit sizes of the ECDLP and the IFP that provide the same level of security. In Table 8, we give an estimation of the strength comparison of the ECDLP and the IFP. In particular, we have the following from Table 8:

- The security of 768-bit IFP is close to that of 113-bit ECDLP over prime field, 113-bit ECDLP over binary field, or 118-bit ECDLP on Koblitz curves. The world records of 2011 for solving the IFP and the ECDLP are 768-bit IFP in 2010 [25,26] and 112-bit ECDLP over prime field in 2009 [15], respectively. Since the times of these two records are close, we consider that these records indicate reasonability of our estimation.

Table 8. Estimation of the bit sizes of the ECDLP and the IFP providing the same level security

Bit sizes of the IFP	Bit sizes of the ECDLP		
	Prime fields	Binary fields	Koblitz curves
512	87	87	92
755	112	112	117
768	113	113	118
894	124	124	129
1024	133	134	139
1308	153	154	159
1413	160	160	166
1536	168	168	174
2048	195	196	202
2671	224	224	231
3241	247	247	254

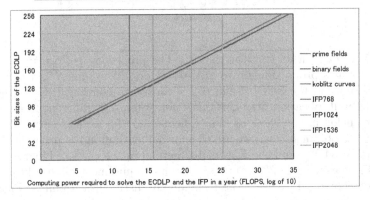

- The security of 1024-bit IFP is close to that of 133-bit ECDLP over prime field, 134-bit ECDLP over binary field, or 139-bit ECDLP on Koblitz curves. Though it is often said that 160-bit ECDLP corresponds to 1024-bit IFP, our estimation indicates that shorter ECC key sizes provide the same level of security.

5   Conclusions

In this paper, we estimated the complexity of the rho method for solving the ECDLP based on state-of-the-art of theory and experiments, and estimated the computing power required to solve the ECDLP in a year (see Table 5). We also estimated the computing power required to solve the IFP based on CRYPTREC Report 2006 result (see Table 7), and gave an estimation of the strength comparison of the ECDLP and the IFP (see Table 8). Although we estimated the complexity of the GNFS under the assumption of unlimited memory size, the bit sizes of the IFP in Table 8 would decrease under the assumption of limited memory size of the GNFS. In particular, we estimated from Table 8 that the security of 1024-bit IFP is close to that of 140-bit ECDLP. If we say 160-bit ECC has 80-bit security because the complexity of the rho method is square root, our estimation indicates that 1024-bit RSA does not reach the 80-bit security.

Acknowledgments. A part of this research is financially supported by a contract research with the National Institute of Information and Communications Technology (NICT), Japan.

References

1. ANSI X9.62, Public Key Cryptography for the Financial Services Industry: The Elliptic Curve Digital Signature Algorithm (ECDSA) (1999)
2. Bailey, D., Baldwin, B., Batina, L., Bernstein, D., Birkner, P., Bos, J., van Damme, G., de Meulenaer, G., Fan, J., Güneysu, T., Gurkaynak, F., Kleinjung, T., Lange, T., Mentens, N., Paar, C., Regazzoni, F., Schwabe, P., Uhsadel, L.: The Certicom Challenges ECC2-X, IACR ePrint Archive, 2009/466 (2009), http://eprint.iacr.org/2009/466
3. Bernstein, D.J.: Curve25519: New Diffie-Hellman Speed Records. In: Yung, M., Dodis, Y., Kiayias, A., Malkin, T. (eds.) PKC 2006. LNCS, vol. 3958, pp. 207–228. Springer, Heidelberg (2006)
4. Bernstein, D.J.: Speed Reports for Elliptic-Curve Cryptography (2010), http://cr.yp.to/ecdh/reports.html
5. Bernstein, D.J., Chen, H.-C., Cheng, C.-M., Lange, T., Niederhagen, R., Schwabe, P., Yang, B.-Y.: ECC2K-130 on NVIDIA GPUs. In: Gong, G., Gupta, K.C. (eds.) INDOCRYPT 2010. LNCS, vol. 6498, pp. 328–346. Springer, Heidelberg (2010)
6. Bernstein, D.J., Lange, T., Schwabe, P.: On the Correct Use of the Negation Map in the Pollard rho Method. In: Catalano, D., Fazio, N., Gennaro, R., Nicolosi, A. (eds.) PKC 2011. LNCS, vol. 6571, pp. 128–146. Springer, Heidelberg (2011)
7. Breaking ECC2K-130, IACR ePrint Achive, 2009/541, http://eprint.iacr.org/2009/541.pdf
8. Brent, R., Pollard, J.: Factorization of the eighth Fermat number. Mathematics of Computation 36, 627–630 (1981)
9. Canfield, E.R., Erdos, P., Pomerance, C.: On a problem of Oppenheim concerning Factorisatio Numerorum. J. Number Theory 17, 1–28 (1983)
10. CRYPTREC, CRYPTREC Report 2006 (2006), http://www.cryptrec.go.jp/report/c06_wat_final.pdf
11. Blake, I., Seroussi, G., Smart, N.: Elliptic Curves in Cryptography. Cambridge University Press (1999)
12. Certicom, Certicom ECC Challenge (1997), http://www.certicom.jp/images/pdfs/cert_ecc_challenge.pdf
13. Certicom, Curves List (1997), http://www.certicom.jp/index.php/curves-list
14. ECRYPT II, ECRYPT II Report on Key Sizes (2011), http://www.keylength.com/en/3/
15. EPFL IC LACAL, PlayStation 3 computing breaks 2^{60} barrier 112-bit prime ECDLP solved (2009), http://lacal.epfl.ch/112bit_prime
16. Galbraith, S.D., Ruprai, R.S.: Using Equivalence Classes to Accelerate Solving the Discrete Logarithm Problem in a Short Interval. In: Nguyen, P.Q., Pointcheval, D. (eds.) PKC 2010. LNCS, vol. 6056, pp. 368–383. Springer, Heidelberg (2010)

17. Gallant, R., Lambert, R., Vanstone, S.: Improving the Parallelized Pollard Lambda Search on Binary Anomalous Curves. Mathematics of Computation 69, 1699–1705 (2000)
18. Güneysu, T., Kasper, T., Novotný, M., Paar, C., Rupp, A.: Cryptanalysis with COPACOBANA. Transactions on Computers 57, 1498–1513 (2008)
19. Granlund, T.: Instruction latencies and throughput for AMD and Intel x86 processors (February 13, 2012 version), http://gmplib.org/~tege/x86-timing.pdf
20. Hankerson, D., Menezes, A., Vanstone, S.: Guide to Elliptic Curve Cryptography. Springer Professional Computing (2004)
21. Harley, R.: Elliptic curve discrete logarithms project,
    http://pauillac.inria.fr/~harley/ecdl/
22. Izu, T., Kogure, J., Shimoyama, T.: CAIRN 2: An FPGA Implementation of the Sieving Step in the Number Field Sieve Method. In: Paillier, P., Verbauwhede, I. (eds.) CHES 2007. LNCS, vol. 4727, pp. 364–377. Springer, Heidelberg (2007)
23. Kleinjung, T.: Estimates for factoring 1024-bit integers. In: Securing Cyberspace: Applications and Foundations of Cryptography and Computer Security, Workshop IV: Special Purpose Hardware for Cryptography: Attacks and Applications, Slides (2006), http://www.ipam.ucla.edu/schedule.aspx?pc=scws4
24. Kleinjung, T.: Evaluation of Complexity of Mathematical Algorithms. CRYPTREC technical report No.0601 in FY 2006 (2007),
    http://www.cryptrec.jp/estimation.html
25. Kleinjung, T., Aoki, K., Franke, J., Lenstra, A.K., Thomé, E., Bos, J.W., Gaudry, P., Kruppa, A., Montgomery, P.L., Osvik, D.A., te Riele, H., Timofeev, A., Zimmermann, P.: Factorization of a 768-Bit RSA Modulus. In: Rabin, T. (ed.) CRYPTO 2010. LNCS, vol. 6223, pp. 333–350. Springer, Heidelberg (2010)
26. Kleinjung, T., Bos, J.W., Lenstra, A.K., Osvik, D.A., Aoki, K., Contini, S., Franke, J., Thomé, E., Jermini, P., Thiémard, M., Leyland, P., Montgomery, P., Timofeev, A., Stockinger, H.: A heterogeneous computing environment to solve the 768-bit RSA. Cluster Computing 15(1), 53–68 (2012)
27. Knuth, D.: The art of computer programming, Seminumerical Algorithms, vol. II. Addison-Wesley, Reading (1969)
28. Koblitz, N.: Elliptic curve cryptosystems. Mathematics of Computation 48, 203–209 (1987)
29. Lenstra, A., Lenstra, H., Manasse, M., Pollard, J.: The Number Field Sieve. In: Symposium on Theory of Computing - STOC 1990, pp. 564–572. ACM (1990)
30. Lenstra, A., Verheul, E.: Selecting Cryptographic Key Sizes. Journal of Cryptology 14(4), 255–293 (2001)
31. Menezes, A., Okamoto, T., Vanstone, S.: Reducing elliptic curve logarithms to logarithms in a finite field. IEEE Transactions on Information Theory 39, 1639–1646 (1993)
32. Miller, V.S.: Use of Elliptic Curves in Cryptography. In: Williams, H.C. (ed.) CRYPTO 1985. LNCS, vol. 218, pp. 417–426. Springer, Heidelberg (1986)
33. NESSIE, NESSIE Security Report (Feburary 2003)
34. NIST Special Publication 800-57, http://csrc.nist.gov/publications/nistpubs/800-57/sp800-57-Part1-revised2_Mar08-2007.pdf
35. Orman, H., Hoffman, P.: Determining Strengths for Public Keys Used for Exchanging Symmetric Keys. IETF RFC 3766/BCP 86 (April 2004)
36. Pollard, J.: Monte Carlo methods for index computation mod p. Mathematics of Computation 32, 918–924 (1978)
37. Pomerance, C.: The Number Field Sieve. In: Proceedings of Symposia in Applied Mathematics, vol. 48, pp. 465–480 (1994)

38. Rivest, R., Shamir, A., Adelman, L.: A method for obtaining digital signatures and public-key cyrptosystems. Communications of the ACM 21, 120–126 (1978)
39. RSA Labs. A Cost-Based Security Analysis of Symmetric and Asymmetric Key Lengths, RSA Labs Bulletin (13) (April 2000) (revised November 2001)
40. Satoh, T., Araki, K.: Fermat quotients and the polynomial time discrete log algorithm for anomalous elliptic curves. Commentarii Mathematici Universitatis Sancti Pauli 47, 81–92 (1998)
41. Semaev, I.: Evaluation of discrete logarithms in a group of p-torsion points of an elliptic curve in characteristic p. Mathematics of Computation 67, 353–356 (1998)
42. Shamir, A.: Factoring Large Numbers with the TWINKLE Device (Extended Abstract). In: Koç, Ç.K., Paar, C. (eds.) CHES 1999. LNCS, vol. 1717, pp. 2–12. Springer, Heidelberg (1999)
43. Shamir, A., Tromer, E.: Factoring Large Numbers with the TWIRL Device. In: Boneh, D. (ed.) CRYPTO 2003. LNCS, vol. 2729, pp. 1–26. Springer, Heidelberg (2003)
44. Smart, N.P.: The discrete logarithm problem on elliptic curves of trace one. Journal of Cryptology 12, 110–125 (1999)
45. Teske, E.: Speeding Up Pollard's Rho Method for Computing Discrete Logarithms. In: Buhler, J.P. (ed.) ANTS 1998. LNCS, vol. 1423, pp. 541–554. Springer, Heidelberg (1998)
46. Teske, E.: On random walks for Pollard's rho method. Mathematics of Computation 70, 809–825 (2001)
47. van Oorschot, P.C., Wiener, M.J.: Parallel collision search with cryptanalytic applications. Journal of Cryptology 12, 1–28 (1999)
48. Wiener, M., Zuccherato, R.J.: Faster Attacks on Elliptic Curve Cryptosystems. In: Tavares, S., Meijer, H. (eds.) SAC 1998. LNCS, vol. 1556, pp. 190–200. Springer, Heidelberg (1999)
49. Yasuda, M., Izu, T., Shimoyama, T., Kogure, J.: On random walks of Pollard's rho method for the ECDLP on Koblitz curves. Journal of Math-for-Industry 3(2011B-3), 107–112 (2011)
50. Yasuda, M., Shimoyma, T., Izu, T., Kogure, J.: On the strength comparison of ECC and RSA. In: Workshop Record of SHARCS 2012, pp. 61–79 (2012), http://2012.sharcs.org/

Appendix A: Experimental Results on the Randomness

A-1: Randomness of f_{TA}

The randomness of f_{TA} depends heavily on the partition number L. To analyze the randomness of f_{TA} with L accurately, we solved the ECDLP over both prime and binary fields of 40 and 50-bits. In the following, we describe our experiments:

- We used the parallelized rho method with $M = 10$ processors and collision detection using distinguished points.
- We used f_{TA} with some $3 \leq L \leq 100$. For each L, we solved the ECDLP for 100 times with randomly chosen starting points. Note that we did not use the speed-up with the negation map in our experiments (hence we have $\text{Exp} = \sqrt{\pi n/2}$).

Table 9 and 10 show our experimental results on the randomness of f_{TA} with $3 \leq L \leq 100$. In Table 9 and 10, we give the following data (In particular, we summarize our experimental results on the average of $\delta(f_{TA})$ in Fig. 4):

- μ: the average number of iterations before obtaining a collision.
- σ: the standard deviation of the number of iterations.
- μ/Exp: the average number of iterations divided by Exp, which is the same as $\delta(f)$.
- σ/Exp: the standard deviation divided by Exp.

In the following, we show parameters of the ECDLP over prime and binary fields.

Prime fields case : Let $E : y^2 = x^3 + ax + b$ be an elliptic curve defined over a prime field $\mathbb{F}_q$. Parameters of the ECDLP over prime fields of 40 and 50-bits are as follows (each data is represented in hexadecimal): Note that $S = (x_S, y_S)$ and $T = (x_T, y_T)$ are two points of E, n is the order of S and k is the cofactor defined by $E(\mathbb{F}_q)/n$.

$$
\begin{cases}
q & = 1000000000F, \\
a & = 58B15FA9BD, \\
b & = 2C053EE7E9, \\
x_S & = 2E6105B3EF, \\
y_S & = 855C930596, \\
x_T & = 6F0F05F8AE, \\
y_T & = A03DF7A253, \\
n & = \text{FFFFFAFEA9} \ (\approx 40\text{-bit}), \\
k & = 1.
\end{cases}
\qquad
\begin{cases}
q & = 5AF3107A4727, \\
a & = 513126EC56EB, \\
b & = 271F6BAD88F1, \\
x_S & = 295ADCF2FC02, \\
y_S & = 47126D966B08, \\
x_T & = 2E5C9B0B2BC8, \\
y_T & = 41B1DD3BEBF0, \\
n & = \text{5AF3114927D9} \ (\approx 50\text{-bit}), \\
k & = 1.
\end{cases}
$$

Binary fields case : Let $E : y^2 + xy = x^3 + ax^2 + b$ be an elliptic curve defined over a binary field $\mathbb{F}_q$. Parameters of the ECDLP over prime fields of 40 and 50-bits are as follows (each data is represented in hexadecimal): In this case, each data of q represents the reduction polynomial which defines the polynomial basis of a binary field $\mathbb{F}_q$.

$$
\begin{cases}
q & = 10008000007, \\
a & = 93E84A3D71, \\
b & = 4C52A09C07, \\
x_S & = F89BE06701, \\
y_S & = 53357B5E9, \\
x_T & = 1834458EB8, \\
y_T & = 77EA789F07, \\
n & = \text{7FFFF92FF1} \ (\approx 40\text{-bit}), \\
k & = 2.
\end{cases}
\qquad
\begin{cases}
q & = 4000000000207, \\
a & = 35D9C8DBE00B2, \\
b & = 2A1F0D81C88F3, \\
x_S & = 1D6C6E2802BB9, \\
y_S & = 100733D4F059E, \\
x_T & = 1BF0F3287E51E, \\
y_T & = 22828E9AE5DA5, \\
n & = \text{1FFFFFED2C77B} \ (\approx 50\text{-bit}), \\
k & = 2.
\end{cases}
$$

Table 9. Experimental results on the randomness of f_{TA} for solving the ECDLP over prime fields of 40 and 50-bits (without the speed-up using the negation map)

40-bit case (Exp = 1314195)				
partition number L	Av. of the number of iterations (μ)	St. deviation of iterations (σ)	Av. of $\delta(f_{TA})$ (μ/Exp)	St. deviation (σ/Exp)
3	3780998.8	1686618.94	2.877046	1.283386
10	1480367.1	771647.108	1.126444	0.587163
15	1332788.1	718925.636	1.014148	0.547046
20	1376661.5	722977.738	1.047532	0.55013
30	1254674.4	696777.35	0.95471	0.530193
50	1321172.9	660277.4	1.00531	0.50242
100	1394145.9	590048.911	1.060836	0.448981

50-bit case (Exp = 12533142)				
partition number L	Av. of the number of iterations (μ)	St. deviation of iterations (σ)	Av. of $\delta(f_{TA})$ (μ/Exp)	St. deviation (σ/Exp)
3	36150929	16451208.7	2.884427	1.312616
10	14018496	6499862.24	1.118514	0.518614
15	12532011	5726785.38	0.99991	0.456931
20	13704980	7750317.31	1.093499	0.618386
30	13370033	5930133.94	1.066774	0.473156
50	13361654	6859717.02	1.066106	0.547326
100	13348175	7163665.54	1.06503	0.571578

A-2: Randomness of $f_{GLV,s}$

The randomness of $f_{GLV,s}$ depends heavily on the parameter s. To analyze the randomness of $f_{GLV,s}$, we solved the ECDLP on Koblitz curves $E(\mathbb{F}_{2^m})$ with $m = 41, 53, 83, 89$ by using $f_{GLV,s}$ for $s = 0, m/5, m/3, m/2$. Similarly to the case of f_{TA}, our experiments are as follows (see [49] for details):

- We used the parallelized rho method with $M = 10$ processors and collision detection using distinguished points.
- For each parameter, we solved the ECDLP for 100 times with randomly chosen starting point. Since $f_{GLV,s}$ is defined on $E/\sim$, we have Exp $= \frac{1}{2}\sqrt{\frac{\pi n}{m}}$.

Table 11 shows our experimental results on the randomness of $f_{GLV,s}$ for $s = 0, m/5, m/3, m/2$. In particular, we summarize our experimental results on the average of $\delta(f_{GLV,s})$ in Table 12. Parameters of the ECDLP on Koblitz curves are showed in [49, Section 4.2].

Table 10. Same as Table 9, but over binary fields

40-bit case (Exp = 929275)				
partition number L	Av. of the number of iterations (μ)	St. deviation of iterations (σ)	Av. of $\delta(f_{\text{TA}})$ (μ/Exp)	St. deviation (σ/Exp)
3	2360560.1	1201327.8	2.540214	1.292757
10	1113151.3	489458.635	1.197869	0.52671
15	1023983	522466.937	1.101915	0.56223
20	987927.74	457815.575	1.063116	0.492658
30	905661.7	508812.744	0.974589	0.547537
50	958556	553241.565	1.031509	0.595347
100	899006.13	488759.614	0.967426	0.525957

50-bit case (Exp = 29736841)				
partition number L	Av. of the number of iterations (μ)	St. deviation of iterations (σ)	Av. of $\delta(f_{\text{TA}})$ (μ/Exp)	St. deviation (σ/Exp)
3	52886657	43926581.2	1.778489	1.477177
10	33894170	17743071.6	1.139804	0.59667
15	32213318	16864852.9	1.08328	0.567137
20	30470124	16128602.2	1.024659	0.542378
30	28145732	15094088.7	0.946494	0.507589
50	32036952	16071089.1	1.077349	0.540444
100	26390118	12484665.3	0.887455	0.419838

Table 11. Experimental results on the randomness of $f_{\text{GLV},s}$ for solving the ECDLP on Koblitz curves $E(\mathbb{F}_{2^m})$ with $m = 41, 53, 83, 89$ (with the speed-up using the Frobenius and the negation maps) [49, Table 2]

	Parameter s	Av. of the number of iterations (μ)	Av. of $\delta(f_{\text{GLV},s})$ (μ/Exp)	St. deviation (σ/Exp)
$m = 41$	$s = 0$	109789	1.06	0.52
	$s = m/5$	117708	1.14	0.64
	$s = m/3$	133100	1.29	0.64
	$s = m/2$	120467	1.17	0.62
$m = 53$	$s = 0$	616273	1.10	0.56
	$s = m/5$	540220	0.96	0.50
	$s = m/3$	628533	1.12	0.59
	$s = m/2$	706519	1.26	0.65
$m = 83$	$s = 0$	9362605	1.03	0.49
	$s = m/5$	8979741	0.99	0.56
	$s = m/3$	11278465	1.25	0.59
	$s = m/2$	10531561	1.16	0.63
$m = 89$	$s = 0$	64270064	1.01	0.48
	$s = m/5$	74819712	1.20	0.62
	$s = m/3$	67569759	1.08	0.58
	$s = m/2$	80869338	1.29	0.60

$\text{Exp} = \frac{1}{2}\sqrt{\frac{\pi n}{m}} = 102620 \ (m = 41), \ 558438 \ (m = 53), \ 905047 \ (m = 83), \ 62348200 \ (m = 89)$

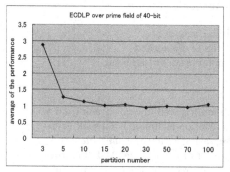
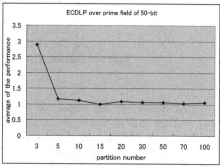
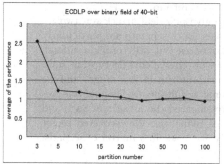
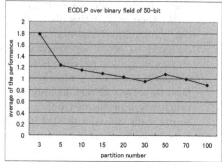

Fig. 4. Experimental results on the average of $\delta(f_{\mathrm{TA}})$ for solving the ECDLP over prime and binary fields of 40 and 50-bits (Exp $= \sqrt{\pi n/2}$, without the speed-up using the negation map)

Table 12. Experimental results on the average of $\delta(f_{\mathrm{GLV},s})$ for $s = 0, m/5, m/3, m/2$ on Koblitz curves $E(\mathbb{F}_{2^m})$ with $m = 41, 53, 83, 89$ (Exp $= \frac{1}{2}\sqrt{\pi n/m}$) [49, Table 3]

	$s = 0$	$s = m/5$	$s = m/3$	$s = m/2$
$m = 41$	1.06	1.14	1.29	1.17
$m = 53$	1.10	0.96	1.12	1.26
$m = 83$	1.03	0.99	1.25	1.16
$m = 89$	1.01	1.20	1.08	1.29
average	1.05	1.07	1.18	1.22

New Attacks for Knapsack Based Cryptosystems

Gottfried Herold and Alexander Meurer[*]

Ruhr-Universität Bochum
Horst Görtz Institut für IT-Sicherheit
{gottfried.herold,alexander.meurer}@rub.de

Abstract. In this paper, we revisit Shamir's well-known attack (and a variant due to Lagarias) on the basic Merkle-Hellman Knapsack cryptosystem (MH scheme). The main observation is that the *superincreasing* property of the secret key sequence $\mathfrak{a}$ used in the original MH construction is not necessary for the attack. More precisely, the attack is applicable as long as there are sufficiently many secret key elements $\mathfrak{a}_i$ whose size is much smaller than the size of the secret modulus M.

We then exploit this observation to give practical attacks on two recently introduced MH-like cryptosystems. Both schemes are particularly designed to avoid superincreasing sequences but still provide enough structure to allow for complete recovery of (equivalent) decryption keys. Similarly to Shamir's attack, our algorithms run in two stages and we need to solve different fixed-dimensional simultaneous Diophantine approximation problems (SDA). We implemented the attacks in Sage and heuristically solved the SDA by lattice reduction. We recovered secret keys for both schemes and various security levels in a matter of seconds.

Keywords: Knapsack Cryptosystem, Merkle-Hellman, Shamir's attack, Diophantine approximation.

1 Introduction

Shortly after Diffie and Hellman proposed the seminal concept of public-key cryptography [1] in 1976, Merkle and Hellman proposed their *knapsack cryptosystem* [2] in 1978 representing one of the first instantiations within the public-key framework. As the name implies, their basic scheme is based on the combinatorial knapsack / subset sum problem, i.e. given a vector of integer weights $a = (a_1, \ldots, a_n)$ and a target sum S, find a selection of the weights that exactly sum up to S, i.e. find $x \in \{0,1\}^n$ such that

$$\sum_{i=1}^{n} x_i a_i = S \ . \tag{1}$$

The public key in the original MH-scheme is exactly such a n-dimensional vector a and a n-bit message $x \in \{0,1\}^n$ is encrypted by simply computing the corresponding sum $S = \sum x_i a_i$.

---

[*] Supported by RURS, Germany Excellence Initiative [DFG GSC 98/1].

I. Visconti and R. De Prisco (Eds.): SCN 2012, LNCS 7485, pp. 326–342, 2012.
© Springer-Verlag Berlin Heidelberg 2012

To achieve *correct* decryption, we only employ certain a's so that at most one solution to (1) for every fixed S exists. In the public key setting, we need to efficiently generate such a public key a together with a secret key $\mathfrak{a}$ that allows for fast decryption (throughout this paper, usage of Fraktur type letters (e.g. $\mathfrak{a}, \mathfrak{b}, \ldots$) will emphasize secret key elements). Thus, the well-known NP-hardness result [3] for the general subset sum problem forces us to embed a special structure both in a and $\mathfrak{a}$. As usual, we intend to hide this special structure in a trapdoor so that only the legitimate receiver is able to decrypt. In the basic MH-scheme, the special structure is given by a so-called *superincreasing sequence* of secret knapsack weights $\mathfrak{a}$, i.e.

$$\mathfrak{a}_k > \sum_{i=1}^{k-1} \mathfrak{a}_i \quad \text{for all } k \in \{2, \ldots, n\} \ . \tag{2}$$

For those sequences, decryption can easily be done by a straightforward greedy algorithm in linear time. To hide the superincreasing property, Merkle and Hellman applied a linear modular transformation to the secret weights, i.e. the public key consists of $a_i = \mathfrak{a}_i \cdot \mathfrak{u} \mod M$ for a large modulus M (not necessarily prime), i.e.

$$M > \sum_{i=1}^{n} \mathfrak{a}_i \ , \tag{3}$$

where $\mathfrak{u} \in \mathbb{Z}_M^*$ is a secret multiplier. The secret key is then given by the modulus M and the inverse multiplier $u = \mathfrak{u}^{-1} \mod M$. To decrypt a ciphertext $S = \sum x_i a_i$, one simply computes $\mathfrak{S} = S \cdot u \mod M = \sum x_i \mathfrak{a}_i \mod M$. The size condition (3) guarantees that this equations holds over $\mathbb{Z}$ and thus the greedy algorithm can be applied due to the superincreasing property of $\mathfrak{a}$ to recover x.

Compared to many other prominent public key schemes, e.g. those based on the factorization or discrete log problem, the original MH-scheme offers an attractive efficiency due to its comparably cheap operations, e.g. no exponentiation is needed. Over the last thirty years, many researchers proposed various knapsack based schemes many of who have been broken and some remained secure, see [13] or [12] for a survey. Recently, there has been progress in constructing *provably secure* schemes connected to the subset-sum problem like the lattice-based schemes of Ajtai and Dwork [16], Regev [17] and Peikert [18] or the remarkably direct and simple construction of Lyubashevsky et al. [21].

Despite these efforts in provable security, there are still many ad-hoc constructions whose security remains questionable. Indeed, there are serious indications for an inherent difficulty of embedding a trapdoor in a knapsack based scheme that stem from several practical attacks on various schemes in the late 1970's culminating in Shamir's polynomial time attack on the basic MH-scheme [10] or Brickell's attack on the multiply-iterated MH system [8]. While those attacks heavily rely on the specific structure of the proposed knapsacks, there are also so-called *low-density* attacks working for generic knapsacks whose weights are rather large, see [4,11,14,15].

Shamir's original result [10] provides an algorithm running in time poly(n) that recovers *equivalent* decryption keys for *almost all* public keys of the basic MH-scheme. Shortly afterwards, Lagarias gave a simplified description of Shamir's attack based on simultaneous Diophantine approximation [6] and provided a rigorous analysis in [9]. As our algorithm heavily relies on those ideas, we start with a revision of [6] in the next section. For the moment, it is enough to think of Lagarias' version of Shamir's attack as the following two step procedure:

i)   Use the public information $\boldsymbol{a}$ to derive a D-dimensional Diophantine approximation problem (SDA) with at least one "unnaturally good" approximation and recover this particular approximation.
ii) Use the approximation of step i) to recover an equivalent decryption key $(\tilde{u}, \tilde{M})$, i.e. the sequence $\tilde{a}_i = a_i \cdot \tilde{u} \mod \tilde{M}$ is also superincreasing and the size condition (3) also holds for $\tilde{M}$ and $\tilde{\mathfrak{a}}$.

Observe that every equivalent key allows for correct decryption. The SDA in step i) is fixed-dimensional and comes with an "unnaturally good" approximation because of the way the $\boldsymbol{a}$ are constructed, i.e. this uses the fact that the sequence $\mathfrak{a}$ is superincreasing. As we will see in Section 2, the superincreasing property itself is *not* necessarily needed for the attack to work; rather one only needs an unnaturally large gap between some of the $\mathfrak{a}_i$ and M. We will exploit this to present attacks on two different recently proposed cryptosystems based on knapsacks, namely [20] and (a generalized version of) [19], both of which were specifically designed to resist Shamir's attack.

Our Contributions.   As a first contribution, we will present an efficient heuristic algorithm that breaks a recently proposed cryptosystem based on multiple knapsacks [20]. This scheme is based on three different knapsacks, i.e. $\boldsymbol{f} = (f_1, \ldots, f_n)$, $\boldsymbol{g} = (g_1, \ldots, g_n)$ and $\boldsymbol{h} = (h_1, \ldots, h_n)$ where

$$f_i = \mathfrak{f}_i \cdot \mathfrak{u} \mod M$$
$$g_i = \mathfrak{g}_i \cdot \mathfrak{v} \mod M \qquad (4)$$
$$h_i = \mathfrak{h}_i \cdot \mathfrak{u} \cdot \mathfrak{v} \mod M$$

with two secret multipliers $\mathfrak{u}, \mathfrak{v} \in \mathbb{Z}_M^*$ and corresponding inverses $u = \mathfrak{u}^{-1} \mod M$ and $v = \mathfrak{v}^{-1} \mod M$. The public key is given by the three vectors $\boldsymbol{f}, \boldsymbol{g}$ and $\boldsymbol{h}$ and the secret key consists of the two inverse multipliers u and v together with the modulus M. Here, the first two knapsacks $\mathfrak{f}$ and $\mathfrak{g}$ are *non-superincreasing* and meant to preclude an attacker from using the structure of the third knapsack $\mathfrak{h}$ which itself is indeed superincreasing[1]. To be more precise, the encryption of a message $\boldsymbol{x} \in \{0, 1\}^n$ is computed as $S := S_{\boldsymbol{f}} \cdot S_{\boldsymbol{g}} + S_{\boldsymbol{h}}$

---

[1] Clearly, Shamir's attack is directly applicable to the third equation of (4) to recover an equivalent secret key $(\tilde{u}\tilde{v}, \tilde{M})$. However, the authors of [20] claim that breaking the scheme requires to find a suitable factorization $\tilde{u}, \tilde{v}$ of $\tilde{u}\tilde{v}$ which is assumed to be hard.

where the subindex indicates the appropriate knapsack used to compute the respective sum, i.e. $S_{\mathfrak{f}} = \sum f_i x_i$. To decrypt S, one first reverses the modular transformations of (4) by multiplying with $u \cdot v$, i.e. one computes

$$u \cdot v \cdot S = S_{\mathfrak{f}} \cdot S_{\mathfrak{g}} + S_{\mathfrak{h}} = \sum_{i=1}^{n} \mathfrak{f}_i x_i \cdot \sum_{i=1}^{n} \mathfrak{g}_i x_i + \sum_{i=1}^{n} \mathfrak{h}_i x_i \mod M \ . \qquad (5)$$

To achieve correct decryption, one intuitively chooses $\mathfrak{f}$ and $\mathfrak{g}$ quite small compared to $\mathfrak{h}$ so that the perturbations caused by $S_{\mathfrak{f}} \cdot S_{\mathfrak{g}}$ do not prevent from recovering x in a greedy fashion. Additionally, the modulus has to fulfill a size condition similar to (3) and hence the $\mathfrak{f}, \mathfrak{g}$ are also rather small compared to M.

This observation is the starting point for our attack: Since $\mathfrak{f}$ and $\mathfrak{g}$ are small compared to M, we can easily derive two independent SDAs of fixed dimension which are both equipped with "unnaturally good" approximations as in Shamir's attack on the basic MH-scheme. Once we find those approximations, we are able to derive two high-quality approximations δ_u and δ_v of $\frac{u}{M}$ and $\frac{v}{M}$ respectively. We can further use those approximations δ_u, δ_v to efficiently reveal the secret key (u, v, M) by just solving another two-dimensional SDA.

As a second contribution, we present an efficient heuristic algorithm that breaks a variant of the cryptosystem of [19]. This cryptosystem uses as the easy knapsack $\mathfrak{a} = (\mathfrak{a}_0, \ldots, \mathfrak{a}_{n-1})$, with

$$\mathfrak{a}_i = 2^i \cdot c_i, \qquad i = 0, \ldots, n-1 \qquad (6)$$

where c_i is a random odd $n - i + l$-bit number. Here $l(n)$ is a parameter of the scheme, where the original version of [19] had $l = 0$. The public knapsack a is again given by $a_i = \mathfrak{u} \cdot \mathfrak{a}_i \mod M$ for some random $n + l + \log n$-bit modulus M and $u \in \mathbb{Z}_M^*$, so the size constraint from Eq.3 is satisfied. a is the public key, whereas $u = \mathfrak{u}^{-1} \mod M$ and M are the secret key. $x \in \{0, 1\}^n$ is again encrypted as $S = \sum x_i a_i$. To decrypt a ciphertext S, one can compute $\mathfrak{S} = u \cdot S \mod M$ and recover x by considering $\sum x_i \mathfrak{a}_i = \mathfrak{S} \mod 2^j$ for $j = 0, \ldots, n-1$.

Although this scheme avoids superincreasing sequences and the $\mathfrak{a}_i$ are indeed rather large, Shamir's attack is still applicable: the easiest way to see this is to consider $\tilde{\mathfrak{a}} = \mathfrak{a} \cdot 2^{-\alpha} \mod M$ as the secret knapsack with secret multiplier $\tilde{\mathfrak{u}} = \mathfrak{u} \cdot 2^{\alpha} \mod M$, where $\alpha = n - \beta$ for small $\beta > 0$.

To conclude, we would like to stress that we heuristically solved all SDA via lattice reduction and we confirmed our heuristic analysis by a large number of experiments. For both schemes we almost always recovered equivalent secret keys in a matter of seconds, see the full version [22] for details.

2 Attacking Knapsack Schemes via Diophantine Approximation

In [6], Lagarias gave a neat representation of Shamir's original attack in terms of Diophantine approximations. Generally, the D-dimensional simultaneous Diophantine approximation problem (SDA) considers the task of approximating a given real vector $\boldsymbol{\alpha} \in \mathbb{R}^D$ by a rational vector $\boldsymbol{\xi} \in \mathbb{Q}^D$ with common denominator $Z \in \mathbb{Z}$, i.e. $\xi_i = \frac{z_i}{Z}$ for all i (where $z_i \in \mathbb{Z}$). In our setting, we are faced with a slightly different scenario: We need to approximate a D-dimensional *rational* vector

$$\boldsymbol{\alpha}_D := \left(\frac{a_2}{a_1}, \ldots, \frac{a_{D+1}}{a_1} \right)$$

with common denominator a_1 with a rational vector $\boldsymbol{\xi}_D = \left(\frac{k_2}{k_1}, \ldots, \frac{k_{D+1}}{k_1} \right)$ with *smaller* denominator k_1.

The crucial cryptographic weakness of the public sequence $\boldsymbol{a}$ of the basic MH-scheme can now be stated as an unusual Diophantine approximation property. To see this, we write the key equations $u \cdot a_i \equiv \mathfrak{a}_i \mod M$ as $\mathfrak{a}_i = u \cdot a_i - k_i \cdot M$ and transform this into

$$\frac{u}{M} - \frac{k_i}{a_i} = \frac{1}{a_i} \cdot \frac{1}{\gamma} \tag{7}$$

for unknown $k_i \in \mathbb{Z}$, where we call $\gamma := \frac{|M|}{|a_i|}$ the *gap*.

For the MH-cryptosystem γ represents the gap between the size of the secret $\mathfrak{a}_i$ and M. Weakening this to $\left| \frac{u}{M} - \frac{k_i}{a_i} \right| \leq \frac{1}{a_i} \cdot \frac{1}{\gamma}$, this inequality constraints $\frac{u}{M} \in [0, 1]$ to a near-integer multiple of $\frac{1}{a_i}$ (up to a small error of $1/\gamma$). The set of possible values for $\frac{u}{M}$ thus is a union of a_i disjoint intervals that cover an $\mathcal{O}(1/\gamma)$-fraction of $[0, 1]$. Heuristically, we expect that by considering this inequality for the $D - 1$ values $i = 2, \ldots, i = D$ of i, $\frac{u}{M}$ is restricted to a $\mathcal{O}(1/\gamma^{D-1})$-fraction of $[0, 1]$, so when considering another D'th value $i = 1$, the corresponding interval and hence k_1 will be unique if $\frac{1}{\gamma^{D-1}} \cdot a_1 = o(1)$.

A crucial point to note here is that we only need to consider a constant number D of a_i's for sufficiently large gaps. To tackle these equation via lattices, we substract Eq.(7) for $i = 1$ and $i \geq 2$, multiplying by a_i and a_1 and obtain

$$|k_i a_1 - k_1 a_i| \leq \frac{|a_1 - a_i|}{\gamma} \tag{8}$$

which we recognize as exactly the SDA problem from above if we would divide by $k_1 a_1$. Note here that $|a_1 - a_i| \approx a_i \approx a_1 \approx M$ as far as orders of magnitude are concerned.

We will now show that one can heuristically recover k_1 by using lattice reduction as long as the lattice dimension D is appropriately chosen (depending on the size of the $a_i \approx M$ and γ), see Sect. 2.1. Once k_1 has been learned, the second step of Shamir's attack recovers an equivalent decryption key (u^*, M^*). Essentially, plugging k_1 and a_1 into Eq.(7) yields a good approximation to $\frac{u}{M}$ and a subsequent refined interval search reveals $\frac{u^*}{M^*}$. Since both of our attacks proceed differently here, we omit a deeper description and refer the interested reader to [6,9,10].

2.1   Solving Simultaneous Diophantine Approximation via Lattices

Our aim is to exploit Eq.(8) in order to recover k_1. Therefore, we briefly recall some basic facts about lattices. Generally, a D-dimensional full-rank lattice $L \subset \mathbb{R}^D$ is a discrete (abelian) subgroup of $\mathbb{R}^D$ with $\text{span}_{\mathbb{R}}(L) = \mathbb{R}^D$. One usually describes L by a basis $\boldsymbol{B} = (\boldsymbol{b}_1, \ldots, \boldsymbol{b}_D)^T \in \mathbb{R}^{D \times D}$, i.e. $L(\boldsymbol{B})$ consists of all linear combination of the basis vectors $\boldsymbol{b}_i$ with integer coefficients. An important invariant of L is its determinant $\det(L)$ which is defined as the absolute value of the determinant of $\boldsymbol{B}$. We denote the length of a shortest vector $\boldsymbol{v} \in L$ by $\lambda_1(L)$, i.e. $\lambda_1(L) := \min_{0 \neq \boldsymbol{v} \in L} \|\boldsymbol{v}\|$ where we use the Euclidean norm for convenience. The following crucial upper bound on $\lambda_1(L)$ was given by Minkowski.

Lemma 1 (Minkowski's First Theorem). *For any D-dimensional full-rank lattice L it holds*

$$\lambda_1(L) \leq \sqrt{D} \det(L)^{\frac{1}{D}} . \tag{9}$$

This upper bound is frequently used in lattice-based cryptanalysis where one often assumes that a lattice vector $\boldsymbol{v}$ fulfilling the Minkowski bound is indeed a shortest vector of the lattice. If so, we can efficiently compute $\boldsymbol{v}$ as long as the dimension of L is fixed by computing a *reduced basis* $\tilde{\boldsymbol{B}}$, i.e. $\tilde{\boldsymbol{B}}$ is a basis of shortest possible vectors. Note that in general $\tilde{\boldsymbol{B}}$ does not contain the D shortest vectors of the lattice L since L is not always spanned by these vectors.

We now show how to construct a lattice L in order to recover k_1. Consider the D-dimensional γ-scaled lattice spanned by the basis

$$\boldsymbol{B} := \begin{pmatrix} \gamma a_1 & & & 0 \\ & \ddots & & \vdots \\ & & \gamma a_1 & 0 \\ -\gamma a_2 & \ldots & -\gamma a_D & 1 \end{pmatrix} .$$

Observe that the lattice $L(\boldsymbol{B})$ contains the vector $\boldsymbol{v} := (k_2, \ldots, k_D, k_1) \cdot \boldsymbol{B}$ whose last coordinate reveals k_1. Suppose $a_1 \approx 2^m$ and $|a_i| < 2^m$ for any i, which will be the bound given by the modulus and write $\gamma = 2^g$ for the gap size. It holds

$$\|\boldsymbol{v}\|^2 = \sum_{i=2}^{D} \gamma^2 |a_1 k_i - a_i k_1|^2 + k_1^2 < D2^{2m}$$

and thus $\|\boldsymbol{v}\| \leq \sqrt{D}2^m$. If we can fix a constant $D > \frac{m+g}{g}$, or equivalently $\frac{1}{\gamma^{D-1}} \cdot a_i = o(1)$, this guarantees $m < (m+g)\frac{D-1}{D}$, which eventually yields

$$\|\boldsymbol{v}\| < \sqrt{D}2^m \ll 2^{(m+g)\frac{D-1}{D}} \approx (\gamma|a_1|)^{\frac{D-1}{D}} = \det(L)^{\frac{1}{D}} .$$

Unfortunately, $L(\boldsymbol{B})$ contains another short vector $\boldsymbol{w} := (a_2, \ldots, a_D, a_1) \cdot \boldsymbol{B} = (0, \ldots, 0, a_1)$ linearly independent of $\boldsymbol{v}$ of roughly the same length $\|\boldsymbol{w}\| \approx |M|$. This implies that a reduced basis $\tilde{\boldsymbol{B}}$ not necessarily contains the wanted vector $\boldsymbol{v}$, but it has been verified experimentally, see e.g. [5], that $\boldsymbol{v}$ can be represented as an integer linear combination of the two shortest basis vectors, i.e. $\boldsymbol{v} \in \text{span}(\tilde{\boldsymbol{b}}_1, \tilde{\boldsymbol{b}}_2)$. Since $\boldsymbol{v}$ itself is rather small the corresponding integer coefficients are also small and can easily be determined by enumeration.

3   The Multiple Knapsack Cryptosystem

In order to show our first result, we first give a precise description of the multiple knapsack scheme (MKS for shorthand) of Kobayashi et al. [20]. Since our algorithm recovers the original secret key by simply exploiting the structure of the public key elements, we do not present the encryption or decryption procedure. Instead, we only discuss the key generation algorithm and some very specific size conditions both on the secret sequences $\mathfrak{f}$, $\mathfrak{g}$, $\mathfrak{h}$ and the modulus M as introduced in Eq.(4). The first condition is intended to avoid Shamir's attack and concerns the two *non-superincreasing* sequences $\mathfrak{f}$ and $\mathfrak{g}$. It essentially complements the usual *superincreasing* property as defined in Eq.(2).

Condition 1. The secret sequences $\mathfrak{f} = (\mathfrak{f}_1, \ldots, \mathfrak{f}_n)$ and $\mathfrak{g} = (\mathfrak{g}_1, \ldots, \mathfrak{g}_n)$ are *non-superincreasing*, i.e.

$$\mathfrak{f}_k \le \sum_{i=1}^{k-1} \mathfrak{f}_i \quad \text{and} \quad \mathfrak{g}_k \le \sum_{i=1}^{k-1} \mathfrak{g}_i \tag{10}$$

for all $k = 2, \ldots, n$.

The second condition is necessary to allow for correct decryption and gives a complicated restriction on the size of the elements $\mathfrak{h}_k$ which depends on the previously chosen elements $\mathfrak{f}_i$, $\mathfrak{g}_i$ for $i \le k$ and $\mathfrak{h}_i$ for $i < k$.

Condition 2. The sequence $\mathfrak{h}$ has to fulfill

$$\mathfrak{h}_k > -\mathfrak{f}_k \mathfrak{g}_k + \sum_{i=1}^{k-1} \mathfrak{f}_i \cdot \sum_{i=1}^{k-1} \mathfrak{g}_i + \sum_{i=1}^{k-1} \mathfrak{h}_i \tag{11}$$

$$-\mathfrak{f}_1 \left(2^n - 2^k\right) \left(\mathfrak{f}_k - \sum_{i=1}^{k-1} \mathfrak{f}_i\right) - \mathfrak{g}_1 \left(2^n - 2^k\right) \left(\mathfrak{g}_k - \sum_{i=1}^{k-1} \mathfrak{g}_i\right)$$

for all $k = 2, \ldots, n$.

For simplicity, we denote the formula on the right hand side of Eq.(11) by Cond2(k). Note that substituting (10) into (11) implicitly gives $\mathfrak{h}_k > \sum_{k=1}^{k-1} \mathfrak{h}_i$, i.e. the sequence $\mathfrak{h}$ is still superincreasing in the usual sense. As already mentioned, one also needs to impose a size condition on the modulus M in order to obtain an equation over $\mathbb{Z}$ when applying the inverse modular transformation as given in Eq.(5). This size condition is explicitly given by

$$M > \sum_{i=1}^{n} \mathfrak{f}_i \cdot \sum_{i=1}^{n} \mathfrak{g}_i + \sum_{i=1}^{n} \mathfrak{h}_i \ . \tag{12}$$

Note that combining Condition 1 and 2 gives a simple way of successively generating the secret sequences. We now give a concrete key generation algorithm realizing this task when picking initial elements $\mathfrak{f}_1$, $\mathfrak{g}_1$ and $\mathfrak{h}_1$ of bit size Fn, Gn and Hn respectively for positive integers $F, G, H \in \mathbb{N}$, see Alg.1.

Algorithm 1. KeyGen

Input: Positive integers $n, F, G, H \in \mathbb{N}$

Choose $\mathfrak{f}_1 \xleftarrow{R} [2^{Fn}, 2^{Fn+1})$, $\mathfrak{g}_1 \xleftarrow{R} [2^{Gn}, 2^{Gn+1})$ and $\mathfrak{h}_1 \xleftarrow{R} [2^{Hn}, 2^{Hn+1})$.

For $k = 2$ **to** n **do**

$\quad \mathfrak{f}_k \xleftarrow{R} [0, \sum_{i=1}^{k-1} \mathfrak{f}_i]$

$\quad \mathfrak{g}_k \xleftarrow{R} [0, \sum_{i=1}^{k-1} \mathfrak{g}_i]$

$\quad \mathfrak{h}_k \xleftarrow{R} [\text{Cond2}(k), 2 \cdot \text{Cond2}(k)]$

Return $\mathfrak{f}, \mathfrak{g}, \mathfrak{h}$ (fulfilling Cond. 1 and Cond. 2)

We would like to stress that this key generation algorithm slightly deviates from the informal description given by the authors in [20]. The main difference is that we allow for a proper parametrization of the size of the secret sequences in the main parameter n. Furthermore we provide concrete intervals where the elements have to be chosen from successively. Alternatively to Alg.1, one could also chose *all* elements of the sequences $\mathfrak{f}$ and $\mathfrak{g}$ of the *same* bit size Fn and Gn respectively and resample unless all conditions are fulfilled. As we will see next, the key observation for our attack is an exponentially large gap between the size of M and the size of the first few elements of $\mathfrak{f}, \mathfrak{g}$. This gap also occurs for the modified key generation algorithm and thus does not avoid our attack.

From the size condition Eq.(12) we expect that M is at least quadratic in the $\mathfrak{f}_i$. Let us make this statement more precise:

Proposition 1. *Let $D > 2 + \max\{\frac{F}{G}, \frac{G}{F}\}$ be a constant. For $i \leq D$, we always have $\log \mathfrak{f}_i < Fn + \mathcal{O}(1)$ and $\log \mathfrak{g}_i < Gn + \mathcal{O}(1)$. Furthermore, $\log M > Fn + Gn$.*

Proof. By construction, $\mathfrak{f}_1 < 2^{Fn+1}$. By the property of being non-increasing, $\mathfrak{f}_i \leq \sum_{j=1}^{i-1} \mathfrak{f}_j$, which shows the first statement by induction on D. Since $M > \mathfrak{f}_1 \cdot \mathfrak{g}_1$, we get $M > 2^{Fn+Gn}$, which proves the claim.

While this already gives us a large enough gap for the first phase, we need a slightly stronger version for the second phase:

Proposition 2. *For almost all keys output by Alg.1 and for some constant c it holds that $M > 2^{Fn+Gn+cn}$.*

Proof. This is more complicated than Prop. 1 and uses $M > \mathfrak{h}_2$. The proof is somewhat technical and can be found in the appendix.

4   Our Attack on the MKS Cryptosystem

We are now ready to describe the two phases of our attack. In the first phase, we merely use the public $\mathfrak{f}_i$ and $\mathfrak{g}_i$ for $1 \leq i \leq D$. The gap between the size of those integers and the modulus M as given by Prop. 1 allows to derive two approximations δ_u and δ_v of $\frac{u}{M}$ and $\frac{v}{M}$ respectively. Once these approximations are known, we will proceed with the second phase which eventually recovers the secret key (M, u, v).

4.1   The First Phase(MKS): Computing Approximations δ_u and δ_v

We only give a detailed description for δ_u, as δ_v can be treated completely similar. As in Shamir's attack in Sect. 2, one rewrites the key equation $\mathfrak{f}_i = \mathfrak{f}_i \cdot \mathbf{u}$ mod M as $u\mathfrak{f}_i = \mathfrak{f}_i + k_i M$ for unknown $k_i \in \mathbb{Z}$, or equivalently

$$\left| \frac{u}{M} - \frac{k_i}{f_i} \right| = \frac{\mathfrak{f}_i}{f_i M} \tag{13}$$

for $1 \le i \le D$. Let us assume that $\frac{M}{f_i}$ is bounded by a constant for $i \le D$, which happens with good probability (in fact, since our analysis is very conservative, we can even use $D = 3$ and we can tolerate a rather large bound here, so this is not a problem in practice). We now use the results from Sect. 2 with $m = \log f_i = \log M + \mathcal{O}(1)$ and $g = \log M - \log \mathfrak{f}_i$. We easily compute, using Prop. 1 and $D > 2 + \max\{\frac{F}{G}, \frac{G}{F}\}$

$$\frac{m+g}{m} = 1 + \frac{\log M}{\log M - \log \mathfrak{f}_i} = 2 + \frac{\log \mathfrak{f}_i}{\log M - \log \mathfrak{f}_i} < 2 + \frac{Fn + \mathcal{O}(1)}{Gn + \mathcal{O}(1)} < D \ .$$

This implies that the technique of Sect. 2 is applicable and gives us approximations δ_u and δ_v for $\frac{u}{M}$ and $\frac{v}{M}$ respectively.

Remarks. A standard technique to complicate Shamir's attack on the original MH scheme is to permute the public key elements. Then the first few elements do not belong any longer to the smallest secret key elements. But since only a constant number of D elements is needed in the first phase of the attack, see Sect. 2, one can simply guess the D smallest elements in time $\mathcal{O}(n^D)$. For our attack the situation is even better: It is possible to show that we can always use $D = 3$ and that *any* selection of public key elements $\mathfrak{f}_i$ can be used for our attack. Thus permuting them does not provide any further security.

4.2   The Second Phase(MKS): Revealing the Secret Key (M, u, v)

In the previous phase, we obtained high-quality approximations $\delta_u := \frac{k_i^u}{f_i}$ and $\delta_v := \frac{k_i^v}{g_1}$ of $\frac{u}{M}$ and $\frac{v}{M}$ respectively. From Eq.(13), we get for the quality of those approximations:

$$\left| \frac{u}{M} - \delta_u \right| < \frac{\mathfrak{f}_i}{f_i M}, \qquad \left| \frac{v}{M} - \delta_v \right| < \frac{\mathfrak{g}_i}{g_i M}$$

or after multiplying by M and using Prop. 1 and that $\frac{M}{f_i}$ is bounded

$$|u - M\delta_u| < 2^{Fn - \log M + \mathcal{O}(1)}, \qquad |v - M\delta_v| < 2^{Gn - \log M + \mathcal{O}(1)} \ .$$

Now let us consider the lattice

$$\mathbf{B} := \begin{pmatrix} \alpha & \beta\delta_u & \gamma\delta_v \\ 0 & \beta & 0 \\ 0 & 0 & \gamma \end{pmatrix}$$

where $\alpha := 2^{-2 \log M}$, $\beta := 2^{-Fn}$ and $\gamma := 2^{-Gn}$. These choices yield a lattice vector

$$v := (M, -u, -v) \cdot B = (\alpha M, \beta(M\delta_u - u), \gamma(M\delta_v - v)) \qquad (14)$$

of length $\|v\| < 2^{-\log M + \mathcal{O}(1)}$ that obviously reveals the secret key (M, u, v). By comparison, for the lattice determinant we get, using Prop. 2

$$\det(L)^{\frac{1}{3}} = (\alpha\beta\gamma)^{\frac{1}{3}} = 2^{\frac{1}{3}(-2\log M - Fn - Gn) + \mathcal{O}(1)} > 2^{-\log M + \frac{c}{3}n + \mathcal{O}(1)} .$$

Since $\det(L)^{\frac{1}{3}}$ is larger than $\|v\|$ by at least an exponetially large factor, heuristically we find the secret key by computing the reduced basis of B whose shortest vector reveals the secret key (M, u, v) according to Eq.(14).

5   The 2-adic Knapsack Cryptosystem

As a second result, we will give a polynomial time attack on (a generalized version) of the 2-adic knapsack cryptosystem (2KS) of Zhang, Wang and Hu [19] that heuristically recovers an equivalent decryption key from the public key. To fix some notation, let us recall the key generation from Section 1: The secret knapsack is given by

$$\mathfrak{a}_i = 2^i \cdot c_i, \qquad i = 0, \ldots, n-1$$

and the public knapsack is given by

$$a_i = \mathfrak{u} \cdot \mathfrak{a}_i \bmod M .$$

The a_i are the public key, whereas $u = \mathfrak{u}^{-1} \bmod M$ and M are the secret key. Here, the c_i are uniformly random odd $n-i+l$-bit integers, such that $\mathfrak{a}_i$ is a $n+l$-bit number with $\mu_2(\mathfrak{a}_i) = i$. M is chosen as a random $n + l + \log n$-bit modulus to ensure $\sum \mathfrak{a}_i < M$ and $u \in \mathbb{Z}_M^*$. By μ_2 we denote the 2-adic weight, i.e. $\mu_2(x)$ is maximal such that $2^{\mu_2(x)}$ divides x. In contrast to the original scheme [19] we introduced an additional parameter $l = o(n)$, whose role will be discussed in the next subsection. Potentially, we may permute the a_i in the public key, so we are only given $b_i = a_{\pi(i)}$ for some unknown permutation π.

Our attack will recover M and u, or at least an equivalent pair $\widetilde{M}$ and $\widetilde{u}$, such that $\widetilde{\mathfrak{a}}_i = a_i \cdot \widetilde{u} \bmod \widetilde{M}$ has the same structure as the $\mathfrak{a}_i$ and $\widetilde{M} > \sum \widetilde{\mathfrak{a}}_i$.

5.1   Attacks on $l = 0$ or l Too Large

Note that the original cryptosystem didn't have the parameter l and explicitly sets $c_{n-1} = 1$. This renders the scheme trivially insecure, which we will only sketch: An adversary can simply guess c_{n-2}, which can be either 1 or 3. Since $c_{n-2} \cdot a_{n-1} \equiv 2c_{n-1} \cdot a_{n-2} \bmod M$, we have $c_{n-2} \cdot a_{n-1} - 2a_{n-2} = \kappa M$, where $|\kappa| \leq 3$. With at least constant probability, $\kappa \neq 0$ and this directly reveals M

(and hence u via $a_{n-1} \cdot u = 2^{n-1} \bmod M$ if M is odd). Note that one can improve the success probability of this attack by guessing more of the c_i's for large i and also note that if the attack fails for a particular pair, this reveals information about those c_i (and also about any potential permutation of the a_i).

We thus introduced l to avoid this kind of attack. In general, the above attack still works if one can correctly guess three adjacent c_i. Since we only get a multiple of M we need the additional third c_i to compute a gcd. In our experiments for the attack below, see [22], we conservatively set $l \geq 40$.

Observe that increasing l will reduce the density of the knapsack, which is given by $\frac{n}{n+l+\log n}$ here, and this can make the scheme vulnerable to low-density attacks [4,11,14,15]. In order to avoid low-density attacks, we will conservatively assume that $l = o(n)$ for our further analysis, although our attack can be easily seen to extend to $l = \mathcal{O}(n)$.

5.2   Our Attack on the 2-adic Knapsack Cryptosystem

Again, our attack consists of 2 phases. In the first phase we solve a SDA problem and use the approximation we obtained to recover an equivalent key in the second phase.

One way to express the underlying idea is to write (for M odd) the public key as $a_i = c_i \cdot 2^{i-\alpha} \cdot 2^{\alpha} u \bmod M$ and consider $2^{\alpha} u$ as the secret multiplier. If we choose α slightly smaller than n, we can use Shamir's attack to obtain an approximation of $\frac{2^{-\alpha} \cdot u \bmod M}{M}$ and proceed from that.

5.3   The First Phase(2KS): Computing Approximations δ_u and Δ_u

For the first phase, let us write the key equations as

$$\mathfrak{a}_i = a_i \cdot u - \ell_i M \tag{15}$$

$$\ell_i = \left\lfloor a_i \cdot \frac{u}{M} \right\rfloor \tag{16}$$

For simplicity, we will assume that M is odd. If not, u and $\mathfrak{u}$ will be odd and all a_i but a_1 (which we may ignore) will be even and we can extend our attack to any bounded $\mu_2(M)$ by just iteratively dividing Eq.(15) by 2. Now, choose $\alpha = n - \beta$ for some small constant β and consider Eq.(15) modulo 2^{α} for any D values of i with $i \geq \alpha$ to obtain

$$\ell_i = a_i \cdot uM^{-1} \bmod 2^{\alpha} \tag{17}$$

We define the rational $\bar{\delta}_u := \frac{u}{M} \in [0,1]$ and the integer $\Delta_u^{(i)} := u \cdot M^{-1} \bmod 2^i$, shorthand writing Δ_u for $\Delta_u^{(n)}$. Here, $\bar{\delta}_u$ is the exact value and not an approximation. Combining Equations (16) and (17) gives us

$$a_i \cdot \bar{\delta}_u - 1 < a_i \cdot \Delta_u^{(\alpha)} - k_i \cdot 2^{\alpha} \leq a_i \cdot \bar{\delta}_u \tag{18}$$

with unknown integers k_i, whenever $i \geq \alpha$. Reorganize those equations gives

$$-\frac{1}{a_i} < (\Delta_u^{(\alpha)} - \bar{\delta}_u) - \frac{2^\alpha}{a_i} \cdot k_i \leq 0 \ . \tag{19}$$

After dividing by 2^α, in the notation of Sect. 2, we have a gap $\gamma = 2^\alpha$ and the a_i are of size $2^{n+l+\log n}$. So $g = \alpha = n - \beta$ and $m = n + l + \log n$. Since $l = o(n)$, we may set $\beta = D = 3$ to satisfy $D > \frac{m+g}{m}$ (due to the heuristics involved, one should choose D as a slightly larger constant) and using the results from Sect. 2, this allows us to recover those k_i in polynomial time with high probability and hence an approximation for $\Delta_u^{(\alpha)} - \bar{\delta}_u$ up to an error of at most $\frac{1}{a_i}$ for the largest a_i considered. Note that if a permutation π is present, we need to guess the position of the D largest a_i, for which there are $\mathcal{O}\left(n^D\right)$ possibilities. In Rmk. 3 we will sketch how to improve that by choosing $D < \beta$.

Since $\Delta_u^{(\alpha)}$ is an integer and $0 \leq \bar{\delta}_u < 1$, our approximation determines $\Delta_u^{(\alpha)}$ completely after guessing at most one bit and we get an approximation δ_u for $\bar{\delta}_u$ with $\left|\delta_u - \bar{\delta}_u\right| \leq \frac{1}{a_i}$. Denote the rational bounds obtained for $\bar{\delta}_u$ by ω and Ω (i.e. $\omega \leq \bar{\delta}_u < \Omega$) and the approximation quality $\Omega - \omega$ as $\frac{\vartheta}{M}$. While our attack can tolerate a very large ϑ, to simplify the further analysis, let us assume that ϑ is bounded by some small constant, which happens with good probability.

5.4   The Second Phase: Computing an Equivalent Secret Key

In the second phase of our attack, we will compute an equivalent secret key from $\Delta_u^{(\alpha)}$ and δ_u. The second phase can be further subdivided into 2 steps. In the first step, we will recover all ℓ_i and the permutation π (if present) and obtain updated rational bounds $\omega \leq \bar{\delta}_u < \Omega$. In the second step, we just read off an equivalent key from the values we previously obtained.

First Step: Recover the Permutation π and the ℓ_i. For the first step, let us begin by just guessing the missing β highest bits of Δ_u. Our aim is to recover the permutation π of the a_i (if present) and all ℓ_i: Recall we are only given $b_i = a_{\pi(i)}$ for some yet unknown permutation. Plugging in $\bar{\delta}_u \in [\omega, \Omega[$ into Eq.(16) directly gives us each $\ell_{\pi^{-1}(j)}$ up to an error of at most $\lceil \vartheta \rceil$. Now, the special structure of our hidden easy knapsack can be expressed as

$$\mathfrak{a}_i = a_i \cdot u - \ell_i M \equiv 2^i \mod 2^{i+1} \tag{20}$$

which, since M is odd, we can rewrite as

$$\mu_2(a_i \cdot \Delta_u - \ell_i) = i \tag{21}$$

For any given b_j with $j = \pi(i)$, we can then simply compute a list $L(j)$ of all possible values of $\mu_2(b_j \cdot \Delta_u - \ell_{\pi^{-1}(j)})$.

Due to the way the 2-adic weight of consecutive numbers behave, whenever $i > \log\lceil \vartheta \rceil$, we can only get the correct value $i \in L(j)$ and additionally some values from $0, \ldots, \lfloor \log\lceil \vartheta \rceil \rfloor$ as possible values in $L(j)$. For $i \leq \log\lceil \vartheta \rceil$, we may get one arbitrarily large wrong value $V(i)$ and some values among $0, \ldots, \lfloor \log\lceil \vartheta \rceil \rfloor$.

As a consequence, any $i > \log \lceil \vartheta \rceil$ that is not among the $V(i)$'s can only appear in exactly one $L(j)$, so we must have $\pi(i) = j$ for these pairs. This also gives us ℓ_i for these pairs, as the 2-adic weight can only be correct for one of the possible values of ℓ_i. So we get ℓ_i and $\pi(i)$ for all but at most $2 \log \lceil \vartheta \rceil$ values of i. For the remaining values of π and the ℓ_i's, the total number of possibilities left is bounded by a constant, so we can simply guess them. Note here that every time we recover any ℓ_i for which there were previously several possibilities, we also get improved updated bounds $\omega \leq \bar{\delta}_u < \Omega$ via Eq.(16). In our experiments, we only ever had to guess at most one bit here.

Second Step: Compute an Equivalent Decryption Key. After having recovered Δ_u, all ℓ_i and π, we can proceed to the final step to procure an equivalent decryption key. To start, note that equivalent keys must additionally satisfy

$$M > \sum \mathfrak{a}_i . \tag{22}$$

This is enforced by the key generation by setting M of appropriate bit size. Since we know the ℓ_i, this can be expressed as $M > \sum a_i \cdot u - \ell_i M$, or equivalently $\delta_u < \frac{1 + \sum \ell_i}{\sum a_i}$, which we incorporate into our bound $\omega \leq \delta_u < \Omega$ by possibly updating Ω.

Note at this point that ω and Ω are both rational numbers in $[0, 1]$. Since they came either from Eq.(16) for fixed ℓ_i or Eq.(22), each denominators is either one of the a_i or $\sum a_i$. In particular, both numerators and denominators can be bounded by $2^{n+l+2 \log n}$. Also note that since the lower bound may be satisfied with equality, whereas the upper may not, we have $\omega < \Omega$ with strict inequality, which implies $0 < \frac{\Omega + \omega}{2} < 1$ and $\frac{\Omega - \omega}{2} > 0$. Due to the size constraints on the numerators and denominators, each of $\frac{\Omega + \omega}{2}$, $1 - \frac{\Omega + \omega}{2}$ and $\frac{\Omega - \omega}{2}$ is bounded by $2^{-2n - 2l - 4 \log n - 1}$.

Now we claim that *any* odd $\widetilde{M}$ and $0 < \tilde{u} < \widetilde{M}$ satisfying both $\omega \leq \frac{\tilde{u}}{\widetilde{M}} < \Omega$ and $\tilde{u} \cdot \widetilde{M}^{-1} \bmod 2^n = \Delta_u$ will be an equivalent decryption key. To see this, note that $\frac{\tilde{u}}{\widetilde{M}} < \Omega$ implies Eq.(22) with u, M replaced by $\tilde{u}, \widetilde{M}$. By construction of our bounds, $\omega \leq \frac{\tilde{u}}{\widetilde{M}} < \Omega$ fixes the ℓ_i defined by Eq.(16) (with $\tilde{u}, \widetilde{M}$ rather that u, M) to exactly the values ℓ_i we obtained in the first step. This in turn implies that for $\tilde{u} \cdot \widetilde{M}^{-1} = \Delta_u$, Eq.(21) and equivalently Eq.(20) (with $\tilde{u}, \widetilde{M}$ rather that u, M) are satisfied, which says that $\tilde{\mathfrak{a}}_i = a_i \cdot \tilde{u} \bmod \widetilde{M}$ has exactly the structure we want. To find such $\tilde{u}, \widetilde{M}$, we just express the conditions as

$$\omega \widetilde{M} < \tilde{u} < \Omega \widetilde{M} \tag{23}$$

$$\tilde{u} = \widetilde{M} \cdot \Delta_u - \kappa \cdot 2^n \tag{24}$$

for some integer κ. By using the second equation, we can restate the first one as

$$\omega < \Delta_u - 2^n \frac{\kappa}{\widetilde{M}} < \Omega \tag{25}$$

Except for $\widetilde{M}$ having to be odd, setting $\frac{\kappa}{M} = \frac{1}{2^n}(\Delta_u - \frac{\omega + \Omega}{2})$ would work. In order to obtain an odd $\widetilde{M}$, let us write $\frac{1}{2^n}(\Delta_u - \frac{\omega + \Omega}{2})$ as a rational $\frac{r}{s}$. By multiplying both r and s by appropriate powers of 2, we can ensure that s is even and $2 \log s - \log r > 6n + 2l + 4 \log n$. Now, we just set $\kappa := r$ and $\widetilde{M} := s + 1$ and define $\widetilde{u}$ by Eq.(24). If we set $\varepsilon := \Delta_u - \frac{\omega + \Omega}{2} - 2^n \frac{\kappa}{M}$, then our large (and conservative) choice of r, s implies $\left| \frac{r}{s} - \frac{\kappa}{M} \right| < 2^{-6n - 2l - 4 \log n}$, so $0 < \varepsilon < 2^{-5n - 2l - 4 \log n}$. The size constraints on the numerators and denominators of ω and Ω then imply $\varepsilon < \frac{\Omega - \omega}{2}$, which implies that Eq.(25) is satisfied. A simple computation gives $\frac{\widetilde{u}}{M} = \frac{\omega + \Omega}{2} + \varepsilon$, from which we infer $0 < \widetilde{u} < \widetilde{M}$, so indeed the $\widetilde{u}, \widetilde{M}$ we constructed form an equivalent key. Let us summarize our findings:

Theorem 1. *Let ϑ_{max} be any constant. Under the heuristic that our lattice-based approach to Eq.(19) uniquely recovers the k_i considered (or at least gives only polynomially many candidates) and under the heuristic that the quality of the approximation thereby obtained satisfies $\Omega - \omega < \frac{\vartheta_{max}}{N}$, we obtain a polynomial-time algorithm that computes an equivalent decryption key $(\widetilde{u}, \widetilde{M})$ from the public key of the 2KS-scheme. The key $(\widetilde{u}, \widetilde{M})$ allows for correct decryption with 2KS's decryption algorithm.*

Proof. This is an immediate consequence of our previous exposition. It is clear that the algorithm implicit above runs in polynomial time. Note that the guessing needed in the algorithm above gives only a polynomial factor $O(n^D)$ (from guessing the position of the D largest i's if a permutation is present) and we can always verify whether we output an equivalent key.

Remark 3. We would like to note that phase 1 can be replaced by Lenstra's pt. integer programming algorithm [7] for fixed dimension (which is much slower in pratice), as originally considered by [10], so we can weaken the first heuristic to require that the k_i are uniquely determined by the equations considered (or at least that there are only polynomially many possibilities). For the second heuristic, recall again that $\Omega - \omega$ is at most $\frac{1}{a_{n-1}}$ (and usually much smaller), so for M prime this provably holds with high probability $\geq \frac{1}{2}$ even for $\vartheta_{max} = 2$.

In our experiments, we did set $\beta = D = 10$ to a rather large value to simplify the first phase (this helps for the heuristic arguments), but did not guess the positions of the 10 largest i's, which would give another polynomial factor of n^D. We would like to remark that one can actually do much better and get rid of this large polynomial factor (under yet another heuristic):

Rather than choosing $\alpha = n - \beta$ and $D = \beta$ in phase 1 of the algorithm, one can also choose $\alpha = \frac{n}{2}$ and so $g = \frac{n}{2}$. We can still choose $D > \frac{m+g}{g} = O(1)$, where in practice we will need to choose a bigger D. Guessing D of the b_j's with $\pi^{-1}(j) > \alpha$ requires only $O(2^D) = O(1)$ effort. We can then proceed with the first step of the second phase, but without guessing the β highest bits of Δ_u. With only $\Delta_u^{(\frac{n}{2})}$ known, this still gives us ℓ_i and $\pi(i)$ for all but $2 \log \vartheta$ of the i's with $i < \frac{n}{2}$. We make the additional heuristic assumption that if we make a wrong choice for the b_j's then the first step of the second phase will give us a contradiction, so we only proceed if we made a correct guess. We can then go back and iteratively repeat the first phase, but with $\alpha = \frac{3n}{4}, \alpha = \frac{7n}{8}, \ldots$ (and always the same D). Using the already known values for π from the previous iteration, guessing a correct set of b_j's only requires at most constant $O(2^D)$ tries on average for each iteration. By this trick, we can actually reduce the factor to the runtime that comes from having to guess a good set of b_i's from $O(n^D)$ down to $O(\log n)$, if we make the heuristic assumption that whenever we guess wrongly in phase 1, step 1 of phase 2 will give us a contradiction with overwhelming probability.

References

1. Diffie, W., Hellman, M.E.: New directions in cryptography. IEEE Transactions on Information Theory 22(6), 644–654 (1976)
2. Merkle, R.C., Hellman, M.E.: Hiding Information and Signatures in Trapdoor Knapsacks. IEEE Transactions on Information Theory IT-24(5) (September 1978)
3. Garey, M.R., Johnson, D.S.: Computers and Intractability: A Guide to the Theory of NP-Completeness
4. Brickell, E.F.: Solving Low Density Knapsacks. In: Chaum, D. (ed.) Advances in Cryptology, Proceedings of CRYPTO 1983, pp. 25–37. Plenum Press, New York (1983)
5. Brickell, E.F., Lagarias, J.C., Odlyzko, A.M.: Evaluation of the Adleman Attack on Multiply Iterated Knapsack Cryptosystems. In: Chaum, D. (ed.) Advances in Cryptology, Proceedings of CRYPTO 1983, pp. 39–42. Plenum Press, New York (1983)
6. Lagarias, J.C.: Knapsack Public Key Cryptosystems and Diophantine Approximation. In: Chaum, D. (ed.) Advances in Cryptology, Proceedings of CRYPTO 1983, pp. 3–23. Plenum Press, New York (1983)
7. Lenstra, H.W.: Integer Programming with a Fixed Number of Variables. Mathematics of Operations Research 8(4) (November 1983)
8. Brickell, E.F.: Breaking Iterated Knapsacks. In: Blakely, G.R., Chaum, D. (eds.) CRYPTO 1984. LNCS, vol. 196, pp. 342–358. Springer, Heidelberg (1985)
9. Lagarias, J.C.: Performance Analysis of Shamir's Attack on the Basic Merkle-Hellman Knapsack Cryptosystem. In: Paredaens, J. (ed.) ICALP 1984. LNCS, vol. 172, pp. 312–323. Springer, Heidelberg (1984)
10. Shamir, A.: A Polynomial-Time Algorithm for Breaking the Basic Merkle-Hellman Cryptosystem. IEEE Transactions on Information Theory IT-30(5) (September 1984)
11. Lagarias, J.C., Odlyzko, A.M.: Solving Low-Density Subset Sum Problems. Journal of the ACM 32(1), 229–246 (1985)
12. Brickel, E.F., Odlyzko, M.: Cryptanalysis: A Survey of Recent Results. Proceedings of the IEEE 76(5), 578–593 (1988)
13. Odlyzko, A.M.: The rise and fall of knapsack cryptosystems. In: Cryptology and Computational Number Theory. Proc. Symp. Appl. Math., vol. 42, pp. 75–88. Am. Math. Soc. (1990)
14. Joux, A., Stern, J.: Improving the Critical Density of the Lagarias-Odlyzko Attack Against Subset Sum Problems. In: Budach, L. (ed.) FCT 1991. LNCS, vol. 529, pp. 258–264. Springer, Heidelberg (1991)

15. Coster, M.J., Joux, A., LaMacchia, B.A., Odlyzko, A.M., Schnorr, C.-P., Stern, J.: Improved Low-Density Subset Sum Algorithms. In: Computational Complexity, vol. 2, pp. 111–128 (1992)
16. Ajtai, M., Dwork, C.: A Public-Key Cryptosystem with Worst-Case/Average-Case Equivalence. In: Proceedings of the Twenty-Ninth Annual ACM Symposium on the Theory of Computing, STOC, pp. 284–293 (1997)
17. Regev, O.: On lattices, learning with errors, random linear codes, and cryptography. In: Proceedings of the 37th Annual ACM Symposium on Theory of Computing, STOC, pp. 84–93 (2005)
18. Peikert, C.: Public-key cryptosystems from the worst-case shortest vector problem: extended abstract. In: Proceedings of the 41st Annual ACM Symposium on Theory of Computing, STOC, pp. 333–342 (2009)
19. Zhang, W., Wang, B., Hu, Y.: A New Knapsack Public-Key Cryptosystem. In: 2009 International Conference on Information Assurance and Security (IAS), vol. 2, pp. 53–56 (2009)
20. Kobayashi, K., Tadaki, K., Kasahara, M., Tsujii, S.: A knapsack cryptosystem based on multiple knapsacks. In: 2010 International Symposium on Information Theory and its Applications (ISITA), pp. 428–432 (October 2010)
21. Lyubashevsky, V., Palacio, A., Segev, G.: Public-Key Cryptographic Primitives Provably as Secure as Subset Sum. In: Micciancio, D. (ed.) TCC 2010. LNCS, vol. 5978, pp. 382–400. Springer, Heidelberg (2010)
22. Herold, G., Meurer, A.: New Attacks for Knapsack Based Cryptosystems. Full Version, http://eprint.iacr.org

A   Proof of Proposition 2

We need to show Prop. 2, which states that for almost all keys output by Alg.1 it holds that $M > 2^{Fn+Gn+cn}$ for some constant c.

In order to show this, let us assume w.l.o.G. that $F \leq G$. We first need a simple lemma:

Lemma 2. *Let* $0 < \tilde{c} < 1$ *be an arbitrary constant. For a randomly chosen sequence* $\mathfrak{g}$ *according to Alg.1 it holds*

$$\mathbf{Pr}\left[\mathfrak{g}_1 - \mathfrak{g}_2 \geq 2^{(1-\tilde{c})Gn}\right] = 1 - \mathrm{negl}(n) \qquad (26)$$

where the probability is taken over the random choice of $\mathfrak{g}_1$ *and the random choice of* $\mathfrak{g}_2$ *conditioned on* $\mathfrak{g}_1 \geq \mathfrak{g}_2$.

Proof. An easy computation shows

$$\mathbf{Pr}\left[\mathfrak{g}_1 - \mathfrak{g}_2 \geq 2^{(1-\tilde{c})Gn}\right] = 1 - \mathbf{Pr}\left[\mathfrak{g}_1 - \mathfrak{g}_2 < 2^{(1-\tilde{c})Gn}\right]$$
$$\geq 1 - \mathbf{Pr}\left[\frac{\mathfrak{g}_2}{\mathfrak{g}_1} > 1 - 2^{-\tilde{c}Gn}\right] = 1 - \mathrm{negl}(n) \ .$$

Note that the expected value of the difference $\mathfrak{g}_1 - \mathfrak{g}_2$ can be easily computed as $\mathbb{E}\left[\mathfrak{g}_1 - \mathfrak{g}_2\right] = \frac{\mathbb{E}[\mathfrak{g}_1]}{2} = \frac{3}{4}2^{Gn}$. Thus, the above lemma states that the key generation algorithm almost always outputs a sequence $\mathfrak{g}$ such that the difference $\mathfrak{g}_1 - \mathfrak{g}_2$ is concentrated around its expectation.

We now examine Condition 2 of the MKS system more carefully for $k = 2$ and use Lem. 2 to argue that the size of $\mathfrak{h}_2$ can be lower bounded by $\approx 2^{(2G+c)n}$ for some positive constant $c > 0$. Then $M > \mathfrak{h}_2$ is already provides a sufficiently good lower bound for M, although one could easily obtain better bounds by estimating the size of $\mathfrak{h}_n$ where one can take the superincreasing property of $\mathfrak{h}$ into account. Formally, since $F \leq G$, proposition 2 follows from

Lemma 3. *For almost all secret keys output by Alg.1 it holds*

$$\frac{\log(M)}{n} \geq 2G + c \tag{27}$$

for some positive constant $c > 0$.

Proof. Consider Cond. 2 for $k = 2$ and first observe that $-\mathfrak{f}_2\mathfrak{g}_2 + \mathfrak{f}_1\mathfrak{g}_1 \geq 0$ and $-\mathfrak{f}_1(2^n - 4)(\mathfrak{f}_2 - \mathfrak{f}_1) \geq 0$ due to Cond. 1. Using $\mathfrak{g}_2 - \mathfrak{g}_1 \leq 0$ we can now lower bound $\mathfrak{h}_2$ as

$$\mathfrak{h}_2 > \mathfrak{g}_1(2^n - 4)(\mathfrak{g}_1 - \mathfrak{g}_2)$$

and applying Lem.2 with $\tilde{c} := \frac{1}{G+1}$ gives

$$\mathfrak{h}_2 > 2^{(2G+1-\frac{G}{G+1})n}$$

which proves the claim for $c := 1 - \frac{G}{G+1} > 0$.

Multiple Differential Cryptanalysis Using LLR and χ^2 Statistics

Céline Blondeau[1,*], Benoît Gérard[2,**], and Kaisa Nyberg[1]

[1] Aalto University School of Science,
Department of Information and Computer Science
[2] UCL Crypto Group, Université catholique de Louvain, ICTEAM Institute

Abstract. Recent block ciphers have been designed to be resistant against differential cryptanalysis. Nevertheless it has been shown that such resistance claims may not be as accurate as wished due to recent advances in this field. One of the main improvements to differential cryptanalysis is the use of many differentials to reduce the data complexity. In this paper we propose a general model for understanding multiple differential cryptanalysis and propose new attacks based on tools used in multidimensional linear cryptanalysis (namely LLR and χ^2 statistical tests). Practical cases to evaluate different approaches for selecting and combining differentials are considered on a reduced version of the cipher PRESENT. We also consider the accuracy of the theoretical estimates corresponding to these attacks.

Keywords: block cipher, multiple differential cryptanalysis, statistical test, data complexity.

1 Introduction

Differential cryptanalysis has been introduced in 1990 by Biham and Shamir [3, 4] in order to break the *Data Encryption Standard* block cipher. This statistical cryptanalysis exploits the existence of a *differential*, *i.e.*, a pair (α, β) of differences such that for a given input difference α, the output difference after encryption equals β with a high probability. This attack has been successfully applied to many ciphers and has been extended to various attacks, such as truncated differential cryptanalysis or impossible differential cryptanalysis, for instance.

In the original version of differential cryptanalysis [3], a unique differential is exploited. Then, Biham and Shamir improved their attack by considering several differentials having the same output difference [4]. Truncated differential cryptanalysis introduced by Knudsen [19] uses differentials with many output differences that are structured as a linear space. A theoretical framework have

---

* The research described in this paper by this author has been funded by the Academy of Finland under project 122736 and was partly supported by the European Commission through the ICT program under contract ICT-2007-216676 ECRYPT II.
** Postdoctoral researcher supported by Walloon region MIPSs project.

I. Visconti and R. De Prisco (Eds.): SCN 2012, LNCS 7485, pp. 343–360, 2012.

recently been proposed to analyze attacks using multiple differentials by summing the corresponding counters [9].

The motivation of this work is to investigate other different techniques for combining information from multiple differentials. As shown in the case of linear cryptanalysis, different approaches may be used depending on the context. In 2004, Biryukov et al. proposed a multiple linear cryptanalysis under the assumption that linear approximations are statistically independent[1] [5]. Later Hermelin et al. introduced the multidimensional linear cryptanalysis [14, 15]. Contrary to previous attacks, the multidimensional technique focuses on the distribution of the vector of parity bits obtained when applying approximations to a single plaintext/ciphertext pair instead of considering the vector of empirical biases. In that case, the independence assumption is removed but some heuristic might be used when theoretically analyzing the attack. For both approaches, classical statistical tools are used to distinguish the statistic corresponding to the correct key guess from wrong ones. Again, the choice of the tool may depend on the context. For instance, in [10], because of the hardness of profiling the distribution corresponding to the correct key, the attack on PRESENT shows better results using χ^2 than using LLR statistic.

Our Contributions. Our contributions are threefold. First, we introduce a general way of formalizing differential attacks by defining the notion of *partition* functions (this corresponds to the way counters corresponding to output differences are gathered). Second, we consider the χ^2 and the LLR statistical tests used in multidimensional linear cryptanalysis as tools for combining information from the groups of differentials determined by the *partition* function. We derive estimates for the data complexities of the corresponding differential attacks. Finally, we present a set of experiments that aim at (i) evaluating the accuracy of the estimates derived, (ii) comparing χ^2 and LLR combining tools and (iii) comparing different *partition* functions.

The paper is organized as follows. In Section 2 we define the notations and recall some results from order statistics that will be used to derive data complexity estimates. Further, in Section 3 we present a general model for multiple differential cryptanalysis, introduce the notion of *partition* function and link this notion with already published differential attacks. Then, in Section 4, we present two tools for combining information based on the LLR and the χ^2 statistical tests. We derive estimates for the corresponding data complexities and also discuss the way of choosing *partition* functions. Finally, Section 5 contains the experiments that have been performed to compare the different methods.

2   Theoretical Background

2.1   Differential Cryptanalysis against SPN Ciphers

In this paper we consider SPN ciphers that form a subclass of iterated block ciphers. Let m be the block size of the considered cipher E and K the key used

---

[1] While not abusive for the DES cipher, this assumption is misleading for new ciphers.

for enciphering samples: $E : \mathbb{F}_2^m \longrightarrow \mathbb{F}_2^m$, $x \mapsto E_K(x)$. Then, since E is an iterated block cipher, it can be expressed as $E_K(x) = F_{K_r} \circ \cdots \circ F_{K_1}(x)$, where F is the round function parameterized by round sub-keys $K_1, \ldots, K_r$.

The attack we are interested in is a member of the so-called last-round attacks, which themselves constitute the major part of statistical cryptanalyses. These last-round[2] attacks use a particular behavior of $F_{K_{r-1}} \circ \cdots \circ F_{K_1}$ (that is often referred as *statistical characteristic*) to partially recover the value of K_r. In the following we will use the compact notation $F_K^{r'} \stackrel{\text{def}}{=} F_{K_{r'}} \circ \cdots \circ F_{K_1}$. The idea is to partially decipher ciphertexts using different values for a part of K_r that we name *candidates* and denote by k. In the case of an incorrect guess we obtain outputs corresponding to $F_k^{-1} \circ F_K^r$ while for the correct key guess k_0 the outputs correspond to F_K^{r-1} and thus the statistical characteristic should be observed if enough samples are available. Such attack relies on the assumption that F_K^{r-1} can be distinguished from the set of functions $F_k^{-1} \circ F_K^r$. In practical situations, the latter functions behave as randomly chosen permutations as stated by the following Wrong Key Randomization Hypothesis.

Hypothesis 1. *(Wrong Key Randomization) Functions $F_k^{-1} \circ F_K^r$ for wrong key candidates k are indistinguishable from randomly chosen permutations.*

Assuming that this hypothesis does not hold would mean that $r + 1$ rounds of the cipher are distinguishable and hence the attacker should be able to attack more rounds. As a consequence, this hypothesis is quite reasonable as soon as the attacker targets the largest number of rounds he is able to attack (which is typically the case). The resulting attack consists of the following three steps.

1 **Distillation.** For each key candidate ciphertexts are partially deciphered. The number of occurrences of the characteristic is stored for each candidate.
2 **Analysis.** Key candidates are ranked according to the counters computed in the Distillation step.
3 **Search.** Finally, all master keys corresponding to the most likely key candidate are exhaustively tested. If the correct master key is not found then the search step is performed again using the second most likely candidate and so on . . .

Differential Cryptanalysis. Here we consider the basic differential cryptanalysis which is a last-round attack where the statistical characteristic is an $(r - 1)$-round differential. It is a pair of input/output differences (δ_0, δ_{r-1}) and the corresponding probability $p(\delta_0 \to \delta_{r-1})$,

$$p(\delta_0 \to \delta_{r-1}) \stackrel{\text{def}}{=} \Pr_{\mathbf{X},\mathbf{K}} \left[F_{\mathbf{K_r}}^{-1}(E_{\mathbf{K}}(\mathbf{X})) \oplus F_{\mathbf{K_r}}^{-1}(E_{\mathbf{K}}(\mathbf{X} \oplus \delta_0)) = \delta_{r-1} \right].$$

Usually, it is assumed that for an incorrect key candidate the probability of observing the differential is $\frac{1}{2^m-1}$. Nevertheless, it has been recalled in [12] that considering that $F_k^{-1} \circ F_K^r$ acts as a random permutation, the distribution of this probability is known to be a Poisson distribution with parameter $\frac{1}{2^m-1}$.

---

[2] Notice that the attacker may be able to consider less rounds than $r - 1$ but for the sake of simplicity we detail the attack assuming one round only is considered.

Using More Than One Characteristic. Using many characteristics allows the attacker to extract more information from available samples what is of interest as soon as the induced overhead (in both distillation and analysis steps) is negligible compared to the gain in the final search step induced by the additional information obtained (due to the better ranking of the correct key). Premise of this approach have already been proposed in some papers by independently considering different differentials [4] (different analysis phases for different characerics) or by summing the information coming from the different characerics to perform all in one step. In the context of linear cryptanalysis, the method known as *multiple linear cryptanalysis* [18, 5, 13] considers each characteristic independently and proposes to analyze the vectors of information for each key candidate. While the question of characteristics combination have been deeply studied for linear cryptanalysis [18, 5, 13–15], the lack of a comprehensive study on this topic in the context of differential cryptanalysis motivates the present work. In the following, and after presenting the required background, we propose a general framework and instantiate it with statistical tools already shown to be useful for linear cryptanalysis. Later on, we present experiments we ran to determine what seems to be the best combining technique in practice.

2.2   Order Statistics for Gaussian Variables

We propose here to recall a result on order statistics for normally distributed random variables that have been used by Selçuk to derive estimates of the data complexity for single linear[3] cryptanalysis [22]. Let us model the attack as follows. We will see later that, due to the tools used, scores obtained will fit into this model.

Model 1. *Let $S(k)$ be the score/statistic obtained for a key candidate k. Then,*

$$S(k) \sim \begin{cases} \mathcal{N}(\mu_R, \sigma_R^2), & \text{if } k = k_0, \\ \mathcal{N}(\mu_W, \sigma_W^2), & \text{otherwise.} \end{cases}$$

Assuming that this model holds then the distributions of ordered wrong-key scores are also normally distributed. This allows expressing the number of required samples for the attack as a function of the minimum rank wished for the correct key and the probability of this rank to be reached. Works have shown that the data complexity of an attack is not influenced by n but by its advantage a [22, 8] that we define now.

Definition 1. *Let 2^n be the number of possible key candidates and ℓ the maximum number of candidates that will be considered in the final search step. Then, the advantage of such attack over exhaustive search is defined as:*

$$a \stackrel{\text{def}}{=} n - \log_2(\ell).$$

---

[3] While single differential cryptanalysis has also been studied in the mentioned paper, results are far from being satisfying as admitted by the author. In that case Poisson distribution is more accurate [12, 7].

The success probability of an attack P_s is the probability that the correct key candidate is ranked among the ℓ first candidates at the output of analysis step.

The following result expresses the success probability of an attack in the Model 1 as a function of the parameters μ_R, σ_R, μ_W and σ_W. This result is the cornerstone of further data complexity estimate derivations.

Lemma 1. *Let a be the advantage of an attack and N_s be the number of available samples, then, the success probability of the attack P_S can be approximated by:*

$$P_S \approx \Phi_{0,1}\left(\frac{\mu_R - \mu_a}{\sqrt{\sigma_a^2 + \sigma_R^2}}\right),$$

where $\mu_a = \mu_W + \sigma_W \Phi_{0,1}^{-1}(1 - 2^{-a})$, and, $\sigma_a^2 \approx \dfrac{\sigma_W^2 \, 2^{-(n+a)}}{\varphi_{0,1}^2(\Phi_{0,1}^{-1}(1-2^{-a}))}$.

Proof. The proof follows the one of Theorem 1 in [22]. □

Remark. For the different applications considered in this paper, σ_a turns out to be negligible compared to σ_r and hence we will consider that $\sigma_a^2 + \sigma_R^2 = \sigma_R^2$. Indeed, it can be proved[4] that $\dfrac{2^{-(n+a)}}{\varphi_{0,1}^2(\Phi_{0,1}^{-1}(1-2^{-a}))} \approx \dfrac{2^{-n}}{\sqrt{2\pi}}$. In typical cases, n will be large enough for σ_a^2 to be small compared to σ_W^2. Since in the worst observed case, $\sigma_R^2 \approx \sigma_W^2$, then σ_a^2 will also be negligible compared to σ_R^2. Hence, we will use the following approximation for P_s:

$$P_S = \Phi_{0,1}\left(\frac{\mu_R - \mu_W - \sigma_W \Phi_{0,1}^{-1}(1 - 2^{-a})}{\sigma_R}\right). \tag{1}$$

We will discuss this last point later in the respective sections and provide observed values.

3   General Model for Multiple Differential Cryptanalysis

In simple differential cryptanalysis, one sample is composed of a pair of plaintexts $(x, x \oplus \delta_0)$ and the corresponding ciphertexts $(y = E_K(x), y' = E_k(x \oplus \delta_0))$. Eventually, multiple input differences may be used to perform an attack and then structures should be use to generate more samples from less plaintexts. In the following, we will study the complexities of different attacks in terms of the number N_s of required samples to avoid ambiguities. In the case where a single input difference is used then the corresponding data complexity N will be $N = 2N_s$. If more than one input difference is used, then plaintexts should be grouped into structures and then the coefficient 2 in the data complexity may change.

---

[4] This result can be derived from the Taylor series of the error function.

3.1 Partition in Differential Cryptanalysis

In this section, we propose a general model for multiple differential cryptanalysis. The aim of such a model is to provide a common language to express various notions of differential cryptanalysis (multiple, improbable, impossible, ...) in such a way that the same analysis tools can be used to evaluate performance of the attacks. This model will also help in the investigation for new techniques that handle multiple characteristics.

From a very abstract point of view, a differential cryptanalysis is composed of two functions.

- First a *sampling function* processes, for each key candidate k, the N_s available samples $(s_i)_{1 \leq i \leq N_s}$ and extracts the corresponding difference distributions q^k by normalizing the counters. This function corresponds to the distillation step.

$$\eta : \quad \mathbb{F}_{2^{2m}}^{N_s} \times \mathcal{K} \to [0,1]^{2^m}, \quad (\{s_1, \ldots, s_{N_s}\}, k) \mapsto q^k = (q_\delta^k)_{\delta \in \mathbb{F}_{2^m}}$$

where

$$q_\delta^k = \frac{1}{N_s} \#\{s_i = (y_i, y_i'), \ F_k^{-1}(y_i) \oplus F_k^{-1}(y_i') = \delta\}.$$

- Second, a *scoring function* extract a score for the candidate k from the empirical distribution q^k of observed differences. This function corresponds to the first part of the analysis step (then candidates are ordered from the most likely to the least one).

$$\psi : \quad [0,1]^{2^m} \to \mathbb{R}, \quad q^k \mapsto \psi(q^k).$$

Since in actual ciphers $m \geq 64$, the storage of distributions q^k is not possible. The solution is to consider smaller distributions. From a general point of view, this can be done by projecting the observed differences on a set of smaller cardinality by partitioning the space of output differences. We will show later how known attacks translate into this model. We denote by π such partition function from $\mathbb{F}_{2^m}$ to a set V (we assume that $V = \mathcal{I}m(\pi)$). We can generalize the sampling and scoring functions by considering the partition function π.

Model 2. *In differential cryptanalysis, the score of a key candidate is obtained composing the following two functions defined for a given mapping π from $\mathbb{F}_{2^m}$ to a set V.*

$$\eta_\pi : \quad \mathbb{F}_{2^{2m}}^{N_s} \times \mathcal{K} \to [0,1]^{|V|}, \quad (\{s_1, \ldots, s_{N_s}\}, k) \mapsto q^k = (q_v^k)_{v \in V}$$

where

$$q_v^k \stackrel{\text{def}}{=} \frac{1}{N_s} \#\{s_i = (y_i, y_i'), \ \pi\left(F_k^{-1}(y_i) \oplus F_k^{-1}(y_i')\right) = v\},$$

and

$$\psi_\pi : \quad [0,1]^{|V|} \to \mathbb{R}, \quad q^k \mapsto \psi_\pi(q^k).$$

Scoring Functions and Difference Distributions. Later in Section 4, we will instantiate different scoring functions ψ_π. Some of them are based on the knowledge of the theoretical behavior of difference distributions q^k. This behavior obviously depends on whether k corresponds to the correct key or not. If yes, the distribution q^k will be determined by differential probabilities, while if not, Hypothesis 1 implies that q^k follows a distribution corresponding to what would be obtained when considering the output of a random permutation. Hence, we place ourselves in the following model.

Model 3. *Let k be a subkey candidate and q^k the corresponding difference distribution obtained by a sampling function η_π. Then,*

$$\Pr\left[q_v^k = x\right] = \begin{cases} \Pr\left[p_v = x\right], & \text{if } k = k_0, \\ \Pr\left[\theta_v = x\right], & \text{otherwise,} \end{cases}$$

where distributions p and θ are defined as

$$p_v = \sum_{d \in \pi^{-1}(v)} p(\delta_0 \rightarrow d) \quad \text{and} \quad \theta_v = \frac{1}{\#\pi^{-1}(v)}.$$

Remark. An attack based on partitioning input and output spaces was proposed by Harpes and Cramer in [17]. We would like to stress that such attack uses a partition of the plaintext (ciphertext, *resp.*) space while we consider in this paper partitions of input (output, *resp.*) difference space.

3.2 Partitions and Actual Attacks

Simple/Impossible/Improbable Differential Attacks. In these attacks, one considers a single differential (δ_0, δ_{r-1}) having an unexected behavior (eg. a too large or too small probability of occurring). Such cryptanalyses can be represented in our model using the following function identifying differences to the set indexed by $V = \{0, 1\}$.

$$\pi(d) = \begin{cases} 1, & \text{if } d = \delta_{r-1}, \\ 0, & \text{otherwise.} \end{cases}$$

The corresponding scoring function is determined by the number of times the characteristic occurred hence only takes into consideration the value q_1 of the projected distribution.

Truncated Differential Attacks. Truncated differential cryptanalysis [19] is similar to differential cryptanalysis in the sense that usually only one truncated differential characteristic (Δ_0, Δ_{r-1}) is used. Such attacks can be represented in our model in the same way that the previous ones *i.e.* using the projected space $V = \{0, 1\}$ and a similar partition function

$$\pi(d) = \begin{cases} 1, & \text{if } d \in \Delta_{r-1}, \\ 0, & \text{otherwise.} \end{cases}$$

Again, the corresponding scoring function only takes into consideration the value q_1 of the projected distribution.

Multiple Differential Attacks. To improve the performances of differential attacks, information coming from different differentials may be combined. We consider here attacks such that differentials used have the same input difference. We discuss at the end of Section 5 how our model can be extended to the use of multiple input differences. Assuming that the collection of differential $\left(\delta_0, \delta_{r-1}^{(i)}\right)_{i=1,\dots,A}$ is used, we model the attack with projected space $V = \{0, 1, \dots, A\}$ and partition function:

$$\pi(d) = \begin{cases} i, \text{ if } d = \delta_{r-1}^{(i)}, \\ 0, \text{ otherwise.} \end{cases}$$

4   Instantiations and Complexity Estimates

In this section, we provide instantiations of *scoring functions* and the corresponding estimates for data complexities. Later, in Section 5 we experiment these *scoring functions* using different *partition functions* by attacking a reduced version of PRESENT [6, 20] and discuss the corresponding time and memory complexities.

4.1   The Sum-of-Counters Scoring Function

This technique consists in summing counters corresponding to considered differentials. Theoretical analysis of this method is done in [9]. Taking notations of the previous section, the scoring function is determined by $\sum_{i=1}^{A} q_i$ or equivalently by the value $1 - q_0$. In this setting the scores cannot be approximated by a Gaussian distribution and even Poisson approximation leads to pessimistic results. This has been explained in [9] where a formula is given to obtain a better estimate than using Poisson distribution. For more details please refer to [9].

4.2   The LLR Scoring Function

The Neyman-Pearson lemma [21] gives the optimal form of the acceptance region on which is derived the LLR method. The optimality requires that both p and θ distributions are known (or at least the values p_v/θ_v).

Definition 2. *Let* $p = [p_v]_{v \in V}$ *be the expected probability distribution vector,* θ *the uniform one and* q^k *the observed one for a key candidate* k. *For a given number of sample* N_s, *the optimal statistical test consists in comparing the following statistic to a fixed threshold.*

$$\mathrm{LLR}(q^k, p, \theta) \stackrel{\mathrm{def}}{=} N_s \sum_{v \in V} q_v \log\left(\frac{p_v}{\theta_v}\right).$$

An important remark here is that, similarly to the case presented in Section 4.1, the LLR statistic can be computed with a memory complexity of one floating-point counter per candidate. Indeed, this statistic is a weighted sum of counters for which weights are known before attacking. This test has been applied in [2] by Baignères et al. in the case of linear cryptanalysis. Applying the law of large numbers, they shown that the LLR statistic tends toward a Gaussian distribution with different means and variances according to the distribution q is extracted from. These means are expressed in terms of relative entropy.

Definition 3. *Let p and p' be two probability distribution vectors over V. The relative entropy (aka. Kullback-Leibler divergence) between p and p' is*

$$D\left(p||p'\right) \stackrel{\text{def}}{=} \sum_{v \in V} p_v \log\left(\frac{p_v}{p'_v}\right).$$

We also define the following metrics

$$D_2\left(p||p'\right) \stackrel{\text{def}}{=} \sum_{v \in V} p_v \log^2\left(\frac{p_v}{p'_v}\right), \quad \text{and} \quad \Delta D\left(p||p'\right) \stackrel{\text{def}}{=} D_2\left(p||p'\right) - D\left(p||p'\right)^2.$$

Lemma 2. *(Proposition 3 in [2]) The distributions of LLR(q^k, p, θ) asymptotically tend toward a Gaussian distribution as the number of samples N_s increases. If samples are obtained from distribution p (θ, resp.), the LLR statistic tends toward $\mathcal{N}(\mu_R, \sigma_R^2)$ ($\mathcal{N}(\mu_W, \sigma_W^2)$, resp.), where*

$$\mu_R = N_s \, D\left(p||\theta\right), \qquad \mu_W = -N_s \, D\left(\theta||p\right),$$
$$\sigma_R^2 = N_s \, \Delta D\left(p||\theta\right), \qquad \sigma_W^2 = N_s \, \Delta D\left(\theta||p\right).$$

Then, we can use Lemma 1 to obtain the following result.

Theorem 1. *Let a be the advantage of an attack then the number N_s of samples required to reach success probability P_S is*

$$N_s = \frac{\left[\sqrt{\Delta D\left(p||\theta\right)} \, \Phi_{0,1}^{-1}(P_S) + \sqrt{\Delta D\left(\theta||p\right)} \, \Phi_{0,1}^{-1}\left(1 - 2^{-a}\right)\right]^2}{\left[D\left(p||\theta\right) + D\left(\theta||p\right)\right]^2}. \tag{2}$$

Proof. The proof is based on Lemma 1 and can be found in [1]. □

4.3   The χ^2 Scoring Function

The aforementioned LLR test is optimal when both distributions are known. In our context, the knowledge of θ relies on Hypothesis 1 and the knowledge of p is based on the possibility of the attacker to theoretically compute differential probabilities. Hence, the use of an alternative statistic may be of interest when one of these two distributions is unknown to the attacker. The χ^2 method has already proved out to be useful particularly in the context of linear cryptanalysis, where the correct-guess distributions vary a lot with the key [10].Also in the differential case, obtaining a good estimate of the correct-guess distribution may be impossible. The idea is then to compare the empirical distribution to the wrong-guess distribution: the vector corresponding to the correct key-guess should end up with one of the largest scores (*i.e.*, the smallest probability of being drawn from θ).

Definition 4. *Let q^k be an empirical distribution vector. The χ^2 statistic used to determine the probability of the vector to correspond to a realization from distribution θ is*

$$\chi^2(q^k, \theta) = N_s \sum_{v \in V} \frac{(q_v^k - \theta_v)^2}{\theta_v}.$$

Notice that using χ^2 method, all the counters should be stored since it is not possible to compute the statistic on-the-fly as it was the case when summing counters or for LLR. This results in an increased memory cost when using this technique. The following quantity appears when considering the parameters of the χ^2 score distributions.

Definition 5. *Let p be a probability distribution vector over V. The capacity of this vector is defined by*

$$C(p) \stackrel{\text{def}}{=} \sum_{v \in V} \frac{(p_v - \theta_v)^2}{\theta_v}.$$

Lemma 3. *[16] The distribution of $\chi^2(q^k, \theta)$ asymptotically tends toward a Gaussian distribution as the number N_s of samples increases. If samples are obtained from distribution p (θ, resp.), the χ^2 statistic tends toward $\mathcal{N}(\mu_R, \sigma_R^2)$ ($\mathcal{N}(\mu_W, \sigma_W^2)$, resp.) where,*

$$\mu_R = |V| + N_s C(p) \quad , \quad \mu_W = |V|,$$
$$\sigma_R^2 = 2|V| + 4N_s C(p) \quad , \quad \sigma_W^2 = 2|V|.$$

In [16], Hermelin *et al.* proposed an approximation of the data complexity of a χ^2 statistical test. It turns out that, at least in the present context, the estimate proposed in the following theorem is tighter.

Theorem 2. *Let $C(p)$ be the capacity of the correct-candidate probability vector p. Then, the number N_s of samples of the corresponding attack with success probability P_S and advantage a can be estimated by*

$$N_s = \frac{\sqrt{2|V|}b + 2t^2 + t(\sqrt{2|V|} + 2b)\sqrt{1 + 4\frac{t^2 - b^2}{(\sqrt{2|V|} + 2b)^2}}}{C(p)}, \quad (3)$$

where $b = \Phi_{0,1}^{-1}(1 - 2^{-a})$ and $t = \Phi_{0,1}^{-1}(P_S)$. Fixing the success probability to 0.5, we obtain the following estimate for the number of samples:

$$N_s = \frac{\sqrt{2|V|}\Phi_{0,1}^{-1}(1 - 2^{-a})}{C(p)}. \quad (4)$$

Proof. The proof is based on Lemma 1 and can be found in [1]. □

4.4 Different Partition Functions

We present here two different types of partition functions. The first one encompass all previously proposed attacks by projecting some considered differences to corresponding elements of V and all others to 0. The second family of partition functions induce a balanced partitioning of the difference space (the sets of differences that are projected to elements of V are all of equal cardinality). This last type of partitioning has (to our knowledge) never been investigated and seems to be the most promising one regarding the motivation of this paper. We will now refer to these two techniques for building partition functions as respectively *balanced* and *unbalanced partitioning*.

Let us recall that we consider that differentials used all have the same input difference, we will explain later how different input differences can be handled.

Unbalanced Partitioning. When the attacker knows the probability of some differentials $(\delta_0, \delta_{r-1}^{(i)})_{1 \leq i \leq A}$, then the natural way of partitioning is to allocate a counter to each of these differentials. A "trash" counter will gather all other output differences.

$$\pi_{unbal}(d) = \begin{cases} i, & \text{if } d = \delta_i, \\ 0, & \text{otherwise.} \end{cases} \tag{5}$$

Let us denote by Δ_{r-1} the set of output differences $\Delta_{r-1} \overset{\text{def}}{=} (\delta_{r-1}^{(i)})_{1 \leq i \leq A}$. It is likely that this set allows early discarding of the so-called *wrong pairs*, i.e., pairs (y, y') such that, for all candidates k, $F_k^{-1}(y) \oplus F_k^{-1}(y') \notin \Delta_{r-1}$. Using such sieving process allows to decrease the number of partial decryptions in the attack and typically results in considering active bits in the difference $y \oplus y'$. In our model such wrong pairs will only account for the counters q_0^k. As $\sum_{v=0}^{|V|-1} q_v^k = 1$ ($|V| = A + 1$), for each candidate k, q_0^k can be derived from the other values. The theoretical probability θ_0 is equal to $\theta_0 = 1 - \sum_{v=1}^{|V|-1} \theta_v = 1 - \frac{|V|-1}{2^m - 1}$.

Balanced Partitioning. This alternative results in a balanced partitioning of the space of differences and hence the sieving process will not be as effective as in the case of unbalanced partitioning (if needed at all). Balanced partition functions consider in the experiments have a particular structure linked to truncated differentials. A support s to indicate the set of targeted difference bits, $s \subset \{0, m-1\}$, is determined ($|V| = 2^{|s|}$) and the partition function consists of considering only bits belonging to this support:

$$\pi_{bal}(d) = d|_s = \sum_{i=0}^{|s|} 2^i \cdot d_{s(i)}, \tag{6}$$

where $s(i)$ denote the i-th bit that belong to the support.

What may be considered as an advantage is that such partition functions make use of all pairs of plaintexts. Hence more information may be available (at the potential cost of higher time or memory requirements). In this *balanced* model the distribution θ of the wrong key is uniform. That means, in the notation of Model 3, that the quantity θ_v is equal, for all $v \in V$: $\theta_v = \frac{2^m}{|V|}$.

The main drawback of this model is that the differentials are grouped, and depending on the way this is done, the attack may be more or less efficient.

5   Experiments

In this section, we experiment different combinations of *partition* and *scoring* functions on nine rounds of SMALLPRESENT-[8][5] a reduced-version of PRESENT presented in [20]. The goal is to investigate the potential improvements mentioned in Section 4 and to test their robustness in a real attack context (that is with potentially badly estimated distributions). More details about the choices of experiment parameters can be found in [1].

5.1   On the Choice of Partition Functions

Depending on the targeted cipher, the structure of the possible partition functions may differ a lot. Nevertheless, using both a *balanced* and an *unbalanced* partitioning, (see Equations (6), and (5)) we expect to cover a large spectrum of attack possibilities in the context of SPN ciphers.

About π_{unbal}. Such unbalanced partition function is generally chosen in such a way that an efficient sieve can be performed to discard wrong pairs. In our settings, see Equation (5) , the discarded pairs correspond to the ones that increment counter q_0 for all key candidates. The use of such sieving process leads to an important gain in the time complexity of the partial decryption phase.

The weakness of this kind of partition function is that only few pairs are really useful to the attack (non-discarded pairs). More precisely, for N_s samples and a given index value $v \neq 0$,

$$\# \left\{ (y, y') | \pi_{unbal} \left(F_k^{-1}(y) \oplus F_k^{-1}(y') \right) = v \right\} = \mathcal{O} \left(\frac{N_s}{2^m} \right), \text{ where } \frac{N_s}{2^m} \leq 1.$$

In the context of classical simple differential cryptanalysis this phenomenon is related to the thresholds that can be observed on curves representing success rate or advantage as a function of the number of available samples. When using scoring techniques as the one proposed in this paper, this may explain part of the discrepancies between theoretical and empirical results, particularly in the context of χ^2.

About π_{bal}. In the case of *balanced* partition functions, the aforementioned behavior is not observed since all pairs are taken into account. Indeed,

$$\# \left\{ (y, y') | \pi_{bal} \left(F_k^{-1}(y) \oplus F_k^{-1}(y') \right) = v \right\} = \mathcal{O} \left(N_s \cdot \theta_v \right), \text{ while } \theta_v = \frac{1}{|V|}.$$

---

[5] It is an SPN cipher that processes 32-bit blocs using a 40-bit master key. One round is composed of a key addition, a non-linear layer of 4-bit S-boxes and a bit permutation.

That means that for *balanced* partition functions, if N_s is larger than $|V|$, the noise is reduced[6]. Nevertheless, in such context we generally cannot use an efficient sieving process hence the time complexity of the resulting attack is more important: for each sample a partial decryption of the last round has to be performed. Part of this drawback is removed due to the smaller data complexity. Hence both approaches may be of interest depending on the context.

5.2 Experimental Results

The present work proposes to model multiple differential cryptanalysis as the combination of a partition and a scoring function. We derived estimates for the data complexity corresponding to different scoring functions and introduced two families of partition functions. Hence, there are many things that experiments may tell us about the relevance of these tools. We will first discuss the accuracy of the estimates for the data complexity we derived. Then, we will focus on the scoring functions and their robustness regarding badly estimated distributions. Thus, we ran experiments in two different contexts:

(i) using "actual" correct-key distribution: this distribution was obtained by experimentally computing differential probabilities for fixed keys and then averaging over 200 different keys[7];

(ii) using estimated correct-key distribution: we model the fact that an attacker may only have access to estimates of the differential probabilities by degrading the actual correct-key distribution for a given error rate.

All experiments have been performed targeting nine rounds of the cipher. The main reason is that the corresponding data complexities are high enough for the attack to make sense and small enough for us to perform enough experiments. For the same reason, we choose size of output spaces $|V|$ in such a way that the counter storage of the resulting attacks can be handled in RAM and that the number of key candidates is at most 2^{16}.

Accuracy of the Data Complexity Estimates. Accuracy of the data complexity estimates presented in Theorem 1 and Theorem 2 depends on different parameters (the size of the output space, the partition function and so on). It also strongly depends on the correctness of estimates used for the distributions. In order to focus on the validity of provided formulas, we ran experiments in the setting (i)[8] correct-key distribution thus any observed deviation should not be attributed to an incorrect estimate of the differential probabilities.

We observe that for both χ^2 (Figure 1) and LLR (Figure 2), formulas provided by Theorem 2 and Theorem 1 give rather good estimates for the data complexity.

---

[6] Intuitively: for a fixed value of $|V|$, the noise is decreasing as the number of sample is increasing

[7] This technique has been shown to provide good results in [7].

[8] Notice that for the χ^2 scoring function, we first computed capacities for different fixed keys and then averaged obtained values.

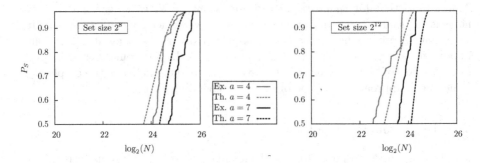

Fig. 1. Data complexities of attacks using χ^2 scoring and balanced partitioning

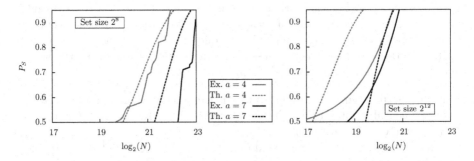

Fig. 2. Data complexities of attacks using LLR scoring and balanced partitioning

Comparison of Scoring Functions (Known Distributions). We now consider Figure 1 and Figure 2 in a different way, since we aim at comparing both χ^2 and LLR scoring functions. Obviously the LLR scoring function has much smaller data requirement. For instance, for an advantage $a = 7$ and an output space size $|V| = 2^{12}$, it only requires $2^{18.7}$ plaintexts to reach a success probability of one half while $2^{23.55}$ is required using χ^2. This is a natural result since LLR attacks are run with actual values of the differential probabilities and hence have more information to process the available data.

Comparison of Scoring Functions (Estimated Distributions). In [10], Cho has shown that if the attacker only has a badly estimated correct-key distribution then using the LLR statistical test is not relevant anymore. We conducted experiments in that direction assuming that the estimated probability distributions were biased. We emulated this phenomenon by adding some random noise to the distribution estimate (that is $\hat{p}_v = p_v \pm \frac{p_v}{100}$) then normalizing $\hat{p}_v$.

We present in Figure 3 the results of our investigation in the case of a *balanced* partition function with $|V| = 2^8$ (case were the best match is obtained between theory and practice) when the attacker only knows a correct estimate of the distribution. Using both LLR or χ^2 scoring functions leads to inaccurate estimations of the data complexity.

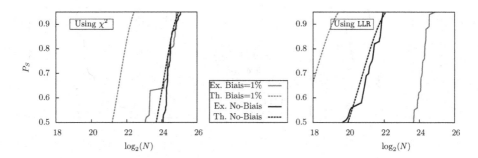

Fig. 3. Data complexities for biased distribution (using balanced partitioning of a set of cardinality $|V| = 2^8$ with advantage $a = 4$)

It turns out that the noised distribution we obtained can be distinguished from the corresponding uniform distribution θ more easily and hence theoretical expectations are optimistic. For χ^2 method, it can be seen by comparing capacities (the noised distribution has a larger capacity than the actual one) and in the case of LLR method this can be seen by looking at the relative entropy between θ and the noised distribution (that is larger). The main information is that this badly estimated distribution does not affect the attack using χ^2 scoring function, what is quite natural since the distribution p is not involved in the process, while for LLR scoring function this induces an overhead in the data complexity. With only a 1% bias, χ^2 scoring function achieve slightly better performance than LLR (in terms of data complexity).

Notice that in practice, when instantiating attacks on real ciphers with large state size, it is not so easy to obtain a good estimation of the correct-key distributions. A folklore result is that the differential probability can be underestimated by adding probabilities of corresponding differential trails found using a Branch-and-Bound algorithm. The main difficulty comes from the choice made by designers known as "wide trail strategy" [11]. Such strategy implies that the number of significant trails in a differential (or linear approximation) exponentially increases with the number of rounds. Experiments made (but not presented in this paper) show that even on SMALLPRESENT-[8] estimating distributions directly using a Branch-and-Bound algorithm leads to an error drastically larger than 1%. Hence in practice, an attacker may favor the χ^2 scoring function.

Comparing Partition Functions. Let us now consider the impact of partition functions used. Figure 1 and Figure 2 are related to experiments that have been performed using the newly introduced *balanced* partitioning. We also ran experiments using the former *unbalanced* partitioning for which an efficient sieving process can be performed (see Figure 4). We chose to perform attacks with an output set of size $|V| = 2^{16}$. The reason is that for smaller sizes corresponding attacks require much more data. Hence, to fairly compare partition functions we used best possible parameters that allow performing enough attacks for plotting results in a given time.

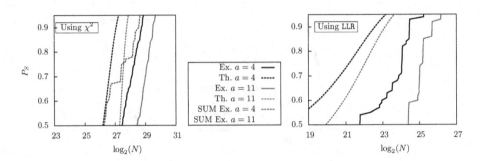

Fig. 4. Data complexities for an unbalanced partitioning (set of cardinality 2^{16})

First we observe that due to the use of a sieving process, the theoretical estimates for the data complexity are pretty optimistic (a sketch of explanation is given in Section 5.1). Focusing on experimental curves, we can conclude that from a purely information theoretical point of view, using *balanced partitioning* allows extracting more information from available samples than using *unbalanced* ones. Nevertheless, also the cost of memory and time, see [1], has to be considered when comparing both types of partition functions.

On the Use of Differentials with Different Input Differences. There are two straightforward ways of extending this work to multiple input differences. The first one is to consider the same *partition* function for each input difference so that only one output distribution is considered. The second technique is orthogonal since it consists in considering independently the distributions coming from different input differences. The corresponding scoring functions boils down to summing scores obtain for each distribution.

We ran experiments using both approaches and surprisingly did not obtained radically better results than using a single input difference. Nevertheless, we observed a strong correlation between the distributions obtained that should be exploited. This is a very promising scope for further improvements of this work.

6   Conclusion

This paper builds on the work made on the topic of linear cryptanalysis using multiple approximations. We investigate different statistical tests (namely LLR and χ^2) to combine information coming from a large number of differentials while, to our knowledge, only summing counters was considered up to now. To analyze these tools, we introduce a formal way of representing multiple differential cryptanalysis using *partition* functions and present two different families of such functions namely *balanced* and *unbalanced* partitioning (previous attacks being modelled as unbalanced partitioning). Finally, we present experiments performed on a reduced version of PRESENT that confirm the accuracy of the data complexity estimates derived in some contexts. These experiments show a relatively good accuracy of the estimates and illustrate the fact that using *balanced* partitioning one is able to take profit of all available pairs.

Further research include exploiting the similarities observed between distributions corresponding to different input differences and solving the challenging problem of estimating correct-key distributions for actual ciphers.

References

1. Blondeau, C., Gérard, B., Nyberg, K.: Multiple Differential Cryptanalysis using LLR and χ^2 Statistics (Extended version),
   http://research.ics.aalto.fi/publications/blondeau/BloGerNyb12.pdf
2. Baignères, T., Junod, P., Vaudenay, S.: How Far Can We Go Beyond Linear Cryptanalysis? In: Lee, P.J. (ed.) ASIACRYPT 2004. LNCS, vol. 3329, pp. 432–450. Springer, Heidelberg (2004)
3. Biham, E., Shamir, A.: Differential Cryptanalysis of DES-like Cryptosystems. In: Menezes, A., Vanstone, S.A. (eds.) CRYPTO 1990. LNCS, vol. 537, pp. 2–21. Springer, Heidelberg (1991)
4. Biham, E., Shamir, A.: Differential cryptanalysis of DES-like cryptosystems. Journal of Cryptology 4, 3–72 (1991)
5. Biryukov, A., De Cannière, C., Quisquater, M.: On Multiple Linear Approximations. In: Franklin, M. (ed.) CRYPTO 2004. LNCS, vol. 3152, pp. 1–22. Springer, Heidelberg (2004)
6. Bogdanov, A., Knudsen, L.R., Leander, G., Paar, C., Poschmann, A., Robshaw, M.J.B., Seurin, Y., Vikkelsoe, C.: PRESENT: An Ultra-Lightweight Block Cipher. In: Paillier, P., Verbauwhede, I. (eds.) CHES 2007. LNCS, vol. 4727, pp. 450–466. Springer, Heidelberg (2007)
7. Blondeau, C., Gérard, B.: Links between theoretical and effective differential probabilities: Experiments on PRESENT. In: TOOLS 2010 (2010),
   http://eprint.iacr.org/2010/261
8. Blondeau, C., Gérard, B., Tillich, J.-P.: Accurate estimates of the data complexity and success probability for various cryptanalyses. In: Charpin, P., Kholosha, S., Rosnes, E., Parker, M.G. (eds.) HRPR 2010, vol. 59(1-3), pp. 3–34. Springer (2011)
9. Blondeau, C., Gérard, B.: Multiple Differential Cryptanalysis: Theory and Practice. In: Joux, A. (ed.) FSE 2011. LNCS, vol. 6733, pp. 35–54. Springer, Heidelberg (2011)
10. Cho, J.Y.: Linear Cryptanalysis of Reduced-Round PRESENT. In: Pieprzyk, J. (ed.) CT-RSA 2010. LNCS, vol. 5985, pp. 302–317. Springer, Heidelberg (2010)
11. Daemen, J., Rijmen, V.: The Wide Trail Design Strategy. In: Honary, B. (ed.) Cryptography and Coding 2001. LNCS, vol. 2260, pp. 222–238. Springer, Heidelberg (2001)
12. Daemen, J., Rijmen, V.: Probability distributions of correlation and differentials in block ciphers. Journal of Mathematical Cryptology 1, 12–35 (2007)
13. Gérard, B., Tillich, J.-P.: On Linear Cryptanalysis with Many Linear Approximations. In: Parker, M.G. (ed.) Cryptography and Coding 2009. LNCS, vol. 5921, pp. 112–132. Springer, Heidelberg (2009)
14. Cho, J.Y., Hermelin, M., Nyberg, K.: A New Technique for Multidimensional Linear Cryptanalysis with Applications on Reduced Round Serpent. In: Lee, P.J., Cheon, J.H. (eds.) ICISC 2008. LNCS, vol. 5461, pp. 383–398. Springer, Heidelberg (2009)

15. Hermelin, M., Cho, J.Y., Nyberg, K.: Multidimensional Linear Cryptanalysis of Reduced Round Serpent. In: Mu, Y., Susilo, W., Seberry, J. (eds.) ACISP 2008. LNCS, vol. 5107, pp. 203–215. Springer, Heidelberg (2008)
16. Hermelin, M., Cho, J.Y., Nyberg, K.: Multidimensional Extension of Matsui's Algorithm 2. In: Dunkelman, O. (ed.) FSE 2009. LNCS, vol. 5665, pp. 209–227. Springer, Heidelberg (2009)
17. Harpes, C., Massey, J.L.: Partitioning Cryptanalysis. In: Biham, E. (ed.) FSE 1997. LNCS, vol. 1267, pp. 13–27. Springer, Heidelberg (1997)
18. Kaliski Jr., B.S., Robshaw, M.J.B.: Linear Cryptanalysis Using Multiple Approximations. In: Desmedt, Y.G. (ed.) CRYPTO 1994. LNCS, vol. 839, pp. 26–39. Springer, Heidelberg (1994)
19. Knudsen, L.R.: Truncated and Higher Order Differentials. In: Preneel, B. (ed.) FSE 1994. LNCS, vol. 1008, pp. 196–211. Springer, Heidelberg (1995)
20. Leander, G.: Small scale variants of the block cipher PRESENT. Cryptology ePrint Archive, Report 2010/143 (2010), http://eprint.iacr.org/2010/143
21. Neyman, P., Pearson, E.: On the problem of the most efficient tests of statistical hypotheses. Philosophical Trans. of the Royal Society of London, 289–337 (1933)
22. Selçuk, A.A.: On probability of success in linear and differential cryptanalysis. Journal of Cryptology 21, 131–147 (2008)
23. Wang, M.: Differential Cryptanalysis of Reduced-Round PRESENT. In: Vaudenay, S. (ed.) AFRICACRYPT 2008. LNCS, vol. 5023, pp. 40–49. Springer, Heidelberg (2008)

Quo Vadis Quaternion? Cryptanalysis of Rainbow over Non-commutative Rings

Enrico Thomae

Horst Görtz Institute for IT-Security
Faculty of Mathematics
Ruhr-University of Bochum, 44780 Bochum, Germany
enrico.thomae@rub.de

Abstract. The Rainbow Signature Scheme is a non-trivial generalization of the well known Unbalanced Oil and Vinegar Signature Scheme (Eurocrypt '99) minimizing the length of the signatures. Recently a new variant based on non-commutative rings, called NC-Rainbow, was introduced at CT-RSA 2012 to further minimize the secret key size. We disprove the claim that NC-Rainbow is as secure as Rainbow in general and show how to reduce the complexity of MinRank attacks from 2^{288} to 2^{192} and of HighRank attacks from 2^{128} to 2^{96} for the proposed instantiation over the ring of Quaternions. We further reveal some facts about Quaternions that increase the complexity of the signing algorithm. We show that NC-Rainbow is just a special case of introducing further structure to the secret key in order to decrease the key size. As the results are comparable with the ones achieved by equivalent keys, which provably do not decrease security, and far worse than just using a PRNG, we recommend not to use NC-Rainbow.

Keywords: Multivariate Cryptography, Algebraic Cryptanalysis, Rainbow, MinRank, HighRank, Non-commutative Rings, Quaternions.

1 Introduction

Rainbow was proposed in 2005 [4] and is a layer-based variant of the well known multivariate quadratic ($\mathcal{MQ}$) signature scheme *Unbalanced Oil and Vinegar* (UOV). UOV itself was proposed by Patarin *et al.* [8] at Eurocrypt 1999 and is one of the oldest $\mathcal{MQ}$-schemes still unbroken. The downside of UOV is a comparably large signature expansion by a factor of 3 for current parameters ($m = 28, n = 84$) [16]. Rainbow improves this to signatures of length $n = 42$ for messages of length $m = 24$, also for current parameters $(2^8, 18, 12, 12)$ [5].

$\mathcal{MQ}$-schemes in general suffer from comparably large key sizes. The Rainbow scheme over non-commutative rings proposed at CT-RSA 2012, also called NC-Rainbow [17], claims to reduce the secret key size by 75% while obtaining the same level of security.

I. Visconti and R. De Prisco (Eds.): SCN 2012, LNCS 7485, pp. 361–373, 2012.

Related Work. The parameter set $(2^8, 6, 6, 5, 5, 11)$ proposed for Rainbow in the original paper [4] was broken by Billet and Gilbert [2] in 2006 using a *Min-Rank* attack. The idea of those attacks was known since 2000 and first proposed in [7]. At Crypto 2008 Faugère *et al.* [6] refined the technique of Billet and Gilbert using Gröbner Bases. Ding *et al.* took this attack into account and proposed new parameters of Rainbow in [5]. For a comprehensive comparison of all known attacks on Rainbow and proposals for secure parameters we refer to [12]. So far there are two different techniques known to reduce the secret key size of Rainbow. On the one hand we can introduce a special structure, such like a cyclic coefficient matrix [11] and on the other hand we can use equivalent keys [13]. The latter exploits that large parts of the key are redundant and do not provide any security, whereas for the first variant it is an open problem to quantify the loss of security.

Achievement and Organization. Section 2 introduces the NC-Rainbow signature scheme as proposed in [17]. For readers unfamiliar with multivariate quadratic schemes, we start by briefly describing the Unbalanced Oil and Vinegar scheme and its layer-based variant Rainbow. Section 3 explains the algebraic structure of the ring of Quaternions and show how these seriously speed up MinRank and HighRank attacks.

2   Basics

In this section we explain the Rainbow signature scheme over non-commutative rings as proposed in [17] and introduce the necessary notation. For a better understanding we first briefly introduce the Unbalanced Oil and Vinegar as well as the Rainbow Signature Scheme.

The general idea of $\mathcal{MQ}$-signature schemes is to use a public multivariate quadratic map $\mathcal{P} : \mathbb{F}_q^n \to \mathbb{F}_q^m$ with

$$\mathcal{P} = \begin{pmatrix} p^{(1)}(x_1, \dots, x_n) \\ \vdots \\ p^{(m)}(x_1, \dots, x_n) \end{pmatrix}$$

and

$$p^{(k)}(x_1, \dots, x_n) := \sum_{1 \le i \le j \le n} \widetilde{\gamma}_{ij}^{(k)} x_i x_j = x^\mathsf{T} \mathfrak{P}^{(k)} x,$$

where $\widetilde{\gamma}_{ij}^{(k)} \in \mathbb{F}_q$ are some coefficients, $\mathfrak{P}^{(k)}$ is the $(n \times n)$ matrix describing the quadratic form of $p^{(k)}$ and $x = (x_1, \dots, x_n)^\mathsf{T}$. Note that we can neglect linear and constant terms as they never mix with quadratic terms and thus have no positive effects on security.

The trapdoor is given by a structured central map $\mathcal{F} : \mathbb{F}_q^n \to \mathbb{F}_q^m$ with

$$\mathcal{F} = \begin{pmatrix} f^{(1)}(u_1, \dots, u_n) \\ \vdots \\ f^{(m)}(u_1, \dots, u_n) \end{pmatrix}$$

and

$$f^{(k)}(u_1, \ldots, u_n) := \sum_{1 \leq i \leq j \leq n} \gamma_{ij}^{(k)} u_i u_j = u^\mathsf{T} \mathfrak{F}^{(k)} u.$$

In order to hide this trapdoor we choose two secret linear transformations S, T and define $\mathcal{P} := T \circ \mathcal{F} \circ S$. See figure 1 for illustration.

Fig. 1. $\mathcal{MQ}$-Scheme in general

For the **Unbalanced Oil and Vinegar (UOV)** signature scheme the variables u_i with $i \in V := \{1, \ldots, v\}$ are called *vinegar variables* and the remaining variables u_i with $i \in O := \{v + 1, \ldots, n\}$ are called *oil variables*. The central map $f^{(k)}$ is given by

$$f^{(k)}(u_1, \ldots, u_n) := \sum_{i \in V, j \in V} \gamma_{ij}^{(k)} u_i u_j + \sum_{i \in V, j \in O} \gamma_{ij}^{(k)} u_i u_j.$$

The corresponding matrix $\mathfrak{F}^{(k)}$ is depicted in figure 2.

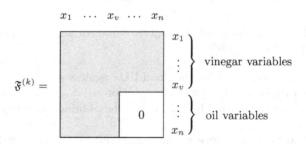

Fig. 2. Central map $\mathfrak{F}^{(k)}$ of UOV. White parts denote zero entries while gray parts denote arbitrary entries.

As we have m equations in $m + v$ variables, fixing v variables will yield a solution with high probability. Due to the structure of $\mathfrak{F}^{(k)}$, *i.e.* there are no quadratic terms of two oil variables, we can fix the vinegar variables at random to obtain a system of linear equations in the oil variables, which is easy to solve. This procedure is not possible for the public key, as the transformation S of variables fully mixes the variables (like oil and vinegar in a salad). Note that for UOV we can discard the transformation T of equations, as the trapdoor is invariant under this linear transformation.

Rainbow uses the same idea as UOV but in different layers. A current choice of parameters is given by $(q, v_1, o_1, o_2) = (2^8, 18, 12, 12)$. In particular the field size $q = 2^8$ and the number of layers is two. Note, two layers seems to be the best choice in order to prevent MinRank attacks and preserve short signatures at the same time. The central map $\mathcal{F}$ of Rainbow is divided into two layers $\mathfrak{F}^{(1)}, \ldots, \mathfrak{F}^{(12)}$ and $\mathfrak{F}^{(13)}, \ldots, \mathfrak{F}^{(24)}$ of form given in figure 3. Let $V_1 := \{1, \ldots, v_1\}, O_1 := \{v_1 + 1, \ldots, v_1 + o_1\}$ and $O_2 := \{v_1 + o_1 + 1, \ldots, v_1 + o_1 + o_2\}$. A formal description of $\mathcal{F}$ is given by the following formula.

$$f^{(k)}(u_1, \ldots, u_n) := \sum_{i \in V_1, j \in V_1} \gamma_{ij}^{(k)} u_i u_j + \sum_{i \in V_1, j \in O_1} \gamma_{ij}^{(k)} u_i u_j$$
$$\text{for } k = 1, \ldots, o_1$$

$$f^{(k)}(u_1, \ldots, u_n) := \sum_{i \in V_1 \cup O_1, j \in V_1 \cup O_1} \gamma_{ij}^{(k)} u_i u_j + \sum_{i \in V_1 \cup O_1, j \in O_2} \gamma_{ij}^{(k)} u_i u_j$$
$$\text{for } k = o_1 + 1, \ldots, o_1 + o_2$$

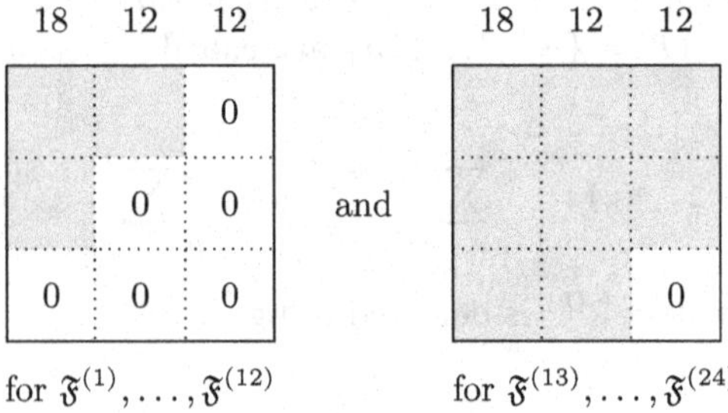

Fig. 3. Central map of Rainbow $(2^8, 18, 12, 12)$. White parts denote zero entries while gray parts denote arbitrary entries.

To use the trapdoor we first solve the small UOV system $\mathfrak{F}^{(1)}, \ldots, \mathfrak{F}^{(o_1)}$ by fixing the v_1 vinegar variables at random. The solution $u_1, \ldots, u_{v_1 + o_1}$ is now used as vinegar variables of the second layer. Solving the obtained linear system yields $u_{v_1 + o_1 + 1}, \ldots, u_{v_1 + o_1 + o_2}$.

The **NC-Rainbow** signature scheme proposed at CT-RSA 2012 [17] uses some non-commutative ring $\mathbb{Q}_q$ with dimension r over $\mathbb{F}_q$ to further decrease the secret key size. Due to the existence of a $\mathbb{F}_q$-linear isomorphism $\phi^{\tilde{n}} : \mathbb{F}_q^{\tilde{n}r} \to \mathbb{Q}_q^{\tilde{n}}$ with $\tilde{n}r := n$ and $\tilde{m}r := m$, the central map $\mathcal{F}$ can be replaced by $\phi^{-\tilde{m}} \circ \tilde{\mathcal{F}} \circ \phi^{\tilde{n}}$ for $\tilde{\mathcal{F}} : \mathbb{Q}_q^{\tilde{n}} \to \mathbb{Q}_q^{\tilde{m}}$. Let $\tilde{V}_1 := \{1, \ldots, \tilde{v}_1\}, \tilde{O}_1 := \{\tilde{v}_1 + 1, \ldots, \tilde{v}_1 + \tilde{o}_1\}$ and $\tilde{O}_2 := \{\tilde{v}_1 + \tilde{o}_1 + 1, \ldots, \tilde{v}_1 + \tilde{o}_1 + \tilde{o}_2\}$ with $r\tilde{v}_1 := v_1, r\tilde{o}_1 := o_1$ and $r\tilde{o}_2 := o_2$. The central map $\tilde{\mathcal{F}}$, as defined in [17], is given by the following polynomials.

$$\tilde{f}^{(k)}(u_1,\ldots,u_n) := \sum_{i\in\tilde{V}_1,j\in\tilde{V}_1} u_i\gamma_{ij}^{(k)}u_j + \sum_{i\in\tilde{V}_1,j\in\tilde{O}_1} u_i\gamma_{ij}^{(k)}u_j + u_j\gamma_{ji}^{(k)}u_i$$

$$\text{for } k = 1,\ldots,\tilde{o}_1$$

$$\tilde{f}^{(k)}(u_1,\ldots,u_n) := \sum_{i\in\tilde{V}_1\cup\tilde{O}_1,j\in\tilde{V}_1\cup\tilde{O}_1} u_i\gamma_{ij}^{(k)}u_j + \sum_{i\in\tilde{V}_1\cup\tilde{O}_1,j\in\tilde{O}_2} u_i\gamma_{ij}^{(k)}u_j + u_j\gamma_{ji}^{(k)}u_i$$

$$\text{for } k = \tilde{o}_1 + 1,\ldots,\tilde{o}_1 + \tilde{o}_2$$

Note that in contrast to [17] we neglect linear and constant terms. As not all coefficients of those terms are chosen uniformly at random over $\mathbb{F}_q$ (cf. section 3) they would provide further equations to speed up the Reconciliation attack (cf. Sec. 5, Eq. 4 in [15]). As we will not investigate Reconciliation attacks, we just forget about this flaw of NC-Rainbow.

3   Cryptanalysis of NC-Rainbow

The authors of [17] claimed that NC-Rainbow is as secure as the original Rainbow scheme, as every instance $(\mathbb{Q}_q,\tilde{v}_1,\tilde{o}_1,\tilde{o}_2)$ of the former can be transformed to an instance $(\mathbb{F}_q,v_1,o_1,o_2)$ of the latter, due to the $\mathbb{F}_q$-linear isomorphism ϕ. Well, as we will see below, this only provides an upper bound on the security.

First, we need the other direction to prove security, which does not hold due to the special choice of $\tilde{\mathcal{F}}$. More precisely, we will see in lemma 2 that the size of $\tilde{\mathcal{F}}$ must be at least as large as the size of $\mathcal{F}$ to obtain exactly the same level of security.

Second, ϕ is *not* $\mathbb{F}_q^r$-linear. So even if the size of $\tilde{\mathcal{F}}$ is large enough, it is not clear at all, if the additional structure of $\mathbb{Q}_q$ can be used to attack the scheme. We will later use the structure of Quaternions to speed up MinRank and HighRank attacks.

Third, the ring used by the authors of [17] is commutative. But we do not restrict our cryptanalysis to this case and also investigate non-commutative rings (cf. remark 1).

In the sequel we explain and attack NC-Rainbow over the ring of Quaternions (cf. definition 1), as proposed by the authors of [17]. Note that the amount of additional structure introduced by $\tilde{\mathcal{F}}$ is independent of the encoding of the non-commutative ring and thus NC-Rainbow is not equally secure to Rainbow for every non-commutative ring (cf. lemma 2). But there might be smarter encodings than Quaternions, which speed up known attacks a little less. We still do not think it is worthwhile to search for those non-commutative rings, as the whole construction is just a special case of reducing key size by introducing some structure to the secret key. Compare [11, 13] for the state of the art.

Definition 1 (Ring of Quaternions). *The non-commutative ring of Quaternions* $(\mathbb{Q}_q, +, \odot)$ *of dimension* $r = 4$ *is defined by*

$$\mathbb{Q}_q := \{(a, b, c, d)^\mathsf{T} \mid a, b, c, d \in \mathbb{F}_q\}$$

with

$$\begin{pmatrix} a_1 \\ b_1 \\ c_1 \\ d_1 \end{pmatrix} + \begin{pmatrix} a_2 \\ b_2 \\ c_2 \\ d_2 \end{pmatrix} := \begin{pmatrix} a_1 + a_2 \\ b_1 + b_2 \\ c_1 + c_2 \\ d_1 + d_2 \end{pmatrix}$$

and

$$\begin{pmatrix} a_1 \\ b_1 \\ c_1 \\ d_1 \end{pmatrix} \odot \begin{pmatrix} a_2 \\ b_2 \\ c_2 \\ d_2 \end{pmatrix} := \begin{pmatrix} a_1 a_2 - b_1 b_2 - c_1 c_2 - d_1 d_2 \\ a_1 b_2 + b_1 a_2 + c_1 d_2 - d_1 c_2 \\ a_1 c_2 - b_1 d_2 + c_1 a_2 + d_1 b_2 \\ a_1 d_2 + b_1 c_2 - c_1 b_2 + d_1 a_2 \end{pmatrix}.$$

The authors of [17] suggested to use the finite field $\mathbb{F}_{2^8}$. Note there exists a $\mathbb{F}_{2^8}$-linear map given by $\phi : \mathbb{F}_{2^8}^4 \to \mathbb{Q}_{256} : (a, b, c, d)^\mathsf{T} \mapsto (a, b, c, d)^\mathsf{T}$.

Remark 1. The ring of Quaternions is commutative over fields of *even* characteristic, by definition of multiplication $\odot$ [14]. Thus we will distinguish between *odd* and *even* characteristic for every single attack in the sequel.

Remark 2. The ring of Quaternions over finite fields is not a division ring (skew field) [1]. This can be easily followed by a theorem of Wedderburn, who proved in 1905 that every finite skew field is a field (cf. theorem 2.55, page 70 in [10]). The authors of [17] did not address the impact of this fact to the signing algorithm. For example the element $(1, 1, 1, 1) \in \mathbb{Q}_{2^k}$ does not have an inverse and thus it might become much harder to find a solution of the linear system of oil variables. Note that the probability of a random element in $\mathbb{Q}_q$ to have no inverse is $1/q$. For the proposed parameters $(\widetilde{v}_1, \widetilde{o}_1, \widetilde{o}_2) = (5, 4, 4)$ we need 12 inversions to perform the Gaussian elimination in both layers and additional 8 inversions to obtain the solution. Hence the probability of finding a solution is $0.996^{20} \approx 0.923$ in $\mathbb{Q}_{2^8}$ and $0.937^{20} \approx 0.272$ in $\mathbb{Q}_{2^4}$. Note that NC-Rainbow over $\mathbb{Q}_2$ has probability 2^{-20} and thus would hardly work in practice.

Hidden Structure of NC-Rainbow. Before we continue to improve MinRank and HighRank attacks, we want to determine the hidden structure of NC-Rainbow over Quaternions in general. Example 1 gives a first impression.

Example 1. To illustrate special structures over $\mathbb{F}_q$ introduced by NC-Rainbow, we use the following example throughout the paper. Let $v_1 = 8, o_1 = 4, o_2 = 4$ and thus $\widetilde{v}_1 = 2, \widetilde{o}_1 = 1, \widetilde{o}_2 = 1$. In figure 4 the central polynomials $\mathfrak{F}_1, \ldots, \mathfrak{F}_8$ of Rainbow are compared to the central polynomials $\widetilde{\mathfrak{F}}_1, \ldots, \widetilde{\mathfrak{F}}_8$ over fields of *odd* characteristic obtained by NC-Rainbow. Thereby crosses denote arbitrary values and empty squares denote systematical zeros. Later we will see that even the crosses of different maps are connected in some way. Further figure 5 shows that the structure is even stronger over fields of *even* characteristic.

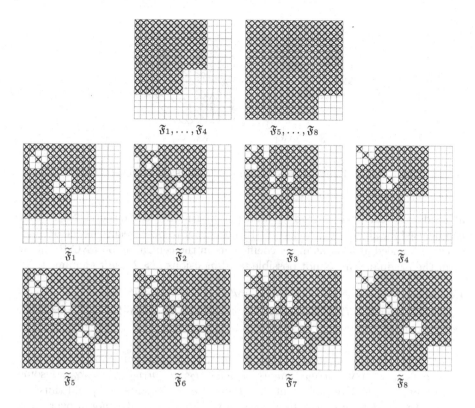

Fig. 4. Central map of Rainbow compared to NC-Rainbow over fields of odd characteristic

To determine *all* the structure over $\mathbb{F}_q$, we have a closer look at $u_i\gamma_{ij}u_j + u_j\gamma_{ji}u_i$ over $\mathbb{Q}$ for $i \neq j$. Let $u_1 := (u_{11}, u_{12}, u_{13}, u_{14})^\mathsf{T}$, $u_2 := (u_{21}, u_{22}, u_{23}, u_{24})^\mathsf{T}$, $\gamma_{12} := (t_1, t_2, t_3, t_4)^\mathsf{T}$ and $\gamma_{21} := (t_5, t_6, t_7, t_8)^\mathsf{T}$. Due to remark 1 we only have to consider $u_i\gamma_{ij}u_j$ in fields of *even* characteristic. We obtain $\phi^{-1} \circ (u_1\gamma_{12}u_2) \circ \phi = u_1^\mathsf{T}(M_1, M_2, M_3, M_4)u_2$ with M_i given below.

$$M_1 = \begin{pmatrix} t_1 & t_2 & t_3 & t_4 \\ t_2 & t_1 & t_4 & t_3 \\ t_3 & t_4 & t_1 & t_2 \\ t_4 & t_3 & t_2 & t_1 \end{pmatrix}, M_2 = \begin{pmatrix} t_2 & t_1 & t_4 & t_3 \\ t_1 & t_2 & t_3 & t_4 \\ t_4 & t_3 & t_2 & t_1 \\ t_3 & t_4 & t_1 & t_2 \end{pmatrix},$$

$$M_3 = \begin{pmatrix} t_3 & t_4 & t_1 & t_2 \\ t_4 & t_3 & t_2 & t_1 \\ t_1 & t_2 & t_3 & t_4 \\ t_2 & t_1 & t_4 & t_3 \end{pmatrix}, M_4 = \begin{pmatrix} t_4 & t_3 & t_2 & t_1 \\ t_3 & t_4 & t_1 & t_2 \\ t_2 & t_1 & t_4 & t_3 \\ t_1 & t_2 & t_3 & t_4 \end{pmatrix}.$$

Note that $\phi^{-1} \circ u_i\gamma_{ij}u_j \circ \phi$ produces 4 polynomials over $\mathbb{F}_q$ with 16 monomials $u_{1i}u_{2j}$, $i, j = 1, 2, 3, 4$. Further for the original Rainbow scheme, all these 64 coefficients of $u_{1i}u_{2j}$ for $1 \leq i, j \leq 4$ in the secret polynomials $f^{(1)}, \ldots, f^{(4)}$ of $\mathcal{F}$ are chosen independently, uniformly at random. But due to the special choice of the central map of NC-Rainbow, now only 4 coefficients t_i are chosen uniformly

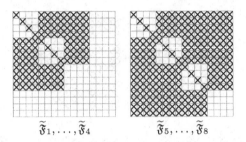

$$\tilde{\mathfrak{F}}_1, \ldots, \tilde{\mathfrak{F}}_4 \qquad\qquad \tilde{\mathfrak{F}}_5, \ldots, \tilde{\mathfrak{F}}_8$$

Fig. 5. Central map of NC-Rainbow over fields of even characteristic

at random. Clearly this introduce additional structure to the secret key $\mathcal{F}$ that can be used for algebraic attacks (cf. [15]). In order to be as secure as the original scheme, we need at least as many coefficients in the central map of NC-Rainbow as in the original. This is not possible for dimensions $r > 2$ due to lemma 1.

Lemma 1. *Let $\mathbb{F}_q$ be any finite field and R a non-commutative ring of dimension $r > 2$ over $\mathbb{F}_q$. Then NC-Rainbow over R with any secret map $\tilde{\mathcal{F}}$ can never be as secure as Rainbow.*

Proof. The maximal number of quadratic monomials containing variables u_1 and u_2 in R is 6, namely $\gamma_1 u_1 u_2$, $\gamma_2 u_2 u_1$, $u_1 \gamma_3 u_2$, $u_2 \gamma_4 u_1$, $u_1 u_2 \gamma_5$, $u_2 u_1 \gamma_6$ for some coefficients $\gamma_i \in R$. Every element $\gamma_i \in R$ encodes r elements of $\mathbb{F}_q$ and thus the maximal number of coefficients we can choose uniformly at random over $\mathbb{F}_q$ is $6r$. On the other hand there are r^2 monomials over $\mathbb{F}_q$ produced by u_1 and u_2. All those monomials occur in r different polynomials and thus are represented by r^3 coefficients in $\mathbb{F}_q$. In the case of Rainbow all these coefficients are chosen independently, uniformly at random. While $r^3 > 6r$ for $r > 2$ this is not possible for NC-Rainbow. $\qquad\square$

Next we observe that the matrices M_i are heavily structured. A simple addition $M_1 + M_2 + M_3 + M_4$ provides a matrix with the same value in every entry and thus with rank 1 instead of 4. We will use this fact later on to improve MinRank attacks.

The following matrices produced by $u_i \gamma_{ii} u_i$ provide even more structure (cf. figure 5).

$$M_1 = \begin{pmatrix} t_1 & 0 & 0 & 0 \\ 0 & t_1 & 0 & 0 \\ 0 & 0 & t_1 & 0 \\ 0 & 0 & 0 & t_1 \end{pmatrix}, M_2 = \begin{pmatrix} t_2 & 0 & 0 & 0 \\ 0 & t_2 & 0 & 0 \\ 0 & 0 & t_2 & 0 \\ 0 & 0 & 0 & t_2 \end{pmatrix},$$

$$M_3 = \begin{pmatrix} t_3 & 0 & 0 & 0 \\ 0 & t_3 & 0 & 0 \\ 0 & 0 & t_3 & 0 \\ 0 & 0 & 0 & t_3 \end{pmatrix}, M_4 = \begin{pmatrix} t_4 & 0 & 0 & 0 \\ 0 & t_4 & 0 & 0 \\ 0 & 0 & t_4 & 0 \\ 0 & 0 & 0 & t_4 \end{pmatrix}.$$

For fields of *odd* characteristic the structure of M_i produced by $u_i\gamma_{ij}u_j + u_j\gamma_{ji}u_i$ becomes slightly more difficult.

$$M_1 = \begin{pmatrix} t_1 + t_5 & -t_2 - t_6 & -t_3 - t_7 & -t_4 - t_8 \\ -t_2 - t_6 & -t_1 - t_5 & t_4 - t_8 & -t_3 + t_7 \\ -t_3 - t_7 & -t_4 + t_8 & -t_1 - t_5 & t_2 - t_6 \\ -t_4 - t_8 & t_3 - t_7 & -t_2 + t_6 & -t_1 - t_5 \end{pmatrix},$$

$$M_2 = \begin{pmatrix} t_2 + t_6 & t_1 + t_5 & -t_4 + t_8 & t_3 - t_7 \\ t_1 + t_5 & -t_2 - t_6 & -t_3 - t_7 & -t_4 - t_8 \\ t_4 - t_8 & -t_3 - t_7 & t_2 + t_6 & t_1 - t_5 \\ -t_3 + t_7 & -t_4 - t_8 & -t_1 + t_5 & t_2 + t_6 \end{pmatrix},$$

$$M_3 = \begin{pmatrix} t_3 + t_7 & t_4 - t_8 & t_1 + t_5 & -t_2 + t_6 \\ -t_4 + t_8 & t_3 + t_7 & -t_2 - t_6 & -t_1 + t_5 \\ t_1 + t_5 & -t_2 - t_6 & -t_3 - t_7 & -t_4 - t_8 \\ t_2 - t_6 & t_1 - t_5 & -t_4 - t_8 & t_3 + t_7 \end{pmatrix},$$

$$M_4 = \begin{pmatrix} t_4 + t_8 & -t_3 + t_7 & t_2 - t_6 & t_1 + t_5 \\ t_3 - t_7 & t_4 + t_8 & t_1 - t_5 & -t_2 - t_6 \\ -t_2 + t_6 & -t_1 + t_5 & t_4 + t_8 & -t_3 - t_7 \\ t_1 + t_5 & -t_2 - t_6 & -t_3 - t_7 & -t_4 - t_8 \end{pmatrix}.$$

Obtaining a generic, *i.e.* independent of the choice of coefficients t_i, linear combination $a_1 M_1 + a_2 M_2 + a_3 M_3 + a_4 M_4 =: N$ with rank less than 4 becomes a little more involved. We now want to show that there always exists a matrix N with rank 3, *i.e.* we can find a linear combination of columns such that $b_1 N_{.1} + b_2 N_{.2} + b_3 N_{.3} + N_{.4} = 0$. Collecting the coefficients of $t_1, \ldots, t_8$ in every of the 4 components and setting them to zero provides 32 quadratic equations in the unknowns a_1, a_2, a_3, a_4 and b_1, b_2, b_3. We obtain the following solution by computing the Gröbner Basis of this system.

$$a_1 = 1, \ a_2 = b_1, \ a_3 = b_2, \ a_4 = b_3 \ \text{and} \ b_1^2 + b_2^2 + b_3^2 = -1$$

Lemma 2 proves that $b_1^2 + b_2^2 + b_3^2 = -1$ with $b_1 = 0$ always has a solution over $\mathbb{F}_p$ with $p > 2$ prime. Note that this implies the existence of a solution also over extension fields.

Lemma 2. *Let $p > 2$ be prime. Then there exists a, b such that*

$$a^2 + b^2 + 1 \equiv 0 \pmod{p}.$$

Proof. This lemma, as well as its proof, is well-known in literature. As the proof itself is very elegant, we give a brief description for readers who are unfamiliar with this topic. Consider the two sets

$$A = \left\{ 0^2, 1^2, \ldots, \left(\frac{p-1}{2}\right)^2 \right\} \ \text{and} \ B = \left\{ -0^2 - 1, -1^2 - 1, \ldots, -\left(\frac{p-1}{2}\right)^2 - 1 \right\}.$$

Obviously all elements of A as well as of B are pairwise distinct. Due to $|A| = |B| = \frac{p+1}{2}$ we obtain a total amount of $|A| + |B| = p + 1$ elements. As $|\mathbb{F}_p| = p$ there must be one element contained in both sets and thus $a^2 \equiv -b^2 - 1 \pmod{p}$. $\square$

To conclude the preparation of our MinRank attack, we give the matrices produced by $u_i \gamma_{ii} u_i$ over fields of *odd* characteristic.

$$M_1 = \begin{pmatrix} 2t_1 & -2t_2 & -2t_3 & -2t_4 \\ -2t_2 & -2t_1 & 0 & 0 \\ -2t_3 & 0 & -2t_1 & 0 \\ -2t_4 & 0 & 0 & -2t_1 \end{pmatrix}, M_2 = \begin{pmatrix} 2t_2 & 2t_1 & 0 & 0 \\ 2t_1 & -2t_2 & -2t_3 & -2t_4 \\ 0 & -2t_3 & 2t_2 & 0 \\ 0 & -2t_4 & 0 & 2t_2 \end{pmatrix},$$

$$M_3 = \begin{pmatrix} 2t_3 & 0 & 2t_1 & 0 \\ 0 & 2t_3 & -2t_2 & 0 \\ 2t_1 & -2t_2 & -2t_3 & -2t_4 \\ 0 & 0 & -2t_4 & 2t_3 \end{pmatrix}, M_4 = \begin{pmatrix} 2t_4 & 0 & 0 & 2t_1 \\ 0 & 2t_4 & 0 & -2t_2 \\ 0 & 0 & 2t_4 & -2t_3 \\ 2t_1 & -2t_2 & -2t_3 & -2t_4 \end{pmatrix}.$$

MinRank Attack. The main idea of rank attacks is that the rank of $\mathfrak{F}^{(k)}$ is invariant under the bijective transformation of variables S but not under the transformation of equations T. Thus we can use the rank as distinguisher to recover T. Note that once T is known, S is also recovered comparably fast by UOV attacks like the one of Kipnis and Shamir [9] due to the special choice of parameters.

A naive way of performing a MinRank attack [2] is to sample a vector $\omega \in_R \mathbb{F}_q^n$ and hope that it lies in the kernel of a linear combination of low-rank matrices. If this is true, solving the linear system of equations

$$\sum_{i=1}^{m} \lambda_i \mathfrak{P}^{(i)} \omega = 0 \text{ for } \omega \in_R \mathbb{F}_q^n, \lambda_i \in \mathbb{F}_q, \mathfrak{P}^{(i)} \in \mathbb{F}_q^{n \times n}$$

reveals a part of the secret transformation T. The complexity of sampling $\omega \in \ker(\mathfrak{F})$ is q^{n-d} with n the number of variables and $d = \dim(\ker(\mathfrak{F}))$. Note $n - d = \text{rank}(\mathfrak{F})$.

Lemma 3. *The complexity of MinRank attacks on NC-Rainbow over fields $\mathbb{F}_q$ of even characteristic is at most $q^{4\tilde{v}_1 + \tilde{o}_1}$ instead of $q^{4\tilde{v}_1 + 4\tilde{o}_1}$.*

Proof. For fields of even characteristic we already showed that $M_1 + M_2 + M_3 + M_4$ has rank 1 instead of 4. Remember that for $\mathfrak{F}^{(1)} + \mathfrak{F}^{(2)} + \mathfrak{F}^{(3)} + \mathfrak{F}^{(4)} =: \mathfrak{F}$ every (4×4) submatrix contains only equal elements, *i.e.* $\mathfrak{F}_{i,j} = \mathfrak{F}_{x,y}$ with $4k \leq i, x \leq 4(k+1), 4\ell \leq j, y \leq 4(\ell+1)$ for some $k \neq \ell$. Adding column $v_1 + 4k$ to the columns $v_1 + 4k - 1, v_1 + 4k - 2, v_1 + 4k - 3$ for $1 \leq k \leq \tilde{o}_1$ vanishes a total of $3\tilde{o}_1$ columns. Hence $\mathfrak{F}$ has rank $4\tilde{v}_1 + \tilde{o}_1$. Compare example 1 for an illustration:

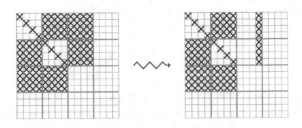

□

Lemma 4. *The complexity of MinRank attacks on NC-Rainbow over fields $\mathbb{F}_q$ of odd characteristic is at most $q^{4\tilde{v}_1+3\tilde{o}_1}$ instead of $q^{4\tilde{v}_1+4\tilde{o}_1}$.*

Proof. Due to lemma 2 there exists a linear combination of every four columns $v_1+4k, v_1+4k-1, v_1+4k-2, v_1+4k-3$ with $1 \le k \le \tilde{o}_1$ of $\mathfrak{F}^{(1)}+\mathfrak{F}^{(2)}+\mathfrak{F}^{(3)}+\mathfrak{F}^{(4)}$, such that one column vanishes.   □

We implemented NC-Rainbow using the software system Magma V2.16-1 [3] and observed that the ranks are even smaller than given by lemma 3 and 4. Table 1 illustrate the ranks of the central polynomials and their linear combination for fields of even characteristic and different sets of parameters. The last two columns give the maximum of all minimal ranks that we brute-forced in several experiments.

Table 1. Ranks of NC-Rainbow over even characteristic, experimentally derived. The last two columns give the maximum of all minimal ranks that we brute-forced in several experiments.

$\tilde{v}_1$	$\tilde{o}_1$	$\tilde{o}_2$	$\mathfrak{F}_i$ $1 \le i \le o_1$	$\mathfrak{F}_i$ $o_1 < i \le m$	$\sum_{i=1}^{4} \mathfrak{F}_i$	$\sum_{i=o_1+1}^{o_1+4} \mathfrak{F}_i$	$\sum_{i=1}^{o_1} \gamma_i\mathfrak{F}_i$	$\sum_{i=o_1+1}^{o_1+o_2} \gamma_i\mathfrak{F}_i$
5	1	1	24	28	20	24	16	20
5	1	2	24	32	20	24	16	18
5	2	1	28	32	20	28	14	24
5	2	2	28	36	20	28	14	20
5	3	3	32	44	20	32	14	22

Table 2. Ranks of NC-Rainbow over odd characteristic, experimentally derived. The last two columns give the maximum of all minimal ranks that we brute-forced in several experiments.

$\tilde{v}_1$	$\tilde{o}_1$	$\tilde{o}_2$	$\mathfrak{F}_i$ $1 \le i \le o_1$	$\mathfrak{F}_i$ $o_1 < i \le m$	$\sum_{i=1}^{o_1} \gamma_i\mathfrak{F}_i$	$\sum_{i=o_1+1}^{o_1+o_2} \gamma_i\mathfrak{F}_i$
5	1	1	24	28	22	26
5	1	2	24	32	22	28
5	2	1	28	32	24	30
5	2	2	28	36	24	31
5	3	3	32	44	27	39

Heuristic: We have experimentally derived that $\mathfrak{F}^{(1)} + \mathfrak{F}^{(2)} + \mathfrak{F}^{(3)} + \mathfrak{F}^{(4)}$ has rank $4\widetilde{v}_1$ instead of $4\widetilde{v}_1 + \widetilde{o}_1$ for even characteristic. Moreover, for $4\widetilde{o}_1 > \widetilde{v}_1$ there always exists a linear combination such that all (4×4) matrices on the diagonal are zero. Experiments suggest that this linear combination has rank $3\widetilde{v}_1 - 1$.

Table 3. Log$_2$ complexity of MinRank attacks against NC-Rainbow over $\mathbb{Q}_q$ with even characteristic

$(\widetilde{v}_1, \widetilde{o}_1, \widetilde{o}_2)$	claimed	real	heuristic
$(5, 4, 4)$	288	192	112
$(7, 5, 5)$	384	264	160
$(9, 6, 6)$	480	336	208

HighRank attack. Our observation regarding HighRank attacks holds both for even and odd characteristic.

Lemma 5. *The complexity of HighRank attacks on NC-Rainbow over $\mathbb{Q}_q$ is at most $q^{o_2 - \widetilde{o}_2}$ instead of q^{o_2}.*

Proof. We already mentioned that there exists a linear combination of high rank matrices such that the rank decrease. In particular for fields of even characteristic $M_1 + M_2 + M_3 + M_4$ has rank 1 instead of 4 and for fields of odd characteristic we showed in lemma 2 that there exists a generic linear combination of M_1, M_2, M_3, M_4 with rank 3. Thus we do not have to remove *all* polynomials $\mathfrak{F}_i$ of high rank to observe a decrease of rank, but only 3 out of 4, *i.e.* in total we have to brute force $4\widetilde{o}_2 - \widetilde{o}_2 = o_2 - \widetilde{o}_2$ linear combinations of public polynomials $\mathfrak{P}_i$.

Table 4. Log$_2$ complexity of HighRank attacks against NC-Rainbow over $\mathbb{Q}_q$

$(\widetilde{v}_1, \widetilde{o}_1, \widetilde{o}_2)$	claimed	real
$(5, 4, 4)$	128	96
$(7, 5, 5)$	160	120
$(9, 6, 6)$	192	144

Acknowledgments. The author wants to thank the anonymous reviewers of SCN 2012 for their helpful remarks and suggestions. He was supported by the German Science Foundation (DFG) through an Emmy Noether grant. Furthermore the author was in part supported by the European Commission through the IST Programme under contract *ICT-2007-216676 Ecrypt II*.

References

[1] Aristidou, M., Demetre, A.: A Note on Quaternion Rings over $\mathbb{Z}_p$. International Journal of Algebra 3, 725–728 (2009)

[2] Billet, O., Gilbert, H.: Cryptanalysis of Rainbow. In: De Prisco, R., Yung, M. (eds.) SCN 2006. LNCS, vol. 4116, pp. 336–347. Springer, Heidelberg (2006)

[3] Computational Algebra Group, University of Sydney. The MAGMA Computational Algebra System for Algebra, Number Theory and Geometry, http://magma.maths.usyd.edu.au/magma/

[4] Ding, J., Schmidt, D.: Rainbow, a New Multivariable Polynomial Signature Scheme. In: Ioannidis, J., Keromytis, A.D., Yung, M. (eds.) ACNS 2005. LNCS, vol. 3531, pp. 164–175. Springer, Heidelberg (2005)

[5] Ding, J., Yang, B.-Y., Chen, C.-H.O., Chen, M.-S., Cheng, C.-M.: New Differential-Algebraic Attacks and Reparametrization of Rainbow. In: Bellovin, S.M., Gennaro, R., Keromytis, A.D., Yung, M. (eds.) ACNS 2008. LNCS, vol. 5037, pp. 242–257. Springer, Heidelberg (2008)

[6] Faugère, J.-C., Levy-dit-Vehel, F., Perret, L.: Cryptanalysis of MinRank. In: Wagner, D. (ed.) CRYPTO 2008. LNCS, vol. 5157, pp. 280–296. Springer, Heidelberg (2008)

[7] Goubin, L., Courtois, N.T.: Cryptanalysis of the TTM Cryptosystem. In: Okamoto, T. (ed.) ASIACRYPT 2000. LNCS, vol. 1976, pp. 44–57. Springer, Heidelberg (2000)

[8] Kipnis, A., Patarin, J., Goubin, L.: Unbalanced Oil and Vinegar Signature Schemes. In: Stern, J. (ed.) EUROCRYPT 1999. LNCS, vol. 1592, pp. 206–222. Springer, Heidelberg (1999)

[9] Kipnis, A., Shamir, A.: Cryptanalysis of the Oil & Vinegar Signature Scheme. In: Krawczyk, H. (ed.) CRYPTO 1998. LNCS, vol. 1462, pp. 257–266. Springer, Heidelberg (1998)

[10] Lidl, R., Niederreiter, H.: Finite Fields, 2nd edn. EMA, vol. 20. CUP, Cambridge (1997)

[11] Petzoldt, A., Bulygin, S., Buchmann, J.: CyclicRainbow – A Multivariate Signature Scheme with a Partially Cyclic Public Key. In: Gong, G., Gupta, K.C. (eds.) INDOCRYPT 2010. LNCS, vol. 6498, pp. 33–48. Springer, Heidelberg (2010)

[12] Petzoldt, A., Bulygin, S., Buchmann, J.: Selecting Parameters for the Rainbow Signature Scheme. In: Sendrier, N. (ed.) PQCrypto 2010. LNCS, vol. 6061, pp. 218–240. Springer, Heidelberg (2010)

[13] Petzoldt, A., Thomae, E., Bulygin, S., Wolf, C.: Small Public Keys and Fast Verification for Multivariate Quadratic Public Key Systems. In: Preneel, B., Takagi, T. (eds.) CHES 2011. LNCS, vol. 6917, pp. 475–490. Springer, Heidelberg (2011)

[14] Pierce, R.S.: Associative Algebras, p. 16. Springer (1982)

[15] Thomae, E.: A Generalization of the Rainbow Band Separation Attack and its Applications to Multivariate Schemes (2012), http://eprint.iacr.org/2012/223

[16] Thomae, E., Wolf, C.: Solving Underdetermined Systems of Multivariate Quadratic Equations Revisited. In: Fischlin, M., Buchmann, J., Manulis, M. (eds.) PKC 2012. LNCS, vol. 7293, pp. 156–171. Springer, Heidelberg (2012)

[17] Yasuda, T., Sakurai, K., Takagi, T.: Reducing the Key Size of Rainbow Using Non-commutative Rings. In: Dunkelman, O. (ed.) CT-RSA 2012. LNCS, vol. 7178, pp. 68–83. Springer, Heidelberg (2012)

Homomorphic Encryption
for Multiplications and Pairing Evaluation

Guilhem Castagnos[1] and Fabien Laguillaumie[2]

[1] Institut de Mathématiques de Bordeaux, Université Bordeaux 1/CNRS
351, cours de la Libération, 33405 Talence cedex, France
`guilhem.castagnos@math.u-bordeaux1.fr`
[2] Université de Caen Basse-Normandie and CNRS/ENSL/INRIA/UCBL LIP
Laboratoire de l'Informatique du Parallélisme
46 Allée d'Italie, 69364 Lyon, France
`fabien.laguillaumie@unicaen.fr`

Abstract. We propose a generic approach to design homomorphic encryption schemes, which extends Gjøsteen's framework. From this generic method, we deduce a new homomorphic encryption scheme in a composite-order subgroup of points of an elliptic curve which admits a pairing $e : \mathbf{G} \times \mathbf{G} \to \mathbf{G}_t$. This scheme has some interesting theoretical and practical properties: it allows an arbitrary number of multiplications in the groups $\mathbf{G}$ *and* $\mathbf{G}_t$, *as well as* a pairing evaluation on the underlying plaintexts. We prove the semantic security under chosen plaintext attack of our scheme under a generalized subgroup membership assumption, and we also prove that it *cannot* achieve ind-cca1 security. We eventually propose an original application to shared decryption. On the theoretical side, this scheme is an example of cryptosystem which can be naturally implemented with groups of prime order, as the homomorphic properties require only a *projecting* pairing using Freeman's terminology. However the application to shared decryption also relies on the fact that the pairing is *cancelling* and therefore does not survive this conversion.

1 Introduction

Homomorphic encryption scheme allows one to operate on plaintexts, only from their given ciphertexts. The Elgamal encryption is a classical example of such a homomorphic encryption, since, given two ciphertexts, it is easy to obtain the encryption of the product of the two corresponding plaintexts. This malleability property is of crucial interest since it is the core of many electronic realizations of real-life applications like electronic voting [BFP+01, DJ01], private information retrieval [Lip05], verifiable encryption [FPS00], mix-nets [NSNK06, Jur03], auction protocols [MMO10], *etc.* In most of these cases, there is a need for an *additively* homomorphic encryption, in the sense that it is possible to obtain the encryption of the sum of plaintexts. Since the introduction of the first probabilistic encryption scheme by Goldwasser and Micali in 1984 [GM84] (where they also formally defined the notion of semantic security for encryption), many

I. Visconti and R. De Prisco (Eds.): SCN 2012, LNCS 7485, pp. 374–392, 2012.
© Springer-Verlag Berlin Heidelberg 2012

schemes were designed along the same lines, like Benaloh [Ben88], Naccache and Stern [NS98], or Okamoto and Uchiyama [OU98]. These cryptosystems are based on modular arithmetic, and use indeed several quotients of $\mathbf{Z}$, so that their one-wayness relies on the hardness of the factorization of (special form of) RSA modulus and their semantic security on distinguishing some powers. Significant improvements appear in the subsequent scheme designed by Paillier [Pai99] in 1999 which is still very popular. Its semantic security is based on the decisional composite residuosity assumption. Paillier's scheme has then been generalized by Damgård and Jurik [DJ01], allowing one to encrypt larger messages. All these schemes fit Gjøsteen's framework around subgroup membership problems [Gjo04, Gjo05], which encompasses also multiplicative schemes like Elgamal. Encryption schemes supporting both additive and multiplicative homomorphisms are of course critical for the design of highly functional cryptosystems. A spectacular breakthrough was made by Gentry who proposed the first *fully homomorphic* encryption scheme [Gen09], which allows to compute *arbitrary* functions over encrypted data without the decryption key. Recent works show that efficiency of such systems could become reality (see for instance some solutions based on the (ring) *learning with error problems* [BV11, BGV12]). On the way towards practical fully homomorphic encryption are schemes that partially support additive and multiplicative homomorphisms, like Boneh, Goh and Nissim's scheme (BGN) [BGN05]. It is based on groups of points of elliptic curves of composite orders which admit a pairing, supports an arbitrary number of additions and only one multiplication. This remains sufficient to make possible the evaluation of a formula in disjunctive normal form where each conjunction has at most 2 literals. In practice, this provides efficient solutions, with quite standard objects, for operations on encrypted data which do not require fully homomorphic schemes, such as search or statistics.

Our Contributions. In this paper, we propose a homomorphic encryption scheme which supports an arbitrary number of group operations and *pairing evaluation* on the underlying plaintexts. We first give a generic construction of a homomorphic scheme which goes a step forward compared to Gjøsteen's framework and extends its properties. We provide an instantiation within groups of composite orders with a pairing which has richer homomorphic properties, and discuss if this instantiation can be moved into a prime-order setting.

One of the features of our new scheme is that it is possible to encrypt *any* element of a subgroup of composite order of the group of points of a pairing-friendly elliptic curve. Moreover, it is publicly possible, given the encryptions of two points, to compute the encryption of the products of these points (if we consider the group of points of the curve as multiplicative). It is as well possible to publicly compute an encryption of the pairing of these two points. To finish, given the encryptions of two pairing evaluations, it is possible to publicly compute an encryption of the product of these values.

Even if the global setting of our scheme (bilinear groups of composite order) is quite similar to the setting of BGN, the malleability properties of our scheme are indeed very different from the ones of BGN. This comes from the fact that the plaintexts of BGN are *small* integers (or elements of $\mathbf{Z}/2\mathbf{Z}$) encoded in elliptic curve points by exponentiation whereas plaintexts of our scheme are just points.

Quite surprisingly, our system is *not* ind $-$ cca1 (cf. Prop. 1). This result proves that even with strong assumptions, there exist homomorphic schemes which cannot reach such a level of security. Moreover, the role of the splitting problem in our system makes it possible to provide a natural and original application to shared decryption, that does not rely on traditional secret sharing techniques. Concerning the conversion in the prime-order setting, we are able to benefit from Freeman's transformation (cf. [Fre10, MSF10, SC12]) from pairing-based schemes in composite-order groups into equivalent ones in prime-order groups: Our basic scheme can be directly converted, which gives a more efficient cryptosystem, based on the Decision Linear Problem. However, the nice result on ind $-$ cca1 security and the application to shared decryption do not survive this conversion. This may give an evidence of the existence of limits to Freeman's transformation.

The paper is organized as follows. In section 2, we give the necessary background to define a homomorphic encryption scheme for multiplications and pairing evaluation. In section 3, we describe a generic construction of a multiplicative homomorphic scheme. This construction gives schemes whose one-wayness is based on a generalization of the splitting problem in finite groups and whose semantic security is based on a generalization of the symmetric subgroup membership problem. These problems have been introduced by Gjøsteen [Gjo04, Gjo05] and our generic construction can be viewed as a generalization of his construction with more than two subgroups. An instantiation of our construction in quotients of $\mathbf{Z}$ can be found in [GBD05]. Section 4 is devoted to an instantiation in bilinear groups of composite order that gives a concrete and efficient homomorphic scheme for multiplications and pairing evaluation. As detailed in that section, it is necessary, contrary to BGN, to use groups whose order is the product of at least *three* prime numbers to get a secure scheme. At the end of this section we give an application to shared decryption. Eventually, we compare our new cryptosystem with existing schemes and discuss the (im)possibility to move our scheme into a prime-order setting.

2   Background

2.1   Encryption Scheme: Definitions

Definition. Let $\lambda \in \mathbf{N}$ be a security parameter. An encryption scheme is a triple of algorithms $\mathcal{E} = (\mathsf{KeyGen}, \mathsf{Encrypt}, \mathsf{Decrypt})$. The probabilistic polynomial-time key generation algorithm KeyGen takes 1^λ as input and returns a pair (pk, sk) of public key and the matching secret key. The probabilistic polynomial-time encryption algorithm $\mathsf{Encrypt}$ takes 1^λ, a public key pk and a message m as inputs, and outputs a ciphertext c. The deterministic polynomial-time decryption algorithm $\mathsf{Decrypt}$ takes 1^λ, a secret key sk and a ciphertext c as inputs and returns either a message m or the symbol $\perp$ which indicates the invalidity of the ciphertext. The scheme must be *correct*, which means that for all security parameters λ, and for all messages m, if $(pk, sk) \xleftarrow{\$} \mathcal{E}.\mathsf{KeyGen}(1^\lambda)$ then $\mathcal{E}.\mathsf{Decrypt}(1^\lambda, sk, \mathcal{E}.\mathsf{Encrypt}(1^\lambda, pk, m)) = m$ with probability (taken on all internal random coins and random choices) 1.

Security Requirements. The *total break* of an encryption scheme is declared if an attacker can recover the secret key from (at least) the public key. Therefore any probabilistic polynomial-time Turing machine $\mathcal{A}$ (the *attacker*) must have a success in recovering the public key arbitrarily small, where the *success* is defined, for an integer λ, as $\mathbf{Succ}_{\mathcal{E}}^{\mathsf{tb}}(\mathcal{A}) = \Pr\big[(pk, sk) \xleftarrow{\$} \mathcal{E}.\mathsf{KeyGen}(1^\lambda) : \mathcal{A}(pk) = sk\big].$

A stronger security notion expected from an encryption scheme is the *one-wayness*, which means that, given only the public data, an adversary cannot recover the message corresponding to a given ciphertext. More precisely, if we denote by $\mathcal{M}$ the set of plaintexts, any probabilistic polynomial-time Turing machine $\mathcal{A}$ has a success in inverting the encryption algorithm arbitrarily small, where the *success* is defined, for an integer λ, as $\mathbf{Succ}_{\mathcal{E}}^{\mathsf{ow}}(\mathcal{A})$ equals to

$$\Pr\big[(pk, sk) \xleftarrow{\$} \mathcal{E}.\mathsf{KeyGen}(1^\lambda), m \xleftarrow{\$} \mathcal{M} : \mathcal{A}(pk, \mathcal{E}.\mathsf{Encrypt}(1^\lambda, pk, m)) = m\big].$$

Note that the previous definition supposes that the attacker has no more information than the public key : the attacker is said to do a *chosen-plaintext attack* (since he can produce the ciphertext of messages of his choice). If he has access to a decryption oracle, the attack is said be a *chosen-ciphertext attack*.

An encryption scheme must indeed reach a stronger notion of security : it must have *semantic security* (a.k.a. *indistinguishability*). This means that an attacker is computationally unable to distinguish between two messages, chosen by himself, which one has been encrypted, with a probability significantly better than one half. The *indistinguishability game* is formally defined as:

Experiment $\mathbf{Exp}_{\mathcal{E}}^{\mathsf{ind-atk}}(\mathcal{A})$

$(pk, sk) \xleftarrow{\$} \mathcal{E}.\mathsf{KeyGen}(1^\lambda)$

$(m_0, m_1, s) \xleftarrow{\$} \mathcal{A}_1^{\mathcal{O}_1}(pk)$

$b^\star \xleftarrow{\$} \{0, 1\}$ with

$c^\star \xleftarrow{\$} \mathcal{E}.\mathsf{Encrypt}(1^\lambda, pk, m_{b^\star})$

$b \xleftarrow{\$} \mathcal{A}_2^{\mathcal{O}_2}(s, c^\star)$

if $b = b^\star$ then return 1

else return 0

- atk = cpa and
  - $\mathcal{O}_1 = \emptyset$
  - $\mathcal{O}_2 = \emptyset$
- atk = cca1 and
  - $\mathcal{O}_1 = \mathcal{E}.\mathsf{Decrypt}(1^\lambda, sk, \cdot)$
  - $\mathcal{O}_2 = \emptyset$
- atk = cca2 and
  - $\mathcal{O}_1 = \mathcal{E}.\mathsf{Decrypt}(1^\lambda, sk, \cdot)$
  - $\mathcal{O}_2 = \mathcal{E}.\mathsf{Decrypt}(1^\lambda, sk, \cdot)$

where the adversary $\mathcal{A}$ is modeled as a 2-stage probabilistic polynomial-time Turing machine $(\mathcal{A}_1, \mathcal{A}_2)$. In the CCA2 game, a natural restriction is imposed to $\mathcal{A}_2$ which is not allowed to query $\mathcal{O}_2$ on $c^\star$. The *advantage* of the attacker is then defined as $\mathbf{Adv}_{\mathcal{E}}^{\mathsf{ind-atk}}(\mathcal{A}) = \left|\Pr\big(\mathbf{Exp}_{\mathcal{E}}^{\mathsf{ind-atk}}(\mathcal{A}) = 1\big) - \frac{1}{2}\right|.$

It is well known that encryption schemes which enjoy homomorphic properties, cannot achieve the highest level of security (namely IND-CCA2 security), but can still achieve IND-CCA1 security (see for instance [APK10]).

2.2 Homomorphic Encryption for Multiplications and Pairing Evaluation

In order to describe more precisely our new encryption scheme with its features, we will use the following less general definition of encryption schemes but more adapted to our setting.

First of all, the set of plaintexts will be composed of two distinct *multiplicative groups* $(\mathbf{M}, \times_{\mathbf{M}})$ and $(\mathbf{M_t}, \times_{\mathbf{M_t}})$. Similarly, the set of ciphertexts is composed of two distinct sets $\mathbf{C}$ and $\mathbf{C_t}$ corresponding respectively to encryptions of elements of $\mathbf{M}$ and $\mathbf{M_t}$. Moreover, a particular characteristic of our encryption scheme is that there is a function e (a *pairing*) mapping elements from $\mathbf{M} \times \mathbf{M}$ onto elements of $\mathbf{M_t}$.

Definition 1. *Let $\lambda \in \mathbf{N}$ be a security parameter. An* homomorphic encryption scheme for multiplications and pairing evaluation *is composed of the following algorithms:*

- KeyGen *is a probabilistic algorithm which takes as input 1^λ and outputs the keys pair (pk, sk) of public and secret key respectively, the groups of plaintexts $\mathbf{M}$ and $\mathbf{M_t}$, the sets of ciphertexts $\mathbf{C}$ and $\mathbf{C_t}$ and the pairing $e : \mathbf{M} \times \mathbf{M} \to \mathbf{M_t}$. The description of the groups $\mathbf{M}, \mathbf{M_t}, \mathbf{C}, \mathbf{C_t}$ and of the pairing e will be common parameters for each of the following algorithms;*
- Encrypt *is a probabilistic algorithm which takes as inputs 1^λ, the public key pk and a plaintext m. If $m \in \mathbf{M}$ it outputs a ciphertext $c \in \mathbf{C}$ else if $m \in \mathbf{M_t}$ it outputs a ciphertext $c \in \mathbf{C_t}$;*
- Decrypt *is a deterministic algorithm which takes as inputs 1^λ, the secret key sk and a ciphertext c. It outputs either a plaintext m (in $\mathbf{M}$ if $c \in \mathbf{C}$ and in $\mathbf{M_t}$ if $c \in \mathbf{C_t}$) or $\perp$;*
- EvalMul *is a probabilistic algorithm which takes as inputs 1^λ, the public key pk and two ciphertexts c and c' of unknown plaintexts m and m' of the same group. If c and c' are elements of $\mathbf{C}$, it outputs an element $c'' \in \mathbf{C}$ which is a random encryption[1] of $m \times_{\mathbf{M}} m'$; else if c and c' are elements of $\mathbf{C_t}$ it outputs a random encryption $c'' \in \mathbf{C_t}$ of $m \times_{\mathbf{M_t}} m'$;*
- EvalPair *is a probabilistic algorithm which takes as inputs 1^λ, a public key pk, and two ciphertexts c and c' of $\mathbf{C}$ of unknown plaintexts m and m' of $\mathbf{M}$. It outputs a random encryption $c'' \in \mathbf{C_t}$ of $e(m, m') \in \mathbf{M_t}$.*

These algorithms must verify the different correctness *properties, defined as follows. For all $\lambda \in \mathbf{N}$,*

$$\Pr\big[(pk, sk) \xleftarrow{\$} \mathsf{KeyGen}(1^\lambda), m \xleftarrow{\$} \mathbf{M} \cup \mathbf{M_t}, c \xleftarrow{\$} \mathsf{Encrypt}(1^\lambda, pk, m) :$$
$$\mathsf{Decrypt}(1^\lambda, sk, c) = m\big] = 1.$$

$$\Pr\big[(pk, sk) \xleftarrow{\$} \mathsf{KeyGen}(1^\lambda), m \xleftarrow{\$} \mathbf{M}, m' \xleftarrow{\$} \mathbf{M},$$
$$c \xleftarrow{\$} \mathsf{Encrypt}(1^\lambda, pk, m), c' \xleftarrow{\$} \mathsf{Encrypt}(1^\lambda, pk, m'), c'' \xleftarrow{\$} \mathsf{EvalMul}(1^\lambda, c, c', pk) :$$
$$\mathsf{Decrypt}(1^k, sk, c'') = m \times_{\mathbf{M}} m'\big] = 1$$

---

[1] By *random encryption*, we mean that the distribution of the outputs c'' of EvalMul is the same as the distribution of the encryption algorithm on inputs $m \times_{\mathbf{M}} m'$.

$$\Pr\big[(pk, sk) \xleftarrow{\$} \mathsf{KeyGen}(1^\lambda), m \xleftarrow{\$} \mathbf{M_t}, m' \xleftarrow{\$} \mathbf{M_t},$$
$$c \xleftarrow{\$} \mathsf{Encrypt}(1^\lambda, pk, m), c' \xleftarrow{\$} \mathsf{Encrypt}(1^\lambda, pk, m'), c'' \xleftarrow{\$} \mathsf{EvalMul}(1^\lambda, c, c', pk) :$$
$$\mathsf{Decrypt}(1^k, sk, c'') = m \times_{\mathbf{M_t}} m'\big] = 1$$

and for pairing evaluation:

$$\Pr\big[(pk, sk) \xleftarrow{\$} \mathsf{KeyGen}(1^\lambda), m \xleftarrow{\$} \mathbf{M}, m' \xleftarrow{\$} \mathbf{M},$$
$$c \xleftarrow{\$} \mathsf{Encrypt}(1^\lambda, pk, m), c' \xleftarrow{\$} \mathsf{Encrypt}(1^\lambda, pk, m'), c'' \xleftarrow{\$} \mathsf{EvalPair}(1^\lambda, c, c', pk) :$$
$$\mathsf{Decrypt}(1^k, sk, c'') = e(m, m)'\big] = 1$$

At that point, it is important to keep in mind that in our scheme, a first level of plaintexts will lie in the group $(\mathbf{M}, \times_{\mathbf{M}})$ and their corresponding ciphertexts will lie in the set $\mathbf{C}$. Once $\mathsf{EvalPair}$ is evaluated on two such ciphertexts, the result is an encryption of the pairing of the original first level plaintexts from $\mathbf{M}$ and so lies in $\mathbf{C_t}$: this gives a second level of ciphertexts, corresponding to the second level of plaintexts $\mathbf{M_t}$. Since the homomorphic property will also apply on the second level, it is possible to obtain the encryption of products of such pairings. This is why our scheme is homomorphic for the two multiplications $\times_{\mathbf{M}}$ *and* $\times_{\mathbf{M_t}}$ *and* for the pairing evaluation.

Another important remark is that the scheme can not be semantically secure for the whole message set: The first stage adversary of the indistinguishability game can pick one plaintext in $\mathbf{M}$ and the other one in $\mathbf{M_t}$. Then the second stage adversary will observe if the challenge ciphertext is in $\mathbf{C}$ or $\mathbf{C_t}$. The semantic security of the scheme will rather hold for plaintexts of $\mathbf{M}$ and for plaintexts of $\mathbf{M_t}$ separately.

3   General Setting

In this section, we first give a natural generic construction of an homomorphic scheme on which our instance of an homomorphic encryption scheme for multiplications and pairing evaluation will be based. This construction is quite natural but the algorithmic problem on which relies the one wayness of the scheme is *not*. That's why we give in Subsection 3.3 a particular setting of this construction for which the one wayness of the scheme is related to a classical splitting problem. This construction generalizes the scheme from [GBD05] in an abstract group with more than 2 subgroups. This generalization actually allows the design of richer cryptosystems: indeed, the scheme from [GBD05] does not support bilinear groups (see Subsection 4.2), whereas it is possible to implement our framework with such specific groups, which leads to an encryption scheme which is more versatile. In the next section, we show how to apply this construction to pairing-friendly elliptic curves to get the homomorphic encryption scheme for multiplications and pairing evaluation.

3.1   A Generic Construction

Let $\lambda \in \mathbf{N}$ be a security parameter and k be a fixed integer. Let $\mathbf{G}$ be a finite Abelian *multiplicative* group and for $i \in \{1, \ldots, k\}$, $\mathbf{H}_i$ is a subgroup of $\mathbf{G}$ of order denoted by $|\mathbf{H}_i|$. We impose that the orders of the subgroups $\mathbf{H}_1, \ldots, \mathbf{H}_k$ are k distinct integers of λ bits such that $\gcd(|\mathbf{H}_1|, \ldots, |\mathbf{H}_k|) = 1$. We denote $(u_1, \ldots, u_k)$ the integers such that $\sum_{i=1}^{k} u_i |\mathbf{H}_i| = 1$. We call Bézout the algorithm which computes these k values from the orders $|\mathbf{H}_1|, \ldots, |\mathbf{H}_k|$.

In the following, whenever a group appears in the input or output of an algorithm, it means that an efficient way to compute the group law is known and that we can sample random elements of this group. For example, the groups are cyclic and a generator is given.

We denote as GroupsGen the probabilistic algorithm that takes as input 1^λ and outputs the tuple $(\mathbf{G}, \mathbf{H}_1, \ldots, \mathbf{H}_k, |\mathbf{H}_1|, \ldots, |\mathbf{H}_k|)$. The public key pk consists of the groups $\mathbf{G}, \mathbf{H}_1, \ldots, \mathbf{H}_k$ whereas the private key sk will consist of their orders and the Bézout coefficients. More precisely, the key generation algorithm is as follows:

Algorithm KeyGen(1^λ)

$(\mathbf{G}, \mathbf{H}_1, \ldots, \mathbf{H}_k, |\mathbf{H}_1|, \ldots, |\mathbf{H}_k|) \xleftarrow{\$} \mathsf{GroupsGen}(1^\lambda)$
$(u_1, \ldots, u_k) \leftarrow \mathsf{Bézout}(|\mathbf{H}_1|, \ldots, |\mathbf{H}_k|)$
$pk \leftarrow (\mathbf{G}, \mathbf{H}_1, \ldots, \mathbf{H}_k)$
$sk \leftarrow (|\mathbf{H}_1|, \ldots, |\mathbf{H}_k|, u_1, \ldots, u_k)$
return (pk, sk)

The encryption algorithm will use the homomorphism $\Pi : \mathbf{G} \to \mathbf{G}/\mathbf{H}_1 \times \cdots \times \mathbf{G}/\mathbf{H}_k$. This homomorphism is the Cartesian product of the surjective homomorphisms $\pi_i : \mathbf{G} \to \mathbf{G}/\mathbf{H}_i$ for $i = 1, \ldots, k$. The set of plaintexts is defined to be $\mathbf{G}$. Let m be an element of $\mathbf{G}$: It is encrypted as a random representative of the k-tuple of classes $\Pi(m) = (m\mathbf{H}_1, \ldots, m\mathbf{H}_k) \in \mathbf{G}/\mathbf{H}_1 \times \cdots \times \mathbf{G}/\mathbf{H}_k$. For example, when generators $(h_1, \ldots, h_k)$ of $(\mathbf{H}_1, \ldots, \mathbf{H}_k)$ are publicly known, an encryption of m consists therefore of $(mh_1^{r_1}, \ldots, mh_k^{r_k})$ for random $r_1, \ldots, r_k \in \{1, \ldots, |\mathbf{G}|\}$. To decrypt $C = (c_1, \ldots, c_k) \in \mathbf{G}^k$, one computes $\prod_{i=1}^{k} c_i^{u_i |\mathbf{H}_i|}$. If C is an encryption of m, then $\prod_{i=1}^{k} c_i^{u_i |\mathbf{H}_i|} = m^{\sum_{i=1}^{k} u_i |\mathbf{H}_i|} = m$, and the encryption scheme is correct.

More formally, the encryption and decryption algorithms are described bellow. It is easy to see that this gives an homomorphic scheme : if C_1 (resp. C_2) is an encryption of m_1 (resp. m_2) then $C_1 C_2$ (with the component-wise multiplication) is an encryption of $m_1 m_2$ that can be randomized by a multiplication by a random element of $(\mathbf{H}_1, \ldots, \mathbf{H}_k)$.

Algorithm Encrypt($1^k, pk, m$)

$(\mathbf{G}, \mathbf{H}_1, \ldots, \mathbf{H}_k) \leftarrow pk$
$C \xleftarrow{\$} \Pi(m)$
return C

Algorithm Decrypt($1^k, sk, C$)

$(c_1, \ldots, c_k) \leftarrow C$
$(|\mathbf{H}_1|, \ldots, |\mathbf{H}_k|, u_1, \ldots, u_k) \leftarrow sk$
$m \leftarrow \prod_{i=1}^{k} c_i^{u_i |\mathbf{H}_i|}$
return m

3.2   Security of the Generic Construction

The *total break* under a *chosen plaintext attack* of the scheme presented in the previous subsection is equivalent to the following problem: given $\mathbf{G}$ and k of its subgroups $\mathbf{H}_1, \ldots, \mathbf{H}_k$, find the orders of $\mathbf{H}_1, \ldots, \mathbf{H}_k$. This is a standard *order-finding problem* which can be solved with standard algorithms for computing discrete logarithms. These algorithms are of complexity either exponential or sub-exponential in the security parameter, depending on context (when the discrete logarithm is supposed to be hard). If the order of $\mathbf{G}$ is given, the total break is equivalent to the factorization of this number, which is at least a λ bit integer (note that not the whole factorization of $|\mathbf{G}|$ might be found). The best algorithms for factoring have a sub-exponential complexity.

The *one wayness* of the scheme under a *chosen plaintext attack* is equivalent to the difficulty of the following problem: Given a random representative of the image $\Pi(m) \in \mathbf{G}/\mathbf{H}_1 \times \cdots \times \mathbf{G}/\mathbf{H}_k$, recover $m \in \mathbf{G}$. In the next subsection, we give a specific setting where this problem is equivalent to a more common problem, namely the *splitting problem* [Gjo05].

Concerning *the indistinguishability* under a *chosen plaintext attack*, we define the following problem, which is generally called a *subgroup membership problem*. In this specific form it is a direct generalization of the *symmetric subgroup membership problem* (cf. [Gjo04, Gjo05]), where $k = 2$, $\mathbf{H}_1 \cap \mathbf{H}_2 = \{1\}$ and $\mathbf{G} = \mathbf{H}_1\mathbf{H}_2$.

Definition 2 (Generalized Symmetric Subgroup Membership Problem). *The* generalized symmetric subgroup membership problem *(GSSMP) consists, given the tuple* $(\mathbf{G}, \mathbf{H}_1, \ldots, \mathbf{H}_k)$ *as input, in distinguishing the two distributions* $\mathbf{G} \times \cdots \times \mathbf{G}$ *and* $\mathbf{H}_1 \times \cdots \times \mathbf{H}_k$. *More formally, let us consider the following random experiment:*

Experiment $\mathbf{Exp}^{\mathsf{GSSMP}}_{\mathsf{GroupsGen}}(\mathcal{A})$

$(\mathbf{G}, \mathbf{H}_1, \ldots, \mathbf{H}_k, |\mathbf{H}_1|, \ldots, |\mathbf{H}_k|) \xleftarrow{\$} \mathsf{GroupsGen}(1^\lambda)$
$b^\star \xleftarrow{\$} \{0,1\}$
if $b^\star = 0$ then $X \xleftarrow{\$} \mathbf{G} \times \cdots \times \mathbf{G}$
   else $X \xleftarrow{\$} \mathbf{H}_1 \times \cdots \times \mathbf{H}_k$
$b \leftarrow \mathcal{A}(\mathbf{G}, \mathbf{H}_1, \ldots, \mathbf{H}_k, X)$
if $b = b^\star$ then return 1
   else return 0

The advantage *of* $\mathcal{A}$ *in solving the generalized symmetric subgroup membership problem is*

$$\mathbf{Adv}^{\mathsf{GSSMP}}_{\mathsf{GroupsGen}}(\mathcal{A}) = \left| \Pr[\mathbf{Exp}^{\mathsf{GSSMP}}_{\mathsf{GroupsGen}}(\mathcal{A}) = 1] - \frac{1}{2} \right|.$$

Theorem 1 (ind − cpa). *Let k be an integer. If there exists an attacker against the indistinguishability of the generic encryption scheme of subsection 3.1 with parameter k in a chosen plaintext attack with security parameter λ, running time τ and advantage ε, then there exists an algorithm for the generalized symmetric subgroup membership problem with the same security parameter, advantage $\varepsilon/2$ and running time $\tau + T_{k\text{-}Mul}$ where $T_{k\text{-}Mul}$ is the time to perform k multiplications in $\mathbf{G}$.*

Remark that conversely, given a distinguisher for the GSSMP, it is trivial to build an attacker for the semantic security. As a result, the two problems are polynomially equivalent.

3.3   A Particular Setting

A particular specialization of the generic construction of subsection 3.1, is when there exists subgroups $\mathbf{G}_1, \ldots, \mathbf{G}_k$ of $\mathbf{G}$ such that $\mathbf{G} = \prod_{i=1}^{k} \mathbf{G}_i$ and $\mathbf{G}_i \cap \mathbf{G}_j = \{1\}$ if $i \neq j$. We suppose that $|\mathbf{G}_1|, \ldots, |\mathbf{G}_k|$ are k distinct primes of $\lambda/(k-1)$ bits. In this case, we define the subgroups $\mathbf{H}_i$ as $\mathbf{H}_i = \prod_{j \neq i} \mathbf{G}_j$ for $i \in \{1, \ldots, k\}$.

We denote as GroupsGen' the algorithm that takes as input 1^λ and outputs the tuple $(\mathbf{G}, \mathbf{H}_1, \ldots, \mathbf{H}_k, |\mathbf{H}_1|, \ldots, |\mathbf{H}_k|, \mathbf{G}_1, \ldots, \mathbf{G}_k)$.

We still suppose that there exists a public method to sample random elements of $\mathbf{G}$ and of the subgroups $\mathbf{H}_1, \ldots, \mathbf{H}_k$. However, it is not necessary that anyone can sample elements of the subgroups $\mathbf{G}_1, \ldots, \mathbf{G}_k$ (as we shall see in subsection 4.2, such an implementation of the construction with elliptic curves equipped with pairings, actually leads to an insecure scheme). The encryption scheme is defined in the same way as in subsection 3.1. Only the construction of the subgroups $\mathbf{H}_1, \ldots, \mathbf{H}_k$ differs (with GroupsGen' instead of GroupsGen).

For each $i \in \{1, \ldots, k\}$, $\mathbf{G}/\mathbf{H}_i$ is isomorphic to $\mathbf{G}_i$. We denote as ϕ_i this isomorphism and as Φ the Cartesian product of the ϕ_i for $i \in \{1, \ldots, k\}$. This map Φ is an isomorphism between $\mathbf{G}/\mathbf{H}_1 \times \cdots \times \mathbf{G}/\mathbf{H}_k$ and $\mathbf{G}_1 \times \cdots \times \mathbf{G}_k$.

We have the following commutative diagram where each map is an isomorphism:

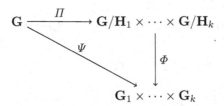

Let m be an element of $\mathbf{G}$, then there is a unique decomposition of m as a k–tuple $(m_1, \ldots, m_k) \in \mathbf{G}_1 \times \cdots \times \mathbf{G}_k$ such that $m = \prod_{i=1}^{k} m_i$. The map Ψ corresponds to this decomposition, and Ψ^{-1} is the computation of the product $\prod_{i=1}^{k} m_i$.

Remark 1. Decrypting a ciphertext $C = (c_1, \ldots, c_k)$ associated to the plaintext m is closely related to the decomposition of Ψ as it corresponds to the computation of $\Psi^{-1} \circ \Phi$. More precisely, let us fix $i \in \{1, \ldots, k\}$ and let us consider a representative $c_i = m h_i \in \mathbf{G}$ of $\pi_i(m)$ with $h_i \in \mathbf{H}_i$. Remember that we have $\sum_{j=1}^{k} u_j |\mathbf{H}_j| = 1$. Modulo $|\mathbf{G}_i|$ this sum gives $u_i |\mathbf{H}_i| = 1$ as $|\mathbf{G}_i|$ divides all $|\mathbf{H}_j|$ with $j \neq i$. As a consequence, if $(m_1, \ldots, m_k) = \Psi(m)$, then $m_j^{u_i |\mathbf{H}_i|} = 1$ if $j \neq i$ and $m_i^{u_i |\mathbf{H}_i|} = m_i$. The decryption $\prod_{i=1}^{k} c_i^{u_i |\mathbf{H}_i|}$ gives $\prod_{i=1}^{k} c_i^{u_i |\mathbf{H}_i|} = \prod_{i=1}^{k} (m h_i)^{u_i |\mathbf{H}_i|} = \prod_{i=1}^{k} (m_1 m_2 \ldots m_k)^{u_i |\mathbf{H}_i|} = \prod_{i=1}^{k} m_i = m$.

To sum up, the decryption process corresponds to the computation of the tuple $(m_1, \ldots, m_k)$ with Φ and making their product with ψ^{-1}.

In this special setting, breaking the one wayness of the encryption scheme is equivalent to solving a direct generalization of a well known problem, the splitting problem defined in (cf. [Gjo04, Gjo05]) where $k = 2$.

Definition 3 (Splitting Problem). *The* splitting problem *consists, given the tuple* $(\mathbf{G}, \mathbf{H}_1, \ldots, \mathbf{H}_k)$ *and* $m \in \mathbf{G}$, *in finding* $(m_1, \ldots, m_k) \in \mathbf{G}_1 \times \cdots \times \mathbf{G}_k$ *such that* $m = \prod_{i=1}^{k} m_i$. *More formally, let us consider the following random experiment:*

Experiment $\mathbf{Exp}_{\mathsf{GroupsGen}'}^{\mathsf{SP}}(\mathcal{A})$

> $(\mathbf{G}, \mathbf{H}_1, \ldots, \mathbf{H}_k, |\mathbf{H}_1|, \ldots, |\mathbf{H}_k|, \mathbf{G}_1, \ldots, \mathbf{G}_k) \leftarrow \mathsf{GroupsGen}'(1^\lambda)$
> $m \xleftarrow{\$} \mathbf{G}$
> $(m_1, \ldots, m_k) \leftarrow \mathcal{A}(\mathbf{G}, \mathbf{H}_1, \ldots, \mathbf{H}_k, m)$
> if $\forall i \in \{1, \ldots, k\}, m_i \in \mathbf{G}_i$ and $\prod_{i=1}^{k} m_i = m$ then return 1
>   else return 0

> *The* success *of* $\mathcal{A}$ *in solving the splitting problem is*

$$\mathbf{Succ}_{\mathsf{GroupsGen}'}^{\mathsf{SP}}(\mathcal{A}) = \Pr\left[\mathbf{Exp}_{\mathsf{GroupsGen}'}^{\mathsf{SP}}(\mathcal{A}) = 1\right].$$

Theorem 2 (One-Wayness-CPA). *If there exists an attacker against the one-wayness under a chosen plaintext attack of the encryption scheme of subsection 3.3 with security parameter* λ, *running time* τ *and success* ε, *then there exists an algorithm for the splitting problem with the same security parameter, success* ε^k *and running time* $\tau + (k+1)T_{k\text{-}Mul} + T_{k\text{-}Inv} + (k+1)T_{k\text{-}Rand}$ *where* $T_{k\text{-}Mul}$ *(resp.* $T_{k\text{-}Inv}$*) is the time to perform a multiplication (resp. an inversion) in* $\mathbf{G} \times \cdots \times \mathbf{G}$, *and* $T_{k\text{-}Rand}$ *the time to sample a random element of* $\mathbf{H}_1 \times \cdots \times \mathbf{H}_k$.

Proof. Let us denote $\mathcal{E}'$ the encryption scheme of this subsection and suppose that there is an attacker $\mathcal{A}$ which succeeds in breaking the one-wayness of the scheme with probability $\varepsilon = \mathbf{Succ}_{\mathcal{E}'}^{\mathsf{OW}}(\mathcal{A})$ and running time τ. We show that this attacker can be used to design a successful algorithm $\mathcal{B}$ which solves the Splitting Problem. The challenge of $\mathcal{B}$ consists of $(\mathbf{G}, \mathbf{H}_1, \ldots, \mathbf{H}_k, m)$. Let us denote $\Psi(m) = (m_1, \ldots, m_k)$, the solution that $\mathcal{B}$ is looking for. The algorithm $\mathcal{B}$ first retrieves m_1 thanks to its oracle $\mathcal{A}$. Let $(h_1, \ldots, h_k)$ be a random element of $\mathbf{H}_1 \times \cdots \times \mathbf{H}_k$ and f another random element of $\mathbf{H}_1$. $\mathcal{B}$ builds the ciphertext $C = (mh_1, h_2f, \ldots, h_kf)$. Denote $(1, f_2, \ldots, f_k) = \Psi(f)$. It is easy to see that C is a random encryption of $m_1 f_2 f_3 \ldots f_k = m_1 f$ where f is known by $\mathcal{B}$. As a result, $\mathcal{B}$ forward the public key $(\mathbf{G}, \mathbf{H}_1, \ldots, \mathbf{H}_k)$ and the ciphertext C to $\mathcal{A}$, and gets m_1 with probability ε. Iterating this procedure, $\mathcal{B}$ outputs $(m_1, \ldots, m_k)$ with probability ε^k, k calls to $\mathcal{A}$, $k+1$ samples of random elements of $\mathbf{H}_1 \times \cdots \times \mathbf{H}_k$ and $(k+1)$ multiplications and one inversion in $\mathbf{G} \times \cdots \times \mathbf{G}$. $\qquad\square$

Again, there is an equivalence between the two problems. Let us denote $C = (c_1, c_2, \ldots, c_k)$ an encryption of m where $c_i = mh_i$, with $h_i \in \mathbf{H}_i$ for all $i \in \{1, \ldots, k\}$ and $(m_1, m_2, \ldots, m_k) = \Psi(m)$. For $i \in \{1, \ldots, k\}$, $\Psi(c_i) = \Psi(m)\Psi(h_i)$ and $\Psi(h_i) = (h_{i,1}, \ldots, h_{i,i-1}, 1, h_{i,i+1}, \ldots, h_{i,k})$ due to the construction of $\mathbf{H}_i$. As a result, an oracle for the Splitting Problem called on the input c_i gives m_i in the i-th coordinate. With k calls to the oracle, one can retrieve $m = m_1 m_2 \ldots m_k$ and break the one wayness of the encryption scheme.

3.4   Known Implementations of the Construction

Let $p = 2n + 1$, $n = q_1 q_2$ where p, q_1, q_2 are distinct primes. The particular setting described in the previous subsection was used in [GBD05] with $\mathbf{G}$ the cyclic subgroup of the multiplicative group $(\mathbf{Z}/p\mathbf{Z})^*$ of order n and $k = 2$. The subgroup $\mathbf{H}_1 = \mathbf{G}_2$ (resp. $\mathbf{H}_2 = \mathbf{G}_1$) is the cyclic subgroup of order q_2 (resp. of order q_1). In this work the Splitting Problem was named Projection Problem. This scheme was generalized in an abstract group $\mathbf{G}$ still with $k = 2$ in [Bro07]. Our construction can thus be viewed as a generalization of this last work with $k \geq 2$. Other schemes based on the Symmetric Subgroup Membership Problem and the Splitting Problem are implementations of this construction, such as the scheme of [Gjo05].

4   A Concrete Homomorphic Scheme for Multiplications and Pairing Evaluation

In this section, we consider the construction of subsection 3.3 in a context of pairing-friendly elliptic curves. This means that there exists a non-degenerate efficiently computable bilinear map $e : \mathbf{G} \times \mathbf{G} \to \mathbf{G_t}$, where $\mathbf{G_t}$ is a group isomorphic to $\mathbf{G}$ called the target group. In this case, $\mathbf{G}$ is essentially a group of points of an elliptic curve. We will then enjoy a double homomorphic property: The homomorphy for the group of points of the elliptic curve and the homomorphy in the target group of the pairing. As a result we will get a secure scheme satisfying Definition 1, which is more versatile than existing schemes.

4.1   Implementation of the Generic Construction with Bilinear Groups with Composite Orders

As in the generic construction, let k be a fixed integer and $\lambda \in \mathbf{N}$ be a security parameter. Let $q_1, \ldots, q_k$ be k distinct prime integers of λ bits and $n = \prod_{i=1}^{k} q_i$ be the product of these primes. The integer ℓ is defined as the smallest integer such that $p = \ell n - 1$ is prime and $p \equiv 2 \pmod 3$. The following construction of a bilinear group with composite order has been initially proposed in [BGN05] with $k = 2$.

Let us consider the supersingular elliptic curve of equation $y^2 = x^3 + 1$ defined over $\mathbf{F}_p$. The $\mathbf{F}_p$-rational points of this curve form a group of cardinality $p + 1 = \ell n$ and we denote by $\mathbf{G}$ its subgroup of order n. Let $\mathbf{G_t}$ be the subgroup of $(\mathbf{F}_{p^2})^*$

of order n. Finally, let $e : \mathbf{G} \times \mathbf{G} \to \mathbf{G_t}$ be the modified Weil Pairing as defined in [BF03, Mil04]. In [BRS11], a method with ordinary curves and embedding degree 1 is also proposed which is quite equivalent in terms of efficiency: For the supersingular curve construction, $\rho := \log p / \log n \approx 1$ (ℓ is less than 10 bits in practice, for a 1500 bits n) and the embedding degree is 2. In [BRS11], the curves constructed with embedding degree 1 have $\rho \approx 2$. So both constructions are close to the minimum $\rho \times \kappa = 2$ where κ is the embedding degree.

As in the construction of subsection 3.3, we denote by $\mathbf{G}_i$ the subgroup of $\mathbf{G}$ of order q_i, for all integers $i \in \{1, \dots, k\}$ and the subgroups $\mathbf{H}_i$ are again defined as $\mathbf{H}_i = \prod_{\substack{j=1 \\ j \neq i}}^{k} \mathbf{G}_j$. With these groups, one can apply the construction of subsection 3.3 to get an homomorphic encryption scheme in $\mathbf{G}$. Moreover, we can define the corresponding subgroups in $\mathbf{G}_t$ and we will get another homomorphic encryption scheme in $\mathbf{G}_t$. With the pairing e, we get an homomorphic encryption scheme for multiplications and pairing evaluation.

We denote as $\mathcal{BG}$ the algorithm which takes as input 1^λ and k and outputs the tuple $(\mathbf{G}, \mathbf{G}_t, e, \mathbf{H}_1, \dots, \mathbf{H}_k, \mathbf{G}_1, \dots, \mathbf{G}_k, q_1, \dots, q_k)$.

4.2   Insecure Instantiation with $k = 2$

If one chooses $k = 2$, then $\mathbf{H}_2 = \mathbf{G}_1$ is of order q_1 and $\mathbf{H}_1 = \mathbf{G}_2$ is of order q_2. In this case, the corresponding encryption scheme in $\mathbf{G}_t$ is a direct generalization of the [GBD05] scheme in $\mathbf{F}_{p^2}$. Unfortunately, in this case, the Generalized Symmetric Subgroup Membership Problem of Definition 2 is tractable and the encryption scheme is therefore not semantically secure. Indeed, as we want to be able to sample random elements of $\mathbf{H}_1$ and $\mathbf{H}_2$ then generators h_1 of order q_2 and h_2 of order q_1, must be public. In that case, we can easily recognize elements of $\mathbf{H}_1 \times \mathbf{H}_2$ thanks to the pairing e: Let $(x_1, x_2) \in \mathbf{G} \times \mathbf{G}$, then

$$(x_1, x_2) \in \mathbf{H}_1 \times \mathbf{H}_2 \iff e(x_1, h_2) = 1 \text{ and } e(x_2, h_1) = 1.$$

To see that fact, let g be a generator of $\mathbf{G}$ and let us write $h_2 = g^{rq_2}$ for some r prime to q_1 and $x_1 = g^{r'}$ for some integer r'. Then x_1 is an element of $\mathbf{H}_1$ if and only if q_1 divides r', if and only if $e(x_1, h_2) = e(g, g)^{rr'q_2} = 1$. The criterion for $x_2 \in \mathbf{H}_2$ holds by symmetry.

In the BGN scheme (cf. [BGN05]), a composite bilinear group with $k = 2$ is actually used. However, in that particular scheme, only a random generator of the subgroup $\mathbf{G}_1$ is given in the public key which makes the previous attack unfeasible. As a result, only messages modulo $\mathbf{G}_1$ can be encrypted. This is not a problem since in the BGN cryptosystem, only *small* plaintext messages m of $\mathbf{N}$ are encoded with the exponentiation $g \mapsto g^m$; the decryption can then be performed by the computation of a small discrete logarithm in basis g modulo $\mathbf{G}_1$. In our scheme, we want to encrypt *any* element of $\mathbf{G}$, that is why we also need to publish a generator of $\mathbf{G}_2$ and this attack is then possible. Therefore we need at least $k = 3$ to get a secure scheme.

4.3 Description of Our Scheme with $k = 3$

As previously said, to design a secure instantiation from our methodology, we need to use the bilinear groups with composite-order generator $\mathcal{BG}$ with k at least equals to 3. For simplicity, we expose our scheme with $k = 3$. This means that the integer n is the product of three primes $n = q_1 q_2 q_3$. We suppose also that h_i are random generators of the groups $\mathbf{H}_i$ of orders n/q_i for $i = 1, 2, 3$. They can be produced by taking a generator g of $\mathbf{G}$ and setting $h_i = g^{\alpha_i q_i}$, for random α_i prime to n.

Note that $e(g, g)$ generates the group $\mathbf{G_t}$ and $e(g, h_i)$ generates the subgroup of $\mathbf{G_t}$ of order n/q_i. We can therefore apply the generic construction in $\mathbf{G}$ and $\mathbf{G_t}$: to encrypt of elements of $\mathbf{G_t}$, instead of multiplying the message by a random power of h_i, one has to multiply by a random power of $e(g, h_i)$.

This gives an homomorphic scheme for multiplications and pairing evaluation with $\mathbf{M} = \mathbf{G}$, $\mathbf{M_t} = \mathbf{G_t}$, $\mathbf{C} = \mathbf{G}^3$ and $\mathbf{C_t} = \mathbf{G_t}^3$. This scheme is presented in Figure 1.

Algorithm KeyGen(1^λ)

$(\mathbf{G}, \mathbf{G}_t, e, \mathbf{H}_1, \mathbf{H}_2, \mathbf{H}_3, \mathbf{G}_1, \mathbf{G}_2, \mathbf{G}_3, q_1, q_2, q_3)$
$\quad \xleftarrow{\$} \mathcal{BG}(1^\lambda, k = 3)$
$g \xleftarrow{\$} \mathbf{G}$ of order n ; $g_t \leftarrow e(g, g)$
for i from 1 to 3 do
$\quad h_i \xleftarrow{\$} \mathbf{H}_i$ of order n/q_i
$\quad h_{t_i} \leftarrow e(g, h_i)$
$(u, v, w) \leftarrow \text{Bézout}(q_2 q_3, q_1 q_3, q_1 q_2)$
$n \leftarrow q_1 q_2 q_3$
$pk \leftarrow (g, h_1, h_2, h_3, g_t, h_{t_1}, h_{t_2}, h_{t_3}, n, \mathbf{G}, \mathbf{G_t}, e)$
$sk \leftarrow pk \cup (q_1, q_2, q_3, u, v, w)$
return (pk, sk)

Algorithm Encrypt$(1^\lambda, pk, m)$

if $m \in \mathbf{G}$ then
$\quad$ for i from 1 to 3 do
$\quad\quad r_i \xleftarrow{\$} \{1, \dots, n\}$
$\quad\quad c_i \leftarrow m h_i^{r_i}$
$\quad C \leftarrow (c_1, c_2, c_3)$
else
$\quad$ for i from 1 to 3 do
$\quad\quad r_i \xleftarrow{\$} \{1, \dots, n\}$
$\quad\quad c_i \leftarrow m h_{t_i}^{r_i}$
$\quad C \leftarrow (c_1, c_2, c_3)$
return C

Algorithm Decrypt$(1^\lambda, sk, C)$

$(c_1, c_2, c_3) \leftarrow C$
$m \leftarrow c_1^{u q_2 q_3} \times c_2^{v q_1 q_3} \times c_3^{w q_1 q_2}$
return m

Algorithm EvalPair$(1^k, pk, C, C')$

$(c_1, c_2, c_3) \leftarrow C$
$(c_1', c_2', c_3') \leftarrow C'$
for i from 1 to 3 do
$\quad r_i \xleftarrow{\$} \{1, \dots, n\}$
$\quad c_i'' \leftarrow e(c_i, c_i') h_{t_i}^{r_i}$
return (c_1'', c_2'', c_3'')

Algorithm EvalMul$(1^\lambda, pk, C, C')$

$(c_1, c_2, c_3) \leftarrow C$
$(c_1', c_2', c_3') \leftarrow C'$
if $C \in \mathbf{G}^3$ then
$\quad$ for i from 1 to 3 do
$\quad\quad r_i \xleftarrow{\$} \{1, \dots, n\}$
$\quad\quad c_i'' \leftarrow c_i c_i' h_i^{r_i}$
else
$\quad$ for i from 1 to 3 do
$\quad\quad r_i \xleftarrow{\$} \{1, \dots, n\}$
$\quad\quad c_i'' \leftarrow c_i c_i' h_{t_i}^{r_i}$
return (c_1'', c_2'', c_3'')

Fig. 1. Our new homomorphic encryption for multiplications and pairing evaluation

Correctness of Decryption and Homomorphic Properties. The correctness of the decryption algorithm follows from the generic construction. The homomorphic property of EvalMul for both multiplication in $\mathbf{G}$ and $\mathbf{G_t}$ can be checked easily. Concerning the pairing evaluation, for $i = 1, 2, 3$, we have

$$e(c_i, c_i') = e(mh_i^{r_i}, m'h_i^{r_i'}) = e(m, m')\underbrace{e(h_i^{r_i}, m')e(m, h_i^{r_i'})e(h_i^{r_i}, h_i^{r_i'})}_{\text{of order } n/q_i}$$

and the element $e(h_i^{r_i}, m')e(m, h_i^{r_i'})e(h_i^{r_i}, h_1^{r_i'})$ lies in the subgroup of $\mathbf{G_t}$ of order n/q_i, therefore $e(c_i, c_i')$ is the i-th part of an encryption of $e(m, m')$.

Security Results. The one-wayness of our scheme against chosen plaintext attacks follows from Theorem 2 if the splitting problem is hard. In $\mathbf{G}$, this means it must be hard to decompose an element m in $m_1, m_2, m_3 \in \mathbf{G_1} \times \mathbf{G_2} \times \mathbf{G_3}$ such that $m = m_1 m_2 m_3$. According to Theorem 1, our encryption scheme is semantically secure against chosen plaintext attacks for messages in $\mathbf{G}$ if the generalized symmetric subgroup membership problem with pairing is hard in $\mathbf{G}$, $i.e.$, if it is hard to distinguish elements of $\mathbf{H_1} \times \mathbf{H_2} \times \mathbf{H_3}$ in $\mathbf{G} \times \mathbf{G} \times \mathbf{G}$, given generators of $\mathbf{G}, \mathbf{H_1}, \mathbf{H_2}$ and $\mathbf{H_3}$ and a pairing $e : \mathbf{G} \times \mathbf{G} \to \mathbf{G_t}$. Given the pairing e, it is easy to see that this GSSMP problem in $\mathbf{G}$ reduces to the GSSMP problem in $\mathbf{G_t}$. As a consequence, under the assumption that the generalized symmetric subgroup membership problem with pairing is hard in $\mathbf{G}$, our encryption scheme is semantically secure against chosen plaintext attacks for both messages in $\mathbf{G}$ and in $\mathbf{G_t}$. This assumption can be proved to hold in the generic group model if factoring n is hard, following the lines of the proofs of [KSW08, Section A.2] and [JS08, Theorem 4].

Regarding the security against adaptive chosen ciphertexts attacks, the cryptosystem being homomorphic, it cannot be even one-way (ow − cca2) in this scenario. Little is known on the security of homomorphic schemes in the cca1 scenario without strong assumptions (cf. [BP04, APK10]). Surprisingly for our cryptosystem, we are able to prove that for messages in $\mathbf{G}$, ind − cca1 security cannot be reached. This result proves that even with strong assumptions, *all* the homomorphic schemes cannot be proved to be ind − cca1 secure.

Proposition 1. *The new homomorphic encryption for multiplications and pairing evaluation of Figure 1 is not* ind − cca1 *secure for plaintext messages in* $\mathbf{G}$.

Proof. Before getting its challenge ciphertext in the ind − cca1 experiment, an adversary can use its decryption oracle to decompose a random $x \in \mathbf{G}$ in $x_1, x_2, x_3 \in \mathbf{G_1} \times \mathbf{G_2} \times \mathbf{G_3}$ such that $x = x_1 x_2 x_3$ following the reduction of the proof of Theorem 2. Knowing elements of $\mathbf{G_1}, \mathbf{G_2}, \mathbf{G_3}$, the subgroups of order q_1, q_2 and q_3, the adversary can now solve the subgroup membership problem like in the case $k = 2$ (see subsection 4.2). Hence, he can break the indistinguishability of the scheme.

As the scheme is not $ind - cca1$ secure in $\mathbf{G}$, from $c = (c_1, c_2, c_3)$ a ciphertext for $m \in \mathbf{G}$, the attacker can get some information on m. For example, the proposition tells us that during a "lunchtime" attack, an attacker can solve the splitting problem and compute elements $x_1, x_2, x_3 \in \mathbf{G}_1 \times \mathbf{G}_2 \times \mathbf{G}_3$. As a result, he can compute, $e(c_i, x_i) = e(m_i, x_i)$ for $i \in \{1, \ldots, 3\}$. The product of these three pairings evaluations gives $e(m, x)$. If x is a generator, the adversary can further get the pairing evaluation of m with elements of $\mathbf{G}$ of his choice. Note that this lunchtime attack in not a full break, the adversary only gets a piece of information on the plaintext. Moreover this attack does not apply in $\mathbf{G_t}$. Note also that Proposition 1 can be generalized for all k.

4.4   Application to Shared Decryption

Our cryptosystem uses three projections whose kernels are subgroups of coprime orders. This particular setting makes it possible to design an original shared decryption process. Suppose that $c = (c_1, c_2, c_3)$ is an encryption of $m \in \mathbf{G}$. The goal is that three entities $\mathcal{A}_1, \mathcal{A}_2, \mathcal{A}_3$, cooperate to decrypt c. Moreover, we want to achieve some kind of robustness, *i.e.*, that each entity can check if the other ones give correct results. The protocol is a simple modification of our cryptosystem (see Figure 1) as follows: at the end of the KeyGen algorithm, performed by a trusted dealer, each $\mathcal{A}_i$ is given the public key together with the prime q_i. The Encrypt, EvalMul and EvalPair algorithms remain unchanged. During the new Decrypt algorithm, each entity recovers $m_i := c_i^{u_i(n/q_i)}$ where u_i is the inverse of n/q_i modulo q_i. Then, in a reconstruction phase, each party broadcasts m_i to the others and each party can recover the plaintext message $m = m_1 m_2 m_3$. The correctness of the decryption follows from Remark 1. Moreover, before the reconstruction, each entity $\mathcal{A}_i$ can check the validity of the message sent by the others. Without loss of generality, $\mathcal{A}_1$ can compute a random element $x_2 \in \mathbf{G}_2$ (resp. $x_3 \in \mathbf{G}_3$) by selecting a random power of $h_3^{q_1}$ (resp. of $h_2^{q_1}$). Following the discussion at the end of the previous subsection, $\mathcal{A}_1$ accepts m_2 and m_3 if and only if $e(c_i, x_i)$ equals $e(m_i, x_i)$ for $i \in \{2, 3\}$.

This process can be easily extended to more participants by using our construction with $k > 3$. We note that in this protocol, each $\mathcal{A}_i$ learns a part of the secret key and can break the semantic security of the scheme as he can generate elements of $\mathbf{G}_1, \mathbf{G}_2, \mathbf{G}_3$ and solve the subgroup membership problem (as in the case $k = 2$). However, we believe that this protocol is of interest because of its simplicity and originality compared to standard secret sharing techniques.

5   Comparison with Other Works and Conclusion

As we saw in subsection 4.2, the BGN scheme from [BGN05] is quite similar to ours but with $k = 2$. In that cryptosystem, only *small* plaintext messages m of $\mathbf{N}$ are encoded with the exponentiation $g \mapsto g^m$. This encoding allows to compute sums of messages by computing product of points and to get products with the pairing evaluations. We can also use this encoding in our cryptosystems to get such homomorphic properties. Contrary to our scheme, in the BGN cryptosystem one cannot get encryption of product of arbitrary points, and one cannot get encryption of pairings and of product of pairings. Thus the properties of our scheme are quite different from the ones of BGN.

In [BWY11, Lew12] a general subgroup decision problem is formulated, unifying several decision assumptions made in bilinear composite groups this past few years in the area of (hierarchical) identity-based encryption. This decision problem is different from GSSMP (see Def. 2): two of the subgroups play a different roles from the others, whereas in the problem we consider the role played by all subgroups $\mathbf{H}_i$ to be the same.

In [Fre10], Freeman provides a framework to translate features of composite-order bilinear groups in the prime-order setting. To this purpose, he defines two kinds of property for pairing: *cancelling* and *projecting*. Projecting intuitively means that the pairing and some projections maps commute. This is the core of our construction: a projection map is used in the decryption algorithm, since a ciphertext is projected in $\mathbf{G}_1 \times \mathbf{G}_2 \times \mathbf{G}_3 \simeq \mathbf{G}/\mathbf{H}_1 \times \mathbf{G}/\mathbf{H}_2 \times \mathbf{G}/\mathbf{H}_3$, and the product of each terms gives the plaintext message (cf. Remark 1). The fact that the projection and the pairing commute ensures that the pairing of two ciphertexts in $\mathbf{G}^3$ decrypts to the pairing of the corresponding plaintexts.

Our cryptosystem can thus be adapted in the prime-order setting following Freeman's construction of a projecting pairing to convert the BGN cryptosystem. For example, we can obtain a cryptosystem satisfying Definition 1 as follows: Let $e : G \times G \to G_t$ be a symmetric pairing where G and G_t are groups of prime order q. Freeman's framework (cf. [Fre10, subsection 3.1]) allows to construct a subgroup $\mathbf{H}$ of $\mathbf{G} = G^3$, a pairing $\hat{e} : \mathbf{G} \times \mathbf{G} \to G_t^9$ and a subgroup $\mathbf{H}_t$ of $\mathbf{G}_t := G_t^9$ such that there exits maps $\pi_1 : \mathbf{G} \to \mathbf{G}$ and $\pi_t : \mathbf{G}_t \to \mathbf{G}_t$ with $\mathbf{H} \subset \ker \pi_1$, $\mathbf{H}_t \subset \ker \pi_t$ and $\hat{e}(\pi_1(x), \pi_1(y)) = \pi_t(\hat{e}(x, y))$, for all $(x, y) \in \mathbf{G}^2$. The public key consists of $\mathbf{G}, \mathbf{H}, \mathbf{G}_t$ and $\mathbf{H}_t$. The private key is the maps (π_1, π_t). To encrypt $m \in G$, one computes $c = (m, m, m)h$ where h is a random element of $\mathbf{H}$. Decryption of c is done by applying π_1, which gives $\pi_1((m, m, m))$. From that, m is recovered as the first element is a power of m, m^s where s is an explicit non zero element of $\mathbf{F}_q$. Decryption in $\mathbf{G}_t$ is carried out in the same way with the map π_t. The scheme is homomorphic for multiplication and for pairing evaluation thanks to the projecting property.

As for the BGN cryptosystem, this conversion gives a more efficient scheme in terms of key size and computation cost. The ind $-$ cpa security of the converted scheme relies on the Decision Linear Problem.

Our framework also uses a pairing with the cancelling property since we have a decomposition $\mathbf{G} = \mathbf{G}_1\mathbf{G}_2\mathbf{G}_3$ such that $e(g_i, g_j) = 1$ if $g_i \in \mathbf{G}_i$ and $g_j \in \mathbf{G}_j$ with $i \neq j$. This cancelling property is needed for the proof of the result on ind $-$ cca1 security of Proposition 1. Moreover, this property and the relation with the splitting problem is also the core of our application to shared decryption. These properties do not remain after the conversion.

In [MSF10, SC12], the problem of the transposition of *all* cryptosystems using composite-order bilinear groups in prime-order groups is discussed. In [SC12] a prime-order construction with both cancelling and projecting properties is given, together with a new security proof of the blind signature scheme of [MSF10] in the prime-order setting, which was believed impossible to get outside composite bilinear group.

We leave as open the problem of proving that the additional properties of our cryptosystem, which need particular projecting *and* cancelling maps, can or can not be instantiated in prime-order groups with a direct approach. An impossible result would answer the open problem left in [SC12].

References

[APK10]   Armknecht, F., Peter, A., Katzenbeisser, S.: Group Homomorphic Encryption: Characterizations, Impossibility Results, and Applications. To appear in Des. Codes Cryptography. IACR e-print 2010/501 (2010), http://eprint.iacr.org/2010/501

[BDPR98]   Bellare, M., Desai, A., Pointcheval, D., Rogaway, P.: Relations among Notions of Security for Public-Key Encryption Schemes. In: Krawczyk, H. (ed.) CRYPTO 1998. LNCS, vol. 1462, pp. 26–45. Springer, Heidelberg (1998)

[Ben88]   Benaloh, J.C.: Verifiable Secret-Ballot Elections. PhD thesis, Yale University (1988)

[BF03]   Boneh, D., Franklin, M.K.: Identity-Based Encryption from the Weil Pairing. SIAM J. Comput. 32(3), 586–615 (2003)

[BFP+01]   Baudron, O., Fouque, P.-A., Pointcheval, D., Poupard, G., Stern, J.: Practical Multi-Candidate Election System. In: Proc. of PODC 2001, pp. 274–283 (2001)

[BGN05]   Boneh, D., Goh, E.-J., Nissim, K.: Evaluating 2-DNF Formulas on Ciphertexts. In: Kilian, J. (ed.) TCC 2005. LNCS, vol. 3378, pp. 325–341. Springer, Heidelberg (2005)

[BP04]   Bellare, M., Palacio, A.: Towards Plaintext-Aware Public-Key Encryption Without Random Oracles. In: Lee, P.J. (ed.) ASIACRYPT 2004. LNCS, vol. 3329, pp. 48–62. Springer, Heidelberg (2004)

[Bro07]   Brown, J.: Secure Public-Key Encryption from Factorisation-related problem. PhD Thesis, Queensland University of Technology (2007)

[BRS11]   Boneh, D., Rubin, K., Silverberg, A.: Finding composite order ordinary elliptic curves using the Cocks-Pinch method. Journal of Number Theory 131(5), 832–841 (2011)

[BWY11]   Bellare, M., Waters, B., Yilek, S.: Identity-Based Encryption Secure against Selective Opening Attack. In: Ishai, Y. (ed.) TCC 2011. LNCS, vol. 6597, pp. 235–252. Springer, Heidelberg (2011)

[BGV12]   Brakerski, Z., Gentry, C., Vaikuntanathan, V.: Fully Homomorphic Encryption without Bootstrapping. To appear in Proc. of Innovations in Theoretical Computer Science (ITCS) (2012)

[BV11]   Brakerski, Z., Vaikuntanathan, V.: Efficient Fully Homomorphic Encryption from (Standard) LWE. In: Proc. of FOCS 2011, pp. 97–106. IEEE (2011)

[DJ01]   Damgård, I., Jurik, M.: A Generalisation, a Simplification and some Applications of Paillier's Probabilistic Public-Key System. In: Kim, K. (ed.) PKC 2001. LNCS, vol. 1992, pp. 119–136. Springer, Heidelberg (2001)

[Fre10]   Freeman, D.M.: Converting Pairing-Based Cryptosystems from Composite-Order Groups to Prime-Order Groups. In: Gilbert, H. (ed.) EUROCRYPT 2010. LNCS, vol. 6110, pp. 44–61. Springer, Heidelberg (2010)

[FPS00]   Fouque, P.-A., Poupard, G., Stern, J.: Sharing Decryption in the Context of Voting or Lotteries. In: Frankel, Y. (ed.) FC 2000. LNCS, vol. 1962, pp. 90–104. Springer, Heidelberg (2001)

[GBD05]   González Nieto, J.M., Boyd, C., Dawson, E.: A Public Key Cryptosystem Based on a Subgroup Membership Problem. Des. Codes Cryptography 36(3), 301–316 (2005)

[Gen09]   Gentry, C.: Fully homomorphic encryption using ideal lattices. In: Proc. of STOC 2009, pp. 169–178. ACM (2009)

[Gjo04]   Gjøsteen, K.: Subgroup membership problems and public key cryptography. PhD Thesis, Norwegian University of Science and Technology (2004)

[Gjo05]   Gjøsteen, K.: Symmetric Subgroup Membership Problems. In: Vaudenay, S. (ed.) PKC 2005. LNCS, vol. 3386, pp. 104–119. Springer, Heidelberg (2005)

[GM84]   Goldwasser, S., Micali, S.: Probabilistic Encryption. JCSS 28(2), 270–299 (1984)

[JS08]   Jager, T., Schwenk, J.: The Generic Hardness of Subset Membership Problems under the Factoring Assumption. IACR e-print 2008/482 (2008), http://eprint.iacr.org/2008/482

[KSW08]   Katz, J., Sahai, A., Waters, B.: Predicate Encryption Supporting Disjunctions, Polynomial Equations, and Inner Products. In: Smart, N.P. (ed.) EUROCRYPT 2008. LNCS, vol. 4965, pp. 146–162. Springer, Heidelberg (2008)

[Jur03]   Jurik, M.: Extensions to the Paillier Cryptosystem with Applications to Cryptological Protocols. PhD thesis, Århus University (2003)

[Lip05]   Lipmaa, H.: An Oblivious Transfer Protocol with Log-Squared Communication. In: Zhou, J., López, J., Deng, R.H., Bao, F. (eds.) ISC 2005. LNCS, vol. 3650, pp. 314–328. Springer, Heidelberg (2005)

[Lew12]   Lewko, A.: Tools for Simulating Features of Composite Order Bilinear Groups in the Prime Order Setting. In: Pointcheval, D., Johansson, T. (eds.) EUROCRYPT 2012. LNCS, vol. 7237, pp. 318–335. Springer, Heidelberg (2012), http://eprint.iacr.org/2011/490.pdf

[Mil04]   Miller, V.S.: The Weil Pairing, and Its Efficient Calculation. J. Cryptology 17(4), 235–261 (2004)

[MMO10]   Mitsunaga, T., Manabe, Y., Okamoto, T.: Efficient Secure Auction Protocols Based on the Boneh-Goh-Nissim Encryption. In: Echizen, I., Kunihiro, N., Sasaki, R. (eds.) IWSEC 2010. LNCS, vol. 6434, pp. 149–163. Springer, Heidelberg (2010)

[MSF10]   Meiklejohn, S., Shacham, H., Freeman, D.M.: Limitations on Transformations from Composite-Order to Prime-Order Groups: The Case of Round-Optimal Blind Signatures. In: Abe, M. (ed.) ASIACRYPT 2010. LNCS, vol. 6477, pp. 519–538. Springer, Heidelberg (2010)

[NS98]   Naccache, D., Stern, J.: A New Public Key Cryptosystem Based on Higher Residues. In: Proc. of CCS 1998, pp. 546–560 (1998)

[NSNK06]   Nguyen, L., Safavi-Naini, R., Kurosawa, K.: Verifiable shuffles: a formal model and a Paillier-based three-round construction with provable security. Int. J. Inf. Secur. 5(4), 241–255 (2006)

[OU98]   Okamoto, T., Uchiyama, S.: A New Public-Key Cryptosystem as Secure as Factoring. In: Nyberg, K. (ed.) EUROCRYPT 1998. LNCS, vol. 1403, pp. 308–318. Springer, Heidelberg (1998)

[Pai99]   Paillier, P.: Public-Key Cryptosystems Based on Composite Degree Residuosity Classes. In: Stern, J. (ed.) EUROCRYPT 1999. LNCS, vol. 1592, pp. 223–238. Springer, Heidelberg (1999)

[SC12]   Seo, J.H., Cheon, J.H.: Beyond the Limitation of Prime-Order Bilinear Groups, and Round Optimal Blind Signatures. In: Cramer, R. (ed.) TCC 2012. LNCS, vol. 7194, pp. 133–150. Springer, Heidelberg (2012)

Publicly Verifiable Ciphertexts

Juan Manuel González Nieto[1], Mark Manulis[2], Bertram Poettering[3],
Jothi Rangasamy[1], and Douglas Stebila[1]

[1] Queensland University of Technology, Brisbane, Australia
{j.gonzaleznieto,j.rangasamy,stebila}@qut.edu.au
[2] University of Surrey, Guildford, United Kingdom
mark@manulis.eu
[3] Royal Holloway, University of London, United Kingdom
bertram.poettering@rhul.ac.uk

Abstract. In many applications where encrypted traffic flows from an open (public) domain to a protected (private) domain there exists a gateway that bridges the two domains and faithfully forwards the incoming traffic to the receiver. We observe that indistinguishability against (adaptive) chosen-ciphertext attacks (IND-CCA), which is a mandatory goal in face of active attacks in a public domain, can be essentially relaxed to indistinguishability against chosen-plaintext attacks (IND-CPA) for ciphertexts once they pass the gateway that acts as an IND-CCA/CPA filter, by first checking the validity of an incoming IND-CCA ciphertext, then transforming it (if valid) into an IND-CPA ciphertext, and finally forwarding the latter to the recipient in the private domain. "Non-trivial filtering" can result in reduced decryption costs on the receiver's side.

We identify a class of encryption schemes with *publicly verifiable ciphertexts* that admit generic constructions of (non-trivial) IND-CCA/CPA filters. These schemes are characterized by existence of public algorithms that can distinguish between valid and invalid ciphertexts. To this end, we formally define (non-trivial) public verifiability of ciphertexts for general encryption schemes, key encapsulation mechanisms, and hybrid encryption schemes, encompassing public-key, identity-based, and tag-based encryption flavors. We further analyze the security impact of public verifiability and discuss generic transformations and concrete constructions that enjoy this property.

1 Introduction

Transmission of sensitive information over public networks necessitates the use of cryptographic protection. Modern cryptography offers various techniques, including public key encryption (PKE) and identity-based encryption (IBE), by which the sender can use public information to encrypt a message only the intended receiver can decrypt. These two encryption flavors can be combined into a common syntax, called *general encryption* (GE) [1], and for longer messages, hybrid encryption schemes based on key and data encapsulation techniques, i.e. the KEM/DEM approach [10], are often more efficient.

I. Visconti and R. De Prisco (Eds.): SCN 2012, LNCS 7485, pp. 393–410, 2012.
© Springer-Verlag Berlin Heidelberg 2012

The most standard security notion for encryption schemes is *indistinguisha-bility* (IND) — a ciphertext may not leak any information about the encrypted message (except possibly its length) — whose definitions consider different types of attacks. The strongest is an *adaptive chosen-ciphertext attack* (CCA), in which an attacker can ask for decryption of ciphertexts of her own choice (other than the target ciphertext). IND-CCA-security hence protects encrypted messages of honest senders despite the threat that receivers may also have to decrypt ci-phertexts constructed by the adversary. More generally, such threat exists if the network is susceptible to active attacks. In contrast, if senders are trustworthy and their messages are delivered over a network that protects authenticity, then security against *chosen-plaintext attacks* (CPA) would already provide sufficient confidentiality guarantees, possibly resulting in better performance.

IND-CCA/CPA FILTERING AND ITS APPLICATIONS. Consider an intermediate party, called a *gateway*, and assume that encrypted sender's messages are trans-mitted over a public network until they reach the gateway and are then forwarded by the gateway over a private network to the receiver, with the gateway being trusted by the receiver to forward faithfully.

By the above reasoning, IND-CCA security would be required for the encrypted traffic from (possibly malicious) senders towards the gateway. But for messages on the internal network — including from the gateway to the receiver — IND-CPA security would be sufficient in practice to preserve confidentiality. If the gateway just forwards all (IND-CCA) ciphertexts from the outside world without modifi-cation, all security goals remain satisfied, but perhaps we can improve efficiency for the receiver by having the gateway do some processing on ciphertexts before forwarding them.

An often observed difference between IND-CPA and IND-CCA schemes is that IND-CPA schemes successfully decrypt every given ciphertext, whereas the ma-jority of IND-CCA schemes typically check ciphertexts for consistency and de-crypt only those that are "well-formed" [8,10,17,18,19]. For such schemes the gateway could act as a filter that would sort out inconsistent IND-CCA cipher-texts. There exist few IND-CCA schemes [4,25,26], that decrypt every ciphertext to a possibly meaningless (random) message. Such schemes are not well-suited to filtering since the gateway would need to know the receiver's private key to de-cide whether the message is meaningful, which would in general be unacceptable since it requires trusting gateways for confidentiality, not just integrity.

In this paper, we are interested in solutions that allow an honest-but-curious gateway to transform IND-CCA-secure traffic from a public network into IND-CPA-secure traffic for a private network at low cost and while fully preserv-ing confidentiality of encrypted messages; the key step is that the gateway is trusted to correctly perform a "validity check" of traffic from the public network before forwarding it on to the private network. Recipient devices on the private network can then use a more efficient decryption procedure.

Many real applications could benefit from this "sender-gateway-receiver" sce-nario: for example, sensor networks often consist of many low-powered nodes that communicate with each other locally and which use a single more powerful gateway device to communicate with the Internet. To protect their local communications, nodes may have shared keys with the sink which they use in highly efficient symmetric key algorithms, only needing to resort to more expensive asymmetric algorithms when communicating with the outside world. In our paradigm, the gateway could take IND-CCA-secure traffic from senders in the outside world, check it for validity, and convert it to a simpler (IND-CPA-secure) format to reduce the processing costs for receiving sensor nodes. As a second example, mail servers (MTAs) generally receive emails over unprotected networks, whereas email recipients typically contact these servers to access their emails after having established an end-to-end authenticated (and possibly encrypted) channel with them. Hence, for encrypted emails or attachments, the mail server could perform a "sanity check" and filter out inconsistent ciphertexts, saving the client from their local processing.

CIPHERTEXT CONSISTENCY CHECKS. IND-CCA-secure schemes where inconsistent ciphertexts can be filtered out based on consistency checks seem very suitable for our purposes. Consistency checks can be either private or public: the check is private if it requires at least partial knowledge of the private key (e.g. in [10]), while public checks do not require any secrets (e.g. in [8,17]).

We will focus on IND-CCA-secure cryptosystems with *publicly verifiable ciphertexts*. Interestingly, public verifiability has been treated so-far in a rather folklore manner, e.g. as a property of concrete schemes, e.g. [8,17,19,18]. To make use of this property in general, for example to enable "black-box" constructions of higher-level security protocols from publicly verifiable encryption schemes, a more formal and thorough characterization of public verifiability is merited. We also note that public verifiability has been extensively addressed in a different context, namely with regard to *threshold encryption*, where as observed initially in [20] and then provably realized in [32,8,7,22], this property is useful to make the threshold decryption process of an IND-CCA-secure threshold encryption scheme non-interactive and robust.

In our applications, public verifiability can immediately be used to detect and filter out invalid IND-CCA ciphertexts, i.e. by trusting the gateway to perform the check. This filtering could also be performed for IND-CCA schemes with private consistency checks, as long as these checks need only parts of the private key that are by themselves not sufficient to break IND-CPA security. Existence of such IND-CCA schemes has been demonstrated by Persiano [27] through his concept of *trapdoor cryptosystems*. For instance, he proved that a trapdoor containing private-key components in Cramer-Shoup PKE [10] that are used in the consistency check cannot be used for an IND-CPA attack (although their disclosure allows malleability attacks). Being concerned about IND-CCA-security, Persiano argued that existence of such trapdoors is a drawback. Taking a look at trapdoor cryptosystems in [27] from the perspective of our work, we observe that the gateway could indeed be given trapdoor information to check IND-CCA consistency *without* losing IND-CPA security. However, this approach would offer somewhat weaker guarantees in contrast to publicly verifiable schemes: if the delegated trapdoor keys are ever leaked, then IND-CCA security can never be recovered. This contrasts with our approach, in which the receiver always has the potential to obtain IND-CCA security at any particular time simply by performing more operations.

CONTRIBUTIONS. We formalize the property of *publicly verifiable ciphertexts* for general encryption, general KEMs, and general KEM/DEM hybrid schemes. Our definitions emphasize the role of public ciphertext consistency checks within the decryption procedure. In our approach, decryption algorithms of publicly verifiable schemes follow a strictly modular design where the consistency check can be performed independently of the remaining "lightweight" decryption procedure. Success or failure of the entire decryption procedure is indicated by the consistency check, which can be performed by any third party without access to any secret information. The only exception is the KEM/DEM approach, where we relax these conditions to account for decryption failures in the DEM part. Our definitions employ the syntax of generalized encryption by Abdalla *et al.* [1] which we extend to also capture *tag-based encryption* (TBE) [3,17] and to address KEMs and the KEM/DEM framework.

With these definitions, we first prove the very general statement that any IND-CCA-secure scheme with publicly verifiable ciphertexts remains at least IND-CPA-secure if the underlying consistency check is outsourced from the decryption procedure. In some sense, this gives us the trivial and well-known result that any IND-CCA-secure ciphertext can be publicly converted into a ciphertext that still guarantees basic IND-CPA protection (since every IND-CCA-secure scheme is also IND-CPA-secure). However, the notion of public verifiability is particular interesting in the case where the verification algorithm is *strictly non-trivial* — the public consistency check fails exactly when the IND-CCA-secure scheme's decryption algorithm fails — as such publicly verifiable schemes can readily be used to build the aforementioned IND-CCA/CPA filters.

We provide several constructions (general and concrete) of IND-CCA-secure schemes with strictly non-trivial publicly verifiability. In addition to existing schemes, e.g. [8,17,19,18], for which public verifiability was discussed informally, we first show that two well-known general ways for obtaining IND-CCA secure schemes offer public verifiability (although not strictly non-trivial public verifiability), namely the Canetti-Halevi-Katz (CHK) transform [9] and the NIZK-based transform [29,23]. The result on CHK contrasts with the related transform by Boneh and Katz [6] that uses a message authentication code (MAC) and does not offer public verifiability. We present a concrete PKE scheme, obtained through a tweak on the KEM of Kiltz [18], that offers an especially lightweight decryption procedure for ciphertexts that passed its strictly non-trivial public verification. In addition to PKE we consider KEMs and give examples of public key-based, identity-based, and tag-based KEMs with strictly non-trivial public verification. Finally, we look into the KEM/DEM paradigm and show that strictly non-trivial public verification of the KEM partially carries over to the hybrid scheme — namely, we define a *somewhat non-trivial* public verification for hybrid encryption schemes by linking a failure in the hybrid decryption process to a verification failure in either the KEM or the DEM, and show that by outsourcing KEM consistency check the hybrid construction remains at least IND-CPA-secure.

2   Publicly Verifiable Ciphertexts in General Encryption

2.1   Definition: General Encryption

A *general encryption* (GE) scheme $\mathsf{GE} = (\mathsf{PG}, \mathsf{KG}, \mathsf{Enc}, \mathsf{Dec})$ consists of four algorithms:

$\mathsf{PG}(1^k)$: The parameter generation algorithm PG takes input a security parameter 1^k, $k \geq 0$, and returns public parameters par and a master secret key msk. Public parameters include a description of the identity space IDSp, the message space MsgSp, and the tag space TagSp.

$\mathsf{KG}(\mathsf{par}, \mathsf{msk}, \mathsf{id})$: On input par, msk, and $\mathsf{id} \in \mathsf{IDSp}$, the key generation algorithm KG produces an encryption key ek and decryption key dk.

$\mathsf{Enc}(\mathsf{par}, \mathsf{ek}, M, t)$: On input par, ek, a message $M \in \mathsf{MsgSp}$, and a tag $t \in \mathsf{TagSp}$, the encryption algorithm Enc outputs a ciphertext C.

$\mathsf{Dec}(\mathsf{par}, \mathsf{ek}, \mathsf{dk}, C, t)$: On input par, ek, dk, C, and a tag t, the deterministic decryption algorithm Dec returns either a plaintext message M or $\perp$ to indicate that it rejects.

This GE formalism encompasses public-key, identity-based, and tag-based encryption schemes:

PKE: Set $\mathsf{msk} = \epsilon$ and assume that IDSp and TagSp contain a single fixed element that can be omitted as implicit input to the algorithms.

IBE: Consider KG that on input id outputs $\mathsf{ek} = \mathsf{id}$ and assume that TagSp contains again a single fixed element that can be omitted as implicit input to the algorithms.

TBE: Set $\mathsf{msk} = \epsilon$ and assume that IDSp contains again a single fixed element that can be omitted as implicit input to the algorithms.

CORRECTNESS. A general encryption scheme $\mathsf{GE} = (\mathsf{PG}, \mathsf{KG}, \mathsf{Enc}, \mathsf{Dec})$ is *correct* if, for all $(\mathsf{par}, \mathsf{msk}) \in [\mathsf{PG}]$, all plaintexts $M \in \mathsf{MsgSp}$, all identities $\mathsf{id} \in \mathsf{IDSp}$, all $(\mathsf{ek}, \mathsf{dk}) \in [\mathsf{KG}(\mathsf{par}, \mathsf{msk}, \mathsf{id})]$, and all tags $t \in \mathsf{TagSp}$, we have $\mathsf{Dec}(\mathsf{par}, \mathsf{ek}, \mathsf{dk}, \mathsf{Enc}(\mathsf{par}, \mathsf{ek}, M, t), t) = M$ with probability one, where the probability is taken over the coins of Enc.

INDISTINGUISHABILITY. The IND-CCA/CPA security games between a challenger and an adversary $\mathcal{A}$ are defined by the experiments in Figure 1 (left column). The advantage of $\mathcal{A}$ in those games is defined as

$$\mathbf{Adv}_{\mathcal{A},\mathsf{GE}}^{\mathsf{IND}\text{-}\mathsf{xxx}}(k) = \left| \Pr\left(\mathbf{Exp}_{\mathcal{A},\mathsf{GE}}^{\mathsf{IND}\text{-}\mathsf{xxx},0}(k) = 1 \right) - \Pr\left(\mathbf{Exp}_{\mathcal{A},\mathsf{GE}}^{\mathsf{IND}\text{-}\mathsf{xxx},1}(k) = 1 \right) \right|,$$

where $\mathsf{xxx} \in \{\mathsf{CPA}, \mathsf{CCA}\}$. A GE scheme is IND-xxx-secure if the advantage of any PPT adversary $\mathcal{A}$ in the corresponding game is negligible in the security parameter k.

$\mathbf{Exp}_{\mathcal{A},\mathsf{GE}}^{\mathsf{IND\text{-}xxx},b}(k)$:

1. $(\mathsf{par},\mathsf{msk}) \stackrel{\$}{\leftarrow} \mathsf{PG}(1^k)$
2. $U, V, KList, DList \leftarrow \emptyset$
3. $(st, M_0, M_1, \mathsf{id}^*, t^*) \stackrel{\$}{\leftarrow} \mathcal{A}_1^{\mathcal{O}_{\mathsf{EK}}, \mathcal{O}_{\mathsf{DK}}[,\mathcal{O}_{\mathsf{Dec}}]}(\mathsf{par})$
   If $\mathcal{A}$ queries $\mathcal{O}_{\mathsf{EK}}(\mathsf{id})$:
   (a) If $\mathsf{id} \in U$ then return $\perp$
   (b) $U \leftarrow U \cup \{\mathsf{id}\}$
   (c) $(\mathsf{ek}[\mathsf{id}], \mathsf{dk}[\mathsf{id}]) \stackrel{\$}{\leftarrow} \mathsf{KG}(\mathsf{par}, \mathsf{msk}, \mathsf{id})$
   (d) Append $(\mathsf{id}, \mathsf{ek}[\mathsf{id}], \mathsf{dk}[\mathsf{id}])$ to $KList$
   (e) Answer $\mathcal{A}$ with $\mathsf{ek}[\mathsf{id}]$
   If $\mathcal{A}$ queries $\mathcal{O}_{\mathsf{DK}}(\mathsf{id})$:
   (a) If $\mathsf{id} \notin U$ then return $\perp$
   (b) $V \leftarrow V \cup \{\mathsf{id}\}$
   (c) Answer $\mathcal{A}$ with $\mathsf{dk}[\mathsf{id}]$ from $KList$
   If $\mathcal{A}$ queries $\mathcal{O}_{\mathsf{Dec}}(C, \mathsf{id}, t)$ (if $\mathsf{xxx} = \mathsf{CCA}$):
   (a) If $\mathsf{id} \notin U$ then return $\perp$
   (b) $M \leftarrow \mathsf{Dec}(\mathsf{par}, \mathsf{ek}[\mathsf{id}], \mathsf{dk}[\mathsf{id}], C, t)$
   (c) Append (C, id, t) to $DList$
   (d) Answer $\mathcal{A}$ with M
4. If $M_0 = M_1$ or $|M_0| \neq |M_1|$ then return $\perp$
5. If $\mathsf{id}^* \notin U$ then return $\perp$
6. $C^* \stackrel{\$}{\leftarrow} \mathsf{Enc}(\mathsf{par}, \mathsf{ek}[\mathsf{id}^*], M_b, t^*)$
7. $b' \stackrel{\$}{\leftarrow} \mathcal{A}_2^{\mathcal{O}_{\mathsf{EK}}, \mathcal{O}_{\mathsf{DK}}[,\mathcal{O}_{\mathsf{Dec}}]}(st, C^*)$
   Answer queries as above
8. If $\mathsf{id}^* \in V$ then return $\perp$
9. If $(C^*, \mathsf{id}^*, t^*) \in DList$ then return $\perp$
10. Return 1 if $b' = b$, else return 0.

$\mathbf{Exp}_{\mathcal{A},\mathsf{GKEM}}^{\mathsf{IND\text{-}xxx},b}(k)$:

1. $(\mathsf{par},\mathsf{msk}) \stackrel{\$}{\leftarrow} \mathsf{PG}(1^k)$
2. $U, V, KList, DList \leftarrow \emptyset$
3. $(st, \mathsf{id}^*, t^*) \stackrel{\$}{\leftarrow} \mathcal{A}_1^{\mathcal{O}_{\mathsf{EK}}, \mathcal{O}_{\mathsf{DK}}[,\mathcal{O}_{\mathsf{Dec}}]}(\mathsf{par})$
   If $\mathcal{A}$ queries $\mathcal{O}_{\mathsf{EK}}(\mathsf{id})$:
   (a) If $\mathsf{id} \in U$ then return $\perp$
   (b) $U \leftarrow U \cup \{\mathsf{id}\}$
   (c) $(\mathsf{ek}[\mathsf{id}], \mathsf{dk}[\mathsf{id}]) \stackrel{\$}{\leftarrow} \mathsf{KG}(\mathsf{par}, \mathsf{msk}, \mathsf{id})$
   (d) Append $(\mathsf{id}, \mathsf{ek}[\mathsf{id}], \mathsf{dk}[\mathsf{id}])$ to $KList$
   (e) Answer $\mathcal{A}$ with $\mathsf{ek}[\mathsf{id}]$
   If $\mathcal{A}$ queries $\mathcal{O}_{\mathsf{DK}}(\mathsf{id})$:
   (a) If $\mathsf{id} \notin U$ then return $\perp$
   (b) $V \leftarrow V \cup \{\mathsf{id}\}$
   (c) Answer $\mathcal{A}$ with $\mathsf{dk}[\mathsf{id}]$ from $KList$
   If $\mathcal{A}$ queries $\mathcal{O}_{\mathsf{Dec}}(C, \mathsf{id}, t)$ (if $\mathsf{xxx} = \mathsf{CCA}$):
   (a) If $\mathsf{id} \notin U$ then return $\perp$
   (b) $K \leftarrow \mathsf{Decap}(\mathsf{par}, \mathsf{ek}[\mathsf{id}], \mathsf{dk}[\mathsf{id}], C, t)$
   (c) Append (C, id, t) to $DList$
   (d) Answer $\mathcal{A}$ with K
4. If $\mathsf{id}^* \notin U$ then return $\perp$
5. $(C^*, K_0^*) \stackrel{\$}{\leftarrow} \mathsf{Encap}(\mathsf{par}, \mathsf{ek}[\mathsf{id}^*], t^*)$
6. $K_1^* \stackrel{\$}{\leftarrow} \mathsf{KeySp}(k)$
7. $b' \stackrel{\$}{\leftarrow} \mathcal{A}_2^{\mathcal{O}_{\mathsf{EK}}, \mathcal{O}_{\mathsf{DK}}[,\mathcal{O}_{\mathsf{Dec}}]}(st, C^*, K_b^*)$
   Answer queries as above.
8. If $\mathsf{id}^* \in V$ then return $\perp$
9. If $(C^*, \mathsf{id}^*, t^*) \in DList$ then return $\perp$
10. Return 1 if $b' = b$, else return 0.

Fig. 1. IND-CCA/CPA security experiments for General Encryption (left) and General Key Encapsulation (right)

2.2 General Encryption with Publicly Verifiable Ciphertexts

In our definition of general encryption with publicly verifiable ciphertexts we require existence of a separate algorithm for ciphertext validation and that the scheme's original decryption procedure can be logically divided into this public validation check followed by a lightweight decryption algorithm.

Definition 1 (Publicly Verifiable GE). *A general encryption scheme* $\mathsf{GE} = (\mathsf{PG}, \mathsf{KG}, \mathsf{Enc}, \mathsf{Dec})$ *is said to be* publicly verifiable *with respect to auxiliary algorithms* Ver *and* Dec' *if* $\mathsf{Dec}(\mathsf{par}, \mathsf{ek}, \mathsf{dk}, C, t)$ *has the same input/output behavior as the following sequence of operations:*

1. $C' \leftarrow \mathsf{Ver}(\mathsf{par}, \mathsf{ek}, C, t)$
2. *If* $C' = \perp$, *then return* $\perp$
3. $M \leftarrow \mathsf{Dec}'(\mathsf{par}, \mathsf{ek}, \mathsf{dk}, C', t)$
4. *Return* M

where Ver *and* Dec' *satisfy the following:*

Ver(par, ek, C, t): *Given public parameters* par, *the encryption key* ek, *a ciphertext C, and a tag t, this algorithm outputs either $\perp$ if the ciphertext fails the validation or a (transformed) ciphertext C'. Note that* Ver *does not take any secrets as input.*

Dec$'$(par, ek, dk, C', t): *This deterministic algorithm takes input public parameters* par, *encryption and decryption keys* (ek, dk), *a ciphertext C', and a tag t, and outputs a message M or $\perp$.*

Hereafter, when we say Dec $=$ Dec$' \circ$ Ver we mean that Dec can be decomposed into two algorithms Ver and Dec$'$ according to the above construction. Note that all IND-CCA-secure general encryption schemes trivially achieve public verifiability with respect to Ver(par, ek, C, t) $:= C$ and Dec$' :=$ Dec. We are often interested in the case where something non-trivial is occurring in Ver, i.e. where the consistency check is essential for successful decryption. Note that this separation does not formally ensure that Dec$'$ is more efficient than Dec, though in practice we are of course interested primarily in such schemes.

Definition 2 (Strictly Non-Trivial Public Verification). *Let* GE $=$ (PG, KG, Enc, Dec) *be a general encryption scheme that is publicly verifiable with respect to auxiliary algorithms* Ver *and* Dec$'$. *Let* (par, msk) $\leftarrow$ PG(1^k). Ver *is said to be* strictly non-trivial *if, for all* id $\in$ IDSp, *all* $t \in$ TagSp, *and* (ek, dk) $\leftarrow$ KG(par, msk, id),

1. Ver(par, ek, C, t) $= \perp \Leftrightarrow$ Dec(par, ek, dk, C, t) $= \perp$ *for all C, and*
2. *there exists a ciphertext C for which* Dec(par, ek, dk, C, t) $= \perp$.

Condition 1 requires that successful public verification is both necessary and sufficient for the decryption algorithm not to fail. Condition 2 formally excludes IND-CCA-secure schemes where Dec never outputs $\perp$ (e.g. [25,26,4] where modified (challenge) ciphertexts decrypt to random messages) to capture the intuition that in order to determine whether C carries some meaningful message one must have at least partial knowledge of the private key (which contradicts the goals of strictly non-trivial public verification).

Theorem 1 (proven in Appendix A) shows that any IND-CCA-secure GE scheme with publicly verifiable ciphertexts remains at least IND-CPA-secure if its decryption algorithm Dec is replaced with Dec$'$. In the original decryption procedure a strictly non-trivial verification process may syntactically modify the ciphertext. For syntactical reasons we must ensure that ciphertexts output by the encryption algorithm of the new scheme can be processed with Dec$'$. This is achieved via post-processing of original ciphertexts using Ver and by viewing this step as part of the new encryption algorithm.

Theorem 1. *Let* GE $=$ (PG, KG, Enc, Dec) *be an* IND-CCA-*secure general encryption scheme that is publicly verifiable with respect to* Ver *and* Dec$'$. *Let* Enc$' :=$ Ver $\circ$ Enc *(where $\circ$ denotes the obvious composition) and let* GE$' :=$ (PG, KG, Enc$'$, Dec$'$). *For every* IND-CPA *adversary $\mathcal{A}$ against* GE$'$ *there exists an* IND-CCA *adversary $\mathcal{B}$ against* GE *such that, for all $k \geq 0$,* $\mathbf{Adv}_{\mathcal{A},\text{GE}'}^{\text{IND-CPA}}(k) \leq \mathbf{Adv}_{\mathcal{B},\text{GE}}^{\text{IND-CCA}}(k)$, *where $\mathcal{B}$ has (asymptotically) the same running time as $\mathcal{A}$.*

2.3   Publicly Verifiable Ciphertexts through CHK Transformation

Canetti, Halevi, and Katz [9] described an method for constructing an IND-CCA-secure public key encryption scheme PKE from any IND-CPA-secure identity-based encryption scheme IBE with identity-space $\{0,1\}^{\ell_s(k)}$ and any strongly unforgeable *one-time signature* scheme OTS $=$ (KG, Sign, Vrfy) with the verification key space $\{0,1\}^{\ell_s(k)}$ (see [9] for the syntax of OTS and the details of the original CHK transform; note that one-time signature schemes can be constructed from any one-way function [28]). Later, Kiltz [17] showed that CHK transform works also if the IND-CPA-secure IBE scheme is replaced by a weakly IND-CCA-secure tag-based encryption scheme TBE with tag-space $\{0,1\}^{\ell_s(k)}$.

Figure 2 (which uses GE notation) shows that in both cases, the resulting PKE is public verification with respect to PKE.Ver and PKE.Dec$'$, but importantly the public verification is *not* strictly non-trivial: the IBE or TBE decryption operation may still fail. In the IBE-based case ek $= \epsilon$ remains empty while dk $=$ msk and par are output by IBE.PG. In the TBE-based case ek and dk are output by TBE.KG using par generated by TBE.PG. Original IBE-based transform from [9] and its TBE-based version from [17] are obtained using PKE.Dec $=$ PKE.Dec$' \circ$ PKE.Ver.

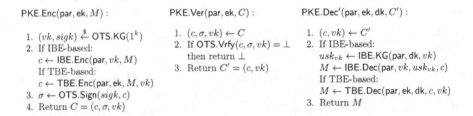

Fig. 2. PKE with Publicly Verifiable Ciphertexts from CHK Transformation

2.4   Publicly Verifiable Ciphertexts Using NIZKs

An IND-CPA-secure public key encryption scheme PKE$' =$ (PG, KG, Enc, Dec) can be converted into an IND-CCA-secure one using a non-interactive zero-knowledge (NIZK) proof (P, V) with simulation soundness, as proven by Sahai [29] based on the Naor-Yung approach [23]. The private/public key pair of the resulting scheme PKE is given by (dk, ek) $=$ ((dk$_1$, dk$_2$), (ek$_1$, ek$_2$, ρ)) where (dk$_i$, ek$_i$), $i \in \{1,2\}$, are obtained from two independent runs of PKE$'$.KG and ρ is the common reference string of the NIZK proof system for languages of the form $(c_1, c_2, \text{ek}_1, \text{ek}_2)$ satisfying $c_1 =$ PKE$'$.Enc(par, ek$_1$, M) $\wedge$ $c_2 =$ PKE$'$.Enc(par, ek$_2$, M) where M (and implicitly random coins used in the encryption process) play the role of the witness. As demonstrated in Figure 3, IND-CCA schemes output by this transformation offer public verifiability, though not strictly non-trivial public verifiability as the PKE$'$.Dec operation in PKE.Dec$'$ may output $\bot$. This reasoning also applies to the NIZK-based constructions from [12] and to the first IND-CCA-secure PKE scheme by Dolev, Dwork, and Naor [11] that uses NIZK-proofs in a slightly different way. Although NIZK-based schemes are regarded as not efficient, we notice that their lightweight decryption procedure Dec' (if the scheme is viewed from the public verifiability perspective) is as efficient as that of CHK-based schemes in Figure 2.

PKE.Enc(par, ek, M) :	PKE.Ver(par, ek, C) :	PKE.Dec$'$(par, ek, dk, C') :
1. $(\mathsf{ek}_1, \mathsf{ek}_2, \rho) \leftarrow \mathsf{ek}$	1. $(\mathsf{ek}_1, \mathsf{ek}_2, \rho) \leftarrow \mathsf{ek}$	1. $(\mathsf{dk}_1, \mathsf{dk}_2) \leftarrow \mathsf{dk}$
2. $c_1 \leftarrow \mathsf{PKE}'.\mathsf{Enc}(\mathsf{par}, \mathsf{ek}_1, M)$	2. $(c_1, c_2, \pi) \leftarrow C$	2. $c_1 \leftarrow C'$
3. $c_2 \leftarrow \mathsf{PKE}'.\mathsf{Enc}(\mathsf{par}, \mathsf{ek}_2, M)$	3. If $V(\rho, (c_1, c_2, \mathsf{ek}_1, \mathsf{ek}_2), \pi) = \bot$	3. $M \leftarrow \mathsf{PKE}'.\mathsf{Dec}(\mathsf{par}, \mathsf{ek}_1, \mathsf{dk}_1,$
4. $\pi \leftarrow P(M, (c_1, c_2, \mathsf{ek}_1, \mathsf{ek}_2), \rho)$	then return $\bot$	$c_1)$
5. Return $C = (c_1, c_2, \pi)$	4. Return $C' = c_1$	4. Return M

Fig. 3. PKE with Publicly Verifiable Ciphertexts from NIZK-based Transformation

2.5 Our PKE Scheme with Strictly Non-trivial Publicly Verifiable Ciphertexts

In this section, we propose a practical IND-CCA-secure PKE scheme, whose public verification is strictly non-trivial and is well-suited for IND-CCA/CPA filters described in the introduction due to an especially light algorithm Dec'. Our construction is inspired by the IND-CCA public-key KEM of Kiltz [18], which when plugged into a KEM/DEM framework would yield an IND-CCA-secure PKE scheme (but loose strictly non-trivial public verification as discussed in Section 4). In contrast, we obtain strictly non-trivial publicly verifiable PKE in a more direct way, by using the encapsulated key in [18] as a one-time pad for the message and by linking the resulting ciphertext components together with a one-time signature, whose verification key is in turn bound to the KEM ciphertext part through a tweak on the original scheme from [18]. Our scheme provides strictly non-trivial public verifiability, unlike the schemes presented in Sections 2.3 and 2.4 based on the CHK and NIZK transformations.

THE SCHEME. Our PG algorithm is similar to [18] except that it uses gap groups: $\mathsf{PG}(1^k)$ outputs public parameters $\mathsf{par} = (\mathbb{G}, p, g, \mathsf{DDH}, \mathsf{H})$ where $\mathbb{G} = \langle g \rangle$ is a multiplicative cyclic group of prime order p, $2^k < p < 2^{k+1}$, DDH is an efficient algorithm such that $\mathsf{DDH}(g^a, g^b, g^c) = 1 \Leftrightarrow c = ab\,(p)$, and $\mathsf{H} : \mathbb{G} \rightarrow \{0,1\}^{\ell_1(k)}$ is a cryptographic hash function such that $\ell_1(k)$ is a polynomial in k. We also use a strong one-time signature scheme $\mathsf{OTS} = (\mathsf{KG}, \mathsf{Sign}, \mathsf{Vrfy})$ with verification key space $\{0,1\}^{\ell_2(k)}$ such that $\ell_2(k)$ is a polynomial in k and a target collision resistant hash function $\mathsf{TCR} : \mathbb{G} \times \{0,1\}^{\ell_2(k)} \rightarrow \mathbb{Z}_p$. The message space is $\mathsf{MsgSp} = \{0,1\}^{\ell_1(k)}$. The scheme works as shown in Figure 4.

SECURITY ANALYSIS. First we give intuition why our scheme is IND-CCA-secure. Let (c^*, σ^*, vk^*) be the challenge ciphertext. As we discussed above, without the CHK transform, the proposed PKE can be seen as a KEM/DEM combination which is at least IND-CPA-secure due to Herranz et al. [15]. As for the KEM, the Hashed Diffie-Hellman (HDH) assumption [2] can be used to prove the IND-CPA

PKE.KG(par) :

1. $x \xleftarrow{\$} \mathbb{Z}_p^*$
2. $u \leftarrow g^x, v \xleftarrow{\$} \mathbb{G}$
3. $ek \leftarrow (u, v)$, $dk \leftarrow x$
4. Return (ek, dk)

PKE.Enc(par, ek, M) :

1. $(u, v) \leftarrow ek$
2. $(vk, sigk) \xleftarrow{\$} \mathsf{OTS.KG}(1^k)$
3. $r \xleftarrow{\$} \mathbb{Z}_p^*$, $c_1 \leftarrow g^r$
4. $t \leftarrow \mathsf{TCR}(c_1, vk)$, $\pi \leftarrow (u^t v)^r$
5. $K \leftarrow \mathsf{H}(u^r)$, $c_2 \leftarrow M \oplus K$
6. $c \leftarrow (c_1, c_2, \pi)$
7. $\sigma \leftarrow \mathsf{OTS.Sign}(sigk, c)$
8. Return $C = (c, \sigma, vk)$

PKE.Ver(par, ek, C) :

1. $(u, v) \leftarrow ek$
2. $(c, \sigma, vk) \leftarrow C$
3. $(c_1, c_2, \pi) \leftarrow c$
4. $t \leftarrow \mathsf{TCR}(c_1, vk)$
5. If $\mathsf{DDH}(c_1, u^t v, \pi) \neq 1$ or
   $\mathsf{OTS.Vrfy}(c, \sigma, vk) = \bot$
   return $\bot$
6. Return $C' = (c_1, c_2)$

PKE.Dec'(par, ek, dk, C') :

1. $(c_1, c_2) \leftarrow C'$
2. $x \leftarrow dk$
3. $K \leftarrow \mathsf{H}(c_1^x)$, $M \leftarrow c_2 \oplus K$
4. Return M

Fig. 4. Our PKE with Strictly Non-Trivial Publicly Verifiable Ciphertexts

security of the resulting PKE. Note that the message does not depend on vk^*, and σ^* is just the signature on c^*. Therefore c^* being an output of the IND-CPA-secure scheme hides the value of the chosen b from the adversary.

We now claim that the IND-CCA adversary $\mathcal{A}$ may access decryption oracle but gains no help in guessing the value of b. Suppose the adversary submits a ciphertext $(c', \sigma', vk') \neq (c^*, \sigma^*, vk^*)$ to the decryption oracle. Now there are two cases: $(a) \, vk' = vk^*$ or $(b) \, vk' \neq vk^*$. When $vk' = vk^*$, the decryption oracle will output $\bot$ as the adversary fails to break the underlying strongly unforgeable one-time signature scheme with respect to vk'. When $vk' \neq vk^*$, the attacker $\mathcal{B}$ against the HDH problem can set the public keys as seen in the IND-CCA security proof for the KEM by Kiltz [18] such that (1) $\mathcal{B}$ can answer except for the challenge ciphertext all decryption queries from $\mathcal{A}$ even without the knowledge of the secret key and (2) $\mathcal{B}$ solves HDH if $\mathcal{A}$ wins. This security is captured by the following theorem, which is proven in the full version [13].

Theorem 2. *Assume that* TCR *is a target collision resistant hash function and* OTS *is a strongly unforgeable one-time signature scheme. Under the Hashed Diffie-Hellman assumption for* $\mathbb{G}$ *and* H, *the PKE scheme* (PKE.KG, PKE.Enc, PKE.Dec = PKE.Dec' $\circ$ PKE.Ver) *based on Figure 4 is* IND-CCA-*secure.*

EFFICIENCY. Our PKE scheme in Figure 4 is more efficient than previous schemes with public consistency checks. In our scheme, public keys consist of 2 group elements, the ciphertext overhead is 2 group elements, a one-time signature and a one-time verification key, encryption requires 3.5 group exponentiations (using simultaneous exponentiation) and 1 one-time signature, verification requires 1 group exponentiation, 2 pairings, and 1 one-time signature verification, and lightweight decryption requires only one exponentiation.

Amongst existing PKE constructions with public consistency checks, only two seem to offer the same efficiency for lightweight decryption: Kiltz [18] describes a (direct) PKE construction (in addition to KEM) that is publicly verifiable with the same lightweight decryption cost of 1 group exponentiation, but at the cost of requiring public keys with the number of group elements being linear in the security parameter, as opposed to only 2 group elements in the public key of our scheme. Hanaoka and Kurosawa [14] describe a publicly verifiable KEM that, when combined with a DEM, would yield a (somewhat non-trivial, cf. Section 4) publicly verifiable PKE. Its lightweight decryption would require 1 group exponentiation (plus any costs from the DEM) but its public keys would contain 3 group elements, compared to 2 group elements in our scheme.

3 Publicly Verifiable Ciphertexts in General KEMs

3.1 Definition: General KEM

A *general key encapsulation* mechanism (GKEM) is a tuple GKEM = (PG, KG, Encap, Decap) of four algorithms such that PG and KG have the same syntax as in case of general encryption (cf. Section 2.1) except that message space is replaced with the key space KeySp, whereas the syntax of Encap and Decap matches that of Enc and Dec, respectively, with the only difference that Encap outputs a ciphertext C and a session key $K \in$ KeySp, while Decap outputs either K or $\perp$.

GKEM correctness and adversarial advantage $\mathbf{Adv}_{\mathcal{A},\mathsf{GKEM}}^{\mathsf{IND}\text{-}\mathsf{xxx}}(k)$, xxx $\in$ {CPA, CCA} in indistinguishability experiments from Figure 1 are also defined analogously to the case of general encryption.

3.2 General KEMs with Public Verifiable Ciphertexts

Definition 3 (Publicly Verifiable GKEM). *A general key encapsulation mechanism* GKEM = (PG, KG, Encap, Decap) *is said to be* publicly verifiable *with respect to auxiliary algorithms* Ver *and* Decap' *if* Decap = Decap' ∘ Ver *where* Ver *and* Decap' *satisfy the following:*

Ver(par, ek, C, t): *Given public parameters* par, *the encryption key* ek, *a ciphertext* C, *and a tag* t, *this algorithm outputs either* $\perp$ *if the ciphertext fails the validation, or a (transformed) ciphertext* C'. *Note that* Ver *does not take any secrets as input.*

Decap'(par, ek, dk, C', t): *This deterministic algorithm takes input public parameters* par, *encryption and decryption keys* (ek, dk), *a ciphertext* C', *and a tag* t, *and outputs a key* K.

Since all IND-CCA-secure general GKEMs trivially achieve public verifiability with respect to Ver(par, ek, C, t) := C and Decap' := Decap we can reuse Definition 2 for GKEMs to define their strictly non-trivial public verification.

Theorem 3 (whose proof is identical to that of Theorem 1 and is omitted here) shows that any publicly verifiable IND-CCA-secure GKEM scheme will remain at least IND-CPA-secure if the verification algorithm Ver is run by an honest-but-curious gateway. To account for a non-trivial verification process that may modify the ciphertext, we again apply post-processing to the output of the encapsulation algorithm (cf. Section 2.2).

Theorem 3. *Let* GKEM $=$ (PG, KG, Encap, Decap) *be an* IND-CCA-*secure general KEM and publicly verifiable with respect to* Ver *and* Decap'. *Let* Encap' $:=$ Ver $\circ$ Encap *and let* GKEM' $:=$ (PG, KG, Encap', Decap'). *For every* IND-CPA *adversary* $\mathcal{A}$ *against* GKEM', *there exists an* IND-CCA *adversary* $\mathcal{B}$ *against* GKEM *such that, for all* $k \geq 0$, $\mathbf{Adv}_{\mathcal{A},\mathsf{GKEM'}}^{\mathsf{IND\text{-}CPA}}(k) \leq \mathbf{Adv}_{\mathcal{B},\mathsf{GKEM}}^{\mathsf{IND\text{-}CCA}}(k)$, *where* $\mathcal{B}$ *has (asymptotically) the same running time as* $\mathcal{A}$.

3.3   Constructions of Strictly Non-trivial Publicly Verifiable KEMs

We now present some examples for KEMs with publicly verifiable ciphertexts. First, we discuss the publicly verifiable construction of an identity-based KEM that we obtain immediately from the IND-CCA-secure IB-KEM proposed by Kiltz and Galindo [19]. Parameters par' $=$ $(\mathbb{G}_1, \mathbb{G}_T, p, g, e, \mathsf{H})$ chosen by parameter generation algorithm PG(1^k), $k \in \mathbb{Z}_{\geq 0}$, are such that $\mathbb{G}_1$ is a multiplicative cyclic group of prime order p : $2^{2k} < p$, $\mathbb{G}_T$ is a multiplicative cyclic group of the same order, g is a random generator of $\mathbb{G}_1$, e : $\mathbb{G}_1 \times \mathbb{G}_1 \rightarrow \mathbb{G}_T$ is a non-degenerate bilinear map, and H : $\{0,1\}^{\ell(k)} \rightarrow \mathbb{G}_1$ is a hash function such that $\ell(k)$ is a polynomial in k. We also use a target collision resistant function TCR : $\mathbb{G}_1 \rightarrow \mathbb{Z}_p$. Figure 5 details the scheme.

Note that by defining KEM.Decap $=$ KEM.Decap' $\circ$ KEM.Ver we immediately obtain the original Kiltz-Galindo IB-KEM [19]. It is easy to see that its public verification algorithm KEM.Ver is strictly non-trivial. Further, Kiltz and Galindo noted that ignoring all operations associated to the identity in their IB-KEM yields a simplified version of the IND-CCA-secure public-key schemes from [8,17]. Therefore, by removing computations related to the ciphertext component c_2 and the key generation algorithm KG from Kiltz-Galindo's IB-KEM, we immediately obtain publicly verifiable constructions of a public-key KEM and a tag-based KEM with strictly non-trivial public verification.

4   Publicly Verifiable Ciphertexts in Hybrid Encryption

Since its invention, the KEM/DEM approach [10,30], being very simple and flexible, has become popular and part of several encryption standards [16,24,31]. It has been shown that if both the KEM and the DEM are secure against chosen-ciphertext attacks, then so is the resulting hybrid encryption scheme [10]. Herranz *et al.* [15] studied necessary and sufficient security conditions for KEMs and DEMs in relation with the security of the hybrid construction. They showed

KEM.PG(1^k) :

1. Generate
   par$' = (\mathbb{G}_1, \mathbb{G}_T, p, g, e, \mathsf{H})$
2. $\alpha \xleftarrow{\$} \mathbb{G}_1$, msk $\leftarrow \alpha$
3. $u, v \xleftarrow{\$} \mathbb{G}_1$, $z \leftarrow e(g, \alpha)$
4. pk $\leftarrow (u, v, z)$
5. par $\leftarrow$ (par$'$, pk)
6. Return (par, msk)

KEM.Encap(par, id) :

1. (par$'$, pk) $\leftarrow$ par
2. Parse par$'$ and pk
3. $r \xleftarrow{\$} \mathbb{Z}_p^*$, $c_1 \leftarrow g^r$
4. $t \leftarrow \mathsf{TCR}(c_1)$
5. $c_2 \leftarrow \mathsf{H}(id)^r$
6. $c_3 \leftarrow (u^t v)^r$
7. $K \leftarrow z^r \in \mathbb{G}_T$
8. $C \leftarrow (c_1, c_2, c_3) \in \mathbb{G}_1^3$
9. Return (C, K)

KEM.KG(par, msk, id) :

1. Parse (par$'$, pk) $\leftarrow$ par and par$'$
2. $s \xleftarrow{\$} \mathbb{Z}_p$, dk[id] $\leftarrow (\alpha \cdot \mathsf{H}(id)^s, g^s)$
3. Return dk[id]

KEM.Ver(par, pk, id, C) :

1. (par$'$, pk) $\leftarrow$ par
2. Parse par$'$ and pk
3. $(c_1, c_2, c_3) \leftarrow C$, $t \leftarrow \mathsf{TCR}(c_1)$
4. If $e(g, c_3) \neq e(c_1, u^t v)$ or
   $e(g, c_2) \neq e(c_1, \mathsf{H}(id))$,
   then return $\perp$
5. Return $C' = (c_1, c_2)$

KEM.Decap$'$(par, id, dk[id], C') :

1. (par$'$, pk) $\leftarrow$ par
2. Parse par$'$
3. $(c_1, c_2) \leftarrow C'$, $(d_1, d_2) \leftarrow$ dk[id]
4. $K \leftarrow e(c_1, d_1)/e(c_2, d_2)$
5. Return K

Fig. 5. Kiltz-Galindo IB-KEM with Publicly Verifiable Ciphertexts

that for the IND-CCA-security of the hybrid scheme, the KEM must be IND-CCA-secure while the security requirement on the DEM can be relaxed from IND-CCA to IND-OTCCA that prevents *one-time* (adaptive) chosen-ciphertext attacks.

Therefore, when dealing with public verifiability of hybrid schemes we must take into account existence of consistency checks in the decryption of DEM (in addition to checks for the KEM part). Since DEM consistency checks are performed using the decapsulated key, hybrid schemes cannot provide strictly non-trivial public verification from Definition 2. We show, however, that these schemes can offer a somewhat relaxed property, where public verifiability refers only to the KEM part, meaning that successful public consistency check of the KEM part is a necessary but not a sufficient condition for the overall success of decryption. In the context of gateway-assisted IND-CCA/CPA conversion this property effectively allows to outsource the consistency check of the KEM part to the gateway. In this way clients would only need to perform private consistency checks for the DEM part, which means negligible costs in comparison to the verification costs for KEMs.

4.1 Definition: Hybrid General Encryption

Let GKEM $=$ (PG, KG, Encap, Decap) be a general KEM scheme (as defined in Section 3.1) and let DEM $=$ (Enc, Dec) be a one-time symmetric key encryption scheme [15]. The two schemes are assumed to be compatible, i.e. session keys output by KEM are appropriate for DEM.

A *hybrid general encryption* (HGE) scheme is a tuple HGE $=$ (PG, KG, Enc, Dec) of four algorithms as defined in Figure 6.

HGE.PG(1^k) :

1. $(\mathsf{par}, \mathsf{msk}) \overset{\$}{\leftarrow} \mathsf{KEM.PG}(1^k)$
2. Return $(\mathsf{par}, \mathsf{msk})$

HGE.Enc($\mathsf{par}, \mathsf{ek}, M, t$) :

1. $(C_1, K) \leftarrow \mathsf{KEM.Encap}(\mathsf{par}, \mathsf{ek}, t)$
2. $C_2 \leftarrow \mathsf{DEM.Enc}(K, M)$
3. Return $C = (C_1, C_2)$

HGE.KG($\mathsf{par}, \mathsf{msk}, \mathsf{id}$) :

1. $(\mathsf{ek}, \mathsf{dk}) \overset{\$}{\leftarrow} \mathsf{KEM.KG}(\mathsf{par}, \mathsf{msk}, \mathsf{id})$
2. Return $(\mathsf{ek}, \mathsf{dk})$

HGE.Dec($\mathsf{par}, \mathsf{ek}, \mathsf{dk}, C, t$) :

1. $(C_1, C_2) \leftarrow C$
2. $K \leftarrow \mathsf{KEM.Decap}(\mathsf{par}, \mathsf{ek}, \mathsf{dk}, C_1, t)$
3. If $K = \bot$ then return $\bot$
4. $M \leftarrow \mathsf{DEM.Dec}(K, C_2)$
5. Return M (possibly as $\bot$)

Fig. 6. Hybrid General Encryption Scheme HGE

CORRECTNESS. A hybrid general encryption scheme $\mathsf{HGE} = (\mathsf{PG}, \mathsf{KG}, \mathsf{Enc}, \mathsf{Dec})$ is *correct* if, for all $(\mathsf{par}, \mathsf{msk}) \in [\mathsf{HGE.PG}]$, all plaintexts M, all identities $\mathsf{id} \in \mathsf{IDSp}$, all $(\mathsf{ek}, \mathsf{dk}) \in [\mathsf{HGE.KG}(\mathsf{par}, \mathsf{msk}, \mathsf{id})]$, and all tags $t \in \mathsf{TagSp}$, we have $\mathsf{HGE.Dec}(\mathsf{par}, \mathsf{ek}, \mathsf{dk}, \mathsf{HGE.Enc}(\mathsf{par}, \mathsf{ek}, M, t), t) = M$ with probability one, where the probability is taken over the coins of HGE.Enc.

4.2   Hybrid General Encryption with Publicly Verifiable Ciphertexts

When defining public verifiability of $\mathsf{HGE} = (\mathsf{PG}, \mathsf{KG}, \mathsf{Enc}, \mathsf{Dec})$ schemes with respect to Ver and Dec′, we can essentially reuse Definition 1 for general encryption. Note that message M output by the lightweight decryption algorithm Dec′ could also be an error symbol $\bot$. As previously mentioned, in general HGE cannot satisfy Definition 2 of strictly non-trivial public verification since failure of the original decryption procedure HGE.Dec may not necessarily imply failure of the verification algorithm Ver′. For this reason we define the following relaxed notion:

Definition 4 (Somewhat Non-trivial Public Verification). *Let* $\mathsf{HGE} = (\mathsf{PG}, \mathsf{KG}, \mathsf{Enc}, \mathsf{Dec})$ *be a hybrid general encryption scheme from Figure 6 that is publicly verifiable with respect to auxiliary algorithms* Ver *and* Dec′. *Let* $(\mathsf{par}, \mathsf{msk}) \leftarrow \mathsf{PG}(1^k)$. Ver *is said to be* somewhat non-trivial *if, for all* $\mathsf{id} \in \mathsf{IDSp}$, *all* $t \in \mathsf{TagSp}$, *and* $(\mathsf{ek}, \mathsf{dk}) \leftarrow \mathsf{KG}(\mathsf{par}, \mathsf{msk}, \mathsf{id})$,

1. $(\mathsf{Ver}(\mathsf{par}, \mathsf{ek}, C, t) = \bot \vee \mathsf{DEM.Dec}(K, C_2) = \bot) \Leftrightarrow \mathsf{Dec}(\mathsf{par}, \mathsf{ek}, \mathsf{dk}, C, t) = \bot$
   for all C, *where* $C = (C_1, C_2)$ *and* $K = \mathsf{KEM.Decap}(\mathsf{par}, \mathsf{ek}, \mathsf{dk}, C_1, t)$, *and*
2. *there exists a ciphertext* C *for which* $\mathsf{Dec}(\mathsf{par}, \mathsf{ek}, \mathsf{dk}, C, t) = \bot$.

Condition 1 requires that successful public verification is necessary but not sufficient for the decryption algorithm to successfully decrypt. In particular, if Ver succeeds then the only reason why HGE.Dec fails is because of a failure in DEM.Dec. Condition 2 remains as in Definition 2.

   Theorem 4 (proven in the full version [13]) shows that if the underlying general KEM is publicly verifiable with strictly non-trivial verification then the hybrid general encryption scheme is publicly verifiable in the somewhat non-trivial way and that by outsourcing verification of the KEM part the hybrid scheme remains at least IND-CPA-secure.

Theorem 4. *Let* GKEM = (PG, KG, Encap, Decap) *be an* IND-CCA-*secure general key encapsulation mechanism that is publicly verifiable with respect to* GKEM. Ver *and* GKEM.Decap′, DEM = (Enc, Dec) *be an* IND-OTCCA-*secure data encapsulation mechanism, and* HGE = (PG, KG, Enc, Dec) *be the resulting hybrid general encryption scheme.*

1. *If* GKEM.Ver *is strictly non-trivial then* HGE *is publicly verifiable with respect to a somewhat non-trivial* HGE.Ver *and an algorithm* HGE.Dec′.

2. *Let* HGE′ := (PG, KG, Enc′, Dec′) *with* HGE′.Enc′ = HGE.Ver ∘ HGE.Enc *and* HGE′.Dec′ = HGE.Dec′. *For any* IND-CPA *adversary* $\mathcal{A}$ *against* HGE′, *there exists an* IND-CPA *adversary* $\mathcal{B}_1$ *against* GKEM′ *and an* IND-OTCCA *adversary* $\mathcal{B}_2$ *against* DEM *such that*

$$\mathbf{Adv}_{\mathcal{A},\mathsf{HGE}'}^{\mathsf{IND\text{-}CPA}}(k) \leq \mathbf{Adv}_{\mathcal{B}_1,\mathsf{GKEM}'}^{\mathsf{IND\text{-}CCA}}(k) + \mathbf{Adv}_{\mathcal{B}_2,\mathsf{DEM}}^{\mathsf{IND\text{-}OTCCA}}(k) \quad \forall k \geq 0$$

and $\mathcal{B}_1$ *and* $\mathcal{B}_2$ *have (asymptotically) the same running time as* $\mathcal{A}$.

4.3   Constructions of Hybrid Encryption with Publicly Verifiable Ciphertexts

Herranz et al. [15] showed that if some IND-CCA-secure KEM is combined with an IND-OTCCA-secure DEM then the resulting hybrid encryption scheme is also IND-CCA-secure. As shown by Cramer and Shoup [10], one can easily construct an IND-OTCCA-secure DEM by adding a one-time MAC to a one-time-secure DEM such as one-time pad. Moreover, Theorem 4 states that if the underlying KEM is publicly verifiable then the resulting hybrid encryption scheme is publicly verifiable as well. We can thus immediately obtain a range of publicly verifiable constructions of hybrid encryption schemes with somewhat non-trivial verification from these two building blocks; for instance, we can apply publicly verifiable KEM constructions from Section 3.3.

In the case of tag-based KEM/DEM approach, Abe *et al.* [3] showed that IND-CCA-secure hybrid encryption can be obtained by combining an IND-CCA-secure tag-based KEM with a one-time secure DEM. They also provide constructions of IND-CCA-secure tag-based KEMs that they obtain generically from IND-CCA-secure public-key KEMs and one-time MACs. Our publicly verifiable public-key-based KEM constructions from Section 3.3 can be used to instantiate their tag-based KEMs, resulting in further publicly verifiable hybrid encryption schemes.

5   Conclusion

In this work we formalized the notion of public verifiability for encryption schemes, KEMs, and hybrid KEM/DEM constructions. By adopting and extending the generalized syntax from [1] our definitions of publicly verifiable schemes and corresponding security results hold for public-key based, identity-based, and tag-based settings. We defined conditions under which public verifiability can be seen as a non-trivial requirement for IND-CCA security and have proven that by outsourcing verification those schemes remain at least IND-CPA secure. We showcased that well-known CHK and NIZK-based transforms offer strictly non-trivial public verification, proposed a new PKE scheme that makes most use of this property, and discussed different flavors of efficient strictly non-trivial publicly verifiable KEMs. With regard to hybrid schemes we showed that although strictly non-trivial verification is not achievable, a relaxed notion of somewhat non-trivial public verifiability can be obtained, which still offers sufficient performance gains in IND-CCA/CPA filters that are useful for applications where outsourcing of ciphertext verification to an honest-but-curios gateway without losing confidentiality is sufficient for practical purposes.

Acknowledgments. This research was supported by the Australian Technology Network (ATN) and German Academic Exchange Service (DAAD) Joint Research Co-operation Scheme. Juan Manuel González Nieto and Douglas Stebila were further supported by the Australia–India Strategic Research Fund project TA020002. Mark Manulis acknowledges support through German Research Foundation (DFG) via grant MA 4957. This work was also supported by the German Federal Ministry of Education and Research (BMBF) within EC SPRIDE and by the Hessian LOEWE excellence initiative within CASED.

References

1. Abdalla, M., Bellare, M., Neven, G.: Robust Encryption. In: Micciancio, D. (ed.) TCC 2010. LNCS, vol. 5978, pp. 480–497. Springer, Heidelberg (2010)
2. Abdalla, M., Bellare, M., Rogaway, P.: The Oracle Diffie-Hellman Assumptions and an Analysis of DHIES. In: Naccache, D. (ed.) CT-RSA 2001. LNCS, vol. 2020, pp. 143–158. Springer, Heidelberg (2001)
3. Abe, M., Gennaro, R., Kurosawa, K.: Tag-KEM/DEM: A New Framework for Hybrid Encryption. Journal of Cryptology 21(1), 97–130 (2008)
4. Abe, M., Kiltz, E., Okamoto, T.: Chosen Ciphertext Security with Optimal Ciphertext Overhead. In: Pieprzyk, J. (ed.) ASIACRYPT 2008. LNCS, vol. 5350, pp. 355–371. Springer, Heidelberg (2008)
5. Bentahar, K., Farshim, P., Malone-Lee, J., Smart, N.P.: Generic Constructions of Identity-Based and Certificateless KEMs. J. Cryptology 21(2), 178–199 (2008)
6. Boneh, D., Katz, J.: Improved Efficiency for CCA-Secure Cryptosystems Built Using Identity-Based Encryption. In: Menezes, A. (ed.) CT-RSA 2005. LNCS, vol. 3376, pp. 87–103. Springer, Heidelberg (2005)
7. Boneh, D., Boyen, X., Halevi, S.: Chosen Ciphertext Secure Public Key Threshold Encryption Without Random Oracles. In: Pointcheval, D. (ed.) CT-RSA 2006. LNCS, vol. 3860, pp. 226–243. Springer, Heidelberg (2006)
8. Boyen, X., Mei, Q., Waters, B.: Direct chosen ciphertext security from identity-based techniques. In: Atluri, V., Meadows, C., Juels, A. (eds.) ACM CCS 2005, pp. 320–329. ACM (2005)

9. Canetti, R., Halevi, S., Katz, J.: Chosen-Ciphertext Security from Identity-Based Encryption. In: Cachin, C., Camenisch, J. (eds.) EUROCRYPT 2004. LNCS, vol. 3027, pp. 207–222. Springer, Heidelberg (2004)

10. Cramer, R., Shoup, V.: Design and analysis of practical public-key encryption schemes secure against adaptive chosen ciphertext attack. SIAM J. Computing 33(1), 167–226 (2003)

11. Dolev, D., Dwork, C., Naor, M.: Non-Malleable Cryptography (Extended Abstract). In: ACM STOC 1991, pp. 542–552. ACM (1991)

12. Elkind, E., Sahai, A.: A unified methodology for constructing public-key encryption schemes secure against adaptive chosen-ciphertext attack. Cryptology ePrint Archive, Report 2002/042 (2002), http://eprint.iacr.org/2002/042

13. González Nieto, J.M., Manulis, M., Poettering, B., Rangasamy, J., Stebila, D.: Publicly Verifiable Ciphertexts. Full version. Cryptology ePrint Archive, Report 2012/357 (2012), http://eprint.iacr.org/2012/357

14. Hanaoka, G., Kurosawa, K.: Efficient Chosen Ciphertext Secure Public Key Encryption under the Computational Diffie-Hellman Assumption. In: Pieprzyk, J. (ed.) ASIACRYPT 2008. LNCS, vol. 5350, pp. 308–325. Springer, Heidelberg (2008)

15. Herranz, J., Hofheinz, D., Kiltz, E.: KEM/DEM: Necessary and sufficient conditions for secure hybrid encryption. Cryptology ePrint Archive, Report 2006/256 (2006), http://eprint.iacr.org/2006/256

16. Imai, H., Yamagishi, A.: CRYPTREC Project - Cryptographic Evaluation Project for the Japanese Electronic Government -. In: Okamoto, T. (ed.) ASIACRYPT 2000. LNCS, vol. 1976, pp. 399–400. Springer, Heidelberg (2000)

17. Kiltz, E.: Chosen-Ciphertext Security from Tag-Based Encryption. In: Halevi, S., Rabin, T. (eds.) TCC 2006. LNCS, vol. 3876, pp. 581–600. Springer, Heidelberg (2006)

18. Kiltz, E.: Chosen-Ciphertext Secure Key-Encapsulation Based on Gap Hashed Diffie-Hellman. In: Okamoto, T., Wang, X. (eds.) PKC 2007. LNCS, vol. 4450, pp. 282–297. Springer, Heidelberg (2007)

19. Kiltz, E., Galindo, D.: Direct Chosen-Ciphertext Secure Identity-Based Key Encapsulation Without Random Oracles. In: Batten, L.M., Safavi-Naini, R. (eds.) ACISP 2006. LNCS, vol. 4058, pp. 336–347. Springer, Heidelberg (2006)

20. Lim, C.H., Lee, P.J.: Another Method for Attaining Security against Adaptively Chosen Ciphertext Attacks. In: Stinson, D.R. (ed.) CRYPTO 1993. LNCS, vol. 773, pp. 420–434. Springer, Heidelberg (1994)

21. Liu, J.K., Chu, C.K., Zhou, J.: Identity-Based Server-Aided Decryption. In: Parampalli, U., Hawkes, P. (eds.) ACISP 2011. LNCS, vol. 6812, pp. 337–352. Springer, Heidelberg (2011)

22. Libert, B., Yung, M.: Adaptively Secure Non-interactive Threshold Cryptosystems. In: Aceto, L., Henzinger, M., Sgall, J. (eds.) ICALP 2011, Part II. LNCS, vol. 6756, pp. 588–600. Springer, Heidelberg (2011)

23. Naor, M., Yung, M.: Public-key Cryptosystems Provably Secure against Chosen Ciphertext Attacks. In: ACM STOC 1990, pp. 427–437. ACM (1990)

24. NESSIE. Final report of European project IST-1999-12324: New European Schemes for Signatures, Integrity, and Encryption (April 2004), https://www.cosic.esat.kuleuven.be/nessie/

25. Phan, D.H., Pointcheval, D.: Chosen-Ciphertext Security without Redundancy. In: Laih, C.-S. (ed.) ASIACRYPT 2003. LNCS, vol. 2894, pp. 1–18. Springer, Heidelberg (2003)

26. Phan, D.H., Pointcheval, D.: OAEP 3-Round:A Generic and Secure Asymmetric Encryption Padding. In: Lee, P.J. (ed.) ASIACRYPT 2004. LNCS, vol. 3329, pp. 63–77. Springer, Heidelberg (2004)
27. Persiano, P.: About the Existence of Trapdoors in Cryptosystems (manuscript), http://libeccio.dia.unisa.it/Papers/Trapdoor/Trapdoor.pdf
28. Rompel, J.: One-Way Functions are Necessary and Sufficient for Secure Signatures. In: STOC 1990, pp. 387–394. ACM (1990)
29. Sahai, A.: Non-malleable non-interactive zero-knowledge and adaptive chosen-ciphertext security. In: FOCS 1999, pp. 543–553. IEEE (1999)
30. Shoup, V.: A proposal for an ISO standard for public key encryption (version 2.1) (2001) (manuscript), http://shoup.net/papers
31. Shoup, V.: ISO 18033-2: An emerging standard for public-key encryption, Final Committee Draft (December 2004), http://shoup.net/iso/std6.pdf
32. Shoup, V., Gennaro, R.: Securing Threshold Cryptosystems against Chosen Ciphertext Attack. In: Nyberg, K. (ed.) EUROCRYPT 1998. LNCS, vol. 1403, pp. 1–16. Springer, Heidelberg (1998)

A   Proof of Theorem 1

Proof. Let A be an adversary that breaks the IND-CPA security of GE′ and runs in time t_A. We build an algorithm B running in time t_B that, using A as a sub-routine, breaks the IND-CCA security of GE. Let C_{GE} denote the challenger in the associated IND-CCA security game for GE.

Algorithm B interacts with C_{GE} and A. With A, B acts as a challenger playing the IND-CPA security game for GE′. In detail, B does the following: On input public par, B forwards them on to A. At some point A outputs the challenge consisting of two messages M_0 and M_1, a target identity id*, and a target tag t^*. B forwards M_0 and M_1 along with id* and t^* to GE challenger C_{GE}, which in turn responds with a ciphertext C^* on M_b^* for a random bit b (unknown to B). Since C^* is publicly verifiable, B hands $\bar{C}^* \leftarrow \text{Ver}(\text{par}, \text{ek}[\text{id}^*], C^*, t^*)$ as the challenge ciphertext over to A. Eventually, A outputs a bit b', which B uses as it own output.

Queries of A to the oracles O_{EK} and O_{DK} are answered by B as follows:

- $O_{EK}(\text{id})$: B queries $O_{EK}(\text{id})$ to C_{GE} and responds to A with whatever it receives from C_{GE}. Note that A is allowed to query O_{EK} on id*.
- $O_{DK}(\text{id})$: B queries $O_{DK}(\text{id})$ to C_{GE} and responds to A with whatever it receives from C_{GE}. Note that A is not allowed to query O_{DK} on id*.

The total running time of B is $t_B \leq t_A + t_{Ver}$ with t_A being the running time of A and t_{Ver} being the execution time of Ver.

Given the above perfect simulation of oracles, B clearly breaks the IND-CCA security of GE whenever A breaks the IND-CPA security of GE′. $\square$

Public-Key Encryption with Lazy Parties*

Kenji Yasunaga

Institute of Systems, Information Technologies and Nanotechnologies, Japan
yasunaga@isit.or.jp

Abstract. In a public-key encryption scheme, if a sender is not concerned about the security of a message and is unwilling to generate costly randomness, the security of the encrypted message can be compromised. This is caused by the *laziness* of the sender. In this work, we characterize *lazy parties* in cryptography. Lazy parties are regarded as honest parties in a protocol, but they are not concerned about the security of the protocol in a certain situation. In such a situation, they behave in an honest-looking way, and are unwilling to do a costly task. We study, in particular, public-key encryption with lazy parties. Specifically, as the first step toward understanding the behavior of lazy parties in public-key encryption, we consider a rather simple setting in which the costly task is to generate randomness used in algorithms, and parties can choose either costly good randomness or cheap bad randomness. We model lazy parties as rational players who behaves rationally to maximize their utilities, and define a security game between lazy parties and an adversary. A secure encryption scheme requires that the game is conducted by lazy parties in a secure way if they follow a prescribed strategy, and the prescribed strategy is a good equilibrium solution for the game. Since a standard secure encryption scheme does not work for lazy parties, we present some public-key encryption schemes that are secure for lazy parties.

1 Introduction

Consider the following situation. Alice is a teacher of a course "Introduction to Cryptography." She promised to inform the students of their grades by using public-key encryption. Each student prepared his/her public key, and sent it to Alice. Since there are many students taking the course, it is very costly to encrypt the grades of all the student. However, since she promised to use public-key encryption, she decided to encrypt the grades. To encrypt messages, she needs to generate randomness. Generating good randomness is also a costly task. While the grades are personal information for the students and thus they want them to be securely transmitted, the grades are not personal information for Alice. The security of the grades is not her concern. She noticed that, even if she used bad randomness for encryption, no one may detect it. Consequently, she used cheap bad randomness for encryption instead of costly good randomness.

The above situation resulted in an undesirable consequence. This example demonstrates that, if some party in a cryptographic protocol is not concerned

---

* Research supported in part by JSPS KAKENHI (23500010).

I. Visconti and R. De Prisco (Eds.): SCN 2012, LNCS 7485, pp. 411–425, 2012.
© Springer-Verlag Berlin Heidelberg 2012

about the security and is unwilling to do a costly task, then the security of the protocol may be compromised. The insecurity is caused by the *laziness* of the party. A traditional cryptography did not consider the laziness of players who are regarded as honest. However, the security should be preserved even if such lazy parties exist.

1.1   This Work

We introduce the notion of *lazy parties*, who may compromise the security of cryptographic protocols. We characterize lazy parties such that (1) they are not concerned about the security of the protocol in a certain situation, and (2) they behave in an honest-looking way and are unwilling to do a costly task. We study, in particular, public-key encryption schemes with lazy parties. As the first step toward understanding the behavior of lazy parties in public-key encryption, we consider the following rather simple setting. The sender and the receiver have their own valuable messages. They want to transmit a message securely if it is valuable for them. However, since both the sender and the receiver are lazy, the sender is not willing to do a costly task if a message is not valuable for him, and the receiver vice versa. The costly task we consider is to generate randomness used in algorithms. For simplicity, we assume that players can choose either costly good randomness or cheap bad randomness. While the costly good randomness is a truly random string, the cheap bad randomness is some fixed string in our setting. Our goal is to design public-key encryption schemes in which valuable messages of the sender or the receiver can be transmitted securely by the lazy sender and receiver who may use bad randomness in algorithms.

Formalizing the Problem. We formalize the security of public-key encryption for lazy parties as follows. First we define a security game between a sender, a receiver, and an adversary. The game is a variant of the usual chosen plaintext attack (CPA) game of public-key encryption. In this game we see the sender and the receiver as rational players. The sender and the receiver have their utility functions, the values of which are determined by the outcome of the game, and they play the game to maximize their utilities. Roughly speaking, we say that an encryption scheme is secure for lazy parties if there is a pair of prescribed strategies of the sender and the receiver for the game, the game is conducted in a secure way if they follow the prescribed pair of strategies, and the pair of strategies is a good equilibrium solution. The solution concepts we consider in this work are Nash equilibrium and strict Nash equilibrium, which is stronger than Nash equilibrium.

Impossibility Results. As impossibility results, we show that to achieve the security for lazy parties with a Nash equilibrium solution in our setting, the sender must generate a secret key, and the encryption phase requires at least two rounds. Neither of them is satisfied in the usual public-key encryption. Therefore, we need to consider encryption schemes in which the sender generates a secret key in the key generation phase, and the sender and the receiver interacts at least two times in encrypting a message.

Constructions. The security for lazy parties varies according to what information each player knows. We consider several situations according to the information each player knows, and present a secure encryption scheme for lazy parties in each situation.

First we consider a basic situation in which the receiver does not know whether a message to be encrypted is valuable for him or not, and the sender knows the value of the message for him. We propose a two-round encryption scheme that is secure for lazy parties with a strict Nash equilibrium solution. The idea is simple. First the receiver generates a random string, encrypts it by the public key of the sender, and sends it to the sender. Next the sender recovers the random string from the ciphertext and uses it to encrypt a message by the one-time pad. Since the receiver does not know whether a message to be encrypted is valuable for him or not, the receiver will generate good randomness.

Next, we consider a situation in which the receiver may know whether a message to be encrypted is valuable for him or not. This captures a real-life situation; If we use encryption, in many cases, it is realized not only by the sender but also the receiver that what kind of message will be sent. Under this situation, the above two-round scheme seems no longer secure since the receiver would not generate good randomness if a message to be encrypted is not valuable for him. We show that for any pair of strategies the above two-round scheme cannot achieve the security for lazy parties with a Nash equilibrium solution. Thus we propose a three-round encryption scheme that is secure in this situation. The encryption phase is conducted as follows. First the sender and the receiver perform a key-agreement protocol to share a random string between them so that the shared string will be good randomness if at least one of them uses good randomness in the key-agreement protocol. Then, the sender uses the shared string as randomness in the encryption algorithm. Finally, after recovering a message, the receiver encrypts the message by the sender's public key and makes it public. At first glance, the final step of making the encrypted message public seems redundant, but our scheme does not achieve the security without this step. Our three-round scheme is secure for lazy parties with a strict Nash equilibrium solution.

We generalize the above situation such that both the sender and the receiver may know that a message to be encrypted is valuable for them. The difference from the previous situation is that the sender may be able to know the value of the message for the receiver, and the receiver vice versa. In this situation, we realized that the above three-round scheme has two different pairs of strategies that achieve the security with a strict Nash equilibrium. There is a situation such that one pair yields a higher utility to the sender, and the other pair yields a higher utility to the receiver. Moreover, if the sender follows a strategy that yields a higher utility to him and the receiver also does so, they will conduct an encryption protocol in an insecure way, which is worse for both of them. Thus, we propose a simple way to avoid such a consequence.

Finally, we consider constructing a non-interactive encryption scheme that is secure for lazy parties. We avoid the impossibility of existing non-interactive schemes by adding some reasonable assumption to lazy parties. The assumption is that players do not want to reveal their secret key to adversaries. Then we employ a *signcryption* scheme for an encryption scheme. A signcryption scheme is a cryptographic primitive that achieves both public-key encryption and signature simultaneously, and thus the sender also has the secret key. Some of signcryption schemes (e.g., [1]) have the *key-exposure property*, which means that the sender's secret key can be efficiently recovered from a ciphertext and its random string. This property seems to be undesirable in a standard setting. However, we show that if a signcryption scheme with the key-exposure property is employed as a public-key encryption scheme, it is secure for lazy parties with a strict Nash equilibrium solution.

1.2   Related Work

Halpern and Pass [2] have introduced *Bayesian machine games* in which players' utilities can depend on the computational costs of their strategies. We could use the framework of Halpern and Pass to define a security of public-key encryption schemes for lazy parties since the utilities of lazy parties depend on their computational cost. We did not use their framework in this work since their framework seems too general for our purpose.

There have been many studies on *rational cryptography* [3,4,5], in which players in cryptographic protocols are considered rational players. Much study has been devoted to designing *rational secret sharing* [6,7,8,9,10,11,12,13]. Recently, the problem of fair two-party computation with rational players was considered [14,15]. The work in this paper also can be seen as a study of rational cryptography. As far as we know, this is the first study of rational behavior in public-key encryption schemes.

In cryptography, there are several characterizations of parties who are neither honest nor malicious [16,17,18]. In particular, the deviations of honest-looking parties were studied in [16,17]. All types of honest-looking parties defined in [16,17] deviate from the protocol in a way that is computationally indistinguishable from the view of external or internal parties. This means that any efficient statistical test cannot tell the difference between honest parties and honest-looking parties. In this study, we consider honest-looking parties who may deviate from the protocol by using a fixed string instead of a truly random string. Since the difference between fixed strings and truly random strings can be told by a simple statistical test, the deviations of lazy parties in this study are bolder than honest-looking parties in [16,17]. Note that all the characterization in [16,17] appeared in the context of general multiparty computation, not in public-key encryption.

A main problem of public-key encryption with lazy parties is that lazy parties might not use good randomness in algorithms. There are many studies on the security of cryptographic tasks when only weak randomness is available. If there are only high min-entropy sources, not including truly random one, many impossibility results are known [19,20]. Bellare et al. [21] introduced hedged public-key encryption, which achieves the usual CPA security if good randomness is used, and achieves a weaker security if bad randomness is used. In this work, we consider only two types of randomness sources, truly random ones and fixed ones. We achieve the security by a mechanism such that lazy parties choose to use good randomness for their purpose.

1.3 Future Work

Possible future work is extending the framework of this work to more general settings. For example, in this work, lazy players can choose either truly random (full entropy) strings or fixed (zero entropy) strings as the randomness in algorithms. Since it seems more realistic for players to be able to choose random strings from general entropy sources, extending the framework to such a general setting and defining a reasonable security on that setting are interesting for future work.

Another possible future work is to explore cryptographic protocols that may be compromised in the presence of lazy parties. Although we consider only generating good randomness as a costly task, it is possible to consider another thing as cost, such as time for computation and delay in the protocol.

1.4 Organization

In Section 2, we introduce the CPA game for lazy parties, define utility functions of lazy parties, and provide a definition of the CPA security for lazy parties. Our secure encryption schemes in various situations are presented in Section 3. All the proofs of propositions and theorems can be found in the full version of this paper.

1.5 Notations

A function $\epsilon(\cdot)$ is called *negligible* if for any constant c, $\epsilon(n) < 1/n^c$ for every sufficiently large n. For two families of random variables $X = \{X_n\}_{n\in\mathbb{N}}$ and $Y = \{Y_n\}_{n\in\mathbb{N}}$, we say that X and Y are *computationally indistinguishable*, denoted by $X \approx_c Y$, if for every probabilistic polynomial-time (PPT) distinguisher D, there is a negligible function $\epsilon(\cdot)$ such that $|\Pr[D(X_n) = 1] - \Pr[D(Y_n) = 1]| \leq \epsilon(n)$ for every sufficiently large n. For a probabilistic algorithm A, the output of A when the input is x is denoted by $A(x)$, and denoted by $A(x; r)$ when the random string r used in A is represented explicitly.

2 Lazy Parties in Public-Key Encryption

We consider the following setting of public-key encryption between a lazy sender and a lazy receiver. Each lazy party has a set of valuable messages, and wants a message to be sent securely if it is valuable for that party. If a message to be encrypted is not valuable for a party, he is not concerned about the security of the message, and does not want to use good randomness in the computation.

In this paper, we consider only two types of randomness, good randomness and bad randomness. Good randomness is a truly random string but costly. Bad randomness is generated with zero cost, but is some fixed string.

We formalize the security as follows. Lazy parties are considered as rational players who have some utility functions and behave rationally to maximize their utilities. We define a security game between a lazy sender, a lazy receiver, and an adversary. Then, we say that an encryption scheme is secure if there is a pair of prescribed strategies of the sender and the receiver for the game, the game is conducted in a secure way if they follow the strategies, and the pair of strategies is a good equilibrium solution.

We define public-key encryption as an *interactive* protocol between a sender and a receiver. The reason is that we cannot achieve the security if the sender does not have a secret key or the encryption phase is conducted in one round, which will be described in the last of this section. In the key generation phase, both the sender and the receiver generate their own public key and secret key, then each public key is distributed to the other player. In the encryption phase, the players conduct an interactive protocol in which the sender has a message as an input. After the encryption phase, the receiver can recover the message by running the decryption algorithm. This definition is much more general than the usual public-key encryption, in which only the receiver generates a public key and a secret key, and the encryption phase is just sending a ciphertext from the sender to the receiver.

Definition 1 (Public-key encryption scheme). *An n-round public-key encryption scheme Π is the tuple $(\{\mathrm{GEN}_w\}_{w \in \{S,R\}}, \{\mathrm{ENC}_i\}_{i \in \{1,\ldots,n\}}, \mathrm{DEC})$ such that*

- **Key generation:** *For each $w \in \{S, R\}$, on input 1^k, GEN_w outputs (pk_w, sk_w). Let $\mathcal{M}$ denote the message space.*

- **Encryption:** *For a message $m \in \mathcal{M}$, set $st_S = (pk_S, pk_R, sk_S, m)$, $st_R = (pk_S, pk_R, sk_R)$, and $c_0 = \bot$. Let $w \in \{S, R\}$ be the first sender, and $\bar{w} \in \{S, R\} \setminus \{w\}$ the second sender. For each round $i \in \{1, \ldots, n\}$, when i is odd, $\mathrm{ENC}_i(c_{i-1}, st_w)$ outputs (c_i, st'_w), and st_w is updated to st'_w, and when i is even, $\mathrm{ENC}_i(c_{i-1}, st_{\bar{w}})$ outputs $(c_i, st'_{\bar{w}})$, and $st_{\bar{w}}$ is updated to $st'_{\bar{w}}$.*

- **Decryption:** *After the encryption phase, on input st_R, DEC outputs $\hat{m}$.*

- **Correctness:** *For any message $m \in \mathcal{M}$, after the encryption phase, $\mathrm{DEC}(st_R) = m$.*

We provide a definition of the chosen plaintext attack (CPA) game for lazy parties. The game is a variant of the usual CPA game for public-key encryption. The game is conducted as follows. The sender S (and the receiver R) has his valuable message space $\mathcal{M}_S$ (and $\mathcal{M}_R$), which is a subset of $\{0, 1\}^*$. First, each player $w \in \{S, R\}$ are asked to choose good randomness or bad randomness for the key generation algorithm. If player w chooses good randomness, a random string r_w^g for key generation is sampled as a truly random string. Otherwise, r_w^g is generated by the adversary of this game. Then, pairs of public and secret keys for the two parties are generated using r_w^g as a random string, and the public keys are distributed to the sender, the receiver, and the adversary. Next, the adversary generates two sequences m_0 and m_1 of challenge messages, where $m_b = (m_{b,1}, \ldots, m_{b,\ell})$ for $b \in \{0,1\}$ and some polynomial ℓ. After that, the challenger chooses $b \in \{0,1\}$ uniformly at random. The sender receives m_b and asked to choose good or bad randomness for the encryption protocol. If he chooses good randomness, random strings $r^e_{i,j}$ for encryption is sampled as truly random strings, where $r^e_{i,j}$ represents a random string used in the j-th round of the encryption for the i-th message $m_{b,i}$. Otherwise, strings $r^e_{i,j}$'s are generated by the adversary. Similarly, the receiver also asked to choose good or bad randomness for the encryption protocol without seeing the challenge messages m_b, and random strings $r^e_{i,j}$'s are generated in the same way as the sender. Then, a sequence of challenge messages are encrypted using $r^e_{i,j}$'s as random strings. Finally, the adversary receives a sequence of challenge ciphertexts, and outputs a guess $b' \in \{0,1\}$. The outcome of the game consists of five values Win, Val_S, Val_R, Num_S, and Num_R. The value Win takes 1 if the guess of the adversary is correct, namely $b = b'$, and 0 otherwise. The value Val_w for player $w \in \{S, R\}$ takes 1 if there is at least one valuable message for player w in the sequence m_b of challenge messages, and 0 otherwise. The value Num_w for player $w \in \{S, R\}$ represents the number of times that player w chose good randomness in the game, which is between 0 and 2.

In the following, we provide a formal definition of the CPA game for lazy parties. For a probabilistic algorithm A, we denote by $\ell(A)$ the length of random bits required in running A. We define $\mathrm{SAMP}(\cdot)$ to be an algorithm such that $\mathrm{SAMP}(A)$ samples a random string from $\{0,1\}^{\ell(A)}$.

Definition 2 (CPA game for lazy parties). *Let $\Pi = (\{\mathrm{GEN}_w\}_{w \in \{S,R\}}, \{\mathrm{ENC}_i\}_{i \in \{1,\ldots,n\}}, \mathrm{DEC})$ be a public-key encryption scheme. For an adversary A, the security parameter k, valuable message spaces $\mathcal{M}_S$ and $\mathcal{M}_R$, and a pair of strategies (σ_S, σ_R), we define the following game.*

$\mathrm{Game}^{\mathrm{cpa}}(\Pi, k, A, \mathcal{M}_S, \mathcal{M}_R, \sigma_S, \sigma_R)$:

1. ***Choice of randomness for key generation:*** *For each $w \in \{S, R\}$, compute $x^g_w \leftarrow \sigma_w(1^k, \mathcal{M}_w)$, where $x^g_w \in \{\mathsf{Good}, \mathsf{Bad}\}$. If $x^g_w = \mathsf{Bad}$, then given $(1^k, w)$, A outputs $r^g_w \in \{0,1\}^{\ell(\mathrm{GEN}_w(1^k))}$. Otherwise sample $r^g_w \leftarrow \mathrm{SAMP}(\mathrm{GEN}_w(1^k))$.*

2. ***Key generation:*** *For each $w \in \{S, R\}$, generate $(pk_w, sk_w) \leftarrow \mathrm{GEN}_w(1^k; r^g_w)$. Let $\mathcal{M}$ be the corresponding message space.*

3. ***Challenge generation:*** *Given (pk_S, pk_R), A outputs $m_0 = (m_{0,1}, \ldots, m_{0,\ell})$ and $m_1 = (m_{1,1}, \ldots, m_{1,\ell})$, where $\ell \in \mathbb{N}$ is a polynomial in k and $m_{i,j} \in \mathcal{M}$ for each $i \in \{0,1\}$ and $j \in \{1,\ldots,\ell\}$. Then sample $b \in \{0,1\}$ uniformly at random.*

4. ***Choice of randomness for encryption:*** *For each $w \in \{S, R\}$, compute $x^e_w \leftarrow \sigma_w(pk_S, pk_R, sk_w, aux_w)$, where $x^e_w \in \{\mathsf{Good}, \mathsf{Bad}\}$, $aux_S = m_b$, and $aux_R = \bot$. If $x^e_w = \mathsf{Bad}$, then given w, A outputs $r^e_{i,j} \in \{0,1\}^{\ell(\mathrm{ENC}_j(\cdot))}$ for each $i \in \{1,\ldots,\ell\}$ and $j \in \{1,\ldots,n\}$. Otherwise sample $r^e_{i,j} \leftarrow$*

SAMP(ENC$_j(\cdot)$) for each $i \in \{1,\ldots,\ell\}$ and $j \in \{1,\ldots,n\}$. Let w be the first sender, and $\bar{w}$ the second sender, which are determined by Π.

5. **Encryption:** For $i \in \{1,\ldots,\ell\}$, do the following. Set $st_S = (pk_S, pk_R, sk_S, m_{b,i})$, $st_R = (pk_S, pk_R, sk_R)$, and $c_{i,0} = \perp$. For $j \in \{1,\ldots,n\}$, when j is odd, compute $(c_{i,j}, st_w') \leftarrow$ ENC$_j(c_{i,j-1}, st_w; r_{i,j}^e)$ and st_w is updated to st_w', and when j is even, compute $s(c_{i,j}, st_{\bar{w}}') \leftarrow$ ENC$_j(c_{i,j-1}, st_{\bar{w}}; r_{i,j}^e)$ and $st_{\bar{w}}$ is updated to $st_{\bar{w}}'$.

6. **Guess:** Given $\{c_{i,j} : i \in \{1,\ldots,\ell\}, j \in \{1,\ldots,n\}\}$, A outputs $b' \in \{0,1\}$.

7. **Output** (Win, Val$_S$, Val$_R$, Num$_S$, Num$_R$), where Win takes 1 if $b' = b$, and 0 otherwise, Val$_w$ takes 1 if $m_{b,i} \in \mathcal{M}_w$ for some $i \in \{1,\ldots,\ell\}$, and 0 otherwise, and Num$_w$ represents the number of times that σ_w output Good in the game.

Next, we define the utility functions of lazy sender and receiver for this game.

Definition 3 (Utility function for CPA game). *Let (σ_S, σ_R) be a pair of strategies of the game* **Game**^{cpa}. *The utility of player $w \in \{S, R\}$ when the outcome* Out $=$ (Win, Val$_S$, Val$_R$, Num$_S$, Num$_R$) *happens is defined by*

$$u_w(\text{Out}) = (-\alpha_w) \cdot \text{Win} \cdot \text{Val}_w + (-\beta_w) \cdot \text{Num}_w,$$

where $\alpha_w, \beta_w \in \mathbb{R}$ are some non-negative constant. Let q_w be the maximum number that Num$_w$ *can take. (q_w is either 0, 1, or 2, depending on the scheme Π.) We say that the utility is valid if $\alpha_w/2 > q_w \cdot \beta_w$ for each $w \in \{S, R\}$.*

The utility when the players follow a pair of strategies (σ_S, σ_R) is defined by

$$U_w(\sigma_S, \sigma_R) = \min_{A, \mathcal{M}_S, \mathcal{M}_R} \{\mathbf{E}[u_w(\text{Out})]\},$$

where Out *is the outcome of the game* **Game**$^{\text{cpa}}(\Pi, k, A, \mathcal{M}_S, \mathcal{M}_R, \sigma_S, \sigma_R)$, *and the minimum is taken over all PPT adversaries A and valuable message spaces $\mathcal{M}_S$ and $\mathcal{M}_R$ for every sufficiently large k.*

Note that, in the above definition, we take the minimum over all possible adversaries (and valuable message spaces) to define the utility when players follow a pair of strategies (σ_S, σ_R). This is because we would like to evaluate a pair of strategies (σ_S, σ_R) by considering the worst-case for possible adversaries and valuable message spaces. In other words, we would like to say that a pair of strategies is good if it is guaranteed to yield high utility for any adversary and players, who are associated with valuable message spaces.

Note that the validity condition of the utility guarantees that players have an incentive to use good randomness for achieving the security. If players do not use good randomness, then there is an adversary such that Win $\cdot$ Val$_w$ is always 1. The best we can hope for is that the expected value of Win $\cdot$ Val$_w$ is $1/2$ (plus some negligible value), which increases the utility by $\alpha_w/2$. Since Num$_w$ takes at most q_w in the game, the inequality $\alpha_w/2 > q_w \cdot \beta_w$ means that achieving the security is worth paying the cost of good randomness. Hereafter, we assume that the utility functions are valid.

As game theoretic solution concepts, we define Nash equilibrium and strict Nash equilibrium. Since any strategy that a player can follow should be computable in a polynomial time and a negligible difference of the outcome of the game should be ignored for PPT algorithms, we consider a computational Nash equilibrium.

Definition 4 (Computational Nash equilibrium). *A pair of PPT strategies* (σ_S, σ_R) *of the game* **Game**^{cpa} *is called a* computational Nash equilibrium *if for each player* $w \in \{S, R\}$, *it holds that*

$$U_w(\sigma_S^*, \sigma_R^*) \leq U_w(\sigma_S, \sigma_R) + \epsilon(k)$$

for every PPT strategy σ_w' *of player* w, *where* $(\sigma_S^*, \sigma_R^*) = (\sigma_S', \sigma_R)$ *if* $w = S$, $(\sigma_S^*, \sigma_R^*) = (\sigma_S, \sigma_R')$ *otherwise, and* $\epsilon(\cdot)$ *is a negligible function.*

Strict Nash equilibrium guarantees that if a player deviates from the strategy, then the utility of the player decreases by a non-negligible amount. The definition is based on that of [22], which appeared in the context of rational secret sharing. To define strict Nash equilibrium, we need to introduce the notion of *equivalent strategy*.

Definition 5 (Equivalent strategy). *Let* (σ_S, σ_R) *be a pair of strategies of the game* **Game**^{cpa}, *and* σ_w' *any strategy of player* $w \in \{S, R\}$. *We say* σ_w' *is equivalent to* σ_w, *denoted by* $\sigma_w' \approx \sigma_w$, *if for any PPT adversary* A *and valuable message spaces* $\mathcal{M}_S$ *and* $\mathcal{M}_R$,

$$\{\mathsf{Trans}(1^k, \sigma_w)\} \approx_c \{\mathsf{Trans}(1^k, \sigma_w')\},$$

where $\mathsf{Trans}(1^k, \rho_w)$ *represents the transcript of the game* **Game**$^{\mathrm{cpa}}(\Pi, k, A, \mathcal{M}_S, \mathcal{M}_R, \sigma_S^*, \sigma_R^*)$, *which includes all values generated in the game except the internal random coin of* σ_w', *and* $(\sigma_S^*, \sigma_R^*) = (\sigma_S', \sigma_R)$ *if* $w = S$, $(\sigma_S^*, \sigma_R^*) = (\sigma_S, \sigma_R')$ *otherwise.*

Definition 6 (Computational strict Nash equilibrium). *A pair of strategies* (σ_S, σ_R) *of the game* **Game**^{cpa} *is called a* computational strict Nash equilibrium *if*

1. (σ_S, σ_R) *is a Nash equilibrium;*
2. *For any* $w \in \{S, R\}$ *and any* $\sigma_w' \not\approx \sigma_w$, *there is a constant* $c > 0$ *such that* $U_w(\sigma_S^*, \sigma_R^*) \leq U_w(\sigma_S, \sigma_R) - 1/k^c$ *for infinitely many* k, *where* $(\sigma_S^*, \sigma_R^*) = (\sigma_S', \sigma_R)$ *if* $w = S$, $(\sigma_S^*, \sigma_R^*) = (\sigma_S, \sigma_R')$ *otherwise.*

We define the security of encryption schemes for lazy parties.

Definition 7 (CPA security for lazy parties). *Let* $\Pi = (\{\mathrm{GEN}_w\}_{w \in \{S, R\}}, \{\mathrm{ENC}_i\}_{i \in \{1, \dots, n\}}, \mathrm{DEC})$ *be a public-key encryption scheme, and* (σ_S, σ_R) *a pair of strategies of the game* **Game**^{cpa}. *We say that* $(\Pi, \sigma_S, \sigma_R)$ *is CPA secure with a (strict) Nash equilibrium for* **Game**^{cpa} *if*

1. *For any PPT adversary A, valuable message spaces $\mathcal{M}_S, \mathcal{M}_R$, and every sufficiently large k, it holds that $\Pr[\text{Win} \cdot (\text{Val}_S + \text{Val}_R) \neq 0] \leq 1/2 + \epsilon(k)$, where $\text{Win}, \text{Val}_S, \text{Val}_R$ are components of the outcome of the game $\textbf{Game}^{\text{cpa}}(\Pi, k, A, \mathcal{M}_S, \mathcal{M}_R, \sigma_S, \sigma_R)$, and $\epsilon(\cdot)$ is a negligible function;*

2. *The pair of strategies (σ_S, σ_R) is a computational (strict) Nash equilibrium.*

In the first condition, we evaluate the value of $\text{Win} \cdot (\text{Val}_S + \text{Val}_R)$ since if $\text{Val}_S + \text{Val}_R = 0$, all the messages chosen by the adversary are not valuable for both the sender and the receiver.

Note that the usual CPA security of usual (non-interactive) public-key encryption is a special case of the above definition. If the scheme Π consists of $(\text{GEN}_R, \text{ENC}_1, \text{DEC})$, a pair of strategies (σ_S, σ_R) is such that both σ_S and σ_R always output Good, and the second condition of the security is not considered, then the above security is equivalent to the usual CPA security of public-key encryption. For a usual encryption scheme $\Pi = (\text{GEN}, \text{ENC}, \text{DEC})$, we say that Π is *CPA secure* if it is CPA secure in this sense.

Impossibility Results. The first observation for achieving the security for lazy parties is that the sender must generate a secret key and the encryption phase requires at least two rounds, neither of them is satisfied in the usual public-key encryption. Roughly speaking, the reason why secure schemes require to generate a secret key for a sender is that if the messages to be encrypted are valuable for the receiver but not for the sender, the sender does not use good randomness and thus the adversary can correctly guess which of the challenge messages was encrypted because she known all the input to the sender. Furthermore, even if the sender has his secret key, if the encryption phase is 1-round, there is an adversary who can guess the challenge correctly. Consider an adversary who submits challenge messages such that one consists of the same two messages and the other consists of different two messages, and all the messages are valuable for the receiver but not for the sender. Then the sender does not use good randomness, and thus the adversary can choose randomness for encryption. If she choose the same random strings for two challenge messages, then although the adversary does not know the secret key of the sender, since the encryption is 1-round, she can correctly guess which of the challenges was encrypted by checking whether given two challenge ciphertexts are the same or not. See the full version for the formal statements and proofs.

3   Secure Encryption Schemes for Lazy Parties

3.1   Two-Round Encryption Scheme

We present a two-round public-key encryption scheme that is CPA secure with a strict Nash equilibrium. The encryption phase is conducted as follows. First the receiver generates a random string, encrypts it by the public key of the sender, and sends it to the sender. Next the sender encrypt a messages by the one-time pad, in which the sender uses the random string received from the receiver. The receiver can recover the message since he knows the random string. Our scheme is based on any CPA-secure public-key encryption scheme $\Pi = (\text{GEN}, \text{ENC}, \text{DEC})$ in which the message space is $\{0,1\}^\mu$ and the length of random bits required in ENC is μ.

The description of our two-round scheme $\Pi_{\text{two}} = (\text{GEN}_S, \{\text{ENC}_i\}_{i \in \{1,2\}}, \text{DEC}_R)$ is the following.

- $\text{GEN}_S(1^k)$: Generate $(pk_S, sk_S) \leftarrow \text{GEN}(1^k)$, and output (pk_S, sk_S).
  Let $\mathcal{M} = \{0,1\}^\mu$ be the message space, where μ is a polynomial in k. Set $st_S = (pk_S, sk_S)$ and $st_R = pk_S$.
- $\text{ENC}_1(st_R)$: Sample $r \in \{0,1\}^\mu$ uniformly at random, compute $c_1 \leftarrow \text{ENC}(pk_S, r)$, and output $(c_1, (sk_R, r))$.
  $\text{ENC}_2(c_1, st_S)$: Compute $\hat{r} \leftarrow \text{DEC}(sk_S, c_1)$ and $c_2 = m \oplus \hat{r}$, and output c_2.
- $\text{DEC}_R(c_2, (sk_R, r))$: Compute $\hat{m} = c_2 \oplus r$ and output $\hat{m}$.

We define a pair of strategies (σ_S, σ_R) such that

- $\sigma_S(1^k, \mathcal{M}_S)$ outputs Good with probability 1. $\sigma_S(pk_S, sk_S, aux_S)$ is not defined.
- $\sigma_R(1^k, \mathcal{M}_R)$ is not defined. $\sigma_R(pk_S, aux_R)$ outputs Good with probability 1.

Theorem 1. *If Π is CPA secure, $(\Pi_{\text{two}}, \sigma_S, \sigma_R)$ is CPA secure with a strict Nash equilibrium for* **Game**^{cpa}.

3.2 Additional Information to the Receiver

In this section, we consider a situation in which the receiver may know whether a message to be encrypted is valuable for the receiver or not. This situation can be reflected by changing the game **Game**^{cpa} such that the adversary can choose either "$aux_R = \bot$" or "$aux_R = \text{Val}_R$" in the challenge generation phase. Let **Game**$_R^{\text{cpa}}$ denote the modified game.

In this situation, the scheme presented in Section 3.1 is no longer secure. Intuitively, this is because the receiver does not generate good randomness if a message to be encrypted is not valuable for him.

Proposition 1. *For any pair of strategies (σ_S, σ_R), $(\Pi_{\text{two}}, \sigma_S, \sigma_R)$ is not CPA secure with a Nash equilibrium for* **Game**$_R^{\text{cpa}}$.

We present a three-round encryption scheme that is secure for **Game**$_R^{\text{cpa}}$. In the encryption phase, first the sender and the receiver perform a key-agreement protocol that generates a random string shared between them. The shared string is good randomness if one of the sender and the receiver uses good randomness in the key-agreement protocol. Then, the sender uses the shared string as randomness to encrypt a message. Finally, after recovering a message, the receiver encrypt the message by the sender's public key and makes it public. As described later, the final step is necessary to achieve the security. Our scheme is based on any CPA-secure public-key encryption scheme $\Pi = (\text{GEN}, \text{ENC}, \text{DEC})$ in which the message space is $\{0,1\}^{2\mu}$ and the length of random bits required in ENC is μ.

The description of the encryption scheme $\Pi_{\text{three}} = (\{\text{GEN}_w\}_{w\in\{S,R\}},$ $\{\text{ENC}_i\}_{i\in\{1,2,3\}})$ is the following. The decryption algorithm does not exist in Π_{three} since the receiver decrypts a message in computing ENC_3.

- $\text{GEN}_w(1^k)$: Generate $(pk_w, sk_w) \leftarrow \text{GEN}(1^k)$, and output (pk_w, sk_w).
  Let $\mathcal{M} = \{0,1\}^{2\mu}$ be the message space, where μ is a polynomial in k. Set $st_S = (pk_S, pk_R, sk_S)$ and $st_R = (pk_S, pk_R, sk_R)$.
- $\text{ENC}_1(st_R)$: Sample $r_1 \in \{0,1\}^\mu$ uniformly at random, compute $c_1 \leftarrow \text{ENC}(pk_S, r_1)$, and output $(c_1, (sk_R, r_1))$.
  $\text{ENC}_2(c_1, st_S)$: Sample $r_2 \in \{0,1\}^\mu$ uniformly at random and compute $c_2 \leftarrow \text{ENC}(pk_R, r_2)$ and $\hat{r}_1 \leftarrow \text{DEC}(sk_S, c_1)$. Then set $r_L \circ r_R = \hat{r}_1 \oplus r_2$ such that $|r_L| = |r_R| = \mu$, compute $c_3 \leftarrow \text{ENC}(pk_R, m; r_L)$, and output $((c_2, c_3), sk_S)$, where $x \circ y$ denote the concatenation of strings x and y.
  $\text{ENC}_3((c_2, c_3), st_R)$: Compute $\hat{r}_2 \leftarrow \text{DEC}(sk_R, c_2)$, set $\hat{r}_L \circ \hat{r}_R = r_1 \oplus \hat{r}_2$, compute $\hat{m} \leftarrow \text{DEC}(sk_S, c_3)$ and $c_4 \leftarrow \text{ENC}(pk_S, \hat{m}; \hat{r}_R)$, and make c_4 public. The decrypted message is $\hat{m}$.

We define a pair of strategies (σ_S, σ_R) such that

- $\sigma_S(1^k, \mathcal{M}_S)$ outputs Good with probability 1. $\sigma_S(pk_S, pk_R, sk_S, aux_S)$ outputs Good if $m_{b,i} \in \mathcal{M}_S$ for some $i \in \{1, \ldots, \ell\}$, and Bad otherwise.
- $\sigma_R(1^k, \mathcal{M}_R)$ outputs Good with probability 1. $\sigma_R(pk_S, pk_R, sk_R, aux_R)$ outputs Good if $aux_R = \bot$ or $\text{Val}_R = 1$, and Bad otherwise.

At first glance, it does not seem necessary to make c_4 public at the third round of the encryption phase. However, it is necessary to do so because if not, the sender can achieve the security without using good randomness in the key generation phase.

Theorem 2. *If Π is CPA secure, $(\Pi_{\text{three}}, \sigma_S, \sigma_R)$ is CPA secure with a strict Nash equilibrium for* $\mathbf{Game}_R^{\text{cpa}}$.

3.3   Additional Information to the Sender and the Receiver

In this section, we consider a situation in which both the sender and the receiver may know that a message to be encrypted is valuable for them. The situation is different from that of the previous section because the sender may be able to know the value of a message for the receiver, and the receiver vice versa. This situation can be reflected by changing the game $\mathbf{Game}_R^{\text{cpa}}$ such that the adversary can choose either "$aux_S = m_b$" or "$aux_S = (m_b, \text{Val}_R)$", and either "$aux_R = \bot$", "$aux_R = \text{Val}_R$", "$aux_R = \text{Val}_S$", or "$aux_R = (\text{Val}_S, \text{Val}_R)$" in the challenge generation phase. Let $\mathbf{Game}_{S,R}^{\text{cpa}}$ denote the modified game.

In this game, the scheme Π_{three} has two different strict Nash equilibria.

Proposition 2. *There are two pairs of strategies* (σ_S, σ_R) *and* (ρ_S, ρ_R) *such that* $\sigma_S \not\approx \rho_S$, $\sigma_R \not\approx \rho_R$, *and both* $(\Pi_{\text{three}}, \sigma_S, \sigma_R)$ *and* $(\Pi_{\text{three}}, \rho_S, \rho_R)$ *are CPA secure with strict Nash equilibrium for* $\mathbf{Game}_{S,R}^{\text{cpa}}$. *Furthermore, there is a PPT adversary A and valuable message spaces* $\mathcal{M}_S$ *and* $\mathcal{M}_R$ *such that* $\mathbf{E}[u_S(\text{Out}_\rho)] - \mathbf{E}[u_S(\text{Out}_\sigma)] \geq \beta_S - \epsilon(k)$ *and* $\mathbf{E}[u_R(\text{Out}_\sigma)] - \mathbf{E}[u_R(\text{Out}_\rho)] \geq \beta_R - \epsilon(k)$ *for every sufficiently large* k, *where* Out_σ *is the outcome of the game* $\mathbf{Game}_{S,R}^{\text{cpa}}$ *in which players follow* (σ_S, σ_R), Out_ρ *is the outcome of the game* $\mathbf{Game}_{S,R}^{\text{cpa}}$ *in which players follow* (ρ_S, ρ_R), *and* $\epsilon(\cdot)$ *is a negligible function.*

As shown in the proof, the difference between outputs of (σ_S, σ_R) and (ρ_S, ρ_R) is only in the case that $aux_S = (m_b, \text{Val}_R)$, $aux_R = (\text{Val}_S, \text{Val}_R)$, and $\text{Val}_S = \text{Val}_R = 1$. In this case, the sender uses good randomness and the receiver uses bad randomness in (σ_S, σ_R), while the sender uses bad randomness and the receiver uses good randomness in (ρ_S, ρ_R). Therefore, the sender prefers to following (ρ_S, ρ_R), while the receiver prefers to following (σ_S, σ_R). It is difficult to determine which pair of strategies the players follow. If the protocol have started, but the sender and the receiver have not agreed on which pair of strategies they follow, the outcome can be worse for both of them. If the sender follows (ρ_S, ρ_R) and the receiver follows (σ_S, σ_R) when $\text{Val}_S = \text{Val}_R = 1$, in this case both players are to use bad randomness in the encryption, thus the adversary can correctly guess b with probability 1. Such an outcome should be avoided for both players.

There is a simple way of avoiding that outcome. In the encryption phase, if $x_R^e \neq \text{Good}$, the receiver uses the all-zero string as a random string. Since the sender can verify if the random string chosen by the receiver is all-zero or not, if so, the sender will use good randomness if a message is valuable. The all-zero string is a signal that the receiver did not used good randomness.

3.4 Signcryption with an Additional Assumption

A signcryption scheme is one of cryptographic primitives that achieves both public-key encryption and signature simultaneously. In particular, a secret key for encryption and a signing key for signature is common, and a public key for encryption and a verification key for signature is also common.

We show that signcryption schemes with some property can achieve the CPA security for lazy parties if we add an assumption for players. The assumption is that players do not want to reveal their secret keys. This is plausible since, if the secret key of some player is revealed, it is equivalent to that the encrypted messages to the player are revealed and the signatures of the player are forged.

Formally, a signcryption scheme Π_{sigenc} consists of three PPT algorithms $(\{\text{GEN}_w\}_{w \in \{S,R\}}, \text{SIGENC}, \text{VERDEC})$ such that

- $\text{GEN}_w(1^k)$: Output a signing/decryption key (secret key) sk_w and a verification/encryption key (public key) pk_w; Let $\mathcal{M}$ denote the message space.
- $\text{SIGENC}(pk_R, sk_S, m)$: For a message $m \in \mathcal{M}$, output the ciphertext c;
- $\text{VERDEC}(pk_S, sk_R, c)$: For a ciphertext c, output $\perp$ if the verification fails, and the decrypted message $\hat{m}$ otherwise.

Some of signcryption schemes (e.g., [1]) have the *key-exposure* property that, if the randomness used in SIGENC is revealed, then the secret key of the sender is efficiently computed from the randomness. This property seems to be undesirable in a standard setting. However, if a signcryption scheme with key-exposure property is used as a public-key encryption scheme, it can achieve the CPA security for lazy parties.

We modify the game **Game**^{cpa} such that the adversary outputs (b', sk'_S) in the guess phase, and Secret is included in the output of the game, where Secret takes 1 if $sk_S = sk'_S$ and 0 otherwise. Let **Game**$^{\text{cpa}}_{\text{secret}}$ denote the modified game.

The utility function for the sender when the outcome Out $=$ (Win, Val$_S$, Val$_R$, Num$_S$, Num$_R$, Secret) happens is defined by

$$u_S(\text{Out}) = (-\alpha_S) \cdot \text{Win} \cdot \text{Val}_S + (-\beta_S) \cdot \text{Num}_S + (-\gamma_S) \cdot \text{Secret},$$

where $\gamma_S \in \mathbb{R}$ is a non-negative constant such that $\gamma_S > \alpha_S/2 + q_S \cdot \beta_S$. The condition on γ_S implies that achieving Secret $= 0$ is the most valuable for the sender.

We define a pair of strategies (σ_S, σ_R) for the game **Game**$^{\text{cpa}}_{\text{secret}}$ such that

- $\sigma_S(1^k, \mathcal{M}_S)$ outputs Good with probability 1. $\sigma_S(pk_S, sk_S, aux_S)$ outputs Good with probability 1.
- $\sigma_R(1^k, \mathcal{M}_R)$ outputs Good with probability 1. $\sigma_R(pk_S, aux_R)$ is not defined.

Theorem 3. *Let* $\Pi_{\text{sigenc}} = (\{\text{GEN}_w\}_{w \in \{S,R\}}, \text{SIGENC}, \text{VERDEC})$ *be a signcryption scheme with CPA security and key-exposure property. Then* $(\Pi_{\text{sigenc}}, \sigma_S, \sigma_R)$ *is CPA secure with a strict Nash equilibrium for the game* **Game**$^{\text{cpa}}_{\text{secret}}$.

Acknowledgments. The author would like to thank Keisuke Tanaka and Keita Xagawa for their constructive comments and suggestions. The author would also like to thank anonymous reviewers for their helpful comments and suggestions.

References

1. Zheng, Y.: Digital Signcryption or How to Achieve Cost (Signature & Encryption) << Cost(Signature) + Cost(Encryption). In: Kaliski Jr., B.S. (ed.) CRYPTO 1997. LNCS, vol. 1294, pp. 165–179. Springer, Heidelberg (1997)
2. Halpern, J.Y., Pass, R.: Game theory with costly computation. In: Innovations in Computer Science, pp. 120–142 (2010)
3. Katz, J.: Bridging Game Theory and Cryptography: Recent Results and Future Directions. In: Canetti, R. (ed.) TCC 2008. LNCS, vol. 4948, pp. 251–272. Springer, Heidelberg (2008)
4. Dodis, Y., Rabin, T.: Cryptography and game theory. In: Nisan, N., Roughgarden, T., Tardos, E., Vazirani, V.V. (eds.) Algorithmic Game Theory, pp. 181–207. Cambridge University Press (2007)
5. Halpern, J.Y.: Computer science and game theory. In: Durlauf, S.N., Blume, L.E. (eds.) The New Palgrave Dictionary of Economics. Palgrave Macmillan (2008)

6. Halpern, J.Y., Teague, V.: Rational secret sharing and multiparty computation: extended abstract. In: Babai, L. (ed.) STOC, pp. 623–632. ACM (2004)
7. Abraham, I., Dolev, D., Gonen, R., Halpern, J.Y.: Distributed computing meets game theory: robust mechanisms for rational secret sharing and multiparty computation. In: Ruppert, E., Malkhi, D. (eds.) PODC, pp. 53–62. ACM (2006)
8. Dov Gordon, S., Katz, J.: Rational Secret Sharing, Revisited. In: De Prisco, R., Yung, M. (eds.) SCN 2006. LNCS, vol. 4116, pp. 229–241. Springer, Heidelberg (2006)
9. Kol, G., Naor, M.: Cryptography and game theory: Designing protocols for exchanging information. In: [23], pp. 320–339
10. Kol, G., Naor, M.: Games for exchanging information. In: Dwork, C. (ed.) STOC, pp. 423–432. ACM (2008)
11. Micali, S., Shelat, A.: Purely rational secret sharing (extended abstract). In: [24], pp. 54–71
12. Ong, S.J., Parkes, D.C., Rosen, A., Vadhan, S.P.: Fairness with an honest minority and a rational majority. In: [24], pp. 36–53
13. Asharov, G., Lindell, Y.: Utility dependence in correct and fair rational secret sharing. J. Cryptology 24(1), 157–202 (2011)
14. Asharov, G., Canetti, R., Hazay, C.: Towards a Game Theoretic View of Secure Computation. In: Paterson, K.G. (ed.) EUROCRYPT 2011. LNCS, vol. 6632, pp. 426–445. Springer, Heidelberg (2011)
15. Groce, A., Katz, J.: Fair Computation with Rational Players. In: Pointcheval, D., Johansson, T. (eds.) EUROCRYPT 2012. LNCS, vol. 7237, pp. 81–98. Springer, Heidelberg (2012)
16. Canetti, R., Feige, U., Goldreich, O., Naor, M.: Adaptively secure multi-party computation. In: STOC, pp. 639–648 (1996)
17. Canetti, R., Ostrovsky, R.: Secure computation with honest-looking parties: What if nobody is truly honest (extended abstract). In: STOC, pp. 255–264 (1999)
18. Aumann, Y., Lindell, Y.: Security against covert adversaries: Efficient protocols for realistic adversaries. Journal of Cryptology 23(2), 281–343 (2010)
19. Dodis, Y., Ong, S.J., Prabhakaran, M., Sahai, A.: On the (im)possibility of cryptography with imperfect randomness. In: FOCS, pp. 196–205 (2004)
20. Bosley, C., Dodis, Y.: Does Privacy Require True Randomness? In: Vadhan, S.P. (ed.) TCC 2007. LNCS, vol. 4392, pp. 1–20. Springer, Heidelberg (2007)
21. Bellare, M., Brakerski, Z., Naor, M., Ristenpart, T., Segev, G., Shacham, H., Yilek, S.: Hedged Public-Key Encryption: How to Protect against Bad Randomness. In: Matsui, M. (ed.) ASIACRYPT 2009. LNCS, vol. 5912, pp. 232–249. Springer, Heidelberg (2009)
22. Fuchsbauer, G., Katz, J., Naccache, D.: Efficient Rational Secret Sharing in Standard Communication Networks. In: Micciancio, D. (ed.) TCC 2010. LNCS, vol. 5978, pp. 419–436. Springer, Heidelberg (2010)
23. Canetti, R. (ed.): TCC 2008. LNCS, vol. 4948. Springer, Heidelberg (2008)
24. Reingold, O. (ed.): TCC 2009. LNCS, vol. 5444. Springer, Heidelberg (2009)

Probabilistically Correct Secure Arithmetic Computation for Modular Conversion, Zero Test, Comparison, MOD and Exponentiation*

Ching-Hua Yu[1,2] and Bo-Yin Yang[2]

[1] National Taiwan University, Taipei, Taiwan
[2] Center for Information Tech. and Innovation,
Academia Sinica, Taipei, Taiwan
chinghua.yu@gmail.com, by@crypto.tw

Abstract. When secure arithmetic is required, computation based on secure multiplication (MULT) is much more efficient than computation based on secure Boolean circuits. However, a typical application may also require other building blocks, such as comparison, exponentiation and the modulo (MOD) operation. Secure solutions for these functions proposed in the literature rely on bit-decomposition or other bit-oriented methods, which require $O(\ell)$ MULTs for ℓ-bit inputs. In the absence of a known bit-length independent solution, the complexity of the whole computation is often dominated by these non-arithmetic functions.

In this paper, we resolve the above problem for the case of two-party protocols against a malicious adversary. We start with a general modular conversion, which converts secret shares over distinct moduli. For this, we propose a probabilistically correct protocol with a complexity that is independent of ℓ. Then, we show that when these non-arithmetic functions are based on secure modular conversions, they can be computed in constant rounds and $O(k)$ MULTs, where k is a parameter with an error rate of $2^{-\Omega(k)}$.

Keywords: secure arithmetic, two-party computation, probabilistically correct algorithm, data privacy.

1 Introduction

Secure two-party computation allows two parties, Alice and Bob, to jointly compute a function $f(x^A, x^B)$ without revealing anything about their inputs, where x^A and x^B are secret vectors held by Alice and Bob respectively. Solutions based on Boolean circuits [7, 12, 21, 34] provide general feasibility results, while solutions based on secure arithmetic computation, constructed by using e.g., homomorphic encryption or oblivious transfer [17, 23, 36], are efficient for addition and multiplication. Specifically, in arithmetic applications, such as data mining, machine learning, auction, and distributed generation of cryptographic keys [4, 8, 10, 16, 24, 25], the second choice is usually considered more efficient in practice.

---

* An extended version of this paper, which is [37], is at IACR e-Print Archive 2011/560.

I. Visconti and R. De Prisco (Eds.): SCN 2012, LNCS 7485, pp. 426–444, 2012.
© Springer-Verlag Berlin Heidelberg 2012

Besides addition and multiplication, several non-arithmetic functions that involve integer comparison, the zero test, which tests whether an input value is zero, the modulo (MOD) operation, which computes the remainder of x divided by a public integer P, while the input and the output are both shares in $\mathbb{Z}_Q$, and exponentiation also play important roles in many arithmetic applications. To realize the best of both worlds, recent works of secure arithmetic computation involve two directions. Some works [17, 23, 27, 36] developed efficient secure arithmetic primitives (i.e., techniques for an efficient secure multiplication); others [14, 22, 30, 33, 36] considered how to compute non-arithmetic functions efficiently based on a secure multiplication. However, the complexity of the existing protocols to these non-arithmetic functions is still much higher than that of secure multiplication. Therefore, even though the arithmetic functions can be computed efficiently, the computation of these non-arithmetic functions may dominate the complexity in many applications. For instance, from the existing results, we can use bit-decomposition, which converts a secret number into a secret binary set [14, 28, 32], as a generic solution to compute non-arithmetic functions in a bit-oriented manner; or we can use more efficient solutions tailored for specific problems, such as integer comparison [30], the MOD operation [22, 28] and modular exponentiation [36]. Unfortunately, the complexity of these solutions is still at least $O(\ell)$ secure multiplications[1], where ℓ is the bit-length of the inputs.

The above limitation raises some interesting questions. First, are there constant round and probabilistically correct solutions to these problems such that the complexity only depends on a correctness parameter k and has an exponentially low error rate of $2^{-\Omega(k)}$? From a theoretical viewpoint, such solutions serve as evidence of a complexity breakthrough regarding non-arithmetic computation using arithmetic operations. They are also in accord with the direction of a recent study [33], on sub-linear secure comparison (whose complexity is $O(\sqrt{\ell}(k + \log \ell))$ secure multiplications and constant rounds). From a practical viewpoint, such solutions provide a trade-off between the efficiency and the error rate. Moreover, is there a unified framework better than bit-decomposition for integer comparison, the zero test, the MOD operation and the modular exponentiation?

1.1   Problem Statement

We study secure two-party computation of several non-arithmetic functions that involve the zero test (equality test), integer comparison, the MOD operation, and modular exponentiation based on the modular conversion protocol. The objective is to find bit-length independent solutions, where the complexity depends on the number of secure multiplications.

Instead of using bit-decomposition as the bridge between the arithmetic functions and the non-arithmetic functions, we use *modular conversion*, which

---

[1] Using the method in [36], integer exponentiation takes $O(1)$ secure multiplications, but modular exponentiation requires an additional comparison and zero test. Thus, in general cases, the complexity is still bounded by $O(\ell)$.

converts the shares in $\mathbb{Z}_Q$ into shares in $\mathbb{Z}_P$. The setting of modular conversion is as follows. Let $Q, P \geq 2$ be two distinct integers, and let x be a secret in $\mathbb{Z}_Q$.[2] In addition, let x^A and x^B be additive shares of x in $\mathbb{Z}_Q$, i.e., $x = x^A + x^B$ mod Q, held by Alice and Bob respectively. Modular conversion converts x^A and x^B into z^A and z^B such that $x = z^A + z^B$ mod P.

On one hand, modular conversion can serve a general purpose. First, modular conversion is related to the MOD operation. We show a simple reduction from modular conversion to the MOD operation in Section 3.7. Second, let ℓ be the bit-length of Q. Then, bit-decomposition can be reduced to $\ell - 1$ parallel MOD operations by computing x mod $2^{\ell-1}, ..., x$ mod 2 and some linear combinations. This implies the general use of modular conversion for binary functions. Moreover, because the MOD operation is reducible to modular conversion, but not vice versa, modular conversion serves as a more general functionality.

On the other hand, for many well used functions like the zero test (equality test), integer comparison, the MOD operation, and modular exponentiation, it may be not necessary to perform full bit-decomposition, as the solutions can be constructed directly by modular conversion.

1.2   Contributions

We propose a new secure two-party modular conversion scheme for general moduli. That is, the input and the output are secret shares in $\mathbb{Z}_Q$ and $\mathbb{Z}_P$ respectively, where Q and P are arbitrary integers greater than or equal to 2. Then, using modular conversion, we derive efficient solutions to several non-arithmetic functions.

Our framework for the general modular conversion protocol is based on a probabilistically correct computation that relies on the manipulation of secret shares. When the secret shares of an input are generated uniformly, the error rate of the computation is constant. Therefore, by using uniformly random re-sharing k times, we can construct a solution with an error rate of $2^{-\Omega(k)}$.

To obtain solutions that would block a malicious adversary, we first construct the protocols of these functions in the passive security model, and then show that these protocols can be enhanced to be actively secure by efficient arithmetic zero-knowledge proofs.

In the passive security model, assuming the existence of a Multiplicative to Additive Sharing Conversion or a secure multiplication, we derive the following protocols and results.

- A general modular conversion protocol that uses $O(k)$ (about $7k + 30$) secure multiplications and $O(1)$ (about 8) rounds, with an error rate of $2^{-\Omega(k)}$ (at most $(7/10)^k$ for all $k \geq 20$).
- A randomized zero-test protocol whose cost is $O(k)$ (about k) secure multiplications and $O(1)$ (about 8) rounds with an error rate of 2^{-k} at most.

---

[2] In this paper, unless otherwise specified, $x \in \mathbb{Z}_Q$ simply means that $x \in \{0, ..., Q-1\}$, and $y = x$ mod Q means that $y \in \{0, ..., Q-1\}$.

– Solutions to the sign function, integer comparison, the MOD operation and modular exponentiation based on modular conversion and the zero test are described. The complexity of all the solutions is $O(k)$ secure multiplications and $O(1)$ rounds, with an error rate of $2^{-\Omega(k)}$ at most.

Our schemes can be adapted to the active security model by $O(k)$ multiplication proofs. See [37] for the implementation detail of this extension.

1.3   Potential Application and Open Problem

In this paper, we proposed the first probabilistically-correct protocols which is non-binary and has an input-independent complexity to several problems of secure two-party computation. In the following, we describe and recall some potential applications for instance.

Let Alice be a bank issuing a credit card CC. Alice wants to know the ratio of their CC users to spend more than 21% of their personal income last year with CC card, as the assessment of whether their policies of interest, rewards, and benefits packages are attractive, as well as adjusts its commercial strategy in accordance with it. In addition, Alice would like to know what ratio of the CC users to borrow more than 73% of their income using CC short-term loan, one of the criteria as a financial risk evaluation in order to judge whether to raise the threshold of issuing and lending conditions. When computing the ratio, Alice also put a weight according to each user's credit level. In the second assessment, Alice needs to compute $\frac{1}{n} \sum_{i=1}^{n} w_i(x_i > 73\% \cdot p_i)$, where x_i, p_i, and $w_i \in [0, 100]$ are the CC card spending, the personal income, and the credit weight of User$_i$ in the last year respectively. Alice owns the credit card spending record and the credit weight of the CC users, which is possibly stored in a confidential way, but the personal income record of the CC users is held by some government agency. Let Bob be such an agency. Hence Alice would like to conduct a cooperative computation with Bob. However most people consider their personal income and spending record as privacy and hope the Government and the bank not to disclose this information to a third party under any circumstances. Hence the computation should be conducted with privacy guarantees. This can be done through secure two-party computation. First, Alice sends Bob secret shares of x_i and w_i over a sufficient large ring/field $\mathbb{Z}_Q$, and Bob sends Alice a secret share of p_i over $\mathbb{Z}_Q$ for each i. Then, Alice and Bob compute $[z]_Q \leftarrow \sum_{i=1}^{n} [w_i]_Q \cdot \mathsf{CMP}_Q(100 \cdot [x_i]_Q > 73 \cdot [p_i]_Q)$, where CMP_Q is a secure comparison protocol with input/output shares over $\mathbb{Z}_Q$. To reveal the output to Alice, Bob simply sends his secret share of z to Alice. Using our CMP_Q protocol, Alice can obtain a probabilistically correct result. Our CMP_Q protocol is implemented by $21k + 90$ MULT_2 and 6 MULT_Q with an error rate $(7/10)^k$, where MULT_2 and MULT_Q are secure multiplication protocols over $\mathbb{Z}_2$ and $\mathbb{Z}_Q$ respectively. Assume $n = 100000$, and set $k = 13$ for an error rate less than 0.01 for each invocation of the CMP_Q protocol. By Chernoff bound, we have $\Pr[error(z/n) \le 0.02] \ge 1 - e^{-10}$. Note that a small k is adequate for a high accurate learning.

In this instance, the computation involves secure operations of addition, multiplication, and comparison; in other cases, the computation can involve a more complex formula or algorithm. In addition, before revealing the output to Alice, a small noise (e.g., noise drawn from the Laplace distribution [19]) can be added to the output to reduce the information of individual items, which is important when many functions are evaluated. This method can have some guarantee of data privacy (e.g., the notion of differential privacy [19]) and encourage individuals to be willing to agree on such revelation. In [18], Dwork et al. show how to generate shares of an approximate exponential noise for this purpose. Recent works on this line involve [6, 26].

Recently in [13], Choi et al. conduct a comparison between secure Boolean circuits and secure arithmetic circuits for implementing their algorithm of an application in on-line marketplace. They show that the GMW protocol [21] (which relies on Boolean-circuit representation) are more efficient than the VIFF protocol [15] and the SEPIA protocol [11] (which rely on arithmetic-circuit representation). On one hand, besides the addition operation, their algorithm is mainly composed of binary operations involving AND, MUX, XOR, and comparison but does not contain multiplication. Hence in their case, it can be more suitable to use a boolean circuit-based solution instead of an arithmetic one, but the result can not be generalized to other applications. In addition, they only tested computation with input length of 16 bits, which may be too small for general cases while the advantage of using secure arithmetic circuits for addition and multiplication gets larger with the input length). On the other hand, their application can serve as another witness of the importance of an efficient comparison protocol. Because unlike addition and multiplication, the comparison has been considered as a very expensive operation and often dominates the complexity of the whole computation for a long time (as also mentioned in [11]), the improvement of its complexity is critical to these practical applications.

More generally, addition, multiplication, zero test, comparison, exponentiation and MOD are basic arithmetic computation. They are extensively used in arithmetic applications, such as data mining, machine learning and distributed generation of cryptographic keys [4, 8, 10, 16, 24, 25]. More projects relying on secure arithmetic computation can be found in the web pages of [1, 2].

Besides these potential applications, future directions involve solutions to other expensive non-arithmetic operations, e.g., whether there is a probabilistically correct protocol with sub-linear complexity for integer division when both the divisor and the dividend are secrets, solutions in the multiparty case, and deterministic solutions with sub-linear complexity. See [35] for a recent study of this line.

1.4   Related Work

Share Conversion is usually regarded as a tool for bridging different kinds of computation. In [14], Damgård et al. proposed a constant-round protocol for bit-decomposition to support integer comparison, the zero test, the MOD operation and exponentiation in arithmetic circuits. The communication complexity of the bit-decomposition protocol in [14] is $O(\ell \log \ell)$ (secure multiplications). Subsequently, it was improved to $O(\ell \log^* \ell)$ in [32]. A statistically secure conversion between integer shares and $\mathbb{Z}_Q$ shares was proposed in [3], and a deterministic conversion from a prime field $\mathbb{Z}_Q$ to $\mathbb{Z}_{Q-1}$ was presented in [36]. Both solutions are efficient compared to secure multiplications; however, the former requires the secret $x < \frac{Q}{16} \cdot \frac{2^{-\sigma}}{n}$, where σ is a security parameter, and the latter requires $x < \frac{Q}{2}$. Although the solutions are not effective for general cases, they motivate the direction of our work. Moreover, in [36], efficient protocols for the transformation between additive and multiplicative shares are proposed to take care of private exponentiation in a non-bit-oriented manner.

Integer Comparison is an important functionality in many arithmetic applications. Besides using bit-decomposition [3, 14], a protocol for secure comparison without bit-decomposition is described in [30]. Recently, Toft [33] proposed a sub-linear protocol for secure two-party comparison (or an extension for two non-colluding parties known in multiple parties). The constant-round protocol involves $\sqrt{\ell}$ equality tests (in parallel), each of which can be performed by using $O(k)$ secure multiplications with a 2^{-k} error rate by using a similar equality test scheme to that in [30]. Hence, the total complexity of the protocol is $O(\sqrt{\ell}(k + \log \ell))$.

MOD Operation. In [28], a protocol that uses constant rounds and $O(\ell)$ secure multiplications is proposed for secure MOD operations without using bit-decomposition. Recently, Guajardo et al. [22] introduced a statistically secure solution for modulo reduction. It requires at most $O(n^2 \sigma \ell_a)$ secure multiplications, where n is the number of parties, σ is a security parameter, and ℓ_a is the bit length of a (public) modulus. However, for general cases, such as $a = Q - 1$ or $a = Q/2$, this solution still requires $O(\ell)$ secure multiplications.

Modular Exponentiation. The first constant-round solution proposed by Damgård et al. [14] was based on bit-decomposition, which dominated the complexity. More recently, Yu et al. [36] developed a constant-round protocol for secure two-party exponentiation using $O(\ell)$ secure multiplications. The protocol's complexity is dominated by modular reduction, which we will improve to derive a better result.

In Table 1, we summarize our results for two-party computation of the general modular conversion, zero test, integer comparison, modular exponentiation and modulo reduction protocols, and compare their complexity with existing solutions. All of the compared solutions are based on a MULT, so the multiparty protocols in [28–30] can also be applied to the two-party case provided there is a secure two-party MULT.

2   Preliminaries

We assume the computation involves two non-colluding parties, Alice and Bob, communicating over a public channel. For a functionality $f(\cdot, \cdot)$, a protocol is said to be *passively secure* or *semi-honest secure* if, for any honest-but-curious

Table 1. Comparison of our results and those of the protocols in [28–30, 33, 36] for computing additive shares over $\mathbb{Z}_Q$. ($\ell = \log Q$ is the length of the elements in the field $\mathbb{Z}_Q$; and k is the correctness parameter for exponentially low error rates.)
* The cost of $\mathsf{ModCNV}_{Q \to P}$ is about $7k + 30$ MULT_P's.
** The cost of CMP_Q is about $21k + 90$ MULT_2's and 6 MULT_Q's, upper-bounded by the complexity of $21k + 96$ MULT_Q's.

Problem	Solution	Rounds	Complexity (MULT_Q)	Error Rate
General Modular Conversion	Section 3.3	8	$7k+30$ *	$(7/10)^k$
Zero Test	[30]	8	81ℓ	deterministic
	[30]	4	$12k$	$(1/2)^k$
	Section 3.4	8	k	$(1/2)^k$
Integer Comparison	[30]	15	$297\ell + 5$	deterministic
	[33]	$O(1)$	$O(\sqrt{\ell}(k + \log \ell))$	$(1/2)^k$
	Section 3.6	11	$21k + 96$ **	$(7/10)^k$
Modular Exponentiation	[29]	24	$162\ell + 46\sqrt{\ell} + 28$	deterministic
	Section 3.6, based on [36]	13	$8k + 36$	$(7/10)^k$
MOD (modulo reduction)	[28]	22	$354\ell + 3$	deterministic
	Section 3.6	8	$7k + 30$	$(7/10)^k$

adversary $\mathcal{A}$ who corrupts Alice, there exists a probabilistic polynomial time simulator $\mathcal{S}$ that, given the inputs and the randomness of $\mathcal{A}$, can produce a view of $\mathcal{A}$ that is (statistically/computationally) indistinguishable from the real interaction with Bob. A similar rationale should hold if Bob is corrupted. For a standard formal definition, readers may refer to [20]. We construct protocols based on arithmetic operations, i.e., additions and multiplications of (sufficiently large) finite fields/rings and assume that all the inputs and outputs of the protocols are secret shares.

Secret Shares and Secure Protocols. To protect a secret, such as a private value, a widely used method hides the secret in secret shares. In two-party computation, secret shares are usually expressed in an additive form. For example, let x be a secret in $\mathbb{Z}_Q$. If Alice and Bob hold x^A and x^B respectively, such that $x = x^A + x^B$ mod Q, Alice's (resp. Bob's) view on x^A (resp. x^B) should be indistinguishable from a uniformly random value in $\mathbb{Z}_Q$, so that Alice (resp. Bob) cannot learn anything about x from x^A (resp. x^B). In this scenario, x is called a shared secret. Note that a linear combination of secret shares can be computed locally, but the multiplication of two secrets would involve communication. To formulate the computation based on secret shares, all the inputs and outputs of a protocol π are expressed as shared secrets as $(y^A, y^B) \leftarrow \pi(A(x^A), B(x^B))$, where the superscript A (resp. B) of x^A (resp. x^B) denotes Alice's (resp. Bob's) share of x, and $A(.)$ (resp. $B(.)$) denotes Alice's (resp. Bob's) inputs.

Multiplicative to Additive Sharing (M2A). M2A is a basic functionality in secure two-party computation. Let x^A and x^B be the secret inputs of Alice and Bob respectively. An M2A protocol outputs y^A and y^B, held by Alice and Bob respectively, such that $y^A + y^B \equiv x^A \cdot x^B \mod Q$. We formulate this procedure as $(y^A, y^B) \leftarrow \mathsf{M2A}_Q(A(x^A), B(x^B))$.

Secure Multiplication (MULT). MULT is a functionality that securely computes the multiplication of two shared secrets. For example, Alice and Bob have x^A, y^A and x^B, y^B respectively as inputs, where $x = x^A + x^B \mod Q$ and $y = y^A + y^B \mod Q$; and they get z^A and z^B respectively as outputs such that $z^A + z^B \mod Q = x \cdot y \mod Q = (x^A + x^B) \cdot (y^A + y^B) \mod Q$. Since $x^A y^A$ and $x^B y^B$ can be computed locally by Alice and Bob respectively, the procedure involves two invocations of M2A for $x^A y^B$ and $x^B y^A$. We formulate the procedure as $(z^A, z^B) \leftarrow \mathsf{MULT}_Q(A(x^A, y^A), B(x^B, y^B))$.

Assumption 1 (M2A or MULT). We assume the existence of a M2A or a MULT. We take them as the cost units and regard the computation of one M2A or MULT as one communication round.

There have been solutions to $\mathsf{M2A}_Q$ and MULT_Q for an arbitrarily modulus Q. The implementation can be based on various cryptographic assumptions such as homomorphic encryption [17, 23, 27, 36] and oblivious transfers [23]. For example, when M2A is constructed using the Paillier cryptosystem [31], it should follow the hardness assumption of *decisional composite residuosity* (DCRA), and there will be a hidden security parameter σ. Nevertheless, M2A and MULT can be implemented by computing $O(1)$ modular exponentiations and communicating $O(1)$ ciphertexts, or equivalently $O(\ell + \sigma)$ bits, in $O(1)$ rounds.

2.1 Some Building Blocks

Polynomial Function Evaluation (POLY). Given a non-zero shared secret $x = x^A + x^B \mod Q$ as the input, POLY computes a polynomial function $f(x) = \sum_{i=1}^{k} c_i x^i$, where $c_1, ..., c_k$ are public constants. We formulate the computation as $(z^A, z^B) \leftarrow \mathsf{POLY}_Q(f(x), A(x^A), B(x^B))$. Note that POLY is only used in cases where the input secret x is non-zero. The POLY protocol for the multiparty case can be found in [5, 14]. Their protocol can be modified for the two-party use by carefully considering required commitments and zero-knowledge proofs. Alternatively, see [37], for a simple implementation of two-party POLY_Q. The total cost is less than $k + 4\mathsf{M2A}_Q$'s and 3 rounds.

m-Fan-In AND (AND_Q^m). Given a set of shared secret $x_i = x_i^A + x_i^B \mod Q$, where $x_i \in \{0, 1\}$ for $i = 1$ to m as the inputs, AND_Q^m computes $x_1 \wedge ... \wedge x_m$. We formulate this protocol as $(z^A, z^B) \leftarrow \mathsf{AND}_Q^m(A(x_1^A, ... x_m^A), B(x_1^B, ..., x_m^B))$. It is similar to the unbounded fan-in multiplication in [5]; however, the latter only supports non-zero inputs and finite fields. By contrast, the inputs of AND_Q^m can be 0, and Q can be an arbitrary integer greater than or equal to 2. An implementation of a two-party AND_Q^m can be found in [37]. The total cost of our implementation is about 5 rounds with $m + 5$ $\mathsf{M2A}_P$'s and 1 $\mathsf{M2A}_Q$, where P is the smallest prime greater than $m + 1$.

3   Probabilistically Correct Protocols with Passive Security

3.1   Our Framework

In this section, we explain how several non-arithmetic functions can be implemented by using secure arithmetic computation in the passive security model.

First, we construct a modular conversion protocol that converts shares in $\mathbb{Z}_Q$ into shares in $\mathbb{Z}_P$. Let x be a secret in $\mathbb{Z}_Q$, and let x^A and x^B be the additive shares of x in $\mathbb{Z}_Q$ (i.e., $x = x^A + x^B \mod Q$) held by Alice and Bob respectively. Modular conversion converts x^A and x^B into z^A and z^B respectively such that $x = z^A + z^B \mod P$.

To obtain a *general* modular conversion, we first build more limited protocols that only work with the input secret in a certain range. Then, we tweak them to ensure their validity regardless of the values of the secret shares. With uniformly random re-sharing, we can derive a probabilistically correct randomized algorithm of modular conversion with no constraint on the input secret.

In addition to the general modular conversion protocol, a randomized zero test protocol can be built by using modular conversion protocols of limited validity. Using the modular protocols as primitives, we also build several applications that involve the sign test, integer comparison and MOD operations. The applications form the centerpiece of an efficient modular exponentiation scheme. Please refer to the protocol hierarchy in [37].

3.2   Modular Conversion with Input Constraints

First, We implement the modular conversion protocols with some constraints on the input secret x. If an input satisfies the constraints, it can be assumed that partial information about the input secret is known. Specifically, when the sign of the input (whether $x < Q/2$ or $x \geq Q/2$) is known, the modular conversion of x from Q to P for arbitrary Q and P can be computed efficiently. By using this information to determine whether a wrap-around modulo Q occurs in $x = x^A + x^B \mod Q$, only one invocation of M2A$_P$ is required. Hence, based on this observation, we implement two function-limited protocols: one $\frac{1}{2}$modular conversion protocol for the case where $x < Q/2$ ($\frac{1}{2}$ModCNV$^{\perp}_{Q \to P}$), and one for the case where $x \geq Q/2$ ($\frac{1}{2}$ModCNV$^{\top}_{Q \to P}$), as shown in Fig. 1. Moreover, when Q is a small constant, the modular conversion of x from Q to an arbitrary P can be computed by using $O(1)$ MULT$_P$'s deterministically and validly without input constraints. Specifically, when $Q = 2$, the implementation of ModCNV$_{2 \to P}$ only requires one M2A$_P$, as shown in Fig. 1.

Correctness. We only reason the case where $x < Q/2$ ($\frac{1}{2}$ModCNV$^{\perp}_{Q \to P}$) because the case where $x \geq Q/2$ ($\frac{1}{2}$ModCNV$^{\top}_{Q \to P}$) is similar, and the correctness of ModCNV$_{2 \to P}$ is easy to follow. First, note that $x^A + x^B$ can only be $x + Q$ or x depending on whether a wrap-around modulo Q occurs. If $x^A, x^B < Q/2$, the outcome must be x, i.e., $x = x^A + x^B$. If $x^A, x^B \geq Q/2$, we can be certain that

Two half valid modular conversion protocols:

- **Inputs:** Alice holds $x^A \in \mathbb{Z}_Q$ and Bob holds $x^B \in \mathbb{Z}_Q$ such that $x = x^A + x^B$ mod Q. Q, P are two public integers, $Q > 2, P \geq 2$.
- **Outputs:** Alice obtains z^A and Bob obtains z^B such that $z^A + z^B = x$ mod P.

Case 1: $\frac{1}{2}\mathsf{ModCNV}^{\perp}_{Q \to P}(A(x^A), B(x^B))$, valid for $x < \frac{Q}{2}$:

1. Alice computes a number b^A locally such that $b^A = 1$ if $x^A < \frac{Q}{2}$, otherwise 0.
2. Bob computes a number b^B locally such that $b^B = 1$ if $x^B < \frac{Q}{2}$, otherwise 0.
3. Run $(z'^A, z'^B) \leftarrow \mathsf{M2A}_P(A(b^A), B(b^B))$.
4. Alice computes $z^A = (x^A + z'^A \cdot Q) \mod P$, and Bob computes $z^B = (x^B + (z'^B - 1) \cdot Q) \mod P$

Case 2: $\frac{1}{2}\mathsf{ModCNV}^{\top}_{Q \to P}(A(x^A), B(x^B))$, valid for $x \geq \frac{Q}{2}$:

1. Alice computes a number b^A locally such that $b^A = 1$ if $x^A \geq \frac{Q}{2}$, otherwise 0.
2. Bob computes a number b^B locally such that $b^B = 1$ if $x^B \geq \frac{Q}{2}$, otherwise 0.
3. Run $(z'^A, z'^B) \leftarrow \mathsf{M2A}_P(A(b^A), B(b^B))$.
4. Alice computes $z^A = (x^A - z'^A \cdot Q) \mod P$, and Bob computes $z^B = (x^B - z'^B \cdot Q) \mod P$

$\mathsf{ModCNV}_{2 \to P}(A(x^A), B(x^B))$ modular conversion protocol for the case where $x \in \mathbb{Z}_2$:

- **Inputs:** Alice holds $x^A \in \mathbb{Z}_2$ and Bob holds $x^B \in \mathbb{Z}_2$ such that $x = x^A + x^B$ mod 2. P is a public integer, $P > 2$.
- **Outputs:** Alice obtains $z^A \in \mathbb{Z}_P$ and Bob obtains $z^B \in \mathbb{Z}_P$ such that $z^A + z^B = x$ mod P.

1. Run $(z'^A, z'^B) \leftarrow \mathsf{M2A}_P(A(x^A), B(x^B))$.
2. Alice computes $z^A = (x^A - 2 \cdot z'^A) \mod P$, and Bob computes $z^B = (x^B - 2 \cdot z'^B) \mod P$.

Fig. 1. Protocol $\frac{1}{2}\mathsf{ModCNV}^{\perp}_{Q \to P}(A(x^A), B(x^B))$, $\frac{1}{2}\mathsf{ModCNV}^{\top}_{Q \to P}(A(x^A), B(x^B))$ and $\mathsf{ModCNV}_{2 \to P}(A(x^A), B(x^B))$

$x = x^A + x^B - Q$. Otherwise, if $x^A < Q/2, x^B \geq Q/2$ or $x^A \geq Q/2, x^B < Q/2$, we have $Q/2 \leq x^A + x^B < Q/2 + Q$. Specifically, when $x < Q/2$, $x^A + x^B$ can only be $x + Q$. Therefore, when $x < Q/2$, only the case where $x^A, x^B < Q/2$ does not involve a wrap-around modulo Q. This corresponds to the Boolean test in Step 3, where $z'^A + z'^B \mod P = b^A b^B = (x^A < Q/2) \wedge (x^B < Q/2)$. Since we have $x = x^A + x^B + ((z'^A + z'^B \mod P) - 1)Q$, which implies that $x \mod P = (x^A + z'^A Q \mod P) + (x^B + (z'^B - 1)Q \mod P) \mod P$, protocol $\frac{1}{2}\mathsf{ModCNV}^{\perp}_{Q \to P}$ is valid for $x < Q/2$.

Security and Complexity. The communication part of the above protocols only involves one invocation of $\mathsf{M2A}_P$, so the security and efficiency follows from those of $\mathsf{M2A}_P$. Note that we assume $\mathsf{M2A}_P$ is secure, and the secret share z'^A

(resp. z'^B) should be indistinguishable from a uniformly random value from Alice's (resp. Bob's) view. Hence, Alice (resp. Bob) does not obtain any additional information from the communication. The detailed security proofs will be provided in the full paper.

3.3 General Modular Conversion

Next, we describe a protocol for general modular conversion based on the protocols for modular conversion with input constraints We focus on the case where Q is an odd number. The extension regarding an arbitrary Q ($Q \geq 2$) is discussed in [37].

Recall that, while $\mathsf{ModCNV}_{2 \to Q}$ is always valid, the validity of $\frac{1}{2}\mathsf{ModCNV}^{\perp}_{Q \to 2}$ is only guaranteed when $x < Q/2$. When $x \geq Q/2$, the validity of $\frac{1}{2}\mathsf{ModCNV}^{\perp}_{Q \to 2}$ depends on the value of the shares. Assume one of the shares is sampled according to the uniformly distribution in $\mathbb{Z}_Q$. Then, for $x \in [Q/2, Q-1]$, the error rate of $\frac{1}{2}\mathsf{ModCNV}^{\perp}_{Q}$ would decree linearly when x gets large. When x is close to $Q/2$, $\frac{1}{2}\mathsf{ModCNV}^{\perp}_{Q}$ would return a correct output with a high probability; when x is close to $Q-1$, $\frac{1}{2}\mathsf{ModCNV}^{\perp}_{Q}$ would return an incorrect output with a high probability. More accurate formula is described in the following lemma.

Lemma 1. *Let $Q > 2, P \geq 2$, where $P \nmid Q$. Assume that $\frac{Q}{2} \leq x < Q$ and let x^A and x^B be a pair of shares of x. If x^A is a random number sampled according to the uniform distribution in $\mathbb{Z}_Q$, then the error rate of $\frac{1}{2}\mathsf{ModCNV}^{\perp}_{Q \to P}(A(x^A), B(x^B))$ would be $\frac{2(x - \lfloor (Q-1)/2 \rfloor)}{Q}$.*

Specifically, when Q is an odd number, for all $\frac{Q}{2} \leq x < Q$, there always exists at least one pair of shares (x^A, x^B) such that $(x^A < \frac{Q}{2}, x^B \geq \frac{Q}{2})$ or $(x^A \geq \frac{Q}{2}, x^B < \frac{Q}{2})$; and there always exists at least one pair of shares such that $(x^A < \frac{Q}{2}, x^B < \frac{Q}{2})$. The former case results in a fault in $\frac{1}{2}\mathsf{ModCNV}^{\perp}_{Q \to P}$, and the latter works properly in $\frac{1}{2}\mathsf{ModCNV}^{\perp}_{Q \to P}$. This implies that $\frac{1}{2}\mathsf{ModCNV}^{\perp}_{Q \to P}$ can serve as a randomized test. Therefore, we use uniformly random re-sharing to generate k pairs of shares of x and run $\frac{1}{2}\mathsf{ModCNV}^{\perp}_{Q \to P}$ k times. If $x < Q/2$, $\frac{1}{2}\mathsf{ModCNV}^{\perp}_{Q \to P}$ would return (random) shares of the correct $x \bmod P$ over $\mathbb{Z}_P$ for all derived pairs of shares; otherwise, with a non-negligible probability, at least one pair of shares would have a wrong and different result from the others. However, if x is close to $Q/2$ (resp. $Q-1$), since the error rate of $\frac{1}{2}\mathsf{ModCNV}^{\perp}_{Q \to P}$ is close to 0 (resp. 1) , all the k tests of $\frac{1}{2}\mathsf{ModCNV}^{\perp}_{Q \to P}$ would be correct (resp. wrong) with high probability. On the other hand, if x is close to $3Q/4$, the error rate of $\frac{1}{2}\mathsf{ModCNV}^{\perp}_{Q \to P}$ would be close to $1/2$; and hence, with high probability, at least one of the k pairs of shares would have a different result. Therefore, we test $x + \lfloor iQ/\rho \rfloor \bmod Q$ for $i = 0, ..., \rho - 1$ in parallel. Because at least one element of $x, x + \lfloor Q/\rho \rfloor ..., x + \lfloor (\rho-1)Q/\rho \rfloor \bmod Q$ is close to $3Q/4$, there is a high probability that we can identify this element successfully (in a private way). Thus, we have the following lemma.

Lemma 2. *Let $Q > 2, P \geq 2$, where $P \nmid Q$, and let $x \in \mathbb{Z}_Q$. For $i = 0, ..., \rho - 1$, let $x_i = x + \left\lfloor i \cdot \frac{Q}{\rho} \right\rfloor$; and let $(x_{i,1}^A, x_{i,1}^B), ..., (x_{i,k}^A, x_{i,k}^B)$ be k pairs of shares of x_i, where for all j, $x_{i,j}^A$ is a uniformly and independently random number in $\mathbb{Z}_Q$. In addition, let $(y_{i,j}^A, y_{i,j}^B)$ be the outputs of $\frac{1}{2}\mathsf{ModCNV}_{Q \to P}^{\perp}(A(x_{i,j}^A), B(x_{i,j}^B))$ and let $y_{i,j} = y_{i,j}^A + y_{i,j}^B \bmod P$. Then, the probability that $y_{i,1} = ... = y_{i,k}$ for all $i = 0, ..., \rho - 1$ is at most $\left(\frac{1}{2} + \frac{1}{\rho}\right)^k$.*

As a result, at least one of $x, x + \lfloor Q/\rho \rfloor, ..., x + \lfloor (\rho - 1)Q/\rho \rfloor \mod Q$ can be identified as greater than or equal to $Q/2$ with high probability (in a private way). Therefore, by utilizing $\frac{1}{2}\mathsf{ModCNV}_{Q \to P}^{\top}$, which is valid in this interval, we can derive a valid modular conversion of x from modulo Q to P with high probability. Our general modular conversion protocol is shown in Fig. 2. In Step 1, note that α_i stands for whether a wrap-around modulo Q occurs when $x_i^A = x^A + \left\lfloor i \cdot \frac{Q}{\sigma} \right\rfloor$ $\mod Q$ is computed; this will be used later in Step 7. As we have explained above, at least one of x_i would be close to $3Q/4$. For the convenience of illustration, we denote any one of such x_i by x_s with index s. In Step 2(a), a public random number is easy to obtain by letting Alice and Bob sample r_j^A and r_j^B respectively and then reveal them to compute $r_j = r_j^A + r_j^B \mod Q$ in the passively secure setting. In Step 3, u_i (resp. v_i) stands for wether $y_{i,1}, ..., y_{i,k}$ are all 1 (resp. all 0). In Step 4, a_i denotes whether there are distinct values among $y_{i,1}, ..., y_{i,k}$. Here we use the fact that $u_i^B - u_i^A = u_i^B + u_i^A \mod 2$ and the fact that u_i and v_i cannot be 1 at the same time. Note that $a_i = 1$ if and only if $x_i \geq \lfloor Q/2 \rfloor$, and from Lemma 7, with high probability, a_s would be 1. In Step 5, because the output shares are required to be in $\mathbb{Z}_P$, they convert the shares of a_i from $\mathbb{Z}_2$ to $\mathbb{Z}_P$. Note that this step is deterministically correct. The conversion in Step 7 is valid when $x_i \geq \lfloor Q/2 \rfloor$, and so the computation of w_s is deterministically correct. Finally, recall there can be multiple i satisfying $x_i \geq \lfloor Q/2 \rfloor$, and in Step 4, there is a non-negligible probability to get $a_i = 1$ (which implies $b_i = 1$) when $x_i \geq \lfloor Q/2 \rfloor$. Because $a_i = 1$ if and only if $x_i \geq \lfloor Q/2 \rfloor$ (which implies w_i is valid), we simply pick the first valid one, which is the computation in Step 8. The following theorem proves the correctness of this randomized protocol.

Theorem 3 (Correctness). *Let $Q > 2$ and $P \geq 2$ be two numbers, where Q is odd; and let $x^A, x^B \in \mathbb{Z}_Q$ be the secret shares of x in $\mathbb{Z}_Q$ i.e., $x = x^A + x^B \mod Q$. $(z^A, z^B) \leftarrow \mathsf{ModCNV}_{Q \to P}(A(x^A), B(x^B), k)$ form shares of x in $\mathbb{Z}_P$ with an error rate at most $\left(\frac{1}{2} + \frac{1}{\rho}\right)^k$, where ρ is the optimum parameter in $\mathsf{ModCNV}_{Q \to P}$.*

Security. Besides of the generation of k public random numbers that do not contain any information about the secret values, the communication only takes place in the sub-protocols whose outputs are all secret shares that are indistinguishable from uniformly random numbers from each party's view. Hence, the security follows from that of the sub-protocols. The detailed proof is deferred to the full version of this paper.

- **Inputs:** Alice holds $x^A \in \mathbb{Z}_Q$ and Bob holds $x^B \in \mathbb{Z}_Q$ such that $x = x^A + x^B$ mod Q. $Q > 2$ and $P \geq 2$ are two public numbers. Q is odd.
- **Outputs:** Alice obtains z^A and Bob obtains z^B such that $z^A + z^B = x$ mod P.

If $P|Q$, Alice and Bob output $z^A = x^A$ mod P and $z^B = x^B$ mod P respectively; else, let ρ be a parameter for the optimum adjustment and k be a parameter for the error rate.

1. For $i = 0, ..., \rho-1$, Alice sets $\alpha_i = (x_i^A + \lfloor i \cdot \frac{Q}{\rho} \rfloor \geq Q)$ and $x_i^A = x^A + \lfloor i \cdot \frac{Q}{\rho} \rfloor - \alpha_i Q$, and Bob sets $x_i^B = x^B$.
2. Alice and Bob run the following procedure for $j = 1, ..., k$ in parallel:
   (a) Generate a public random number r_j (uniformly and independently).
   (b) For each i, Alice and Bob locally compute $x_{i,j}^A \leftarrow x_i^A + r_j$ mod Q and $x_{i,j}^B \leftarrow x_i^B - r_j$ mod Q respectively.
   (c) For each i, run $(y_{i,j}^A, y_{i,j}^B) \leftarrow \frac{1}{2}\mathsf{ModCNV}_{Q\to 2}^{\perp}(A(x_{i,j}^A), B(x_{i,j}^B))$.
3. For each i, compute $(u_i^A, u_i^B) \leftarrow \mathsf{AND}_2^k(A(y_{i,1}^A, ..., y_{i,k}^A)), B(y_{i,1}^B, ..., y_{i,k}^B))$ and $(v_i^A, v_i^B) \leftarrow \mathsf{AND}_2^k(A(1 - y_{i,1}^A, ..., 1 - y_{i,k}^A)), B(-y_{i,1}^B, ..., -y_{i,k}^B))$.
4. For each i, Alice sets $a_i^A = 1 - u_i^A - v_i^A$, and Bob sets $a_i^B = 0$;
5. For each i, run $(b_i^A, b_i^B) \leftarrow \mathsf{ModCNV}_{2\to P}(a_i^A, a_i^B)$.
6. For each i, run $(w_i'^A, w_i'^B) \leftarrow \frac{1}{2}\mathsf{ModCNV}_{Q\to P}^{\top}(A(x_i^A), B(x_i^B))$.
7. For each i, Alice sets $w_i^A = w_i'^A - \lfloor i \cdot \frac{Q}{\rho} \rfloor + \alpha_i Q$ mod P, and Bob sets $w^B = w'^B$.
8. Compute z^A and z^B such that $z^A + z^B = b_0 w_0 + \bar{b}_0 b_1 w_1 + ... + (\bar{b}_0 ... \bar{b}_{\rho-2} b_{\rho-1} w_{\rho-1})$ mod P using $(1+\rho)\rho/2$ MULT_P (where $\bar{b}_i = 1 - b_i$, $b_i = b_i^A + b_i^B$ mod P and $w_i = w_i^A + w_i^B$ mod P).

Fig. 2. General modular conversion protocol: $\mathsf{ModCNV}_{Q\to P}(A(x^A), B(x^B), k)$

Complexity and Parameter Optimization. Note that Step 8 can be computed by using $(1+\rho)\rho/2$ MULT_P in $\log_2 \rho$ parallel rounds, and Steps 5 and 6 can be computed in parallel. The communication part of the protocol involves generating k random public numbers, $k\rho \frac{1}{2}\mathsf{ModCNV}_{Q\to P}^{\perp}$, ρ AND_2^k, k MULT_2, k $\mathsf{ModCNV}_{2\to P}$, $k \frac{1}{2}\mathsf{ModCNV}_{Q\to P}^{\top}$, and $(1+\rho)\rho/2$ MULT_P. For simplicity, we estimate the cost by the number of MULT_P, counting the cost of 2 $\mathsf{M2A}_P$ as 1 MULT_P. Note that the cost of MULT_2 is no more than MULT_P; and the total cost is at most $(1+\rho)\rho/2 + k\rho + 2k + 3\rho$ MULT_P and $5 + \lceil \log_2 \rho \rceil$ rounds. Since ρ is a constant, the complexity is $O(k)$ MULT_P and $O(1)$ rounds.

Furthermore, ρ (and k) can be chosen to optimize the cost. Suppose we expect that the protocol to have an error rate of at most $2^{-c}, c > 0$. Then, according to Theorem 3,

$$\left(\frac{1}{2} + \frac{1}{\rho}\right)^k \leq 2^{-c} \implies k \geq \frac{-c}{\log_2(\frac{1}{2} + \frac{1}{\rho})},$$

so the total cost would be at most

$$\frac{(7+\rho)\rho}{2} + \frac{-c(\rho+2)}{\log_2(\frac{1}{2}+\frac{1}{\rho})} \quad \text{MULT}_P\text{'s.}$$

Hence, for optimization purposes, we choose $\rho = 3$ for $0 < c \le 1$, $\rho = 4$ for $2 \le c \le 9$ and $\rho = 5$ for all $c \ge 10$. We summarize the complexity of this optimization strategy in the following lemma.

Lemma 4. *The optimum parameter ρ in* $\text{ModCNV}_{Q\to P}$ *is always less than or equal to 5; and the cost of* $\text{ModCNV}_{Q\to P}$ *is at most $7k + 30$ MULT$_P$'s and 8 rounds with an error rate of at most $\left(\frac{7}{10}\right)^k$ when $k \ge 20$.*

3.4 Zero Test

Nishide and Ohta [30] proposed a non-bitwise zero test that calculates the Legendre symbol multiple times. Given an odd prime Q, the solution is based on the observation that if $a = 0$, " $\left(\frac{a+r}{Q}\right) = \left(\frac{r}{Q}\right)$ " is always true; and if $a \ne 0$, " $\left(\frac{a+r}{Q}\right) = \left(\frac{r}{Q}\right)$ " is valid with a probability of about $1/2$ for a random value r uniformly sampled from $\mathbb{Z}_Q$. The method requires $12k$ MULT$_Q$'s with an error rate of $\left(\frac{1}{2}\right)^k$. Instead of comparing the Legendre symbol, we provide an even more lightweight solution for two-party computation based on $\frac{1}{2}\text{ModCNV}_{Q\to 2}^{\perp}$. Here, we consider the case where Q is a prime. An extension for an arbitrary modulus is described in [37].

First, note that the validity of $\frac{1}{2}\text{ModCNV}_{Q\to 2}^{\perp}$ is only guaranteed when the input secret is less than $Q/2$. In addition, by Lemma 1, the error rate increases linearly with x when $x \ge Q/2$ (when the shares of x are sampled uniformly from $\mathbb{Z}_Q$). However, because the counts of odd and even numbers in $[Q/2, Q-1]$ are the same, when x is sampled uniformly from $\mathbb{Z}_Q$ (or $\mathbb{Z}_Q^*$), $\frac{1}{2}\text{ModCNV}_{Q\to 2}^{\perp}$ has approximately the same probability of returning 1 or 0. The following lemma states the condition more accurately.

Lemma 5. *Let Q be an odd number ($Q > 2$), r be a random number uniformly sampled from $\mathbb{Z}_Q^*$, r^A be a random number uniformly sampled from $\mathbb{Z}_Q$, and $r^B = r - r^A \bmod Q$. In addition, let (z^A, z^B) be an output of $\frac{1}{2}\text{ModCNV}_{Q\to 2}^{\perp}(A(r^A), B(r^B))$ and $z = z^A + z^B \bmod 2$. Then, when $Q = 4a + 1$, $Pr[z = 1] = \frac{Q+1}{2Q}$; otherwise, (when $Q = 4a - 1$), $Pr[z = 1] = \frac{Q^2+1}{2Q(Q-1)}$.*

Combining this with the fact that, because Q is a prime, $f(r) = rx : \mathbb{Z}_Q^* \to \mathbb{Z}_Q^*$ is an isomorphism. Therefore, we provide an efficient randomized protocol through random re-sharing, as shown in Fig. 3. Note that when $Q = 2$, ($x{=}0$) is simply $1 - x \bmod 2$. Otherwise, when Q is an odd prime, the correctness of ZeroTest_Q is proved by the following theorem.

Theorem 6 (Correctness). *Let Q be an odd prime, and let (x^A, x^B) be a pair of shares of x in $\mathbb{Z}_Q$. Then, $(z^A, z^B) \leftarrow \text{ZeroTest}_Q(A(x^A), B(x^B), k)$ forms a pair of shares of $(x{=}0)$ with an error rate less than $\left(\frac{1}{2}\right)^k$.*

- **Inputs:** Alice holds $x^A \in \mathbb{Z}_Q$ and Bob holds $x^B \in \mathbb{Z}_Q$, such that $x = x^A + x^B$ mod Q. Q is a public prime.
- **Outputs:** Alice obtains z^A and Bob obtains z^B such that $z^A + z^B \mod Q = 1$ if $x = 0$, otherwise 0.

When $Q = 2$: output $z^A \leftarrow 1 - x^A$ and $z^B \leftarrow x^B$,
else (when $Q > 2$):

1. Alice and Bob run the following procedure for $i = 1, ..., k$ in parallel:
   (a) Generate a public random number s_i (uniformly and independently).
   (b) Generate a public non-zero random number r_i (uniformly and independently).
   (c) Alice and Bob locally compute $x_i^A \leftarrow r_i x^A + s_i \mod Q$ and $x_i^B \leftarrow r_i x^B - s_i \mod Q$ respectively.
   (d) Run $(w_i^A, w_i^B) \leftarrow \frac{1}{2}\mathsf{ModCNV}_{Q \to 2}^{\perp}(A(x_i^A), B(x_i^B))$.
2. Run $(w'^A, w'^B) \leftarrow \mathsf{AND}_2^k(A(1 - w_1^A, ..., 1 - w_k^A), B(-w_1^A, ..., -w_k^A))$.
3. Run $(z^A, z^B) \leftarrow \mathsf{ModCNV}_{2 \to Q}(A(w'^A), B(w'^B))$.

Fig. 3. Zero test protocol: $\mathsf{ZeroTest}_Q(A(x^A), B(x^B), k)$

Security and Complexity. The communication part of the protocol comprises generating k public $s_i \in_R \mathbb{Z}_Q$ and k public $r_i \in_R \mathbb{Z}_Q^*$, k $\frac{1}{2}\mathsf{ModCNV}_{Q \to 2}^{\perp}$, 1 AND_2^k, and 1 $\mathsf{ModCNV}_{2 \to Q}$. Since no public s_i or r_i contain any information about the secrets, the security of the protocol follows from that of the sub-protocols. Besides, since the cost of $\mathsf{M2A}_2$ is not more than that of $\mathsf{M2A}_Q$, and a MULT_Q involves two $\mathsf{M2A}_Q$'s, for simplicity, we estimate the cost by the number of MULT_Q. The total cost is approximately k MULT_Q's and 8 rounds.

- **Inputs:** Alice holds $x^A \in \mathbb{Z}_Q$ and Bob holds $x^B \in \mathbb{Z}_Q$ such that $x = x^A + x^B$ mod Q, where Q is a public odd number.
- **Outputs:** Alice obtains z^A and Bob obtains z^B such that $z^A + z^B \mod Q = 1$ if $x \leq \lfloor \frac{Q}{2} \rfloor$, otherwise 0.

1. Alice and Bob locally compute $x'^A = 2x^A \mod Q$ and $x'^B = 2x^B \mod Q$ respectively.
2. Run $(y^A, y^B) \leftarrow \mathsf{ModCNV}_{Q \to 2}(A(x'^A), B(x'^B), k)$.
3. Run $(z^A, z^B) \leftarrow \mathsf{ModCNV}_{2 \to Q}(A(1 - y^A), B(y^B))$.

Fig. 4. Sign test protocol: $\mathsf{SIGN}_Q(A(x^A), B(x^B))$

3.5   Sign Test

Let $1, ..., \lfloor Q/2 \rfloor$ correspond to positive numbers, and let $\lceil (Q + 1)/2 \rceil, ..., Q - 1$ correspond to negative numbers $(- \lceil (Q + 1)/2 \rceil, ..., -1)$. For all x in $\mathbb{Z}_Q$, we compute the sign of x through general modular conversion. Here, we consider the case where Q is an odd number. An extension for an arbitrary Q is discussed in [37].

A simple implementation of the protocol is described in Fig. 4. The protocol's validity follows that of $\mathsf{ModCNV}_{Q\to 2}$ and $\mathsf{ModCNV}_{2\to Q}$ and the fact that, for all $x < Q/2$, $2x$ $(0 \le 2x < Q)$ is even; and for all $x \ge Q/2$, $2x - Q$ $(0 \le 2x - Q < Q)$ is odd.

Security and Complexity. SIGN_Q only involves $\mathsf{ModCNV}_{Q\to 2}$ and $\mathsf{ModCNV}_{2\to Q}$, so the security follows from those sub-protocols. Hence, by Lemma 4, the output of SIGN_Q is valid with a probability of at least $1 - (7/10)^k$; and the cost is about $7k + 30$ MULT_2's and 1 $\mathsf{M2A}_Q$ and 9 rounds.

3.6 Applications

In this section, we consider several applications of the modular conversion protocols and the zero test protocol. Using our implementation of SIGN_Q, the complexity of the applications is at most $O(k)$ MULT_Q's and $O(1)$ rounds, with an error rate of $2^{-\Omega(k)}$ at most.

Integer Comparison (CMP_Q). Integer comparison assesses whether $(x \le y)$ or $(x \ge y)$, etc. When the input secrets x and y are known to be in the interval $[0, Q/2]$, the computation is just $Sign_Q(A(x^A - y^A \mod Q), B(x^B - y^B \mod Q))$. Otherwise, if x and y are known to be in Z_Q, similar to the derivation in [30], CMP_Q can be reduced to a cubic combination of $Sign_Q(A(x^A), B(x^B))$, $Sign_Q(A(y^A), B(y^B))$ and $Sign_Q(A(x^A - y^A \mod Q), B(x^B - y^B \mod Q))$ by 2 rounds and 3 MULT_Q's[3]. Hence, the whole computation mainly requires 3 invocations of SIGN_Q.

Exponentiation (EXP_Q). Yu et al. [36] proposed an efficient method for performing secure two-party modular exponentiation in an arithmetic way. Under their scheme, the secret base is first converted into multiplicative shares over $\mathbb{Z}_Q^*$ and the secret exponent is converted into additive shares over $\mathbb{Z}_{Q-1}$. Then, the computation can be expressed as $(x + (x{=}0))^{(y \mod Q-1)} - (x{=}0) \mod Q$. In the authors' implementation, the scheme can be computed efficiently except the zero test $(x{=}0)$ and modular conversion (converting the shares of y from Q to $Q - 1$) components. The cost of the computation is estimated to be 5 rounds and 12 $\mathsf{M2A}_Q$'s, or equivalently about 6 MULT_Q's. Hence, our zero test and general modular conversion solutions can complement the implementation in [36].

MOD Operation ($\mathsf{MOD}_{Q,P}$). Here, the MOD operation is defined as the remainder of an integer division of a secret x, shared over $\mathbb{Z}_Q$, with a public divisor P. In [14, 28], this function is called modulo reduction, which is related to modular conversion. With input $x^A, x^B \in \mathbb{Z}_Q$, $\mathsf{MOD}_{Q,P}$ is expected to output $z^A, z^B \in \mathbb{Z}_Q$

---

[3] Let $\alpha = (x{\le}Q/2)$, $\beta = (y{\le}Q/2)$ and $\gamma = (x - y{\le}Q/2)$. We have $(x{\le}y) = \alpha\overline{\beta} + \overline{\alpha}\overline{\beta}\overline{\gamma} + \alpha\beta\overline{\gamma} = \alpha(\beta + \gamma - 2\beta\gamma) + 1 - \beta - \gamma + \beta\gamma$.

such that $z^A + z^B \mod Q = x \mod P$, where $x = x^A + x^B \mod Q$. That is, the input and the output are both shares in $\mathbb{Z}_Q$. However, it can be reduced to two invocations of the general modular conversion protocols, $\mathsf{ModCNV}_{Q \to P}$ and $\mathsf{ModCNV}_{P \to Q}$.

Acknowledgement. The authors would like to thank Kai-Min Chung and Feng-Hao Liu for their helpful discussion and promotion of this study. They also thank the anonymous referees for valuable feedback. Finally, they thank National Science Council for partial sponsorship under grants 100-2218-E-001-002 and 100-2628-E-001-004-MY3.

References

1. SEPIA, http://sepia.ee.ethz.ch/
2. VIFF, http://viff.dk/doc/applications.html
3. Algesheimer, J., Camenisch, J.L., Shoup, V.: Efficient Computation Modulo a Shared Secret with Application to the Generation of Shared Safe-Prime Products. In: Yung, M. (ed.) CRYPTO 2002. LNCS, vol. 2442, pp. 417–432. Springer, Heidelberg (2002)
4. Avidan, S., Elbaz, A., Malkin, T.: Privacy preserving pattern classification. In: 15th ICIP, pp. 1684–1687 (2008)
5. Bar-Ilan, J., Beaver, D.: Non-cryptographic fault-tolerant computing in a constant number of rounds of interaction. In: Proc. 8th PODC, pp. 201–209 (1989)
6. Beimel, A., Nissim, K., Omri, E.: Distributed Private Data Analysis: Simultaneously Solving How and What. In: Wagner, D. (ed.) CRYPTO 2008. LNCS, vol. 5157, pp. 451–468. Springer, Heidelberg (2008)
7. Ben-Or, M., Goldwasser, S., Wigderson, A.: Completeness theorems for non-cryptographic fault-tolerant distributed computation. In: STOC 1988, pp. 1–10 (1988)
8. Bogetoft, P., Christensen, D.L., Damgård, I., Geisler, M., Jakobsen, T., Krøigaard, M., Nielsen, J.D., Nielsen, J.B., Nielsen, K., Pagter, J., Schwartzbach, M., Toft, T.: Secure Multiparty Computation Goes Live. In: Dingledine, R., Golle, P. (eds.) FC 2009. LNCS, vol. 5628, pp. 325–343. Springer, Heidelberg (2009)
9. Boudot, F.: Efficient Proofs that a Committed Number Lies in an Interval. In: Preneel, B. (ed.) EUROCRYPT 2000. LNCS, vol. 1807, pp. 431–444. Springer, Heidelberg (2000)
10. Bunn, P., Ostrovsky, R.: Secure two-party k-means clustering. In: Proc. 14th CCS, pp. 486–497. ACM (2007)
11. Burkhart, M., Strasser, M., Many, D., Dimitropoulos, X.: SEPIA: privacy-preserving aggregation of multi-domain network events and statistics. In: 19th USENIX, pp. 223–240 (2010)
12. Chaum, D., Crepéau, C., Damgård, I.: Multiparty unconditionally secure protocols. In: Proc. 20th STOC, vol. 47, pp. 11–19. ACM (1988)
13. Choi, S.G., Hwang, K.-W., Katz, J., Malkin, T., Rubenstein, D.: Secure Multi-Party Computation of Boolean Circuits with Applications to Privacy in On-Line Marketplaces. In: Dunkelman, O. (ed.) CT-RSA 2012. LNCS, vol. 7178, pp. 416–432. Springer, Heidelberg (2012)

14. Damgård, I., Fitzi, M., Kiltz, E., Nielsen, J.B., Toft, T.: Unconditionally Secure Constant-Rounds Multi-party Computation for Equality, Comparison, Bits and Exponentiation. In: Halevi, S., Rabin, T. (eds.) TCC 2006. LNCS, vol. 3876, pp. 285–304. Springer, Heidelberg (2006)
15. Damgård, I., Geisler, M., Krøigaard, M., Nielsen, J.B.: Asynchronous Multi-party Computation: Theory and Implementation. In: Jarecki, S., Tsudik, G. (eds.) PKC 2009. LNCS, vol. 5443, pp. 160–179. Springer, Heidelberg (2009)
16. Damgård, I., Mikkelsen, G.L.: Efficient, Robust and Constant-Round Distributed RSA Key Generation. In: Micciancio, D. (ed.) TCC 2010. LNCS, vol. 5978, pp. 183–200. Springer, Heidelberg (2010)
17. Damgård, I., Orlandi, C.: Multiparty Computation for Dishonest Majority: From Passive to Active Security at Low Cost. In: Rabin, T. (ed.) CRYPTO 2010. LNCS, vol. 6223, pp. 558–576. Springer, Heidelberg (2010)
18. Dwork, C., Kenthapadi, K., McSherry, F., Mironov, I., Naor, M.: Our Data, Ourselves: Privacy Via Distributed Noise Generation. In: Vaudenay, S. (ed.) EUROCRYPT 2006. LNCS, vol. 4004, pp. 486–503. Springer, Heidelberg (2006)
19. Dwork, C., McSherry, F., Nissim, K., Smith, A.: Calibrating Noise to Sensitivity in Private Data Analysis. In: Halevi, S., Rabin, T. (eds.) TCC 2006. LNCS, vol. 3876, pp. 265–284. Springer, Heidelberg (2006)
20. Goldreich, O.: Foundations of Cryptography - vol. II, Basic Applications. Cambridge University Press (2004)
21. Goldreich, O., Micali, S., Wigderson, A.: How to play any mental game - A completeness theorem for protocols with honest majority. In: Proc. 19th STOC, pp. 218–229. ACM (1987)
22. Guajardo, J., Mennink, B., Schoenmakers, B.: Modulo Reduction for Paillier Encryptions and Application to Secure Statistical Analysis. In: Sion, R. (ed.) FC 2010. LNCS, vol. 6052, pp. 375–382. Springer, Heidelberg (2010)
23. Ishai, Y., Prabhakaran, M., Sahai, A.: Secure Arithmetic Computation with No Honest Majority. In: Reingold, O. (ed.) TCC 2009. LNCS, vol. 5444, pp. 294–314. Springer, Heidelberg (2009)
24. Lindell, Y., Pinkas, B.: Privacy-preserving data mining. Journal of the Cryptology 15(3), 177–206 (2002)
25. Lindell, Y., Pinkas, B.: Secure multiparty computation for privacy-preserving data mining. Journal of the ACM 1(1), 59–98 (2009)
26. Mironov, I., Pandey, O., Reingold, O., Vadhan, S.: Computational Differential Privacy. In: Halevi, S. (ed.) CRYPTO 2009. LNCS, vol. 5677, pp. 126–142. Springer, Heidelberg (2009)
27. Mohassel, P., Weinreb, E.: Efficient Secure Linear Algebra in the Presence of Covert or Computationally Unbounded Adversaries. In: Wagner, D. (ed.) CRYPTO 2008. LNCS, vol. 5157, pp. 481–496. Springer, Heidelberg (2008)
28. Ning, C., Xu, Q.: Multiparty Computation for Modulo Reduction without Bit-Decomposition and a Generalization to Bit-Decomposition. In: Abe, M. (ed.) ASIACRYPT 2010. LNCS, vol. 6477, pp. 483–500. Springer, Heidelberg (2010)
29. Ning, C., Xu, Q.: Constant-rounds, linear multi-party computation for exponentiation and modulo reduction with perfect security. In: Lee, D.H. (ed.) ASIACRYPT 2011. LNCS, vol. 7073, pp. 572–589. Springer, Heidelberg (2011)
30. Nishide, T., Ohta, K.: Multiparty Computation for Interval, Equality, and Comparison Without Bit-Decomposition Protocol. In: Okamoto, T., Wang, X. (eds.) PKC 2007. LNCS, vol. 4450, pp. 343–360. Springer, Heidelberg (2007)

31. Paillier, P.: Public-Key Cryptosystems Based on Composite Degree Residuosity Classes. In: Stern, J. (ed.) EUROCRYPT 1999. LNCS, vol. 1592, pp. 223–238. Springer, Heidelberg (1999)
32. Toft, T.: Constant-Rounds, Almost-Linear Bit-Decomposition of Secret Shared Values. In: Fischlin, M. (ed.) CT-RSA 2009. LNCS, vol. 5473, pp. 357–371. Springer, Heidelberg (2009)
33. Toft, T.: Sub-linear, Secure Comparison with Two Non-colluding Parties. In: Catalano, D., Fazio, N., Gennaro, R., Nicolosi, A. (eds.) PKC 2011. LNCS, vol. 6571, pp. 174–191. Springer, Heidelberg (2011)
34. Yao, A.C.-C.: How to generate and exchange secrets. In: Proc. 27th FOCS, pp. 162–167. IEEE Computer Society (1986)
35. Yu, C.-H.: Sign Modules in Secure Arithmetic Circuits. IACR Cryptology ePrint Archive, 539 (2011)
36. Yu, C.-H., Chow, S.S.M., Chung, K.-M., Liu, F.-H.: Efficient Secure Two-Party Exponentiation. In: Kiayias, A. (ed.) CT-RSA 2011. LNCS, vol. 6558, pp. 17–32. Springer, Heidelberg (2011)
37. Yu, C.-H., Yang, B.-Y.: Probabilistically Correct Secure Arithmetic Computation for Modular Conversion, Zero Test, Comparison, MOD and Exponentiation. IACR Cryptology ePrint Archive, 560 (2011)

MAC Aggregation with Message Multiplicity

Vladimir Kolesnikov

Bell Labs, Murray Hill, NJ 07974, USA
kolesnikov@research.bell-labs.com

Abstract. Wireless sensor networks (WSN) collect and report measurements, such as temperature, to a central node. Because sensors are usually low-powered devices, data is transmitted hop-by-hop, through neighboring nodes, before it reaches the destination.

Each nodes' messages are authenticated with a MAC (Message Authentication Code), keyed with a key known to the generating sensor and the control node. Because transmission channel capacity is often small, MACs represent a significant overhead. Indeed, a typical 128-bit MAC is as much as an order of magnitude larger than the data it authenticates – a temperature or consumption reading, even with a timestamp, can be stored in 10-15 bits. To mitigate these overheads, methods to compute *aggregate* MACs, of length much shorter than the concatenation of constituent MACs, were proposed.

Unfortunately, known MAC aggregation techniques require that any message may not appear twice in the aggregate MAC. This is entrenched both in the definitions and constructions/proofs. This is a significant impediment in many typical practical deployments of WSNs. Indeed, one typical message relay strategy, *flooding*, relies on each node retransmitting received packets to all neighbors, almost certainly causing message repetition and inability to aggregate MACs. Further, we are not aware of any WSN protocols that guarantee non-duplication of messages.

We propose a simple and very practical new way of MAC aggregation which allows message duplicates, and hence is usable in many more deployment scenarios. We derive a new security definition of this type of aggregate MAC, and discuss several variants of our construction and additional benefits such as Denial-of-Service resilience.

1 Introduction

In many of today's and future applications, both military (e.g., surveillance) and civilian (e.g., building management systems), scores of cheap low-power sensors report measurements, such as motion, vibration, radiation, temperature, electricity consumption and other parameters, to a control node. To save power and reduce deployment costs, it is often the case that data is sent wirelessly, and sensors serve as relay nodes that retransmit messages from other, more remote sensors. These types of wireless sensor networks (WSN) is a very rapidly developing research area, due to the utility WSNs provide at a very low cost.

To prevent *en route* accidental and malicious data corruption, nodes' messages are authenticated with a MAC (Message Authentication Code), keyed

I. Visconti and R. De Prisco (Eds.): SCN 2012, LNCS 7485, pp. 445–460, 2012.

with a key known to the generating sensor and the control node. Because transmission channel capacity is often small, MACs represent a significant overhead. Indeed, a typical 128-bit MAC is as much as an order of magnitude larger than the data it authenticates – a temperature or consumption reading, even with a timestamp, can be stored in 10-15 bits. To mitigate these overheads, methods to compute *aggregate* MACs (AggMAC), of length much shorter than the concatenation of constituent MACs, were proposed [KL08, EFG+10]. One of the important assumptions of these AggMAC schemes is that no message may appear twice in the aggregate MAC. This is entrenched both in the definitions and constructions/proofs (cf. Section 2).

We next argue that this is is a significant use restriction for AggMAC in WSNs.

1.1   The Need for AggMAC with Message Multiplicity and Aggregation of Already-Aggregated MACs

We now argue that AggMAC which allows for aggregation of identical messages is *critical* in many typical practical deployments of WSNs. Conversely, existing AggMAC restriction of aggregation of distinct messages only is a *significant* impediment in many (but not all – see below) practical scenarios. We refer the interested reader to [DP10, SMZ07] for thorough WSN overview; here we briefly summarize relevant discussion from WSN network design literature.

We first argue that message duplication/multiplicity (we will use the terms interchangeably) is very hard to avoid (and often is a feature) in network design, and especially in WSN design.

Ubiquity of Message Duplication. The underlying reason for message duplication is the message forwarding techniques in WSNs, and, more generally, in many multi-hop mesh networks, which often rely on sending the same message on more than one path, and almost certainly *do not guarantee* that a particular message does not follow several paths. In turn, some of the reasons for such routing are

1. non-central, distributed knowledge of the network structure,
2. need for robustness in dealing with message loss and adversarial intervention, and
3. standard routing techniques, which require resending message thought to be lost (but which might in fact be buffered somewhere), multiple paths between nodes, etc.

We now consider these in some more detail, and provide examples to further substantiate our claim.

We start with noting one popular WSN message forwarding technique *flooding*. The idea here is that when a node wants to send a message, it sends it down to all available paths (or, in geographic routing, only to nodes who are physically closer to the receiver). We note that overheads here are not as dramatic as it may seem at the first glance, since, firstly, duplicate messages are discarded before forwarding (of course, if aggregate authentication is desired, a count of the number of dropped copies of a particular message will need to be maintained). Further, transmission to several nodes incurs no overhead as compared to a single node transmission, due to the properties of wireless broadcast.

Complete network flooding is a rather extreme use of the technique; it is often used in critical paths and parts of the network where more robustness is desired. Such use constitutes a frequent compromise in network design. We stress that in some applications, such as some military applications, where there are concerns of adversarial or even accidental interference with the network, the robustness property of flooding (or other duplication approaches) is a critical architectural feature.

Further, we note that WSNs are frequently deployed with *a priori* unknown and, furthermore, constantly changing network structure, similarly to MANETs (Mobile Ad-hoc Networks). As such, routing paths and their properties often change, forcing messages to be sent and delivered via multiple paths.

Finally, in the scenarios where in normal operation a protocol *never* sends a message on more than one path, error conditions will often cause messages to be duplicated. For example, if a message is thought to be lost, it will be retransmitted, perhaps after a delay, and it may take a different path. Hovever, it is probable that a message in fact was not lost, but buffered (longish-term buffering is essential in WSNs, since sensors must be in sleep mode most of the time for power conservation). In this case, the two messages are duplicated.

Protocol Message Duplication Disrupts Existing AggMAC Schemes.
We now argue that message duplication is in fact very disruptive to application of AggMACs which do not support message multiplicity.

At the first glance, it may seem that message duplication may be technically avoided by randomizing a part of the message or inserting a counter. This way, a message m would each time be viewed as (m, r), where r may be discarded by the receiver. There are several problems with this approach. Firstly, r incurs transmission overhead. More important, however, is the fact that only the node that generated m can generate (m, r). That is, if an intermediate node needs to retransmit a message, it will not be able to generate an authenticated (m, r'), and must resend (m, r), causing duplication.

Hence, when an intermediate node receives two sets of messages M_1, M_2 and two AggMACs σ_1, σ_2, it will not be able to aggregate them, if *at least one message is duplicated*, i.e. if $M_1 \cap M_2 \neq \emptyset$.

Use Cases for Existing AggMAC Approaches. Existing AggMAC algorithms, which do not allow message duplication, are sufficient for certain types of manually deployed WSNs where there is a layer of intermediate aggregator nodes, with a fixed and centrally known connectivity matrix (and hence with fixed routing tables), and where sensors talk directly to these intermediate application. We stress that the non-duplication assumption is an expensive one to enforce in many network types and protocols, and it is highly desirable not to burden network and routing designers with meeting this requirement.

The Need for Aggregation of AggMACs of Sets. From the above discussion it immediately follows that it is highly desirable for the AggMAC aggregation function to be able to aggregate the already aggregated MACs, rather than simply being able to incorporate a single MAC into the aggregate.

1.2   Our Contributions and Outline of the Work

Addressing the need discussed above, we present two simple and very practical solutions which allow duplicate messages to be securely aggregated in an aggregate MAC. Importantly, our AggMAC functions accept as input *sets* of messages and corresponding aggregate MACs. We mention additional benefits of one of our constructions, such as Denial-of-Service resilience, and their trade-offs.

We start with the discussion of related work in Section 2. We then informally present our two constructions in Section 3:

In our main construction, we achieve our stronger notion of AggMAC, while keeping the size of aggregate MAC equal to that of the size of a single constituent MAC. This construction achieves optimal MAC size, and gives a complete use flexibility.

Our second construction offers Denial-of-Service (DoS) resilience, i.e., limits the disruption of an authentication failure of the entire message chain forced by a transmission error or an active attacker anywhere in the delivery path. In contrast with [KL08] (and similarly to [EFG+10]), this construction requires the order of AggMAC application to be maintained to enable verification.

In Section 4, we formalize our (until then) informal discussion. In Section 4.1, taking as the base the definition of [KL08], we derive a new security definition of this type of aggregate MAC, simply by allowing sets with element multiplicity, and removing the [KL08]'s restriction that the two aggregated sets must not have common elements. We then formally present our constructions, and state and prove corresponding security theorems in Section 4.2.

Performance. The performance characteristics of our first scheme are the same as those of [KL08] (which are shown optimal by [KL08]). Specifically, the size of our AggMAC is equal to the size of a single MAC, it takes small constant time to aggregate two AggMACs, and verification is linear in the number of MACs incorporated in AggMAC.

Our second construction offers similar performance, with the exception of AggMAC size, which starts at the size of a MAC tag, and grows by one bit per incorporated tag.

2   Related Work

There is a large body of work on security of data transmission in wireless networks, and specifically in WSNs, a very rapidly developing area today. Vast majority of this work is only tangentially related to cryptography.

MAC aggregation was considered in security literature, e.g., [CPS06, HE03], but without a model or proof of security[1]. Bhaskar et al. [BHL07] considered aggregate MAC as a tool in constructing aggregate designated-verifier signatures. They proposed XOR-based aggregate MAC as in [KL08], but did not model its security properties formally.

We are not aware of the issue of message multiplicity in aggregate MAC being considered even informally, nor we are aware of prior constructions, even those presented only with informal security argument, that satisfy our notion of security. At the same time, analogously to this work, Bellare et al. [BNN07] showed how to lift the restrictions of distinct message and distinct message per signer in the context of aggregate signatures.

Here we review in detail only the works [KL08, EFG+10, KLH11], which formally address MAC aggregation. We show that not only existing definitions, but also constructions, do not allow for message multiplicity.

[KL08]. Katz and Lindell [KL08] were the first to map the idea of authenticator aggregation from public-key signatures [BGLS03] to symmetric-key MACs. They suggested an efficient construction that allows to aggregate any number of MACs (generated under different keys) into the aggregate short MAC which will validate the integrity of the entire data set. The main idea of their construction is to simply bitwise XOR the constituent MACs, as shown on Figure 1. Katz and Lindell also consider scenarios where only a particular message, and not all the messages in the set, needs to be authenticated by the receiver. They suggest a variant of their approach, where they create several "XOR buckets", or AggMACs, each authenticating up to ℓ messages. This trade-off allows faster individual MAC verification at the expense of extra communication.

We note that the scheme of [KL08] cannot be used if message sets may contain duplicates. The definition of [KL08] explicitly disallows message multiplicity, and this is inherent in their contruction. Indeed, it is easy to see that the XOR-based scheme of [KL08] is insecure when one duplicate MAC is aggregated, since this MAC simply cancels its already-aggregated duplicate (hence, duplicate messages must be considered unauthenticated by AggMAC).

[EFG+10]. Eikemeier et al. [EFG+10] extended the security guarantees of [KL08]. They included subtle optional aggregate MAC security properties, such as putting the order of the message chain under the protection of aggregate MAC, and proposed simple constructions achieving their definition. The main idea of their *sequential aggregation* construction is that each node, when adding its message to the set of authenticated messages, computes (with its key) the MAC of the concatenation of its message and previous aggregated MAC. The model and the proof of security is quite involved, and requires a *partially invertible* MAC. (Roughly, a partially invertible MAC allows to obtain the last block of the MAC'ed message, given the tag and rest of the message.) This type of MAC is needed in the proof, to be able to compute a basic MAC forgery from aggregate MAC forgery.

---

[1] [CPS06]'s XOR-based scheme is essentially the same as [KL08], and [HE03]'s scheme is similar to that of [EFG+10].

As in [KL08], the definition of security of [EFG+10] prohibits message duplication. While their construction is not clearly insecure in the presence of duplicate messages, their proof (or, more specifically, the reduction from aggregate to basic MAC), seems to inherently rely on non-duplication of constituent MACs, and we don't immediately see how remove this requirement. Further, their AggMAC construction takes the tuple (k, m, M, σ) of the secret key, message, set of MAC'ed messages, and the current aggregate MAC as input. It does not aggregate two already-aggregated MACs. However, we note that their construction guarantees the ordering of the aggregated messages, which we (and other works) do not.

[KLH11]. Kolesnikov et al. [KLH11] and its full version [KL12] consider protection against denial-of-service (DoS) attacks and line transmission errors. To this effect, they prove security (in the sense of [KL08]) for a large class of aggregation functions, which are one-to-one and efficiently computable on their components (i.e. constituent MAC inputs). They also describe several interesting aggregation functions, such as XOR shifted in the staircase manner (shown on Figure 2), and discuss their DoS-resilient properties. We note that their constructed family is not secure in the presence of message multiplicity, and counterexamples can be readily constructed (e.g., the [KL08] construction is a member of the family proven secure in [KLH11]).

Our second construction, the "staircase XOR", is a special case of the family considered in [KLH11]. In this work, we prove that it has stronger security properties than claimed in [KLH11], namely, that it is secure in the presence of message multiplicity.

To summarize, in contrast with all prior work, we allow message multiplicity in secure aggregate MAC. Further, in contrast with [EFG+10], we also allow aggregation of two already-aggregated MACs.

3   Our Constructions at the High Level

For the sake of presentation, we take the simple construction of [KL08] (illustrated in Figure 1) as our starting point; we provide several modifications and discuss their benefits and trade offs.

The simple idea of [KL08] (which nevertheless involves non-trivial modeling and proof) is that bitwise XORing the constituent (standard) *deterministic* MACs will result in unforgeable aggregate MAC of the same length as one constituent MAC. At the very high level, their proof of security of aggregate MAC is as follows. Suppose an adversary can forge the aggregate MAC computed by XORing basic MACs. Then, such an adversary can be used to break the security of a constituent MAC: given a forged aggregate MAC, we "XOR out" all but one constituent MACs, to obtain a valid MAC on the remaining message. Since we assume basic MACs are unforgeable, we arrive at a contradiction.

Construction 1. Let τ be a deterministic MAC tag. The simplest and very practically useful idea we propose is to replace the bitwise XOR in the AggMAC of [KL08] with field addition. More specifically, consider a field F_p, where $p \geq 2^{|\tau|}$.

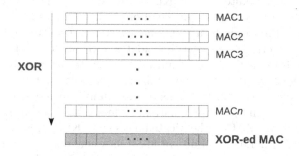

Fig. 1. Bitwise XOR AggMAC of [KL08]

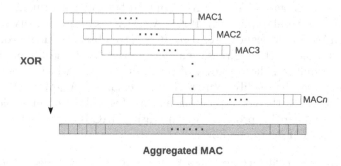

Fig. 2. The staircase AggMAC

We will view the MAC tag τ as an element in F_p in the natural way. When aggregating two message sets M_1, M_2 with AggMACs τ_1, τ_2, we simply compute new $AggMAC(M_1, M_2) = \tau_1 + \tau_2 \pmod{p}$. Jumping ahead, we note that we will not need to translate elements of F_p back into the domain of MAC tags, since **Vrfy** can compare tags in F_p.

The proof of security of our aggregate MAC is as follows. Suppose an adversary can forge the aggregate MAC computed as above. Then such an adversary can be used to break the security of a constituent MAC: given a forged aggregate MAC, we subtract out all but one constituent MACs (or AggMAC of its several duplicates). We then obtain a valid MAC on the remaining message m_j by dividing the remaining MAC by the multiplicity of m_j in aggregate MAC. All operations are performed in the field F_p. Since we assume basic MACs are unforgeable, we arrive at a contradiction.

Theorem 1. *(Informal; see Section 4.2 for formal statement and proof.)   MAC aggregation scheme informally described above is a secure aggregation function of deterministic MACs, even when message multiplicity is allowed.*

Construction 2. As pointed out in [KLH11, KL12], existing AggMAC schemes [KL08, EFG+10] are vulnerable to denial-of-service (DoS) attacks and simply to transmission errors. Indeed, a single incorrectly transmitted bit (i.e., which is not corrected by error-correction) invalidates authenticity of the entire set of messages. To help remedy this, the authors proved security of a large class of AggMAC functions, among them the "staircase" aggregation function, shown on Figure 2. This and other constructions of the family provide a useful trade off between message length and error isolation, so that a bit-error invalidates only a limited number of AggMAC-authenticated messages. [KLH11, KL12] prove security in the model of [KL08], and do not allow message multiplicity in AggMAC.

In this work, we prove that specifically the "staircase" AggMAC is secure even if message multiplicity is allowed. The intuition for the proof is as follows. Suppose an adversary can forge the aggregate MAC as above. Then, such an adversary can be used to break the security of any constituent MAC: as before, given a forged aggregate MAC, we XOR out all but one constituent MACs (or AggMAC of its several duplicates). If this AggMAC is of multiplicity $mult = 1$, we have a MAC forgery candidate. If $mult > 1$, we observe that its constituent MACs are stacked in the staircase manner, and at least one bit of the MAC (one "sticking out" on the top level of the staircase, and which is not XORed with anything) can be readily computed from remaining AggMAC. We thus fix this bit (which fixes the corresponding bits in this MAC's other copies of the staircase). We repeat this process until the entire MAC is computed, and we use this as basic MAC forgery candidate.

Theorem 2. *(Informal; see Section 4.2 for formal statement and proof.)   The "staircase" MAC aggregation scheme informally described above and shown on Figure 2 is a secure aggregation function of deterministic MACs, even when message multiplicity is allowed.*

4   MAC Aggregation with Message Multiplicity: Formal Constructions and Theorems

4.1   Preliminaries: Notation, Conventions and Definitions

In this section we discuss some of the required preliminaries, such as definitions and notation.

In our definitions and constructions, we always consider sets with element multiplicity. Such sets are usually referred to as *multisets*. However, because our discussion is intertwined with prior work, which specifically excluded multisets, we chose to refer to both notions as "sets", or "sets (possibly with multiplicity)". Similarly, we will sometimes overload the term aggregate MAC to mean either our notion or that of [KL08], depending on the context.

We now give the basic definition of Message Authentication Code (MAC). MAC is a tool for ensuring authenticity of messages. It is commonly used in authenticating communication: two parties have shared a random private key k of length n; later, one of them wants to use k to authenticate messages by generating corresponding tags. The tag generation function is stateless and deterministic, and verification is done by applying the tagging function to compute the correct tag of the given message, and comparing it with the candidate tag. More formally:

Definition 1. *A* Message Authentication Code (MAC) *is a stateless deterministic algorithm* $\mathbf{MAC} : \{0,1\}^n \times \{0,1\}^* \mapsto TAG$. *On input key* $k \in \{0,1\}^n$ *and a message* $m \in \{0,1\}^*$, $\mathbf{MAC}$ *outputs a tag* $\tau \in TAG$. *(Here TAG is the domain of tags, which depends on* n, *and is independent of the signed message length.) We will sometimes write* $\mathbf{MAC}_k(m)$ *to mean* $\mathbf{MAC}(k,m)$.

Let $k \in_R \{0,1\}^n$. *Let Adv be a polytime adversary with an access to the MAC oracle* $O(m) = \mathbf{MAC}_k(m)$. *Adv outputs a message* m' *and its alleged authentication tag* τ', *and must never call* $O(m')$. *We say that MAC is secure, if for every such Adv,* $Prob(\tau' = \mathbf{MAC}_k(m')) < 1/n^c$ *for every* c *and sufficiently large* n.

We note that MAC is a special case of the more general notion of message authentication schemes. MAC satisfies the strongest requirements of message authentication schemes [BGM04], and is sufficient for our purposes.

Aggregate MAC with Message Multiplicity. An important notion of aggregate MACs was introduced in [KL08]. We prove security with respect to the following stronger definition, derived from [KL08][2], with the only difference that it allows message multiplicity.

Definition 2. *(Aggregate MAC with Message Multiplicity.) An aggregate message authentication code is a tuple of probabilistic polynomial-time algorithms* (**MAC**, **Agg**, **Vrfy**) *such that:*

- *Authentication algorithm* **MAC**: *upon input a key* $k \in \{0,1\}^n$ *and a message* $m \in \{0,1\}^*$, *algorithm* **MAC** *outputs a tag* τ.
- *Aggregation algorithm* **Agg**: *upon input two sets of message/identifier pairs* $M^1 = \{(m_1^1, \mathrm{id}_1^1), ..., (m_{i_1}^1, \mathrm{id}_{i_1}^1)\}, M^2 = \{(m_1^2, \mathrm{id}_1^2), ..., (m_{i_2}^2, \mathrm{id}_{i_2}^2)\}$, *and associated tags* τ^1, τ^2, *algorithm* **Agg** *outputs a new tag* τ. *We stress that* **Agg** *is unkeyed.*
- *Verification algorithm* **Vrfy**: *upon receiving a set of key/identifier pairs* $\{(k_1, \mathrm{id}_1), ..., (k_t, \mathrm{id}_t)\}$, *a set (possibly with multiplicity) of message/identifier pairs* $M = \{(m_1, id_1'), ..., (m_i, id_i')\}$, *and a tag* τ, *algorithm* **Vrfy** *outputs a single bit, with '1' denoting acceptance and '0' denoting rejection. We denote this procedure by* $\mathbf{Vrfy}_{(k_1, \mathrm{id}_1), ..., (k_n, \mathrm{id}_t)}(M, \tau)$. *(In normal usage,* $id_i' \in \{\mathrm{id}_1, ..., \mathrm{id}_t\}$ *for all* i.)

---

[2] [EFG+10] proposed additional aggregate MAC security properties, such as including the order of the messages under the protection of aggregate MAC. We view these properties as optional in a the majority of scenarios. Further, the definition of [EFG+10] does not provide for aggregation of two already-aggregated MACs, a property we find extremely useful in practice.

The following correctness conditions are required to hold:

- *For all $k, \text{id}, m \in \{0,1\}^*$, it holds that $\mathbf{Vrfy}_{k,id}(m, \mathbf{MAC}_k(m)) = 1$. (This is essentially the correctness condition for standard MACs.)*
- *(Aggregation of MAC tags enables correct verification.) Let M^1, M^2 be two sets of message/identifier pairs (possibly with element multiplicity and further possibly with $M^1 \cap M^2 \neq \emptyset$), and let $M = M^1 \cup M^2$, with element multiplicity. If:*
  1. *$\mathbf{Vrfy}_{(k_1,\text{id}_1),...,(k_t,\text{id}_t)}(M^1, \tau^1) = 1$, and*
  2. *$\mathbf{Vrfy}_{(k_1,\text{id}_1),...,(k_t,\text{id}_t)}(M^2, \tau^2) = 1$, then*
  $\mathbf{Vrfy}_{(k_1,\text{id}_1),...,(k_n,\text{id}_n)}(M, \mathbf{Agg}(M^1, M^2, \tau^1, \tau^2)) = 1$.

We now present the security part of the definition.

Definition 3. *(Security properties of Aggregate MAC with Message Multiplicity.) Let Adv be a non-uniform probabilistic polynomial-time adversary, and consider the following experiment involving Adv and parameterized by a security parameter n:*

- *Key generation: Keys $k_1, ..., k_t \in \{0,1\}^n$, for $t = poly(n)$, are generated.*
- *Attack phase: Adv may query the following oracles:*
  - *Message authentication oracle Mac: On input (i, m), the oracle returns $\mathbf{MAC}_{k_i}(m)$.*
  - *Corruption oracle Corrupt: upon input i, the oracle returns k_i.*
- *Output: The adversary Adv outputs a set of message/identifier pairs $M = \{(m_1, \text{id}_1), ..., (m_i, \text{id}_i)\}$ (possibly with multiplicity) and a tag τ.*
- *Success determination: We say Adv succeeds if (1) $\mathbf{Vrfy}_{k_1,...,k_t}(M, \tau) = 1$ and (2) there exists a pair $(m_{i*}, \text{id}_{i*}) \in M$ such that*
  1. *Adv never queried Corrupt(id_{i*}), and*
  2. *Adv never queried Mac(id_{i*}, m_{i*}).*

We say that the aggregate MAC scheme (**MAC**, **Agg**, **Vrfy**) is secure if for all $t = poly(n)$ and all non-uniform probabilistic polynomial-time adversaries Adv, the probability that Adv succeeds in the above experiment is negligible.

Observation 1. *Message multiplicity in AggMAC is not guaranteed. That is, an adversary is allowed to create AggMAC which incorporates additional (or fewer) copies of honestly generated and MAC'ed messages.*

   This, of course, is not a security weakness, as message duplicates only represent message forwarding inefficiencies, and are simply discarded, leaving a single authenticated copy of the message. Further, such duplicates can always be generated by the adversary simply by replaying the entire MAC or AggMAC in any MAC/AggMAC scheme.

Observation 2. *We note that our constructions also satisfy natural variants of the Definition 3, such as the one where the the adversary is allowed to set all but one of the keys k_i (on which he must later produce a forgery). This, in particular, holds because we don't rely in our proofs on the fact that the opened keys were properly sampled.*

4.2   Constructions and Security Theorems

We now present our constructions and theorems.

The Main Construction

Construction 1. *(Aggregate MAC Scheme with Message Multiplicity) Let* **MAC** *be a deterministic algorithm producing tags from domain* $\{0,1\}^n$. *Let* $p > 2^n$ *be a prime. We define* (**MAC**,**Agg**,**Vrfy**) *as follows:*

- *Algorithm* **MAC**: *upon input* $k \in \{0,1\}^n$ *and* $m \in \{0,1\}^*$, *outputs* $\tau = $ **MAC**$_k(m)$. *We will naturally view the tag* τ *as an element of* F_p, *whose binary representation in* F_p *is equal to the string* τ.
- *Algorithm* **Agg**: *upon input two sets (possibly with element multiplicity)* M^1, M^2 *of message/identifier pairs, two tags* $\tau^1, \tau^2 \in F_p$, *the algorithm outputs* $\tau = \tau^1 + \tau^2 \pmod p$.
- *Algorithm* **Vrfy**: *upon input a set of keys* $k_1, ..., k_t \in \{0,1\}^n$, *a set* $M = \{(m_1, i_1), ..., (m_j, i_j)\}$ *of message/identifier pairs (possibly with multiplicity) where* $i_j \in \{1, ..., t\}$ *for all* j, *algorithm* **Vrfy** *computes* τ' *by computing individual message tags* **MAC**$_k(m)$, *and applying the aggregation algorithm.* **Vrfy** *outputs 1 if and only if* $\tau' = \tau$.

Theorem 3. *Assume* **MAC** *is a secure deterministic message authentication code according to Definition 1. Then Construction 1 is a secure aggregate MAC with message multiplicity scheme according to Definition 3.*

Proof. Our proof is similar to that of [KL08].

Fix a probabilistic polynomial-time adversary Adv and some $t = poly(n)$ as in Definition 2. We construct a probabilistic polynomial-time MAC forgery algorithm F that interacts with an instance of MAC, i.e. its oracles **MAC** and **Vrfy** with unknown key k, and attempts to produce a valid forgery for a previously-unauthenticated message.

The main idea of the reduction is as follows. F will execute Adv and answer its queries of the game of Definition 3. Since, by assumption, Adv wins the aggregate-MAC game by constructing a forgery, our goal is to translate this win into the MAC game, which F will also win. We will do this by obtaining the challenge from the MAC game, and using it to construct the aggregate-MAC game challenge to Adv. We do it in a way that, firstly, Adv will not know that he is playing a doctored game (this is needed to prevent Adv from "losing on purpose"), and secondly, Adv's winning advantage can be readily translated into the winning advantage of F.

F proceeds as follows:

- F chooses a random $i' \in \{t_1, ..., t(n)\}$. This will be F's guess of under which key k_i Adv will attempt forgery.
- For $i = 1$ to $t(n)$:
  - If $i' \neq i$, choose random $k_i \in \{0,1\}$ (F will use this key to respond to Mac and Corrupt queries of the game of Definition 3).

- If $i' = i$, do nothing (we will redirect the MAC queries associated with this key to the MAC game that F is trying to win).
- Run Adv, answering its queries as follows:
  - Query $\mathtt{Mac}(i, m)$: If $i \neq i'$ then F answers the query using the known key k_i. If $i = i'$ then F queries its own MAC oracle $\mathbf{MAC}_k(m)$ and returns the result.
  - Query $\mathtt{Corrupt}(i)$: If $i \neq i'$ then give Adv the known key k_i. If $i = i'$ then abort (F gives up on attempting to win this game. This is not a problem, since, as we show below, F will still have a non-negligible advantage in winning).
- At some point, Adv outputs the set (possibly with message multiplicity) $M = \{(m_1, id_1'), ..., (m_k, id_k')\}$ and aggregate tag τ. Let j be the first index such that (1) Adv never queried $\mathtt{Corrupt}(id_j')$ and (2) Adv never queried $\mathtt{Mac}(id_j', m_j)$. (We assume without loss of generality that some such j exists.) Here, if $id_j = i'$, then we will be able to translate the Adv's presumably winning response to the MAC game F is playing. Thus, if $id_j' \neq i'$ then abort; otherwise, proceed as described below.
- What remains is to see how to translate Adv's response to the MAC game F is playing. Recall, Adv gave F the set of messages (with multiplicity) M and the aggregate tag τ. F can obtain the MACs of all the individual messages m_i, with the exception of m_j, since F is not allowed query the oracle $\mathtt{Mac}(j, m_j)$ or to corrupt the corresponding player. Denote by $mult_i$ the multiplicity of message $m_i \in M$. Then, F computes tag $\tau_j = \mathbf{MAC}(j, m_j)$ from the value of the function τ and all other constituent MAC tags:

$$\tau_j = \frac{\tau - \sum_{i \neq j} mult_i \cdot \tau_i}{mult_j} \pmod{p}. \tag{1}$$

Now, F simply submits (m_j, τ_j) as his MAC forgery, treating τ_j as element of $\{0, 1\}^n$. (If τ_j cannot be represented in $\{0, 1\}^n$ – which means aggregate tag τ was not valid – F outputs a random string in $\{0, 1\}^n$.)

The proof now follows from the observation that the probability that F does not abort (i.e. that Adv will select $i' = i$) is exactly $1/t(n)$. It is easy to see that, if in such non-aborting execution, Adv's output (M, τ) is a valid aggregate MAC, then the computed τ_j is a valid MAC of message m_j in the MAC game F wants to win (this is because all operations are done in the field F_p). Finally, it is easy to see that manipulations with the (unsecured) message ordering information can be also effected by corresponding message substitution; this theorem and the proof applies in this case as well. In sum, we have constructed F that wins the MAC game with non-negligible advantage if the aggregate-MAC adversary Adv wins the corresponding game non-negligibly often. This completes the proof. $\square$

The "Staircase" Construction. Let $\oplus^{i\leftrightarrow}$ be the string XOR operation with partial string overlap of length i, as follows (see also Figure 3). Given two strings $s_1, s_2 \in \{0, 1\}^*$ and $0 \leq i \leq \min\{|s_1|, |s_2|\}$, we compute $s_1 \oplus^{i\leftrightarrow} s_2$ as follows. We

Fig. 3. The $\oplus^{i\leftrightarrow}$ operation with overlap $i = |s_1| - 3 = |s_2| - 2$

append $j_1 = |s_2| - i$ zeros to the string s_1 and then XOR it with s_2 (prepended with $j_2 = |s_1| - i$ zeros). That is, $s_1 \oplus^{i\leftrightarrow} s_2 = \{s_1 || \langle j_1 \quad \text{zeros} \rangle\} \oplus \{\langle j_2 \quad \text{zeros} \rangle || s_2\}$. It is easy to check that this ensures that original strings s_1, s_2 overlap in i positions in the applied XOR operation, and the length of the output string is $|s_1| + |s_2| - i$.

We note that we need to define $\oplus^{i\leftrightarrow}$ on two strings of different sizes, since we will aggregate already-aggregated MACs. Further, of course, the order of operands matters in the $\oplus^{i\leftrightarrow}$ operation.

In the following construction, we slightly abuse the notation, and allow the verification algorithm to additionally take the message ordering information sufficient replicate the application sequence of aggregation algorithms **Agg**.

Construction 2. *(Staircase AggMAC Scheme with Message Multiplicity) Let* **MAC** *be a deterministic algorithm with tags of size n. Let $i \in \{0, ..., n-1\}$ be the "staircase overlap" parameter. We define (***MAC**,**Agg**,**Vrfy***) as follows:*

- *Algorithm* **MAC***: upon input $k \in \{0,1\}^n$ and $m \in \{0,1\}^*$, outputs* $\text{MAC}_k(m)$.
- *Algorithm* **Agg***: upon input two sets (M^1, M^2) of message/identifier pairs, possibly with element multiplicity, and two tags τ^1, τ^2, the algorithm outputs* $\tau = \tau^1 \oplus^{i\leftrightarrow} \tau^2$.
- *Algorithm* **Vrfy***: upon input a set of keys $k_1, ..., k_t \in \{0,1\}^n$, a set (possibly with multiplicity) $M = \{(m_1, i_1), ..., (m_j, i_j)\}$ of message/identifier pairs, where $i_j \in \{1, ..., t\}$ for all j, and ordering information sufficient replicate the application sequence of aggregation algorithms* **Agg***, algorithm* **Vrfy** *computes τ' by computing individual message tags $\text{MAC}_k(m)$, and applying aggregation algorithms in the specified order.* **Vrfy** *outputs 1 if and only if* $\tau' = \tau$.

Kolesnikov et al. [KLH11, KL12] discuss in detail several message transmission algorithms that take advantage of the "staircase" MAC aggregation to achieve denial-of-service resilience. The main idea of their general approach is that a single bit of AggMAC only depends on a constant number of constituent MACs. This way, if a bit is incorrectly transmitted, MACs which did not contribute to it can still be successfully verified. Further, by having nodes set only specific bits of AggMAC, they allow for basic tools allowing to isolate the source of errors/attack. We refer the interested reader to their work for more details.

Theorem 4. *Assume* **MAC** *is a secure deterministic message authentication code according to Definition 1. Then, for any* $i \in \{0, ..., n-1\}$, *Construction 2 is a secure aggregate MAC with message multiplicity scheme according to Definition 3.*

Proof. Our proof is similar to that of Theorem 3.

Fix a probabilistic polynomial-time adversary Adv and some $t = poly(n)$ as in Definition 2. We construct a probabilistic polynomial-time MAC forgery algorithm F that interacts with an instance of MAC, i.e. its oracles **MAC** and **Vrfy** with unknown key k, and attempts to produce a valid forgery for a previously-unauthenticated message.

The main idea of the reduction is as follows. F will execute Adv and answer its queries of the game of Definition 3. Since, by assumption, Adv wins the aggregate-MAC game by constructing a forgery, our goal is to translate this win into the MAC game, which F will also win. We will do this by obtaining the challenge from the MAC game, and using it to construct the aggregate-MAC game challenge to Adv. We do it in a way that, firstly, Adv will not know that he is playing a doctored game (this is needed to prevent Adv from "losing on purpose"), and secondly, Adv's winning advantage can be readily translated into the winning advantage of F.

F proceeds as follows:

- F chooses a random $i' \in \{t_1, ..., t(n)\}$. This will be F's guess of under which key k_i Adv will attempt forgery.
- For $i = 1$ to $t(n)$:
  - If $i' \neq i$, choose random $k_i \in \{0, 1\}$ (F will use this key to respond to Mac and Corrupt queries of the game of Definition 3).
  - If $i' = i$, do nothing (we will redirect the MAC queries associated with this key to the MAC game that F is trying to win).
- Run Adv, answering its queries as follows:
  - Query Mac(i, m): If $i \neq i'$ then F answers the query using the known key k_i. If $i = i'$ then F queries its own MAC oracle $\mathbf{MAC}_k(m)$ and returns the result.
  - Query Corrupt(i): If $i \neq i'$ then give Adv the known key k_i. If $i = i'$ then abort (F gives up on attempting to win this game. This is not a problem, since, as we show below, F will still have a non-negligible advantage in winning).
- At some point, Adv outputs the set (possibly with message multiplicity) $M = \{(m_1, id_1'), ..., (m_k, id_k')\}$, ordering information sufficient to reproduce MAC aggregation sequence, and aggregate tag τ. Let j be the first index such that (1) Adv never queried Corrupt(id_j') and (2) Adv never queried Mac(id_j', m_j). (We assume without loss of generality that some such j exists.) Here, if $id_j = i'$, then we will be able to translate the Adv's presumably winning response to the MAC game F is playing. Thus, if $id_j' \neq i'$ then abort; otherwise, proceed as described below.

- What remains is to see how to translate Adv's response to the MAC game F is playing. Recall, Adv gave F the set of messages (with multiplicity) M and the aggregate tag τ. F can obtain the MACs of all the individual messages m_i, with the exception of m_j, since F is not allowed to query the oracle $\mathtt{Mac}(j, m_j)$. F then XORs out all but one constituent MACs, with appropriate multiplicity, in appropriate positions specified in ordering information. This operation leaves aggregate MAC of (possibly several identical messages) $m_j{}^3$. Denote this AggMAC by τ. If this AggMAC is just a MAC (i.e. m_j is of multiplicity $mult = 1$), we have a MAC forgery candidate. If $mult > 1$, we observe that $\tau's$ constituent MACs are stacked in the staircase manner (possibly with different overlaps, or with no overlap at all), and at least one bit of the MAC (one on the top of the staircase, which is not XORed with anything) can be readily computed from τ. We thus compute and fix this bit (which fixes the corresponding bits in this MAC's other copies of the staircase). We repeat this process until the entire MAC is computed (it is always possible to repeat as above bit fixing together with τ will determine another bit of the MAC, due to the staircase construction). We use the obtained MAC as the forgery candidate.

The proof now follows from the observation that the probability that F does not abort (i.e. that Adv will select $i' = i$) is exactly $1/t(n)$. It is easy to see that, if in such non-aborting execution, Adv's output (M, τ) is a valid aggregate MAC, then the computed τ_j is a valid MAC of message m_j in the MAC game F wants to win. In sum, we have constructed F that wins the MAC game with non-negligible advantage if the aggregate-MAC adversary Adv wins the corresponding game non-negligibly often. This completes the proof.

Acknowledgment. I would like to thank Georg Hampel for discussions on WSNs message forwarding architectures, Wonsuck Lee for discussions on applications of aggregate MAC in SmartGrid, and the anonymous reviewers of SCN 2012 for helpful comments.

References

[BGLS03] Boneh, D., Gentry, C., Lynn, B., Shacham, H.: Aggregate and Verifiably Encrypted Signatures from Bilinear Maps. In: Biham, E. (ed.) EUROCRYPT 2003. LNCS, vol. 2656, pp. 416–432. Springer, Heidelberg (2003)

[BGM04] Bellare, M., Goldreich, O., Mityagin, A.: The power of verification queries in message authentication and authenticated encryption. Cryptology ePrint Archive, Report 2004/309 (2004), http://eprint.iacr.org/

[BHL07] Bhaskar, R., Herranz, J., Laguillaumie, F.: Aggregate designated verifier signatures and application to secure routing. IJSN 2(3/4), 192–201 (2007)

---

^{3} Again, we slightly abuse notation here, as the obtained aggregate MAC may not have been obtained by applying **Agg** due to the "missing staircase steps". We note that the missing staircase steps are not a problem for our argument.

460   V. Kolesnikov

[BNN07]   Bellare, M., Namprempre, C., Neven, G.: Unrestricted Aggregate Sig-
           natures. In: Arge, L., Cachin, C., Jurdziński, T., Tarlecki, A. (eds.)
           ICALP 2007. LNCS, vol. 4596, pp. 411–422. Springer, Heidelberg (2007)
[CPS06]   Chan, H., Perrig, A., Song, D.: Secure hierarchical in-network aggregation
           in sensor networks. In: Juels, A., Wright, R.N., De Capitani di Vimercati,
           S. (eds.) 13th Conference on Computer and Communications Security,
           ACM CCS 2006, pp. 278–287. ACM Press (October/November 2006)
[DP10]   Dargie, W., Poellabauer, C.: Fundamentals of wireless sensor networks:
           theory and practice. John Wiley and Sons (2010)
[EFG+10]   Eikemeier, O., Fischlin, M., Götzmann, J.-F., Lehmann, A., Schröder, D.,
           Schröder, P., Wagner, D.: History-Free Aggregate Message Authentication
           Codes. In: Garay, J.A., De Prisco, R. (eds.) SCN 2010. LNCS, vol. 6280,
           pp. 309–328. Springer, Heidelberg (2010)
[HE03]   Hu, L., Evans, D.: Secure aggregation for wireless networks. In: Proceed-
           ings of the 2003 Symposium on Applications and the Internet Workshops
           (SAINT 2003 Workshops), SAINT-W 2003, p. 384. IEEE Computer Soci-
           ety, Washington, DC (2003)
[KL08]   Katz, J., Lindell, A.Y.: Aggregate Message Authentication Codes. In:
           Malkin, T. (ed.) CT-RSA 2008. LNCS, vol. 4964, pp. 155–169. Springer,
           Heidelberg (2008)
[KL12]   Kolesnikov, V., Lee, W.: MAC aggregation protocols resilient to DoS at-
           tacks. International Journal of Security and Networks (IJSN) (to appear,
           2012)
[KLH11]   Kolesnikov, V., Lee, W., Hong, J.: MAC aggregation resilient to DoS at-
           tacks. In: 2011 IEEE International Conference on Smart Grid Communi-
           cations (SmartGridComm), pp. 226–231 (October 2011)
[SMZ07]   Sohraby, K., Minoli, D., Znati, T.: Wireless sensor networks: technology,
           protocols, and applications. John Wiley and Sons (2007)

Efficiency Limitations of Σ-Protocols
for Group Homomorphisms Revisited

Björn Terelius and Douglas Wikström

KTH Royal Institute of Technology, Stockholm, Sweden
{terelius,dog}@csc.kth.se

Abstract. We study the problem of constructing efficient proofs of knowledge of preimages of general group homomorphisms. We simplify and extend the recent negative results of Bangerter et al. (TCC 2010) to *constant round* (from three-message) generic protocols over *concrete* (instead of generic) groups, i.e., we prove lower bounds on both the soundness error and the knowledge error of such protocols. We also give a precise characterization of what can be extracted from the prover in the direct (common) generalization of the Guillou-Quisquater and Schnorr protocols to the setting of general group homomorphisms.

Then we consider some settings in which these bounds can be circumvented. For groups with no subgroups of small order we present: (1) a three-move honest verifier zero-knowledge argument under some set-up assumptions and the *standard* discrete logarithm assumption, and (2) a Σ-proof of both the order of the group and the preimage. The former may be viewed as an offline/online protocol, where all slow cut-and-choose protocols can be moved to an offline phase.

1 Introduction

An honest-verifier zero-knowledge proof of knowledge is a two party protocol where a prover demonstrates knowledge of a secret and the verifier does not learn anything he can not compute himself. A protocol is complete if the honest verifier accepts when interacting with the honest prover. The prover is honest-verifier zero-knowledge if the view of the honest verifier interacting with the prover can be simulated efficiently.

The probability that a malicious prover convinces the verifier of a false statement is called the *soundness error*. The prover is said to *know* the secret when there exists an efficient *extractor* which after interacting with the prover outputs the secret. On the other hand, a malicious prover who does not know the secret still has some probability, called the *knowledge error*, of convincing the verifier. Making the knowledge error as small as possible at low computational and communication costs is an important goal in the construction of protocols.

Guillou's and Quisquater's [12] protocol for proving knowledge of an RSA root and Schnorr's well-known proof of knowledge of a discrete logarithm [14] in a group of prime order q are particularly nice proofs of knowledge. Recall that in Schnorr's proof of knowledge of w such that $y = g^w$, the prover first

I. Visconti and R. De Prisco (Eds.): SCN 2012, LNCS 7485, pp. 461–476, 2012.

commits to randomness $r \in \mathbb{Z}_q$ by sending $\alpha = g^r$ to the verifier. The verifier then sends a random challenge $c \in \mathbb{Z}_q$ and the prover responds with $d = cw + r \bmod q$. To extract the secret w, the extractor only needs to sample interactions until it finds two accepting transcripts (α, c, d) and (α, c', d'), where $c' \neq c$, and compute $w = (d - d')(c - c')^{-1} \bmod q$. Similar protocols with exponentially small knowledge errors can be constructed for statements involving several group elements. The protocols exhibiting this form, with three messages, extraction from two accepting transcripts sharing the first message, and a strong form of honest-verifier simulation, are called Σ-proofs [7].

There is a simple and well-known generalization of Schnorr's protocol that can be executed over a group of unknown order, or even prove knowledge of a preimage $w \in \mathcal{G}$ of an element $y \in \mathcal{H}$ under a group homomorphism $\phi : \mathcal{G} \to \mathcal{H}$. Unfortunately, the resulting protocol has soundness and knowledge error $1/2$. These errors can be reduced to 2^{-n} by n repetitions, but this approach is impractical because it increases both the computation and communication costs considerably. Thus, a natural question is whether there exist protocols with small knowledge error and a structure similar to the Guillou-Quisquater and Schnorr proofs, but which works for any groups $\mathcal{G}$ and $\mathcal{H}$ and group homomorphism ϕ.

1.1   Previous Work

Proofs of knowledge over groups of unknown order have been studied before and both positive and negative results are known. Shoup [15] gave a three-message protocol for proving knowledge of w such that $y = w^{2^m}$ in an RSA group and showed that a knowledge error of $1/2$ is optimal.

Bangerter, Camenisch and Krenn [1] considered generic Σ-protocols, i.e., three-message protocols where the prover computes integer linear combinations of the secret witness and random elements, and possibly applies the homomorphism. They proved a lower bound on the knowledge error of such protocols in the *generic group model*. They also showed that the lower bounds hold for some natural generalizations of Schnorr's protocol in concrete groups. Specifically, they generalized Shoup's result on powers in RSA groups to arbitrary exponents and proved a lower bound of the knowledge error of exponentiation homomorphisms $\phi(w) = g^w$ in groups of unknown order, under mild assumptions on the extractor.

There is a vast literature on constructing protocols for specific groups and homomorphisms, with and without computational assumptions, and we only mention a few. Fujisaki and Okamoto [9] created an integer commitment scheme (subsequently generalized and corrected by Damgård and Fujisaki [8]) along with an argument of knowledge of the opening of the commitment under the strong RSA assumption. The argument of knowledge is actually a Σ-protocol of $(w, r) \in \mathbb{Z}^2$ such that $y = g^w h^r$. Other protocols [3] have been proposed based on the same principles.

Bangerter, Camenisch and Maurer [2] proposed two protocols for proving knowledge of a preimage in a group with unknown order. The first protocol assumed that the players are given an auxiliary *pseudo-preimage* (e', u') such that $y^{e'} = \phi(u')$ where e' is a prime larger than any challenge. Thus, if the ordinary extractor has found a pseudo-preimage (e, u) such that $y^e = \phi(u)$, one knows that $\gcd(e, e') = 1$, which implies that there exist integers a, b such that $ae + be' = 1$. Hence $y = \phi(u)^a \phi(u')^b = \phi(au + bu')$. This method of finding a proper preimage is sometimes called "Shamir's trick". Their second protocol is based on running two Σ-protocols in parallel, one being a Damgård-Fujisaki commitment. This protocol was later criticized by Kunz-Jacques et al. [13], since a verifier can choose a bad RSA-modulus. The prefix protocol of Wikström [16] used to establish a safe modulus suffers from the same flaw, though his main protocol remains secure.

Groups of unknown order have been used in several identification schemes. Brickell and McCurley [5] constructed an identification scheme that is secure as long as either discrete logarithms or factoring is hard. In their scheme, the prover knows the (prime) order of the generator g but the verifier does not. Their protocol share some similarities with our Protocol 3 for proving knowledge of a multiple of the order and subsequent proof of knowledge of the discrete logarithm in Protocol 4. Girault et al. [10] suggested an identification scheme that uses Schnorr's protocol in a group of unknown order (cf. our Protocol 1) to prove knowledge of a secret w for the public identity g^w. However, the security model in [10] only requires the extractor to output a witness if the attacker can forge the proof for a *randomly chosen* public identity with non-negligible probability, and they note that this protocol is not a proof of knowledge.

Cramer and Damgård [6] recently gave a method for *amortizing* the cost of cut-and-choose protocols over *several instances*, which reduces both the computational complexity and the size of the proof. This does not contradict our lower bounds since we only consider a single instance of the problem of proving knowledge of w such that $y = \phi(w)$.

1.2   Our Results

We begin by giving a precise characterization of the knowledge of the prover in the well-known generalization of the Guillou-Quisquater and Schnorr-protocols to the setting of group homomorphisms. We essentially prove that if a prover convinces the honest verifier with probability p, then we can extract $e \approx 1/p$ and u such that $y^e = \phi(u)$ in time $O(T(n)e)$ for some polynomial $T(n)$.

Then we consider a generalization of Bangerter et al.'s [1] class of generic Σ-protocols for proving knowledge of a preimage of a group homomorphism. We extend their model from three-message protocols to protocols with any *constant number of rounds* with challenges that could depend on previous messages and we prove lower bounds on both the knowledge error and the soundness error of protocols from this class.

- Under mild assumptions, we show that a malicious prover who knows a pseudo-preimage $u = 2w + \sigma$ of $y = \phi(w)$, where $\phi(\sigma) = 1$, can convince the verifier with some *constant* probability, where the constant depends on the protocol. Thus, an efficient extractor for w can, in general, not be constructed unless w can be computed from $(2, u)$. This generalizes the result for *three-message* protocols given in [1] to *constant-round* protocols. Furthermore, our analysis is simpler and does not rely on the generic group model.

- We show that if the group $\mathcal{H}$ has an element γ of small order and the verifier uses a natural type of verification test, then the proof does not even need to be sound. In particular, we construct a malicious prover who knows γ and w such that $y = \gamma\phi(w)$, yet manages to convince the verifier that $y = \phi(w')$ for some w'. The technique is similar to that of Kunz-Jacques et al. [13].

These results shed some new light on what is needed from a protocol for proving knowledge of a preimage.

Finally, we investigate two ways of circumventing the negative results. We present two honest-verifier zero-knowledge protocols that allow (a precisely characterized) partial knowledge extractor in general, and a proper knowledge extractor under assumptions on the order of the underlying group.

- Our first protocol, Protocol 2, only works for the exponentiation homomorphism under the *standard* discrete logarithm assumption in a different group of *known prime order*, and requires set-up assumptions. We show that if a prover convinces the verifier with probability p, then we can extract $e \approx 1/p$ and u such that $y^e = g^{eu}$. In contrast to the basic protocol, Protocol 1, this may, loosely, be viewed as an argument of knowledge of the preimage up to small subgroups, and an argument of knowledge of w when the order of the underlying group contains no small factors. The set-up assumptions require cut-and-choose protocols, but these can be executed in an offline phase.
- Our second protocol, Protocol 4, works for any group homomorphism, but requires that the prover knows the order of the underlying group (in fact it proves knowledge of both a multiple of the order and the preimage). We show that if a prover convinces the verifier with probability p, then we can extract $e \approx 1/p$ and u such that $y^e = \phi(u)$ and every factor of e divides the order of y. Again, if the order of the group contains no small factors, this gives a proof of knowledge.

Although neither protocol solves the problem of constructing an efficient proof of knowledge of a preimage in general, our protocols suffice in certain situations. The first protocol can, e.g., be used to prove knowledge of an integer w such that $y_0 = g_0^w$ and $y_1 = g_1^w$, where g_0 and g_1 are generators of two groups of *distinct* large prime orders.

1.3   Notation

Throughout the paper, we use the standard definitions of zero-knowledge protocols [11] and proofs of knowledge [4]. Let n and n_c to denote the security parameter and bit-size of challenges. When executing proofs of knowledge of exponents, we denote by n_w the bit-size of the exponent and n_r the additional bits in the randomizer. We let $\mathcal{G}$ and $\mathcal{H}$ denote abelian groups and let $\phi : \mathcal{G} \to \mathcal{H}$ be a group homomorphism. Since ϕ will often be an exponentiation homomorphism, we will write $\mathcal{G}$ additively and $\mathcal{H}$ multiplicatively.

We sometimes use overlining to indicate that something is a vector or a list, e.g., $\overline{z} \in \mathcal{G}^n$ is a list of n elements in $\mathcal{G}$. We write $\phi(\overline{z})$ as a short-hand for the list obtained by applying the homomorphism to each component of $\overline{z}$. Similarly, if $w \in \mathcal{G}$ and $\overline{\alpha} \in \mathbb{Z}^n$, we use the convention that $w^{\overline{\alpha}} = (w^{\alpha_1}, \ldots, w^{\alpha_n})$. For a list or vector $\overline{v}$, the number of components is denoted by $dim(\overline{v})$. We adopt the definition of a *pseudo-preimage* of Bangerter et al. [1].

Definition 1. *Let $\phi : \mathcal{G} \to \mathcal{H}$ be a group homomorphism and let y be an element of $\mathcal{H}$. A* pseudo-preimage *of y is a pair $(e, u) \in \mathbb{Z} \times \mathcal{G}$ such that $y^e = \phi(u)$.*

The following observation follows immediately from the definition.

Lemma 1. *Let $y = \phi(w)$. Any pseudo-preimage (e, u) of y must have the form $u = ew + \sigma$, where $\phi(\sigma) = 1$, i.e., σ is an element in the kernel of ϕ.*

2   Tight Analysis of the Basic Protocol

Below we recall the natural generalization of Schnorr's protocol for proving knowledge of a discrete logarithm to the setting where the prover instead needs to show that it knows a preimage $w \in \mathcal{G}$ of $y \in \mathcal{H}$ under a homomorphism $\phi : \mathcal{G} \to \mathcal{H}$.

Protocol 1 (Basic Protocol)
COMMON INPUT. An element $y \in \mathcal{H}$ and a homomorphism $\phi : \mathcal{G} \to \mathcal{H}$ of abelian groups $\mathcal{G}$ and $\mathcal{H}$.
PRIVATE INPUT. An element $w \in \mathcal{G}$ such that $y = \phi(w)$.

1. $\mathcal{P}$ chooses $r \in \mathcal{G}$ randomly[1] and hands $\alpha = \phi(r)$ to $\mathcal{V}$.
2. $\mathcal{V}$ chooses $c \in [0, 2^{n_c} - 1]$ randomly and hands c to $\mathcal{P}$.
3. $\mathcal{P}$ computes $d = cw + r$ in $\mathcal{G}$ and hands d to $\mathcal{V}$.
4. $\mathcal{V}$ verifies that $y^c \alpha = \phi(d)$

We obtain Schnorr's proof of knowledge of a discrete logarithm in a group $\langle g \rangle$ of prime order q by setting $\mathcal{G} = \mathbb{Z}_q$, $\mathcal{H} = \langle g \rangle$ and $\phi(w) = g^w$. When the order of g is unknown, we treat $\phi(w) = g^w$ as a homomorphism from $\mathcal{G} = \mathbb{Z}$ to $\langle g \rangle$. More precisely, we assume that $w \in [0, 2^{n_w} - 1]$ and choose $r \in [0, 2^{n_w + n_c + n_r} - 1]$ which is statistically close to uniform modulo the order of g if n_r is large enough. As a slight generalization, we may let the verifier check that $d \in [0, 2^{n_w + n_c + n_r} - 1]$. This modification does not affect Theorem 1 and 2 below, except that the protocol is overwhelmingly complete rather than perfectly complete. We use this variant in Protocol 3.

---

[1] It is sufficient that the distribution of r is statistically close to uniform in $\mathcal{G}$ or even that the distribution of $cw + r$ is statistically close to $c'w' + r'$ for any c, c', w, w' allowed in the protocol.

It is well-known that Protocol 1 is honest-verifier zero-knowledge, so we state that theorem without proof. It is also well-known that the protocol, in general, is not a proof of knowledge of w such that $y = \phi(w)$. On the other hand, it is clear that the prover shows that it knows *something* related to w and as far as we know there is no *precise* characterization in the literature of what can, and can not, be extracted from a convincing prover. Such a characterization is useful in the rest of the paper.

Theorem 1 (Zero-Knowledge). *Protocol 1 is complete and honest-verifier statistical (perfect) zero-knowledge if for each w and each $c \in [0, 2^{n_c} - 1]$, the distributions of $cw + r$ and r are statistically close (identical).*

Informally, the following theorem says that if a prover convinces the verifier with probability p, then we can extract $e \approx 1/p$ and u such that $y^e = \phi(u)$. In other words, the more successful a prover is, the more it needs to know about the preimage of y. The extractor depends on a parameter ϵ that controls how close e is to $1/p$. The reader may think of $\epsilon = \frac{1}{4}$. The proof of Theorem 2 is given in the full version.

Theorem 2 (Extraction and Soundness). *There exists an extractor $\mathcal{E}_\epsilon$, parameterized by $\epsilon < 1/2$ with $\epsilon^{-1} \in \mathsf{Poly}(n)$, using any PPT prover $\mathcal{P}^*$ as an oracle such that if $\mathcal{P}^*$ convinces $\mathcal{V}$ with probability $\Delta > \kappa$ on common input (y, ϕ), then $\mathcal{E}_\epsilon(y, \phi)$ extracts an integer $0 < e \leq \frac{1}{(1-\epsilon)^2 \Delta}$ and $u \in \mathcal{G}$ such that $y^e = \phi(u)$. The extractor runs in expected time $O(\epsilon^{-2} T(n)/(\Delta - \kappa))$, where $T(n)$ is a polynomial (independent of ϵ) and the knowledge error κ is defined as $\kappa = 2^{1-n_c}/\epsilon$.*

The following theorem shows that we can not hope to find an extractor which extracts significantly more. This theorem is very similar to a theorem in [1], but differs in that their formulation concerns a *restricted* class of extractors.

Theorem 3. *A malicious prover knowing only y, e and $ew + \sigma$ such that $y^e = \phi(ew+\sigma)$, where $\phi(\sigma) = 1$, can convince the verifier with probability $1/e - \mathsf{negl}(n)$ if the distributions of $r + \frac{c}{e}\sigma$ and r are statistically close for each $c \in [0, 2^{n_c} - 1]$ such that $e \mid c$.*

Proof. The prover chooses r and sends $\phi(r)$ as usual. After receiving the challenge c, the prover halts if $e \nmid c$, and responds with

$$d' = \frac{c}{e}(ew + \sigma) + r = cw + r + \frac{c}{e}\sigma$$

otherwise. We clearly have $\phi(d') = \phi(d)$, since $d = cw + r$. Furthermore, the verifier notices that the prover is cheating with negligible probability, since d' is statistically close in distribution to a correctly formed response.   □

If c is not chosen uniformly from an interval as in Protocol 1, e.g., if e never divides c, we are not able to apply the previous theorem directly. However, it is always possible to find c^* such that $e \mid (c - c^*)$ with probability $1/e$. The malicious prover can then answer with $d' = r + \frac{(c - c^*)}{e}(ew + \sigma) = r - c^*w + \frac{(c - c^*)}{e}\sigma + cw$ whenever e divides $c - c^*$. This is indistinguishable from the real response provided that the distributions of $r - c^*w + \frac{(c - c^*)}{e}\sigma$ and r are statistically close, which happens for example if r is chosen from a sufficiently large interval. We generalize this approach in the next section.

3   Lower Bound on the Knowledge Error

Suppose that we wish to prove knowledge of w such that $y = \phi(w)$ in a group of unknown order. Bangerter et al. [1] defined generic Σ-protocols as the class of protocols where the verifier only sends random challenges and the prover only uses the homomorphism and linear combinations of group elements to generate his responses. They proved a lower bound on the knowledge error in the *generic group model* for such protocols and gave concrete examples of protocols where the bounds hold in the plain model.

In this section we generalize their result to any *constant round* protocol of the same type (Σ-protocols have three messages) and give the verifier more freedom in how it chooses its challenges. We also provide a novel analysis that does not rely on the generic group model.

Definition 2. *Consider a protocol for proving knowledge of a preimage, executed by a prover $\mathcal{P}$ and a verifier $\mathcal{V}$ with common input $\mathcal{G}$, $\mathcal{H}$, a group homomorphism $\phi : \mathcal{G} \to \mathcal{H}$ and $y \in \mathcal{H}$, and private input w such that $y = \phi(w)$. We call it a constant-round generic protocol if in the ith round:*

1. *$\mathcal{V}$ sends integer vectors $\overline{\alpha}^{(i)}$, $\overline{\beta}^{(i)}$ chosen according to some distributions, possibly depending on the messages in the earlier rounds, and*
2. *$\mathcal{P}$ responds with $\overline{t}^{(i)} = \phi\big(A^{(i)}\overline{r} + \overline{\alpha}^{(i)}w\big)$ and $\overline{s}^{(i)} = B^{(i)}\overline{r} + \overline{\beta}^{(i)}w$,*

where $A^{(i)}$ and $B^{(i)}$ are public integer matrices and $\overline{r}$ denotes the random tape, viewed as a vector of elements in $\mathcal{G}$, given to the prover. The verifier may use any polynomial time test to decide whether or not to accept the proof.

Remark 1. Readers familiar with the generic Σ-protocols in [1] may notice that their definition is a special case of Definition 2, obtained by restricting the protocol to two rounds. In the first round, $\overline{\alpha}^{(0)}$ and $\overline{\beta}^{(0)}$ are part of the protocol specification. In the second round, $\overline{\alpha}^{(1)}$ and $\overline{\beta}^{(1)}$ are defined (using the notation of [1]) as

$$\overline{\alpha}_j^{(1)} = f_j + \sum g_{ji}c_i \quad \text{and} \quad \overline{\beta}_j^{(1)} = d_j + \sum e_{ji}c_i ,$$

where f_j, d_j, g_{ji} and e_{ji} are public constants and $c_1, \ldots, c_p$ are the challenges chosen by the verifier.

In the following, we consider all of the rounds simultaneously. To simplify the exposition, we define $\overline{\alpha}$ and $\overline{t}$ as the column vectors formed by all elements of $\overline{\alpha}^{(i)}$ and $\overline{t}^{(i)}$ respectively, and let A be the matrix formed by the rows of all $A^{(i)}$. We define B, $\overline{\beta}$ and $\overline{s}$ analogously. This permits us to write all the equations concisely as

$$\overline{t} = \phi(A\overline{r} + \overline{\alpha}w) \quad \text{and} \quad \overline{s} = B\overline{r} + \overline{\beta}w \ .$$

Note that a malicious prover can generate $\overline{t}$ as $t_i = \phi\left((A\overline{r})_i\right)\phi(w)^{\alpha_i}$. This shows that the protocol could equivalently have been designed to just send $\phi\left((A\overline{r})_i\right)$ since the powers of $\phi(w)$ can be computed from the public information and added or removed from whatever the prover sends. It is, however, not as easy to generate $\overline{s}$, since the prover does not know w. Intuitively, we want to avoid this problem by constructing a prover that "almost" knows $2w$ and only answers when the challenge has a given parity.

Theorem 4. *Let $(\mathcal{P}, \mathcal{V})$ be a constant-round generic protocol as in Definition 2. There exists a prover $\mathcal{P}^*$ that takes as input the groups $\mathcal{G}$, $\mathcal{H}$, a homomorphism $\phi : \mathcal{G} \to \mathcal{H}$, an integer vector $\overline{v}^*$, a group element $y \in \mathcal{H}$, and a pseudo-preimage $(2, u)$ such that $u = 2w + \sigma$ where $y = \phi(w)$ and $\phi(\sigma) = 1$.*

Define $S = \{\overline{\beta} : \exists \overline{v} \text{ such that } \overline{\beta} = B\overline{v}\}$ as the set of challenges $\overline{\beta}$ in the protocol that have preimages under B. For each $\overline{\beta} \in S$, let $\overline{v}_{\overline{\beta}}$ denote a preimage[2] of $\overline{\beta}$ under B, i.e., $\overline{\beta} = B\overline{v}_{\overline{\beta}}$. Let $T \subset \{\overline{v}_{\overline{\beta}} : \overline{\beta} \in S\}$ be a subset of the preimages $\overline{v}_{\overline{\beta}}$ such that for every $\overline{v}, \overline{v}' \in T$ for which $\overline{v} = \overline{v}' \bmod 2$, the statistical distance between the distributions of $\overline{r}$ and $\overline{r}^* = \overline{r} + \overline{v}'w - \frac{\overline{v} - \overline{v}'}{2}\sigma$ is at most ϵ.

If the integer vector $\overline{v}^* \in T$ is chosen such that $\Pr[\overline{v}_{\overline{\beta}} = \overline{v}^* \bmod 2] \geq 2^{-\dim(\overline{v})}$, when the probability is taken over the choice of $\overline{\beta}$ conditioned on $\overline{\beta} \in S$ and $\overline{v}_{\overline{\beta}} \in T$, then $\mathcal{P}^*$ convinces $\mathcal{V}$ with probability at least

$$\Pr[\overline{\beta} \in S] \cdot \Pr[\overline{v}_{\overline{\beta}} \in T \mid \overline{\beta} \in S] \cdot 2^{-\dim(\overline{v})} - \epsilon \ ,$$

where $\dim(\overline{v})$ is the (constant) number of components in $\overline{v}$.

About the Assumptions. To ensure that $\overline{\beta}w$ is completely hidden in $B\overline{r} + \overline{\beta}w$, we expect that every integer vector $\overline{\beta}$ has a preimage under B, or in other words that the lattice spanned by B contains all points with integer coordinates. If this is the case, then $\Pr[\overline{\beta} \in S] = 1$ and moreover, the preimages $\overline{v}_{\overline{\beta}}$ can be chosen such that $\overline{v}_{\overline{\beta}} = \overline{v}_{\overline{\beta}'} \bmod 2$ whenever $\overline{\beta} = \overline{\beta}' \bmod 2$. Hence we can choose $\overline{v}^*$ such that $\Pr[\overline{v}_{\overline{\beta}} = \overline{v}^* \bmod 2] \geq 2^{-\dim(\overline{\beta})}$ rather that $\Pr[\overline{v}_{\overline{\beta}} = \overline{v}^* \bmod 2] \geq 2^{-\dim(\overline{v})}$.

The set T encodes a subset of preimages $\overline{v}_{\overline{\beta}}$ for which the distributions $\overline{r}$ and $\overline{r}^*$ are statistically close. If the components of $\overline{r}$ are chosen from a sufficiently large subset of $\mathcal{G}$, then T contains all preimages, so $\Pr[\overline{v}_{\overline{\beta}} \in T \mid \overline{\beta} \in S] = 1$. This

---

[2] There may be several integer vectors $\overline{v}$ such that $\overline{\beta} = B\overline{v}$. Let $\overline{v}_{\overline{\beta}}$ be some choice among those preimages.

happens for example if $\bar{r}$ is chosen uniformly from a finite group, or if $\mathcal{G} = \mathbb{Z}$ and $\bar{r}$ is chosen from a large interval. We remark that this assumption was also made implicitly for $\mathcal{G} = \mathbb{Z}$ by Bangerter et al. [1]. Using these two stronger assumptions gives us the following corollary.

Corollary 1. *Let $(\mathcal{P}, \mathcal{V})$ be a constant-round generic protocol as in Theorem 4 and suppose that every integer vector has a preimage under B and that the randomness $\bar{r}$ is chosen from a sufficiently large subset of $\mathcal{G}$ so that $T = \{\bar{v}_{\bar{\beta}} : \bar{\beta} \in S\}$. Then the malicious prover $\mathcal{P}^*$, who knows $\bar{v}^*$, $y = \phi(w)$, and a pseudo-preimage $(2, u)$, convinces $\mathcal{V}$ with probability at least $2^{-\dim(\bar{\beta})} - \epsilon$.*

Interpretation of Theorem 4. Recall that Protocol 1 and Theorem 2 showed that we can extract a pseudo-preimage in any group. This is sufficient if a preimage can be computed from the pseudo-preimage, which is the case in groups of known prime order, for example. On the other hand, computing w from $2w + \sigma$ in $\mathbb{Z}_N^*$ where N is a safe RSA modulus, would imply computing a multiple of the group order $\phi(N)$. This is believed to be infeasible, even for machines running in expected polynomial time. Theorem 4 shows that (under some plausible assumptions) we can not extract more than the pseudo-preimage, since that is all the malicious prover is given. In particular, it gives a lower bound on the knowledge error *assuming* that it is infeasible to compute a preimage from the pseudo-preimage. (To see this, suppose that there is an extractor which after interacting with any prover outputs a true preimage in expected time $T(n)/(\Delta - \kappa)$ where Δ is the prover's success probability and κ is the knowledge error. Running this extractor with e.g. the malicious prover of Corollary 1 gives an algorithm which takes a pseudo-preimage and outputs a preimage in expected time $T(n)/(2^{-\dim(\bar{\beta})} - \epsilon - \kappa)$. Since it was assumed hard to compute a preimage, the distance between κ and $2^{-\dim(\bar{\beta})}$ must be negligible.) We note, however, that it may be possible to construct an efficient protocol by violating the hypothesis of the theorem. Thus, like many other negative results in cryptography, the result should be viewed as a guide for future research, and not as the final answer.

Proof (of Theorem 4). We consider only the case where $\bar{\beta} \in S$ and $\bar{v}_{\bar{\beta}} \in T$, which explains the factor

$$\Pr[\bar{\beta} \in S]\, \Pr[\bar{v}_{\bar{\beta}} \in T \mid \bar{\beta} \in S]$$

in the success probability of our adversary. There exists a $\bar{v}^* \in T$ such that

$$\Pr[\bar{v}_{\bar{\beta}} = \bar{v}^* \bmod 2 \mid \bar{\beta} \in S \wedge \bar{v}_{\bar{\beta}} \in T] \geq 2^{-\dim(\bar{v})} \ ,$$

where the probability is taken over the choice of $\bar{\beta}$. This follows, since there are at most $2^{\dim(\bar{v})}$ possibilities for the parities. If each had probability less than $2^{-\dim(\bar{v})}$, the probabilities would not sum to 1.

Define $\bar{v}$ as $\bar{v} = \bar{v}_{\bar{\beta}}$. The malicious prover $\mathcal{P}^*$ samples $\bar{r}'$ with the distribution of $\bar{r}$ in the protocol and then generates $\bar{s}'$ and $\bar{t}'$ as follows

$$\bar{t}' = \phi(A\bar{r}')y^{\bar{\alpha} - A\bar{v}^*} \quad \text{and} \quad \bar{s}' = B\bar{r}' + \frac{\bar{\beta} - \bar{\beta}^*}{2}u \ ,$$

where $\overline{\beta}^* = B\overline{v}^*$. Consider now an $\overline{s}$ formed in an execution with the honest prover, conditioned on $\overline{\beta} \in S$, $\overline{v} \in T$, and $\overline{v} = \overline{v}^* \bmod 2$. It can be expressed as

$$\overline{s} = B\overline{r} + \overline{\beta}w = B(\overline{r} + \overline{v}^*w) + \frac{\overline{\beta} - \overline{\beta}^*}{2} 2w$$

$$= B\left(\overline{r} + \overline{v}^*w - \frac{\overline{v} - \overline{v}^*}{2}\sigma\right) + \frac{\overline{\beta} - \overline{\beta}^*}{2}u$$

$$= B\overline{r}^* + \frac{\overline{\beta} - \overline{\beta}^*}{2}u \ ,$$

where $\overline{r}^* = \overline{r} + \overline{v}^*w - \frac{\overline{v}-\overline{v}^*}{2}\sigma$. We may similarly express $\overline{t}$ as

$$\overline{t} = \phi(A\overline{r} + \overline{\alpha}w) = \phi\left(A\overline{r}^* - A\overline{v}^*w + A\frac{\overline{v} - \overline{v}^*}{2}\sigma + \overline{\alpha}w\right)$$

$$= \phi(A\overline{r}^*)\phi(w)^{\overline{\alpha} - A\overline{v}^*} \ .$$

To conclude the proof, we note that the statistical distance between $(\overline{s}', \overline{t}')$ and $(\overline{s}, \overline{t})$ is at most ϵ since the statistical distance between the distributions of $\overline{r}^*$ and $\overline{r}$ is at most ϵ.   □

4   Lower Bound on the Soundness Error

Next, we show that if the group has a subgroup of small order and the verifier uses a constant round generic protocol with a natural type of acceptance test, then the proof does not even need to be sound. In particular, we show that a malicious prover knowing an element γ of small order and w such that $\tilde{y} = \gamma\phi(w)$ can convince the verifier that $\tilde{y} = \phi(w')$ for some w'. Note that γ does not have to be in the image of ϕ.

Recall that Cauchy's theorem states that if $\mathcal{H}$ is a finite group and q is a prime dividing the order of $\mathcal{H}$, then there is an element of order q in $\mathcal{H}$. Thus, when the order of $\mathcal{H}$ is unknown, we can not exclude the possibility of elements of small order.

Theorem 5. *Let $\mathcal{H}$ be an abelian group, let $\phi : \mathbb{Z} \to \mathcal{H}$ be a group homomorphism, and let $\gamma \in \mathcal{H}$ be an element of prime order q. Define $\overline{s}$, $\overline{t}$, $\overline{\alpha}$, and $\overline{\beta}$ as in Definition 2 except that we only allow $\overline{\alpha}$ and $\overline{\beta}$ to depend on $\overline{s}$, not on $\overline{t}$. Let $f_i(\cdot, \cdot, \cdot)$ and $g_{ij}(\cdot, \cdot, \cdot)$ be polynomials and let $h_i(\cdot, \cdot, \cdot)$ be a polynomial time computable function. If the verifier's acceptance test is of the form*

$$y^{f_i(\overline{s}, \overline{\alpha}, \overline{\beta})} \prod_j t_j^{g_{ij}(\overline{s}, \overline{\alpha}, \overline{\beta})} = \phi(h_i(\overline{s}, \overline{\alpha}, \overline{\beta})) \quad \forall i \in I \ ,$$

where the product is taken over all components of $\overline{t}$, then there exists a PPT prover $\mathcal{P}^*$, a PPT algorithm M_σ, and a PPT algorithm $M_{\mathcal{V}^*}$ such that at least one of the following holds for each γ, w and $y = \phi(w)$, where $\Delta = q^{-(\dim \overline{s} + \dim \overline{\beta} + \dim \overline{\alpha})}/3$:

1. On input γ and w, $\mathcal{P}^*$ convinces the honest verifier on common input $\tilde{y} = \gamma\phi(w)$ with probability at least Δ over the random tapes of the prover and verifier.

2. On input w, M_σ outputs a non-zero element in the kernel of ϕ with probability at least Δ over the random tape of M_σ.

3. On input q and a transcript of an execution between an honest prover and an honest verifier on private input w and common input $y = \phi(w)$, $M_{\mathcal{V}^*}$ outputs either $w \bmod q$ or $\perp$, where $w \bmod q$ is output with probability at least Δ over the random tapes of the prover and verifier.

The intuition is that the malicious prover $\mathcal{P}^*$ can guess the residue modulo q of $f_i(\overline{s}, \overline{\alpha}, \overline{\beta})$ and $g_{ij}(\overline{s}, \overline{\alpha}, \overline{\beta})$ and be correct with probability 3Δ. $\mathcal{P}^*$ then generates $(\overline{s}, \overline{t})$ as if producing a correct proof for $y = \phi(w)$, but modifies $\overline{t}$ to cancel any factors γ that appear in the verifier's acceptance test when run with $\tilde{y} = \gamma y$. This modification can be done as long as a certain linear system is solvable. Case 2 and 3 in the theorem give the possibilities when this system is not solvable. The full proof of Theorem 5 is given in the full version of this paper.

To see why it may be hard to compute an element in the kernel, note that for, e.g., the exponentiation homomorphism, finding an element in the kernel corresponds to finding a multiple of the order of the underlying group.

We require that $\overline{\alpha}$ and $\overline{\beta}$ do not depend on $\overline{t}$ in order to be able to take a valid transcript and modify $\overline{t}$ without changing anything else. On the other hand, the requirement that f_i and g_{ij} are polynomials is only used to express the probability that we correctly guess the residue modulo q in terms of the number of messages. This requirement can be relaxed to allow any polynomial time computable functions if there are not too many functions f_i and g_{ij}.

5 On Circumventing the Limitations

The previous work mentioned in the introduction, and the results in previous sections, give considerable evidence that an efficient zero-knowledge proof (of knowledge) of a preimage of a group homomorphism can not be constructed. In this section we consider two settings where we nevertheless are able to construct efficient protocols for proving knowledge of something more than a pseudo-preimage.

5.1 When We Know That a Committed Integer Is Small

In this section we restrict our attention to the exponentiation homomorphism $\phi(w) = g^w$, where $g \in \mathcal{H}$. Our protocol can be used to prove knowledge of e and u such that $y^e = g^{eu}$ and $e = \mathsf{Poly}(n)$. The small remaining exponent e is needed to circumvent Theorem 5.

Note that if the order of (y, g), considered as an element in $\mathcal{H} \times \mathcal{H}$, contains no factors of polynomial size, then this shows that the prover knows u such that $y = g^u$. An example of an application where this is the case is a prover that needs to show knowledge of an integer w of bounded size, such that $y_0 = g_0^w$ and $y_1 = g_1^w$, where g_i generates a group of prime order q_i and $q_0 \neq q_1$.

Our protocol takes a commitment $C(w, s)$ of the witness w as additional input and the prover is given the randomness s used to form the commitment. Before the protocol is executed, the verifier must be convinced that the committed value is an integer with bounded absolute value. We postpone the discussion of how this can be enforced to Section 5.1 below.

We use a statistically hiding homomorphic commitment scheme with an efficient Σ-proof of the committed value, e.g., Pedersen's commitment scheme, and write $C_{ck}(w, s)$ for a commitment of $w \in \mathbb{Z}_m$ using randomness $s \in \mathcal{R}$, where $\mathbb{Z}_m$ and $\mathcal{R}$ are the message space and randomizer spaces of the commitment scheme. We stress that the message space $\mathbb{Z}_m$ of the commitment scheme can depend on the commitment parameter ck and that there are no restrictions on m except that $2^{n_w + n_c + n_r} < m/2$. In particular, *we do not need an integer commitment scheme* and we can rely on the standard discrete logarithm assumption.

Similarly to standard Σ-proofs over groups of prime order, our protocol can easily be generalized to prove various more complicated statements involving multiple exponents.

Protocol 2 (Proof of Knowledge of Logarithm)

COMMON INPUT. Elements y and g of an abelian group $\mathcal{H}$, a joint commitment parameter ck, and a commitment W.

PRIVATE INPUT. An exponent $w \in [0, 2^{n_w} - 1]$ such that $y = g^w$, and $s \in \mathcal{R}$ such that $W = C_{ck}(w, s)$.

1. $\mathcal{P}$ chooses $r \in [0, 2^{n_w + n_c + n_r} - 1]$ and $t \in \mathcal{R}$ randomly, computes $\alpha = g^r$ and $R = C(r, t)$, and hands (α, R) to $\mathcal{V}$.
2. $\mathcal{P}$ proves knowledge of u, s, r, and t such that $W = C(u, s)$ and $R = C(r, t)$. This is done in parallel with the remaining three rounds (the honest prover sets $u = w$).
3. $\mathcal{V}$ hands a randomly chosen challenge $c \in [0, 2^{n_c} - 1]$ to $\mathcal{P}$.
4. $\mathcal{P}$ computes $d_0 = cw + r$ over $\mathbb{Z}$ and $d_1 = cs + t$ over $\mathcal{R}$, and hands (d_0, d_1) to $\mathcal{V}$.
5. $\mathcal{V}$ verifies that $d_0 \in [0, 2^{n_w + n_c + n_r} - 1]$, $W^c R = C(d_0, d_1)$, and $y^c \alpha = g^{d_0}$.

Theorem 6 (Zero-Knowledge). *Protocol 2 is overwhelmingly complete and honest-verifier statistical zero-knowledge.*

The proof of Theorem 6 is given in the full version.

Informally, if a prover convinces the verifier with probability p, then we can extract integers e and u such that $y^e = g^{eu}$ and $e \approx 1/p$. Formally, we need to take care of the commitment parameter ck and commitment W given as additional inputs. In our theorem, the adversary may in a first phase choose the instance (y, g, W) based on the commitment parameter. This is formalized as a PPT instance chooser $\mathcal{I}$. In an application the instance chooser represents the events occurring before the protocol is executed.

Theorem 7 (Soundness and Knowledge Extraction). *Let ck be a random commitment parameter. Given a PPT instance chooser $\mathcal{I}$, we define $(y, g, u, s, z) = \mathcal{I}(ck)$ and $W = \mathsf{C}(u, s)$, where u is an integer satisfying $|u| \in [0, 2^{n_w} - 1]$.*

There exists an extractor $\mathcal{E}_\epsilon$, parametrized by $\epsilon < 1/2$, with $\epsilon^{-1} \in \mathsf{Poly}(n)$, using any prover $\mathcal{P}^*(z)$ as an oracle such that if $\mathcal{P}^*(z)$ convinces $\mathcal{V}(y, g, ck, W)$ with non-negligible probability Δ, then the extractor $\mathcal{E}_\epsilon(y, g, ck, W)$ outputs (e, u) such that $0 < e \le \frac{1}{(1-\epsilon)^2 \Delta}$ and $y^e = g^{eu}$ with overwhelming probability under the assumption that the commitment scheme is binding. The extractor runs in expected time $O\big(\epsilon^{-2} T(n)/(\Delta - \kappa)\big)$ for some polynomial $T(n)$ and negligible κ.

The proof of Theorem 7 is given in the full version.

Enforcing Small Exponents. We could of course construct a cut-and-choose protocol for proving that a committed value is small when viewed as an integer, but then we could just as well prove knowledge of the exponent *directly* using this approach. Similarly, it makes little sense to let a trusted party certify a commitment of the secret exponent w, when it can just as well certify (y, g) directly. For Protocol 2 to be of interest we need to *decouple the size-guarantee* of the committed value *from the choice of a particular exponent w*.

A trusted party certifies several commitments $Z_1, \ldots, Z_k$ with $Z_i = \mathsf{C}_{ck}(z_i, t_i)$, where both $z_i \in [0, 2^{n_w + n_r} - 1]$ and $t_i \in \mathcal{R}$ are randomly chosen and handed to the prover. Then it is easy to prove that another commitment $W = \mathsf{C}(w, s)$ contains an integer with absolute value less than $2^{n_w + n_r}$ by simply revealing $(z, t) = (w + z_i, s + t_i)$ such that $Z_i W = \mathsf{C}_{ck}(z, t)$. The receiver verifies the certificate of Z_i and that $0 < z < 2^{n_w + n_r}$. Note that using this method, we must effectively reduce the maximum size of w by n_r bits, i.e., the security parameters in Protocol 2 must be modified slightly. The trusted party can go offline after publishing the commitments, but $z = w + z_i$ reveals w, so the trusted party learns w. The latter can be avoided by instead letting the prover register its commitments with the trusted party (or directly with the receiver) and prove that they are correctly formed using a (slow) cut-and-choose protocol in a preliminary phase.

5.2   When the Prover Knows the Order of the Group

We consider the problem of constructing a protocol for proving knowledge of a preimage of a homomorphism, when the prover knows (a multiple of) the order of y. From here on, we use σ to denote the group order rather than any element in the kernel.

Recall that in the protocol for proving knowledge of a discrete logarithm in groups of unknown order, Bangerter et al. [2] assume that the prover has been given a pseudo-preimage (e, u) such that $y^e = g^u$ and $e > 2^{n_c}$ is a large prime such that $e \nmid u$. The reason that the prime is large is to ensure that when a pair of accepting transcripts are extracted in the basic protocol, we have a relation $y^{c-c'} = \phi(u - u')$ and $\gcd(c - c', e)$ is already one, effectively terminating the extraction procedure of Theorem 2 in a single step.

We observe that if the prover knows such a pseudo-preimage and a proper witness w such that $y = g^w$ as well, then it can actually compute a multiple $ew - u \neq 0$ of the order of g. Thus, it seems that the prover essentially knows the order of g in their setting.

The idea of the main protocol of this section is that the prover first proves knowledge of the group order and then proves knowledge of a preimage using the basic protocol (Protocol 1). Combining knowledge of a pseudo-preimage (e, u) with small e with knowledge of the order σ of the group allows the extractor to simplify both quantities.

Proof of Knowledge of a Multiple of the Order of an Element. We do not know how to construct an efficient proof of knowledge of the order of a group element, but it turns out that a proof of knowledge of a *multiple* of the order suffices for our purposes. The proofs of the following theorems appear in the full version of this paper.

Protocol 3 (Knowledge of Multiple of the Order of an Element)
COMMON INPUT. An element g of an abelian group $\mathcal{H}$ and an upper bound 2^{n_w} of $|\langle g \rangle|$.
PRIVATE INPUT. The order $|\langle g \rangle|$ of g.

1. $\mathcal{P}$ and $\mathcal{V}$ compute $u = 2^{n_w + 2n_c + n_r + 2}$ and $y = g^u$.
2. $\mathcal{P}$ computes $w = u \bmod |\langle g \rangle|$.
3. Using Protocol 1, $\mathcal{P}$ proves knowledge of integers e and u' (e.g., 1 and w) such that $|e| < 2^{n_c + 1}$, $|u'| < 2^{n_w + n_c + n_r + 1}$, and $y^e = g^{u'}$.

Theorem 8. *Protocol 3 is complete and an honest-verifier statistical zero-knowledge proof of knowledge of a multiple of the order of g.*

Proof of Knowledge of a Preimage. Using the above protocol for proving knowledge of a multiple of the order of a group element, we now construct a proof of knowledge of a preimage for provers that know the order of y.

Protocol 4 (Proof of Knowledge of a Preimage)
COMMON INPUT. An element $y \in \mathcal{H}$ and a homomorphism $\phi : \mathcal{G} \to \mathcal{H}$ of abelian groups $\mathcal{G}$ and $\mathcal{H}$.
PRIVATE INPUT. A preimage $w \in \mathcal{G}$ such that $y = \phi(w)$ and the order σ of y.

1. $\mathcal{P}$ and $\mathcal{V}$ execute Protocol 3 on common input y and an upper bound 2^{n_w} of the order $\sigma = |\langle y \rangle|$, and private input σ, i.e., $\mathcal{P}$ proves knowledge of a multiple of σ.
2. $\mathcal{P}$ and $\mathcal{V}$ execute Protocol 1 on common input y and private input w, i.e., $\mathcal{P}$ proves knowledge of a pseudo-preimage of y under ϕ.

Theorem 9. *Protocol 4 is complete and honest-verifier statistical zero-knowledge.*

The only difference between the results below and Theorem 2 is that here we can not only bound the size of e, we can also reduce it further until all its factors appear in σ, the order of y. When σ has no small factors, the result is a proper proof of knowledge.

Theorem 10 (Extraction and Soundness). *There exists an extractor $\mathcal{E}_\epsilon$, parameterized by $\epsilon < 1/2$ with $\epsilon^{-1} \in \mathsf{Poly}(n)$, such that for every (y, ϕ), and every PPT prover $\mathcal{P}^*$ which convinces $\mathcal{V}(y, \phi)$ with probability $\Delta > \kappa$, $\mathcal{E}_\epsilon(y, \phi)$, using $\mathcal{P}^*$ as an oracle, extracts an integer $0 < e \leq \frac{1}{(1-\epsilon)^2 \Delta}$ and $u \in \mathcal{G}$ such that $y^e = \phi(u)$ and each factor of e divides σ. The extractor runs in expected time $O\big(\epsilon^{-2} T(n)/(\Delta - \kappa)\big)$, where $T(n)$ is a polynomial and κ is defined as $\kappa = 2^{1-n_c}/\epsilon$.*

Corollary 2. *If every factor of σ is greater than 2^{n_c}, then Protocol 4 is a proof of knowledge with negligible soundness/knowledge error of a preimage w such that $y = \phi(w)$.*

References

1. Bangerter, E., Camenisch, J., Krenn, S.: Efficiency Limitations for Σ-Protocols for Group Homomorphisms. In: Micciancio, D. (ed.) TCC 2010. LNCS, vol. 5978, pp. 553–571. Springer, Heidelberg (2010)
2. Bangerter, E., Camenisch, J., Maurer, U.M.: Efficient Proofs of Knowledge of Discrete Logarithms and Representations in Groups with Hidden Order. In: Vaudenay, S. (ed.) PKC 2005. LNCS, vol. 3386, pp. 154–171. Springer, Heidelberg (2005)
3. Bangerter, E., Krenn, S., Sadeghi, A.-R., Schneider, T., Tsay, J.-K.: On the design and implementation of efficient zero-knowledge proofs of knowledge. In: ECRYPT Workshop on Software Performance Enhancements for Encryption and Decryption and Cryptographic Compilers, SPEED-CC 2009 (2009)
4. Bellare, M., Goldreich, O.: On Defining Proofs of Knowledge. In: Brickell, E.F. (ed.) CRYPTO 1992. LNCS, vol. 740, pp. 390–420. Springer, Heidelberg (1993)
5. Brickell, E.F., McCurley, K.S.: An interactive identification scheme based on discrete logarithms and factoring. J. Cryptology 5(1), 29–39 (1992)
6. Cramer, R., Damgård, I.: On the Amortized Complexity of Zero-Knowledge Protocols. In: Halevi, S. (ed.) CRYPTO 2009. LNCS, vol. 5677, pp. 177–191. Springer, Heidelberg (2009)
7. Cramer, R., Damgård, I., Schoenmakers, B.: Proof of Partial Knowledge and Simplified Design of Witness Hiding Protocols. In: Desmedt, Y.G. (ed.) CRYPTO 1994. LNCS, vol. 839, pp. 174–187. Springer, Heidelberg (1994)
8. Damgård, I., Fujisaki, E.: A Statistically-Hiding Integer Commitment Scheme Based on Groups with Hidden Order. In: Zheng, Y. (ed.) ASIACRYPT 2002. LNCS, vol. 2501, pp. 125–142. Springer, Heidelberg (2002)
9. Fujisaki, E., Okamoto, T.: Statistical Zero Knowledge Protocols to Prove Modular Polynomial Relations. In: Kaliski Jr., B.S. (ed.) CRYPTO 1997. LNCS, vol. 1294, pp. 16–30. Springer, Heidelberg (1997)
10. Girault, M., Poupard, G., Stern, J.: On the fly authentication and signature schemes based on groups of unknown order. J. Cryptology 19(4), 463–487 (2006)
11. Goldwasser, S., Micali, S., Rackoff, C.: The knowledge complexity of interactive proof systems. SIAM J. Comput. 18(1), 186–208 (1989)

12. Guillou, L.C., Quisquater, J.-J.: A Practical Zero-Knowledge Protocol Fitted to Security Microprocessor Minimizing Both Transmission and Memory. In: Günther, C.G. (ed.) EUROCRYPT 1988. LNCS, vol. 330, pp. 123–128. Springer, Heidelberg (1988)
13. Kunz-Jacques, S., Martinet, G., Poupard, G., Stern, J.: Cryptanalysis of an Efficient Proof of Knowledge of Discrete Logarithm. In: Yung, M., Dodis, Y., Kiayias, A., Malkin, T. (eds.) PKC 2006. LNCS, vol. 3958, pp. 27–43. Springer, Heidelberg (2006)
14. Schnorr, C.-P.: Efficient signature generation by smart cards. J. Cryptology 4(3), 161–174 (1991)
15. Shoup, V.: On the security of a practical identification scheme. J. Cryptology 12(4), 247–260 (1999)
16. Wikström, D.: Designated Confirmer Signatures Revisited. In: Vadhan, S.P. (ed.) TCC 2007. LNCS, vol. 4392, pp. 342–361. Springer, Heidelberg (2007)

A More Efficient Computationally Sound Non-Interactive Zero-Knowledge Shuffle Argument

Helger Lipmaa[1] and Bingsheng Zhang[2]

[1] University of Tartu, Estonia
[2] State University of New York at Buffalo, USA

Abstract. We propose a new non-interactive (perfect) zero-knowledge (NIZK) shuffle argument that, when compared the only previously known efficient NIZK shuffle argument by Groth and Lu, has a small constant factor times smaller computation and communication, and is based on more standard computational assumptions. Differently from Groth and Lu who only prove the co-soundness of their argument under purely computational assumptions, we prove computational soundness under a necessary knowledge assumption. We also present a general transformation that results in a shuffle argument that has a quadratically smaller common reference string (CRS) and a small constant factor times times longer argument than the original shuffle.

Keywords: Bilinear pairings, cryptographic shuffle, non-interactive zero-knowledge, progression-free sets.

1 Introduction

In a shuffle argument, the prover proves that two tuples of randomized ciphertexts encrypt the same multiset of plaintexts. Such an argument is needed in e-voting and anonymous broadcast. In the case of e-voting, shuffles are used to destroy the relation between the voters and their ballots. There, the voters first encrypt their ballots. The ciphertexts are then sequentially shuffled by several independent mix servers, where every server also produces a zero-knowledge shuffle argument. At the end, all shuffle arguments are verified and the final ciphertexts are threshold-decrypted. If all arguments are accepted, then the shuffle is correct. Moreover, as long as one mix server is honest, the shuffle remains private (that is, one cannot relate the voters and their ballots).

A lot of research has been conducted in the area of constructing secure and efficient shuffle arguments, with recent work resulting in shuffles that have sublinear communication and very competitive computational complexity. However, it is also important that the shuffle argument is non-interactive, due to the fact that non-interactive arguments are transferable (create once, verify many times without interacting with the prover). This is especially important in e-voting, where the correctness of e-voting (and thus of the shuffle) should be verifiable

I. Visconti and R. De Prisco (Eds.): SCN 2012, LNCS 7485, pp. 477–502, 2012.

Table 1. Brief comparison of existing (not random-oracle based) and new (two last ones) NIZK shuffle arguments. Here, the communication complexity and the CRS length are given in group elements, prover's computation is given in exponentiations, and verifier's computation is given in (symmetric or asymmetric) bilinear pairings.

	|CRS|	Comm.	$\mathcal{P}$'s comp.	$\mathcal{V}$'s comp.	Pairing	Sound	Assumption
[14]	$2n+8$	$15n+120$	$51n+246$	$75n+282$	Sym.	Co-	PPA + SPA + DLIN
Sect. 5	$7n+6$	$6n+11$	$17n+16$	$28n+18$	Asym.	Sound	PKE + PSDL + DLIN
[19]	$7\sqrt{n}+6$	$30n+33\sqrt{n}$	$63n+48\sqrt{n}$	$84n+54\sqrt{n}$	Asym.	Sound	PKE + PSDL + DLIN

in years to come. Practically all previous shuffle arguments are interactive, and can only be made non-interactive by using the Fiat-Shamir heuristic, that is, in the random oracle model. For example, Groth and Ishai [13], Groth [11], and Bayer and Groth [2] have constructed shuffle arguments with communication $\Theta(n^{2/3})$, $\Theta(n^{1/2})$, and $\Theta(n^{1/2})$ respectively, where n is the number of ciphertexts. Unfortunately, they make use of the Schwartz-Zippel lemma that requires the verifier to first provide a random input. The only known way to make the Schwartz-Zippel lemma based arguments non-interactive is to use the random oracle model. Unfortunately, it is well-known that there are protocols that are secure in the random oracle model but not in the plain model. Even if there are no similar distinguishing attacks against any of the existing shuffle arguments, it is prudent to design alternative non-interactive shuffle arguments that are not based on random oracle model.

The only known (not random-oracle based) efficient non-interactive zero-knowledge (NIZK) shuffle argument (for the BBS cryptosystem [3]) was proposed by Groth and Lu in [14]. The security of the Groth-Lu argument is based on the common reference string model and on two new computational assumptions, the permutation pairing assumption (PPA, see [14]) and the simultaneous pairing assumption (SPA). While Groth and Lu proved that their assumptions are secure in the generic group model, one can argue that their assumptions are specifically constructed so as the concrete shuffle argument will be co-sound [16] (see [14] and Sect. 2 for discussions on co-soundness). It is therefore interesting to construct a shuffle argument from "more standard" assumptions. Moreover, their shuffle argument has a relatively large computational complexity and communication complexity. (See Tbl. 1 for a comparison.)

We construct a new non-interactive shuffle argument that has better communication and is based on more standard computational security assumptions than the Groth-Lu argument. Full comparison between the Groth-Lu and the new argument is given later. Recall that permutation matrix is a Boolean matrix that has exactly one 1 in every row and column. From a very high-level point of view, following [9] and subsequent papers, we let the prover to commit to a permutation matrix and then present an efficient permutation matrix argument (given commitments commit to a permutation matrix). We then prove that the plaintext vector corresponding to the output ciphertext vector is equal to the product of this matrix and the plaintext vector corresponding to the input ciphertext vector, and thus is correctly formed. Both parts are involved. In particular, coming up with a characterization of permutation matrices that allows for an efficient cryptographic implementation was not a trivial task.

Terelius and Wikström [23] constructed an interactive permutation matrix argument based on the fact that a matrix is a permutation matrix iff its every column sums to 1 and its every row has exactly one non-zero element. To verify that the committed matrix satisfies these properties, they used the Schwartz-Zippel lemma with the verifier sending a random vector to the prover. This introduces interaction (or the use of a random oracle). We do not know how to prove efficiently in NIZK that a commitment commits to a unit vector; how to construct such an *efficient* argument is an interesting open problem. We propose a superficially similar permutation matrix argument that is based on the (related) fact that a matrix is a permutation matrix exactly if every column sums to 1 and every row has *at most* one non-zero element. However, we do not explicitly use the Schwartz-Zippel lemma, and this makes it possible for us to create a NIZK argument without using the random oracle model.

Cryptographically, the new permutation matrix argument is based on recent techniques of Groth [12] and Lipmaa [18] who proposed an NIZK argument for circuit satisfiability based on two subarguments, for Hadamard — that is, entry-wise — product and permutation. (The same basic arguments were then used in [4] to construct an efficient non-interactive range proof.) Unfortunately, in their subarguments, the prover has quadratic (or quasilinear $O(n2^{2\sqrt{2\log_2 n}})$, if one only counts the group operations) computational complexity. This is not acceptable in our case, and therefore *we do not use any of the arguments that were constructed in [12,18]*.

We propose 2 new basic arguments (a zero argument, see Sect. 3.1, and a 1-sparsity argument, see Sect. 3.2), and then combine them in Sect. 3.3 to form a permutation matrix argument. The zero argument (the prover can open the given commitment to the zero tuple) can be interpreted as a knowledge of the discrete logarithm argument, and is a special case of Groth's restriction argument from [12]. On the other hand, the 1-sparsity argument (the prover can open the given commitment to a tuple $a = (a_1, \ldots, a_n)$, where at most one coordinate a_i is non-zero) is conceptually new.

Like the basic arguments of [18], the new 1-sparsity argument relies on the existence of a dense progression-free set. However, the costs of the 1-sparsity argument do not depend explicitly on the size of the used progression-free sets. Briefly, in [18] and the new 1-sparsity argument, the discrete logarithm of the non-interactive argument is equal to the sum of two polynomials $F_{con}(x)$ and $F_\pi(x)$, where x is the secret key. The first polynomial F_{con} has exactly one monomial per constraint that a honest prover has to satisfy. The number of constraints is linear (for any i, $a_i \cdot b_i = c_i$) in [18] and quadratic (for any two different coefficients a_i and a_j, $a_i \cdot a_j = 0$) in the new 1-sparsity argument. The second polynomial consists of monomials (a quasilinear number $O(n2^{2\sqrt{2\log_2 n}})$ in [18] and a linear number in the new 1-sparsity argument) that have to be computed by a honest prover during the argument, and this is the main reason why both the CRS length and the prover's computational complexity are lower in the 1-sparsity argument compared to the arguments in [18]. We find this to be an interesting result by itself, leading to an obvious question whether similar arguments (that have a superlinear number of constraints and a linear number of spurious monomials) can be used as an underlying engine to construct other interesting NIZK proofs.

In Sect. 5, we combine the permutation matrix argument with a knowledge version of the BBS [3] cryptosystem to obtain an efficient NIZK shuffle argument. Informally, by the KE assumption [6], in the knowledge BBS cryptosystem (defined in Sect. 4) the ciphertext creator knows both the used plaintext and the randomizer. Since it is usually not required that the ciphertext creator also knows the randomizer, the knowledge BBS cryptosystem satisfies a stronger than usual version of plaintext-awareness. While this version of plaintext-awareness has not been considered in the literature before, it is also satisfied by the Damgård's Elgamal cryptosystem from [6].

According to [1], only languages in **P/poly** can have direct black-box *perfect* NIZK arguments.[1] Since all known constructions of NIZK arguments use direct black-box reductions, one can argue that the "natural" definition of soundness is not the right definition of soundness for perfect NIZK arguments, see [14] for more discussion. To overcome the impossibility results of [1], Groth and Lu [14] proved co-soundness [14,16] of their argument under purely computational assumptions.

Our subarguments (the zero argument, the 1-sparsity argument, and the permutation matrix argument) are not computationally sound since their languages are based on a perfectly hiding commitment scheme, see Sect. 3. Instead, we prove that these arguments satisfy a weak version of soundness [12,18] under purely computational assumptions. We could use a similar definition of the weak soundness of the shuffle argument and prove that the new shuffle argument is (weakly) sound by using only standard computational assumptions. Instead (mostly since computational soundness is a considerably more standard security requirement), we prove computational soundness of the shuffle argument under a (known) knowledge assumption. This is also the reason why we need to use the *knowledge* BBS cryptosystem.

Apart from the knowledge assumption, the security of the new shuffle argument is based on the DLIN assumption [3] (which is required for the CPA-security of the BBS cryptosystem), and on the power symmetric discrete logarithm (PSDL, see Sect. 2) assumption from [18]. The PSDL assumption is much more standard(-looking) than the SPA and PPA assumptions from [14].

---

[1] It is not necessary to have a perfect NIZK argument for a shuffle (one could instead construct a computational NIZK proof), but the techniques of both [14] and especially of the current paper are better suited to construct *efficient* perfect NIZK arguments. We leave it as an open question to construct a computational NIZK proof for shuffle with a comparable efficiency.

Tbl. 1 provides a comparison between [14] and the new shuffle argument. Since it was not stated in [14], we have calculated ourselves[2] the computational complexity of the Groth-Lu argument. As seen from Tbl. 1, the new argument is computationally about 2.5 to 3 times more efficient and communication-wise about 2 times more efficient, if one just counts the number of exponentiations (in the case of the prover's computation), pairings (verifier's computation), or group elements (communication). In addition, the new argument uses asymmetric pairings $\hat{e} : \mathbb{G}_1 \times \mathbb{G}_2 \to \mathbb{G}_T$, while [14] uses symmetric pairings with $\mathbb{G}_1 = \mathbb{G}_2$. This means in particular that the difference in efficiency is larger than seen from Tbl. 1. First, asymmetric pairings themselves are much more efficient than symmetric pairings. Second, if asymmetric pairings were used in the Groth-Lu shuffle, one would have to communicate two different versions (one in group $\mathbb{G}_1$ and another one in group $\mathbb{G}_2$) of some of the group elements.

The main drawback of the new shuffle argument is that its soundness relies additionally on a knowledge assumption. However, a non-standard assumption is necessary to achieve perfect zero-knowledge [1]. Differently from the random oracle assumption that is known to be false in general, knowledge assumptions are just known to be non-falsifiable and thus might be true for any practical purposes. (In comparison, the Groth-Lu argument was proven to be co-sound, which is a weaker version of computational soundness, under purely computational assumptions.)

Moreover, the Groth-Lu shuffle uses the BBS cryptosystem (where one ciphertext is 3 group elements), while we use the new knowledge BBS cryptosystem (6 group elements). This difference is small compared to the reduction in the argument size. The use of knowledge BBS cryptosystem corresponds to adding a proof of knowledge of the plaintexts (and the randomizers) by the voters. However, it means that in the proof of soundness, we show security only against (white-box) adversaries who have access to the secret coins of all voters and mixservers. It is a reasonable compromise, comparable to the case in interactive (or Fiat-Shamir heuristic based) shuffles where the ballots are accompanied by a proof of knowledge of the ballot, from which either the adversary of the simulator can obtain the actual votes, but without the use of a random oracle, see Sect. 5 for more discussion. As we note there, our soundness definition follows that of [14], but the mentioned issues are due to the use of a knowledge assumption. We hope that the current work will motivate more research on clarifying such issues.

Another drawback of our scheme as compared to [14] is that it uses a lifted cryptosystem, and thus can be only used to shuffle small plaintexts. This is fine in applications like e-voting (where the plaintext is a candidate number). Many of the existing e-voting schemes are based on (lifted) Elgamal and thus require the plaintexts to be small. We note that significant speedups can be achieved in both cases by using efficient multi-exponentiation algorithms and thus for a meaningful computational comparison, one should implement the shuffle arguments.

---

[2] Our calculations are based on the Groth-Sahai proofs [17] that were published after the Groth-Lu shuffle argument. The calculations may be slightly imprecise.

In the full version [19], we show that one can transform both the Groth-Lu argument and the new argument, by using the Clos network [5], to have a CRS of size $\Theta(\sqrt{n})$ while increasing the communication and computation by a small constant factor. This version of the new argument is computationally/communication-wise only slightly less efficient than the Groth-Lu argument but has a quadratically smaller CRS, see Tbl. 1. This transformation can be applied to any shuffle argument that has linear communication and computation, and a CRS of length $f(n) = \Omega(1)$. We pose it as an open problem to construct (may be using similar techniques) an NIZK shuffle argument where both the CRS and the communication are sublinear.

Due to the lack of space, some proofs are only given in the full version [19].

2   Preliminaries

Let $[n] = \{1, 2, \ldots, n\}$. If $y = h^x$, then let $\log_h y := x$. To help readability in cases like $g_2^{r_i + x^{\lambda_{\psi^{-1}(i)}}}$, we sometimes write $\exp(h, x)$ instead of h^x. Let κ be the security parameter. PPT denotes probabilistic polynomial time. For a tuple of integers $\Lambda = (\lambda_1, \ldots, \lambda_n)$ with $\lambda_i < \lambda_{i+1}$, let $(a_i)_{i \in \Lambda} = (a_{\lambda_1}, \ldots, a_{\lambda_n})$. We sometimes denote $(a_i)_{i \in [n]}$ as $\boldsymbol{a}$. We say that $\Lambda = (\lambda_1, \ldots, \lambda_n) \subset \mathbb{Z}$ is an (n, κ)-nice tuple, if $0 < \lambda_1 < \cdots < \lambda_i < \cdots < \lambda_n = \text{poly}(\kappa)$. Let S_n be the set of permutations from $[n]$ to $[n]$.

By using notation that is common in additive combinatorics [22], if Λ_1 and Λ_2 are subsets of some additive group ($\mathbb{Z}$ or $\mathbb{Z}_p$ within this paper), then $\Lambda_1 + \Lambda_2 = \{\lambda_1 + \lambda_2 : \lambda_1 \in \Lambda_1 \wedge \lambda_2 \in \Lambda_2\}$ is their *sum set* and $\Lambda_1 - \Lambda_2 = \{\lambda_1 - \lambda_2 : \lambda_1 \in \Lambda_1 \wedge \lambda_2 \in \Lambda_2\}$ is their *difference set*. In particular, if Λ is a set, then $k\Lambda = \{\sum_{i=1}^k \lambda_i : \lambda_i \in \Lambda\}$ is an *iterated sumset*. On the other hand, $k \cdot \Lambda = \{k\lambda : \lambda \in \Lambda\}$ is a *dilation* of Λ. We also let $2\hat{}\Lambda = \{\lambda_1 + \lambda_2 : \lambda_1 \in \Lambda \wedge \lambda_2 \in \Lambda \wedge \lambda_1 \neq \lambda_2\} \subseteq \Lambda + \Lambda$ to denote a *restricted sumset*.

A set $\Lambda = \{\lambda_1, \ldots, \lambda_n\}$ of integers is *progression-free* [22], if no three elements of Λ are in arithmetic progression, that is, $\lambda_i + \lambda_j = 2\lambda_k$ only if $i = j = k$. Let $r_3(N)$ denote the cardinality of the largest progression-free set that belongs to $[N]$. Recently, Elkin [7] showed that $r_3(N) = \Omega((N \cdot \log^{1/4} N)/2^{2\sqrt{2 \log_2 N}})$. On the other hand, it is known that $r_3(N) = O(N(\log \log N)^5/\log N)$ [21]. Thus, according to [21], the minimal N such that $r_3(N) = n$ is $\omega(n)$, while according to Elkin, $N = O(n2^{2\sqrt{2 \log_2 n}}) = n^{1+o(1)}$. Thus, for any fixed $n > 0$, there exists $N = n^{1+o(1)}$, such that $[N]$ contains an n-element progression-free subset [18].

While the efficiency of arguments from [18] directly depended on the choice of the progression-free set, in our case the only thing dependent on this choice is the tightness of most of our security reductions; see the definition of PSDL below, or the proofs of Thm. 2, Thm. 4 and Thm. 5. Due to this, one may opt to use a less dense (but easy to construct) progression-free set. As an example, Erdős and Turán [8] defined a set $T(n)$ of all integers up to n that have no number 2 in their ternary presentation. Clearly, $|T(n)| \approx n^{\log_3 2} \approx n^{0.63}$ and $T(n)$ is progression-free. One can obtain a dense set of progression-free odd positive integers by mapping every a in $T(n)$ to $2a + 1$.

A *bilinear group generator* $\mathcal{G}_{bp}(1^\kappa)$ outputs gk := $(p, \mathbb{G}_1, \mathbb{G}_2, \mathbb{G}_T, \hat{e}, g_1, g_2) \leftarrow$ $\mathcal{G}_{bp}(1^\kappa)$ such that p is a κ-bit prime, $\mathbb{G}_1$, $\mathbb{G}_2$ and $\mathbb{G}_T$ are multiplicative cyclic groups of order p, $\hat{e} : \mathbb{G}_1 \times \mathbb{G}_2 \to \mathbb{G}_T$ is a bilinear map (pairing), and $g_t \leftarrow \mathbb{G}_t \setminus \{1\}$ is a random generator of $\mathbb{G}_t$ for $t \in \{1, 2\}$. Additionally, it is required that (a) $\forall a, b \in \mathbb{Z}$, $\hat{e}(g_1^a, g_2^b) = \hat{e}(g_1, g_2)^{ab}$, (b) $\hat{e}(g_1, g_2)$ generates $\mathbb{G}_T$, and (c) it is efficient to decide the membership in $\mathbb{G}_1$, $\mathbb{G}_2$ and $\mathbb{G}_T$, the group operations and the pairing $\hat{e}$ are efficiently computable, generators of $\mathbb{G}_1$ and $\mathbb{G}_2$ are efficiently sampleable, and the descriptions of the groups and group elements each are $O(\kappa)$ bit long. One can represent an element of $\mathbb{G}_1/\mathbb{G}_2/\mathbb{G}_T$ in respectively 512/256/3072 bits, by using an optimal (asymmetric) Ate pairing over a subclass of Barreto-Naehrig curves.

A *public-key cryptosystem* $(\mathcal{G}_{bp}, \mathcal{G}_{pkc}, \mathcal{E}nc, \mathcal{D}ec)$ is a tuple of efficient algorithms, where $\mathcal{G}_{bp}$ is a bilinear group generator that outputs gk, $\mathcal{G}_{pkc}(gk)$ generates a secret/public key pair (sk, pk), randomized encryption algorithm $\mathcal{E}nc_{pk}(\mu; r)$ produces a ciphertext c, and deterministic decryption algorithm $\mathcal{D}ec_{sk}(c)$ produces a plaintext μ. It is required that for all gk $\leftarrow \mathcal{G}_{bp}(1^\kappa)$, (sk, pk) $\in \mathcal{G}_{pkc}(gk)$ and for all valid μ and r, $\mathcal{D}ec_{sk}(\mathcal{E}nc_{pk}(\mu; r)) = \mu$. Assume that the randomizer space $\mathcal{R}$ is efficiently sampleable. A public-key cryptosystem $(\mathcal{G}_{bp}, \mathcal{G}_{pkc}, \mathcal{E}nc, \mathcal{D}ec)$ is *CPA-secure*, if for all stateful non-uniform PPT adversaries $\mathcal{A}$, the following probability is negligible in κ:

$$\left| \Pr \left[\begin{array}{l} \text{gk} \leftarrow \mathcal{G}_{bp}(1^\kappa), (\text{sk}, \text{pk}) \leftarrow \mathcal{G}_{pkc}(\text{gk}), (\mu_0, \mu_1) \leftarrow \mathcal{A}(\text{pk}), \\ b \leftarrow \{0, 1\}, r \leftarrow \mathcal{R} : \mathcal{A}(\mathcal{E}nc_{pk}(\mu_b; r)) = b \end{array} \right] - \frac{1}{2} \right| .$$

Let Λ be an (n, κ)-nice tuple for $n = \text{poly}(\kappa)$. A bilinear group generator $\mathcal{G}_{bp}$ is Λ-*PSDL secure* [18], if for any non-uniform PPT adversary $\mathcal{A}$,

$$\Pr[\text{gk} := (p, \mathbb{G}_1, \mathbb{G}_2, \mathbb{G}_T, \hat{e}, g_1, g_2) \leftarrow \mathcal{G}_{bp}(1^\kappa), x \leftarrow \mathbb{Z}_p : \mathcal{A}(\text{gk}; (g_1^{x^\ell}, g_2^{x^\ell})_{\ell \in \Lambda}) = x]$$

is negligible in κ. (Note that $\mathcal{A}$ also has access to $g_t^{x^0}$ since it belongs to gk.) A version of PSDL assumption in a non pairing-based group was defined in [10]. Lipmaa [18] proved that the Λ-PSDL assumption holds in the generic group model for any (n, κ)-nice tuple Λ given that $n = \text{poly}(\kappa)$. More precisely, any successful generic adversary for Λ-PSDL requires time $\Omega(\sqrt{p/\lambda_n})$ where λ_n is the largest element of Λ. Thus, the choice of the actual security parameter depends on λ_n and thus also on Λ.

Let $\mathcal{G}_{bp}$ be a bilinear group generator, and let gk := $(p, \mathbb{G}_1, \mathbb{G}_2, \mathbb{G}_T, \hat{e}, g_1, g_2) \leftarrow \mathcal{G}_{bp}(1^\kappa)$. Let $R = \{(\text{gk}; C, w)\}$ be an efficiently computable group-specific binary relation such that $|w| = \text{poly}(|C|)$. Here, C is a statement, and w is a witness. Let $L = \{(\text{gk}; C) : (\exists w)(\text{gk}; C, w) \in R\}$ be a group-specific **NP**-language. Shuffle (see Sect. 5) has a natural corresponding group-specific language, since one proves a relation between elements of the same group.

A *non-interactive argument* for R consists of the following PPT algorithms: a bilinear group generator $\mathcal{G}_{bp}$, a common reference string (CRS) generator $\mathcal{G}_{crs}$, a prover $\mathcal{P}$, and a verifier $\mathcal{V}$. For gk $\leftarrow \mathcal{G}_{bp}(1^\kappa)$ and crs $\leftarrow \mathcal{G}_{crs}(\text{gk})$, $\mathcal{P}(\text{gk}, \text{crs}; C, w)$ produces an argument π. The verifier $\mathcal{V}(\text{gk}, \text{crs}; C, \pi)$ outputs either 1 (accept) or 0 (reject). If the verifier only accesses a small part crs_v of crs, we say that crs_v is the verifier's part of the CRS and we will give just crs_v as an input to $\mathcal{V}$. When efficiency is not important (e.g., in the security definitions), we give the entire crs to $\mathcal{V}$.

An argument $(\mathcal{G}_{\mathsf{bp}}, \mathcal{G}_{\mathsf{crs}}, \mathcal{P}, \mathcal{V})$ is *perfectly complete*, if for all $\mathsf{gk} \leftarrow \mathcal{G}_{\mathsf{bp}}(1^\kappa)$, all $\mathsf{crs} \leftarrow \mathcal{G}_{\mathsf{crs}}(\mathsf{gk})$ and all (C, w) such that $(\mathsf{gk}; C, w) \in R$, $\mathcal{V}(\mathsf{gk}, \mathsf{crs}; C, \mathcal{P}(\mathsf{gk}, \mathsf{crs}; C, w)) = 1$. An argument $(\mathcal{G}_{\mathsf{bp}}, \mathcal{G}_{\mathsf{crs}}, \mathcal{P}, \mathcal{V})$ is *adaptively computationally sound*, if for all non-uniform PPT adversaries $\mathcal{A}$, the probability

$$\Pr\left[\begin{array}{l} \mathsf{gk} \leftarrow \mathcal{G}_{\mathsf{bp}}(1^\kappa), \mathsf{crs} \leftarrow \mathcal{G}_{\mathsf{crs}}(\mathsf{gk}), (C, \pi) \leftarrow \mathcal{A}(\mathsf{gk}, \mathsf{crs}) : \\ (\mathsf{gk}; C) \notin L \wedge \mathcal{V}(\mathsf{gk}, \mathsf{crs}; C, \pi) = 1 \end{array}\right]$$

is negligible in κ. The soundness is adaptive in the sense that the adversary sees the CRS before producing the statement C. An argument $(\mathcal{G}_{\mathsf{bp}}, \mathcal{G}_{\mathsf{crs}}, \mathcal{P}, \mathcal{V})$ is *perfectly witness-indistinguishable*, if for all $\mathsf{gk} \in \mathcal{G}_{\mathsf{bp}}(1^\kappa)$, $\mathsf{crs} \in \mathcal{G}_{\mathsf{crs}}(\mathsf{gk})$ and $((\mathsf{gk}; C, w_0), (\mathsf{gk}; C, w_1)) \in R^2$, the distributions $\mathcal{P}(\mathsf{gk}, \mathsf{crs}; C, w_0)$ and $\mathcal{P}(\mathsf{gk}, \mathsf{crs}; C, w_1)$ are equal. An argument $(\mathcal{G}_{\mathsf{bp}}, \mathcal{G}_{\mathsf{crs}}, \mathcal{P}, \mathcal{V})$ is *perfectly zero-knowledge*, if there exists a PPT simulator $\mathcal{S} = (\mathcal{S}_1, \mathcal{S}_2)$, such that for all stateful interactive non-uniform PPT adversaries $\mathcal{A}$,

$$\Pr\left[\begin{array}{l} \mathsf{gk} \leftarrow \mathcal{G}_{\mathsf{bp}}(1^\kappa), \mathsf{crs} \leftarrow \mathcal{G}_{\mathsf{crs}}(\mathsf{gk}), \\ (C, w) \leftarrow \mathcal{A}(\mathsf{gk}, \mathsf{crs}), \\ \pi \leftarrow \mathcal{P}(\mathsf{gk}, \mathsf{crs}; C, w) : \\ (\mathsf{gk}; C, w) \in R \wedge \mathcal{A}(\pi) = 1 \end{array}\right] = \Pr\left[\begin{array}{l} \mathsf{gk} \leftarrow \mathcal{G}_{\mathsf{bp}}(1^\kappa), (\mathsf{crs}, \mathsf{td}) \leftarrow \mathcal{S}_1(\mathsf{gk}), \\ (C, w) \leftarrow \mathcal{A}(\mathsf{gk}, \mathsf{crs}), \\ \pi \leftarrow \mathcal{S}_2(\mathsf{gk}, \mathsf{crs}, \mathsf{td}; C) : \\ (\mathsf{gk}; C, w) \in R \wedge \mathcal{A}(\pi) = 1 \end{array}\right].$$

Here, td is the *simulation trapdoor*.

The soundness of NIZK arguments (for example, an argument that a computationally binding commitment scheme commits to 0) seems to be an unfalsifiable assumption in general. We will use a weaker version of soundness in the sub-arguments, but in the case of the shuffle argument, we will prove soundness. Similarly to [12,18], we will base the soundness of that argument on an explicit knowledge assumption.

For two algorithms $\mathcal{A}$ and $X_{\mathcal{A}}$, we write $(y; z) \leftarrow (\mathcal{A}\|X_{\mathcal{A}})(x)$ if $\mathcal{A}$ on input x outputs y, and $X_{\mathcal{A}}$ on the same input (including the random tape of $\mathcal{A}$) outputs z. Let Λ be an (n, κ)-nice tuple for some $n = \mathrm{poly}(\kappa)$. Consider $t \in \{1, 2\}$. The bilinear group generator $\mathcal{G}_{\mathsf{bp}}$ is Λ-*PKE secure in group* $\mathbb{G}_t$ if for any non-uniform PPT adversary $\mathcal{A}$ there exists a non-uniform PPT extractor $X_{\mathcal{A}}$, such that

$$\Pr\left[\begin{array}{l} \mathsf{gk} := (p, \mathbb{G}_1, \mathbb{G}_2, \mathbb{G}_T, \hat{e}, g_1, g_2) \leftarrow \mathcal{G}_{\mathsf{bp}}(1^\kappa), (\alpha, x) \leftarrow \mathbb{Z}_p^2, \\ \mathsf{crs} \leftarrow (g_t^\alpha, (g_t^{x^\ell}, g_t^{\alpha x^\ell})_{\ell \in \Lambda}), (c, \hat{c}; (a_\ell)_{\ell \in \{0\} \cup \Lambda}) \leftarrow (\mathcal{A}\|X_{\mathcal{A}})(\mathsf{gk}, \mathsf{crs}) : \\ \hat{c} = c^\alpha \wedge c \neq \prod_{\ell \in \{0\} \cup \Lambda} g_t^{a_\ell x^\ell} \end{array}\right]$$

is negligible in κ. Note that the element a_0 is output since g_t belongs to the CRS, and thus the adversary has access to $(g_t^{x^\ell}, g_t^{\alpha x^\ell})$ for $\ell \in \{0\} \cup \Lambda$. Groth [12] proved that the Λ-PKE assumption holds in the generic group model in the case $\Lambda = [n]$; his proof can be straightforwardly modified to the general case. We later need the special case where $\Lambda = \emptyset$, that is, the CRS contains only g_t^α, and the extractor returns a_0 such that $c = g_t^{a_0}$. This *KE assumption (in a bilinear group)* is similar to Damgård's KE assumption [6], except that it is made in a bilinear group setting.

A (tuple) commitment scheme $(\mathcal{G}_{\mathsf{com}}, \mathcal{C}om)$ consists of two PPT algorithms: a randomized CRS generation algorithm $\mathcal{G}_{\mathsf{com}}$, and a randomized commitment algorithm $\mathcal{C}om$. Here, $\mathcal{G}_{\mathsf{com}}^t(1^\kappa, n)$, $t \in \{1, 2\}$, produces a CRS ck_t, and $\mathcal{C}om^t(\mathsf{ck}_t; \boldsymbol{a}; r)$, with $\boldsymbol{a} = (a_1, \ldots, a_n)$, outputs a commitment value $A \in \mathbb{G}_t$. Within this paper, we open a commitment $\mathcal{C}om^t(\mathsf{ck}_t; \boldsymbol{a}; r)$ by publishing the values $\boldsymbol{a}$ and r.

A commitment scheme $(\mathcal{G}_{\mathsf{com}}, \mathcal{C}om)$ is *computationally binding in group* $\mathbb{G}_t$, if for every non-uniform PPT adversary $\mathcal{A}$ and positive integer $n = \mathrm{poly}(\kappa)$, the probability

$$\Pr \left[\begin{array}{l} \mathsf{ck}_t \leftarrow \mathcal{G}_{\mathsf{com}}^t(1^\kappa, n), (\boldsymbol{a_1}, r_1, \boldsymbol{a_2}, r_2) \leftarrow \mathcal{A}(\mathsf{ck}_t) : \\ (\boldsymbol{a_1}, r_1) \neq (\boldsymbol{a_2}, r_2) \wedge \mathcal{C}om^t(\mathsf{ck}_t; \boldsymbol{a_1}; r_1) = \mathcal{C}om^t(\mathsf{ck}_t; \boldsymbol{a_2}; r_2) \end{array} \right]$$

is negligible in κ. A commitment scheme $(\mathcal{G}_{\mathsf{com}}, \mathcal{C}om)$ is *perfectly hiding in group* $\mathbb{G}_t$, if for any positive integer $n = \mathrm{poly}(\kappa)$ and $\mathsf{ck}_t \in \mathcal{G}_{\mathsf{com}}^t(1^\kappa, n)$ and any two messages $\boldsymbol{a_1}$ and $\boldsymbol{a_2}$, the distributions $\mathcal{C}om^t(\mathsf{ck}_t; \boldsymbol{a_1}; \cdot)$ and $\mathcal{C}om^t(\mathsf{ck}_t; \boldsymbol{a_2}; \cdot)$ are equal. We use the following variant of the *knowledge commitment scheme* from [12] as modified by Lipmaa [18]:

CRS Generation $\mathcal{G}_{\mathsf{com}}^t(1^\kappa, n)$: Let Λ be an (n, κ)-nice tuple with $n = \mathrm{poly}(\kappa)$. Define $\lambda_0 = 0$. Given a bilinear group generator $\mathcal{G}_{\mathsf{bp}}$, set $\mathsf{gk} := (p, \mathbb{G}_1, \mathbb{G}_2, \mathbb{G}_T, \hat{e}, g_1, g_2) \leftarrow \mathcal{G}_{\mathsf{bp}}(1^\kappa)$. Choose random $\alpha, x \leftarrow \mathbb{Z}_p$. The CRS is $\mathsf{ck}_t \leftarrow (\mathsf{gk}; \hat{g}_t, (g_{ti}, \hat{g}_{ti})_{i \in [n]})$, where $g_{ti} = g_t^{x^{\lambda_i}}$ and $\hat{g}_{ti} = g_t^{\alpha x^{\lambda_i}}$. Note that $g_t = g_{t0}$ is a part of gk.

Commitment: To commit to $\boldsymbol{a} = (a_1, \ldots, a_n) \in \mathbb{Z}_p^n$ in group $\mathbb{G}_t$, the committing party chooses a random $r \leftarrow \mathbb{Z}_p$, and defines $\mathcal{C}om^t(\mathsf{ck}_t; \boldsymbol{a}; r) := (g_t^r \cdot \prod_{i=1}^n g_{ti}^{a_i}, \hat{g}_t^r \cdot \prod_{i=1}^n \hat{g}_{ti}^{a_i})$.

Let $t = 1$. Fix a commitment key ck_1 that in particular specifies $g_2, \hat{g}_2 \in \mathbb{G}_2$. A commitment $(A, \hat{A}) \in \mathbb{G}_1^2$ is *valid*, if $e(A, \hat{g}_2) = e(\hat{A}, g_2)$. The case of $t = 2$ is dual.

As shown in [18], the knowledge commitment scheme in group $\mathbb{G}_t$ is perfectly hiding, and computationally binding under the Λ-PSDL assumption in group $\mathbb{G}_t$. If the Λ-PKE assumption holds in group $\mathbb{G}_t$, then for any non-uniform PPT algorithm $\mathcal{A}$, that outputs some valid knowledge commitments there exists a non-uniform PPT extractor $X_\mathcal{A}$ that, given as an input the input of $\mathcal{A}$ together with $\mathcal{A}$'s random coins, extracts the contents of these commitments.

A trapdoor commitment scheme has 3 additional efficient algorithms: (a) A trapdoor CRS generation algorithm inputs t, n and 1^κ and outputs a CRS ck^* (that has the same distribution as $\mathcal{G}_{\mathsf{com}}^t(1^\kappa, n)$) and a trapdoor td, (b) a randomized trapdoor commitment that takes ck^* and a randomizer r as inputs and outputs the value $\mathcal{C}om^t(\mathsf{ck}^*; \mathbf{0}; r)$, and (c) a trapdoor opening algorithm that takes ck^*, td, $\boldsymbol{a}$ and r as an input and outputs an r', s.t. $\mathcal{C}om^t(\mathsf{ck}^*; \mathbf{0}; r) = \mathcal{C}om^t(\mathsf{ck}^*; \boldsymbol{a}; r')$. The knowledge commitment scheme is trapdoor, with the trapdoor being $\mathsf{td} = x$: after trapdoor-committing $A \leftarrow \mathcal{C}om^t(\mathsf{ck}; \mathbf{0}; r) = g_t^r$ for $r \leftarrow \mathbb{Z}_p$, the committer can open it to $(\boldsymbol{a}; r - \sum_{i=1}^n a_i x^{\lambda_i})$ for any $\boldsymbol{a}$ [12,18].

To avoid knowledge assumptions, one can relax the notion of soundness. Following [16] and [14], R_{co}-soundness is a weaker version of soundness, where it is required that an adversary who *knows* that $(\mathsf{gk}; C) \notin L$ should not be able to produce a witness w_{co} such that $(\mathsf{gk}; C, w_{co}) \in R_{co}$ (see [14] or [16] for a longer explanation). More formally, let $R = \{(\mathsf{gk}; C, w)\}$ and $L = \{(\mathsf{gk}; C) : (\exists w)(\mathsf{gk}; C, w) \in R\}$ be defined as earlier. Let $R_{co} = \{(\mathsf{gk}; C, w_{co})\}$ be an efficiently computable binary relation. An argument $(\mathcal{G}_{\mathsf{bp}}, \mathcal{G}_{\mathsf{crs}}, \mathcal{P}, \mathcal{V})$ is (adaptively) R_{co}-*sound*, if for all non-uniform PPT adversaries $\mathcal{A}$, the following probability is negligible in κ:

$$\Pr\left[\begin{array}{l} \mathsf{gk} \leftarrow \mathcal{G}_{\mathsf{bp}}(1^\kappa), \mathsf{crs} \leftarrow \mathcal{G}_{\mathsf{crs}}(\mathsf{gk}), (C, w_{co}, \pi) \leftarrow \mathcal{A}(\mathsf{gk}, \mathsf{crs}) : \\ (\mathsf{gk}; C, w_{co}) \in R_{co} \wedge \mathcal{V}(\mathsf{gk}, \mathsf{crs}; C, \pi) = 1 \end{array}\right] .$$

In [12], Groth proposed efficient NIZK arguments that he proved to be sound under the power computational Diffie-Hellman assumption and the PKE assumption. Groth's arguments were later made more efficient by Lipmaa [18], who also showed that one can use somewhat weaker security assumptions (PSDL instead of PCDH). Groth [12] and Lipmaa [18] proposed two basic arguments (for Hadamard product and permutation). In both cases, Lipmaa showed that by using results about progression-free sets one can construct a set Λ_2 with $|\Lambda_2| = O(n2^{2\sqrt{2\log_2 n}}) = n^{1+o(1)}$. Together with a trivial Hadamard sum argument, one obtains a complete set of arguments that can be used to construct NIZK arguments for any NP language. (See [12,18] for discussion.) However, this is always not the most efficient way to obtain a NIZK argument for a concrete language. In Sect. 3 we define new basic arguments that enable us to construct a very efficient permutation matrix argument and thus also a very efficient shuffle argument.

3   New Subarguments

In this section we present some subarguments that are required to construct the final shuffle argument. However, we expect them to have independent applications and thus we will handle each of them separately.

3.1   New Zero Argument

In a zero argument, the prover aims to convince the verifier that he knows how to open knowledge commitment $A_t \in \mathbb{G}_t$ to the all-zero message tuple $\mathbf{0} = (0, \ldots, 0)$. Alternatively, one aims to prove the knowledge of the discrete logarithm of A_t, that is, that $A_t = g_t^r$ for some r. By using the homomorphic

---

CRS generation $\mathcal{G}_{crs}(1^\kappa)$: Let $\mathsf{gk} := (p, \mathbb{G}_1, \mathbb{G}_2, \mathbb{G}_T, \hat{e}, g_1, g_2) \leftarrow \mathcal{G}_{bp}(1^\kappa)$. Let $\mathring{\alpha} \leftarrow \mathbb{Z}_p$. Denote $\mathring{g}_t \leftarrow g_t^{\mathring{\alpha}}$ for $t \in \{1, 2\}$. The CRS is $\mathsf{crs} \leftarrow (\mathring{g}_1, \mathring{g}_2)$. The commitment key is $\mathsf{ck}_2 \leftarrow (\mathsf{gk}; \mathring{g}_2)$, and the verifier's part of the CRS is $\mathsf{crs}_v \leftarrow \mathring{g}_1$.
Common input: $A_2 \leftarrow g_2^r \in \mathbb{G}_2$.
Argument generation $\mathcal{P}_0(\mathsf{gk}, \mathsf{crs}; A_2, r)$: The prover defines $\mathring{A}_2 \leftarrow \mathring{g}_2^r$, and sends $\pi \leftarrow \mathring{A}_2 \in \mathbb{G}_2$ to $\mathcal{V}$ as the argument.
Verification $\mathcal{V}_0(\mathsf{gk}, \mathsf{crs}_v; A_2, \pi = \mathring{A}_2)$: The verifier accepts if $\hat{e}(\mathring{g}_1, A_2) = \hat{e}(g_1, \mathring{A}_2)$.

Protocol 1: New zero argument in group $\mathbb{G}_2$

properties of the knowledge commitment scheme, the prover can use the zero argument to show that A_t can be opened to an arbitrary constant.

This argument can be derived from [12,18]. Intuitively, we set (only for this argument) $n = 0$ and show that $A = A_2$ is a commitment to a length-0 tuple. For this, we only have to include to the CRS the elements $\mathring{g}_1$ and $\mathring{g}_2$. (The case $t = 1$ can be handled dually.) The following theorem is basically a tautology, since the KE assumption states that the prover knows r. However, since any $(A_2, \mathring{A}_2)$, where $\mathring{A}_2 = A_2^{\mathring{\alpha}}$, is a commitment of $\mathbf{0}$ (and thus, $(\mathsf{gk}; A_2) \in L$) for *some* r, we cannot claim that Prot. 1 is computationally sound (even under a knowledge assumption). Instead, analogously to [12,18], we prove a weaker version of soundness (which is however sufficient to achieve soundness of the shuffle argument). Note that the last statement of the theorem basically says that no efficient adversary can output an input to the product argument together with an accepting argument and openings to all commitments and all other pairs of type $(y, \bar{y})$ that are present in the argument, such that $a_i b_i \neq c_i$ for some i.

Theorem 1. *The non-interactive zero argument in Prot. 1 is perfectly complete, perfectly zero-knowledge. Any non-uniform probabilistic-polynomial time adversary has a negligible chance of returning an input $inp^0 = A_2$ and a satisfying argument $\pi^0 = \mathring{A}_2$ together with a opening witness $w^0 = (\boldsymbol{a}, r)$, such that $(A_2, \mathring{A}_2) = \mathcal{C}om^2(\mathsf{ck}_2; \boldsymbol{a}; r)$, $\boldsymbol{a} \neq 0$ but the verification $\mathcal{V}_0(\mathsf{gk}, \mathsf{crs}; A_2, \mathring{A}_2)$ accepts.*

Proof. PERFECT COMPLETENESS is straightforward, since $\hat{e}(\mathring{g}_1, A_2) = \hat{e}(g_1^{\mathring{\alpha}}, A_2) = \hat{e}(g_1, A_2^{\mathring{\alpha}}) = \hat{e}(g_1, \mathring{A}_2)$. PERFECT ZERO-KNOWLEDGE: we construct the following simulator $\mathcal{S} = (\mathcal{S}_1, \mathcal{S}_2)$. The simulator $\mathcal{S}_1$ generates first $\mathsf{td} = \mathring{\alpha} \leftarrow \mathbb{Z}_p$, and then $\mathsf{crs} \leftarrow (\mathring{g}_1 \leftarrow g_1^{\mathring{\alpha}}, \mathring{g}_2 \leftarrow g_2^{\mathring{\alpha}})$, and saves td. Since the simulator $\mathcal{S}_2$ later knows $\mathring{\alpha}$, it can compute a satisfying argument $\mathring{A}_2$ as $\mathring{A}_2 \leftarrow A_2^{\mathring{\alpha}}$. Clearly, $\mathring{A}_2$ has the same distribution as in the real argument.

WEAKER VERSION OF SOUNDNESS: assume that there exists an adversary $\mathcal{A}$ that can break the last statement of the theorem. That is, $\mathcal{A}$ can create $(A_2, (\boldsymbol{a}, r), \mathring{A}_2)$ such that $(A_2, \mathring{A}_2) = \mathcal{C}om^2(\boldsymbol{a}; r)$, $\boldsymbol{a} \neq \mathbf{0}$, and $\hat{e}(\mathring{g}_1, A_2) = \hat{e}(g_1, \mathring{A}_2)$. But then $(A_2, \mathring{A}_2) = (g_2^r \cdot \prod_{i=1}^n g_2^{a_i x^{\lambda_i}}, \mathring{g}_2^r \cdot \prod_{i=1}^n \mathring{g}_2^{a_i x^{\lambda_i}})$ with $\lambda_I \neq 0$ for some $I \in [n]$. Since $(\mathsf{gk}, \mathsf{crs})$ contains $\mathring{g}_2^{x^\ell}$ only for $\ell \in \{0\}$, the adversary has thus broken the $\emptyset$-PSDL assumption. But the $\emptyset$-PSDL assumption is straightforwardly true, since then the input of the adversary does not depend on x at all. Thus, the argument in Prot. 1 satisfies the last statement of the theorem. $\square$

The fact that the weaker version of soundness of this argument does not require any (non-trivial) assumption is, while somewhat surprising, also a logical consequence of CRS including $\mathring{g}_2^{x^\ell}$ only for $\ell \neq 0$. In fact, if the CRS contained $\mathring{g}_2^{x^\ell}$ for some other value of ℓ then the argument would not be sound under any (reasonable) computational assumption. The proof of the following lemma is straightforward.

Lemma 1. *The CRS length in Prot. 1 is 1 element from the group $\mathbb{G}_1$ and 1 element from the group $\mathbb{G}_2$. The argument size in Prot. 1 is 1 element from the group $\mathbb{G}_2$. Prover's computational complexity is dominated by 1 exponentiation. The verifier's computational complexity is dominated by 2 bilinear pairings.*

3.2   New 1-Sparsity Argument

Assume that $A_2 \in \mathbb{G}_2$. A vector $\boldsymbol{a} \in \mathbb{Z}_p^n$ is k-*sparse*, if it has at most k non-zero coefficients. In a 1-*sparsity argument* in $\mathbb{G}_2$, the prover aims to convince the verifier that he knows an opening $A_2 = g_2^r \cdot \prod_{i=1}^n g_{2,\lambda_i}^{a_i}$ such that $\boldsymbol{a}$ is 1-sparse, that is, there exists $I \in [n]$ such that for $i \neq I$, $a_i = 0$, while a_I can take any value, including 0. Alternatively, since $\mathbb{Z}_p$ has no zero divisors, this means that the prover aims to convince the verifier that $a_i a_j = 0$ for every $i, j \in [n]$ such that $i \neq j$. (Note that the zero argument can seen as a 0-sparsity argument.) A new 1-sparsity argument is depicted by Prot. 2; 1-sparsity argument in $\mathbb{G}_1$ is defined dually.

Intuitively, the new 1-sparsity argument is constructed by following the same main ideas as the basic arguments (for Hadamard product and permutation) from [18]. That is, we start with a verification equation $\hat{e}(A_1, A_2) = \hat{e}(g_1, F)$, where the discrete logarithm of the left-hand side, see Eq. (1), is a sum of two polynomials $F_{con}(x)$ and $F_\pi(x)$, where x is the secret key. In this case, $F_{con}(x)$ has $n(n-1)$ monomials (with coefficients $a_i a_j$ with $i \neq j$) that all vanish exactly if the prover is honest. On the other hand, the polynomial $F_\pi(x)$ has only $2n+1$ monomials. Therefore, a honest prover can compute the argument given $2n+1$ pairs $(g_{2\ell}, \bar{g}_{2\ell})$. Moreover, the prover can construct F by using 10 exponentiations. For comparison, in the basic arguments (the Hadamard product argument and the permutation argument) of [18], the polynomial $F_{con}(x)$ had n monomials, and the polynomial $F_\pi(x)$ had $O(n2^{2\sqrt{2\log_2 n}}) = n^{1+o(1)}$ monomials. Thus, the CRS had $O(n2^{2\sqrt{2\log_2 n}}) = n^{1+o(1)}$ group elements and the prover's computational complexity was dominated by $O(n2^{2\sqrt{2\log_2 n}}) = n^{1+o(1)}$ exponentiations.

Similarly to the zero argument, we cannot prove the computational soundness of this argument, since for every $\boldsymbol{a}$, there exists r such that $A_2 = g_2^r \prod_{i\in[n]} g_2^{a_i x^{\lambda_i}}$. Instead, following [12,18], we prove a weaker version of knowledge. Intuitively, the theorem statement includes f'_ℓ only for $\ell \in \bar{\Lambda}$ (resp., a_ℓ for $\ell \in \Lambda$ together with r) since $\bar{g}_{2\ell}$ (resp., $\bar{g}_{1\ell}$) belongs to the CRS only for $\ell \in \bar{\Lambda}$ (resp., $\ell \in \{0\} \cup \Lambda$).

Theorem 2. *The 1-sparsity argument in Prot. 2 is perfectly complete and perfectly witness-indistinguishable. Let Λ be a progression-free set of odd positive integers. If the $\mathcal{G}_{bp}$ is $\bar{\Lambda}$-PSDL secure, then any non-uniform PPT adversary has negligible chance of outputting $inp^{spa} \leftarrow (A_2, \bar{A}_2)$ and a satisfying argument $\pi^{spa} \leftarrow (A_1, \bar{A}_1, F, \bar{F})$ together with an opening witness $w^{spa} \leftarrow ((a_\ell)_{\ell \in \Lambda}, r, (f'_\ell)_{\ell \in \bar{\Lambda}})$, such that $(A_2, \bar{A}_2) = \mathcal{C}om^2(\mathsf{ck}_2; \boldsymbol{a}; r)$, $(F, \bar{F}) = (g_2^{\sum_{\ell \in \bar{\Lambda}} f'_\ell x_\ell}, \bar{g}_2^{\sum_{\ell \in \bar{\Lambda}} f'_\ell x_\ell})$, for some $i \neq j \in [n]$, $a_i a_j \neq 0$, and the verification $\mathcal{V}_{spa}(\mathsf{gk}, \mathsf{crs}; (A_2, \bar{A}_2), \pi^{spa})$ accepts.*

The (weak) soundness reduction is tight, except that it requires to factor a polynomial of degree $2\lambda_n = \max\{i \in \bar{\Lambda}\}$.

Proof. Let $\eta \leftarrow \hat{e}(A_1, A_2)$ and $h \leftarrow \hat{e}(g_1, g_2)$. PERFECT WITNESS-INDISTINGUISHABILITY: since satisfying argument π^{spa} is uniquely determined, all witnesses result in the same argument, and thus this argument is witness-indistinguishable.

PERFECT COMPLETENESS. All verifications but the last one are straightforward. For the last verification $\hat{e}(A_1, A_2) = \hat{e}(g_1, F)$, note that $\log_h \eta = (r + \sum_{i=1}^n a_i x^{\lambda_i})(r + \sum_{j=1}^n a_j x^{\lambda_j}) = F_{con}(x) + F_\pi(x)$, where

$$
F_{con}(x) = \underbrace{\sum_{i=1}^n \sum_{j=1: j \neq i}^n a_i a_j x^{\lambda_i + \lambda_j}}_{\delta \in 2\Lambda} \text{ and } F_\pi(x) = \underbrace{r^2 + 2r \sum_{i=1}^n a_i x^{\lambda_i} + \sum_{i=1}^n a_i^2 x^{2\lambda_i}}_{\delta \in \bar{\Lambda}} .
$$
(1)

Thus, $\log_h \eta$ is equal to a sum of x^δ for $\delta \in 2\Lambda$ and $\delta \in \bar{\Lambda}$. If the prover is honest, then $a_i a_j = 0$ for $i \neq j$, and thus $\log_h \eta$ is a formal polynomial that has non-zero monomials γx^δ with only $\delta \in \bar{\Lambda}$. Since then $a_i = 0$ for $i \neq I$, we have $\log_h \eta = r^2 + 2r a_I x^{\lambda_I} + a_I^2 x^{2\lambda_I} = \log_{g_2} F$. Thus, if the prover is honest, then the third verification succeeds.

WEAKER VERSION OF SOUNDNESS: Assume that $\mathcal{A}$ is an adversary that can break the last statement of the theorem. Next, we construct an adversary $\mathcal{A}'$ against the $\bar{\Lambda}$-PSDL assumption. Let $\mathsf{gk} \leftarrow \mathcal{G}_{bp}(1^\kappa)$ and $x \leftarrow \mathbb{Z}_p$. The adversary $\mathcal{A}'$ receives $\mathsf{crs} \leftarrow (\mathsf{gk}; (g_1^{x^\ell}, g_2^{x^\ell})_{\ell \in \bar{\Lambda}})$ as her input, and her task is to output x. She sets $\bar{\alpha} \leftarrow \mathbb{Z}_p$, $\mathsf{crs}' \leftarrow (\bar{g}_1, \bar{g}_2, (g_1^{x^\ell}, g_1^{\bar{\alpha} x^\ell})_{\ell \in \Lambda}, (g_2^{x^\ell}, g_2^{\bar{\alpha} x^\ell})_{\ell \in \Lambda \cup (2 \cdot \Lambda)})$, and then forwards crs' to $\mathcal{A}$. Clearly, crs' follows the distribution imposed by $\mathcal{G}_{crs}(1^\kappa)$. Denote $\mathsf{ck}_2 \leftarrow (\mathsf{gk}; \bar{g}_2, (g_2^{x^\ell}, g_2^{\bar{\alpha} x^\ell})_{\ell \in \Lambda})$. According to the last statement of the theorem, $\mathcal{A}(\mathsf{gk}; \mathsf{crs}')$ returns $((A_2, \bar{A}_2), w^{spa} = ((a_\ell)_{\ell \in \Lambda}, r, (f'_\ell)_{\ell \in \bar{\Lambda}}), \pi^{spa} = (A_1, \bar{A}_1, F, \bar{F}))$.

Assume that $\mathcal{A}$ was successful, that is, for some $i, j \in [n]$ and $i \neq j$, $a_i a_j \neq 0$. Since $(A_2, \bar{A}_2) = \mathcal{C}om^2(\mathsf{ck}_2; \boldsymbol{a}; r)$ and $\mathcal{V}_{spa}(\mathsf{gk}, \mathsf{crs}'; (A_2, \bar{A}_2), \pi^{spa}) = 1$, $\mathcal{A}'$ has expressed $\log_h \eta = \log_{g_2} F$ as a polynomial $f(x)$, where at least for some $\ell \in 2\Lambda$, x^ℓ has a non-zero coefficient.

On the other hand, $\log_{g_2} F = \sum_{\ell \in \bar{\Lambda}} f'_\ell x^\ell = f'(x)$. Since Λ is a progression-free set of odd positive integers, then $2\Lambda \cap \bar{\Lambda} = \emptyset$ and thus if $\ell \in \bar{\Lambda}$ then $\ell \notin 2\Lambda$. Therefore, all coefficients of $f'(x)$ corresponding to any x^ℓ, $\ell \in 2\Lambda$, are equal to

---

System parameters: Let $n = \text{poly}(\kappa)$. Let $\Lambda = \{\lambda_i : i \in [n]\}$ be an (n, κ)-nice progression-free set of odd positive integers. Denote $\lambda_0 := 0$. Let $\bar{\Lambda} = \{0\} \cup \Lambda \cup (2 \cdot \Lambda)$.

CRS generation $\mathcal{G}_{\text{crs}}(1^\kappa)$: Let $\text{gk} := (p, \mathbb{G}_1, \mathbb{G}_2, \mathbb{G}_T, \hat{e}, g_1, g_2) \leftarrow \mathcal{G}_{\text{bp}}(1^\kappa)$. Let $\bar{\alpha}, x \leftarrow \mathbb{Z}_p$. Denote $\bar{g}_t \leftarrow g_t^{\bar{\alpha}}$, $g_{t\ell} \leftarrow g_t^{x^\ell}$ and $\bar{g}_{t\ell} \leftarrow g_t^{\bar{\alpha}x^\ell}$ for $t \in \{1, 2\}$ and $\ell \in \bar{\Lambda}$. The CRS is $\text{crs} \leftarrow (\bar{g}_1, \bar{g}_2, (g_{1\ell}, \bar{g}_{1\ell})_{\ell \in \Lambda}, (g_{2\ell}, \bar{g}_{2\ell})_{\ell \in \Lambda \cup (2 \cdot \Lambda)})$. Set $\text{ck}_2 \leftarrow (\text{gk}; \bar{g}_2, (g_{2\ell}, \bar{g}_{2\ell})_{\ell \in \Lambda})$, and let $\text{crs}_v \leftarrow (\bar{g}_1, \bar{g}_2)$ be the verifier's part of crs.

Common input: $(A_2, \bar{A}_2) = \mathcal{C}om^2(\text{ck}_2; a; r) = (g_2^r \cdot g_{2,\lambda_I}^{a_I}, \bar{g}_2^r \cdot \bar{g}_{2,\lambda_I}^{a_I}) \in \mathbb{G}_2^2$, with $I \in [n]$.

Argument generation $\mathcal{P}_{spa}(\text{gk}, \text{crs}; (A_2, \bar{A}_2), (a, r))$: The prover defines $A_1 \leftarrow g_1^r \cdot g_{1,\lambda_I}^{a_I}$, $\bar{A}_1 \leftarrow \bar{g}_1^r \cdot \bar{g}_{1,\lambda_I}^{a_I}$, $F \leftarrow g_2^{r^2} \cdot g_{2,\lambda_I}^{2ra_I} \cdot g_{2,2\lambda_I}^{a_I^2}$, and $\bar{F} \leftarrow \bar{g}_2^{r^2} \cdot \bar{g}_{2,\lambda_I}^{2ra_I} \cdot \bar{g}_{2,2\lambda_I}^{a_I^2}$. The prover sends $\pi^{spa} \leftarrow (A_1, \bar{A}_1, F, \bar{F}) \in \mathbb{G}_1^2 \times \mathbb{G}_2^2$ to the verifier as the argument.

Verification $\mathcal{V}_{spa}(\text{gk}, \text{crs}_v; (A_2, \bar{A}_2), \pi^{spa})$: $\mathcal{V}_{spa}$ accepts iff $\hat{e}(A_1, g_2) = \hat{e}(g_1, A_2)$, $\hat{e}(\bar{A}_1, g_2) = \hat{e}(A_1, \bar{g}_2)$, $\hat{e}(g_1, \bar{A}_2) = \hat{e}(\bar{g}_1, A_2)$, $\hat{e}(g_1, \bar{F}) = \hat{e}(\bar{g}_1, F)$, and $\hat{e}(A_1, A_2) = \hat{e}(g_1, F)$.

Protocol 2: New 1-sparsity argument

0. Thus $f(X) = \sum f_\ell X^\ell$ and $f'(X) = \sum_{\ell \in \bar{\Lambda}} f'_\ell X^\ell$ are different polynomials with

$$f(x) = f'(x) = \log_{g_2} F .$$

Therefore, $\mathcal{A}'$ has succeeded in creating a non-zero polynomial $d = f - f'$, such that $d(x) = \sum_{\ell \in \bar{\Lambda}} d_\ell x^\ell = 0$.

Next, $\mathcal{A}'$ can use an efficient polynomial factorization algorithm in $\mathbb{Z}_p[X]$ to efficiently compute all $2\lambda_n + 1$ roots of $d(x)$. For some root y, $g_1^{x^\ell} = g_1^{y^\ell}$. $\mathcal{A}'$ sets $x \leftarrow y$, thus violating the $\bar{\Lambda}$-PSDL assumption. $\square$

The 1-sparsity argument is not perfectly zero-knowledge. The problem is that the simulator knows $\text{td} = (\bar{\alpha}, x)$, but given td and $(A_2, \bar{A}_2)$ she will not be able to generate π^{spa}. E.g., she has to compute $A_1 = g_1^r \cdot g_1^{a_I x^{\lambda_I}}$ based on $A_2 = g_2^r \cdot g_2^{a_I x^{\lambda_I}}$ and x, but without knowing r, I or a_I. This seems to be impossible without knowing an efficient isomorphism $\mathbb{G}_1 \rightarrow \mathbb{G}_2$. Computing F and $\bar{F}$ is even more difficult, since in this case the simulator does not even know the corresponding elements in $\mathbb{G}_1$. Technically, the problem is that due to the knowledge of the trapdoor, the simulator can, knowing one opening (a, r), produce an opening (a', r') to any other a'. However, here she does not know any openings. For the same reason, the permutation matrix argument of Sect. 3.3 will not be zero-knowledge. On the other hand, in the final shuffle argument of Sect. 5, the simulator creates all commitments by herself and can thus properly simulate the argument. By the same reason, the subarguments of [12,18] are not zero-knowledge but their final argument (for circuit satisfiability) is.

Theorem 3. *Consider Prot. 2. The CRS consists of $2n + 1$ elements of $\mathbb{G}_1$ and $4n + 1$ elements of $\mathbb{G}_2$, with the verifier's part of the CRS consisting of only 1 element of $\mathbb{G}_1$ and 1 element of $\mathbb{G}_2$. The communication complexity (argument size) of the argument in Prot. 2 is 2 elements from $\mathbb{G}_1$ and 2 elements from $\mathbb{G}_2$. Prover's computational complexity is dominated by 10 exponentiations. Verifier's computational complexity is dominated by 10 bilinear pairings.*

Setup: let $\mathsf{gk} := (p, \mathbb{G}_1, \mathbb{G}_2, \mathbb{G}_T, \hat{e}, g_1, g_2) \leftarrow \mathcal{G}_{\mathsf{bp}}(1^\kappa)$.
Common reference string $\mathcal{G}_{\mathsf{crs}}(\mathsf{gk})$: Let $\bar{\alpha}, \mathring{\alpha}, x \leftarrow \mathbb{Z}_p$, $\bar{g}_t \leftarrow g_t^{\bar{\alpha}}$, $\mathring{g}_t \leftarrow g_t^{\mathring{\alpha}}$, $g_{t\ell} \leftarrow g_t^{x^\ell}$, and $\bar{g}_{t\ell} \leftarrow \bar{g}_t^{x^\ell}$. Let $D \leftarrow \prod_{i=1}^n g_{2, \lambda_i}$. Let $\mathsf{crs} \leftarrow (\bar{g}_1, \bar{g}_2, \mathring{g}_1, \mathring{g}_2, (g_{1\ell}, \bar{g}_{1\ell})_{\ell \in \Lambda}, (g_{2\ell}, \bar{g}_{2\ell})_{\ell \in \Lambda \cup (2 \cdot \Lambda)}, D)$, $\mathsf{ck}_2 = (\mathsf{gk}; \bar{g}_2, (g_{2\ell}, \bar{g}_{2\ell})_{\ell \in \Lambda})$, $\mathring{\mathsf{ck}}_2 = (\mathsf{gk}; g_2, \mathring{g}_2)$, and $\mathsf{crs}_v = (\bar{g}_1, \bar{g}_2, \mathring{g}_1)$.
Common input: $(c_{2i}, \bar{c}_{2i}) = \mathcal{C}om^2(\mathsf{ck}_2; \boldsymbol{P}_i; r_i) = (g_2^{r_i} \cdot g_{2, \lambda_{\psi(i)}}, \bar{g}_2^{r_i} \cdot \bar{g}_{2, \lambda_{\psi(i)}})$ for $i \in [n]$.
Argument Generation $\mathcal{P}_{pm}(\mathsf{gk}, \mathsf{crs}; (\boldsymbol{c_2}, \boldsymbol{\bar{c}_2}), (P, \boldsymbol{r}))$: Construct a zero argument $\pi^0 \leftarrow \mathring{g}_2^{\sum_{i=1}^n r_i}$ that $(\prod_{i=1}^n c_{2i})/D$ commits to $\boldsymbol{0}$. For $i \in [n]$, construct a 1-sparsity argument $\pi_i^{spa} = (c_{1i}, \bar{c}_{1i}, F_i, \bar{F}_i)$ that $(c_{2i}, \bar{c}_{2i})$ commits to a 1-sparse row. Send $\pi^{pm} \leftarrow (\pi^0, \boldsymbol{\pi^{spa}})$ to the verifier.
Verification $\mathcal{V}_{pm}(\mathsf{gk}, \mathsf{crs}_v; (\boldsymbol{c_2}, \boldsymbol{\bar{c}_2}); \pi^{pm})$: The verifier checks $n + 1$ arguments $(\pi^0, \boldsymbol{\pi^{spa}})$.

Protocol 3: New permutation matrix argument in group $\mathbb{G}_2$ with $P = P_\psi$

3.3 New Permutation Matrix Argument

In this section, we will design a new *permutation matrix argument* where the prover aims to convince the verifier that he knows a permutation matrix P such that $(c_{2i}, \bar{c}_{2i}) \in \mathbb{G}_2^2$ are knowledge commitments to P's rows. Recall that a permutation matrix is a Boolean matrix with exactly one 1 in every row and column: if ψ is a permutation then the corresponding permutation matrix P_ψ is such that $(P_\psi)_{ij} = 1$ iff $j = \psi(i)$. Thus $(P_{\psi^{-1}})_{ij} = 1$ iff $i = \psi(j)$. We base our argument on the following lemma.

Lemma 2. *An $n \times n$ matrix P is a permutation matrix if and only if the following two conditions hold: (a) the sum of elements in any single column is equal to 1, and (b) no row has more than 1 non-zero elements.*

Proof. First, assume that P is a permutation matrix. Then every column has exactly one non-zero element (namely, with value 1), and thus both claims hold. Second, assume that (a) and (b) are true. Due to (a), every column must have at least one non-zero element, and thus the matrix has at least n non-zero elements. Due to (b), no row has more than 1 non-zero elements, and thus the matrix has at most n non-zero elements. Thus the matrix has exactly n non-zero elements, one in each column. Due to (a), all non-zero elements are equal to 1, and thus P is a permutation matrix. $\square$

We now use the 1-sparsity argument and the zero argument to show that the committed matrix satisfies the claims of Lem. 2. Therefore, by Lem. 2, P is a permutation matrix. Following [12,18] and similarly to the case of the zero and 1-sparsity arguments, we prove that the permutation argument satisfies a "weaker" version of soundness.

Theorem 4. *The argument in Prot. 3 is a perfectly complete and perfectly witness-indistinguishable permutation matrix argument. Let Λ be a progression-free set of odd positive integers. If the $\bar{\Lambda}$-PSDL assumption holds, then any non-uniform PPT adversary has a negligible chance in outputting an input $\mathsf{inp}^{pm} \leftarrow$*

$(c_2, \bar{c}_2)$ and a satisfying argument $\pi^{pm} \leftarrow (\pi^0, (c_{1i}, \bar{c}_{1i}, F_i, \bar{F}_i)_{i \in [n]})$ together with an opening witness $w^{pm} \leftarrow ((a_i)_{i \in \Lambda}, r_a, (\boldsymbol{P_i}, r_i, (f'_{ij})_{j \in \bar{\Lambda}})_{i \in [n]})$, such that $((\prod_{i=1}^n c_{2i})/D, \pi^0) = \mathcal{C}om^2(\mathsf{ck}_2; \boldsymbol{a}; r_a)$, $(\forall i \in [n])(c_{2i}, \bar{c}_{2i}) = \mathcal{C}om^2(\mathsf{ck}_2; \boldsymbol{P_i}; r_i)$, $(\forall i \in [n]) \log_{g_2} F_i = \sum_{j \in \bar{\Lambda}} f'_{ij} x^j$, $(\boldsymbol{a} \neq \boldsymbol{0} \vee (\exists i \in [n]) \boldsymbol{P_i}$ is not 1-sparse), and the verification $\mathcal{V}_{pm}(\mathsf{gk}, \mathsf{crs}; (c_2, \bar{c}_2), \pi^{pm})$ accepts.

Proof. PERFECT COMPLETENESS: follows from the completeness of the 1-sparsity and zero arguments and from Lem. 2, if we note that $\prod_{i=1}^n c_{2i}/D = g_2^{\sum_{i=1}^n r_i}$, and thus $(\prod_{i=1}^n c_{2i}/D, \pi^0)$ commits to $\boldsymbol{0}$ iff every column of P sums to 1.

WEAKER VERSION OF SOUNDNESS: Let $\mathcal{A}$ be a non-uniform PPT adversary that creates $(c_2, \bar{c}_2)$, an opening witness $((a_\ell)_{\ell \in \Lambda}, r_a, (P_i, r_i, (f'_{ij})_{j \in \bar{\Lambda}})_{i \in [n]})$, and an accepting NIZK argument π^{spa}.

Since the zero argument is (weakly) sound, verification of the argument π^0 shows that every column of P sums to 1. Here the witness is $w^0 = (\boldsymbol{a}, r_a)$ with $\boldsymbol{a} = \sum_{i=1}^n \boldsymbol{P_i} - \boldsymbol{1}$. By the $\bar{\Lambda}$-PSDL assumption, the 1-sparsity assumption is (weakly) sound. Therefore, verification of the arguments $\boldsymbol{\pi^{spa}}$ shows that every row of P has exactly one 1 (here the witness is $w_i^{spa} = (P_i, r_i, (f'_{ij})_{j \in \bar{\Lambda}})$). Therefore, by Lem. 2 and by the (weak) soundness of the 1-sparsity and zero arguments, P is a permutation matrix.

PERFECT WITNESS-INDISTINGUISHABILITY: since satisfying argument π^{pm} is uniquely determined, all witnesses result in the same argument, and therefore the permutation matrix argument is witness-indistinguishable.   □

Lemma 3. *Consider Prot. 3. The CRS consists of $2n + 2$ elements of $\mathbb{G}_1$ and $5n + 4$ elements of $\mathbb{G}_2$. The verifier's part of the CRS consists of 2 elements of $\mathbb{G}_1$ and of 2 elements of $\mathbb{G}_2$. The communication complexity is $2n$ elements of $\mathbb{G}_1$ and $2n + 1$ elements of $\mathbb{G}_2$. The prover's computational complexity is dominated by $10n + 1$ exponentiations. The verifier's computational complexity is dominated by $10n + 2$ pairings.*

4   Knowledge BBS Cryptosystem

Boneh, Boyen and Shacham [3] proposed the BBS cryptosystem $\Pi = (\mathcal{G}_{bp}, \mathcal{G}_{pkc}, \mathcal{E}nc, \mathcal{D}ec)$. We will use a (publicly verifiable) "knowledge" version of this cryptosystem so that according to the KE (that is, the $\emptyset$-PKE) assumption, the party who produces a valid ciphertext must know both the plaintext and the randomizer. We give a definition for group $\mathbb{G}_1$, the knowledge BBS cryptosystem for group $\mathbb{G}_2$ can be defined dually.

Setup (1^κ): Let $\mathsf{gk} \leftarrow (p, \mathbb{G}_1, \mathbb{G}_2, \mathbb{G}_T, \hat{e}, g_1, g_2) \leftarrow \mathcal{G}_{bp}(1^\kappa)$.
Key Generation $\mathcal{G}_{pkc}(\mathsf{gk})$: Set $(\tilde{\alpha}_1, \tilde{\alpha}_2, \tilde{\alpha}_3) \leftarrow \mathbb{Z}_p^3$, $\tilde{g}_1 \leftarrow g_1^{\tilde{\alpha}_3}$, $\tilde{g}_2^{(1)} \leftarrow g_2^{\tilde{\alpha}_1}$, $\tilde{g}_2^{(2)} \leftarrow g_2^{\tilde{\alpha}_2}$, $\tilde{g}_2^{(3)} \leftarrow g_2^{\tilde{\alpha}_3}$. The secret key is $\mathsf{sk} := (\mathsf{sk}_1, \mathsf{sk}_2) \leftarrow (\mathbb{Z}_p^*)^2$, and the public key is $\mathsf{pk} \leftarrow (\mathsf{gk}; \tilde{g}_1, \tilde{g}_2^{(1)}, \tilde{g}_2^{(2)}, \tilde{g}_2^{(3)}, f, \tilde{f}, h, \tilde{h})$, where $f = g_1^{1/\mathsf{sk}_1}$, $\tilde{f} = f^{\tilde{\alpha}_1}$, $h = g_1^{1/\mathsf{sk}_2}$, and $\tilde{h} = h^{\tilde{\alpha}_2}$.

Encryption $\mathcal{E}\mathsf{nc}_{\mathsf{pk}}(\mu; \sigma, \tau)$: To encrypt a message $\mu \in \mathbb{Z}_p$ with randomizer $(\sigma, \tau) \in \mathbb{Z}_p^2$, output the ciphertext $\mathsf{u} = (\mathsf{u}_1, \mathsf{u}_2, \mathsf{u}_3, \tilde{\mathsf{u}}_1, \tilde{\mathsf{u}}_2, \tilde{\mathsf{u}}_3)$, where $\mathsf{u}_1 = f^\sigma$, $\mathsf{u}_2 = h^\tau$, $\mathsf{u}_3 = g_1^{\mu+\sigma+\tau}$, $\tilde{\mathsf{u}}_1 = \tilde{f}^\sigma$, and $\tilde{\mathsf{u}}_2 = \tilde{h}^\tau$, and $\tilde{\mathsf{u}}_3 = \tilde{g}_1^{\mu+\sigma+\tau}$.

Decryption $\mathcal{D}\mathsf{ec}_{\mathsf{sk}}(\mathsf{u}_1, \mathsf{u}_2, \mathsf{u}_3, \tilde{\mathsf{u}}_1, \tilde{\mathsf{u}}_2, \tilde{\mathsf{u}}_3)$: if $\hat{e}(\mathsf{u}_1, \tilde{g}_2^{(1)}) = \hat{e}(\tilde{\mathsf{u}}_1, g_2)$, $\hat{e}(\mathsf{u}_2, \tilde{g}_2^{(2)}) = \hat{e}(\tilde{\mathsf{u}}_2, g_2)$ and $\hat{e}(\mathsf{u}_3, \tilde{g}_2^{(3)}) = \hat{e}(\tilde{\mathsf{u}}_3, g_2)$, then return the discrete logarithm of $g_1^\mu \leftarrow \mathsf{u}_3/(\mathsf{u}_1^{\mathsf{sk}_1}\mathsf{u}_2^{\mathsf{sk}_2})$. Otherwise, return $\perp$.

Since $\mathcal{E}\mathsf{nc}_{\mathsf{pk}}(\mu_1; \sigma_1, \tau_1) \cdot \mathcal{E}\mathsf{nc}_{\mathsf{pk}}(\mu_2; \sigma_2, \tau_2) = \mathcal{E}\mathsf{nc}_{\mathsf{pk}}(\mu_1 + \mu_2; \sigma_1 + \sigma_2, \tau_1 + \tau_2)$, the knowledge BBS cryptosystem is additively homomorphic (with respect to element-wise multiplication of the ciphertexts). In particular, one can re-encrypt (that is, blind) a ciphertext efficiently: if σ_2 and τ_2 are random, then $\mathcal{E}\mathsf{nc}_{\mathsf{pk}}(\mu; \sigma_1, \tau_1) \cdot \mathcal{E}\mathsf{nc}_{\mathsf{pk}}(0; \sigma_2, \tau_2) = \mathcal{E}\mathsf{nc}_{\mathsf{pk}}(\mu; \sigma_1 + \sigma_2, \tau_1 + \tau_2)$ is a random encryption of μ, independently of σ_1 and τ_1.

The cryptosystem has to be lifted (i.e., the value μ be in exponent) for the soundness proof of the new shuffle argument in Sect. 5 to go through; see there for a discussion. Thus, to decrypt, one has to compute discrete logarithms. Since this the latter is intractable, in real applications one has to assume that μ is small. Consider for example the e-voting scenario where μ is the number of the candidate (usually a small number).

One can now use one of the following approaches. First, discard the ballots if the ciphertext does not decrypt. (This can be checked publicly.) Second, use a (non-interactive) range proof [20,4] (in the e-voting scenario, range proofs are only given by the voters and not by the voting servers, and thus the range proof can be relatively less efficient compared to the shuffle argument) to guarantee that the ballots are correctly formed. In this case, invalid ballots can be removed from the system before starting to shuffle (saving thus valuable time otherwise wasted to shuffle invalid ciphertexts). Both approaches have their benefits, and either one can be used depending on the application.

The inclusion of $\tilde{\mathsf{u}}_3$ to the ciphertext is required because of our proof technique. Without it, the extractor in the proof of of the soundness of the new shuffle argument can extract μ only if μ is small. Thus, security would not be guaranteed against an adversary who chooses u_3 without actually knowing the element μ.

It is easy to see that the knowledge BBS cryptosystem, like the original BBS cryptosystem, is CPA-secure under the DLIN assumption (see Sect. A for the definition of the latter).

5   New Shuffle Argument

Let $\Pi = (\mathcal{G}_{\mathsf{pkc}}, \mathcal{E}\mathsf{nc}, \mathcal{D}\mathsf{ec})$ be an additively homomorphic cryptosystem. Assume that u_i and u_i' are valid ciphertexts of Π. We say that $(\mathsf{u}_1', \dots, \mathsf{u}_n')$ is a *shuffle* of $(\mathsf{u}_1, \dots, \mathsf{u}_n)$ iff there exists a permutation $\psi \in S_n$ and randomizers $r_1, \dots, r_n$ such that $\mathsf{u}_i' = \mathsf{u}_{\psi(i)} \cdot \mathcal{E}\mathsf{nc}_{\mathsf{pk}}(0; r_i)$ for $i \in [n]$. (In the case of the knowledge BBS cryptosystem, $r_i = (\sigma_i, \tau_i)$.) In a shuffle argument, the prover aims to convince the verifier in zero-knowledge that given $(\mathsf{pk}, (\mathsf{u}_i, \mathsf{u}_i')_{i \in [n]})$, he knows a permutation $\psi \in S_n$ and randomizers r_i such that $\mathsf{u}_i' = \mathsf{u}_{\psi(i)} \cdot \mathcal{E}\mathsf{nc}_{\mathsf{pk}}(0; r_i)$ for

$i \in [n]$. More precisely, we define the group-specific binary relation R^{sh} exactly as in [14]: $R^{sh} := \{((p, \mathbb{G}_1, \mathbb{G}_2, \mathbb{G}_T, \hat{e}, g_1, g_2), (\mathsf{pk}, \{u_i\}, \{u_i'\}), (\psi, \{r_i\})) : \psi \in S_n \wedge (\forall i : u_i' = u_{\psi(i)} \cdot \mathcal{E}\mathsf{nc}_{\mathsf{pk}}(0; r_i))\}$ Note that both according to the corresponding computational soundness definition and the Groth-Lu co-soundness definition (see App. B), the adversary picks not only the final ciphertexts u_i' but also the initial ciphertexts u_i.

In a real life application of the shuffle argument, the adversary (e.g., a malicious mix server) usually gets the ciphertexts u_i from a third party (from voters, or from another mix server), and thus does not know their discrete logarithms. However, in such a case we can still prove soundness of the full e-voting system (including the voters and all mix servers) if we give the adversary access to secret coins of all relevant parties. The use of knowledge BBS guarantees that the encrypters (voters) know the plaintexts and the randomizers, and thus the use of knowledge BBS can be seen as a white-box non-interactive knowledge argument. This corresponds to the case in several interactive (or Fiat-Shamir heuristic based) shuffles, where the ballots are accompanied by a proof of knowledge of the actual vote, from what the (black-box) simulator obtains the actual plaintexts necessary to complete the simulation. We thus think that soundness in our model is relevant, and corresponds to the established cryptographic practice with a twist. We leave the question of whether this model is necessary in applications like e-voting (where initial ciphertexts are not provided by the mixservers), and when co-soundness is undesired, as an interesting open problem. Using the Groth-Lu co-soundness definition avoids this issue, since in that case the adversary does not have access to the random coins of the participants.

We note that Groth and Lu made in addition a similar assumption in [14] where they prove co-soundness against adversaries who also output and thus know the secret key of the cryptosystem. (See App. B for a precise definition.) Thus, the adversary can decrypt all the ciphertexts, and thus knows the plaintexts (but does not have to know the randomizers). As argued in [14], this is reasonable in the setting of mixnet where the servers can usually threshold-decrypt all the results. Their approach is however not applicable in our case, since the knowledge of the secret key enables the adversary to obtain the plaintexts and the randomizers in exponents, while to prove the soundness in Thm. 5 the adversary has to know the plaintexts and the randomizers themselves.

Next, we construct an efficient shuffle argument that works with the knowledge BBS cryptosystem of Sect. 4. Assume that the ciphertexts $(u_{i1}, u_{i2}, u_{i3}, \tilde{u}_{i1}, \tilde{u}_{i2}, \tilde{u}_{i3})$, where $i \in [n]$, are created as in Sect. 4. The shuffled ciphertexts with permutation $\psi \in S_n$ and randomizers $(\sigma_i', \tau_i')_{i \in [n]}$ are $u_i' = (u_{i1}', u_{i2}', u_{i3}', \tilde{u}_{i1}', \tilde{u}_{i2}', \tilde{u}_{i3}') = u_{\psi(i)} \cdot \mathcal{E}\mathsf{nc}_{\mathsf{pk}}(0; \sigma_i', \tau_i') = \mathcal{E}\mathsf{nc}_{\mathsf{pk}}(\mu_{\psi(i)}; \sigma_{\psi(i)} + \sigma_i', \tau_{\psi(i)} + \tau_i')$. Let $P = P_{\psi^{-1}}$ denote the permutation matrix corresponding to the permutation ψ^{-1}.

The new shuffle argument is described in Prot. 4. Here, the prover first constructs a permutation matrix and a permutation matrix argument π^{pm}. After that, he shows that the plaintext vector of u_i' is equal to the product of this permutation matrix and the plaintext vector of u_i. Importantly, we can prove the adaptive computational soundness of the shuffle argument. This is since while in the previous arguments one only relied on (perfectly hiding) knowledge commitment scheme and thus any commitment could commit at the same time to the correct value (for example, to a permutation matrix) and to an incorrect value (for example, to an all-zero matrix), here the group-dependent language contains statements about a public-key cryptosystem where any ciphertext can be uniquely decrypted. Thus, it makes sense to state that $(\mathsf{pk}, (\mathsf{u}_i, \mathsf{u}_i')_{i \in [n]})$ is *not a shuffle*. To prove computational soundness, we need to rely on the PKE assumption. It is also nice to have a shuffle argument that satisfies a standard security notion.

Theorem 5. *Prot. 4 is a non-interactive perfectly complete and perfectly zero-knowledge shuffle argument of the knowledge BBS ciphertexts. Assume that μ is sufficiently small so that $\log_{g_1} g_1^{\mu}$ can be computed in polynomial time. If the Λ-PSDL, the DLIN, the KE (in group $\mathbb{G}_1$), and the $\bar{\Lambda}$-PKE (in group $\mathbb{G}_2$) assumptions hold, then the argument is also adaptively computationally sound.*

We recall that $\emptyset$-PKE is equal to the KE assumption (in the same bilinear group). Thus, if $\bar{\Lambda}$-PKE is hard then also Λ-PKE and KE are hard (in the same group).

Proof. PERFECT COMPLETENESS: To verify the proof, the verifier first checks the consistency of the commitments, ciphertexts and the permutation matrix argument; here one needs that the permutation matrix argument is perfectly complete. Assume that the prover is honest. The verification equation in step 5a holds since

$$
\begin{aligned}
\hat{e}(f, c_\sigma) \cdot \prod_{i=1}^{n} \hat{e}(\mathsf{u}_{i1}, c_{2i}) =& \hat{e}(f, g_2^{R_\sigma} \cdot \prod_{i=1}^{n} g_{2,\lambda_i}^{\sigma_i'}) \cdot \prod_{i=1}^{n} (\hat{e}(\mathsf{u}_{i1}, g_2^{r_i}) \cdot \hat{e}(f^{\sigma_i}, g_{2,\lambda_{\psi^{-1}(i)}})) \\
=& \hat{e}(f^{R_\sigma} \cdot \prod_{i=1}^{n} \mathsf{u}_{i1}^{r_i}, g_2) \cdot \prod_{i=1}^{n} \hat{e}(f^{\sigma_{\psi(i)} + \sigma_i'}, g_{2,\lambda_i}) \\
=& \hat{e}(\mathsf{u}_\sigma, g_2) \cdot \prod_{i=1}^{n} \hat{e}(\mathsf{u}_{i1}', g_{2,\lambda_i}) \ .
\end{aligned}
$$

The equations in steps 5b and 5c can be verified similarly.

ADAPTIVE COMPUTATIONAL SOUNDNESS: Let $\mathcal{A}$ be a non-uniform PPT adversary that, given gk and a crs, creates a statement $(\mathsf{pk} = (\mathsf{gk}; \tilde{g}_1, \tilde{g}_2^{(1)}, \tilde{g}_2^{(2)}, \tilde{g}_2^{(3)}, f, \tilde{f}, h, \tilde{h}), (\mathsf{u}_i, \mathsf{u}_i')_{i \in [n]})$ and an accepting NIZK argument π^{sh} (as in Eq. (2) in Prot. 4), such that the plaintext vector $(\mathsf{u}_i')_{i \in [n]}$ is not a permutation of the plaintext vector $(\mathsf{u}_i)_{i \in [n]}$. Assume that the DLIN assumption holds in $\mathbb{G}_1$, the KE assumption holds in $\mathbb{G}_1$ and $\bar{\Lambda}$-PKE (and thus also Λ-PKE and KE) assumption holds in $\mathbb{G}_2$. We now construct an adversary $\mathcal{A}'$ that breaks the Λ-PSDL assumption.

Recall that π^{pm} contains values π^0 and $\pi_i^{spa} = (c_{1i}, \bar{c}_{1i}, F_i, \bar{F}_i)$. By applying the relevant knowledge assumption, we can postulate the existence of the following non-uniform PPT knowledge extractors that, with all but a negligible probability, return certain values:

Common reference string: Similarly to the permutation matrix argument, let
$\bar{\alpha}, \mathring{\alpha}, x \leftarrow \mathbb{Z}_p$, $\bar{g}_t \leftarrow g_t^{\bar{\alpha}}$, $\mathring{g}_t \leftarrow g_t^{\mathring{\alpha}}$, $g_{t\ell} \leftarrow g_t^{x^\ell}$, and $\bar{g}_{t\ell} \leftarrow \bar{g}_t^{x^\ell}$. Let $D \leftarrow \prod_{i=1}^n g_{2,\lambda_i}$.
In addition, let $\mathsf{sk}_1, \mathsf{sk}_2 \leftarrow \mathbb{Z}_p^*$ and $\tilde{\alpha}_1, \tilde{\alpha}_2, \tilde{\alpha}_3 \leftarrow \mathbb{Z}_p$. Let $f \leftarrow g_1^{1/\mathsf{sk}_1}$, $h \leftarrow g_1^{1/\mathsf{sk}_2}$,
$\tilde{f} \leftarrow f^{\tilde{\alpha}_1}$, $\tilde{h} \leftarrow h^{\tilde{\alpha}_2}$, $\tilde{g}_1 \leftarrow g_1^{\tilde{\alpha}_3}$, $\tilde{g}_2^{(1)} \leftarrow g_2^{\tilde{\alpha}_1}$, $\tilde{g}_2^{(2)} \leftarrow g_2^{\tilde{\alpha}_2}$, and $\tilde{g}_2^{(3)} \leftarrow g_2^{\tilde{\alpha}_3}$.
The CRS is $\mathsf{crs} := (\bar{g}_1, \bar{g}_2, \mathring{g}_1, \mathring{g}_2, (g_{1\ell}, \bar{g}_{1\ell})_{\ell \in \Lambda}, (g_{2\ell}, \bar{g}_{2\ell})_{\ell \in \Lambda \cup (2 \cdot \Lambda)}, D)$. The commitment keys are $\mathsf{ck}_t \leftarrow (\mathsf{gk}; \bar{g}_t, (g_{t\ell}, \bar{g}_{t\ell})_{\ell \in \Lambda})$ and $\mathring{\mathsf{ck}}_2 \leftarrow (\mathsf{gk}; \mathring{g}_2)$. The public key is
$\mathsf{pk} = (\mathsf{gk}; \tilde{g}_1, \tilde{g}_2^{(1)}, \tilde{g}_2^{(2)}, \tilde{g}_2^{(3)}, f, \tilde{f}, h, \tilde{h})$, and the secret key is $\mathsf{sk} = (\mathsf{sk}_1, \mathsf{sk}_2)$.

Common input: $(\mathsf{pk}, (\mathsf{u}_i, \mathsf{u}_i')_{i \in [n]})$, where $\mathsf{u}_i = \mathcal{E}\mathsf{nc}_{\mathsf{pk}}(\mu_i; \sigma_i, \tau_i) \in \mathbb{G}_1^3$ and $\mathsf{u}_i' = \mathcal{E}\mathsf{nc}_{\mathsf{pk}}(\mu_{\psi(i)}; \sigma_{\psi(i)} + \sigma_i', \tau_{\psi(i)} + \tau_i') \in \mathbb{G}_1^3$.

Argument $\mathcal{P}_{sh}(\mathsf{gk}, \mathsf{crs}; (\mathsf{pk}, (\mathsf{u}_i, \mathsf{u}_i')_{i \in [n]}), (\psi, (\sigma_i', \tau_i')_{i \in [n]}))$: the prover does the following.

1. Let $P = P_{\psi^{-1}}$ be the $n \times n$ permutation matrix corresponding to the permutation ψ^{-1}.
2. For $i \in [n]$, let $r_i \leftarrow \mathbb{Z}_p$ and $(c_{2i}, \bar{c}_{2i}) \leftarrow \mathcal{C}\mathsf{om}^2(\mathsf{ck}_2; \boldsymbol{P}_i; r_i) = (g_2^{r_i} \cdot g_{2,\lambda_{\psi^{-1}(i)}}, \bar{g}_2^{r_i} \cdot \bar{g}_{2,\lambda_{\psi^{-1}(i)}})$.
3. Generate a permutation matrix argument π^{pm} for inputs $(c_2, \bar{c}_2)$.
4. Set $(R_\sigma, R_\tau) \leftarrow \mathbb{Z}_p^2$, $(c_\sigma, \bar{c}_\sigma) \leftarrow \mathcal{C}\mathsf{om}^2(\mathsf{ck}_2; \sigma_1', \ldots, \sigma_n'; R_\sigma)$, and $(c_\tau, \bar{c}_\tau) \leftarrow \mathcal{C}\mathsf{om}^2(\mathsf{ck}_2; \tau_1', \ldots, \tau_n'; R_\tau)$.
5. Compute $(\mathsf{u}_\sigma, \tilde{\mathsf{u}}_\sigma) \leftarrow (f^{R_\sigma} \cdot \prod_{i=1}^n \mathsf{u}_{i1}^{r_i}, \tilde{f}^{R_\sigma} \cdot \prod_{i=1}^n \tilde{\mathsf{u}}_{i1}^{r_i})$, $(\mathsf{u}_\tau, \tilde{\mathsf{u}}_\tau) \leftarrow (h^{R_\tau} \cdot \prod_{i=1}^n \mathsf{u}_{i2}^{r_i}, \tilde{h}^{R_\tau} \cdot \prod_{i=1}^n \tilde{\mathsf{u}}_{i2}^{r_i})$, $(\mathsf{u}_\mu, \tilde{\mathsf{u}}_\mu) \leftarrow (g_1^{R_\sigma + R_\tau} \cdot \prod_{i=1}^n \mathsf{u}_{i3}^{r_i}, \tilde{g}_1^{R_\sigma + R_\tau} \cdot \prod_{i=1}^n \tilde{\mathsf{u}}_{i3}^{r_i})$.
6. The argument is

$$\pi^{sh} \leftarrow ((c_{2i}, \bar{c}_{2i})_{i \in [n]}, \pi^{pm}, c_\sigma, \bar{c}_\sigma, c_\tau, \bar{c}_\tau, \mathsf{u}_\sigma, \tilde{\mathsf{u}}_\sigma, \mathsf{u}_\tau, \tilde{\mathsf{u}}_\tau, \mathsf{u}_\mu, \tilde{\mathsf{u}}_\mu) . \tag{2}$$

Verification $\mathcal{V}_{sh}(\mathsf{gk}, \mathsf{crs}; (\mathsf{pk}, (\mathsf{u}_i, \mathsf{u}_i')_{i \in [n]}), \pi^{sh})$: the verifier does the following.

1. Check that $\hat{e}(\bar{g}_1, c_\sigma) = \hat{e}(g_1, \bar{c}_\sigma)$ and $\hat{e}(\bar{g}_1, c_\tau) = \hat{e}(g_1, \bar{c}_\tau)$.
2. Check that $\hat{e}(\mathsf{u}_\sigma, \tilde{g}_2^{(1)}) = \hat{e}(\tilde{\mathsf{u}}_\sigma, g_2)$, $\hat{e}(\mathsf{u}_\tau, \tilde{g}_2^{(2)}) = \hat{e}(\tilde{\mathsf{u}}_\tau, g_2)$, and $\hat{e}(\mathsf{u}_\mu, \tilde{g}_2^{(3)}) = \hat{e}(\tilde{\mathsf{u}}_\mu, g_2)$.
3. For $i \in [n]$, check that $\hat{e}(\mathsf{u}_{i1}, \tilde{g}_2^{(1)}) = \hat{e}(\tilde{\mathsf{u}}_{i1}, g_2)$, $\hat{e}(\mathsf{u}_{i2}, \tilde{g}_2^{(2)}) = \hat{e}(\tilde{\mathsf{u}}_{i2}, g_2)$, $\hat{e}(\mathsf{u}_{i3}, \tilde{g}_2^{(3)}) = \hat{e}(\tilde{\mathsf{u}}_{i3}, g_2)$, $\hat{e}(\mathsf{u}_{i1}', \tilde{g}_2^{(1)}) = \hat{e}(\tilde{\mathsf{u}}_{i1}', g_2)$, $\hat{e}(\mathsf{u}_{i2}', \tilde{g}_2^{(2)}) = \hat{e}(\tilde{\mathsf{u}}_{i2}', g_2)$, and $\hat{e}(\mathsf{u}_{i3}', \tilde{g}_2^{(3)}) = \hat{e}(\tilde{\mathsf{u}}_{i3}', g_2)$.
4. Check the permutation matrix argument π^{pm}.
5. Check that the following three equations hold:
   (a) $\hat{e}(f, c_\sigma) \cdot \prod_{i=1}^n \hat{e}(\mathsf{u}_{i1}, c_{2i}) = \hat{e}(\mathsf{u}_\sigma, g_2) \cdot \prod_{i=1}^n \hat{e}(\mathsf{u}_{i1}', g_{2,\lambda_i})$,
   (b) $\hat{e}(h, c_\tau) \cdot \prod_{i=1}^n \hat{e}(\mathsf{u}_{i2}, c_{2i}) = \hat{e}(\mathsf{u}_\tau, g_2) \cdot \prod_{i=1}^n \hat{e}(\mathsf{u}_{i2}', g_{2,\lambda_i})$, and
   (c) $\hat{e}(g_1, c_\sigma c_\tau) \cdot \prod_{i=1}^n \hat{e}(\mathsf{u}_{i3}, c_{2i}) = \hat{e}(\mathsf{u}_\mu, g_2) \cdot \prod_{i=1}^n \hat{e}(\mathsf{u}_{i3}', g_{2,\lambda_i})$.

Protocol 4: New shuffle argument

- By the KE assumption in group $\mathbb{G}_1$, there exists a knowledge extractor that, given $(\mathfrak{u}_{ij}, \tilde{\mathfrak{u}}_{ij}, \mathfrak{u}'_{ij}, \tilde{\mathfrak{u}}'_{ij})_{j \in [3]}$ and access to $\mathcal{A}$'s random coins, returns the values μ_i, σ_i, τ_i, μ'_i, σ'_i and τ'_i, such that $\mathfrak{u}_i = \mathcal{E}\mathsf{nc}_{\mathsf{pk}}(\mu_i; \sigma_i, \tau_i)$ and $\mathfrak{u}'_i = \mathcal{E}\mathsf{nc}_{\mathsf{pk}}(\mu'_i; \sigma'_i, \tau'_i)$. Note that it might be the case that $\mu'_i \neq \mu_{\varrho(i)}$.
- By the Λ-PKE assumption in group $\mathbb{G}_2$, there exists a knowledge extractor that, given $(c_\sigma, \bar{c}_\sigma, c_\tau, \bar{c}_\tau)$ and access to $\mathcal{A}$'s random coins, returns openings $(\boldsymbol{\sigma}^*, R_\sigma)$ and $(\boldsymbol{\tau}^*, R_\tau)$, such that $(c_\sigma, \bar{c}_\sigma) = \mathcal{C}\mathsf{om}^2(\mathsf{ck}_2; \boldsymbol{\sigma}^*; R_\sigma)$ and $(c_\tau, \bar{c}_\tau) = \mathcal{C}\mathsf{om}^2(\mathsf{ck}_2; \boldsymbol{\tau}^*; R_\tau)$. It does not have to hold that $\sigma'_i = \sigma_{\psi(i)} + \sigma^*_i$ and $\tau'_i = \tau_{\psi(i)} + \tau^*_i$ for $i \in [n]$.
- By the KE assumption in group $\mathbb{G}_1$, there exists a knowledge extractor that, given $(\mathfrak{u}_\sigma, \tilde{\mathfrak{u}}_\sigma, \mathfrak{u}_\tau, \tilde{\mathfrak{u}}_\tau, \mathfrak{u}_\mu, \tilde{\mathfrak{u}}_\mu)$ and access to $\mathcal{A}$'s random coins, returns openings $(v_\sigma, v_\tau, v_\mu)$, such that $(\mathfrak{u}_\sigma, \tilde{\mathfrak{u}}_\sigma) = (f^{v_\sigma}, \tilde{f}^{v_\sigma})$, $(\mathfrak{u}_\tau, \tilde{\mathfrak{u}}_\tau) = (h^{v_\tau}, \tilde{h}^{v_\tau})$, and $(\mathfrak{u}_\mu, \tilde{\mathfrak{u}}_\mu) = (g_1^{v_\mu}, \tilde{g}_1^{v_\mu})$. (Thus, it is not necessary that the adversary created the values $\mathfrak{u}_\sigma$, $\mathfrak{u}_\tau$ and $\mathfrak{u}_\mu$ correctly, it is just needed that she knows their discrete logarithms.)
- By the KE assumption in group $\mathbb{G}_2$, there exists a knowledge extractor that, given $((\prod_{i=1}^n c_{2i})/D, \pi^0)$ and access to $\mathcal{A}$'s random coins, returns an opening $((a_i)_{i \in [n]}, r_a)$, such that $((\prod_{i=1}^n c_{2i})/D, \pi^0) = \mathcal{C}\mathsf{om}^2(\mathsf{ck}_2; \boldsymbol{a}; r_a)$.
- By the Λ-PKE assumption in group $\mathbb{G}_2$, for every $i \in [n]$ there exists a knowledge extractor that, given $(c_{2i}, \bar{c}_{21})$ and access to $\mathcal{A}$'s random coins, returns an opening $((P_{ij})_{j \in [n]}, r_i)$ such that $(c_{2i}, \bar{c}_{2i}) = \mathcal{C}\mathsf{om}^2(\mathsf{ck}_2; \boldsymbol{P_i}; r_i)$.
- By the $\bar{\Lambda}$-PKE assumption in group $\mathbb{G}_2$, for every i there exists a knowledge extractor that, given $(F_i, \bar{F}_i)$ and access to $\mathcal{A}$'s random coins, returns openings $(f'_{ij})_{j \in \bar{\Lambda}}$ such that $\log_{g_2} F_i = \sum_{j \in \bar{\Lambda}} f'_{ij} x^j$.

The probability that any of these extractors fails is negligible, in this case we can abort. In the following, we will assume that all extractors succeeded.

Let $\mathfrak{a}$ be $\mathcal{A}$'s output. Based on $\mathcal{A}$ and the last three type of extractors, we can build an adversary $\mathcal{A}'$ that returns $\mathfrak{a}$ together with $((a_i)_{i \in [n]}, r_a, (\boldsymbol{P_i}, r_i, (f'_{ij})_{j \in \bar{\Lambda}})_{i \in [n]})$. Since the permutation matrix argument is (weakly) sound (as defined in the last statement of Thm. 4) and π^{pm} verifies, we have that $\boldsymbol{c_2} = (c_{2i})_{i \in [n]}$ commits to a permutation matrix. Thus, there exists $\psi \in S_n$ such that for every $i \in [n]$, $c_{2i} = \exp(g_2, r_i + x^{\lambda_{(\psi^{-1}(i))}})$.

Assume now that the equation in step 5a holds. Then

$$\hat{e}(\mathfrak{u}_\sigma, g_2) = \hat{e}(f, c_\sigma) \cdot \prod_{i=1}^n \hat{e}(\mathfrak{u}_{i1}, c_{2i}) / \prod_{i=1}^n \hat{e}(\mathfrak{u}'_{i1}, g_{2,\lambda_i})$$

$$= \hat{e}(f, g_2^{R_\sigma + \sum_{i=1}^n \sigma^*_i x^{\lambda_i}}) \cdot \prod_{i=1}^n \hat{e}(f^{\sigma_i}, g_2^{r_i + x^{\lambda_{\psi^{-1}(i)}}}) / \prod_{i=1}^n \hat{e}(f^{\sigma'_i}, g_2^{x^{\lambda_i}})$$

$$= \hat{e}(f^{R_\sigma + \sum_{i=1}^n \sigma_i r_i + \sum_{i=1}^n (\sigma_{\psi(i)} + \sigma^*_i - \sigma'_i) x^{\lambda_i}}, g_2) .$$

Since $\mathfrak{u}_\sigma = f^{v_\sigma}$, $\sum_{i=1}^n (\sigma_{\psi(i)} + \sigma^*_i - \sigma'_i) x^{\lambda_i} + R_\sigma + \sum_{i=1}^n \sigma_i r_i - v_\sigma = 0$. If $\sigma'_i \neq \sigma_{\psi(i)} + \sigma^*_i$ for some $i \in [n]$, then the adversary has succeeded in creating a non-trivial polynomial $f^*(X) = \sum_{i=1}^n f^*_i X^{\lambda_i} + f^*_0$, with $f^*_i = \sigma_{\psi(i)} + \sigma^*_i - \sigma'_i$ and

$f_0^* = R_\sigma + \sum_{i=1}^n \sigma_i r_i - v_\sigma$, such that $f^*(x) = 0$. By using an efficient polynomial factorization algorithm, one can now find all $\lambda_n + 1$ roots of $f^*(X)$. For one of those roots, say y, we have $g_2^y = g_2^x$. $\mathcal{A}'$ can now return $y = x$. Since $(\mathsf{gk}, \mathsf{crs})$ only contains f^{x^ℓ} for $\ell = 0$, the adversary has thus broken the $\emptyset$-PSDL assumption, an assumption that is true unconditionally since the adversary's input does not depend on x at all. Thus, $\sigma_i' = \sigma_{\psi(i)} + \sigma_i^*$ for $i \in [n]$.

Analogously, by the verification in step 5b, $\sum_{i=1}^n (\tau_{\psi(i)} + \tau_i^* - \tau_i') x^{\lambda_i} + R_\tau + \sum_{i=1}^n \tau_i r_i - v_\tau = 0$, and thus, $\tau_i' = \tau_{\psi(i)} + \tau_i^*$ for all $i \in [n]$.

Finally, by the verification in step 5c,

$$\hat{e}(\mathsf{u}_\mu, g_2) = \hat{e}(g_1, c_\sigma c_\tau) \cdot \prod_{i=1}^n \hat{e}(u_{i3}, c_{2i}) / \prod_{i=1}^n \hat{e}(u_{i3}', g_{2,\lambda_i})$$

$$= \hat{e}(g_1, g_2^{R_\sigma + R_\tau + \sum_{i=1}^n (\sigma_i^* + \tau_i^*) x^{\lambda_i}}) \cdot$$

$$\prod_{i=1}^n \hat{e}(g_1^{\mu_i + \sigma_i + \tau_i}, \exp(g_2, r_i + x^{\lambda_{\psi^{-1}(i)}})) / \prod_{i=1}^n \hat{e}(g_1^{\mu_i' + \sigma_i' + \tau_i'}, g_2^{x^{\lambda_i}}) \ .$$

Thus,

$$\log_{g_1} \mathsf{u}_\mu = R_\sigma + R_\tau + \sum_{i=1}^n (\sigma_i^* + \tau_i^*) x^{\lambda_i} + \sum_{i=1}^n (\mu_i + \sigma_i + \tau_i)(r_i + x^{\lambda_{\psi^{-1}(i)}}) -$$

$$\sum_{i=1}^n (\mu_i' + \sigma_i' + \tau_i') x^{\lambda_i}$$

$$= R_\sigma + R_\tau + \sum_{i=1}^n (\mu_i + \sigma_i + \tau_i) r_i +$$

$$\sum_{i=1}^n (\mu_{\psi(i)} - \mu_i' + \sigma_{\psi(i)} + \sigma_i^* - \sigma_i' + \tau_{\psi(i)} + \tau_i^* - \tau_i') x^{\lambda_i}$$

$$= R_\sigma + R_\tau + \sum_{i=1}^n (\mu_i + \sigma_i + \tau_i) r_i + \sum_{i=1}^n (\mu_{\psi(i)} - \mu_i') x^{\lambda_i} \ .$$

If $\mu_i' \neq \mu_{\psi(i)}$ for some $i \in [n]$, then the adversary has succeeded in creating a non-trivial polynomial $f^*(X) = \sum_{i=1}^n f_i^* X^{\lambda_i} + f_0^*$, with $f_i^* = \sum_{i=1}^n (\mu_{\psi(i)} - \mu_i')$ and $f_0^* = R_\sigma + R_\tau + \sum_{i=1}^n (\mu_i + \sigma_i + \tau_i) r_i - v_\mu$, such that $f^*(x) = 0$. By using an efficient polynomial factorization algorithm, one can now find all $\lambda_n + 1$ roots of f^*. For one of those roots, say y, we have $g_2^y = g_2^x$. Since $(\mathsf{gk}, \mathsf{crs})$ only contains $g_1^{x^\ell}$ for $\ell \in \Lambda$, the adversary has thus broken the Λ-PSDL assumption. Therefore, due to the Λ-PSDL assumption, $\mu_i' = \mu_{\psi(i)}$ for $i \in [n]$.[3]

---

[3] For the argument in this paragraph to go through, we need the knowledge BBS cryptosystem to be lifted and the plaintexts to be small. Otherwise, the adversary will not know the coefficients of $f'(X)$, and thus one could not use a polynomial factorization algorithm to break the Λ-PSDL assumption. Thus, a crafty adversary might be able to break soundness by choosing g_1^μ from which she cannot compute μ.

Inputs: gk and CRS as in Prot. 4, trapdoor td $= (\mathring{\alpha}, \bar{\alpha}, x)$, and $(\mathsf{pk}, (\mathsf{u}_i, \mathsf{u}'_i)_{i \in [n]})$
Output: π^{sh}
Simulation:

1. Pick random $z_i, r_{i1}, r_{i2} \leftarrow \mathbb{Z}_p$ for $i \in [n]$.
2. Set $c_\sigma \leftarrow \prod_{i=1}^n g_2^{r_{i1}}$, $c_\tau \leftarrow \prod_{i=1}^n g_2^{r_{i2}}$, $c_{2i} \leftarrow g_2^{z_i}$ and $\bar{c}_{2i} \leftarrow \bar{g}_2^{z_i}$ for $i \in [n]$.
3. Set $(\mathsf{u}_\sigma, \tilde{\mathsf{u}}_\sigma) \leftarrow (\prod_{i=1}^n (f^{r_{i1}} \cdot \mathsf{u}_{i1}^{z_i} \cdot (\mathsf{u}'_{i1})^{-x^{\lambda_i}}), \prod_{i=1}^n (\tilde{f}^{r_{i1}} \cdot \tilde{\mathsf{u}}_{i1}^{z_i} \cdot (\tilde{\mathsf{u}}'_{i1})^{-x^{\lambda_i}}))$, $(\mathsf{u}_\tau, \tilde{\mathsf{u}}_\tau) \leftarrow$
   $(\prod_{i=1}^n (h^{r_{i2}} \cdot \mathsf{u}_{i2}^{z_i} \cdot (\mathsf{u}'_{i2})^{-x^{\lambda_i}}), \prod_{i=1}^n (\tilde{h}^{r_{i2}} \cdot \tilde{\mathsf{u}}_{i2}^{z_i} \cdot (\tilde{\mathsf{u}}'_{i2})^{-x^{\lambda_i}}))$, $(\mathsf{u}_\mu, \tilde{\mathsf{u}}_\mu) \leftarrow (\prod_{i=1}^n (g_1^{r_{i1}+r_{i2}} \cdot$
   $\mathsf{u}_{i3}^{z_i} \cdot (\mathsf{u}'_{i3})^{-x^{\lambda_i}}), \prod_{i=1}^n (\tilde{g}_1^{r_{i1}+r_{i2}} \cdot \tilde{\mathsf{u}}_{i3}^{z_i} \cdot (\tilde{\mathsf{u}}'_{i3})^{-x^{\lambda_i}}))$.
4. Complete the remaining part of the proof.
5. Simulate π^{pm} by using the trapdoor opening of commitments as follows:
   (a) Let $\pi^0 \leftarrow ((\prod_{i=1}^n c_{2i})/D)^{\mathring{\alpha}}$.
   (b) Let π_i^{spa} be a 1-sparsity argument that $(c_{2i}, \bar{c}_{2i})$ commits to a 1-sparse vector.
       That is, $\pi_i^{spa} = (c_{1i}, \bar{c}_{1i}, F_i, \bar{F}_i)$ for $c_{1i} \leftarrow g_1^{z_i}$, $\bar{c}_{1i} \leftarrow \bar{g}_1^{z_i}$, $F_i \leftarrow g_2^{z_i^2}$, $\bar{F}_i \leftarrow \bar{g}_2^{z_i^2}$.
   (c) Let $\pi^{pm} \leftarrow (\pi^0, \boldsymbol{\pi}^{spa})$.
6. Set $\pi^{sh} \leftarrow ((c_{2i}, \bar{c}_{2i})_{i \in [n]}, \pi^{pm}, c_\sigma, \bar{c}_\sigma, c_\tau, \bar{c}_\tau, \mathsf{u}_\sigma, \tilde{\mathsf{u}}_\sigma, \mathsf{u}_\tau, \tilde{\mathsf{u}}_\tau, \mathsf{u}_\mu, \tilde{\mathsf{u}}_\mu)$.

Protocol 5: Simulator $\mathcal{S}_2$: construction

Thus, $\mathsf{u}'_{i1} = f^{\sigma_{\psi(i)}+\sigma_i^*}$, $\mathsf{u}'_{i2} = h^{\tau_{\psi(i)}+\tau_i^*}$, $\mathsf{u}'_{i3} = g_1^{\mu_{\psi(i)}+\sigma_{\psi(i)}+\sigma_i^*+\tau_{\psi(i)}+\tau_i^*}$ and similarly for elements $\tilde{\mathsf{u}}'_{ij}$, and therefore, $\{\mathsf{u}'_i\}$ is indeed a correct shuffle of $\{\mathsf{u}_i\}$.

PERFECT ZERO-KNOWLEDGE: We construct a simulator $\mathcal{S} = (\mathcal{S}_1, \mathcal{S}_2)$ as follows. First, $\mathcal{S}_1$ generates random $\mathring{a}, \bar{a}, x \leftarrow \mathbb{Z}_q$, and sets td $\leftarrow (\mathring{a}, \bar{a}, x)$. He then creates crs as in Prot. 4, and stores td. The construction of $\mathcal{S}_2$ is given in Prot. 5. Next, we give an analysis of the simulated proof. Note that c_σ, c_τ and c_{2i} are independent and random variables in $\mathbb{G}$, exactly as in the real run of the protocol. With respect to those variables, we define u_σ, u_τ and u_μ so that they satisfy the verification equations. Thus, we are now only left to show that the verification equations in steps 5a, 5b and 5c hold.

Clearly, π^{pm} is simulated correctly, since $\hat{e}(\mathring{g}_1, (\prod_{i=1}^n c_{2i})/D) = \hat{e}(g_1, \pi^0)$, $\hat{e}(c_{1i}, g_2) = \hat{e}(g_1, c_{2i})$, $\hat{e}(\bar{c}_{1i}, g_2) = \hat{e}(c_{1i}, \bar{g}_2)$, $\hat{e}(g_1, \bar{c}_{2i}) = \hat{e}(\bar{g}_1, c_{2i})$, $\hat{e}(g_1, \bar{F}_i) = \hat{e}(\bar{g}_1, F_i)$, and $\hat{e}(c_{1i}, c_{2i}) = \hat{e}(g_1^{z_i}, g_2^{z_i}) = \hat{e}(g_1, g_2^{z_i^2}) = \hat{e}(g_1, F_i)$.

Finally, we have

$$\hat{e}(f, c_\sigma) \cdot \prod_{i=1}^n \hat{e}(\mathsf{u}_{i1}, c_{2i}) = \hat{e}(f, \prod_{i=1}^n g_2^{r_{i1}}) \cdot \prod_{i=1}^n \hat{e}(\mathsf{u}_{i1}, g_2^{z_i}) = \hat{e}(\prod_{i=1}^n f^{r_{i1}} \cdot \prod_{i=1}^n \mathsf{u}_{i1}^{z_i}, g_2)$$

$$= \hat{e}(\prod_{i=1}^n (f^{r_{i1}} \mathsf{u}_{i1}^{z_i}(\mathsf{u}'_{i1})^{-x^{\lambda_i}}), g_2) \cdot \prod_{i=1}^n \hat{e}(\mathsf{u}'_{i1}, g_{2,\lambda_i})$$

$$= \hat{e}(\mathsf{u}_\sigma, g_2) \cdot \prod_{i=1}^n \hat{e}(\mathsf{u}'_{i1}, g_{2,\lambda_i}) .$$

Similarly, $\hat{e}(h, c_\tau) \cdot \prod_{i=1}^n \hat{e}(\mathsf{u}_{i2}, c_{2i}) = \hat{e}(\mathsf{u}_\tau, g_2) \cdot \prod_{i=1}^n \hat{e}(\mathsf{u}'_{i2}, g_{2,\lambda_i})$ and $\hat{e}(g_1, c_\sigma c_\tau) \cdot \prod_{i=1}^n \hat{e}(\mathsf{u}_{i3}, c_{2i}) = \hat{e}(\mathsf{u}_\mu, g_2) \cdot \prod_{i=1}^n \hat{e}(\mathsf{u}'_{i3}, g_{2,\lambda_i})$. Thus all three verification equations hold, and therefore the simulator has succeeded in generating an argument that has the same distribution as the real argument.   □

Theorem 6. *Consider Prot. 4. The CRS consists of $2n + 2$ elements of $\mathbb{G}_1$ and $5n + 4$ elements of $\mathbb{G}_2$, in total $7n + 6$ group elements. The communication complexity is $2n + 6$ elements of $\mathbb{G}_1$ and $4n + 5$ elements of $\mathbb{G}_2$, in total $6n + 11$ group elements. The prover's computational complexity is dominated by $17n + 16$ exponentiations. The verifier's computational complexity is dominated by $28n + 18$ pairings.*

We note that in a mix server-like application where several shuffles are done sequentially, one can get somewhat smaller amortized cost. Namely, the output ciphertext u_i' of one shuffle is equal to the input ciphertext u_i of the following shuffle. Therefore, in step 3, one only has to check the correctness of the ciphertexts u_i' in the case of the very last shuffle. This means that the verifier's amortized computational complexity is dominated by $22n + 18$ pairings (that is, one has thus saved $6n$ pairings).

Acknowledgments. We would like to thank Jens Groth for insightful comments. The work was done while the second author was working at the University of Tartu. The authors were supported by Estonian Science Foundation, grant #9303, and European Union through the European Regional Development Fund.

References

1. Abe, M., Fehr, S.: Perfect NIZK with Adaptive Soundness. In: Vadhan, S.P. (ed.) TCC 2007. LNCS, vol. 4392, pp. 118–136. Springer, Heidelberg (2007)
2. Bayer, S., Groth, J.: Efficient Zero-Knowledge Argument for Correctness of a Shuffle. In: Pointcheval, D., Johansson, T. (eds.) EUROCRYPT 2012. LNCS, vol. 7237, pp. 263–280. Springer, Heidelberg (2012)
3. Boneh, D., Boyen, X., Shacham, H.: Short Group Signatures. In: Franklin, M. (ed.) CRYPTO 2004. LNCS, vol. 3152, pp. 41–55. Springer, Heidelberg (2004)
4. Chaabouni, R., Lipmaa, H., Zhang, B.: A Non-Interactive Range Proof with Constant Communication. In: Keromytis, A. (ed.) FC 2012, February 27-March 2. LNCS. Springer, Heidelberg (2012)
5. Clos, C.: A Study of Non-Blocking Switching Networks. Bell System Technical Journal 32(2), 406–424 (1953)
6. Damgård, I.: Towards Practical Public Key Systems Secure against Chosen Ciphertext Attacks. In: Feigenbaum, J. (ed.) CRYPTO 1991. LNCS, vol. 576, pp. 445–456. Springer, Heidelberg (1992)
7. Elkin, M.: An Improved Construction of Progression-Free Sets. Israeli Journal of Mathematics 184, 93–128 (2011)
8. Erdős, P., Turán, P.: On Some Sequences of Integers. Journal of the London Mathematical Society 11(4), 261–263 (1936)
9. Furukawa, J., Sako, K.: An Efficient Scheme for Proving a Shuffle. In: Kilian, J. (ed.) CRYPTO 2001. LNCS, vol. 2139, pp. 368–387. Springer, Heidelberg (2001)

10. Golle, P., Jarecki, S., Mironov, I.: Cryptographic Primitives Enforcing Communication and Storage Complexity. In: Blaze, M. (ed.) FC 2002. LNCS, vol. 2357, pp. 120–135. Springer, Heidelberg (2003)
11. Groth, J.: Linear Algebra with Sub-linear Zero-Knowledge Arguments. In: Halevi, S. (ed.) CRYPTO 2009. LNCS, vol. 5677, pp. 192–208. Springer, Heidelberg (2009)
12. Groth, J.: Short Pairing-Based Non-interactive Zero-Knowledge Arguments. In: Abe, M. (ed.) ASIACRYPT 2010. LNCS, vol. 6477, pp. 321–340. Springer, Heidelberg (2010)
13. Groth, J., Ishai, Y.: Sub-linear Zero-Knowledge Argument for Correctness of a Shuffle. In: Smart, N. (ed.) EUROCRYPT 2008. LNCS, vol. 4965, pp. 379–396. Springer, Heidelberg (2008)
14. Groth, J., Lu, S.: A Non-interactive Shuffle with Pairing Based Verifiability. In: Kurosawa, K. (ed.) ASIACRYPT 2007. LNCS, vol. 4833, pp. 51–67. Springer, Heidelberg (2007)
15. Groth, J., Ostrovsky, R., Sahai, A.: Perfect Non-interactive Zero Knowledge for NP. In: Vaudenay, S. (ed.) EUROCRYPT 2006. LNCS, vol. 4004, pp. 339–358. Springer, Heidelberg (2006)
16. Groth, J., Ostrovsky, R., Sahai, A.: New Techniques for Non-interactive Zero Knowledge (March 7, 2011), full version of [15]. Draft, available from the authors
17. Groth, J., Sahai, A.: Efficient Non-interactive Proof Systems for Bilinear Groups. In: Smart, N. (ed.) EUROCRYPT 2008. LNCS, vol. 4965, pp. 415–432. Springer, Heidelberg (2008)
18. Lipmaa, H.: Progression-Free Sets and Sublinear Pairing-Based Non-Interactive Zero-Knowledge Arguments. In: Cramer, R. (ed.) TCC 2012. LNCS, vol. 7194, pp. 169–189. Springer, Heidelberg (2012)
19. Lipmaa, H., Zhang, B.: A More Efficient Computationally Sound Non-Interactive Zero-Knowledge Shuffle Argument. Tech. Rep. 2011/394, International Association for Cryptologic Research (July 21, 2011), http://eprint.iacr.org/2011/394
20. Rial, A., Kohlweiss, M., Preneel, B.: Universally Composable Adaptive Priced Oblivious Transfer. In: Shacham, H., Waters, B. (eds.) Pairing 2009. LNCS, vol. 5671, pp. 231–247. Springer, Heidelberg (2009)
21. Sanders, T.: On Roth's Theorem on Progressions. Annals of Mathematics 174(1), 619–636 (2011)
22. Tao, T., Vu, V.: Additive Combinatorics. Cambridge Studies in Advanced Mathematics. Cambridge University Press (2006)
23. Terelius, B., Wikström, D.: Proofs of Restricted Shuffles. In: Bernstein, D.J., Lange, T. (eds.) AFRICACRYPT 2010. LNCS, vol. 6055, pp. 100–113. Springer, Heidelberg (2010)

A   Decisional Linear Assumption

We say that a bilinear group generator $\mathcal{G}_{\mathsf{bp}}$ is DLIN (decisional linear) secure [3] in group $\mathbb{G}_t$, for $t \in \{1, 2\}$, if for all non-uniform polynomial time adversaries $\mathcal{A}$, the following probability is negligible in κ:

$$\left| \Pr \begin{bmatrix} \mathsf{gk} \leftarrow \mathcal{G}_{\mathsf{bp}}(1^\kappa), \\ (f, h) \leftarrow (\mathbb{G}_t^*)^2, (\sigma, \tau) \leftarrow \mathbb{Z}_p^2 : \\ \mathcal{A}(\mathsf{gk}; f, h, f^\sigma, h^\tau, g_t^{\sigma+\tau}) = 1 \end{bmatrix} - \Pr \begin{bmatrix} \mathsf{gk} \leftarrow \mathcal{G}_{\mathsf{bp}}(1^\kappa), \\ (f, h) \leftarrow (\mathbb{G}_t^*)^2, (\sigma, \tau, z) \leftarrow \mathbb{Z}_p^3 : \\ \mathcal{A}(\mathsf{gk}; f, h, f^\sigma, h^\tau, g_t^z) = 1 \end{bmatrix} \right| .$$

B   Groth-Lu Co-soundness Definition

The Groth-Lu shuffle argument is proven to be R_{co}^{sh}-sound with respect to the next language [14] (here, as in [14], we assume the setting of symmetric pairings $\hat{e} : \mathbb{G} \times \mathbb{G} \to \mathbb{G}_T$, and like [14] we give the definition with respect to the BBS cryptosystem only):

$$R_{co}^{sh} := \left\{ \begin{array}{l} ((p, \mathbb{G}, \mathbb{G}_T, \hat{e}, g), (f, h, \{u_i\}, \{u_i'\}), \mathsf{sk} = (\mathsf{sk}_1, \mathsf{sk}_2)) : (x, y) \in (\mathbb{Z}_p^*)^2 \wedge \\ f = g^{\mathsf{sk}_1} \wedge h = g^{\mathsf{sk}_2} \wedge (\forall \psi \in S_n \exists i : \mathcal{Dec}_{\mathsf{sk}}(u_i') \neq \mathcal{Dec}_{\mathsf{sk}}(u_{\psi(i)})) \end{array} \right\}.$$

That is, the adversary is required to return not only a non-shuffle ($\{u_i\}, \{u_i'\}$), but also a secret key sk that makes it possible to verify efficiently that ($\{u_i\}, \{u_i'\}$) is really not a shuffle. As argued in [14], this definition of R_{co}^{sh} makes sense in practice, since there is always some coalition of the parties who knows the secret key. See [14] for more.

Active Security in Multiparty Computation over Black-Box Groups

Yvo Desmedt[1], Josef Pieprzyk[2], and Ron Steinfeld[3,*]

[1] Dept. of Computer Science, University College London, UK
y.desmedt@cs.ucl.ac.uk
[2] Centre for Advanced Computing – Algorithms and Cryptography (ACAC)
Dept. of Computing, Macquarie University, North Ryde, Australia
josef.pieprzyk@mq.edu.au
[3] Clayton School of Information Technology,
Monash University, Clayton, Australia
ron.steinfeld@monash.edu

Abstract. Most previous work on unconditionally secure multiparty computation has focused on computing over a finite field (or ring). Multiparty computation over other algebraic structures has not received much attention, but is an interesting topic whose study may provide new and improved tools for certain applications. At CRYPTO 2007, Desmedt et al introduced a construction for a passive-secure multiparty multiplication protocol for black-box groups, reducing it to a certain graph coloring problem, leaving as an open problem to achieve security against *active* attacks.

We present the first n-party protocol for unconditionally secure multiparty computation over a black-box group which is secure under an *active* attack model, tolerating any adversary structure Δ satisfying the Q^3 property (in which no union of three subsets from Δ covers the whole player set), which is known to be necessary for achieving security in the active setting. Our protocol uses Maurer's Verifiable Secret Sharing (VSS) but preserves the essential simplicity of the graph-based approach of Desmedt et al, which avoids each shareholder having to rerun the full VSS protocol after each local computation. A corollary of our result is a new active-secure protocol for general multiparty computation of an arbitrary Boolean circuit.

Keywords: Multi-Party Computation, General Adversary Structures, Non-Abelian Group, Black-Box, Graph Colouring, Active Security.

1 Introduction

Multiparty computation in the unconditionally secure model has been extensively studied in the cryptographic literature. The classical works [3,4] established secure protocols against threshold adversary structures (with the number

---

* Most of this work was done while R.S. was with Macquarie University.

I. Visconti and R. De Prisco (Eds.): SCN 2012, LNCS 7485, pp. 503–521, 2012.
© Springer-Verlag Berlin Heidelberg 2012

of corrupted parties $t < n/3$, which was shown optimal), and later protocols with improved efficiency and security against general adversary structures were presented [15,10,11,6,16,18,17,19,2,7]. Yet a common feature of those protocols is that they reduce general multiparty computation to performing addition and multiplication computations over a *field*. This raises the natural problem of realizing multiparty computation over other algebraic structures. The question is interesting not only intrinsically from a theoretical point of view, but may lead to new techniques that may have advantages over those used for multiparty computation over fields. Generalizations of the field-based protocols to work over a *ring* have been investigated (e.g. [5]), but the problem of performing multiparty computation over an arbitrary *group* has received less attention so far, with only passive-secure protocols known [9]. The problem of multiparty computation over a *non-abelian* group is of particular interest, since, as pointed out in [8], a result due to Barrington [1] (see Sec. 3.4) implies that multiparty computation over the non-abelian symmetric group S_5 is *complete* for general multiparty computation, i.e. it allows construction of secure computation protocols for *arbitrary* functions.

Let G denote a finite (multiplicatively written) group, and C denote a G-circuit, i.e. a circuit in which the inputs are elements of G and the allowed circuit gates are either a multiplication gate (taking two inputs in G and outputting their product in G) or a constant multiplication gate (taking an input in G and returning the input multiplied by some constant in G). A multiparty computation protocol for C over a black box group G [8] is an n-party protocol in which, for $i = 1, \ldots, m$, input $x_i \in G$ is held by one of the n parties, and at the end of the protocol, all parties hold $y = f_C(x_1, \ldots, x_m) \in G$, where f_C is the function over G computed by the G-circuit C. The protocol is said to be *black-box* if it treats the group G as a black-box: the only operations performed in the protocol are sampling random elements in G, multiplying elements in G and computing inverses in G.

Desmedt et al [9,8] introduced a novel construction for a black-box protocol for f_C, by reducing it to a certain graph coloring problem. The approach of [9] differs in an interesting way from classical multiparty computation protocols that work over fields and rings [3,4]. The latter protocols designed to handle an adversary structure Δ (specifying the collection of party subsets that may be corrupted) make use of a secret sharing scheme SS_Δ secure against adversary structure Δ; to multiply two circuit values shared among the parties using SS_Δ, each party does a local multiplication operation on its shares, and then performs a full SS_Δ sharing to reshare the result among *all* parties, who then perform a recombination operation to compute their new share. In contrast, in the group-based protocol of [9], two circuit values shared by a secret sharing scheme SS_Δ are multiplied by a sequence of *simple* resharing and combining operations specified by a colored communication graph; each of these sharing operations are typically much simpler that running a full resharing operation for SS_Δ (for instance, in the scheme of [9], a sharing operation just involves computing a 2-of-2 sharing of a group element and sending the two shares to two parties).

Unfortunately, the protocol of [9] only achieves security against passive adversaries, since it does not provide a way of verifying the correctness of the computations performed. It thus left the natural open problem of designing multiparty protocols over a black-box group secure against *active* adversaries.

Our Results. In this paper, we address the above-mentioned open problem. We present the first n-party protocol for unconditionally secure multiparty computation over a black-box group G which is secure under an *active* attack model. Our protocol achieves the *optimal* resilience in the active setting, namely it is can tolerate any adversary structure Δ satisfying the Q^3 property, in which no union of three subsets from Δ covers the whole player set, which is known to be necessary for achieving security in the active setting [15]. The communication complexity of our protocol for computing a G-circuit C is $O(|C| \cdot M(\Delta)^2 \cdot \text{poly}(n))$ group elements, where $M(\Delta)$ denotes the number of maximal sets in the adversary structure Δ, and $|C|$ denotes the size of C.

A corollary of our result is a new active-secure protocol for securely computing an arbitrary Boolean circuit C, via Barrington's result mentioned above, with communication complexity $O(|C| \cdot M(\Delta)^2 \cdot \text{poly}(n))$ bits. Note that a similar communication complexity proportional to $M(\Delta)^2$ is achieved in [20] but using a completely different field-based approach.

Our construction is based on an extension of the communication graph approach used in [9]. However, whereas in [9] each node in the graph is assigned a single color corresponding to the party that performs a multiplication and resharing computation at that node, in our protocol each edge is assigned a *subset* of colors corresponding to a subset of players that send or receive shares along the edge and jointly participate in the computation performed at the graph nodes adjacent to the edge. To ensure the validity of the initial input sharing, we use Maurer's simple construction of a Verifiable Secret Sharing (VSS) scheme [19], which works over a black-box group. At each internal node of our graph, the correctness of the computation is verified by a multiparty pairwise comparison protocol inspired by Maurer's field-based multiplication protocol from [19].

Interestingly, unlike Maurer's field-based multiplication protocol in [19], our protocol retains the essential simplicity of the resharing operations used at each node of the graph in the protocol of [9]: each party in the subset of players assigned to a node in our protocol does *not* rerun the VSS sharing protocol for resharing the intermediate protocol multiplication values at each node, but uses just a 2-of-2 sharing of its output value, and consequently has an efficiency advantage over Maurer's protocol when applied to computing Boolean circuits (see Sec. 3.4 for more details). Please note however, that similarly to Maurer's protocol in [19], we do not claim that our Boolean circuit protocol offers any asymptotic complexity advantages over previous field-based protocols for Boolean circuit computation. Indeed, the field-based protocol from [20] offers a similar asymptotic complexity for general adversary structures, and the protocols from [3,4] are asymptotically significantly more efficient for threshold structures.

Rather, we view it mainly as an illustration of the power of our protocols over black-box groups.

Due to limited space, the proofs of some results have been omitted from this version of the paper. They can be found the full version, available from the authors' web page.

Open Problems. A central and interesting open problem left by our work is to construct an active-secure protocol over black box groups tolerating a more restricted but useful class of adversary structures, such as a t-of-n threshold adversary structure, while achieving a communication complexity *polynomial* in n. Currently, we do not see how to adapt our approach to achieve this goal, and it seems to require new ideas. In particular, there seems to be an inherent contradiction between the requirement to have at least $2t + 1$ colors assigned to each edge in our protocol graph (in order to achieve an honest majority at the node and thus ensure correctness of the computation at the node) and the optimal resilience condition $n = 3t + 1$, which means that each edge excludes a *unique* t-subset of parties. The security of our approach (like that of [9]) against a t-subset I of parties requires the existence of an I-avoiding path in the graph whose edges exclude I. Thus if each edge excludes only a unique t-subset, that edge can be used for only one I-avoiding path, whereas in a polynomial-sized graph, each edge must be re-used for exponentially many paths, since there are exponentially many t-subsets I.

Other Related Work. Sun et al [21] gave improvements to the graph coloring constructions of Desmedt et al [9], showing them to be polynomial-sized for certain resilience cases. These apply to the 't-reliable' coloring notion needed for the passive-secure protocols in [9], but do not seem applicable to our stronger 'Δ-active-reliable' coloring notion that we use to achieve active-security, and involves coloring the graph edges with $2t+1$-subsets of colors. As discussed above, this notion seems to require exponential-sized graphs. Barrington's encoding of Boolean circuits into S_5 was used in secure multiparty computation already in 1987 [14]. However, the security achieved in [14] was in the computationally bounded attack model, while in [8] and in this paper, the security achieved is against computationally unbounded attacks.

2   Preliminaries

2.1   Active Attack Model

We first recall the formal definition of secure multi-party computation in the active (malicious), computationally unbounded attack model, restricted to deterministic symmetric functionalities and perfect emulation [13]. The number of parties participating in the protocol is denoted by n, and the parties are denoted by $P_1, \ldots, P_n$. We assume a general static party corruption model specified an *adversary structure* Δ, which is a (monotone) collection of subsets of the player index set $[n] = \{1, \ldots, n\}$, corresponding to the player subsets that may be corrupted. It is known [15] that secure multiparty computation in the active computationally unbounded model is possible for an adversary structure Δ if and only if Δ has the Q^3 property, i.e. $[n] \neq I_1 \cup I_2 \cup I_3$ for all $I_1, I_2, I_3 \in \Delta$.

The uncorrupted players are assumed to correctly follow the protocol, whereas the corrupted players can behave arbitrarily and are allowed to communicate with each other. Also, every pair of parties can communicate via a private authenticated channel (meaning that communication between two parties P_i and P_j cannot be eavesdropped by any other party, and that when P_i receives a message from P_j, P_i knows that the message was sent by P_j; moreover, an honest player P_i can detect that an expected message from P_j has not arrived - in this case, we assume that P_i substitutes a certain 'default' message, as specified in the protocol).

Security in the active model must guarantee not only the *privacy* of the inputs held by the honest parties (as in the passive case), but also the *correctness* of the protocol output computed by the honest parties. But note that perfect correctness can never be achieved in the following sense: regardless of the protocol, nothing can prevent an adversary-controlled party P_i from ignoring its protocol input x_i and *substituting* a different value x_i' when participating in the protocol. Accordingly, the security definition is constructed to ensure that this *substitution* "attack" is essentially the only attack possible on correctness of the protocol (in particular, it ensures that the substituted value x_i' cannot depend on the values of honest party inputs). To achieve this, the security definition compares the execution of the real protocol in question (called the REAL model), to the execution of an idealized protocol involving an honest trusted entity in addition to the parties running the protocol (called the IDEAL model). In the IDEAL model, each party privately sends its (possibly substituted) protocol input to the honest trusted entity. The trusted entity evaluates the desired function f on the inputs it received and sends the result back to all parties. It is clear that in the IDEAL model, the 'substitution' attack is the only possible attack. So, a protocol is said to be secure if for every adversary $\mathcal{A}$ in the REAL model, there is an adversary B in the IDEAL model which produces the same output distribution (for the honest parties and the adversary). We now present the formal definition.

Definition 1. *Let $f : (\{0,1\}^*)^n \to \{0,1\}^*$ denote an n-input, single-output function, and let $\prod$ be an n-party protocol for computing f. We denote the party input sequence by $\boldsymbol{x} = (x_1, \ldots, x_n)$, and the projection of the n-ary sequence $\boldsymbol{x}$ on the coordinates in $I \subseteq [n]$ by $\boldsymbol{x}_I$. Let $\mathcal{A}$ denote a REAL model adversary against protocol $\prod$, where $\mathcal{A}$ controls a subset $I \in \Delta$ of corrupted parties. Let $\mathrm{OUT}^{\prod}_{I,A}(\boldsymbol{x})$ (respectively $\mathrm{OUT}^{\prod}_{[n]\setminus I,A}(\boldsymbol{x})$) denote the vector of outputs of the corrupted players P_i with $i \in I$ using some standard ordering (respectively, the list of outputs of honest players P_i with $i \in [n] \setminus I$ using some standard ordering) after running protocol $\prod$ on input $\boldsymbol{x}$, with $\mathcal{A}$ run on input $(\boldsymbol{x}_I, I)$ and controlling parties P_i for $i \in I$.*

We say that $\prod$ is a Δ-secure protocol for computing f if, for every REAL model adversary $\mathcal{A}$, there exists an IDEAL model adversary $B = (B_1, B_2)$ such that, for all $I \in \Delta$ and for all $\boldsymbol{x} \in (\{0,1\}^*)^n$, the random variables $\mathrm{REAL}^{\prod}_{I,A}(\boldsymbol{x})$

and $\mathsf{IDEAL}^f_{I,B}(x)$ are identically distributed, where we define:

$$\mathsf{REAL}^\Pi_{I,A}(x) = (\mathsf{OUT}^\Pi_{[n]\setminus I,A}(x), \mathsf{OUT}^\Pi_{I,A}(x))$$

and

$$\mathsf{IDEAL}^f_{I,B}(x) = (f(x')^{n-t}, B_2(x_I, I, f(x'); r))$$

with $x' = (x'_1, \ldots, x'_n)$, $x'_i = B_1(x_I, I, i; r)$ for $i \in I$ and $x'_i = x_i$ for $i \in [n] \setminus I$. Here, r is the (common) uniformly random coins input of deterministic algorithms B_1 and B_2.

Note that in the IDEAL model adversary $B = (B_1, B_2)$ in the above definition, algorithm B_1 performs the substitution of corrupted player inputs, whereas B_2 simulates the output of the corrupted players. The first component of $\mathsf{IDEAL}_{I,B}(x)$, namely $f(x')^{n-t}$ represents the $n-t$ outputs of the honest players indexed by $[n] \setminus I$ in the IDEAL model; these outputs are all equal to $f(x')$.

2.2 Maurer's Simple Verifiable Secret Sharing Scheme

Our protocol makes use of a Verifiable Secret Sharing (VSS) scheme due to Maurer [19], which works over any black-box group. We now recall this scheme.

First, we recall the definition of VSS. It is an adaptation of standard secret sharing to the active-security setting, in which both the dealer and some shareholders may be actively corrupted.

Definition 2 (VSS). *A VSS scheme is run among n parties $P_1, \ldots, P_n$, one of which is the* dealer. *The players with indices in $I \in \Delta$ (possibly including the dealer) are actively corrupted, and all other players honestly follow the protocol. It consists of two protocols: a sharing protocol* **VSS Share** *used by the dealer to distribute shares of his secret among all parties, and a* **VSS Reconstruct** *protocol used by the shareholders to reconstruct the secret. The protocols satisfy the following conditions:*

- *Unique Reconstruction: At the end of a run of the* **VSS Share** *protocol, the dealer is committed to a unique secret s, in the following sense: a subsequent run of* **VSS Reconstruct** *ends with all honest parties returning the value s.*
- *Honest Dealer Correctness: If the dealer is honest with secret s,* **VSS Reconstruct** *ends with all honest parties returning the value s.*
- *Honest Dealer Privacy: If the dealer is honest, the distribution of the adversary's view during the* **VSS Share** *protocol is independent of the dealer's secret s.*

Let us now recall Maurer's simple VSS scheme [19] for adversary structure Δ. We denote by $M(\Delta)$ the number of *maximal* sets in Δ. Below, G denotes any (black-box) group. Also note that, if Δ is Q^3, a broadcast from one player to all players (as used below) can be simulated with communication polynomial in n using only point to point communication links between any pair of players [12].

Protocol 1 Maurer's **VSS Share**

Input: Dealer holds a secret $s \in G$.

1: Let $\ell = M(\Delta)$ and $I_1, \ldots, I_\ell$ denote the sequence of all maximal sets in Δ (in some ordering).
2: Dealer chooses uniformly random shares $s_1, \ldots, s_\ell$ in G such that $s_1 s_2 \cdots s_\ell = s$.
3: For $i \in [\ell]$, dealer sends s_i to each party P_j with $j \in [n] \setminus I_i$.
4: For $i \in [\ell]$, every pair of parties P_j, P_k with $j, k \in [n] \setminus I_i$ check (by exchanging values) whether their received values of s_i agree. If any party detects a disagreement, it broadcasts a complaint.
5: Dealer broadcasts to all parties all shares s_i for which a complaint was broadcast.

Output: Party P_j holds shares $\{s_i : j \in [n] \setminus I_i\}$, for $j \in [n]$.

Protocol 2 Maurer's **VSS Reconstruct**

Input: Party P_j holds shares $\{s_i : j \in [n] \setminus I_i\}$, for $j \in [n]$.

1: For $j \in [n]$, party P_j sends its shares $\{s_i : j \in [n] \setminus I_i\}$, to every other party.
2: For $i \in [\ell]$, each party P reconstructs s_i as the unique value v for which there exists a $J \in \Delta$ such that P received v as the value of s_i in the previous step from all parties P_j with $j \in [n] \setminus (I_i \cup J)$.
3: Each party reconstructs $s = s_1 \cdots s_\ell$, where for $i \in [\ell]$, s_i is the value reconstructed in the previous step.

Output: Party P_j holds secret s, for $j \in [n]$.

Theorem 1 ([19]). *If Δ is Q^3, then Maurer's **VSS Share** and **VSS Reconstruct** protocols form a VSS scheme (i.e. secure against adversary structure Δ). The communication complexity of **VSS Share** and **VSS Reconstruct** is $O(M(\Delta) \cdot poly(n))$ group elements.*

2.3 G-Circuits

We recall the definition of G-circuits. In the following, for a group G, we define an m-input 1-output G-circuit C as a circuit (directed acyclic graph) with m input nodes, one output node, and two types of gates (corresponding to all other circuit nodes):

1. Mult: Given two inputs x and y in G, the gate output is $x \cdot y \in G$[1]
2. CMult$_{\alpha,\beta}$: Given one input $x \in G$, the gate output is $\alpha \cdot x \cdot \beta \in G$ (note that the constants $\alpha, \beta \in G$ are built into the gate).

We denote by $f_C : G^m \to G$ the function computed by the G-circuit C.

---

[1] The incoming edges to Mult gates need to be labeled to indicate which one is the left input.

3 Our New Protocol

First, in Sec. 3.1, we reduce the G-circuit computation protocol problem (in which at the beginning, each party holds $x_i \in G$, and at the end each party holds the circuit output) to the Shared 2-Product protocol problem (in which at the beginning, the parties hold shares of two elements $x, y \in G$, and at the end, the parties holds shares of $z = x \cdot y$). This part of our protocol is almost identical to that of [9]. Then, in Sec. 3.2, we show how to construct a Shared 2-Product protocol, using a suitable coloring of a certain planar graph. In this part we introduce significant modifications to the protocol in [9] to handle active attacks.

3.1 Construction of G-Circuit Protocol from a Shared 2-Product Subprotocol

We begin by reducing the problem of constructing a Δ-private protocol for computing an m-input G-circuit computing a function $f_C(x_1, \ldots, x_m)$ (where each input x_i is held by one of the parties), to the problem of constructing a subprotocol for the *Shared* 2-Product function $f'_G(x, y) = x \cdot y$, where inputs x, y and output $z = x \cdot y$ are shared among the parties. We define for this subprotocol *active* correctness and strong Δ-security properties, which strengthen the correctness and strong Δ-privacy of the passive model in [9] to the active case. In the definition below, the share ownership functions $\mathcal{O}_x, \mathcal{O}_y, \mathcal{O}_z$ specify for each share index $j \in [\ell]$, the indices of the sets of players $\mathcal{O}_x(j), \mathcal{O}_y(j), \mathcal{O}_z(j) \subseteq [n]$ which hold the jth input shares $s_x(j)$ and $s_y(j)$ and jth output share $s_z(j)$, respectively.

Definition 3 (Shared n-Party 2-Product Subprotocol). *A n-Party Shared 2-Product subprotocol $\prod_S$ with sharing parameter ℓ and share ownership functions $\mathcal{O}_x, \mathcal{O}_y, \mathcal{O}_z : [\ell] \to 2^{[n]}$ has the following features:*

- *Input: For $j \in [\ell]$, each party in set $\mathcal{O}_x(j)$ holds jth share $s_x(j) \in G$ of x, and each party in set $\mathcal{O}_y(j)$ holds jth share $s_y(j) \in G$ of y, where $x \overset{\mathrm{def}}{=} s_x(1) \cdot s_x(2) \cdots s_x(\ell)$ and $y \overset{\mathrm{def}}{=} s_y(1) \cdot s_y(2) \cdots s_y(\ell)$, respectively.*
- *Output: For $j \in [\ell]$, each party in set $\mathcal{O}_z(j)$ holds jth share $s_z(j)$ of output $z \overset{\mathrm{def}}{=} s_z(1) \cdots s_z(\ell)$.*
- *Active-Correctness: We say that $\prod_S$ is **active-correct** if it has the following property. Suppose that, at the beginning of the protocol, for $j \in [\ell]$, all honest parties in set $\mathcal{O}_x(j)$ (resp. $\mathcal{O}_y(j)$) hold the same input share $s_x(j)$ (resp. $s_y(j)$), defining protocol inputs $x = s_x(1) \cdots s_x(\ell)$ and $y = s_y(1) \cdots s_y(\ell)$. Then, at the end of the protocol, for each $j \in [\ell]$, all honest parties in set $\mathcal{O}_z(j)$ hold the same output share $s_z(j)$ defining protocol output $z = s_z(1) \cdots s_z(\ell)$, and $z = x \cdot y$ holds.*
- *Strong Δ-Security: Let $\mathcal{A}$ denote a REAL model adversary against subprotocol $\prod_S$, where $\mathcal{A}$ controls a subset $I \in \Delta$ of corrupted parties. Let $I_x = \{j \in [\ell] : (\mathcal{O}_x(j) \cap I) \neq \emptyset\}$ and $I_y = \{j \in [\ell] : (\mathcal{O}_y(j) \cap I) \neq \emptyset\}$.*

Let $\mathcal{A}^{\prod_S(s_x, s_y)}(\{s_x(j)\}_{j \in I_x}, \{s_y(j)\}_{j \in I_y}, z_{aux})$ denote the output state of $\mathcal{A}$ at the end of a run of subprotocol $\prod_S$ with protocol inputs s_x, s_y, in which $\mathcal{A}$ is run on input $(\{s_x(j)\}_{j \in I_x}, \{s_y(j)\}_{j \in I_y}, z_{aux})$, where z_{aux} is an auxiliary input (representing the adversary's input state), and let $s_z(j)$ denote the jth output share held by the honest parties in set $\mathcal{O}_z(j)$ at the end of this run. We say that $\prod_S$ achieves **strong Δ-security** if, for every $I \in \Delta$, there exist $j_x^*, j_y^*, j_z^* \in [\ell]$ with $j_z^* \in \{j_x^*, j_y^*\}$ and sets $\mathcal{O}_x(j_x^*), \mathcal{O}_y(j_y^*), \mathcal{O}_z(j_z^*)$ all disjoint from I, such that for every active adversary $\mathcal{A}$ against $\prod_S$ corrupting parties P_i for $i \in I$, there exists a probabilistic simulator algorithm S such that for all protocol inputs s_x, s_y and auxiliary inputs z_{aux}, the random variables $\mathsf{REAL}_{I,\mathcal{A}}^{\prod_S}$ and $\mathsf{SIM}_{I,S}^{\prod_S}$ are identically distributed. Here, we define:

$$\mathsf{REAL}_{I,\mathcal{A}}^{\prod_S} = \langle \mathcal{A}^{\prod_S(s_x, s_y)}(\{s_x(j)\}_{j \in I_x}, \{s_y(j)\}_{j \in I_y}, z_{aux}), \{s_z(j)\}_{j \in [\ell] \setminus \{j_z^*\}} \rangle,$$

$$\mathsf{SIM}_{I,S}^{\prod_S} = \mathsf{S}(I, \{\mathbf{s}_x(j)\}_{j \in [\ell] \setminus \{j_x^*\}}, \{\mathbf{s}_y(j)\}_{j \in [\ell] \setminus \{j_y^*\}}, z_{aux}).$$

If $j_z^* = j_x^*$ (resp. $j_z^* = j_y^*$) then we say $\prod_S$ achieves x-**preserving strong Δ-security** (resp. y-**preserving strong Δ-security**). If $j_z^* = j_x^* = j_y^*$ for all I, then we say $\prod_S$ achieves **symmetric strong Δ-security**.

Remark. In the above definition, the simulator S must simulate both the output of $\mathcal{A}$ and all but one of the output shares $s_z(j)$, given all but one of the x-input (resp. y-input) shares $s_x(j)$ (resp. $s_y(j)$).

Our construction of an active-secure G-circuit computation protocol $\prod_a(C, \prod_S)$ given a G-circuit C with m input nodes, and a Shared 2-Product subprotocol $\prod_S$, runs similarly to the corresponding passive construction in [9], except that here, the secrets x_i are shared out using Maurer's VSS scheme, and each share is held by a set of parties, rather than a single party. Due to space limitations, we defer the formal specification of protocol $\prod_a(C, \prod_S)$ to the full version of the paper. We assume that $\prod_S$ satisfies symmetric strong Δ-security, with sharing parameter ℓ and share ownership functions $\mathcal{O}_x = \mathcal{O}_y = \mathcal{O}_z$ (for simplicity, we do not consider here the more general case of x-preserving or y-preserving strong Δ-security as in [9] since our constructions for Π_S in later sections satisfy symmetric strong Δ-security). Since our protocol makes use of Maurer's VSS scheme (see Sec. 2.2), we also assume here for compatibility that the sharing parameter $\ell = M(\Delta)$, and that $\mathcal{O}_x(i) = [n] \setminus I_i$, for $i \in [\ell]$, where I_i is the ith t-subset of $[n]$ (in some ordering), as used in Maurer's VSS scheme. Below, for $i \in [m]$, we let $j(i) \in [n]$ denote the index of the party holding the ith circuit input x_i.

The following lemma establishes the Δ-security of protocol $\prod_a(T, \prod_S)$, assuming the active-correctness and strong Δ-security of subprotocol $\prod_S$. The IDEAL model adversary in the proof makes use of the unique reconstruction property of the VSS scheme to reconstruct from the shares held by the honest parties, the 'substituted' input values x_i' committed by the corrupted players during the dealing phase of the VSS. The IDEAL model adversary then simulates the view of the corrupted parties at each node of the tree T by using the known inputs to the subprotocol run at the node as input to the simulator associated to subprotocol Π_S thanks to its strong Δ-security. This lemma can be viewed as an extension of Lemma 3 in [9] to the active attack setting. Its proof can be found in the full version.

Lemma 1. *For any G-circuit C, if the n-party Shared 2-Product subprotocol $\prod_S$ satisfies active-correctness and symmetric strong Δ-security, then the protocol $\prod_a(C, \prod_S)$ is an n-party Δ-secure protocol for computing function f_C computed by C.*

3.2   Construction of a *t*-Secure Shared 2-Product Subprotocol from a *t*-Active-Reliable Coloring

We now show how to reduce the problem of constructing a t-Private n-Party Shared 2-Product Subprotocol $\prod_S$ to a certain combinatorial coloring problem for a planar graph. In contrast to the coloring in [9] in which graph *nodes* are assigned colors, our coloring assigns colors to graph *edges*. More significantly, whereas in [9] each node was assigned a *single color* from $[n]$ denoting the index of the party performing computation at that node, we assign a *subset* of colors from $[n]$ to each edge, denoting the indices of parties receiving the share sent along the edge, and participating in the computation at the node that the edge is directed towards. Our construction is specific to the PDAG $\mathcal{G}_{grid}(\ell)$ shown in Fig. 1, with $\ell = M(\Delta)$, the number of maximal sets in the adversary structure Δ. The node rows (resp. columns) of $\mathcal{G}_{grid}(\ell)$ are numbered consecutively from

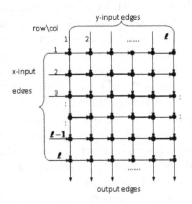

Fig. 1. The PDAG $\mathcal{G}_{grid}(\ell)$

1 to ℓ from top to bottom (resp. left to right). We label the edges of $\mathcal{G}_{grid}(\ell)$ as follows: the label (i, j, d) denotes the edge of $\mathcal{G}_{grid}(\ell)$ which is directed into the node in the ith row and jth column in the direction $d \in \{H, V\}$ (horizontal if $d = H$ or vertical if $d = V$). An exception is that $(\ell + 1, j, V)$ denotes the jth outgoing edge of the node in row ℓ and column j. Note also that the nodes on column ℓ do not have horizontal outgoing edges. We call the horizontal incoming

edges to the leftmost column the *x-input edges* (and edge $(\ell+1-j, 1, H)$ is called the jth x-input edge), the vertical incoming edges to the top row the *y-input edges* (and edge $(1, j, V)$ is called the jth y-input edge), and the vertical outgoing edges in the bottom row the *output edges* (and edge $(\ell+1, j, V)$ is called the jth output edge).

Let $C : [\ell+1] \times [\ell] \times \{H, V\} \rightarrow 2^{[n]}$ be an n-Active-Reliable coloring function that associates to each edge (i, j, d) a color subset $C(i, j, d)$ from the set of n possible colors $[n]$. We now define the notion of a Δ-active-reliable n-coloring, which may be viewed as an 'active' variant of the t-reliable coloring in [9].

Definition 4 (Δ-active-reliable n-coloring). *We say that $C : [\ell+1] \times [\ell] \times \{H, V\} \rightarrow 2^{[n]}$ is a Δ-active-reliable n-coloring for PDAG $\mathcal{G}_{grid}(\ell)$ if $C(i, j, H) \cap C(i, j, V) \notin \Delta$ and $C(i, j, d) \neq I_1 \cup I_2$ for all i, j, d and $I_1, I_2 \in \Delta$, and, for each $I \in \Delta$, there exists $j^* \in [\ell]$ and:*

- *A path $PATH_x$ in $\mathcal{G}_{grid}(\ell)$ from the j^*th x-input edge (i.e. edge $(\ell+1-j^*, 1, H)$) to the j^*th output edge (i.e. edge $(\ell+1, j^*, V)$), such that all edges (i, j, d) along the path have color sets $C(i, j, d)$ disjoint from the subset I (we call such a path I-avoiding), and*
- *An I-avoiding path $PATH_y$ in $\mathcal{G}_{grid}(\ell)$ from the j^*th y-input edge (i.e. edge $(1, j^*, V)$) and the j^*th output edge (i.e. edge $(\ell+1, j^*, V)$).*

If the jth x-input, y-input and output edges are assigned the same color subset by C for all $j \in [\ell]$ (i.e. $C(1, j, V) = C(\ell+1-j, 1, H) = C(\ell+1, j, V)$ for $j \in [\ell]$), then we say that C is a symmetric Δ-active-reliable n-coloring.

Given a Δ-active-reliable coloring for PDAG $\mathcal{G}_{grid}$, our Shared 2-Product protocol $\Pi_S(\mathcal{G}_{grid}, C)$ is given below as Protocol 3.

Our protocol makes use of a subprotocol **NodeMult** that is run at each node of the graph $\mathcal{G}_{grid}$ and given below as Protocol 4. At each protocol step, if a party P_i expects to receive a group element a from some other party P_j, and P_i does not receive the group element (because P_j is corrupted and sends nothing), we assume that P_i substitutes the default value 1 for the element a.

Theorem 2. *If C is a symmetric Δ-active-reliable n-coloring for $\mathcal{G}_{grid}(\ell)$ then Shared 2-Product protocol $\prod_S(\mathcal{G}_{grid}(\ell), C)$ achieves active-correctness and strong Δ-security.*

The proof of Theorem 2 is based on the properties of the **NodeMult** protocol stated in Lemma 2 below. Due to limited space, the proofs of Lemma 2 and Theorem 2 are deferred to the full version of this paper. Here, we provide an informal overview of the protocol and its security analysis.

Informal overview of protocol $\Pi_S(\mathcal{G}_{grid}, C)$. The edges of $\mathcal{G}_{grid}$ are labeled with shares sent in the protocol, the nodes of $\mathcal{G}_{grid}$ represent multiplication operations on the shares labelling the incoming edges to the node, and the node product is then reshared along the node outgoing edges. The color subsets assigned by coloring C indicate the indices of players receiving the shares sent along the edge, and the multiplication and resharing computations at each node are performed by the subprotocol **NodeMult** among these parties.

Given a simulatable **NodeMult** subprotocol that produces at each node's outgoing edges a fresh resharing of the product of the incoming edge shares, the Δ-security of $\Pi_S(\mathcal{G}_{grid}, C)$ follows from the existence of adversary-avoiding input-output paths in PDAG $\mathcal{G}_{grid}$ (these paths are guaranteed to exist by the Δ-active-reliable property of coloring C). Thanks to the fresh resharing at each node, the output shares sent along outgoing edges not on the adversary-avoiding paths can be simulated by independent random elements.

The main novelty in our protocol versus the passive-secure protocol in [9] is in the design of the **NodeMult** subprotocol. The fact that each edge share is held by a set of parties containing a sufficiently large subset of honest parties, allows us to design appropriate correctness verification checks in **NodeMult** (reminiscent of those in Maurer's robust multiplication protocol [19] over a field) that ensure the correctness of the computation at each node (whereas in the protocol in [9], each node computation is performed by a single party and may fail if the corresponding party is actively corrupted). An interesting aspect of our protocol is that **NodeMult** verification checks can ensure the correctness of the computation *without* having to rerun the full VSS resharing protocol at each node (only a simple 2-of-2 resharing is needed), whereas in Maurer's multiplication protocol, each pairwise product of shares has to be reshared with a VSS, leading to a lower efficiency. The **NodeMult** protocol is run at each internal node of the graph $\mathcal{G}_{grid}(\ell)$. Before the protocol is run, the parties in the set S (labeling the horizontal incoming edge to the node) each hold a share $s \in G$ and the parties in the set T (labeling the vertical incoming edge to the node) each hold a share $t \in G$. The purpose of the protocol is to compute $s \cdot t$ and reshare this product as $a \cdot b$ where a and b are fresh shares. Accordingly, at the end of the protocol, each of the parties in the set A (labeling the outgoing vertical edge) all hold the share $a \in G$ and each of the parties in the set B (labeling the outgoing horizontal edge) all hold the share $b \in G$, such that $a \cdot b = s \cdot t$. Note that in the coloring construction presented in the next section, we have $A = T$ and $B = S$. The protocol runs in two phases.

In the first phase (lines 1 to 11), each party P_k that holds *both* incoming shares s and t (i.e. each party P_k in $S \cap T$) computes $s \cdot t$ and a fresh resharing of this value (a_k, b_k) with $a_k \cdot b_k = s \cdot t$ (note that by construction of S and T from the Δ-active-reliable coloring it is guaranteed that $S \cap T \notin \Delta$ so $S \cap T$ contains at least one *honest* party). Each P_k privately sends its share a_k (resp. b_k) to each party in A (resp. B), and then the parties in A (resp. B) check by doing pairwise comparisons that they all hold the same value of a_k (resp. b_k) for all k. If an inconsistency is detected, the value of a_k (resp. b_k) is broadcast by P_k to all parties. This doesn't violate privacy because it only happens when some party who received or sent a_k (resp. b_k) was corrupted. In the second phase (lines 12 to 26), the parties in A and B check that the sharings (a_k, b_k) define the same secret for all values of k, i.e. $a_k \cdot b_k = a_1 \cdot b_1$ for all k. This check is equivalent to checking that $a_k^{-1} \cdot a_1 = b_k \cdot b_1^{-1}$ for all k and the latter check is done (in lines 12-16) by a pairwise comparison between every pair of parties, one from A (who holds $a_k^{-1} \cdot a_1$) and one from B (who holds $b_k b_1^{-1}$). If the tests pass then a_1, b_1 is taken to be the protocol output sharing, which is known to be correct, since one of the a_k, b_k have been correctly shared by the honest party in $S \cap T$, and $a_k \cdot b_k = a_1 \cdot b_1$ (and privacy is preserved since the parties only receive values they already have). Otherwise, if the test fails for some k, the players in A (resp. B) broadcast the values of $a_k^{-1} \cdot a_1$ (resp. $b_k b_1^{-1}$) and the values broadcast by the honest parties in A (resp. B) are compared. The values Hon_A^k (resp. Hon_B^k) broadcast by the honest parties can be deduced uniquely by the assumption that A (resp. B) cannot be covered by a union of two subsets in Δ (which in turn follows from the Δ-active-reliable property of coloring C). If they are equal, the test failure complaint was made falsely by a corrupted party, so it is ignored. Otherwise, if they are not equal, one of the parties P_k in $S \cap T$ must be corrupted. In this case, the corrupted parties already know both s and t so there is no privacy requirement, and the protocol *backtracks*: the parties in S (resp. T) broadcast the value of s (resp. t) to all parties, and output shares are defined to be $s \cdot t$ and 1, respectively, using the values of s and t broadcast by honest parties in S (resp. T).

Protocol 3 Shared 2-Product Protocol $\prod_S(\mathcal{G}_{grid}(\ell), C)$

Input: For $j = 1, \ldots, \ell$, parties P_i with $i \in \mathcal{O}_x(j)$ hold jth share $s_x(j) \in G$ of x and jth share $s_y(j) \in G$ of y, where $\mathbf{s}_x = (s_x(1), s_x(2), \ldots, s_x(\ell))$ and $\mathbf{s}_y = (s_y(1), s_y(2), \ldots, s_y(\ell))$ denote ℓ-of-ℓ sharing of $x \stackrel{\text{def}}{=} s_x(1) \cdot s_x(2) \cdots s_x(\ell)$ and $y \stackrel{\text{def}}{=} s_y(1) \cdot s_y(2) \cdots s_y(\ell)$, respectively. (We assume that C is a symmetric Δ-active-reliable n-coloring of $\mathcal{G}_{grid}(\ell)$, and define $\mathcal{O}_x(j) \stackrel{\text{def}}{=} C(1, j, V) = C(\ell+1-j, 1, H) = C(\ell+1, j, V)$).

1: Define input edge labels $v(\ell+1-j, 1, H) = s_x(j)$ and $v(1, j, V) = s_y(j)$ for $j \in [\ell]$.

2:

3: **for** $i = 1$ to ℓ **do**

4:

5:   **for** $j = 1$ to ℓ **do**

6:     Run protocol **NodeMult** with input share $s = v(i, j, H)$ held by party set $S = C(i, j, H)$ and input share $t = v(i, j, V)$ held by party set $T = C(i, j, V)$, and output party sets $A = C(i+1, j, V)$ and $B = C(i, j+1, H)$ if $j < \ell$ or $B = A$ if $j = \ell$. The protocol ends with output share a held by party set A and output share b held by party set B, with $a \cdot b = s \cdot t$.

7:     Define labels $v(i+1, j, V) \stackrel{\text{def}}{=} a$ for edge $(i+1, j, V)$ (or $v(i+1, j, V) = a \cdot b$ if $j = \ell$) and, if $j < \ell$, label $v(i, j+1, H) \stackrel{\text{def}}{=} b$ for edge $(i, j+1, H)$.

8:   **end for**

9: **end for**

Output: For $j = 1, \ldots, \ell$, parties P_i with $i \in \mathcal{O}_x(j)$ hold jth share $s_z(j) \stackrel{\text{def}}{=} v(\ell+1, j, V) \in G$ of $z = x \cdot y$.

Lemma 2. *Assume that $S \cap T \notin \Delta$ and none of S, T, A, B are equal to the union of two sets from Δ. Then protocol **NodeMult**(s, t, S, T, A, B) satisfies the following properties, for all protocol inputs s, t, all $I \in \Delta$ and every active adversary $\mathcal{A}$ corrupting parties P_i for $i \in I$:*

– *Correctness: If, at the beginning of the protocol, all honest parties P_i with $i \in S$ (resp. $i \in T$) hold the same share s (resp. t), then at the end of the* *protocol, all honest parties P_i with $i \in A$ (resp. $i \in B$) hold the same share a (resp. b), with $a \cdot b = s \cdot t$.*

- *Security: Let $in_{\mathcal{A}}^I \subseteq \{s, t\}$ denote the protocol inputs given to $\mathcal{A}$, i.e. $s \in in_{\mathcal{A}}^I$ (resp. $t \in in_{\mathcal{A}}^I$) if $S \cap I \neq \emptyset$ (resp. if $T \cap I \neq \emptyset$). Similarly, let $out_{\mathcal{A}}^I \subseteq \{a, b\}$ denote the protocol outputs given to $\mathcal{A}$, i.e. $a \in out_{\mathcal{A}}^I$ (resp. $b \in out_{\mathcal{A}}^I$) if $A \cap I \neq \emptyset$ (resp. if $B \cap I \neq \emptyset$). Let $\mathcal{A}^{(s,t)}(in_{\mathcal{A}}^I, z_{aux})$ denote the output state of $\mathcal{A}$ on input $(in_{\mathcal{A}}^I, z_{aux})$ at the end of a run of **NodeMult**(s, t, S, T, A, B) (here z_{aux} is an auxiliary input representing the adversary's input state). Then, if $|out_{\mathcal{A}}^I| \leq 1$, there exists a probabilistic simulator algorithm S such that the random variables $\mathsf{REAL} \stackrel{\text{def}}{=} \langle \mathcal{A}^{(s,t)}(in_{\mathcal{A}}^I, z_{aux}), out_{\mathcal{A}}^I \rangle$ (representing the output state of $\mathcal{A}$ and protocol output given to $\mathcal{A}$) and $\mathsf{SIM} \stackrel{\text{def}}{=} \mathsf{S}(in_{\mathcal{A}}^I, z_{aux})$ (representing the simulated output state of $\mathcal{A}$ and protocol output given to $\mathcal{A}$) are identically distributed.*

3.3 Construction of a Δ-Active-Reliable Coloring of Graph $\mathcal{G}_{grid}(\ell)$

To complete our protocol construction, it remains to describe a Δ-active-reliable coloring of the graph $\mathcal{G}_{grid}(\ell)$. Our deterministic construction of such a coloring is given in Algorithm 5. It may be viewed as an adaptation of the deterministic t-reliable coloring of $\mathcal{G}_{grid}(\ell)$ from [9].

Lemma 3. *If Δ is Q^3, the coloring C returned by **DetCol** is a Δ-active-reliable n-coloring for $\mathcal{G}_{grid}(\ell)$.*

Proof. First, notice that $C(i, j, H) \cap C(i, j, V) = [n] \setminus (I_{\ell+1-i} \cup I_j)$ cannot be in Δ for any i, j since otherwise, it would imply that $[n]$ is the union of three sets $I_{\ell+1-i}, I_j, [n] \setminus (I_{\ell+1-i} \cup I_j)$ from Δ, contradicting the Q^3 property. Similarly, we must have $C(i, j, d)$ cannot be a union of two sets from Δ, otherwise again it would contradict the Q^3 property. For each $i \in [\ell]$, observe that the edges along the $(\ell+1-i)$th row and ith column of $\mathcal{G}_{grid}(\ell)$ are I_i-avoiding under the coloring C. The path $PATH_y$ for I_i is formed by the i'th column, while the path $PATH_x$ is formed by the portion of the $(\ell + 1 - i)$th row to the left of its intersection with $PATH_y$, with the rest of $PATH_x$ being the part of $PATH_y$ below the ith row. Finally, notice that $C(1, j, V) = C(\ell + 1 - j, 1, H) = C(\ell + 1, j, V)$ for all $j \in [\ell]$ so C is a symmetric Δ-active-reliable n-coloring, as claimed. $\square$

Putting together the results of Lemma 1, Theorem 2 and Lemma 3, we get our main result.

Corollary 1. *If Δ is Q^3, there exists a Shared 2-Product black box Protocol for G satisfying active-correctness and strong Δ-security and with communication complexity $O(M(\Delta)^2 poly(n))$ group elements, a black box Δ-secure protocol for any G-circuit C with communication complexity $O(|C| \cdot M(\Delta)^2 \cdot poly(n))$ group elements.*

Protocol 4 NodeMult(s, t, S, T, A, B)

Input: Parties P_i with $i \in S$ hold share $s \in G$, Parties P_i with $i \in T$ hold share $t \in G$.

1: Let $c = |S \cap T|$. Without loss of generality, assume $S \cap T = \{1, \ldots, c\}$.
2: **for** $k = 1$ to c **do**
3:     Party P_k computes $u = s \cdot t$ (since $k \in S \cap T$, P_k holds both s and t).
4:     Party P_k chooses uniformly random $a_k, b_k \in G$ such that $a_k \cdot b_k = u$.
5:     Party P_k sends a_k to each party P_i with $i \in A$.
6:     Every pair of parties P_i, P_j with $i, j \in A$ send to each other the values $a_{k,i}, a_{k,j}$ of
        a_k that P_i (resp. P_j) received from P_k. If either P_i or P_j detects an inconsistency
        (i.e. $a_{k,i} \neq a_{k,j}$), it broadcasts a complaint against P_k.
7:     If a complaint was broadcast in previous step against P_k, party P_k broadcasts
        a_k to all n parties, and all parties accept this value as the correct value of a_k.
8:     Party P_k sends b_k to each party P_i with $i \in B$.
9:     Every pair of parties P_i, P_j with $i, j \in B$ send to each other the values $b_{k,i}, b_{k,j}$ of
        b_k that P_i (resp. P_j) received from P_k. If either P_i or P_j detects an inconsistency
        (i.e. $b_{k,i} \neq b_{k,j}$), it broadcasts a complaint against P_k.
10:    If a complaint was broadcast in previous step against P_k, party P_k broadcasts
        b_k to all n parties, and all parties accept this value as the correct value of b_k.
11: **end for**
12: **for** $k = 2$ to c **do**
13:    **for all** $i \in A$ and $j \in B$ **do**
14:        Party P_i sends to P_j the value $a_k^{-1} \cdot a_1$, and P_j sends to P_i the value $b_k \cdot b_1^{-1}$.
15:        If either P_i or P_j detects an inconsistency (i.e. $a_k^{-1} \cdot a_1 \neq b_k \cdot b_1^{-1}$), it broadcasts
            a complaint k.
16:    **end for**
17:    **if** a complaint k was broadcast in previous step **then**
18:        All parties P_i with $i \in A$ broadcast $a_k^{-1} \cdot a_1$ to all n parties. Let Hon_A^k denote
            the value v such that all parties P_i with $i \in A \setminus J$ broadcasted the value v, for
            some $J \in \Delta$. (such v exists and is unique, see proof of Lemma 2).
19:        All parties P_i with $i \in B$ broadcast $b_k \cdot b_1^{-1}$ to all n parties. Let Hon_B^k denote
            the value v such that all parties P_i with $i \in B \setminus J$ broadcasted the value v,
            for some $J \in \Delta$. (such v exists and is unique, see proof of Lemma 2).
20:        **if** $Hon_A^k \neq Hon_B^k$ **then**
21:            Each party P_i with $i \in S$ broadcasts s to all n parties. Let Hon_s denote
                the value v such that all parties P_i with $i \in S \setminus J$ broadcasted the value v,
                for some $J \in \Delta$. (such v exists and is unique, see proof of Lemma 2).
22:            Each party P_i with $i \in T$ broadcasts t to all n parties. Let Hon_t denote
                the value v such that all parties P_i with $i \in S \setminus J$ broadcasted the value v,
                for some $J \in \Delta$. (such v exists and is unique, see proof of Lemma 2).
23:            **return** with each party P_i with $i \in A$ holding output share $a = Hon_s \cdot$
                Hon_t, and each party P_i with $i \in B$ holding output share $b = 1$.
24:        **end if**
25:    **end if**
26: **end for**
27: **return** with each party P_i with $i \in A$ holding output share $a = a_1$, and each
    party P_i with $i \in B$ holding output share $b = b_1$.

Output: Parties P_i with $i \in A$ hold share $a \in G$, Parties P_i with $i \in B$ hold share
$b \in G$, with $a \cdot b = s \cdot t$.

Algorithm 5 Algorithm **DetCol**

Input: Graph $\mathcal{G}_{grid}(\ell)$ (see Fig. 1), where $\ell = M(\Delta)$.

Let $I_1, \ldots, I_\ell$ denote the sequence of all maximal sets Δ (in some ordering).

For $(i, j) \in [\ell + 1] \times [\ell]$, $C(i, j, V) \overset{\text{def}}{=} [n] \setminus I_j$ and, if $i \leq \ell$, $C(i, j, H) \overset{\text{def}}{=} [n] \setminus I_{\ell+1-i}$.

Output: A Δ-active-reliable coloring C of Graph $\mathcal{G}_{grid}(\ell)$.

3.4   Application to Active-Secure General Multiparty Computation

In this Section, we explain how to apply our protocol for black-box groups to obtain a new approach for constructing actively-secure multiparty computation protocols for arbitrary Boolean circuits.

We begin by recalling a result of Barrington [1] that was used in the passive attack setting of [8] to reduce multiparty computation of arbitrary Boolean circuits to an S_5-circuit. Let C denote a G-circuit and let $f_C : G^m \to G$ be the function computed by C. Let 1_G denote the identity element of G. For some fixed $\sigma \in G \setminus \{1_G\}$, let $\phi_\sigma : \{0, 1\} \to G$ denote the encoding function mapping 0 to 1_G and 1 to σ. We say that a G-circuit C *computes* a Boolean function g if there exists $\sigma \in G$ such that $g(x_1, \ldots, x_n) = \phi_\sigma^{-1}(f_C(\phi_\sigma(x_1), \ldots, \phi_\sigma(x_n)))$ for all $(x_1, \ldots, x_n) \in \{0, 1\}^n$. Barrington's result can be stated as follows (see [8]).

Theorem 3 (Adapted from [1]). *Let C be a Boolean circuit consisting of N_A 2-input AND gates, N_N NOT gates, and depth d. Then there exists an S_5-circuit C' which computes the Boolean function computed by C. The circuit C' contains $N'_M = 3N_A$ Mult gates and $N'_{CM} = 4N_A + N_N$ CMult gates, and has depth $d' \leq 4d$.*

The S_5-circuit C' constructed in the proof of Theorem 3 computes the Boolean circuit C using the encoding function $\phi_\sigma : \{0, 1\} \to S_5$ mapping 0 to 1_{S_5} and 1 to the 5-cycle $\sigma = (1, 2, 3, 4, 5)$. In the passive attack setting of [8], all parties are assumed to honestly follow the protocol and correctly encode their Boolean inputs into the set $\{1_{S_5}, \sigma\}$, which are then used as input to the protocol for computing the S_5-circuit C'. However, in the active attack setting we study in this paper, one cannot directly apply our G-circuit protocol from the previous section to C', since the corrupted parties may choose as their inputs to circuit C' elements outside the set $\{1_{S_5}, \sigma\}$ in order to corrupt the protocol output. To fix this problem, we modify our protocol from the previous section for this application, by adding an additional input verification step. This verification step allows the parties to interactively check that the VSS'ed input elements of all parties are in the set $\{1_{S_5}, \sigma\}$, without revealing anything else about the shared inputs when they are indeed in the set $\{1_{S_5}, \sigma\}$. If a shared input is found by the check to be outside the set $\{1_{S_5}, \sigma\}$, the party who shared the input is declared corrupted, and the corresponding shared input is redefined to be a VSS sharing of the default value 1_{S_5}. The correctness of the test in Protocol 6 is shown by Lemma 4. It uses elementary properties of the group S_5, and its proof can be found in the full version of the paper.

Lemma 4. *For each $i \in [m]$, the tests $y_1 = 1_{S_5}$ and $y_2 = 1_{S_5}$ are both verified if and only if $x_i \in \{1_{S_5}, \sigma\}$.*

Protocol 6 Verification Step (inserted into Protocol $\prod_a(C, \prod_S)$).

Input: For $i \in [m]$, the parties hold a VSS sharing $\mathbf{s}_{x_i} = (s_{x_i}(1), \ldots, s_{x_i}(\ell))$ of input $x_i \in S_5$ shared by party $P_{j(i)}$, where, for each $j \in [\ell]$, share $s_{x_i}(j)$ is held by players in set $\mathcal{O}_x(j) = [n] \setminus I_j$.

for $i = 1$ to m **do**

    1. The parties jointly compute, using G-circuit protocol from Sec. 3.1 on the VSS'ed input $x_i \in S_5$, the value $y_1 = E_1(x_i)$, where $E_1(x) = x \cdot \sigma \cdot x^{-1} \cdot \sigma^{-1}$.

    2. The parties jointly compute, using G-circuit protocol from Sec. 3.1 on the VSS'ed input $x_i \in S_5$, the value $y_2 = E_2(x_i)$, where $E_2(x) = x \cdot g_1 \cdot x^2 \cdot g_2 \cdot x^3 \cdot (g_1 \cdot g_2)^{-1}$, $g_1 = (1)(2,3)(4)(5)$ and $g_2 = (1,2,5,4,3)$.

    3. If $y_1 = 1_{S_5}$ and $y_2 = 1_{S_5}$, the parties conclude that $x_i \in \{1_{S_5}, \sigma\}$. Else, the parties conclude that $x_i \notin \{1_{S_5}, \sigma\}$, declare party $P_{j(i)}$ as corrupted, and set $x_i = 1_{S_5}$, with all VSS shares $s_{x_i}(j) = 1_{S_5}$ for $j \in [\ell]$.

end for

Output: For $i \in [m]$, the parties hold a VSS sharing $\mathbf{s}_{x_i} = (s_{x_i}(1), \ldots, s_{x_i}(\ell))$ of input $x_i \in S_5$ with $x_i \in \{1_{S_5}, \sigma\}$ and for $j \in [\ell]$, share $s_{x_i}(j)$ is held by set $\mathcal{O}_x(j) = [n] \setminus I_j$.

By adding the verification Protocol 6 to our protocol in Sec. 3.1 and applying it to the S_5-circuit C' produced by Theorem 3, we obtain an active-secure protocol for computing any Boolean function. The correctness follows from Lemma 4 and the correctness of our G-circuit protocol, and the security follows from the simulatability of our G-circuit protocol. The proof follows by a straightforward modification of the proof of Lemma 1 and is omitted.

Corollary 2. *If Δ is Q^3, the above protocol is a Δ-secure protocol for any Boolean circuit C, with communication complexity $O(|C| \cdot M(\Delta)^2 \cdot poly(n))$ bits.*

Our protocol works quite differently from previous approaches to general secure multiparty computation that work over a field. The latter can achieve a similar communication complexity of $O(M(\Delta)^2)$ bits [20]. Because our protocol only runs the full VSS sharing protocol at the beginning but not at each intermediate graph node, its communication complexity is only $O(\ell^2 \cdot poly(n))$ group elements for multiplying two VSSed group elements whereas the complexity of the field-based protocol of Maurer [19], which is also based on Maurer's VSS, is $O(\ell^3 \cdot poly(n))$ field elements for multiplying two VSSed field elements where $\ell = M(\Delta)$, i.e. our protocol saves a factor of order $\Omega(\ell)$ (ignoring the dependance on n) in communication complexity over Maurer's protocol when applied to computing the same Boolean circuit C (with Maurer's protocol over $GF(2)$ and our protocol over S_5).

Acknowledgements. We thank Huaxiong Wang for encouraging us to address the problem. We also thank Yuval Ishai for pointing out the problem (addressed in Sec. 3.4) of incorrectly encoded inputs in applying our protocol to the computation of Boolean circuits. Part of this work was done while Y. Desmedt was visiting Macquarie University, funded by BT as "BT Chair of Information Security". The research of J. Pieprzyk and R. Steinfeld was supported by an Australian Research Fellowship (ARF) from the Australian Research Council (ARC), and ARC Discovery Grants DP0987734 and DP110100628.

References

1. Barrington, D.A.: Bounded-Width Polynomial-Size Branching Programs Recognize Exactly Those Languages in NC^1. In: STOC 1986, pp. 1–5 (1986)
2. Beerliová-Trubíniová, Z., Hirt, M.: Perfectly-Secure MPC with Linear Communication Complexity. In: Canetti, R. (ed.) TCC 2008. LNCS, vol. 4948, pp. 213–230. Springer, Heidelberg (2008)
3. Ben-Or, M., Goldwasser, S., Wigderson, A.: Completeness Theorems for Non-Cryptographic Fault-Tolerant Distributed Computation. In: STOC 1988, pp. 1–10 (1988)
4. Chaum, D., Crépeau, C., Damgård, I.: Multiparty unconditionally secure protocols. In: STOC 1988, pp. 11–19 (1988)
5. Cramer, R., Fehr, S., Ishai, Y., Kushilevitz, E.: Efficient Multi-Party Computation Over Rings. In: Biham, E. (ed.) EUROCRYPT 2003. LNCS, vol. 2656, pp. 596–613. Springer, Heidelberg (2003)
6. Cramer, R., Damgård, I., Maurer, U.: General Secure Multi-party Computation from any Linear Secret-Sharing Scheme. In: Preneel, B. (ed.) EUROCRYPT 2000. LNCS, vol. 1807, pp. 316–334. Springer, Heidelberg (2000)
7. Damgård, I., Ishai, Y., Krøigaard, M.: Perfectly Secure Multiparty Computation and the Computational Overhead of Cryptography. In: Gilbert, H. (ed.) EUROCRYPT 2010. LNCS, vol. 6110, pp. 445–465. Springer, Heidelberg (2010)
8. Desmedt, Y., Pieprzyk, J., Steinfeld, R., Sun, X., Tartary, C., Wang, H., Yao, A.C.-C.: Graph coloring applied to secure computation in non-abelian groups. J. Cryptology (to appear, 2011)
9. Desmedt, Y., Pieprzyk, J., Steinfeld, R., Wang, H.: On Secure Multi-party Computation in Black-Box Groups. In: Menezes, A. (ed.) CRYPTO 2007. LNCS, vol. 4622, pp. 591–612. Springer, Heidelberg (2007)
10. Fitzi, M., Hirt, M., Maurer, U.M.: Trading Correctness for Privacy in Unconditional Multi-party Computation. In: Krawczyk, H. (ed.) CRYPTO 1998. LNCS, vol. 1462, pp. 121–136. Springer, Heidelberg (1998)
11. Fitzi, M., Hirt, M., Maurer, U.M.: General Adversaries in Unconditional Multi-party Computation. In: Lam, K.-Y., Okamoto, E., Xing, C. (eds.) ASIACRYPT 1999. LNCS, vol. 1716, pp. 232–246. Springer, Heidelberg (1999)
12. Fitzi, M., Maurer, U.: Efficient Byzantine Agreement Secure against General Adversaries. In: Kutten, S. (ed.) DISC 1998. LNCS, vol. 1499, pp. 134–148. Springer, Heidelberg (1998)
13. Goldreich, O.: Foundations of Cryptography: vol. II - Basic Applications. Cambridge University Press (2004)
14. Goldreich, O., Micali, S., Wigderson, A.: How to Play Any Mental Game. In: STOC 1987, pp. 218–229 (1987)
15. Hirt, M., Maurer, U.: Complete Characterization of Adversaries Tolerable in Secure Multi-Party Computation. In: PODC 1997, pp. 25–34 (1997)
16. Hirt, M., Maurer, U.: Player simulation and general adversary structures in perfect multiparty computation. J. Cryptology 13(1), 31–60 (2000)
17. Hirt, M., Maurer, U.: Robustness for Free in Unconditional Multi-party Computation. In: Kilian, J. (ed.) CRYPTO 2001. LNCS, vol. 2139, pp. 101–118. Springer, Heidelberg (2001)

18. Hirt, M., Maurer, U., Przydatek, B.: Efficient Secure Multi-party Computation. In: Okamoto, T. (ed.) ASIACRYPT 2000. LNCS, vol. 1976, pp. 143–161. Springer, Heidelberg (2000)
19. Maurer, U.: Secure multi-party computation made simple. Discrete Applied Mathematics 154, 370–381 (2006)
20. Prabhu, B.S., Srinathan, K., Pandu Rangan, C.: Trading Players for Efficiency in Unconditional Multiparty Computation. In: Cimato, S., Galdi, C., Persiano, G. (eds.) SCN 2002. LNCS, vol. 2576, pp. 342–353. Springer, Heidelberg (2003)
21. Sun, X., Yao, A.C.-C., Tartary, C.: Graph Design for Secure Multiparty Computation over Non-Abelian Groups. In: Pieprzyk, J. (ed.) ASIACRYPT 2008. LNCS, vol. 5350, pp. 37–53. Springer, Heidelberg (2008)

Hash Combiners for Second Pre-image Resistance, Target Collision Resistance and Pre-image Resistance Have Long Output

Arno Mittelbach

Darmstadt University of Technology, Germany
http://www.cryptoplexity.de
arno.mittelbach@cased.de

Abstract. A (k, l) hash-function combiner for property P is a construction that, given access to l hash functions, yields a single cryptographic hash function which has property P as long as at least k out of the l hash functions have that property. Hash function combiners are used to hedge against the failure of one or more of the individual components. One example of the application of hash function combiners are the previous versions of the TLS and SSL protocols [7,6].

The concatenation combiner which simply concatenates the outputs of all hash functions is an example of a robust combiner for collision resistance. However, its output length is, naturally, significantly longer than each individual hash-function output, while the security bounds are not necessarily stronger than that of the strongest input hash-function. In 2006 Boneh and Boyen asked whether a robust black-box combiner for collision resistance can exist that has an output length which is significantly less than that of the concatenation combiner [2]. Regrettably, this question has since been answered in the negative for fully black-box constructions (where hash function and adversary access is being treated as black-box), that is, combiners (in this setting) for collision resistance roughly need at least the length of the concatenation combiner to be robust [2,3,11,12].

In this paper we examine weaker notions of collision resistance, namely: *second pre-image resistance* and *target collision resistance* [15] and *pre-image resistance*. As a generic brute-force attack against any of these would take roughly 2^n queries to an n-bit hash function, in contrast to only $2^{n/2}$ queries it would take to break collision resistance (due to the birthday bound), this might indicate that combiners for weaker notions of collision resistance can exist which have a significantly shorter output than the concatenation combiner (which is, naturally, also robust for these properties). Regrettably, this is not the case.

Keywords: hash functions, combiners, collision resistance, second pre-image resistance, target collision resistance, pre-image resistance.

I. Visconti and R. De Prisco (Eds.): SCN 2012, LNCS 7485, pp. 522–539, 2012.

1   Introduction

In theory, hash functions are usually treated as ideal objects, that is, they are assumed to be random oracles or to hold certain properties such as collision resistance (it is difficult to find two messages that hash to the same value) or pre-image resistance (it is difficult, given an image, to find any pre-image). Assuming that these properties hold, this then allows us to prove protocols or constructions to be secure when instantiated with such a function. However, finding functions that provably hold any of the properties usually demanded of good hash functions is a difficult problem. Consequently, in practice, hash functions are heuristics that come only with a very limited number of guarantees. Thus it is not surprising that with time, attacks against practical hash functions are usually found that drastically lower the bounds assumed in theory. Many attacks have been presented for MD5 [20,18,16], and also for SHA-1 first attacks have been published [19,5,1,4]. This, in turn, led NIST to hold a competition to find a successor to the SHA-1 and SHA-2 families.

Combiners. Hash function combiners can be used to hedge against the failure of one (or more) of the components. A (k, l)-combiner is a construction that given access to l primitives implements the same primitive while guaranteeing that a certain property or multiple properties hold as long as a these are held by k out of the l input primitives. If the combiner ensures this for some property then it is said to be *robust* for that property.

Combiners are usually considered as black-box combiners, that is, the combiner only gets black-box access to its input hash functions. This is due to that i) this allows us the use the combiner with any hash functions; and ii) we are (so far) ignorant as to properly modeling white-box access. Consider, for example, the somewhat "pathological" combiner C^{H_1, H_2} with two input hash functions which on input M returns $H_1(M)$ if H_1 is collision resistant and $H_2(M)$ otherwise. Naturally, this combiner does all we want from a combiner for hash functions, but we have no idea, of how such a combiner could be implemented. In this paper, we limit our investigation to black-box combiners and speak henceforth only of combiner.

For hash functions the classical combiner robust for collision resistance is the concatenation combiner, i.e., $C_{||}(M) = H_1(M)||H_2(M)$ is a robust $(1,2)$-combiner for collision resistance as naturally any two messages (M, M') that collide under $C_{||}$ also collide under both hash functions (i.e., $H_b(M) = H_b(M')$ for $b = \{1, 2\}$).

However, when simply concatenating the outputs of several hash functions, the output length grows significantly, while the security guarantee of the combined hash function does not necessarily increase. That is, we expect an adversary to find collisions for a hash function with output length n after roughly $2^{n/2}$ queries to the function (due to the generic birthday attack), a bound which can only be met by the concatenation combiner if all input functions were "ideal" hash functions to begin with (for which naturally a combiner would not be needed in the first place). Thus, Boneh and Boyen asked whether robust combiners for collision resistance exist that have a significantly shorter output length than the concatenation combiner [2]. This question has since been answered negatively [2,3,11,12].

Weaker Than Collision Resistance. In practice, "full" collision resistance is not always required, i.e., for many applications a suitable level of security can be achieved with weaker notions such as second pre-image or target collision resistance. Here an adversary has to find a collision for a specific message. Think for example of checksums for programs. If an adversary wants to maliciously change the program then it has to make sure not to change the checksum in the process. Thus, the first part of the collision is fixed. Another example of a weaker property is pre-image resistance where given an image the best strategy for an adversary of finding a corresponding pre-image should be exhaustive search. Think password storage, for an application where pre-image resistance yields sufficient security.

For these variants of collision resistance the concatenation combiner is, naturally, also robust. While the generic birthday attack gives us an estimate of $2^{n/2}$ queries an adversary has to perform to find a (random) collision for an ideal function, an adversary would have to search the entire domain to break any of the properties second pre-image-, target collision- or pre-image resistance when considering ideal functions. It is thus interesting to study the question of finding combiners with short output that are robust for any of these weaker properties. A promising indication is also that short output combiners exist for the related (but privately-keyed) properties *message authentication codes* and *pseudo-randomness*. Regrettably, we will show that, as for the collision resistance case, such combiners cannot exist.

Impossibility Results. For our definitions and proofs we closely follow Pietrzak's elegant proof for the collision resistance case [12,10]. We will define combiners in the style of [2] as a pair of algorithms (C, P) where C implements the combiner logic and P provides a reduction from attacks on the combiner to attacks on the input functions. To prove the non-existence of a black-box combiner C with short output we will design an attack oracle $\mathcal{B}$ (that we will call breaking oracle) which breaks the investigated property (e.g., second pre-image resistance) for the combiner with noticeable probability but which does not help the security reduction P too much in breaking the property for the necessary number of input hash functions (2 in the case of a $(1, 2)$-combiner). The intuition is, that if the combiner compresses too much, than collisions appear on the combiner due to the compression and not due to collisions on the input hash functions. If we can guarantee that the breaking oracle only outputs such collisions, then the reduction P has to find collisions without the aid of the breaking oracle. However, if the combiner was indeed robust then the reduction P must, also with access to this specific breaking oracle, be able to break the property (e.g., find second pre-images) for all input hash functions (in case of a

$(1,2)$-combiner). Such a reduction P, on the other hand, allows us to compress a uniformly chosen random function $R : \{0,1\}^w \to \{0,1\}^v$ to below $2^w v$ bits. As this violates a corollary of Shannon's source coding theorem [17] we can argue that such combiners cannot exist.

The main contribution of our paper is to extend Theorem 1 given by Pietrzak [12] for the properties second pre-image resistance, target collision resistance and pre-image resistance. That is, randomized combiners robust for collision resistance, second pre-image resistance, target collision resistance or pre-image resistance have to have long output. We give an informal version of our main theorem for the case of deterministic combiners for two hash functions:

Theorem 1 (informal). *For some $n, m, v, w \in \mathbb{N}$ assume $C : \{0,1\}^m \to \{0,1\}^n$ is an efficient black-box-combiner for two hash functions of the form $H : \{0,1\}^w \to \{0,1\}^v$ that is robust for collision resistance, second pre-image resistance, target collision resistance or pre-image resistance. Then the combiner's output length n is bounded by:*

$$n \geq 2v - \mathcal{O}(\omega) \tag{1}$$

where ω is logarithmic in the number of hash function queries by the combiner.

Note that the bound roughly corresponds to the concatenation combiner's output length of $2v$. As Canetti et al. showed in [3], it is however possible to chop off a logarithmic number of bits (logarithmic in the number of oracle calls by the combiner) of the concatenation combiner while staying robust. As their combiner achieves the bound given in equation (1) the bound is tight.

Further note that we will prove the result for finite domain hash functions. However, as this is an impossibility result, proving it for a finite domain actually makes the result stronger, as every secure hash function that takes arbitrary length messages also has to be secure when considering the subset of only fixed length input messages.

Related Work. Combiners for the properties second pre-image resistance and pre-image resistance with short output length have been studied by Rjasko [14] who gives an impossibility result for a special case of deterministic combiners where the reduction can query the breaking oracle only once. As shown in [12] this simplification allows for a much simpler proof than the general case for probabilistic combiners where the reduction can query the adversary (or breaking oracle in our terminology) multiple times.

2 Preliminaries

2.1 Notation

Unless stated otherwise, lower-case letters such as $n \in \mathbb{N}$ represent natural numbers. With 1^n we denote the unary representation of n and with $\langle n \rangle_b$ its binary representation padded with zeros to length b. Upper-case letters in standard typeface like M stand for bit strings. We denote with $\{0,1\}^n$ the set of all bit strings M of length $|M| = n$, while $\{0,1\}^*$ denotes the set of all bit strings. For bit strings $X, Y \in \{0,1\}^*$ we denote with $X||Y$ the concatenation. If $\mathcal{X}$ is a set then by $|\mathcal{X}|$ we denote its cardinality. By $M \leftarrow \mathcal{X}$ we mean that M is chosen uniformly from $\mathcal{X}$, if $\mathcal{X}$ is a distribution then $M \leftarrow \mathcal{X}$ denotes that M is chosen accordingly. The logarithm log is always to base 2.

PTM stands for Polynomial time Turing Machine and PPTM for Probabilistic Polynomial time Turing Machine. Upper-case letters in calligraphy like $\mathcal{A}$ usually denote a PPTM. We will often simply call them adversary or algorithm and we write $\mathcal{A}(M)$ if M is initially written on the Turing Machine's input tape (i.e., the algorithm runs with input M). By $X \leftarrow \mathcal{A}$ we denote that X is output by algorithm $\mathcal{A}$. If the Turing Machine has black-box access to one or more oracles $\mathcal{O}_1, ..., \mathcal{O}_z$ (these will usually be hash functions), we denote this by adding the oracles in superscript: $\mathcal{A}^{\mathcal{O}_1,...,\mathcal{O}_z}$.[1]

By $\text{qry}^{\mathcal{O}_i}(\mathcal{A}^{\mathcal{O}_1,...,\mathcal{O}_z}(M))$ we denote the set of all of $\mathcal{A}$'s queries to oracle $\mathcal{O}_i$ when algorithm $\mathcal{A}$ runs on input M.

If X and Z are random variables then $Pr[X = y]$ denotes the probability that X takes on the value of y. By $Pr[X = y|Z]$ we denote the conditional probability of $X = y$ given Z. If $\mathbf{pre}$ is a predicate or event then $Pr[\mathbf{pre}]$ denotes the probability that the predicate is true (the event occurs)

We write $Pr[\text{step}_1; ...; \text{step}_i : \text{condition}]$ which describes a random experiment and which should be read as: the probability that the condition holds after the steps were executed in consecutive order.

If A is an event then by $\neg A$ we denote the complementary event, that is, $Pr[\neg A] = 1 - Pr[A]$. By $\wedge$ (resp. $\vee$) we denote the conjunction (resp. disjunction) of events: if A and B are events then $Pr[A \wedge B]$ is the probability that both events A and B occur and $Pr[A \vee B]$ is the probability that at least one of the events A or B does occur.

2.2   Hash Functions and Their Properties

Formally hash functions are defined as a family of functions together with a key generation algorithm HKGen that picks one of the functions to be used. That is, A *hash function* (family) is a pair of efficient algorithms $\mathcal{H} = (\text{HKGen}, H)$ where $\text{HKGen}(1^n)$ is a probabilistic algorithm that takes as input the security parameter 1^n and outputs a key K (note that the security parameter is implicit in K) and $H(K, M) := H_K(M)$ is a deterministic algorithm that takes a key K and message $M \in \{0,1\}^*$ as input and outputs a hash value $H_K(M) \in \{0,1\}^n$. We will drop the subscript and write $H(M)$ if it is clear from context which key the function gets.

We require different properties from hash functions depending on the application. The properties that we are interested in in this paper are *collision resistance*

---

[1] In this case the Turing Machine has extra oracle tapes (one per oracle). $\mathcal{A}$ can write query X on oracle tape i and gets the oracle's answer $\mathcal{O}_i$ in the next step written on the tape.

(CR, it should be difficult to find two messages that hash to the same value), *second pre-image resistance* (SPR, it should be difficult given a message to find a second message that hashes to the same value) its variant *target collision resistance*[2] (TCR) and *pre-image resistance* (OW, given an image it should be difficult to find a corresponding pre-image).

In this extended abstract we will give the necessary definitions and proofs for the case of second pre-image resistance. Please refer to the full version [8] for the cases target collision resistance and pre-image resistance.

Definition 1 (Second Pre-image Resistance). *We call a hash function $\mathcal{H} = (HKGen, H)$ second pre-image resistant (SPR) with respect to distribution $\mathcal{M}$, if the advantage for every efficient adversary $\mathcal{A}$ in the following experiment is negligible in n:*

$$Adv_{\mathcal{A}}^{spr}(n) = Pr \left[\begin{array}{cc} K \leftarrow HKGen(1^n); M \leftarrow \mathcal{M}(1^n); & M \neq M' \wedge \\ M' \leftarrow \mathcal{A}(K, M) & : H_K(M) = H_K(M') \end{array} \right] \approx 0$$

The probability is over the selection of $K \leftarrow HKGen(1^n)$, the choice of $M \leftarrow \mathcal{M}$ and $\mathcal{A}$'s internal coin tosses.

2.3 Predicates Capturing Events

In the upcoming proofs and in our definition of a robust combiner we need to formalize the event that an adversary finds second pre-images. For this we examine a random experiment $\mathcal{A}^{H_1,\ldots,H_l}$ where an adversary plays against hash functions $H_1,\ldots,H_l$. For this, we define predicate **spr** to be true if and only if the adversary in the course of the experiment finds a second pre-image. By finding we mean that the adversary actually performs one query to a hash function H_i which yields the second pre-image in respect to some target message. The definitions are closely related to Pietrzak's definition for collision resistance [12].

Definition 2. *The predicate $spr^{H_i(X_i)}(\mathcal{A}^{H_1,\ldots,H_l})$ is defined for the random experiment $\mathcal{A}^{H_1,\ldots,H_l}$ and target message X_i and holds if $\mathcal{A}$ finds a second pre-image for X_i for function H_i; that is, in the course of the computation of $\mathcal{A}^{H_1,\ldots,H_l}$ an oracle call to H_i is made with messages (X_{spr}) for which $H_i(X_i) = H_i(X_{spr})$ and $X_i \neq X_{spr}$. Formally:*

$$spr^{H_i(X_i)}(\mathcal{A}^{H_1,\ldots,H_l}) \Longleftrightarrow$$
$$\exists X_{spr} \in qry^{H_i}(\mathcal{A}^{H_1,\ldots,H_l}) : X_i \neq X_{spr} \wedge H_i(X_i) = H_i(X_{spr})$$

For subset $\mathcal{H} \subseteq \{H_1,...,H_l\}$ and target messages $X_1,...,X_l$ we define the predicate $spr_{X_1,...,X_l}^{\mathcal{H}}(\mathcal{A}^{H_1,\ldots,H_l})$ to hold if second pre-images are found for all hash functions in $\mathcal{H}$ (for corresponding target message X_i):

$$spr_{X_1,...,X_l}^{\mathcal{H}}(\mathcal{A}^{H_1,\ldots,H_l}) \Longleftrightarrow \forall H_i \in \mathcal{H} : spr^{H_i(X_i)}(\mathcal{A}^{H_1,\ldots,H_l})$$

---

[2] Target collision resistant hash functions are often also referred to as *universal one-way hash functions* [9].

For $1 \leq n \leq l$ we define the predicate $\mathbf{spr}_{n,X_1,...,X_l}(\mathcal{A}^{H_1,...,H_l})$ to hold if a second pre-image is found for n of the l hash oracles:

$$\mathbf{spr}_{n,X_1,...,X_l}(\mathcal{A}^{H_1,...,H_l}) \iff \exists \mathcal{H} \subseteq \{H_1, ..., H_l\}, |\mathcal{H}| \geq n : \mathbf{spr}_{X_1,...,X_l}^{\mathcal{H}}(\mathcal{A}^{H_1,...,H_l})$$

2.4   Randomized Black-Box Combiners for Cryptographic Hash Functions

As usual for impossibility results we want to be as general as possible about the capabilities of the considered combiners. We consider randomized black-box combiners after Pietrzak [12] in the non-uniform setting. This means that the combiners get as additional input their randomness R which can be regarded as some sort of public key. The (k, l) combiner is formalized as a pair of algorithms (C, P) where C is a non-uniform circuit implementing the logic of the combiner and P provides a security reduction. For this C gets access to the l hash functions $H_1, \ldots, H_l$ and P gets access to a breaking oracle[3] $\mathcal{B}$ which can produce second pre-images with a certain success probability ρ. If security reduction $P^{\mathcal{B},H_1,...,H_l}$ finds second pre-images for $l - k + 1$ of the input hash functions with noticeable probability (with respect to the breaking oracle's success rate ρ), we call the combiner ρ-robust for second pre-image resistance. Thus a combiner is ρ-robust if and only if such a breaking oracle cannot exist if at least k out of the l input hash functions hold the property.

Definition 3. *A randomized (k, l)-combiner for hash functions $H_1, ..., H_l$ of the forms $\{0, 1\}^w \rightarrow \{0, 1\}^v$ is a pair of efficient algorithms (C, P) where $C : \mathcal{R} \times \{0, 1\}^m \rightarrow \{0, 1\}^n$ is an oracle circuit and P is an oPPTM[4] providing the security reduction for C.*

Let $0 \leq \rho \leq 1$. Oracle $\mathcal{B}^{spr}$ ρ-breaks $C^{H_1,...,H_l}$ (for SPR) if it outputs a second pre-image to input message $M \leftarrow \{0, 1\}^m$ for $C^{H_1,...,H_l}(R, M)$ with probability ρ (over the choice of message and randomness). If no second pre-image is found it outputs $\perp$.

*The combiner is called ρ-**robust for SPR** if for some non-negligible $0 < \epsilon \leq 1$ and any choice of functions $H_1, ..., H_l$ and for any breaking oracle $\mathcal{B}^{spr}$ that ρ-breaks $C^{H_1,...,H_l}$, the random experiment $P^{\mathcal{B}^{spr},H_1,...,H_l}$ on input $(M_1, ..., M_l)$ with $M_i \leftarrow \{0, 1\}^m$ (for $i = 1, ..., l$) finds second pre-images for $l - k + 1$ input hash functions with probability:*

$$Pr[\mathbf{spr}_{l-k+1,M_1,...,M_l}(P^{\mathcal{B}^{spr},H_1,...,H_l}(M_1, ..., M_l))] \geq \epsilon \tag{2}$$

The combiner is called robust for SPR if it is efficient and ρ-robust for every non negligible $\rho(v)$.

Note that the breaking oracle's success probability ρ can be a function of $v \in \mathbb{N}$, i.e., the hash functions' output length. Further note, that we could have fixed the reduction's success probability ϵ to a constant value, due to the fact that we are

---

[3] Think of the breaking oracle as the best known adversary against the combiner.

[4] See [12] for how to treat non-uniform reductions.

considering randomized combiners. Given some combiner (C, P) that satisfies equation (2) for some non-negligible ϵ, we can easily construct a new combiner C, P^* that satisfies equation (2) with probability $\epsilon^* > \epsilon$ by simply repeatedly calling P with renewed random coins. We will later fix ϵ to $2/3$ (an arbitrary choice) to simplify notation.

Definition 4 (Efficiency). *Let q_C be the number of oracle queries performed by C and q_P an upper bound for the number of oracle calls made by P, then the combiner (C, P) is called* efficient *if both q_P and q_C are polynomial in v.*

Remark 1 (On efficiency definition). Note that it is sufficient to only count successful calls to the breaking oracle, that is, we do not need to count queries to $\mathcal{B}$ where the answer is $\perp$. By not counting unsuccessful calls to the breaking oracle we actually make the impossibility result stronger as even then, as we will see the reduction P will have to make exponentially many calls to the hash function oracle to succeed. This can be done as, unsuccessful even the successful queries to $\mathcal{B}$ will not help P (too much) in its task and unsuccessful queries cannot be used by P to hide hash function calls.

Further note that throughout this paper we assume that q_C, q_P^H and q_P^B are at least one. This can be safely assumed as the contrary would be rather uninteresting: consider for example a combiner which does not use its hash functions. It is trivially non-robust as collisions for the combiner cannot be reduced to collisions on any of the input functions.

3   Robust Combiners Have Long Output

In this section we will give the formal definition of Theorem 1 together with its proof for the case of second pre-image resistance. Please refer to the full version of this extended abstract [8] for the necessary adaptations for the cases of target collision resistance and pre-image resistance:

Theorem 2. *For some $n, m, v, w \in \mathbb{N}$ assume (C, P) is an efficient (k, l)-black-box-combiner for hash functions of the form $\{0, 1\}^w \to \{0, 1\}^v$. Let $C : \mathcal{R} \times \{0, 1\}^m \to \{0, 1\}^n$ be robust for collision resistance, second pre-image resistance, target collision resistance or pre-image resistance. Then the combiner's output length n is bounded by:*

$$n \geq (l - k + 1)v - \mathcal{O}(\log q_C) \tag{3}$$

where q_C is the number of hash function queries performed by C.

3.1   Additional Definitions

For the upcoming proof of our main theorem we need a notion of second pre-images that are *safe* for the combiner. "Safe for the combiner" means that the evaluation of the message pair (M, M') on a specific combiner C does not yield a trivial second pre-image for hash function H and target message X. Trivial in the sense that during the evaluation combiner C on messages M and M' queries hash function H on a message $X_{\mathbf{spr}}$ for which $X \neq X_{\mathbf{spr}}$ and $H(X) = H(X_{\mathbf{spr}})$:

Definition 5 (Safe Second Pre-Image). *Let* $H : \{0,1\}^w \to \{0,1\}^v$ *be a hash function and* $C : \{0,1\}^m \to \{0,1\}^n$ *some oPPTM. Let* $X_{target} \in \{0,1\}^w$*. We say that the message* $M_{spr} \in \{0,1\}^m$ *is a safe second pre-image with respect to message* $M \in \{0,1\}^m$ *and function* H *(with respect to* C^H *and* X_{target}*) if*

1. $C^H(M) = C^H(M_{spr})$ *(but not necessarily* $M \neq M_{spr}$, *that is,* (M, M_{spr}) *may be a pseudocollision)*
2. *the evaluation of* $C^H(\cdot)$ *on inputs* M *and* M_{spr} *does not involve a call to* $H(X)$ *with* $X \neq X_{target}$ *and* $H(X) = H(X_{target})$:

$$\forall X \in qry^H(C^H(M)) \cup qry^H(C^H(M_{spr})) : X = X_{target} \vee H(X) \neq H(X_{target})$$

We define the predicate $\mathbf{safeSpr}_{H,X}^{C^H}(M, M_{spr})$ *iff* (M, M_{spr}) *is a safe second pre-image for hash function* H *and target message* X.

For $k \in \mathbb{N}$ *we denote with* $\mathbf{safeSpr}_{k,X_1,...,X_l}^{C^{H_1,...,H_l}}(M, M_{spr})$ *that* (M, M_{spr}) *is a safe second pre-image for messages* $X_1, .., X_l$ *for k out of C's l oracles* H_i *($i = 1, ..., l$). Here* X_i *is the target message for function* H_i *($i = 1, ..., l$).*

Compressibility. The main idea in the upcoming proof is to show that if a robust combiner with short output exists then we can compress a uniformly random function $H : \{0,1\}^w \to \{0,1\}^v$ below $2^w v$ bits. This, however, is not possible due to a result proved by Shannon (which we will present in Proposition 2) and hence such a combiner cannot exist. To express this we need a notion of compressibility:

Definition 6 (Compressibility)
A random variable H *can be compressed to s bits, if two functions* **com** *and* **dec** *(for compression, resp. decompression) exist such that on average the size of* com($\tilde{H}$) *(where* $\tilde{H}$ *is an instantiation of the random variable) is less or equal to s bits and that the probability of* **dec**(**com**($\tilde{H}$)) *is exactly 1; that is* **dec**($\cdot$) *is always able to completely restore* $\tilde{H}$:

$$E[\|\mathbf{com}(\tilde{H})\|] \leq s \qquad and \qquad Pr[\mathbf{dec}(\mathbf{com}(\tilde{H})) = \tilde{H}] = 1$$

3.2   Proof of Theorem 2

We will now present the proof of our main theorem for the case of second-preimage resistance. Our argument follows Pietrzak's in [12,10] where he proves the theorem for collision resistance. We are going to prove Theorem 2 indirectly by proving a proposition which informally says that if the output length of a combiner (C, P) is short, then it cannot be efficient, as P will have to make exponentially many queries to its hash oracle for (C, P) to be robust:

Proposition 1. *For some $n, m, w, v, l, k \in \mathbb{N}$ Let $C : \mathcal{R} \times \{0,1\}^m \to \{0,1\}^n$ be an oracle circuit with input domain $m := l \cdot (v+1)$, with q_C oracle gates for every hash function $H_i : \{0,1\}^w \to \{0,1\}^v$ (for $i = 1, ..., l$) and with output range*

$$n := (l - k + 1) \cdot (v - \log q_C) - t \qquad (t > 0) \qquad (4)$$

Let $\rho := (1 - 2^{-t+l+2})/\binom{l}{k}$. If (C, P) is a ρ-robust (for SPR, TCR or OW) (k, l)-combiner where reduction P has success probability at least $2/3$, making $q_P^{\mathcal{B}}$ queries to the breaking oracle and q_P^H queries to its hash functions then

$$v \le \log q_P^H + 2 + \log l \qquad (5)$$

or equivalently

$$2^v \le q_P^H \cdot 4 \cdot l \qquad (6)$$

Before we prove the proposition, let us show how it implies Theorem 2:

Proof (of Theorem 2). Proposition 1 states that if a (k, l) combiner (C, P) is ρ-robust with $\rho = (1 - 2^{-t+l+2})/\binom{l}{k}$ and the combiner has domain $m := l \cdot (v+1)$ and range $n := (l - k + 1) \cdot (v - \log q_C) - t$ for some $t > 0$, then it needs to make exponentially many calls to its oracles as $q_P^H \ge 2^{v-2-l}$. That is, P is not efficient. As every robust combiner is also ρ-robust for $\rho = (1 - 2^{-t+l+2})/\binom{l}{k}$ this proves Theorem 2 for the special case where the combiner is shrinking by $m - n = l \cdot (v + 1) - (l - k + 1) \cdot (v - \log q_C) + t$ as the combiner is either not efficient or not robust. However, as a combiner for arbitrary length hash functions necessarily has to work for fixed length functions as well the result presented here directly applies for arbitrary and infinite domain combiners. □

3.3   An Outline

To prove Proposition 1 we have to find oracles $H_1, \ldots, H_l$ and $\mathcal{B}$ such that the breaking oracle $\mathcal{B}$ finds second pre-images for combiner $C^{H_1, \ldots, H_l} : \{0,1\}^m \to \{0,1\}^n$ with range $n < (l-k+1)v - \mathcal{O}(\log q_C)$ while k out of the l hash functions stay second pre-image resistant in relation to $P^{\mathcal{B}, H_1, \ldots, H_l}$; that is, $P^{\mathcal{B}, H_1, \ldots, H_l}$ is not able to find second pre-images for more than $l - k + 1$ hash functions even with access to the powerful breaking oracle $\mathcal{B}$.

For this we are going to use hash functions chosen uniformly at random from the space of all functions of the form $\{0,1\}^w \to \{0,1\}^v$. For the breaking oracle $\mathcal{B}$ we are going to carefully design a function which outputs only safe second pre-images (cf. Definition 5) with respect to the target messages $X_1, \ldots, X_l \in \{0,1\}^w$ (denoted by $\mathcal{B}^{X_1, \ldots, X_l}$) given to the security reduction P; that is, P cannot simply use the breaking oracle to get all the necessary second pre-images.

After proving that such a breaking oracle initialized to message $X_1, \ldots, X_l \in \{0,1\}^w$ does indeed break the security of any (k, l)-combiner with high probability it remains to prove that the reduction $P^{\mathcal{B}, H_1, \ldots, H_l}$ with access to our breaking oracle and the (uniformly random) hash functions makes a poor job in finding second pre-images. For this we will use a corollary from Claude E. Shannon's source coding theorem (see any good introduction to information theory or Shannon's original [17]):

Proposition 2. *A uniformly random function* $H : \{0,1\}^w \rightarrow \{0,1\}^v$ *(with prefix-free domain[5]) cannot be compressed to less than* $2^w v$ *bits.*

What we will show is that if $P^{\mathcal{B},H_1,\ldots,H_l}$ is able to find enough (i.e., more than $l-k$) second pre-images for $H_1,\ldots,H_l$ with noticeable probability, then we are able to compress $H_1,\ldots,H_l$ to less than $l2^w v$ bits. That is, we are going to design a custom compression (**com**) and decompression (**dec**) algorithm that given $H_1,\ldots,H_l$, P and $\mathcal{B}$ uses P to compress the hash functions $H_1,\ldots,H_l$. As these are uniformly random, this forms a contradiction to Proposition 2 and hence such a P cannot exist. What is left to show is that in our case **com** and **dec** can initialize the breaking oracle with the target messages given to P before P is given access to the breaking oracle (remember that our breaking oracle $\mathcal{B}^{X_1,\ldots,X_l}$ outputs only second pre-images that are safe for the specific messages $X_1,\ldots,X_l$). We will see that this is in fact the case and that thus $\mathcal{B}$ will not be of too much use for P.

3.4   The Proof

The Oracles. To prove Proposition 1 we begin by defining the $l+1$ oracles $H_1,\ldots,H_l$ and $\mathcal{B}$. The hash functions H_i $(i = 1,\ldots,l)$ are each sampled uniformly at random from the set of all functions of the form $\{0,1\}^w \rightarrow \{0,1\}^v$. The breaking oracle $\mathcal{B}$ will be defined by a function $\phi : \{0,1\}^* \rightarrow \{0,1\}^m$ which is also sampled uniformly at random from all functions of the form $\{0,1\}^* \rightarrow \{0,1\}^m$. Function ϕ defines for a message $M \in \{0,1\}^m$ and randomness $R \in \mathcal{R}$ a pseudo-second pre-image $M_{\mathbf{spr}}$ for $C^{H_1,\ldots,H_l}(R,M)$ as $M_{\mathbf{spr}} := \phi(R||\langle i \rangle)$, where i is the smallest integer such that $C^{H_1,\ldots,H_l}(R,M) = C^{H_1,\ldots,H_l}(R,M_{\mathbf{spr}})$.

Our goal is to make sure that the breaking oracle outputs only safe second pre-images (with respect to some target messages $X_1,\ldots,X_l$) where by safe we mean that the oracle's output second pre-images should be safe for k out of the l hash functions (i.e., $\mathbf{safeSpr}_{k,X_1,\ldots,X_l}^{C^{H_1,\ldots,H_l}}(M,M_{\mathbf{spr}})$, compare Definition 5). Furthermore, each second pre-image output by $\mathcal{B}$ has to be safe for exactly the same k hash functions.

Let us assume that $\mathcal{B}^{X_1,\ldots,X_l}$ was initialized with target messages $X_1,\ldots,X_l$. As abbreviation we will simply write $\mathcal{B}$ when we mean a breaking oracle that was initialized with fixed but random target messages. We now introduce sets S_i (for $i = 1,\ldots,l$) that comprise all safe message, randomness pairs for hash function H_i. If $M_{\mathbf{spr}}$ is defined through ϕ as described above then we can define sets S_i as:

$$S_i := \{(R,M) \in \mathcal{R} \times \{0,1\}^m : \mathbf{safeSpr}_{H_i,X_i}^{C^{H_1,\ldots,H_l}}(M,M_{\mathbf{spr}})\} \quad \text{for } i \in \{1,\ldots,l\}$$

---

[5] Note that all functions $\{0,1\}^w \rightarrow \{0,1\}^v$ have a prefix-free domain and range, as all elements in either set have the same length.

We now define the intersection of k out of the l sets S_i such as to maximize the number of elements in the intersection. Let therefor

$$\Gamma_{\max} := \operatorname*{argmax}_{\substack{\Gamma \subseteq \{1,\dots,l\} \\ |\Gamma|=k}} \left| \bigcap_{i \in \Gamma} S_i \right| .$$

With $\Gamma_{\max}$ we can define the maximal intersection

$$\mathcal{R}_\Gamma := \bigcap_{i \in \Gamma_{\max}} S_i$$

which allows us to formalize the breaking oracle $\mathcal{B}$ as:

$$\mathcal{B}^{X_1,\dots,X_l}(R, M) := \begin{cases} M_{spr} & \text{if } (R, M) \in \mathcal{R}_\Gamma \\ \bot & \text{otherwise} \end{cases}$$

Thus, on input (R, M) our breaking oracle $\mathcal{B}^{X_1,\dots,X_l}$ will output a second pre-image $M_{\mathbf{spr}}$ such that $C^{H_1,\dots,H_l}(R, M) = C^{H_1,\dots,H_l}(R, M_{\mathbf{spr}})$ only if it is safe for at least k of the l hash functions in regard to the target messages $X_1, \dots, X_l$. Also note that two second pre-images for inputs (R, M) and (R', M') will be safe for (at least) the same k hash functions.

The Breaking Oracle $\mathcal{B}$ is ρ-Robust for All (k, l)-Combiners. We will now show that our breaking oracle ρ-breaks every (k, l)-combiner with some noticeable ρ. Note that, by definition, the breaking oracle ρ-breaks $C^{H_1,\dots,H_l}$ with

$$\rho = \frac{|\mathcal{R}_\Gamma|}{|\mathcal{R}| \cdot 2^m}$$

This we will prove using the following lemma stating informally that sampled second pre-images will be safe for at least k out of l hash functions for (k, l)-combiners most of the time.[6] (See the full version [8] for a proof for Lemma 1.).

Lemma 1. Let $C : \{0,1\}^m \to \{0,1\}^n$ be any oracle machine with q_C oracle gates per hash function $H_i : \{0,1\}^w \to \{0,1\}^v$ (with $i = 1, .., l$). Let $X_1, \dots, X_l \in \{0,1\}^w$ be target messages for functions $H_1, \dots, H_l$. For messages M, M_{spr} sampled as $M \leftarrow \{0,1\}^m$ and $M_{spr} \leftarrow (C^{H_1,\dots,H_l})^{-1}(M)$ we have:

$$Pr[\boldsymbol{safeSpr}_{k,X_1,\dots,X_l}^{C^{H_1,\dots,H_l}(\cdot)}(M, M_{spr})] \geq 1 - q_C^{l-k+1} \cdot \binom{l}{l-k+1} \cdot 2^{n-(v+1)(l-k+1)}$$

---

[6] Note that this lemma is essentially the only place where we need that the combiner's output length is significantly less than that of the concatenation combiner, $n = (l - k + 1)(v - \log(q_C)) - t$ (see equation (4)).

From Lemma 1 we will now deduce a lower bound for ρ. Let $I_{R,M} := 1$ if (R, M) is safe for at least k of the l hash functions H_i and $I_{R,M} = 0$ otherwise. Formally:

$$I_{R,M} := \begin{cases} 1 & \text{if } \mathbf{safeSpr}_{k,X_1,\ldots,X_l}^{C^{H_1,\ldots,H_l}(R,\cdot)}(M, M_{\mathbf{spr}}) \\ 0 & \text{otherwise} \end{cases}$$

Lemma 1 gives us a lower bound on the probability for event $I_{R,M} = 1$ as our breaking oracle samples random second pre-images. Using an upper bound of 2^l on the binomial coefficient we have that

$$Pr[I_{R,M} = 1] \geq 1 - q_C^{l-k+1} \cdot 2^{n-(v+1)(l-k+1)+l}$$

Now with $n := (l - k + 1) \cdot (v - \log q_C) - t$ (see equation 4) we get

$$Pr[I_{R,M} = 1] \geq 1 - q_C^{l-k+1} \cdot 2^{n-(v+1)(l-k+1)+l}$$
$$\geq 1 - q_C^{l-k+1} \cdot 2^{(l-k+1)\cdot(v-\log q_C)-t-(v+1)(l-k+1)+l}$$
$$= 1 - q_C^{l-k+1} \cdot 2^{\log q_C^{-(l-k+1)}} \cdot 2^{-(l-k+1)} \cdot 2^{-t+l}$$
$$\geq 1 - 2^{-t+l}$$

Remember that, by definition, the breaking oracle $\mathcal{B}$ has an inherent set $\mathcal{R}_\Gamma$ and only outputs second pre-images if the input (R, M) is an element of $\mathcal{R}_\Gamma$. With Γ we have fixed the set of k hash functions H_i ($i \in \Gamma_{\max}$) such that $\mathcal{R}_\Gamma$ is maximized. The indicator $I_{R,M}$ equals 1, if we have a safe second pre-image for k hash functions but not necessarily for the k hash functions specified by $\Gamma_{\max}$. We can however safely assume that ρ is greater than the probability of a safe second pre-image ($Pr[I_{R,M} = 1]$) divided by the possibilities of choosing k out of l elements (as $\Gamma_{\max}$ was designed to maximize this probability). Thus, with the expectation value for event $I_{R,M}$ (note that $E[I_{R,M}] = Pr[I_{R,M} = 1]$) we can lowerbound $\rho \geq E[I_{R,M}]/\binom{l}{k}$.

Setting $\tilde{e} := 1 - E[I_{R,M}]$ and applying the reverse Markov inequality, we have that:

$$Pr[E[I_{R,M}] < 1 - \gamma 2^{-t+l}] = Pr[\tilde{e} \geq \gamma 2^{-t+l}]$$
$$\leq \frac{1 - E[I_{R,M}]}{1 - 1 + \gamma 2^{-t+l}}$$
$$\leq \frac{1 - 1 + 2^{-t+l}}{1 - 1 + \gamma 2^{-t+l}} = \frac{1}{\gamma}$$

Setting $\gamma := 4$ yields: $Pr[E[I_{R,M}] < 1 - 2^{-t+l+2}] \leq \frac{1}{4}$. Using the estimate $\rho \geq E[I_{R,M}]/\binom{l}{k}$ we thus have:

$$Pr\left[\rho < (1 - 2^{-t+l+2})/\binom{l}{k}\right] \leq Pr\left[E[I_{R,M}]/\binom{l}{k} < (1 - 2^{-t+l+2})/\binom{l}{k}\right]$$
$$\leq \frac{1}{4} \tag{7}$$

We proved that with probability of at least 0.75, our breaking oracle ρ-breaks a (k, l)-combiner with $\rho = (1 - 2^{-t+l+2})/\binom{l}{k}$.

3.5 $\mathcal{B}$ Does Not Help P

We will now present the lemma that allows us to prove Proposition 1. Informally this lemma states that if the range of the combiner is as in the proposition and the reduction $P^{\mathcal{B},H_1,...,H_l}$ finds second pre-images with some probability then we can use this to compress the combined function table of hash functions $H_1, ..., H_l$ below $l2^w v$ bits. This can then be used to prove Proposition 1 as the H_i $(i = 1, ..., l)$ were chosen uniformly at random and therefore, by Proposition 2, cannot be compressed below $l2^w v$ bits.

Lemma 2. *Let (C,P) be as in Proposition 1 with*

$$v > \log q_P^H + \log l + 2 \tag{8}$$

Also let for any set of target messages $X_1, ..., X_l \in \{0,1\}^w$

$$Pr[\boldsymbol{spr}_{l-k+1,X_1,...,X_l}(P^{\mathcal{B}^{X_1,...,X_l},H_1,...,H_l}(X_1, ..., X_l))] \geq 0.5 \tag{9}$$

Then $H_1, ..., H_l$ can be compressed below $l2^w v$ bits.

Let us show how we can now prove our main proposition, Proposition 1:

Proof (of Proposition 1). Let Δ denote the event that $\mathcal{B}$ ρ-breaks C^H with $\rho \geq (1-2^{-t+3})/\binom{l}{k}$ (note that $Pr[\Delta] \geq 0.75$). With equation (7) and the bound on P from the definition of robust second-pre-image combiners (see Proposition 1 and the discussion following Definition 3), we can derive the following bound for any collection X^l of input messages:

$$\forall X^l \in \overbrace{\{0,1\}^w \times ... \times \{0,1\}^w}^{l \text{ times}}:$$

$$Pr[\boldsymbol{spr}_{l-k+1,X^l}(P^{\mathcal{B},H_1,...,H_l}(X^l))] = Pr[\Delta] \cdot Pr[\boldsymbol{spr}_{l-k+1,X^l}(P^{\mathcal{B},H_1,...,H_l}(X^l))|\Delta]$$

$$\geq \frac{3}{4} \cdot \frac{2}{3} = 0.5$$

Assume the $H_1, ..., H_l$ are uniformly random, then by Lemma 2 the combined function table for $H_1, ..., H_l$ can be compressed below $l2^w v$ bits. This contradicts Proposition 2 and hence equation (8) must be wrong. Thus:

$$v \leq \log q_P^H + 2 + \log l$$

which concludes the proof.   □

Compressing $H_1, ..., H_l$ with Second Pre-images by $P^{\mathcal{B},H_1,...,H_l}$

We will here only present a proof sketch for Lemma 2 (please refer to the full version [8] for a detailed proof).

Let us first take a closer look at the second pre-images sampled by the breaking oracle. By definition $\mathcal{B}(R, M)$ will only output a (pseudo) second pre-image if it is a safe one. Let's assume that $P^{\mathcal{B},H_1,\ldots,H_l}$ was given the target messages $X_1,\ldots,X_l$ and that the breaking oracle $\mathcal{B}^{X_1,\ldots,X_l}$ was initialized with exactly these. For now think of P as being a fair player who honestly is telling $\mathcal{B}$ its target values (we will later see why this can be assumed).

The breaking oracle $\mathcal{B}^{X_1,\ldots,X_l}$ now only outputs safe second pre-images that are safe for k of the l hash functions. For the reduction $P^{\mathcal{B}^{X^l},H^l}$ (for notational simplicity we write $P^{\mathcal{B}^{X^l},H^l}$ instead of $P^{\mathcal{B}^{X_1,\ldots,X_l},H_1,\ldots,H_l}$) to be successful it has for its input $(X_1,\ldots,X_l)$ to find second pre-images for $l-k+1$ of the l hash functions where X_i is the first part of the collision for hash function H_i ($i=1,\ldots,l$). This, however, directly implies that if $P^{\mathcal{B}^{X^l},H^l}(X_1,\ldots,X_l)$ succeeds and outputs $l-k+1$ second-pre-images then at least for one of the $l-k+1$ hash functions the second pre-image was not generated by the breaking oracle directly.

Let s denote the index of the hash function H_s ($s \in \{1,\ldots,l\}$) for which the second pre-image output by $P^{\mathcal{B}^{X^l},H^l}$ was not trivially created via the breaking oracle $\mathcal{B}^{X^l}$. Let $X_{\mathbf{spr}}^s$ be the second pre-image for hash function H_s for message X_s, i.e., $H_s(X_s) = H_s(X_{\mathbf{spr}})$ and $X_s \neq X_{\mathbf{spr}}$. What we now know is that the oracle query $H_s(X_{\mathbf{spr}}^s)$ which resulted in this second pre-image is made by P directly and not by the breaking oracle $\mathcal{B}^{X^l}$. Hence, $X_{\mathbf{spr}}^s$ is not present in any of the queries to H_s resulting from calls to the the breaking oracle. Let us by

$$\mathrm{qry}^{H_i}_{\mathcal{B}^{X^l}(R,M)} = \mathrm{qry}^{H_i}(C^{H^l}(R,M)) \cup \mathrm{qry}^{H_i}(C^{H^l}(R,M^{\mathcal{B}}_{spr})) \qquad (10)$$

denote all the queries to hash function H_i that occur in the evaluation of a $\mathcal{B}^{X^l}$ query on input (R,M), i.e. the queries resulting from evaluating the combiner $C^{H^l}(\cdot)$ with input (R,M) (the request to the breaking oracle) and $(R,M^{\mathcal{B}}_{spr})$ (the oracle's answer). Then we can rephrase the above statement about the second pre-image $X_{\mathbf{spr}}^s$ found by $P^{\mathcal{B}^{X^l},H^l}$ for hash function H_s:

$$X_{\mathbf{spr}}^s \notin \mathrm{qry}^{H_s}_{\mathcal{B}^{X^l}(M_B)} \quad \forall\, M_B \in \mathrm{qry}^{\mathcal{B}}(P^{\mathcal{B}^{X^l},H^l}(M)) \qquad (11)$$

This could again be rephrased as: $P^{\mathcal{B}^{X^l},H^l}(M_1,\ldots,M_l)$ cannot find trivial second-pre-images for all $l-k+1$ hash functions; $P^{\mathcal{B}^{X^l},H^l}$ cannot simply let $\mathcal{B}^{X^l}$ do all the work.

Now how does this help in compressing the function table of $H_1,\ldots,H_l$? The idea is to design a compression algorithm **com** together with a corresponding decompression algorithm **dec**. Both algorithms **com** and **dec** share a common, combined target message $X_\tau = (X_1,\ldots,X_l)$ with $(X_i \in \{0,1\}^w$ for $i=1,\ldots,l)$. The algorithms make use of the security reduction P and provide P with the input X_τ and the oracles that P expects: a breaking oracle $\mathcal{B}$ and hash functions $H_1,\ldots,H_l$.

If P succeeds in generating a second-preimage $X_{\mathbf{spr}}$, the compression algorithm **com** reduces the combined function table of $H_1,\ldots,H_l$ by X_τ. It further removes all the calls from P and $\mathcal{B}$ to any of the hash functions H_i (note that as **com** provided P and $\mathcal{B}$ with the hash functions it can easily track all those queries). The compression algorithm **com** then prepends the reduced function table with the hash values that P and $\mathcal{B}$ request during the execution of P. The new function table now contains one hash value less (the one from the second pre-image for one of the target messages in X_τ) than the original function table and we have thus compressed the function table by v bits. For decompression we can simply again simulate P (with the same random coins) and if we can identify the query with the second pre-image we can reconstruct the function table.

The difficulty will be to identify the call $X_{\mathbf{spr}}^s$ from P to hash function H^s which yields the second pre-image as it may not be P's last call. As we have said, **com** and **dec** can track which query goes to which hash function. Thus if we store the index of the call to H_s which yielded the second pre-image relative to the number of calls made by P (we know that this is bound by q_P, compare Definition 4).

Finally we have to make sure that the breaking oracle $\mathcal{B}$ given to P is initialized with the correct messages $(X_1, \ldots, X_l) = X_\tau$. Again, as **com** and **dec** provide the breaking oracle to P they can simply initialize the breaking oracle before "handing it over". $\Diamond$

With this we have completed the proof of Theorem 2 for the case of second pre-images. We refer to the full version of this extended abstract [8] for the omitted proofs as well as for the analyses for the properties target collision resistance and pre-image resistance.

4 Conclusion and Outlook

We have given a strong indication that combiners with short output robust for second pre-image resistance, target collision resistance or pre-image resistance do not exist. By this, we have extended Pietrzak's Theorem where he gave the result for the case of plain collision resistance [12]. Note that our work, as well as Pietrzak's only applies to fully black-box reductions in the terminology of Reingold et al. [13]. One possibility of bypassing such an impossibility result, is to consider white-box access to the hash functions (resp. the breaking oracle). A different approach would be to consider combiners only for a specific class of hash functions (e.g., efficiently implementable functions) instead of combiners that need to be robust for any choice of functions. Ideally, this class of hash functions should contain functions used in practice, such as the SHA familiy.

Acknowledgments. I thank the anonymous reviewers for valuable comments. I would like to especially thank Christina Brzuska and Marc Fischlin for insightful discussions. This work was supported by CASED (`www.cased.de`).

References

1. Aoki, K., Sasaki, Y.: Meet-in-the-Middle Preimage Attacks Against Reduced SHA-0 and SHA-1. In: Halevi, S. (ed.) CRYPTO 2009. LNCS, vol. 5677, pp. 70–89. Springer, Heidelberg (2009)

2. Boneh, D., Boyen, X.: On the Impossibility of Efficiently Combining Collision Resistant Hash Functions. In: Dwork, C. (ed.) CRYPTO 2006. LNCS, vol. 4117, pp. 570–583. Springer, Heidelberg (2006)

3. Canetti, R., Rivest, R., Sudan, M., Trevisan, L., Vadhan, S., Wee, H.: Amplifying Collision Resistance: A Complexity-Theoretic Treatment. In: Menezes, A. (ed.) CRYPTO 2007. LNCS, vol. 4622, pp. 264–283. Springer, Heidelberg (2007)

4. De Cannière, C., Rechberger, C.: Preimages for Reduced SHA-0 and SHA-1. In: Wagner, D. (ed.) CRYPTO 2008. LNCS, vol. 5157, pp. 179–202. Springer, Heidelberg (2008)

5. De Cannière, C., Rechberger, C.: Finding SHA-1 Characteristics: General Results and Applications. In: Lai, X., Chen, K. (eds.) ASIACRYPT 2006. LNCS, vol. 4284, pp. 1–20. Springer, Heidelberg (2006)

6. Dierks, T., Rescorla, E.: The Transport Layer Security (TLS) Protocol Version 1.2. RFC 5246 (Proposed Standard) (August 2008), http://www.ietf.org/rfc/rfc5246.txt, updated by RFCs 5746, 5878, 6176

7. Freier, A., Karlton, P., Kocher, P.: The Secure Sockets Layer (SSL) Protocol Version 3.0. RFC 6101 (Historic) (August 2011), http://www.ietf.org/rfc/rfc6101.txt

8. Mittelbach, A.: Hash combiners for second pre-image resistance, target collision resistance and pre-image resistance have long output (full version). Cryptology ePrint Archive, Report 2012/354 (2012), http://eprint.iacr.org/

9. Naor, M., Yung, M.: Universal one-way hash functions and their cryptographic applications. In: 21st ACM STOC Annual ACM Symposium on Theory of Computing, May 15–17, pp. 33–43. ACM Press, Seattle (1989)

10. Pietrzak, K.: Compression from collisions, or why CRHF combiners have a long output (full version)

11. Pietrzak, K.: Non-trivial Black-Box Combiners for Collision-Resistant Hash-Functions Don't Exist. In: Naor, M. (ed.) EUROCRYPT 2007. LNCS, vol. 4515, pp. 23–33. Springer, Heidelberg (2007)

12. Pietrzak, K.: Compression from Collisions, or Why CRHF Combiners Have a Long Output. In: Wagner, D. (ed.) CRYPTO 2008. LNCS, vol. 5157, pp. 413–432. Springer, Heidelberg (2008)

13. Reingold, O., Trevisan, L., Vadhan, S.P.: Notions of Reducibility between Cryptographic Primitives. In: Naor, M. (ed.) TCC 2004. LNCS, vol. 2951, pp. 1–20. Springer, Heidelberg (2004)

14. Rjaško, M.: On existence of robust combiners for cryptographic hash functions. In: ITAT, pp. 71–76 (2009)

15. Rogaway, P., Shrimpton, T.: Cryptographic Hash-Function Basics: Definitions, Implications, and Separations for Preimage Resistance, Second-Preimage Resistance, and Collision Resistance. In: Roy, B., Meier, W. (eds.) FSE 2004. LNCS, vol. 3017, pp. 371–388. Springer, Heidelberg (2004)

16. Sasaki, Y., Aoki, K.: Finding Preimages in Full MD5 Faster Than Exhaustive Search. In: Joux, A. (ed.) EUROCRYPT 2009. LNCS, vol. 5479, pp. 134–152. Springer, Heidelberg (2009)

17. Shannon, C., Petigara, N., Seshasai, S.: A mathematical theory of Communication. Bell System Technical Journal 27, 379–423 (1948)
18. Stevens, M., Sotirov, A., Appelbaum, J., Lenstra, A., Molnar, D., Osvik, D.A., de Weger, B.: Short Chosen-Prefix Collisions for MD5 and the Creation of a Rogue CA Certificate. In: Halevi, S. (ed.) CRYPTO 2009. LNCS, vol. 5677, pp. 55–69. Springer, Heidelberg (2009)
19. Wang, X., Yin, Y.L., Yu, H.: Finding Collisions in the Full SHA-1. In: Shoup, V. (ed.) CRYPTO 2005. LNCS, vol. 3621, pp. 17–36. Springer, Heidelberg (2005)
20. Wang, X., Yu, H.: How to Break MD5 and Other Hash Functions. In: Cramer, R. (ed.) EUROCRYPT 2005. LNCS, vol. 3494, pp. 19–35. Springer, Heidelberg (2005)

Human Perfectly Secure Message Transmission Protocols and Their Applications

Stelios Erotokritou[1,2,*] and Yvo Desmedt[1,**]

[1] Department of Computer Science, University College London, UK
{s.erotokritou,y.desmedt}@cs.ucl.ac.uk

[2] Computation-based Science and Technology Research Center, The Cyprus Institute

Abstract. Perfectly secure message transmission (PSMT) schemes have been studied in the field of cryptography for nearly 20 years.

In this paper we introduce a new aspect to PSMT. We consider the case when the hardware/software used by the receiver might be corrupted by the adversary. To address this, we replace the receiver by a human (the dual of this is when the sender is a human). Because of this, any proposed protocols should be computationally efficient for a human to carry out. Additionally, they should be as simple as possible, requiring minimal amount of thought and effort for someone to use them correctly.

Taking the above into consideration, we propose two different constructions of such protocols. These have been designed to be secure and to be *usable* - so as to be easy and accurate when human parties use them.

Experiments were carried out with human participants to evaluate what humans can compute.

Keywords: PSMT, Secret Sharing, Information Theoretic Security, Privacy, Combinatorics.

1 Introduction

Perfectly secure message transmission (PSMT) schemes were introduced in [13]. In such protocols, a sender is connected to a receiver over an underlying network through a number of node disjoint network paths, otherwise known as wires. Since their introduction, PSMT protocols have been the focus of much research [7,11,15,20] where protocols have been made more efficient with regards to computational and communication complexity [9,21,26]. Protocols have also been considered in various network models [12,14,19] and different adversary models have been considered [24,29].

Nearly all of these protocols consider the sender and receiver of a communication to be a Turing machine capable of complex mathematical operations

---

* The author would like to thank EPSRC and BT for their funding of part of this research.
** Part of this work was done while funded by EPSRC EP/C538285/1 and by BT, as BT Chair of Information Security.

I. Visconti and R. De Prisco (Eds.): SCN 2012, LNCS 7485, pp. 540–558, 2012.

such as Lagrange interpolation for the reconstruction of shared secrets [27], Reed Solomon error correction techniques [5] amongst others.

But what if one of these two parties is not capable of such operations? What if the receiver of the communication is a human who cannot execute such computationally intensive and hard (for humans) operations? This could arise when a computational device is not available or indeed cannot be trusted.

A computational device may not be trusted when perhaps it is infected with some form of malware. As seen in [4], when computer systems were infected by malware, key facilities had to be taken offline to prevent any problems that could arise from this. When such a situation arises, it is important that operations of a plant still continue. To allow for this, it is important that human operatives continue with key required operations in a correct and precise manner. Alternatively, computational devices may not be trusted as a result of malfunctions.

Another motivation behind this aspect of PSMT could also be electronic code voting. Code voting was proposed by Chaum in [6] and in such a voting scheme each voter receives a unique PIN per candidate by *postal mail*. By making the PINs, considered over all different voters and all different candidates, unique, the PIN can be used to vote. To vote, the voter just enters the PIN received corresponding to the candidate of his/her choice. The breakthrough of Chaum's approach is that one can use a possibly hacked computer to perform a secure operation. Furthermore, it has been shown to be user friendly [3]. But what if contrary to Chaum's assumptions the postal mail cannot be trusted? If that is the case, adversarial collaborations can violate key election properties such as identifying a voter's vote, ballot stuffing, amongst others. In such a case, to make electronic code voting secure, human voters would have to receive shares of their voting codes from a number of possibly corrupt (by malware) computational devices. Reconstruction of the voting codes in such a scenario would have to be carried out by the human voters themselves as their devices are not necessarily trusted. For this to occur correctly, schemes used would have be simple and easy enough for humans to carry out the required computations with a very high percentage of accuracy.

Taking the above into consideration, we propose two different constructions of such protocols. These have been designed to be secure and usable - so as to be easy and accurate when human parties use them. One of these constructions is based on mod10 arithmetic whilst the other is based on using permutations to perform such modulo addition.

We base our constructions on experiments with human participants.

2   Background and Preliminary Results

2.1   Adversary Model and Security Definition

We now give a general outline of the security model which will be considered throughout the text.

The adversary is assumed to be present in the underlying network which connects the sender and the receiver of a message transmission protocol. The adversary is assumed to know the complete protocol specification, message space $\mathcal{M}$ and the complete structure of the network graph. Throughout the text, a static t-threshold bounded, computationally unlimited adversary will be considered. Both passive and active adversaries will be considered. The adversary is assumed to be able to corrupt up to t number of nodes of the underlying network connecting the sender and receiver and thus the adversary is capable of corrupting up to t node disjoint paths (otherwise known as wires) which connect the sender and receiver.

Throughout the text we want to achieve perfect security, i.e. information theoretic security. We want the communication between a sender and a receiver to be achieved with probability 1. The message a receiver accepts is denoted by M^R and should always be the same value as the message transmitted by a sender, denoted by M^S.

2.2   Secret Sharing Friendly to Humans

In this section we describe the secret sharing scheme that will be used in two of the protocols to be presented.

An n-out-of-n secret sharing scheme allows for a secret message M to be distributed as a selection of n number of shares $\{s_1, \ldots, s_n\}$ so that the following properties are achieved:

- From the collection of n shares one is able to reconstruct M.
- Any subset of $(n-1)$ or less shares reveals no information about M.

Various secret sharing schemes exist in the literature such as those presented in [18,27]. These schemes though require computation which is difficult for a human receiver (as we consider in this text) to carry out. Any secret sharing schemes that will be used should thus be easy for humans to use. In Section 3, secret sharing mod10 will be the only computation that will be used. We now describe this scheme.

In secret sharing mod10, when a secret (quantified by a number composed of a number of digits) is shared to a number of shares (each of which is also a number of equal length to the secret), the sum of all respective digits from all shares mod10 will be equal to the respective digit of the original shared secret.

Human friendly secret sharing mod10 can be explained by the following:

$$\forall i \in \{1, \ldots, k\} : D_i(s) = \sum_{j=1}^{n} D_i(s_j) \bmod 10$$

Where s denotes the secret, s_j denotes one of the n shares $(1 \leq j \leq n)$, k denotes the length in digits of the secret s (and subsequently the length in digits of all shares both of which are elements of $(Z_{10})^k$), and D_i denotes digit i $(1 \leq i \leq k)$ of the secret or share (D_2 would thus identify the second digit of the secret or share). The above can be read as "For every i, the sum of digit i over all shares, mod10, results in the same value as digit i of the secret".

It is easy to see that the described scheme is a secret sharing scheme. Without knowing all n shares one cannot reconstruct a shared secret. Additionally, knowledge of a lower number of shares (than what are required to reconstruct a secret) does not reveal any information of the shared secret. This is due to Shannon's proof of the one time pad [28]. Because of this, all messages in $\mathcal{M}$ are possible when less than n shares are known. This is equivalent to information theoretic secrecy as defined in [28]. Reconstruction of a secret can be carried out in a simple to use manner - as described in Appendix A.

2.3   Set Systems

In this section we overview set systems which are the key combinatorial structures used in the construction of PSMT protocols with a human receiver to be presented in Section 3.

In [10], Desmedt-Kurosawa defined the following:

Definition 1 ([25]). *A set system is a pair* $(X, \mathcal{B})$, *where* $X \triangleq \{1, 2, \ldots, n\}$ *and* $\mathcal{B}$ *is a collection of blocks* $B_i \subset X$ *with* $i = 1, 2, \ldots, b$.

In the above definition the symbol $\triangleq$ means "is equal to by definition".

Definition 2 ([10]). *We label* $(X, \mathcal{B})$ *as an* (n, b, t)-*verifiers set system if:*

1. $|X| = n$,
2. $|B_i| = t + 1$ *for* $i = 1, 2, \ldots, b$, *and*
3. *For any subset* $F \subset X$ *with* $|F| \leq t$, $\exists B_i \in \mathcal{B}$ *such that* $F \cap B_i = \emptyset$.

We generalize the definition of (n, b, t)-verifiers set systems as follows:

Definition 3. *We say that* $(X, \mathcal{B})$ *is a generalized* (n, b, t', t)-*verifiers set system if the following conditions are satisfied:*

1. $|X| = n$,
2. $|B_i| = t' + 1$ *for* $i = 1, 2, \ldots, b$, *and*
3. *For any subset* $F \subset X$ *with* $|F| \leq t$, $\exists B_i \in \mathcal{B}$ *such that* $F \cap B_i = \emptyset$.

The definitions of both verifiers set systems and generalized verifiers set systems ensure the *key* property that for a set of blocks (each block of size $(t + 1)$ or $(t' + 1)$ respectively), at least one block does not contain any elements of *any* (at most) t sized subset of elements.

The generalized (n, b, t', t)-verifiers set system will be important in the construction of our PSMT protocols with a human receiver. We will assume X represents the set of wires connecting the sender to the human receiver and $\mathcal{B}$ will be different subsets of these wires. As the adversary is t-bounded, this ensures that at least one block will be free from any adversary presence.

Generalized Verifier Set Systems and Covering Designs. We now explain the connection between generalized verifier set systems and covering designs.

Definition 4. *A collection* $\mathcal{C}$ *of* k-*subsets of* $\{1, \ldots, n\}$ *called blocks is an* (n, k, t)-*cover design if every* t-*subset of* $\{1, \ldots, n\}$ *is contained in at least one block.*

The definitions of generalized verifier set systems and covering designs identify them to essentially be equivalent by taking complements. In other words, one can use cover designs to construct generalized verifier set systems (and vice versa). The following lemma from [10] shows this - the proof of which is clear.

Lemma 1. $(X, \mathcal{B})$ *is a* (v, b, t)*-verifiers set system if and only if the set system* $(X, \mathcal{B}^c)$ *is a* $(v, v - t - 1, t)$*-covering, where* $\mathcal{B}^c \triangleq \{X \backslash B_i \mid B_i \in \mathcal{B}\}$.

Corollary 1. *Similarly,* $(X, \mathcal{B})$ *is a generalized* (n, b, t', t)*-verifiers set system if and only if the set system* $(X, \mathcal{B}^c)$ *is a* $(v, v - t' - 1, t)$*-covering, where* $\mathcal{B}^c \triangleq \{X \backslash B_i \mid B_i \in \mathcal{B}\}$.

Constructing Set Systems. We now describe the simplest construction of a generalized verifier sets which will be used as a reference for protocols to be presented in Section 3. We will refer to this construction as "Disjoint Set System". Further constructions result from the extensive work in covering designs such as those of [1,2,16,17,23,25] amongst others.

Lemma 2. *When* $n = b \times (t' + 1)$ *and* $b \geq t + 1$, *a generalized* (n, b, t', t)*-verifier set system* $(X, \mathcal{B})$ *can be constructed when each block is disjoint to all others.*

Proof. From [23, p. 221], as $\mathcal{B}$ is composed of $(t + 1)$ disjoint $(t' + 1)$-sized blocks, it is easy to see that a t-threshold bounded adversary can be present in at most t blocks - satisfying the properties of generalized verifier sets. □

Similarly, the following is a construction for an (n, b, t)-verifiers set system.

Lemma 3. *When* $n = b \times (t + 1)$ *and* $b = t + 1$, *an* (n, b, t)*-verifiers set system* $(X, \mathcal{B})$ *can be constructed when each block is disjoint to all others.*

The proof of this is similar to that of Lemma 2.

We refer to verifiers and generalized verifier set systems constructed as in Lemma 2 and Lemma 3 as *Disjoint Set Systems*.

2.4 $t + 1$-out-of-n Human Friendly Secret Sharing

A link between covering designs (and due to Lemma 1 verifiers set systems) and secret sharing was made in [25] (see also [22] for a special case). We now briefly survey this link.

Assume $(X, \mathcal{B})$ is an (n, b, t)-verifiers set system. We now explain how to use it as a $t + 1$-out-of-n secret sharing scheme. First, we let $X = \mathcal{P}$, the set of participants. Let M be the secret. We first use a b-out-of-b secret sharing scheme as explained in Section 2.2. This provides us with shares s_i $(1 \leq i \leq b)$. For each i $(1 \leq i \leq b)$ we give share s_i to the participants that belong to block B_i.

As any $t + 1$ parties are present in all b blocks, they can reconstruct the secret by pooling together the shares they received.

In essence, we prove the above claim formally in the proof of Theorem 1.

Generalization of Secret Sharing Scheme. The secret sharing scheme presented in this section can be generalized using an Abelian group. It should be noted that a quasigroup suffices. Care though is needed when using a quasigroup to take into account the potential lack of associativity and commutativity.

In such a case, the sharing of a secret from the group will be explained by the following:

$$\forall i \in \{1, \ldots, k\} : D_i(s) = \sum_{j=1}^{n} D_i(s_j) \bmod |A|$$

For the above, the definitions of s, s_j, n, k and D_i are similar to those of when human friendly secret sharing mod10 was explained in Section 2.2.

When $A = \{0, 1\}$, the generalization of the secret sharing scheme describes XOR-sharing. In this paper, we assume the case of when $A = \{0, \ldots, 9\}$ as it has the favorable property of being easy to evaluate when used by humans.

3   Mod 10 Human PSMT Protocols against Active Adversary

In this section we present two human PSMT protocols based on mod10 arithmetic. We consider an active adversary and present a one phase (non-interactive) and two phase (interactive) protocol. We denote with n the number of wires used to connect the sender and the receiver.

3.1   One-Phase Mod 10 PSMT with a Human Receiver

In the one phase protocol the human receiver cannot communicate with the sender. Transmission of data only occurs from the sender to the receiver. The protocol we present is based on the concept of generalized (n, b, t', t)-verifier set systems and mod10 arithmetic (see Section 2.4). As shown in [13] one phase PSMT can only occur when $n \geq 3t + 1$ wires are used. We assume that wires connecting the sender and the receiver correspond to points in a generalized $(n, b, 2t + 1, t)$-verifier set system to be used.

The main idea of the protocol is as follows. The secret message will be secret shared in a similar manner as described in Section 2.4 - but instead a b-out-of-b secret sharing scheme will be used (where b denotes the number of blocks to be be used). Each shares will then be transmitted over a block of wires with each share transmitted over one block only. Each block will be of size at least $(2t + 1)$ so a majority can always be received correctly by the receiver. By sending shares over blocks of wires which chosen so that the adversary is not present in at least one of these blocks, the correctness of the protocol will be achieved.

The protocol is formally presented as follows - denoting with M^S the secret of the communication.

Protocol 1. *One-Phase Transmission Protocol with a Human.*

Protocol Setup. Selection of b number of blocks $B_1, \ldots, B_b$ of size $|B_i| \geq 2t+1$ and which satisfy the key property that for any (at most) t sized subset F of elements, there exists at least one block B_i such that $B_i \cap F = \emptyset$.

Phase 1. The sender generates secret shares of M^S using a b-out-of-b secret sharing scheme as outlined in Section 2.4 and sends share s_i ($1 \leq i \leq b$) over all wires which correspond to points for block B_i.

End of Phase 1. The receiver obtains the secret message M^S by using all correct shares and using the reconstruction process outlined in Section 2.4. By summing the digits over all correct shares mod10 the receiver will reconstruct the secret. The receiver identifies correct shares using a majority vote - correct shares are received at least $(t+1)$ times.

Theorem 1. *The One-Phase* mod10 *Transmission Protocol with a human receiver is a PSMT protocol.*

Proof. The protocol achieves perfect privacy as due to Condition 3 of generalized verifier set systems, there will exist at least one block of wires free of the t-bounded adversary. In this way, the adversary lacks at least one share transmitted by the sender and perfect privacy is achieved. Perfect reliability is achieved as the protocol uses blocks of size at least $(2t+1)$. As the adversary is t-bounded, this ensures that the human receiver accepts a majority of the correct share transmitted by the sender for all blocks. The human receiver thus correctly accepts the secret by reconstructing the secret using majority received shares. Furthermore, as a majority is used to confirm the correctness of a share and as this is always achieved, the adversary cannot cause the protocol to fail in any way. The protocol thus achieves perfectly secure message transmission.□

One-Phase PSMT with a Human Using a Disjoint Set System. We may assume the case of when all blocks are truly disjoint between them - as described by Lemma 2, as this construction is the simplest and easiest construction for a human party to use. Using this construction, the parameters of the protocol are as follows - there are $b = t + 1$ blocks with the size of each block $|B_i| \geq 2t + 1$ (although $|B_i| = 2t + 1$ suffices).

Assuming the use of the construction described in Lemma 2, the sender's computational complexity is $O(t^2)$. This is because the sender has to transmit a field element in $(Z_{10})^k$ on each of the $O(t^2)$ wires connecting sender and receiver.The computational complexity of the receiver is $O(t^2 \log t)$, because the receiver at the end of Phase 1 accepts $O(t^2)$ field elements in $(Z_{10})^k$ and because the correctness of these elements needs to be checked to identify the correct $t+1$ shares of the secret. It is easy to see that the communication complexity of the protocol is also $O(t^2)$ - as the sender transmit a single field element in $(Z_{10})^k$ over each of the $O(t^2)$ wires[1].

---

[1] It is important to note that using any of the known set systems constructions will always result in the same communication and computational complexities - as all state of the art constructions will require $O(t^2)$ wires connecting sender and receiver.

Optimally Connected One-Phase PSMT with a Human. As shown in [13] the optimal number of wires for one-phase PSMT is $n = 3t + 1$. Using this number, there exist a trivial generalized $(3t + 1, \binom{3t + 1}{2t + 1}, 2t + 1, t)$-verifier set. A protocol initiated with these parameters is identical to a protocol presented in [12] when using a threshold adversary structure. In such a protocol, all possible $(2t + 1)$ subsets of wires from $(3t + 1)$ wires are used as blocks. Such a protocol though is impractical for use when a human party is involved as the number of required blocks increases greatly as the value of t increases.

It should be noted that for small values of t (say $t = 1$, 2) the number of subsets of wires which will be used as blocks will be relatively low, allowing for such a protocol to be simple and practically feasible for a human party to use. This secret sharing scheme was first presented by Liu in 1968 [22].

3.2   Two-Phase Mod 10 PSMT with a Human Receiver

For two phase PSMT protocols, the receiver and sender are able to interact over a network with a *lower number of wires* $n \geq 2t + 1$ connecting the two parties - when compared to the $n \geq 3t + 1$ number of wires required for one phase PSMT protocols. The solution we present is based on the concept of (n, b, t)-verifier sets. We assume that wires connecting the sender and receiver correspond to points in the (n, b, t)-verifier set system to be used.

The main idea of the protocol is as follows. The protocol is initiated by the receiver who transmits different random values to the sender upon different sets of wires of size at least $(t+1)$ - transmitting the same value over wires in the same set. This ensures that if the adversary is active, the sender is able to identify sets of wires for which *different* values are received. Such sets are blacklisted. The sender uses the values received from non-blacklisted sets to privately send the secret of the communication. The protocol is formally presented as follows - denoting with M^S the secret of the communication.

Protocol 2. *Two-Phase Transmission Protocol with a Human.*

Protocol Setup. An (n, b, t)-verifier set system with b number of blocks $B_1, \ldots,$ B_b all of which are of size $|B_i| \geq t+1 = t'$ and which satisfy the key property that at least one block does not contain elements of *any* (at most) t sized subset of elements will have to be constructed. $\mathcal{B}$ will be used to denote the set of all blocks used.

Step 1. For each block $B_1, \ldots, B_b$, the receiver chooses a uniformly random field element r_i from $(Z_{10})^k$. When $B_i = \{x_{i_1}, x_{i_2}, \ldots x_{i_{t'}}\}$, the sender sends the value of r_i on wire x_{i_j} (for all x_{i_j} in B_i where $1 \leq j \leq t'$).

Step 2. If the received values that should correspond to r_i on wires $B_i = \{x_{i_1}, x_{i_2}, \ldots x_{i_{t'}}\}$ are different, the sender black lists B_i (and checks this for all $1 \leq i \leq b$). The sender broadcasts the complete black list of such B_i to the receiver. We call this list $\mathcal{B}'$.

The sender then computes $\mathcal{B}'' = \mathcal{B} \setminus \mathcal{B}'$. The sender adds the random values r_i corresponding with the blocks in $\mathcal{B}''$. So, if $\mathcal{B}'' = \{B_{j_1}, B_{j_2}, \ldots, B_{j_l}\}$, the sender computes $r = r_{j_1} + r_{j_2} + \cdots + r_{j_i}$ and sends to the receiver $V = r + M^S$ using broadcast. (The addition of the random values to calculate r occurs using mod 10 arithmetic for each digit and likewise for the evaluation of V.)

Step 3 The receiver is able to decode M^S in a similar manner to the actions of the sender in Step 2. $\mathcal{B}''$ will first be found using the received broadcast value of $\mathcal{B}'$ and then the value of r will be calculated. M^S can then be decoded as $M^S = V - r$. (The addition of the random values to calculate r occurs using mod 10 arithmetic and likewise for the subtraction which occurs for the evaluation of M^S.)

Note: One should note that the broadcast which occurs in Step 2 does not have to be carried out by transmitting the information to broadcast over all wires connecting the sender and the receiver. Instead, this information can be sent on any $2t + 1$ wires. As there are at most t faulty wires, this ensures that the correct information will be correctly received by the receiver at the end of Step 2.

Theorem 2. *The Two-Phase* mod 10 *Transmission Protocol with a human receiver is a PSMT protocol.*

Proof. The protocol achieves perfect privacy as due to Condition 3 of verifier set systems, there exists at least one block with wires free of the adversary. As this block is free of the adversary, a single value will be received from it which will be used in the calculation of r and since the adversary does not learn it, perfect privacy is achieved. Perfect reliability is achieved as the sender only considers blocks from which a single value was received. As blocks are of size $(t + 1)$, a t-bounded adversary cannot make the sender consider a value the receiver did not send. This in addition to the broadcast of the list of blacklisted blocks $\mathcal{B}'$, allows for perfect reliability to be achieved and for perfectly secure message transmission also.   □

Two-Phase PSMT with a Human Using a Disjoint Set System. We may assume the case of when all these sets are truly disjoint between them - as shown in the construction of Lemma 3, as this construction is the simplest and easiest construction for a human party to use. Using this construction, the parameters of the protocol are as follows - there are $b = t + 1$ blocks with the size of each block $|B_i| \geq t + 1$ (although $|B_i| = t + 1$ suffices).

Assuming the use of the construction described in Lemma 3, the receiver's computational complexity is $O(t^2)$. This is because the receiver has to transmit a field element in $(Z_{10})^k$ on each of the $O(t^2)$ wires connecting the two parties in the first phase[2]. In the second phase of the protocol, the receiver may have to accept $O(t^2)$ field elements in $(Z_{10})^k$ - from the broadcast of the black list $\mathcal{B}'$ of 'faulty' blocks which can be of maximum size t. The computational complexity of the sender is $O(t^2)$, for the same reasons. The sender accepts $O(t^2)$ field elements in $(Z_{10})^k$ at the end of the first step and has to evaluate and broadcast black

---

[2] The receiver also has to select $t + 1$ random elements and evaluate $\mathcal{B}''$.

list $\mathcal{B}'$. The communication complexity of the protocol is $O(t^2)$ because of the broadcast of the $O(t)$ sized set of black-listed blocks over any $O(2t+1)$ wires.

Optimally Connected Two-Phase PSMT with a Human. As shown in [13] the optimal number of wires for two-phase PSMT is $n = 2t + 1$. Similar to one phase transmission protocols with a human, there also exists a trivial $(2t+1, \binom{2t+1}{t+1}, t)$-verifier set. In such a protocol, all possible $(t+1)$ subsets of wires from $(2t + 1)$ wires are used as blocks. Such a protocol though is impractical for use when a human party is involved as the number of required blocks increases greatly as the value of t increases.

It should be noted that for small values of t (say $t = 1, 2, 3$) the number of subsets of wires which will be used as blocks will be relatively low, allowing for such a protocol to be simple and practically feasible for a human party to use.

3.3   Practically Feasible Protocols for Small Values of t

A slight weakness of the one and two phase protocols presented is the rather sub-optimal number of wires required to tolerate a t-bounded adversary. In this section we identify parameters that could be used for natural practical use case scenarios where the value of t is relatively small - up to $t = 3$.

For both the one and two phase protocols we identified an alternative set system comprised of all $(2t + 1)$ and $(t + 1)$ subset of wires from the respective optimal number of wires. We now comment on the set systems which could be used for these alternative protocols for small values of t.

For the one phase case, $n = 3t + 1$ number of wires will be required. The generalized verifier set system to be used will consist of all possible $(2t+1)$ sized subsets. For $t = 1$ and $n = 4$ the number of blocks will be $C(4, 3) = 4$. For $t = 2$ and $n = 7$ the number of blocks will be $C(7, 5) = 21$. Beyond $t = 2$ the number of blocks for the human receiver to use becomes impractical (for $t = 3$ $C(10, 7) = 120$).

Similarly, for the two phase case, $n = 2t + 1$ number of wires will be required. The verifier set system to be used will consist of all possible $(t+1)$ sized subsets. For $t = 1$ and $n = 3$ the number of blocks will be $C(3, 2) = 3$. For $t = 2$ and $n = 5$ the number of blocks will be $C(5, 3) = 10$ and for $t = 3$ and $n = 7$ the number of blocks will be $C(7, 4) = 35$. Beyond $t = 3$ the number of blocks for the human receiver to use becomes impractical (for $t = 4$ $C(9, 5) = 126$).

Further to the above, we also present examples of practically feasible set systems for small values of t which could be used by the protocols presented in the earlier two sections. We identify the number of required blocks and the size of set X of the set system. For the one phase protocol, we require the blocks to be of size at least 2t+1. Similarly, for the two phase protocol, blocks size must be at least t+1. Specifics on how such set systems can be constructed follow from the source of the data which is the La Jolla Covering Repository [1] (please note that other similar examples found in the repository could also be used).

Table 1. Examples of various generalized verifier sets which could be used in the one-phase protocol for small values of t using Corollary 1

Value of t	Size of Blocks	Number of Required Blocks	$\|X\| = n$	$n = 3t + 1$
1	3	4	4	Yes
2	5	11	8	No
2	5	21	7	Yes
3	7	21	13	No

Table 2. Examples of various verifier sets which could be used in the two-phase protocol for small values of t using Lemma 1

Value of t	Size of Blocks	Number of Required Blocks	$\|X\| = n$	$n = 2t + 1$
1	2	3	3	Yes
2	3	6	6	No
2	3	10	5	Yes
3	4	12	9	No
3	4	35	7	Yes

4   Human Friendly Addition Mod 10

The protocols presented in Section 3 required the human receiver to execute some computation. Despite the computational and seemingly mathematical simplicity, some users may find these operations confusing and difficult to execute correctly.

In this section we present an alternative PSMT protocol with a human receiver. The protocol is more user friendly and easier for human receivers to use as no *apparent* form of mathematical operations need to be carried out. Instead, all receivers have to do is to follow a path traced by joined lines over some figures - as will be detailed in Section 4.2. This alternative protocol represents addition mod10 using permutations to make the addition mod10 operation friendlier to humans. We regard $Z_{10}(+)$ as a subgroup of the symmetric group S_{10}.

4.1   Addition Mod 10 Using Permutations

Suppose that one wants to carry out the addition mod10 of $x + s$ (where $0 \leq s, x, \leq 9$). Furthermore, lets assume that this addition should use secret sharing - as s is a secret that should not be transmitted over a single channel. This in effect means that when carrying out addition mod 10 and provided that $s_1 + s_2 + s_3 = s$, $x + s \equiv x + s_1 + s_2 + s_3$.

In effect, shares s_1, s_2 and s_3 denote how x should progressively shift (upwards due to addition mod 10). We now describe how this can be represented as permutations and (importantly to achieve user friendliness) pictures of shifts.

Suppose that the value of $x = 6$ and that the value of $s = 5$. This means that after the addition mod10 of $x + s$, the result should be $(6 + 5) \mod 10 = 1$. A picture of the shift should thus point from 6 to 5.

Furthermore, lets assume that s is secret shared to $s_1 = 8$, $s_2 = 4$ and $s_3 = 3$. This means that the value of x should shift from its original value of 6 to $((6 + 8) \bmod 10 =)4$ when added $\bmod 10$ with s_1. When this result is added $\bmod 10$ to s_2 it should then shift to $((4 + 4) \bmod 10 =)8$ and when this second result is added $\bmod 10$ to s_3 is should result to $((8 + 3) \bmod 10 =)1$.

4.2   Human PSMT Permutation Protocol against a Passive Adversary

We now present the more user friendly PSMT protocol with a human receiver considering a t-threshold bounded passive adversary. In the background the scheme uses permutations to add modulo a number as described in Section 4.1. Despite this, all human receivers have to execute is the simple task of tracing a line amongst other lines in a diagram.

For the protocol to be presented the number of wires n required to connect the sender and a human receiver equal $n = t + 1$. In Section 4.3 we outline how such protocols can be used against an active adversary.

Protocol 3. *Human Permutation Protocol.*

Protocol Setup. The sender constructs a random permutation π and shares this permutation over n other random permutations - $\pi_1, \ldots, \pi_n$, such that these permutation placed in order reconstruct π. Each π_i $(1 \leq i \leq n)$ will be a *diagram* which is part of π.

Phase 1. The sender transmits $\pi_i \in_R S_c$ over wire w_i $(1 \leq i \leq n)$.

End of Phase 1. The human receiver receives shares of a permutation - each of which is a diagram. The human receiver brings all diagrams (all the shares of a permutation) together in their right order (π_1 first, π_2 second, $\ldots$, π_n last), and is able to view the complete permutation.

Theorem 3. *The Human Permutation Protocol is a PSMT protocol.*

Proof. Perfect privacy is achieved as the adversary will not learn the permutation transmitted on the wire which the adversary does not control. As these permutations are randomly constructed, perfect privacy is achieved. Perfect reliability is achieved as a passive adversary is considered.   □

For clarity, we also present and explain the protocol through the use of diagrams. We assume the value of $t = 1$ and that the secret to be transmitted from the sender to the receiver is a single digit.

The human receiver starts of with the same initial handout of instructions similar to that shown in Figure 1. Such a handout could be made readily available before any such protocol execution is required.

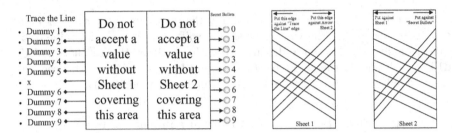

Fig. 1. Initial view of human receiver

Fig. 2. Two diagrams corresponding to shares to be received by the receiver

We assume that the two diagrams that will be transmitted by the sender will be those shown in Figure 2.

The human receiver will receive the first diagram from one of the two wires which connect the sender to the receiver. This will be placed in the position indicated by the handout as shown in Figure 3.

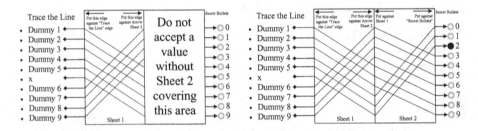

Fig. 3. The human receiver will place the first diagram in the appropriate position

Fig. 4. The receiver traces the radio button corresponding to the start of the line

Similarly, the human receiver will receive the second diagram from the second wire and place it in the position indicated by the handout. The digit secret will then be identified by tracing the line over the two permutation sheets to the radio button number corresponding to the start of the traced line (the human receiver will begin tracing from the radio button marked with "x"). The radio button number will correspond to the digit secret. This is shown in Figure 4 (for the example, the secret digit is 2).

Once the human receiver identifies the radio button corresponding to the start of the traced line, they accept the secret digit of the communication as the number which corresponds to the final radio button.

From the description, this protocol seems easy for a human receiver to use without errors. In Section 5 we assess the way human participants used a variant of this protocol by discussing the results of experimental evaluation carried out.

The protocol is a PSMT protocol as a t-bounded passive adversary can learn at most t of the diagrams sent to the human receiver. *Given that the generation of these diagrams are carried out in a random manner by the sender*, then by not knowing one of these $t + 1$ in number diagrams, it is easy to see that the adversary cannot know the value of the secret.

Note: If a secret to be sent to a human receiver is a number with more than one digit, the above process will have to be carried out in independent executions for each of the digits corresponding to the secret.

4.3   Active Adversary Human PSMT Permutation Protocols

It is easy to see that the constructions used for the protocols of Section 3 can also be used for human PSMT permutation protocols against an active adversary. The only way in which the protocols will differ, is that instead of transmission of shares, transmission of diagrams will occur.

For the one phase active adversary protocol the changes are very apparent (transmit diagrams in the place of shares). For the two phase case, the changes would be very similar but some extra steps will be required[3].

5   Experimental Evaluation of Human Friendly Addition

To assess the usability of the proposed human PSMT protocols we carried out experiments with participants. It should be noted that these experiments were carried out in the context of another paper [8]. However, the focus of the paper was how humans interact with electronic voting protocols. The experiments are the only form of overlap between the two papers.

Although our original experiments were directed to check how user friendly our alternatives [8] to Chaum's code voting [6] are, the same experiments allow us to compare the classical approach used to add integers mod10, versus our alternative. Due to space reasons, and since the original focus of the experiment is different, details of the experiments and the experimental evaluation that was carried out can be found in Section 5 of [8].

5.1   Relativity of Experiments to PSMT Protocols and Discussion of Results

In this section we explain how the experiments were carried out, although in the context of another paper [8], they are also valid in the context of this paper.

It is easy to see that the experiments carried out in the context of the mod 10 voting schemes are very relative to the protocols presented in Section 3. This because both the mod10 voting scheme and the protocols presented in Section 3 use the same secret sharing scheme as described in Section 2.4. In the experiments that were carried out, each participant had to reconstruct two different secrets - based on the instructions which can be found in Appendix A.

---

[3] This will include ordering non blacklisted diagrams in some order and possibly sending a correction deviance value to precisely define the secret digit. All of this information can be sent via broadcast. As set systems are used and as the adversary will not know at least one diagram the security of the protocols will be achieved.

The experiments carried out showed that human participants were able to use the secret sharing scheme correctly with a 95% success rate.

To be more precise, only five people (out of one hundred) made errors. Two of these got both experimental instances (secret reconstruction) wrong whereas the other three only got one wrong. Considering there were 200 experimental instances, one can say that the success rate of the experiments was 96.5%.

This indicates that human receivers will also use the protocols presented in Section 3 correctly. Identifying a majority was not tested in the experiments that were carried out. But this seems a relatively easy operation that humans can carry out. So with confidence we can state that human receivers will be able to use protocols similar to those presented in Section 3 with high accuracy.

The relationship between the experiments referred to as permutation voting schemes with the PSMT protocol with a human presented in Section 4 is also clear. In the experiments carried out, participants were asked to identify bullets corresponding to four different identified candidates - in a similar way as the description of the protocol presented in Section 4.2. One can consider that 400 experimental instances were carried out of which only a single error occurred.

Based on the very high 99.75% accuracy of correctness for the experiments, this suggests that human receivers will use the protocol presented in Section 4 correctly in most cases also.

When comparing the two techniques between them, it is apparent from the results of the experiments that the human participants had a greater success rate with the permutation based mod10 addition than with the regular addition mod10. In fact, it was a common comment from the participants that the permutation based mod10 addition was extremely easy - whereas the other experiment was rather challenging for some people.

6   Conclusions and Future Work

In this text we have presented a new concept to perfectly secure message transmission protocols. For various applications and purposes, it may be required that one of the communicating parties be a human. This brings about the need for PSMT protocols with a human receiver. For humans to be able to use such protocols, it is important that they be computationally efficient and simple to be executed correctly with high accuracy of success by the human parties.

We have presented two different constructions of such protocols and commented on the high accuracy with which human participants have correctly carried out experiments which are based on similar concepts used by the protocols presented. This suggests that human parties will be able to use the proposed protocols with a high accuracy of correctness.

Protocols based on the construction of using permutations to add modulo a number were used with a very high accuracy by human participants compared to when using the classical mod10 arithmetic construction. This suggests that humans can add numbers (which can denote secrets) correctly using such constructions - especially our permutation construction. This high accuracy identifies these constructions as good tools for designing PSMT protocols with humans.

However, the protocols that were presented might still be improved. The constructions of Section 3 are based on set systems. When choosing the values given as parameters for the proposed protocols, the complexity on the number of wires required (size of X) without requiring many blocks is $O(t^2)$. As future work, the protocols presented could be made more efficient regarding communication and computational complexities - where less data need to be sent and less computation needs to be carried out by the communicating parties. To achieve this, more efficient constructions of set systems - which require a lower than $O(t^2)$ complexity on the number of wires required (size of X), whilst still achieving secure and polynomial time protocols, is an interesting question to solve. This is important to study further as currently all known constructions have a complexity of $O(t^2)$.

Further work could be done concerning the testing of the proposed protocols. This could include a greater proportion of the population. Even though we had 100 participants, their ages did not surpass 65. Thus further experiments of the proposed protocols should include older participants to assess accurately how older human receivers could use the proposed human PSMT protocols.

Acknowledgements. The authors would like to thank Rene Peralta (NIST) for suggesting to use a subgroup of the permutation group. This suggestion inspired us to use permutations to achieve human friendly additions mod 10.

Additionally, the authors would like to thank the anonymous referees for their valuable comments on improving the presentation of this paper.

The authors would also like to thank the 100 anonymous participants for their contribution in the experimental evaluation of the proposed protocols.

References

1. La Jolla Covering Repository, http://www.ccrwest.org/cover.html
2. Abel, R.J.R., Assaf, A.M., Bennett, F.E., Bluskov, I., Greig, M.: Pair covering designs with block size 5. Discrete Mathematics 307(14), 1776–1791 (2007)
3. Ansper, A., Heiberg, S., Lipmaa, H., Øverland, T.A., van Laenen, F.: Security and Trust for the Norwegian E-Voting Pilot Project *E-valg 2011*. In: Jøsang, A., Maseng, T., Knapskog, S.J. (eds.) NordSec 2009. LNCS, vol. 5838, pp. 207–222. Springer, Heidelberg (2009)
4. BBC News. Iranian oil terminal 'offline' after 'malware attack', http://www.bbc.com/news/technology-17811565
5. Berlekamp, E.R.: Factoring polynomials over large finite fields*. In: SYMSAC 1971, p. 223. ACM (1971)
6. Chaum, D.: SureVote: Technical Overview. In: Proceedings of the Workshop on Trustworthy Elections (WOTE 2001), Tomales Bay, CA, USA, August 26-29 (2001)
7. Choudhury, A., Patra, A., Ashwinkumar, B.V., Srinathan, K., Rangan, C.P.: Secure message transmission in asynchronous networks. Journal Parallel Distributed Computing 71(8), 1067–1074 (2011)
8. Desmedt, Y., Erotokritou, S.: Towards Usable and Secure Internet Voting, http://www.cyi.ac.cy/images/ResearchProjects/SteliosE/towUsSecIntVoting.pdf
9. Desmedt, Y., Erotokritou, S., Safavi-Naini, R.: Simple and Communication Complexity Efficient Almost Secure and Perfectly Secure Message Transmission Schemes. In: Bernstein, D.J., Lange, T. (eds.) AFRICACRYPT 2010. LNCS, vol. 6055, pp. 166–183. Springer, Heidelberg (2010)

10. Desmedt, Y., Kurosawa, K.: How to Break a Practical MIX and Design a New One. In: Preneel, B. (ed.) EUROCRYPT 2000. LNCS, vol. 1807, pp. 557–572. Springer, Heidelberg (2000)
11. Desmedt, Y., Wang, Y.: Perfectly Secure Message Transmission Revisited. In: Knudsen, L.R. (ed.) EUROCRYPT 2002. LNCS, vol. 2332, pp. 502–517. Springer, Heidelberg (2002)
12. Desmedt, Y., Kurosawa, K.: How to Break a Practical MIX and Design a New One. In: Preneel, B. (ed.) EUROCRYPT 2000. LNCS, vol. 1807, pp. 277–287. Springer, Heidelberg (2000)
13. Dolev, D., Dwork, C., Waarts, O., Yung, M.: Perfectly Secure Message Transmission. Journal of the ACM 40(1), 17–47 (1993)
14. Franklin, M., Wright, R.N.: Secure Communication in Minimal Connectivity Models. In: Nyberg, K. (ed.) EUROCRYPT 1998. LNCS, vol. 1403, pp. 346–360. Springer, Heidelberg (1998)
15. Franklin, M., Yung, M.: Secure hypergraphs: Privacy from partial broadcast. SIAM J. Discrete Math. 18(3), 437–450 (2004)
16. Gordon, D.M., Kuperberg, G., Patashnik, O.: New Constructions for Covering Designs. J. Combin. Designs 3, 269–284 (1995)
17. Gordon, D.M., Kuperberg, G., Patashnik, O., Spencer, J.H.: Asymptotically optimal covering designs. Journal of Combinatorial Theory, Series A
18. Ito, M., Saito, A., Nishizeki, T.: Secret sharing schemes realizing general access structures. In: Proc. IEEE Global Telecommunications Conf., Globecom 1987, pp. 99–102. IEEE Communications Soc. Press (1987)
19. Kumar, M., Goundan, P., Srinathan, K., Rangan, C.: On perfectly secure communication over arbitrary networks. In: Proceedings of the Annual ACM Symposium on Principles of Distributed Computing (PODC), pp. 193–202 (2002)
20. Kurosawa, K., Suzuki, K.: Almost Secure (1-Round, n-Channel) Message Transmission Scheme. In: Desmedt, Y. (ed.) ICITS 2007. LNCS, vol. 4883, pp. 99–112. Springer, Heidelberg (2009)
21. Kurosawa, K., Suzuki, K.: Truly Efficient 2-Round Perfectly Secure Message Transmission Scheme. In: Smart, N. (ed.) EUROCRYPT 2008. LNCS, vol. 4965, pp. 324–340. Springer, Heidelberg (2008)
22. Liu, C.L.: Introduction to Combinatorial Mathematics. McGraw-Hill (1968)
23. Mills, W.H.: Covering designs I: Coverings by a small number of subsets. Ars Combinatoria 8, 199–315 (1979)
24. Patra, A., Choudhury, A., Rangan, C.P.: Brief announcement: Perfectly secure message transmission tolerating mobile mixed adversary with reduced phase complexity. In: PODC 2010, Zurich, Switzerland, July 25-28, pp. 245–246 (2010)
25. Rees, R., Stinson, D.R., Wei, R., Rees, G.H.J.V.: An Application of Covering Designs: Determining the Maximum Consistent Set of Shares in a Threshold Scheme. Ars Comb. 53, 225–237 (1999)
26. Sayeed, H.M., Abu-Amara, H.: Efficient Perfectly Secure Message Transmission in Synchronous Networks. Information and Computation 126(1), 53–61 (1996)
27. Shamir, A.: How to share a secret. Commun. ACM 22(11), 612–613 (1979)
28. Shannon, C.E.: Communication Theory of Secrecy Systems. Bell Systems Technical Journal 28, 656–715 (1949)
29. Yang, Q., Desmedt, Y.: General Perfectly Secure Message Transmission Using Linear Codes. In: Abe, M. (ed.) ASIACRYPT 2010. LNCS, vol. 6477, pp. 448–465. Springer, Heidelberg (2010)

A   Reconstruction of Mod 10 Secret Shared Secrets

We provide the instructions and their associated diagrammatic interpretation given to participants on how to reconstruct a Mod 10 shared secret.

Instructions: We explain how to reconstruct a secret through an example. Supposing the five 4-digit shares are the following:

$$\boxed{72\underline{9}1}\ \boxed{16\underline{5}8}\ \boxed{9\mathbf{2}0\mathit{2}}\ \boxed{748\underline{4}}\ \boxed{81\underline{7}\mathit{2}}$$

To reconstruct the secret you have to:

- Add all digits corresponding to units for the five numbers. In the example, these are all *emphasized* digits. Please note down the digit corresponding to the sum's number of units. $1 + 8 + 2 + 4 + 2 = 1\underline{7}$. Here we note down **7**
- Add all digits corresponding to tens for the five numbers. In the example, these are all underlined digits. Please note down the digit corresponding to the sum's number of units. $9 + 5 + 0 + 8 + 7 = 2\underline{9}$. Here we note down **9**
- Add all digits corresponding to hundreds for the five numbers. In the example, these are all **bold** digits. Please note down the digit corresponding to the sum's number of units. $2 + 6 + 2 + 4 + 1 = 1\underline{5}$. Here we note down **5**

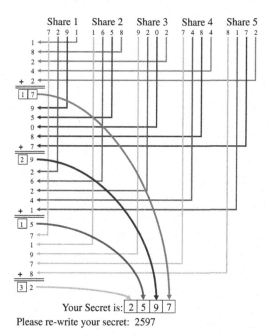

Fig. 5. Detailed instructions on how to reconstruct a mod10 secret shared secret in figure format (colors and size modified to satisfy the requirements of the publisher)

- Add all digits corresponding to thousands for the five numbers. In the example, these are all digits with no styling. Please note down the digit corresponding to the sum's number of units. $7 + 1 + 9 + 7 + 8 = 3\underline{2}$. Here we note down **2**

The secret is reconstructed by correctly ordering the noted numbers. For the example, we would reconstruct the secret to be equal to 2597.

Oblivious Transfer with Hidden Access Control from Attribute-Based Encryption

Jan Camenisch[1], Maria Dubovitskaya[1,2],
Robert R. Enderlein[1,2], and Gregory Neven[1]

[1] IBM Research – Zurich, Säumerstrasse 4,
CH-8803 Rüschlikon, Switzerland
[2] Department of Computer Science,
Swiss Federal Institute of Technology (ETH Zürich),
CH-8092 Zürich, Switzerland

Abstract. The notion of oblivious transfer with hidden access control policies (HACOT) was recently proposed by Camenisch et al. (Public-Key Cryptography 2011). This primitive allows a user to anonymously query a database where each record is protected by a hidden attribute-based access control policy. At each query, the user either learns the value of a single record if the attributes in his key satisfy the policy, or the mere fact that his attributes do not satisfy the policy. The database, even when colluding with the key issuer, learns nothing about the identity of the user, the index or the access policy of the record, or whether access was granted or denied. At the same time, the database can keep an eye on the overall access frequency to prevent the data from being "crawled".

In this paper, we present a new HACOT scheme which is more efficient and offers more expressive policies than the scheme presented by Camenisch et al. We construct our HACOT protocol based on a hidden ciphertext-policy attribute-based encryption (HP-ABE) scheme by Nishide et al.: users are issued HACOT decryption keys based on HP-ABE attributes and HACOT records are encrypted under HP-ABE policies. However, as we will see, this simple approach does not work and we need to extend the Nishide et al. scheme as follows. First, we add protocols that allows users to verify that the public key of the issuer and ciphertexts are correctly formed. Second, we reserve one attribute and give the corresponding decryption key only to the database. Thereby users can no longer decrypt records by themselves but require the help of the database. Third, we provide a joint decryption protocol between the user and the database, so that the database does not learn which ciphertext is decrypted. The latter will also allow one to optionally add revocation of the users' access. We prove our construction secure by a reduction to the security of Nishide et al.'s scheme, the Symmetric External Diffie-Hellman (SXDH) and Simultaneous Flexible Pairing (SFP) assumptions.

Keywords: Privacy, Oblivious Transfer, Attribute-Based Encryption.

I. Visconti and R. De Prisco (Eds.): SCN 2012, LNCS 7485, pp. 559–579, 2012.
© Springer-Verlag Berlin Heidelberg 2012

1 Introduction

Consider a medical database containing patients' medical records. Clearly, proper encryption and access control mechanisms need to be in place to protect such sensitive data. Different access control policies may apply to different records, ensuring for example that only relevant specialists and the treating medical staff have access to a patient's record. Given the frequent changes in medical personnel at hospitals, a role-based or attribute-based approach seems a natural solution.

Mere access control may not be enough, however. First, the access control policy by itself may leak sensitive information about a patient's illness. For example, the nature of a patient's health problem is pretty clear if an oncologist, a psychiatrist, or a plastic surgeon has access to his or her record. The treating medical staff may also have an interest in hiding the access control policies, e.g., to avoid being approached by the press when treating celebrities. Second, the query pattern for a particular record may reveal considerable information about the seriousness of the patient's condition or the phase of treatment. It is therefore desirable that the database can be queried anonymously, so that the database administrator remains oblivious as to who accesses which record at which time. Third, the database owner may want to prevent its users from abusing their anonymity to "crawl" the database and re-create a copy outside the owner's control. The database must therefore be able to detect unusual query activity to throttle requests, e.g., by inserting time delays or by presenting CAPTCHAs.

Narayan et al. [21] proposed a privacy-preserving Electronic Health Records (EHR) system that allows one to share patient data among healthcare providers in the cloud, using attribute-based encryption. However, the cloud provider still learns which files get downloaded (the scheme does not provide oblivious access to the data), the access control policy of records is not hidden, and revocation only works when all data is deleted from the user's device after each query.

A full-fledged solution is given by Camenisch et al. [8], who combine adaptive oblivious transfer (OT), anonymous credentials, and zero-knowledge proofs to build a primitive called Oblivious Transfer with Hidden Access Control Policies (HACOT).

As observed by Camenisch et al. [8], attribute-based encryption with hidden ciphertext policies (HP-ABE) [17,23,18] is a similar primitive: a user's decryption key is associated with a list of attributes, while a ciphertext is associated with a hidden access control policy so that it can only be decrypted by users whose attributes satisfy the policy. Thus one could attempt to apply an HP-ABE scheme in the scenario above: issuing decryption keys to the medical personnel, encrypting each patient's record under the appropriate policy, and sending all ciphertexts to all users, all mentioned security requirements are met. However, this approach does not offer all the necessary security features, as we will discuss in detail in this paper. For example, it allows users to crawl the database and "bulk-decrypt" all records to which they have access offline. Also, it is not possible to revoke access, an indispensable feature in a changing environment such as a hospital's workforce.

Revocation is notoriously difficult to implement in identity-based and attribute-based encryption systems, with most practical solutions requiring a painful trade-off to be made between security and frequency of key updates and database re-encryptions. Finally, as we will explain in more detail later, a HP-ABE scheme does not exclude that a single ciphertext decrypts to different plaintexts for different users, leading to anonymity problems. So, a plain application of HP-ABE is not satisfactory and, indeed, the construction of an HACOT scheme based on HP-ABE was left as an open problem by Camenisch et al. [8].

Our Contributions. In this paper, we extend the HP-ABE scheme by Nishide et al. [23,22] as follows into an HACOT scheme to bring it to the same level of functionality as the HACOT protocol of [8]. First, we add protocols that allow users to verify that the public key of the issuer and ciphertexts are correctly formed. Second, we reserve one attribute and give the corresponding decryption key only to the database so that users can no longer decrypt records by themselves but require the help of the database. Instead, we provide a joint decryption protocol between the user and the database, so that users can again decrypt records under the control of the database but with the database not learning which particular ciphertext is decrypted. The latter will also allow to optionally add revocation of the users' access. Thus, when using our functionality/scheme with an authenticated encryption scheme [3], one indeed obtains the required solution.

We also address a deficiency in the definition and protocol by Camenisch et al. [8]: in their ideal functionality, users are returned $\perp$ if they do not have the necessary access rights, but in their protocol, they receive a random message in this case. We address this as follows: we define the ideal functionality 1) to handle only encryption keys that can then be used to derive keys for a symmetric encryption scheme and 2) in case a user has no access, the functionality will return a random key to the user.

Our construction relies on interactive zero-knowledge proofs of knowledge [13], Groth-Sahai non-interactive proofs [16], the privacy-friendly signature scheme by Abe et al. [1] and an HP-ABE scheme that allows transformations described in Section 4. Our HACOT protocol offers several advantages over that of Camenisch et al. [8]. First, access control policies in our protocol are specified as vectors of subsets of polynomial-size attribute universes, which is more expressive than the boolean attributes of their scheme. Communication and computation by the database in the decryption protocol is independent of the number of attributes in our scheme, versus linear in theirs. Indeed, already for 3 attributes all operations are more efficient in our scheme except the key generation where ours is costly (using realistic security parameters for both schemes).

We prove our construction secure in the common reference string (CRS) model under the Symmetric eXternal Diffie-Hellman (SXDH) assumption, the Simultaneous Flexible Pairing (SFP) [1] assumption, and the security of the underlying HP-ABE scheme (in the case of Nishide et al.'s scheme: generic bilinear group model). We also implemented a prototype of our protocol and provide a theoretical efficiency analysis and experimental performance results. Notice that database updates are also supported in our scheme, and records can be added to the database without having to re-encrypt the whole database. The database provider just distributes an update containing the ciphertexts of the new records.

Related Work. All attribute-based [28,4,23,18] and predicate [17,18] encryption schemes allow for offline decryption, and can therefore not be used as such for the scenario we envisage. Some of these schemes [17,23,18] are *policy-hiding*, meaning that users cannot deduce anything about the policy of a ciphertext except whether their key satisfies it. The schemes of Katz et al. and Lewko et al. [17,18] allow for conjunctions and disjunctions in the policy, but require composite-order bilinear groups. The scheme of Nishide et al. [23] allows for slightly less powerful policies but works in a prime-order group setting. The scheme of Lewko et al. [18] and the second construction of Nishide et al. [23] are fully secure in the generic group model [22], whereas the other schemes are only selectively secure.

There is an extensive body of literature on the subject of oblivious transfer [27]. In this paper we use the adaptive k-out-of-n variant [20,9], where a user may query for up to k records from a database of n records. The user does not learn anything about the $(n-k)$ records he did not query, while the database does not learn which records were queried. The goal is to "amortize" communication costs so that the encrypted database of size linear in n is transmitted once, but each transfer afterwards has communication cost independent of n. Several extensions to adaptive k-out-of-n OT have been proposed, including pricing [7] and access control with known [6,12] and hidden [8] policies. Our protocol is an alternative instantiation of the latter primitive.

Zhang et al. [29] have proposed a scheme that combines the OT protocol of Camenisch el al. [9] with the attribute based encryption scheme of Lewko et al. [18] and achieves oblivious transfer with access control functionality, but their scheme does not cover the hidden policy case and does not provide revocation of users. We also show in Section 4 that this scheme cannot be extended to a hidden policy while preserving our HACOT security properties.

Green et al. [15] propose a way to outsource the main computation for decrypting ABE ciphertexts to a (possibly passively malicious) proxy, however their approach does not fit well with our real-world/ideal-world security notions since it is not clear what guarantees the user has if the proxy maliciously deviates from its specifications.

2   Definitions

An oblivious transfer protocol with hidden access control policies (HACOT) is run between an *issuer*, who sets up the system, and generates keys of users; one or more *databases*, who publish records and control users' access rights to the database by setting access policies; and *users*, who anonymously fetch records that they are entitled to access. Let $\mathcal{I}$ denote the issuer, $\mathcal{DB}$ the set of all databases, $\mathcal{DB}_\varrho$ the database with index ϱ, $\mathcal{U}$ the set of all users, $\mathcal{U}_\varphi$ the user with index φ.

2.1 Syntax and Basic Terminology

By $\mathbb{N}$ we denote the set of natural numbers, by $\mathbb{N}_n$ the set of all natural numbers between 0 and $(n-1)$. By $\mathbb{Z}_p$ we denote the ring of integers modulo p. We use $\mathbb{N}_n^*$ and $\mathbb{Z}_p^*$ to denote $\mathbb{N}_n \setminus \{0\}$ and $\mathbb{Z}_p \setminus \{0\}$, respectively. By $e\colon \mathbb{G}_1 \times \mathbb{G}_2 \mapsto \mathbb{G}_T$ we denote a bilinear map. If $\kappa \in \mathbb{N}$, then $\mathbf{1}^\kappa$ denotes the string consisting of κ ones.

If $\mathbb{A}$ is a set, then $a \xleftarrow{\$} \mathbb{A}$ means we set a to a random element of that set. If $\mathcal{A}$ is a Probabilistic Polynomial-Time (PPT) algorithm or interactive machine, then $y \xleftarrow{\$} \mathcal{A}(x)$ means we assign y to the output of $\mathcal{A}$ when run with fresh random coins on input x. If $\mathcal{A}$ and $\mathcal{B}$ are two interactive machines, then let $(In_\mathcal{A}\|In_\mathcal{B}) \rightarrow (Out_\mathcal{A}\|Out_\mathcal{B})$ denote the sets of inputs and outputs of $\mathcal{A}$ and $\mathcal{B}$ during the interaction between these two machines.

2.2 Record Policies and User Attributes

Our HACOT scheme uses the same policy framework as the HP-ABE scheme by Nishide et al. [23]. We recall the notation below for convenience.

All records in the database are encrypted. The database $\mathcal{DB}_\varrho$ can specify an access policy for an encrypted record $C_{\varrho,\psi}$, which is called a ciphertext policy $(W_{\varrho,\psi})$. The issuer gives $\mathcal{U}_\varphi$ a secret decryption key corresponding to the set of access attributes (L_φ) granted to the user.

We denote languages for the attributes and policies as $\mathcal{L}_L$ and $\mathcal{L}_W$ respectively. We write $L \models W$ to mean that W is satisfied by L, and $L \not\models W$ if not (i.e., a user key corresponding to L, respectively can and cannot decrypt a ciphertext with policy W).

We now describe the structure of attributes and policies in more detail. The keys issued to users are associated with a list of attributes $L = (L_1, \ldots, L_n)$ from n different categories. Let $n_i \in \mathbb{N}$ be the (finite and polynomial) number of possible attribute values in the i-th category. Without loss of generality, we can encode the n_i attributes of category i as elements of $\mathbb{N}_{n_i}$, so that $L_i \in \mathbb{N}_{n_i}$. For example, in a hospital scenario, the $n = 3$ categories could be (Job Title, Department, Gender), where Job Title can take any of the $n_1 = 5$ attributes {student, nurse, doctor, surgeon, administration}, Department can take any of the $n_2 = 4$ attributes {cardiology, maternity, neurology, oncology}, and Gender can be any of the $n_3 = 2$ attributes {male, female}.

Each record in the database has an access control policy associated with it. A policy $W = (W_1, \ldots, W_n)$ is expressed as a list of n subsets of attributes $W_i \subseteq \mathbb{N}_{n_i}$. A key endowed with the attribute list L is authorized to access a record if and only if all attributes in the key are also in the ciphertext policy, i.e., $L \models W \Leftrightarrow \forall i \in \mathbb{N}_{n+1}^* : L_i \in W_i$. For example, Alice may be a surgeon in the oncology department, so that her key is associated with (surgeon, oncology, female), while Bob, who is an administrative assistant in the maternity department, has key (administration, maternity, male). If a patient's medical record is protected by a policy $W =(\{\text{doctor, surgeon}\}, \{\text{cardiology, oncology}\}, \{\text{male, female}\})$, then Alice can access the record, but Bob cannot.

One could view the ciphertext policy as implementing a limited version of conjunctive normal form: within a category, the policy specifies an OR condition on the attribute the user key has for that category; and all attributes of the key have to be in the access structure, basically an AND condition. Note that the access structure is hidden from the user, meaning that he cannot recover it from the ciphertext alone.

2.3   Definition of **HACOT** without Revocation

A HACOT scheme is a tuple of the following eight PPT algorithms and protocols:

- IssuerSetup$(\mathcal{L}_L, \mathcal{L}_W) \xrightarrow{\$} (pk_{\mathcal{I}}, sk_{\mathcal{I}})$.   This algorithm generates the system-wide issuer public key $pk_{\mathcal{I}}$ and corresponding secret key $sk_{\mathcal{I}}$. The input to this algorithm is a description of the set of attributes $\mathcal{L}_L$ that keys can be endowed with, and a description of the set of ciphertext policies $\mathcal{L}_W$.
- VerifyIssuerKey$\big((pk_{\mathcal{I}})||(pk_{\mathcal{I}}, sk_{\mathcal{I}})\big) \xrightarrow{\$} (b||\varepsilon)$.   Upon receiving the public key of the issuer, each user and each database runs this protocol with the issuer, so that the latter can prove that the issuer keys are correctly formed. The common input is the issuer's public key, the issuer's private input is his secret key. The output is a bit b indicating whether the user or database accepts the issuer's key.
- DBSetup$(pk_{\mathcal{I}}) \xrightarrow{\$} (pk_{\mathcal{DB}_\varrho}, sk_{\mathcal{DB}_\varrho})$.   The database with index ϱ runs this algorithm to generate its public key $pk_{\mathcal{DB}_\varrho}$ and corresponding private key $sk_{\mathcal{DB}_\varrho}$.
- VerifyDBKey$\big((pk_{\mathcal{I}}, pk_{\mathcal{DB}_\varrho})||(pk_{\mathcal{I}}, pk_{\mathcal{DB}_\varrho}, sk_{\mathcal{DB}_\varrho})\big) \xrightarrow{\$} (b||\varepsilon)$.   Upon receiving the public key of $\mathcal{DB}_\varrho$, each user runs this protocol with the database $\mathcal{DB}_\varrho$, so that the latter can prove in zero-knowledge that it knows the secret key corresponding to its public key. The common input consists of the issuer's and the database's public keys. The database's private input is its secret key. The output is a bit b indicating whether the public key $pk_{\mathcal{DB}_\varrho}$ is accepted.
- IssueRecord$(pk_{\mathcal{I}}, pk_{\mathcal{DB}_\varrho}, sk_{\mathcal{DB}_\varrho}, K_{\varrho,\psi}, W_{\varrho,\psi}) \xrightarrow{\$} C_{\varrho,\psi}$. The database $\mathcal{DB}_\varrho$ runs this algorithm to publish a new record with index ψ. The input are the database's key pair, the issuer's public key, the plaintext $K_{\varrho,\psi} \in \mathbb{G}_T$, and the ciphertext policy $W_{\varrho,\psi} \in \mathcal{L}_W$. The output is the ciphertext $C_{\varrho,\psi}$.
- CheckRecord$(pk_{\mathcal{I}}, pk_{\mathcal{DB}_\varrho}, C_{\varrho,\psi}) \xrightarrow{\$} b$.   Upon receiving a ciphertext $C_{\varrho,\psi}$, each user performs a check to test whether it is correctly formed. The output bit b indicates the result of that check.
- Escrow$(sk_{\mathcal{I}}, pk_{\mathcal{I}}, pk_{\mathcal{DB}_\varrho}, C_{\varrho,\psi}) \xrightarrow{\$} (K_{\varrho,\psi}, W_{\varrho,\psi})$.   With this algorithm, $\mathcal{I}$ can efficiently recover the plaintext and the policy of the ciphertext $C_{\varrho,\psi}$ without interacting with $\mathcal{DB}_\varrho$. This algorithm models the fact that in most HP-ABE systems, the issuer can recover a great deal of information from all ciphertexts by using his private key.
- IssueUserKey$\big((pk_{\mathcal{I}}, \varphi, L_\varphi)||(pk_{\mathcal{I}}, sk_{\mathcal{I}}, \varphi, L_\varphi)\big) \xrightarrow{\$} (sk_{\mathcal{U}_\varphi}||\varepsilon)$.   The user with index φ and the issuer run this interactive protocol to generate a new secret key $sk_{\mathcal{U}_\varphi}$ for $\mathcal{U}_\varphi$. We assume that the protocol is run over an authenticated channel. Common inputs are φ, attributes $L_\varphi \in \mathcal{L}_L$, and the public key of the issuer. The issuer has his secret key as private input. Only the user receives output from this protocol, namely his secret key $sk_{\mathcal{U}_\varphi}$.

- Query$\big((sk_{\mathcal{U}\varphi}, pk_{\mathcal{I}}, pk_{\mathcal{DB}\varrho}, C_{\varrho,\psi}) \| (pk_{\mathcal{I}}, pk_{\mathcal{DB}\varrho}, sk_{\mathcal{DB}\varrho})\big) \xrightarrow{\$} (K'\|\varepsilon).$ The user $\mathcal{U}_\varphi$ queries database $\mathcal{DB}_\varrho$ to attempt to decrypt record ψ. The common input contains the public keys of the issuer and database. The user's private input is his secret key and the ciphertext $C_{\varrho,\psi}$. (A more general definition would include the entire encrypted database in the user's input, but the most efficient schemes should not need this.) The database's secret input is its private key. Only the user receives output from this protocol, namely the recovered plaintext K'. If decryption was successful, then $K' = K_{\varrho,\psi}$, otherwise K' is a random element of $\mathbb{G}_T$. Queries take place over anonymous channels so that the database does not know with which user it interacts.

We assume that the CRS and system parameters are generated according to the appropriate distributions and are made available to all participants.

This definition is similar to the definition of HACOT in [8]. The differences are as follows: 1) our definition allows for more expressive policies; 2) records can be added individually instead of setting them up all at once at system startup; 3) our system allows for multiple independent databases; and 4) we explicitly model the level of access that the issuer has in our system though the Escrow functionality. With respect to the last point, our scheme is at a disadvantage compared to [8]: while the issuer in [8] can always generate for himself a user key that decrypts all records, he must interact with the database to recover the plaintext of a record; to recover the policy, one interaction with the database per attribute is necessary.

2.4 Security Definitions

To define the security of our protocol we take an approach from [9,8] which is inspired by universal composability [11] and reactive systems [25,26]. Namely, we prove a HACOT protocol secure through an indistinguishability argument between the instantiation of HACOT in the real world $\mathcal{R}_{\text{HACOT}}$, where players run the set of cryptographic protocols, and an ideal world functionality $\mathcal{F}_{\text{HACOT}}$, which applies the functionality the cryptographic protocols are supposed to realize.

In the real world after receiving a message from the environment $\mathcal{E}$ all parties run the corresponding cryptographic algorithms or engage in the protocols described in Section 2.3.

We briefly describe the $\mathcal{F}_{\text{HACOT}}$ functionality below and provide a formal ideal world definition in the full version [5]. We note that the interfaces between the environment $\mathcal{E}$ and $\mathcal{R}_{\text{HACOT}}$ and between $\mathcal{E}$ and $\mathcal{F}_{\text{HACOT}}$ are identical.

Ideal World (sketch). In the ideal world, $\mathcal{F}_{\text{HACOT}}$ performs all actions only after relaying all received messages to the simulator $\mathcal{S}$ and getting an approval from $\mathcal{S}$. After receiving a first message from the issuer, $\mathcal{F}_{\text{HACOT}}$ fixes the set of possible attributes and policies. It further relays all messages between users, databases and issuer during the Issuer and Database Setup phases and creates a list of all databases and users. Note that after Setup is completed, it is not possible to add users or databases. Later, during Record Issuance, $\mathcal{F}_{\text{HACOT}}$ stores records and their policies upon request from the database. This can be repeated any number of times, meaning that the records can be added at any time. When receiving a key request from a user, $\mathcal{F}_{\text{HACOT}}$ stores an entry with the set of attributes for that user's key. Finally, during a Query, $\mathcal{F}_{\text{HACOT}}$ removes the user and record identifier from the user's request before forwarding it to $\mathcal{S}$ and to the corresponding database. After the database replies with a bit b, $\mathcal{F}_{\text{HACOT}}$ checks whether the set of user's attributes satisfies the policy of the requested record; if $b = 0$, then it sends $\bot$ to the user; if $b = 1$ and the policy is satisfied, it sends the stored record back to the user, otherwise, it sends back a random group element.

Discussion of Security Properties. Informally, the specification of the ideal functionality $\mathcal{F}_{\text{HACOT}}$ is such that the following security properties are trivially satisfied. Hence, any real-world implementation of the scheme must satisfy the same properties.

Database security. Users need to contact the database for each record that they want to access, so the database can keep an eye on the overall access frequency and throttle too-frequent requests. Users cannot determine whether their key satisfies the access policy of the record before the interaction. They cannot deduce anything about the contents of a record if they did not query it with a valid key that satisfies the policy. After a successful interaction, users cannot deduce anything about the policy except whether their key satisfies it or not. Cheating and colluding users cannot query any records that one of them could not have queried individually. In particular, they cannot "combine" or "rearrange" attributes in their keys.

User security. The only information that the database sees during a query is the mere fact that a query takes place. In particular, it cannot determine which user queries which record, which policy is associated to the record, which attributes the user has, and whether access to the record was granted or not. User security is valid even if the database colludes with the issuer and other users. If the query protocol completes successfully, honest users are guaranteed that 1) if access was granted, then their key satisfies the policy of the record and 2) if access was denied, then their key does not satisfy the policy of the record.

3   Preliminaries

In this section we describe the security assumptions and building blocks used in our scheme.

3.1   Assumptions

Decisional Diffie-Hellman (DDH) Assumption. Let $\mathbb{G}$ be either $\mathbb{G}_1$, $\mathbb{G}_2$ or $\mathbb{G}_T$ (and let g be the corresponding generator of the group, viz. g_1, g_2, g_T). Let $a, b, z \xleftarrow{\$} \mathbb{Z}_p$. DDH is hard in $\mathbb{G}$ if for every PPT algorithm $\mathcal{A}$:

$$\text{Adv}_{\mathbb{G}}^{\text{DDH}} \overset{\text{def}}{=} \left| \Pr\left[\mathcal{A}(g, g^a, g^b, g^{ab}) \overset{\$?}{=} 1 \right] - \Pr\left[\mathcal{A}(g, g^a, g^b, g^z) \overset{\$?}{=} 1 \right] \right| = negl. \quad (1)$$

Symmetric External Diffie-Hellman (SXDH) Assumption. We say that the SXDH assumption holds if DDH holds in $\mathbb{G}_1$, $\mathbb{G}_2$ and $\mathbb{G}_T$. This assumption holds only for type-3 [14] bilinear maps: this means there exists no efficiently computable homomorphism from $\mathbb{G}_1$ to $\mathbb{G}_2$ or vice-versa. It is believed SXDH holds in certain subgroups of MNT elliptic curves.

ℓ-Simultaneous Flexible Pairing (SFP) Assumption. Let $A, B \xleftarrow{\$} \mathbb{G}_1$, $\tilde{A}, \tilde{B} \xleftarrow{\$} \mathbb{G}_2$ and $g_Z, f_Z, g_R, f_U \xleftarrow{\$} \mathbb{G}_1^*$. For $j \in \mathbb{N}_{\ell+1}^*$ let $P_j \stackrel{\text{def}}{=} (Z_j, R_j, S_j, T_j, U_j, V_j, W_j)$ that satisfies:

$$
\begin{aligned}
e(A, \tilde{A}) &= e(g_Z, Z_j) \, e(g_R, R_j) \, e(S_j, T_j) \, \wedge \\
e(B, \tilde{B}) &= e(f_Z, Z_j) \, e(f_U, U_j) \, e(V_j, W_j) \ .
\end{aligned}
\tag{2}
$$

We say that the ℓ-SFP assumptions holds in $\mathbb{G}_1$ if for all PPT algorithms $\mathcal{A}$ (3) is satisfied [1,2], where $P_{\ell+1}$ satisfies (2) and $Z_{\ell+1} \neq 1 \wedge \forall i \in \mathbb{N}_{\ell+1}^* : Z_{\ell+1} \neq Z_i$.

$$
\mathrm{Adv}_{\mathbb{G}_1}^{\ell-\mathrm{SFP}} \stackrel{\text{def}}{=} \Pr\left[\mathcal{A}\left(g_Z, f_Z, g_R, f_U, A, B, \tilde{A}, \tilde{B}, (P_j)_{j=1}^{\ell}\right) \stackrel{\$?}{=} P_{\ell+1} \right] = negl. \tag{3}
$$

We define ℓ-SFP in $\mathbb{G}_2$ analogously by exchanging the groups $\mathbb{G}_1$ and $\mathbb{G}_2$ above.

This assumption is parameterized by ℓ (unlike the other assumptions which are static), where a larger ℓ means a stronger assumption. This assumption was proven to hold in the generic bilinear group model [2], as long as $\ell \ll \sqrt{p}$ (quadratic bound).

3.2 Zero-Knowledge Proofs

ZKPK denotes an interactive zero-knowledge proof (or argument) of knowledge [13], while NIZK denotes a non-interactive zero-knowledge proof [16]. We will use the Camenisch-Stadler notation [10] to describe what is being proven, for example:

ZKPK$\{(\alpha, \beta) : y = g^\alpha \wedge z = g^\beta h^\alpha\}$. Variables in parenthesis denote the elements knowledge is proven about, such that the formula after the colon is true.

3.3 Hidden-Policy Attribute-Based Encryption

A HP-ABE scheme is a tuple of the following four PPT algorithms:

• IssuerSetup$(1^\kappa, \mathcal{L}_L, \mathcal{L}_W) \xrightarrow{\$} (pkh_{\mathcal{I}}, skh_{\mathcal{I}})$.   Using $\mathcal{L}_L, \mathcal{L}_W$, and a security parameter as input, this algorithm outputs the public and secret keys of $\mathcal{I}$.

• IssueUserKey$(skh_{\mathcal{I}}, pkh_{\mathcal{I}}, L) \xrightarrow{\$} skh_{\mathcal{U}}$.   Given a permissible set of attributes $L \in \mathcal{L}_L$ and the issuer's key pair, this generates a new user key $skh_{\mathcal{U}}$ endowed with L.

• Encrypt$(pkh_{\mathcal{I}}, K, W) \xrightarrow{\$} C$.   Given a plaintext $K \in \mathbb{G}_T$, a permissible ciphertext policy $W \in \mathcal{L}_W$, and the issuer's public key $pkh_{\mathcal{I}}$, this algorithm generates a corresponding ciphertext C.

- Decrypt($skh_\mathcal{U}, pkh_\mathcal{I}, C$) → K'.   Given a ciphertext C, the user's secret key $skh_\mathcal{U}$, and the issuer's public key $pkh_\mathcal{I}$, this algorithm decrypts the ciphertext with the user's secret key. If the key satisfies the policy ($L \models W$), then the correct plaintext is recovered ($K' = K$). If the key does not satisfy the policy then $K' \neq K$ with overwhelming probability.

Security of HP-ABE. Informally, an HP-ABE scheme is secure if an adversary, who can adaptively get as many keys issued as he wants, cannot tell if a given challenge ciphertext decrypts to some plaintext M_0 under policy W_0 or to some other plaintext M_1 under W_1 of his choosing (modulo the trivial cases). A precise definition is given in the full version [5]. Note that some HP-ABE schemes are only *selectively* secure (meaning the adversary must fix the challenge plaintexts and policies before he receives the issuer's key), but this is not sufficient for our scheme.

We use the second construction of Nishide et al.'s HP-ABE [23] scheme. It is proven secure in the generic bilinear group setting [22], and requires Type-3 pairings. It allows the issuer to add attributes and categories after system setup. In their scheme the issuer is assumed to be trusted, unlike our HACOT scheme.

3.4   Structure-Preserving Signatures

To hide the record index during a query, but at the same time make sure that the user is asking to decrypt a correct ciphertext, we need a signature scheme that allows for zero-knowledge proof-of-possession. As the ciphertext is a set of group elements, we use the basic signature scheme by Abe et al. [1] for signing group elements. This scheme does not require the signer to know the discrete logarithm of the group elements he is signing. It is existentially unforgeable against adaptive chosen message attacks if the Simultaneous Flexible Pairing assumption [1] holds.

This signature scheme Sig allows the user to re-randomize (blind) the signature and prove in zero-knowledge that this is still a correct signature. The user's anonymity is thus preserved, and the database has the guarantee that it is not helping the user to decrypt invalid ciphertexts. The scheme consists of a key generation algorithm Sig.KeyGen; a signing algorithm Sig.Sign; a verification algorithm Sig.Verify; a re-randomization algorithm Sig.Rerand, that takes as input a signature σ of a message m and outputs a re-randomized signature σ', which is also a valid signature on m; and two algorithms Sig.KeyProve and Sig.Prove for proving in zero-knowledge the validity of the key and the signature respectively.

4   Achieving HACOT from HP-ABE

Let us give some intuition and a high-level description of our scheme, in particular how to extend a HP-ABE scheme into an oblivious access control system with hidden policies. In our protocol we use a concrete HP-ABE scheme by Nishide et al. [23], but one can apply a similar trick to other HP-ABE schemes. Recall that in HP-ABE, a user's decryption key is associated with a list of attributes, while a ciphertext is associated with a hidden access control policy. A user can decrypt a ciphertext offline only if the attributes from his key satisfy the cipertext policy. Assume a database would just employ an HP-ABE scheme to encrypt all records and then publish these encryptions. Users would be issued the HP-ABE decryption keys corresponding to their attributes. In this approach, the access control policies would indeed be hidden and also users would only be able to access the records for which their attributes match the access control policies. Unfortunately, this solution does not provide all the properties that HACOT requires:

- First, somewhat counterintuitively, anonymity of the users is not guaranteed: in case the database and the issuer are malicious, they could deviate from the key issuance and encryption procedures so that if two users with the same attributes decrypt a record their result will still be different; hence, the scheme would not satisfy our ideal world definition. In a higher-level protocol, the two users might be distinguishable.

- Second, users can immediately decrypt all the records for which they have the necessary attributes. This will allow colluding users to derive information about the policies. Furthermore, the database has no control over the access frequency of records and cannot revoke access rights.

To address the first issue, we make the operations by the issuer and the database verifiable. We add an additional protocol (VerifyIssuerKey) in which the issuer proves that its keys were generated correctly, we turn the IssueUserKey algorithm that generates users' decryption keys into a two-party computation between the issuer and the user, and we provide a protocol VerifyEncryption allowing users to check that the ciphertexts are correctly formed.

Addressing the second issue is a bit trickier. A first idea to ensure that users cannot decrypt without the help of the database could be to combine a standard OT protocol to encrypt records twice, first under the OT protocol and then under the appropriate policies using the HP-ABE scheme. (Zhang et al. [29] used a similar approach to obtain an OT protocol with public access control policies.) This does not suffice, however, as users can perform the outer HP-ABE decryption step without interacting with the database and learn information about the access policies by observing whether decryption succeeds. Encrypting first under the HP-ABE scheme does not work either, since colluding users could start by doing a single OT query, and then attempt decrypting the inner HP-ABE ciphertext without oversight. Besides violating our ideal world definition, such a scheme excludes any interactive revocation scheme.

On a high level, our approach is the following. We create a dedicated "zeroth" attribute category of the HP-ABE scheme so that the issuer only issues decryption keys for one particular attribute $\mathcal{W}_{\mathcal{I}}$ in this zeroth category, but each database encrypts records under policies that require a different attribute $\mathcal{W}_{\mathcal{DB}_\varrho}$ for the zeroth category. The database has a "transformation key" that allows it to convert a ciphertext encrypted for $\mathcal{W}_{\mathcal{DB}_\varrho}$ into one for $\mathcal{W}_{\mathcal{I}}$. When the user wants to decrypt a record, she blinds the ciphertext and engages in a joint decryption protocol with the database to obtain a transformed ciphertext for $\mathcal{W}_\mathcal{I}$. To make sure that the user blinded a ciphertext that was previously published by the database, the database signs all of its ciphertexts. During the decryption protocol, the user proves knowledge of a valid signature for her blinded ciphertext—without revealing the signature, of course.

Now that the database is involved in the decryption process of the user, it becomes much easier to add revocation. Users are issued an anonymous credential and the database will only run the joint decryption protocol if the user's credential has not been revoked. There are a number of possible schemes to employ here and we will follow the choice by Camenisch et al. for their HACOT scheme [8].

5   Our Construction without Revocation

In this section we describe in detail how to construct our HACOT protocol (without the optional revocation mechanism) when instantiated with the second HP-ABE scheme by Nishide et al. [23]. The description of the construction will be followed by a discussion about asymptotic complexity. The changes needed to handle revocation are described in the full version [5].

5.1   Detailed Construction

We now present the realizations of all algorithms and protocols of our scheme listed in Section 2.3 in detail.

System Parameters. We assume that the following parameters are generated by a trusted third party (or alternatively generated jointly via a multiparty computation) and are an extra (implicit) input to all algorithms and protocols. Concretely, all primitives we use require a common bilinear map setting: $(p, \mathbb{G}_1, \mathbb{G}_2, \mathbb{G}_T, g_1 \in \mathbb{G}_1, g_2 \in \mathbb{G}_2, e) \leftarrow \text{Gen}(1^\kappa)$. We denote $g_T \stackrel{\text{def}}{=} e(g_1, g_2)$. For the Groth-Sahai proofs we also need a common reference string $CRS \leftarrow \{\mathfrak{U}_{1,2} \leftarrow g_2^\mathfrak{a}, \mathfrak{U}_{2,1} \leftarrow g_2^\mathfrak{t}, \mathfrak{U}_{2,2} \leftarrow g_2^{\mathfrak{a}\mathfrak{t}}\}$, where $\mathfrak{a}, \mathfrak{t} \stackrel{\$}{\leftarrow} \mathbb{Z}_p^*$.

Issuer Key Generation and Verification. In addition to the n regular categories, the issuer creates an additional zeroth category, and creates one attribute $\mathcal{W}_\mathcal{I}$ in that category. Let $A_{0,0} = g_1^{a_{0,0}}$ be the public key component associated to that attribute ($a_{0,0}$ is the private key component). All the users' keys he issues will contain this $\mathcal{W}_\mathcal{I}$ attribute (that is $L_0 = 0$). The key generation algorithm IssuerSetup is depicted in Figure 1, and takes as input the number of categories n and the number of attributes possible per category $\{n_i\}_{i=1}^n$; $n_0 = 1$.

Each party who receives the issuer's public key checks that the latter's key was generated correctly by running the VerifyIssuerKey protocol, which consists of checking that $Y \neq 1$, $B \neq 1$, $A_{i,t} \neq 1$, and running the following proof of knowledge with the issuer: $\text{ZKPK}_1 \stackrel{\text{def}}{=} \text{ZKPK}\{(sgk_\mathcal{I}, w, \beta, \{\{a_{i,t}\}\}) : Y = g_T^w \wedge B = g_1^\beta \wedge \bigwedge_{i=0}^n (\bigwedge_{t=0}^{n_i-1} (A_{i,t} = g_1^{a_{i,t}})) \wedge \text{Sig.KeyProve}(sgk_\mathcal{I}, vk_\mathcal{I})\}$.

1. Generate HP-ABE key:

$w, \beta \xleftarrow{\$} \mathbb{Z}_p^* ; Y \leftarrow g_T^w ; B \leftarrow g_1^\beta ;$

$\{\{a_{i,t} \xleftarrow{\$} \mathbb{Z}_p^* ; A_{i,t} \leftarrow g_1^{a_{i,t}}\}_{t=0}^{n_i-1}\}_{i=0}^n ;$

$skh_\mathcal{I} \leftarrow (\{a_{i,t}\}, w, \beta) ;$

$pkh_\mathcal{I} \leftarrow (\{A_{i,t}\}, Y, B).$

2. Generate signing keys:

$(sgk_\mathcal{I}, vk_\mathcal{I}) \xleftarrow{\$} \mathsf{Sig.KeyGen}(1^\kappa) ;$

Output $sk_\mathcal{I} \leftarrow (skh_\mathcal{I}, sgk_\mathcal{I}) ;$

$\qquad pk_\mathcal{I} \leftarrow (pkh_\mathcal{I}, vk_\mathcal{I}).$

Fig. 1. IssuerSetup algorithm

1. Generate HP-ABE keys for the DB-specific attribute:

$k_\varrho \xleftarrow{\$} \mathbb{Z}_p ;$

$A_{0,\varrho} \leftarrow A_{0,0}^{k_\varrho} = g_1^{a_{0,0}k_\varrho} ;$

$skh_{\mathcal{DB}_\varrho} \leftarrow k_\varrho ; pkh_{\mathcal{DB}_\varrho} \leftarrow A_{0,\varrho}.$

2. Generate signing keys:

$(sgk_{\mathcal{DB}_\varrho}, vk_{\mathcal{DB}_\varrho}) \xleftarrow{\$} \mathsf{Sig.KeyGen}(1^\kappa) ;$

Output $sk_{\mathcal{DB}_\varrho} \leftarrow (skh_{\mathcal{DB}_\varrho}, sgk_{\mathcal{DB}_\varrho}) ;$

$\qquad pk_{\mathcal{DB}_\varrho} \leftarrow (pkh_{\mathcal{DB}_\varrho}, vk_{\mathcal{DB}_\varrho}).$

Fig. 2. DBSetup algorithm

Database Key Generation and Verification. Recall that ϱ is the implicit database identifier. Each database $\mathcal{DB}_\varrho$ that joins the system extends the zeroth category with a new attribute, $\mathcal{W}_{\mathcal{DB}_\varrho}$. The public key component associated to that attribute is $A_{0,\varrho} = A_{0,0}^{k_\varrho}$, where k_ϱ is part of the database's private key. The value $A_{0,\varrho} = g_1^{a_{0,0}k_\varrho}$ can be considered as part of the public key of the "related" HP-ABE scheme, i.e., the secret key component corresponding to $\mathcal{W}_{\mathcal{DB}_\varrho}$ thereby implicitly becomes $a_{0,\varrho} = a_{0,0}k_\varrho \pmod{p}$.

The database setup consists of an algorithm DBSetup shown in Figure 2 to generate the database's key pair.

Each user receiving $pk_{\mathcal{DB}_\varrho}$ checks that the database's public was generated correctly with the protocol VerifyDBKey, which consists of first checking that $A_{0,\varrho} \neq 1$, and then running the following proof of knowledge with the database:

$$\mathsf{ZKPK}_2 \stackrel{\text{def}}{=} \mathsf{ZKPK}\{(sgk_{\mathcal{DB}_\varrho}, k_\varrho) : A_{0,\varrho} = A_{0,0}^{k_\varrho} \wedge \mathsf{Sig.KeyProve}(sgk_{\mathcal{DB}_\varrho}, vk_{\mathcal{DB}_\varrho})\}.$$

Verifiable Encryption of Records. To encrypt a record with (implicit) index ψ, containing the plaintext $K \in \mathbb{G}_T$ and the hidden ciphertext policy $W_{\varrho,\psi} = [W_0, \ldots, W_n]$, where $\forall i : W_i \subseteq \mathbb{N}_{n_i}$, the database runs IssueRecord as shown in Figure 3. If one wants to use messages $M \in \{0,1\}^*$ instead, one can use an authenticated encryption [3] algorithm AuthEnc that uses elements from $\mathbb{G}_T$ as symmetric keys to encrypt M using the key K.

For the zeroth category, only the ciphertext component $C_{0,\varrho,2}$ for the $\mathcal{W}_{\mathcal{DB}_\varrho}$ attribute is published and not $C_{0,0,2}$ for the $\mathcal{W}_\mathcal{I}$ attribute. For the latter the users will have the decryption key but not for the former. However, as $C_{0,0,2} = (C_{0,\varrho,2})^{k_\varrho^{-1}}$, users can decrypt a record if (and only if) the database helps them.

Users need to verify all ciphertexts by running CheckRecord, which for each record verifies correctness of the GS proof π and the signature σ' on $C_{0,\varrho,2}$.

Issuing Decryption Keys to Users. Let $(L_1, \ldots, L_n)$, $L_i \in \mathbb{N}_{n_i}$, be the attributes of the user. We add to these $L_0 = 0$ (corresponding to $\mathcal{W}_\mathcal{I}$) and set $L_\varphi = (L_0, L_1, \ldots L_n)$. The protocol depicted in Figure 4 ensures that the keys are

1. Encrypt the record with respect to the policy with the HP-ABE scheme:
   $(\hat{C}, C_0, C_{0,1}, C_{0,\varrho,2}, \{\{C_{i,t}\}_{t=0}^{n_i-1}\}_{i=1}^n) \xleftarrow{\$} \mathsf{Encrypt}(pkh_{\mathcal{I}}, K_{\varrho,\psi}, W_{\varrho,\psi})$, that is:
      Choose $\{r_i \xleftarrow{\$} \mathbb{Z}_p^*\}_{i=0}^n$; $\{\epsilon_{i,t} \xleftarrow{\$} \mathbb{Z}_p^*$ for all $t \in (\mathbb{N}_{n_i} \setminus W_i)\}_{i=1}^n$.
      Set $r = \sum_{i=0}^n r_i \bmod p$; $\{\epsilon_{i,t} \leftarrow 0$ for all $t \in W_i\}_{i=1}^n$; $\hat{C} \leftarrow KY^r$;
      $C_0 \leftarrow B^r$; $C_{0,\varrho,2} \leftarrow A_{0,\varrho}^{r_0}$; $\{C_{i,1} \leftarrow g_1^{r_i}\}_{i=0}^n$; $\{\{C_{i,t,2} \leftarrow A_{i,t}^{r_i} g_1^{\epsilon_{i,t}}\}_{t=0}^{n_i-1}\}_{i=1}^n$.
2. Generate a Groth-Sahai proof $\pi = \mathsf{NIZK}_3$ to assert correctness of the encryption:
   $\pi \overset{\text{def}}{=} \mathsf{NIZK}\{(\{r_i\}_{i=0}^n) : \bigwedge_{i=0}^n (C_{i,1} = g_1^{r_i}) \wedge C_0 = \prod_{i=0}^n B^{r_i} \wedge C_{0,\varrho,2} = A_{0,\varrho}^{r_0}\}$.
3. Sign the ciphertext component $C_{0,\varrho,2} : \sigma' \xleftarrow{\$} \mathsf{Sig.Sign}_{sgk_{DB_\varrho}}(C_{0,\varrho,2})$.
   Output $C_{\varrho,\psi} \leftarrow (\pi, \sigma', \hat{C}, C_0, C_{0,1}, C_{0,\varrho,2}, \{\{C_{i,t}\}_{t=0}^{n_i-1}\}_{i=1}^n)$.

Fig. 3. IssueRecord algorithm

generated in an honest way, i.e., that the $D_{i,j}$'s are computed correctly with respect to L_i and contain a random λ_i. To this end, the user chooses an ephemeral ElGamal key pair and a random λ_i'' and sends the issuer encryptions of $g_2^{\lambda_i''}$. As discussed in Section 4, this will ensure the anonymity for the user during decryption. The issuer then chooses his own values of λ_i' and then computes the encryptions of the HP-ABE keys by modifying the received encryptions so that $\lambda_i \equiv \lambda_i' + \lambda_i'' \pmod{p}$ will hold. For this to work, the user and the issuer have to prove to each other that they did their computation correctly with the following two proof protocols. With the first protocol $\mathsf{ZKPK}_4 \overset{\text{def}}{=} \mathsf{ZKPK}\{(x, \{\lambda_i'', r_i\}_{i=1}^n) : X = g_2^x \wedge (\bigwedge_{i=1}^n (E_i = g_2^{\lambda_i''} X^{r_i} \wedge F_i = g_2^{r_i}))\}$ the user proves to the issuer that (E_i, F_i) is a valid encryption of the value $g_2^{\lambda_i''}$. With the second proof of knowledge $\mathsf{ZKPK}_5 \overset{\text{def}}{=} \mathsf{ZKPK}\{(w, \beta, s, \{\lambda_i', \tilde{a}_i\}_{i=0}^n, \{\tilde{r}_i\}_{i=1}^n) : Y = g_T^w \wedge B = g_1^\beta \wedge 1 = g_2^w g_2^s (D_0^{-1})^\beta \wedge D_{0,2} = g_2^{\lambda_0''} g_2^{\lambda_0'} \wedge D_{0,1} = g_2^s D_{0,2}^{\tilde{a}_0} \wedge (\bigwedge_{i=0}^n (A_{i,L_i} = g_1^{\tilde{a}_i})) \wedge (\bigwedge_{i=1}^n (\tilde{E}_i = g_2^{\lambda_i'} E_i \wedge \hat{E}_i = g_2^s \tilde{E}_i^{\tilde{a}_i} X^{\tilde{r}_i} \wedge \hat{F}_i = F_i^{\tilde{a}_i} g_2^{r_{5,i}}))\}$ the issuer proves to the user that the encryptions he sent 1) were computed correctly and were based on the values he received from the user; 2) indeed encode the correct attributes, i.e., those defined by the A_{i,L_i}'s contained in the issuer's public key. Finally, the issuer signs the value $D_{0,2}$ using the Abe et al. signature scheme, such that the user can prove to the database that he uses the correct input in the Query protocol.

Decryption of a Record. Assume a user wants to decrypt a record; HP-ABE decryption would work as in Equation 4 assuming the user's key satisfies the ciphertext policy (cf. [23]).

$$K' \leftarrow \frac{\hat{C} \prod_{i=0}^n \mathsf{e}(C_{i,1}, D_{i,1})}{\mathsf{e}(C_0, D_0) \prod_{i=0}^n \mathsf{e}(C_{i,L_i,2}, D_{i,2})} \tag{4}$$

Intuitively, each key component $D_{i,2}$ allows the user to decrypt a ciphertext component $C_{i,L_i,2}$ if $D_{i,2}$ corresponds to attribute L_i. However, in our scheme, even if the attributes $(L_1, \ldots L_n)$ in the user's key all satisfy the policy, he could by construction not decrypt the ciphertext component $C_{0,\varrho,2}$, because all users lack the

User φ $(pk_{\mathcal{I}}, \varphi, L_\varphi)$:   Authenticated channel   Issuer $(pk_{\mathcal{I}}, sk_{\mathcal{I}}, \varphi, L_\varphi)$:

$(\lambda_0'', x) \xleftarrow{\$} (\mathbb{Z}_p^*)^2$; $X \leftarrow g_2^x$; $s \xleftarrow{\$} \mathbb{Z}_p^*$;

$\{\lambda_i'', r_i \xleftarrow{\$} (\mathbb{Z}_p)^2\}_{i=1}^n$; $\{\tilde{a}_i \stackrel{\text{def}}{=} a_{i,L_i} ; \tilde{r}_i \xleftarrow{\$} \mathbb{Z}_p\}_{i=1}^n$;

$\{(E_i, F_i) \leftarrow (g_2^{\lambda_i''} X^{r_i}, g_2^{r_i})\}_{i=1}^n.$ $\{\lambda_i' \xleftarrow{\$} \mathbb{Z}_p\}_{i=0}^n$.

$\qquad\qquad\qquad\qquad\qquad X, \lambda_0'',$

$\qquad\qquad\qquad\qquad \{E_i, F_i\}_{i=1}^n, \mathsf{ZKPK}_4$
$\overrightarrow{\qquad\qquad\qquad\qquad\qquad\qquad\qquad}$ $\{\tilde{E}_i \leftarrow g_2^{\lambda_i'} E_i\}_{i=1}^n$; $D_{0,2} \leftarrow g_2^{\lambda_0' + \lambda_0''}$;

$\qquad\qquad\qquad\qquad\qquad\qquad\qquad$ $\{\hat{E}_i \leftarrow g_2^s \tilde{E}_i^{\tilde{a}_i} X^{\tilde{r}_i} ; \hat{F}_i \leftarrow F_i^{\tilde{a}_i} g_2^{\tilde{r}_i}\}_{i=1}^n$;

$\qquad\qquad\qquad\qquad\qquad\qquad\qquad$ $\sigma'' \leftarrow \mathsf{Sig.Sign}_{sgk\mathcal{I}}(D_{0,2})$;

$\qquad\qquad\qquad D_0, D_{0,1}, D_{0,2}, \sigma'',$ $D_0 \leftarrow g_2^{\frac{w+s}{\beta}}$; $D_{0,1} \leftarrow g_2^s D_{0,2}^{a_{0,0}}.$

$\qquad\qquad\qquad \{\tilde{E}_i, \hat{E}_i, \hat{F}_i\}_{i=1}^n, \mathsf{ZKPK}_5$
$\overleftarrow{\qquad\qquad\qquad\qquad\qquad\qquad\qquad}$

$\{D_{i,1} \leftarrow \hat{E}_i \hat{F}_i^{-x}\}_{i=1}^n$;

$\{D_{i,2} \leftarrow \tilde{E}_i F_i^{-x}\}_{i=1}^n.$

Return $sk_{\mathcal{U}_\varphi} \leftarrow (L_\varphi, \sigma'', D_0, \{D_{i,1}, D_{i,2}\}_{i=0}^n).$ **Return** ε.

Fig. 4. Interactive issuing of a user's decryption keys. The proofs ZKPK_4 and ZKPK_5 are defined in the text.

key component for this zeroth attribute. Indeed, the key for this would be $D_{0,2}^{k_\varrho^{-1}}$, where k_ϱ is the database's secret. Thus, to decrypt, the user has to run the Query protocol with the database to compute $P \stackrel{\text{def}}{=} \mathrm{e}(C_{0,\varrho,2}, D_{0,2}^{k_\varrho^{-1}}) = \mathrm{e}(C_{0,\varrho,2}, D_{0,2})^{k_\varrho^{-1}}$ and then run the HP-ABE decryption. This protocol is given in Figure 5. It is of course important that 1) the database cannot learn $C_{0,\varrho,2}$ nor $D_{0,2}$ because otherwise it would learn which record a user attempts to decrypt and 2) the database is nevertheless ensured that the user indeed wants to compute this expression on valid inputs. The latter is achieved by having the user prove that he knows signatures on $C_{0,\varrho,2}$ and $D_{0,2}$ from the database and the issuer, and the former is ensured by proper blinding of these two inputs. Note that if the user does not possess the necessary decryption keys, decryption will result in a random symmetric key K' to be recovered (which will make the authenticated decryption algorithm $\mathsf{AuthDec}$ return $\bot$).

The user proves possession of signatures on $C_{0,\varrho,2}$ and $D_{0,2}$, specific to the record ψ and user φ respectively, by the proof protocol $\mathsf{ZKPK}_6 \stackrel{\text{def}}{=} \mathsf{ZKPK}\{(k_c^{-1}, k_d^{-1}, \tilde{\sigma}', \tilde{\sigma}'') :$ $\mathsf{Sig.Prove}(vk_{\mathcal{DB}_\varrho}, C'^{k_c^{-1}}, \tilde{\sigma}') \wedge \mathsf{Sig.Prove}(vk_{\mathcal{I}}, D''^{k_d^{-1}}, \tilde{\sigma}'')\}.$ By the proof protocol $\mathsf{ZKPK}_7 \stackrel{\text{def}}{=} \mathsf{ZKPK}\{(k_\varrho) : (P')^{k_\varrho} = \mathrm{e}(C', D'') \wedge A_{0,\varrho} = A_{0,0}^{k_\varrho}\}$ the database proves to the user that P' is indeed correctly computed with respect to its secret key k_ϱ that is defined by $A_{0,\varrho}$.

Real-World Escrow. The issuer can recover the plaintext from a given ciphertext C with the help of $sk_{\mathcal{I}}$: $K' \leftarrow \hat{C} \, \mathrm{e}(C_0, g_2)^{-w\beta^{-1}} = K g_{\mathrm{T}}^{wr} \, \mathrm{e}(g_1^{\beta r}, g_2)^{-w\beta^{-1}} = K.$ The issuer now checks if the authenticated ciphertext can be decrypted with $\mathsf{AuthDec}$ with key K. If $\mathsf{AuthDec}$ succeeded, the issuer can recover the ciphertext policy thus: $\{W_i \leftarrow \{t \in \mathbb{N}_{n_i} | C_{i,1}^{a_{i,t}} = C_{i,t,2}\}\}_{i=1}^n.$ For $i = 0$, the perfect

User φ $(sk_{\mathcal{U}\varphi},\ pk_{\mathcal{I}},\ pk_{\mathcal{DB}_\varrho},\ C_{\varrho,\psi})$:Anonymous channel Database ϱ $(pk_{\mathcal{I}},\ pk_{\mathcal{DB}_\varrho},\ sk_{\mathcal{DB}_\varrho})$:

Blind $C_{0,\varrho,2}$ of record ψ and $D_{0,2}$
of user φ :

$k_c, k_d \xleftarrow{\$} \mathbb{Z}_p^*$;

$C' \leftarrow C_{0,\varrho,2}^{k_c}$; $D'' \leftarrow D_{0,2}^{k_d}$.

Re-randomize sigantures:

$\tilde{\sigma}' \xleftarrow{\$} \mathsf{Sig.Rerand}(\sigma')$;

$\tilde{\sigma}'' \xleftarrow{\$} \mathsf{Sig.Rerand}(\sigma'')$.

$$\xrightarrow{\quad C', D'', \mathsf{ZKPK}_6 \quad}$$

$$\xleftarrow{\quad P', \mathsf{ZKPK}_7 \quad}$$

Transform input: $P' \leftarrow \mathrm{e}(C', D'')^{k_\varrho^{-1}}.$

Unblind P': $P \leftarrow P'^{k_c^{-1} k_d^{-1}}$.

Return $K' \leftarrow \dfrac{\hat{C} \prod_{i=0}^n \mathrm{e}(C_{i,1}, D_{i,1})}{P\,\mathrm{e}(C_0, D_0) \prod_{i=1}^n \mathrm{e}(C_{i,L_i,2}, D_{i,2})}.$

Return ε.

Fig. 5. The Query protocol. The proofs ZKPK_6 and ZKPK_7 are defined in the text.

soundness of the NIZK_3 proof guarantees that $C_{0,\varrho,2}$ is well-formed and that $r = \sum r_i$, therefore $W_0 \leftarrow \{\varrho\}$. If $\mathsf{AuthDec}$ failed, the issuer simply sets $W_1 = \emptyset$ (the message can never be decrypted).

5.2 Protocol Complexity

A significant amount of work is done during setup and record issuing phases. Let N_{users}, N_{records}, and V denote the number of users, records, and attributes respectively. The players have to perform computations in time linear either to $N_{\mathrm{users}} \cdot V$, or to $N_{\mathrm{records}} \cdot V$, but never linear to the product of the three $N_{\mathrm{users}} \cdot N_{\mathrm{records}} \cdot V$, similarly to [8].

For each query, the user has to do work linear in n (number of categories), while the database has to do only a constant[1] amount of work (in contrast, in [8] both the user and the database have to do work linear in n). In the worst case, each user will query each ciphertext, so it is very important to ensure a fast query protocol for the database, which has to bear most of the work.

Adding revocation does not have a big influence on the complexity analysis: the complexity of the query phase remains the same. The public key of the issuer however will increase linearly in size to N_{users}.

6 Security Analysis

Theorem 1. *If the* HP-ABE *scheme by Nishide et al. is secure, the SXDH assumption holds, and the* $\max(N_{\mathrm{users}}, N_{\mathrm{records}})$-*SFP assumption holds in the chosen bilinear group, then our scheme presented in Section 5.1 securely implements the* HACOT *functionality described in Section 2.*

Corollary 2. *Our* HACOT *scheme is secure in the generic bilinear group model.*

---

[1] Constant assuming we fix the security parameter κ. If κ varies, then the run time is $O(\kappa^3)$.

The corollary trivially follows from security of the Nishide et al. scheme in the generic group model [22]. We prove the theorem by demonstrating indistinguishability between adversarial actions in the real protocol and the ideal world for static corruptions: for every real-world adversary $\mathcal{A}$, we show how to construct an ideal-world adversary $\mathcal{S}$, such that for every environment $\mathcal{E}$: $\mathcal{E}$ cannot distinguish whether it is interacting with $\mathcal{A}$ in the real world or with $\mathcal{S}$ in the ideal world, i.e.,

$$\forall \mathcal{A} : \exists \mathcal{S} : \forall \mathcal{E} : \mathrm{Adv}_{\mathcal{E},\mathcal{A}}^{\mathsf{HACOT}} \overset{\mathrm{def}}{=}$$
$$\left| \Pr\left[\mathrm{Exec}(\mathcal{E}, \mathcal{A}, \mathcal{R}_{\mathrm{HACOT}}) \overset{\$?}{=} 1 \right] - \Pr\left[\mathrm{Exec}(\mathcal{E}, \mathcal{S}, \mathcal{F}_{\mathrm{HACOT}}) \overset{\$?}{=} 1 \right] \right| = negl. \ , \quad (5)$$

where $\mathrm{Exec}(\mathcal{E}, \mathcal{A}, \mathcal{R}_{\mathrm{HACOT}})$ denotes the binary random variable given by the output of $\mathcal{E}$ when interacting with $\mathcal{A}$ and $\mathcal{R}_{\mathrm{HACOT}}$ in the real world; and analogously for $\mathrm{Exec}(\mathcal{E}, \mathcal{S}, \mathcal{F}_{\mathrm{HACOT}})$ in the ideal world.

Proof Sketch. Due to space constraints we only sketch the proof here; details are given in the full version [5]. In case all parties are honest, the real and ideal worlds are indistinguishable by construction. To handle the case where some parties misbehave, we need to show how to construct a simulator $\mathcal{S}$. The construction of $\mathcal{S}$ is mostly straightforward: $\mathcal{S}$ extracts the witnesses from all interactive zero-knowledge proofs so that $\mathcal{S}$ can extract blinding factors and signature forgeries from $\mathcal{A}$ in the query protocol. $\mathcal{S}$ also simulates all interactive zero-knowledge proofs and GS proofs, which gives it the "wiggle room" to encrypt bogus plaintexts instead of the real records, and later manipulate the query protocol so that honest users still recover the correct record. We show that dishonest users cannot detect the deception based on the security of the HP-ABE scheme plus the SXDH assumption, where the latter is needed because of our tweaks in the "zeroth category" of the HP-ABE scheme. Another delicate point in the proof is that a dishonest issuer should not be able to issue to an honest user a malformed key that permits correct decryption even if access should be denied. We prove that the joint randomness in the issuance protocol prevents this under the SXDH assumption.

7 Implementation

We implemented the scheme presented in Section 5 in C++ using the PBC Library [19]. Our implementation uses "D"-type curves [19], on which the SDXH assumption is believed to hold. Keys and records are stored as files on disk. Records can be files of arbitrary size. We use the NIST standard AES-256-CGM as the authenticated encryption scheme.

Our program currently does not support revocation.

We have observed run times of around 0.5–3 seconds for most algorithms/ protocols when run with groups of order $\approx 2^{158}$ and 5 categories and 22 attributes, except the IssueUserKey protocol, which took around 11.5 seconds. Overall, the measured run times confirm our theoretical predictions.

8   Comparison with HACOT by Camenisch et al. at PKC 2011

In this section, we will compare the scheme presented by Camenisch et al. at PKC 2011 [8] (CDNZ) with our scheme (without revocation). We first show that the class of expressible policies in both schemes is the same, and that there is an efficient transformation from CDNZ-policies to our policies (the transformation from our policies to CDNZ-polices is inefficient, as it may require an exponential number of categories. We omit it due to space constraints). We then compare the communications and runtime costs of both schemes in "steady state" (after setup) when they are used with CDNZ-policies, and show that our scheme is faster and needs less bandwidth.

Explanation of CDNZ-Policies. In CDNZ, the keys issued to users are associated with a list of bits of length ℓ: $d = (d_0, \ldots, d_{\ell-1})$ and $d_i \in \mathbb{N}_2$. Each record in the database has an access control policy associated with it. A policy $c = (c_0, \ldots, c_{\ell-1})$ is also expressed as a list of ℓ bits ($c_i \in \mathbb{N}_2$). The index of a bit in that list is called its "category". A key is authorized to access a record if and only if $\sum_{i=0}^{\ell-1} c_i d_i = \sum_{i=0}^{\ell-1} c_i$.

Expressing CDNZ Policies in our Scheme. It is easy to emulate CDNZ-policies in our scheme: simply set the same number of categories ($n \leftarrow \ell$), and create two attributes per category $\forall i \in \mathbb{N}_{n+1}^* : n_i = 2$. Users' keys are endowed with the following attributes, and policies are formed thus: $\forall i \in \mathbb{N}_{n+1}^* : L_i \leftarrow d_i$; if $c_i = 0 : W_i \leftarrow \{0,1\}$; else $W_i \leftarrow \{1\}$. We will use this transformation as the basis for comparing the two schemes.

Efficiency Comparison. The scheme presented in this paper has lower communication and computation costs than CDNZ in "steady state" (after setup). Detailed results are given in the full version [5]. Assuming we use our scheme to express CDNZ-policies ($n = \ell$, $V = 2\ell$), our records are (asymptotically) 1.6 times smaller, the database can generate them (asympotically) 1.8 times faster, and users can check them (asymptotically) twice as fast. The communication costs in the query protocol are constant in our scheme, versus linear in CDNZ. The user's computational costs during the query protocol are (asymptotically) five times lower in our scheme; and the database's computational costs are constant-time in our scheme (versus linear in CDNZ).

Our scheme becomes faster and requires less bandwidth than CDNZ when there are three categories or more.

It must be said however, that our scheme trades more efficient "steady state" communication, storage, and computational costs with more expensive setup costs: for example, it takes about 18 seconds (for $n = 10$) to issue a user's key in our scheme, while this operation is nearly instantaneous in CDNZ.

9   Conclusions and Future Work

We created a scheme that allows a database to publish records that are protected by a hidden access control policy, and that users can access without revealing their identity or choice of record. Extensions to our scheme allow the key issuer to revoke the user's keys. We have proved our scheme secure in the generic bilinear group model.

Our construction uses attribute-based encryption and, in comparison to the prior work based on anonymous credentials, offers more expressive policies and improved efficiency. Finally, we have implemented our scheme. Timing results of a prototype implementation show that the scheme is scalable and sufficiently performant to be used in practical settings.

Recently, Okamoto and Takashima [24] have proposed an HP-ABE scheme that is secure under the decision linear assumption. It seems that one could extend their scheme into a HACOT scheme similarly as we have done it for the Nishide el al. scheme, i.e., by splitting the attribute keys between the database and the users. As this approach does not use the HP-ABE scheme as a block box, the security of such an extension of the Okamoto and Takashima scheme will have to be proven from scratch. We leave this as future work.

Other future work is investigating how to remove the unfettered access the issuer has over the published records.

Acknowledgements. The research leading to these results has received funding from the European Community's Seventh Framework Programme (FP7/2007-2013) as part of the "ICT Trust and Security Research", under grant agreements n°257782 for the project ABC4Trust and n°216676 for the project Ecrypt II.

References

1. Abe, M., Fuchsbauer, G., Groth, J., Haralambiev, K., Ohkubo, M.: Structure-Preserving Signatures and Commitments to Group Elements. In: Rabin, T. (ed.) CRYPTO 2010. LNCS, vol. 6223, pp. 209–236. Springer, Heidelberg (2010)
2. Abe, M., Haralambiev, K., Ohkubo, M.: Signing on Elements in Bilinear Groups for Modular Protocol Design. IACR Cryptology ePrint Archive, 133 (2010)
3. Bellare, M., Namprempre, C.: Authenticated Encryption: Relations among Notions and Analysis of the Generic Composition Paradigm. J. Cryptology 21(4), 469–491 (2008)
4. Bethencourt, J., Sahai, A., Waters, B.: Ciphertext-Policy Attribute-Based Encryption. In: IEEE Symposium on Security and Privacy, pp. 321–334. IEEE Computer Society (2007)
5. Camenisch, J., Dubovitskaya, M., Enderlein, R.R., Neven, G.: Oblivious Transfer with Hidden Access Control from Attribute-Based Encryption. IACR Cryptology ePrint Archive, 348 (2012)
6. Camenisch, J., Dubovitskaya, M., Neven, G.: Oblivious Transfer with Access Control. In: Al-Shaer, E., Jha, S., Keromytis, A.D. (eds.) ACM Conference on Computer and Communications Security, pp. 131–140. ACM (2009)

7. Camenisch, J., Dubovitskaya, M., Neven, G.: Unlinkable Priced Oblivious Transfer with Rechargeable Wallets. In: Sion, R. (ed.) FC 2010. LNCS, vol. 6052, pp. 66–81. Springer, Heidelberg (2010)

8. Camenisch, J., Dubovitskaya, M., Neven, G., Zaverucha, G.M.: Oblivious Transfer with Hidden Access Control Policies. In: Catalano, D., Fazio, N., Gennaro, R., Nicolosi, A. (eds.) PKC 2011. LNCS, vol. 6571, pp. 192–209. Springer, Heidelberg (2011)

9. Camenisch, J.L., Neven, G., Shelat, A.: Simulatable Adaptive Oblivious Transfer. In: Naor, M. (ed.) EUROCRYPT 2007. LNCS, vol. 4515, pp. 573–590. Springer, Heidelberg (2007)

10. Camenisch, J., Stadler, M.: Efficient Group Signature Schemes for Large Groups (Extended Abstract). In: Kaliski Jr., B.S. (ed.) CRYPTO 1997. LNCS, vol. 1294, pp. 410–424. Springer, Heidelberg (1997)

11. Canetti, R.: Universally Composable Security: A New Paradigm for Cryptographic Protocols. IACR Cryptology ePrint Archive, 67 (2000)

12. Coull, S., Green, M., Hohenberger, S.: Controlling Access to an Oblivious Database Using Stateful Anonymous Credentials. In: Jarecki, S., Tsudik, G. (eds.) PKC 2009. LNCS, vol. 5443, pp. 501–520. Springer, Heidelberg (2009)

13. Cramer, R., Damgård, I., MacKenzie, P.D.: Efficient Zero-Knowledge Proofs of Knowledge without Intractability Assumptions. In: Imai, H., Zheng, Y. (eds.) PKC 2000. LNCS, vol. 1751, pp. 354–373. Springer, Heidelberg (2000)

14. Galbraith, S.D., Paterson, K.G., Smart, N.P.: Pairings for Cryptographers. Discrete Applied Mathematics 156(16), 3113–3121 (2008)

15. Green, M., Hohenberger, S., Waters, B.: Outsourcing the Decryption of ABE Ciphertexts. In: USENIX Security Symposium. USENIX Association (2011)

16. Groth, J., Sahai, A.: Efficient Non-interactive Proof Systems for Bilinear Groups. In: Smart, N.P. (ed.) EUROCRYPT 2008. LNCS, vol. 4965, pp. 415–432. Springer, Heidelberg (2008)

17. Katz, J., Sahai, A., Waters, B.: Predicate Encryption Supporting Disjunctions, Polynomial Equations, and Inner Products. In: Smart, N.P. (ed.) EUROCRYPT 2008. LNCS, vol. 4965, pp. 146–162. Springer, Heidelberg (2008)

18. Lewko, A., Okamoto, T., Sahai, A., Takashima, K., Waters, B.: Fully Secure Functional Encryption: Attribute-Based Encryption and (Hierarchical) Inner Product Encryption. In: Gilbert, H. (ed.) EUROCRYPT 2010. LNCS, vol. 6110, pp. 62–91. Springer, Heidelberg (2010)

19. Lynn, B.: On the Implementation of Pairing-Based Cryptography. PhD thesis, Stanford University, PBC library (2007), http://crypto.stanford.edu/pbc/

20. Naor, M., Pinkas, B.: Oblivious Transfer with Adaptive Queries. In: Wiener, M. (ed.) CRYPTO 1999. LNCS, vol. 1666, pp. 573–590. Springer, Heidelberg (1999)

21. Narayan, S., Gagné, M., Safavi-Naini, R.: Privacy Preserving EHR System Using Attribute-based Infrastructure. In: Perrig, A., Sion, R. (eds.) CCSW, pp. 47–52. ACM (2010)

22. Nishide, T.: Cryptographic Schemes with Minimum Disclosure of Private Information in Attribute-Based Encryption and Multiparty Computation. PhD thesis, University of Electro-Communications (2008)

23. Nishide, T., Yoneyama, K., Ohta, K.: Attribute-Based Encryption with Partially Hidden Encryptor-Specified Access Structures. In: Bellovin, S.M., Gennaro, R., Keromytis, A.D., Yung, M. (eds.) ACNS 2008. LNCS, vol. 5037, pp. 111–129. Springer, Heidelberg (2008)

24. Okamoto, T., Takashima, K.: Adaptively Attribute-Hiding (Hierarchical) Inner Product Encryption. In: Pointcheval, D., Johansson, T. (eds.) EUROCRYPT 2012. LNCS, vol. 7237, pp. 591–608. Springer, Heidelberg (2012)
25. Pfitzmann, B., Waidner, M.: Composition and Integrity Preservation of Secure Reactive Systems. In: Gritzalis, D., Jajodia, S., Samarati, P. (eds.) ACM Conference on Computer and Communications Security, pp. 245–254. ACM (2000)
26. Pfitzmann, B., Waidner, M.: A Model for Asynchronous Reactive Systems and its Application to Secure Message Transmission. In: IEEE Symposium on Security and Privacy, p. 184 (2001)
27. Rabin, M.O.: How to Exchange Secrets by Oblivious Transfer. Technical Report TR-81, Harvard Aiken Computation Laboratory (1981)
28. Sahai, A., Waters, B.: Fuzzy Identity-Based Encryption. In: Cramer, R. (ed.) EUROCRYPT 2005. LNCS, vol. 3494, pp. 457–473. Springer, Heidelberg (2005)
29. Zhang, Y., Au, M.H., Wong, D.S., Huang, Q., Mamoulis, N., Cheung, D.W., Yiu, S.-M.: Oblivious Transfer with Access Control: Realizing Disjunction without Duplication. In: Joye, M., Miyaji, A., Otsuka, A. (eds.) Pairing 2010. LNCS, vol. 6487, pp. 96–115. Springer, Heidelberg (2010)

Author Index